M.-C. Gaudel J.-P. Jouannaud (Eds.)

TAPSOFT '93:
Theory and Practice
of Software Development

4th International Joint Conference CAAP/FASE,
Orsay, France, April 13-17, 1993
Proceedings

Springer-Verlag

Berlin Heidelberg New York
London Paris Tokyo
Hong Kong Barcelona
Budapest

Series Editors

Gerhard Goos
Universität Karlsruhe
Postfach 69 80
Vincenz-Priessnitz-Straße 1
W-7500 Karlsruhe, FRG

Juris Hartmanis
Cornell University
Department of Computer Science
4130 Upson Hall
Ithaca, NY 14853, USA

Volume Editors

Marie-Claude Gaudel
Jean-Pierre Jouannaud
LRI, Université de Paris-Sud et CNRS (UA 410)
Bâtiment 490, 91405 Orsay Cedex, France

CR Subject Classification (1991): D.1-3, F.1-3

ISBN 3-540-56610-4 Springer-Verlag Berlin Heidelberg New York
ISBN 0-387-56610-4 Springer-Verlag New York Berlin Heidelberg

© Springer-Verlag Berlin Heidelberg 1993
Printed in Germany

Typesetting: Camera ready by author/editor
Printing and binding: Druckhaus Beltz, Hemsbach/Bergstr.
45/3140-543210 - Printed on acid-free paper

Preface

This volume contains the proceedings of the fourth International Joint Conference on the Theory and Practice of Software Development, TAPSOFT'93. Its predecessors were held in Berlin (1985), Pisa (1987), Barcelona (1989) and Brighton (1991). TAPSOFT'93 is being held from April 13 to April 17, 1993, in Orsay.

Since its creation in 1985, the aim of this conference has been to bring together theoretical computer scientists and researchers in software engineering with a view to discussing how formal methods can usefully be applied in software development.

Continuing with this tradition, TAPSOFT'93 consists of three parts: an advanced seminar, and two colloquiums, CAAP and FASE.

• The 1993 issue of the *Advanced Seminar* includes invited surveys by :

H-D. Ehrich, J. Guttag, C. Jones, B. Mahr, W. Thomas,

and invited conferences by:

A. Arnold, P-P. Degano, N. Dershowitz, G. Longo.

• The *Colloquium on Trees in Algebra and Programming* (CAAP) is held annually in conjunction either with TAPSOFT or ESOP and focuses on the theories underlying the overall theme of TAPSOFT. This year, the selected papers are organised in seven sessions: Specifications and Proofs, Concurrency, Automata and Counting, Constraints Solving, Rewriting, Logic and Trees, Analysis of Algorithms, plus a common session with FASE on Type Inference.

The program committee of CAAP'93 is the following: A. Arnold*, N. Dershowitz, H. Ganzinger*, J. Goguen, J-P. Jouannaud* (Chair), J-W. Klop*, D. Kosen, U. Montanari*, M. Nivat*, L. Pacholski*, B. Rovan*, W. Thomas*.

• The *Colloquium on Formal Approaches of Software Engineering* (FASE) focuses on formal methods and techniques for innovative software development. The selected papers are presented in the following sessions: Case Studies in Formal Design and Development, Compositionality Modules and Development, Formal Development, Foundations and Analysis of Formal Specifications, Verification of Concurrent Systems, Model Checking, Parallel Calculus, plus a common session with CAAP on Type Inference.

The program committee of FASE is the following: E. Astesiano*, M. Dincbas*, H. Erhig*, M-C. Gaudel*(Chair), S. Gerhart, D. Jacobs*, C. Jones*, T. Maibaum*, F. Orejas*, J. Sifakis, A. Tarlecki*.

The TAPSOFT'93 proceedings are published in a single volume, which departs from the tradition. It reflects the convergence of topics in the two colloquiums and in the advanced seminar; most lectures in the seminar are of keen interest for both the audiences of CAAP and FASE; moreover it turned out that papers on type inference were submitted and accepted in both conferences and this has resulted in a common session. We consider this as a success of TAPSOFT in being a link between theoretically inclined and methodogically inclined research.

Nearly 150 papers were submitted to TAPSOFT'93. Like a number of major conferences this year, we have noticed a very significant increase in the number of submitted papers and in their overall quality as well. This has resulted, of course, in a strong selection of 42 papers. We thank sincerely all the program committee members, especially those who managed to attend the final meeting (marked with a * in the two lists above), and the referees listed on the next page for their care and advice (we apologize for possible omissions). Special thanks are due to Claude Marché for his help in computerizing the collection of the review forms. Besides being quite useful, it pointed out that interoperability of computer systems is still an open issue...

Thanks are also due to the organising committee of TAPSOFT: A. Finkel, M-C. Gaudel (general chair), J-P. Jouannaud, B. Rozoy, M.-F. Kalogera (AFCET). Special thanks are due to Corinne Sweeney of AFCET and to Evelyne Jorion of LRI for helping us efficiently.

TAPSOFT'93 has been supported by CNRS, the ESPRIT Basic Research Working Group COMPASS, DRET-DGA, EATCS, GI, LRI, the Ministère des Affaires Etrangères, the Ministère de la Recherche et de l'Espace, the PRC Programmation et Outils pour l'Intelligence Artificielle, Université de Paris-Sud (Division Recherche).

Orsay, February 1993 Marie-Claude Gaudel
Jean-Pierre Jouannaud

List of Reviewers

Amadio R.
Anderson Stuart
Asperti A.
Astesiano E.
Badouel E.
Baldamus Michael
Basin David
Baumeister H.
Beaudouin-Lafon Michel
Bellia Marco
Bergstra J.A.
Berlioux Pierre
Bernot Gilles
Bertossi Alan
Beyer
Billaud M.
Bockmayr A.
Borzyszkowski Andrzej
Bouajjani Ahmed
Boudet A.
Brandenburg F.J.
Cardelli Luca
Caspi Paul
Clement T.
Comon H
Compton K.
Corradini Andrea
Costa G.
Cottam Ian
Courcelle B.
Curien P-L.
Dahn B.I.
De Francesco Nicoletta
De Nicola Rocco
de Frutos David
Degano P.
Dershowitz N.
de Simone Robert
de Vink Erik
de Vries Fer-Jan
Diekert V.
Drossopoulou Sophia
Durand I.
Farinas del Cerro Luis
Faulhaber Joachim
Fedou J.M.
Félix P.

Fernandez de la Vega W.
Ferrari G.
Fey Werner
Finkel Alain
Fisher M.D.
Gabarro Joaquim
Ganascia A.
Garavel Hubert
Gnesi Stefania
Getzinger Thomas
Gogolla Martin
Götzke K.
Grädel Erich
Graf Susanne
Grieskamp Wolfgang
Gruska D.
Hermann Miki
Hui Shi
Hussman Heinrich
Inverardi Paola
Jaehnichen
Kahrs Stefan
Kent S.
Kindler Andrea
Klein H.J.
Klop Jan-Willem
Kok Joost
Korff M.
Kreowski Hans-Joerg
Krieg-Brückner Bernd
Krob D.
Kucherov Gregory
Langen Anno
Lescanne Pierre
Lindenstrauss Naomi
Liskiewicz Maciej
Litovsky I.
Lugiez Denis
Longo G.
Luo Zahohui
Magee J.
Maggiolo-Schettini Andrea
Maranguet L.
Marché C.
Marre Bruno
Mirkowska Grazyna
Moggi Eugenio

Möller Bernhard
Moller Faron
Monahan B.
Moore R
Mosses Peter.
Murphy C.
Nicollin Xavier
Nieuwenhuis Robert
Nipkow Tobias
Niwinski Damian
Noll Thomas
Ohlbach H.J.
Padawitz Peter
Palamidessi C.
Parisi-Presicce Francesco
Pawlowski Wieslaw
Pena Ricardo
Pepper Peter
Phillips I.C.C
Plaisted David A.
Plesnik J.
Potthoff A.
Privara Igor
Puel L.
Ramakrishnan Iv.
Reggio Gianna
Remy J.L.
Reingold Edward
Reinhardt Klaus
Rodriguez-Artalego Mario
Rossi Francesca
Rusinowitch Michael
Rutter J.J.M.M.
Ruzicka P.
Ryan Mark
Sagiv Y.
Sannella Don
Santen
Sargeant J.

Sassone Vladimiro
Savadovsky P.
Schieferdecker I.
Schott R.
Scollo Giuseppe
Seibert S.
Seese D.
Sergot M.J.
Serpette B.
Siegel M.
Siroky A.
Snyder W
Socher-Ambrosius Rolf
Sopena E.
Soria M.
Sotteau Dominique
Stalzer Mark
Steffen Bernhard
Stickel Mark E.
Stuber Jürgen
Sturc J.
Tönne A.
Tulipani Sandro
Valkema E.
van Oostrom V.
van Raamsdonk F.
Waldmann U.
Wiedermann J.
Wilke Th.
Wills A.
Wolczko M.
Wolff Burkhart
Wolz Dietmar
Yelick K.
Zhang Hantao
Zimmermann Paul
Zlatos P.
Zucca E.

Contents

FASE: Model Checking

Invited Conference

CAAP-FASE: Type Inference

CAAP: Analysis of Algorithms

FASE: Parallel Calculus

Goldilocks and the Three Specifications

John V. Guttag*

Massachusetts Institute of Technology
Cambridge, MA 02139 USA
Email: guttag@lcs.mit.edu

Abstract. A young girl enters Threads Forest. She becomes lost. She searches for enlightenment.

1 Prolog

Goldilocks' mother had often warned her not to enter Threads Forest. It was a strange and sometimes dangerous place. On the floor of the forest, where the sun never penetrated, grew toxic fungi. Dangerous beasts lurked everywhere.

There were many paths through the forest, and since they often crossed and frequently dead ended it was easy to get lost, even to starve. Furthermore from time to time old paths disappeared and new ones appeared. Wise men and women asserted that some paths would always be there, but were cryptic about which ones.

Despite her mother's repeated warnings, Goldi ventured into the forest. She soon became hopelessly lost. After giving her plight a moment's thought, she took the only rational course of action. "Help, get me out of here," she screamed.

Somewhat to her surprise, her plea was answered almost immediately. Three strangers slipped from behind three graceful deciduous conifers. "What seems to be the problem?" they asked in unison. "I can't find my way out of this stupid forest," Goldi replied. "Not to worry," said the shortest of the strangers. "You're in luck. It just so happens that we're cartographers, and we've each just completed a map of the forest."

With that, the cartographers each handed Goldi a map. Upon examining them, Goldi discovered (to her disgust) that they were all different. "Of course they are," exclaimed the cartographers. "One is too weak, one is too strong, and one is juuuuust right."

For some reason, that explanation didn't satisfy Goldi. Seeing her puzzlement, the smallest cartographer tried to explain. "All of the paths on the too

---

*Support for this research has been provided in part by the Advanced Research Projects Agency of the Department of Defense, monitored by the Office of Naval Research Research under contract N00014-89-J-1988, and in part by the National Science Foundation under grant 9115797-CCR.

weak map exist at present and will continue to exist forever. However, there are many paths through the forest that don't appear on the map. The too strong map contains all of the useful paths through the forest at the present time. However, some of these paths may disappear in the future. The just right map contains all of the paths that will always be available."

Again, the explanation did not satisfy Goldi. "Why," she demanded, "do you insist on confusing me by giving me three maps?" The tallest cartographer, who was more patient than the others, made one more attempt at educating Goldi. "The too weak map is easier to follow than either of the others, and does contain some paths (albeit often longer than necessary) through the forest. The too strong map contains the shortest paths through the forest today. The problem is that you may not be able to use them tomorrow. The just right map, well that's juuuuust right."

Goldi was still puzzled. "Perhaps," she pleaded, a tear glistening in the corner of one eye, "you could give me formal specifications of all this?" "Ok," chortled the middle-sized cartographer, with a mocking glint in his eye, "you asked for it."

2   Introduction

In designing an interface, there is sometimes a tradeoff between making it easy to implement and making it easy to use. This tradeoff often centers, particularly in concurrent programs, around the amount of nondeterminism allowed. More nondeterminism leaves freedom for the implementor to choose a simpler or more efficient implementation. Less nondeterminism may support the development of simpler or more efficient client programs.

This paper presents three alternative formal specifications of part of a threads interface. The specifications presented here differ in the amount of nondeterminism allowed, and describe a hierarchy of implementations: the implementations satisfying the "too strong" specification are a strict subset of those satisfying the "just right" specification which, in turn, are a strict subset of those satisfying the "too weak" specification.

The specifications presented here are based upon work the author did in conjunction with Andrew Birrell, Jim Horning, Roy Levin and Garret Swart— all of the Digital Equipment Corporation Systems Research Center (SRC). In [1] we published what purported to be a formal specification of the threads synchronization primitives implemented as part of the Topaz operating system on the Firefly multi-processor. To the best of our knowledge, the implementation of Topaz indeed satisfied these specifications. However, the specifications were simultaneously too weak and too strong. The specifications were too weak in that they could not be used to justify some reasonable uses of the specified primitives in client programs, because the specifications permitted paths that could not actually arise in the implementation. The specifications were too strong in that they would not be satisfied by contemplated remote procedure call (RPC) implementations, because the specifications guaranteed the existence of paths that would disappear in those implementations.

The next section presents a short overview of Larch interface specifications. The section after that presents a short overview of what threads are about, lays out the issues involved in choosing the degree and types of non-determinism to be allowed, and presents formal specifications of three interesting alternatives in that space. The note concludes with a brief discussion of how the specifications were derived and the utility of the process and the specifications.

3   Larch Interface Specifications

Larch is a family of languages for writing formal specifications of interfaces in digital systems. The basic approach is described in [4].

The Larch family of languages supports a *two-tiered*, definitional style of specification. Each specification has components written in two languages: one language that is designed for a specific programming language and another language that is independent of any programming language. We call the former kind *Larch interface languages*, and the latter the *Larch Shared Language* (LSL).

Interface languages are used to specify the interfaces between program components. Each specification provides the information needed to use an interface. Each interface language deals with what can be observed by client programs written in a particular programming language. It provides a way to write assertions about program states, and it incorporates programming-language-specific notations for features such as side effects, exception handling, iterators, and concurrency.

Larch interface languages encourage a style of programming that emphasizes the use of abstractions, and each provides a mechanism for specifying abstract types. If its programming language provides direct support for abstract types, the interface language facility is modeled on that of the programming language; if its programming language does not, the facility is designed to be compatible with other aspects of the programming language.

An interface specification can describe exported types, constants, variables, and procedures. The specification of each procedure in an interface can be studied, understood, and used without reference to the specifications of other procedures. A specification consists of a procedure header (declaring the types of its arguments, results, and any global variables it may access) followed by a body of the form:

```
requires Predicate
modifies Target list
ensures  Predicate
```

A specification places constraints on both clients and implementations of the procedure. The *requires clause* is used to state restrictions on the state, including the values of any parameters, at the time of any call. The *modifies* and *ensures clauses* place constraints on the procedure's behavior when it is called properly. When specifying sequential programs, they relate two states, the state when

```
uses TaskQueue;
mutable type queue;
immutable type task;

task *getTask(queue q) {
  modifies q;
  ensures
    if isEmpty(q^)
      then result = NIL ∧ unchanged(q)
      else (*result)' = first(q^) ∧ q' = tail(q^);
}
```

Figure 1: An LCL interface specification

the procedure is called, the *pre-state*, and the state when it terminates, the *post-state*.

A modifies clause says what objects a procedure is allowed to change. It says that the procedure must not change the value of any objects visible to the client except for those in the target list. Any other object must have the same value in the pre and post-states. If there is no modifies clause, then no externally visible object can be changed.

Figure 1 contains a sample interface specification. The specification is written in LCL (a Larch interface language for C). This fragment introduces two abstract types and a procedure (function in C parlance) for selecting a task from a task queue. Briefly, * means pointer to (as in C), **result** refers to the value returned by the function, the symbol ˆ is used to refer to the value of an object in the pre-state, and the symbol ' to refer to its value in the post-state.

The specification of **getTask** is not self-contained. For example, looking only at this specification there is no way to know which task **getTask** selects, because the meaning of the operators **first** and **tail** are not given. Is **first(q^)** the task that has been in q the longest? Is it is the one in q with the highest priority?

Interface specifications rely on definitions from *auxiliary specifications*, written in LSL, to provide semantics for the primitive terms they use. Specifiers are not limited to a fixed set of notations, but can use LSL to define specialized vocabularies suitable for particular interface specifications or classes of specifications. The **uses** clause in Figure 1 incorporates the LSL specification **TaskQueue** (not shown), which defines the operators **first** and **tail**.

The logical basis for Larch's treatment of concurrency is described in [1] and is similar to the one discussed in [7]. Our specifications deal only with safety, not with liveness.

Specifications of procedures for concurrent programs are similar to specifications of procedures for sequential programs. In both cases, the specifications prescribe the observable effects of procedures, without saying how they are to be achieved. In a sequential program, the states between a procedure call and its return cannot be observed in the calling environment. Thus one can specify a procedure by giving a predicate relating just the state when the procedure is called and the state when it returns [5]. Similarly, an *atomic action* in a concurrent program has no visible internal structure; its observable effects can also be specified by a predicate on just two states.

Any behavior of a concurrent system can be described as the execution of a sequence of atomic actions. In specifying atomic actions, we don't specify how atomicity is to be achieved, only that it must be. In an implementation, atomic actions may proceed concurrently as long as the concurrency isn't observable.

Atomic procedures execute just one atomic action per call. Each can be specified in terms of just two states: the state immediately preceding and the state immediately following the action. Note that, when dealing with concurrent programs, the pre-state of the action corresponding to a procedure body is not necessarily the state in which the procedure call was initiated; actions by other threads may have intervened. Similarly, the post-state of the action is not necessarily the state in which the caller resumes execution.

The observable effects of a *non-atomic procedure* cannot be described in terms of just two states. Its effects may span more states, and actions of other threads may be interleaved with its atomic actions. However, each execution of a non-atomic procedure can be viewed as a sequence of atomic actions. We specify a non-atomic procedure by giving a predicate that defines the allowable sequences of atomic actions (i.e., sequences of pre-post state pairs). Each execution of the procedure must be equivalent to such a sequence. Although it is sometimes necessary to specify constraints on the sequence as a whole, it often suffices to specify the atomic actions separately.

In addition to the constructs used to specify sequential interaces, we use the following constructs in specifying the procedures in the threads' interface:

- **when** clauses stating conditions that must be satisfied for atomic actions to take place. They place constraints not on the client but on the called procedure, which is obligated to make sure that its condition holds before taking any externally visible action. A **when** clause may thus impose a delay until actions of other threads make its predicate true. An omitted **when** clause is equivalent to **when** true, that is, no delay is required.

- **action** clauses specifying named actions. They are within the scope of the procedure header, and may refer to the procedure's formal parameters, results, and specification variables.

- **composition of** clauses indicating that any execution of a non-atomic procedure must be equivalent to execution of the named actions in the given order, possibly interleaved with actions of other threads.

- The reserved word **self**, standing for the identity of the thread executing the specified action.

```
mutable type mutex;

uses Mutex;

mutex mutex_create(void) {
  ensures fresh(result) ∧ result' = free;
}

void acquire(mutex m) {
  modifies m;
  when isFree(m^) ensures m' = grantMutex(self);
}

void release(mutex m) {
  requires holder(m^) = self;
  modifies m;
  ensures m' = free;
}
```

Figure 2: Specification of mutexes

4 The threads interface

The threads interface provides facilities for creating and controlling threads, which may or may not share memory. This note is concerned only with the facilities used for synchronizing threads.[1] Some of these are rather simple, and are derived from the concepts of *monitors* and *condition variables* described by Hoare[6]. Their semantics is similar to that provided by Mesa [8].

As far as clients of threads are concerned, all threads can execute concurrently. The threads implementation is responsible for assigning threads to real processors. The way in which this assignment is made affects performance, but does not affect the semantics of the synchronization primitives. The programmer can reason as if there were as many processors as threads.

Mutexes

A *mutex* [3] is the basic tool enabling threads to cooperate on access to shared variables. A mutex is normally used to achieve an effect similar to monitors, ensuring that a set of actions on a group of variables can be made *atomic* relative to any other thread's actions on these variables. A mutex is associated with the set of variables, and each critical section is bracketed by calls of the procedures acquire and release. The semantics of acquire and release ensure that these critical sections are indeed mutually exclusive.

There seems to be little controversy about the appropriate semantics for mutexes, so we give only one specification, Figure 2. The interface specification

---

[1] For more extensive descriptions of how threads are intended to be used and how they can be implemented see [1] and [2].

begins by asserting that `mutex` is a mutable abstract type. It then incorporates an LSL specification, `Mutex` that provides the operators `isFree`, `holder`, `grantMutex`, and `free` used in specifying the procedures exported by the interface. This LSL specification contains the axioms

```
holder(grantMutex(t)) = t
¬ isFree(grantMutex(t))
isFree(free)
```

Condition Variables

Condition variables make it possible for a thread to suspend its execution while awaiting an action by some other thread. The normal paradigm for using condition variables is as follows. A condition variable `c` is associated with some shared variables protected by a mutex `m` and a predicate based on those shared variables. A thread acquires `m` (i.e., enters a critical section) and evaluates the predicate to see if it should call `wait(m, c)` to suspend its execution. This call atomically releases the mutex (i.e., ends the critical section) and suspends execution of that thread.

After any thread changes the shared variables so that `c`'s predicate might be satisfied, it calls `signal(c)` to awaken one thread or `broadcast(c)` to awaken all of them. `Signal` and `broadcast` allow blocked threads to resume execution and re-acquire the mutex. When a thread returns from `wait` it is in a new critical section. It re-evaluates the predicate and determines whether to proceed or to call `wait` again.

There are several subtleties in the semantics of these procedures, e.g., even if threads take care to call `signal` only when the predicate is true, the predicate may become false before a waiting thread resumes execution. These subtleties, and the utility of formal specifications in clarifying them, are discussed at some length in [1].

Figure 3 contains a specification of condition variables. It begins by importing the specification of the `mutex` interface. Next, type `condition` is specified to be a mutable abstract type. The `uses` clause incorporates an LSL specification of finite sets, and asserts that objects of type `condition` will be modeled in the specification as sets of objects of type `thread`. When a thread executes `wait(m, c)` it notionally inserts itself in the set `c` and waits for some other thread to remove it by calling `signal` or `broadcast`. We sat "notionally" because while it is convenient in the specification to model a condition variable as a set of threads, it need not be implemented that way.

Note that the specification of `broadcast` implies the specification of `signal`. `Broadcast` must unblock all threads waiting on the condition variable, whereas `signal` unblocks one or more threads (assuming that there are any waiting on the condition). This means that any implementation that satisfies `broadcast`'s specification will also satisfy `signal`'s. Of course, a good implementation of `signal` should strive to unblock exactly one thread. The difficulty in guaranteeing this stronger specification arises from the possibility of a race between calls

```
imports mutex;

mutable type condition;

uses Set(thread, condition);

condition condition_create(void) {
   ensures fresh(result) ∧ result' = { };
}

void signal(condition c) {
   modifies c;
   ensures if c^ = { } then c' = { } else c' ⊂ c^;
}

void broadcast(condition c) {
   modifies c;
   ensures c' = { };
}

void wait(mutex m, condition c) {
   = composition of Enqueue; Resume
   requires holder(m^) = self;
   modifies m, c;
   action Enqueue
      ensures m' = free ∧ c' = insert(self, c^);
   action Resume
      when isFree(m^) ∧ self ∉ c^
      ensures m' = grantMutex(self) ∧ c' = c^;
}
```

Figure 3: Specification of condition variables

to **signal** and **wait**. It is a limitation of the specification technique that we specify only what is guaranteed, and not what should happen most of the time.

Alerts

Alerts provide a polite form of interrupt. They are most often used to request termination of a long-running computation or a long-term wait.

The procedure call **alert(t)** is used to request that the thread **t** respond to an alert. A thread can check whether it has been alerted by calling **testAlert**. It is considered good practice for threads executing long-running computations to occasionally call **testAlert**. Similarly, threads executing waits that may last for a long time should block themselves by calling **alertWait** rather than **wait**. The function **alertWait** is similar to **wait**, except that

1. The wait can be terminated by an alert even if the condition on which the

```
imports condition;

typedef enum {alerted, signaled} alertStatus;

spec immutable type pendingAlerts;

uses Set(thread, pendingAlerts);

spec pendingAlerts pa = { };

void alert(thread t) pendingAlerts pa; {
    modifies pa;
    ensures pa' = insert(t, pa^);
}
```

Figure 4: Common part of specification of alerts

thread is waiting has not been signaled, and

2. alertWait returns a value indicating whether it is responding to a signal or to an alert.

A key issue in the design of a threads package with alerts is the amount of nondeterminism allowed in testAlert. If a thread executes alert(t) before the thread t executes testAlert, will testAlert necessarily return true? Clients would prefer an unqualified "yes." However, in a distributed system with remote procedure calls, t may migrate from node to node and alert may have to chase t. Guaranteeing that testAlert will always return true may be unacceptably inefficient, and clients may have to settle for "sometimes."

A similar question arises with alertWait. Things are straightforward when a blocked thread receives only a signal or an alert, but if a thread receives both, what is guaranteed about the outcome? Must it always return signaled if possible? Always return alerted if possible? Respond to whichever comes first? Or can the choice be nondeterministic?

The three specifications Goldilocks was given by the cartographers deal with these issues. Figure 4 contains material common to all three.

The specification uses a specification variable, pa, to keep track of pending alerts. Specification variables are declared solely to facilitate writing specifications. Like other global variables, they appear in the headers and bodies of specification. However, they are not exported by the interface, therefore client code cannot refer to them.

The weakest, and simplest, specification considered here, Figure 5, allows considerable nondeterminism. It allows testAlert to return true only if the thread has been alerted, but to return false any time. The specification allows alertWait to return signaled only if the thread has been removed from c, and to return alerted only if the thread has a pending alert. However, since the two when clauses of the AlertResume action are not mutually exclusive, the

```
bool testAlert(void) pendingAlerts pa; {
   modifies pa;
   ensures
     if result
       then self ∈ paˆ ∧ pa' = delete(self, paˆ)
       else pa' = paˆ;
}

alertStatus alertWait(mutex m, condition c) pendingAlerts pa; {
     = composition of Enqueue; AlertResume
   requires holder(mˆ) = self;
   modifies m, c, pa;
   action Enqueue ensures
     m' = free ∧ c' = insert(self, cˆ) ∧ pa' = paˆ;
   action AlertResume
     when isFree(mˆ) ∧ self ∉ cˆ
       ensures result = signaled ∧ m' = grantMutex(self)
         ∧ c' = cˆ ∧ pa' = paˆ;
     when isFree(mˆ) ∧ self ∈ paˆ
       ensures result = alerted ∧ m' = grantMutex(self)
         ∧ c' = delete(self, cˆ) ∧ pa' = delete(self, paˆ);
```

Figure 5: Too weak specification

```
alertStatus alertWait(mutex m, condition c) pendingAlerts pa; {
    = composition of Enqueue; ChooseOutcome; GetMutex

  requires holder(m^) = self;
  modifies m, c, pa;

  spec bool signalChosen;

  action Enqueue
    ensures m' = free ∧ c' = insert(self, c^) ∧ pa' = pa^;
  action ChooseOutcome
    when self ∉ c^ ∨ self ∈ pa^
      ensures signalChosen' = self ∉ c^
        ∧ c' = delete(self, c^) ∧ m' = m^
        ∧ pa' = (if signalChosen' then pa^
                  else delete(self, pa^));
    action GetMutex
      when isFree(m^)
        ensures m' = grantMutex(self) ∧ c' = c^ ∧ pa' = pa^
          ∧ result = (if signalChosen then signaled else alerted);
}
```

Figure 6: Just right specification of alertWait

procedure can return either **signaled** or **alerted** when the thread has been alerted and the condition variable signaled. Therefore, this specification does not rule out the possibility that a signal will be lost by being delivered only to a thread that subsequently returns **alerted** rather than **signaled**. Since it fails to provide this guarantee, which is useful to clients without causing implementation problems, we label this specification "too weak."

The "just right" specification, Figure 6, provides a stronger guarantee for **alertWait**. It introduces a local specification variable, **signalChosen** and an extra action, **ChooseOutcome**. Here **alertWait** must return **signaled** when a signal comes first, but either outcome is allowed when an alert comes before a signal. This specification does not allow signals to be lost; clients of **signal** can rely on a waiting thread being unblocked, if there are any.

The "too strong" specification, Figure 7, strengthens **testAlert**'s specification by requiring that it return true if the thread has been alerted. Although this guarantee is appropriate for uniprocessors, it is unlikely to be valid in an RPC implementation in a distributed environment. The specification strengthens the "too weak" specification of **alertWait** by adding the conjunct **self $\in$ c** to the second **when** clause of the action **AlertResume**. This ensures that signals are not lost. As it happens, however, this specification is "way too strong" in that we know of no efficient implementation that satisfies it.

```
bool testAlert(void) pendingAlerts pa; {
  modifies pa;
  ensures result = (self ∈ paˆ) ∧ pa' = delete(self, paˆ);
}

alertStatus alertWait(mutex m, condition c) pendingAlerts pa; {
    = composition of Enqueue; AlertResume
  requires holder(mˆ) = self;
  modifies m, c, pa;
  action Enqueue ensures
    m' = free ∧ c' = insert(self, cˆ) ∧ pa' = paˆ;
  action AlertResume
    when isFree(mˆ) ∧ self ∉ cˆ
      ensures result = signaled ∧ m' = grantMutex(self)
        ∧ c' = cˆ ∧ pa' = paˆ;
    when isFree(mˆ) ∧ self ∈ paˆ ∧ self ∈ cˆ
      ensures result = alerted ∧ m' = grantMutex(self)
        ∧ c' = delete(self, cˆ) ∧ pa' = delete(self, paˆ);
```

Figure 7: Too strong specification

5   Discussion

An important aspect of the work discussed here was the interplay among clients, implementors, and specifiers. We wrote a great many more specifications than the three discussed here. Some were rejected because they didn't ensure properties needed by clients, others because they promised more than the implementors knew how to provide efficiently.

Formalizability was never the bottleneck. Although the process of formalizing something we thought we understood often revealed a lack of precision in that understanding, we never found that we couldn't formalize something that we truly understood. Many times when we had seemingly reached agreement in oral discussion, the attempt to record that agreement in a specification revealed ambiguity or incompleteness. On those occasions the specifiers would come back to the clients or implementors with some precisely formulated alternatives and ask "Which do you want?"

We now have specifications that both clients and implementors have accepted. Does this mean that they are necessarily perfect, or even perfect for some purpose? No, but that isn't the issue.

In this exercise, we wanted to use formal specification as a tool to better understand a set of possible threads interfaces. The formal specifications helped us formulate precise questions about which design decisions were sensible, which were reflected in an existing implementation, and which were likely to persist in future implementations. Comparing alternative specifications helped us to explore a portion of the design space. Others may not agree with our definition of "just right" but at least we have clarified some of the choices.

6 Epilog

Shortly after parting from the cartographers, Goldi came upon a lone man, frantically chopping away at the forest with a dull machete. Upon spotting Goldi, he ceased his work and asked her what it was she held in her hand. Upon being told that they were specifications, he immediately seized and then ate them.

"What have you done?" protested Goldi, "Now I'll never find my way out of here." "Real hackers don't use specifications," thundered the man. With that, he handed Goldi a machete and a piece of paper. "You should be able to beat your way out on your own. However, if you decide to wimp out, you can always call the number on this paper, and ask to speak to the wizard who created this place."

Goldi, by now wise to the ways of the forest, wasted no time in dialing the number. "The number you have reached is no longer in service," the computer-generated voice informed her.

Acknowledgements

Most of the material in this paper is drawn from an earlier note co-authored with Jim Horning. I appreciate his graciousness in allowing me to use it here.

Steve Garland played a major role in designing the specification language used in this paper, and in adapting the original Modula-2 specifications to C.

Barbara Liskov, Sharon Perl, and Bill Weihl all provided useful and timely comments on an earlier draft of this paper. Jim Horning provided many useful comments on several versions of this paper.

References

[1] A.D. Birrell, J.V. Guttag, J.J. Horning, and R. Levin. "Synchronization primitives for a multiprocessor: a formal specification." *Operating Systems Review* 21(5), Nov. 1987. Revised version in [9].

[2] Andrew Birrell, "An Introduction to Programming with Threads," Report 35, Digital Equipment Corporation Systems Research Center, Palo Alto, January 1989. Revised version in [9].

[3] Edsger W. Dijkstra, "The Structure of the 'THE'—Multiprogramming System," *Comm. ACM*, vol. 11, no. 5, 341–346, 1968.

[4] J.V. Guttag and J.J Horning, with S.J. Garland, K.D. Jones, A. Modet and J.M. Wing, *Larch: Languages and Tools for Formal Specification*, Springer-Verlag, New York, 1993.

[5] C. A. R. Hoare, "Procedures and Parameters: An Axiomatic Approach," Symposium on Semantics of Algorithmic Languages, Springer-Verlag, 1971.

[6] C. A. R. Hoare, "Monitors: An Operating System Structuring Concept," *Comm. ACM*, vol. 17, no. 10, 549–557, 1974.

[7] Leslie Lamport, "A Simple Approach To Specifying Concurrent Systems," Report 15, Digital Equipment Corporation, Systems Research Center, Palo Alto, 1986.

[8] B. W. Lampson and D. D. Redell, "Experiences with Processes and Monitors in Mesa," *Comm. ACM*, vol. 23, no. 2, 105–117.

[9] Greg Nelson (ed.). *Systems Programming with Modula-3*, Prentice Hall, 1991.

On Relating Some Models for Concurrency

Pierpaolo Degano*   Roberto Gorrieri†   Sebastiano Vigna‡

1   Introduction

The activities of concurrent distributed processes are commonly considered as events that are atomic and occur instantaneously; they often carry a label, indicating the kind of activity performed. Instead, many different ways are proposed in the literature to compose and organize events in order to represent the runs of a process, i.e., its *behaviour*. A coarse classification divides these descriptions according to two orthogonal axes: *interleaving* vs. *causality-based* representations, and *linear* vs. *branching time* ones. In the interleaving models, the events of a run simply occur one after the other, and there is no way to express whether there is any causal link between them, due, e.g., to some shared resource or because they happen in the same place. The causality-based representations generally use a partial ordering relation on the events in order to reflect these potential causal dependencies and independencies. Once chosen the favourite representation of the runs of a process, its behaviour is obtained by giving them some structure. When these descriptions form a set, we get the so-called linear time models. In the branching time models, the representation of process runs are organized as a tree by identifying those events shared by different runs, thus making explicit when a choice occurred.

In order to exemplify, we mention Hoare's *traces* [Hoa85] as an example of interleaving, linear time model: a process behaviour is a language, the words of which are sequences of labels. In this way the temporal (or *generation*) ordering in which the events occur is recorded by the sequence of their labels. Milner's *synchronization trees* [Mil80] are an example of interleaving, branching time model; they are trees with labelled arcs, that represent event occurrences, so the choices and the generation ordering are explicitly represented. *Partial orderings* of (labelled) events are quite popular a causality-based linear time model (see, e.g., Pratt's *pomsets* [Pra86]). In these models, the causal dependencies are explicitly represented by the partial ordering relation, and absence of ordering is interpreted as causal independence. The most studied causality-based, branching time model are (labelled) *events structures* [Win87] that are essentially partial orderings of events plus an additional relation, called conflict: two events are in conflict if the occurrence of one of them in a run excludes the other to occur in the same run.

*Dipartimento di Matematica, Università di Parma, Via M. d'Azeglio 85, I-43100 Parma PR, Italy, Fax: +39-521-902350, and Dipartimento di Informatica, Università di Pisa, Corso Italia 40, I-56125 Pisa PI, Italy, Fax: +39-50-510226; e_mail: degano@di.unipi.it.

†Dipartimento di Matematica, Università di Bologna, Piazza di Porta San Donato 5, I-40127 Bologna BO, Italy, Fax: +39-51-354490; e_mail: gorrieri@cs.unibo.it.

‡Dipartimento di Scienze dell'Informazione, Università di Milano, Via Comelico 39/41, I-20135 Milano MI, Italy, Fax: +39-2-55006276; e_mail: vigna@ghost.sm.dsi.unimi.it.

There are no absolute criteria to prefer one among the above models. Indeed, the choice of one of them depends on which aspects of processes are of interest, on the mathematical and mechanical tools available for analysing process behaviour, and also on personal taste. This paper aims at making the choice a little bit less arbitrary, by formally relating the four classes arising from the combination of interleaving or causality-based models with the linear or branching time ones. Intuitively, it is easy to compare these classes, but only few papers address formally this issue, among the others [SNW, Roz90]. Also, establishing formal relationships reveals some subtle differences between causality-based models.

For example, you may go from a branching time representation to a linear time representation of a process just by taking the "path language" of the former. Similarly, it may seem easy to go from a partial ordering of events to a set of traces, by taking all the total orderings, i.e., all the sequences of (labels of) events that are compatible with the partial ordering (containing it, in set-theoretical terms). However, this is not always the case, because the absence of ordering between two events does not necessarily imply that they may occur in any temporal order, although this is quite common an assumption (e.g., see Kahn'-Plotkin's Q axiom, the semantics of asynchronous composition in CCS and similar languages, the representation theorem of prime event structures as domains of configurations). Indeed, a relation of *priority*, both on conflicting and on causally independent events, has been recently advocated [JG88] in order to compactly specify the behaviour of processes in critical situations, e.g., to prevent faults or to cope with them. Therefore, it may well happen that two causally unrelated events may occur only in a fixed temporal ordering.

Thus, partial orderings of events and event structures are not fully satisfactory when priorities are of interest, while (not surprisingly!) *causal trees* [DD90] are such. Recall that causal trees are arc-labelled trees with enriched labels that, beside the performed activity, supply also indication of its causes. As a matter of fact, causal trees extend synchronization trees with a relation of causality (and the generation ordering is inherited), while event structures extend synchronization trees with a relation of causal independence, with no regard to the generation ordering (*cf.* how a prime event structure is recovered from a domain of configurations).

Our main contribution is a first step towards a formal characterization of which information is lost when passing from the causality-based, branching time models to the interleaving, branching time and the causality-based, linear time ones, and from these to the interleaving, linear time models. Said in the other way around, we establish which is the necessary and sufficient information that enables us to reconstruct the causality-based, branching time behaviour of a process from those behaviours lacking the information about the causal or about the branching structures, provided that the latter two agree when interpreted in the interleaving, linear time setting.

A more precise synopsis of our paper follows. We chose a representative for each of the four classes of behaviour discussed above, and we present them as four categories: **TL, ST, MOL, CT**. The objects of the category **TL** are Hoare's trace languages, while those of **ST** are Milner's synchronization trees. Category **MOL** has the so-called *mixed orderings* of events as objects [DDM90]. A mixed ordering is a partial ordering of events with an additional total ordering to be interpreted as the *generation* ordering, that "sequentializes" also the occurrences of events not causally related. The fourth category **CT** has causal trees as objects. Actually, each run of a process is indexed and so is its representation. E.g., an object of **TL** is an indexed set of traces, rather than a language. The morphisms of these categories preserve to some extent the structure of their objects. There are obvious forgetful functors from **CT** to **ST** and **MOL**, and from these to **TL**, that always have left and right adjoints. For example, the left adjoint to the forgetful functor from **ST** to **TL** makes the trivial synchronization tree that has a branching only at its root, while the right adjoint glues the traces as much as possible. The forgetful functors have also an axiomatic characterization. The main theorem says that the four categories above form a pullback. More accurately, **CT** is a reflective and coreflective subcategory of $\mathbf{ST} \times_{\mathbf{TL}} \mathbf{MOL}$, because of pathological cases descibed in Section 3. We think that other models for concurrency (such as Mazurkiewicz's *traces*, Pratt's *pomsets* [Pra86], Janicki' and Koutny's *composets* [JK91], Rabinovitch' and Trakhtenbrot's *behaviour structures* [RT88]) can be recast with minor efforts in our framework by establishing pairs of adjoints, one of which is usually an obvious forgetful functor.

In Section 5, we compare event structures and causal trees. It is easy to pass from an event structure to a causal tree, but this transformation is fully invertible only when causally independent events may occur in any temporal ordering and there is no auto-concurrency (no two causally independent events have the same label). This is mainly because event structures are not fully satisfactory when priority has to be expressed. In order to increase their expressive power, we add to event structures a priority relation, besides the causal and the conflict ones. Of course, priority cannot interfere with causality, but it may dictate which event has to be fired in a set of enabled conflicting ones, and which among enabled concurrent events has to occur first. Prioritized event structures are a conservative extension of prime event structures in that their configurations are finitary, coherent, prime algebraic partial orderings, namely *domains*. Therefore, it is possible to reconstruct a prime event structure with the same "dynamics" of a prioritized one. Essentially, what is lost is that some events may disappear or may be duplicated, and that the priority links may be transformed into causality links. Eventually, the category of causal trees is shown to be a coreflective sub-category of that of prioritized event structures. Additionally, the coreflection shows that the expressive power of the two models is the same.

The last section briefly introduces denotational operators for prioritized nondeterminism and prioritized asynchrony, in terms of event structures and their counterparts in terms of causal trees. The latter helps in defining a causality-based, branching time operational semantics, given in the SOS style, for concurrent languages with priority, omitted here because of lack of space. The operational and denotational semantics in the other classes are recovered easily, by factoring the causality-based semantics with the obvious counterparts of the axioms characterizing the forgetful functors from **CT** to **ST**, **MOL**, and **TL**.

2 Prime Event Structures

We assume that the reader is familiar with basic domain theory; we only recall that a poset $(P, \leq)$ is a *Scott domain* if P is consistently complete and algebraic. The order structure we are interested in is a particular kind of Scott domains; it is a finitary, coherent, prime algebraic poset, that we will simply call a *domain*.

The notion we recall from the literature is that of a prime event structure [NPW81, Win87] (we will often omit the attribute prime). They form a well-studied semantic model for true concurrency in the branching-time approach.

An event structure $\mathcal{E} = \langle E, \leq, \# \rangle$ consists of a poset $(E, \leq)$ and an irreflexive relation $\# \subseteq E \times E$ of conflict (disjoint from $\leq$) such that

(i) E is a countable set of events,

(ii) for every $e \in E$, e is *finitely preceded*, i.e., $\{e' \mid e' \leq e\}$ is finite,

(iii) the conflict relation is *hereditary*, i.e., $e\#e' \leq e'' \Rightarrow e\#e''$, for every $e, e', e'' \in E$.

One usually calls *events* the elements of E and says that e' causes e if $e' \leq e$; we use $e \geq e'$ iff $e' \leq e$. Another derived relation is the concurrency relation $co = E \times E \setminus (\leq \cup \geq \cup \#)$: two events are *concurrent* if they are not related in either relation.

Given a set of events X, the sets of the minimal events, denoted $\min(X)$, is defined as follows:

$$\min(X) = \{e \in X \mid (e' \in X \wedge e' \leq e) \Rightarrow e = e'\},$$

A subset $X \subseteq E$ is a *configuration* when it satisfies the following conditions:

- X is a *cone*, i.e., $\forall x \in X. \forall y \in E. y \leq x \Rightarrow y \in X$.

- X is *conflict-free*, i.e., $X \times X \cap \# = \emptyset$.

Conf$(\mathcal{E})$ denotes the set of configurations of E.

Another way of characterizing a cone is through the notion of *securing sequence*. An event e is secured in X if there exists a sequence $e_0 e_1 \ldots e_n$ of events in X such that $e_n = e$ and $e_i \in \min(E \setminus \{e_0, e_1, \ldots e_{i-1}\})$. A set X is a cone if for all e in X, e is secured in X.

Since a principal configuration $\downarrow e = \{e' \in E \mid e' \leq e\}$ is contained into another configuration X if and only if $e \in X$, every configuration is the union ($= \sup$ in **Conf**$(\mathcal{E})$) of the principal configurations contained in it. When ordered by inclusion, **Conf**$(\mathcal{E})$ is a domain, where the complete primes are the principal configurations. We are now in a position to state the representation theorem for prime event structures [NPW81].

Theorem 2.1 *If $\mathcal{E}$ is a prime event structure, then* **Conf**$(\mathcal{E})$ *is a domain. Moreover any domain $\mathcal{D}$ is of the form* **Conf**$(\mathcal{E})$ *for some event structure $\mathcal{E}$.*

The event structure $\mathcal{E}$ mentioned in the statement above is built on the set of complete prime elements of $\mathcal{D}$, with the induced order and with the conflict relation defined by $p\#q$ if $\neg \exists x \in \mathcal{D} \, (p \leq x \wedge q \leq x)$. Note that two events are set concurrent if and only if they may occur in any order.

When events carry labels over an alphabet Σ, we obtain labelled event structures, i.e., quadruples of the form $\mathcal{E} = \langle E, \leq, \#, \ell \rangle$, where $\ell : E \longrightarrow \Sigma$.

3 Some useful categories

In this section we describe some categories which we will use in order to relate some classical models of concurrency. As anticipated in the introduction, we will consider a representative for each class of process behaviour arising from the combination of the interleaving/causality-based and linear/branching time parameters. Hoare's traces are the representative for interleaving, linear time models, and describe the behaviour of a process as a set of sequences of event labels. Then, synchronization trees are considered for the interleaving, branching time case. Adding a causality relation on the sequence of events of a run yields mixed ordering of events, the representative of causality-based, linear time models. Finally, we consider causal trees, that are synchronization trees enriched with a causality information as our last model. Actually, in any model we index the runs of a process, in order to distinguish those that are represented in the same way. For example, a process that may perform in two different runs the same sequence of events labelled, say, α and β is rendered in our interleaving, linear representative as $\{\langle 0, \alpha\beta \rangle, \langle 1, \alpha\beta \rangle\}$. Similarly, the two mixed orderings of events it originates carry indexes. In the branching time representatives, indexes are attached to paths of trees. We assume in the sequel a fixed alphabet Σ. The letter J, possibly with subscripts, will be always used to denote sets of indexes.

We first give a categorical structure to multi-sets of Hoare's traces.

Definition 3.1 *The category* **TL** *of sequences on Σ has as objects extent functions $J_S \xrightarrow{S} \Sigma^*$. Morphisms from S to S' are given by maps*

$$f : J_S \longrightarrow J_{S'}$$

such that $S(j)$ is a prefix of $S'(f(j))$.

The next definition is a categorical version of synchronization trees, defined on top of traces by providing a "glueing" function that identifies part of the common prefix of two traces.

Definition 3.2 *The category* **ST** *of synchronization trees labelled on Σ has as objects pairs $T = \langle e_T, g_T \rangle$, where e_T is an extent function $J_T \xrightarrow{e_T} \Sigma^*$, and g_T is a glueing function $g_T : J_T \times J_T \longrightarrow \Sigma^*$ satisfying*

$$g_T(j_1, j_2) = g_T(j_2, j_1)$$
$$g_T(j_1, j_2) \leq e_T(j_1), e_T(j_2)$$
$$g_T(j_1, j_2) \wedge g_T(j_2, j_3) \leq g_T(j_1, j_3) \; \textit{(triangular inequality)}$$

where $\leq$ denotes the prefix ordering and $\wedge$ denotes the respective meet operation.

Morphisms $T \longrightarrow T'$ are functions $f : J_T \longrightarrow J_{T'}$ which increase extent and glueing, i.e.,

$$e_T(j) \leq e_{T'}(f(j))$$
$$g_T(j_1, j_2) \leq g_{T'}(f(j_1), f(j_2)).$$

Technically speaking, the above is equivalent to defining a *symmetric category enriched over a bicategory*, introduced by R.F.C. Walters in [Wal82] and applied to concurrency in [KLP90]. However, we will not need the full bicategorical machinery in our treatment. Note also that the morphisms we define are slightly more general than functors: indeed, they are functors into the Cauchy-completion (in the sense of Lawvere [Law74]) of the codomain.

We now recall the notion of labelled mixed orderings of events, and then we define the category of their languages as the representative for the causality-based, linear time models. We will use an extended alphabet $\Sigma \times \mathbf{Pfin}(\mathbf{N})$ (where $\mathbf{Pfin}(\mathbf{N})$ denotes the finite parts of the natural numbers): in each label $\langle \sigma, K \rangle$, the set of natural numbers K specifies the causes of σ, and it is interpreted as a set of backwards pointers to the preceding labels. These pointers encode a partial ordering under obvious consistency conditions (they must point to some labels, and they must reflect transitivity of causality).

When dealing with these strings, we will write

$$\langle \sigma_0, K_0 \rangle \langle \sigma_1, K_1 \rangle \cdots \langle \sigma_n, K_n \rangle \trianglelefteq \langle \sigma'_0, K'_0 \rangle \langle \sigma'_1, K'_1 \rangle \cdots \langle \sigma'_{n'}, K'_{n'} \rangle$$

iff $n \leq n'$, and $\sigma_j = \sigma'_j$, $K_j \subseteq K'_j$ for all $0 \leq j \leq n$.

Definition 3.3 *The category* **MO** *of* mixed ordering labelled on Σ *has as objects* M *strings in the alphabet* $\Sigma \times \mathbf{Pfin}(\mathbf{N})$ *satisfying the following conditions: if*

$$M = \langle \sigma_0, K_0 \rangle \langle \sigma_1, K_1 \rangle \cdots \langle \sigma_n, K_n \rangle,$$

then

- *for all* $p \in K_j$, $0 < p \leq j$ *(pointers are well-defined), and*

- *if* $p \in K_j$, $q \in K_{j-p}$ *then* $p + q \in K_j$ *(transitivity of causality).*

There is a (unique) morphism $M \longrightarrow M'$ *if* $M \trianglelefteq M'$.

This definition is equivalent to specify a finite, totally ordered set which is labelled on Σ and endowed with a partial ordering which is contained in the total one. Morphisms are then inclusions which preserve both orders and have a prefix of the target as image.

Note that the preservation of one of the orders does not imply in general the preservation of the other one. If you consider a map whose source has the trivial partial ordering (i.e., the identity relation), any set map will preserve this ordering, but could not preserve the total one. On the other hand, a map whose target has the trivial partial ordering cannot preserve a non-trivial partial ordering.

Definition 3.4 *The category* **MOL** *of languages of mixed ordering labelled on Σ has as objects functions* $J_O \xrightarrow{O} \mathrm{Obj}(\mathbf{MO})$. *Morphisms* $O \longrightarrow O'$ *are defined by a function* $f : J_O \longrightarrow J_{O'}$ *such that* $O(j) \trianglelefteq O'(f(j))$.

The representative for causality-based, branching time models we choose is that of causal trees. The present definition is formulated in terms of glueing of mixed orderings.

Definition 3.5 *The category* **CT** *of* causal trees labelled on Σ *has as objects pairs* $C = \langle e_C, g_C \rangle$, *where* e_C *is an extent function* $J_C \xrightarrow{e_C} \mathrm{Obj}(\mathbf{MOL})$ *and* g_C *is a glueing function* $g_C : J_C \times J_C \longrightarrow \mathrm{Obj}(\mathbf{MOL})$ *satisfying*

$$
\begin{aligned}
g_C(j_1, j_2) &= g_C(j_2, j_1) \\
g_C(j_1, j_2) &\leq e_C(j_1), e_C(j_2) \\
g_C(j_1, j_2) \wedge g_C(j_2, j_3) &\leq g_C(j_1, j_3) \ \textit{(triangular inequality)}
\end{aligned}
$$

Morphisms $C \longrightarrow C'$ *are functions*

$$f : J_C \longrightarrow J_{C'}$$

such that

$$e_T(j) \trianglelefteq e_{T'}(f(j))$$
$$g_T(j_1, j_2) \trianglelefteq g_{T'}(f(j_1), f(j_2)).$$

The above four main categories are related by a number of forgetful functors, which have right and left adjoints. There is clearly a forgetful functor **ST** $\longrightarrow$ **TL** which forgets the glueing information contained in a tree, and a forgetful functor **MOL** $\longrightarrow$ **TL** which forgets the causal information. Note that the two causally independent events described by the mixed ordering $\langle \alpha, \emptyset \rangle \langle \beta, \emptyset \rangle$ originate a single trace $\alpha\beta$, thus reflecting our intuition about priority. Instead, if we take partial orderings in place of mixed ones, the two traces $\alpha\beta$ and $\beta\alpha$ are obtained by forgetting the causal relation.

The left adjoint to the forgetful functor **ST** $\longrightarrow$ **TL** makes a tree out of a trace language by specifying no glueing, while the right adjoint adds the maximum glueing. Formally,

Proposition 3.1 *The forgetful functor* $U : $ **ST** $\longrightarrow$ **TL** *has a right and a left adjoint* R *and* L, *defined by*

$$e_{L(S)}(j) = e_{R(S)}(j) = S(j)$$
$$g_{L(S)}(j_1, j_2) = \varepsilon$$
$$g_{R(S)}(j_1, j_2) = S(j_1) \wedge S(j_2)$$

The left adjoint to the forgetful functor **MOL** $\longrightarrow$ **TL** adds no causal information, while the right adjoint adds all the possible causal information. Formally,

Proposition 3.2 *The forgetful functor* $U : $ **MOL** $\longrightarrow$ **TL** *has a right and a left adjoint* R *and* L. *For any object* $S \in$ **TL**, *if* $S(j) = \sigma_0\sigma_1 \cdots \sigma_n$ *they are defined by*

$$L(S)(j) = \langle \sigma_0, \emptyset \rangle \langle \sigma_1, \emptyset \rangle \cdots \langle \sigma_n, \emptyset \rangle$$
$$R(S)(j) = \langle \sigma_0, \emptyset \rangle \langle \sigma_1, \{1\} \rangle \cdots \langle \sigma_n, \{1, 2, \ldots, n\} \rangle$$

Causal trees have two trivial forgetful functors on **MOL** and **ST**: the first one forgets the conflict information, while the second one forgets the causal information (also this two functors have obvious left and right adjoints). It is easy to check that we have indeed a commutative diagram

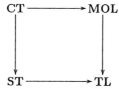

of forgetful functors. The obvious question is if this diagram is a pullback, i.e., if, given a tree (providing conflict information) plus a mixed ordering language (providing causal information) which describe the same set of paths, we can rebuild uniquely a causal tree that expresses concisely all the information.

As it stands, the diagram is not a pullback, as the following example shows: take two paths $\langle 0, \alpha\beta\gamma \rangle$ and $\langle 1, \alpha\beta\delta \rangle$ with $g(0,1) = \alpha\beta$. Consider then the mixed ordering language

$$\{\langle 0, \langle \alpha, \emptyset \rangle\langle \beta, \emptyset \rangle\langle \gamma, \emptyset \rangle \rangle, \langle 1, \langle \alpha, \emptyset \rangle\langle \beta, \{1\} \rangle\langle \delta, \emptyset \rangle \rangle\}.$$

There is no obvious way to turn this pair into a causal tree, because the causality information specified by the mixed ordering language contradicts the conflict information given by the tree (indeed, the glueing information of the tree says that the two observation were *completely coincident in the first two steps*, so that we could not *observe different causal relations*).

However, the pullback $\mathbf{ST} \times_{\mathbf{TL}} \mathbf{MOL}$ has a strict relation with $\mathbf{CT}$, because the functor $\mathbf{CT} \longrightarrow \mathbf{ST} \times_{\mathbf{TL}} \mathbf{MOL}$ induced by the universal property of the pullback sends a causal tree to the pair given by the underlying Σ-labelled tree, and by the mixed ordering language specified by its extent function. Since a causal tree is completely defined by these data, the mapping is injective.

Moreover, this functor has two adjoints, which deal with pairs of mixed orderings which have a different causal information in the initial segment glued by g_C. When such a conflict occurs, the right adjoint takes the *intersection* of the two causal orders. Intuitively, the extra causal information is considered spurious, because another run sharing the same prefix does not show it. On the contrary, the left adjoint takes the *least order generated by the union* of the two causal orderings. In this case, the extra information is considered valid, as if it were "skipped" while representing one run.

Theorem 3.1 $\mathbf{CT}$ *is a reflective and coreflective subcategory of* $\mathbf{ST} \times_{\mathbf{TL}} \mathbf{MOL}$.

Note that the two adjoints behave well with respect to objects of $\mathbf{ST} \times_{\mathbf{TL}} \mathbf{MOL}$ which are image of the inclusion functor from $\mathbf{CT}$. This condition simply means that no glueing is made of labels of mixed orderings reporting inconsistent information. When this is the case, the left and the right adjoints do coincide, and re-construct a causal tree isomorphic to the original one.

The forgetful functors of the previous commutative diagram can be described algebraically, when trees are represented as algebras generated by the empty tree, prefixing and summation (of course, two new categories should be defined for trees, equivalent to $\mathbf{CT}$ and $\mathbf{ST}$). It is well-known that passing from a branching time representation to a linear one is expressed by the axiom

$$\lambda \cdot (Z + Z') = \lambda \cdot Z + \lambda \cdot Z',$$

for any kind of label λ. Of course, when $\lambda \in \Sigma$, we get an algebraic characterization of the forgetful functor $\mathbf{ST} \longrightarrow \mathbf{TL}$, while the one $\mathbf{CT} \longrightarrow \mathbf{MOL}$ is captured when $\lambda \in \Sigma \times \mathbf{Pfin}(\mathbf{N})$. Instead, in order to forget causality one can use the axiom

$$\langle \sigma, K \rangle \cdot Z = \langle \sigma, K' \rangle \cdot Z,$$

that, when Z is instantiated to a (causal) tree, characterizes the forgetful functor $\mathbf{CT} \longrightarrow \mathbf{ST}$, and that describes the forgetful functor $\mathbf{MOL} \longrightarrow \mathbf{TL}$, when Z is a mixed ordering.

In our setting, it is also straightforward to axiomatize the obvious forgetful functor from mixed orderings to pomsets, that discards the generation ordering and enforces the assumption that concurrent events may occur in any order. The following equation expresses precisely this fact:

$$\langle \sigma, K \rangle \langle \rho, K' + 1 \rangle M = \langle \rho, K' \rangle \langle \sigma, K + 1 \rangle M.$$

4   Adding Priorities to Event Structures

Nondeterminism is a powerful notion which permits to have compact descriptions of systems with a large number of details which, when taken into account, may turn it into a deterministic systems. Similarly, we see priority as a tool for abstracting from complex relations among events that are visible only when the description of the system is given at a low level. As a matter of fact, these relations have mainly to do with a combination of temporal constraints and a shared use of limited resources. Almost all these details may be ignored when compactly describing a system at a high level, except for those concerning the common resources. Priority gives an obvious discipline for breaking the tie between conflicting events. Instead, when two events are considered concurrent at a high level, priority imposes on them a timing order, but *not* a causality one; if unfortunately the timing order is violated, the prioritized event will never occur.

As an example, consider Pierpaolo and Roberto who wish to take the same plane, but only the latter has a reservation. So, Roberto has priority over Pierpaolo, who is standing by. If both are at the airport in time and a single seat is free, Roberto gets it. Abstractly, this situation is represented by a prioritized conflict between the events *Roberto-flies* and *Pierpaolo-flies*. Instead, if there are seats enough, first Roberto and then Pierpaolo get their places (and no causal relation holds between the two events). If however Roberto is not at the check-in desk in time, while Pierpaolo is there, only the latter is accomodated and the former will never have a seat on that flight (Sebastiano has wings...).

The main aim of this section is the extension of the model of prime event structures in which a priority relation, i.e. a partial ordering $\ll$ between events is accomodated smoothly. The only constraints on $\ll$ are that it does not interfere with $\leq$ and it should enjoy the property of being a finitely preceding relation. Formally, we have the following.

Definition 4.1 *A prioritized labelled event structure (ples, for short) is a quintuple* $\mathcal{E} = \langle E, \leq, \#, \ll, \ell \rangle$ *where:*

- $\mathcal{E}' = \langle E, \leq, \#, \ell \rangle$ *is an event structure (its associated prime event structure),*

- $\ll$ *is a partial ordering on E such that*

  (i) $\ll \cap \geq = \{ \langle e, e \rangle \mid e \in E \}$,

  (ii) *for every $e \in E$, e is finitely prioritized, i.e., $\{ e' \mid e' \ll e \}$ is finite.*

According to the above intuition, if $e \ll e'$ (e has priority on e') and $e \# e'$, whenever both are enabled e is chosen and e' is discarded; if instead only e' is enabled, then it may be executed. When $e \ll e'$ and e *co* e', whenever both are enabled e is executed first and e' is delayed; if instead only e' is enabled, then it may be executed, but its occurrence prevents e to be executed, even if enabled later on. Therefore, the configurations of prioritized labelled event structures, called *pri*-configurations, require a stronger version of cone. The additional constraint takes into account the priority relation. Let us first consider two simple examples.

Example 4.1 *The ples in Figure 1.a) represents two independent events, α and β, where β has priority over α. Its intended poset of pri-configurations is given in b); note that the unique configuration which is not a pri-one is $\{\alpha\}$. In Figure 1.c) we have another ples; all of its configurations are pri-configurations, but there is no arc from $\{\gamma\}$ to $\{\alpha, \gamma\}$, due to the priority of β over α.*

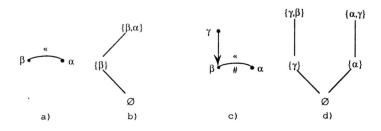

Figure 1: Posets of pri-configurations for two simple ples's

We need an auxiliary definition. Given a ples and a set X of events, let pri-min(X) be the set of the events in it which are minimal w.r.t. both the causality and priority relations, i.e.,

$$\text{pri-min}(X) = \{e \in X \mid (e' \in X \wedge e' \leq e) \Rightarrow e = e'\} \cap$$
$$\{e \in X \mid (e' \in X \wedge e' \ll e) \Rightarrow e = e'\}.$$

Definition 4.2 *Given the ples $\mathcal{E} = \langle E, \leq, \#, \ll, \ell \rangle$, a subset $X \subseteq E$ and an event $e \in X$, we say that e is* pri-secured *in X if there exists a sequence (often called a* pri-proof*) $e_0 e_1 \ldots e_n$ of events in X such that $e_n = e$ and $e_i \in pri\text{-}min(E \setminus \{e_0, e_1, \ldots e_{i-1}\})$.*

As an example, consider the pri-configuration $\{\alpha, \beta\}$ in Figure 1.b); there is a unique pri-securing sequence of α in it, namely $\beta\alpha$. In the pri-configuration $\{\alpha, \gamma\}$ in Figure 1.d), both $\alpha\gamma$ and γ are pri-proofs of γ; instead $\gamma\alpha$ is not a pri-proof for α. (Note that there is no need to introduce infinite pri-proofs, because the causality and priority relations are finitely preceded.)

Definition 4.3 *Given the ples $\mathcal{E} = \langle E, \leq, \#, \ll, \ell \rangle$, a subset $X \subseteq E$ is a* pri-configuration *if the following hold:*

(i) X is conflict-free, and

(ii) $\forall e \in X. e$ is pri-secured in X.

Let **Pconf**($\mathcal{E}$) *be the family of the pri-configurations of $\mathcal{E}$.*

Obviously, every pri-configuration of a ples is also a configuration of its associated les. The *vice versa* does not hold, as shown in Figure 1.*b*). Also, Figure 1.*d*) shows that the partial ordering on pri-configurations is contained in set inclusion. Indeed, an event can be added to a pri-configuration X, if it belongs to pri-min$(E \setminus X)$ and if, additionally, it has no priority over the elements of X.

Definition 4.4 *Let* $X, X \cup \{e\} \in \mathbf{Pconf}(\mathcal{E})$. *Define* $X \prec X \cup \{e\}$ *if*

(*i*) $e \in pri\text{-}min(E \setminus X)$ *and*

(*ii*) $\forall e' \in pri\text{-}min(E \setminus X)$, $e \not\ll e'$.

Finally, let $\sqsubseteq$ *be the reflexive, transitive closure of* $\prec$, *i.e.,* $\sqsubseteq = \prec^*$.

Note that for all pri-configurations $X \in \mathbf{Pconf}(\mathcal{E})$, $\emptyset \sqsubseteq X$.

Example 4.2 *Consider the ples and its poset of configurations depicted in Figure 2. In this case, several configurations (e.g., $\{\beta, \delta\}$) are not pri-ones, but $\sqsubseteq = \subseteq$. This is no more the case for the ples in Figure 3. After the execution of the event ρ, there is only one pri-minimal event, namely α, hence $\{\rho\} \not\sqsubseteq \{\beta, \rho\}$. Condition (ii) above makes $\{\beta, \rho\} \not\sqsubseteq \{\beta, \rho, \alpha\}$, because α cannot be executed after the execution of the less prioritized event β.*

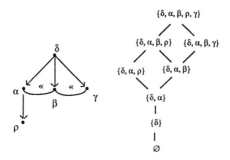

Figure 2: A prioritized event structure and its intended poset of configurations. Note that $\alpha \ll \gamma$, by transitivity of $\ll$.

Theorem 4.1 *The partially ordered set* $\mathcal{F} = \langle \mathbf{Pconf}(\mathcal{E}), \sqsubseteq \rangle$ *is finitary, coherent and prime algebraic, i.e., a domain.*

Proof. (Sketch) Coherence is easy to establish, because pri-proofs are preserved under union of compatible configurations. The poset is finitary because both causality and priority relations are finitely preceded. Prime algebraicity requires to resort to the easier fact that $\mathcal{D} = \langle \mathbf{Pconf}(\mathcal{E}), \subseteq \rangle$ is a domain, too. Actually, given a pri-configuration X, for every P complete prime in $\mathcal{D}$, $P \subseteq X$, there exists a Q complete prime in $\mathcal{F}$, $Q \sqsubseteq X$, such that $P \subseteq Q$. $\square$

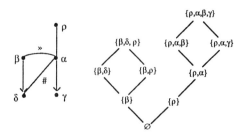

Figure 3: A prioritized event structure and its intended poset of pri-configurations. Note that no arc connects $\{\rho\}$ to $\{\beta, \rho\}$, nor $\{\beta, \rho\}$ to $\{\rho, \alpha, \beta\}$.

The above theorem permits to build a prime event structure from the domain of pri-configurations of a prioritized one, by applying the construction of the representation theorem. However, the relevant information about the causal independence of temporal dependent events is lost. Indeed, from the domain in Figure 1.b), we get the prime event structure in Figure 4.a), in which the priority relation has been tranformed in a causal one. From the domain in Figure 1.d) one obtains the les in Figure 4.b), where the original event γ has been duplicated, because γ and α cannot occur in any order, although independent (firing γ first, excludes α to occur). As last example, consider the les in Figure 4.c), originated from the domain in Figure 3. Note that the original event β has been duplicated: one of the new events is in conflict with α, the other is caused by α.

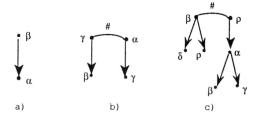

Figure 4: Prime event structures obtained from the domains of pri-configurations of the ples's in Figure 1.b), 1.d) and 3, respectively.

5 Relating Causal Trees and Prioritized LES

It is easy to associate to an event structure a causal tree by suitably labelling the unfolding of its domain of configurations. Here we define an adjunction between the categories of causal trees and prioritized event structures, as defined below.

Definition 5.1 *The category* **PLES** *has as objects prioritized labelled event structures and as morphisms maps $f : E \longrightarrow E'$ which preserve causality and labelling, and which* *induce a map* $\mathbf{Pconf}(\mathcal{E}) \longrightarrow \mathbf{Pconf}(\mathcal{E}')$ *(by direct image) preserving the bottom and* $\prec$.

Note that these maps may identify conflicting events with the same label.

Now we turn to the definition of the **Unf** functor, which unfolds a ples $\mathcal{E}$ to a causal tree: recall that for all $X, X' \in \mathbf{Pconf}(\mathcal{E})$, if $X \prec X'$ then $X' = X \cup \{e\}$. Thus, the set of finite $\prec$-paths starting from the bottom of the domain of pri-configurations gives us the indexing set J of the tree $\mathbf{Unf}(\mathcal{E})$; each index is mapped to the string of labels of the events occurring along the path paired with backpointers to their causes. The glueing function is given by $g(j_1, j_2) = j_1 \wedge j_2$ (i.e., the greatest common subpath of j_1 and j_2).

Given a ples morphism $f : \mathcal{E} \longrightarrow \mathcal{E}'$, we have to show it induces a causal tree morphism $\mathbf{Unf}(f) : \mathbf{Unf}(\mathcal{E}) \longrightarrow \mathbf{Unf}(\mathcal{E}')$. Each path in $\mathbf{Pconf}(\mathcal{E})$ is given by a sequence of pri-configurations $\emptyset \prec X_1 \prec X_2 \prec \ldots \prec X_n$, which is mapped on a sequence $f(\emptyset) = \emptyset \prec f(X_1) \prec f(X_2) \prec \ldots \prec f(X_n)$, defining a path labelled in the same way (possibly with more causes) because $\prec$, $\leq$ and labelling are preserved. The glueing increases because f is a function.

Theorem 5.1 Unf *has a left adjoint* **L**.

Proof. The action of **L** on the objects of **CT** is rather simple: each arc of the tree (which can be identified *via* a pair $\langle j, k \rangle$, where j belongs to the indexing set of the tree and k is a natural number expressing the depth of the arc in the tree; note that many pairs correspond to a single arc because of glueing) is an event; the back pointers along each path induces the causality ordering of the ples, the total ordering of the path induces the priority ordering and two arcs on different paths are always in conflict.

Given a tree morphism $f : C \longrightarrow C'$, the corresponding morphism on ples $\mathbf{L}(f) : \mathbf{L}(C) \longrightarrow \mathbf{L}(C')$ is defined by $\langle j, k \rangle \mapsto \langle f(j), k \rangle$ (the triangular inequality guarantees that $\mathbf{L}(f)$ is well defined). The reader can check that this morphism is an arrow of **PLES**.

In order to show that the just decribed constructions define a left adjoint **L**, we build a universal arrow for each causal tree C, i.e., a tree morphism

$$C \longrightarrow \mathbf{Unf}(\mathbf{L}(C))$$

which factors bijectively and naturally all morphisms $\mathbf{L}(C) \longrightarrow \mathcal{E}$, for any prioritized event structure $\mathcal{E}$.

Since each finite configuration $X \in \mathbf{Pconf}(\mathbf{L}(C))$ is of the form $\{\langle j, 0 \rangle, \langle j, 1 \rangle, \ldots, \langle j, n \rangle\}$, with $n < |e_C(j)|$ (for $n = -1$ we get the empty configuration), and since

$$\{\langle j, 0 \rangle, \langle j, 1 \rangle, \ldots, \langle j, n-1 \rangle\} \prec \{\langle j, 0 \rangle, \langle j, 1 \rangle, \ldots, \langle j, n \rangle\},$$

we can define the universal arrow $C \longrightarrow \mathbf{Unf}(\mathbf{L}(C))$ as

$$j \mapsto \emptyset, \{\langle j, 0 \rangle\}, \{\langle j, 0 \rangle, \langle j, 1 \rangle\}, \ldots, \{\langle j, 0 \rangle, \langle j, 1 \rangle, \ldots \langle j, |e_C(j)| - 1 \rangle\}.$$

For any morphism $f : C \longrightarrow \mathbf{Unf}(\mathcal{E})$, if

$$j \mapsto \emptyset \prec X_1^j \prec X_2^j \prec \ldots \prec X_n^j$$

then we define the associated morphism $g : \mathbf{L}(C) \longrightarrow \mathcal{E}$ by letting

$$\langle j, k \rangle \mapsto X_k^j \setminus X_{k-1}^j.$$

It is then easy to show that the composition with the universal arrow induces a natural bijection. $\square$

Note that **L** is an inclusion. Thus,

Theorem 5.2 CT *is a coreflective subcategory of* **PLES**.

6   Semantic Priority Operators

We claim that the new model of prioritized labelled event structures can be used quite profitably for giving denotational semantics to process algebras enriched with operators of priority. Furthermore, with the "equivalent" model of causal trees we equip these prioritized constructs with an inductive definition in denotational (and operational) styles.

For the sake of brevity, we consider the semantics of a prioritized nondeterministic choice and of a prioritized parallel composition,[1] only. We introduce a family of semantic operators of the form $\mathcal{E}_0 +_{\mathcal{R}} \mathcal{E}_1$ and $\mathcal{E}_0||_{\mathcal{R}}\mathcal{E}_1$, respectively. The index $\mathcal{R}$ is a partial ordering on the labels of events that induces a priority relation $\ll$ on the events of $\mathcal{E}_0$ and $\mathcal{E}_1$. Note that a notion of "dynamic" priority can be expressed easily through the indexing. When $\mathcal{R} = \emptyset$, the standard choice and parallel operators are recovered. This approach is in the line of [Jan87, CH89, BK92]; a priority determined by textual position, similar to the one used in PRIALT of occam [JG88, Cam89], can be accomodated smoothly.

The operations $\mathcal{E}_0 +_{\mathcal{R}} \mathcal{E}_1$ and $\mathcal{E}_0||_{\mathcal{R}}\mathcal{E}_1$ over ples's are defined as follows, assuming $\mathcal{E}_i = \langle E_i, \leq_i, \#_i, \ll_i, \ell_i \rangle$, $i = 0, 1$, with $E_0 \cap E_1 = \emptyset$:

pri-sum: $\mathcal{E}_0 +_{\mathcal{R}} \mathcal{E}_1 \overset{\text{def}}{=} \langle E_0 \cup E_1, \leq_0 \cup \leq_1, \#, \ll, \ell_1 \cup \ell_2 \rangle$ where

$$\# = \#_0 \cup \#_1 \cup (E_0 \times E_1) \cup (E_1 \times E_0)$$

$$\ll = \ll_0 \ \cup \ \ll_1 \ \cup \{\langle e, e' \rangle \mid \langle \ell_i(e), \ell_{i+1 \bmod 2}(e') \rangle \in \mathcal{R}, \ i = 0, 1\}.$$

pri-parallel: $\mathcal{E}_0||_{\mathcal{R}}\mathcal{E}_1 \overset{\text{def}}{=} \langle E_0 \cup E_1, \leq_0 \cup \leq_1, \#, \ll, \ell_0 \cup \ell_1 \rangle$, where

$$\# = \#_0 \cup \#_1$$

$$\ll = \ll_0 \cup \ll_1 \cup \{\langle e, e' \rangle \mid \langle \ell_i(e), \ell_{i+1 \bmod 2}(e') \rangle \in \mathcal{R}, \ i = 0, 1\}.$$

Moreover, prioritized choice and parallel operators can be defined directly over causal trees, thus facilitating the definition of an operational SOS semantics for a concurrent language equipped with priority (see [DD89] for other usual semantic operations).

Let $\mathcal{R} \subseteq \Sigma \times \Sigma$ be a priority relation; let I and J be disjoint sets of indexes; and let $T = \sum_I \langle \sigma_i, K_i \rangle \cdot T_i$ and $U = \sum_J \langle \nu_j, H_j \rangle \cdot U_j$ be causal trees, represented in algebraic style. Finally, let $I' = \{i \in I \mid \neg \exists j \in J. \ \langle \nu_j, \sigma_i \rangle \in \mathcal{R}$ and $J' = \{j \in J \mid \neg \exists i \in I. \ \langle \sigma_i, \nu_j \rangle \in \mathcal{R}\}$. Then, the operators of prioritized nondeterministic choice, $\oplus_{\mathcal{R}}$, and of asynchronous parallel composition, $\backslash\backslash_{\mathcal{R}}$, are defined as follows.

$$T \oplus_{\mathcal{R}} U = \sum_{I'} \langle \sigma_i, K_i \rangle \cdot T_i \ + \ \sum_{J'} \langle \nu_j, H_j \rangle \cdot U_j$$

and

$$T \backslash\backslash_{\mathcal{R}} U = \sum_{I'} \langle \sigma_i, K_i \rangle \cdot (T_i \backslash\backslash_{\mathcal{R}} (\delta(U) \setminus A)) \ + \ \sum_{J'} \langle \nu_j, H_j \rangle \cdot ((\delta(T) \setminus B) \backslash\backslash_{\mathcal{R}} U_j)$$

where

---

[1]Communication is not considered as it is orthogonal to priority, and can be dealt with following the techniques developed for prime event structures, see, e.g., [Vaa89].

- $A = \{\nu_j \mid j \in J,\ \exists i \in I.\langle \nu_j, \sigma_i \rangle \in \mathcal{R}\}$, and $B = \{\sigma_i \mid i \in I,\ \exists j \in J.\langle \sigma_i, \nu_j \rangle \in \mathcal{R}\}$,

- $\delta(T)$ increments all the causes in T pointing behind its root (see [DD89] for details),

- $T \setminus A$ is the usual pruning operation over the set of labels $\langle \sigma, K \rangle$, with $\sigma \in A \subseteq \Sigma$.

Lack of space prevents us from inductively defining the operational semantics of the two operators, in the style of [DD89]. However, the task is easy; we just mention that the constraints expressed by sets I' and J' are reflected by negative premises in the inference rules.

The following proposition states that the above operations on ples's and on causal trees agree in a strong sense. It provides the basis for proving that the causal tree operational semantics and the ples denotational one coincide, up to strong bisimulation.

Proposition 6.1 *Given two ples's $\mathcal{E}_0$ and $\mathcal{E}_1$, the following hold:*

- $\mathrm{Unf}(\mathcal{E}_0) \oplus_{\mathcal{R}} \mathrm{Unf}(\mathcal{E}_1)$ *is isomorphic to* $\mathrm{Unf}(\mathcal{E}_0 +_{\mathcal{R}} \mathcal{E}_1)$,

- $\mathrm{Unf}(\mathcal{E}_0) \backslash\!\backslash_{\mathcal{R}} \mathrm{Unf}(\mathcal{E}_1)$ *is isomorphic to* $\mathrm{Unf}(\mathcal{E}_0 \|_{\mathcal{R}} \mathcal{E}_1)$.

7 Acknowledgements

The authors would like to acknowledge the useful discussions with S. Kasangian and V. Sassone. Pierpaolo Degano was partially supported by C.N.R. project "Progetto finalizzato sistemi informatici e calcolo parallelo" and by project MASK SC1-CT92-00776, founded by C.E.C.. Roberto Gorrieri was partially supported by C.E.C. Esprit Programme Basic Research Action Number 6360 (BROADCAST). The authors were also partially supported by M.U.R.S.T. 40%.

References

[BK92]   E. Best and M. Koutny. Petri net semantics of priority systems. *Theoretical Computer Science*, 96:175–215, 1992.

[Cam89] J. Camilleri. An operational semantics for occam. *International Journal of Parallel Programming*, 18(5), 1989.

[CH89]   R. Cleaveland and M. Hennessy. Priorities in process algebras. In *Proc. LICS '89*, pages 193–202, Edinburgh, 1989.

[DD89]   Ph. Darondeau and P. Degano. Causal trees. In *Proc. 11th Int. Coll. on Automata and Languages ICALP*, number 372 in LNCS, pages 234–248. Springer-Verlag, 1989.

[DD90]   Ph. Darondeau and P. Degano. Causal trees: Interleaving + causality. In *Proc. 18th École de Printemps sur la Semantique de Parallelism*, number 469 in LNCS, pages 239–255. Springer-Verlag, 1990.

[DDM90] P. Degano, R. De Nicola, and U. Montanari. A partial ordering semantics for CCS. *Theoretical Computer Science*, 75:223–262, 1990.

[Hoa85]   C.A.R. Hoare. *Communicating Sequential Processes*. Prentice Hall, Englewood Cliffs, NJ, 1985.

[Jan87]   R. Janicki. A formal semantics of concurrent systems with a priority relation. *Acta Informatica*, 24:33–55, 1987.

[JG88]   G. Jones and M. Goldsmith. *Programming in* occam-2. Prentice-Hall, Englewood Cliffs, NJ, 1988.

[JK91]   R. Janicki and M. Koutny. Invariant semantics with inhibitor arcs. In *Proc. CONCUR '91*, number 527 in LNCS, pages 317–331. Springer-Verlag, 1991.

[KLP90]   S. Kasangian, A. Labella, and A. Pettorossi. Observers, experiments and agents: a comprehensive approach to concurrency. In I. Guessarian, editor, *Semantics of Systems of Concurrent Processes*, number 469 in LNCS. Springer-Verlag, 1990.

[Law74]   F.W. Lawvere. Metric spaces, generalized logic, and closed categories. *Rendiconti Seminario Mat. e Fis. di Milano*, 43:135–166, 1974.

[Mil80]   R. Milner. *A Calculus of Communicating Systems*. Number 92 in LNCS. Springer-Verlag, 1980.

[NPW81]   M. Nielsen, G. Plotkin, and G. Winskel. Petri nets, event structures, and domains, part I. *Theoretical Computer Science*, 13:85–108, 1981.

[Pra86]   V.R. Pratt. Modeling concurrency with partial orders. *International Journal of Parallel Programming*, 15(1):33–71, 1986.

[Roz90]   B. Rozoy. On distributed languages and models for distributed computations. In I. Guessarian, editor, *Semantics of Systems of Concurrent Processes*, number 469 in LNCS, pages 434–456. Springer-Verlag, 1990.

[RT88]   A. Rabinovich and B.A. Trakhtenbrot. Behavior structures and nets. *Fundamenta Informaticae*, 11(4):357–404, 1988.

[SNW]   V. Sassone, M. Nielsen, and G. Winskel. A hierarchy of models for concurrency. Technical report. Draft.

[Vaa89]   F.W. Vaandrager. A simple definition for parallel composition of prime event structures. Technical Report CS-R 8903, CWI, Amsterdam, 1989.

[Wal82]   R.F.C. Walters. Sheaves on sites as Cauchy-complete categories. *Journal of Pure and Applied Algebra*, 24:95–102, 1982.

[Win87]   G. Winskel. Event structures. In *Petri Nets: Applications and Relationships to Other Models of Concurrency, Advances in Petri Nets 1986, Part II*, number 255 in LNCS, pages 325–392. Springer-Verlag, 1987.

Compositionality Results for Different Types of Parameterization and Parameter Passing in Specification Languages

H. Ehrig, Technical University Berlin

R. M. Jimenez, Universitat Politecnica de Catalunya

F. Orejas, Universitat Politecnica de Catalunya

1 Introduction

In the literature on specification several notions of parameterization have been studied. Some of these notions regard parameterizations only at the model level, i.e as functors or parameterized algebras that are used to build data types from other given data types in a well-specified manner. Examples in this sense are the pioneering approach of [TWW 82], where parameterized data types are defined as persistent free functors specified by inclusions of specifications, and the Extended-ML modules [ST 89]. A different approach consists in seeing parameterizations as parametric specification transformations. This view has been taken in [BG 80, Ehc 82], where parameterized specifications are defined as inclusions of specifications and where the transformation associated to parameter passing is "computed" by means of a pushout construction. A rather more general approach along this line can be found in [SW 83, Wir 86], where parameterizations are allowed to be arbitrary λ-expressions built over the ASL specification-building operations and parameter passing is defined as a form of β-reduction.

[EKTWW 84] provided the first synthesis of the two different lines by defining parameterizations both as specifications of parameterized data types and as parametric specification transformations in a compatible manner. However, the results of [EKTWW 84] applied only to the initial framework and to the case where parameterizations are defined as inclusions of specifications (i.e. [TWW 82] and [BG 80, Ehc 82, Li 83]).

Recently, in [SST 90], Sannella, Sokolowski and Tarlecki have studied the general case (i.e. parameterizations defined by arbitrary λ-expressions), within the loose framework, and have found that the two notions of parametric transformation of specifications (from now on, parameterized specifications) and specification of parameterized data types would not only be based on different intuitions, but would also be semantically different. Essentially, their point of view is that parameterized specifications are not proper specifications in the sense that they are not necessarily intended to describe a software unit but a specification transformation, i.e. their aim is to be useful at the specification design level, since they may be seen as user-defined specification-building operations. Conversely, specifications of parameterized data types are true specifications in the sense that are intended to describe (generic) software units. As a consequence the two notions denote different constructions: a parameterized specification denotes a function that maps specifications into specifications (or classes of models into classes of models), whereas a specification of parameterized data types describes a class of "parameterized programs", i.e. functions that map "programs" into "programs" (or models into models). To be more precise, we may consider that a "program" is a specification having a single model (up to isomorphism).

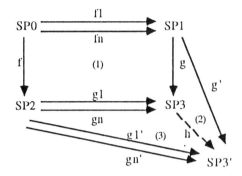

Remarks

1. Note that SP3 is not the colimit object in diagram (1).

2. In the case n = 1 a multiple pushout is a pushout.

3. In the case n = 0 the multiple pushout object SP3 is equal to SP1 with $g = 1_{SP1}$.

As a consequence of the fact that finite coproducts can be constructed using pushouts and initial objects and of the fact that multiple pushouts can be constructed using finite coproducts and pushouts we have:

2.3 Proposition

If SF = (SPEC, Catmod) is a specification frame then **SPEC** has multiple pushouts.

In the same way that amalgamations are the semantic counter-parts of pushouts, we may define multiple amalgamation as the semantic construction associated to multiple pushouts.

2.4 Definition

An indexed category SF has __multiple amalgamation__ if for every multiple pushout as above we have the following properties:

1. For all objects A1 in Catmod(SP1) and all families of objects $A2^* = (A2_1,...,A2_n)$ in Catmod(SP2) and $A0^* = (A0_1,...,A0_n)$ in Catmod(SP0) with $V_{fi}(A1) = A0_i = V_f(A2_i)$, for i = 1,...,n there is a unique object A3 in Catmod(SP3), called multiple amalgamation of A1 and $A2^*$ via $A0^*$, written $A3 = A1 +_{A0*}A2^*$ such that $V_g(A3) = A1$ and $V_{gi}(A3) = A2_i$ for i = 1,...,n.

2. A similar property for morphisms h1, $h2^*$, $h0^*$, defining $h3 = h1 +_{h0*} h2^*$.

Multiple amalgamation is equivalent to the fact that Catmod transforms multiple pushouts in **SPEC** into multiple pullbacks in **CATCAT** (where multiple pullbacks are the dual construction to multiple pushouts). On the other hand, as a consequence of the fact that if (SPEC, Catmod) is a specification frame then Catmod transforms pushouts into pullbacks and initial into terminal objects, we have that:

2.5 Theorem

Specification frames have multiple amalgamation.

Multiple extensions can be constructed using multiple amalgamation, in a similar way as extensions can be constructed using amalgamation [EBCO 91]

2.6 Definition

An indexed category SF has <u>multiple extension</u> if for every multiple pushout in **SPEC** and every strongly multiple persistent mapping F: Catmod(SP0) → Catmod(SP1) w.r.t. (f1,...,fn), i.e. for every A1 in Catmod(SP1) and every i $V_{fi}(F(A1)) = A1$, there is a strongly multiple persistent mapping F^*:Catmod(SP2) → Catmod(SP3) w.r.t. (g1,...,gn) s.t. the following diagram commutes

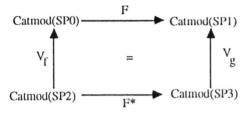

Moreover, if F is a functor then also F^* is a functor.

2.7 Theorem

Specification frames have multiple extension.

3 Basic Specifications and Specification Building Operations

In this section we present the kind of specifications and specification-building operations with which we deal in the rest of the paper. With respect to the specifications, we assume that the logic used for specification is a specification frame, SF = (**SPEC**,Catmod). However, we will not consider that a specification is just an object in **SPEC**. Instead, we will consider that a specification SPC is a pair (SP, C) formed by an object SP in **SPEC** and a set of *constraints* C. Constraints are semantic constructions restricting the possible interpretations of a specification, i.e. a constraint restricts the class of models of a specification to those satisfying the constraint. Different kinds of constraints have been defined and used in the literature [Rei 80, BG 80, SW 82, SW 83, EWT 82, Ehr 81, ON 90, BG 92]. The importance of constraints is a consequence, on the one hand, of the additional expressive power that they provide to specifications and, on the other, because they are the basis of a number of structuring concepts and constructions found in specification languages [BG 80, BG 92, OSC 89].

It can be proved (for details see e.g. [EBCO 91]) that, given a specification frame SF = (**SPEC**,Catmod), the pair SFC = (**SPECC**, CatmodC) is also a specification frame, called <u>induced specification frame with constraints</u>, where **SPECC** is the category of specifications with constraints and CatmodC is the functor that maps every pair (SP, C) to the full subcategory of Catmod(SP) of all models of SP satisfying the constraints in C.

There are mainly two reasons for working with an induced specification frame with constraints instead of with an arbitrary specification frame. The first one is of a methodological nature: we wanted to handle constraints explicitly by one specification-building operation (i.e. **impose**, see below), because some kinds of constraints are a major structuring semantic tool (see [BG80, Rei 80, OSC 89, Bau 91, GB 92]) which, in our opinion, have to be dealt with at the specification language level, rather than considering them embedded in the underlying specification frame. The second reason is of a technical nature: at some points of the paper we need to consider specifications over *unitary* constraints which can be handled more uniformly if we consider that they already belong to the associated logic of constraints. In particular, an unitary constraint is a constraint that restricts a specification to a single model. Being more precise, given a specification SP and a model A in Catmod(SP), the unitary constraint C_A is defined: $\forall B \in$ Catmod(SP) B satisfies C_A iff $B \cong A$

The syntax for writing specifications is given by a set of specification expressions over a set of specification-building operations, i.e. a specification expression is a term built by applying a number of specification-building operations to "constant" specification expressions. As a consequence, every specification expression E denotes a basic specification $[E]_{Spec}$. In particular, expressions are defined as follows:

3.1 Definition

The set of <u>specification expressions</u> over SFC is the least set satisfying:

1. If SP0 $\in$ **SPEC** then SP0 is a specification expression. The specification denoted by SP0 is SP0 together with an empty set of constraints, i.e. $[SP0]_{Spec} = (SP0, \emptyset)$.

2. **impose** C **on** E, where E is a specification expression and C is set of constraints over $[E]_{Spec}$, is a specification expression. In this case $[\textbf{impose } C' \textbf{ on } E]_{Spec} = (SP, C \cup C')$, where $[E]_{Spec} = (SP, C)$.

3. **enrich** E **by** f, where f is a morphism from $[E]_{Spec}$ to a given SPC' in **SPECC**, is a specification expression. In this case, $[\textbf{enrich } E \textbf{ by } f]_{Spec} = SPC'$.

4. E1 $+_{(E0, f1, f2)}$ E2, fi : $[E0]_{Spec} \to [Ei]_{Spec}$ is a morphism in Mor(**SPECC**) ($\forall$ i = 0,...,2) is a specification expression. In this case, $[E1 +_{(E0, f1, f2)} E2]_{Spec} = (SP3, C3)$ defined as the result of the pushout:

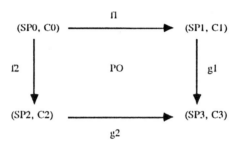

where $[Ei]_{Spec} = (SPi, Ci)$ ($\forall$ i = 0,...,2).

Obviously, at the model level, the meaning of these expressions may be defined by considering the model classes of the specifications denoted by the expressions, i.e. CatmodC($[E]_{Spec}$), but we can also define a model level semantics by providing meaning to all the specification-building operations in terms of operations on the model classes:

3.2 Definition

The <u>semantics at the model level for specification expressions</u> is defined as follows:

1. $[SP0]_{Mod} = Catmod(SP0)$

2. $[\textbf{impose } C' \textbf{ on } E]_{Mod} = \{A \in [E]_{Mod} \,/\, A |= C'\}$.

3. $[\textbf{enrich } E \textbf{ by } f]_{Mod} = CatmodC(SPC')$.

4. $[E1 +_{(E0, f1, f2)} E2]_{Mod} = [E1]_{Mod} +_{[E0]_{Mod}} [E2]_{Mod} = CatmodC(SP3,C3)$

Remarks

1. The two definitions are compatible in the sense that $\text{CatmodC}([E]_{Spec}) = [E]_{Mod}$, for every expression E. This is a consequence of the properties of specification frames.

2. Following the Module Algebra approach [BHK 90] we can consider the specification-building operations as operators of an abstract signature $\Sigma SPEC$ over two sorts (specifications and morphisms). In this sense, specification expressions are just terms in $T_{\Sigma SPEC}$ and the two semantic definitions $[\_]_{Spec}$ and $[\_]_{Mod}$ can be seen just as the definition of two $\Sigma SPEC$-algebras in terms of $SPECC$ and $\text{CatmodC}(SPECC)$, respectively. This fact is used below to define specification expressions over variables, i.e. terms in $T_{\Sigma SPEC}(X)$, and variable substitution.

3. Comparing our specification-building operations, and the ones considered in [SST 90], essentially two differences may be found. The first one is that they consider an operation to close (up to isomorphism) the class of models of a given specification. We do not consider such an operation since we assume (although it is not explicitly stated) that in our framework model classes are already closed up to isomorphism. Actually we think that having the possibility of defining a specification that excludes some isomorphic models is a quite awkward choice, either for the specification frame or for the specification language. The second difference is that they consider a *derive* operation that allows the hiding or forgetting of parts of a specification. Our opinion is that this kind of operation should only be considered in a second layer of a specification language. Being specific, hiding parts of a specification should only be possible through the use of a notion of module with well-defined import and export interfaces describing the "visible" parts of a specification. Actually this is the main feature of modules systems such as the ones found in Extended ML and ACT TWO [ST 89, EM 90].

4 Parameterizations

As said in the introduction, following [SST 90] we consider two kinds of parameterizations: parameterized specifications and specifications of parameterized data types. The main difference is methodological: when designing a software system, specifications of parameterized data types are intended to be descriptions of software units that will eventually "exist" in the system; conversely parameterized specifications are user-defined specification-building operations that are just utilized in the specification design phase. A typical example of a specification of parameterized data types may be the ubiquitous STACK[X] specification, describing generic stacks. Obviously, this specification can be used for building arbitrary stack specifications and, in this sense, can be considered as a parameterized specification. But we can better see STACK[X] as the specification of a generic module for building program units implementing arbitrary stacks. A typical example of a parameterized specification can be the specification COMMUT[X] that, given a specification of a data type including a binary operation, yields as result the parameter specification enriched with the commutativity axiom for that operation. For instance, passing as parameter a specification of Groups would produce as result the specification of Abelian Groups. COMMUT[X] can hardly be seen as the description of a software unit.

As in [SST 90], we consider that parameterizations are defined as arbitrary specification expressions over a specification variable. This generalizes a number of previous approaches (e.g. [TWW 78, BG 80, Ehc 82, EM 85]) where only an enrichment of the parameter specification was allowed. In particular, also as in [SST 90], the notation used is the following one: $\lambda X{:}SPC.E[X]$ denotes a parameterized specification mapping classes of SPC-models into classes of E[X/SPC]-models, where SPC is a specification with constraints, E[X/SPC] is the expression obtained by substituting in E the variable X by SPC, with E[X]∈$T_{\Sigma SPEC}(\{X\})$ (see remark 3.2.2); similarly, ΠX:SPC.E is the specification of a parameterized data type denoting mappings that associate E[X/SPC]-models to SPC-models.

In the rest of the section we study the semantics of both kinds of parameterizations. Moreover we provide two levels of semantics. At the model level, the definitions follow the intuitions discussed above. At the specification level, the definitions can be seen as a form of abstract syntax for the two parameterization mechanisms. This specification level semantics is needed in section 5 for defining the semantics of parameter passing.

In the most simple approaches to parameterization (e.g.[TWW 82, BG 80, Ehc 82, EKTWW 84]) a parameterized specification is seen as an inclusion of specifications, SPC⊆SPC'. This is sometimes slightly generalized to arbitrary morphisms f: SPC → SPC'. However, in our context, the semantics at the specification level of a parameterized specification is going to be defined as a set of morphisms from the formal parameter into the result specification. The intuition for this is that, if parameterized specifications are defined by arbitrary specification-building operations, then the formal parameter specification "may occur" several times inside the body specification. A simple example of this is the λ-expression λX:SPC.(enrich X by f)+(enrich X by f'). More realistic examples can be found easily, especially when dealing with higher-order parameterizations. In this example, the specification level semantics is represented by the following diagram:

$$SPC \underset{f2}{\overset{f1}{\Longrightarrow}} SPC'$$

where SPC' contains two copies of SPC and f1 and f2 are, respectively, two morphisms mapping SPC into each of the copies.

4.1 Definition

Given a parameterized specification λX:SPC.E[X] its semantics at the specification level, [λX:SPC.E[X]]$_{Spec}$, is defined as a triple (SPC, SPC', F), where SPC', usually called the *body specification*, is the specification denoted by E[X/SPC], i.e. [E[X/SPC]]$_{Spec}$ and F is a set of n morphisms, with n≥0, from SPC to SPC', i.e.:

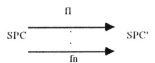

Depending on the form of E (see def. 3.1), [λX:SPC.E[X]]$_{Spec}$ is defined as follows:

1. If E[X]=SP0 then [λX:SPC.E[X]]$_{Spec}$ = (SPC,SP0,Ø)

2. If E[X]=X then [λX:SPC.E[X]]$_{Spec}$ = (SPC,SPC,{id: SPC → SPC})

3. If E[X]=**impose** C **on** E'[X] and [λX:SPC.E'[X]]$_{Spec}$ = (SPC, (SP',C'), F') then [λX:SPC.E[X]]$_{Spec}$ = (SPC,(SP',C'∪C),{i ∘ f: SPC → (SP',C'∪C)/ f∈F'}) where i denotes the inclusion : (SP',C') → (SP',C'∪C).

4. If E[X] = **enrich** E'[X] **by** f, [λX:SPC.E'[X]]$_{Spec}$ = (SPC, SPC', F') and f: SPC'→ SPC" then [λX:SPC.E[X]]$_{Spec}$ = (SPC,SPC",{f ∘ g: SPC → SPC"/ g∈F'}).

5. If $E[X] = E1[X] +_{(E0[X],\ f1,\ f2)} E2[X]$, $[\lambda X{:}SPC.Ei[X]]_{Spec}= (SPC, SPCi, Fi)$ $(0{\leq}i{\leq}2)$ and f1 and f2 are morphisms from SPC0 to SPC1 and SPC2, resp., then $[\lambda X{:}SPC.E[X]]_{Spec}= (SPC,SPC3,F3)$, where F3= {g1∘h1: SPC → SPC3/ h1∈ F1} ∪ {g2∘h2: SPC → SPC3/ h2∈ F2}) where SPC3, g1 and g2 are defined by the following pushout diagram.

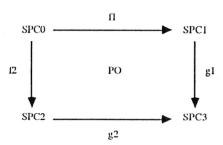

The specification level semantics of $\Pi X{:}SPC.E[X]$ is defined as the one for the corresponding parameterized specification, i.e. $[\Pi X{:}SPC.E[X]]_{Spec} = [\lambda X{:}SPC.E[X]]_{Spec}$

According to the intuitions discussed above, the second level semantics of parameterized specifications is a function mapping model classes into model classes. In particular, given a parameterized specification $\lambda X{:}SPC.E[X]$, this function can be defined, for every class of SPC-models M, as the evaluation at the model level of the expression E over M.

4.2 Definition

Given a parameterized specification $\lambda X{:}SPC.E[X]$, its <u>semantics at the model level</u>, $[\lambda X{:}SPC.E[X]]_{Mod}$, is a function from $2^{CatmodC(SPC)}$ to $2^{CatmodC(E[X/SPC])}$ defined for every M⊆CatmodC(SPC) as the *evaluation* of E over M, denoted E[X/M] (although the abuse of notation), where:

1. If E[X] = SP0 then E[X/M] = CatmodC(SP0)

2. If E[X] = X then E[X/M] = M

3. If E[X] = impose C on E'[X] then E[X/M] = {A∈ E'[X/M] / A⊨ C}.

4. If E[X] = enrich E'[X] by f and f is a morphism from E'[X/SPC] to SPC', then E[X/M] = {A∈CatmodC(SPC') / V_f(A)∈ E'[X/M]}.

5. If $E[X] = E1[X] +_{(E0[X],f1,f2)} E2[X]$, then $E[X/M] = E1[X/M] +_{E0[X/M]} E2[X/M]$

It may be noticed that, due to technical problems, we cannot directly define E[X/M] as the evaluation at the model level of the "constant" expression E[X/impose {C_M} on SPC], i.e. $[E[X/impose \{C_M\}\ on\ SPC]]_{Mod}$, where C_M denotes the constraint that is only satisfied by the models in M. The reason is that if E[X] is (for instance) enrich E'[X] by f, then we know that f is a morphism defined on E'[X/SPC], but not on E[X/impose {C_M} on SPC].

4.3 Proposition

Given $\lambda X{:}SPC.E[X]$, with $[\lambda X{:}SPC.E[X]]_{Spec}=(SPC,SPC',F)$, and M⊆ CatmodC(SPC) we have:

$$[\lambda X{:}SPC.E[X]]_{Mod}(M) = \{A\in CatmodC(SPC') / \forall f\in F\ \ V_f(A)\in M\}$$

4.4 Properties of $[\_]_{Mod}$

For every parameterized specification $\lambda X{:}SPC.E[X]$ we have that:

1. $[\lambda X{:}SPC.E[X]]_{Mod}$ is monotonic, in the sense that for every $M1, M2 \subseteq$ CatmodC(SPC), $M1 \subseteq M2$ implies $[\lambda X{:}SPC.E[X]]_{Mod}(M1) \subseteq [\lambda X{:}SPC.E[X]]_{Mod}(M2)$.

2. In general $[\lambda X{:}SPC.E[X]]_{Mod}$ is not additive, in the sense that for every $M \subseteq$ CatmodC(SPC) $[\lambda X{:}SPC.E[X]]_{Mod}(M) \neq \cup_{A \in M} [\lambda X{:}SPC.E[X]]_{Mod}(\{A\})$.

3. If $[\lambda X{:}SPC.E[X]]_{Spec} = (SPC,SPC',F)$ and $Card(F) \leq 1$ then $[\lambda X{:}SPC.E[X]]_{Mod}$ is additive.

Proof Sketch

The proofs of properties 1 and 3 are trivial. For the second property it is enough to consider the following counter-example. Let SPC and SPC' be the following specifications:

SPC = **sorts** s	SPC' = **sorts** s'
opns a,b	**opns** a',b'

let A and B be two SPC-algebras defined: $A_s = \{0,1\}$, $a_A = 0$, $b_A = 1$ and $B_s = \{0\}$, $a_B = 0 = b_B$ and consider the parameterized specification $\lambda X{:}SPC.X + (\text{enrich } X \text{ by } f)$ where f is the morphism from SPC to SPC' associating s', a' and b' to s, a and b, respectively.

Now, the algebra C defined $C_s = \{0,1\}$, $C_{s'} = \{0\}$, $a_C = 0$, $b_C = 1$, $a'_C = 0 = b'_C$ is in $F(\{A,B\})$ but not in $F(\{A\}) \cup F(\{B\})$, where $F = [\lambda X{:}SPC.X + (\text{enrich } X \text{ by } f)]_{Mod}$. ∎

A similar (though slightly more complex) counter-example can be found in [SST 90]. Now the model level semantics of parameterized data types specifications is defined as the class of all mappings F such that, for every model A, F(A) is in the result of evaluating the parameterization over A.

4.5 Definition

Given a specification of parameterized data types $\Pi X{:}SPC.E[X]$, its semantics at the model level, $[\Pi X{:}SPC.E[X]]_{Mod}$, is the class of all mappings F from CatmodC(SPC) to CatmodC(E[X/SPC]) such that for every $A \in$ CatmodC(SPC), $F(A) \in E[X/\{A\}]$

4.6 Remarks

1. Let $[\Pi X{:}SPC.E[X]]_{Spec}$ be (SPC, SPC', F) if $F \in [\Pi X{:}SPC.E[X]]_{Mod}$ then F is strongly multiple persistent with respect to F, i.e. $\forall A \in$ CatmodC(SPC) and $\forall f \in F$ $V_f \circ F(A) = A$.

2. It may seen also sensible to restrict $[\Pi X{:}SPC.E[X]]_{Mod}$ to the class of "structure-preserving" mappings (i.e. functors) from CatmodC(SPC) to CatmodC(E[X/SPC]), but this restriction has some undesirable consequences that are discussed further in 4.9.

An important issue concerning specifications consists in finding an adequate notion of (internal) correctness. For non-parameterized specification a reasonable and simple correctness condition is consistency, i.e. existence of models. In this sense, a similar condition for specifications of parameterized data types would be asking for $[\Pi X{:}SPC.E[X]]_{Mod} \neq \emptyset$. With respect to parameterized specifications, since they are intended for building specifications, we can base their correctness on their "ability" to build correct specifications. Then, we can define two different correctness conditions: a strong one, if every result of applying the parameterization is consistent, and a weak one, if only some results are consistent.

4.7 Definitions

A parameterized specification $\lambda X{:}SPC.E[X]$ is strongly correct (resp. weakly correct) iff $\forall M \subseteq CatmodC(SPC)$, with $M \neq \varnothing$, $[\lambda X{:}SPC.E[X]]_{Mod}(M) \neq \varnothing$ (resp. $\exists M \subseteq CatmodC(SPC)$ $[\lambda X{:}SPC.E[X]]_{Mod}(M) \neq \varnothing$).

A specification of parameterized data types $\Pi X{:}SPC.E[X]$ is correct iff $[\Pi X{:}SPC.E[X]]_{Mod} \neq \varnothing$.

4.8 Facts

1. $\lambda X{:}SPC.E[X]$ is weakly correct iff $CatmodC(E[X/SPC]) \neq \varnothing$.

2. $\Pi X{:}SPC.E[X]$ is correct iff $\lambda X{:}SPC.E[X]$ is strongly correct.

4.9 Remark

It must be noted that if the model level semantics of specifications of parameterized data types would have been restricted to functor classes then some "reasonable" specifications of this kind would be considered incorrect. This can be seen in the following counter-example:

Let SPC and SPC' be the following first order logic specifications:

$$
\begin{array}{ll}
\text{SPC} = & \textbf{sorts}\ s1 \\
& \textbf{opns}\ a,b{:}\ s1
\end{array}
\qquad
\begin{array}{ll}
\text{SPC'} = \text{SPC} + & \textbf{sorts}\ s2 \\
& \textbf{opns}\ c,d{:}\ s2 \\
& \textbf{axms}\ a=b \Rightarrow c \neq d \\
& \phantom{\textbf{axms}\ } a \neq b \Rightarrow c=d
\end{array}
$$

and let us consider the parameterized data type $\Pi X{:}$ SPC.enrich X by i, where i is the inclusion from SPC to SPC'. This specification may be seen as the loose specification of a family of parameterized data types defining a type s2, with two constants c and d, from a type s1, also with two constants a and b, in such a way that c and d must have a different value if a and b have the same one, and vice-versa. However, there are no functors from Catmod(SPC) to Catmod(SPC'): if we consider the two algebras A and B in Catmod(SPC) defined $A_{s1} = \{0,1\}$, $B_{s1} = \{2\}$ with $a_A = 0$, $b_A = 1$ and $a_B = b_B = 2$, then we have an obvious homomorphism from A to B. However for any A', B' in Catmod(SPC'), such that $V_i(A') = A$ and $V_i(B') = B$, there cannot exist any homomorphism from A' to B'.

4.10 Remark (The Initial Case)

All the results presented in this and the following section can be directly applied to the initial approach to algebraic specification [GTW 78, EM 85]. It is enough to consider that specifications carry an initial or free constraint. In this sense, the results in this paper can be applied to generalize all known results for parameterizations in the initial framework.

5 Parameter Passing

In the previous section we have studied the syntax and semantics for the two kinds of parameterizations, in this section we will study the mechanisms for parameter passing. In particular, this consists in describing the result of applying a parameterization to an actual parameter specification that "matches" the formal parameter, this matching being done (as usual) through a fitting morphism. Note that this is not just evaluating the expression associated to the parameterization over the actual parameter, since this may be meaningless: a similar problem was already discussed for a simpler case after definition 4.2, which was then solved in a quite ad-hoc manner. In this section we find a more systematic solution by using the "multiple constructions" introduced in this paper, that can be found in section 2.

The result of parameter passing is described at the specification and at the model levels showing compositionality results, namely that the class of models of the resulting specification of a parameter passing operation coincides with the model-level semantics of that operation. It has sometimes been argued that describing parameter passing (and, in general, any other specification building operation) at the specification level is methodologically inadequate, since this means "flattening" (losing the structure of) the given specification. We think that this may be true in some cases but not in this one. The reason is that, in our framework, the "structure" of a specification is defined at two levels: at the higher one, the structure is defined by means of modules, which are not treated in this paper, and at the lower level the structure is defined in terms of the constraints associated to the specification (e.g. see [OSC 89]). In this sense, providing a semantic definition at the specification level is methodologically fully adequate.

5.1 Definition

The syntax of parameter passing for a parameterized specification is given by

$$(\lambda X: SPC.E[X]) (SPC_{act})h$$

where $\lambda X: SPC.E[X]$ is the given parameterized specification, SPC_{act} is the actual parameter and h is the parameter passing morphism h: $SPC \rightarrow SPC_{act}$.

For defining the result of parameter passing (at the specification level) of both kinds of parameterizations we use a multiple pushout construction. This construction works as a pushout but taking care that the "multiple occurrences" of the formal parameter in the body of the parameterization are substituted by multiple occurrences of the actual parameter.

5.2 Definition

The result at the specification level of the parameter passing expression $(\lambda X: SPC.E[X])$ $(SPC_{act})h$ is the specification SPC_{res}, denoted $[(\lambda X: SPC.E[X]) (SPC_{act})h]_{Spec}$, obtained as the result of the following *multiple pushout diagram*:

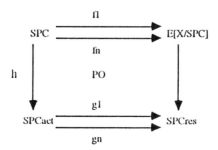

The model level semantics must be defined in terms of the meaning of the parameterized specification and the actual parameter given. This is done by using multiple amalgamation .

5.3 Definition

The result at the model level of the parameter passing expression $(\lambda X: SPC.E[X])$ $(SPC_{act})h$, denoted $[(\lambda X: SPC.E[X])(SPC_{act})h]_{Mod}$, is defined as the *multiple amalgamation* with respect to the above multiple pushout diagram of the following model classes:

$$[(\lambda X:\ SPC.E[X])(SPC_{act})h]_{Mod} = [(\lambda X:\ SPC.E[X])]_{Mod}(M) +_{M} *CatmodC(SPC_{act})^*$$

where $M = V_h(CatmodC(SPC_{act}))$

A compositionality theorem can be proved by showing (by induction on the structure of specification expressions) that $[E[X/SPC]]_{Mod} + CatmodC(SPC)^* \ CatmodC(SPC_{act})^*$ and $[(\lambda X:SPC.E[X])]_{Mod}(M) +_M *CatmodC(SPC_{act})^*$ coincide.

5.4 Theorem

$$CatmodC([(\lambda X:\ SPC.E[X])\ (SPC_{act})h]_{Spec}) = [(\lambda X:\ SPC.E[X])\ (SPC_{act})h]_{Mod}$$

Given the parameter passing expression $(\lambda X:\ SPC.E[X])\ (SPC_{act})h$, the following facts hold concerning the correctness and consistency of the specifications involved:

5.5 Facts

1. If $\lambda X:\ SPC.E[X]$ is strongly correct and SPC_{act} is consistent then SPC_{res} is consistent.

2. If $[(\lambda X:\ SPC.E[X])]_{Spec} = (SPC,\ SPC',\ F)$, $card(F) > 0$ and SPC_{res} is consistent then $\lambda X:SPC.E[X]$ is weakly correct and SPC_{act} is consistent.

3. If $[(\lambda X:\ SPC.E[X])]_{Spec} = (SPC,\ SPC',\ F)$ and $card(F) = 0$ then SPC_{res} is consistent iff SPC' is consistent.

The syntax of parameter passing for specifications of parameterized data types shows the fact that only models are admissible actual parameters. However, not only formal parameter models are acceptable, but also models of any specification matching the formal parameter are considered. Then, to define the result of parameter passing at the specification level, we identify the given model with its specification, including a corresponding unitary constraint.

5.6 Definition

The syntax of parameter passing for a specification of parameterized data types is given by:

$$(\Pi X:\ SPC.E[X])\ (A)_h$$

where $A \in CatmodC(SPC_{act})$ and h is teh parameter passing morphism $h : SPC \rightarrow SPC_{act}$.

5.7 Definition

The result at the specification level of the parameter passing expression $(\Pi X:\ SPC.E[X])$ $(A)_h$ is the specification SPC_{res} obtained as the result $[(\Pi X:\ SPC.E[X])(A)_h]_{Spec}$ of the following multiple pushout diagram:

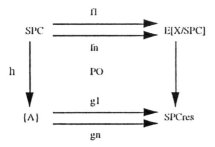

where {A} denotes the specification **impose** C_A **on** SPC_{act}.

Proving Ground Confluence and Inductive Validity in Constructor Based Equational Specifications

Klaus Becker

Fachbereich Informatik, Universität Kaiserslautern
6750 Kaiserslautern, Germany
email: klbecker@informatik.uni-kl.de

Abstract

We study ground confluence and inductive validity in equational specifications that are interpreted in a constructor based way. By defining semantics of the specification in an appropriate way, we are able to transfer the proof-by-consistency concepts from unstructured specifications to constructor based specifications, where the unstructured specifications with their usual semantics are included as a special case. We further show that the proof-by-consistency concepts not only apply to inductive theorem proving, but can as well be employed to prove ground confluence of rewrite systems. So we present a refutationally complete prover for ground confluence and inductive validity that applies to unstructured as well as constructor based equational specifications.

1 Introduction

Equational specifications can be considered as the programs of an applicative programming language with rewriting being its computation mechanism. Semantics is assigned to such specification programs using canonical term algebras. Usually all ground terms of the given signature contribute to the construction of the carrier set. Sometimes however it is convenient to introduce so-called constructors in order to capture the intuition of the specifier. In that case the operations given by the signature are split into two groups: those which are used to construct the domain of computation — the constructors — and those which do not contribute to this construction, but which are to be (possibly partially) defined over the domain of interest — the defined operators.

To consider an example, let 0 ("zero") and s ("successor") be the constructor symbols that introduce the natural numbers. Then the following equations $(R1)\ldots(R4)$ define addition and subtraction over the natural numbers. Note that subtraction is not a totally defined operation with respect to the constructors, as there is no constructor term that is equivalent to (e.g.) $0 - s(0)$.

$(R1)$	$x + 0$	$=$	x	$(R3)$	$x - 0$	$=$	x
$(R2)$	$x + s(y)$	$=$	$s(x + y)$	$(R4)$	$s(x) - s(y)$	$=$	$x - y$

When choosing this kind of predefined split of operators, it is reasonable to interprete those equations that define non-constructor symbols in a constructor restricted way: variables occuring in these equations are to be instantiated only by constructor terms. We call the result of such an interpretation of the specification, which is in the spirit of Kapur&Musser [KaMu86, KaMu87], "constructor semantics". In order to model the variable restrictions we use a suitable order-sorted interpretation of the syntactical objects (see also [SNGM89]).

When specifying with equations, ground confluence and inductive validity are of special interest. Ground confluence can be considered as a kind of correctness property of the specification, whenever the equations of the specification are used as rewrite rules. The notion of inductive validity is used to describe those equations that are valid in the standard model of the specification.

Whereas little work has been done on proving ground confluence (see [Pl85, Fr86, Go87]), several methods have been developed to prove inductive validity in various contexts (see e.g. [Bu69, BoMo79, Mu80, HuHu82, KaMu87, Ba88, KoRu90, Ly92]).

The constructor approach we are concerned with is treated in [KaMu86, KaMu87] using the so-called proof-by-consistency method. Problems usually occur in this approach if partially defined functions are present. Take for instance in the example above the equation $(x - y) + y = x$, where the left hand side $(x - y) + y$ is not totally defined wrt. the constructors. Of course, the question, whether this equation is an inductive theorem or not, depends on how the notion of inductive validity is defined.

Using our definition of semantics we are given a simple and canonical way to introduce inductive validity, causing no particular problems when partially defined functions are present. An equation is said to be inductively valid, if it is valid in the standard (constructor-based) model of the specification. We thus propose a quite simple solution to the problem mentioned in [KNZ91].

Our approach to treat ground confluence is based on the observation (which is also stated in [Pa92]), that the methods to prove inductive validity can as well be employed to prove ground confluence. Our method thus totally differs from the existing ones.

To summarize, we develop a theorem prover for inductive validity and ground confluence which is based on constructor semantics. This prover is designed along the lines of [Ba88], thus leading to a refutationally complete method. That means, if the given set of hypotheses is not inductively valid, or if the given rewrite system is not ground confluent, then this fact will be indicated after a finite number of steps. Finally note that our approach is designed in such a way that it contains the case of unstructured specifications with their usual semantics as a special case, as one always can decide to consider all symbols as constructors.

The paper is organized as follows: Section 2 introduces constructor based specifications, section 3 constructor semantics and some basic notions. Section 4 analyses the key notion of ground reducibility in the constructor based context. In section 5 we describe the prover from an abstract point of view. The specific inference rules are developed in section 6. Finally, in the last section we put together previous results and illustrate them with some examples.

We assume that the reader is familiar with the basic concepts of term rewriting (see [AvMa90, DeJo90]) and mathematical logic. Notions and notations not defined here are standard. Proofs have to be omitted for lack of space.

2 Constructor based specifications

A specification $(\Sigma, \mathcal{R})$ is given by a signature Σ and a set $\mathcal{R}$ of equations. These equations will be interpreted as rewrite rules throughout the paper. Following the lines of Kapur & Musser [KaMu86, KaMu87] we fix the terms that are to be considered as constructors in advance. Technically, we assume that Σ is a signature enrichment $\Sigma_0 + \Sigma_1$ and that $\mathcal{R}$ is a rule enrichment $\mathcal{R}_0 + \mathcal{R}_1$ compatible with the signature enrichment (see below). . Σ_0 introduces the sorts and basic constructor operations and $\mathcal{R}_0$ defines the relations among the basic objects. Σ_1 introduces new function symbols that are defined by $\mathcal{R}_1$ wrt. the constructor domain. The latter means that the variables in $\mathcal{R}_1$ are to be instantiated only by constructor terms.

In order to model this kind of variable restriction we use an order-sorted interpretation of Σ (see also [SNGM89]). This approach enables us to model partial functions in a canonical way.

A *(hierarchical) signature* $\Sigma = (S, F, D)$ consists of a set S of sort symbols, a set F of function symbols and a set D of function declarations $f : s_1, \ldots, s_n \rightarrow s$ ($f \in F; s_i, s \in S$) and subsort declarations $s_1 \lhd s_2$ ($s_1, s_2 \in S$), where $\lhd$ denotes the ordering relation between the sorts.

A signature $\Sigma = (S, F, D)$ is said to be *flat* iff D contains no subsort declarations, and for any $f \in F$ there exists exactly one function declaration in D.

A *functional signature enrichment* $\Sigma_0 + \Sigma_1$ consists of a signature $\Sigma_0 = (S_0, F_0, D_0)$ and a triple $\Sigma_1 = (\emptyset, F_1, D_1)$ with $F_0 \cap F_1 = \emptyset$ such that (S_0, F_1, D_1) is a signature too. Note that there are introduced no new sorts by Σ_1.

We assume in the sequel that $\Sigma = \Sigma_0 + \Sigma_1$ is a given flat functional signature enrichment. Further we assume that $V = \bigcup_{s \in S_0} V_s$ is the union of disjoint infinitary sets V_s of variables for the sorts introduced by Σ_0.

Next we construct the *(hierarchical) constructor signature* $\Sigma^\wedge = \Sigma_0^\wedge + \Sigma_1^\wedge$ *induced by the (flat) functional signature enrichment* $\Sigma = \Sigma_0 + \Sigma_1$. Let $F_0^{(\geq 1)}$ be the set of function symbols of F_0 that have an arity greater or equal than 1. Then let

- $\Sigma_0^\wedge = (S_0 \cup S_0^\wedge, F_0, D_0 \cup D_0^\wedge \cup D_{sort})$, where

$$
\begin{aligned}
S_0^\wedge &= \{s^\wedge \mid s \in S_0\} \\
D_0^\wedge &= \{f : s_1^\wedge, \ldots, s_n^\wedge \rightarrow s^\wedge \mid f \in F_0^{(\geq 1)}, \; f : s_1, \ldots, s_n \rightarrow s \; \in D_0\} \\
D_{sort} &= \{s \lhd s^\wedge \mid s \in S_0\},
\end{aligned}
$$

- $\Sigma_1^\wedge = (\emptyset, F_1, D_1^\wedge)$, where

$$
D_1^\wedge = \{f : s_1^\wedge, \ldots, s_n^\wedge \rightarrow s^\wedge \mid f \in F_1, \; f : s_1, \ldots, s_n \rightarrow s \; \in D_1\}.
$$

Now every flat Σ-term can be regarded as a hierarchical $\Sigma^\wedge$-term and vice versa. In the sequel we interpret all terms over the hierarchical signature $\Sigma^\wedge$. As a consequence, the range of the variables that are introduced for the sorts in S_0 is restricted. Note that no variables are introduced for the new sorts in $S_0^\wedge$.

Let $TERM(\Sigma^\wedge, V)$ denote the set of $\Sigma^\wedge$-terms, $TERM_0(\Sigma^\wedge, V)$ the set of terms of a sort in S_0 — the so-called base terms — and $TERM^\wedge(\Sigma^\wedge, V)$ the terms of a sort in $S_0^\wedge$ — the mixed terms.

A $\Sigma^\wedge$-*compatible rule enrichment* $\mathcal{R} = \mathcal{R}_0 + \mathcal{R}_1$ is the union of the sets of rules $\mathcal{R}_0$ and $\mathcal{R}_1$ (satisfying the usual variable condition $VAR(v) \subseteq VAR(u)$ for $u = v \in \mathcal{R}$) such that (i) $\mathcal{R}_0$ is a set of rules over Σ_0 and (ii) $\mathcal{R}_1$ is a set of rules over $\Sigma^\wedge$, where the left hand side of every rule in $\mathcal{R}_1$ contains a new symbol of F_1 (or is an element of $TERM^\wedge(\Sigma^\wedge, V)$).

Finally, a *constructor based specification* $(\Sigma^\wedge, \mathcal{R})$ consists of a constructor signature $\Sigma^\wedge = \Sigma_0^\wedge + \Sigma_1^\wedge$ induced by a flat functional signature enrichment $\Sigma = \Sigma_0 + \Sigma_1$ and a $\Sigma^\wedge$-compatible rule enrichment $\mathcal{R} = \mathcal{R}_0 + \mathcal{R}_1$.

We finish this section with some remarks about the kind of specifications just introduced. First, the order-sorted approach is well-suited to capture a "constructor based intuition" in a rather simple and natural way. Special technical problems do not occur, as the sort hierarchy is such simple that all the basic notions to be defined below remain decidable. In particular, the rules introduced by the specification are always sort-decreasing, thus leading to a well-behaved rewrite relation.

There is one point that always should be kept in mind: Variables do only exist for the base sorts. Consequently, to be sort-compatible, all the substitutions used throughout the paper (including matching substitutions and unifiers) have to instantiate variables by base terms. In order to get rid of this restriction, we introduce what we call quasi-substitutions (see section 6). However these "substitutions" are only used to formulate appropriate inference rules, they do not occur elsewhere in the paper.

3 Inductive validity and ground confluence

We assume throughout this paper that $(\Sigma^\wedge, \mathcal{R})$ is a given constructor based specification (induced by $\Sigma = \Sigma_0 + \Sigma_1$). To define the basic notions we first introduce the rewrite relation induced by $(\Sigma^\wedge, \mathcal{R})$.

Definition 3.1 *Let* $s \longrightarrow_\mathcal{R} t$ *for* $s, t \in TERM(\Sigma^\wedge, V)$ *iff there exists a position* $p \in O(s)$, *a substitution* σ *(that respects the sort hierarchy restriction) and a rule* $u = v \in \mathcal{R}$ *such that* $s/p \equiv \sigma(u)$ *and* $t \equiv s[\sigma(v)]_p$.

Note that — due to the variable restriction — rewriting has to be performed in a kind of innermost fashion.

One easily proves that $\overset{*}{\longleftrightarrow}_\mathcal{R}$ is a congruence relation on $TERM(\Sigma^\wedge, V)$. Let $\mathcal{T}_{(\Sigma^\wedge, \mathcal{R})}$ denote the canonical (hierarchical) term algebra induced by the congruence relation $\overset{*}{\longleftrightarrow}_\mathcal{R}$ on $TERM(\Sigma^\wedge)$. One easily shows that $\mathcal{T}_{(\Sigma^\wedge, \mathcal{R})}$ is initial in the class of hierarchical $\Sigma^\wedge$-algebras that are models of $\mathcal{R}$. So $\mathcal{T}_{(\Sigma^\wedge, \mathcal{R})}$ represents a kind of *constructor semantics* of the specification $(\Sigma^\wedge, \mathcal{R})$. In [AvBe92] it is shown (in a more general context including built-in structures) that the above definition of semantics is sound.

Next we define the basic notions this paper is concerned with. In order to make apparent the difference between our constructor approach and the usual one we always emphasize the given order-sorted specification.

Definition 3.2 *A* $\Sigma^\wedge$-*equation* $s = t$ *is called an* inductive theorem *(wrt.* $(\Sigma^\wedge, \mathcal{R})$*) or* inductively valid *(wrt.* $(\Sigma^\wedge, \mathcal{R})$*) iff* $\mathcal{T}_{(\Sigma^\wedge, \mathcal{R})}$ *is a model of* $s = t$.

Definition 3.3 $\mathcal{R}$ *is said to be* $(\Sigma^{\wedge}\text{-})$*ground confluent* *iff for any terms* $s, s_1, s_2 \in TERM(\Sigma^{\wedge})$, *if* $s_1 \;_{\mathcal{R}}{\overset{*}{\longleftarrow}}\; s \overset{*}{\longrightarrow}_{\mathcal{R}} s_2$, *then* $s_1 \downarrow_{\mathcal{R}} s_2$. $\mathcal{R}$ *is said to be* locally $(\Sigma^{\wedge}\text{-})$*ground confluent iff* $s_1 \downarrow_{\mathcal{R}} s_2$ *whenever* $s_1 \;_{\mathcal{R}}{\longleftarrow}\; s \longrightarrow_{\mathcal{R}} s_2$.

Next we relate both notions to ground joinability. This enables us to develop a uniform treatment of inductive validity and ground confluence.

A $\Sigma^{\wedge}$-ground equation $s = t$ is *joinable* (*wrt.* $(\Sigma^{\wedge}, \mathcal{R})$) iff $s \downarrow_{\mathcal{R}} t$. An arbitrary $\Sigma^{\wedge}$-equation $s = t$ is *ground joinable* (*wrt.* $(\Sigma^{\wedge}, \mathcal{R})$) iff $\tau(s) \downarrow_{\mathcal{R}} \tau(t)$ for all ground substitutions τ. Finally, a set S of $\Sigma^{\wedge}$-equations is ground joinable (wrt. $(\Sigma^{\wedge}, \mathcal{R})$) iff all equations from S are ground joinable (wrt. $(\Sigma^{\wedge}, \mathcal{R})$).

Lemma 3.1 *Let* $\mathcal{R}$ *be ground confluent. Let* S *be a set of* $\Sigma^{\wedge}$-*equations. Then* S *is inductively valid wrt.* $(\Sigma^{\wedge}, \mathcal{R})$ *iff* S *is ground joinable wrt.* $(\Sigma^{\wedge}, \mathcal{R})$.

In order to relate ground confluence to ground joinability we first review the notion of critical pairs. Let $u = v$ and $u' = v'$ be two rules of $\mathcal{R}$ that share no variables. Let p be a non-variable position of u and let u/p and u' be unifiable with most general unifier (mgu) μ. Then $\mu(u)[\mu(v')]_p = \mu(v)$ is called a *critical pair between the two rules*. Again note that μ is a $\Sigma^{\wedge}$-substitution and thus has to respect the sort hierarchy. Let $CRIT(\mathcal{R})$ denote the set of all critical pairs resulting from the rules of $\mathcal{R}$. The following critical pair lemma is proved just as in the non-constructor case.

Lemma 3.2 $\mathcal{R}$ *is locally* $\Sigma^{\wedge}$-*ground confluent iff* $CRIT(\mathcal{R})$ *is ground joinable wrt.* $(\Sigma^{\wedge}, \mathcal{R})$.

By Newmans lemma, ground confuence and local ground confluence are equivalent, provided $\mathcal{R}$ is (ground) terminating, i.e. $\overset{+}{\longrightarrow}_{\mathcal{R}}$ is a well-founded relation on $TERM(\Sigma^{\wedge})$.

To guarantee the latter, we assume that we are given a reduction ordering $>$ on $TERM(\Sigma, V)$ (and thus on $TERM(\Sigma^{\wedge}, V)$) such that $\mathcal{R}$ is compatible with $>$, i.e. $u > v$ for any $u = v \in \mathcal{R}$. Some considerations to be made below require orderings that in addition have the subterm property. For that reason we assume that $>$ is *ground subterm compatible*, meaning that there exists a well-founded partial ordering $\succ$ on $TERM(\Sigma)$ such that (i) for all $s, t \in TERM(\Sigma)$, if $s > t$ then $s \succ t$ and (ii) $s[t] \succ t$ for all $s, t \in TERM(\Sigma)$ with $s \not\equiv t$. Then, as a consequence, the following statement needed below is true: if $s_1 \;_{\mathcal{R}}{\longleftarrow}\; s \longrightarrow_{\mathcal{R}} s_2$, then $s_1 \downarrow_{\mathcal{R}} s_2$, or there exists a critical pair $u = v$ and a ground substitution τ such that $\{s\} \succ\succ \{\tau(u), \tau(v)\}$.

4 Ground reducibility

The prover to be developed below is based on the notion of ground reducibility.

Definition 4.1 *A* $\Sigma^{\wedge}$-*term* t *is said to be* ground reducible (wrt. $(\Sigma^{\wedge}, \mathcal{R})$) *iff* $\tau(t)$ *is reducible by* $\mathcal{R}$ *for any ground substitution* τ.

Ground reducibility is decidable in the flat case (see [Pl85, KNZ87]). We show that this result carries over to the constructor based approach (without taking efficiency into consideration).

In the constructor based setting instantiation of a variable by a term involving a function symbol of F_1 is not allowed. We introduce a new flat setting where the symbols of F_1 are replaced in a certain sense by new function symbols that map into a new sort. The variable restriction then can be modeled using the requirement of flat sort compatibility.

First let t be an arbitrary $\Sigma^\wedge$-term. A *maximal Σ_0-subterm of t* is a subterm $t/p \in TERM_0(\Sigma, V)$ of t such that t/p' contains a new symbol of F_1 for any position p' above p. Let $w_1, \ldots, w_n$ be the sequence of the maximal Σ_0-subterms of t in the "natural ordering from left to right" (i.e. if $i < j$ and $w_i \equiv t/p_i$ as well as $w_j \equiv t/p_j$, then $p_i <_{lex} p_j$, where $<_{lex}$ is the usual lexicographic ordering). Note that two terms that are unifiable have the same number of maximal Σ_0-subterms.

Now let t be a given $\Sigma^\wedge$-term. We construct a new signature $\Sigma^\#$, which is a flat enrichment of Σ_0, a new $\Sigma^\#$-term $t^\$$ and a new set $\mathcal{R}^\#$ of rules over $\Sigma^\#$ such that t is ground reducible wrt. $(\Sigma^\wedge, \mathcal{R})$ iff $t^\$$ is ground reducible wrt. $(\Sigma^\#, \mathcal{R}_0 \cup \mathcal{R}^\#)$.

Let $t_1, \ldots, t_k$ be the $\Sigma^\wedge$-subterms of t that are unifiable with a left hand side of a rule of $\mathcal{R}_1$. In particular let t_i be unifiable with u_i where $u_i = v_i \in \mathcal{R}_1$. Further let $t_0 \equiv t$.

In a first step we define the new signature. Let $s_\#$ be a new sort symbol and let $c_\#$ be a constant of sort $s_\#$. Let $\$$ be a new function symbol with arity $k + 1$ with declaration $\$: s_\#, \ldots, s_\# \longrightarrow s_\#$. For any $i \in \{0, \ldots, k\}$ let $w_{i1}, \ldots, w_{in_i}$ be the sequence of maximal Σ_0-subterms of t_i. Let $\#_i$ $(i = 0, \ldots, k)$ be a new function symbol with declaration $\#_i : s_{i1}, \ldots, s_{in_i} \longrightarrow s_\#$, where $s_{ij} = sort(w_{ij})$ $(j = 1, \ldots, n_i)$. Let $\Sigma^\#$ result from Σ_0 by adding all the new symbols.

Next we construct the $\Sigma^\#$-term $t^\$$ and the set $\mathcal{R}^\#$ of $\Sigma^\#$-rules. Let $t_i^\# \equiv \#_i(w_{i1}, \ldots, w_{in_i})$ $(i = 0, \ldots, k)$. Analogously, let $u_i^\# \equiv \#_i(w'_{i1}, \ldots, w'_{in_i})$ $(i = 1, \ldots, k)$, where $w'_{i1}, \ldots, w'_{in_i}$ is the sequence of maximal Σ_0-subterms of u_i. Now let $t^\$ \equiv \$(t_0^\#, \ldots, t_k^\#)$ and let $\mathcal{R}^\# = \{u_i^\# = c_\# \mid i = 1, \ldots, k\}$.

Using the following lemma as well as the decidability result concerning the usual unstructured setting we obtain decidability of ground reducibility in the constructor based setting.

Lemma 4.1 *The hierarchical $\Sigma^\wedge$-term t is ground reducible wrt. $(\Sigma^\wedge, \mathcal{R})$ iff the flat $\Sigma^\#$-term $t^\$$ is ground reducible wrt. $(\Sigma^\#, \mathcal{R}_0 \cup \mathcal{R}^\#)$.*

To illustrate the above considerations we continue our example from the introduction. Let $\mathcal{R}_0$ be empty and $\mathcal{R}_1$ consist of the rules $(R1) \ldots (R4)$. Let $t \equiv (x - y) + y$. Then $t^\$ \equiv \$(\#_0(x, y, y), \#_1(x, y), \#_2(x, y))$ and $\mathcal{R}^\# = \{\#_1(x, 0) = c_\#; \#_2(s(x), s(y)) = c_\#\}$. Now $t^\$$ is not ground reducible wrt. $\mathcal{R}^\#$. Take for instance the ground substitution that instantiates x by 0 and y by $s(0)$. Using the lemma one obtains that t is not ground reducible wrt. $\mathcal{R}$ in the hierachical setting.

Next we consider ground reducibility of $\Sigma^\wedge$-equations.

Definition 4.2 *A $\Sigma^\wedge$-equation $s = t$ is ground reducible wrt. $(\Sigma^\wedge, \mathcal{R})$ iff for any ground substitution τ, if $\tau(s) \not\equiv \tau(t)$, then $\tau(s)$ or $\tau(t)$ is reducible by $\mathcal{R}$.*

Ground reducibility of an equation $s = t$ is usually encoded by introducing a new symbol $\approx$ and a new rule with left hand side $\approx (x, x)$ and considering the "new term" $s \approx t$. In our context we have to respect the variable restriction. Let $\approx_s$ be a new

exists an index k such that $(\mathcal{G}_0, \mathcal{H}_0) \vdash_{\mathcal{I}} \cdots \vdash_{\mathcal{I}} (\mathcal{G}_k, \mathcal{H}_k)$ and $fail(\mathcal{H}_k)$ is true, or for all k we have $(\mathcal{G}_k, \mathcal{H}_k) \vdash_{\mathcal{I}} (\mathcal{G}_{k+1}, \mathcal{H}_{k+1})$ and $\bigcup_i \bigcap_{j \geq i} \mathcal{H}_j = \emptyset$.

Lemma 5.4 *Let the pair $(\mathcal{G}, \mathcal{H})$ preserve unjoinability. Let the sequence $(\mathcal{G}, \mathcal{H}) = (\mathcal{G}_0, \mathcal{H}_0), (\mathcal{G}_1, \mathcal{H}_1), \ldots$ represent a fair derivation that as well preserves unjoinability. If $\mathcal{G}$ is not ground joinable, then there exists an index k such that $fail(\mathcal{H}_k)$ is true.*

In order to assure the existence of fair derivations we introduce the following notion. The inference system $\mathcal{I}$ *allows continuation wrt. fail* iff for any $H \in \mathcal{H}$, if $fail(H)$ is not true, then there exists a set $\mathcal{H}'$ such that $(\mathcal{G}, \mathcal{H}) \vdash_{\mathcal{I}} (\mathcal{G}', \mathcal{H}')$ and $H \notin \mathcal{H}'$.

Lemma 5.5 *Let $\mathcal{I}$ allow continuation wrt. fail. Then for any $(\mathcal{G}, \mathcal{H})$ there exists a sequence $(\mathcal{G}, \mathcal{H}) = (\mathcal{G}_0, \mathcal{H}_0), (\mathcal{G}_1, \mathcal{H}_1), \ldots$ that represents a fair derivation wrt. fail.*

6   The inference system

In section 5 we have developed the basic concepts of our prover. Here we show the details: We make precise the inference system $\mathcal{I}$, we define the failure predicate *fail*, and we prove the properties to make applicable the lemmas of section 5. That will immediately define our proof procedure.

The first rule uses superposition in order to propagate hypotheses. Let $H : (s = t, (C, \rho))$ be an equation (with C-reference) and $u = v$ a rule of $\mathcal{R}$ such that H and $u = v$ share no variables. If s/p (t/p is treated analogously) and u are unifiable with mgu μ and if s/p is not a variable, then $(\mu(s)[\mu(v)]_p = \mu(t), (C, \mu\rho))$ is a *superposition result between H and $\mathcal{R}$ (at the position p)*. Let $SUP(H, \mathcal{R})$ (resp $SUP(H, p, \mathcal{R})$) be the set of all superposition results between H and $\mathcal{R}$ (at the position p).

Rule 1 (Superposition) *Let $\mathcal{S} \subseteq SUP(H, \mathcal{R})$ be a covering set for $\{H\}$. Then*

$$\frac{(\mathcal{G}, \mathcal{H} \cup \{H\})}{(\mathcal{G} \cup \{H\}, \mathcal{H} \cup \mathcal{S})}.$$

As every equation of $\mathcal{H}$ has to be treated by the inference system, the set $\mathcal{S} \subseteq SUP(H, \mathcal{R})$ of superposition results should be kept small. In many cases it suffices to superpose at a "complete" single position: Let $H : (s = t, (C, \rho))$. A position $p \in O(s)$ (or $p \in O(t)$) is said to be *complete wrt. $\mathcal{R}$* iff $SUP(H, p, \mathcal{R})$ is a covering set for H.

Next we make precise the *fail*-predicate exactly in the same way as in [Ba88].

Definition 6.1 *For $H : (s = t, (C, \rho))$ let $fail(H)$ be true iff either $s > t$ and s is not ground reducible wrt. $(\Sigma^\wedge, \mathcal{R})$, or $t > s$ and t is not ground reducible wrt. $(\Sigma^\wedge, \mathcal{R})$, or $s <> t$ and $s = t$ is not ground reducible wrt. $(\Sigma^\wedge, \mathcal{R})$. Let $fail(\mathcal{H})$ be true iff there exists a hypothesis $H \in \mathcal{H}$ such that $fail(H)$ is true.*

One easily proves that *fail* is correct wrt. joinability. The following lemma shows that $\mathcal{I}$ allows continuation wrt. *fail*, provided Rule 1 is a member of $\mathcal{I}$.

Lemma 6.1 *If $fail(H)$ is false, then $SUP(H, \mathcal{R})$ is a covering set for $\{H\}$.*

The simplification and deletion rules to be defined below use instantiation of equations. These equations may be rules from $\mathcal{R}$, hypotheses from $\mathcal{G}$ or lemmata from $\mathcal{L}$, where $\mathcal{L}$ is a set of equations which are known to be ground joinable. Instantiation by substitutions is too weak a concept, as substitutions have to respect the sort hierarchy and so variables can only be replaced by terms without new function symbols. In order to get rid of this restriction we introduce what we call quasi-substitutions.

Definition 6.2 *A $\Sigma^\wedge$-term t is said to be Σ_0-defined (wrt. $(\Sigma^\wedge, \mathcal{R})$) iff for any ground substitution τ there exists an element w in $TERM_0(\Sigma^\wedge)$ such that $\tau(t) \xrightarrow{*}_\mathcal{R} w$.*

In section 7 we show how to test whether a term is Σ_0-defined.

Definition 6.3 *A mapping $\sigma : V \to TERM(\Sigma^\wedge, V)$ is said to be a quasi-substitution wrt. $(\Sigma^\wedge, \mathcal{R})$ iff (i) $DOM(\sigma) = \{x \mid \sigma(x) \neq x\}$ is finite, (ii) $sort(x) \trianglelefteq sort(\sigma(x))$ for all $x \in DOM(\sigma)$ and (iii) $\sigma(x)$ is Σ_0-defined wrt. $(\Sigma^\wedge, \mathcal{R})$ for any $x \in DOM(\sigma)$.*

Rule 2 (Simplification) *Let $H : (s = t, (C, \rho))$. Let $u = v$ be an equation with $u = v \in \mathcal{R} \cup \mathcal{L}$ or $(u = v, (C', \rho')) \in \mathcal{G}$. Let $p \in O(s)$ (analogously for t) and σ be a quasi-substitution wrt. $(\Sigma^\wedge, \mathcal{R})$ such that (i) $s/p \equiv \sigma(u)$, (ii) $\sigma(u) > \sigma(v)$ and (iii) $\rho(C) >> \sigma\rho'(C')$ provided $(u = v, (C', \rho')) \in \mathcal{G}$. Let $H' : (s[\sigma(v)]_p = t, (C, \rho))$. Then*

$$\frac{(\mathcal{G}, \mathcal{H} \cup \{H\})}{(\mathcal{G}, \mathcal{H} \cup \{H'\})}.$$

To be able to formulate a quite general deletion rule we first introduce two new notations. First, two $\Sigma^\wedge$-terms s and t are *quasi-equationally related by $\mathcal{R} \cup \mathcal{G} \cup \mathcal{L}$ below* (C, ρ) iff there exists an equation $u = v$ with $u = v \in \mathcal{R} \cup \mathcal{L}$ or $(u = v, (C', \rho')) \in \mathcal{G}$ and a quasi-substitution σ wrt. $(\Sigma^\wedge, \mathcal{R})$ such that (i) $s \equiv w[\sigma(u)]_p$ and $t \equiv w[\sigma(v)]_p$ (for appropriate w and p) and (ii) $\rho(C) >> \sigma\rho'(C')$ provided $(u = v, (C', \rho')) \in \mathcal{G}$. Second, two $\Sigma^\wedge$-terms s and t are *quasi-subconnected by $\mathcal{R} \cup \mathcal{G} \cup \mathcal{L}$ below* (C, ρ) iff there exist a number $n \geq 0$ and terms $s_0, \ldots, s_n \in TERM(\Sigma^\wedge, V)$ such that (i) $s \equiv s_0$ and $t \equiv s_n$, (ii) s_i and s_{i+1} are quasi-equationally related by $\mathcal{R} \cup \mathcal{G} \cup \mathcal{L}$ below (C, ρ) for $i = 0, \ldots, n - 1$ and (iii) $\rho(C) \gg \{s_i\}$ for $i = 1, \ldots, n - 1$.

Rule 3 (Deletion) *Let $H : (s = t, (C, \rho))$. Let s and t be quasi-subconnected by $\mathcal{R} \cup \mathcal{G} \cup \mathcal{L}$ below (C, ρ). Then*

$$\frac{(\mathcal{G}, \mathcal{H} \cup \{H\})}{(\mathcal{G}, \mathcal{H})}.$$

The following deletion rules (deletion of trivial equations and deletion by subsumption) can be obtained as special cases of Rule 3.

Rule 4 (Equality Check) *Let $H : (s = t, (C, \rho))$ be such that $s \equiv t$. Then*

$$\frac{(\mathcal{G}, \mathcal{H} \cup \{H\})}{(\mathcal{G}, \mathcal{H})}.$$

Rule 5 (Subsumption) *Let $H : (s = t, (C, \rho))$. Let s and t be quasi-equationally related by $\mathcal{R} \cup \mathcal{G} \cup \mathcal{L}$ below (C, ρ). Then*

$$\frac{(\mathcal{G}, \mathcal{H} \cup \{H\})}{(\mathcal{G}, \mathcal{H})}.$$

The following lemma sums up all the "correctness properties" of the rules. Let $\mathcal{I}$ consist of Rule 1, Rule 2 and Rule 3.

Lemma 6.2

(a) *Every inference step* $(\mathcal{G}, \mathcal{H}) \vdash_{\mathcal{I}} (\mathcal{G}', \mathcal{H}')$ *is generic.*

(b) *Every inference step* $(\mathcal{G}, \mathcal{H}) \vdash_{\mathcal{I}} (\mathcal{G}', \mathcal{H}')$ *preserves admissibility.*

(c) *Let* $\mathcal{R}$ *be ground confluent and let* $\mathcal{G}$ *be ground joinable. Then every inference step* $(\mathcal{G}, \mathcal{H}) \vdash_{\mathcal{I}} (\mathcal{G}', \mathcal{H}')$ *preserves joinability.*

(d) *Let* $\mathcal{R}$ *be ground confluent or* $CRIT(\mathcal{R}) \subseteq \mathcal{G}$. *Let* $\mathcal{H}$ *be admissible. Then every inference step* $(\mathcal{G}, \mathcal{H}) \vdash_{\mathcal{I}} (\mathcal{G}', \mathcal{H}')$ *inductively preserves unjoinability.*

7 Results and examples

In this section we present our proof procedures and illustrate them by examples. In theorem 7.1 we show how to prove $\Sigma^\wedge$-ground confluence of $\mathcal{R}$.

Theorem 7.1

(a) *Let* $CRIT(\mathcal{R}) \subseteq \mathcal{C}$. *If* $(\mathcal{C}, \mathcal{C}) \vdash_{\mathcal{I}} \cdots \vdash_{\mathcal{I}} (\mathcal{G}', \emptyset)$, *then* $\mathcal{R}$ *is* $\Sigma^\wedge$-*ground confluent.*

(b) *Let* $\mathcal{C} = CRIT(\mathcal{R})$. *If* $(\mathcal{C}, \mathcal{C}) \vdash_{\mathcal{I}} \cdots \vdash_{\mathcal{I}} (\mathcal{G}', \mathcal{H}')$ *such that* $fail(\mathcal{H}')$ *is true, then* $\mathcal{R}$ *is not* $\Sigma^\wedge$-*ground confluent.*

(c) *Let* $\mathcal{C} = CRIT(\mathcal{R})$. *If* $(\mathcal{C}, \mathcal{C}) = (\mathcal{G}_0, \mathcal{H}_0), (\mathcal{G}_1, \mathcal{H}_1), \ldots$ *represents a fair derivation wrt. fail and if* $\mathcal{R}$ *is not* $\Sigma^\wedge$-*ground confluent, then there exists an index* k *such that* $fail(\mathcal{H}_k)$ *is true.*

The following example is taken from [NRS89]. Note again that all terms have to be interpreted hierarchically and that variables are of a "low sort".

Example 7.1 *Let* $F_0 = \{0, s, p\}$ *be the set of constructors and* $F_1 = \{+, -, *\}$ *the set of new symbols. Further let* $\mathcal{R}_0 = \{R1, R2\}$ *define integers and let* $\mathcal{R}_1 = \{R3, \ldots, R11\}$.

(R1)	$s(p(x))$	$=$	x	(R6)	$x - 0$	$=$	x
(R2)	$p(s(x))$	$=$	x	(R7)	$x - s(y)$	$=$	$p(x - y)$
				(R8)	$x - p(y)$	$=$	$s(x - y)$
(R3)	$x + 0$	$=$	x	(R9)	$x * 0$	$=$	0
(R4)	$x + s(y)$	$=$	$s(x + y)$	(R10)	$x * s(y)$	$=$	$(x * y) + x$
(R5)	$x + p(y)$	$=$	$p(x + y)$	(R11)	$x * p(y)$	$=$	$(x * y) - x$

We obtain the following set $CRIT(\mathcal{R}) = \{C1, \ldots, C8\}$ *of critical pairs:*

$(C1)$	$s(x)$	$=$	$s(x)$	$(C5)$	$p(x - p(y))$	$=$	$x - y$
$(C2)$	$p(x)$	$=$	$p(x)$	$(C6)$	$s(x - s(y))$	$=$	$x - y$
$(C3)$	$s(x + p(y))$	$=$	$x + y$	$(C7)$	$(x * p(y)) + x$	$=$	$x * y$
$(C4)$	$p(x + s(y))$	$=$	$x + y$	$(C8)$	$(x * s(y)) - y$	$=$	$x * y$

In order to show that $\mathcal{R}$ is ground confluent, we add the following equations $\mathcal{A} = \{A1, \ldots, A6\}$:

$(A1)$	$p(x) + y$ $\cdot$	$=$	$p(x + y)$	$(A4)$	$p(x) - y$	$=$	$p(x - y)$
$(A2)$	$s(x) + y$	$=$	$s(x + y)$	$(A5)$	$s(x) - y$	$=$	$s(x - y)$
$(A3)$	$(x - y) + y$	$=$	x	$(A6)$	$(x + y) - y$	$=$	x

Now, using the fact that all $\Sigma^{\wedge}$-terms are Σ_0-defined wrt. $(\Sigma^{\wedge}, \mathcal{R})$, we easily show that $(\mathcal{C}, \mathcal{C}) \stackrel{*}{\vdash}_{\mathcal{I}} (\mathcal{G}', \emptyset)$ where $\mathcal{C} = CRIT(\mathcal{R}) \cup \mathcal{A}$. Thus $\mathcal{R} = \mathcal{R}_0 + \mathcal{R}_1$ is $\Sigma^{\wedge}$-ground confluent (in the constructor approach). In addition we obtain by the following theorem that the equations in $\mathcal{A}$ are inductively valid wrt. $(\Sigma^{\wedge}, \mathcal{R})$.

Next we turn to inductive theorem proving.

Theorem 7.2

(a) *Let $\mathcal{R}$ be ground confluent. If $(\mathcal{C}, \mathcal{C}) \vdash_{\mathcal{I}} \cdots \vdash_{\mathcal{I}} (\mathcal{G}', \emptyset)$, then $\mathcal{C}$ is inductively valid wrt. $(\Sigma^{\wedge}, \mathcal{R})$.*

(b) *Let $\mathcal{R}$ be ground confluent. If $(\mathcal{C}, \mathcal{C}) \vdash_{\mathcal{I}} \cdots \vdash_{\mathcal{I}} (\mathcal{G}', \mathcal{H}')$ such that $fail(\mathcal{H}')$ is true, then $\mathcal{C}$ is not inductively valid wrt. $(\Sigma^{\wedge}, \mathcal{R})$.*

(c) *Let $\mathcal{R}$ be ground confluent. If $(\mathcal{C}, \mathcal{C}) = (\mathcal{G}_0, \mathcal{H}_0), (\mathcal{G}_1, \mathcal{H}_1), \ldots$ represents a fair derivation wrt. fail and if $\mathcal{C}$ is not inductively valid wrt. $(\Sigma^{\wedge}, \mathcal{R})$, then there exists an index k such that $fail(\mathcal{H}_k)$ is true.*

Using preservingness properties that are based on inductive validity instead of joinability we can even drop the condition of $\mathcal{R}$ being ground confluent in the "positive case (a)" of theorem 7.2.

Theorem 7.3 *If $(\mathcal{C}, \mathcal{C}) \vdash_{\mathcal{I}} \cdots \vdash_{\mathcal{I}} (\mathcal{G}', \emptyset)$, then $\mathcal{C}$ is inductively valid wrt. $(\Sigma^{\wedge}, \mathcal{R})$.*

We again consider the example introduced in the introduction.

Example 7.2 *Let $F_0 = \{0, s\}$ and $F_1 = \{+, -\}$. Let $\mathcal{R}_0 = \emptyset$ and $\mathcal{R}_1 = \{R1, \ldots, R4\}$. $\mathcal{R}$ is $\Sigma^{\wedge}$-ground confluent as $CRIT(\mathcal{R}) = \emptyset$.*

$(R1)$	$x + 0$	$=$	x	$(R3)$	$x - 0$	$=$	x
$(R2)$	$x + s(y)$	$=$	$s(x + y)$	$(R4)$	$s(x) - s(y)$	$=$	$x - y$

We analyse whether the following hypotheses are inductively valid wrt. $(\Sigma^{\wedge}, \mathcal{R})$ or not. The references will be dropped if we do not have to take them into consideration.

$(H1)$	$(x + y) - y$	$=$	x	$(H2)$	$(x - y) + y$	$=$	x

To show that $H1 : (x + y) - y = x$ is an inductive theorem wrt. $(\Sigma^{\wedge}, \mathcal{R})$ we first use superposition. Note that by the variable restriction we only have to overlap with rule $(R1)$ and $(R2)$. The superposition results are (i) $x - 0 = x$, which can be further *simplified and then deleted, and (ii)* $(s(x' + y') - s(y') = x', ((x + y) - y = x, \{x \leftarrow x', y \leftarrow s(y')\}))$. *The latter hypothesis can be simplified by (R4) using the fact that* $x' + y'$ *is* Σ_0-*defined. The result* $((x' + y') - y' = x', ((x + y) - y = x, \{x \leftarrow x', y \leftarrow s(y')\}))$ *then can be deleted by the subsumption rule.*

The hypothesis H2 : $(x - y) + y = x$ *can directly be refuted, as* $(x - y) + y > x$ *(by an appropriate ordering* $>$*) and* $(x - y) + y$ *is not ground reducible (see section 4).*

The following result (obtained by J. Avenhaus) shows that our prover as well can be used to show that a term is Σ_0-defined. This fact is needed to apply Rule 2 and Rule 3. For that purpose we introduce new constants $*_s$ for all $s \in S_0$. Let $\Sigma_*^\wedge$ be the resulting signature. For simplicity we drop the sort subscripts. Let $\mathcal{R}^* = \{f(x_1, \ldots, x_n) = * \mid f \in F_0\}$.

Lemma 7.1 *Let* $TERM(\Sigma^\wedge) \neq \emptyset$. *Then the* $\Sigma^\wedge$-*term* t *is* Σ_0-*defined wrt.* $(\Sigma^\wedge, \mathcal{R})$ *iff the* $\Sigma_*^\wedge$-*equation* $t = *$ *is an inductive theorem wrt.* $(\Sigma_*^\wedge, \mathcal{R} \cup \mathcal{R}^*)$.

Thus we can use the methods just developed to prove Σ_0-definedness. Let us consider again example 7.1. We have $\mathcal{R}^* = \{0 = *, s(x) = *, p(x) = *\}$. It is easy to show that the equations $x + y = *$, $x - y = *$ and $x * y = *$ are inductive theorems wrt. $(\Sigma_*^\wedge, \mathcal{R} \cup \mathcal{R}^*)$. Then of course all $\Sigma^\wedge$-terms are Σ_0-defined wrt. $\mathcal{R}$. So we can fill the gap in the argumentation concerning example 7.1.

To finish we briefly comment on the relationship between constructor based and unstructured specifications. Of course, the unstructured case is totally covered by our approach, as we always can decide to consider all symbols as constructors. The next result shows that, even if we are only interested in non-constructor results, it may be useful to switch over to constructor semantics, provided we have sufficient completeness.

Definition 7.1 *The constructor based specification* $(\Sigma^\wedge, \mathcal{R})$ *is said to be* sufficiently complete *iff every* $\Sigma^\wedge$-*term* t *is* Σ_0-*defined wrt.* $(\Sigma^\wedge, \mathcal{R})$.

Lemma 7.2 *Let* $(\Sigma^\wedge, \mathcal{R})$ *be a sufficiently complete constructor based specification induced by* Σ. *Then:*

(a) If $\mathcal{R}$ *is* $\Sigma^\wedge$-*ground confluent, then* $\mathcal{R}$ *is also* Σ-*ground confluent.*

(b) If $s = t$ *is an inductive theorem wrt.* $(\Sigma^\wedge, \mathcal{R})$, *then* $s = t$ *is also an inductive theorem wrt.* $(\Sigma, \mathcal{R})$.

Note that using this lemma we obtain "full" ground confluence in example 7.1. In an additional example (taken from [Go87] and also discussed in [Fr86]) we show that it may be convenient to switch over to the constructor based approach as one may gain efficiency.

Example 7.3 *Let* $\mathcal{R} = \{R1, R2, R3\}$.

$$
\begin{array}{llll}
(R1) & 0 + y & = & y \\
(R2) & s(x) + y & = & s(x + y) \\
(R3) & x + (y + z) & = & (x + y) + z
\end{array}
$$

To show that $\mathcal{R}$ is Σ-ground confluent (in the non-constructor approach) we have to consider the following critical pairs $C1, \ldots, C5$.

$$
\begin{array}{llll}
(C1) & (x + 0) + z & = & x + z \\
(C2) & (0 + y) + z & = & y + z \\
(C3) & x + s(y + z) & = & (x + s(y)) + z \\
(C4) & s(x + (y + z)) & = & (s(x) + y) + z \\
(C5) & x + ((y + u) + v) & = & (x + y) + (u + v)
\end{array}
$$

In the constructor approach however (with the usual signature split) we only have to consider $C1$ and $C3$. As the specification is sufficiently complete, it suffices to prove $\Sigma^\wedge$-ground confluence of $C1$ and $C3$.

Acknowledgements: I would like to thank J. Avenhaus for some useful hints and for many discussions on earlier drafts of the paper.

References

[AvBe92]   J. Avenhaus and K. Becker, Conditional rewriting modulo a built-in algebra, SEKI Report SR-92-11.

[AvMa90]   J. Avenhaus and K. Madlener, Term rewriting and equational reasoning, in: R. B. Banerji, ed., *Formal Techniques in Artificial Intelligence* (North-Holland, Amsterdam, 1990) pp. 1-43.

[Ba88]   L. Bachmair, Proof by Consistency in Equational Theories, in: *3rd LICS* (1988) pp. 228-233.

[BoMo79]   R.S. Boyer and J.S. Moore, *A Computational Logic* (Academic Press, New York, 1979).

[Bu69]   R. Burstall, Proving properties of programs by structural induction, *Computer Journal* 12 (1969) pp. 41-48.

[DeJo90]   N. Dershowitz and J. P. Jouannaud, Rewriting systems, in: J. van Leeuwen, ed., *Handbook of Theoretical Computer Science, Vol. B* (Elsevier, Amsterdam, 1990) pp. 241-320.

[Fr86]   L. Fribourg, A strong restriction of the inductive completion procedure, *13th ICALP 86*, LNCS 266 (Springer, Berlin, 1991) pp. 105-115.

[Go87]   R. Göbel, Ground confluence, in: *2nd RTA 87* LNCS 256 (Springer, Berlin, 1991) pp. 156-167.

[HuHu82]   G. Huet and J. M. Hullot, Proofs by Induction in Equational Theories with Constructors, *J. Comput. Syst. Sci* 25 (1982) pp. 239-266.

[KaCh86]   S. Kaplan and M. Choquer, On the decidability of quasi-reducability, in: *Bull. EATCS* 28 (1986) pp. 32-34.

[KaMu86]   D. Kapur and D.R. Musser, Inductive reasoning for incomplete specifications, in: *Proc. IEEE Symposium on Logic in Computer Science* (Cambridge MA, 1986) pp. 367-377.

[KaMu87]   D. Kapur and D.R. Musser, Proof by consistency, *Artificial Intelligence* 31(2) (1987) pp. 125-157.

[KNZ87]   D. Kapur, P. Narendran and H. Zhang, On sufficient completeness and related properties of term rewriting systems, *Acta Informatica* 24(4) (1987), pp. 395-415.

[KNZ91]   D. Kapur, P. Narendran and H. Zhang, Automating inductionless induction using test sets, *J. Symbolic Computation* 11 (1991), pp. 83-111.

[KoRu90]   E. Kounalis and M. Rusinowitch, Mechanizing Inductive Reasoning, in: *Proc. of 8th AAAI '90* (MIT Press, 1990) pp. 240-245.

[Ly92]   O. Lysne, Proof by consistency in constructive systems with final algebra semantics, in: *Proc. of 3rd ALP '92*, LNCS 632, (Springer, Berlin 1992) pp. 276-290.

[Mu80]   D. R. Musser, On Proving Inductive Properties of Abstract Data Types, in: *Proc. 7th ACM Symp. on Principles of Programming Languages* (1980) pp. 154-162.

[NRS89]   W. Nutt, P. Réty and G. Smolka, Basic narrowing revisited, *Journal of Symbolic Computation* 7(3& 4) 1989, pp. 295-318.

[Pa92]   P. Padawitz, Generic induction proofs, to appear in *CTRS 92*.

[Pl85]   D. Plaisted, Semantic confluence tests and completion methods, *Inform. and Control* 65(2/3) 1985, pp. 182-215.

[SNGM89]   G. Smolka, W. Nutt, J.A. Goguen and J. Meseguer, Order-sorted equational computation, in: H. Ait-Kaci and M. Nivat, eds., *Resolution of Equations in Algebraic Structures, Vol. 2* (Academic Press, San Diego CA, 1989) pp. 297-367.

[Wi91]   C.-P. Wirth, Inductive theorem proving in theories specified by positive/negative conditional equations, Diplomarbeit, Universität Kaiserslautern, Fachbereich Informatik, 1991.

Associative-Commutative Discrimination Nets

Leo Bachmair   Ta Chen   I. V. Ramakrishnan

Department of Computer Science, SUNY at Stony Brook
Stony Brook, NY 11794, U.S.A.

Abstract. Use of discrimination nets for many-to-one pattern matching has been shown to dramatically improve the performance of the Knuth-Bendix completion procedure used in rewriting. Many important applications of rewriting require associative-commutative (*AC*) function symbols and it is therefore quite natural to expect performance gains by using similar techniques for *AC*-completion. In this paper we propose such a technique, called *AC*-discrimination net, that is a natural generalization of the standard discrimination net in the sense that if no *AC*-symbols are present in the pattern, it specializes to the standard discrimination net. Moreover we show how *AC*-discrimination nets can be augmented so as to further improve the performance of *AC*-matching on problems that are typically seen in practice.

1   Introduction

Term matching is a fundamental operation in equational and functional programming and in various theorem proving methods, such as the many variants of the completion procedure [3]. In these applications the problem usually occurs in the form of many-to-one matching, where one has to determine for a given set of terms $t_1, \ldots, t_n$, also called *patterns*, if one matches a specified term s, called the *subject*. For instance, in a completion procedure the patterns to be considered are the left-hand sides of current rewrite rules, which may dynamically change.

The most efficient many-to-one matching algorithms use trie-like data structures, called *discrimination nets*, and corresponding tree automata, that allow one to factor out common expressions in a given set of patterns. Since completion procedures spend most of their time on normalization of terms (which consists of repeated steps of matching followed by term replacement), sophisticated matching algorithms based on discrimination nets may result in dramatic speedups, as has been demonstrated by Christian [1].

An important application of completion is to associative-commutative rewrite systems, which require a suitably modified operation, called associative-commutative matching (or *AC*-matching). One-to-one *AC*-matching is an *NP*-complete problem, but can be solved in polynomial time if patterns are restricted to linear terms (without multiple occurrences of variables) [2]. The essential component of the one-to-one *AC*-matching algorithm described by Benanav, Kapur, and Narendran [2] is the application of maximum bipartite graph matching. In fact, Verma and Ramakrishnan [13] showed that the two problems, associative-commutative matching and maximum bipartite graph matching are mutually reducible, so that complexity bounds for one problem also apply to the other. The best currently known lower bound for AC-matching is $O(mn^{1.5})$, where m refers to the size of the pattern and n to the size of the subject.

In many applications, however, many-to-one matching is needed. Since AC-matching takes up most of the computation time in associative-commutative completion procedures—and discrimination nets had resulted in considerable speedups of standard completion—there have been attempts to adapt discrimination nets to AC-matching. These attempts have not been entirely satisfactory. In this paper, we demonstrate that discrimination nets, in combination with bipartite graph matching, can indeed be applied to do AC-matching efficiently. We propose associative-commutative discrimination nets, which are hierarchically structured collections of standard discrimination nets, with bipartite graph matching being used to combine the results from one level of the hierarchy so as to make them available to the next higher level. This approach applies to all different kinds of discrimination nets that have been proposed in the literature (deterministic or nondeterministic, adaptive or non-adaptive), and an associative-commutative net specializes to a standard discrimination net if applied to terms with no associative-commutative operators. The algorithm solves the many-to-one matching problem, but is of the same asymptotic complexity as the best current algorithm for the simpler problem of one-to-one matching.

The paper is organized as follows. In the next section we introduce some terminology and give a general definition of discrimination nets. In Section 3 we briefly discuss the reduction of associative-commutative matching to a matching problem on flattened terms. In Section 4 we introduce associative-commutative discrimination nets, design a corresponding matching algorithm, and analyse its complexity. In practical applications of associative-commutative matching, the bipartite graph matching problems that need to be solved are of a special form, which we exploit in Section 5 to improve the algorithm. Nonlinear matching is briefly discussed in Section 6. In the concluding section we summarize our results and compare them to other recent work.

2   Discrimination Nets

We shall consider terms built from a given finite set of function symbols $\mathcal{F}$ and a (countable) set of variables $\mathcal{V}$. We use the symbols s and t to denote terms, f and g to denote function symbols, and x, y, and z to denote variables. The *arity* of a function symbol f is denoted by $\alpha(f)$. If t is a term $f(t_1, \ldots, t_n)$, then $t_1, \ldots, t_n$ are called the *top-level arguments* of t.

The expression $t|_p$ denotes the subterm of t at position p. Positions may, for instance, be represented as sequences of integers. So, if $p' = pq'$ (that is, p is a *prefix* of p'), then $t|_{p'}$ is a subterm of $t|_p$. We use Λ for the top-most position $(t|_\Lambda = t)$. By $t(p)$ we denote the symbol at position p in t. The symbol $t(\Lambda)$ is also called the top-most, or root, symbol of t. For example, 2 is a position in $t = f(a, g(a, b))$ and $t|_2 = g(a, b)$, while $t(2) = g$.

The application of a substitution σ to a term t is written $t\sigma$. A term t is said to *match* another term s (and s is called an *instance* of t) if there is a substitution σ such that $s = t\sigma$.

In term rewriting, efficient matching algorithms have been designed that employ an indexing technique similar to tries based on so-called *discrimination nets*. In defining discrimination nets, we have to refer to "partially constructed" terms. By a *skeleton* we mean a set S of pairs (p, f_p) of positions and function symbols, where (i) S contains a pair with first component p whenever it contains one with first component $p.i$, and (ii) if $p.i$ is a first component of some pair in S, then $i \leq \alpha(f_p)$. Given a (non-empty) skeleton S, we define its *fringe* to be the set of all positions $p.i$, such that S contains a pair (p, f_p), where $1 \leq i \leq \alpha(f_p)$, but contains no pair with first component $p.i$. The fringe of the empty skeleton is defined to be $\{\Lambda\}$. Skeletons and corresponding fringes can conveniently be represented as terms built from function symbols and some special constant $\square$ not contained in $\mathcal{F}$: the fringe consists of all positions at which $\square$ occurs, while the remaining positions, with their corresponding function symbols, determine the skeleton. For example, the term $f(\square, g(a, \square))$ represents the skeleton $\{(\Lambda, f), (2, g), (2.1, a)\}$ with corresponding fringe $\{1, 2.2\}$.

A term t is said to be *compatible* with a skeleton S if for every pair (p, f_p) in S either p is a position in t and $t(p) = f_p$, or else some prefix of p is a variable position in t. A set M of terms is said to be compatible with S if each term in M is. If M is compatible with S, we say that p is a *discrimination position* (for M and S) if it is a position in the fringe of S and $t(p)$ is a function symbol (not a variable), for some term t in M.

Let ω be a new constant not contained in $\mathcal{F}$. A *matching tree* is a tree where the edges are labelled by symbols from $\mathcal{F} \cup \{\omega\}$ and with each node u is associated a non-empty set of terms M_u (the match set), a skeleton S_u (the partial match), and, if u is not a leaf, a position p_u (the discrimination position), such that (i) the empty skeleton is associated with the root of the tree; (ii) p_u is a discrimination position for M_u and S_u, for each non-leaf node u; and (iii) for each edge (u, v), $S_v = S_u \cup \{(p_u, f)\}$, where f is the label of (u, v), and M_v is the set of all terms in M_u that are compatible with S_v. Note that, for each node u, the match set M_u is compatible with the skeleton S_u.

A *discrimination net* is a maximal matching tree that contains no duplicate nodes. (A node v' is a duplicate of another node v, if there are two edges (u, v) and (u, v') that are labelled by the same symbol.) In other words, a discrimination net is a matching tree to which no edges can be added. Thus, in a discrimination net there is no discrimination position for M_u and S_u, for any leaf u. We also say that D is a discrimination net for the set of terms M associated with its root. Observe that, if D is a discrimination net for M, all discrimination positions p_u must be positions in some term t of M. Furthermore the discrimination positions along any branch in D are distinct, so that any discrimination net for a finite set of terms M has to be finite.

The construction of a discrimination net for a given (finite) set of terms T is straightforward. An initial matching tree consists of a single node u labelled by $M_u = M$ and $S_u = \emptyset$. If for some leaf v in a given matching tree there exists a discrimination position p_v for M_v and S_v, then the tree can be expanded correspondingly. If there are no further discrimination positions, the process terminates with a discrimination net. Since for any given leaf, there may be different discrimination positions to choose from, different discrimination nets may be obtained from a given initial set of terms M. In this sense our definition characterizes *adaptive* discrimination nets. Discrimination nets have typically been constructed according to some fixed order in which positions are chosen, e.g., left-to-right preorder as in [4]. The construction of discrimination nets can be optimized via a suitable choice of discrimination positions, in order to improve the matching time and decrease the size of the discrimination net, see [11]. A discrimination net for the set of terms $\{f(a, a), f(a, x)\}$ is shown in Figure 1(a).

Let T be a set of *linear* terms (that is, terms without multiple occurrences of the same variable) and D be a discrimination net for T. We define a corresponding *matching automaton* A as follows. The nodes of D are the states of A, with the root being the initial state and the leaves being final states. On a given input term s, the automaton makes a transition $u \to v$, if D contains an edge (u, v) labelled by the symbol f and either $s(p_u) = f$ or else $s(p_u)$ is a variable and $f = \omega$. The automaton is said to *succeed*, if it reaches a final state, and is said to *fail*, otherwise.

We emphasize that these matching automata are deterministic (at any given moment an automaton may make at most one transition) and inspect each input symbol at most once. It can be proved that if an automaton reaches a final state v, then M_v contains exactly those terms of T which match s. If the automaton fails, then the input term s is matched by no term in T. There are obvious optimizations of matching automata, such as merging equivalent states (which may be expressed in the discrimination net by labelling edges by sets of symbols); for further details see [11]. For example, Figure 1(b) shows an optimized version of the above net.

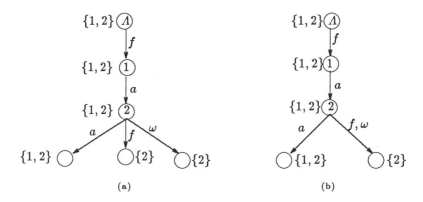

Fig. 1. (a) A discrimination net for $\{1 : f(a, a), 2 : f(a, x)\}$ and (b) its optimization.

In dealing with nonlinear patterns one would first apply discrimination nets to linearized versions of the given terms, where different occurrences of the same variable are considered different, and in a second phase check whether the proposed instantiations for all occurrences of the same variable are consistent; see also Section 6.

It is possible to slightly change the definition of discrimination nets. We say that a term t is *strongly compatible* with a skeleton S if for every pair (p, f_p) in S, p is a position in t and either $t(p) = f_p$ or else $t(p)$ is a variable and $f_p = \omega$. If t is compatible with S, then some instance of t, but not necessarily t itself, is strongly compatible with S. For example, both $f(x, a, b)$ and $f(b, a, a)$ are compatible with the skeleton $\{(\Lambda, f), (1, b)\}$, but only the second term is strongly compatible.

Let discrimination nets be defined as before, but with condition (iii) replaced by: (iii') for each edge (u, v), $S_v = S_u \cup \{(p_u, f)\}$, where f is the label of (u, v), and M_v is the set of all terms in M_u that are *strongly* compatible with S_v. Such discrimination nets can be used as *nondeterministic* automata, as follows. There is a transition $u \to v$ if D contains an edge (u, v) labelled either by the symbol ω or else by the symbol f, where $s(p_u) = f$. Thus, there may be different transitions from a state on the same input. Whenever a final state is reached, the corresponding match set contains only patterns that match the input term, but may not contain *all* such patterns. For further details see Christian [1]. Figure 2 illustrates the differences between the deterministic and nondeterministic versions of a discrimination net.

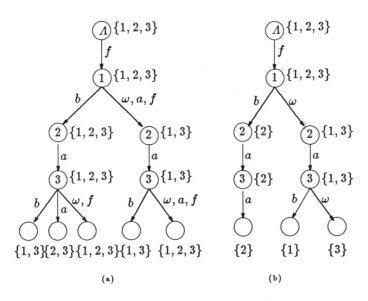

(a)   (b)

Fig. 2. Deterministic (a) and nondeterministic (b) discrimination nets for $\{1 : f(x, a, b),\ 2 : f(b, a, a),\ 3 : f(x, a, y)\}$

Nondeterministic automata may require that all possible computation sequences be enumerated, so that the same symbol of the input term s may have to be inspected repeatedly, as often as once for every pattern. Therefore they may be less efficient than deterministic automata in practice. On the other hand, they are smaller in size and can often be more easily updated, as patterns can readily be added to or deleted from T. Thus, in applications where the set of terms to match with keeps changing (such as in completion procedures), nondeterministic automata may be preferable, while for fixed sets T deterministic automata are more efficient.

The associative-commutative matching algorithm proposed in this paper is based on the use of discrimination nets, but applies to any version thereof, whether deterministic or nondeterministic, adaptive or non-adaptive. For reasons of simplicity, our exposition is given in terms of deterministic automata.

3 Associative-Commutative Matching

Let AC be a set of associativity and commutativity axioms

$$f(x, f(y, z)) = f(f(x, y), z)$$
$$f(x, y) = f(y, x)$$

for some function symbols f. We write $f \in AC$ to indicate that f is such an associative-commutative symbol, and denote by $=_{AC}$ the equational theory induced by the set of equations AC. Thus, $s =_{AC} t$ if and only if s and t are equivalent under associativity and commutativity.

A term t is said to *AC-match* another term s if there exists a substitution σ, such that $t\sigma =_{AC} s$. We shall first consider the problem of deciding, for given linear terms $t_1, \ldots, t_n$, which ones AC-match a specified term s.

In dealing with associativity and commutativity it is of advantage to "flatten" terms and allow varying arity for AC-symbols. More precisely, if f is an AC-symbol, then $f(X)$ is a syntactically valid term, if the sequence of terms X consists of at least two terms. (We denote the length of a sequence X by $|X|$.)

By L we denote the set of all rewrite rules (also called *flattening rules*) of the form

$$f(X, f(Y), Z) \rightarrow f(X, Y, Z), \qquad f \in AC, \ |X| + |Z| \geq 1, \ |Y| \geq 2.$$

Terms that can not be rewritten by L are said to be *flat*. The normal form of a term t under the flattening rules is denoted by $\bar{t}$. Let us denote by $\sim$ the smallest symmetric rewrite relation (also called the *permutation congruence*) for which

$$f(X, u, Y, v, Z) \sim f(X, v, Y, u, Z), \qquad \text{if } f \in AC.$$

It is well-known that the flattened versions of terms equivalent under AC are unique up to the permutation congruence. Consequently, a term t AC-matches a term s if and only if there exists a substitution σ, such that $\overline{t\sigma} \sim \bar{s}$. If we assume that $x\sigma$ is a flat term, for all variables x, then $\overline{t\sigma}$ is almost a flat term as well. The only subterms to which a flattening rule can be applied are of the form $f(Y, x\sigma, Y')$, where $f \in AC$ and $x\sigma = f(Z)$, for some AC-symbol f, in which case $f(Y, f(Z), Y')$ will be flattened to $f(Y, Z, Y')$. The same effect is achieved by substituting for x, not the term $f(Z)$, but instead the *sequence* of terms Z. Denoting by $\bar{\sigma}$ this substitution, with sequences of terms substituted for variable arguments of AC-symbols, we find that $\overline{t\sigma} \sim \bar{s}$ is equivalent to $\bar{t}\bar{\sigma} \sim \bar{s}$.

In sum, the AC-matching problem can essentially be reduced to ordinary matching up to permutation of arguments of AC-symbols, provided terms are flattened first. Henceforth, we shall consider only flattened linear terms and speak of AC-matching to refer matching up to permutation. In the next section we apply discrimination nets to this problem.

4 Associative-Commutative Discrimination Nets

The AC-*nesting depth* at a position in a term is recursively defined as follows. The AC-nesting depth at Λ is 0. If n is the AC-nesting depth at position p in t, then the AC-nesting depth at a position $p.i$ in t is $n + 1$, if $t(p)$ is an AC-symbol, and n, otherwise. The AC-nesting depth of a term is the maximum AC-nesting depth of any of its positions. By the *top-layer* $\hat{t}$ of a term t we mean the expression obtained from t by removing all subterms at positions with non-zero AC-nesting depth. For example, if $f \in AC$ and $g \notin AC$, then the top-layer of $g(a, f(b, c))$ is $g(a, f)$. Observe that the top-layer of a term is a syntactically valid term if AC-symbols are regarded as constants. If t contains no AC-symbols, then $\hat{t} = t$. Furthermore, if $s \sim t$, then $\hat{s} = \hat{t}$.

Now suppose s and t are flat terms, such that $t\sigma \sim s$, where $x\sigma$ may be a sequence of terms, if x occurs as argument of an AC-symbol in t. Then (i) $\hat{t}$ matches $\hat{s}$ and (ii) for all positions p of AC-nesting depth 0 in t, if $t(p)$ is an AC-symbol, then $(t|_p)\sigma \sim s|_p$. Conversely, if (i) and (ii) are satisfied for some substitution σ, then $t\sigma \sim s$. In other words, AC-matching can be characterized in terms of conditions (i) and (ii).

Condition (i) represents a standard matching problem. Let us consider condition (ii). Suppose $t|_p = f(t_1, \ldots, t_m)$ and $s|_p = f(s_1, \ldots, s_n)$, where $f \in AC$. Let us also assume, without loss of generality, that for some k, $0 \le k \le m$, no term $t_1, \ldots, t_k$ is a variable, while all terms $t_{k+1}, \ldots, t_m$ are variables. Define a bipartite graph $G = (V_1 \cup V_2, E)$, with $V_1 = \{s_1, \ldots, s_n\}$, $V_2 = \{t_1, \ldots, t_k\}$, and E consisting of all pairs (s_i, t_j), such that $s_i\sigma \sim t_j$, for some substitution σ. It can easily be seen that if (a) either $n = m$ or $n > m > k$, and (b) there is a matching of size k in the bipartite graph G, then $f(t_1, \ldots, t_m)\sigma \sim f(s_1, \ldots, s_n)$, for some substitution σ and hence condition (ii) is satisfied. (Recall that we consider only linear terms.)

In sum, a flat term t AC-matches another flat term s if and only if (i) the top-layer of t matches the top-layer of s and (ii) maximal AC-subterms of s are AC-matched by corresponding subterms of t. The second condition can be checked by AC-matching proper subterms of t and s and using bipartite graph matching. The above observations motivate the following definitions.

If T is a set of terms, we denote by $\hat{T}$ the set of all top-layers of terms in T. In a discrimination net for such a set $\hat{T}$, nodes v, for which there is an edge (u, v) labelled by an AC-symbol, are called AC-*nodes*. Furthermore, we denote by L_v the set of all terms $t|_{p_u}$, for which $t \in T$, $\hat{t} \in M_v$, and p_u is a non-variable position in t; and by R_v the set of all non-variable terms that occur as top-level arguments of terms in L_v.

An AC-*discrimination net* is a hierarchically structured collection of standard discrimination nets. Formally, an AC-discrimination net for a set of flat terms T consists of (i) a standard discrimination net D (the *top-level net*) for the set $\hat{T}$ of top-layers of T, and (ii) associated with each AC-node v in D, an AC-discrimination net (an AC-*subnet*) for the set R_v. By the *depth* of an AC-discrimination net for T we mean the maximal AC-nesting depth of any term in T.

An AC-discrimination net for a set of terms T defines an AC-matching automaton, which is deterministic and inspects each input symbol at most once, but differs from a standard matching automaton in that it dynamically computes current match sets.

The algorithm AC-match, which accepts as input a flat term s and an associative-commutative discrimination net D for a set of flat terms T, is defined as follows:

1. Let u be the root of D, D' its top-level standard discrimination net, and M'_u be T.
2. If u is leaf, then return $M_u \cap M'_u$.
3. Otherwise, let (u, v) be the edge in D' corresponding to the symbol $f = s(p_u)$. (If f is a variable, the corresponding edge is the one labelled by ω.)
4. If v is an AC-node, then $s|_{p_u}$ is a term $f(s_1, \ldots, s_n)$. Recursively apply the algorithm AC-match to each term s_i and the AC-subnet D_v associated with v, to determine which terms in R_v AC-match s_i.
   Define, for each term $t = f(t_1, \ldots, t_k, x_{k+1}, \ldots, x_m)$ in L_v with non-variable arguments $t_1, \ldots, t_k$, a bipartite graph G_t with vertices $s_1, \ldots, s_n$ and $t_1, \ldots, t_k$ and with all pairs (s_i, t_j), for which s_i AC-matches t_j, as edges. If (a) either $n = m$ or else $n > m > k$, and (b) there is a matching of size k in the graph G_t, then t AC-matches $f(s_1, \ldots, s_n)$.
   Let L'_v be the set of all terms in L_v that AC-match $f(s_1, \ldots, s_n)$. Let M'_v be the set of all terms in M'_u, such that either $t|_{p'}$ is a variable, for some prefix p' of p_u, or else $t|_{p_u}$ is in L'_v.
5. Let u be v and M'_u be M'_v and go to step 2.

This algorithm is correct:

Theorem 1. *Let D be an associative-commutative discrimination net for a set of flat terms T, and let s be a flat term. Then the algorithm AC-match returns, for input D and s, the set of all terms in T that AC-match s.*

Proof. The proof is by induction on the depth of D. Let T' be the set returned by AC-match for input D and s and let t be a term in T'. We first prove that (i)

$\hat{t}$ matches $\hat{s}$ and (ii) for all positions p of AC-nesting depth 0 in t, if $t(p)$ is an AC-symbol, then $t|_p$ AC-matches $s|_p$.

Let u be the root of the top-layer discrimination net D' of D and let v be the final state that is reached by the matching automaton A' defined by D' on input $\hat{s}$. The same node v is the last one reached by AC-match. Since t is in M_v, we may infer that $\hat{t}$ matches $\hat{s}$.

Let p be a position of AC-nesting depth 0 in t, and suppose $t|_p = f(t_1, \ldots, t_m)$ and $s|_p = f(s_1, \ldots, s_n)$, for some AC-symbol f. Let (u', v') be the edge considered in step 3 of AC-match at the time when the symbol at position p in s is inspected. Since any AC-subnet of D is of smaller depth, we may use the induction hypothesis to infer that the set M'_v computed in the succeeding step 4 contains only terms t' such that $t'|_p$ AC-matches $s|_p$. Thus, conditions (i) and (ii) are indeed satisfied for t.

On the other hand, it can easily be seen that that if a term t is contained in T but not in T', then t does not AC-match s. This completes the proof. $\square$

Theorem 2. *Let D be an associative-commutative discrimination net for a set of flat terms T, and let s be a flat term. The algorithm AC-match determines the set of all terms in T that AC-match s in time $O(n) + O(mn^{1.5})$, where n is the size of the subject term s and m is the sum of the sizes of all pattern terms in T.*

Proof. First note that each symbol in the input term s is inspected at most once. If the symbol inspected is not AC, then its processing takes only a constant amount of time (steps 3 and 5).

In the case of an AC-symbol, which is the root of a subterm $f(s_1, \ldots, s_{n_i})$ of s, we need to apply a bipartite graph matching algorithm to graphs G_t, for certain sets of patterns t, all of which are subterms of terms in the initial set T. Let $n_i + m_t$ be the number of vertices in G_t. Then the number of edges is at most $n_i m_t$, and a maximum bipartite matching on G_t can be computed in time $O(m_t n_i \sqrt{n_i})$. The total time for all bipartite matchings on graphs with $V_1 = \{s_1, \ldots, s_{n_i}\}$ is thus no more than $O(mn_i^{1.5})$. Since $\sum_i n_i \leq n$, the total time for all bipartite graph matchings done during the course of the algorithm is no more than $O(mn^{1.5})$.

Furthermore, the computation of current match sets M'_v and returned match sets $M_u \cap M'_u$ can be done in time proportional to the size of the sets involved, which is no more than m. Therefore the total time for all of these operations cannot exceed $O(nm)$. We have thus established the desired bound of $O(n) + O(mn^{1.5})$ on the running time of AC-match. $\square$

Finally, a few remarks about the space complexity of the discrimination net. The time to build the discrimination net is directly related to its space complexity, and the size of the discrimination net can become quite large. In fact, the worst-case lower bound on space of a discrimination net is exponential in the number of terms [11]. However, at the expense of increasing the matching time it is possible to reduce the space complexity. One approach is to build a nondeterministic net based on strong compatibility. Another approach that can yield much bigger space reductions is to build a different kind of discrimination net based on root-to-leaf path sequences which contain both positions and function symbols. Details about such nets appear in [10, 12, 8].

5 Secondary Automata

In the above AC-matching algorithm we have applied indexing techniques to the non-AC portions of given pattern terms, and have used bipartite graph matching to deal with AC-subterms. The running time of the algorithm is dominated by the cost of bipartite graph matching. The bipartite graphs that have to be considered are of the form $G = (V_1 \cup V_2, E)$, where $V_1 = \{s_1, \ldots, s_l\}$ is a set of input subterms, $V_2 = \{t_1, \ldots, t_k\}$ is a set of pattern subterms, and E contains an edge (s_i, t_j) if and only if t_j AC-matches s_i.

More precisely, the terms $t_1, \ldots, t_k$ are the non-variable top-level arguments of some occurrence of an AC-operator in a pattern term. It appears that in practice the number k is usually quite small. For instance, in all the associative-commutative rewrite systems listed by Hullot [5], there are no AC-subterms with more than *two* non-variable arguments. We have also analysed several benchmark problems for AC-completion, such as certain group examples similar to the ones used by Christian [1]. In one typical example, a total of 128 rewrite rules were generated during the completion of a canonical system of 35 rules. There were 183 occurrences of AC-symbols on the left-hand sides of these rules, of which 81 had only variables as arguments, while the remaining ones had only one non-variable argument. In the examples we looked at, there was only one instance of an AC-subterm with more than two non-variable arguments. (The number of non-variable arguments in that case was four.)

These observations have led us to design special techniques, called secondary automata, to efficiently handle bipartite graph matching for cases where V_2 is small, say $k \leq 4$.

Suppose graphs are represented by adjacency matrices, with rows corresponding to nodes s_i and columns corresponding to nodes t_j. The edge set E is computed row by row, as the algorithm AC-match is applied to each term s_i. Let us denote by G_i the subgraph of G consisting of the first i rows.

For example, suppose we have one pattern $f(g(a,b), g(a,x), y))$, where only f is an AC-symbol. We need to look at bipartite graphs $G = (V_1 \cup V_2, E)$, with $V_2 = \{g(a,b), g(a,x)\}$. The sets V_1 and E depend on the input term. For an input term $f(g(a,d), g(a,c), g(a,b))$, we have $V_1 = \{g(a,d), g(a,c), g(a,b)\}$. The two terms $g(a,d)$ and $g(a,c)$ are AC-matched only by the second term in V_2, while $g(a,b)$ is AC-matched by both pattern subterms, so that we obtain adjacency matrices

$$G_1 = (0\ 1),\ G_2 = \begin{pmatrix} 0 & 1 \\ 0 & 1 \end{pmatrix},\ G = G_3 = \begin{pmatrix} 0 & 1 \\ 0 & 1 \\ 1 & 1 \end{pmatrix}.$$

The maximum graph matching is of size 2.

Let us classify bipartite graphs $G = (V_1 \cup V_2, E)$ with $|V_2| = k$, according to the size of a maximum matching and the subset of vertices in V_2 matched in a maximum matching. More precisely, a *matching characteristic* is a collection δ of d-element subsets of V_2, where $d \le k$. We say that G has matching characteristic δ if, for every set $M \in \delta$, there exists a maximum matching of G on which each vertex in M, but no vertex in $V_2 \setminus M$, is incident. (Thus, the size of the maximum matching is d.) Note that there are only finitely many different sets δ, for any fixed number k.

For example, graphs G_1 and G_2 above have matching characteristic $\{2\}$, while G_3 has matching characteristic $\{1, 2\}$.

We define an automaton S_k, for each k, as follows. Each matching characteristic δ is represented by a unique state of S_k. The input symbols for S_k are bitstrings b of length k (each such bitstring representing a possible row in adjacency matrix). There is a transition from δ to δ' on input b if there is some graph G of matching characteristic δ and with adjacency matrix A, such that the graph G' defined by the adjacency matrix obtained from A by adding row b, has matching characteristic δ'. There is exactly one state δ_0 with $|\delta_0| = 0$, which is taken as the initial state of S_k; and exactly one state δ_k with $|\delta_k| = k$, which is taken as the only final state of S_k. We call S_k a *secondary automaton*.

The secondary automata S_2 is shown in Figure 3. The states are numbered, with matching characteristic as indicated. For instance, state 3 has matching characteristic $\{\{1\}, \{2\}\}$, which is the property of any graph $G = (V_1 \cup V_2, E)$, where V_2 has two elements, E is non-empty, and all edges are incident on the same element (either the first or the second) of V_2.

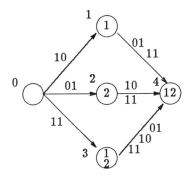

Fig. 3. Secondary automaton of depth 2.

Observe that all transitions lead from a state representing matchings of size d to a state representing matchings of size $d + 1$. In fact, we have:

Lemma 3. *Let* $G = (V_1 \cup V_2, E)$ *and* $G' = (V_1' \cup V_2, E')$ *be bipartite graphs, such that* $V_1' = V_1 \cup \{v\}$ *and* $E' = E \cup E_v$, *where* E_v *is a set of edges* (v, v'), *with* $v' \in V_2$. *Also, let* d *be the size of a maximum matching in* G. *Then* G' *has either* *a maximum matching of size $d+1$, or else has the same matching characteristics as G.*

Proof. Let the matching characteristics of G and G' be δ and δ' respectively. Suppose G' has a maximum matching of size d, $\delta \neq \delta'$ and $M' \in \delta' \setminus \delta$. For any $M \in \delta$, there must be a vertex $w \in M'$ such that $w \notin M$. Clearly, v is matched with a vertex $u \in M$ because otherwise M' would be either of size $d+1$ or included in δ. Let v' be the vertex matched with u in a matching characterized by M. If v' is not matched with any vertex in M', then $M' \in \delta$, which is a contradiction. Suppose u' is v''s match in M'. If $u' \in M$, one can repeat the above argument until a vertex $w \in V_2$ but $w \notin M$ is found; otherwise, we take $w = u'$. In both cases, we have shown for G' the existence of maximum matchings of size $d+1$ incident upon the subset $M \cup \{w\}$ of V_2. A contradiction. □

As an immediate corollary we obtain:

Corollary 4. *Let $G = (V_1 \cup V_2, E)$ be a bipartite graph with $|V_1| = l$ and $|V_2| = k$. Let A be the corresponding adjacency matrix, and A_i be the i-th row of A. Then the secondary automaton S_k, for input $A_1 \ldots A_l$, will reach the state δ that represents the matching characteristics of G.*

In the context of the algorithm AC-match the secondary automata can be used in step 4, to determine whether there exists a bipartite matching of the required size. The number of states in a secondary automaton increases exponentially with k, so that these automata are only practical for small values of k. (The automaton S_1 has only two states, while S_2 has five, and S_3 sixteen.) Fortunately, the value of k tends to be small enough in practical examples, as we have mentioned above.

Secondary automata can also be adapted to yield the actual matching substitutions. If, in traversing a secondary automaton, one can not move to a new state on a row of the adjacency matrix, the input subterm corresponding to the row is a candidate term for the substitution of some variable $x_{k+1}, \cdots, x_m$. By keeping track of such candidates, once the AC-matching is done, one can find consistent substitutions for all the variables in a pattern. For instance, in the pattern $f(g(a, x), g(b, y))$ and the subject $f(g(a, b), g(b, c))$, where both f and g are in AC, y has two candidate substitutions a and c while x has only b. From these candidates, one can determine the final substitution $x \mapsto b$ and $y \mapsto c$ once the algorithm has finished.

Theorem 5. *All bipartite matching problems at all AC-nodes visited during traversal of an AC-discrimination net for a set of flat terms, with total size m, on behalf of an input term of size n can be done in $O(mn)$ time.*

Proof. Since the transition function at each state of a secondary automaton of depth k can be implemented as a k-dimensional table, each transition takes $O(k)$. Thus, using the notation as in proof of Theorem 2, a maximum bipartite matching on G_t can be computed in time $O(m_t n_i)$. Therefore, the time to compute maximum bipartite matchings on graphs with $V_1 = \{s_1, \cdots, s_{n_i}\}$ is no more than $O(mn_i)$ and the total time for all bipartite matchings done during the course of AC-match is no more than $O(mn)$. □

6   Nonlinear Matching

The above (polynomial-time) algorithm applies to linear pattern terms. In its simplest form, the algorithm just determines which patterns AC-match a given input term. In situations where most match attempts are likely to fail (as is typical of theorem proving applications), it may thus make sense to use this version of the algorithm as a "filter," to quickly sort out failed matching attempts. In case of success, a *single* substitution for a pattern can easily be extracted during the algorithm, which is sufficient for the purpose of rewriting with linear terms.

In the case of nonlinear terms, we apply the matching algorithm to linearized versions of patterns in a first phase, and, in a second phase, check whether the proposed substitutions for different occurrences of the same variable are consistent. This requires that *all* matching substitutions be computed, and the AC-matching algorithm has to be extended correspondingly. In particular, we have to compute all maximal bipartite graph matchings—instead of just determining whether a maximum-sized matching exists. (The nonlinear AC-matching problem is NP-complete, so that a considerable increase in computing time, as compared to linear AC-matching, is not surprising.)

7   Concluding Remarks

In this paper, we have proposed a new data structure, called AC-discrimination nets, and used it to speed up many-to-one AC-matching. In any set of patterns the nesting depth of AC-symbols defines a number of levels of non-AC-parts. An AC-discrimination net is a collection of standard discrimination nets, structured in a way that reflects this hierarchy. The AC-matching algorithm, recursively traversing the levels of the net, uses bipartite graph matching on each level to interpret and combine the AC-matching results from lower levels. If no AC-symbols are present in the patterns, the AC-discrimination net specializes to a standard discrimination net.

We have also proposed secondary automata as a novel data structure for further speeding up matching of AC-patterns typically encountered in practice. Secondary automata are only dependent on the number of non-variable arguments within AC-subterms of the pattern, so that all AC-subterms having the same number of non-variable arguments can be handled by a single secondary automaton. This feature makes it attractive for completion as there is no need to create them dynamically when patterns change.

Let us briefly discuss some of the other proposals for many-to-one AC-matching. Lugiez and Kounalis [6] proposed an algorithm to compile pattern matching of AC function definitions in functional languages. In their approach a complete pattern tree (that guides matching) is constructed by enumerating certain AC terms. Such an enumeration appears to be prohibitively expensive in terms of both time and space. Nicolaita [9] described a method which is based on Christian's discrimination net [1]. The main drawback with his method is that it requires that the arguments of AC-subterms in the patterns as well as in the subject be ordered. It is not clear whether the ordering constraints can be efficiently maintained in completion, where both the patterns and the subjects keep changing dynamically. (The kind of ordering to be used is left unspecified and the complexity of the algorithm is left open.) Lugiez and Moysset describe a bottom-up procedure for AC-matching in which patterns are preprocessed into a large nondeterministic tree automaton [7]. The running time of the algorithms is not analysed, but the construction of a deterministic automaton (from the nondeterministic one) is bound to be expensive.

Finally we remark that our linear matching algorithm can be directly used to deal with function symbols that are only commutative, in which case no flattening rules are applied to such function symbols. For function symbols that are only associative we simply need to replace bipartite graph matching with ordered bipartite matching.

Acknowledgments. We wish to thank the referees for their comments. This research has been supported in part by NSF grant CCR-9102159.

References

1. J. Christian. Fast Knuth-Bendix completion : Summary. In *RTA'89*, pages 551–555. Springer-Verlag LNCS 355, 1989.
2. D. Kapur D. Benanav and P. Narendran. Complexity of matching problems. *Journal of Symbolic Computation*, 3:203–216, 1987.
3. N. Dershowitz and J.-P. Jouannaud. Rewrite systems. In *Handbook of Theoretical Computer Science*, volume B, chapter 6, pages 243–309. Elsevier, 1990.
4. A. Graf. Left-to-right tree pattern matching. In *RTA'91*, pages 323–334. Springer-Verlag LNCS 488, 1991.
5. J.-M. Hullot. A catalogue of canonical term rewriting systems. Technical Report CSL-113, SRI International, April 1980.
6. E. Kounalis and D. Lugiez. Compilation of pattern matching with associative-commutative functions. In *TAPSOFT'91*, pages 57–73. Springer-Verlag LNCS 493, 1991.
7. D. Lugiez and J.L. Moysset. Complement problems and tree automata in AC-like theories. To appear in *STACS'93*.
8. W. McCune. Experiments with discrimination-tree indexing and path indexing for term retrieval. Technical Report MCS-P191-1190, Argonne National Laboratory, Argonne, Illinois, USA, January 1991.
9. D. Nicolaita. An indexing scheme for AC-equational theories. Technical report, Research Institute for Infomatics, Bucharest, Romania, February 1992.
10. R. Ramesh, I.V. Ramakrishnan, and D.S. Warren. Automata-driven indexing of prolog clauses. In *Seventh Annual ACM Symposium on Principles of Programming Languages*, pages 281–290, San Francisco, 1990.
11. R.C. Sekar, R. Ramesh, and I.V. Ramakrishnan. Adaptive pattern matching. In *ICALP'92*, pages 247–260. Springer-Verlag LNCS 623, 1992.
12. M. E. Stickel. The path-indexing method for indexing terms. Technical Report 473, SRI International, Menlo Park, California, USA, October 1989.
13. R. M. Verma and I.V. Ramakrishnan. Tight complexity bounds for term matching problems. *Information and Computation*, 101(1):33–69, November 1992.

Algebraic Specification and Development in Geometric Modeling*

Y. Bertrand, J.-F. Dufourd, J. Françon, P. Lienhardt

Département d'Informatique, Université Louis-Pasteur / CNRS
7, rue René-Descartes, 67084 Strasbourg Cedex, France, tel: 33 88 61 43 00,
e-mail: {bertrand, dufourd, françon, lienhardt} @dpt-info.u-strasbg.fr

Abstract. For several years now, the Geometric Modeling Group of Strasbourg has been working on new formal concepts and tools for describing and manipulating the boundary representation of geometric objects. In a large project of an interactive modeller for volumic objects, the description of which is based on generalized maps, it attempts to cover the whole process from mathematical modeling to efficient implementation, via a complete algebraic specification. Basic concepts and results of this experiment in horizontal and vertical software specification and development are presented along with several illustrations. Advances in algebraic specification methodology are highlighted, specially hierarchical construction of ordered sorts and operations.

1 Introduction

For geometrical applications, algebraic specifications improve modeling and software development processes. We try to show it through the report of a large-size project.

Several methods have been proposed for describing and manipulating geometric objects on computers [41, 42]. One of them, namely boundary representation [2, 38, 39], consists in describing objects by their subdivisions, in vertices, edges, faces and volumes. In this frame, mathematical combinatorial models have been proposed. The oldest one is the combinatorial map [16], well studied in [28, 44, 43, 8]. It has numerous uses in geometric modeling [1, 31, 21, 11]. New combinatorial topological models of n-dimensional objects rely on map extensions [9, 29, 32, 13]. Among them, we have proposed the n-dimensional generalized map, or n-g-map [33, 34, 35]. It is a particularly efficient model to deal with topology of manifolds. When completed by an embedding model, it allows to describe the entire geometry of n-dimensional manifold objects.

Furthermore, for a long time, it has been attempted to improve the computer graphics programming techniques by functional [40], logical [20], or object-oriented [26] approaches. But we think that decisive progress will come above all from formal specification techniques, particularly algebraic ones [17, 3, 46]. Their first outstanding use was in [36, 37] where graphical basic objects and operations were algebraically specified . Other works normalize libraries of graphical interactive primitives, like GKS [10], or describe particular algorithms [30]. Note also the attempt of [25] which specifies elementary geometric constructions with an extended OBJ3. In [12, 13, 14], we give the basis of an algebraic specification of maps and extensions. However using algebraic specifications has never been reported for computer graphics real-size applications.

So, for a full-scale test of both the operationality of the n-g-map model and the efficiency of the algebraic specification techniques, our group has designed and developed original and complex software, namely an interactive volumic modeller, i.e., a program which helps to interactively build and handle 3D geometrical objects, with topological basis [5]. The algebraic specification of this software is the continuation of our preceeding work. It gives us a rigorous hierarchical description of object sorts and operations, with a functional constructive point of view, an horizontal structuring, a vertical development

---

* This research has been supported by the GDR *Programmation*, CNRS, France.

[18], and even a logical prototyping [3] and a real implementation. As far as we know, this is the first attempt to develop an interactive volumic modeller on a topological basis, and, moreover, with the help of a complete algebraic specification. This kind of product is the kernel of specialized software for industrial applications, e.g., mechanical CAD, 3D meshing, design, architecture.

We present here the n-g-maps and the modeller. However, the paper is especially centered on the specification problem and on the solutions supplied. We insist on the theoretical fundamentals, the methodology of construction of the ordered sorts and the specification of the main operations. We rapidly discuss a few choices we made on realization, interactivity and implementation. The power of the modeller is illustrated by complex geometric objects.

Section 2 describes the embedded n-g-maps, derived notions and properties. Section 3 presents the main functionalities and user operations of the modeller. Section 4 proposes an order-sorted kernel of algebraic specification for the modeller. Section 5 deals with the vertical development. Section 6 treats the horizontal structuring. Section 7 presents technical features of the modeller. Section 8 summarizes this experiment and gives future prospects. An Appendix shows screen pictures of objects built by the modeller.

2 A Geometrical Model

2.1 A Topological Model

The *n-dimensional generalized map*, *n-g-map* for short, is a combinatorial notion, which is used as a general basis for the topological modeling in dimension n. The mathematical elements we give here are only those used in the following. A complete study as well as justifications for modeling and mathematical proofs of soundness are in [33, 34, 35].

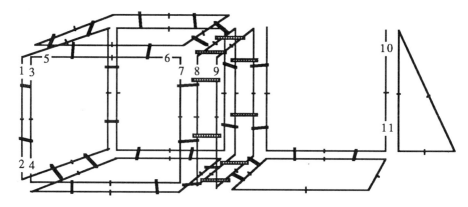

Fig. 1. An example of a 3-g-map with 2 connected components.

Recall that an *involution* α in a set D is a bijection such that $\alpha(\alpha(x)) = x$ for any x in D. Let $n \geq -1$. An *n-g-map* $G = (D, \alpha_0, ..., \alpha_n)$ consists of a finite set D of *darts* with n+1 companion involutions α_k in D, $0 \leq k \leq n$, with the constraints: $\alpha_k \circ \alpha_j$ is an involution, for $k+2 \leq j \leq n$. Darts x and y are said to be *k-sewn* in G if $\alpha_k(x) = y$ (and $\alpha_k(y) = x$).

Fig. 1 (and Picture 1 in Appendix) shows a 3-g-map represented, or *embedded*, in $\mathbf{R}^3$. Darts are natural numbers (only partially written in the drawing for clarity) embedded as half straight line segments in $\mathbf{R}^3$. Involution α_0 is symbolized by thin strokes between half segments, α_1 by their junctions, α_2 by thicker black strokes, and α_3 by hatched strokes. Thus $\alpha_0(1) = 2$, $\alpha_0(2) = 1$, $\alpha_1(3) = 5$, $\alpha_2(1) = 3$, $\alpha_2(8) = 7$, $\alpha_3(8) = 9$, $\alpha_3(9) = 8$, $\alpha_1(10) = 10$, $\alpha_2(9) = 9$, $\alpha_3(1) = 1$, etc.

An n-g-map can be viewed as a *multigraph* in D with n+1 companion symmetric binary relations determined by the α_k, for $0 \leq k \leq n$. The result is a notion of *(strong) connected component* for n-g-map as in multigraphs (cf. Fig. 1). The connected component of dart x in G is denoted $\langle\alpha_0, ..., \alpha_n\rangle(x)$. New simple notions can also be introduced.

For $0 \leq k \leq n$, the *(n-1)-g-map of k-cells* of the n-g-map $G = (D, \alpha_0, ..., \alpha_n)$ is defined by $G_k = (D, \alpha_0, ..., \alpha_{k-1}, \alpha_{k+1}, ..., \alpha_n)$. The *k-cell* of G incident to dart x is the connected component of x in G_k. The 0-cells, 1-cells, 2-cells and 3-cells of G are respectively called the *vertices, edges, faces* and *volumes* of G (Fig. 2).

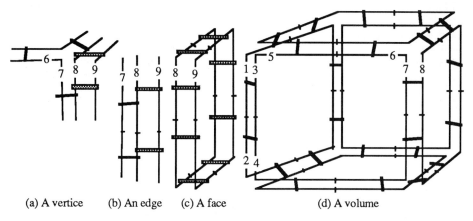

(a) A vertice   (b) An edge   (c) A face   (d) A volume

Fig. 2. K-cells incident to dart 8 of the 3-g-map in Fig. 1.

Similarly, for $0 \leq k \leq n$, the *(k-1)-g-map of simple k-cells* of G is defined by $G'_k = (D, \alpha_0, ..., \alpha_{k-1})$. The *simple k-cell* of G incident to dart x is the connected component of x in G'_k (Fig. 3). So, constraints $\alpha_k \circ \alpha_j$ is an involution of the n-g-map definition say that k-sewings are always done in n-g-maps for *all* the darts of *isomorphic* simple k-cells.

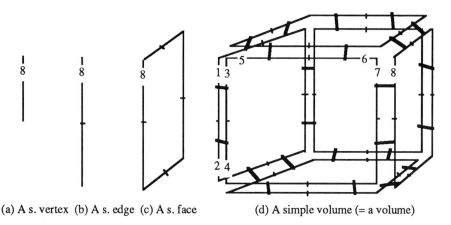

(a) A s. vertex (b) A s. edge (c) A s. face   (d) A simple volume (= a volume)

Fig. 3. Simple (or s.) k-cells incident to dart 8 of the 3-g-map in Fig. 1.

2.2 A Geometrical Embedding Model

For any dimension k, $0 \leq k \leq n$, the geometric *k-embedding* of an n-g-map in an n-dimensional Euclidean space $\mathbf{R}^n$ is fixed by labels associated with k-cells, in fact by a single dart per k-cell.

More precisely, for $0 \leq k \leq n$, k-embedding labels are *manifolds* of dimension k, i.e., in dimensions 0, 1, 2, etc, respectively points, Jordan arcs, disc homeomorphic patches, etc. In Fig. 1, each vertex is 0-embedded in a point of $\mathbf{R}^3$, each edge as a straight line segment, each face as a plane patch, and each volume as a polyhedron. Note that the display often splits the cells, to show darts and sewings, as in Fig. 1 and Picture 1.

2.3 Properties of the Generalized Maps

Many interesting *properties* about the topology of objects can be obtained from a modeling by n-g-maps. The principal ones concern 2-g-maps which modelize surfaces. Indeed, with a given 2-g-map may always be associated the topology of a *subdivision* of a surface, open or closed, orientable or not, with or without boundaries. Conversely, a 2-g-map may always be associated with the topology of any surface subdivision [27, 33].

Three *characteristics* of a 2-g-map are typical of the subdivision of the surface whose topology is represented by the 2-g-map. They are the *number of boundaries*, the *orientability factor* (the value of which is 0 if the surface is orientable, 1 or 2 otherwise), the *genus* (i.e., the number of holes) [27]. For instance, the triplet of characteristics of a disk, a sphere, a torus, a Moëbius strip, a Klein bottle, respectively are (1, 0, 0), (0, 0, 0), (0, 0, 1), (1, 1, 0), (0, 2, 0). These characteristics can be computed from a 2-g-map associated with the surface. Picture 2 shows non orientable open and closed surfaces.

3 Functionalities of the Modeller

The modeller is a program which allows interactively to construct, modify, manipulate, display and record geometric 3D objects, thanks to numerous original facilities.

3.1 Modeled Objects

The end user of the modeller manipulates embedded 3-g-maps with some additional constraints. They modelize objects composed of vertices, edges, faces and volumes, which are *regularized* or *not* [45]. Thus, dangling edges, open faces or volumes, non orientable faces can intentionally be manipulated, efficiently detected and possibly discarded.

More precisely, the following additional *topological constraints* are adopted for the 3-g-maps handled by the user: (1) α_0 is an involution with no fixed point; (2) $\alpha_0 \circ \alpha_1$ has no fixed point; (3) $\alpha_0 \circ \alpha_2$ has no fixed point; (4) $\alpha_1(x) = x$ implies $\alpha_3(x) = x$; (5) $<\alpha_0, \alpha_1>(x)$ and $<\alpha_0, \alpha_1>(\alpha_3(x))$ are disjoint for any dart x.

The intuitive meaning of these constraints is: (1) *dangling* darts are forbidden; (2) *loops* are forbidden; (3) *bent* edges, i.e., simple edges 2-sewn to themselves, are forbidden; (4) only *closed* simple faces can be sewn; (5) *folded* simple faces, i.e., simple faces 3-sewn to themselves, are forbidden. The 3-g-map in Fig. 1 satisfies these properties.

A very simple *embedding* is adopted: each vertex is embedded as a point of $\mathbf{Q}^3$. Thus, an edge is implicitly embedded as the *line segment* joining the two points associated with the vertices that bound the edge. Similarly, a face is implicitly embedded as a *surface patch* joining the line segments associated with the edges which bound the face. If the face is bounded by three edges, the patch is planar. Otherwise its exact form is not essential in our application. Such a patch, which is only defined by its boundary, is easily handled by most basic graphics libraries, for instance to fill it or to render it.

3.2 High-level Operations

About 150 high-level operations can be used through menus. Creation, deletion, duplication, subdivision, sewing and unsewing of k-cells and connected components of embedded 3-g-maps are among the main supplied facilities. Production and sewing of linearized cubic curves, bicubic surfaces, tricubic volumes, revolution and sweeping curves and surfaces are very useful operations offered for building quickly realistic objects.

Motion and deformation with constant topology of designated parts of an object are possible under an interactive control. Immediate computing of the three characteristics of built surfaces allows the user to permanently check their quality. Visualization, coloring, picking, files, undo-redo, press book, etc, complete the functionalities.

Despite the simplicity of the topological and embedding models, it is possible to build complex objects with these operations, as displayed in Pictures 3 to 8 of Appendix. In traditional modellers, such objects sometimes need *Boolean shape operations* [41], which are brute force and time consuming. The clear distinction between topology and embedding in the geometrical model often allows us to avoid these operations. Moreover this distinction is a basic principle of the following formal specifications.

4 Algebraic Specification of an N-g-map Basic Kernel

We formalize a kernel of n-g-maps manipulations. It is more general than what is strictly needed for the modeller in order to make specification, subsequent programmation and future re-using more easy, clear and safe. In this section, the specification is mainly an *horizontal structuring* by *extensions without parameter*, and without explicitly *importing/exporting modules* [18]. The specification is *order-sorted* [23] and *equational*, with the usual *if_then_else_* and == (for comparison) polymorphic functional symbols [17]. We always adopt an *initial semantics* point of view [17, 23]. Specifications of Booleans, non null natural, natural and rational numbers, i.e., *Boolean, nznat, nat* and *rat* sorts, are built-in, with the *constraint* to be in the *initial* semantics [18].

4.1 Topology

The dart sort is named *dart*. An erroneous dart *err_dart* is introduced with the *dart?* sort as such that *dart < dart?*, in the sense of the ordered sorts [23]. We choose atomic n-g-map *generators* to facilitate the building of other operations by composition, particularly sewings and unsewings of k-cells. That leads to sorts which are *greater* than necessary and which are called by the generic name *map*. The specification of the most general sort, *map0*, begins by that of the topological generators, *v*, *i*, and *l*:

> **sorts** *dart dart? map0*
> **subsort** *dart < dart?*
> **operations**
>   *err_dart : → dart?*
>   *v : → map0*
>   *i : map0 dart → map0*
>   *l : map0 **nat** dart dart → map0*

For simplification's sake, we identify here *dart* sort and **nznat**, *err_dart* and 0, and *dart?* and **nat**. This enables us to stay in the *initial semantics* avoiding both parameters and functorial considerations [17]. In fact, darts are actually represented by pointers in the modeller implementation. The symbol of constant *v* corresponds to the empty map, *i(m, x)* inserts a dart *x* in a map *m*, *l(m, k, x, y)* associates *y* to *x* with label (in *dimension*) *k*, in a "semi-sewing". These operations are total. So, we can insert by *i* several times the same dart in a map, and apply *l* anyhow. In initial semantics, the sort *map0* is interpreted as the set of all the closed terms which are generated by these operators.

The following operator *a* formalizes the n-g-map functions α_k (cf. section 2) extended to the maps: *a(m, k, x)* returns the *successor* at dimension *k* of *x* in the map *m*:

> **operation**
>   *a : map0 **nat** dart → dart?*
> **axioms** *(m : map0, k j : **nat**, x y z : dart)*
>   *a(v, k, z) = err_dart*
>   *a(i(m, x), k, z) = **if** z == x **then** x **else** a(m, k, z)*
>   *a(l(m, j, x, y), k, z) = **if** k == j **and** z == x **then** y **else** a(m, k, z)*

To retrieve the usual cases, we define a new *map1* sort, with *map1* < *map0*, interpreted as a set of *directed multigraphs* on darts, with edges labelled in **nat**. The invariant *inv_map1* characterizes the maps of *map0* which belong to *map1*. The operation *i(m, x)* is interpreted as the insertion of a graph node *x* in *m*, and *l(m, k, x, y)* as the addition of an edge *(x, y)* labelled by *k*. The Boolean operation *ex_dart(m, x)* returns **true** iff *x* is in *m*:

> **sort** *map1*
> **subsort** *map1 = map0 [inv_map1]*
> **operations**
>   *ex_dart : map0 dart → **Boolean***
>   *inv_map1 : map0 → **Boolean***
> **preconditions** *(m : map1, k : nat, x y : dart)*
>   **prec** *[map1] i(m, x)* ≡ **not** *ex_dart(m, x)*
>   **prec** *[map1] l(m, k, x, y)* ≡ *ex_dart(m, x)* **and** *ex_dart(m, y)*
> **axioms** *(m : map0, k n : nat, x y z : dart)*
>   *ex_dart(v, z) =* **false**
>   *ex_dart(i(m, x), z) = z == x* **or** *ex_dart(m, z)*
>   *ex_dart(l(m, k, x, y), z) = ex_dart(m, z)*
>   *inv_map1(v) =* **true**
>   *inv_map1(i(m, x)) =* **not** *ex_dart(m, x)* **and** *inv_map1(m)*
>   *inv_map1(l(m, k, x, y)) = ex_dart(m, x)* **and** *ex_dart(m, y)*
>   **and** *inv_map1(m)*

Preconditions for *i* and *l* derive from the invariant *inv_map1*: when applied to *map1 m*, *i(m, x)* returns a legal element of *map1* iff *x* does not belong to *m*, and *l(m, k, x, y)* iff *x* and *y* belong to *m*. Each precondition definition is indexed by the target sort of the operator between square brackets, e.g., *[map1]* for *i*. In fact, the above preconditions are the *weakest ones* to satisfy the invariant, which can be proven. The new operations *i* and *l* are restrictions of the old ones: they have exactly the same semantics as previously on the domain defined by the invariant. This satisfies the *monotonicity condition* of [23].

A *hierarchy* of about 40 ordered map sorts with invariants and operations with preconditions has been defined. Constraints get more and more restrictive: sorts with α_k injective, with α_k a permutation, with α_k an involution, with k ≤ 3, with embedding constraints, etc. For instance, the sort *map3* take into account the *permutativity* of *i* and *l*:

> **sort** *map3*
> **subsort** *map3 < map2*
> **axioms** *(m : map2, k k' n : nat, x y x' y' z : dart)*
>   *i(i(m, x), x') = i(i(m, x'), x)*
>   *l(l(m, k, x, y), k', x', y') = l(l(m, k', x', y'), k, x, y)*
>   *i(l(m, k, x, y), z) = l(i(m, z), k, x, y)*

The sort hierarchy meets the order-sorted signature constraints: it is *regular* and *coherent*, in the sense of [23]. It is completely described in [4].

4.2 Embedding

We extend the specification with an *embedding generator em*. Thus, *em(m, k, x, q)* embeds the *k*-cell of *m* containing dart *x* on a geometric object *q* of sort *embed* and of dimension *k*:

> **sort** *embed*
> **operation**
>   *em : map0 **nat** dart embed → map0*
> **precondition** *(m : map0, k : nat, x : dart, q : embed)*
>   **prec** *em(m, k, x, q)* ≡ *inv_embed(q, k)*

To meet this constraint, we introduce sorts *embedk* of geometric objects of dimension *k*, with *embedk < embed*. We also define an invariant *inv_embed(q, k)*, **true** iff *q* belongs to sort *embedk*, which is the precondition for *em*. In fact, only 0-embeddings are explicit in the modeller. They are 3D points, i.e., triplets of **rat** coordinates, built by the 0-embedding generator *genembed0*. Thus we have in this simple case:

> **operations**
> $genembed0 : \mathbf{rat}^3 \rightarrow embed0$
> $inv\_embed : embed \rightarrow \mathbf{Boolean}$
> **axiom** $(x\,y\,z\,x1 : \mathbf{rat}, k : \mathbf{nat})$
> $inv\_embed(genembed0(x, y, z), k) = k == 0$

The introduction of the map generator *em* enriches the set of *map0* terms. It also forces to complete the previous specifications. For instance, a new axiom is needed for *a*:

> **axiom** $(m : map0, k\,j : \mathbf{nat}, x\,z : dart, q : embed)$
> $a(em(m, k, x, q), j, z) = a(m, j, z)$

Such axioms can always be automatically added, and wont be written here anymore. In fact, as there are thousands in the modeller specification, it is impossible to write them by hand. They are called *implicit axioms* in [37]. As previously, only darts present in a map can be embedded. This property restricts the *map0* sort to a new sort *mape1 < map0*. Furthermore, for the modeller, *at most one* dart per k-cell is k-embedded. Thus, we introduce again a new sort *mape2 < mape1*, defined by an invariant *inv_mape2*, in fact *free_embed(m, k, x)*, that is **true** iff no dart of the k-cell of x is k-embedded in *m*:

> **sort** *mape2*
> **subsort** *mape2 = mape1 [inv_mape2]*
> **axiom** $(m : mape1, k : \mathbf{nat}, x : dart, q : embed)$
> $inv\_mape2(em(m, k, x, q)) = free\_embed(m, k, x)$

We immediately deduce from this invariant the weakest precondition of operator *em* for the *mape2* sort. At this level, the precondition for *l* is more tricky to obtain: *l(m, k, x, y)* is legal w.r.t. the embedding constraints only if, for all $j \neq k$, the *j*-cells of *x* and *y* are still the same ones, or one of them is not *j*-embedded. The auxiliary operation *free_embedl(m, k, x, y)* returns **true** iff this condition holds. Its formal specification is not given here.

4.3 Geometric Operators

We impose to the final objects of the modeller *exactly one* k-embedding per k-cell. A new sort *mape3 < mape2* derives. To maintain the *mape3* invariant, operator *l* might be called by a new operator *ll* which removes some embeddings to avoid two distinct k-embeddings for a k-cell. Thus, operation *ll(m, k, x, y)* removes, if necessary, the embeddings of the cells which contains *y*, and k-sews *x* and *y* by *l(l(m, k, x, y), k, y, x)*. Precisely, before the k-sewing, for all $j \neq k$, it calls a function *llk(m, j, x, y)* which removes if necessary the *j*-embedding associated with the *j*-cell containing *y*.

Symmetrically, function *rr(m, k, x)* first unsews in *m* darts *x* and *y = a(m, k, x)*, then duplicates if necessary the *j*-embeddings for all $j \neq k$ if *x* is *j*-embedded in *m*. It calls for all *j* $\neq k$ a function *rrk(m, k, j, x, y)* which duplicates the *j*-embedding if necessary.

4.4 Sort Hierarchy and Initial Semantics

This leads us to a rather complex map *sort hierarchy*, with the top level *map0*. Several branches go down: one for topology, with ... *map2 < map1 < map0*, one for embedding, with ...< *mape2 < mape1 < map0*, and other ones for cell *markers* (cf. Section 5). Note that new map generators are always introduced at top level, with automatical repercussions on the lower levels by implicit axioms. The *3-g-map* sort of the embedded 3-g-maps with the modeller constraints of Section 3 is at the bottom of the hierarchy. In an initial semantics, it can be interpreted as the *intersection* of all its upper sorts, in other words, as the set of the *map0* terms which exactly satisfy the invariants of the whole hierarchy [4].

With *order-sorted algebras* [23] it is easy to describe step by step numerous geometric models, starting from a unique model with atomic generators. *Invariants* and *preconditions* help to easily limit ordered geometric sorts, as pointed out by [25]. Intermediate models correspond to intermediate states when building geometric objects [13]. They facilitate defining total operations. They can also be used in modeling as such, when extending the class of handled objects beyond the strict 3-g-maps [4].

However, our specifications might be considered as *over-specified* [6]. It is the case with any specification where generators are chosen, sometimes rather early for practical reasons, because some implementations and algorithms are favoured. In fact, an early decision about the choice of the generators allows us to properly define the sort hierarchy and to make the kernel runable, which is essential for debugging.

Moreover, our aim is that the last level of specification be isomorphic with the implementation. That is an additional reason why, contrary to other approaches, as for instance *loose semantics* [46], we have favoured an *initial semantics* approach during the whole development of the specifications.

The properties of the 3-g-maps, for instance α_k being an involution, for $0 \leq k \leq 3$, α_0 being an involution with no fixed point, $\alpha_0 \circ \alpha_1$ having no fixed point, etc, can be obtained from the specification as *inductive theorems*. That agrees with the initial semantics. These theorems can be proven by a mechanized inductive reasoning [14, 15].

5 Vertical Development

The previous operators are combined to obtain new ones. Their definitions can be given first at a high level of abstraction, appropriate for logical prototyping, but often inefficient for a realistic implementation. The new operators have to be *refined* in a progressive *vertical development*. Our aim is to keep the same specification framework for this refinement. We examine this process through an example.

We specify operator *cc* of cell traversal: *cc(m, x)* extracts the connected component of *m* of sort *map1* containing dart *x*. We start with a short abstract definition *à la Kruskal* using other operators, the specification of which is simple and only given in comments:

> **operation**
>   *cc : map1 dart → map1*
> **precondition** *(m : map1, x : dart)*
>   **prec** *cc(m, x) ≡ ex_dart(m, x)*
> **axioms** *(m : map1, k : nat, x y z : dart)*
>   *cc(i(m, x), z) = if x == z then i(v, z) else cc(m, z)*
>   *cc(l(m, k, x, y), z) = if islink(l(m, k, x, y), z, x)*
>   **then if** *islink(m, x, y) then l(cc(m, z), k, x, y)*
>   **else** *l(union(cc(m, x), cc(m, y)), k, x, y)*
>   **else** *cc(m, z)*
> /* *union(m1, m2) merges m1 et m2;*
>   *islink(m, x, y) is* **true** *iff the connected components of x and y in m are the same ones* */

A straight implementation of *cc* as specified (a logical prototyping) will always have a time complexity exponential w.r.t. *p*, the number of darts in the map (in the best, average and worst cases). In fact, an acceptable response time imposes a complexity of *cc* in *O(p)* in the worst case.

We improve this situation by a refinement of the specification. Thanks to a new *map0 generator of dart marking*, named *mark*, we specify a *depth-first* traversal *mkcc(m, x)*, which marks the connected component of *x* in *m* instead of extracting it. The complexity in maximum time of this new operator is in *O(p)*, when supposing an *O(1)* complexity for the implemented basic operators, which is true in the actual implementation of the modeller. To simplify, we directly pass to a new sort of marked maps, named *mapc*, such that *mapc < map1*. The objects of this sort meet the following constraint of *strict connectivity*: existence of a path from a dart *x* to a dart *y* implies existence of another one from *y* to *x*. This property also holds for n-g-maps, so *3-g-map < mapc < map1*:

operation
    mkcc : mapc dart → mapc
precondition *(m : mapc, x : dart)*
    prec *mkcc(m, x) ≡ ex_dart(m, x)* **and** *not_mark(m)*
axioms *(m m1 : mapc, n : nat, x : dart)*
    mkcc(m, x) = mkcc_aux(mark(m, x), dim(m), x)
      with *mkcc_aux(m, n, x) =* **if** *n < 0* **then** *m* **else** *mkcc_aux(m1, n - 1, x)*
        with *m1 =* **if** *ismark(m, a(m, n, x))* **then** *m* **else** *mkcc(m, a(m, n, x))*
/* *mark(m, x) marks the dart x in m;*
  ismark(m, x) is true iff dart x is marked in map m;
  not_mark(m) is **true** *iff no dart of m is marked;*
  dim(m) gives the dimension of map m */

For a final non recursive implementation, we refine once more the specification into another one, which is *tail recursive*, and directly implementable in $O(p)$ time. Actually, it is easier to realize this traversal in a *breadth-first* way, the queue of marked darts being explicitly linked in the map itself thanks to another *map generator*, called *markcc*:

axioms *(m m0 m1 m2 : mapc, n : nat, x x0 y z z1 t t0 t1 t2 : dart)*
    mkcc(m, x) = mkcc_list(m0, x0, t0)
      with *(m0, t0) = mkcc_aux(markcc(m, x, x), dim(m), x, x)*
        x0 = succ_markcc(m1, x)
    mkcc_list(m, z, t) = **if** *z == z1* **then** *m* **else** *mkcc_list(m1, z1, t1)*
      with *z1 = succ_markcc(m, z)*
        (m1, t1) = mkcc_aux(m, n, z1, t)
        mkcc_aux(m, n, z, t) = **if** *n < 0* **then** *(m, t)*
                             else *mkcc_aux(m2, n - 1, z, t2)*
          with *(m2, t2) = endmarkcc(m, t, a(m, n, z))*
/* *succ_markcc(m, x) is the successor of dart x in the queue of marked darts;*
  endmarkcc(m, t, x) takes dart x after dart t in this queue */

Note that the *map0* sort enrichment by new mark generators is only realized with the last version of the generators, i.e., in the example, with *markcc*. In fact, when we go down the sort hierarchy, for instance fixing $n = 3$, or imposing that some involutions be without fixed points, we can write specialized traversal functions still more efficient than the ones above. Thus, an edge traversal in a 3-g-map can be realized by direct compositions of *a*, for dimensions 2 and 3, without explicit depth- or breadth-first traversal. Finally, through factorizing definitions by **with** and using iterators (cf. Section 6), the specification can be directly translated into a procedural language.

6 Horizontal Structuring

6.1 Sewing Operators

At *3-g-map* level, we can write functions to create, remove, sew and unsew k-cells. We distinguish between *topological operators*, with strong topological and embedding preconditions, and *geometrical* (i.e., topological *and* embedding) *operators* of higher level, that only have topological preconditions. Particularly, sewing operators which meet the 3-g-maps constraints of the modeller can be defined this way.

We present three examples: topological sewing, *se*, geometric sewing, *gse*, and insertion, *gie2*, of two simple edges, with only the formal specifications of *se* and *gse*:

operations
    se, gse : 3-g-map dart dart → 3-g-map
preconditions *(g : 3-g-map, x y : dart)*
    prec *gse(g, x, y) ≡ ex_dart(g, x)* **and** *ex_dart(g, y)* **and** *a(g, 2, x) == x*
                and *a(g, 2, y) == y* **and** *x ≠ a(g, 0, y)* **and** *x ≠ y*
    prec *se(g, x, y) ≡* **prec** *(gse(g, x, y))* **and** *free_embedl(g, 2, x, y)*
                and *free_embedl(g, 2, a(g, 0, x), a(g, 0, y))*

axioms *(g : 3-g-map, x y : dart)*
   se(g, x, y) = L(L(g, 2, x, y), 2, a(g, 0, x), a(g, 0, y))
   with *L(g, k, x, y) = l(l(g, k, x, y), k, y, x)*
   gse(g, x, y) = se(llk(llk(llk(llk(g, 1, x, y), 3, x, y), 0, x, y),
                0, a(g, 0, x), a(g, 0, y)), x, y)

Operator *gse* is written efficiently by using, instead of the general operator *ll*, operator *llk* at the appropriate dimensions to remove superfluous embeddings (cf. subsection 4.3). Operation *gie2(g, x, y)*, which uses *se*, is rather surprising. It allows us to subdivide one face or to merge two faces, depending on whether the faces of *x* and *y* are the same ones or not (Fig. 4, (a) and (b), and Pictures 9 and 10 in Appendix).

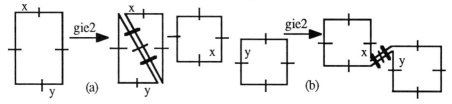

Fig. 4. Insertion of two simple sewn edges.

In the modeller, several useful operators are defined the same way, in particular *Euler operators*, which keep the surface genus unchanged [39].

6.2 Meshes, Second Order and Iterators

We now briefly present the specification of a high-level operator, namely a *mesh contructor* [4]. The interest lies in the way this operator is specified. It clearly distinguishes between topology and embedding, and reduces the required number of operations. Moreover, it makes possible to justify the introduction of second order functions and iterators in specifications. We propose here to create simple meshes, which can be completed by poles afterwards (Fig. 5, Picture 11, and Picture 12 for an extension).

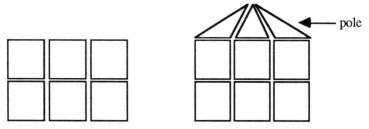

Fig. 5. A simple mesh and a mesh with pole (the 0 and 2-sewings are omitted).

A *simple mesh* is made of simple quadrangles sewn together by operator *se*. The mesh topology is progressively created and embedded thanks to a function $f: nat^4 \rightarrow embed$ which 0-embeds a dart per quadrangle. The 4 variables of *f* are *n* and *p*, which give the mesh size, and $i \in [0, n]$ and $j \in [0, p]$, which give the columns and lines of the mesh points.

The mesh function, denoted *grid*, uses auxiliary creations of squares, i.e., *sqrgrid*, *sqrgridll*, *sqrgridnl* and *sqrgridlp*, whose specification is omitted (cf. [4] for details):

operation
   grid : 3-g-map $(nat^4 \rightarrow embed)$ $nat^2 \rightarrow 3$-g-map
  axioms *(g : 3-g-map, f : $nat^4 \rightarrow embed$, i j k n p : nat)*
   grid(g, f, n, p) = grid2(grid1(sqrgrid11(g, f, n, p), f, 2, n, p), f, 2, 2, n, p
   with *grid1(g, f, k, n, p) =*
        if *k > n* **then** *g* **else** *grid1(sqrgridn1(g, f, k, n, p), f, k + 1, n, p)*
       grid2(g, f, i, j, n, p) =

if $i > n$ *then if* $j \geq p$ *then* g *else* $grid2(sqrgrid1p(g, f, j, n, p), 2, j + 1, n, p)$
else $grid2(sqrgrid(g, f, i, j, n, p), i + 1, j, n, p)$

Second order functions, like *grid*, are out of the strict frame of traditional algebraic specifications. They could be avoided by using parameterized modules as in OBJ3 [24]. But it is a heavy solution when the parameters concern only a few functions as it is here the case, where, moreover, the semantics does not create any problems.

The use of auxiliary functions *grid1* and *grid2* to simulate two embedded iterations on the mesh squares by a *tail recursion* makes the specification heavy and reduces its readability. To remove them, we use *iterators*, considered as macro-definitions. For instance, $v = v0$; *while not* $cond(v)$ *do* $succ(v)$ defines by induction the last value v of a sequence of values, where the initial, current and next ones are respectively $v0$, v and $succ(v)$, and the stop condition $cond(v)$. It textually replaces the following *iter* function defined by: $v = iter(v0)$ *with* $iter(v) = if$ $cond(v)$ *then* v *else* $iter(succ(v))$.

The following specification which redefines *grid* with two embedded iterators, simplifies the specifications and brings us closer to functional and procedural languages:

axioms $(g\,g1\,g2\,gj : 3\text{-}g\text{-}map, f : nat^4 \rightarrow embed, i\,j\ k\,n\,p : nat)$
 $grid(g, f, n, p) = g2$
 with $(i, g2) = (2, g1)$; *while* $i \leq n$ *do* $(i{+}1, gj)$
   with $(j, gj) = (2, sqrgrid1p(g2, f, j, n, p))$;
      while $j \leq p$ *do* $(j{+}1, sqrgrid(gj, f, i, j, n, p))$
   $(k, g1) = (2, sqrgrid11(g, f, n, p))$;
      while $k \leq n$ *do* $(k{+}1, sqrgridn1(g1, f, k, n, p))$

6.3 Miscellaneous: User Interaction, Errors, Libraries

Classical algebraic specifications do not conveniently deal with *user interactions* [37] which can be seen as a distinct process, concurrent with the modeller process. A formalism suited to the description of concurrency, like LOTOS, could be used. In our case, it is a heavy solution, since the entry of external events is strictly limited to a small specification part. We have prefered to describe user interactions by a *meta-specification*, i.e., a second level of specifications, which manipulate the first level ones by simple axiom modifications [4].

In a modeller, *errors* are linked to user interaction. Operators with preconditions have been implemented in the way they were specified, i.e., without testing the preconditions in their bodies. They have been encapsulated in high-level functions, algebraically specified too, which deal with computer-human interactions, preconditions and errors.

Today, graphical software development makes an intensive use of built-in graphical *libraries*. We have formally specified the library we use (Silicon Graphics GL), by an arbitrary choice of basic generators and by expressing other operators w.r.t. them. Such a task was difficult, given the imperfections of the documentation.

7 Some Technical Features of the Modeller

The modeller includes about 1800 operations: 1400 for geometric modeling and 400 for the environment and the interface. Most of them, except for 100 mathematical or trivial functions, were developed from complete algebraic specifications. The operations of the basic kernel were translated into PROLOG and tested by *logical prototyping* [4]. Only 150 parameterized operations are visible for the user through the interface.

The modeller is currently implemented in C for Silicon Graphics workstations. Thanks to the map concepts, the data structures that are used are very simple. Except for the upper ones, all the map and dart sorts of the hierarchy are really implemented with *the same unified C types*. A unified map structure consists mainly of a linked linear list of similar dart records, the fields of which are more or less constrained, depending on the invariants of the corresponding map sort. Each dart record contains 1 dart pointer to the successor in the list, 4 dart pointers to represent the k-sewings, for $0 \leq k \leq 3$, one pointer to the optional 0-embedding, and several markers for traversal and interactive selections. The program contains about 25 000 lines of C, a rather small number for software of this type. This is mainly due to the conciseness and reusability induced by algebraic techniques.

Response time is comparable with those of commercial products with similar features and may be even better. The main operations, particularly the traversals, have a time complexity in $O(p)$, where p is the number of darts. This is not the case in many commercial modellers which often take $O(p^2)$, because they lack directly accessible topological data. Other classical data structures, such as those derived from the "winged edge" [2], often take comparable memory space for a more restricted modeling area.

8 Conclusion

The n-g-map is a general and efficient model that helps to describe and handle the topology of n-dimensional objects. With embeddings, this model can be implemented in any dimension. For example, we chose to derive 3-g-maps with 0-embedding for a geometric modeller of complex manifold objects embedded in Q^3. Other choices could be made with other map extensions and embeddings. But the handling of *non manifold* objects [45] requires even more general mathematical concepts, cellular complexes [19] for instance.

With the above algebraic specification and its ordered sorts and invariants, we obtain a formal, functional, hierarchized, and homogeneous description of objects and operations. As often [22], genericity has not been necessary. In the future for instance, it may become interesting, to parameterize the modeller by topological or embedding constraints. Finally, we expect to recover a specification language well suited to the needs above [7].

Proofs of *correctness* of our horizontal structurings are possible and will be undertaken, with a mechanical help [24]. But, the proofs of correctness of our vertical developments, which involve techniques of program transformation and synthesis, are more difficult to bring into play. Moreover, work about using algebraic specifications in semi-automatical proofs of geometric properties is in progress [14, 15].

The concrete results of our study is an interactive modeller of 3D objects. Private firms are already interested by its functionalities. However, it must be adapted and extended in order to be used in real applications. Algebraic specifications give a basis which makes those extentions easier. Among the next fundamental ones, there is the cellular complexes [19] and the Boolean shape operators [41].

Our experiment illustrates how algebraic specifications help to elaborate and study models in geometry, and to design and develop software in this area. Conversely, the spectacular workbench of geometric modeling is convenient to understand how algebraic specifications improve axiomatization and programming processes in a complex field.

References

1. Baudelaire, P and Gangnet, M: Planar Maps: An Interaction Paradigm for Graphic Design. *Proc. CHI'89* (1989) 313–318
2. Baumgart, B: A Polyhedron Representation for Computer Vision. *Proc. AFIPS Nat. Conf.* Proc. 44 (1975) 589–596
3. Bergstra, J A, Heering, J and Klint, P: *Algebraic Specification*. ACM, Addison-Wesley (1988)
4. Bertrand, Y: Spécification Algébrique et Réalisation d'un Modeleur Interactif de Subdivisions Tridimensionnelles. *Thèse de Doctorat*, CRI-ULP, Strasbourg (1992)
5. Bertrand, Y, Dufourd, J-F, Françon, J et Lienhardt P: Modélisation Volumique à Base Topologique. *Proc. Micad*, Paris (1992)
6. Bidoit, M: Development of Modular Specification by Stepwise Refinements using the PLUSS Specification Language. *Tech. rep. LIENS* 91-9 (1991),
7. Bidoit, M, Kreowski, H-J, Lescanne, P, Orejas, F and Sannella, D: *Algebraic System Specification and Development*. LNCS n°501, Springer-Verlag (1991)

8. Bryant, R and Singerman, D: Foundations of the Theory of Maps on Surfaces with Boundaries. *Quart. Journal of Math. Oxford* Vol 2 n° 36 (1985) 17–41
9. Cori, R: Un code pour les graphes planaires et ses applications. *Astérisque* n° 27 (1975)
10. Duce, D A , Fielding, E V C and Marshall, L S: Formal Specification of a Small Example based on GKS. *ACM Trans. on Graphics* Vol 7 n° 3 (1988) 180-197
11. Dufourd, J-F, Gross, C and Spehner, J-C: A Digitisation Algorithm for the Entry of Planar Maps. *Proc. Comp. Graphics Int.* Leeds, Springer-Verlag (1989) 649-662
12. Dufourd, J-F: Algebraic Map-Based Topological Kernel for Polyhedron Modelers. *Proc. Eurographics*, Hamburg, Elsevier (1989) 301-312
13. Dufourd, J-F: Formal Specification of Subdivisions using Hypermaps. *Computer Aided Design*, Butterworth-Heinemann Vol 23 n° 2 (1991) 99-116
14. Dufourd, J-F: An OBJ3 Functional Specification for the Boundary Representation. *Proc. ACM-Siggraph Symp. on Solid Modeling Foundations & CAD/CAM Appl.*, Austin (1991) 61-72
15. Dufourd, J-F: Foundations of Boundary Representation Revisited with a New Foremap Axiomatics. *Proc. Eurographics Work. on Formal Spec. in Comp. Graphics*, Marina di Carrara (1991)
16. Edmonds, J: A Combinatorial Representation for Polyhedral Surfaces. *Not. AMS* Vol 7 (1960)
17. Ehrig, H and Mahr, B: *Fundamentals of Algebraic Specifications Vol 1 : Equations and Initial Semantics.* Springer-Verlag (1985)
18. Ehrig, H and Mahr, B: *Fundamentals of Algebraic Specifications Vol 2 : Module Specifications and Constraints.* Springer-Verlag (1990)
19. Elter, H et Lienhardt, P: Extension de la Notion de Carte pour la Représentation de la Topologie d'Objets Géométriques Complexes. *Proc. Journées Gros-Plan*, Lille (1991)
20. Franklin, W R, Wu , P Y F & Samaddar, S: Prolog & Geometry Projects. *IEEE CG & A* Vol 6 (1986)
21. Gangnet, M, Hervé, J-C, Pudet, T and Van Thong, J-M: Incremental Computation of Planar Maps. *ACM Computer Graphics* Vol 23 n° 3 (1989) 345–354
22. Gaudel, M-C: Structuring and Modularizing Algebraic Specifications. *R. 01-92* LRI, Orsay (1992)
23. Goguen, J A & Meseguer, J: Order-Sorted Algebra I: Equational Deduction for Multiple Inheritance, Overloading, Exceptions, and Partial Operations. *Tech. Rep.n° 89-10* SRI-CSL (1989)
24. Goguen, J A and Winkler, T: Introducing OBJ3. *Tech. Rep. n° 88-9*, SRI-CSL Menlo Park (1988)
25. Goguen, J A: Modular Algebraic Specification of Some Basic Geometrical Constructions. *Artificial Intelligence* Vol 37 (1988) 123-153
26. Grant, E, Amburn, P and Whitted, T: Exploiting Classes in Modeling and Display Software. *IEEE CG&A* Vol 6 (1986) 13-20
27. Griffiths, H-B: *Surfaces,* Cambridge Univ. Press, Cambridge (1981)
28. Jacques, A: Constellations et Graphes Topologiques. *Coll. Math. Soc. J. Bolyai* (1970) 657–672
29. James, L: Maps and Hypermaps: Operations and Symmetry. *PhD thesis*, Dep. of Mathematics, Univ. of Southampton (1985)
30. Lakshminarasimhan and A L, Srivas, M: A Framework for Functional Specification and Transformation of Hidden Surface Elimination Algorithms. *CG. Forum* Vol 8 n° 2 (1989) 75-98
31. Lienhardt, P: Free-Form Surfaces Modeling by Evolution Simulation. *Proc. Eurographics,* Nice, Elsevier (1988) 327–341
32. Lienhardt, P: Extension of the Notion of Map and Subdivision of Three Dimensional Space. *Proc. STACS*, Bordeaux, *LNCS* Vol 294, Springer-Verlag (1988) 301-311
33. Lienhardt, P : Subdivisions of Surfaces and Generalized Maps. *Proc. Eurographics*, Hamburg, Elsevier (1989) 439–452
34. Lienhardt, P: Subdivisions of N-Dimensional Spaces and N-Dimensional Generalized Maps. *Proc. 5° ACM Symp. on Comp. Geometry* , Saarbrücken (1989) 228–236
35. Lienhardt, P: Topological Models for Boundary Representation : A Comparison with N-dimensional Generalized Maps. *Comp.-Aided Design* Vol 23 n° 1, Butterworth-H. (1991) 59–82
36. Mallgren, W R: Formal Specification of Graphic Data Types. *ACM TOPLAS* Vol 4 n°4 (1982) 687-710.
37. Mallgren, W R: Formal Specification of Interactive Graphics Programming Languages. *ACM Distinguished Dissertation*, MIT Press (1982)
38. Mäntylä, M and Sulonen, R: GWB : A Solid Modeler with Euler Operators. *IEEE CG & A* Vol 2 n° 7 (1982) 17-31
39. Mäntylä, M: *An Introduction to Solid Modeling.* Computer Science Press, Rockville (1988)
40. Parsons, M S: Image Representations Using Miranda Laws. *Comp. Graphics Forum* Vol 8 n°2, North-Holland (1989) 99-106
41. Requicha, A: Representations for Rigid Solids : Theory, Methods and Systems. *ACM Computing Surveys* Vol 12 n° 4 (1980) 437–464
42. Requicha, A A G and Voelker, H B: Solid Modeling: Current Status and Research Directions. *IEEE CG & A* Vol 3 n° 7 (1983) 25-37
43. Tutte, W: *Graph Theory.* Encyclop. of Mathematics and its Applications, Addison–Wesley (1984)
44. Vince, A: Combinatorial Maps. *J. of Combinatorial Theory* Series B n° 34 (1983) 1–21
45. Weiler, K: The Radial Edge Structure: A Topological Representation for Non-Manifold Geometric Boundary Modeling. in *Geometric Modeling for CAD Applications*, Elsevier (1988) 3-36
46. Wirsing, M: Algebraic Specification. *Handbook of Theoretical Computer Science, Vol 2 : Formal Models and Semantics*, Elsevier (1990) 675-788

Appendix

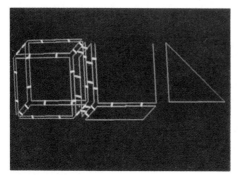

Picture 1: The 3-g-map of Figure 1

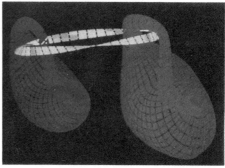

Picture 2: A Moëbius band and 2 Klein bottles

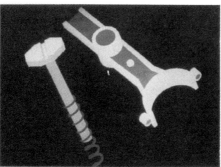

Picture 3: Mechanical parts

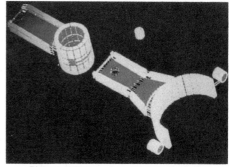

Picture 4: Details of a splitted mechanical part

Picture 5: A surfacic teapot

Picture 6: A volumic teapot

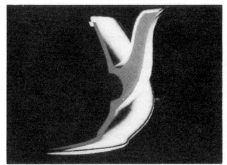

Picture 7: Spout of the volumic teapot

Picture 8: Handle of the volumic teapot

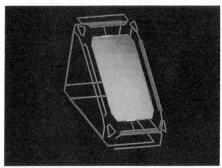

Picture 9: A face to be split

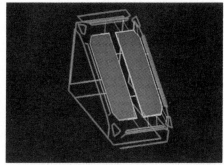

Picture 10: The splitted face

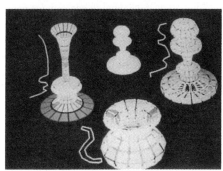

Picture 11: Surfacic meshes

Picture 12: Volumic meshes

A Case Study in
Transformational Design of Concurrent Systems*

Ernst-Rüdiger Olderog   Stephan Rössig

FB Informatik, Universität Oldenburg
Postfach 2503, 2900 Oldenburg, Germany[†]

Abstract. We explain a transformational approach to the design and verification of communicating concurrent systems. The transformations start form specifications that combine trace-based with state-based assertional reasoning about the desired communication behaviour, and yield concurrent implementations. We illustrate our approach by a case study proving correctness of implementations of safe and regular registers allowing concurrent writing and reading phases, originally due to Lamport.

1   Introduction

For concurrent systems a variety of specification formalisms have been developed, among them Temporal Logic [MP91], iterative programs like action systems [Bac90] or UNITY programs [CM88], input/output automata [LT89], and process algebra [Mil89, BW90]. However, it remains a difficult task to design correct implementations starting from such specifications. It is here that we wish to make a contribution.

We are developing a novel transformational approach to the design of communicating concurrent systems. Our work originates from the ESPRIT Basic Research Action "ProCoS". ProCoS stands for "Provably Correct Systems" and is a wide-spectrum verification project where embedded communicating systems are studied at various levels of abstraction ranging from requirements' capture over specification language and programming language down to the machine language [Bjø89].

We use a specification language SL that combines trace-based with state-based assertional reasoning. The *trace part* specifies in a modular fashion in which order communications on the channels may occur. To this end, regular expressions over channel alphabets are used. In the trace part we build on ideas of pure process algebra with uninterpreted action symbols. Of course in any realistic application one has also to reason about values that are communicated. In SL the communication values are specified with the help of a *state part* which consists of state variables and communication assertions describing when a channel is enabled for communication and what the effect of such a communication is. The state part corresponds to an iterative program in the style of action systems or UNITY extended by communication through explicit message passing.

The specification language SL is not as high-level as temporal logic can be, but it has the advantage that it allows us to formulate transformation rules for the stepwise design of implementations. In the ProCoS project we have developed a set of transformation rules that is complete for transforming a large class of specifications into sequential occam-like programs [ORSS92]. In this paper we present further transformation rules that enable us to derive distributed concurrent systems with components communicating by synchronous message passing.

Our work on transformational design is in the tradition of the work originated by Burstall and Darlington and pursued fur-

---

*This research was partially supported by the CEC with the ESPRIT Basic Research Project No. 7071 ProCoS II and by the German Ministry of Research and Technologie (BMFT) as part of the project KORSO (Korrekte Software) under grant No. 01 IS 203 N.

[†]{olderog,roessig}@informatik.uni-oldenburg.de

ther to practical application in projects like CIP (standing for Computer-aided Intuition-guided Programming) [Bau87] and PROSPECTRA (standing for PROgram development by SPECification and TRAnsformation) [Kri89]. While these approaches were concerned with conventional sequential programs, we study here concurrency and communication.

Central to our approach is the concept of a *mixed term* [Old91b], i.e. a construct that mixes programming and specification constructs. Mixed terms are well suited to express intermediate stages of a design where some implementation details are fixed and others are still open. Mixed terms arise naturally as a formalization of the method of stepwise refinement originally advocated by Dijkstra and Wirth. They appear also in the refinement calculi of [Mor90, Bac90], but these calculi deal with sequential or iterative programs without explicit communication.

In this paper we illustrate our approach by a case study that is concerned with one of the basic assumptions of many distributed algorithms, viz. the correct interprocess communication. In his article [Lam86], Lamport analyzes interprocess communication through registers that can be accessed by writers and readers in a possibly concurrent, i.e. overlapping fashion. The assumptions that distributed algorithms make about interprocess communication is mirrored by the values that a reader of the register may obtain in case of an overlapping writing phase. Lamport defines three classes of registers called safe, regular and atomic where safe registers are the weakest and atomic are the strongest class. The main contribution of [Lam86] are several constructions of stronger register types from weaker ones together with correctness proofs in a specific formalism. The topic of concurrent registers has excited quite some interest in the literature on distributed algorithms. A good overview can be found in [LG89].

In this paper we specify safe and regular registers in the language SL and systematically derive one of Lamport's concurrent implementations using our transformational approach.

2 Specifications

In this section we use the example of registers to provide an introduction to the specification language SL. As in [Lam86] we consider registers that can store a value of some value set V and that are shared by one writer and possibly several readers. We begin with the case of only one reader. Following [LG89] such a register can be modelled as a system communicating through directed channels with its environment consisting of a writer and a reader as shown in Figure 1. The writer initiates a

Figure1: Register as communicating system

writing phase by sending a value from the set V along the input channel W. This phase ends when a corresponding acknowledgement signal is output on channel A. Conversely, the reader initiates a *reading phase* by sending a signal along the input channel R. This phase ends when a value from the set V is returned along the output channel T.

It remains to be specified what value is returned at the end of a reading phase. For a reading phase that does not overlap with any writing phase there is only one correct value to be returned, viz. the most recently written one. However, it is not clear what should happen in the case of concurrent, i.e. overlapping reading and writing phases. Therefore Lamport distinguishes three classes of registers called safe, regular and atomic [Lam86].

For a *safe* register, *any* value of the value set V may be returned. For a *regular* register, either the value *before* or *after* the overlapping write must be returned. More generally, a read that overlaps with several writes, one of the values before or after these writes must be returned. For an *atomic* register, overlapping reads and writes must have the same effect as if they occur in some non-overlapping order. We shall consider here only safe and regular registers.

2.1 Safe Registers

Let us first explain how to specify a safe register in SL. An SL specification describes a communicating system using several parts.

Interface. This part lists the communication channels of the system with their direction (input or output) and value type. For the register the interface is given by

> input W of V
> output A of signal
> input R of signal
> output T of V.

Trace Part. This part specifies the sequencing constraints on the interface channels whereas the communicated values are ignored. This is done by stating one or more *trace assertions*, each one consisting of an alphabet, i.e. a subset of the interface channels, and a regular expression over these channels. The regular expression describes the sequencing constraints on the channels mentioned in the alphabet. By stating several such trace assertions, we can specify different aspects of the intended system behaviour in a modular fashion.

For the register the trace part is given by

> trace W, A in $pref(W.A)^*$
> trace R, T in $pref(R.T)^*$.

The first trace assertion concerns the writer. It states that communications on the channels W and A should occur in alternating order starting with W. In other words, at each moment the trace of channels W and A should be a prefix of some word in the regular language $(W.A)^*$. The second trace assertion states a similar requirement for the reader.

The informal semantics of this part of an SL specification is that the described behaviour must satisfy the sequencing constraints of all trace assertions simultaneously. The trace part of an SL specification corresponds to *path expressions* in the sense of [CH74] or to a regular fragment of *trace logic* in the sense of [Zwi89] and [Old91a].

State Part. This part describes what the exact values are that can be exchanged over the interface channels. To this end, this part may introduce local state variables. These variables constitute the state space of the specification and are used in so-called communication assertions specifying the link between values and channels. However, these variables need not appear in an implementation of the specified system.

For the register we use the following state variables:

> var v of V
> var m of bool
> var c of bool.

The variable v represents the current *value* of the register. The boolean variable m stands for write *modus* and expresses whether the register is currently engaged in a writing phase. The boolean variable c indicates whether a reading phase has to return the *correct* value, i.e. the one currently stored in v.

A *communication assertion* for a channel ch is of the form

com ch write $\overline{w}$ read $\overline{r}$ when wh then th

where $\overline{w}$ and $\overline{r}$ are disjoint lists of state variables, the list $\overline{w}$ of *write* variables and the list $\overline{r}$ of *read* variables, and two predicates, the *when* or *enable* predicate wh describing when a channel is enabled for communication and the *then* or *effect* predicate th describing the communication value and the effect of this communication on the state variables.

The enable predicate may only use variables from $\overline{w}$ and $\overline{r}$. The effect predicate may additionally use primed versions of the write variables and the distinguished variable @ch obtained by prefixing the channel name ch by the symbol @. As in the specification language Z [Spi89], a primed variable x' refers to the value of the variable x at the moment of termination. The read variables are not changed. The variable @ch refers to the communication value on the channel ch.

If one of the variable lists is empty or one of the predicates is true, these components are omitted from the communication assertion. In general, there can be several communication assertions for the same channel. We require that the set of all write variables in these assertions is disjoint from the set of all read variables.

For the channels W, A, R, T of the register we state the following communication assertions.

com W write v, m, c
　　then $m' \wedge v' = @W \wedge \neg c'$

asserts that each communication on channel W updates the state variables v, m and c as follows: the write modus m is set, the value v of the register becomes the current communication value $@W$, and c is set to false to indicate for a possibly overlapping reading phase that an arbitrary value may be returned.

Simpler is the communication assertion for channel A:

com A write m then $\neg m'$

just asserts that a communication on A switches off the write modus. For channel R,

com R write c read m then $c' = \neg m$

asserts that in c it is recorded whether the register is currently outside a write modus. For channel T,

com T read c, v then $c \Rightarrow @T = v$

asserts that when c is set the communication value on channel T has to be the correct value as given by v.

Putting these parts together, we arrive at the SL specification of a safe register for one reader and value set V shown in Figure 2.

Informally, this SL specification describes the set of all traces of communications along the channels W, A, R and T that satisfy the constraints given by the trace assertions and communication assertions simultaneously. Communications are denoted by pairs (ch, k) where ch is a channel name and

spec input W of V
　　output A of signal
　　input R of signal
　　output T of V
　　trace W, A in $pref(W.A)^*$
　　trace R, T in $pref(R.T)^*$
　　var m of bool
　　var c of bool
　　var v of V
　　com W write v, m, c
　　　　then $m' \wedge v' = @W \wedge \neg c'$
　　com A write m then $\neg m'$
　　com R write c read m
　　　　then $c' = \neg m$
　　com T read c, v then $c \Rightarrow @T = v$
end

Figure 2: Specification 1-reader-V-safe

k is the communication value. Communications on channels ch of type signal will be simply denoted by the channel name ch itself. For example, for V={1,2,3,4,5} the communication trace

$tr = (W,3).A.R.(T,3).R.(W,5).A.(T,4).R.(T,5)$

satisfies 1-reader-V-safe. Note that within the second reading phase a writing phase occurs which sets the state variable c to false. Hence at the end of this reading phase an arbitrary value from V may be output on channel T. Here we have chosen the value 4. On the other hand, the last reading phase ends with c evaluating to true and thus outputs the most recently written value, which is 5.

The formal semantics of the specification language SL is defined in a *predicative style* in [Old91b] and [ORSS92] and is beyond the scope of this paper. We mention only that in this semantics each SL specification S is identified with a pair $\Delta : P$ where Δ is the interface of S and P is a predicate describing the behaviour specified by S in terms of communication traces, ready sets and some other ingredients that are not important here.

A *ready set* is a set of channels that are ready for communication. The formal semantics of an SL specification S requires that each communication trace of a system satisfying S should be ready on all channels that may occur next according to the trace and communication assertions of S. For example, after the above trace tr the specification 1-reader-V-safe requires that a register should be ready for communication on the channels W and R. In particular, a register may not refuse to interact with its writer or reader after the trace tr.

In principle, the trace part of specification 1-reader-V-safe can be eliminated in favour of an extended state part. However, this would result in a specification that is more difficult to understand. In general, we strive to express the data independent aspects of a system behaviour in the trace part.

For each given n, the above specification can be extended to one specifiying a safe register with n readers using communication channels R_i and T_i for $i \in 1..n$ (Figure 3).

```
spec input W of V
     output A of signal
     input R_1, ..., R_n of signal
     output T_1, ..., T_n of V
     trace W, A in pref(W.A)*
i∈1..n: trace R_i, T_i in pref(R_i.T_i)*
     var m of bool
     var c_1, ..., c_n of bool
     var v of V
     com W write v, m, c_1, ..., c_n
        then m' ∧ v' = @W ∧ ⋀_{i=1}^n ¬c_i'
     com A write m then ¬m'
i∈1..n: com R_i write c_i read m
             then c_i' = ¬m
i∈1..n: com T_i read c_i, v then c_i ⇒ @T_i = v
end
```

Figure3: Specification n-reader-V-safe

Since each of the readers can have different overlappings with writing phases, we introduce separate state variables c_i to record whether at the end of a reading phase the reader i should get the correct value of the register as stored in variable v. This is specified in the communication assertion for channel T_i.

2.2 Regular Registers

Let us now specify the behaviour of a regular register for n readers and the value set V in the language SL. We can reuse a large part of the specification n-reader-V-safe above. Only the specification of the value returned at the end of a reading phase need to be changed. The idea is here to replace the boolean variables c_i by *set valued* variables C_i which at each moment represent the set of values from V that may be returned. Thus we declare

$$\text{var } C_1, ..., C_n \text{ of } V - set$$

and change the communication assertion for T_i to

$$\text{com } T_i \text{ read } C_i \text{ then } @T_i \in C_i.$$

It remains to be specified how to update the state variables C_i. Since by the regularity condition a reading phase overlapping a writing phase should either return the value before or after the write, we keep track of the *old* value of the register with every write. Thus we introduce the state variable

$$\text{var } old \text{ of } V$$

and use the following communication assertions for channels R_i and W:

$$\begin{aligned}
\text{com } R_i \text{ write } C_i \text{ read } m, old, v \\
\text{then } (\neg m \Rightarrow C_i' = \{v\}) \\
\wedge (m \Rightarrow C_i' = \{v, old\})
\end{aligned}$$

$$\begin{aligned}
\text{com } W \text{ write } v, m, C_1, ..., C_n, old \\
\text{then } m' \wedge v' = @W \wedge old' = v \\
\wedge \bigwedge_{i=1}^n C_i' = C_i \cup \{@W\} \, .
\end{aligned}$$

Thus at the start of a reading phase through R_i the set of correct values depends on whether the register is in a write modus. If not, only the current value is the correct one. Otherwise the current and the old value are both correct. If during the reading phase new writing phases are initiated by a communication on channel W, each time the set of correct values is enlarged by the newly written value $@W$.

```
spec input W of V
    output A of signal
    input R₁,..., Rₙ of signal
    output T₁,..., Tₙ of V
    trace W,A in pref(W.A)*
i∈1..n: trace Rᵢ,Tᵢ in pref(Rᵢ.Tᵢ)*
    var m of bool
    var C₁,..., Cₙ of V − set
    var v of V
    var old of V
    com W write v,m,C₁,...,Cₙ,old
        then m' ∧ v' = @W ∧ old' = v
            ∧ ⋀ⁿᵢ₌₁ Cᵢ' = Cᵢ ∪ {@W}
    com A write m then ¬m'
i∈1..n: com Rᵢ write Cᵢ read m,old,v
        then (¬m ⇒ Cᵢ' = {v})
            ∧ (m ⇒ Cᵢ' = {v,old})
i∈1..n: com Tᵢ read Cᵢ then @Tᵢ ∈ Cᵢ
end
```

Figure4: Specification n-reader-V-regular

Altogether we obtain the specification shown by Figure 4. Examples of communication traces satisfying n-reader-V-regular are

$$(W,3).A.R.(T,3).R.(W,5).A.(W,1).A.(T,k)$$

where $k \in \{1,3,5\}$. After each of these traces the register is ready to engage in communications on channels W and R.

3 Transformational Approach

The standard setting for a transformational approach is that specifications are transformed stepwise into programs. For example, our aim in ProCoS is to transform specifications of the language SL into programs of an occam-like programming language PL. In our present study we do not aim at occam-like programs but wish to show how to construct complex registers from simpler ones.

Such a construction can be conveniently expressed in the language MIX of *mixed terms*. MIX comprises *n*-ary programming operators OP that can be applied to specifications or other mixed terms $S_1,...,S_n$ yielding a mixed term $OP[S_1,...,S_n]$. In general, MIX

serves to express the intermediate stages of a transformational design from SL to PL and thus contains SL and PL as proper subsets. Here MIX is used as a language for expressing implementations of registers.

Under the predicative semantics described in [Old91b] and [ORSS92], specifications, programs and mixed terms are all identified with so-called *systems*. These are pairs $\Delta : P$ where Δ is an interface and P is a predicate describing the communication behaviour on the interface channels in Δ. Logical implication and equivalence on predicates are lifted to systems as follows:

- system implication: $\Delta_1 : P_1 \Longrightarrow \Delta_2 : P_2$
  if $\Delta_1 = \Delta_2$ and $\models P_1 \Rightarrow P_2$,

- system equivalence: $\Delta_1 : P_1 \equiv \Delta_2 : P_2$
  if $\Delta_1 = \Delta_2$ and $\models P_1 \Leftrightarrow P_2$.

We also write $\Delta_2 : P_2 <\equiv \Delta_1 : P_1$ instead of $\Delta_1 : P_1 \Longrightarrow \Delta_2 : P_2$. Under the predicative semantics, system implication models the *satisfaction* or *implementation* or *refinement* relation. Thus a program or mixed term Q *is correct w.r.t.* or *satisfies* or *implements* or *refines* a specification S iff $Q \Longrightarrow S$ holds. Note that system equivalence is a special case of refinement.

In the transformational approach a design of a program or mixed term Q from a specification S is a sequence

$$S \equiv R_1 <\equiv ... <\equiv R_n \equiv Q$$

of system implications between mixed terms $R_1,...,R_n$ where R_1 is the given specification S and R_n is the desired result Q. The transitivity of the relation $\Longrightarrow$ ensures the desired correctness result $Q \Longrightarrow S$.

Each of the implications $R_i <\equiv R_{i+1}$ in the design sequence is generated by an application of a transformation rule. We distinguish two classes of transformation rules. Rules preserving system equivalence $\equiv$ do not modify the system behaviour but only its syntactic representation. By contrast, *implementation* or *strengthening* rules relate systems of different behaviour by $\Longrightarrow$. An application of such a rule represents an irreversible design decision: nondeterminism within the behaviour may be removed or an over-specification is obtained.

3.1 Transforming the State Part

As a first contact with our transformational approach we present four groups of transformation rules dealing exclusively with the state part of a specification. As an application we shall then formally derive (the intuitively clear statement) that regular registers refine safe registers.

Specification format. It is convenient to extend the specification format by introducing *invariant declarations* of the form

$$\text{inv } p$$

where p is a predicate such that all free variables are declared within the specification considered. Such a declaration postulates that p holds in the initial state and after each communication.

Thus an SL specification can be represented as a tuple **spec** Δ *TA Va CA I* **end** where the components are as follows:

Δ	– a set of interface channels,
TA	– a set of trace assertions,
Va	– a set of variable declarations,
CA	– a set of communication assertions,
I	– a set of invariants.

Conjunction. These transformations reveal the conjunctive nature of communication assertions and invariants; their application always yield equivalent specifications.

T 3.1 (*conjunction of communication assertions*) Two communication assertions

$$\text{com } ch \text{ write } \overline{w}_i \text{ read } \overline{r}_i$$
$$\text{when } wh_i \text{ then } th_i$$

($i \in \{1, 2\}$) for the same channel ch are equivalent to a single one:

$$\text{com } ch \text{ write } \overline{w}_1 \cup \overline{w}_2 \text{ read } \overline{r}_1 \cup \overline{r}_2$$
$$\text{when } wh_1 \wedge wh_2 \text{ then } th_1 \wedge th_2.$$
∎

The conjunction of all communication assertions for a channel ch within *CA* yields the *unique communication assertion* for ch:

$$\text{com } ch \text{ write } \overline{w}_{ch} \text{ read } \overline{r}_{ch}$$
$$\text{when } wh_{ch} \text{ then } th_{ch}.$$

T 3.2 (*conjunction of invariants*) Two invariant declarations **inv** p_1 and **inv** p_2 are equivalent to a single one: **inv** $p_1 \wedge p_2$. ∎

In the following we denote by $\bigwedge I$ the conjunction of all invariant predicates. If I is empty, we put $\bigwedge I = \text{true}$.

Strengthening. These transformations strengthen the system behaviour by restricting the initial state, the state space or the effect of a communication. They either remove some nondeterminism or lead to over-specification. It requires creativity to find the right degree of strengthening within the design process.

T 3.3 (*initialization*) Any variable declaration **var** x of ty_x may be extended to an initialized declaration **var** x of ty_x **init** e thereby defining e as initial value of x. ∎

T 3.4 (*invariant strengthening*) An invariant predicate p may be replaced by any predicate q over free variables *Va* such that $q \Rightarrow p$ holds. ∎

Introducing an invariant declaration in a specification without invariants is included as the special case of strengthening **inv true**.

T 3.5 (*effect strengthening*) An effect predicate p may be replaced by any predicate q such that $q \wedge \bigwedge I \Rightarrow p$ holds and its free variables agree with the read and write list. ∎

Modifying specification components. These transformations describe the interaction of several specification components. Their application always yield equivalent specifications.

T 3.6 (*communication assertion modifications*) An enable or effect predicate p may be replaced by any predicate q with $\bigwedge I \Rightarrow (p \Leftrightarrow q)$ as far as the static semantics conditions are not violated. ∎

Thus dependent on the specification invariant a single enable or effect predicate can be strengthened or weakened without changing the behaviour.

The counterpart of this transformation allows to modify an invariant dependent on the initial state and CA. To this end we need the notion of stability. A predicate q with free variables in Va is *stable for a channel* ch if the unique communication assertion of ch guarantees the following: q holds in all termination states of communications on ch that start in a state satisfying q. Formally, we have

$$stable(q, ch)$$

$$\Leftrightarrow_{df}$$

$$wh_{ch} \wedge th_{ch} \wedge q \Rightarrow q[\overline{w}'_{ch}/\overline{w}_{ch}]$$

where the substitution $q[\overline{w}'_{ch}/\overline{w}_{ch}]$ replaces the write variables $\overline{w}_{ch}$ by their primed versions. Note that disjointness of $\overline{w}_{ch}$ and $free(q)$ guarantees $stable(q, ch)$.

T 3.7 (*invariant modifications*) Let q be a predicate which holds in the initial state and is stable for all channels in Δ. Then any invariant predicate p may be weakened to the implication $q \Rightarrow p$ or strengthened to the conjunction $q \wedge p$. ∎

Removing a declaration inv p is done by weakening to $p \Rightarrow p$.

Local variables. Here we consider how read and write lists of a communication assertions and the set of local variable declarations can be changed by equivalence transformations.

T 3.8 (*read list modification*) Any variable $x \in Va$ may be added to the read list of a communication assertion of channel ch provided x does not occur in the write list $\overline{w}_{ch}$. A variable occurring free neither in the enable nor in the effect predicate of a communication assertion may be removed from its read list. ∎

The following two rules are corollaries of a quite complex equivalence transformation dealing with the combined modification of variable declarations, invariants and communication assertions. They allow us to add and remove variable declarations together with modifications of communication assertions.

T 3.9 (*state space extension*) The state space can be extended by declaration of a new local variable. In addition the write lists of any communication assertions may be extended by this variable. ∎

T 3.10 (*removing write only variables*) A variable declaration var x of $ty_x[$ init $e]$ may be removed from a specification if x does not occur free in any invariant, enable or effect predicate. In that case x must be removed from the variable lists of the communication assertions and their effect predicates must be changed such that

$$th_{ch}^{new} \quad \Leftrightarrow \quad \exists x' \bullet th_{ch}^{old}$$

holds for all channels ch where x appears in the write list. ∎

3.2 Regular Implements Safe

From their informal description it seems obvious that a regular register implements a safe one. Here we will prove this relation formally for the SL specifications given in Section 2. Since both specifications agree on their interface and trace parts, we need to relate only their state parts. To this end, we shall apply the above transformation rules and massage the specification n-reader-V-safe until specification n-reader-V-regular is obtained. We proceed in three steps:

1. The communication assertions of T_i are modified to the pattern of the regular register specification. Therefore the state space is extended by set-valued variables $C_1, ..., C_n$ and the invariant $\bigwedge_{i=1}^{n} c_i \Rightarrow (C_i = \{v\})$ is introduced.

2. By appropriate initialization and effect strengthening the invariant of Step 1 is made redundant. This allows to remove the same and afterwards all variables $c_1, ..., c_n$.

3. The variable *old* is added and channels W and R_i are strengthened to achieve the regular specification pattern.

In the following we give a detailed account of this refinement by referring to the numbers of applied transformation rules. Starting point is the specification n-reader-V-safe.

Step 1 We extend the internal state space by new local variables $C_1, ..., C_n$ where write accesses are restricted to channels W and $R_1, ..., R_n$ [T3.9]:

> var $C_1, ..., C_n$ of $V - set$
> com W write $C_1, ..., C_n$
> com R_i write C_i.

The values of $C_1, ..., C_n$ are related to those of $c_1, ..., c_n$ by the following invariant [T3.4]:

$$\text{inv} \bigwedge_{i=1}^{n} (c_i \Rightarrow C_i = \{v\}).$$

Thus whenever T_i has to return the correct register value then variable C_i holds value $\{v\}$. The effect predicates of channels R_i are now strengthened [T3.5] to $@T_i \in C_i$ based on implication

$$@T_i \in C_i \land \bigwedge_{i=1}^{n} (c_i \Rightarrow C_i = \{v\})$$
$$\Rightarrow (c_i \Rightarrow @T_i = v).$$

Accordingly the read lists are modified [T3.8] by appending C_i and removing c_i. Thus in total the old communication assertions of $T_1, ..., T_n$ are replaced by the following ones for each $i \in 1..n$:

> com T_i read C_i then $@T_i \in C_i$.

Step 2 We strengthen the system behaviour in such a way that the invariant becomes redundant and thus may be removed. Firstly, all variables c_i are initialized with false [T3.3]:

> var $c_1, ..., c_n$ of bool init false.

Therefore the invariant holds initially. Secondly, the effect predicates of channels R_i are strengthened [T3.5]:

> com R_i write C_i, c_i read m, v
> then $c_i' = \neg m \land (\neg m \Rightarrow C_i' = \{v\})$.

Since any communication on W assigns false to all c_i, its termination state satisfies the invariant. All remaining channels $A, T_1, ..., T_n$ do not write variables occurring in the invariant predicate. Thus the invariant holds and its declaration can be removed [T3.7].

This leads to a specification without read accesses to variables $c_1, ..., c_n$. By transformation [T3.10] their declarations are removed and the communication assertions of W and $R_1, ..., R_n$ are modified using the logical equivalences $\exists c_1', ..., c_n' \bullet \bigwedge_{i=1}^{n} \neg c_i' \Leftrightarrow$ **true** and $\exists c_i' \bullet c_i' = \neg m \Leftrightarrow$ **true**. We thus obtain the following specification:

> spec ... *interface and trace assertions* ...
> var m of bool
> var $C_1, ..., C_n$ of $V - set$
> var v of V
> com W write $v, m, C_1, ..., C_n$
>   then $m' \land v' = @W$
> com A write m then $\neg m'$
> $_{i \in 1..n:}$ com R_i write C_i read m, v
>   then $\neg m \Rightarrow C_i' = \{v\}$
> $_{i \in 1..n:}$ com T_i read C_i then $@T_i \in C_i$
> end

Step 3 We introduce the local variable *old* of type V and allow write access to it by W [T3.9]:

> var *old* of V
> com W write *old*.

Strengthening W by conjunct $\bigwedge_{i=1}^{n} C_i' = C_i \cup \{@W\} \land old' = v$ [T3.5] and extending the read lists of all R_i by *old* [T3.8] together with strengthening their effects by conjuncts $m \Rightarrow C_i' = \{v, old\}$ [T3.5] delivers the target specification n-reader-V-regular.

4 Concurrent Implementations

In this section we study the implementation of a specification as a system of concurrently working subsystems synchronized via internal communication. When designing such a system one first decides on its architecture, i.e. which tasks should be performed concurrently and how subsystems should communicate. The transformational refinement process is then guided by these decisions.

As an example we consider the implementation of an n-reader-V-safe register using n copies $X_1, ..., X_n$ of 1-reader-V-safe registers and an auxiliary write process WP due to [Lam86, LG89]. The architecture of this implementation is shown in Figure 5. Thus

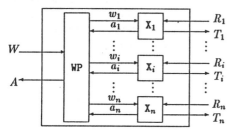

Figure5: Implementation of n-reader-V-safe

each of the n readers can communicate directly via the channels R_i and T_i with a private single reader register X_i. By contrast, the writer communicates via W and A with the auxiliary process WP which is linked with the single reader registers X_i via the internal channels w_i and a_i. The idea is that a write access to the n-reader register is implemented in several stages. After having received a new value by communication on W the process WP transmits this value via potentially parallel internal writes to all X_i. The external acknowledge on A is offered as soon as all internal writes have indicated their termination by the acknowledge events a_i.

We now present a formal transformational design of this implementation consisting of the following steps:

- Local channels are declared and their global sequencing is constrained.

- The state space is extended to cover the state spaces of the n single reader register. The behaviour is strengthened to achieve the effects of the 1-reader-V-safe specification.

- The whole specification is decomposed into the subsystems WP and $X_1, ..., X_n$.

4.1   Local Channels

A communication on a local channel is independent from and invisible to the environment. It may be performed as soon as its enable predicate holds in the current internal state and the extended trace satisfies the sequencing constraints of all trace assertions. Thus in contrast to external channels there is no synchronization with the environment.

Interface channels $ch_1, ..., ch_k$ of a specification S are localized applying to S the declaration operator CHAN with parameters $ch_1, ..., ch_k$:

$$S_1 = \text{CHAN } ch_1, ..., ch_k\ S.$$

CHAN is one of the operators of the language MIX so that S_1 is a mixed term. The semantics of CHAN implies that the system S_1 avoids engaging in unboundedly many communications on the local channels $ch_1, ..., ch_k$. Thus CHAN is a so-called "angelic" operator which is difficult to implement.

To avoid non-implementability we additionally use the operator HIDE from MIX:

$$S_2 = \text{CHAN } ch_1, ..., ch_k \text{ HIDE } ch_1, ..., ch_k\ S.$$

Systems S_1 and S_2 behave the same as long as S does not allow unbounded communication on $ch_1, ..., ch_k$. But in contrast to S_1 unbounded communication on these channels leads to divergence of S_2. For a more detailed analysis see [ORSS92].

Here we present a rule dealing with the combined effect of introducing local channels with hiding.

T 4.1 (*introducing local channels*)
Let $S = \text{spec } \Delta\ TA\ Va\ CA\ I$ end be a specification and $ch_1, ..., ch_k$ channel names not in Δ. Then S is equivalent to any mixed term

$$T = \text{CHAN } ch_1, ..., ch_k \text{ HIDE } ch_1, ..., ch_k$$
$$\text{spec } \Delta_T\ TA_T\ Va\ CA\ I \text{ end}$$

where the interface Δ_T is given by[1]

Δ input ch_1 of $ty_{ch_1}, ...$input ch_k of ty_{ch_k}
output ch_1 of $ty_{ch_1}, ...$output ch_k of ty_{ch_k}

---

[1] For technical reasons the local channels are declared with both directions.

and the trace part TA_T satisfies the following conditions:

1. it prevents unbounded communication on the new channels,

2. its projection onto the old channels allows exactly the same traces as TA,

3. for each prefix t of one of its traces and for each trace assertion $ta \in TA_T$ the intersection of all extensions of t with the alphabet of ta contains at most one of the new channels.

∎

Condition 1 implies that T describes a divergence free system. Conditions 2 and 3 imply that semantically S and T describe the same traces and ready sets. An application of this rule requires to find a right extension of the trace part meeting both these conditions and the overall development idea.

In our example we introduce the local channels $w_1, ..., w_n, a_1, ..., a_n$. As mentioned above communications on w_i and a_i are always enclosed by a preceding W and a finishing A communication. Hence the application conditions 1–3 of [T4.1] are satisfied. No restrictions are required between write and acknowledge channels of different single readers. Thus we replace the specification n-reader-V-safe by the following mixed term:

```
CHAN  w₁, ..., wₙ, a₁, ..., aₙ
HIDE  w₁, ..., wₙ, a₁, ..., aₙ
spec input w₁, ..., wₙ of V
     output w₁, ..., wₙ of V
     input a₁, ..., aₙ of signal
     output a₁, ..., aₙ of signal
```

... all n-reader-V-safe components ...
$i \in 1..n$:

$\quad$ trace W, A, w_i, a_i in $pref(W.w_i.a_i.A)^*$
end

4.2 Trace Assertions and Invariants

Now we aim at the behaviour of the single reader registers. This requires an extended reasoning about modifications of the state

part where in addition to the rules presented in 3.1 also the trace part is taken into account.

The following rule provides a generalization of the invariant reasoning based on [T3.6] and [T3.7]. It checks whether a predicate q holds whenever the system may engage in a communication on channel ch and allows us to modify its communication assertion appropriately. We say that a channel ch^* establishes q if it holds in the terminating state of each ch^* communication:

$$establish(q, ch^*)$$

$$\Leftrightarrow_{df}$$

$$wh_{ch^*} \wedge th_{ch^*} \Rightarrow q[\overline{w}'_{ch^*}/\overline{w}_{ch^*}].$$

T 4.2 (effect modifications under trace assertions) Let trace $ch_1, ..., ch_k$ in re be a trace assertion and q be a predicate which is stable for all channels of $\Delta \setminus \{ch_1, ..., ch_k\}$. Let $ch \in \{ch_1, ..., ch_k\}$ be a channel such that in every word of the regular language of re each occurrence of ch is preceded by a channel ch^* establishing q. If further all intermediate channels between ch^* and ch are stable for q then the effect th_{ch} may be weakened to $q \Rightarrow th_{ch}$ or strengthened to $q \wedge th_{ch}$ without changing the behaviour. ∎

For the moment the design process proceeds by the same technique shown in detail in 3.2: the state space is changed and communication assertions are strengthened; invariants are introduced to modify communication assertions and are removed afterwards.

At first we introduce new local variables m_i, lc_i, v_i which shall correspond to the local variables m, c, v of an 1-reader-V-safe register specification. Write and read access to these new variables is restricted as follows:

```
var m₁, ..., mₙ, lc₁, ..., lcₙ of bool
var v₁, ..., vₙ of V
com wᵢ write vᵢ, mᵢ, lcᵢ
com aᵢ write mᵢ
com Rᵢ write lcᵢ read mᵢ
com Tᵢ read lcᵢ, vᵢ.
```

Then the effect predicates of theses channels are strengthened. The additional restrictions are motivated by the corresponding predicates in 1-reader-V-safe.

com w_i write $v_i, m_i, \ell c_i$ read v
    then $m_i' \wedge v_i' = v \wedge \neg \ell c_i'$
com a_i write m_i then $\neg m_i'$
com R_i write $c_i, \ell c_i$ read m, m_i
    then $c_i' = \neg m \wedge \ell c_i' = \neg m_i$
com T_i read $c_i, v, \ell c_i, v_i$
    then $(c_i \Rightarrow @T_i = v) \wedge (\ell c_i \Rightarrow @T_i = v_i)$

In the following steps the effect predicates are modified such that they become independent from variables m and $c_1, ..., c_n$. This is done by iterated application of the invariant technique shown in the previous example. New invariants are introduced and some effects are modified under them. After that effect predicates of other channels are strengthened to make the invariant redundant.

Firstly we deal with channels T_i whose effect predicates are simplified under the following invariant:

$$\text{inv } \bigwedge_{i=1}^{n} (c_i \Rightarrow \ell c_i \wedge v_i = v).$$

Thus communication assertions of T_i can be replaced by the following ones:

com T_i read $\ell c_i, v_i$ then $\ell c_i \Rightarrow @T_i = v_i.$

Consideration of the single effect predicates shows that this invariant is established by any communication on W, since all c_i are set to false, and is a stable property of channels T_i, a_i, A. The initialization of variables $c_1, ..., c_n$ by false makes it also valid in the initial state. The effect predicates of channels w_i and R_i are strengthened by the conjuncts $\neg c_i$ and $\neg m \Rightarrow (\neg m_i \wedge v_i = v)$, respectively, and thus the invariant becomes redundant.

var $c_1, ..., c_n$ of bool init false
com w_i write $v_i, m_i, \ell c_i$ read v, c_i
    then $m_i' \wedge v_i' = v \wedge \neg \ell c_i' \wedge \neg c_i$
com R_i write $c_i, \ell c_i$ read m, m_i, v_i, v
    then $c_i' = \neg m \wedge \ell c_i' = \neg m_i \wedge$
        $(\neg m \Rightarrow \neg m_i \wedge v_i = v)$

Next all read accesses to variables c_i are removed using the invariant $m \Rightarrow \bigwedge_{i=1}^{n} \neg c_i.$

It allows us to strengthen the effects of all w_i by replacing conjuncts $\neg c_i$ with m:

com w_i write $v_i, m_i, \ell c_i$ read v, m
    then $m_i' \wedge v_i' = v \wedge \neg \ell c_i' \wedge m.$

The invariant predicate used here holds in the initial state and is stable for all channels. Thus it can be removed without any further changes.

Then the local variables $c_1, ..., c_n$ are removed and we obtain the following reduced state part:

var $m, m_1, ..., m_n, \ell c_1, ..., \ell c_n$ of bool
var $v, v_1, ..., v_n$ of V
com W write v, m then $m' \wedge v' = @W$
com A write m then $\neg m'$
com w_i write $v_i, m_i, \ell c_i$ read v, m
    then $m_i' \wedge v_i' = v \wedge \neg \ell c_i' \wedge m$
com a_i write m_i then $\neg m_i'$
com R_i write ℓc_i read m, m_i, v_i, v
    then $\ell c_i' = \neg m_i \wedge$
        $(\neg m \Rightarrow \neg m_i \wedge v_i = v)$
com T_i read $\ell c_i, v_i$ then $\ell c_i \Rightarrow @T_i = v_i.$

Now we pursue the elimination of variable m. To remove the read accesses to variable m the newly introduced rule [T4.2] is applied. Each communication on W assigns true to m and each one on A sets m to false and no other communication modifies the value of m. Thus predicate $m = \text{true}$ is established by W and is stable for all channels but A. We conclude from trace assertion

trace A, W, a_i, w_i in $pref(W.w_i.a_i.A)^*$

that each w_i communication is preceded by an W communication and there cannot occur an A communication between W and the following w_i. Thus the effect th_{w_i} can be weakened and the communication assertions of all w_i are replaced by

com w_i write $v_i, m_i, \ell c_i$ read v
    then $m_i' \wedge v_i' = v \wedge \neg \ell c_i'.$

To deal with the occurrence of m in the effect of channels R_i the behaviour is strengthened by

$$\text{inv } \neg m \Rightarrow \bigwedge_{i=1}^{n} (\neg m_i \wedge v_i = v).$$

Under this invariant the communication assertions of all R_i are modified to

com R_i write lc_i read m, m_i, v_i, v
    then $lc_i' = \neg m_i$.

The initialization

    var m of bool init true

delivers the validity of the above invariant predicate in the initial state. The ·channels a_i, R_i, T_i do not write any variable of the invariant while the effect predicates of W and w_i always establish this invariant. Thus only channel A must be strengthened to achieve the redundancy of the invariant:

com A write m
    read $m_1, ..., m_n, v_1, ..., v_n, v$
    then $\neg m' \wedge \bigwedge_{i=1}^{n} (\neg m_i \wedge v_i = v)$.

Based on the sequencing constraints given by $pref(W.w_i.a_i.A)$ we eliminate by multiple application of [T4.2] all conjuncts $\neg m_i$ and $v_i = v$. The former ones are established by communications a_i and are stable for all channels R_i and T_i. Thus th_A can be weakened by removing conjunct $\bigwedge_{i=1}^{n} \neg m_i$. The other conjuncts $v_i = v$ are established by the w_i's and are stable for all R_i, T_i and a_i. Thus $\bigwedge_{i=1}^{n} v_i = v$ can also be removed. Moreover, since there is no more a read access to m, this local variable can be removed and the communication assertions of W and A are simplified to

    com W write v then $v' = @W$
    com A .

4.3 Parallel Decomposition

A major goal of the definition of SL and MIX was to support the development of concurrent implementations. The result is a parallel decomposition rule based on the n-ary synchronization operator SYN of MIX. According to this rule, interface components, invariants, trace assertions and communication assertions may be divided over the subspecifications in an arbitrary fashion. Only each local variable declaration has to occur in exactly one S_i.

T 4.3 (*parallel decomposition*)
Let $S = \text{spec } \Delta\ TA\ Va\ CA\ I$ end and $S_i = \text{spec } \Delta_i\ TA_i\ Va_i\ CA_i\ I_i$ end for $i \in 1..n$ be specifications where $\Delta = \bigcup_{i=1}^{n} \Delta_i$, $TA = \bigcup_{i=1}^{n} TA_i$, $Va = \biguplus_{i=1}^{n} Va_i{}^2$, $CA = \bigcup_{i=1}^{n} CA_i$ and $I = \bigcup_{i=1}^{n} I_i$. Then

$$S \quad \equiv \quad \text{SYN}[\ S_1, \cdots, S_n\ ]\ ,$$

i.e. S is equivalent to a mixed term where synchronization is applied to all S_i.   ∎

We remark that TA enforces synchronization of all communications that appear on channels in more than one of the local trace assertions TA_i. The disjointness condition on the local variables Va_i reflects distributed concurrency. Thus a parallel decomposition must be prepared by rearranging specification components to achieve disjointness. To this end, we shall use the transformations [T3.1] and [T3.2].

Semantically the meaning of TA is a regular language over the set of all channels. Thus modifications of the set of all trace assertions do not change the specified system behaviour as long as the same language is described. The trace merging algorithm [RS91, ORSS92] provides a transformation to join several trace assertions into a single one. A special case of trace merging is given by the following rule.

T 4.4 (*trace projection*)
Let trace $ch_1, ..., ch_k$ in re be a trace assertion within TA and let $ch_{l_1}, .. ch_{l_m}$ be a subset of its alphabet. Let $\widetilde{re}$ be a regular expression equivalent to re where all occurrences of names $\{ch_1, ..., ch_k\} \backslash \{ch_{l_1}, .. ch_{l_m}\}$ are replaced by nil[3]. Then the addition of the projected trace assertion

$$\text{trace } ch_{l_1}, .. ch_{l_m} \text{ in } \widetilde{re}$$

to TA does not change the behaviour.   ∎

Let us now consider the example. The intended architecture (cf. Figure 5) determines the allocation of the interface components and variable declarations to the subsystems. As mentioned above, each single reader

---

[2] Union of pairwise disjoint sets.

[3] The constant nil denotes the regular language consisting of the empty word.

register X_i shall get the variables $m_i, \ell c_i, v_i$ and therefore variable v must be placed in WP. Since the write list of a communication assertion w_i consists of variables $m_i, \ell c_i, v_i$ and v, we must achieve a conjunctive form of the effect predicate such that the former three and the latter one variable are not accessed in the same conjunct. Restricting the communication value $@w_i$ to v by [T3.5] gives the effect predicate

$$m_i' \wedge \neg \ell c_i' \wedge v_i' = @w_i \wedge @w_i = v.$$

Then by [T3.1] the unique communication assertion is replaced by the following two:

```
com w_i read v then @w_i = v
com w_i write v_i, m_i, ℓc_i
        then m_i' ∧ ¬ℓc_i' ∧ v_i' = @w_i.
```

The specification of a single reader register requires an alternation between write and acknowledge communications. Thus for each $i \in 1..n$ we add by [T4.4] the projections

$$\text{trace } w_i, a_i \text{ in } pref(w_i.a_i)^*$$

of trace assertions

$$\text{trace } W, A, w_i, a_i \text{ in } pref(W.w_i.a_i.A)^*$$

on channels w_i and a_i to TA. After these preparations the whole specification is decomposed by [T4.3] yielding the following mixed term:

```
        CHAN w_1, ..., w_k, a_1, ..., a_n
        HIDE w_1, ..., w_n, a_1, ..., a_n
        SYN[ WP, X_1, ..., X_n ]
where
WP =
    spec input W of V
        output A of signal
        output w_1, ..., w_n of V
        input a_1, ..., a_n of signal
        trace W, A in pref(W.A)*
    i ∈ 1..n :
    trace A, W, a_i, w_i in pref(W.w_i.a_i.A)*
        var v of V
        com W write v then v' = @W
        com w_i read v then @w_i = v
    end
```

```
X_i = spec input w_i of V
        output a_i of signal
        input R_i of signal
        output T_i of V
        trace w_i, a_i in pref(w_i.a_i)*
        trace R_i, T_i in pref(R_i.T_i)*
        var m_i of bool
        var ℓc_i of bool
        var v_i of V
        com w_i write v_i, m_i, ℓc_i
            then m_i' ∧ ¬ℓc_i' ∧ v_i' = @w_i
        com a_i write m_i then ¬m_i'
        com R_i write ℓc_i read m_i
            then ℓc_i' = ¬m_i
        com T_i read ℓc_i, v_i
            then ℓc_i ⇒ @T_i = v_i
    end
```

Note that each X_i is a copy of the 1-reader-V-safe specification with the interface channels W, A, R, T renamed into w_i, a_i, R_i, T_i. This concludes the construction of an n-reader-V-safe register from n copies of a 1-reader-V-safe register and an auxiliary write process WP.

By applying further transformations from [ORSS92, Ch. 8], we can obtain an occam-like implementation of WP with the following program body:

```
WHILE true SEQ[W?v,
            PAR[SEQ[w_1!v,a_1?],...,
                SEQ[w_n!v,a_n?]  ],
            A!].
```

5   Discussion

Our work on transformational design of concurrent systems is close in spirit to the work on UNITY [CM88] and to Back's work on refinement calculus [Bac90]. One of the differences is that UNITY and Back start from iterative programs akin to Dijkstra's do-od loops whereas we start from SL specifications with an explicit treatment of communication. This leads us also to consider a richer class of programming operators and hence transformation rules than previous work.

The case study deals with one of the simpler concurrent implementations of registers originally due to Lamport [Lam86]. Whereas

Lamport gives a correctness proof in some special formalism, we use here a specification formalism combining standard ideas from process algebra, in particular about the semantics of CSP-like communicating processes [Hoa85, Old91a], and from state-based assertional reasoning. Our communication-based specification of the register is inspired by [LG89].

New is our transformational derivation of the concurrent implementation of the n reader safe register. We have applied the same transformational approach to derive also other implementations of register due to [Lam86]: n reader *regular* register implemented by one reader regular registers and by one reader safe registers; safe registers for a finite value set V implemented by safe registers for *binary* values. These transformations rely on further rules dealing with renaming and branching in the flow of control. We have not yet attacked the really difficult constructions for atomic registers. This would be a challenging task for a transformational design.

Acknowledgement. We are grateful to Andrea Sprock who performed an initial study on transformational design of safe and regular registers [Spr92]. This paper is influenced by her work but our proofs are different.

References

[Bac90] R.J.R. Back. Refinement calculus, Part II: Parallel and Reactive Programs. In J.W. de Bakker, W.P. de Roever, and G. Rozenberg, editors, *Stepwise Refinement of Distributed Systems - Models, Formalisms, Correctness*, LNCS 430, pages 67–93. Springer-Verlag, 1990.

[Bau87] F.L. Bauer et al. *The Munich Project CIP, Vol. II: The Transformation System CIP-S.* LNCS 292. Springer-Verlag, 1987.

[Bjø89] D. Bjørner et al. A ProCoS project description - ESPRIT BRA 3104. *EATCS Bulletin*, 39:60–73, 1989.

[BW90] J.C.M. Baeten and P. Weijland. *Process Algebra*. Cambridge University Press, 1990.

[CH74] R.H. Campbell and A.N. Habermann. The specification of process synchronisation by path expressions. LNCS 16. Springer-Verlag, 1974.

[CM88] K.M. Chandy and J. Misra. *Parallel Program Design - A Foundation*. Addison-Wesley, 1988.

[Hoa85] C.A.R. Hoare. *Communicating Sequential Processes*. Prentice-Hall, London, 1985.

[Kri89] B. Krieg-Brückner. Algebraic specification and functionals for transformational program and meta program development. In J. Diaz and F. Orejas, editors, *Proc. TAPSOFT '89*, LNCS 352. Springer-Verlag, 1989.

[Lam86] L. Lamport. On interprocess communications II. *Distributed Comp.*, 1:86–101, 1986.

[LG89] N.A. Lynch and K.J. Goldman. Distributed algorithms. Technical Report MIT/LCS/RSS 5 6.852 Fall 1988, MIT, 1989.

[LT89] N.A. Lynch and M.R. Tuttle. An introduction to input/ouput automata. Technical Report CWI-Quaterly 2(3), CWI, 1989.

[Mil89] R. Milner. *Communication and Concurrency*. Prentice Hall, London, 1989.

[Mor90] C. Morgan. *Programming from Specifications*. Prentice Hall, London, 1990.

[MP91] Z. Manna and A. Pnueli. *The Temporal Logic of Reactive and Concurrent Systems – Specification*. Springer-Verlag, 1991.

[Old91a] E.-R. Olderog. *Nets, Terms and Formulas: Three Views of Concurrent Processes and Their Relationship*. Cambridge University Press, 1991.

[Old91b] E.-R. Olderog. Towards a Design Calculus for Communicating Programs. In J.C.M. Baeten and J.F. Groote, editors, *Proc. CONCUR '91*, LNCS 527, pages 61–77. Springer-Verlag, 1991. invited paper.

[ORSS92] E.-R. Olderog, S. Rössig, J. Sander, and M. Schenke. ProCoS at Oldenburg: The Interface between Specification Language and occam-like Programming Language. Technical Report Bericht 3/92, Univ. Oldenburg, Fachbereich Informatik, 1992.

[RS91] S. Rössig and M. Schenke. Specification and stepwise development of communicating systems. In S. Prehn and W.J. Toetenel, editors, *VDM'91 Formal Software Development Methods*, LNCS 551, pages 149–163. Springer-Verlag, 1991.

[Spi89] J.M. Spivey. *The Z Notation: A Reference Manual*. Prentice Hall, London, 1989.

[Spr92] A. Sprock. Spezifikation von Registern und Verifikation der Implementation von Registern. Studienarbeit, Univ. Oldenburg, 1992.

[Zwi89] J. Zwiers. *Compositionalty, Concurrency and Partial Correctness - Proof Theories for Networks of Processes and Their Relationship*. LNCS 321. Springer-Verlag, 1989.

Yeast: A case study for a practical use of formal methods

Paola Inverardi [1] Balachander Krishnamurthy[2]
Daniel Yankelevich[3]

Abstract

This paper discusses a formal semantics for an existent event-action system, Yeast, developed at AT&T Bell Laboratories. Yeast is a good case study for the use of (true-concurrent) semantic techniques since causal dependence among events, concurrency, nondeterminism and conflicting behaviour of specifications can all be modeled in Yeast. We discuss the use of the formalization in the verification of correctness of real Yeast applications with respect to various properties.

1 Introduction

In this paper we present a formal semantics for an existent event-action system, Yeast, developed at AT&T Bell Laboratories[1]. Yeast supports cooperative work in a distributed computing environment. It allows users to define event-driven specifications which when matched can trigger actions. Yeast manages events through a global space shared among all the users. Some of the events are asynchronous since they can come from the external environment. Yeast is used for a variety of applications, from deadline notification to software configuration management. A Yeast application consists of the set of specifications written to model the domain as well as the events that match the specifications.

The motivation for our work is twofold: i) From the theoretical side, Yeast represents a good case study for the use of (true-concurrent) semantic techniques [7]. Despite their conceptual simplicity, Yeast specifications exhibit a number of interesting behaviours such as causal dependence among events, concurrency, nondeterminism and conflict; ii) From the applicative side, we are interested in verifying the correctness of Yeast applications with respect to various properties. Along with creating Yeast applications we would like to be able to identify specifications that could be enabled by conflicting events, or perform a run-time ordering of specifications. A practical need thus emerges for a formal basis on which to carry out reasoning over Yeast applications.

We define the Yeast semantics in two steps: First, we provide a distributed operational semantics by means of structured inference rules. This operational semantics is distributed in the sense that in each rule only the requirements (pieces of the state) to enable it are expressed, i.e. no global information is required. The second step defines how to retrieve a Petri net representation of Yeast applications from the operational description. A Petri net allows dependency (causality), independency (concurrency) and contraposition (conflict) among a collection of Yeast specifications to be clearly represented. At this second semantic level, we formally define some properties a Yeast user may want to verify on the application.

[1]I.E.I–C.N.R., Pisa, Italy. Research partially funded by Progetto Finalizzato Sistemi Informatici e Calcolo Parallelo
[2]AT&T Bell Laboratories, Murray Hill, NJ 07974 USA
[3]Dipartimento di Informatica, Università di Pisa, Italy

Once the semantics has been provided, there are two approaches to verifying the correctness of Yeast applications. The first one is to perform analysis and verification on the Petri net. This approach relies entirely on the Petri net representation. Given the state of the art, we do not think that this approach is always practical due to the strong limitations in the ability to translate reasonable scale applications efficiently into the net semantic description. Even when the translation has been accomplished, the management of the net description both in terms of computational and space complexity can be hard.

The second approach is to build verification tools that perform the required analysis directly at the application level, i.e. over Yeast source specifications based on the semantic description we have provided. In this work we are interested in pursuing this approach. This is not a simple task and one cannot expect to be completely successful. There can be a price to be paid in terms of completeness of the verification process. In fact, in order to be practical, sometimes it may be convenient to apply heuristics or ask for user intervention.

We first describe Yeast briefly and then discuss a scenario of a Yeast application together with properties of interest. We then review operational semantics and Petri net preliminary definitions and results. The formal model section provides the operational semantics and Petri net representation of the subset of Yeast we consider. Then, this is applied on the specifications in the scenario along with an analysis of the properties of interest. In the same section, the approach we are taking to check these properties on Yeast specifications together with hints on our prototypal implementation in Prolog of two simple analysis tools are presented. We conclude with a section on current and future work.

2 Yeast

Yeast (Yet another Event-Action Specification Tool) is a general-purpose platform for constructing distributed event-action applications using high-level specifications. Yeast supports a wide variety of applications, including calendar and notification systems, computer network management, software configuration management, software process automation, software process measurement, and coordination of wide-area software development. A general-purpose event-action system makes it easier for arbitrary applications to eliminate special purpose event-action matchings.

Yeast was designed with some requirements in mind:

- The specification language must be simple, yet powerful.

- There should be no restriction on the actions that users can specify to be performed in response to the occurrence of user-specified event patterns.

- Users of the system must be able to interactively query the status of specifications they have registered with the system.

Yeast is based on a client-server architecture in which distributed clients register, manipulate and query event-action specifications, and a server performs specification matching and management. A Yeast specification consists of an event pattern along with an action; the server triggers the action whenever it detects an occurrence of the associated event pattern. The action part of a specification can perform any number of actions in response to the matching of the event pattern, including Yeast-related actions.

Event patterns consist of either temporal events or object events. Temporal events are the familiar calendar events (e.g., *at* a particular time) whereas object events are changes in attribute values of an object. Example objects that Yeast knows about are *files*, *directories* and *machines*. Example attributes of files are *size*, *owner*, etc. Yeast can match patterns that are connected by the connectives *and*, *or*, and *then*, which have straightforward semantics (e.g. both sides of an *and* pattern have to be true for the pattern to be true). The *then* connective implies that the left hand side must be true before checking is performed on the right hand side.

The significant difference between other event-action tools such as *cron*, and Yeast is that Yeast can be told about new events. Users can define new object classes and attributes for them. Since change in values of user defined attributes cannot be detected, they have to be *announced* to Yeast.

A simple example shows the extensibility of Yeast. The *defattr* command (part of Yeast) defines a new attribute of a particular type.

```
defattr file debugged boolean
```

Users can now make specifications that are matched when the *debugged* attribute attains a particular value. For example,

```
addspec file libx debugged == true do make system
```

Once Yeast is notified that the file *libx* has been debugged, the system is automatically rebuilt via the *make system* action. The user who has authentication over the attribute *debugged*, after debugging the *libx* file, sends the following announcement:

```
announce file libx debugged = true
```

The announcement facility makes Yeast extensible and thus applicable to a wide range of tasks.

3   A Software Development Scenario

In this section we present a small Yeast application that attempts to model a portion of a software development process. We then present a set of questions of interest which, while specific to the scenario, outline hints at the general properties of specifications that we would like to analyze.

3.1   Scenario

In a software development environment, change that needs to be done as a result of suspected problems or enhancement requests is labeled Modification Request or MR for short. Typically MRs are reviewed by an MR review board who decide which version of the software needs to be changed and which developers are responsible for each change. The MR is assigned to the responsible developers who fix the problem. After testing their changes locally, the developers *submit* the MR, upon which the modified software is rebuilt by an integrator. An approval team typically then approves the modified software, enabling it to be distributed.

For the purposes of this scenario we will consider a simplified example skipping over the MR review process and selection of the appropriate version of the software.

When a MR comes in, it is assigned a number and its status is set to *active*. Suppose it is assigned to a group of three people who have authority to fix the problem. Theoretically they are supposed to agree amongst themselves that the problem has been fixed and then notify the integrator of this fact.

The steps in the portion of the process we model via Yeast are:

- Submitting an MR,

- Rebuilding of software component by the integrator.

- Approval by the approver.

Additionally, suppose that there are temporal constraints in the process. Say, the MR has been assigned at 8AM Monday; developers have until 5PM Wednesday to fix the problem; the integrator then has until 5PM Thursday to rebuild it and the approver must approve it by 5PM Friday. The dependencies are clear: software cannot be approved until it is rebuilt, and rebuilding cannot occur until the MR has been submitted.

With this as background, let us look at a Yeast model of the above process. We consider some potential problems with this model later. For the scenario, let us assume MR23 is the MR in question on the software module m1, and that it was assigned to developers Anna, Bala, and Chico, the integrator is Dan and the approver is Eduardo. The Yeast command `defobj` defines a new object class, and `defattr` defines a new attribute for an object class.

```
defobj MR                       # models a modification request
defattr MR status string        # string attribute of  MR status

defobj module                   # module that has associated MR
defattr module rebuilt boolean  # boolean attr of module status
defattr module approved boolean # boolean attr of module status
```

After the developers test their changes, any of them can send an announcement stating that the MR has been submitted by the developer as follows:

```
announce MR MR23 status = devsub
```

The specification that the above announcement would match is made by the integrator Dan:

```
addspec MR MR23 status == devsub do rebuild m1         (s1)
```

where rebuild is presumably a script for rebuilding software modules. If the *rebuild* script succeeds in rebuilding m1, then the following announcements are generated as part of the script.

```
announce module m1 rebuilt = true
announce MR MR23 status = submitted
```

If the *rebuild* script fails then the following announcement is sent

```
announce module m1 rebuilt = false
```

Likewise, the following specification is made by the approver Eduardo

```
addspec module m1 rebuilt == true do TestAndApprove m1   (s2)
```

where TestAndApprove is a script that tests the module and if the tests are successful generates the following announcements

```
announce module m1 approved = true
announce MR MR23 status = approved
```

Only Dan has the necessary authentication on the attribute *rebuilt* of the object-class module. Similarly, only Eduardo has authentication on the attribute `approved`.

If the status of the MR is still active at 5PM Wednesday then the integrator needs to be notified about this. Likewise, if the module m1 has not been rebuilt by 5PM Thursday the approver needs to be notified. These are the temporal constraints in this mini-process.

```
addspec at 5pm Wednesday and MR MR23 status == active do
    Nobuild dan m1                                          (s3)
```

where Nobuild is a script that notifies the integrator via mail and announces the failure of the rebuild:

```
Mail -s missed_MR23_deadline dan
announce module m1 rebuilt = false
```

```
addspec at 5pm Thursday and module m1 rebuilt == false do
    Noapprove eduardo m1                                    (s4)
```

where Noapprove is a script that notifies the approver Eduardo and announces the failure of the approval:

```
Mail -s missed_MR23_deadline eduardo
announce module m1 approved = false
```

3.2   Properties of interest

The Yeast modeling of the process has potential problems and some properties of interest. An analysis of the specifications should bring these out.

Since any of the three developers (Anna, Bala, Chico) can set the *status* attribute of MR23, there is a possibility that one person may set it to be *devsub* which matches specification S1 triggering a rebuild of m1. If another developer sets the status to *active* later, that will match S3 at 5PM Wednesday triggering a m1 `rebuilt = false` announcement. We would like to know about such possibilities *a priori*.

The following questions are of interest as it relates to analysis of the specifications:

- What is the dependency pattern on the specification/events?
- Is there a time ordering of the specification matching times?
- What are the contrary events possible that could cause a deadlock or lead to potentially erroneous conclusions?
- Which specifications will be the last to be matched?
- Which specification will be matched/attempted to be matched first?

4 The Formal Model

In this section we present the formal model we have defined for the Yeast language. Before introducing the model we recall the preliminary definitions and notions we need. In the following section we introduce the notion of Place/Transitions nets and operational semantics. For a detailed presentation of these topics the reader should refer to [5] and [6] respectively.

4.1 Preliminary Definitions

In this section, we review the main definitions of Place/Transition (P/T) nets and of operational semantics.

Definition 1 P/T Net
A net $N = (S, T, W, M_0)$ consists of disjoint sets S and T of places and transitions, the weight function $W : S \times T \cup T \times S \to I\!N$ and the initial marking $M_0 : S \to I\!N$, where $I\!N$ is the set of natural numbers.

Definition 2 Pre- and post- sets
Given a net $N = (S, T, W, M_0)$ and an element $x \in S \cup T$,

- *the pre-set of x is $^\bullet x = \{y \in S \cup T \mid W(y, x) \neq 0\}$*
- *the post-set of x is $x^\bullet = \{y \in S \cup T \mid W(x, y) \neq 0\}$*

Definition 3 Markings and enabling
Given a net $N = (S, T, W, M_0)$, a marking is a function $M : S \to I\!N$. A transition $t \in T$ is enabled under a marking M, denoted $M[t >$ if for all $s \in {}^\bullet t$, we have $M(s) \geq W(s, t)$. An enabled transition may occur, producing a follower marking M', written $M[t > M'$, if $M[t >$ and $M'(s) = M(s) - W(s, t) + W(t, s)$ for all $s \in S$. In this case, $M[t > M'$ is called a step.

A marking M is called *reachable* if for some sequence of steps $t_1 \ldots t_n$, $M_0[t_1 > M_1 \ldots M_{n-1}[t_n > M$.

As far as the operational semantics is concerned we take the usual SOS approach [6]. That is we describe the operational behaviour of a system in terms of inference rules which define a relation between states of the system.

Definition 4 Operational Semantics
Let S denote the states of the system under description and Act the actions produced by the system when evolving from a state to another state. Then an operational semantics OP is a set of inference rules of the form $\dfrac{Premises}{Conclusion}$ defining a relation $D \subseteq S \times Act \times S$; D is the least relation satisfying the rules.

In the following section we precisely define what are, in our case, states and actions.

4.2 Operational Semantics

In this section we develop the operational semantics reflecting the dynamic behaviour of the language. The operational semantics is defined starting from a syntactic presentation of the language which is slightly different from the grammar presented in the Appendix. The main differences are on the representation of events and of actions. Events are to be considered as unique. That is, two specifications which *use* the same event give rise to two distinct events. In practice, this is realised by subscripting the event with the specification identifier. As far as actions are concerned, we introduce the notion of action with parameters with the convention that action sequences are built with the ';' operator, and () denotes the empty action sequence (i.e. do nothing). When an action has more than one parameter, it indicates a branching upon a condition, and depending on the condition one among the actions (or action sequences) is executed. In this way complex *scripts*, or the intervention of a user, are modelled as a nondeterministic choice, i.e. a branch which depends on a condition that is outside of the system. For instance, the complex script described as TestandApprove in the specification s2 of the SDS example in section 3.1 can be modelled as T&A ()(announce(m1.approved =true); announce(mr23.status = approved)), which reflects the fact that if the test fails, nothing is done otherwise two announcements are issued. Actually this is exactly the formalization we will use in Section 4.4 when modelling the whole SDS example.

Before introducing the rules of the operational semantics we define what is a state and an action of the system. Informally, a **state** of the system is given by a set of specifications plus the conditions that are fulfilled at a particular moment, that is, events that are true and which enable a specification.

Notice that Yeast attributes are not variables, i.e. the value of an attribute is not persistent. For example, if an announcement of the event *att1 = false* is done and after that, a specification of the form *att1 == false do mail(vladimiro)* is included, the mail to vladimiro is not sent, since the announcement of *att1 = false* has been done previously and the system does not remember it.

Definition 5 *Let A be a Yeast event and s be a Yeast specification. Then, A_s is a state component. Moreover, if A is of the form objectattribute = value, then $att(A_s) = objectattribute$ and $val(A_s) = value$.*

For instance, $att((mr23.status = active)_{s3}) = mr23.status$
and $val((mr23.status = active)_{s3}) = active$.

A state component is an event with a subscript identifying which specification it (partially) enables. We define the subindex cl for clock, and events subscripted with a cl are consumed by the system clock to produce new time events. Sub-indexes are omitted when they are obvious from the context, for example if the event corresponds to just one specification.

The state of the system is composed of the current set of specifications plus the set of possible enablings, i.e. the events which are valid; which leads to our next definition.

Definition 6 *The states of the system are pairs (S, E), where S is a set of specifications and E is a set of state components.*

The set $\{s_1, s_2, \ldots s_n\}$ is denoted by $s_1 \oplus s_2 \ldots \oplus s_n$. Similarly $\{e_1, e_2, \ldots e_n\}$ is denoted by $e_1 \oplus e_2 \ldots \oplus e_n$. Notice that $\oplus$ is associative and commutative. The sets

S and E have ϕ_S and ϕ_E as neutral element respectively; furthermore $\oplus$ is idempotent with respect to these neutral elements.

As far as **actions** are concerned, we just take the action part of Yeast specifications. Therefore the rules we are going to present define a relation among states of the system, i.e. $OP \subseteq (S \times E) \times Act \times (S \times E)$.

The operational semantics is defined by means of one inference rule schema. This rule schema stands for different rules which are obtained by instantiating the ACT parameter with the action parameters of the yc function and substituting the bottom left part with the corresponding output value of the yc function. The rule schema is:

$$\frac{E \vdash e, S \vdash addspec(e, ACT)}{S, E \xrightarrow{ACT} yc(ACT, S - addspec(e, ACT), E - e)}$$

where yc is recursively defined as follows:

$$yc : ACT \times S \times E \to S \times E$$
$$yc(\{a_1, \ldots, a_n\}, S, E) = yc(a_n, yc(\{a_1, \ldots, a_{n-1}\}, S, E))$$
$$yc(spec, S, E) = (S \cup spec), E$$
$$yc(defobj, S, E) = yc(defattr, S, E) = S, E$$
$$yc(announce(e), S, E) = S, E \cup e$$
$$yc(shell\_cmd, S, E) = S, E$$

and

$$\frac{e \in E}{E \vdash e} \qquad \frac{s \in S}{S \vdash s}$$

$$\frac{E \vdash e}{E \vdash e \text{ or } e'} \qquad \frac{E \vdash e, e'}{E \vdash e \text{ and } e'}$$

For example, an instance of the rule schema for $ACT = addspec(e', A)$ is:

$$\frac{E \vdash e, S \vdash addspec(e, addspec(e', A))}{S, E \xrightarrow{addspec(e', A)} (S \cup \{addspec(e', A)\}), E}$$

The obvious semantics of these rules is that if the preconditions (i.e. all the expressions which appear in the upper part of the inference rule) are true then it is possible to infer the conclusions (what appears in the bottom part of the rule). In our case we say that if from the set of events E it is possible to derive the existence of the event e and similarly, from the set of specifications S it is possible to derive the existence of the specification $addspec(e, ACT)$ then it is possible to activate the specification. This amounts in executing its action part, thus resulting in a new state of the system in which the enabled specification has been removed from the set of specifications S and in the set of events E the event which has caused the enabling has been consumed.

The last four inference rules define the notion of derivability ($\vdash$) in terms of set membership ($\in$). In general, more complex notions of derivability can be defined, for example when tackling the full Yeast language we must be able to deal with more complex event patterns which may require different assumptions to be verified.

Note that the definition of yc shows that in our model the action part of a specification is atomic. This fact is justified since it reflects the actual behaviour of the Yeast system.

Since Yeast includes timing facilities, an important point is how time is modeled. The optimum would be a model where time is specified only when it is needed, and ignored otherwise. And since time in Yeast applications can be considered discrete, we model time explicitly in the operational semantics. Thus, time events are ordered, and for each pair e, e' of time events such that e' is a immediate successor of e in the (total) timing ordering, a rule of the form $S, E \oplus e \xrightarrow{clock} S, E \oplus e'$ is considered.

Some actions are identified to be *external*, i.e. actions that a user or an external agent may perform. Such actions can occur at any moment. For instance, a user can make an announcement based on the success or failure of his/her work. Clearly it is a nondeterministic choice for the system, and this is modeled by *external* rules. So, for each external event e a rule of the form $S, E \xrightarrow{user} S, E \oplus e$ is included. To choose such a transition represents the fact that a user intervention has produced the event e.

A *computation* is just a sequence of states and rules of the form $S_1, E_1 \xrightarrow{label_1} S_2, E_2 \xrightarrow{label_2} \ldots S_n, E_n$.

4.3 A Petri Net for Yeast

The operational semantics of the language has been given in such a way that it is possible to obtain a Petri net from the rules above. In fact, in [4] it is shown that transition systems whose set of states have monoidal structure (that is, a binary operation that is associative, commutative and idempotent with respect to a zero) are in fact P/T Petri nets. We use this result here in order to derive a Petri net representation for Yeast specifications. As has been pointed out earlier, Petri nets provide a natural representation, since the properties we want to check involve *causal dependencies* among events and require a clear distinction between nondeterminism and concurrency.

Many proposals have been made for Real-time Petri nets (see for example [2]). Timed Petri nets are more complex than the model we are proposing. Here, the clock is considered a process that updates the events associated with time. Places are associated with times that are used in specifications, and the treatment of time is homogeneous since, for instance, the restrictions about time are included in the partial order associated with the net.

The Petri net corresponding to a Yeast specification is obtained directly from the operational semantic rules, since by replacing the comma with the $\oplus$ operator a transition system with monoidal structure on states is obtained.

However, only places which appear as causes of some transitions are considered in the net. In fact, no "dead places" (i.e. places with no outgoing transitions) are taken into account.

We first show how to specialize the meta-rule given in the previous section to a particular set of Yeast specifications.

Definition 7 *Let Y be a set of Yeast specifications. Let Y' be Y plus all the specifications appearing as addspec(E, A) actions in the specifications of Y. Let EY be the set of state components appearing in Y' (either as preconditions or inside actions). Then, the rules associated with Y are obtained by getting all the instances of the meta-rule choosing a specification s and an state component e for the premises such that $s \in Y'$ and $e \in EY$, and S and E are chosen to be minimal with respect to set inclusion.*

Moreover, for each external state component $e \in EY$, a rule $\phi_S, \phi_E \longrightarrow \phi_S, e$ is added, and for each pair of time state components $e_1, e_2 \in EY$ such that e_2 is the immediate *successor of e_1 in EY with respect to the time ordering, a rule $\phi_S, e_1 \longrightarrow \phi_S, e_2$ is added.*

Notice that the rules obtained are axioms of the form $S, E \xrightarrow{ACT} S', E'$. The rules of the case study given in section 4.4 are obtained in this way.

Definition 8 *Given a set of rules defining a Yeast specification Y, with EY and Y' as in the previous definition, the corresponding net N is $N = (S, T, W, M_0)$ where $S \subseteq Y' \cup EY$ is the set of state components and specifications which appear at the left of a rule, T is the set of rules, $W(s, t) = 1$ iff s appears at the left of the arrow in t and $W(t, s) = 1$ iff s appears at the right of the arrow in t, and $M_0 = Y$.*

From a brief analysis, it is easy to observe that contradictory situations may arise from a computation of the net. We call *inconsistent markings* these contradictory markings containing more than one value for an attribute.

Definition 9 *A marking $s_1 \oplus s_2 \oplus \ldots \oplus s_n$ is said to be inconsistent iff there exist i and j such that s_i and s_j are state components and $att(s_i) = att(s_j)$ and $val(s_i) \neq val(s_j)$.*

4.4   Case Study

In the following we show the operational semantics reflecting the dynamic behaviour the sub-processes under consideration.

In the case of our example the object under consideration are modelled as follows:

```
Event  ::= mr23.status = Valstat | m1.rebuilt = Bool
         | m1.approved = Bool | 5pmWed | 5pmThu
Action ::= announce(Event) | mail(User) | rebuild(Action)(Action)
         | T&A(Action)(Action) | Action ; Action | ()
Valstat ::= devsub | submitted | active | approved
Bool   ::= true | false
User   ::= eduardo | dan | ...
```

We recall here that action T&A is used in the specification with two parameters, T&A ()(announce(m1.approved =true); announce(mr23.status = approved)), which reflects the fact that if the test fails, nothing is done, else two announcements are sent.

The system consists of four specifications:

(s1)   mr23.status = devsub   do   rebuild ()(announce(m1.rebuilt = true); announce(mr23.status = submitted))

(s2)   m1.rebuilt = true   do   T&A ()(announce(m1.approved = true); announce(mr23.status = approved))

(s3)   5pmW ∧ mr23.status = active   do   mail(dan); announce(m1.rebuilt = false)

(s4)   5pmT ∧ m1.rebuilt = false   do   mail(eduardo); announce(m1.approved = false)

The initial state of the system is composed of the four specifications. Formally, the initial state is the pair (s1 $\oplus$ s2 $\oplus$ s3 $\oplus$ s4, ϕ_E).

The rules for the system are shown in Table 1. Each transition has a label, which is the set of actions performed when the transition is executed. In this way, *side effects* (as

Table 1: Transition Rules for SDS		
t1)	ϕ_S , ϕ_E $\xrightarrow{user}$	ϕ_S, mr23.status = devsub
t2)	ϕS , ϕ_E $\xrightarrow{user}$	ϕ_S, mr23.status = active
t31)	s1 , mr23.status = devsub $\xrightarrow{rebuild}$	ϕ_S, ϕ_E
t4)	s1 , mr23.status = devsub $\xrightarrow{rebuild}$	ϕ_S, mr23.status = submitted $\oplus$ m1.rebuilt = true
t5)	s2, m1.rebuilt = true $\xrightarrow{T\&A}$	ϕ_S, ϕ_E
t6)	s2, m1.rebuilt = true $\xrightarrow{T\&A}$	ϕ_S , m1.approved = true $\oplus$ mr23.status = approved
t7)	s3, 5pmW$_{s3}$ $\oplus$ mr23.status = active $\xrightarrow{notify}$	ϕ_S, m1.rebuilt = false
t8)	s4 , 5pmT $\oplus$ m1.rebuilt = false $\xrightarrow{noapprove}$	ϕ_S, m1.approved = false
t9)	ϕ_S , ϕ_E $\xrightarrow{clock}$	ϕ_S, 5pmWed$_{cl}$ $\oplus$ 5pmWed$_{s3}$
t10)	ϕ_S , 5pmWed$_{cl}$ $\xrightarrow{clock}$	ϕ_S , 5pmThu

sending a mail, or compiling a file) are modeled as labels of transitions, and hence can be easily identified in any execution.

Each rule specifies only its *requirements* (i.e. what does it need to be enabled) on the left hand side, and its *output* (i.e. what does it produce when it is enabled). Hence, the condition that enables a rule of the form $s, e \xrightarrow{label} s', e'$ in a state (S, E) is that $s \subseteq S$ and $e \subseteq E$. The *matching* of the left hand side of the rules with the current state is done modulo associativity and commutativity of the $\oplus$.

Hence, the clock has a number of rules (t9, t10 in the table) which relate the time events which appear in the specification. In the example we are considering, only 5pm Wednesday and 5pm Thursday appear, and hence only they are considered in the rules: (t9) shows that 5pm Wednesday will be eventually true and (t10) simply says that Wednesday precedes Thursday.

The initial marking is $M_0 = s1 \oplus s2 \oplus s3 \oplus s4$.

For example, suppose that a user announces *mr23.status = active*, and after that another user announces *mr23.status = devsub*. After that, at 5pm Wednesday, specification s3 will be matched, in spite of the fact that the last announcement involving the value of *mr23.status* has set it to be *devsub*. However, there is still a token on the place *mr23.status = active*. In fact, the marking reached after the execution of both events contains two values for *mr23.status*.

4.5 Properties Analysis

We now formally specify the properties we want to analyze.

- What is the dependency pattern on the events of a specification S?
  > Let N[S] be the net derived from S. Then, the dependency pattern on Yeast events corresponds to the set of partial orderings of Yeast events obtained from the partial orderings of the places in the net by substituting each place with its label. Notice that more than one pattern is possible. For instance, if the system has three specifications:

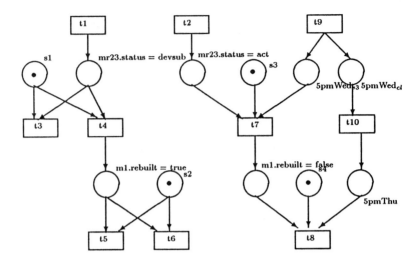

Figure 1: The Petri net for SDS

- E do script(announce(x=1))(announce(y=1))
- x=1 do announce(y=1)
- y=1 do announce(x=1)

there are two different patterns of dependencies: in one of them x=1 depends on y=1 and in the other y=1 depends on x=1.

- Which specification will be the last/first to be matched/attempted to be matched?
  > Find the set of specifications corresponding to the greatest/least events in an admissible partial order.

- What are the possible contrary events that could cause a deadlock or lead to potentially erroneous conclusions?
  > As far as deadlock is concerned, some known techniques can be used (see for example [5]). For "erroneous conclusions" we assimilate them to the generation of *inconsistent markings*, thus a specification can end up with an erroneous conclusion iff its net allows a computation to reach an inconsistent marking. For instance, in the example in correspondence with the conflict situation described in the previous section, there is a step sequence, namely

$$s1 \oplus s2 \oplus s3 \oplus s4[ext2 > s1 \oplus s2 \oplus s3 \oplus s4 \oplus m23.status = active[ext1 >$$

$$s1 \oplus s2 \oplus s3 \oplus s4 \oplus m23.status = active \oplus m23.status = devsub$$

which ends up in a state (marking) containing both *m23.status = devsub* and *m23.status = active*. This conflict is propagated in the net and the step sequence above can be extended to reach a marking containing both *m1.rebuilt = true* and *m1.rebuilt = false*.

4.6   Checking Yeast Properties

In the previous section we have identified the properties of the net that correspond to the desired properties of Yeast specifications. However, as has been pointed out in the introduction, our aim is to check properties directly on the Yeast specification: we do not want to build the net and then to verify the net, since this strategy would be too hard for a real verification tool. Moreover, checking some net properties can in many cases be very difficult. For instance, checking the absence of *inconsistent states*, which is the translation in the net of "no possible erroneous conclusions exist", implies to verify that some markings are not reachable, which can be very complex. In fact, the reachability problem, even for restricted classes of nets, has been shown to have a very high complexity [3]. Thus, the strategy of building the net and subsequent checking for reachable inconsistent states is infeasible. Our strategy is to build correct tools for the system, based on the formal model but not working directly on it.

Many interesting properties can be dealt with just by using *non standard* operational semantics, i.e. by deriving from the rules of the operational semantics more abstract interpreters [10]. An abstract interpreter, based on the net description, filters some pieces of information out and presents an abstract view of the computation. In our case one possibility is to build an abstract interpreter for the construction of *dependency patterns of specifications/events*. For instance, let C be the computation of the SDS system corresponding to the conflict situation (and to the step sequence) of subsection 4.5. The (labeled) graph of specifications/events dependencies we want to obtain from our tool is the following:

We have tested this approach with a prototype implementation of an interpreter of the operational semantics and of an abstract interpreter for detecting dependencies among specifications/events of a given set of Yeast specifications. The implementation of the two interpreters is in Prolog whose input are a set of specifications to be analyzed obtained by directly interfacing the Yeast environment. Since Yeast specifications are dynamic (i.e. they constantly shrink as event patterns are matched and grow when new specifications are added), to generate a snapshot of the current set of specifications, we wrote a new Yeast client command called *dumpspec*. Actually, it was a trivial modification of an existing client command that was used to dump the contents of a set of specifications. The only modification needed was the format. *Dumpspec* merely has to traverse the specification data structure and output the contents.

More precisely, what is obtained is a list of the specifications, for example the input generated in correspondence of the SDS system is:

```
[addspec(object(MR, 'MR23', userdefined,tba),'rebuild m1 ',1),
 addspec(object(module, 'm1', userdefined,tba),'TestAndApprove m1 ',2),
 addspec(and(time(718477200),object(MR, 'MR23', userdefined,tba)),
        'Mail -s missed_MR23_deadline dan ',3),
```

```
addspec(and(time(718563600), object(module, 'm1', userdefined,tba)),
        'Mail -s missed_MR23_deadline eduardo ',4)]
```

A Yeast specification, as mentioned earlier, consists of an event pattern portion and an action portion. The event pattern consists of either a simple event pattern or a combination of two or more simple patterns connected with connectors *and, or.* A simple event is either a temporal event or an object event. The output of a temporal event simply contains "time" and the absolute time at which the event would match. Output of an object event has three components: object class, object and the attribute. If the attribute was user defined then an extra field was output to indicate the fact that the value of the attribute is to be announced ("tba"). The final element is the specification label since it is a crucial item for analysis.

The structure of the Prolog programs is very simple since they straighforwardly reflect the structure of the operational semantics rules. The abstract interpreter is of course more abstract: it does not perform an execution of the Yeast program i.e. it is not concerned with the modification of the state S, E. The control flow among specifications is simulated in order to capture the dependency relationships.

However, not all properties can be checked in this way. Checking for reachability of inconsistent states seems to be as difficult as in the net. It is still possible to use our tools to approach the problem in a more flexible and interactive way. In general, the Yeast specifier has a certain degree of knowledge of which can be weak points of his/her set of specifications. In this context the OS interpreter we have realized can be used to implement the following strategy:

- Construct a set of hypothetical conflicting states, either by proper knowledge or via an algorithm that checks all possible pairs of conflicting attribute/values that appear in the specification.

- Use the *two ways* property of logical variables to run the OS interpreter with a partially instantiated goal where the output state contains a conflicting condition. In this way we can check if there exists a final state containing this condition.

- If the partially instantiated goal succedes then a possible conflict has been detected. Otherwise, the system is safe.

This is just an outline of the technique that we expect to use in order to perform verification of complex properties. Notice that (1) it works directly on specifications using the standard operational rules, and (2) the use of heuristics in the search can help in dealing with an otherwise intractable problem.

5   Conclusions

We have examined a way to formally study a practical event-action system, Yeast, which is presently being used for a variety of applications. We have presented a formal model of Yeast applications, and through the model we were able to answer several interesting properties about the specifications, which would otherwise be hard. Further, the model has already provided insights into the operation of the system pointing out potential conflicts in the construction of future Yeast applications.

We have also started the experimentation of building verification tools based on the formal model, the choice of Prolog as the prototypal language has been mainly of convenience since we wanted high flexibility in experimenting different verification strategies.

The next step will be moving towards ML as implementation language in order to achieve a better integration with the AT&T software development environment in which Yeast is largely used.

References

[1] Balachander Krishnamurthy and David Rosenblum. An Event-Action Model of Computer-Supported Cooperative Work: Design and Implementation In International Workshop on Computer Supported Cooperative Work, Berlin, April 1991

[2] C. Ghezzi, D. Mandrioli, S. Morasca, M.Pezze. A General Way To Put Time In Petri Nets In 5th International Workshop on Software Specification and Design, IEEE, May 1989.

[3] N.D. Jones, L.H. Landweber and Y.E. Lien. Complexity of some Problems in Petri Nets Theoret. Comp. Sci.,4,(1977), 277-299

[4] J. Meseguer and U. Montanari. Petri nets are monoids. *Information and Computation*, 88:105–155, 1990.

[5] W. Reisig. *Petri nets – an introduction*. EATCS Monographs on Theoretical Computer Science, Volume 4. Springer-Verlag, 1985.

[6] G.D. Plotkin. A structural approach to operational semantics. Report DAIMI FN-19, Computer Science Department, Aarhus University, 1981.

[7] J. W. de Bakker, W.P. de Roever and G. Rozenmberg (Eds.) Linear Time, Branching Time and Partial Order in Logics and Models for Concurrency Lecture Notes in Computer Science 354, Springer -Verlag, June 1988

[8] V. S. Alagar and G. Ramanathan. Functional Specifications and Proof of Correctness for Time Dependent Behaviour of Reactive Systems. *Formal Aspects of Computing*, 3:253–283, 1991.

[9] F. Jahanian and A. K. Mok. Safety Analysis of Timing Properties in Real-Time Systems. *IEEE Transactions on Software Engineering*, 12(9):890–904, 1986.

[10] N. De Francesco and P. Inverardi. Proving Fineteness of CCS Processes by Non-Standard Semantics In Proc. CAV 91 Workshop Lecture Notes in Computer Science 575, Springer -Verlag, pp. 266–276, 1992.

Appendix A: Yeast Grammar

Following is the grammar of the subset of the Yeast language we consider.

```
yeast_prog ::= yeast_prog  yeast_cmd
yeast_cmd ::= spec
| DEFOBJ object_class
| DEFATTR object_class obj_attribute type
| ANNOUNCE object_class obj_attribute ASSIGN value
type ::= CHARSTRING | INTEGER | BOOLEAN
spec   ::= ADDSPEC event_pat DO action
action ::= shell_cmd | yeast_cmd
```

```
event_pat ::= event_pat AND event_pat
| event_pat OR event_pat | simple_event
simple_event ::= time_event | object_event
time_event ::= AT absolute_time
absolute_time ::= time_of_day
| time_of_day day_of_week /* 3p mon */
| time_of_day day_number /* 3p 3 */
| time_of_day month day_number  /* 3p jan 2 */
time_of_day ::= hour AM | hour minute AM | hour PM | hour minute PM
hour ::= 1 .. 12
minute ::= 0 .. 59
day_of_week ::= sun .. sat
day_number ::= 1 .. 31
month ::= 1 .. 12
object_event ::= object_class object_name obj_attribute rel_test
object_class ::= string
object_name ::= string
obj_attribute ::= string
rel_test ::= rel_op attr_value
rel_op ::= EQUAL | NE | GT | GE | LT | LE
attr_value ::= string | integer | boolean
```

Verification and Comparison of Transition Systems

André Arnold
LaBRI *
Université Bordeaux I

—

Abstract

The notion of a transition system is of fundamental importance for studying the semantics of systems of interacting processes. Firstly, this notion is convenient for modeling these systems. In particular, the synchronized product of transition systems allows us to describe a system from the description, by transition systems, of its components, and from a description of the interactions between these components by giving the actions or events that may simultaneously occur in the system. Secondly, the notion of a transition system is the basis on which one can develop semantic notions such as verification of properties, by designing logics having transition systems as models, or comparison of transition systems, by structural equivalences defined by homomorphisms or logical equivalences related to logics for transition systems.

In this paper we present a short survey of these basic notions.

Introduction

Most of the works on the semantics of "concurrent", or "communicating", or "interacting" processes, rely on the notion of an automaton. This notion allows us not only to model more or less precisely the behaviour of a system, but to develop tools for verifying the modeled system: from its representation as an automaton, it is easy to observe and to verify some of its properties, like deadlocks, or to compare it with some others.

Although automata theory was mainly developed in relation to formal language theory and its application to lexical and syntactic analysis, this theory was also used in other domains, in particular in the semantics of sequential while-programs [22, 30]. The well-known flowcharts are finite automata describing the control flow of programs. More generally, a finite automaton, consisting of states and labeled transitions, allows us to describe a system whose state evolves over time. Indeed, automata were introduced for this reason, as pointed out by Minsky [27], since they originate with the modeling of neurons, and the celebrated Kleene's theorem

---

*Research Unit of the Centre National de la Recherche Scientifique n° 1304

characterizing languages recognized by a finite automaton refer to behaviours of nerve nets.

In the case of a flowchart the state of a system is the program counter, but the modeling of a sequential program can be enriched by considering the state consisting not only in the program counter but also in the values of some (or all) of its variables (as long as they have a finite range; otherwise the associated automaton will obviously be no longer finite); each action possibly performed by the program is actually performed only when the program is in some particular states, and this action implies a change of state; thus, actions are represented by transitions of an automaton.

This way of representing, by an automaton, a system whose state evolves because of some actions or because of the occurrences of some events applies to many situations, among which systems of processes appear quite naturally. For systems of processes interacting by shared variables, Karp and Miller [23] have extended the model of sequential processes proposed by Ianov [22] by taking into account the fact that some actions performed by the processes of the system can modify disjoint parts of the common storage. The control of the system remains centralized; it is still represented by a finite automaton. But the actions which test or modify the content of the storage test or modify only a part of this storage. Adding the states of the storage to the states of the control, one gets a description of the whole system by a finite automaton, provided, of course that the storage can contain only a finite number of different values. If the control is itself distributed, that is to say if the program counter is, like the storage, a vector, and if action modifies only some components of this vector, the automaton modeling such a system belongs to a remarkable class of automata defined and studied by Zielonka [32], the so-called asynchronous automata.

Other models of systems of processes have been proposed; among them are Petri nets [7], and process calculi à la Milner, like CCS [25, 26, 19] and Meije [6]. Without going into the details, one can admit that all these models amount to specifying sets of states and of transitions between these states. For instance, the states of a Petri net are its markings and transitions are realized by firing one or several transitions of the net. In process calculi, states are terms of a process algebra and transitions are defined by the operational semantics of the calculus which explains how a term is rewritten into another one.

One can therefore consider that the fundamental notion for formally describing a system of processes is the one of an automaton. To emphasize the fact that these automata are not devices used to recognize languages, but that they are formalizations of a structure consisting of states and transitions, we call them *transition systems*. In contrast with transition systems introduced by Keller [24] to model systems of processes, the transitions of transition systems we are using are *labeled* by action or event names, although it is not absolutely necessary: as we shall see it later on, what we need is to distinguish some particular sets of transitions, for instance the set of all transitions caused by a given event. Also, while the definition of a classical automaton includes one or several initial states and a set of final states, the definition of a transition system does not imply the existence of such states, or, more precisely, it is possible to distinguish any number of sets of states according to the need of the modeling. For instance, when modeling a CSP program [21] by a transition system, we need to define the set of success states corresponding to a normal termination of the program, and the set of failure states.

In the first section of this paper, we introduce transition systems and we explain how they allow us to express the behaviour of processes. We also explain how to model the interactions between the processes of a system by explicitly giving the sets of vectors of actions or events that can occur simultaneously in the system. The importance of this operation comes from the fact that all the communication and synchronization constraints can be expressed this way. Then, we define a fundamental operation on transition systems, the *synchronized product*. This operation, introduced by Arnold and Nivat [28, 5, 2], is used to construct a transition system modeling a system of concurrent processes from the transition systems modeling each component process and from a description of the interactions between these components.

To express properties of a transition system, one needs a formal language, called a *logic* (although this name is somewhat abusive, since we are not interested in any notion of a proof in these logics). In the second section, we introduce some of these logics, and we show how it is possible to verify the properties stated in these logics.

One of the main consequences of the existence of a formal definition of the semantics of a system of processes is that it is a basis for a precise definition of the *equivalence* of systems. It becomes possibles to compare two systems directly or to check that an implementation of a system obeys its specification when both can be expressed in the same formalism, namely as transition systems. In the third section, we introduce two kinds of equivalences: *structural equivalences* defined via transition system homomorphisms, and *logical equivalences* defined in relation with the satisfiability of logical formulas. Then we show how these two kinds of equivalences can be related.

1 Modeling interacting systems of processes

1.1 Modeling processes

1.1.1 Labeled transition systems

A *labeled transition system* over an alphabet A of *actions* or *events* is a tuple $\mathcal{A} = < S, T, \alpha, \beta, \lambda >$ where

- S is a finite set of *states*,

- T is a finite set of *transitions*,

- $\alpha, \beta : T \longrightarrow S$ are the mappings which associate with every transition t its *source state* $\alpha(t)$ and its *target state* $\beta(t)$,

- $\lambda : T \longrightarrow A$ labels a transition t by the action or event $\lambda(t)$ which causes this transition.

We assume that there never exist two different transitions with the same label between the same two states, i.e. the mapping $< \alpha, \lambda, \beta >: T \longrightarrow S \times A \times S$ is injective.

1.1.2 Parameterized transition systems

A parameterized transition system is a labeled transition system given with some sets of designed states and some sets of designed transitions, called parameters. The role of these parameters is to give some additional informations on the transition system; it is the case when some states play a special role or when some transitions play a special role which is not specified by the label of the transition. Some example of such situations will be given below.

Example 1. A boolean variable   Let us consider a boolean variable. It has two states, denoted by 0 and 1, according to the current value (0 or 1) of the variable. The set A of actions performed by such a boolean variable contains

to0 which means that the variable is set to 0,

to1 which means that the variable is set to 1,

is0 which tests whether the value of the variable is 0,

is1 which tests whether the value of the variable is 1,

e which does nothing.

The first two actions modify the value of the variable, i.e. its state, in an obvious way. The two tests can be executed only if the variable has the tested value, and this value is not modified. The last action, when executed, does not change the value of the variable. As we shall see later on (example 3), this null action is a way to express the possibility of occurrence of events which does not modify the state of the variable. Therefore the transition system has eight transitions: for each one of these transitions we give, in the following table, its source state, its label, and its target state.

$$
\begin{aligned}
t_1 &: \quad 0 \mapsto \text{e} \rightarrow 0 \\
t_2 &: \quad 0 \mapsto \text{to0} \rightarrow 0 \\
t_3 &: \quad 0 \mapsto \text{to1} \rightarrow 1 \\
t_4 &: \quad 0 \mapsto \text{is0} \rightarrow 0 \\
t_5 &: \quad 1 \mapsto \text{e} \rightarrow 1 \\
t_6 &: \quad 1 \mapsto \text{to0} \rightarrow 0 \\
t_7 &: \quad 1 \mapsto \text{to1} \rightarrow 1 \\
t_8 &: \quad 1 \mapsto \text{is1} \rightarrow 1
\end{aligned}
$$

Example 2. A sequential program   Let us consider the program fragment

```
while true do
 1:if not b then begin
                2:b:=true;
                3:proc;
                4:b:=false
            end
```

With this program, we associate a transition system $\mathcal{P}$ having four states: **1 2**, **3** et **4** (the values of "program counter"). Actions performed by $\mathcal{P}$ are **b:=false** and **b:=true**, **proc**, and the two tests, denoted by **b=true?** and **b=false?** which correspond to the cases where the tested value of **b** has been found respectively equal to **true** and **false**. Thus we get the following transitions

$$
\begin{array}{lllll}
t_1' & : & \mathbf{1} & \mapsto \mathbf{b} = \mathbf{true?} \to & \mathbf{1} \\
t_2' & : & \mathbf{1} & \mapsto \mathbf{b} = \mathbf{false?} \to & \mathbf{2} \\
t_3' & : & \mathbf{2} & \mapsto \mathbf{b} := \mathbf{true} \to & \mathbf{3} \\
t_4' & : & \mathbf{3} & \mapsto \mathbf{proc} \to & \mathbf{4} \\
t_5' & : & \mathbf{4} & \mapsto \mathbf{b} := \mathbf{false} \to & \mathbf{1}
\end{array}
$$

Each component of a system of processes as well the processes themselves as some other ressources such as shared variables, communication channels, etc., can be modelized by transition systems.

1.2   Modeling interactions

Before explaining how to model the interactions between the components of a system of processes, we show how one can obtain the transition system modeling the whole system, when there is no interaction at all.

1.2.1   Free products of transition systems.

Let us consider n transition systems $\mathcal{A}_i = \langle S_i, T_i, \alpha_i, \beta_i, \lambda_i \rangle$ labeled by A_i, for $i = 1, \ldots, n$. The *free product* $\mathcal{A}_1 \times \cdots \times \mathcal{A}_n$ of these n transition systems is the transition system $\mathcal{A} = \langle S, T, \alpha, \beta, \lambda \rangle$ labeled by $A_1 \times \cdots \times A_n$, defined by

$$
\begin{aligned}
S &= S_1 \times \cdots \times S_n, \\
T &= T_1 \times \cdots \times T_n, \\
\alpha(t_1, \ldots, t_n) &= \langle \alpha_1(t_1), \ldots, \alpha_n(t_n) \rangle, \\
\beta(t_1, \ldots, t_n) &= \langle \beta_1(t_1), \ldots, \beta_n(t_n) \rangle, \\
\lambda(t_1, \ldots, t_n) &= \langle \lambda_1(t_1), \ldots, \lambda_n(t_n) \rangle.
\end{aligned}
$$

If the transition system $\mathcal{A}$ is in the *global state* $s = \langle s_1, \ldots, s_n \rangle$, each component transition system, $\mathcal{A}_i$, is in the state s_i; it can perform, independently of every other component, a transition t_i which will set it in the state s_i'. Then, the transition system $\mathcal{A}$ is in the global state $s' = \langle s_1', \ldots, s_n' \rangle$ after having performed the *global transition* $t = \langle t_1, \ldots, t_n \rangle$, corresponding to the *global action* $\lambda(t)$.

Such a definition makes sense if we assume that in a system all components simultaneously execute a transition, i.e., there is a sequence of time slices such that in each slice, each component executes one and only one transition.

1.2.2 Synchronization vectors

When processes interact, it is no longer true that any global action can occur in the system. Indeed, interactions can be described by giving those global actions that may occur in the system and those that may not.

Let us consider the transition system B of Example 1 representing a boolean variable and the transition system $\mathcal{P}$ of Example 2 representing a program which uses this variable.

Since B has two states and eight transitions and $\mathcal{P}$ has four states and five transitions, their free product has eight states and forty transitions and contains, for instance, the global transition consisting of t_2 of B and t'_3 of $\mathcal{P}$ from the global state $\langle\, 0\, ,\, 2\, \rangle$ to $\langle\, 0\, ,\, 3\, \rangle$ labeled by the global action $\langle\, \text{to0}\, ,\, \text{b} := \textbf{true}\, \rangle$.

But the intuitive meaning of b:=true, executed by $\mathcal{P}$, is to set the boolean variable to 1. This variable must simultaneously execute a transition labeled by to1. Conversely, if the variable executes to1, it is being set to 1 by $\mathcal{P}$, which executes b:=true. In other words, $\langle\, \text{to1}\, ,\, \text{b} := \textbf{true}\, \rangle$ is the only global action whose first component is to1; it is also the only one whose second component is b:=true. In the same way, if $\mathcal{P}$ executes b=false? which means that the value of the variable has been found equal to 0, the variable must simultaneously execute an action returning this value, that is is0, and the only global action having is0 as first component, or b=false? as second component, is $\langle\, \text{is0}\, ,\, \text{b} = \textbf{false?}\, \rangle$.

Finally, $\mathcal{P}$ does not interact with the variable when executing **proc**; thus the variable does nothing, i.e., executes e.

Thus, allowed global actions are:

$$\langle \text{to1}, \text{b:=true} \rangle$$
$$\langle \text{to0}, \text{b:=false} \rangle$$
$$\langle \text{is1}, \text{b=false?} \rangle$$
$$\langle \text{is0}, \text{b=true?} \rangle$$
$$\langle\ \text{e}\ ,\quad \textbf{proc}\ \ \rangle$$

Now, we formally define interactions between components of a system. If $A_1, \ldots, A_n$ are alphabets of actions or events, a *synchronization constraint* is a subset of the cartesian product $A_1 \times \cdots \times A_n$. Each member of this subset is a *synchronization vector* and represents an allowed global action of the system.

1.3 Synchronized products of transition systems

If $\mathcal{A}_i, i = 1, \ldots, n$ are transition systems respectively labeled by the alphabets A_i, and if $I \subseteq A_1 \times \cdots \times A_n$ is a synchronization constraint, the *synchronized product* of the $\mathcal{A}_i$ with respect to I, is the sub-transition system of the free product of the $\mathcal{A}_i$, containing only the global transitions labeled by a member of I.

Therefore, a system of processes is also modeled by a transition system.

Example 3. The synchronized product of $\mathcal{B}$ and $\mathcal{P}$ with respect to the synchronization constraint given above is

$$
\begin{array}{llll}
\langle\, 1\,,\,1\,\rangle & \mapsto \langle\, \text{is1} \,,\, b = \text{true?} \,\rangle \to & \langle\, 1\,,\,1\,\rangle \\
\langle\, 1\,,\,2\,\rangle & \mapsto \langle\, \text{to1} \,,\, b := \text{true} \,\rangle \to & \langle\, 1\,,\,3\,\rangle \\
\langle\, 1\,,\,3\,\rangle & \mapsto \langle\, e \,,\, \text{proc} \,\rangle \to & \langle\, 1\,,\,4\,\rangle \\
\langle\, 1\,,\,4\,\rangle & \mapsto \langle\, \text{to0} \,,\, b := \text{false} \,\rangle \to & \langle\, 0\,,\,1\,\rangle \\
\langle\, 0\,,\,1\,\rangle & \mapsto \langle\, \text{is0} \,,\, b = \text{false?} \,\rangle \to & \langle\, 0\,,\,2\,\rangle \\
\langle\, 0\,,\,2\,\rangle & \mapsto \langle\, \text{to1} \,,\, b := \text{true} \,\rangle \to & \langle\, 1\,,\,3\,\rangle \\
\langle\, 0\,,\,3\,\rangle & \mapsto \langle\, e \,,\, \text{proc} \,\rangle \to & \langle\, 0\,,\,4\,\rangle \\
\langle\, 0\,,\,4\,\rangle & \mapsto \langle\, \text{to0} \,,\, b := \text{false} \,\rangle \to & \langle\, 0\,,\,1\,\rangle
\end{array}
$$

2 Logics for transition systems

In order to check the correctness of a system of processes described by a transition system, one has to explicitly express the properties it must have: without such informations the answer to the question "is this system correct?" is always "yes".

Thus, checking correctness of a system requires

- a language to express properties, and

- a definition of whether or not a given transition system has a given property.

This is typically what logics are made for: properties are expressed by formulas, and the satisfaction relation correspond to the second point. On the other hand, we need not any proof system, so that the term of "logic" is used in a wider sense than usual.

2.1 Propositional logics

Let us start with two classical examples of propositional logics for transition systems.

2.1.1 Hennessy–Milner logic

The formulas of the Hennessy–Milner logic [20] are built up from

- the constants **1** et **0** (*true* and *false*), and the usual logical operators $\lor$, $\land$, $\neg$,

- a unary operator $\langle a \rangle$, for each letter a of the alphabet A.

Let $\mathcal{A} = \langle S, T, \alpha, \beta, \lambda \rangle$ be a given transition system and F be a given formula. For any state s of S we define the satisfaction relation $\mathcal{A}, s \models F$ by induction on the construction of F:

- $\mathcal{A}, s \models 1$, $\mathcal{A}, s \not\models 0$,
- $\mathcal{A}, s \models F \vee F'$ iff $\mathcal{A}, s \models F$ or $\mathcal{A}, s \models F'$,
- $\mathcal{A}, s \models F \wedge F'$ iff $\mathcal{A}, s \models F$ and $\mathcal{A}, s \models F'$,
- $\mathcal{A}, s \models \neg F$ iff $\mathcal{A}, s \not\models F$,
- $\mathcal{A}, s \models \langle a \rangle F$ iff there is a transition $s \mapsto a \to s' \in T$ such that $\mathcal{A}, s' \models F$.

2.1.2 CTL*

CTL* [15, 14] is a logic with two kinds of formulas: state formulas and path formulas, and does not take the labels of transitions into account. On the other hand it uses a given set of propositional symbols.

A *path* in a transition system $\mathcal{A} = < S, T, \alpha, \beta, \lambda >$ is a finite or infinite sequence $p = t_1, t_2, \ldots$, of transitions such that for all i, $\beta(t_i) = \alpha(t_{i+1})$. The *source* of this path, denoted by $\alpha(p)$, is $\alpha(t_1)$.

Formulas are built up according to the following rules: a state formula is

- a propositional symbol, or the constants **1** or **0**,
- $F \vee F'$, $F \wedge F'$, and $\neg F$, where F and F' are state formulas,
- EG where G is a path formula;

a path formula is

- the constants **1** or **0**,
- $G \vee G'$, $G \wedge G'$, and $\neg G$, where G and G' are path formulas,
- NG and GUG', where G and G' are path formulas,
- BF, where F is a state formula.

Let us consider a transition system $\mathcal{A}$ and subset $P_{\mathcal{A}}$ of S for any propositional symbol P. The satisfaction relation is defined by

- $\mathcal{A}, s \models P$ iff $s \in P_{\mathcal{A}}$, $\mathcal{A}, s \models 1$, $\mathcal{A}, s \not\models 0$,
- $\mathcal{A}, s \models F \vee F'$ iff $\mathcal{A}, s \models F$ or $\mathcal{A}, s \models F'$,
- $\mathcal{A}, s \models F \wedge F'$ iff $\mathcal{A}, s \models F$ and $\mathcal{A}, s \models F'$,
- $\mathcal{A}, s \models \neg F$ iff $\mathcal{A}, s \not\models F$,
- $\mathcal{A}, s \models EG$ iff there is an infinite path p of source s such that $\mathcal{A}, p \models G$,
- $\mathcal{A}, p \models 1$, $\mathcal{A}, p \not\models 0$,
- $\mathcal{A}, p \models G \vee G'$ iff $\mathcal{A}, p \models G$ or $\mathcal{A}, p \models G'$,
- $\mathcal{A}, p \models G \wedge G'$ iff $\mathcal{A}, p \models G$ and $\mathcal{A}, p \models G'$,
- $\mathcal{A}, p \models \neg G$ iff $\mathcal{A}, p \not\models G$,
- $\mathcal{A}, p \models NG$ iff $p = t \cdot p'$ and $\mathcal{A}, p' \models G$,
- $\mathcal{A}, p \models GUG'$ iff

  - $\mathcal{A}, p \models G'$ or

  - $p = t_1 t_2 \cdots t_n \cdot p'$ with $\mathcal{A}, p' \models G'$ and $\forall i \in \{1, \ldots, n\}$, $\mathcal{A}, t_i \cdots t_n \cdot p' \models G$,

- $\mathcal{A}, p \models BF$ iff $\mathcal{A}, \alpha(p) \models F$.

2.1.3 Propositional logics as free algebras

These two logics, and many others, (see [13] for a survey) fall in the scope of the following definition.

Let $\mathcal{R}$ be a set of sorts and Ω be a set of sorted operators, i.e., each operator ω has an arity $\delta(\omega)$ and a sort $\rho_1 \cdots \rho_{\delta(\omega)} \to \rho$. A formula is a well-formed ground term over Ω.

An Ω-poweralgebra $\mathcal{A}$ is a family $(E_\rho)_{\rho \in \mathcal{R}}$ of sets together with a mapping $\omega_\mathcal{A} : \mathcal{P}(E_{\rho_1}) \times \cdots \times \mathcal{P}(E_{\rho_n}) \to \mathcal{P}(E_\rho)$ for any $\omega \in \Omega$ of sort $\rho_1 \cdots \rho_n \to \rho$.

Therefore, each formula F of sort ρ has an interpretation $F_\mathcal{A} \subseteq E_\rho$ and the satisfaction relation is defined by $\mathcal{A}, r \models F$ iff $r \in F_\mathcal{A}$.

For instance, Hennessy–Milner logic can be defined by the union of the two set of operators $\{1, 0, \vee, \wedge, \neg\}$ and $\{\langle a \rangle \mid a \in A\}$, with only one sort. The interpretation of logical operators in a transition system $\mathcal{A}$ are set-theoretical operations on $\mathcal{P}(\mathcal{S})$, while the interpretation of $\langle a \rangle$ is defined by

$$\langle a \rangle_\mathcal{A}(X) = \{s \in S \mid \exists s' \in X, \exists t \in T : t = s \mapsto a \to s'\}.$$

The logic CTL* can be defined in the same way, it has two sorts: states and paths, so that to be quite rigorous, it must contain two sets of logical operators, one for each sort, but the sort of such an operator can be determined from its context. As another example, we introduce the logic proposed by Dicky [12]. It has two sorts, states and transitions, denoted by σ and τ. it contains usual logical operators and constants, of both sorts, and the specific unary operators src and tgt of sort $\tau \to \sigma$, and in and out of sort $\sigma \to \tau$. Their interpretation in a transition system $\mathcal{A}$ is defined by

- $src_\mathcal{A}(R) = \{\alpha(t) \mid t \in R\}$, $\quad tgt_\mathcal{A}(R) = \{\beta(t) \mid t \in R\}$,
- $in_\mathcal{A}(Q) = \{t \in T \mid \beta(t) \in Q\}$, $\quad out_\mathcal{A}(Q) = \{t \in T \mid \alpha(t) \in Q\}$.

In this algebra, we can generalize the operator $\langle a \rangle$ of Hennessy–Milner logic: we define the new binary operator $\langle Y_\tau \rangle X_\sigma$, of sort $\tau \sigma \to \sigma$, by $src(Y_\tau \wedge in(X_\sigma))$. In a transition system $\mathcal{A}$, $\langle R \rangle Q$ is interpreted as the set

$$\{s \in S \mid \exists a \in A, \exists t = s \mapsto a \to s' \in R : s' \in Q\},$$

and if R is the set of all transitions labeled by a, this is obviously equal to the interpretation of $\langle a \rangle$.

2.2 μ-calculi

Let us consider the state formula $F = E(BPUBP')$ of CTL* and its interpretation $F_\mathcal{A}$ in a transition system $\mathcal{A}$ where P and P' are respectively interpreted as $P_\mathcal{A}$ and $P'_\mathcal{A}$. It can be easily shown that $F_\mathcal{A}$ is the least fixpoint for inclusion of the equation $X = P'_\mathcal{A} \cup (P \cap \mathsf{N}_\mathcal{A} X)$.

More generally, let us consider an Ω-term $t(X_0, X_1, \ldots, X_n)$ of sort ρ_0 over the set $\{X_0, X_1, \ldots, X_n\}$ of variables, where X_i is of sort ρ_i. Let us assume that for any Ω-poweralgebra $\mathcal{A}$, the mapping $t_\mathcal{A} : \mathcal{P}(E_{\rho_0}) \times \mathcal{P}(E_{\rho_1}) \times \cdots \times \mathcal{P}(E_{\rho_n}) \to \mathcal{P}(E_{\rho_0})$ is monotonic for inclusion with respect to all its argument (for the logics considered above, there is a syntactically defined set of terms having this property). Then there exists two monotonic mappings

$$t^*_\mathcal{A} : \mathcal{P}(E_{\rho_1}) \times \cdots \times \mathcal{P}(E_{\rho_n}) \to \mathcal{P}(E_{\rho_0}) \text{ and } t^\infty_\mathcal{A} : \mathcal{P}(E_{\rho_1}) \times \cdots \times \mathcal{P}(E_{\rho_n}) \to \mathcal{P}(E_{\rho_0})$$

such that $t^*_\mathcal{A}(P_1, \ldots, P_n)$ (resp. $t^\infty_\mathcal{A}(P_1, \ldots, P_n)$) is the least (resp. greatest) fixpoint of $X = t_\mathcal{A}(X, P_1, \ldots, P_n)$. Thus we form new formulas by prefixing terms by μX or νX where the interpretation of $\mu X.t(X, X_1, \ldots, X_n)$ (resp. $\nu X.t(X, X_1, \ldots, X_n)$) in $\mathcal{A}$ is $t^*_\mathcal{A}(X_1, \ldots, X_n)$ (resp. $t^\infty_\mathcal{A}(X_1, \ldots, X_n)$).

For instance, the formula $E(BPUBP')$ can be rewritten as $\mu X.P' \vee (P \wedge NX)$.

By iterating this process, one can define a whole hierarchy of new operators.

Example 4. Let us define the following operators

$$
\begin{aligned}
\mathrm{Pred}(X) &= \mathrm{src}(\mathrm{in}(X)), \\
\mathrm{Coreach}(X) &= \mu Y.\mathrm{Pred}(X \vee Y), \\
\mathrm{Live}(X) &= \nu Y.\mathrm{Coreach}(X \wedge Y).
\end{aligned}
$$

The interpretation of $\mathrm{Live}(X)$ in $\mathcal{A}$ is the set of sources of paths going through the interpretation of X infinitely often.

2.3   Verification of formulas

Now, the problem of verification of a transition system $\mathcal{A}$ amounts to computing the interpretation in $\mathcal{A}$ of formulas of a given logic. To do that it is sufficient to be able to compute $\omega_\mathcal{A}(P_1, \ldots, P_n)$ when the sets $P_1, \ldots, P_n$ are given. For most of the usual logics for transition systems, this can be done in time linear in the the size of the transition system $\mathcal{A}$ (cf. [8] for instance). Moreover, it has been shown in [3] that computing $\mu X.t(X, X_1, \ldots, X_n)$ in $\mathcal{A}$ can be also be done in time linear in the size of $\mathcal{A}$ for terms t of the Dicky's logic; this algorithm, which is quadratic in the size of t, has been improved independently in [9], [1], and [31], where it is also linear in the size of t.

3   Comparison of transition systems

When comparing transition systems, an important point to consider is in which respect they may be considered to be equivalent. Very roughly speaking one can say that two transition systems are equivalent if they share common characteristic features. Then the point is to define what a common characteristic feature is. We propose two ways of defining such a notion. The first one is based upon the very "structure" of a transition system, characterized by homomorphisms; the second one is based upon the logical properties of a transition system. Then we show that in some cases these two definitions can be related.

3.1 Structural equivalences

As it is usual in mathematics, one can consider that the characteristic features of a transition system are those that are preserved under morphisms of a given family. The image of a transition system under such a morphism is called its quotient and two objects are equivalent if they have a common quotient. This leads us to the following definitions.

Let $\mathcal{A} = \langle S, T, \alpha, \beta, \lambda \rangle$ and $\mathcal{A}' = \langle S', T', \alpha', \beta', \lambda' \rangle$ be two labeled transition systems. A *homomorphism* h from $\mathcal{A}$ into $\mathcal{A}'$ is a pair of mappings $(h_\sigma : S \to S'$, $h_\tau : T \to T')$ such that $\forall t \in T, \alpha'(h_\tau(t)) = h_\sigma(\alpha(t)), \beta'(h_\tau(t)) = h_\sigma(\beta(t))$, $\lambda'(h_\tau(t)) = \lambda(t)$.

We consider a family $\mathcal{H}$ of *surjective* homomorphisms that has the following properties:

- it contains all identities,
- it is closed under composition,
- it has the *diamond property*: if $h_1 : \mathcal{A} \to \mathcal{A}_1$ and $h_2 : \mathcal{A} \to \mathcal{A}_2$ are in $\mathcal{H}$, there exist $h'_1 : \mathcal{A}_1 \to \mathcal{A}'$ and $h'_2 : \mathcal{A}_2 \to \mathcal{A}'$ in $\mathcal{H}$ such that $h'_1 \circ h_1 = h'_2 \circ h_2$.

Under these hypothesis the relation $\mathcal{A}_1 \sim_\mathcal{H} \mathcal{A}_2$ defined by $\exists h_1, h_2 \in \mathcal{H} :$ $h_1(\mathcal{A}_1) = h_2(\mathcal{A}_2)$ is an equivalence relation.

It follows from the definition that each equivalence class for $\sim_\mathcal{H}$ contains a unique minimal transition system.

Example 5. Bisimulation homomorphisms The following family of homomorphisms was introduced in [4], and in [11, 16, 17] (under the name of transition preserving homomorphisms), to characterize the *bisimulation* relation between two transition systems([29, 25, 20].

A surjective homomorphism $h : \mathcal{A} \to \mathcal{A}'$ is a bisimulation homomorphism if

$$\forall s_1 \in S, \forall t' = h_\sigma(s_1) \mapsto a \to s'_2 \in T', \exists t = s_1 \mapsto a \to s_2 : h_\sigma(s_2) = s'_2.$$

It is easy to show that this family has the above properties and that $\mathcal{A} \sim_\mathcal{H} \mathcal{A}'$ iff there is a bisimulation between $\mathcal{A}$ and $\mathcal{A}'$.

3.2 Logical equivalences

Two transition systems are said to be logically equivalent with respect to some logic L if they satisfy the same set of properties expressible in this logic. Restricting ourself to the logics introduced in the previous section, formulas of which are ground terms built up from a set Ω of sorted operators, we give the following definition: two transition systems $\mathcal{A}$ and $\mathcal{A}'$ are *logically equivalent* with respect to L, denoted by $\mathcal{A} \sim_L \mathcal{A}'$, if $\forall F \in L, F_\mathcal{A} \neq \emptyset \Leftrightarrow F_{\mathcal{A}'} \neq \emptyset$.

3.2.1 Indistinguishability

This notion of logical equivalence is tightly related to the notion of L-type. Given a transition system $\mathcal{A}$ and an object r of $\mathcal{A}$ of sort ρ, the *L-type* of r is the set of formulas $\{F \mid r \in F_{\mathcal{A}}\}$. Two objects of the same sort are are said to be *L-indistinguishable* if they have the same L-type.

Obviously, if two transition systems $\mathcal{A}$ and $\mathcal{A}'$ have the same sets of L-types (i.e., for each object r of $\mathcal{A}$ there exists an object r' of $\mathcal{A}'$ of the same L-type as r) then $\mathcal{A} \sim_L \mathcal{A}'$.

Conversely, let us assume that the sorts of Ω are such that any transition system $\mathcal{A}$ has only finitely many objects of each sort (it is the case for the sorts "states" and "transitions", not for the sort "paths"), and that Ω contains negation for all of its sorts. In this case, if $\mathcal{A} \sim_L \mathcal{A}'$ then $\mathcal{A}$ and $\mathcal{A}'$ have the same set of L-types. Let us assume that there is an object r of $\mathcal{A}$ such that no object r' of $\mathcal{A}'$ has the same L-type. For every object r' of $\mathcal{A}'$ there is a formula $F_{r'}$ such that $r \in (F_{r'})_{\mathcal{A}}$ and $r' \notin (F_{r'})_{\mathcal{A}'}$. Let us consider the finite conjunction F of these $F_{r'}$. Obviously $r \in F_{\mathcal{A}}$ while $F_{\mathcal{A}'}$ is empty, a contradiction.

Let us remark that, under the same hypothesis, the same kind of reasoning allows us to prove that each L-type of $\mathcal{A}$ contains a *characteristic formula* F in the sense that an object r has this L-type iff $r \in F_{\mathcal{A}}$.

Let us also mention that, under these hypothesis, extending a logic with operators defined as least or greatest fixpoints does not extend its indistinguishability power: if the sort of the term $t(X, X_1, \ldots, X_n)$ contains only k objects in $\mathcal{A}$, then $(\mu X.t(X, X_1, \ldots, X_n))_{\mathcal{A}}$ is equal to $(\bigvee_{i=0}^{k} t_i)_{\mathcal{A}}$ where $t_0 = 0$, $t_{i+1} = t(t_i, X_1, \ldots, X_n)$. Therefore, the logical equivalence associated with this extension is the same as the original one.

3.2.2   Quotients under indistinguishability

In any transition system $\mathcal{A}$, the indistinguishability class of an object r is the set of all objects of the same sort and of the same L-type.

Let us consider a logic L containing only the sorts σ and τ (if a logic contains only the sort τ we can extend it by adding transition formulas in the form $F \rightsquigarrow_a F'$ interpreted in a transition system $\mathcal{A}$ as the set of all transitions $s \mapsto a \rightarrow s'$ such that $s \in F_{\mathcal{A}}$ and $s' \in F'_{\mathcal{A}}$). Let us consider the mapping $h = (h_\sigma, h_\tau)$ which sends each state and each transition on its indistinguishability class. We say that L is *adequate* if this mapping is always a transition system homomorphism. We say that it is *fully adequate* if, moreover, r and $h(r)$ have always the same L-type. In this case, $h(\mathcal{A})$ is the unique minimal transition system logically equivalent to $\mathcal{A}$ with respect to L.

Unfortunately, it is not always the case that a logic is fully adequate. However, fortunately, Hennessy-Milner logic as well as Dicky logic are fully adequate.

3.3   Saturating homomorphisms

The well known Hennessy-Milner theorem [20] asserts that the structural equivalence defined by the bisimulation relation is the same as the logical equivalence associated with the Hennessy-Milner logic.

Along the line suggested by the notion of quotient under indistinguishability we are going to investigate the relation between the notions of structural and logical equivalence.

The main tool for studying this relation is the notion of a saturating homomorphism. Let Ω be a set of sorted operators containing only the sorts σ and τ. Let $\mathcal{A}$ and $\mathcal{A}'$ be two transition systems. A surjective homomorphism $h = (h_\sigma, h_\tau) : \mathcal{A} \to \mathcal{A}'$ *saturates* Ω if for all $\omega \in \Omega$ of sort $\rho_1 \cdots \rho_n \to \rho$ and for all $P'_i \subseteq E'_{\rho_i}$,

$$h_\rho^{-1}(\omega_{\mathcal{A}'}(P'_1, \ldots, P'_n)) = \omega_{\mathcal{A}}(h_{\rho_1}^{-1}(P'_1), \ldots, h_{\rho_n}^{-1}(P'_n)).$$

It is obvious that a surjective homomorphism always saturates the logical operators. The only interesting point is the saturation of the other operators.

Example 6. For instance, it is easy to see that a homomorphism is a bisimulation homomorphism iff it saturates the operators $\langle a \rangle$, for all $a \in A$.

For transition systems with unobservable transitions, labeled by ε, there is a notion of *branching bisimulation* (cf. [18, 10]). In exactly the same way as bisimulation is related to bisimulation homomorphisms, branching bisimulation is related to those homomorphisms that saturates the operator $\mathrm{src}_\varepsilon(Y_\tau)$, of sort $\tau \to \sigma$, defined as the least fixpoint of $X_\sigma = \mathrm{src}(Y_\tau) \vee \langle \varepsilon \rangle X_\sigma$.

It is a straightforward consequence of the definition of saturation that if $h : \mathcal{A} \to \mathcal{A}'$ saturates Ω, then, for every formula F of the logic L_Ω built over Ω, $h^{-1}(F_{\mathcal{A}'}) = F_{\mathcal{A}}$; thus, $\mathcal{A}$ and $\mathcal{A}'$ are logically equivalent with respect to L_Ω.

It can be shown that the family $\mathcal{S}_\Omega$ of all homomorphisms saturating Ω contains identities and is closed under composition. If it has also the diamond property, it defines a structural equivalence $\sim_{\mathcal{S}_\Omega}$ which is included in the logical equivalence $\sim_{L_\Omega}$.

We have previously outlined the notion of a fully adequate logic. Indeed these logics have the nice following properties

- the canonical homomorphism from a transition system $\mathcal{A}$ onto its quotient under indistinguishability saturates Ω,

from which we derive

- the family $\mathcal{S}_\Omega$ has the diamond property.

Therefore, for fully adequate logics, the structural equivalence $\sim_{\mathcal{S}_\Omega}$ and the logical equivalence $\sim_{L_\Omega}$ are equal.

References

[1] H. R. Andersen. Model checking and boolean graphs. In B. Krieg-Brückner, editor, *ESOP '92*, pages 1–19, Rennes, 1992. Lect. Notes Comput. Sci. 582.

[2] A. Arnold. Transition systems and concurrent processes. In *Mathematical problems in Computation theory*. Banach Center Publications,vol. 21, 1987.

[3] A. Arnold and P. Crubillé. A linear algorithm to solve fixed point equations on transition systems. *Inf. Process. Lett.*, 29:57–66, 1988.

[4] A. Arnold and A. Dicky. An algebraic characterization of transition system equivalences. *Information and Computation*, 82:198–229, 1989.

[5] A. Arnold and M. Nivat. Comportements de processus. In *Colloque AFCET "Les Mathématiques de l'Informatique"*, pages 35–68, 1982.

[6] G. Boudol. Notes on algebraic calculi of processes. In *Logic and Models of Concurrent Systems*, pages 261–303. NATO ASI Series F-13, Springer Verlag, 1985.

[7] G. W. Brams. *Réseaux de Petri: théorie et pratique*. Masson, Paris, 1982.

[8] E. M. Clarke, E. A. Emerson, and A. P. Sistla. Automatic verification of finite state concurrent systems using temporal logics specifications. *ACM Trans. Prog. Lang. Syst.*, 8:244–263, 1986.

[9] R. Cleaveland and B. Steffen. Computing behavioural relations, logically. In *18th Int. Coll. on Automata, Languages and Programming*, pages 127–138. Lect. Notes Comput. Sci. 510, 1991.

[10] R. de Nicola and F. Vaandrager. Three logics for branching bisimulation. In *5th Symp. on Logic in Comput. Sci.*, pages 118–129, 1990.

[11] P. Degano, R. D. Nicola, and U. Montanari. A partial ordering semantics for CCS based on condition/event systems. *Acta Informatica*, 26:59–91, 1988.

[12] A. Dicky. An algebraic and algorithmic method for analysing transition systems. *Theoretical Comput. Sci.*, 46:285–303, 1986.

[13] E. A. Emerson. Temporal and modal logic. In J. Van Leeuwen, editor, *Handbook of Theoretical Computer Science (vol. B)*, pages 995–1072. Elsevier, 1990.

[14] E. A. Emerson and J. Y. Halpern. "Sometimes" and "Not Never" revisited : on branching versus linear time temporal logic. *J. Assoc. Comput. Mach.*, 33:151–178, 1986.

[15] E. A. Emerson and A. P. Sistla. Deciding full branching time logic. *Information and Control*, 61:175–201, 1984.

[16] G. L. Ferrari. *Unifying models of concurrency*. PhD thesis, Università di Pisa, 1990.

[17] G. L. Ferrari and U. Montanari. Towards the unification of models for concurrency. In A. Arnold, editor, *CAAP '90*, pages 162–176. Lect. Notes Comput. Sci. 431, 1990.

[18] J. F. Groote and F. W. Vaandrager. An efficient algorithm for branching bisimulation and stuttering equivalence. Technical Report CS-R9001, Centre for Math. and Comput. Sci., Amsterdam, 1990.

[19] M. Hennessy. *Algebraic theory of processes*. The MIT Press, 1988.

[20] M. Hennessy and R.Milner. Algebraic laws for nondeterminism and concurrency. *J. Assoc. Comput. Mach.*, 32:137–161, 1985.

[21] C. A. R. Hoare. Communicating sequential processes. *Commun. ACM*, 21:666–677, 1978.

[22] I. I. Ianov. The logical schemes of algorithms. In *Problems of Cybernetics*, volume 1, pages 75–127. Pergamon Press, 1960.

[23] R. M. Karp and R. E. Miller. Parallel program schemata. *J. Comput. Syst. Sci.*, 3:147–195, 1969.

[24] R. M. Keller. Formal verification of parallel programs. *Commun. ACM*, 19:371–384, 1976.

[25] R. Milner. *A calculus of communicating systems*. Lect. Notes Comput. Sci. 92, 1980.

[26] R. Milner. *Communication and concurrency*. Prentice-Hall, 1989.

[27] M. L. Minsky. *Computation: Finite and infinite machines*. Prentice–Hall, 1967.

[28] M. Nivat. Sur la synchronisation des processus. *Revue Technique Thomson–CSF*, 11:899–919, 1979.

[29] D. Park. Concurrency and automata on infinite sequences. In *5th GI Conf. on Theoret. Comput. Sci.*, pages 167–183, Karlsruhe, 1981. Lect. Notes Comput. Sci. 104.

[30] J. D. Rutledge. On Ianov's program schemes. *J. Assoc. Comput. Mach*, 11:1–9, 1964.

[31] B. Vergauwen and J. Lewi. A linear algorithm for solving fixed point equations on transition systems. In J. Raoult, editor, *CAAP '92*, pages 321–341, Rennes, 1992. Lect. Notes Comput. Sci. 581.

[32] W. Zielonka. Notes on asynchronous automata. *RAIRO Inform. Théor.*, 21:99–135, 1987.

Constraining Interference in an Object-Based Design Method

C. B. Jones

Department of Computer Science
Manchester University, M13 9PL, UK
cbj@cs.man.ac.uk

Abstract. This paper is the first of a series which are intended to contribute to tractable development methods for concurrent programs by exploring ways in which object-based language concepts can be used to provide a compositional development method for concurrent programs. The property of a (formal) development method which gives the development process the potential for productivity is compositionality; interference is what makes it difficult to find compositional development methods for concurrent systems. This paper shows how object-based concepts can be used to provide a designer with control over interference; it also proposes a transformational style of development (for systems with limited interference) in which concurrency is introduced only in the final stages of design. The essential idea here is to show that certain object graphs limit interference.

A companion paper discusses the problems of interference more fully and shows how a suitable logic can be used to reason about those systems where interference plays an essential role. There again, concepts are used in the design notation which are taken from object-oriented languages since they offer control of granularity and way of pinpointing interference. A third paper is in preparation which defines the semantics of the object-based design notation.

1 Introduction

The most difficult aspect of finding tractable development methods for concurrent systems is to provide a useful notion of compositionality which facilitates the division of work. Compositionality can be defined as follows (adapted from [Zwi88])

> A development method is *compositional* if the fact that a design step satisfies a given specification can be justified on the basis of the specifications of any constituent components without knowledge of their construction

Earlier work on shared-variable concurrency (see [Jon83] which is significantly extended in [Stø90, Stø91a, Stø91b]) used rely and guarantee conditions both to describe and to reason about *interference*. The fixed format of these specifications was rejected in [Jon91] in favour of a logic with operators which use predicates of pairs of states (this is similar to Lamport's TLA [Lam90, Lam91]). But the proofs in [Jon91] remain long-winded and earlier work has been dogged by issues like atomicity (granularity) and questions about where invariants etc. are supposed to hold.

In common with many others, the current author sees language restrictions as a way of constraining concurrency; in particular, the aim here is to reduce the number of proof obligations in development. The current approach uses concepts of object-oriented languages in order to constrain interference and fix a level of granularity.[1] It is not, however, the aim to add yet one more language to those claiming to be object-oriented; the development method envisaged here ought to be usable for programs in languages such as ABCL [Yon90], Modula-3 [Nel91], Beta [KMMN91] or UFO [Sar92]. The claim is that some carefully chosen subset of object-oriented concepts makes the design of concurrent programs more tractable than in arbitrary shared-variable languages (or even languages like CSP). The move to an object-based language has not made the interference logic redundant it has only reduced the need for interference arguments; [Jon93b] explores the situation where interference is essential.

The design notation used in this paper is heavily influenced by the programming language 'POOL' (see Section 4 for references and some comparative notes); it also reflects discussions with colleagues at Manchester University. Most of the features of the language are presented by examples. Points of interest include the following. *Classes* have *methods* only one of which may be active at any one time (for a particular instance); invocation of methods is synchronous but methods can return before they complete and this releases the invoking process from the *rendezvous*. Consider Figure 1: this can be read as an object-oriented program (which is actually developed from a specification in Section 2). The programming task which is considered concerns sorting: a priority queue delivers – and removes – its smallest value via a remove method (rem); new values can be added by another method (add). Programs obtain a reference to (an instance of) a priority queue with a new $Priq$ statement. In fact, the created queue can be a linked list of instances of $Priq$ but the using program would have no way of detecting this. Each instance has two variables containing a value and a link (possibly nil) to the next element.

```
Priq class
vars m: [N] ← nil; l: private ref(Priq) ← nil
add(e: N) method
   return
   if m = nil then (m ← e; l ← new Priq)
   elif m < e then l!add(e)
   else (l!add(m); m ← e)
   fi
rem() method r: N
   return m
   if m ≠ nil then m ← l!rem()
                  if m = nil then l ← nil
                  fi
   fi
```

Fig. 1. Example $\pi o \beta \lambda$ program: $Priq$

---

[1] The idea to use object-oriented languages was made more tempting by the positive experience of building a theorem proving assistant [JJLM91] in Smalltalk and more recent discussions about exploiting parallel hardware and tackling a multi-user version of *mural*.

In the class $Priq$, the *new* method is implicit; all that happens when an instance is created is that the instance variables (m and l) are initialized. Once created, there are two methods which can be invoked for an instance of the $Priq$ class: *add* puts its argument into the queue and *rem* – which takes no arguments – returns the smallest value contained in the queue. Methods are invoked by expressions like $l!add(7)$ (where l is a reference to an instance of $Priq$). The semantics dictates that only one method can be active at any time in a particular instance of $Priq$.[2] Notice that the return statements occur at the the beginning of the *add* and *rem* methods. This releases the user from the *rendezvous* and lets the remaining code of the method run in parallel with other activity of the invoking program. Furthermore, once – say – the call to the next *add* has been released, the method terminates and its instance is available for other method calls. One can picture a whole sequence of *add* and *rem* methods rippling along the linked-list structure. The fact that the activity can never get out of order is important and results from the object graph which is created. Marking the contained references as private makes it easier to establish results about the object graphs. Were $\pi o\beta\lambda$ a programming language, all sorts of concrete syntax details would have to be resolved – here, a rather relaxed syntax is used with line breaks playing a meaningful part. (The abstract syntax of the language used here is given in an appendix of [Jon92].) The reader should remember that $\pi o\beta\lambda$ is intended as a design notation to be used to develop programs in a language where issues like parsing have received due attention.

In addition to the return statement, there is a yield statement which provides a way of delegating the responsibility to answer a method invocation. As in Figure 1, objects (instances of classes) are created by activating new for a class name; in $\pi o\beta\lambda$ explicit methods for new can be written; the language does not offer inheritance.

In addition to the language presentation herein, it is to some extent true that the search for a development method has been driven by examples: the approach has been to find plausible development steps and then to look for formal rules which justify them. This is largely motivated by the experience which shows that the thing which makes formal development work like mathematics is finding the right steps of development; detailing the proofs of individual steps is less rewarding. One key insight was the realization that assertions (invariants etc.) about the object graphs created by object references are central to the explanation of many algorithms. This paper looks at two topologies in Sections 2 and 3; both use decompositions which are justified by rules which support a 'promotion' of properties about instances to properties about collections of instances. This can be compared with the way in which an inference rule for a while statement can be used to infer results about a composite statement from properties of its components. The need – in the case of more general (DAG-like) topologies – to cope with interference is studied in [Jon93b].

There are at least two options for giving the semantics: mapping to Milner's Polyadic π-calculus [Mil92] or a resumption semantics which fits the way methods work here (cf. [AR89, pp111]; see also [Wol88, AR92]). Since the mapping to the π-calculus is quite far advanced (see [Jon93a]), the working name for the design notation is $\pi o\beta\lambda$.

---

[2] It can be useful to think of classes as blocks which can be multiply instantiated; each instance has local (instance) variables and procedures (methods); the instance variables can only be accessed or changed by the methods; methods are called (invoked) by sending messages.

2 Linked-lists of objects

The first development example in this paper illustrates the object-based nature of the programming language and the role that this plays in developing programs. What follows is a step-wise development of a program which stores each element of a queue as a local variable in an instance of an object; these objects are organized into a linked-list. Because the specifications are simpler, the first steps of development assume sequential execution within a queue (there might – however – be other concurrent threads); concurrency within a queue is considered in the final development step where its use is justified by arguing that it provides the same visible behaviour as the sequential implementation.

Specification

As in a Larch [GHW85, GH93] 'interface language', the design notation is used here to provide a framework for the specification which is given as a class definition. The methods are specified by pre- and post-conditions in a style similar to that used in VDM [Jon90].[3] The separation of the assumptions that a developer can make into pre-conditions should be noted; this is mirrored by the separation of assumptions about interference in [Jon93b]. In post-conditions, hooked identifiers refer to the value of the instance variables before execution of the method and undecorated identifiers refer to the values after execution of the method. Thus

$$b = \overleftarrow{b} \cup \{e\}$$

requires that the value of the instance variable b after an invocation of add is the bag union of the value of that variable before execution of the method with a unit bag containing the value of the parameter. Notice that rem is a partial method and – as in VDM – the post-condition can be undefined if its pre-condition is not satisfied. (The external clauses from VDM operations are barely necessary in the context of a class but there are places where one really ought note that some variables are read-only.) Values of type bag etc. and operators like $\cup$ are part of the specification language.

> $Priq$ class
> vars b: $\mathbb{N}$-bag $\leftarrow \{\}$
> $add(e: \mathbb{N})$ method
>   post $b = \overleftarrow{b} \cup \{e\}$
> $rem()$ method r: $\mathbb{N}$
>   pre $b \neq \{\}$
>   post $r = min(\overleftarrow{b}) \wedge b = \overleftarrow{b} - \{r\}$

Just as in VDM, 'satisfiability' proof obligations can be generated for each method specification.

Straightforward data reification

It is possible to represent the bag abstraction b by an ascending sequence. This step of data reification is sketched here in order to afford comparison with the reification to a linked-list which follows. The objects concerned are

---

[3] The classes here can be compared with modules in VDM-SL [BSI92, Daw91].

$AscSeq = \mathbb{N}^*$

inv $(b) \triangleq is\text{-}ascending(b)$

The invariant is a restriction on the elements which are in the set $AscSeq$ ($is\text{-}ascending$ – and other simple functions – are taken to be obvious).[4]

The relationship between this representation and the abstract objects is defined

$retr : AscSeq \rightarrow \mathbb{N}\text{-}Bag$

$retr(b) \triangleq bagof(b)$

$bagof : X^* \rightarrow X\text{-}Bag$

$bagof(t) \triangleq \{e \mapsto \mathsf{card}\,\{i \in \mathsf{inds}\,t \mid t(i) = e\} \mid e \in \mathsf{elems}\,t\}$

This representation is 'adequate' (there is at least one element of $AscSeq$ which corresponds – under $retr$ – to each element of $\mathbb{N}$-bag). The methods of $Priq$ can be specified on this representation as follows.

$Priq$ class
vars $b: AscSeq \leftarrow []$
$add(e: \mathbb{N})$ method
  post $\exists i \in \mathsf{inds}\,b \cdot b(i) = e \wedge del(b, i) = \overleftarrow{b}$
$rem()$ method $r: \mathbb{N}$
  pre $b \neq []$
  post $r = \mathsf{hd}\,\overleftarrow{b} \wedge b = \mathsf{tl}\,\overleftarrow{b}$

$del(t, i) \triangleq t(1, \ldots, i-1) \frown t(i+1, \ldots, \mathsf{len}\,t)$

The correctness of such a step can be justified by further rules (operation domain/result) of [Jon90].

It is worth taking this opportunity to reflect on where the invariant must hold: a user would presumably accept an implementation of add which put new elements at the end of a list and then sorted it. Thus an invariant does not have to be true mid-operation: it is really a way of abbreviating pre-/post-conditions. It would be possible to develop a sequential implementation – using decomposition rules to justify that the use of while statements etc. – which satisfies this intermediate specification.

Reification involving class instances

The main line of object-based development is now considered (i.e. the reification to $AscSeq$ is ignored and the reference point for this step is the initial specification in terms of a bag). Here again, the first design step focuses on the development of the data structure and finding an appropriate invariant is a key issue. This development step employs multiple instances of class $Priq$; they form a linked-list with the l variable in one instance pointing to the next; the local variables (m) of the instances collectively represent the bag b. The use of references

---

[4] Throughout this paper, VDM notation [Jon90] is used for sequences, maps etc.

necessitates talking about a global state ($\sigma \in \Sigma$). This is viewed as a map from references to instances

$$\Sigma = Ref \xrightarrow{m} Inst$$

and variable names are applied as selectors to objects of $Inst$ (e.g. if p is a reference to an instance of $Priq$, then $m(\sigma(p))$ is a natural number). The state is a Curried argument to functions which depend on the global state. The predicate $is\text{-}linked\text{-}list(p, l)(\sigma)$ is true if the instance pointed to by p (in σ) is the start of a linked-list via the references contained in the l variables of each instance. Although the objective here is to talk about linked-lists etc. without needing to think at the reference level, this predicate can be defined in terms of Σ as follows.[5]

$is\text{-}linked\text{-}list : Ref \times Name \rightarrow \Sigma \rightarrow \mathbb{B}$

$is\text{-}linked\text{-}list(p, l)(\sigma) \quad \triangleq$
$\quad \exists pl \in Ref^* \cdot$
$\qquad pl(1) = p \wedge l(\sigma(pl(\text{len } pl))) = \text{nil} \wedge$
$\qquad \forall i \in \{1, \ldots, \text{len } pl - 1\} \cdot pl(i + 1) = l(\sigma(pl(i)))$

Similarly, a function to extract a sequence from a linked list is $extract\text{-}seq(p, l, n)$ which generates a sequence of the (non-nil) n values from instances linked by the l references.

$extract\text{-}seq : Ref \times Name \times Name \rightarrow \Sigma \rightarrow X^*$

$extract\text{-}seq(p, l, n)(\sigma) \quad \triangleq$
$\quad \text{if } p = \text{nil then } []$
$\quad \text{elif } n(\sigma(p)) = \text{nil then } extract\text{-}seq(l(\sigma(p)), l, n)(\sigma)$
$\quad \text{else } [n(\sigma(p))] \frown extract\text{-}seq(l(\sigma(p)), l, n)(\sigma)$
$\quad \text{fi}$

This can be used to define the set of references which can be reached from a reference.

$reach : Ref \times Name \rightarrow \Sigma \rightarrow X^*$

$reach(p, l)(\sigma) \quad \triangleq \quad \text{elems } extract\text{-}seq(p, l, l)(\sigma)$

The data type invariant can then be defined as follows.

$inv : Ref \rightarrow \Sigma \rightarrow \mathbb{B}$

$inv(p)(\sigma) \quad \triangleq$
$\quad is\text{-}linked\text{-}list(p, l)(\sigma) \wedge is\text{-}ascending(extract\text{-}seq(p, l, m)(\sigma)) \wedge$
$\quad \forall r \in reach(p, l)(\sigma) \cdot l(\sigma(r)) = \text{nil} \Leftrightarrow m(\sigma(r)) = \text{nil}$

---

[5] It would be possible to pass a lambda expression (or simply make l a constant) in order to avoid passing a name to $is\text{-}linked\text{-}list$.

The invariant is considered to be true only between method invocations (rather than during the execution of a method). The retrieve function is as follows.

$$retr : Ref \rightarrow \Sigma \rightarrow \mathbb{N}\text{-}Bag$$

$$retr(p)(\sigma) \quad \triangleq \quad bagof(extract\text{-}seq(p, l, m)(\sigma))$$

It is now possible to specify $Priq$ on the linked-lists.[6]

$Priq$ class
vars m: $[\mathbb{N}] \leftarrow$ nil; l: private ref($Priq$) $\leftarrow$ nil
$add(e: \mathbb{N})$ method
   post let $\overleftarrow{b} = extract\text{-}seq(\text{self}, l, m)(\overleftarrow{\sigma})$ in
     let $b = extract\text{-}seq(\text{self}, l, m)(\sigma)$ in
      $\exists i \in$ inds $b \cdot b(i) = e \land del(b, i) = \overleftarrow{b}$
$rem()$ method $r: \mathbb{N}$
   pre $extract\text{-}seq(\text{self}, l, m)(\sigma) \neq []$
   post let $\overleftarrow{b} = extract\text{-}seq(\text{self}, l, m)(\overleftarrow{\sigma})$ in
     let $b = extract\text{-}seq(\text{self}, l, m)(\sigma)$ in
      $r = $ hd $\overleftarrow{b} \land b = $ tl $\overleftarrow{b}$

Any user of a $Priq$ would be unaware that the implementation involved multiple instances; since the references are private (cannot be copied) they are invisible and free from danger of interference. In order to state the pre- and post-conditions, the sequences are extracted from the state with a reference to the current instance (self) providing the start of the list. A simple generalization of standard refinement rules covers such reification steps.

Operation decomposition

The next step of development is to look at code which satisfies the above specifications: they are decomposed into executable statements.

---

[6] Notice m can contain a VDM-like nil; for the Ref type, a nil value is a normal null reference; there is a sort of pun here since a 'real' object-oriented language would anyway make all values into objects.

```
Priq class
vars m: [ℕ] ← nil; l: private ref(Priq) ← nil
add(e: ℕ) method
    if m = nil then (m ← e; l ← new Priq)
    elif m < e then l!add(e)
    else (l!add(m); m ← e)
    fi
    return
rem() method r: ℕ
    t: ℕ
    t ← m
    if t ≠ nil then m ← l!rem()
                    if m = nil then l ← nil
                    fi
    fi
    return t
```

The inductive justification of this decomposition relies on rules which promote assumptions on one instance of the class to collections of such instances; the linear reference topology allows a structural induction argument about the recursive calls to methods. The base case for add – which starts with b as the empty sequence – is straightforward (p and l are both nil). The inductive step assumes that the recursive call to $l!add(m)$ performs according to specification. Notice that inv above implies that there can not be a loop in the reference chain which is important since otherwise calls to add would deadlock. Notice also that it is not necessary to rely on pre-rem: the implementation happens to deliver a nil result if the method is used outside its intended domain.

Equivalent code

As mentioned above, the initial steps of this development have not employed concurrency within a queue: in the preceding code, add and rem hold the invoking process in a *rendezvous* until they complete and a method call at the head of the list does not complete until all recursive calls terminate. (Recall that only one method can be active in each instance of a method at any one time.) Parallelism can be achieved by letting – for example – rem return the local m before it ripples through bringing up values as required; the invoking process is released from the *rendezvous* and its subsequent code can run in parallel with the $Priq$ methods. Furthermore, this applies to instances of $Priq$ within one queue: once rem has obtained a value from the next element in the queue, it can terminate making it possible for either of the methods of this instance to be invoked. Because of the linear reference topology controlled by private refs, no other thread of control can interfere with the queue.

The argument for the correctness of this step follows from a transformation which permits moving statements

$$S; \text{return } e \quad \leadsto \quad \text{return } e; S \tag{1}$$

providing e is not affected by S and S only changes (other than its own state) states reachable by private references. Thus the preceding code is equivalent to that in Figure 1 of Section 1.

This step uses algebraic laws to re-order code to give an observationally equivalent parallel program to the one which was first specified. Apart from offering what is hopefully an intuitive development route, this has obviated the need to write post-conditions for the concurrent behaviour of the methods. It is not immediately obvious how to write such post-conditions because at the point at which an execution of a method begins, methods on other instances might still be active (such post-conditions appear to need something like Lamport's 'prophesy variables').

The final code behaves in much the same way as $BUBLAT$ (cf. [CLW79]) did in earlier work on 'interference' proofs (e.g. [Stø90]) but there is much less 'mechanism' visible here – further steps of development could bring in the extra variables of the earlier code if so desired.

Alternatives

A couple of general observations can be made even after this simple example. There is a reliance above on the fact that the values (in $\mathbb{N}$) are immutable; while this is taken for granted in non-OO-languages, it is not the norm in the OO-world (cf. open issue 2 in Section 4). If the element values could change, such changes would need to be constrained by interference assertions like those used in [Jon93b].

It must be conceded that – thus far – it would be possible to use a development method in which objects can be guarded from interference by encapsulation and then to have a compiler generate the actual class instances. The reason for taking the approach of creating the instances and reasoning about (non-)interference is that it prepares for the more general approach in [Jon93b]. It is – for example – interesting to consider what would go wrong with the above development if a 'fast path' vector of pointers to every tenth element in the list existed. The sharing of pointers which would result would undermine the transformation shown in Equation 1 and observational equivalence would not be guaranteed. Extensions to reason about such interference would need extra variables in which counts of readers and writers could be maintained.

3   Tree-structured topologies

The programming task specified below is similar to that in the preceding section but it shows that references defining a tree-like object graph can be used as a basis for reasoning; the developed program also introduces a new statement of the language.

Specification

The example of building a simple symbol table is used in [Ame89]; its specification is very simple.

> $Symtab$ class
> vars st: $(Key \xrightarrow{m} Data) \leftarrow \{\}$
> $insert(k: Key, d: Data)$ method
>   post $st = \overleftarrow{st} \dagger \{k \mapsto d\}$
> $search(k: Key)$ method $res: Data$
>   pre $k \in$ dom st
>   post $res = st(k)$

Reification

The first design idea is to represent the map as a binary tree.

$$Tree :: \; mk \; : \; [Key]$$
$$md \; : \; [Data]$$
$$l \quad : \; [Tree]$$
$$r \quad : \; [Tree]$$

$$\text{inv} \, (mk\text{-}Tree(mk, md, l, r)) \; \triangleq$$
$$(mk = \text{nil} \; \Leftrightarrow \; md = \text{nil}) \wedge (mk = \text{nil} \; \Rightarrow \; l = r = \text{nil})$$

Over which an invariant might be defined

$$is\text{-}ordered\text{-}tree : Tree \rightarrow \mathbb{B}$$

$$is\text{-}ordered\text{-}tree(mk\text{-}Tree(mk, md, l, r)) \;\; \triangleq$$
$$\quad \text{if } mk = \text{nil}$$
$$\quad \text{then true}$$
$$\quad \text{else } (\forall lk \in coll(l) \cdot lk < mk) \wedge (\forall rk \in coll(r) \cdot mk < rk) \wedge$$
$$\qquad (l \neq \text{nil} \; \Rightarrow \; is\text{-}ordered\text{-}tree(l)) \wedge (r \neq \text{nil} \; \Rightarrow \; is\text{-}ordered\text{-}tree(r))$$
$$\quad \text{fi}$$

where the *coll* function simply collects the set of *Keys*

$$coll : [Tree] \rightarrow Key\text{-set}$$

$$coll(t) \;\; \triangleq$$
$$\quad \text{cases } t \text{ of}$$
$$\quad \text{nil} \qquad\qquad\qquad\quad \rightarrow \{ \, \},$$
$$\quad mk\text{-}Tree(\text{nil}, md, l, r) \rightarrow \{ \, \},$$
$$\quad mk\text{-}Tree(mk, md, l, r) \rightarrow coll(l) \cup \{mk\} \cup coll(r)$$
$$\quad \text{end}$$

Nested objects like *Tree* have, in $\pi o \beta \lambda$, to be represented by structures built with references. An invariant must specify that the reference structure forms a genuine tree (*is-linked-tree*) and that the *Tree* obtained by using *extract-tree* on the instances satisfies *is-ordered-tree*.

$$inv : Ref \rightarrow \Sigma \rightarrow \mathbb{B}$$

$$inv(p)(\sigma) \;\; \triangleq$$
$$\quad is\text{-}linked\text{-}tree(p, l, r)(\sigma) \wedge is\text{-}ordered\text{-}tree(extract\text{-}tree(p, l, r, mk)(\sigma))$$

The functions *is-linked-tree* and *extract-tree* can be defined in a similar way to *is-linked-list* above.[7] The retrieve function follows.

$$retr : Ref \rightarrow \Sigma \rightarrow (Key \xrightarrow{m} Data)$$

$$retr(p)(\sigma) \;\; \triangleq \;\; retrm(extract\text{-}tree(p, l, r, km)(\sigma))$$

---

[7] It might, however, be worth passing lambda expressions rather than names to define the link tracing.

$$retrm : [Tree] \to (Key \xrightarrow{m} Data)$$

$retrm(t) \quad \triangle$
  cases t of
  nil $\qquad\qquad\qquad \to \{\ \}$,
  $mk\text{-}Tree(\text{nil}, md, l, r) \to \{\ \}$,
  $mk\text{-}Tree(mk, md, l, r) \to retrm(l) \cup \{mk \mapsto md\} \cup retrm(r)$
  end

The methods are respecified as follows.

$Symtab$ class
vars mk: $Key \gets$ nil; md: $Data \gets$ nil;
$\qquad\qquad\qquad\qquad$ l: private ref($Symtab$) $\gets$ nil; r: private ref($Symtab$) $\gets$ nil
$insert(k$: Key, d: $Data)$ method
  post $retr(extract\text{-}tree(\text{self}, l, r, mk)(\sigma)) =$
  $\qquad\qquad\qquad\qquad\qquad retr(extract\text{-}tree(\text{self}, l, r, mk)(\overleftarrow{\sigma})) \dagger \{k \mapsto d\}$
$search(k$: $Key)$ method res: $Data$
  pre $k \in$ dom $retr(extract\text{-}tree(\text{self}, l, r, mk)(\sigma))$
  post $res = (retr(extract\text{-}tree(\text{self}, l, r, mk)(\sigma)))(k)$

Operation decomposition

It is straightforward to provide code which satisfies the specifications above.

$Symtab$ class
vars mk: $Key \gets$ nil; md: $Data \gets$ nil;
$\qquad\qquad\qquad\qquad$ l: private ref($Symtab$) $\gets$ nil; r: private ref($Symtab$) $\gets$ nil
$insert(k$: Key, d: $Data)$ method
  if $mk =$ nil then $(mk \gets k; \ md \gets d)$
  elif $mk = k$ then $md \gets d$
  elif $k < mk$ then (if $l =$ nil then $l \gets$ new $Symtab$ fi $l!insert(k, d)$)
  else (if $r =$ nil then $r \gets$ new $Symtab$ fi $r!insert(k, d)$)
  fi
  return
$search(k$: $Key)$ method res: $Data$
  pre $k \in$ dom $retr(\text{self})$
  if $k = mk$ then return md
  elif $k < mk$ then return $l!search(k)$
  else return $r!search(k)$
  fi

The argument that this code satisfies its specification uses structural induction over the tree topology.

Equivalent code

As in Section 3, the above code is sequential (within one instance of a tree). The transformation in Equation 1 can be used to justify moving the return to the beginning of $insert$.

There is, however, a problem with re-ordering the statements of *search*: no result can be returned until it has been found so the caller of the method has to be held up. But an instance of *Symtab* can be used by another process if the task of delivering a result is delegated (to another instance). This is exactly the semantics of the yield statement. The equivalence used is

$$\text{return } l!m(x) \quad \leadsto \quad \text{yield } l!m(x) \tag{2}$$

providing l is a private reference and only references via private references. Thus the above code can be transformed into the following.

```
Symtab class
vars mk: Key ← nil; md: Data ← nil;
                    l: private ref(Symtab) ← nil; r: private ref(Symtab) ← nil
insert(k: Key, d: Data) method
   return
   if mk = nil then (mk ← k; md ← d)
   elif mk = k then md ← d
   elif k < mk then (if l = nil then l ← new Symtab fi l!insert(k, d))
   else (if r = nil then r ← new Symtab fi r!insert(k, d))
   fi
search(k: Key) method res: Data
   if k = mk then return md
   elif k < mk then yield l!search(k)
   else yield r!search(k)
   fi
```

4 Relationship of $\pi o \beta \lambda$ to POOL

This section comments on the differences between $\pi o \beta \lambda$ and the language which inspired its creation. A useful overview of the work on POOL is [Ame89]. Pierre America and Jan Rutten produced a combined doctoral thesis [AR89] which contains a collection of papers (some published elsewhere) on the formal aspects of the POOL project including their work on (metric) denotational semantics. A proof theory for a sequential version of POOL is given in [Ame86], while [AdB90] addresses proofs about process creation in a language called P which is more like CSP or CCS in the way that communication is a single event without any way to return a value. A proof method for the full *rendezvous* mechanism of POOL is given in [dB91]: but this multi-level approach is not compositional in a useful sense.

The main changes from POOL (see [Ame89, Ame91]) are:

1. In $\pi o \beta \lambda$, methods do not have a body (which, in POOL, is a statement which shows – for instances of the class – when a *rendezvous* can occur as well as executing autonomous code between method invocations); the examples here were longer with a body and it rarely did anything interesting; one can simulate the effect of this body by code in methods and switches etc.
2. The new message to a class can be defined by an explicit method in $\pi o \beta \lambda$.
3. Methods in $\pi o \beta \lambda$ which do not return a value are distinguished from those which do.
4. The *yield* statement is new in $\pi o \beta \lambda$.

5. The *Parallel* statement is also new but is an obvious extension.
6. References in $\pi o\beta\lambda$ are typed.
7. POOL has a local call; this could easily be added to $\pi o\beta\lambda$.
8. Clearly, $\pi o\beta\lambda$ needs some way of controlling conditional 'firing' of methods.

The development method presented here is not like any in the POOL literature. The approach illustrated in the current paper is the way that developments can first employ normal sequential reasoning based on pre-/post-conditions and then use transformations to admit concurrency (similar ideas are present in the works of Lipton [Lip75], Lengauer [Len82], Zwiers [JPZ91], Xu/He [XH91, Xu92] and the well-known UNITY approach [CM88]; equivalence laws are given in [HHJ+87, RH86]; see [OA91]).

Some open issues in $\pi o\beta\lambda$ are:

1. Methods could be divided into those which have a side-effect and those which are purely functional – this is done in UFO [Sar92].
2. It is not clear whether it would be worth distinguishing mutable values from what are constants in other languages – this affects the need for interference assertions (cf. the infamous *ordered-collection* example).
3. So far, $\pi o\beta\lambda$ has not used the (ST) trick of defining operators (e.g. $+, \neg$) as methods; since there are no 'block expressions' the option to do the same for while does not exist.
4. Block statements and exceptions might be added (exceptions could be in the style of VDM's exit).
5. The language has no inheritance yet (it is tempting to try something like 'theory morphisms' – cf. [JJLM91] – because inheritance is often used to solve too many problems at once).
6. There is some case for adding constant (e.g. numeric) channel names (cf. [Jon93b]).

5 Discussion

Clearly there is much more work to be done. Apart from considering other examples, the major activity is to complete the companion paper which provides a semantics for $\pi o\beta\lambda$ in terms of the π-calculus (this approach results from technical difficulties with a more conventional operational or denotational semantics which are discussed further in [Jon93a]). This will be the basis on which the proof obligations are to be justified.

Acknowledgements

The author is grateful to Mario Wolczko, Carlos Figueiredo, Trevor Hopkins, John Sargeant, Michael Fisher and John Gurd for stimulating discussions on topics related to the implementation of object-based languages and machine architectures. The incentive provided by the discussions with the 'Object-Z' group at the University of Queensland is also remembered. Ketil Stølen prompted the use of predicates like *is-linked-list* during an enjoyable visit to Munich. Anders Ravn made useful comments on a draft of this paper and Kohei Honda provided a detailed criticism of both content and presentation style. Feedback from the 1992 meeting of IFIP WG 2.3 was stimulating as were the questions on a trip to NWPC in Bergen and at a seminar in Oslo. The support of a Senior Fellowship from the SERC is gratefully acknowledged.

References

[AdB90]   P. America and F. de Boer. A proof system for process creation. In *[BJ90]*, pages 303–332, 1990.

[Ame86]   Pierre America. A proof theory for a sequential version of POOL. Technical Report 0188, Philips Research Laboratories, Philips Research Laboratories, Nederlandse Philips Bedrijven, B.V., September 1986.

[Ame89]   Pierre America. Issues in the design of a parallel object-oriented language. *Formal Aspects of Computing*, 1(4), 1989.

[Ame91]   P. America. Formal techniques for parallel object-oriented languages. In *[BG91]*, pages 1–17, 1991.

[AR89]   Pierre América and Jan Rutten. *A Parallel Object-Oriented Language: Design and Semantic Foundations*. PhD thesis, Free University of Amsterdam, 1989.

[AR92]   Pierre America and Jan Rutten. A layered semantics for a parallel object-oriented language. *Formal Aspects of Computing*, 4(4):376–408, 1992.

[BF91]   J. A. Bergstra and L. M. G. Feijs, editors. *Algebraic Methods II: Theory Tools and Applications*, volume 490 of *Lecture Notes in Computer Science*. Springer-Verlag, 1991.

[BG91]   J. C. M. Baeten and J. F. Groote, editors. *CONCUR'91 – Proceedings of the 2nd International Conference on Concurrency Theory*, volume 527 of *Lecture Notes in Computer Science*. Springer-Verlag, 1991.

[BJ90]   M. Broy and C. B. Jones, editors. *Programming Concepts and Methods*. North-Holland, 1990.

[BSI92]   BSI. VDM specification language protostandard. Technical Report N-231, BSI IST/5/19, 1992.

[CLW79]   K. M. Chung, F. Luccio, and C. K. Wong. A new permutation algorithm for bubble memories. Technical Report RC 7633, IBM Research Division, 1979.

[CM88]   K. M. Chandy and J. Misra. *Parallel Program Design: A Foundation*. Addison-Wesley, 1988.

[Daw91]   J. Dawes. *The VDM-SL Reference Guide*. Pitman, 1991.

[dB91]   Frank S. de Boer. *Reasoning about Dynamically Evolving Process Structure*. PhD thesis, Free University of Amsterdam, 1991.

[GH93]   J. V. Guttag and J. J. Horning. *Larch: Languages and Tools for Formal Specification*. Springer-Verlag, 1993.

[GHW85]   J. V. Guttag, J. J. Horning, and J. M. Wing. Larch in five easy pieces. Technical Report 5, DEC, SRC, July 1985.

[HHJ+87] C. A. R. Hoare, I. J. Hayes, He Jifeng, C. C. Morgan, A. W. Roscoe, J. W. Sanders, I. H. Sørensen, J. M. Spivey, and B. A. Sufrin. The laws of programming. *Communications of the ACM*, 30(8):672–687, August 1987. see Corrigenda in Communications of the ACM, 30(9): 770.

[JJLM91] C. B. Jones, K. D. Jones, P. A. Lindsay, and R. Moore. *mural: A Formal Development Support System*. Springer-Verlag, 1991.

[Jon83]   C. B. Jones. Specification and design of (parallel) programs. In *Proceedings of IFIP'83*, pages 321–332. North-Holland, 1983.

[Jon90]   C. B. Jones. *Systematic Software Development using VDM*. Prentice Hall International, second edition, 1990.

[Jon91]   C. B. Jones. Interference resumed. In P. Bailes, editor, *Engineering Safe Software*, pages 31–56. Australian Computer Society, 1991.

[Jon92]   C. B. Jones. An object-based design method for concurrent programs. Technical Report UMCS-92-12-1, Manchester University, 1992.

[Jon93a] C. B. Jones. Giving semantics to an object-based design notation. In *CONCUR'93*, Lecture Notes in Computer Science. Springer-Verlag, 1993.

[Jon93b]   C. B. Jones. Reasoning about interference in an object-based design method. In *FME'93*, Lecture Notes in Computer Science. Springer-Verlag, 1993.

[JPZ91]   W. Janssen, M. Poel, and J. Zwiers. Action systems and action refinement in the development of parallel systems. In *[BG91]*, pages 298–316, 1991.

[KMMN91]   B. B. Kristensen, O. L. Madsen, B. Møller-Pedersen, and K. Nygaard. Object oriented programming in the Beta programming language. Technical report, University of Oslo and others, September 1991.

[Lam90]   L. Lamport. A temporal logic of actions. Technical Report 57, Digital Equipment Corporation, Systems Research Center, 1990.

[Lam91]   L. Lamport. The temporal logic of actions. Technical Report 79, Digital, SRC, 1991.

[Len82]   C. Lengauer. *A Methodology for Programming with Concurrency*. PhD thesis, Computer Systems Research Group, University of Toronto, 1982.

[Lip75]   R. J. Lipton. Reduction: A method of proving properties of parallel programs. *Communications of the ACM*, 12:717–721, 1975.

[Mil92]   R. Milner. The polyadic π-calculus: A tutorial. In *Logic and Algebra of Specification*. Springer-Verlag, 1992.

[Nel91]   G. Nelson, editor. *Systems Programming with Modula-3*. Prentice Hall, 1991.

[OA91]   E.-R. Olderog and K. R. Apt. Using transformations to verify parallel programs. In *[BF91]*, pages 55–82, 1991.

[PT91]   S. Prehn and W. J. Toetenel, editors. *VDM'91 – Formal Software Development Methods. Proceedings of the 4th International Symposium of VDM Europe, Noordwijkerhout, The Netherlands, October 1991. Vol.1: Conference Contributions*, volume 551 of *Lecture Notes in Computer Science*. Springer-Verlag, 1991.

[RH86]   A. W. Roscoe and C. A. R. Hoare. Laws of occam programming. Monograph PRG-53, Oxford University Computing Laboratory, Programming Research Group, February 1986.

[Sar92]   J. Sargeant. UFO – united functions and objects draft language description. Technical Report UMCS-92-4-3, Manchester University, 1992.

[Stø90]   K. Stølen. *Development of Parallel Programs on Shared Data-Structures*. PhD thesis, Manchester University, 1990. available as UMCS-91-1-1.

[Stø91a]   K. Stølen. A Method for the Development of Totally Correct Shared-State Parallel Programs. In *[BG91]*, pages 510–525, 1991.

[Stø91b]   K. Stølen. An Attempt to Reason About Shared-State Concurrency in the Style of VDM. In *[PT91]*, pages 324–342, 1991.

[Wol88]   Mario I. Wolczko. *Semantics of Object-Oriented Languages*. PhD thesis, Department of Computer Science, University of Manchester, January 1988.

[XH91]   Qiwen Xu and Jifeng He. A theory of state-based parallel programming by refinement: Part I. In J. Morris, editor, *Proceedings of The Fourth BCS-FACS Refinement Workshop*. Springer-Verlag, 1991.

[Xu92]   Qiwen Xu. *A Theory of State-based Parallel Programming*. PhD thesis, Oxford University, 1992.

[Yon90]   Akinori Yonezawa, editor. *ABCL: An Object-Oriented Concurrent System*. MIT Press, 1990.

[Zwi88]   J. Zwiers. *Compositionality, Concurrency and Partial Correctness: Proof theories for networks of processes, and their connections*. PhD thesis, Technical University Eindhoven, 1988. available as LNCS 321, Springer-Verlag.

From π-calculus to Higher-Order π-calculus — and back

Davide Sangiorgi[1]

Abstract. We compare the first-order and the higher-order paradigms
for the representation of mobility in process algebras. The prototypical
calculus in the first-order paradigm is the *π-calculus*. By generalising its
sort mechanism we derive an ω-order extension, called *Higher-Order π-
calculus*. We give examples of its use, including the encoding of λ-calculus.
Surprisingly, we show that such an extension does not add expressiveness:
Higher-order processes can be faithfully represented at first order. We
conclude that the first-order paradigm, which enjoys a simpler and more
intuitive theory, should be taken as *basic*. Nevertheless, the study of the
λ-calculus encodings shows that a higher-order calculus can be very useful
for reasoning at a more abstract level.

1 Introduction

A *mobile system* is a system with a dynamically changing communication topology. Examples from operating systems are a resource which has a single owner at
any time but whose ownership can be changed as time passes, or process migra-
tion, in which tasks or processes can be exchanged among processors to optimise
their load balance.

There are two approaches to represent mobility in process algebra. In the
higher-order paradigm mobility is achieved by allowing agents to be passed as values in a communication; Thomsen's Plain CHOCS [19] and Boudol's γ-calculus [8]
belong to this category. In the *first-order paradigm* only ports can be transmitted
(we shall use interchangeably the words port, name and channel). The π-calculus
is the prototypical first-order calculus. It was introduced by Milner, Parrow and
Walker in [15] and later refined by Milner [13] with the addition of *sorts* and
of communication of tuples (*polyadic π-calculus*). The choice of the first-order
paradigm for π-calculus was motivated — among other reasons — by the belief that reference passing is enough to represent more involved operations like
process passing. Our goal here is to validate this claim. To this end, we introduce a new calculus, called *Higher-Order π-calculus* (HOπ), which enriches
the π-calculus with explicit higher-order communications. In the HOπ not only
names, but also processes and parametrised processes of arbitrarily high order,
can be transmitted. In this sense, if the ordinary π-calculus is of first order and
Plain CHOCS is of second order, then HOπ is of ω order. We show that HOπ is
representable within π-calculus.

But what does it mean that a given source language is representable within
a given target language? Typically there are three phases:

[1]address: Dep. Comp. Science, University Edinburgh, JCMB, Mayfield road, Edinburgh
EH9 3JZ, U.K. Email: sad@dcs.ed.ac.uk. Work supported by the ESPRIT BRA project
"CONFER".

(1)   Formal definition of the semantics of the two languages;

(2)   Definition of the encoding from the source to the target language;

(3)   Proof of the correctness of the encoding w.r.t. the semantics given.

The predominant approach to the semantics of concurrent systems is *operational*. The possible evolutions of processes are inductively described in terms of *transition systems* which then are quotiented by *equivalence relations* to abstract away from unwanted details. W.r.t. denotational semantics, the operational method necessitates a different approach to translation-correctness, where behaviours rather than meanings are compared. The choice of the behavioural equivalence, besides being "interesting", should be uniform on the calculi. Moreover, we want the encoding to be *fully abstract*, i.e. two source language terms should be equivalent if and only if their translations are equivalent. But since this does not reveal *how* this respectfulness is achieved, the result should be completed with the *operational correspondence* between a term and its translation (i.e. the connection between their transitions).

With the full abstraction demand, we have taken a *strong* point of view on representability. Indeed, while soundness is a necessary property, one might well consider milder forms of completeness, for instance by limiting the testing on target terms to encodings of source contexts. We asked for full abstraction because we wish to use the target terms in *any* contexts; and when two source terms are indistinguishable, their encodings should *always* be interchangeable. In other words, we want to be able to switch freely between the two calculi. In our case, where the source language is HOπ and the target language is π-calculus, this allows us on the one hand to make use of the abstraction power of HOπ, which comes from its ω-order nature. On the other hand, to rely on the more elementary and intuitive theory of π-calculus when reasoning over agents; in virtue of the representability result this theory can be lifted up to HOπ.

This paper is an extract of the core of the author's Ph.D. thesis [18]. We have tried to keep the presentation rather informal, often preferring examples to meticulous technical details. We review π-calculus in Section 2 and introduce HOπ in Section 3. The behavioural equivalence adopted is defined in Section 4; we explain our choice and we outline the problem of defining a natural bisimulation equivalence in a higher-order calculus. In Section 5 we present the compilation from HOπ to π-calculus, whose correctness is examined in Section 6. In Section 7 we look at some uses of the compilation, in particular the study of Milner's encodings of λ-calculus into π-calculus. In Section 8 we survey related work and directions for future research.

2   The polyadic π-calculus

2.1   Syntax

The letters $a, b, \ldots, x, y, \ldots$ stand for names, and P, Q for processes. We add a tilde to mean a possibly empty tuple. The class of π-calculus processes is built from names using the operators of prefixing, sum, parallel composition, restriction, matching and constant application:

$$P \quad :: \quad \sum_{i \in I} \alpha_i.P_i \quad | \quad P_1 \,|\, P_2 \quad | \quad \nu x\, P \quad | \quad [x = y]P \quad | \quad D\langle \widetilde{x} \rangle$$

α is called *prefix* and can be either an input or an output:

$$\alpha \quad :: \quad x(\widetilde{y}) \quad | \quad \overline{x}\langle \widetilde{y} \rangle$$

Each constant D has a defining equation of the form $D \stackrel{\text{def}}{=} (\widetilde{x})P$; the expression $(\widetilde{x})P$ is like a procedure, in which $\widetilde{x}$ represents the parameters. Therefore the operators emulate those of CCS [12]; in addition, there is matching to test for equality of names. We refer to [15, 13] for the intended interpretation of the operators. Application has the highest precedence; sum and parallel composition the lowest. In the sum, I represents a finite indexing set. When I is empty, we get the inactive process, written as 0; sometimes we abbreviate $\alpha.0$ as α. As usual, $+$ is taken to represent binary sum. As Milner does in [13], our sums are *guarded*, i.e. the outermost operator of the summands is prefixing. Guarded sums simplify the reduction semantics of Section 2.3 and smooth the comparison between higher-order and first-order processes that we shall make in Section 5.

The operators $a(\widetilde{b}).P$, $(\widetilde{b})P$ and $\nu b\, P$ bind all free occurrences of the names $\widetilde{b}$ and b in P. These binders give rise in the expected way to the definitions of *free names* of a term. The definitions of substitution and α-conversion are standard too, with renaming possibly involved to avoid capture of free names.

Sometimes *replication* is included in π-calculus in place of constants [13]. The replication $!\,P$ intuitively represents $P\,|\,P \ldots$, i.e. an unbounded number of copies of P in parallel. It is easy to code it up using constants; and if the number of these is finite, the other way round holds too.

2.2 Sorting

All realistic systems which have been described with the π-calculus seem to obey some discipline in the use of names. The introduction of sorts and sortings into the π-calculus [13] intends to make this name discipline explicit. In the polyadic π-calculus, sorts are also essential to avoid disagreement in the arities of tuples carried by a given name, or to be used by a given constant.

Names are partitioned into a collection of *subject sorts*, each of which contains an infinite number of names. We write $x : s$ to mean that x belongs to the subject sort s; this notation is extended to tuples componentwise. Then *object sorts*, ranged over by S, are just sequences over subject sorts, such as $(s_1, \ldots, s_n)$ or (s). Finally, a *sorting* is a function Ob mapping each subject sort to an object sort. We write $s \mapsto (\widetilde{s}) \in Ob$, if Ob assigns the object sort $(\widetilde{s})$ to s; in this case we say that $(\widetilde{s})$ *appears* in Ob. By assigning the object sort (s_1, s_2) to the subject sort s, one forces the object part of any name in s to be a pair whose first component is a name of s_1 and whose second component is a name of s_2. CCS and the monadic unsorted π-calculus can be derived by imposing the sortings $\{\text{NAME} \mapsto ()\}$ and $\{\text{NAME} \mapsto (\text{NAME})\}$ respectively, in which all names belong to the same subject sort NAME.

If $a : s \mapsto (s_1, s_2)$, then for $a(\widetilde{x}).P$ and $\overline{a}\langle\widetilde{x}\rangle.P$ to respect Ob, it must be that $\widetilde{x} = x_1, x_2$, for some $x_1 : s_1$ and $x_2 : s_2$. Moreover, in a matching $[a = b]$, we require that the tested names a and b belong to the same sort. Finally, we have to guarantee the correctness of applications. To this end, we assign an object sort to agents: Processes take the sort $()$, whereas if $D \stackrel{\text{def}}{=} (\widetilde{x})P$ and $\widetilde{x} : \widetilde{s}$, then D, and $(\widetilde{x})P$ take the sort $(\widetilde{s})$. Now, the requirement on $D\langle\widetilde{y}\rangle$ is that $\widetilde{s}$ exists s.t. $\widetilde{y} : \widetilde{s}$ and $D : (\widetilde{s})$. To sum up, a term is *well-sorted* for Ob if all its prefixes and applications obey the discipline given by Ob, as described above. We call an expression of sort $(\widetilde{s})$, for $\widetilde{s}$ non-empty, *abstraction*. Processes and abstractions are *agents*. We use F, G to range over abstractions and A to range over agents.

2.3   Operational Semantics

Following Milner [14, 13], we shall give the operational semantics of the language in terms of a *reduction system* (as opposed to the "traditional" *labelled transition system*). In this technique, inspired by Berry and Boudol's Chemical Abstract Machine [6], axioms for a structural congruence relation are introduced prior to the reduction rules, in order to break a rigid, geometrical vision of concurrency and to allow for redexes as subterms. The interpretation of the operators of the language comes out neatly with reduction semantics, due to the compelling naturalness of each structural congruence and reduction rule.

Structural congruence, written $\equiv$, is the smallest congruence over the class of π-calculus agents which satisfies the rules below. (The symbol $\equiv$ should not be confused with $=$, the latter meaning syntactic equality between processes.)

1. $P \equiv Q$ if P is α-convertible to Q;

2. abelian monoid laws for $+$: $P + Q \equiv Q + P$, $P + (Q + R) \equiv (P + Q) + R$, $P + 0 \equiv P$;

3. abelian monoid laws for $|$: $P \,|\, Q \equiv Q \,|\, P$, $P \,|\, (Q \,|\, R) \equiv (P \,|\, Q) \,|\, R$, $P \,|\, 0 \equiv P$;

4. $\nu x \, 0 \equiv 0$, $\nu x \, \nu y \, P \equiv \nu y \, \nu x \, P$, $(\nu x \, P) \,|\, Q \equiv \nu x \, (P \,|\, Q)$, if x is not free in Q;

5. $[x = x]P \equiv P$;

6. if $D \stackrel{\text{def}}{=} (\widetilde{x})P$, then $D \equiv (\widetilde{x})P$ (or, if instead replication is used, $!\,P \equiv P \,|\, !\,P$).

Now the *reduction rules*, expressing the notion of interaction:

$$\text{COM: } (\cdots + x(\widetilde{y}).P) \,|\, (\cdots + \overline{x}\langle\widetilde{z}\rangle.Q) \longrightarrow P\{\widetilde{z}/\widetilde{y}\} \,|\, Q$$

$$\text{PAR: } \frac{P \longrightarrow P'}{P \,|\, Q \longrightarrow P' \,|\, Q} \qquad\qquad \text{RES: } \frac{P \longrightarrow P'}{\nu x \, P \longrightarrow \nu x \, P'}$$

$$\text{STRUCT: } \frac{Q \equiv P \quad P \longrightarrow P' \quad P' \equiv Q'}{Q \longrightarrow Q'}$$

3 Higher Order π-calculus

3.1 Examples

In the π-calculus only object sorts of the form $(\widetilde{s})$ are allowed. The sortings so obtained are first order, as indicated by the level of bracket nesting, which is limited to one. The *Higher-Order π-calculus* (HOπ) is essentially derived by dropping this limitation. Thus one may enforce processes to be communicated along a name x by declaring $x : s \mapsto (())$. Then an "executer", which receives a process at x and executes it, can be written as $x(X).X$; when put in parallel with $\overline{x}\langle P\rangle.Q$, it gives rise to the interaction

$$\overline{x}\langle P\rangle.Q \mid x(X).X \longrightarrow Q \mid P$$

Before formally defining the syntax and the semantics, let us look at more interesting examples.

Numerals. In [13], Milner shows how to encode numbers in the π-calculus. If $\overline{y}^n$ represents the sequence $\overline{y}. \cdots .\overline{y}$ of length n, and $y, z : s \mapsto ()$, then the natural number n is encoded as follows:

$$[n] \overset{\text{def}}{=} (y, z)\overline{y}^n.\overline{z} : (s, s)$$

We want now to write an agent *Plus* capable of performing the sum of two numbers. Consider the process $\boldsymbol{\nu}\, x\left([n]\langle y, x\rangle \mid x.[m]\langle y, z\rangle\right)$: If we abstract from possible internal reductions, this behaves exactly like $[n + m]\langle y, z\rangle$. Accordingly, if X and Y are variables of the same sort as numerals, we can define

$$Plus \overset{\text{def}}{=} (X, Y, y, z)\left(\boldsymbol{\nu}\, x\left(X\langle y, x\rangle \mid x.Y\langle y, z\rangle\right)\right) : ((s, s), (s, s), s, s)$$

Plus is a higher-order abstraction, because it abstracts on agent-variables (to be precise *Plus* is a second-order abstraction). This is also indicated by the bracket nesting in the definition of *Plus*, which is greater than one. The machinery can be iterated, for instance by defining abstractions on variables of the same sort as *Plus* and so forth, progressively increasing the order of the resulting agents.

An adder which repeatedly takes two numbers at ports a_1, a_2 and outputs their sum at a_3 can be represented as:

$$Add \overset{\text{def}}{=} a_1(X).a_2(Y).\overline{a}_3\Big\langle Plus\,\langle X, Y\rangle\Big\rangle.Add$$

Encoding of the λ-calculus. The idea common to all various attempts at embedding λ-calculus into a process calculus [8, 14, 19] is to view functional application as a particular parallel combination of two agents, the function and its argument, and β-reduction as a particular case of communication. Our encoding into HOπ makes very transparent this idea. For convenience, a variable x of the λ-calculus is mapped into its upper-case variable X in HOπ. We take for granted the basic concepts of λ-calculus. As evaluation strategy, we adopt the one of

Abramsky's *lazy λ-calculus* [1] in which reductions occur only at the extreme left of a term.

$$\mathcal{H}[\![\lambda x.M]\!] \stackrel{\text{def}}{=} (p)p(X,q).\mathcal{H}[\![M]\!]\langle q\rangle$$

$$\mathcal{H}[\![x]\!] \stackrel{\text{def}}{=} X$$

$$\mathcal{H}[\![MN]\!] \stackrel{\text{def}}{=} (p)\boldsymbol{\nu}\, q\left(\mathcal{H}[\![M]\!]\langle q\rangle \mid \overline{q}\langle\mathcal{H}[\![N]\!],p\rangle\right)$$

If s is the sort of the names p, q, then the translation of a λ-term is an abstraction of sort (s). This abstracted name will be the only access to that agent and will be used to interact with the appropriate λ-term. Thus $\mathcal{H}[\![\lambda x.M]\!]\langle p\rangle$ receives at p its λ-argument and the name q which will give access to M. In the translation of application, the restriction on q prevents interferences from other processes.

The higher-order features of HOπ allow us a simpler encoding than Milner's into π-calculus [14]. Indeed, there is a one-to-one correspondence between reductions in λ-terms and in their HOπ counterparts. Therefore, following Boudol's terminology [8], we can claim that *lazy λ-calculus is a subcalculus of HOπ*.

Proposition 3.1 (operational correspondence for $\mathcal{H}$)
Let M and M' be closed λ-terms:

1. *If $M \longrightarrow M'$, then $\mathcal{H}[\![M]\!]\langle p\rangle \longrightarrow \mathcal{H}[\![M']\!]\langle p\rangle$, and conversely,*
2. *if $\mathcal{H}[\![M]\!]\langle p\rangle \longrightarrow Q$, then $\exists M'$ s.t. $Q \equiv \mathcal{H}[\![M']\!]\langle p\rangle$ and $M \longrightarrow M'$.* □

3.2 The syntax of HOπ

We shall maintain the notation introduced in Section 2. Furthermore, we need a set of *agent-variables*, ranged over by X, Y. There are two modifications to bring into the syntax of the π-calculus. First, variable application should be allowed too, so that an abstraction received as input can be provided with the appropriate arguments. Secondly, tuples in prefixing, applications and abstractions may also contain agents or agent-variables. To simplify the notation, in the grammar we use K to stand for an agent or a name and U to stand for a variable or a name.

$$P \quad :: \quad \sum_{i\in I}\alpha_i.P_i \quad \mid \quad P_1 \mid P_2 \quad \mid \quad \boldsymbol{\nu}\,x\,P \quad \mid \quad [x=y]P \quad \mid \quad D\langle\widetilde{K}\rangle \quad \mid \quad X\langle\widetilde{K}\rangle$$
$$\alpha \quad :: \quad \overline{x}\langle\widetilde{K}\rangle \quad \mid \quad x(\widetilde{U})$$

Remember that K may be an agent; hence it may be a process, but also an abstraction of arbitrary high order. An *open* agent is an agent possibly containing free variables. It is worth pointing out that we do not lose expressiveness by having application only with variables and constants. In fact, every well-sorted expression $A\langle\widetilde{K}\rangle$ can be put into this form by "executing" the applications it contains; for instance from $\big((X)Y\langle X\rangle\big)\langle P\rangle$, we get $Y\langle P\rangle$. This makes the definition of substitution more elaborated but facilitates the proofs in the calculus.

3.3 Sorting and operational semantics

In the HOπ the need for sorts is even more compelling than in π-calculus. It is not only now a question of arities, but we have also to avoid any confusion between instantiation to names and to agents as well as instantiation to agents of different order.

W.r.t. the π-calculus sorts, the difference is that the sequences representing object sorts do not have to be made only of subject sorts; but object sorts themselves can appear too. Therefore, using El for a subject or an object sort, the grammar for sorts becomes:

$$
\begin{aligned}
El &:: \quad s \quad | \quad S \\
S &:: \quad (\widetilde{El}) \quad | \quad ()
\end{aligned}
$$

For each object sort S we suppose the existence of an infinite number of variables of sort S. The definition of well-sorted agent is easy and we leave it to the reader. The special case of second-order sorting $\{\text{NAME} \mapsto (())\}$ corresponds to Thomsen's Plain CHOCS.

As an aside, let us point out an alternative notation for sorts which seems fairly effective in HOπ. Consider the abstraction $G \stackrel{\text{def}}{=} (X)F$, for $X : S'$, $F : S$. It represents a function which takes an argument of sort S' and gives back an argument of sort S. From a function-theoretic point of view, G has type $S' \longrightarrow S$. Following such intuition, we could explicitly introduce the arrow-sort and say that $G : S' \longrightarrow S$.

As regards the operational semantics, no modification is necessary in the rules for structural congruence. In the reduction rules only the COM rule is affected; since values exchanged do not have to be only names, it becomes:

$$\text{COM:} \ (\cdots + x(\widetilde{U}).P) \,|\, (\cdots + \overline{x}\langle\widetilde{K}\rangle) \longrightarrow P\{\widetilde{K}/\widetilde{U}\} \,|\, Q$$

4 Behavioural equivalence

We concentrate on bisimulation, probably the most studied behavioural equivalence in process algebra. Both in π-calculus and in HOπ we adopt the congruence induced by *barbed bisimulation* [16, 18]. There are three main reasons for the interest in barbed bisimulation.

1. It allows us to recover from reduction semantics the well-known bisimulation-based equivalences which are defined on the labelled transition system;

2. It can be defined uniformly in different calculi and thus provides us with a fundamental tool for comparing them, the kind of issue on which this paper is mainly concerned;

3. It gives us a natural bisimulation equivalence for higher-order calculi.

Some further comment on (3) is worthwhile. The definition of a natural bisimulation equivalence in a higher-order calculus is not straightforward. The habitual definition of bisimulation, based on the labelled transition system, requires that an action be matched by another only if they have *identical* labels.

This also works for π-calculus if we concede α-convertibility. But it does *not* in a higher-order calculus. Obvious algebraic laws such as the commutativity of parallel composition are lost: For instance, the processes $\overline{a}\langle P|Q\rangle.0$ and $\overline{a}\langle Q|P\rangle.0$ are distinguished since the agents emitted in their respective outputs are syntactically different.

The approach taken by Astesiano, Boudol and Thomsen [4, 8, 19], is to require *bisimilarity* rather than *identity* of the processes emitted in a higher-order output action. But this gives rise to counterintuitive equalities when restriction is a formal binder. The problems are due to the fact that the object part and the continuation are examined separately, thus preventing a satisfactory treatment of the channels private to the two. See [18] for precise examples.

Barbed bisimulation focuses on the reduction or interaction relation, a concept common to different calculi. It goes a little further though, since the reduction relation by itself is not enough to yield the desired discriminanting power. The choice in [18] was to introduce, for each name a, an *observation predicate* $\downarrow_a$ which detects the possibility of performing a communication with the environment along a. A simple syntactic condition is enough to know whether $P \downarrow_a$ holds: there must be in P a prefix $a(\widetilde{x})$ or $\overline{a}\langle\widetilde{x}\rangle$ which is not underneath another prefix and not in the scope of a restriction on a. For example, If P is $(\boldsymbol{\nu}c)(\overline{c}\,.\,b\,|\,d\,.\,a)$, then $P\downarrow_a$, but not $P\downarrow_c$, $P\downarrow_b$ or $P\downarrow_d$.

Definition 4.1 Strong barbed bisimulation, *written* $\overset{\cdot}{\sim}$, *is the largest symmetrical relation on the class of processes of the language s.t. $P \overset{\cdot}{\sim} Q$ implies:*

1. *whenever $P \longrightarrow P'$ then $Q \longrightarrow Q'$ and $P' \overset{\cdot}{\sim} Q'$;*
2. *for each channel a, if $P \downarrow_a$ then $Q \downarrow_a$.* □

The weak version of the equivalence, in which one abstracts away from the length of the reductions in two matching actions, is obtained in the standard way: If $\Longrightarrow$ is the reflexive and transitive closure of $\longrightarrow$ and $\Downarrow_a$ is $\Longrightarrow\downarrow_a$ (the composition of the two relations), then *weak barbed bisimulation*, written $\overset{\cdot}{\approx}$, is defined by replacing the transition $Q \longrightarrow Q'$ with $Q \Longrightarrow Q'$ and the predicate $Q \downarrow_a$ with $Q \Downarrow_a$.

By itself, barbed bisimulation is rather weak (it is not even preserved by parallel composition). By parametrisation over contexts, we get a finer relation.

Definition 4.2 *Two processes P and Q are strong barbed-congruent, written $P \sim^c Q$, if for each context $C[\cdot]$, it holds that $C[P] \overset{\cdot}{\sim} C[Q]$.* □

To obtain *weak barbed congruence*, written $\approx^c$, replace $\overset{\cdot}{\sim}$ with $\overset{\cdot}{\approx}$. The reader familiar with process algebra might remark that most of the common weak bisimulations of labelled transition systems are not preserved by *dynamic* operators, i.e. operators like sum and prefix which are discharged when an action is produced. To recover them, one can parametrise barbed bisimulation over the subclass of contexts which are built by composing the hole $[\cdot]$ and the processes by means of only non-dynamic operators. The resulting equivalence is called *barbed equivalence*.

To test the discriminatory power of barbed bisimulation, we have proved in [18] that in the strong and in the weak case barbed equivalence and congruence coincide in CCS and π-calculus with the ordinary bisimulation-based equivalences. We have also obtained fairly simple direct characterisations of barbed equivalence and congruence in HOπ. In this paper, we shall only deal explicitly with weak barbed congruence; however all results stated hold for weak barbed equivalence too.

5 The compilation from HOπ to π-calculus

We present the compilation into π-calculus on a subclass of the HOπ agents. We make two simplifications. The first regards the arities of the sorts: we allow *one* only value — a name or an abstraction — to be transmitted, and we only allow unary abstractions. This is purely for convenience in the definition of the compilation and of the operational correspondence for it — the generalisation to the calculus with arbitrary arities does not give problems. The second simplification is that we compile into π-calculus only those HOπ agents whose definition use a *finite* number of constants (from a practical point of view, this is a perfectly reasonable assumption). Moreover, since as mentioned in Section 2.1, a finite number of constants can be coded up using replication, we shall adopt replication in place of constants; replication is useful in the definition of the compilation and facilitates the reasoning by structural induction in the proofs. We keep '$\stackrel{\text{def}}{=}$' as abbreviation mechanism, to assign names to expressions to which we want to refer later.

We use $P \{m := F\}$ to stand for $\nu m (P \mid !m(U).F\langle U\rangle)$, where U is a name or a variable, depending upon the sort. We chose curly brackets for this notation because under a certain condition on the use of m in P and F, m acts in P as a pointer to F and $\{m := F\}$ as a "local environment" for P. We shall allow ourselves a free use of this abbreviation. Formally, since only guarded sums are admitted in the language, it is not legal to use it in a context like $[\cdot]+Q$. However there are obvious transformations which convert any misuse of this into a correct process expression, and we leave them implicit.

Intuitively, the compilation $\mathcal{C}$ replaces the communication of an agent with the communication of the *access* to that agent. Thus $P_1 \stackrel{\text{def}}{=} \overline{a}\langle F\rangle.Q$ is replaced by $P_2 \stackrel{\text{def}}{=} (\overline{a}\langle m\rangle.Q) \{m := F\}$. Whereas an agent interacting with P_1 may use F directly with, say, argument b, an agent interacting with P_2 uses m to activate F and provide it with the argument b. The name m is called *name-trigger*.

The compilation has also to modify the sorting Ob. We suppose that Ob is *downward-closed*, that is if $s \mapsto (S) \in Ob$, then s' exists s.t. $s' \mapsto S \in Ob$. If Ob is not already downward-closed, then it can easily be extended to make it so. The *downward-closed* property is used to select a subsorting SOb of Ob from which to draw the name-triggers. There might be different ways of defining SOb: Our sole requirement is that SOb has one and only one subject sort with object sort S, for each object sort S which appears in Ob; we use SOb_S to denote this subject sort. The compilation shall replace agents of sort S with names of sort

$$\mathcal{C}[\![X]\!] \stackrel{\text{def}}{=} \begin{cases} \mathcal{C}[\![(Y)X\langle Y\rangle]\!] & \text{if } X \text{ is a higher-order abstraction} \\ \mathcal{C}[\![(a)X\langle a\rangle]\!] & \text{otherwise} \end{cases}$$

$$\mathcal{C}[\![\alpha.P]\!] \stackrel{\text{def}}{=} \begin{cases} (\overline{a}\langle m\rangle.\mathcal{C}[\![P]\!])\,\{m := \mathcal{C}[\![F]\!]\} & \text{if } \alpha = \overline{a}\langle F\rangle \\ a(x).\mathcal{C}[\![P]\!] & \text{if } \alpha = a(X) \\ \alpha.\mathcal{C}[\![P]\!] & \text{otherwise} \end{cases}$$

$$\mathcal{C}[\![X\langle F\rangle]\!] \stackrel{\text{def}}{=} (\overline{x}\langle m\rangle.0)\,\{m := \mathcal{C}[\![F]\!]\} \qquad \mathcal{C}[\![X\langle b\rangle]\!] \stackrel{\text{def}}{=} \overline{x}\langle b\rangle.0 \qquad \mathcal{C}[\![!\,P]\!] \stackrel{\text{def}}{=} !\,\mathcal{C}[\![P]\!]$$

$$\mathcal{C}[\![P \mid Q]\!] \stackrel{\text{def}}{=} \mathcal{C}[\![P]\!] \mid \mathcal{C}[\![Q]\!] \qquad \mathcal{C}[\![P + Q]\!] \stackrel{\text{def}}{=} \mathcal{C}[\![P]\!] + \mathcal{C}[\![Q]\!] \qquad \mathcal{C}[\![\nu\,a\,P]\!] \stackrel{\text{def}}{=} \nu\,a\,\mathcal{C}[\![P]\!]$$

$$\mathcal{C}[\![\,[a=b]P\,]\!] \stackrel{\text{def}}{=} [a=b]\,\mathcal{C}[\![P]\!] \qquad \mathcal{C}[\![(X)P]\!] \stackrel{\text{def}}{=} (x)\mathcal{C}[\![P]\!] \qquad \mathcal{C}[\![(a)P]\!] \stackrel{\text{def}}{=} (a)\mathcal{C}[\![P]\!]$$

Table 1: The compilation $\mathcal{C}$

$SObs$; indeed, if $A : S = (El)$, then a trigger which has to convey the argument for A carries values of sort El, i.e. its object sort is precisely (El). Therefore we have:

$$\mathcal{C}[\![Ob]\!] = \{s \mapsto (s') \in Ob\} \bigcup \{s \mapsto (SObs) \;:\; s \mapsto (S) \in Ob\}.$$

The behaviour of $\mathcal{C}$ on agents is described in Table 1. To respect the definition on the sorting, we assume that if X is a variable of sort S, then its lower case letter x is a name from $SObs$. Moreover, both this name x and the name-trigger m are taken to be fresh, i.e. not occurring in the source agent.

Besides the above sketched treatment of higher-order outputs, the other interesting rules of Table 1 are those for application and for variable. Consider the application $X\langle K\rangle$: When X is instantiated to an agent G, it becomes $G\langle K\rangle$. Translating it, we expect to receive just a name-trigger to G, and we are expected to use it to activate G with its argument K. This is legal when K is a name (and leads to our rule for for first-order application), but it is not when K is an agent, since we cannot pass it at first order. As in the rule for outputs, this is resolved by sending a name-trigger for K. In the rule for higher-order variable (and for uniformity, also in the rule for first-order variable) an η-conversion is employed. This is to make explicit all possible applications and hence introduce all necessary name-triggers; we shall see later, discussing tentative optimisations for $\mathcal{C}$, that the use of full triggered forms is necessary to get soundness. Note that in this rule the distinction between first-order and higher-order variables introduces a dependency from the sorting. Moreover the latter, for which the sort of Y must be "smaller" than the sort of X, guarantees that $\mathcal{C}$ is well-defined. The compilation acts as an homomorphism in all other cases.

Let us illustrate how $\mathcal{C}$ works on reductions. There are two dimensions at which the number of interactions is expanded. One is *horizontal*. If a transmitted agent F is used by its recipient n times, n interactions are required at first-order to activate the copies of F.

Example 5.1 Let $P \stackrel{\text{def}}{=} \overline{a}\langle F\rangle.Q \mid a(Y).(Y\langle b\rangle \mid Y\langle c\rangle)$. Then $P \longrightarrow P' \stackrel{\text{def}}{=} Q \mid F\langle b\rangle \mid F\langle c\rangle$. In $\mathcal{C}[\![P]\!]$ this is simulated using three reductions:

$$\mathcal{C}[\![P]\!] \quad \overset{\text{def}}{=} \quad (\overline{a}\langle m\rangle.\mathcal{C}[\![Q]\!]) \{m := \mathcal{C}[\![F]\!]\} \mid a(y).(\overline{y}\langle b\rangle \mid \overline{y}\langle c\rangle)$$
$$\longrightarrow \quad (\mathcal{C}[\![Q]\!] \mid \overline{m}\langle b\rangle \mid \overline{m}\langle c\rangle) \{m := \mathcal{C}[\![F]\!]\}$$
$$\longrightarrow\longrightarrow \quad (\mathcal{C}[\![Q]\!] \mid \mathcal{C}[\![F]\!]\langle b\rangle \mid \mathcal{C}[\![F]\!]\langle c\rangle) \{m := \mathcal{C}[\![F]\!]\}$$
$$\sim^{c} \quad \mathcal{C}[\![Q]\!] \mid \mathcal{C}[\![F]\!]\langle b\rangle \mid \mathcal{C}[\![F]\!]\langle c\rangle \ = \ \mathcal{C}[\![P']\!]$$

where the last equality holds because m is not free in the body. $\qquad\square$

The other way to add interactions is *vertical* and takes its significance from the ω-order nature of HOπ. It arises with higher-order abstractions when, after the abstraction itself, one has also to trigger its arguments. This may give rise to interesting chains of activations. To see a simple case, take $P \overset{\text{def}}{=} \overline{a}\langle G\rangle \mid a(Y).Y\langle F\rangle$, where G is a second-order abstraction. We have $P \longrightarrow G\langle F\rangle$. To achieve the same effect $\mathcal{C}[\![P]\!]$ requires two further interactions, one to activate a copy of G and another to activate a copy of F.

6 Correctness of the compilation

Before tackling the question of the semantic correctness of the compilation $\mathcal{C}$, we have to check that its definition is syntactically meaningful by ensuring that it returns first-order agents and that there is agreement between the definitions of $\mathcal{C}$ on sorts and agents. The former is straightforward; the latter holds too because all new names which are introduced (in the rule for application) or whose object part is modified (in the rule for prefixing), respect the sorting $\mathcal{C}[\![Ob]\!]$.

Theorem 6.1 *For each open agent A, it holds that $\mathcal{C}[\![A]\!]$ is a first-order agent and well-sorted for $\mathcal{C}[\![Ob]\!]$.* $\qquad\square$

By contrast, the proof that $\mathcal{C}$ is faithful w.r.t. $\approx^{c}$ is not at all trivial. We limit ourselves to summarising the schema used in [18], to which we refer for the details. The compilation $\mathcal{C}$ is derived into two steps. The first is a mapping $\mathcal{T}$ which transforms an agent into a *triggered agent*. These are "normalised" HOπ agents in which every agent emitted in an output or "expected" in an input has a very simplified form and the same functionality of name-triggers. Thus higher-order communications have become homogeneous and have lost all their potential richness and variety. This greatly simplifies the reasoning over agents. Triggered agents have a few interesting properties, in particular a quite simple characterisation of barbed congruence.

The agent $\mathcal{T}[\![A]\!]$ already has the same structure as $\mathcal{C}[\![A]\!]$. The real difference is that $\mathcal{T}$ is an *endo*-encoding, that is, it remains within the same calculus. This facilitates the correctness proof and prepares the way for the next step, the mapping $\mathcal{F}$, which leads us down to first order. Syntactically, $\mathcal{F}$ is a fairly simple transformation. But semantically it is more delicate because it modifies the object sort of names. The correctness proofs of $\mathcal{T}$ and $\mathcal{F}$ are obtained using direct characterisations of barbed congruence on labelled transition systems plus the "local environment" properties for $\{m := F\}$.

Theorem 6.2 (full abstraction for $\mathcal{C}$) *For each pair of open agents A_1 and A_2, it holds that $A_1 \approx^c A_2$ iff $\mathcal{C}[\![A_1]\!] \approx^c \mathcal{C}[\![A_2]\!]$.* □

The definition of barbed congruence on abstractions and open agents is given in the expected way, by requiring instantiation of variables and of abstracted names with all agents or names of the right sort. Thus $(X)P \approx^c (X)Q$ if for each F of the same sort as X, $P\{F/X\} \approx^c Q\{F/X\}$.

A few considerations to emphasise the faithfulness of $\mathcal{C}$ are worthwhile. By itself, Theorem 6.2 does not reveal anything about how closely $\mathcal{C}[\![P]\!]$ simulates P; actually, nothing prevents us from obtaining the same result with a very bizarre encoding! First of all, let us show the operational correspondence existing between P and $\mathcal{C}[\![P]\!]$. We only look here at reductions; but a similar result holds for the visible actions of the labelled transition system [18].

In clause (1) below, an interaction is *first order* (resp. *higher order*) if the transmitted value is a name (resp. an agent). In clause (2) an interaction is *converted* if it comes from a communication along a name whose object sort has been modified by $\mathcal{C}$, i.e. a name which carries agents in Ob. In clauses (b), F represents the abstraction which is exchanged in P and m the trigger which is exchanged in $\mathcal{C}[\![P]\!]$.

Proposition 6.3 (operational correspondence for $\mathcal{C}$)
Suppose m not free in P and $\mathcal{C}[\![P]\!]$:

1. (a) If $P \longrightarrow P'$ is a first-order interaction, then $\mathcal{C}[\![P]\!] \longrightarrow \mathcal{C}[\![P']\!]$;

    (b) If $P \longrightarrow P'$ is a higher-order interaction, then there are $\widetilde{b}, G, F$ s.t.
    $$P' \equiv \nu\widetilde{b}\,(G\langle F\rangle) \text{ and } \mathcal{C}[\![P]\!] \longrightarrow \nu\widetilde{b}\,\big(\mathcal{C}[\![G]\!]\langle m\rangle\,\{m := \mathcal{C}[\![F]\!]\}\big).$$

2. *the converse of (1), i.e:*

    (a) If $\mathcal{C}[\![P]\!] \longrightarrow P''$ is a non-converted interaction, then P' exists s.t.
    $P \longrightarrow P'$, and $P'' = \mathcal{C}[\![P']\!]$;

    (b) If $\mathcal{C}[\![P]\!] \longrightarrow P''$ is a converted interaction, then there are $\widetilde{b}, G, F$ s.t.
    $P \longrightarrow \nu\widetilde{b}\,(G\langle F\rangle)$ and $P'' \equiv \nu\widetilde{b}\,\big(\mathcal{C}[\![G]\!]\langle m\rangle\,\{m := \mathcal{C}[\![F]\!]\}\big).$ □

Secondly, let us point out that by definitions of $\mathcal{C}$, if P is a first-order process then it is not modified by $\mathcal{C}$, i.e.

$$\mathcal{C}[\![P]\!] = P$$

Thirdly, suppose that P is an HOπ process which can only perform first-order actions. This does not imply that P is also a π-calculus process, as *internally* P could perform communications of agents. But if we relax the definition of well-sorted agent, then we can think of comparing directly P with $\mathcal{C}[\![P]\!]$, and we would get

$$\mathcal{C}[\![P]\!] \approx^c P$$

Optimisations? There are critical points in the definition of $\mathcal{C}$ on agents which is worth indicating. We doubt that non-trivial improvements are possible without loosing full abstraction. The first optimisation one might be tempted of, is on the output of agent-variables, defining

$$\mathcal{C}[\![\overline{a}\langle X\rangle.Q]\!] \stackrel{\text{def}}{=} \overline{a}\langle x\rangle.\mathcal{C}[\![Q]\!] \qquad (*)$$

After all, since all communications of higher-order values are transformed by $\mathcal{C}$ into communications of name-triggers, we already know that x will always be instantiated with one of these; then it seems that the original rule, introducing another name-trigger m is just adding a further level of indirection. But rule $(*)$ in general is *not* sound. Consider in fact

$$P \stackrel{\text{def}}{=} \boldsymbol{\nu}\, a\left(\overline{a}\langle F\rangle \mid a(X).\overline{b}\langle X\rangle.\overline{b}\langle X\rangle\right)$$
$$Q \stackrel{\text{def}}{=} \boldsymbol{\nu}\, a\left(\overline{a}\langle F\rangle \mid a(X).\overline{b}\langle F\rangle.\overline{b}\langle F\rangle\right)$$

Clearly P and Q are equivalent (they are strong barbed-congruent). But adopting rule $(*)$ their translation are not! In fact we have

$$\mathcal{C}[\![P]\!] \stackrel{\text{def}}{=} \boldsymbol{\nu}\, a\left(\overline{a}\langle m\rangle \{m := F\} \mid a(x).\overline{b}\langle x\rangle.\overline{b}\langle x\rangle\right)$$
$$\mathcal{C}[\![Q]\!] \stackrel{\text{def}}{=} \boldsymbol{\nu}\, a\left(\overline{a}\langle m\rangle \{m := F\} \mid a(x).(\overline{b}\langle m_1\rangle.\overline{b}\langle m_2\rangle \{m_2 := F\}) \{m_1 := F\}\right)$$

which can be distinguished since after the initial interaction, $\mathcal{C}[\![Q]\!]$ can perform two outputs of private (and hence distinct) names at b, whereas in $\mathcal{C}[\![P]\!]$ the two outputs at b communicate the same name. For similar reasons, the optimisation

$$\mathcal{C}[\![X\langle Y\rangle]\!] \stackrel{\text{def}}{=} \overline{x}\langle y\rangle.0$$

is not sound. For this, take the HOπ processes $c(X).\boldsymbol{\nu}\, a\left(a(Y).(X\langle Y\rangle \mid X\langle Y\rangle) \mid \overline{a}\langle F\rangle\right)$ and $c(X).\boldsymbol{\nu}\, a\left(a(Y).(X\langle F\rangle \mid X\langle F\rangle) \mid \overline{a}\langle F\rangle\right)$. They are equivalent, but their π-calculus translations would be distinguished by reasoning similarly as above.

There are however situations when the above optimisations are indeed sound; we leave for future work more precise answers to this issue.

7 Some uses of the compilation

We have given the faithfulness of $\mathcal{C}$ only w.r.t. barbed congruence. But we believe that $\mathcal{C}$ respects most of the well-known weak equivalences which admit a uniform definition over higher-order and first-order calculi, such as *testing equivalence* [10], or *refusal equivalence* [17]. The reason is the close operational correspondence between source and target agents of $\mathcal{C}$.

Indeed $\mathcal{C}$ might even be used to *define* equivalences in HOπ. Take for instance *trace semantics* [11], or *causal bisimulation* [9]. These, originally proposed for calculi without mobility, can easily be adapted to π-calculus. More delicate is their extension to a higher-order calculus; as usual, it is not obvious the condition to impose on higher-order outputs. However, if P and Q are HOπ processes and $\ll\gg$ is weak trace equivalence or weak causal bisimulation, we might define:

$$P \ll\gg Q \text{ if } \mathcal{C}[\![P]\!] \ll\gg \mathcal{C}[\![Q]\!]$$

and then look for a direct characterisation (i.e. not mentioning $\mathcal{C}$) of $\ll\gg$.

A nice application of Theorem 6.2 comes from the study of the λ-calculus encodings. We presented the encoding into HOπ in Section 3 (for the lazy λ-calculus). By applying compilation $\mathcal{C}$ we can turn this into a π-calculus encoding. The outcome is precisely Milner's [14]. This commutativity strengthens the naturalness of the translations involved. It means also that we can infer for Milner's encoding all results we can prove working with HOπ. We have used this in [18] to show that both encodings give rise to a λ-model in which a weak form of extensionality holds, and to obtain a direct characterisation of the equivalence induced on the λ-terms by the behavioural equivalence adopted on the process terms.

HOπ has been useful also to understand Milner's encoding of call-by-value λ-calculus into π-calculus. In his original work [14] two encodings were given, and it was not obvious which one should be preferred. When we tried to see if they factor through $\mathcal{C}$ and an encoding into HOπ, the relationship between the two became clear: We could pass from the first to the second encoding using the "false" optimisation ($*$) in section 6. Building on this and on the nonsoundness of ($*$), we have been able to prove that β reduction is not valid for the second encoding (i.e. the encodings of a term and of a β-derivative of its are not equivalent), which fairly reduces its importance. We doubt we could have obtained the rather sophisticated counterexample without going through HOπ.

8 Related work and directions for future research

The first attempt at encoding a higher-order process calculus into π-calculus was made by Thomsen. For this, he used Plain CHOCS (PC) which, as mentioned in Section 3.3, is a subcalculus of HOπ for the sorting $\{Name \mapsto (())\}$. Thomsen's study acted as stimulus and basis for our work. When applied to PC, our compilation $\mathcal{C}$ coincides with Thomsen's translation and in this sense can be seen as an extension of it. Recently, Thomsen's work has been resumed by Amadio [5], which adopts a different equivalence on PC. Our analysis, however, strengthens and completes both Amadio's and Thomsen's in various aspects. First, PC is a special case of a second-order language, whereas HOπ is of ω order. Second, to establish an operational correspondence between PC processes and their π-calculus encodings, they have to modify the semantics of the calculi; this seems rather arbitrary and obscures the meaning of the results obtained. Thirdly they do not get a full abstraction result, as we did in Theorem 6.2.

Expressiveness of π-calculus. Our study on the translation of HOπ and λ-calculus into π-calculus may be seen as just one aspect of a more general investigation into the expressiveness of π-calculus. For instance, it is not clear to us at what extent the results for compilation $\mathcal{C}$ depend upon the choice of the operators in HOπ and π-calculus. We think that in general we cannot remove the restriction on guardness for the sum. But we do not see this as a strong limitation. Besides yielding a simpler reduction semantics, guarded sums are easier to implement. Furthermore, in process algebras guarded sums are usually necessary to make a number of well-known equivalences, congruences w.r.t. the sum operator. Last but not least, they are justified by practical applications, which show that they give all needed expressiveness.

In general, it seems that the problems for the compilation mainly arise with *dynamic* operators, to which sum belongs (another example of dynamic operator is Lotos's disabling [7]).

Adding data to HOπ. The study conducted with the λ-calculus illustrates the usefulness of the abstraction power of HOπ w.r.t. the π-calculus. Such abstraction power could be increased by adding some (simple) form of data, like integers, booleans, or lists. Accordingly, the format of object sorts should be enriched to allow for data communications. Data should be taken into account also in the definition of the equivalences. The interesting thing is that $\mathcal{C}$ is easily generalisable to the extended HOπ, since data can be encoded in the π-calculus ([13, 15]). Then the proof that the faithfulness of $\mathcal{C}$ is maintained would give us confidence that what we are developing is sensible.

Semantics of object-oriented languages. Two interesting approaches to the denotational semantics of parallel object-oriented languages are exhibited in [2] and [20], using metric spaces and by translation into π-calculus, respectively. In both cases the source language is POOL [3]. Let us point out here their weaknesses. In the former, a heavy mathematical machinery, needed to ensure the well-definedness of the semantics. In the latter, the "flatness": There is no concept of type to give an overall idea of the use and the purpose of the various agents defined; and since π-calculus is "low-level", the protocols implementing interactions among different components sometimes are burdensome.

We would like to see if it is possible to gain some benefit by using the HOπ as target language. Higher-order sorts would play the role of types in [2]. The theory developed for the HOπ could be employed to reason on the semantic objects. The representation should be more succinct and readable than the one in [20], even more if data are added to HOπ as suggested above. As for λ-calculus, using $\mathcal{C}$ the two translations could be compared to see if and where they are different.

Acknowledgements.

I am most grateful to Robin Milner. This material was developed through a series of discussions with him. I wish to thank Matthew Hennessy, Benjamin Pierce and Gordon Plotkin for insightful comments; and Jean-Jacques Levy for having invited me to INRIA-Rocquencourt, where the paper has been written.

References

[1] Abramsky, S., The Lazy Lambda Calculus, *Research Topics in Functional Programming*, pp65–116, Addison Wesley, 1989.

[2] America, P. and de Bakker, J. and Kok, J. and Rutten, J., Denotational Semantics of a Parallel Object-Oriented Language, *Information and Computation*, 83(2), 1989.

[3] America, P., Issues in the Design of a Parallel Object-Oriented Language, *Formal Aspects of Computing*, 1(4), pp366–411, 1989.

[4] Astesiano, E. and Giovini, A., Generalized Bisimulation in Relational Specifications, *STACS 88*, LNCS 294, pp207–226, 1988.

[5] Amadio, R., A Uniform Presentation of CHOCS and π-calculus, Rapport de Recherche 1726, INRIA-Lorraine, Nancy, 1992.

[6] Berry, G. and Boudol, G., The Chemical Abstract Machine, *17th POPL*, 1990.

[7] Bolognesi, T. and Brinksma, E., Introduction to the ISO Specification Language LOTOS, in *The Formal Description Technique LOTOS*, North Holland, 1989.

[8] Boudol, G., Towards a Lambda Calculus for Concurrent and Communicating Systems, *TAPSOFT 89*, LNCS 351, pp149–161, 1989.

[9] Degano, P. and Darondeau, P., Causal Trees, *15th ICALP*, LNCS 372, pp234–248, 1989.

[10] De Nicola, R. and Hennessy, R., Testing Equivalences for Processes, *Theor. Comp. Sci.* 34, pp83–133, 1984.

[11] Hoare, C.A.R., *Communicating Sequential Processes*, Prentice Hall, 1985.

[12] Milner, R., *Communication and Concurrency*, Prentice Hall, 1989.

[13] Milner, R., The polyadic π-calculus: a tutorial, Technical Report ECS–LFCS–91–180, LFCS, Dept. of Comp. Sci. Edinburgh Univ., 1991.

[14] Milner, R., Functions as Processes, Technical Report 1154, INRIA Sofia-Antipolis, 1990. Final version in *Journal of Mathem. Structures in Computer Science* 2(2), pp119–141, 1992.

[15] Milner, R. and Parrow, J. and Walker, D., A Calculus of Mobile Processes, (Parts I and II), *Information and Computation*, 100, pp1-77, 1992.

[16] Milner, R. and Sangiorgi, D., Barbed Bisimulation, *19th ICALP*, LNCS 623, pp685–695, 1992.

[17] Phillips, I.C.C., Refusal Testings, *Theor. Comp. Sci.*, 50, pp241–284, 1987.

[18] Sangiorgi, D. *Expressing Mobility in Process Algebras: First-Order and Higher-Order Paradigms*, PhD thesis, Edinburgh Univ., 1992, to appear.

[19] Thomsen, B., *Calculi for Higher Order Communicating Systems*, PhD thesis, Dept. of Computing, Imperial College, 1990.

[20] Walker, D., π-calculus Semantics of Object-Oriented Programming Languages, Technical Report ECS-LFCS-90-122 LFCS, Dept. of Comp. Sci. Edinburgh Univ., 1990. Also in *Proc. Conference on Theoretical Aspects of Computer Software*, Tohoku University, Japan, Sept. 1991.

Hyperedge Replacement with Rendezvous

Gnanamalar David[†]
Frank Drewes[††]
Hans–Jörg Kreowski[††]

Universität Bremen
FB Mathematik und Informatik
Postfach 33 04 40
D-2800 Bremen 33

Abstract
In this paper, we introduce and study a rendezvous mechanism for parallel replacements of hyperedges by (hyperedge–decorated) graphs that allows some merging of the replacing graphs if the attachment of the replaced hyperedges shares some nodes. The main result shows that the rendezvous mechanism can increase the generative power of table–controlled parallel hyperedge replacement graph grammars (which themselves are more powerful than ordinary hyperedge replacement graph grammars).

0   Introduction

Hyperedge replacement (as introduced by Feder [Fed71], Pavlidis [Pav72] and others under various synonyms) is one of the easiest and best studied types of graph rewriting (see, e.g., Bauderon and Courcelle [BC87], Lengauer and Wanke [LW88] and Habel, Kreowski and Vogler [Hab89], [HK87], [HKV89]). Hyperedge replacement graph grammars combine an attractive generative power with interesting structural and decidability properties. To some extend, these nice properties result from the fact that hyperedge replacement is context–free in the sense of Courcelle [Cou87] (see also Habel [Hab89]). On the other hand, the generative power is not only restricted as one must expect from a context–free mode of rewriting, but also because the nature of hyperedge replacement causes certain limitations. For each generated graph language, for example, there is a positive integer k such that no member of the language is k-fold connected. Hence the set of all graphs, the set of all complete graphs, the set of all bipartite graphs and other graph languages of this kind cannot be generated by either sequential or parallel hyperedge replacement graph grammars.

In this paper, we introduce a rendezvous mechanism for parallel hyperedge replacement to overcome these limitations. If the attachments of some hyperedges share some nodes (called a "rendezvous"), their replacing graphs may be merged with each other

---

[†]The author thanks ÖSW, Bochum for its financial support which made his stay in Bremen possible.

[††]Partially supported by the ESPRIT Basic Research WG 3299 (COMPUGRAPH).

according to a predefined rendezvous specification. We show that the rendezvous mechanism can increase the generative power of table–controlled parallel hyperedge replacement graph grammars (which themselves are more powerful than ordinary hyperedge replacement grammars). Actually, we present a hyperedge replacement graph grammar with rendezvous generating the set of all complete graphs and one with a single table for the set of all graphs. The latter one uses only hyperedges of type 1, that is, hyperedges that point to only one node. Moreover, we show that for each table–controlled parallel hyperedge replacement graph grammar there exists a rendezvous table–controlled parallel hyperedge replacement graph grammar of order 2, that is, those using only hyperedges of type 2.

We use a parallel notion of replacement because this seems natural in order to explain the effect of the rendezvous specification. For other approaches to parallelism in the context of formal languages and graph grammars, see, e.g., Herman and Rozenberg [HR75], Ehrig, Kreowski and Taentzer [EK76], [ET92], Bailey, Cuny and Fisher [BCF91], and Nagl [Nag87].

1 Hyperedge Replacement

In this section, we recall the basic notions hyperedge replacement is built upon. We choose ordinary unlabelled undirected graphs without loops and multiple edges as basic structures of interest. To generate sets of graphs, these graphs become decorated with hyperedges each of which has a label and is attached to several nodes of the graph. Further, every such (hyperedge–)decorated graph has a sequence of so-called external nodes. These external nodes are needed to define the replacement of a hyperedge by a (decorated) graph. Every hyperedge of a decorated graph serves as a placeholder for a graph or — recursively — for another decorated graph, which can replace the hyperedge by fusing its external nodes with those the hyperedge is attached to.

1.1 Definition (graph)
A *graph* is a pair (V, E) where V is a finite set of *nodes* (or *vertices*) and E is a set of 2–elements subsets of V, called *edges*. The set of all graphs is denoted by $\mathcal{G}_0$. □

1.2 Definition (decorated graph)
Let N be a set of *nonterminal labels* each element A of which is associated with a natural number, its *type*, denoted by $type(A)$.

A (hyperedge–)*decorated graph* (over N) is a system $H = (V, E, Y, lab, att, ext)$ where

- (V, E) is in $\mathcal{G}_0$, called the *underlying graph* $U(H)$ of H,
- Y is a finite set of *hyperedges*,
- $lab : Y \rightarrow N$ is a mapping, called the *labelling*,
- $att : Y \rightarrow V^*$ is a mapping (called the *attachment*) such that $|att(y)|^1 = type(lab(y))$ for all $y \in Y$,
- $ext \in V^*$, called the (sequence of) *external nodes*.

---

[1]Given $v \in V^*, |v|$ denotes the length of v.

Remarks.

1. If H is a decorated graph we denote its components by V_H, E_H, Y_H, lab_H, att_H and ext_H (unless they are explicitly named).

2. A set N of nonterminals as above will be called *typed* in the following.

3. We let $type(H) = |ext|$ and for every $y \in Y_H$ we define $type_H(y) = type(lab(y))$.

4. The set of all decorated graphs of type k over N is denoted by $\mathcal{G}_k(N)$, and $\mathcal{G}(N)$ denotes $\bigcup_{k \in \mathbb{N}} \mathcal{G}_k(N)$.

5. For every label A we set $[A] = \{1, \ldots, type(A)\}$. Accordingly, for a hyperedge $y \in Y_H$, let $[y]_H = [lab_H(y)]$.

6. For $A \in N$ the decorated graph $([A], \emptyset, \{y\}, lab, att, ext)$ with $lab(y) = A$ and $att(y) = ext = 1 \ldots type(A)$ is called a *handle* and denoted by $A^\bullet$. □

Two decorated graphs are said to be isomorphic if there is an isomorphism between the underlying graphs preserving external nodes, and there is a bijective mapping between their hyperedges which is consistent with the graph isomorphism.

1.3 Definition (isomorphic decorated graphs)
Two decorated graphs H and H' are *isomorphic*, denoted by $H \cong H'$, if there are bijective mappings $f : V_H \to V_{H'}$ and $g : Y_H \to Y_{H'}$ such that $E_{H'} = \{\{f(x), f(y)\} \mid \{x, y\} \in E_H\}$, $lab_H(y) = lab_{H'}(g(y))$ and $f^*(att_H(y)) = att_{H'}(g(y))$ for all $y \in Y_H$, and $f^*(ext_H) = ext_{H'}$, where f^* is the natural extension of f to sequences. □

1.4 Example (hyperedge–decorated graph)
The picture below shows a decorated graph consisting of a graph on six vertices having six edges together with four hyperedges. Its external nodes are drawn with numbers inside which indicate their order. The hyperedges are labelled with A, B, and C, and the order on their tentacles is again indicated by numbers. The type of this decorated graph as well as that of the A–labelled hyperedge is 3, while the hyperedges labelled with B are of type 2 and the one labelled with C is of type 1.

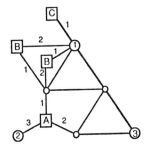

□

Next we define some frequently used operations on decorated graphs.

1.5 Definition (operations on decorated graphs)
Let $H, H' \in \mathcal{G}(N)$.

1. Let $B \subseteq Y_H$. Then the *removal* of B from H yields the decorated graph

$$H - B = (V_H, E_H, Y_H - B, lab, att, ext_H)$$

with $lab(y) = lab_H(y)$ and $att(y) = att_H(y)$ for all $y \in Y_H - B$.

2. The *disjoint union* of H and H' is the decorated graph

$$H + H' = (V_H \mathbin{\mathring{\cup}} V_{H'}, E_H \mathbin{\mathring{\cup}} E_{H'}, Y_H \mathbin{\mathring{\cup}} Y_{H'}, lab, att, ext_H)$$

with $lab(y) = lab_H(y)$ and $att(y) = att_H(y)$ for all $y \in Y_H$ and $lab(y) = lab_{H'}(y)$ and $att(y) = att_{H'}(y)$ for all $y \in Y_{H'}$. Here $\mathring{\cup}$ denotes the disjoint union of sets. (Observe that the disjoint union of decorated graphs is not commutative.) For $H_1, \ldots, H_n \in \mathcal{G}(N)$, $\sum_{i=1}^{n} H_i$ means $H_1 + H_2 + \ldots + H_n$.

3. Let $f : V_H \to V$ be a mapping for some set V. Then the *nodes–set exchange* in H through f yields the decorated graph

$$H/f = (V, E, Y_H, lab_H, att, ext)$$

with $E = \{\{f(x), f(y)\} \mid \{x, y\} \in E_H, f(x) \neq f(y)\}$, $att(y) = f^*(att_H(y))$ for all $y \in Y_H$, and $ext = f^*(ext_H)$, where f^* is the natural extension of f to sequences.

4. Let δ be a binary relation on V_H, let V be the quotient set of V_H through the equivalence relation generated by δ with natural mapping $nat : V_H \to V$. Then H/nat is called the *nodes fusion* according to δ, and is also denoted by H/δ. If $u, v \in V_H^*$, $u = u_1 \cdots u_n$ and $v = v_1 \cdots v_n$, and $\delta = \{(u_i, v_i) \mid 1 \leq i \leq n\}$, we also write $H/(u = v)$ instead of H/δ. $\square$

With the help of the operations just defined we now explain hyperedge replacement. We will restrict ourselves to the parallel mode of rewriting, i.e., we always replace all hyperedges occurring in a decorated graph simultaneously.

1.6 Definition (parallel hyperedge replacement)
Let $H \in \mathcal{G}(N)$ and let $repl : Y_H \to \mathcal{G}(N)$ be a mapping with $type_H(y) = type(repl(y))$ for $y \in Y_H$.

The *replacement* of $Y_H = \{y_1, \ldots, y_n\}$ in H through $repl$ yields the decorated graph

$$\mathrm{REPLACE}(H, repl) = \left((H - Y_H) + \sum_{i=1}^{n} repl(y_i) \right) \Big/ (att = ext)$$

with $att = att(y_1) \cdots att(y_n)$ and $ext = ext_{repl(y_1)} \cdots ext_{repl(y_n)}$.

Remarks.

1. Parallel hyperedge replacement is a simple construction where the hyperedges of a decorated graph are removed, the associated decorated graphs are added disjointly and their external nodes are fused with the corresponding nodes formerly attached to the replaced hyperedges.

2. Note that the component graphs replacing the hyperedges are fully embedded into the resulting graph where their external nodes loose this status.

3. If a mapping $repl : Y_H \to \mathcal{G}(N)$ meets the assumption of the definition, it will be referred to as *well-typed*. $\square$

2 Parallel hyperedge replacement grammars

In this section hyperedge replacement with rendezvous is introduced. The basic model to which the notion of rendezvous is added is HTOL hyperedge replacement. The letter H refers to the hybrid type of graphs where hyperedges are rewritten while undirected edges remain unchanged. The letter T indicates that the considered grammars provide sets of tables where each table is a set of productions, and OL refers to the type of rewriting of OL systems (see, e.g., Rozenberg and Salomaa [RS80]) which was adapted to hyperedge replacement by Kreowski [Kre92].

We first define rendezvous functions. These are functions between binary relations.

2.1 Definition (rendezvous function)
Let I, I', J, J' be sets.

A *rendezvous function* is a function $r : \mathcal{P}(I \times I') \rightarrow \mathcal{P}(J \times J')$.

Here, $\mathcal{P}(S)$ denotes the powerset of a set S.

Remark.

The constant rendezvous function that always yields some fixed binary relation B is denoted by B itself.[2] In particular, $\emptyset$ denotes the rendezvous function assigning $\emptyset$ to every argument. □

2.2 Definition (production, table set, rendezvous specification)
1. A *production* (over N) is a pair $p = (A, R)$ with $A \in N$ and $R \in \mathcal{G}(N)$. A is called the *left-hand side* of p and denoted by $lhs(p)$. R is called the *right-hand side* and denoted by $rhs(p)$. A finite set of productions is called a *table*, and a set of such tables is a *table set*.

2. Let $\mathcal{T}$ be a table set. A *rendezvous specification* for $\mathcal{T}$ is a function $\mathcal{R}$ which assigns to every table $P \in \mathcal{T}$ and every pair $(p, p') \in P \times P$ a rendezvous function $\mathcal{R}_P(p, p')$ from $\mathcal{P}([lhs(p)] \times [lhs(p')])$ to $\mathcal{P}(V_{rhs(p)} \times V_{rhs(p')})$.

Remarks.
1. For every decorated graph H and all $y, y' \in Y_H$ we denote by $\rho_H(y, y')$ the binary relation
$$\rho_H(y, y') = \{(i, j) \in [y]_H \times [y']_H \mid att_H(y)_i = att_H(y')_j\}.$$
We call $\rho_H(y, y')$ the *rendezvous* of y and y' (in H). It is the binary relation describing which of the tentacles of y and y' are attached to the same node in H.

2. If $P \in \mathcal{T}$ and $\mathcal{R}_P(p, p') = r$ for some rendezvous function r and all $p, p' \in P$ we may write $\mathcal{R}_P = r$. □

A rendezvous specification will be used as follows. Whenever the hyperedges of a decorated graph are replaced, for each pair of these hyperedges their rendezvous is determined. Afterwards, the hyperedges are replaced by the right-hand sides of the productions. In addition, nodes are fused if they are related to each other by

---

[2]Of course, this notation is ambiguous since it does not distinguish between rendezvous functions having different domains and/or ranges. However, for our purposes it is not necessary to make a difference here.

$\mathcal{R}_P(p, p')(\rho)$, for every pair of productions applied, and where ρ is the rendezvous of the replaced hyperedges.

We now define hyperedge replacement with rendezvous formally.

2.3 Definition (hyperedge replacement with rendezvous)

Let $H, H' \in \mathcal{G}(N)$, let $\mathcal{T}$ be a table set and let $\mathcal{R}$ be some rendezvous specification for $\mathcal{T}$.

1. A mapping $b : Y_H \to P$ with $P \in \mathcal{T}$ is called an *L-base* (over $\mathcal{T}$) in H if the mapping $repl$ defined by $repl(y) = rhs(b(y))$ for all $y \in Y_H$ is well-typed.

2. For every L-base $b : Y_H \to P$ over $\mathcal{T}$ we define

$$\mathcal{R}(H, b) = \bigcup_{y, y' \in Y_H} \mathcal{R}_P(b(y), b(y'))(\rho_H(y, y')).$$

3. Let $b : Y_H \to P$ an L-base over $\mathcal{T}$ in H. Then there is a *direct derivation* $H \underset{P, \mathcal{R}}{\Longrightarrow} H'$ *through* b if

$$H' \cong \mathrm{REPLACE}(H, repl)/\mathcal{R}(H, b),$$

with $repl : Y_H \to \mathcal{G}(N)$ defined by $repl(y) = rhs(b(y))$ for all $y \in Y_H$.

4. A sequence of direct derivations of the form $H_0 \underset{P_1, \mathcal{R}}{\Longrightarrow} H_1 \underset{P_2, \mathcal{R}}{\Longrightarrow} \cdots \underset{P_k, \mathcal{R}}{\Longrightarrow} H_k$ with $P_1, \ldots, P_k \in \mathcal{T}$ is called a *derivation* (of *length* k) from H_0 to H_k and is denoted by $H_0 \underset{\mathcal{T}, \mathcal{R}}{\overset{k}{\Longrightarrow}} H_k$. If $H \cong H'$, this may be denoted by $H \underset{\mathcal{T}, \mathcal{R}}{\overset{0}{\Longrightarrow}} H'$. If k in $H \underset{\mathcal{T}, \mathcal{R}}{\overset{k}{\Longrightarrow}} H'$ does not matter, it may be replaced by a star symbol. $\square$

2.4 Definition (hyperedge-replacement grammars with rendezvous)

1. A *hybrid table–controlled OL hyperedge replacement grammar with rendezvous* (an *RHTOL HR grammar*) is a system $G = (N, \mathcal{T}, \mathcal{R}, Z)$ where N is a typed set of nonterminals, $\mathcal{T}$ is a finite table set, $\mathcal{R}$ is a rendezvous specification for $\mathcal{T}$, and $Z \in \mathcal{G}_0(N)$, called the *axiom*. If $Z = S^\bullet$ for some $S \in N$ we may denote G by $(N, \mathcal{T}, \mathcal{R}, S)$.

2. Given such a grammar, the *generated graph language* consists of all graphs derivable from Z, i.e.,

$$L(G) = \{H \in \mathcal{G}_0 \mid Z \underset{\mathcal{T}, \mathcal{R}}{\overset{*}{\Longrightarrow}} H\}.$$

Remarks.

1. G is said to be *of order k* if k is the least natural number satisfying $type(A) \le k$ for all $A \in N$.

2. If $\mathcal{C}$ is a class of RHTOL HR grammars we denote by $\mathcal{L}(\mathcal{C})$ the set $\{L(G) \mid G \in \mathcal{C}\}$ and by $\mathcal{C}_i$ the set of all grammars in $\mathcal{C}$ of order not greater than i.

3. $\mathcal{HTOL}$ denotes the class of RHTOL HR grammars with trivial rendezvous specification. That is, $\mathcal{R}_P = \emptyset$ for all tables. $\mathcal{RHOL}$ denotes the class of RHTOL HR grammars with a single table and $\mathcal{HOL}$ denotes the intersection of $\mathcal{HTOL}$ and $\mathcal{RHOL}$. $\square$

The classes $\mathcal{HTOL}$ and $\mathcal{HOL}$ compare to the respective classes introduced by Kreowski [Kre92]. Kreowski proves in particular that $\mathcal{L}(\mathcal{HOL})$ is properly included in $\mathcal{L}(\mathcal{HTOL})$. HOL HR grammars in turn have the same language generative power as ordinary sequential hyperedge replacement grammars.[3]

The construction used for the rendezvous mechanism reminds of earlier work on amalgamation of graph productions by Boehm, Fonio and Habel [BFH87] (see also Degano and Montanari [DM87]). However, whereas amalgamation is used to build new productions out of given ones (and new derivations out of given ones), the rendezvous mechanism influences the result of a (parallel) rewriting step. Whereas the main theorem obtained by Boehm, Fonio and Habel is that amalgamation does not change the generated graphs the idea behind rendezvous is to increase the generative power of hyperedge replacement. So, rendezvous and amalgamation are actually not as closely related as it could seem at first sight.

3 Examples

In this section we present some examples of RHTOL HR grammars. The first grammar generates all square grids, the second one all complete graphs and the third one all graphs.

3.1 Example (generation of square grids)
The RHTOL HR grammar $GRID = (\{A, B\}, \{P_1, P_2\}, \mathcal{R}, Z)$, which generates the set of all square grids, is defined as follows.

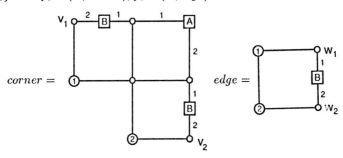

$P_1 = \{p_c, p_e\}$ with $p_c = (A, corner)$, $p_e = (B, edge)$ and

$$\mathcal{R}_{P_1}(p_c, p_e)(\rho) = \begin{cases} \{(v_i, w_1)\} & \text{if } \rho = \{(i, 1)\} \\ \emptyset & \text{otherwise,} \end{cases}$$

---

[3]To be precise, one ought to say that $\mathcal{HOL}$ compares to the set of all hyperedge-replacement grammars where only *canonical derivations* in the sense of Kreowski [Kre87] are allowed. From the viewpoint of generated languages, however, this makes no difference.

$$\mathcal{R}_{P_1}(p_c, p_e)(\rho) = \begin{cases} \{(w_1, w_2)\} & \text{if } \rho = \{(1,2)\} \\ \emptyset & \text{otherwise} \end{cases}$$

and $\mathcal{R}_{P_1} = \emptyset$ otherwise.

$P_2 = \{p'_c, p'_e\}$ with $p'_c = (A, corner')$, $p'_e = (B, edge')$ and

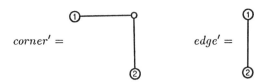

and $\mathcal{R}_{P_2} = \emptyset$.

The first three derivations in $GRID$ are illustrated below.

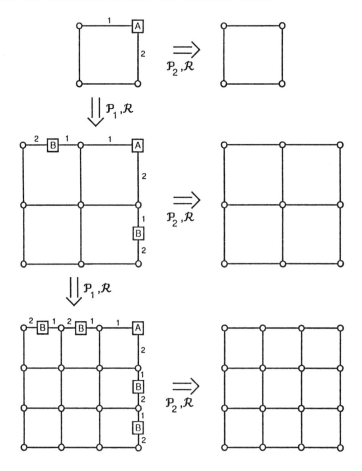

If we take the empty rendezvous specification $\emptyset$ instead of $\mathcal{R}$ (i.e., if we consider the derivations without rendezvous) we get instead derivations of the following kind.

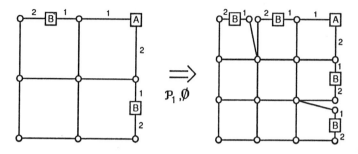

The language generated by $GRID$ is the set of all square grids:

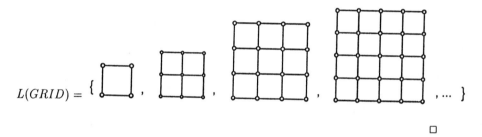

$$L(GRID) = \{ \quad , \quad , \quad , \quad , \ldots \}$$

$\square$

3.2 Example (generation of all complete graphs)
In order to generate the set of all complete graphs the RHTOL HR grammar K given by $K = (\{A\}, \{P_1, P_2\}, \mathcal{R}, A)$ can be used. Its components are defined as follows.

$P_1 = \{p_{new}\}$, $P_2 = \{p_{del}\}$ where $p_{new} = (A, new)$ and $p_{del} = (A, del)$ with

$$new = \qquad\qquad del = \textcircled{1}_V$$

and $\mathcal{R}_{P_1} = \{(v, v)\}$, $\mathcal{R}_{P_2} = \emptyset$.

This grammar generates the set of all complete graphs in the following way. In every intermediate graph, all nodes carry at least one A-labelled hyperedge. Each such hyperedge generates a new node v which is connected with the old one by an edge. By the rendezvous specification, all the new nodes are merged into one, which is thus connected with every old one. $\square$

3.3 Example (generation of all graphs)

Using basically the same idea as above we obtain $ALL = (\{A\}, \{P_1, P_2\}, \mathcal{R}, A)$ which generates the set of all graphs. We let P_2 be as in K, $P_1 = \{p_{new}, p'_{new}\}$, with p_{new} as above and $p'_{new} = (A, new')$ where

$$v \circ\!\!-\!\!-\!\!-\!\!-\!\!\boxed{A}$$

$$new' =$$

$$\textcircled{1}\!\!-\!\!-\!\!-\!\!-\!\!\boxed{A}$$

and, again, $\mathcal{R}_{P_1} = \{(v, v)\}$, $\mathcal{R}_{P_2} = \emptyset$. $\qquad\square$

4 Internal Rendezvous

As mentioned in the introduction one of the main limitations of hyperedge replacement stems from the fact that, if two hyperedges are replaced by some graphs, the newly introduced parts cannot be connected directly. The examples in Section 3 indicate that the rendezvous mechanism enables us to overcome this disadvantage. On the other hand, the examples do not fully exploit the power of the new notion because we never merge "old" parts, that is, external nodes of the right-hand sides. In fact, rendezvous in its most general form seems to exceed our initial intention: Not only are we able to introduce dependencies between new nodes created from different hyperedges in a parallel step; it is also possible to let the graph shrink by fusing old nodes. This is why it is quite unclear how the membership problem can be solved for arbitrary RHTOL HR languages. Because of these reasons the class of RHTOL HR grammars in which only internal nodes (that is, nodes that are not external ones) are merged by the rendezvous specification is of special interest.

4.1 Definition (hyperedge replacement with internal rendezvous)

The class $\mathcal{IHTOL}$ is the set of all RHTOL HR grammars with internal rendezvous (IHTOL HR grammars). An RHTOL HR grammar $(N, \mathcal{T}, \mathcal{R}, Z)$ is in $\mathcal{IHTOL}$ if we have for all $P \in \mathcal{T}$, $p_1, p_2 \in P$, $\rho \subseteq [lhs(p_1)] \times [lhs(p_2)]$ and $(v_1, v_2) \in \mathcal{R}_P(p_1, p_2)(\rho)$ that v_i is an internal node of p_i (for $i = 1, 2$).

We have the following theorem.

4.2 Theorem

Let $G \in \mathcal{IHTOL}$ be such that every right-hand side of a production in G contains at least one internal node. Then the membership problem for G is decidable.

Proof. In each parallel step in G the size (= number of nodes) of the generated graph increases because only internal nodes are affected by the rendezvous and every right-hand side contains (at least) one internal node. (The "worst case" is that all the internal nodes get merged, yielding one new node.) But this means that an easy modification of the well-known algorithm to recognize context-sensitive string languages can be used to recognize $L(G)$. This algorithm produces all derivations that yield graphs of the input graph's size and decides whether one of the generated graphs is isomorphic to the input graph. $\qquad\square$

The reader should notice that all our examples are of the form required by Theorem 4.2. It is an interesting question whether the theorem can be extended to all IHTOL HR grammars, without the requirement of producing at least one new node in each step.

5 The generating power of RHTOL HR grammars

In this section we investigate the power of RHTOL HR grammars. In particular, we prove two theorems. The first one states that there are languages which can be generated by grammars in $\mathcal{IHOL}_1$, i.e., very restricted IHTOL HR grammars that generate languages which cannot be generated by HTOL HR grammars. As a second result of this section we prove that every language generated by an HTOL HR grammar can also be generated by an RHTOL HR grammar of order 2.

The theorem below follows from the fact that — as shown in Example 3.3 — there is a grammar $G \in \mathcal{IHTOL}_1$ generating $\mathcal{G}_0$.

5.1 Theorem

$$\mathcal{L}(\mathcal{IHOL}_1) \setminus \mathcal{L}(\mathcal{HTOL}) \neq \emptyset$$

Proof. For every $G = (N, T, \mathcal{R}, Z) \in \mathcal{IHTOL}$ let $G_\mathsf{U} = (N, \{P\}, \mathcal{R}', Z)$, where $P = \bigcup T$ and

$$\mathcal{R}'_P(p, p') = \begin{cases} \mathcal{R}_{P'}(p, p') & \text{if } p, p' \in P' \text{ for some } P' \in T \\ \emptyset & \text{if there is no such } P' \in T. \end{cases}$$

Obviously, G_U is in $\mathcal{IHOL}$ and we have $L(G) \subseteq L(G_\mathsf{U})$ since every derivation in G is also admissible in G_U. Applying this to the IHTOL HR grammar ALL from Example 3.3 we get $L(ALL) \subseteq L(ALL_\mathsf{U}) \in \mathcal{IHOL}_1$. Since $L(ALL) = \mathcal{G}_0$ this means $L(ALL) = L(ALL_\mathsf{U}) = \mathcal{G}_0$. It remains to show that there is no $G' \in \mathcal{HTOL}$ generating $\mathcal{G}_0$. By the above for all $G' \in \mathcal{HTOL}$ we have $L(G') \subseteq L(G'_\mathsf{U}) \in \mathcal{HOL}$. However, it is well-known that there is no hyperedge-replacement grammar generating $\mathcal{G}_0$ [Hab89], that is, no grammar in $\mathcal{HOL}$ generates $\mathcal{G}_0$. □

Our next theorem states that for every IITOL HR grammar there is an equivalent RHTOL HR grammar of order 2.

5.2 Theorem

$$\mathcal{L}(\mathcal{HTOL}) \subseteq \mathcal{L}(\mathcal{RHTOL}_2)$$

Proof. Let $G = (N, T, \mathcal{R}, Z)$ be of order k. In the following we will define the components of the RHTOL HR grammar $G' = (N', T', \mathcal{R}', Z')$ satisfying $L(G') = L(G)$. Let $N' = \{\hat{A} \mid A \in N\} \mathring{\cup} \{1, \ldots, k\}$, where all labels are of type 2.

The basic idea of the proof is as follows. Consider any A-labelled hyperedge y of type m occurring in Z or in a production, such as the one depicted in the left-hand side below.

This hyperedge will be replaced by the "bipartite" decorated graph in the right-hand side above. Here, the middle node is an auxiliary, new node. The hyperedge labelled $\hat{A}$ (which is attached to the first attached node of y) now gets replaced as y got before, but with the slight modification that only the first external node of the replacing right-hand side remains an external node. All others become ordinary nodes. Hence additional identifications are necessary: the ith attached node of y has to be fused with the node which was the ith external one of the right-hand side before. This is easily done by a rendezvous relation for a $(1,1)$-rendezvous between the $\hat{A}$-labelled and the i-labelled hyperedge.

For each decorated graph $H = (V, E, Y, lab, att, ext)$ let $f(H) = (V', E, Y', lab', att', ext)$, where

$$V' \quad = \quad V \mathbin{\mathring{\cup}} \{v_y \mid y \in Y\}$$

$$Y' \quad = \quad \bigcup_{y \in Y} \{y_i \mid i \in [y]_H\}$$

$$att'(y_i) \quad = \quad v_y att(y)_i \text{ and}$$

$$lab'(y_i) \quad = \quad \begin{cases} \widehat{lab(y)} & \text{if } i = 1 \\ i & \text{if } 2 \le i \le type_H(y). \end{cases}$$

Now define for each production $p = (A, R) \in P \in \mathcal{T}$ a production $\hat{p} = (\hat{A}, \hat{R})$ as follows. If $f(R) = (V, E, Y, lab, att, ext)$ then

$$\hat{R} = (V \mathbin{\mathring{\cup}} \{mid\}, E, Y, lab, att, mid\, ext_1)$$

Furthermore, let $q_i = (i, i^\bullet - Y_{i\bullet})$, for $i = 2, \ldots, k$. For every $P \in \mathcal{T}$ we set

$$\hat{P} = \{\hat{p} \mid p \in P\} \cup \{q_i \mid i = 2, \ldots, k\}.$$

Now $\mathcal{T}' = \{\hat{P} \mid P \in \mathcal{T}\}$. For every $\hat{p} \in \hat{P} \in \mathcal{T}'$ and for all q_i, $2 \le i \le m$, where $ext_{rhs(p)} = v_1 \ldots v_m$ and $ext_{rhs(q_i)} = v\, v'$, we define

$$\mathcal{R}'_P(\hat{p}, q_i)(eq) = \begin{cases} \{(v_i, v'), (v_1, v)\} & \text{if } eq = \{(1,1)\} \\ \emptyset & \text{otherwise.} \end{cases}$$

For all other pairs $p, p' \in P$ we let $\mathcal{R}'_P(p, p') = \emptyset$. Finally, let $Z' = f(Z)$.

It remains to prove that $L(G') = L(G)$. For this, it suffices to show that for all decorated graphs $H, H' \in \mathcal{G}(N)$ there is a direct derivation $H \underset{\mathcal{T}, \mathcal{R}}{\Longrightarrow} H'$ if and only if $f(H) \underset{\mathcal{T}', \mathcal{R}'}{\Longrightarrow} f(H')$, since by definition of f we have $f(H) = H$ if $Y_H = \emptyset$.

Since $\mathcal{R}'$ is empty except for the rendezvous $\{(1,1)\}$ two replacements of hyperedges $y_1, y_2 \in Y_{f(H)}$ are not affected by the rendezvous unless they stem from the same hyperedge in H. Hence by context-freeness of hyperedge replacement we may without loss of generality assume that H is a handle $A^\bullet$. Let $f(R) = (V, E, Y, lab, att, ext)$ and let $p = (A, R) \in P$ be the production applied to $A^\bullet$ in order to derive H'. Then $H' \cong R$, hence $f(H') \cong f(R)$. Let $b : Y_{f(H)} \to \hat{P}$ be defined by

$$repl(y) = \begin{cases} \hat{p} & \text{if } lab_{f(H)}(y) = \hat{A} \\ q_i & \text{if } lab_{f(H)}(y) = i. \end{cases}$$

With $m = type(A)$, $ext_H = v_1 \ldots v_m$, and $Y_H = \{y\}$ we have

$$f(H) \underset{T,\emptyset}{\Longrightarrow} (V \mathbin{\overset{\circ}{\cup}} \{v_y, v_2, \ldots, v_m\}, E, Y, lab, att, v_1 \ldots v_m)$$

through b. Since the rendezvous of each two hyeredges of $f(H)$ is $\{(1,1)\}$, $\mathcal{R}'(f(H), b)$ identifies v_y with v_1 and every v_i with ext_i, for $i = 2, \ldots, m$. (Observe that $v_1 = ext_1$, anyway.) Thus

$$f(H) \underset{T,\mathcal{R}'}{\Longrightarrow} (V, E, Y, lab, att, ext_1 \ldots ext_m) = f(R) \cong f(H')$$

as asserted.

For the other direction let $f(H) = f(A^\bullet) \underset{T',\mathcal{R}'}{\Longrightarrow} H''$. Then $Y_{f(H)} = \{y_1, \ldots, y_m\}$, where y_1 is labelled by $\hat{A}$ and for each i, $2 \le i \le m$, y_i is labelled by i. So the L-base b' used in this direct derivation must have the form

$$b'(y_i) = \begin{cases} \hat{p} & \text{if } i = 1 \\ q_i & \text{if } i > 1 \end{cases}$$

for some $\hat{p}$ and $\hat{P}$ with $\hat{p} \in \hat{P} \in T'$. Hence b defined by $b(y) = p$ is an L-base over T in $H = A^\bullet$ since $p \in P \in T$. Now $H \underset{T,\mathcal{R}}{\Longrightarrow} H'$ through b, for some $H' \in \mathcal{G}(N)$. By the first part of the proof this means $f(H) \underset{T',\mathcal{R}'}{\Longrightarrow} f(H')$ through b', so $H'' \cong f(H')$. $\square$

Observe that the proof of Theorem 5.2 relies heavily on the fact that external nodes are merged by the rendezvous specification. There seems to be no way to achive this effect using an IHTOL$_2$ HR grammar. We have the following corollary summerizing the (proper) inclusions known so far.

5.3 Corollary

1. $\mathcal{L}(\mathcal{HOL}) \subset \mathcal{L}(\mathcal{HTOL}) \subset \dfrac{\mathcal{L}(\mathcal{IHTOL})}{\mathcal{L}(\mathcal{RHTOL}_2)} \subseteq \mathcal{L}(\mathcal{RHTOL})$

2. $\mathcal{L}(\mathcal{HOL}) \subset \mathcal{L}(\mathcal{IHOL}) \subseteq \mathcal{L}(\mathcal{RHOL}) \subseteq \mathcal{L}(\mathcal{RHTOL})$.

Proof. The properness of $\mathcal{L}(\mathcal{HOL}) \subseteq \mathcal{L}(\mathcal{HTOL})$ was shown by Kreowski [Kre92]. Theorem 5.1 yields both $\mathcal{L}(\mathcal{HTOL}) \subset \mathcal{L}(\mathcal{IHTOL})$ and $\mathcal{L}(\mathcal{HOL}) \subset \mathcal{L}(\mathcal{IHOL})$ and $\mathcal{L}(\mathcal{HTOL}) \subset \mathcal{L}(\mathcal{RHTOL}_2)$ is the statement of Theorem 5.2. $\square$

6 Conclusion

This paper presents the very first steps of the investigation of hyperedge replacement with rendezvous. The rendezvous mechanism allows to overcome certain limitations of the generative power of hyperedge replacement grammars without rendezvous. The following are open problems for further consideration:

1. The summarizing Corollary 5.3 leaves the following questions: Are $\mathcal{L}(\mathcal{RHOL})$ and $\mathcal{L}(\mathcal{IHTOL})$ properly included in $\mathcal{L}(\mathcal{RHTOL})$ or not? Is $\mathcal{L}(\mathcal{HTOL})$ included in $\mathcal{L}(\mathcal{RHOL})$ or even in $\mathcal{L}(\mathcal{IHOL})$?

2. The generative power of ordinary hyperedge–replacement graph grammars increases with the order. Is this also the case if the grammars employ the rendezvous mechanism? The authors conjecture that this should be true for $\mathcal{IHTOL}$ but false for $\mathcal{RHTOL}$. (For the latter a proof similar to the one for Theorem 5.2 may be possible but the extension is not trivial.)

3. Is there a sort of "context-freeness lemma" for $\mathcal{IHTOL}$? Which are other interesting special cases of the rendezvous mechanism that increase the generative power of hyperedge replacement but do not destroy all the theory?

4. More explicitly speaking, which of the rich structural and decidability results of hyperedge–replacement grammars and languages can be carried over or adapted to the case of grammars with rendezvous or subclasses of it?

References

[BC87]   M. Bauderon, B. Courcelle. *Graph Expressions and Graph Rewriting. Mathematical Systems Theory*, 20, 83–127, 1987.

[BCF91] D. Bailey, J. Cuny, C. Fischer. *Programming with Very Large Graphs. Lecture Notes in Computer Science*, volume 532, 84–97, 1991.

[BFH87] P. Boehm, H.-R. Fonio, A. Habel. *Amalgamation of Graph Transformations: A Synchronization Mechanism. Journal of Computer and System Sciences*, 34, 377–408, 1987.

[Cou87] B. Courcelle. *An Axiomatic Definition of Context-Free Rewriting and its Application to NLC Graph Grammars. Theoretical Computer Science*, 55, 141–1812, 1987.

[DM87]   P. Degano, U. Montanari. *A Model of Distributed Systems based on Graph Rewriting. Journ. ACM*, 34, 411–449, 1987.

[EK76]   H. Ehrig, H.-J. Kreowski. *Parallel Graph Grammars*. In A. Lindenmayer, G. Rozenberg, editors, *Automata, Languages, Development*, 425–442. North Holland, Amsterdam, 1976.

[ET92]   H. Ehrig, G. Taentzer. *From Parallel Graph Grammars to Parallel High-Level Replacement Systems*. In G. Rozenberg, A. Salomaa, editors, *Lindenmayer Systems*, 283–304. Springer, 1992.

[Fed71]   J. Feder. *Plex Languages. Inform. Sci.*, 3, 225–241, 1971.

[Hab89]   A. Habel. *Hyperedge Replacement: Grammars and Languages*. PhD thesis, Bremen, 1989.

[HK87]   A. Habel, H.-J. Kreowski. *Some Structural Aspects of Hypergraph Languages Generated by Hyperedge Replacement. Lecture Notes in Computer Science*, volume 247, 207–219, 1987.

[HKV89]   A. Habel, H.-J. Kreowski, W. Vogler. *Metatheorems for Decision Problems on Hyperedge Replacement Graph Languages. Acta Informatica*, 26, 657–677, 1989.

[HR75]   G.T. Herman, G Rozenberg. *Developmental Systems and Languages*. North Holland/American Elsevier, New York, 1975.

[Kre87]   H.-J. Kreowski. *Is Parallelism Already Concurrency? Part 1: Derivations in Graph Grammars. Lecture Notes in Computer Science*, volume 291, 343–360, 1987.

[Kre92]   H.-J. Kreowski. *Parallel Hyperedge Replacement*. In G. Rozenberg, A. Salomaa, editors, *Lindenmayer Systems*, 271–282. Springer, 1992.

[LW88]   T. Lengauer, E. Wanke. *Efficient Analysis of Graph Properties on Context–Free Graph Languages. Lecture Notes in Computer Science*, volume 317, 379–393, 1988.

[Nag87]   M. Nagl. *Set Theoretic Approaches to Graph Grammars. Lecture Notes in Computer Science*, volume 291, 41–54, 1987.

[Pav72]   T. Pavlidis. *Linear and Context–Free Graph Grammars. Journ. ACM*, 19(1), 11–23, 1972.

[RS80]   G. Rozenberg, A. Salomaa. *The Mathematical Theory of L Systems*. Academic Press, New York, 1980.

True Concurrency Semantics for a Linear Logic Programming Language with Broadcast Communication

Jean-Marc Andreoli, Lone Leth, Remo Pareschi and Bent Thomsen

European Computer-Industry Research Center,
Arabellastrasse 17, D-8000 Munich 81 (Germany)
{jeanmarc,lone,bt,remo}@ecrc.de

Abstract. We define a true concurrency semantics for *LO*, a reactive programming language characterized by dynamically reconfigurable agents (processes), with interagent communication implemented as broadcasting and logical operators corresponding to Linear Logic connectives. Our semantic model is given by the well-known Chemical Abstract Machine formalism, where concurrent events happen in the form of chemical-like reactions. Our approach consists of mapping *LO* computations into *CHAM* computations and is easily generalizable to *CHAM*-related models like *CHARMs*, rewriting logics etc. We propose two mappings from *LO* to *CHAMs*, both making use of the "membrane" mechanism of the *CHAM*, but differing in the choice of active elements: in one case, the messages are passive and the agents are the active entities which perform read and write operations; by contrast, in the second case, the agents are passive with respect to communication and the messages themselves move around the solution to deliver their content to each agent. The results in the paper show the effectiveness of the *CHAM* and related formalisms as abstract frameworks for modeling the implementation of practical languages on parallel architectures. Furthermore, they provide insight on the two following issues: (*i*) the amount of synchronization needed to add broadcasting to one-to-one communication primitives; (*ii*) the problem of parallel searching for Linear Logic proofs.
Keywords: True Concurrency, Concurrent Rewriting, Chemical Abstract Machines, Broadcasting, Linear Logic.

1 Introduction

In this paper, we provide a true concurrency semantic characterization for *LO* [AP91b, AP91a, ACP92], a language designed for programming reactive systems. *LO* is finding applications in such fields as parallel algorithms [AP91a, APB91], distributed simulations [ACP92] and as a *coordination* language for extending the capabilities of object-oriented languages [BAP92].

LO views the computation as performed by concurrent agents that are themselves characterized by multiple concurrent internal threads of computation; agents can self-replicate, and their primary form of communication is broadcasting. *LO*'s operators correspond to Linear Logic connectives [Gir87]; hence, *LO* can be viewed as a "linear logic programming language".

One main motivation for giving a true concurrency semantics to *LO* is that it provides us with an exact picture of the different options available for its parallel implementation. More generally, we want also to gain insight on synchronization problems related to broadcasting and on the subject of parallel search of Linear Logic proofs. As far as broadcasting in *LO* is concerned, a major issue is *soundness* (that is, the requirement that every message is delivered exactly once to each receiver), under the assumption that the number of receiving agents may change at run time; this situation is common to other reactive systems, be they concurrent programming languages or operating systems. As far as proofs in Linear Logic are concerned, we shall show that *CHAMs* provide proof encodings characterized by a similar degree of parallelism as Proof Nets [Gir87], but better suited for practical implementation in the context of linear logic programming.

Our model of true concurrency is given by the well-known Chemical Abstract Machine (*CHAM*) framework [BB90], which extends the Gamma model [BCLM88], and where concurrent events take the form of chemical-like reactions. Our approach consists of mapping *LO* computations into *CHAM* rewrite sequences and is easily generalizable to formalisms related to the *CHAM* like *CHARMs* [CMR92], rewriting logics [Mes92a] etc.

The rest of this paper is structured as follows. Section 2 recalls the main points about the *CHAM*. Section 3 formally describes *LO* and its model of concurrent computation. In section 4 we show how *LO* computations can be encoded into *CHAM* computations. We start from the basic case of *LO* computations where no broadcasting is involved, and then we consider how things change once broadcasting has to be taken into account; in terms of the corresponding *CHAM* encodings, this will typically imply, with respect to the situation characterized by absence of broadcasting, the introduction of a notion of "time", to indicate that a given agent has already seen, or has not yet seen, a certain message. Different choices will be possible here, by making time either linear or branching; for all cases, theorems will be provided to show the correctness and the completeness of the encodings. Finally, we shall devote section 5 to the discussion of the results.

Remark: due to space restrictions, the proofs of the theorems are omitted. They are available in the technical report version of this paper.

2 *CHAM* Preliminaries

The basic idea of the *CHAM* [BB90] is that the state of a system is like a chemical solution where molecules float around. These molecules can interact with each other according to some reaction rules. Possible contact between molecules is provided for by some means of a stirring mechanism. The solution transformation process is truly parallel since any number of transformations can be performed at the same time, when several rules can be applied to the solution simultaneously and no molecule is involved in more than one rule. Subsolutions can also be transformed in parallel. Solutions are shown using membrane delimiters {| |} and can be treated as molecules or appear as subsolutions in a molecule. In the following m ranges over molecules and $\mathcal{S}$ ranges over solutions, with $\uplus$ being multiset union.

There are certain laws associated with a *CHAM*. The reaction laws comprise the rewrite rules of the *CHAM*, and these rules are specific to each *CHAM*. The rewrite rules only apply to molecules in solutions, not within molecules. Using the *CHAM* rewrite rules a multiset of molecules is related to a multiset of molecules. A solution consisting of an instance of a left hand side of a reaction rule can be substituted by a solution consisting of the corresponding instance of the rules right hand side. In addition to the reaction laws there are three meta rules [BB90]:

1. The chemical law

$$\frac{\mathcal{S} \longrightarrow \mathcal{S}'}{\mathcal{S} \uplus \mathcal{S}'' \longrightarrow \mathcal{S}' \uplus \mathcal{S}''}$$

   describes how parts of a multiset can be rewritten.
2. The membrane law

$$\frac{\mathcal{S} \longrightarrow \mathcal{S}'}{\{\!| \, C[\mathcal{S}] \, |\!\} \longrightarrow \{\!| \, C[\mathcal{S}'] \, |\!\}}$$

   states that a solution can be rewritten inside any context.
3. The reversible airlock law, presented in some *CHAM*'s,

$$\frac{}{\{\!| \, \{m\} \uplus \mathcal{S} \, |\!\} \longleftrightarrow \{\!| \, m \triangleleft \mathcal{S} \, |\!\}}$$

converts any arbitrary solution into a singleton solution, isolating the molecule m. This rule adds a means for introducing some sequentiality into the otherwise extremely parallel *CHAM* model.

Apart from these meta rules a *CHAM* will consist of axioms for transforming molecules on the form $m_1, \ldots, m_p \longrightarrow m'_1, \ldots, m'_q$.

3   LO

3.1   Programs, Resources, Proofs

LO programs are built from the following operators: "par" (written $\mathfrak{P}$), "with" (written $\&$), "becomes" (written $\circ\!\!-$) and "top" (written $\top$). We assume an initial (possibly infinite) set of atomic formulae A from which we can recursively define two classes of expressions: "resource formulae" R and "program formulae" P.

$$R = A \mid R \, \mathfrak{P} \, R \mid R \, \& \, R \mid \top$$
$$P = A \circ\!\!- R \mid A \, \mathfrak{P} \, P$$

A "program" is a set of program formulae and a "context" is a finite multiset of resource formulae. An *LO* sequent is a pair written as $\mathcal{P} \vdash \mathcal{C}$ where $\mathcal{P}$ is a program and $\mathcal{C}$ is a context.

A "proof" is a tree structure whose nodes are labeled with *LO* sequents. By convention, a proof tree is graphically represented with its root at the bottom and growing upward. Its branches are obtained as instances of the following inference figures.

- Decomposition inference figures

$$[\mathbin{\mathscr{R}}] \frac{\mathcal{P} \vdash \mathcal{C}, R_1, R_2}{\mathcal{P} \vdash \mathcal{C}, R_1 \mathbin{\mathscr{R}} R_2} \qquad [\top] \frac{}{\mathcal{P} \vdash \mathcal{C}, \top} \qquad [\&] \frac{\mathcal{P} \vdash \mathcal{C}, R_1 \quad \mathcal{P} \vdash \mathcal{C}, R_2}{\mathcal{P} \vdash \mathcal{C}, R_1 \& R_2}$$

- Progression inference figure

$$[\multimap] \frac{\mathcal{P} \vdash \mathcal{C}, R}{\mathcal{P} \vdash \mathcal{C}, A_1, \ldots, A_n} \quad \text{if } (A_1 \mathbin{\mathscr{R}} \cdots \mathbin{\mathscr{R}} A_n \multimap R) \in \mathcal{P}$$

In these figures, $\mathcal{P}$ and $\mathcal{C}$ denote, respectively, a program and a context. R, R_1, R_2 denote resource formulae and the expression $\mathcal{C}, R$ denotes the context obtained as the multiset union of $\mathcal{C}$ and the singleton R. Notice that, by definition, the elements of a multiset are not ordered. Therefore, the order of the atoms in the left-hand side of a program formula is not relevant.

3.2 Operational Interpretation of the Inference Figures

Read bottom-up, a proof with root sequent $\mathcal{P} \vdash \mathcal{C}$ gives us a static representation (a "snapshot") of the overall evolution of a system of agents working on the initial set of resources $\mathcal{C}$ under program $\mathcal{P}$. Each branch of proof represents the evolution of one agent: the nodes are the agent states while the edges are the state transitions. The open leaves are the agents still living at the time of the snapshot.

Program formulae define the allowed state transitions. They can be thought of as composed of two parts, an *input* part (left-hand side of the symbol $\multimap$) and an *output* part (right-hand side of the symbol $\multimap$), implementing, respectively, the consumption and the production of resources from/to the agent's state. However, the operation of producing new resources is here more complex than in standard multiset rewriting, and may in fact involve the creation of new agents, or the termination of existing ones. Indeed, when the output part of a program formula is produced into a context by application of the progression inference figure $[\multimap]$, it is recursively decomposed by application of the decomposition inference figures, which will either terminate the agent (inference figure $[\top]$) or create a new agent by cloning (inference figure $[\&]$) or simply add new components in the context of the agent (inference figure $[\mathbin{\mathscr{R}}]$).

However, we have not yet explained how broadcast communication among agents is realized: as a matter of fact, this is not done in terms of an explicit inference figure but is instead achieved as a side effect of how proof trees are constructed. We detail the mechanism of proof construction in the next section.

3.3 Proof Construction

A "program call" is a pair $\langle \mathcal{P}; R \rangle$ consisting of an LO program $\mathcal{P}$ and a resource formula R.

Definition 1. A target proof for a program call $\langle \mathcal{P}; R \rangle$ is a proof such that its root is a sequent of the form $\mathcal{P} \vdash \mathcal{C}, R$, where $\mathcal{C}$ is a context containing only atoms.

In other words, target proofs are searched in such a way that the context at their root node may *properly contain* the initial resource of the program call.

We consider two proof construction mechanisms. Let Π be any LO proof.

- Expansion:
  Let ν be an open leaf of Π whose sequent matches the lower sequent of an inference figure. Let Π' be the proof obtained by expanding Π at node ν with branches to new open leaves labeled with the upper sequent(s) of the selected inference figure. We write $\Pi \implies_e \Pi'$
- Instantiation:
  Let Π' be the proof obtained by adding an occurrence of a given atom to the context at each node of Π. We write $\Pi \implies_i \Pi'$.

Clearly, these proof construction mechanisms are sound in the following sense:

Theorem 2. *If Π is a target proof for a given program call, and $\Pi \implies_e \Pi'$ or $\Pi \implies_i \Pi'$ then Π' is also a target proof for that program call.*

Definition 3. A proof construction sequence is a sequence of proofs $\Pi_1, \ldots, \Pi_n$ such that

$$\forall k = 1, \ldots, n-1 \quad \begin{cases} \Pi_k \implies_e \Pi_{k+1} \\ \text{or} \\ \Pi_k \implies_i \Pi_{k+1} \end{cases}$$

The trivial proof Π_o reduced to the single node $\mathcal{P} \vdash R$ is obviously a target proof for the program call $\langle \mathcal{P}; R \rangle$. Hence, by application of theorem 2, so is any proof Π such that there exists a proof construction sequence leading from Π_o to Π. Furthermore, it can be shown that the proofs obtained by this method are all the possible target proofs for the program call, so that the two construction mechanisms introduced above are also complete.

In the agent-oriented computational interpretation of proof construction, an expansion step corresponds to an agent state transition whereas an instantiation step corresponds to a form of communication by broadcasting; indeed, the atom which is added to all the nodes in an instantiation step acts as a message broadcast to all the living agents in the system.

3.4   Control of Broadcast Communication

Unfortunately, the two mechanisms of expansion (i.e. state transition) and instantiation (i.e. broadcast communication) are here completely disconnected: indeed, it can be shown that any expansion step permutes with any instantiation step. In order to allow a form of synchronization between the two mechanisms, required in most applications, we introduce a pragmatic tool which gives the programmer some control over the order of execution of expansion steps and instantiation steps in proof constructions (we loose completeness here).

Let $^\wedge$ be a special symbol, called the "broadcast" marker, which can be used to prefix any atom in the input part of a program formula. Consider then the following program formula:

$$p \, \mathfrak{F} \, {}^\wedge a \multimap r$$

This means that, to apply this program formula in an expansion step using the progression inference figure, the atom p (unmarked) must be found in the context of the selected node, while the atom a is added to this context by performing beforehand an instantiation step adding a to all the nodes of the proof[1]. Except in this situation, no other instantiation steps are allowed. A proof construction sequence satisfying this requirement is called "regular". In the rest of this paper, we consider only regular proof construction sequences, and we take the phrase "proof construction" to mean "regular proof construction".

Definition 4. Let Π, Π' be proofs. We write $\Pi \implies \Pi'$ if there exists a (regular) proof construction sequence from Π to Π'.

Clearly, the relation $\implies$ is reflexive transitive. Consider for example the following LO program

$$\{ \ p \,\mathbf{?}\, a \,\mathbf{o-}\, \top \ ; \ q \,\mathbf{?}\, a \,\mathbf{o-}\, q1 \ ; \ r \,\mathbf{?}\, a \,\mathbf{o-}\, \top \ ; \ s \,\mathbf{?}^\wedge a \,\mathbf{o-}\, \top \ \}$$

Then, as the reader may easily verify,

$$\Pi_1 \implies \Pi_2 \implies \Pi_3 \implies \Pi_4$$

where Π_1, Π_2, Π_3 and Π_4 are the proofs in Fig. 1. (In the figure, the program is omitted from the left-hand side of the sequents.) The step between Π_2 and Π_3 consists of an instantiation step (broadcasting a), prior to an expansion step using the progression inference figure with the fourth program formula on the rightmost open leaf of Π_2. This instantiation step is indeed allowed by the presence of the broadcast marker in the program formula used.

4 Encoding LO Computations into $CHAM$ Computations

In this section we show how LO computations can be mapped into corresponding $CHAM$ computations. The basic idea is that each open leaf of an LO proof, which represents a living agent of the system, is mapped into a sub-solution in the $CHAM$.

The following definition, which will be exploited later on in the translation schemes, maps a resource formula into the set of multisets of atoms which it yields when decomposed (by application of the Decomposition inference figures).

Definition 5. Let R be a resource formula, we take $\|R\|$ to be the set of "par-components" of R defined inductively as follows. Each par-component is a multiset of atoms.

---

[1] Notice the difference here between our broadcast marker and the "tell" mechanism of Concurrent Constraint Logic Programming Languages [Sar89]: in our case, a copy of each broadcast message is delivered to each receiver which can locally consume it; on the other hand, told constraints are added to the global constraint store from where they cannot be removed.

$$\Pi_1 \;=\; \vdash (p \,\mathfrak{F}\, q) \,\&\, r \,\&\, s$$

$$\Pi_2 \;=\; [\&] \;\dfrac{[\mathfrak{F}]\;\dfrac{\vdash p,q}{\vdash p \,\mathfrak{F}\, q} \quad [\&]\;\dfrac{\vdash r \quad \vdash s}{\vdash r \,\&\, s}}{\vdash (p \,\mathfrak{F}\, q) \,\&\, r \,\&\, s}$$

$$\Pi_3 \;=\; [\&] \;\dfrac{[\mathfrak{F}]\;\dfrac{\vdash p,q,a}{\vdash p \,\mathfrak{F}\, q,a} \quad [\&]\;\dfrac{\vdash r,a \quad [\mathrm{o-}]\;\dfrac{[\mathsf{T}]\;\dfrac{}{\vdash \mathsf{T}}}{\vdash s,a}}{\vdash r \,\&\, s,a}}{\vdash (p \,\mathfrak{F}\, q) \,\&\, r \,\&\, s,a}$$

$$\Pi_4 \;=\; [\&] \;\dfrac{[\mathfrak{F}]\;\dfrac{[\mathrm{o-}]\;\dfrac{[\mathsf{T}]\;\dfrac{}{\vdash \mathsf{T},q}}{\vdash p,q,a}}{\vdash p \,\mathfrak{F}\, q,a} \quad [\&]\;\dfrac{[\mathrm{o-}]\;\dfrac{[\mathsf{T}]\;\dfrac{}{\vdash \mathsf{T}}}{\vdash r,a} \quad [\mathrm{o-}]\;\dfrac{[\mathsf{T}]\;\dfrac{}{\vdash \mathsf{T}}}{\vdash s,a}}{\vdash r \,\&\, s,a}}{\vdash (p \,\mathfrak{F}\, q) \,\&\, r \,\&\, s,a}$$

Fig. 1. A subsequence of a regular proof construction sequence

If	Then
$R = R_1 \,\mathfrak{F}\, R_2$	$\|R\| = \{\alpha_1 \uplus \alpha_2 \ \text{s.t.}\ \alpha_1 \in \|R_1\| \ \text{and}\ \alpha_2 \in \|R_2\|\}$
$R = R_1 \,\&\, R_2$	$\|R\| = \|R_1\| \cup \|R_2\|$
$R = \mathsf{T}$	$\|R\| = \emptyset$
R is an atom A	$\|R\| = \{\{A\}\}$

Thus, for example, if R is the resource formula $(p \,\&\, q) \,\mathfrak{F}\, r$, then recursive application of the definition above yields two par-components, respectively $\{p,r\}$ and $\{q,r\}$. These are indeed the multisets of resources which replace the resource R in the two branches of proof obtained in its decomposition.

We first give the translation from LO to $CHAM$ computations in the simple case of programs without occurrences of the broadcast marker, and then, we extend the basic mapping scheme with the broadcast mechanism.

4.1 The Basic Case: No Broadcasting

The $CHAM$ used here is simply composed of a set of subsolutions. Each subsolution represents an open node in the proof (i.e. a living agent), and contains a multiset of resource formulae (i.e. the state of the corresponding agent).

Definition 6. Let Π be a proof. We take $\mathrm{CHAM}(\Pi)$ to be the $CHAM$ solution consisting of the subsolutions of the form $\{\!\mid\! \mathcal{C} \!\mid\!\}$ where $\mathcal{C}$ is the context at an open leaf of Π.

The following definitions provide translation schemes for mapping progression and decomposition inference figures into $CHAM$ rules in the case of LO programs where no program formula is decorated with the broadcast marker $\wedge$.

Definition 7 Progression rules. Let $P = A_1 \,\mathscr{B} \cdots \mathscr{B}\, A_r \multimap R$ be a program formula; we take $\overline{P}$ to be the following *CHAM* rule:

$$A_1, \ldots, A_r \longrightarrow R$$

Thus, according to this definition, the progression inference figure [$\multimap$] disappears altogether in the *CHAM* formulation, as the application of each program formula according to this inference figure gets directly compiled into a corresponding *CHAM* rule.

Definition 8 Decomposition rules. Let R be a resource formula; we take $\overline{R}$ to be the following *CHAM* rule:

If	Then $\overline{R}$ is the rule
$\|R\| = \emptyset$	$\{\!\|\ R \triangleleft \mathcal{S}\ \|\!\} \longrightarrow \cdot$
$\|R\| = \{\alpha\}$	$R \longrightarrow \alpha$
$\|R\| = \{\alpha_1, \ldots, \alpha_n\}$ with $n \geq 2$	$\{\!\|\ R \triangleleft \mathcal{S}\ \|\!\} \longrightarrow \{\!\|\ \mathcal{S} \uplus \alpha_1\ \|\!\}, \ldots, \{\!\|\ \mathcal{S} \uplus \alpha_n\ \|\!\}$

Just as above, the decomposition inference figures are compiled away into *CHAM* rules for each resource formula to which they apply. By definition 5, the par-components of a resource formula R are the multisets of atoms obtained by recursively applying the decomposition inference figures to R till only atomic formulae remain. When there is only one par-component (second line of the table in the definition above), the decomposition is purely local to the subsolution in which it occurs. On the other hand, when there are zero or more than one par-components (first and third line, respectively, in the table), the content of the global solution is modified, as the whole subsolution where the decomposition applies may disappear or may be cloned a number of times; this global behavior is achieved via the use of the airlock mechanism of the *CHAM*, which involves a form of sequentialization.

We can now formally state the equivalence between *LO* computations and *CHAM* computations as follows:

Theorem 9. *Let $\mathcal{P}$ be an LO program (with no occurrence of the broadcast marker $^\wedge$) and let Π and Π' be two proofs based on $\mathcal{P}$. We consider on one hand (regular) proof construction sequences based on $\mathcal{P}$ and on the other hand the CHAM consisting of the set of rules*

$$\{\overline{P}\}_{P \in \mathcal{P}} \cup \{\overline{R}\}_R$$

We have

$$\Pi \Longrightarrow \Pi' \text{ if and only if } \text{CHAM}(\Pi) \longrightarrow^{\star} \text{CHAM}(\Pi')$$

4.2 Implementation of the Broadcast Mechanism

The definition of the *CHAM* rules implementing the progression inference figure is first modified to account for the broadcast markers.

Definition 10. Let $P = A_1 \,\mathfrak{V} \cdots \mathfrak{V}\, A_p \,\mathfrak{V}\, {}^\wedge A_{p+1} \,\mathfrak{V} \cdots {}^\wedge A_r \,\circ\!\!-\, R$ be a program formula, we take $\overline{P}$ to be the following $CHAM$ rule:

$$A_1 \,,\, \ldots \,,\, A_p \;\longrightarrow\; R^{\wedge}\{A_{p+1}, \ldots, A_r\}$$

Notice that the output part and the broadcast atoms of the input part of the formula are coupled together within molecules of a new kind, of the form $R^{\wedge}\alpha$ (where R is a resource formula and α a multiset of atoms), so as to express the synchronization condition captured by the regularity requirement of proof construction.

The $CHAM$ rules implementing decomposition and broadcasting are presented below, using two alternative "time stamp" mechanisms. In both cases, the subsolutions representing the living agents are indexed with a time stamp, but, in the first case, time stamps form a totally ordered linear sequence, whereas the second case makes use of a partial order with a branching structure.

Linear Time Here, the global solution contains, besides the subsolutions corresponding to the living agents, a (unique) global clock written $t!$ (where t is the current global time encoded as a non negative integer) together with blocks of messages of the form $t!\alpha$ where t is a time stamp and α a multiset of atoms. These blocks represent broadcast messages and need to be prefixed with a time stamp in order to ensure that agents read them only once. For each time stamp t lower than the current global time, there is one and only one block of messages prefixed with t, and there are no blocks of messages prefixed with time stamps larger than or equal to the current global time. The idea is that each agent indexed with a given time stamp t has already read all the messages prefixed with time stamps lower than or equal to t, and still need to read the messages prefixed with time stamps greater than t. The synchronization is achieved as follows.

– When an agent is indexed with a time stamp t lower than the current global time, and hence attached to a unique block of messages, this block of messages is read by the agent, i.e. it is added to its current state. This is achieved by the following $CHAM$ rule. We take *broadcast-rule* to be the set consisting of this single rule.

$$\{\!|\, \mathcal{S} \,|\!\}^t \,,\, t!\alpha \;\longrightarrow\; \{\!|\, \mathcal{S} \uplus \alpha \,|\!\}^{(t+1)} \,,\, t!\alpha$$

Notice that the time stamp of the agent is incremented, so that it will never read the block of messages again. On the other hand, the block of messages itself is not discarded, as other agents may still have to read it.

– If an agent is indexed with the current global time, then, and only then, it is allowed to broadcast messages (prefixed with the global time, which then gets incremented) and decompose resource formulae.

Definition 11. Let R be a resource formula, and α_o be a multiset of atoms, we take $\overline{R^{\wedge}\alpha_o}$ to be the following $CHAM$ rule:

$$\{\!|\, R^{\wedge}\alpha_o \triangleleft \mathcal{S} \,|\!\}^t \,,\, t! \;\longrightarrow\; t!\alpha_o \,,\, \{\!|\, \mathcal{S} \uplus \alpha_1 \,|\!\}^{(t+1)} \,,\, \ldots \,,\, \{\!|\, \mathcal{S} \uplus \alpha_n \,|\!\}^{(t+1)} \,,\, (t+1)!$$

where $\|R\| = \{\alpha_1, \ldots, \alpha_n\}$.

Notice that each application of any of these rules grabs the global clock, so that broadcast operations are here sequentialized. Furthermore, the agent(s) resulting from the decomposition of R is (are) indexed with the time stamp $t + 1$, so that they cannot read the messages in α_o, which are prefixed with t. This is indeed required since, in LO, broadcast messages are immediately discarded from the state of the agent which initiates the broadcast, before the transition specified by R is performed.

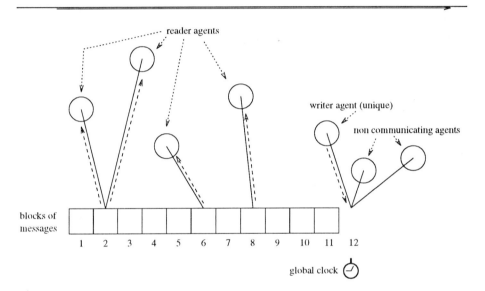

Fig. 2. The linear-time *CHAM* at work

Figure 2 shows the system of agents at work. At any time, each agent can either be a reader, a writer or non-communicating. There might be several simultaneous read operations[2], whereas only one write operation is allowed at a time. Of course, evolutions inside the agents (subsolutions) are completely independent and may occur in parallel.

---

[2] It could be argued that simultaneous reading is not implemented by the *CHAM* described above, because the block of messages in the *broadcast-rule* is grabbed by the reading agent. This is in fact an instance of a general problem of the *CHAM* framework: as mentioned in [CMR92] the *CHAM* cannot distinguish between the situation where some item is preserved by a rewrite rule (as intended for the block of messages in the *broadcast-rule*) and the situation where the same item is cancelled and then generated again (in which case one could argue that simultaneous reading is excluded). The CHARM framework [CMR92], offers a solution to this problem. We have left a study of using the CHARM framework instead of the *CHAM* framework for future research.

We now map *LO* proofs into *CHAM* solutions.

Definition 12. Let Π be a proof and t be a time stamp. We take $\text{CHAM}(\Pi, t)$ to be the *CHAM* solution consisting of the molecule $t!$ together with the subsolutions of the form $\{\!\!|\ \mathcal{C}\ |\!\!\}^t$ where $\mathcal{C}$ is the context at an open leaf of Π.

In other words, this mapping assumes that each open leaf of the proof is mapped into a subsolution indexed with the global time (this amounts to a global synchronization of all the agents). Furthermore, given a solution $\mathcal{S}$, we take $\text{FILTER}(\mathcal{S})$ to be the solution obtained by deleting from $\mathcal{S}$ all the blocks of messages (of the form $u \char`^\alpha$). We can now formally state the equivalence between *LO* computations and *CHAM* computations as follows:

Theorem 13. *Let $\mathcal{P}$ be an LO program, let Π and Π' be two proofs based on $\mathcal{P}$ and let t be any time stamp. We consider on one hand (regular) proof construction sequences based on $\mathcal{P}$ and on the other hand the CHAM consisting of the set of rules*

$$\{\overline{P}\}_{P \in \mathcal{P}} \cup \{\overline{R \char`^\alpha}\}_{R, \alpha} \cup broadcast\text{-}rule$$

We have

$$\Pi \implies \Pi' \text{ if and only if } \exists t', \mathcal{S} \text{ s.t. } \begin{cases} \text{CHAM}(\Pi, t) \longrightarrow^\star \mathcal{S} \\ \text{CHAM}(\Pi', t') = \text{FILTER}(\mathcal{S}) \end{cases}$$

Branching Time Here, the time stamps are finite ordered sequences of positive integers. The empty sequence is written ϵ and the expression $k.t$ denotes the sequence with first element k (an integer) and tail t (a sequence itself). The global solution contains, besides the subsolutions corresponding to the living agents, four kinds of floating molecules:

- Branching points of the form $\&_n^t$ (where $n \geq 2$) encoding a transition, at time t, with n output states (creation by cloning).
- Terminating points of the form $\top^t$ encoding a transition, at time t, with no output state (termination).
- Upward and downward blocks of messages of the form, respectively $t \uparrow \alpha$ and $t \downarrow \alpha$ where t is a time stamp and α is a multiset of atoms, implementing message propagation.

In fact, the structure of the time stamps mimics that of the proof tree: each time stamp identifies a unique node in the proof. Notice that we consider here the possibility of branching points with more than two branches, since decomposition of resource formulae is executed at once and may yield any number of par-components.

Definition 14. Let R be a resource formula, and α_o be a multiset of atoms, we take $\overline{R \char`^\alpha_o}$ to be the following *CHAM* rule:

If	Then $\overline{R^\wedge\alpha_o}$ is the rule
$\|R\| = \emptyset$	$\{\!\| R^\wedge\alpha_o \vartriangleleft \mathcal{S} \|\!\}^t \;\longrightarrow\; t\!\downarrow\!\alpha_o \,,\; T^t$
$\|R\| = \{\alpha\}$	$\{\!\| R^\wedge\alpha_o \vartriangleleft \mathcal{S} \|\!\}^t \;\longrightarrow\; t\!\downarrow\!\alpha_o \,,\; \{\!\| \mathcal{S} \uplus \alpha \|\!\}^t$
$\|R\| = \{\alpha_1,\ldots,\alpha_n\}\ (n \geq 2)$	$\{\!\| R^\wedge\alpha_o \vartriangleleft \mathcal{S} \|\!\}^t \;\longrightarrow\; t\!\downarrow\!\alpha_o \,,\; \&_n^t \,,\; \{\!\| \mathcal{S} \uplus \alpha_1 \|\!\}^{1.t} \,,\ldots,\; \{\!\| \mathcal{S} \uplus \alpha_n \|\!\}^{n.t}$

The propagation of the broadcast messages is achieved by the set *broadcast-rules* consisting of the following four *CHAM* rules.

$$
\begin{aligned}
j.t\!\downarrow\!\alpha \,,\; \&_n^t &\;\longrightarrow\; \{i.t\!\uparrow\!\alpha\}_{i=1\ldots n \wedge i\neq j} \,,\; t\!\downarrow\!\alpha \,,\; \&_n^t \\
t\!\uparrow\!\alpha \,,\; \&_n^t &\;\longrightarrow\; \{i.t\!\uparrow\!\alpha\}_{i=1\ldots n} \,,\; \&_n^t \\
t\!\uparrow\!\alpha \,,\; T^t &\;\longrightarrow\; T^t \\
t\!\uparrow\!\alpha \,,\; \{\!\| \mathcal{S} \|\!\}^t &\;\longrightarrow\; \{\!\| \mathcal{S} \uplus \alpha \|\!\}^t
\end{aligned}
$$

The broadcast mechanism works in the following way; The "broadcaster" is always a living agent, hence an open leaf of the proof tree mapped into a sub-solution of the *CHAM*, indexed with a time stamp t identifying the position of the leaf in the proof tree. In order to broadcast a block of messages to the entire tree, the block is recursively propagated downwards in the tree, using the information of the time stamp, to all the ancestors of the agent. Furthermore each time a downward propagation step is performed at a node, upward propagation steps are triggered at that node. Of course, upward propagation is not initiated on the branch where the downward propagation takes place, but only on sibling branches. This is captured by the first rule in *broadcast-rules*. The last three rules implement in an obvious way upward propagation.

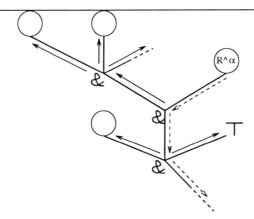

Fig. 3. The branching-time *CHAM* at work

Figure 3 illustrates the propagation mechanism. Dashed arrows represent downward propagation steps along the branch of the ancestors of the agent requesting the broadcast. Plain arrows represent the upward propagation steps — ultimately reaching the whole tree — triggered by these ancestors. Propagation and delivery of messages may here take place simultaneously; multiple concurrent writer agents are allowed as well as multiple concurrent readers[3].

We now map LO proofs into $CHAM$ solutions.

Definition 15. Let Π be a proof. We take $\mathrm{CHAM}(\Pi)$ to be the $CHAM$ solution consisting, for each node at position t in Π, of a molecule of the form $\&_n^t$ if the node is a branching node of Π, or a molecule of the form $\top^t$ if the node is a termination node of Π, or a subsolutions of the form $\{\!| \, \mathcal{C} \, |\!\}^t$ if the node is an open leaf labeled with the context $\mathcal{C}$.

Thus, the whole structure of the proof tree is mapped into the $CHAM$ solution. We can now formally state the equivalence between LO computations and $CHAM$ computations as follows:

Theorem 16. *Let $\mathcal{P}$ be an LO program, let Π and Π' be two proofs based on $\mathcal{P}$. We consider on one hand (regular) proof construction sequences based on $\mathcal{P}$ and on the other hand the $CHAM$ consisting of the set of rules*

$$\{\overline{P}\}_{P \in \mathcal{P}} \cup \{\overline{R^\wedge \alpha}\}_{R,\alpha} \cup broadcast\text{-}rules$$

We have

$$\Pi \Longrightarrow \Pi' \text{ if and only if } \mathrm{CHAM}(\Pi) \longrightarrow^\star \mathrm{CHAM}(\Pi')$$

5 Discussion

5.1 Constructing Proofs in Linear Logic

As shown in [AP91a, And92], LO, without the mechanism for broadcast communication, is sound and complete with respect to Linear Logic [Gir87]; in other words, (i) any proof in LO can be trivially mapped into a proof in Linear Logic, and (ii) any proof in Linear Logic can be transformed, by permutation of the inference figures, into a proof in normal form (called a "focusing" proof in [And92]) which can then be represented by a proof in LO[4]. As a matter of fact, LO, by trading explicit exponentials (responsible in Linear Logic for marking "reusable" formulae) with a "spatial" separation in sequents (permanent entities, i.e., program formulae, on the left of the provability symbol $\vdash$ and non-permanent entities, i.e., resource formulae, on the right) allows searching for Linear Logic proofs under a particularly efficient strategy, described in [And92] (see also Sec. 3); a spatial separation of a similar kind has also been adopted in some more recent developments of the Linear Logic enterprise [Gir91a, Gir91b].

On the other hand, the LO operational semantics is still given in terms of sequent inference figures, and thus maintains those aspects of artificial serialization of the computation which are inherent to sequent proofs: namely, the fact

---

[3] Considerations similar to those of footnote 2 apply here too

[4] In fact, in a slight extension of LO described in [And92] under the name LinLog

that all inference steps on a branch of proof must appear in sequence, although in principle many of them could be performed in parallel. This problem is tackled within Linear Logic itself, where the concept of "Proof Nets" has been proposed as an alternative to sequent proofs in [Gir87]: Proof Nets permit a highly parallel encoding of Linear Logic proofs. However, they are based on a well-formedness criterion (the "short trip" condition) which is rather cumbersome to handle in the process of proof construction; thus, they appear better suited for computational frameworks (e.g. Interaction Nets [Laf90]) where proofs are *normalized* (perhaps by multiple normalization steps taking place simultaneously) rather then directly searched and constructed. Our *CHAM* encoding of *LO* computations retains some aspects of desequentialization offered by Proof Nets, but is better suited to the case of proof construction.

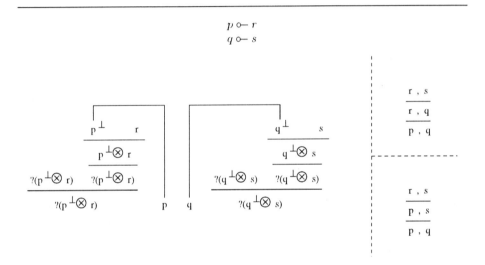

Fig. 4. A potentially simultaneous multiple transition is represented as a single proof net (left) or as two sequent proofs (right).

In particular, program formulae which are purely multiplicative (i.e. contain no occurrence of the additive connective &) can be applied simultaneously in the *CHAM* solution — provided they do not share a resource in their input part. Consider for example the program of Fig. 4. In the *CHAM* encoding, the two formulae may apply simultaneously to any solution of the form {| p, q, S |}, and lead to the solution {| r, s, S |}. This is captured in the proof net representation of the same transition (see Fig. 4), where the application of the two formulae[5] are performed in two distinct parts of the net and hence are not sequentialized. In

---

[5] The program formulae are represented by $?(p^\perp \otimes r)$ and $?(q^\perp \otimes s)$ in the Proof Net.

the sequent proof system, on the other hand, two syntactically distinct proofs are possible (see Fig. 4), which differ only inessentially in the (arbitrary) sequence of application of the formulae.

On the other hand, program formulae containing the additive & must be sequentialized. In our *CHAM* based true concurrency operational semantics, this is realized by the use of the airlock mechanism in the expression of the rules for the decomposition of resource formulae containing the additive, allowing the duplication of whole subsolutions. Similarly, proof nets introduce the concept of "box" to deal with this problem.

Clearly, one could experiment also with other frameworks related to *CHAM*s to implement our approach: suitable candidates are CHARMs [CMR92] (see footnote 2), rewriting logics [Mes92a] [6], contextual nets [MR91] etc.

The proof construction mechanism called "instantiation" in section 3.3, can be shown sound and complete with respect to Linear Logic, as shown in [AP91a], via the Phase Semantics, introduced in [Gir87] to provide a model-theoretic (tarskjian) characterization of Linear Logic. Basically, soundness and complete-ness rely on the idea that generating contexts through proof construction amounts to enumerating phases in the phase space corresponding to the denotation of the given program. In this way, the "copying" operational meaning of the & con-nective is exploited not just for duplicating preexisting information, but also for propagating new information. However, in order to make this approach practical, there is need of the broadcast marker $^\wedge$ to give the user control on which phases are effectively generated; as a consequence, this creates a form of incomplete-ness. Still, the "focusing" strategy for searching proofs can be maintained, by intertwining it with synchronization mechanisms to handle communication; this is directly reflected in the fact that the *CHAM* encodings for *LO* with broad-casting are simple extensions of the non-broadcasting case, where the extensions specifically concern the delivery and the reception of information.

5.2 Broadcasting

We have seen that the main challenges about implementing broadcasting in *LO* are in keeping track of the dynamic reconfigurability of the system (creation and deletion of agents at run-time), and ensuring soundness in the delivery of the messages. This kind of challenges is in general to be met in adding broad-casting to systems based on one-to-one communication. We have proposed two solutions which both make use of a notion of time to overcome such difficulties; thus, messages are time-stamped, and agents themselves have an internal time through which it can be checked whether a given message must or must not be delivered to a given agent. The "linear time" solution relies on the idea that agents regulate their own clocks with respect to a global clock, through which messages are also time-stamped; agents can only read messages which are not in their present or in their past; the internal clock of an agent advances each time

---

[6] As a matter of fact, a broadcast mechanism has been recently implemented on top of the rewriting logic programming language MAUDE [Mes92b].

an agent reads a message or writes one, in which case the global clock gets itself updated through the action of writing. The "branching time" solution relies on the idea of time-stamping agents at the time of their creation; sibling agents all get different stamps, initiating alternative futures evolving from a common past; messages are themselves time-stamped with the stamp of their creator, and cannot be read by any agent who belongs to the same present or the same future of the broadcast message. In this case, there is no global clock, but only local times, starting from the time of the oldest agent, which is stamped with ϵ. Both solutions have their advantages and their trade-offs: linear time is very simple, and entails a straightforward way of implementing parallel reading, but is completely sequential in the writing, as each writer agent must first take possession of the global clock and release it after the write is performed; branching time permits more parallelism in the writing, as there is no notion of a unique global clock, but is more complicated from the point of view of reading, as information must flow through a sideway-downward/upward propagation scheme along the branches of the proof tree. We can make conjectures about which machine architectures are more appropriate for each solution: shared memory architectures appear particularly well-suited for linear time, as the time stamps could be seen as different locations in the memory where the messages are stored and agents actively go and fetch them; highly distributed, message passing architectures fit well instead with branching time, as open nodes in the proof (agents) can be identified with nodes in a network and their ancestors with communication points handling the routing information.

The type of broadcasting in LO programs is closely related to the model studied in [Pra91]. These studies are concerned with the externally observable behavior of processes communicating via broadcasting, thus assuming broadcasting as a primitive mode of communication. However, it is seldom (if ever) the case that parallel or distributed implementation platforms provide broadcast communication as a primitive. Instead one-to-one asynchronous message passing seems to be predominant, and we have therefore focused on how to implement (in an abstract sense) broadcast communication when one-to-one asynchronous message passing is assumed. Recently in the (theoretical) object oriented community the asynchronous one-to-one message passing paradigm has been studied in its own right [HT91, Nie91].

Acknowledgement

Acknowledgements are due to the anonymous Tapsoft referees for their insightful comments.

References

[ACP92]   J-M. Andreoli, P. Ciancarini, and R. Pareschi. Interaction abstract machines. In G. Agha, A. Yonezawa, and P. Wegner, editors, *Research Directions in Concurrent Object Oriented Programming*. MIT Press, 1992. To appear.

[And92]   J-M. Andreoli. Logic programming with focusing proofs in linear logic. *Journal of Logic and Computation*, 2(3), 1992.

[AP91a]   J-M. Andreoli and R. Pareschi. Communication as fair distribution of knowledge. In *Proc. of OOPSLA '91*, Phoenix, Az, U.S.A., 1991.

[AP91b]   J-M. Andreoli and R. Pareschi. Linear objects: Logical processes with built-in inheritance. *New Generation Computing*, 9(3+4):445–473, 1991.

[APB91]   J-M. Andreoli, R. Pareschi, and M. Bourgois. Dynamic programming as multi-agent programming. In *Proc. of the OOPSLA '90/ECOOP'91 workshop on Object-based concurrent computing*, Lecture Notes in Computer Science (612), Genève, Switzerland, 1991. Springer Verlag.

[BAP92]   M. Bourgois, J-M. Andreoli, and R. Pareschi. Extending objects with rules, composition and concurrency: the lo experience. In *Proc. of the OOPSLA '92 workshop on Object-Oriented Programming Languages — The Next Generation*, Vancouver, Canada, 1992.

[BB90]   G. Berry and G. Boudol. The chemical abstract machine. In *Proc. of the 17th ACM Symposium on Principles of Programming Languages*, San Francisco, Ca, U.S.A., 1990.

[BCLM88] J-P. Banâtre, A. Coutant, and D. Le Metayer. A parallel machine for multiset transformation and its programming style. *Future Generation Computer Systems*, 4(2):133–145, 1988.

[CMR92]   A. Corradini, U. Montanari, and F. Rossi. Concurrency and hiding in an abstract rewrite machine. In *Proc. of the International Conference on 5th Generation Computer Systems*, Tokyo, Japan, 1992.

[Gir87]   J-Y. Girard. Linear logic. *Theoretical Computer Science*, 50:1–102, 1987.

[Gir91a] J-Y. Girard. A new constructive logic: Classical logic. *Mathematical Structures in Computer Science*, 1(3), 1991.

[Gir91b] J-Y. Girard. On the unity of logic, 1991. Preprint, Université de Paris 7.

[HT91]   K. Honda and M. Tokoro. An object calculus for asynchronous communication. In *Proc. of ECOOP'91*, Genève, Switzerland, 1991.

[Laf90]   Y. Lafont. Interaction nets. In *Proc. of 17th ACM Symposium on Principles of Programming Languages*, San Francisco, Ca, U.S.A., 1990.

[Mes92a] J. Meseguer. Conditional rewriting logic as a unified model of concurrency. *Theoretical Computer Science*, 93:73–155, 1992.

[Mes92b] J. Meseguer. A logical theory of concurrent objects and its realization in the MAUDE language. In G. Agha, A. Yonezawa, and P. Wegner, editors, *Research Directions in Concurrent Object Oriented Programming*. MIT Press, 1992. To appear.

[MR91]   U. Montanari and F. Rossi. Contextual nets. Technical report, Università di Pisa, Pisa, Italy, 1991.

[Nie91]   O. Nierstrasz. Towards an object calculus. In *Proc. of the OOPSLA '90/ECOOP'91 workshop on Object-based concurrent computing*, Lecture Notes in Computer Science (612), Genève, Switzerland, 1991. Springer Verlag.

[Pra91]   K.V.S. Prasad. A calculus of broadcasting systems. In *Proc. of the 16th Colloquium on Trees in Algebra and Programming*, 1991.

[Sar89]   V.A. Saraswat. *Concurrent Constraint Programming Languages*. PhD thesis, Carnegie-Mellon University, Pittsburg, Pa, U.S.A., 1989.

A General Framework for Modular Implementations of Modular System Specifications

Michel Bidoit*, Rolf Hennicker**

*LIENS, CNRS & Ecole Normale Supérieure
45, Rue d'Ulm, 75230 Paris Cedex, FRANCE
**Institut für Informatik, Ludwig-Maximilians-Universität München
Leopoldstr. 11b, D-8000 München 40, GERMANY

Abstract. We investigate the impact of modularity on the semantics and on the implementation of software specifications. Based on the stratified loose semantics approach we develop a suitable specification framework which meets our basic requirements: the independent construction of implementations for the single constituent parts (modules) of a system specification and the encapsulated development of each implementation part using the principle of stepwise refinement.

Our paper is not aimed at providing an elaborated specification language but rather to concentrate on the modularity issues of system development. Hence, only few but powerful constructs are provided which can be seen as a kernel for further extensions. In particular, we will show that implementation and parameterization can be handled within a uniform concept and we will prove compatibility theorems like the horizontal composition property. All constructs are defined on top of a very general logical framework thus being applicable to various kinds of specification formalisms.

1 Introduction

The modular design of software systems has obvious advantages: it increases the understandability of a software system, supports the reuse of single modules in different applications and allows the independent realization of modules by different programmer teams. But not only the modular design is important: It is crucial that each implementation of a single module meets its requirements. Hence a safe development methodology is needed which allows to split the construction of a single implementation task into well defined steps, each step being manageable more easily than an ad hoc construction of a realization from scratch. This is commonly called the principle of *stepwise refinement.*

In this paper we will develop a suitable specification framework which allows both, the independent construction of implementations for the single constituent parts (modules) of a system specification and the separate development of single implementations by stepwise refinement. We set out from the stratified loose semantics approach of [Bidoit 87] which reflects the modular properties of a specification at the semantical level. In particular, only those realizations of a system specification are accepted which are constructable by the "composition" of single realizations, each single realization being compatible with arbitrary implementations of the other constituent parts of the specification. As a consequence we use a clean distinction between specification modules and their associated system specifications: modules are interpreted by classes of functors while system specifications are interpreted by classes of algebras.

In [Bidoit 87] implementations are treated at the semantical level as models or functors of a specification (module). Hence it is not possible to deal with the development of implementations by stepwise refinements of their abstract specifications. In the present paper we overcome this problem by introducing an implementation relation for system specifications and for specification modules which is based on the stratified loose semantics. Due to the loose semantics approach the implementation ·definition is straightforward by requiring that an implementing module restricts the class of possible realizations (functors) of an abstract specification module. An analogous definition is used for implementations of system specifications considering algebras instead of functors. Since implementations are now handled at the specification level we have provided a suitable basis for the development of formal proof calculi for correctness proofs but this is not in the scope of this paper.

It turns out that our implementation definition has exactly all the properties required for modular system design: it allows independent implementations of modules and sub-systems, it ensures that the properties of "local" implementations are preserved by global ones and it supports the reusability of existing implementations in different contexts. In particular, it guarantees that exchanging a sub-system implementation by another one still produces a globally correct system implementation.

Usually implementations are built on top of already existing specifications of standard data structures (such as arrays, lists, trees etc.). Hence, in general, implementation relations will be established by connecting the signatures of abstract and concrete system specifications (modules resp.) by a signature morphism which maps, if we consider algebraic signatures, abstract sorts and operations to their concrete representations. This shows that there is a close relationship between implementation and parameter actualization (in the classical sense of parameterized specifications). Indeed, in the loose semantics approach, not only syntactically but even semantically there is conceptually no difference between implementation and parameter actualization since in both cases the requirements of an abstract specification, a formal parameter specification resp., must be satisfied by an implementation, by an actual parameter resp.. Hence, in our approach, sub-system specifications can be seen as formal parameters and the implementation of sub-system specifications can be viewed as actualization (parameter passing). As a consequence we deal with both aspects in one uniform framework and the various correlations between implementation and parameterization will be studied using the same formal techniques.

This indicates already that our aim is not the development of an elaborated specification language with a couple of syntactic concepts. On the contrary, we want to concentrate ourselves on the investigation of modularity and implementation issues using only a few but powerful constructs. For the same reason, our approach is developed within a very general logical framework such that it can be instantiated by a series of particular specification formalisms.

2 Assumptions on the Underlying Logical Framework

The approach on modular system design presented in this paper works in a very general setting. In this section we will summarize our assumptions on the underlying logical framework. Note that we do not intend to propose a new powerful framework as an alternative to institutions or specification logics. On the contrary, we will see that we can use such frameworks as a particular basis for our approach. What we need is:

1. A category SIGN of signatures which has inclusions and pushouts [Schoett 87]. We assume that SIGN has an initial object $\emptyset$, called *empty signature*. If $\Sigma, \Sigma' \in$ SIGN and $\iota: \Sigma \to \Sigma'$ is an inclusion morphism we also write $\Sigma \subseteq \Sigma'$. Pushout diagrams are of the

form

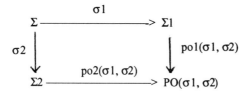

2. A functor Alg: SIGN → CAT^{op} where CAT is the category of all categories. For any signature morphism $\sigma: \Sigma \to \Sigma'$ the functor Alg(σ): Alg(Σ') → Alg(Σ) is called *forgetful functor* associated to σ. It will be denoted by U_σ (or simply by U if σ is clear from the context).

The functor Alg translates any pushout diagram into the following diagram in CAT^{op}:

$$
\begin{array}{ccc}
Alg(\Sigma) & \xleftarrow{\quad U_{\sigma1} \quad} & Alg(\Sigma1) \\
\Big\uparrow U_{\sigma2} & & \Big\uparrow U_{pol(\sigma1,\sigma2)} \\
Alg(\Sigma2) & \xleftarrow{\quad U_{po2(\sigma1,\,\sigma2)} \quad} & Alg(PO(\sigma1,\sigma2))
\end{array}
$$

We assume that any pushout diagram in SIGN as given above has amalgamations w.r.t. Alg. In particular this means that for any two objects A1 ∈ Alg(Σ1), A2 ∈ Alg(Σ2) with $U_{\sigma1}$(A1) = $U_{\sigma2}$(A2) there exists a unique object A2 ⊕ A1 ∈ Alg(PO(σ1, σ2)) such that $U_{po2(\sigma1,\,\sigma2)}$(A2 ⊕ A1) = A2 and $U_{pol(\sigma1,\,\sigma2)}$(A2 ⊕ A1) = A1. For a precise definition of amalgamations see e.g. [Ehrig et al. 89], [Ehrig et al. 91].

Lemma 1   Assume that a pushout diagram is given as above.
If M ⊆ Alg(Σ) and M2 ⊆ Alg(Σ2) are subcategories such that $U_{\sigma2}$(M2) ⊆ M and if
$$F: M \to Alg(\Sigma1)$$
is a functor such that $U_{\sigma1}$(F(A)) = A for all A ∈ M then there exists a unique functor
$$F': M2 \to Alg(PO(\sigma1, \sigma2))$$
such that F'(A2) = A2 ⊕ F($U_{\sigma2}$(A2)). F' is called *extension* of F w.r.t. σ2.

Proof: The proof can be done by a slight generalization of the extension lemma (cf. e.g. [Ehrig et al. 89]).   ♦

3. Finally we assume a class SPEC of specifications and two functions Sig: SPEC → SIGN and Mod: SPEC → CAT^{op} such that for all SP ∈ SPEC, Mod(SP) is a subcategory of Alg(Sig(SP)). The objects of Mod(SP) are called *models* of SP.

Examples   1. All specifications constructed in an arbitrary institution (c.f. [Goguen, Burstall 84]) by the specification building primitives of [Sannella, Tarlecki 84] can be used as the underlying specification language SPEC of our approach if pushouts, inclusions and amalgamations exist. In particular, semiexact reasonable institutions as defined in [Diaconescu et al. 91] provide a suitable basis.

2. The behavioural specification approaches of [Bernot, Bidoit 91] and [Hennicker 92] can be used as a basis for the present framework although they do not provide an institution.

3. Let (ASPEC, Catmod) be a specification logic in the sense of [Ehrig et al. 89] which has pushouts and amalgamations. Moreover, let SIGN be a subcategory of ASPEC which has inclusions and is closed under pushouts and let Sig: ASPEC → SIGN be a function such that for all SP ∈ ASPEC, Catmod(SP) is a subcategory of

Catmod(Sig(SP). Then we have obtained a logical framework for our approach where SPEC = ASPEC, Mod = Catmod and Alg = Catmod restricted to SIGN. For instance, the equational algebraic specification logic where SIGN is the category of algebraic signatures (considered as specifications with no axioms) provides such a framework. If we consider behavioural specifications in the sense of [Orejas et al. 89] then amalgamations only exist if their corresponding pushouts have the "observation preserving property" (cf. [Orejas et al. 89]). Hence, in this case, our constructions will work only if this condition is satisfied.

Note also that the first order specification logic (with arbitrary first order axioms) provides a suitable framework for our approach if SIGN is the category of first order signatures.

3 System Specifications and Modules: The Stratified Loose Approach Revisited

Based on the general logical framework described in the last section we will develop a theory for the modular construction of implementations of modular system specifications. As a main objective of our approach we will provide a semantical basis which allows the separate implementation of the single modules of a system specification such that the local correctness of each "implementation piece" automatically implies the global correctness of the whole system implementation (*principle of modular implementation*).

In order to provide the motivation and the formal background of our general concept we consider in this section the particular case where a modular system specification is constructed by a hierarchy of enrichments. Our presentation follows the ideas of the stratified loose approach to the semantics of modular system specifications as proposed by [Bidoit 87]. Any enrichment step is denoted by a specification module of the form M = (SYS, SP) where SYS is a modular (sub-)system specification and SP is a specification in SPEC (cf. Section 2), called module body, which defines the properties of the enrichment. Since we do not assume anything on the particular form of specifications in SPEC the module body must be a specification and cannot be a specification fragment. However, for particular instantiations of SPEC, a module body could also be defined by some explicit enrichment ΔSP. For instance, in PLUSS (cf. [Bidoit 89]) and in ASL (cf. [Wirsing 86]) an explicit enrichment ΔSP would consist of some sorts, operations and axioms. It is necessary to remark that any specification in SPEC defines a system specification but not vice versa. The difference will be pointed out in the following when developing our syntactical and semantical basis for modular system design.

According to the modularity principle described above an implementation of a system specification should be constructed by separate implementations of each enrichment step, i.e. each module used for the construction of the system specification should be implementable independently from each other. Hence it is necessary to strongly distinguish on the syntactical and on the semantical level between a module M = (SYS, SP) defining an enrichment of SYS and the system specification Sys(M) resulting from the enrichment. In order to start the process of constructing system specifications by successive enrichments of already given system specifications we need an empty system specification, denoted by *Emp*. Then the (abstract) syntax of modules and their associated system specifications is defined as follows: (Note that the syntax of system specifications will be generalized in definition 5 and definition 7 in order to take into account module application.)

Definition 1
(0) *Emp* is a system specification with signature Sig(Emp) =$_{def}$ Ø. Emp is called the *empty system specification*.
(1) If SYS is a system specification and SP is a specification in SPEC such that Sig(SYS) ⊆ Sig(SP), then
$$M = (SYS, SP)$$
is a *specification module* (also called *module* for short) with signature Sig(M) =$_{def}$ Sig(SP).
(2) If M = (SYS, SP) is a specification module, then
$$Sys(M)$$
is a *system specification* with signature Sig(Sys(M)) =$_{def}$ Sig(M). Sys(M) is called the "resulting system specification obtained by applying the enrichment M to SYS". ♦

Notation: Any specification SP in SPEC defines an associated system specification Sys(SP) =$_{def}$ Sys(M) where M = (Emp, SP).

As a consequence of the above definition system specifications are of the form Sys(…Sys(Sys(Sys(SP1), SP2), SP3)…, SPn) where SP1, …, SPn are specifications in SPEC. A more general construction of system specifications will be defined in the next sections. Note that if SPEC allows to define reachability constraints (as e.g. in PLUSS or ASL) then system specifications provide a flexible setting describing data structures with constraints.

According to the loose approach, the semantics of a modular system specification SYS will be defined as some class 𝓜(SYS) of Sig(SYS)-algebras, called the *model class* of SYS. Given some realization (program) P, its correctness w.r.t. a system specification SYS can then be established by relating the program P to one of the models of SYS. In order to study the impact of modularity on the semantics of modules and system specifications we will, for the moment, adopt a simplified view where implementations are treated as models of a specification. A more general framework of implementations will be developed in the next section.
In order to define the semantics of modules and system specifications we first summarize our basic requirements w.r.t. the modular development of modular software systems:

Requirements for modular system development:

1. The various specification modules of a system specification should be implementable independently of each other, possibly by different programmer teams. This means that it should be possible to implement a module M = (SYS, SP) without knowing which specific realization of the sub-system specification SYS has been (or will be) chosen. Hence, replacing some correct realization, say P1, of the system specification SYS by another correct realization of SYS, say P2, should still produce a correct realization of the whole system, without modification of the realization of the module M.
2. Any correct realization of a system specification should also provide a correct realization of each sub-system specification (if it is restricted to the signature of the

sub-system).

3. Any piece of software P that is a correct realization of a sub-system should be reusable (as it is) for a realization of an overall system specification, i.e. no recoding of P should be performed.

4. Global system implementations should be constructed in a modular way using realizations of the single modules.

According to the first requirement a realization of a module M = (SYS, SP) is considered to be a functor F mapping any realization A of SYS to a model of SP[1]. Hence, once a realization of M is provided, it will produce an algebra with the desired properties independently from the particular choice of the realization of SYS. But note that this is not sufficient for satisfying our second requirement from above since the restriction U(F(A)) w.r.t. the forgetful functor U (mapping Sig(SP)-algebras to Sig(SYS)-algebras) may not be a model of SYS. But even if we require U(F(A)) ∈ $\mathcal{M}$(SYS) for all A ∈ $\mathcal{M}$(SYS) the third requirement could be violated if U(F(A)) ≠ A because in this case the functor F has modified the realization A of SYS. These considerations lead to the definition of module semantics as given below.

Now, taking into account the fourth requirement, there is only one canonical way to define the semantics of a system specification Sys(M) with M = (SYS, SP): The semantics of Sys(M) is defined to be the class of all Sig(SP)-algebras F(A) which are obtained by application of some realization F of M to some model A of SYS. Hence all realizations of the system specification Sys(M) are constructed using realizations of M and of SYS. As already indicated above the semantics of a system specification SYS will be denoted by $\mathcal{M}$(SYS). For the semantics of a module M we use the notation SEM(M).

Definition 2

(0) Let *Emp* be the empty system specification. Then $\mathcal{M}$(Emp) =$_{def}$ **1** where **1** denotes the category which contains only one object.

(1) Let M = (SYS, SP) be a specification module. Then

$$\text{SEM(M)} =_{def} \{ \text{ F: } \mathcal{M}(\text{SYS}) \rightarrow \text{Alg(Sig(SP))} \mid \text{F is a functor such that}$$
$$\text{for all A} \in \mathcal{M}(\text{SYS}): \text{F(A)} \in \text{Mod(SP) and U(F(A))} = \text{A,}$$
$$\text{where U is the forgetful functor} \}.$$

The functors of SEM(M) are called *functorial models* of M.[1]

(2) Let Sys(M) be a system specification associated to a module M = (SYS, SP). Then

$$\mathcal{M}(\text{Sys(M)}) =_{def} \{\text{F(A)} \mid \text{F} \in \text{SEM(M), A} \in \mathcal{M}(\text{SYS}) \} ◆$$

System specifications and specification modules are called correct if they have at least one realization:

Definition 3 A system specification SYS is *correct* if and only if $\mathcal{M}$(SYS) ≠ Ø. A specification module M is *correct* if and only if SEM(M) ≠ Ø. ◆

From the semantic definitions follows that for any specification SP in SPEC the semantics of the associated system specification Sys(SP) is the model class of SP, i.e. $\mathcal{M}$(Sys(SP)) = Mod(SP). More generally, the semantics of a system specification Sys(...Sys(Sys(Sys(SP1), SP2), SP3)..., SPn) with specifications SP1, ..., SPn in SPEC is included in the semantics of SPn, i.e. $\mathcal{M}$(Sys(...Sys(Sys(Sys(SP1), SP2), SP3)..., SPn)) ⊆ Mod(SPn). The following simple example shows that this inclusion

---

[1] Note that an alternative would be to consider only functions instead of functors, as discussed e.g. in [Gaudel 92].

may be a proper one. Intuitively the reason for this fact is that the semantics of system specifications takes into account our needs w.r.t. modular software development while the semantics of specifications is mainly property oriented, i.e. it accepts all algebras which satisfy the properties of a specification.

Example Consider the logical framework of equational algebraic specifications (with loose semantics) and two specifications SP1 and SP2 with exactly one sort s and two constants a, b: $\to$ s. Let SP2 have the axiom a = b while SP1 has no axiom. Then the module M = (Sys(SP1), SP2) has no realization since, obviously, no functor F: $\mathcal{M}$(Sys(SP1)) $\to$ Mod(SP2) exists with U(F(A)) = A for all A $\in$ $\mathcal{M}$(Sys(SP1)) = Mod(SP1). Hence no realization of Sys(M) can be produced, i.e. Sys(M) has no model. On the other hand SP2 has all algebras where a, b are interpreted as the same object as models.

4 Implementation of Specification Modules and System Specifications

In the last section we have essentially recalled the basic motivations and definitions of the stratified loose semantics approach introduced in [Bidoit 87]. A methodologically important objective which was not addressed there concerns the stepwise construction of implementations. After splitting an implementation task into several subtasks (according to the modular structure of a system specification) it should be possible to implement each subtask stepwise by a series of design decisions. The principle of stepwise refinement allows to separate implementation constructions into encapsulated implementation units thus leading to a programming discipline which increases the reliability of a final software product. Moreover, it provides means to document single design decision thus facilitating the maintenance of software systems.

In order to allow stepwise refinements in the stratified loose approach we cannot keep the simplified view of the last section where implementations were considered as models of a specification (or functors of a module). We have to provide means which allow to restrict successively the class of admissible realizations of modules and system specifications according to particular design decisions, like choice of algorithms, choice of data structures etc.. As a consequence, an implementation of a system specification must be a system specification as well which just has less models than its corresponding abstract specification. Analogously, an implementation of a specification module M is a module as well which specifies less functors than M. In particular, this implies that the functors of an implementing module have the same domain as the functors of the abstract module. Hence we require that concrete and abstract modules are built on the same sub-system specification. (Note that one could even allow that the sub-system specification SYS' of an implementing module M' has more realizations than the sub-system specification SYS of the corresponding abstract module M since it is sufficient that all functorial models of M' accept all realizations of SYS. For sake of simplicity we do not consider this more general condition here.)

Definition 4 (1) Let SYS and SYS' be system specifications such that Sig(SYS) = Sig(SYS'). Then SYS' is called *system implementation* of SYS (written SYS $\sim\sim\sim>_{sys}$ SYS') if $\mathcal{M}$(SYS') $\subseteq$ $\mathcal{M}$(SYS).
(2) Let M = (SYS, SP) and M' = (SYS, SP') be specification modules such that Sig(M) = Sig(M'). Then M' is called *module implementation* of M (written M $\sim\sim\sim>_{mod}$ M') if SEM(M') $\subseteq$ SEM(M). $\blacklozenge$

In the above implementation definitions it is required that the signatures of concrete and abstract specifications (modules resp.) coincide. A more general concept which allows to define implementations relatively to a signature morphism from an abstract signature to a concrete one will be considered in the next section.

The power of our implementation mechanism depends on the underlying specification language SPEC. For instance, if SPEC incorporates features for behavioural abstractions (like in ASL or in [Sannella, Tarlecki 87]) or if it is directly equipped with behavioural semantics (cf. e.g. [Bernot, Bidoit 91], [Hennicker 92]) then the implementation definition reflects the intuitive idea that a realization is correct if it satisfies the desired input/output behaviour.

The following fact is an immediate consequence of the definitions. It says that module implementations induce system implementations for their associated systems:

Fact 1 Let $M = (SYS, SP)$ and $M' = (SYS, SP')$ be modules such that $M \sim\sim\sim>_{mod}$ M'. Then $Sys(M) \sim\sim\sim>_{sys} Sys(M')$.

We will now analyze how a modular implementation of a system specification will be constructed with the help of our implementation mechanism. Since a system specification is built up by a sequence of modules, each single module enriching a given sub-system specification, it should be enough to implement each module in order to obtain a global system implementation. According to the inductive construction of system specifications this problem can be reduced to the following case: Let SYS1 be a system specification which is constructed by applying a module $M = (SYS, SP)$ to a sub-system specification SYS, i.e. SYS1 = Sys(M). Assume that a system implementation SYS' of the subsystem SYS is already given. The question is how to construct a system implementation for SYS1 using SYS' and a given module implementation $M \sim\sim\sim>_{mod} M'$ where $M' = (SYS, SP')$. Although, according to the above fact, Sys(M') provides a system implementation of SYS1 this is not the implementation we want since it does not use SYS'.

As a solution we propose to introduce a new operation on modules which allows to instantiate sub-system specifications by sub-system implementations. The result of the application of the module $M' = (SYS, SP')$ to the implementation SYS' of SYS yields a system specification which contains as models all algebras which can be produced by the application of functorial models of M' to realizations of SYS'. Before giving the formal definition of the application we will discuss another attempt for solving the problem of sub-system implementation which, however, is not successful:

Remark: Considering the above situation one could try to textually replace within the module M' the sub-system specification SYS by its implementation SYS' thus yielding a module $M_{repl} = (SYS', SP')$. But then it is not guaranteed that $Sys(M_{repl})$ is a system implementation of SYS1. The reason is that, since $\mathcal{M}(SYS') \subseteq \mathcal{M}(SYS)$, there might exist functorial models $F_{repl}: \mathcal{M}(SYS') \to Alg(Sig(SP'))$ of M_{repl} which cannot be extended to functorial models $F: \mathcal{M}(SYS) \to Alg(Sig(SP'))$ of M'. (In other words F_{repl} may not be a restriction of some functorial model F of M'.) Consequently, such functors might produce algebras which cannot be produced by functorial models of M' and hence do not belong to the models of the system specification SYS1 to be implemented.

Definition 5 Let M = (SYS, SP) be a specification module and SYS $\sim\sim\sim>_{sys}$ SYS' be a system implementation.

Then M[SYS ==> SYS'] is a system specification, called *the application of M to SYS'*, with signature Sig(M[SYS ==> SYS']) =$_{def}$ Sig(SP) and with semantics

$$\mathcal{M}(\text{M[SYS ==> SYS']}) =_{def} \{F(A) \mid F \in \text{SEM(M)}, A \in \mathcal{M}(\text{SYS'})\} \quad \blacklozenge$$

Note that $\mathcal{M}$(M[SYS ==> SYS]) = $\mathcal{M}$(Sys(M)), i.e. the system specification associated to a module M has the same semantics as the application of M to its own sub-system specification SYS.

The following lemma states some important properties of module application which can be easily derived from the definitions:

Lemma 2 Let M = (SYS, SP), M' = (SYS, SP') be modules with M $\sim\sim\sim>_{mod}$ M' and let SYS and SYS' be system specifications such that SYS $\sim\sim\sim>_{sys}$ SYS'. Then the following holds:

(1) M[SYS ==> SYS'] is a correct system specification if and only if M is a correct specification module and SYS' is a correct system specification.

(2) Sys(M) $\sim\sim\sim>_{sys}$ M'[SYS ==> SYS']

(3) If M' is correct then $\mathcal{M}$(SYS') = U($\mathcal{M}$(M'[SYS ==> SYS'])) where U: Alg(Sig(M')) $\rightarrow$ Alg(Sig(SYS')) is the forgetful functor. $\quad \blacklozenge$

We shall give a short interpretation of the above properties:

Property (1) shows that the application of a correct module to a correct system specification yields again a correct system specification. In connection with property (2) this means that "locally" correct implementations can be composed to a "globally" correct implementation of a system specification. In particular, property (2) says that implementations can be developed independently from each other, i.e. an implementation of the module M can be constructed without knowing which implementation of the sub-system specification SYS will be provided and vice versa. This is exactly what we have postulated in our first requirement for modular system design in Section 3.

Property (3) ensures that the application of a module implementation M' to a sub-system implementation SYS' does not change (the semantics of) the sub-system implementation. Hence sub-system implementations will be reused without modification. In particular, the application of M' to SYS' yields also an implementation of the smaller system SYS' if it is restricted to the signature of SYS'. This is exactly what we have postulated in the second and third requirement for modular system design in Section 3. Note that the application of a module to a system specification corresponds to the application of a functor to an algebra. Having this correspondence in mind we see that property (3) corresponds at the specification level exactly to the semantical functor property "U(F(A)) = A" required for the functorial models F of a module.

5 A Uniform Concept for Implementation and Parameterization

In the previous section we have assumed that the signatures of implementations and abstract system specifications (modules resp.) coincide. We will now drop this assumption thus leading to a generalized implementation concept which turns out to capture our ideas on the parameterization of system specifications as well.

In practice implementations are usually built on top of already existing, standard data structures. Hence the connection between an abstract specification and the implementation has usually to be provided by a signature morphism which maps the abstract types (sorts) and operations to concrete ones. In order to incorporate this idea in our approach we extend the implementation definitions given in the last section as follows:

Definition 6 (1) Let SYS and SYS' be system specifications and σ: Sig(SYS) $\rightarrow$ Sig(SYS') be a signature morphism. Then SYS' is called σ-*system implementation* of SYS (written SYS $_\sigma\!\!\sim\!\!\sim\!\!\sim\!\!>_{sys}$ SYS') if $U_\sigma(\mathcal{M}(SYS')) \subseteq \mathcal{M}(SYS)$.
(2) Let M = (SYS, SP) and M' = (SYS, SP') be specification modules and τ: Sig(M) $\rightarrow$ Sig(M') be a signature morphism. Then M' is called τ-*module implementation* of M (written M $_\tau\!\!\sim\!\!\sim\!\!\sim\!\!>_{mod}$ M') if $U_\tau(SEM(M')) \subseteq SEM(M)$ where
$$U_\tau(SEM(M')) =_{def} \{U_\tau \bullet F' \mid F' \in SEM(M')\} \quad \blacklozenge$$

Fact 2 If SYS $_\sigma\!\!\sim\!\!\sim\!\!\sim\!\!>_{sys}$ SYS' and SYS' $_{\sigma'}\!\!\sim\!\!\sim\!\!\sim\!\!>_{sys}$ SYS'' then SYS $_{\sigma'\bullet\sigma}\!\!\sim\!\!\sim\!\!\sim\!\!>_{sys}$ SYS''. If M $_\tau\!\!\sim\!\!\sim\!\!\sim\!\!>_{mod}$ M' and M' $_{\tau'}\!\!\sim\!\!\sim\!\!\sim\!\!>_{mod}$ M'' then M $_{\tau'\bullet\tau}\!\!\sim\!\!\sim\!\!\sim\!\!>_{mod}$ M''.

We can now extend the definition of module application to the case of σ-system implementations:

Definition 7 Let M = (SYS, SP) be a specification module and SYS $_\sigma\!\!\sim\!\!\sim\!\!\sim\!\!>_{sys}$ SYS' be a σ-system implementation.
Then M[SYS =σ=> SYS'] is a system specification, called *the application of M to SYS' w.r.t.* σ.
The signature Sig(M[SYS =σ=> SYS']) =$_{def}$ PO(ι, σ) is the pushout of the following diagram in the category SIGN of signatures where ι denotes the inclusion morphism:

$$
\begin{array}{ccc}
Sig(SYS) & \xrightarrow{\ \iota\ } & Sig(SP) \\
\sigma \downarrow & & \downarrow pol(\iota, \sigma) \\
Sig(SYS') & \xrightarrow{\ po2(\iota, \sigma)\ } & PO(\iota, \sigma)
\end{array}
$$

The semantics of the module application is defined by
$$\mathcal{M}(M[SYS =\sigma=> SYS']) =_{def} \{F'(A') \mid A' \in \mathcal{M}(SYS') \text{ and } F': \mathcal{M}(SYS') \rightarrow$$
Alg(PO(ι, σ)) is the unique extension of some $F \in SEM(M)$ w.r.t. $\sigma\}$ $\blacklozenge$

By lemma 1, the unique extension F' of F in the above definition exists since $U_\sigma(\mathcal{M}(SYS')) \subseteq \mathcal{M}(SYS)$ and since for all functorial models $F \in SEM(M)$, $U(F(A)) = A$ holds (where $U = U_\iota$). Moreover, by lemma 1, the semantics of the application of the module M to a system specification SYS' can be characterized by all amalgamations which can be constructed by the models of SYS' and by the functorial models of M, i.e. we have the following fact:

Fact 3 $\mathcal{M}(M[SYS =\sigma=> SYS']) = \{A \in Alg(PO(\iota, \sigma)) \mid A = A' \oplus F(U_\sigma(A'))$
where $A' \in \mathcal{M}(SYS')$ and $F \in SEM(M)\}$

Note that the result signature of the application is not Sig(SP) but PO(ι, σ) since the instantiation of the subsystem SYS by an implementation SYS' should produce an implementation of the overall system specification Sys(M) via a signature morphism that preserves (i.e. extends) the signature morphism σ used for the implementation of the subsystem SYS. Using our constructions one can show that M[SYS =σ=> SYS'] is indeed an implementation of Sys(M) via the pushout morphism po1(ι, σ) which extends σ to Sig(SP). (The proof is a particular consequence of theorem 1 below using the property $\mathcal{M}$(Sys(M)) = $\mathcal{M}$(M[SYS =id=> SYS]) where id denotes the identity morphism.)

Notation: In order to avoid syntactical overhead we will also write M[SYS'] instead of M[SYS =σ=> SYS'] if the explicit denotation of SYS and σ is not important or clear from the context.

An obvious, but important property of the application operation is that it preserves the correctness of the single constituent parts of a system specification:

Fact 4   M[SYS =σ=> SYS'] is a correct system specification if and only if M is a correct specification module and SYS' is a correct system specification.

The above formalism allows to apply a module to an implementation of its sub-system specification. Since implementations are specializations which, on the one hand, may add "something" (usually some sorts and operations) to the signature of the abstract specification and, on the other hand, may rename some parts of the abstract signature, there is, due to the loose semantics approach, conceptually no difference between implementation and parameter actualization (in the classical sense of parameterized specifications). Hence our general framework can be interpreted in two ways:
First, a module may be seen to define an extension of a sub-system specification. Then the application operation is used for instantiating the sub-system specification by an implementation. Secondly, a module M = (SYS, SP) may be interpreted as a parameterized specification with formal parameter specification SYS. In this case, the application of a module is viewed as actualization (or parameter passing). Instead of sub-system implementations we then speak of actual parameters. For instance, the following specification module STACK-MOD is supposed to specify stacks over arbitrary elements. The formal parameter is defined by a specification ELEM for the elements and the stack operations are specified in the specification STACK:
    STACK-MOD = (Sys(ELEM), STACK).
Then, if INT is a specification of integers, stacks of integers can be defined by the following actualization: STACK-MOD[Sys(INT)].
The actualization is performed w.r.t. an appropriate signature morphism which is not explicitly denoted here. Due to the pushout construction no name conflicts will occur in the actualization.

In the following we will neither concentrate only on the implementation aspect nor only on the parameterization aspect of our approach but we will discuss the various correlations between both.
As a first example, let M = (SYS, SP) be a specification module where SYS is considered as a formal parameter specification. Then it is an important question whether applications of M to actual parameters preserve implementation relations between the actual parameters. This property is well known as *monotonicity* of parameterized specifications. For instance, if Sys(INT-IMPL) is an implementation of Sys(INT) (e.g. implementing integers by bit strings) then STACK-MOD[Sys(INT-IMPL)] should be automatically an implementation of STACK-MOD[Sys(INT)]. The

following theorem states that this is indeed true for arbitrary modules and arbitrary implementation relations for actual parameters:

Theorem 1 *(Monotonicity)*
Let M = (SYS, SP) be a specification module and let SYS, SYS' and SYS'' be system specifications such that SYS $_\sigma$~~~>$_{sys}$ SYS' (where SYS' is seen as an actual parameter) and SYS' $_\sigma$~~~>$_{sys}$ SYS'' (where SYS'' is seen as an implementation of the actual parameter).
Then M[SYS $=\sigma=>$ SYS'] $_\kappa$~~~>$_{sys}$ M[SYS $=\sigma'\bullet\sigma=>$ SYS''] is a system implementation where κ is the unique signature morphism determined by the following pushout diagrams:

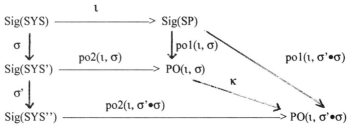

Proof: First, note that M[SYS $=\sigma'\bullet\sigma=>$ SYS''] is well defined since system implementation is transitive (cf. fact 2). We have to show that $U_\kappa(\mathcal{M}(M[SYS =\sigma'\bullet\sigma=> SYS'']))\subseteq \mathcal{M}(M[SYS =\sigma=> SYS'])$. By fact 3,
$\mathcal{M}(M[SYS =\sigma'\bullet\sigma=> SYS'']) = \{A \in Alg(PO(\iota, \sigma'\bullet\sigma)) \mid A = A'' \oplus F(U_{\sigma'\bullet\sigma}(A''))$ where A'' $\in \mathcal{M}(SYS'')$ and $F \in SEM(M)\}$ and
$\mathcal{M}(M[SYS =\sigma=> SYS']) = \{A \in Alg(PO(\iota, \sigma)) \mid A = A' \oplus F(U_\sigma(A'))$ where A' $\in \mathcal{M}(SYS')$ and $F \in SEM(M)\}$.
Now, let A'' $\oplus F(U_{\sigma'\bullet\sigma}(A'')) \in \mathcal{M}(M[SYS =\sigma'\bullet\sigma=> SYS''])$ with A'' $\in \mathcal{M}(SYS'')$ and $F \in SEM(M)$.
Then, by the commutativity of the diagrams and by the properties of amalgamated unions, $U_{po2(\iota,\sigma)}(U_\kappa(A'' \oplus F(U_{\sigma'\bullet\sigma}(A'')))) = U_{\sigma'}(U_{po2(\iota,\sigma'\bullet\sigma)}(A'' \oplus F(U_{\sigma'\bullet\sigma}(A'')))) = U_{\sigma'}(A'')$ and
$U_{po1(\iota,\sigma)}(U_\kappa(A'' \oplus F(U_{\sigma'\bullet\sigma}(A'')))) = U_{po1(\iota,\sigma'\bullet\sigma)}(A'' \oplus F(U_{\sigma'\bullet\sigma}(A''))) = F(U_\sigma(U_{\sigma'}(A'')))$. Hence, by the uniqueness of amalgamations, we know that $U_\kappa(A'' \oplus F(U_{\sigma'\bullet\sigma}(A''))) = U_{\sigma'}(A'') \oplus F(U_\sigma(U_{\sigma'}(A'')))$. Since $U_{\sigma'}(A'') \in \mathcal{M}(SYS')$ and $F \in SEM(M)$ we then know (by fact 3) that $U_\kappa(A'' \oplus F(U_{\sigma'\bullet\sigma}(A''))) \in \mathcal{M}(M[SYS =\sigma=> SYS'])$ and we are done. ◆

We will now consider the relationship between module implementations and parameter passing. An important question is whether module implementations induce automatically system implementations for arbitrary actualizations, i.e. whether parameter passing is compatible with module implementation. For instance, given a module implementation STACK-MOD-IMPL = (Sys(ELEM), STACK-IMPL) of the module STACK-MOD (e.g. implementing stacks by arrays with pointers) and an arbitrary actual parameter, e.g. Sys(INT), of both modules, then we would like that the actualization STACK-MOD-IMPL[Sys(INT)] yields automatically a system implementation of the actualization STACK-MOD[Sys(INT)]. The next theorem states the compatibility of module implementation with parameter passing:

Theorem 2 *(Compatibility of module implementation with parameter passing)*
Let M = (SYS, SP), M' = (SYS, SP') be specification modules such that M $_\tau$~~~>$_{mod}$
M' and let SYS' be a system specification such that SYS $_\sigma$~~~>$_{sys}$ SYS'.
Then M[SYS =σ=> SYS'] $_\mu$~~~>$_{sys}$ M'[SYS =σ=> SYS'] is a system implementation
where μ is the unique signature morphism determined by the following pushout
diagrams:

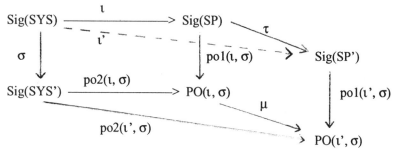

Proof: We have to show that $U_\mu(\mathcal{M}(M'[SYS =\sigma=> SYS'])) \subseteq \mathcal{M}(M[SYS =\sigma=> SYS'])$. By fact 3,
$\mathcal{M}(M'[SYS =\sigma=> SYS']) = \{A \in Alg(PO(\iota', \sigma)) \mid A = A' \oplus F'(U_\sigma(A'))$ where $A' \in \mathcal{M}(SYS')$ and $F' \in SEM(M')\}$ and
$\mathcal{M}(M[SYS =\sigma=> SYS']) = \{A \in Alg(PO(\iota, \sigma)) \mid A = A' \oplus F(U_\sigma(A'))$ where $A' \in \mathcal{M}(SYS')$ and $F \in SEM(M)\}$.
Now, let $A' \oplus F'(U_\sigma(A')) \in \mathcal{M}(M'[SYS =\sigma=> SYS'])$ with $A' \in \mathcal{M}(SYS')$ and $F' \in SEM(M')$.
Then, by the commutativity of the lower triangle and by the properties of amalgamated unions, $U_{po2(\iota, \sigma)}(U_\mu(A' \oplus F'(U_\sigma(A')))) = U_{po2(\iota', \sigma)}(A' \oplus F'(U_\sigma(A'))) = A'$.
We will now show:
(#) $U_{pol(\iota, \sigma)}(U_\mu(A' \oplus F'(U_\sigma(A')))) = F(U_\sigma(A'))$ where $F: \mathcal{M}(SYS) \rightarrow Alg(Sig(SP))$
is defined by $F(A) =_{def} U_\tau(F'(A))$ for all $A \in \mathcal{M}(SYS)$, i.e. $F = U_\tau \bullet F'$.
First, note that $F \in SEM(M)$ since it is assumed that M $_\tau$~~~>$_{mod}$ M'.
Now (#) can be proved using the commutativity of the right square and the properties
of the amalgamated union: $U_{pol(\iota, \sigma)}(U_\mu(A' \oplus F'(U_\sigma(A')))) = U_\tau(U_{pol(\iota', \sigma)}(A' \oplus F'(U_\sigma(A')))) = U_\tau(F'(U_\sigma(A'))) = F(U_\sigma(A'))$, by definition of F. (Note that
$F(U_\sigma(A'))$ is well defined, since SYS $_\sigma$~~~>$_{sys}$ SYS' is assumed and therefore
$U_\sigma(A') \in \mathcal{M}(SYS)$.) The uniqueness of the amalgamated union now implies that
$U_\mu(A' \oplus F'(U_\sigma(A'))) = A' \oplus F(U_\sigma(A'))$. Hence, by fact 3, $U_\mu(A' \oplus F'(U_\sigma(A')))$
$\in \mathcal{M}(M[SYS =\sigma=> SYS'])$ and we are done. ◆

As a consequence of the above theorems we obtain the so-called *horizontal
composition property* for module and system implementations. For instance, if
STACK-MOD, STACK-MOD-IMPL, Sys(INT) and Sys(INT-IMPL) are as above,
then STACK-MOD-IMPL[Sys(INT-IMPL)] yields a system implementation of
STACK-MOD[Sys(INT)].

Corollary 1 *(Horizontal composition property)*
Let M = (SYS, SP), M' = (SYS, SP') be specification modules such that M $_\tau$~~~>$_{mod}$
M'. Moreover, let SYS, SYS' and SYS'' be system specifications such that SYS
$_\sigma$~~~>$_{sys}$ SYS' (where SYS' is seen as an actual parameter) and SYS' $_{\sigma'}$~~~>$_{sys}$
SYS'' (where SYS'' is seen as an implementation of the actual parameter).

Then we have the following diagram of system implementations:

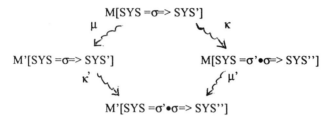

$$M[SYS =\sigma=> SYS']$$

μ ⟵ κ ⟶

$$M'[SYS =\sigma=> SYS'] \qquad\qquad M[SYS =\sigma'\bullet\sigma=> SYS'']$$

κ' ⟶ μ' ⟵

$$M'[SYS =\sigma'\bullet\sigma=> SYS'']$$

with appropriate signature morphisms μ, μ', κ, κ' as defined in the pushout diagrams of theorem 1 and theorem 2.

Proof: The implementations w.r.t. κ and κ' are direct consequences of theorem 1 and the implementations w.r.t. μ and μ' are direct consequences of theorem 2. ♦

Example As an example consider the following system specification SSI of sets of stacks of integers which is built by the following systems and modules:

Sys(INT) and STACK-MOD = (Sys(ELEM), STACK) are given as above,

SET-MOD = (Sys(ELEM), SET) has the same formal parameter as the stack module and the specification SET defines the set operations w.r.t. arbitrary elements.
Then SSI is defined as SSI = SET-MOD[STACK-MOD[Sys(INT)]].

Now suppose that the following implementation modules are given (implementing e.g. stacks by arrays with pointers and sets by lists) and that Sys(INT-IMPL) is an implementation of Sys(INT):

STACK-MOD-IMPL = (Sys(ELEM), STACK-IMPL),

SET-MOD-IMPL = (Sys(ELEM), SET-IMPL).
Then SSI-IMPL = SET-MOD-IMPL[STACK-MOD-IMPL[Sys(INT-IMPL)]]
is a system implementation of SSI.

We will convince ourselves that this is true by considering the following implementation steps:
1. Since Sys(INT-IMPL) implements SYS(INT) and STACK-MOD-IMPL implements STACK-MOD, we know by the corollary that STACK-MOD-IMPL[Sys(INT-IMPL)] is a system implementation of STACK-MOD[Sys(INT)].
2. From 1. and from the fact that SET-MOD-IMPL is a module implementation of SET-MOD follows, again using the corollary, that SSI-IMPL is a system implementation of SSI.

Remark: A particular application of corollary 1 is the case where SYS' = SYS, σ = id (and SYS'' = SYS', σ' = σ). Since $\mathcal{M}$(Sys(M)) = $\mathcal{M}$(M[SYS =id=> SYS]) we then obtain that M'[SYS =σ=> SYS'] is a system implementation of Sys(M). If SYS is not considered as a formal parameter but as a sub-system specification enriched by M, then this fact ensures the independent construction of implementations for sub-system specifications and modules.

5 Concluding Remarks

We have presented a uniform framework for the construction of modular implementations which incorporates the separation of implementation tasks into smaller units and the stepwise development of single "implementation pieces". In order to achieve the independent development of implementations we have introduced two basic specification units: specification modules and system specifications. Semantically, a specification module denotes a class of (algebra-valued) functors and a system specification denotes the class of all algebras which can be constructed by (successive) functor applications according to the modular structure of the specification. Hence, the semantics of a system specification reflects the modular construction of realizations and therefore is different from ASL-like specifications. In particular this means that system specifications are different from 0th-order specifications as defined in [Sannella et al. 90]. On the other hand the semantics of a specification module corresponds to the first-order case of specifications of parametric algebras in the sense of [Sannella et al. 90] because in both concepts realizations are considered to be parameterized programs. However it is important to notice that in our approach specification modules are used as the fundamental tool for building structured (hierarchical) system specifications which makes an essential difference between specification modules and specifications of parametric algebras.

According to the loose approach we have introduced an implementation relation for modules and for system specifications and we have introduced a basic operation on modules (module application) which allows to instantiate the sub-system specification of a module by an implementation. We have discussed the close relationship between system implementation and parameterization and, in fact, we have proposed to use the same constructs for both concepts. A similar suggestion, based on behavioural semantics with constraints, is elaborated in [Orejas, Nivela 90]. The concept of vertical refinement of [Orejas, Nivela 90] corresponds to our concept of module application.

In the presented approach only few assumptions were made on the underlying logical framework, i.e. the developed concepts on modularity, parameterization and implementation can be "reused" for several particular specification theories. However, it should be clear that our concepts will not have the same power in any particular logical framework. For instance, in a behavioural framework the implementation relation defined here would be much more powerful than in standard theories because in the behavioural case our implementation definition would accept all concrete realizations which satisfy the desired observable behaviour of an abstract specification.
Similarly, the complexity of an appropriate proof theory for proving implementation relations will depend on the particular logical framework in which our approach is used. Since we are especially interested in behavioural specifications (cf. [Bernot, Bidoit 91], [Hennicker 92]) we plan to investigate proof criteria for implementations of modules and of system specifications in the behavioural case. As an appropriate basis we could use e.g. the proof theoretic characterization of behavioural implementations given in [Hennicker 90].
An important further objective of future research is the integration of our concepts into a theory of software reusability. For instance, the approach of [Gaudel, Moineau 88] to software reuse is already based on the stratified loose semantics and hence it would

be interesting to apply this approach to the case where implementations are treated at the specification level.

Acknowledgement We would like to thank anonymous referees for several helpful comments and suggestions. This work is partially sponsored by the French-German cooperation programme PROCOPE, by the ESPRIT Working Group COMPASS, and by the German BMFT project KORSO.

References

[Bernot, Bidoit 91] G. Bernot, M. Bidoit: Proving the correctness of algebraically specified software: modularity and observability issues. Proc. AMAST '91, 2nd International Conference on Algebraic Methodology of Software Technology, Techn. Report of the University of Iowa, 1991.

[Bidoit 87] M. Bidoit: The stratified loose approach: A generalization of initial and loose semantics. In: Recent Trends in Data Type Specification, Selected Papers of the 5th Workshop on Specifications of Abstract Data Types, Lecture Notes in Computer Science 332, 1-22, 1987.

[Bidoit 89] M. Bidoit: Pluss, un language pour le développement de spécifications algébriques modulaires. These d'État, Université Paris-Sud, 1989.

[Diaconescu et al. 91] R. Diaconescu, J. Goguen, P. Stefaneas: Logical support for modularisation. To appear in: Proc. of Workshop on Logical Frameworks, Edinburgh, 1991.

[Ehrig et al. 89] H. Ehrig, P. Pepper, F. Orejas: On recent trends in algebraic specification. Proc. ICALP '89, Lecture Notes in Computer Science 372, 263-288, 1989.

[Ehrig et al. 91] H. Ehrig, M. Baldamus, F. Orejas: New concepts of amalgamation and extension for a general theory of specification. Proc. of the 8th Workshop on Specifications of Abstract Data Types, 1991, to appear in: Lecture Notes in Computer Science.

[Gaudel 92] M. C. Gaudel: Structuring and modularizing algebraic specifications: the PLUSS specification language, evolution and perspectives. Proc. STACS '92, Lecture Notes in Computer Science 577, 3-20, 1992.

[Gaudel, Moineau 88] M. C. Gaudel, Th. Moineau: A theory of software reusability. Proc. ESOP '88. Lecture Notes in Computer Science 300, 115-130, 1988.

[Goguen, Burstall 84] J. A. Goguen, R. M. Burstall: Introducing institutions. Logic of Programs, Lecture Notes in Computer Science 164, 221-255, 1984.

[Hennicker 90] R. Hennicker: Context induction: a proof principle for behavioural abstractions and algebraic implementations. Formal Aspects of Computing 4 (3), 326-345, 1990.

[Hennicker 92] R. Hennicker: Behavioural specification and implementation of modular software systems. Technical Report MIP-9203, University of Passau, 1992.

[Orejas et al. 89] F. Orejas, P. Nivela, H. Ehrig: Semantical constructions for categories of behavioral specifications. Proc. Int. Workshop on Categorical Methods in Computer Science with Applications to Topology. Lecture Notes in Computer Science 393, 1989.

[Orejas, Nivela 90] F. Orejas, M. P. Nivela: Constraints for behavioural specifications. Proc. 7th Workshop on Specification of Abstract Data Types. Lecture Notes in Computer Science 534, 220-245, 1990.

[Sannella, Tarlecki 84] D. T. Sannella, A. Tarlecki: Building specifications in an arbitrary institution. Proc. of the Int. Symposium on Semantics of Data Types. Lecture Notes in Computer Science 173, 337-356, 1984.

[Sannella, Tarlecki 87] D. T. Sannella, A. Tarlecki: Toward formal development of programs from algebraic specifications: implementations revisited. Proc. TAPSOFT '87, Lecture Notes in Computer Science 249, 96-110, 1984.

[Sannella et al. 90] D. T. Sannella, A. Tarlecki, S. Sokolowski: Toward formal development of programs from algebraic specifications: parameterisation revisited. Forschungsberichte des Studiengangs Informatik 6/90, Universität Bremen, 1990.

[Schoett 87] O. Schoett: Data abstraction and correctness of modular programming. Ph. D. thesis, CST-42-87, University of Edinburgh, 1987.

[Wirsing 86] M. Wirsing: Structured algebraic specifications: a kernel language. Theoretical Computer Science 42, 123-249, 1986.

Specifications Can Make Programs Run Faster

Mark T. Vandevoorde

Massachusetts Institute of Technology
Cambridge, MA 02139 USA
Email: mtv@lcs.mit.edu

Abstract. This paper describes a strategy for using the information contained in formal specifications to enhance a compiler's ability to perform optimizations. Because specifications are simpler than code and because they abstract away irrelevant implementation details, a compiler with access to specifications can determine that an optimization is safe more often than compilers that analyze only code. Furthermore, formal specifications can be used to allow programmers to define new optimizations.

Our strategy has been implemented in a prototype compiler that incorporates theorem proving technology. The compiler identifies opportunities to perform conventional and programmer-defined optimizations.

1   Introduction

Many approaches to programming emphasize the use of abstractions. The basic idea is to make it easier to understand programs by achieving a separation of concerns. The *client* of an abstraction looks at its specification and writes code that uses the abstraction. He need not concern himself with how the specified behavior is achieved. The *implementor*'s job is to provide an implementation that satisfies the specification. Often, the implementation is substantially more complex than the specification, e.g., for reasons of efficiency, so the specification allows the client to reason about the abstraction at a simpler level.

Although programmers benefit from abstraction and specification when reasoning about programs, existing compilers do not. Compilers should be able to make good use of the information in specifications when optimizing programs, since determining if an optimization is safe requires reasoning about programs.

In this paper, we investigate how to exploit formal specifications to enhance optimization. We use specifications in three ways:

1. to allow programmers to define new optimizations that make abstractions more efficient to use,

2. to relax the preconditions for performing conventional optimizations, and

3. to improve a compiler's ability to recognize that the precondition for performing an optimization is satisfied.

Ultimately, the aim of this research is to make programs built using abstraction and specification more efficient.

Our approach has been implemented in a prototype compiler that incorporates theorem-proving technology to optimize programs written in a strongly typed, imperative language. Early experience with the compiler is encouraging. Performance improvements were obtained in parts of mature programs, and the compiler is able to detect opportunities for optimization that cannot be detected without looking at specifications.

In Section 2 we discuss how specifications can enhance three kinds of optimizations and then briefly discuss related work. In Section 3 we describe the specifications used in Speckle, the source language for our compiler, and we give proof rules for Speckle programs. In Section 4 we describe how our prototype compiler uses the proof rules to identify safe optimizations. Finally, in Section 5 we discuss how our approach fits in the context of software development and report on a case-study of optimizing a program.

2 Optimizations

2.1 Specialized Procedures

Specialized procedures are one kind of programmer-defined optimization for making general procedures run faster in special cases. The basic idea is that a procedure presents one simple specification but has multiple implementations. One implementation is general enough to work in any context, while the others are more efficient but work in fewer contexts. The compiler substitutes one of the faster implementations for the general one when it can prove (using specifications) that a calling context satisfies the stronger pre-condition of the faster implementation.

For example, consider the specification in Fig. 1 for Table_Enter, which enters the value for a key into a table. Suppose that the specifications in Fig. 1 are implemented using an unsorted list of key-value pairs with the invariant that no key appears more than once. Thus, Table_Enter must in general check whether k appears in the list. However, we would like to specialize Table_Enter to avoid this check in contexts where k cannot appear in the list, e.g., in Fig. 2.

Our approach is to have the programmer write the dual implementation for Table_Enter shown in Fig. 3. The "*specialize when*" construct directs the compiler to use the second implementation of Table_Enter when it can discharge the pre-condition not(defined(t^,k)). Specifications are required both to express the pre-condition and to discharge it in contexts like that in Fig. 1.

2.2 Common Subexpression Elimination

Common subexpression elimination (CSE) is a standard optimization to avoid recomputing an expression when its value is already available. For example, in the code fragment

```
x := a[i]; ...; y := a[i]
```

```
Table_Enter = proc (t: Table, k: Key, v: Value)
    modifies t
    ensures t' = bind(t^, k, v)

Table_Lookup = proc (t: Table, k: Key) returns (v: Value)
    modifies --
    ensures v = image(t^, k)
    except signals missing when not(defined(t^, k))
```

Fig. 1: Table Specification

```
v: Value := Table_Lookup(t, k)
    except when missing:
                v := Value_Create()
                Table_Enter(t, k, v)
          end
```

Fig. 2: A Context to Specialize Table_Enter

there is no need to recompute a[i] because its value is available, unless the code between the two occurrences of a[i] changes a or i.

Although compilers are very good at eliminating expressions that use only primitive operations like __+__ and __[__], they are less effective at eliminating procedures calls. The problem is that in imperative programs, a procedure may perform a visible side effect, so eliminating a procedure call, even when its result is available, may alter the program's behavior.

Specifications make it easier to eliminate procedure calls by explicitly stating whether a procedure performs any visible side effects. For example, in Fig. 1 the specification of Table_Lookup states that Table_Lookup performs no visible side effect. Thus, it is safe to eliminate calls to Table_Lookup, but it isn't safe to eliminate calls to Table_Enter, which may modify its first argument.

Specifications also make it easier to recognize equal expressions that are not syntactically identical. For example, in the code fragment

```
Table_Enter(t, k, v1)
v2 := Table_Lookup(t, k)
```

the call to Table_Lookup can be replaced by v1. Although it is impractical to perform this optimization by analyzing the implementations of Table_Lookup and Table_Enter, the optimization is easy to do given the specifications in Fig. 1 and the axiom about tables

∀ t: Table, k: Key, v: Value [image(bind(t, k, v), k) == v]

Currently, compilers only eliminate an expression when an˘ *equal* value is available. With specifications, it is possible to relax this condition. Consider,

```
Table_Enter = proc (t: Table, k: Key, v: Value)
        p: pair := FindPair(t, k)
           except when none: InsertPair(t, k, v)
                            return
                    end
        p.val := v
    specialize when not(defined(t^, k)):
        InsertPair(t, k, v)
    end Table_Enter
```

Fig. 3: A Dual Implementation for Table_Enter

for example, the code

```
i1 := IntSet_Least(s)
i2 := IntSet_AnyElement(s)
```

where **Least** is specified to return the smallest element of the set **s** while the specification of **AnyElement** allows it to return any element. With the specifications, it is possible to recognize that the call to **AnyElement** can be replaced by **i1**, even when **AnyElement** would have returned a different element. Without the specifications, this optimization appears unsafe because it might alter the value computed for **i2**.

2.3 Identifying Loop-Constant Expressions

When a compiler can determine that an expression is a loop constant, it can optimize the loop to compute the expression once rather than once per iteration.

Most of the enhancements to common subexpression elimination also apply to identifying loop-constant expressions. Expressions can be generalized to include procedure calls that perform no visible side effects. Furthermore, the called procedure may be non-deterministic: it need not compute the same value each iteration, but the value returned for the first iteration must be substitutable for the values returned on the other iterations. For example, it is safe to treat **AnyElement(s)** as a loop "constant" when the body of loop does not modify **s**.

2.4 Side Effect Analysis

All of the optimizations discussed above require the compiler to reason about side effects. For common subexpression elimination, it must determine that the code executed between the expressions does not change their value. To identify a loop constant expression, the compiler must determine if the body of the loop affects the value of the expression. To call a specialized implementation, the compiler must often determine that a pre-condition established at one point in the program is still true at a later point, e.g., that in Fig. 2, the pre-condition not(defined(t^,k)) established when **Table_Lookup** signals missing is not invalidated by a side effect of **Value_Create**.

Specifications improve the analysis of side effects. Only specifications can distinguish between side effects that are visible to the client's code from those that are invisible. E.g., a procedure might cache previously computed results in a private data structure—changes to this data structure are invisible to clients.

Specifications of data abstractions also make some side effects invisible because they abstract away parts of data structures used to implement values of a data type. E.g., if tables are represented as lists of key-value pairs, an operation of the table type might sort the list. This side effect is invisible to clients.

Data abstractions are also useful because they introduce new types that, in a strongly typed language, can be used to bound side effects. For example, suppose a user defines the types `IntSet`, `IntQueue`, `IntStack` and implements each one using integer arrays. Because a user-defined type must guarantee that the representation of a value is never directly accessible outside of the implementation of the type, the compiler can assume that a procedure that can only access an `IntSet` cannot modify an `IntQueue` even though both are represented using the same type.

Finally, a data abstraction may specify that the data type is *immutable*, i.e., that no visible side effect is possible on instances of the data type.[1] This eliminates the need to analyze side effects for instances of the type.

2.5 Related Work

The idea of allowing programmers to define new optimizations has been suggested before. In [15], Scherlis allows programmers to enhance performance by writing "expression procedures" for a functional language of recursive equations. In [8], Hisgen presents an unimplemented design of a language where the author of a module provides transformation rules used to restructure the program for efficiency. However, his approach is not modular since, in general, the user must consider how procedures from different modules interact.

Our extensions to standard optimizations are not intended to replace traditional compilation techniques that deal with register allocation and other machine-level issues. The extensions are complementary to code analysis [3], which can perform standard optimizations that span procedure boundaries, e.g., identifying redundant code in different procedures. However, even interprocedural code analysis techniques like [2, 10] can be foiled by invisible side effects that are concealed by specifications in our approach. Furthermore, many code analysis techniques simplify the problem of estimating side effects by either not supporting procedures, not supporting pointers, or restricting pointers to one level of indirection [1, 9, 13, 14, 16]. Because specifications contain information that is useful for bounding side effects, we do not need to make such restrictions. Our handling of side effects is more like the FX language, which augments an imperative dialect of LISP with specifications describing side effects [12]. However, FX specifications cannot express user-defined optimizations.

---

[1] For example, integers and bignums are immutable in Common LISP, but cons cells are mutable.

3   Speckle

Speckle is a strongly typed, imperative programming language based on CLU [11] and designed to experiment with specification-based optimization. We chose CLU as a starting point because it has many of the features of modern programming languages, including data abstraction, exceptions, and (implicit) pointers. Speckle programs are specified using Larch [7], which uses first order predicate logic. To simplify reasoning about programs, some features of CLU are omitted: polymorphism and non-local variables.[2] We also omit first class procedures (procedures as data) because they are difficult to specify in first-order logic.

First, we describe Speckle specifications. Next, we give inference rules, based on specifications, that will be used to prove that optimizations are safe.

3.1   Larch/Speckle Specifications

Larch is a two-tiered specification language. The Larch Shared Language (LSL) is used to define useful mathematical functions in a fragment of multisorted, first-order logic. Functions and sorts defined in LSL are independent of any programming language.

The semantics of LSL defines a first-order *theory*—an infinite set of formulae—for LSL specifications. The theory is the consequence closure of the specification's axioms and inference rules, which include the normal inference rules of predicate logic. For our purposes, it suffices that LSL specifications provide useful axioms in the form of equations.

The Larch/Speckle interface language is the glue between a Speckle program and LSL. Larch/Speckle formalizes the notion of a program state and provides a language for specifying data type and procedure interfaces. These interfaces refer to LSL sorts and functions, e.g., Fig. 1 refers to the LSL functions **image** and **bind**.

A Speckle program state consists of an environment and a store:

$$\textit{Prog State} = \textit{Env X Store}$$
$$\textit{Env} \quad\;\; = \textit{Ident} \rightarrow (\textit{ImmValue} + \textit{Loc})$$
$$\textit{Store} \quad\; = \textit{Loc} \rightarrow \textit{MutValue}$$

σ^{Env} denotes the environment of program state σ, and σ^{Str} denotes its store.

Values are divided into three domains. ImmValues are used to represent values of immutable types, and MutValues are used for values of mutable types. A Loc represents the location (address) of a mutable data structure. A procedure *modifies* a Loc l if $\sigma^{\text{Str}}_{\text{pre}}(l) \neq \sigma^{\text{Str}}_{\text{post}}(l)$.

---

[2]CLU does not have fully global variables, but it has "own" variables. A module's "own" variables are accessible by any procedure in the module but are inaccessible outside the module.

In the absence of procedure variables, techniques based on interprocedural code analysis could effectively bound the set of global variables read or written by a Speckle procedure, e.g., [1]. These variables would be treated like additional arguments to the procedure. Alternatively, Speckle could require the user to list any global variable that a procedure could read or write, e.g., in a fashion similar to Euclid and Modula.

$\forall \ \sigma_{\text{pre}}, \ \sigma_{\text{post}}$: *Prog State, t: TableLoc, k: Key, v: Value*

Table_Enter:

$Norm(\sigma_{\text{pre}}^{\text{Str}}, \sigma_{\text{post}}^{\text{Str}}, t, k, v) == \sigma_{\text{post}}^{\text{Str}}(t) = bind(\sigma_{\text{pre}}^{\text{Str}}(t), k, v)$

$$\wedge \ \forall \ l\text{: } TableLoc \ [l \neq t \Longrightarrow \sigma_{\text{post}}^{\text{Str}}(l) = \sigma_{\text{pre}}^{\text{Str}}(l)]$$

Table_Lookup:

$Norm(\sigma_{\text{pre}}^{\text{Str}}, \sigma_{\text{post}}^{\text{Str}}, t, k, v) == v = image(\sigma_{\text{pre}}^{\text{Str}}(t), k, v) \wedge \sigma_{\text{post}}^{\text{Str}} = \sigma_{\text{pre}}^{\text{Str}}$

$Excpt(\sigma_{\text{pre}}^{\text{Str}}, \sigma_{\text{post}}^{\text{Str}}, t, k) == \sigma_{\text{post}}^{\text{Str}} = \sigma_{\text{pre}}^{\text{Str}}$

$Guard(\sigma_{\text{pre}}^{\text{Str}}, t, k) == not(defined(\sigma_{\text{pre}}^{\text{Str}}(t), k))$

Fig. 4: Procedure Predicates

There may be several aliases for a given Loc *l*. For example, the environment may map any number of Idents to *l*. Also, any MutValue in the range of the store or any ImmValue in the range of the environment may contain *l*. For example, a value for an array of mutable data contains the Loc of each (mutable) element. Similarly, a record value contains the Loc of each mutable field.

Aliasing is not possible for Idents because ImmValues and MutValues may not contain Idents.

Data Type Interfaces. A data type interface names an LSL sort used to represent values of the type and indicates whether the type is mutable—this determines whether the sort is an ImmValue or a MutValue. When a type is specified as mutable, a *location sort* is implicitly defined for the type, e.g., *TableLoc* for locations of **Tables**. In procedure specifications, a term *l* denoting a location may be suffixed by ^ to denote $\sigma_{\text{pre}}^{\text{Str}}(l)$ or by ' to denote $\sigma_{\text{post}}^{\text{Str}}(l)$. A formal parameter whose type is mutable denotes a location; a formal parameter whose type is immutable denotes an ImmValue.

Procedure Interfaces. Specifications of procedures, which may signal exceptions, are written as pre- and post-conditions in a stylized fashion. The **requires** clause defines the pre-condition, *Req* (if any). The **modifies** clause restricts the side-effects of the procedure by defining the set of locations that the procedure is allowed to modify; this restriction is part of every post-condition. The post-condition for a normal return, *Norm*, is further specified by the **ensures** clause, which typically defines the results in terms of the arguments. All procedures are assumed to terminate.

For the sake of brevity, here we allow at most one exception. The **when** clause defines a second condition on the pre-state, *Guard*. The procedure must signal the exception exactly when *Guard* is true. The post-condition for an exceptional return, *Excpt*, is defined by the **modifies** clause and an optional **ensuring** clause.

Fig. 4 lists the result of translating the interface specifications of Fig. 1 into predicates when `Table` is the only mutable type used by the program. For every other mutable type T, the assertion "$\forall\ l\colon TLoc\ [\sigma_{\text{post}}^{\text{Str}}(l) = \sigma_{\text{pre}}^{\text{Str}}(l)]$" would be added as a conjunct to the post-conditions of `Table_Enter`. Note that the post-conditions constrain only the store; the environment is defined by the semantics of the programming language. Pre- and post-conditions may not refer to environments because Speckle does not allow global variables.

3.2 Proof Rules for Speckle Programs

Hoare rules are a standard way of defining proof rules for programs in the form of a parse tree. However, in language with exceptions, it is awkward to use parse trees for the same reason that it is hard to give Hoare rules for statements like `break` and `continue`. Therefore, we use Floyd's approach [4] and define proof rules for Speckle programs that are in the form of a control flow graph (CFG). The proof rules have not been checked against a language semantics.

Each program has a unique entering edge labeled *enter*, one or more exiting edges, and zero or more internal edges. A program is the body of a single procedure, and each exiting edge corresponds to either a normal return or signaling an exception. There are four kinds of nodes: assignment, procedure call, merge, and loop.

We assume that the pre-condition of the program ensures that the program terminates, only calls procedures whose pre-conditions are satisfied, and uses no uninitialized variables. We also assume that all specifications are correct, i.e., they accurately describe their implementations.

Associated with each CFG edge e is an LSL theory, $\mathcal{T}_e$. To prove that some predicate P holds at the program point denoted by an edge e, one must prove that the formula $P(\sigma_e) = true$ is in $\mathcal{T}_e$. The relation $\in$ is used to define the theories at each edge: $F \in \mathcal{T}_e$ means that formula F is in theory $\mathcal{T}_e$. Proof rules define $\in$ inductively, i.e., the theory of each internal and exiting edge is determined by the structure of the CFG and the theory of the entering edge.

The theory $\mathcal{T}_{\text{enter}}$ of the entering edge comes from the specifications of of procedures and data types used in the CFG. $\mathcal{T}_{\text{enter}}$ is the consequence closure of the union of: the theories of all LSL specifications used; the theory of the program state, and procedure predicates defined by Larch/Speckle; and the precondition for entering the CFG specified by the user, if any.

Fig. 5 and Fig. 6 list the proof rules for Speckle. We extend the notation for the hypothesis of a proof rule to include a template of a subgraph appearing in the program. The first proof rule is that each theory is closed under the usual inference rules of predicate logic.

The second proof rule is that the theory of an edge j is an extension of the theories of each edge i that dominates j.[3] This rule propagates the formulae defining σ_i in $\mathcal{T}_i$ to $\mathcal{T}_j$, so it allows $\mathcal{T}_j$ to define σ_j in terms of σ_i. For example, if

---

[3]Edge i *dominates* edge j if every path from the entering edge to j must pass through i. Every edge dominates itself. Edge i *strictly dominates* edge j if i dominates j and $i \neq j$.

$$F \in ConsequenceClosure(\mathcal{T}_e)$$

$$\overline{F \in \mathcal{T}_e}$$

$$F \in \mathcal{T}_i$$
$$\text{Edge } i \text{ dominates edge } j$$

$$\overline{F \in \mathcal{T}_j}$$

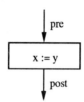

$\sigma_{post}^{Env}(\text{`}\mathbf{x}\text{'}) = \sigma_{pre}^{Env}(\text{`}\mathbf{y}\text{'})$	$\in \mathcal{T}_{post}$
$\forall var : Ident[var \neq \text{`}\mathbf{x}\text{'} \Longrightarrow \sigma_{post}^{Env}(var) = \sigma_{pre}^{Env}(var)]$	$\in \mathcal{T}_{post}$
$\sigma_{post}^{Str} = \sigma_{pre}^{Str}$	$\in \mathcal{T}_{post}$

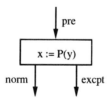

$Norm(\sigma_{pre}^{Str}, \sigma_{norm}^{Str}, \sigma_{pre}^{Env}(\text{`}\mathbf{y}\text{'}), \sigma_{norm}^{Env}(\text{`}\mathbf{x}\text{'}))$	$\in \mathcal{T}_{norm}$
$\neg\, Guard(\sigma_{pre}^{Str}, \sigma_{pre}^{Env}(\text{`}\mathbf{y}\text{'}))$	$\in \mathcal{T}_{norm}$
$\forall var : Ident[var \neq \text{`}\mathbf{x}\text{'} \Longrightarrow \sigma_{norm}^{Env}(var) = \sigma_{pre}^{Env}(var)]$	$\in \mathcal{T}_{norm}$
$Excpt(\sigma_{pre}^{Str}, \sigma_{excpt}^{Str}, \sigma_{pre}^{Env}(\text{`}\mathbf{y}\text{'}))$	$\in \mathcal{T}_{excpt}$
$Guard(\sigma_{pre}^{Str}, \sigma_{pre}^{Env}(\text{`}\mathbf{y}\text{'}))$	$\in \mathcal{T}_{excpt}$
$\sigma_{excpt}^{Env} = \sigma_{pre}^{Env}$	$\in \mathcal{T}_{excpt}$

Fig. 5: Proof Rules for Speckle

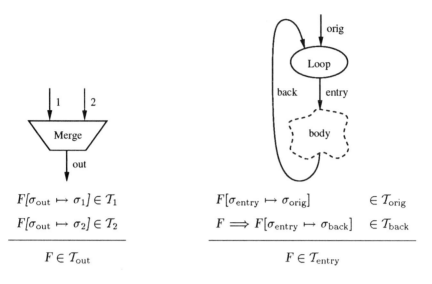

$$F[\sigma_{\text{out}} \mapsto \sigma_1] \in \mathcal{T}_1$$

$$F[\sigma_{\text{out}} \mapsto \sigma_2] \in \mathcal{T}_2$$

$$F \in \mathcal{T}_{\text{out}}$$

$$F[\sigma_{\text{entry}} \mapsto \sigma_{\text{orig}}] \qquad \in \mathcal{T}_{\text{orig}}$$

$$F \implies F[\sigma_{\text{entry}} \mapsto \sigma_{\text{back}}] \quad \in \mathcal{T}_{\text{back}}$$

$$F \in \mathcal{T}_{\text{entry}}$$

Fig. 6: Proof Rules for Speckle, continued

i and j are the edges before and after the statement $\mathbf{x} := \mathbf{x+1}$, $\sigma_j^{\text{Env}}(\mathbf{'x'})$ can be defined in terms of $\sigma_i^{\text{Env}}(\mathbf{'x'})$.

The rule for an assignment states that the only variable affected by the assignment is the one named on the left of ":=", so assignment to '$\mathbf{x}$' never affects '$\mathbf{z}$'. Furthermore, the store is unchanged.

The rule for a procedure call node[4] uses the predicates from the procedure's specification to define the post-state in terms of the pre-state. When the procedure returns normally, the only variable affected by a call is the one that is assigned the result of the call. If the procedure signals an exception, the environment is unchanged. Note that the theories of the exiting edges contain control-dependent information derived from the exception guard.

Because procedures can signal exceptions, a branch can be treated as a call to a procedure that takes a boolean argument and signals an exception exactly when the argument is true.

The merge and loop rule rules correspond to the familiar rules for proof-by-cases and proof-by-induction. The notation $F[\sigma_i \mapsto \sigma]$ denotes F with σ substituted for σ_i and with bound variables renamed to avoid capture.

Note that the theory of edge e is inconsistent ($\textit{true} = \textit{false} \in \mathcal{T}_e$) precisely when the edge is unreachable at run-time. E.g., if a procedure is called in a context where it cannot signal an exception ($\neg \textit{Guard} \in \mathcal{T}_{\text{pre}}$), $\mathcal{T}_{\text{excpt}}$ is inconsistent because it contains both $\textit{Guard}$ and $\neg \textit{Guard}$. The second proof rule propagates the inconsistency to each edge dominated by $\textit{excpt}$, and this is correct: $\textit{excpt}$ is unreachable, so any edge dominated by $\textit{excpt}$ is also unreachable.

---

[4]The rule shown is for a procedure with a single argument and result. We rely on the reader's intuition to extend the rule for different numbers of arguments and results.

4 Prototype Compiler

We constructed a prototype compiler for Speckle that identifies optimizations using the LP theorem-prover [5] and the proof rules from the previous section. The compiler does not generate any code. LP is particularly well-suited for our purpose because it was designed to work with LSL and because it fails quickly when trying to prove a difficult conjecture rather than attempting expensive proof strategies. This is particularly important because many conjectures a compiler wants to prove are false, e.g., most procedure calls cannot be eliminated.

In Section 2, we gave informal pre-conditions for performing various kinds of optimizations. Each of these can be stated formally using the framework of the previous section. For example, to replace a procedure call $\mathtt{x := P(y)}$ by an assignment $\mathtt{x := z}$, the compiler must prove that the available value $\mathtt{z}$ satisfies the post-condition of $\mathtt{P}$, i.e.,

$$Norm(\sigma_{\mathrm{pre}}^{\mathrm{Str}},\ \sigma_{\mathrm{pre}}^{\mathrm{Str}},\ \sigma_{\mathrm{pre}}^{\mathrm{Env}}(\text{`}\mathtt{y}\text{'}),\ \sigma_e^{\mathrm{Env}}(\text{`}\mathtt{z}\text{'})) \in \mathcal{T}_{\mathrm{pre}}$$

where $Norm$ is the post-condition of $\mathtt{P}$, pre is the edge entering the call node, and post is the exiting edge for the normal return, and e is an edge that dominates pre.[5] The compiler must also prove that the call does not signal an exception, i.e.,

$$\neg Guard(\sigma_{\mathrm{pre}},\ \sigma_{\mathrm{pre}}^{\mathrm{Env}}(\text{`}\mathtt{y}\text{'})) \in \mathcal{T}_{\mathrm{pre}}$$

The Speckle compiler uses LP to discharge the proof obligations for optimizations. LP is primarily based on conditional term rewriting, which it uses to simplify terms to normal forms. To prove a conjecture by rewriting, one must simplify it to the term *true*.

LP can automatically convert a set of assertions like those found in LSL and Larch/Speckle specifications into a conditional term rewriting system. In general, a rewriting system only approximates the consequence closure of a set of assertions because a rewriting system is usually incomplete: it may not simplify some formulae in $\mathcal{T}_e$ to *true*.

The compiler uses LP to approximate each theory $\mathcal{T}_e$ by a conditional term rewriting system $\mathcal{R}_e$. The strategy is to simplify a term containing a program state symbol σ_e into either a term that contains no program state symbols or one that contains only program state symbols of edges that dominate e. The net effect is to try to simplify a term into one expressed using at most σ_{enter}, the program state symbol for the entering edge.

The first step in building the term rewriting systems is to construct $\mathcal{R}_{\mathrm{enter}}$, the rewriting system for the entering edge. $\mathcal{R}_{\mathrm{enter}}$ is derived mechanically from the LSL specifications referenced by the program using the LSL Checker, which automatically translates LSL specifications into LP input, which LP then converts into a rewriting system. The compiler also adds assertions to axiomatize program states, location sorts, and predicates derived from Larch/Speckle specifications of procedure interfaces.

---

[5] If z is assigned between edge e and pre, the compiler must introduce a temporary variable to store the available value.

The next step is to construct rewriting systems for the other edges in the program in depth-first order. When edge e exiting node n is visited, $\mathcal{R}_e$ is constructed by extending the rewriting system of the edge entering n. The extensions are determined by n: if n is an assignment node, the conclusions from the assignment rule in Fig. 3 are added to $\mathcal{R}_e$; if n is a procedure call node, the procedure call rule is used. Nothing is added for merge or loop nodes.

Merge and loop nodes must be handled differently from the others because the hypotheses of these rules include subgoals that must be discharged using the theories of other edges. The basic strategy for proving $F \in \mathcal{T}_e$ is to first simplify F using $\mathcal{R}_e$; let t be the simplified form of F. If t contains a program state symbol for an edge that exits a merge or loop node, the compiler automatically attempts proof-by-cases or proof-by-induction.[6]

4.1 An Example

Fig. 7 is an example that illustrates our strategy. Procedure `RemoveDuplicates` uses two user-defined data types: `IntSet`, a type for mutable integer sets, and `IntArray`, a type for integer arrays that can grow and shrink dynamically. The syntactic expressions `a.low, a[i]`, and `a[j] :=...` are shorthands for calls to the procedures `IntArray_GetLow`, `IntArray_Fetch`, and `IntArray_Store`. `IntArray_Trim` takes an array, a starting index, and an element count and discards all other elements.

Using formal specifications and specializations of `IntSet` and `IntArray`, the compiler identifies the following optimizations automatically:[7]

1. The expressions `a[i]` on lines 5 and 6 can be replaced by the value computed for `a[i]` on line 4.

   This optimization relies on the `modifies` clauses of `Member` and `Insert` to show that `a` is unchanged since the call to `Fetch` on line 4.

2. The call to `Insert` need not check whether `a[i]` is in `s`. This is a specialization of `Insert`.

   This optimization relies on the semantics of `if`, the `modifies` clause of `Fetch` to show that `s` is unchanged, and the specification of `Member`.

3. The bounds checks for `a[i]` on line 4 and for `a[j]` on line 6 are unnecessary. These are specializations defined by `Fetch` and `Store`.

4. The two expressions `a.low` on line 10 can be replaced by the value computed for `a.low` on line 1.

Optimizations 3 and 4 require proof-by-cases, proof-by-induction, and array axioms to determine that the bounds of the array are invariant over the loop.

---

[6] If t contains more than one such symbol, the one for the edge closest to e is handled first.

[7] Many of the array optimizations are similar to those in [6]. However, there the semantics of arrays is fixed by the compiler. Here, the semantics of dynamic arrays is defined by the specifier.

```
RemoveDuplicates = proc (a: IntArray)
  1    j: Int := a.low
  2    s: IntSet := IntSet_Create()

  3    for i: Int in IntArray_Indexes(a) do
  4        if not IntSet_Member(s, a[i])
  5           then IntSet_Insert(s, a[i])
  6                  a[j] := a[i]
  7                  j := j + 1
  8              end
  9        end

 10    IntArray_Trim(a, a.low, j - a.low)
       end RemoveDuplicates
```

Fig. 7: Procedure RemoveDuplicates

5 Discussion

All of the optimizations that we have considered here can be hand-coded by the user at the source level. Why, therefore, should one bother using specifications to optimize programs? One reason is that other optimizations that are not expressible at the source level could also benefit from specifications.

Another reason is that relying on the compiler to perform optimizations makes programs easier to build, understand, and maintain. For example, to get the benefit of specialized procedures without using an optimizer, one must introduce a separate interface for each specialized implementation. Each client must decide which interface is appropriate. If they choose an overly general interface, they sacrifice performance, and if they choose an inappropriate specialized interface, they introduce an error. Suppose that later in the life cycle of the program, the reason for the specialized implementation disappears. (E.g., in the original example of Fig. 3, suppose the representation for tables is changed to use binary trees.) Either all interfaces will have to be maintained, or all client code will have to be updated.

Ultimately, the question of whether to use specifications to optimize code boils down to whether the costs of writing formal specifications and running the optimizer justify the benefits of elegant and efficient code. To avoid the cost of writing formal specifications for the entire program, Speckle has features to support partial or missing specifications [17]. This allows a user to amortize costs by focusing on widely-used, lower-level abstractions. Currently, the prototype compiler is too expensive to run outside a research lab; making it practical will require more research.

To guage the potential benefits, we have applied our optimizer to pieces of existing programs. Our initial experience is encouraging. In a study of a program that performs AC-unification, we identified four different specializations whose pre-conditions were discharged by our compiler in several contexts. Optimizing these contexts resulted in an 11% improvement in speed.

5.1 Debugging

All optimizing compilers complicate debugging because an optimized program differs from the unoptimized one. The only new wrinkle added by our strategy is that the optimized program sometimes calls specialized implementations whose existence was unknown to client code.

A more difficult problem is how to identify bugs in specifications. Because the compiler relies on specifications, bugs in specifications can lead to unsound optimizations. One way to eliminate such errors is to verify the specifications, but there are other possibilities too. The compiler could perform sanity checks on specifications. For example, an interface cannot modify an immutable value. Another possibility is for the user to supply code to check the pre-condition of a specialization and for the debugger to insert this code wherever the optimizer has "proved" that the pre-condition is satisfied. The compiler might list the optimizations and/or the proof obligations that it discharges so that the user could check the list for suspicious ones. Finally, the user could direct the compiler to ignore suspect specifications and see if the problem disappears.

5.2 Status

The Speckle compiler demonstrates that our strategy can improve the efficiency of programs that use abstraction. The compiler detects optimizations that are impossible to find without specifications as well as optimizations that, to our knowledge, no other optimization technique discovers because the optimizations are too difficult. The reason is that specifications conceal irrelevant implementation details, such as benevolent side effects and overly deterministic implementations, which foil techniques based only on code analysis.

Initial experience indicates that when our strategy for defining new optimizations is used, the compiler is able to detect optimizations that improve the performance of mature programs. We are continuing to test the compiler to measure how often it detects legal optimizations and how much the optimizations impact efficiency.

Acknowledgements

We thank John Guttag for his many useful suggestions for both improving this work and improving this paper. We also thank William Weihl, Jeannette Wing, the members of the MIT Systematic Program Development Group, and the referees for their comments on earlier drafts.

Support for this research has been provided in part by the Advanced Research Projects Agency of the Department of Defense, monitored by the Office of Naval Research Research under contract N00014-89-J-1988, and in part by the National Science Foundation under grant 9115797-CCR.

[1] J. P. Banning. An efficient way to find the side effects of procedure calls and the aliases of variables. In *POPL*, pages 29–41. ACM, January 1979.

[2] D. R. Chase, M. Wegman, and F. K. Zadeck. Analysis of pointers and structures. In *PLDI*, pages 296–310. ACM, June 1990.

[3] J. Ferrante, K. J. Ottenstein, and J. D. Warren. The program dependence graph and its use in optimization. *ACM TOPLAS*, 9(3):319–349, July 1987.

[4] R. W. Floyd. Assigning meanings to programs. In *Proceedings of Symposia in Applied Mathematics*, volume 19, pages 19–31. AMS, 1967.

[5] S. Garland and J. Guttag. A guide to LP, The Larch Prover. TR 82, DEC Systems Research Center, Palo Alto, CA, December 1991.

[6] R. Gupta. A fresh look at optimizing array bound checking. In *PLDI*, pages 272–282. ACM, June 1990.

[7] J. Guttag, J. Horning (eds.), with S. Garland, K. Jones, A. Modet, and J. Wing. *Larch: Languages and Tools for Formal Specification*. Springer-Verlag, 1993.

[8] A. Hisgen. *Optimization of User-Defined Abstract Data Types: A Program Transformation Approach*. PhD thesis, Carnegie-Mellon University, 1985.

[9] N. D. Jones and S. S. Muchnick. Flow analysis and optimization of LISP-like structures. In *Program Flow Analysis: Theory and Application*, pages 102–131. Prentice-Hall, 1981.

[10] J. R. Larus and P. N. Hilfinger. Detecting conflicts between structure accesses. In *PLDI*, pages 21–34. ACM, June 1988.

[11] B. Liskov and J. Guttag. *Abstraction and Specification in Program Development*. MIT Press, Cambridge, Ma, 1986.

[12] J. M. Lucassen. Types and effects: Towards the integration of functional and imperative programming. MIT/LCS/TR 408, August 1987.

[13] A. Neirynck, P. Panangaden, and A. J. Demers. Computation of aliases and support sets. In *POPL*. ACM, 1987.

[14] B. K. Rosen, M. N. Wegman, and F. K. Zadeck. Global value numbers and redundant computations. In *POPL*. ACM, 1988.

[15] W. L. Scherlis. Program improvement by internal specialization. In *POPL*, pages 41–49. ACM, 1981.

[16] B. Steffen, J. Knoop, and O. Rüthing. Efficient code motion and an adaption to strength reduction. In *TAPSOFT '91 (LNCS 494)*, pages 394–415. Springer-Verlag, April 1991.

[17] M. T. Vandevoorde. Optimizing programs with partial specifications. In *Proceedings of the 1992 Larch Workshop*. Springer Verlag. To appear.

Application of the Composition Principle to Unity-like Specifications

Pierre Collette*

Université Catholique de Louvain, Unité d'Informatique, Place Sainte-Barbe,
B-1348 Louvain-la-Neuve, Belgium

Abstract. The problem of composing mutually dependent rely-guarantee specifications arises in the hierarchical development of reactive or concurrent systems. The composition principle has been proposed as a logic-independent solution to this problem. In this paper, we apply it to Unity-like rely-guarantee specifications. For that purpose, we interpret Unity formulas in Abadi and Lamport's compositional model. Then, the premises of the composition rule are reduced to proof obligations that can be carried out in the existing Unity proof system. The approach is illustrated by an example, the composition of mutually dependent specifications of concurrent buffers.

1 Introduction

Several specification methods [2, 10, 14] for the development of reactive or concurrent systems may be classified as rely-guarantee or assumption-commitment methods. Intuitively, a rely-guarantee specification $R \Rightarrow G$ states that a system satisfies the guarantee condition G if it operates in an environment that satisfies a rely condition R. We consider specification triples (R, G, G^S) where the safety condition G^S is implied by the full (including liveness) guarantee condition G and R is restricted to a safety condition.

Hierarchical specification methods for concurrent systems generally require composition rules. In the rely-guarantee paradigm, the composition principle of [2, 14] provides a way of combining mutually dependent specifications. If $[\![S]\!]$ denotes the set of behaviours allowed by a specification S, this principle may be stated as follows:

$$\frac{P_1 \text{ sat } (R_1 \Rightarrow G_1) \quad [\![R]\!] \cap [\![G_2^S]\!] \subseteq [\![R_1]\!] \quad [\![R]\!] \cap [\![G_1^S]\!] \cap [\![G_2^S]\!] \subseteq [\![G^S]\!]}{P_1 \| P_2 \text{ sat } (R \Rightarrow G)}$$

$$P_2 \text{ sat } (R_2 \Rightarrow G_2) \quad [\![R]\!] \cap [\![G_1^S]\!] \subseteq [\![R_2]\!] \quad [\![R]\!] \cap [\![G_1]\!] \cap [\![G_2]\!] \subseteq [\![G]\!]$$

Basically, the premises correspond the reliance, co-existence, guarantee and strength proof obligations of [10, 20]. Informally, they read:

1. Reliance/Co-existence: $[\![R]\!] \cap [\![G_2^S]\!] \subseteq [\![R_1]\!]$. P_1 does not rely on more than $P_1 \| P_2$ does, nor on more than P_2 guarantees.
2. Reliance/Co-existence: $[\![R]\!] \cap [\![G_1^S]\!] \subseteq [\![R_2]\!]$. P_2 does not rely on more than $P_1 \| P_2$ does, nor on more than P_1 guarantees.

---

* National Fund for Scientific Research (Belgium)

3. Guarantee: $[\![R]\!] \cap [\![G_1^S]\!] \cap [\![G_2^S]\!] \subseteq [\![G^S]\!]$. Under the assumptions on the environment of $P_1 \| P_2$, the safety guarantee conditions of P_1 and P_2 must imply the safety guarantee conditions of $P_1 \| P_2$.

4. Strength: $[\![R]\!] \cap [\![G_1]\!] \cap [\![G_2]\!] \subseteq [\![G]\!]$. Under the assumptions on the environment of $P_1 \| P_2$, the guarantee conditions of P_1 and P_2 must imply the guarantee condition of $P_1 \| P_2$, especially the liveness guarantee conditions.

These four conditions are stated exclusively in semantic terms (sets of allowed behaviours). Our objective is to apply them in a particular development framework. The language we have chosen is Unity logic [6] because it yields workable specifications that may be scaled up to specify large problems [15, 16, 17]. Its operators `initially`, `unless`, and `leadsto` specify initial conditions, next-state relations, and liveness requirements respectively.

Thus, the aim of this paper is to show how the composition rule may be applied to Unity-like specifications. More precisely, we interpret the specifications in Abadi and Lamport's compositional model [2, 4] and then restate the above conditions in terms of the Unity proof obligations $R, G_2^S \vdash R_1$, $R, G_1^S \vdash R_2$, $R, G_1^S, G_2^S \vdash G^S$, and $R, G_1, G_2 \vdash G$.

As discussed in [2, 4], soundness of the composition principle is reached under the hypotheses that G^S and R respectively constrain the specified system and its environment. Therefore, to reach soundness, we propose a new version of `unless` which distinguishes system from environment transitions. Essentially, this modification is similar to what is done in [3, 5] when designing compositional versions of temporal logic.

Throughout the paper, we *preserve* the Unity style of reasoning about specifications and *reuse* the Unity proof rules. This work should thus not be viewed as 'yet another language' but rather as an attempt to combine Abadi-Lamport's work [2] and Chandy-Misra's work [6, 15].

2 Logic

In this section, we interpret Unity-like specifications in Abadi and Lamport's semantic model. Then, we recall some inference rules.

2.1 Semantic Model

In temporal-logic based approaches, the set of variables is usually divided into two classes: the class of *dynamic* variables and the class of *static* variables. Dynamic variables (also called state variables) represent quantities that can vary with time, like x in the Hoare triple $\{x = n\} x := x + 1 \{x > n\}$. A *state* is then defined as a function assigning to each dynamic variable a value in its domain. In contrast, static variables represent quantities that remain constant with time, like n in the above Hoare triple. A *static valuation* is then defined as a function assigning to each static variable a value in its domain.

Abadi and Lamport interpret a specification S as a set $[\![S]\!]$ of allowed behaviours [2]. A behaviour is a sequence

$$\sigma = s_1 \xrightarrow{a_1} s_2 \xrightarrow{a_2} s_3 \xrightarrow{a_3} \dots$$

where each s_k is a state, as defined above, and each a_k is an *agent*. By convention, $|\sigma|$, $s_k.\sigma$, $a_k.\sigma$, and $\sigma|_k$ denote the length of σ, the kth state of σ, the agent responsible for the kth transition, and the finite prefix of σ ending with $s_k.\sigma$ respectively. Agents must be thought as the entities responsible for state transitions. Although two agents (program and environment) would suffice in any particular specification, considering sets of agents eases the composition problem because the parallel composition of programs corresponds to the union of their composing agents. As discussed in [2], it may help the reader to think of the agents as elementary circuit components or individual machine-language instructions but the actual identity of the individual agents never matters. What matters is whether an agent belongs to the specified system or to its environment. Let μ be a set of agents and $\bar{\mu}$ be its complement. Informally, the correctness formula $P \ sat_\mu \ S$ is valid if all the behaviours of P are allowed by $[\![S]\!]$ when the agents in μ are considered to form the program P and the agents in $\bar{\mu}$ are considered to form its environment.

2.2 Syntax and Semantics

Since Abadi and Lamport's model includes both program agents and environment agents, the logic must include formulas which distinguish transitions performed by different sets of agents. For that purpose, we replace the operator `unless` with the operator `unless`$_\mu$ to obtain formulas that constrain the transitions performed by agents in μ only. Informally, $\sigma \in [\![p \ \text{unless}_\mu \ q]\!]$ if and only if every transition of σ performed by a μ-agent transforms a $p \wedge \neg q$ state into a $p \vee q$ state. In other words, if $p \wedge \neg q$ holds before a μ-transition, then p holds after the transition, unless q holds. For example, if x and n are respectively dynamic and static variables, the formula

$$x = n \ \text{unless}_\mu \ x > n$$

asserts that a μ-agent may not decrease the value of x.

Throughout the definitions of this section, p, q are first-order assertions, and the notation $s \models_\xi p$ indicates that p holds on state s, under the static valuation ξ. Note that ξ is always submitted to a universal quantification, meaning that a Unity specification must hold for all the possible assignments to the static variables. In the above example, n may take any arbitrary value.

$$[\![p \ \text{unless}_\mu \ q]\!] =$$
$$\{\sigma \mid \forall \xi : \forall k < |\sigma| : (s_k.\sigma \models_\xi p \wedge \neg q) \wedge (a_k.\sigma \in \mu) \Rightarrow (s_{k+1}.\sigma \models_\xi p \vee q)\}$$

In addition to `unless` used for specifying safety properties, the Unity logic is built upon a second operator `leadsto` used for specifying liveness properties. The formula $p \ \text{leadsto} \ q$ is equivalent to $\Box(p \Rightarrow \Diamond q)$ in temporal logic [13]: if p holds at some point in a behaviour, then q eventually holds. For example, if x and n are respectively dynamic and static variables, the formula

$$x = n \ \text{leadsto} \ x = 2n$$

asserts that x eventually doubles. Finally, the operator `initially` specifies initial conditions.

$$[\![p \ \text{leadsto} \ q]\!] = \{\sigma \mid \forall \xi : \forall k \leq |\sigma| : (s_k.\sigma \models_\xi p) \Rightarrow (\exists j : k \leq j \leq |\sigma| : s_j.\sigma \models_\xi q)\}$$
$$[\![\text{initially} \ p]\!] = \{\sigma \mid \forall \xi : s_1.\sigma \models_\xi p\}$$

Although three operators suffice, it is helpful to introduce the following shorthands:

$$\texttt{stable}_\mu\; p \;\equiv\; p\,\texttt{unless}_\mu\; \mathit{false}$$
$$\texttt{constant}_\mu\; e \;\equiv\; \texttt{stable}_\mu\; e\!=\!n$$

where n is a static variable of the same sort as the expression e. Intuitively, $\texttt{stable}_\mu\; p$ asserts that no μ-agent violates a p state (p is a μ-invariant [3]), and $\texttt{constant}_\mu\; e$ asserts that no μ-agent modifies the value of an expression e.

$$[\![\texttt{stable}_\mu\; p]\!] = \{\sigma \mid \forall \xi : \forall k < |\sigma| : (s_k.\sigma \models_\xi p) \land (a_k.\sigma \in \mu) \Rightarrow (s_{k+1}.\sigma \models_\xi p)\}$$

The Unity operator $\texttt{invariant}$ will never appear in rely-guarantee specifications; it will appear in proofs only. Intuitively, an assertion is an invariant if it holds on every state of a behaviour.

$$[\![\texttt{invariant}\; p]\!] = \{\sigma \mid \forall \xi : \forall k \le |\sigma| : s_k.\sigma \models_\xi p\}$$

The generalisation to a set $\mathcal{S} = \{f_i\}$ of formulas is straightforward:

$$[\![\mathcal{S}]\!] = \cap_i [\![f_i]\!]$$

2.3 Proof Rules

As mentioned in the introduction, we reuse the Unity proof system. Among others, the following weakening, transitivity, conjunction and progress-safety-progress rules are directly drawn from the corresponding rules in [6]:

$$\frac{p\,\texttt{unless}_\mu\; q \quad \texttt{invariant}\; q \Rightarrow r}{p\,\texttt{unless}_\mu\; r} \qquad \frac{p\,\texttt{leadsto}\; q, \quad q\,\texttt{leadsto}\; r}{p\,\texttt{leadsto}\; r}$$

$$\frac{p_1\,\texttt{unless}_\mu\; q_1, \quad p_2\,\texttt{unless}_\mu\; q_2}{p_1 \land p_2\,\texttt{unless}_\mu\,(p_1 \land q_2) \lor (p_2 \land q_1) \lor (q_1 \land q_2)}$$

$$\frac{p\,\texttt{leadsto}\; q, \quad r\,\texttt{unless}_\mu\; b, \quad r\,\texttt{unless}_{\overline\mu}\; b}{p \land r\,\texttt{leadsto}\,(q \land r) \lor b}$$

Similarly, the union theorem of [6] yields the union and decomposition rules:

$$\frac{p\,\texttt{unless}_{\mu_1}\; q, \quad p\,\texttt{unless}_{\mu_2}\; q}{p\,\texttt{unless}_{\mu_1 \cup \mu_2}\; q} \qquad \frac{p\,\texttt{unless}_\mu\; q}{p\,\texttt{unless}_\nu\; q}\; \nu \subseteq \mu$$

The construction rules for invariants are:

$$\frac{\models p}{\texttt{invariant}\; p} \qquad \frac{\texttt{initially}\; p, \quad \texttt{stable}_\mu\; p, \quad \texttt{stable}_{\overline\mu}\; p}{\texttt{invariant}\; p}$$

where $\models p$ means that p is a valid assertion.

All the rules can be proved sound w.r.t. the semantic model: $[\![f_1]\!] \cap \ldots [\![f_n]\!] \subseteq [\![g]\!]$ holds for any rule with premises $f_1, \ldots, f_n$ and conclusion g.

3 Rely-Guarantee

In this section, we first recall the meaning of a rely-guarantee specification $R \Rightarrow G$. Then, we show how the subscripted `unless` formulas of Sect. 2 can be used to restrict a safety specification to system or environment transitions. Finally, we give a rely-guarantee specification of a concurrent buffer.

3.1 Definitions

Let R, G be sets of formulas. Then, the rely-guarantee specification $R \Rightarrow G$ asserts that G holds when R holds.

$$[\![R \Rightarrow G]\!] = \{\sigma \mid \sigma \in [\![R]\!] \Rightarrow \sigma \in [\![G]\!]\}$$

To make sense, the rely condition R should restrict the environment transitions only [2]. Therefore, when specifying a system composed of μ-agents, the rely condition R is restricted to `initially` and `unless`$_{\overline{\mu}}$ formulas. Formally, $R \trianglelefteq \overline{\mu}$ holds (R does not constrain μ [3, 8]):

$$R \trianglelefteq \overline{\mu} \text{ iff } \forall \sigma : \forall k < |\sigma| : \sigma|_k \in [\![R]\!] \wedge a_k.\sigma \in \mu \Rightarrow \sigma|_{k+1} \in [\![R]\!]$$

By convention, G^S denotes the safety formulas of G. Since G^S should restrict the system transitions only, we use `unless`$_\mu$ formulas in G^S when specifying a system composed of μ-agents. No `initially` formula may appear in G^S, that is initial states are determined by the environment (included in the rely condition), not by the system. Formally, $G^S \triangleleft \mu$ holds (G^S constrains at most μ [3, 4]):

$$G^S \trianglelefteq \mu \text{ iff } \forall \sigma : \forall k < |\sigma| : \sigma|_k \in [\![G^S]\!] \wedge a_k.\sigma \notin \mu \Rightarrow \sigma|_{k+1} \in [\![G^S]\!]$$
$$G^S \triangleleft \mu \text{ iff } G^S \trianglelefteq \mu \text{ and } \forall \sigma : \sigma|_1 \in [\![G^S]\!]$$

Due to the use of a unique agent symbol, such specifications distinguish between the system and its environment but not between their composing agents (μ-abstractness is preserved [2]).

3.2 Example

To highlight the use of subscripted formulas, we specify a bounded concurrent buffer that we assume to be composed of μ-agents. A buffer receives messages in the variable *in* and eventually produces them into the variable *out*.

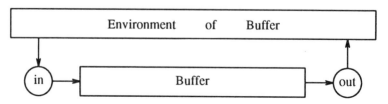

The specification $R \Rightarrow G$ says that if the environment respects some access protocol (rely condition R), then the buffer behaves properly (guarantee condition G): no message is lost, no message is created, messages are delivered in the right order, at most N messages are buffered, input messages are eventually consumed, and buffered messages are eventually produced.

As in [1, 15, 18], we introduce an *auxiliary* variable b to represent the sequence of messages currently buffered. The formula $\texttt{constant}_{\overline{\pi}}\, b$ asserts that b is local to the buffer, hence not modified by $\overline{\pi}$ agents. For the sake of simplicity, this formula has been stated explicitly in the examples. However, it could be considered as a part of the semantics of the auxiliary variables, hence implicitly defined. Formally, the variable b is submitted to existential quantification [1, 4]; consequently, $G^S \lhd \mu$ holds although it includes the formulas $\texttt{initially}\ b = \bot$ and $\texttt{constant}_{\overline{\pi}}\, b$.

The static variable m ranges over messages, the special value $\bot$ denotes the absence of messages, and the operator $\bullet$ stands for sequence concatenation. Observe how the formula $\texttt{constant}_{\mu}\ \langle in \rangle \bullet b \bullet \langle out \rangle$ suffices to specify that no message is either created or lost by the buffer and that messages are delivered in the right order[2].

Specification $\mathbf{R} \Rightarrow \mathbf{G}$

Rely R	Guarantee G	Aux.Variable
$\texttt{initially}\ in = \bot$	$in = m\ \texttt{unless}_{\mu}\ in = \bot$	$\texttt{initially}\ b = \bot$
$\texttt{initially}\ out = \bot$	$\texttt{stable}_{\mu}\ in = \bot$	$\texttt{constant}_{\overline{\pi}}\, b$
$out = m\ \texttt{unless}_{\overline{\pi}}\ out = \bot$	$\texttt{stable}_{\mu}\ out = m$	
$\texttt{stable}_{\overline{\pi}}\ out = \bot$	$\texttt{stable}_{\mu}\ |b| \leq N$	
$\texttt{stable}_{\overline{\pi}}\ in = m$	$\texttt{constant}_{\mu}\ \langle in \rangle \bullet b \bullet \langle out \rangle$	
	$|b| < N\ \texttt{leadsto}\ in = \bot$	
	$|b| > 0\ \texttt{leadsto}\ out \neq \bot$	

The Unity style is preserved in writing specifications as well as in reasoning about them. For example, the following deductions can be rewritten from [15]:

$$G^S \vdash \texttt{invariant}\ |b| \leq N \tag{1}$$

$$G^S \vdash out = \bot\ \texttt{unless}_{\mu}\ |b| < N \vee in = \bot \tag{2}$$

$$H, G \vdash out = \bot\ \texttt{leadsto}\ |b| < N \vee in = \bot \tag{3}$$

where $H = \{\texttt{stable}_{\overline{\pi}}\ out = \bot\}$. Detailed proof examples will be given in next section.

4 Composition

In this section, we show that the syntactic restrictions imposed on the rely-guarantee specifications of Sect. 3 match the hypotheses of the composition rule. We then put this rule into practice by replacing the premises expressed in semantic terms with suitable Unity proof obligations. We finally illustrate the rule by composing mutually-dependent rely-guarantee specifications of concurrent buffers.

---

[2] It also ensures that b does not introduce infinite invisible nondeterminism, a sufficient condition for existential quantification to preserve safety [1]

4.1 Parallel Composition Rule

Let $\mu = \mu_1 \cup \mu_2$ with $\mu_1 \cap \mu_2 = \emptyset$. Formulated in terms of correctness formulas, the composition principle becomes the rule

$$\frac{P_1 \text{ sat}_{\mu_1} (R_1 \Rightarrow G_1) \quad [\![R]\!] \cap [\![G_2^S]\!] \subseteq [\![R_1]\!] \quad [\![R]\!] \cap [\![G_1^S]\!] \cap [\![G_2^S]\!] \subseteq [\![G^S]\!]}{P_2 \text{ sat}_{\mu_2} (R_2 \Rightarrow G_2) \quad [\![R]\!] \cap [\![G_1^S]\!] \subseteq [\![R_2]\!] \quad [\![R]\!] \cap [\![G_1]\!] \cap [\![G_2]\!] \subseteq [\![G]\!]}{P_1 \| P_2 \text{ sat}_\mu (R \Rightarrow G)}$$

According to [2], this rule is sound under the hypotheses $R_1 \lhd \overline{\mu_1}$, $G_1^S \lhd \mu_1$, $R_2 \lhd \overline{\mu_2}$, $G_2^S \lhd \mu_2$, $R \lhd \overline{\mu}$, and $G^S \lhd \mu$. As stated in Sect. 3, a very simple syntactic restriction suffices: the subscripts appearing in the unless formulas of R_1, G_1^S, R_2, G_2^S, R, and G^S are $\overline{\mu_1}$, μ_1, $\overline{\mu_2}$, μ_2, $\overline{\mu}$, and μ respectively. Since the Unity proof system is sound, we may replace set inclusion with proof obligations in the premises:

$$\frac{P_1 \text{ sat}_{\mu_1} (R_1 \Rightarrow G_1) \quad R, G_2^S \vdash R_1 \quad R, G_1^S, G_2^S \vdash G^S}{P_2 \text{ sat}_{\mu_2} (R_2 \Rightarrow G_2) \quad R, G_1^S \vdash R_2 \quad R, G_1, G_2 \vdash G}{P_1 \| P_2 \text{ sat}_\mu (R \Rightarrow G)}$$

4.2 Specification of Concurrent Buffers

$Buffer_1$ transmits messages from the variable in to the intermediate variable mid and $Buffer_2$ transmits messages from the variable mid to the variable out. The specifications $R_1 \Rightarrow G_1$ and $R_2 \Rightarrow G_2$ are drawn from the specification $R \Rightarrow G$ by suitable renaming. Since $\mu_2 \subseteq \overline{\mu_1}$ and $\mu_1 \subseteq \overline{\mu_2}$, the rely conditions R_1, R_2 depend on the guarantee conditions G_2, G_1 respectively. So the proposed rely-guarantee specifications are mutually dependent.

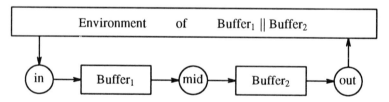

Specification $R_1 \Rightarrow G_1$

Rely R_1	Guarantee G_1	Aux.Variable
initially $in = \bot$	$in = m$ unless$_{\mu_1}$ $in = \bot$	initially $b_1 = \bot$
initially $mid = \bot$	stable$_{\mu_1}$ $in = \bot$	constant$_{\overline{\mu_1}}$ b_1
$mid = m$ unless$_{\overline{\mu_1}}$ $mid = \bot$	stable$_{\mu_1}$ $mid = m$	
stable$_{\overline{\mu_1}}$ $mid = \bot$	stable$_{\mu_1}$ $|b_1| \leq N_1$	
stable$_{\overline{\mu_1}}$ $in = m$	constant$_{\mu_1}$ $\langle in \rangle \bullet b_1 \bullet \langle mid \rangle$	
	$|b_1| < N_1$ leadsto $in = \bot$	
	$|b_1| > 0$ leadsto $mid \neq \bot$	

Specification $R_2 \Rightarrow G_2$

Rely R_2	Guarantee G_2	Aux.Variable
initially $mid = \bot$	$mid = m$ unless$_{\mu_2}$ $mid = \bot$	initially $b_2 = \bot$
initially $out = \bot$	stable$_{\mu_2}$ $mid = \bot$	constant$_{\overline{\mu_2}}$ b_2
$out = m$ unless$_{\overline{\mu_2}}$ $out = \bot$	stable$_{\mu_2}$ $out = m$	
stable$_{\overline{\mu_2}}$ $out = \bot$	stable$_{\mu_2}$ $|b_2| \leq N_2$	
stable$_{\overline{\mu_2}}$ $mid = m$	constant$_{\mu_2}$ $\langle mid \rangle \bullet b_2 \bullet \langle out \rangle$	
	$|b_2| < N_2$ leadsto $mid = \bot$	
	$|b_2| > 0$ leadsto $out \neq \bot$	

4.3 Hiding and Access Restrictions

The program *Buffer* is the parallel composition of *Buffer$_1$* and *Buffer$_2$* where the variable mid, initially empty, is made local.

$$Buffer \equiv (\text{initially } mid = \bot \text{ in } Buffer_1 \| Buffer_2) \setminus \{mid\}$$

To cope with such hiding [7, 9, 19], it suffices to extend the rely condition with the hypotheses that the environment does not modify the local variables and that the program starts with correct initial values for its local variables.

$$\frac{P \text{ sat}_\mu \ (\underline{R} \Rightarrow G)}{P \setminus \{v\} \text{ sat}_\mu \ (R \Rightarrow G)} \quad \underline{R} = R \cup \{\text{constant}_{\overline{\mu}} \ v\}$$

$$\frac{P \text{ sat}_\mu \ (\underline{R} \Rightarrow G)}{(\text{initially } v = e \text{ in } P) \text{ sat}_\mu \ (R \Rightarrow G)} \quad \underline{R} = R \cup \{\text{initially } v = e\}$$

We also need the information that *Buffer$_1$* does not access the variable out and *Buffer$_2$* does not access the variable in. To cope with such access restrictions [7, 19], it suffices to extend the guarantee condition with a constant formula stating that a program does not modify a variable that it does not access.

$$\frac{P \text{ sat}_\mu \ (R \Rightarrow G)}{P \text{ sat}_\mu \ (R \Rightarrow \underline{G})} \quad v \notin Var(P), \ \underline{G} = G \cup \{\text{constant}_\mu \ v\}$$

4.4 Composition of Mutually Dependent Specifications

Assuming *Buffer$_1$* and *Buffer$_2$* satisfy $R_1 \Rightarrow G_1$ and $R_2 \Rightarrow G_2$ respectively, we prove that *Buffer* satisfies $R \Rightarrow G$ provided that $N = N_1 + N_2 + 1$. The following rule is easily derived from the above parallel, hiding and access restrictions rules:

$$\frac{\begin{array}{ccc} Buffer_1 \text{ sat}_{\mu_1} (R_1 \Rightarrow G_1) & R, G_1^S, G_2^S \vdash R_1 & R, G_1^S, G_2^S \vdash G^S \\ Buffer_2 \text{ sat}_{\mu_2} (R_2 \Rightarrow G_2) & R, G_1^S, G_2^S \vdash R_2 & R, G_1, G_2 \vdash G \end{array}}{Buffer \text{ sat}_\mu \ (R \Rightarrow G)}$$

Proof obligations: Jones' work. Based on Jones' earlier work [10], the parallel rules of [19, 20, 21] can be viewed as applications of the composition principle for terminating programs. Although carried out in another framework, the proof obligations can be related to ours:

- In [19, 21], the safety proof obligations look like $R \vee G_2^S \vdash R_1$. These cannot be expressed in our framework: no disjunction is allowed between Unity formulas. However, even if we write $R, G_2^S \vdash R_1$, there is an implicit disjunction between R and G_2^S because they are specifications over distinct sets of agents. More precisely, the disjunction is eventually made explicit in the proof of $R, G_2^S \vdash R_1$ when applying the union rule: the disjunction appears as the union of the sets of agents (see proof of (4) in Sect. 4).
- The liveness proof obligation in [10, 20] requires the construction of a dynamic invariant linking successive states in a behaviour; this binary relation must be preserved by both the environment and the system transitions. In the Unity framework, it basically corresponds to using the progress-safety-progress rule for `leadsto` (see proof of (6) in Sect. 4): its premises r `unless`$_{\overline{\mu}}$ b and r `unless`$_{\mu}$ b express that the associate binary relation must be preserved by both the environment agents and the system agents.

TLA rely-guarantee specifications. We contribute to the rely-guarantee paradigm by using explicit distinct subscripts to distinguish the rely and the guarantee parts of a specification. For example, the $\overline{\mu}$ subscripts indicate that the rely condition constrains the environment only. Similar syntactic restrictions appear in the Temporal Logic of Actions (TLA) for open systems [3, 12]: the disjunction $\mu \vee F$ restricts the transition formula F to environment transitions, and the disjunction $\overline{\mu} \vee F$ restricts the same formula to system transitions. In TLA, unprimed and primed formulas refer to the state before respectively after the transition; with this convention, the formula p `unless`$_{\mu}$ q corresponds to the binary state relation described by $\overline{\mu} \vee (p \wedge \neg q \Rightarrow p' \vee q')$ in TLA. Although they can be expressed in TLA, our specifications are not in TLA canonical form [3]: we specify a *conjunction of restrictions* on the system transitions instead of a *disjunction of allowed* system transitions.

Action-based specifications. Consequently, compared to TLA and other action-based specifications of concurrent objects [3, 9, 11, 18], the Unity approach preserves the *conjunctive character* of a specification: an omitted requirement can simply be added to the conjunction. For instance, the specification of a bounded buffer is obtained from the specification of an unbounded one simply by adding the formula `stable`$_{\mu}$ $|b| < N$. Adding this requirement in action-based specifications implies revising the definition of each action. Furthermore, invariant-looking properties such as `constant`$_{\mu}$ $in \bullet b \bullet out$ appear explicitly. As a drawback w.r.t. action-based specifications, we note that unrealizable specifications are not excluded when using `leadsto`; in action-based approaches, unrealizable specifications may be avoided by replacing the liveness requirements with suitable fairness requirements on the actions. Actually, the two approaches may appear at different stages of the development process: once the Unity specification is established, it may be refined until identifying the system actions becomes necessary. A possible extension of this work is thus the development of proof rules, based on [6], to prove the validity of an action-based specification w.r.t. a Unity rely-guarantee specification. Then, the formal development process goes on, using established refinement method for action-based specifications, e.g. [11].

Temporal operators versus auxiliary variables. Applying the composition principle of [2, 4] requires specifications that can be interpreted in the proposed model. Another candidate specification language would be the compositional version of the linear time temporal logic [5]. Unfortunately, the more powerful operators of temporal logic raise the complexity of reasoning about specifications [18]. By choosing the Unity logic, we follow the alternative approach of *e.g.* [9, 12, 18, 19]: the specification language is simple and the necessary expressive power is obtained by using auxiliary variables. Actually, only `leadsto` is a temporal operator and temporal reasoning is then avoided whenever possible. As claimed in [12, 18], this approach yields more natural specifications: a specification is made of an initial condition (`initially`), a set of allowed transitions (`unless`), and a set of liveness requirements (`leadsto`).

6   Conclusion

In order to reuse Abadi and Lamport's results on mutually dependent rely-guarantee specifications, we have adapted the `unless` operator of Unity. By simple syntactic restrictions, we have obtained formulas that constrain either the system transitions or the environment transitions. Then, we have illustrated the approach on an example, by applying the rule to compose mutually dependent rely-guarantee specifications of concurrent buffers.

An advantage of the approach lies in keeping the Unity style of reasoning about specifications: since the language is simple (short formal description), it yields rather intuitive proof rules, hence workable specifications. However, as discussed in [2], reasoning about concurrent systems remains a lengthy task, because of detailed calculations. Even the simple example of concurrent buffers generates lengthy proofs. Redoing proofs in response to changes in the initial specification could thus be a problem when scaling the approach to real-size developments [16].

Acknowledgements

I am grateful to Pierre-Yves Schobbens, Michel Sintzoff, and Ketil Stølen for their valuable comments on earlier drafts of this paper. I also thank Mete Celitkin, Yves Ledru, Philippe Massonet, and Thanh Tung Nguyen for their helpful suggestions.

References

1. M. Abadi and L. Lamport, The Existence of Refinement Mappings, in *Proceedings of the 3rd Annual Symposium on Logic In Computer Science*, 1988, pp. 165-175.
2. M. Abadi and L. Lamport, Composing Specifications, in J.W. de Bakker, W.-P. de Roever, and G. Rozenberg eds., *Stepwise Refinement of Distributed Systems*, Springer-Verlag, 1990, LNCS 430, pp. 1-41.

3. M. Abadi and L. Lamport, An Old-Fashioned Recipe for Real Time, in J.W. de Bakker, C. Huizing, W.-P. de Roever, and G. Rozenberg eds., *Real Time: Theory in Practice*, Springer-Verlag, 1992, LNCS 600, pp 1-27.

4. M. Abadi and G.D. Plotkin, A Logical View of Composition and Refinement, in *Proceedings of the 18th Annual ACM Symposium on Principles of Programming Languages*, 1991, pp 323-332.

5. H. Barringer, R. Kuiper, and A. Pnueli, Now you may Compose Temporal Logic Specifications, in *Proceedings of the 16th ACM Symposium on Theory of Computing*, 1984, pp. 51-63.

6. K.M. Chandy and J. Misra, Parallel Program Design: a Foundation, Addison-Wesley, 1988.

7. P. Collette, Semantic Rules to Compose Rely-Guarantee Specifications, Research Report RR 92-25, Université Catholique de Louvain, 1992, Belgium.

8. F. Dederichs, System and Environment: The Philosophers Revisited, Technical Report TUM-I9040, Institut für Informatik, Technische Universität München, 1990, Germany.

9. P. Grønning, T.Q. Nielsen and H.H. Lovengreen, Refinement and Composition of Transition-based Rely-Guarantee Specifications with Auxiliary Variables, in K.V. Nori and C.E. Veni Madhavan eds., *Foundations of Software Technology and Theoretical Computer Science*, Springer-Verlag, 1991, LNCS 472, pp 332-348.

10. C.B. Jones, Tentative Steps Towards a Development Method for Interfering Programs, in *ACM Transactions on Programming Languages And Systems*, 1983, Vol 5, 4, pp 596-619.

11. B. Jonsson, On Decomposing and Refining Specifications of Distributed Systems, in J.W. de Bakker, W-P. de Roever, and G. Rozenberg eds, *Stepwise Refinement of Distributed Systems*, Springer-Verlag, 1990, LNCS 430, pp. 261-385.

12. L. Lamport, The Temporal Logic of Actions, Research Report 57, Digital Equipment Corporation Systems Research Center, 1990.

13. Z. Manna and A. Pnueli, The Anchored Version of the Temporal Framework, in J.W. de Bakker, W.-P. de Roever, and G. Rozenberg eds., *Linear Time, Branching Time and Partial Orders in Logics and Models for Concurrency*, Springer-Verlag, 1989, LNCS 354, pp. 201-284.

14. J. Misra and K.M. Chandy, Proofs of Networks of Processes, in *IEEE Transactions on Software Engineering*, 1981, Vol 7, 4, pp 417-426.

15. J. Misra, Specifying Concurrent Objects as Communicating Processes, in *Science of Computer Programming*, 1990, Vol 14, 2-3, pp. 159-184.

16. A. Pizzarello, An Industrial Experience in the use of UNITY, in J.P. Banâtre and D. Le Métayer eds., *Research Directions in High-Level Parallel Programming Languages*, Springer-Verlag, 1991, LNCS 574, pp 39-49.

17. A.K. Singh, Specification of Concurrent Objects Using Auxiliary Variables, in *Science of Computer Programming*, 1991, Vol 16, pp 49-88.

18. E.G. Stark, Proving Entailment Between Conceptual State Specifications, in *Theoretical Computer Science*, 1988, Vol 56, pp 135-154.

19. K. Stølen, A Method for the Development of Totally Correct Shared-State Parallel Programs, in J.C.M. Baeten and J.F. Groote eds., *Proceedings of Concur'91*, Springer-Verlag, 1991, LNCS 527, pp 510-525.

20. J.C.P. Woodcock and B. Dickinson, Using VDM with Rely and Guarantee-Conditions, in R. Bloomfield, L. Marshall and R. Jones eds., *Proceedings of VDM'88: The Way Ahead*, Springer-Verlag, 1988, LNCS 328, pp 434-458.

21. Q. Xu and H. Jifeng, A Theory of State-based Parallel Programming: Part I, in J. Morris ed., *4th BCS-FACS Refinement Workshop*, Springer-Verlag, 1991, pp 326-359.

Trees, ordinals and termination*

Nachum Dershowitz
Department of Computer Science

University of Illinois   The Weizmann Institute of Science
Urbana, IL 61801   Rehovot 76100
U.S.A.   Israel

nachum@cs.uiuc.edu

Know that one is the secret and source of all the cardinals.

— Abraham ibn Ezra (1153)

Abstract

Trees are a natural representation for countable ordinals. In particular, finite trees provide a convenient notation the predicative ones. Processes that transform trees or terms can often be proved terminating by viewing the tree or the tree representation of the term as an ordinal.

1 Introduction

Cantor invented the ordinal numbers

$$0, 1, 2, \ldots \omega, \omega + 1, \ldots \omega 2, \ldots \omega n,$$
$$\ldots \omega^2, \ldots \omega^n, \ldots \omega^\omega, \ldots \omega \uparrow n, \ldots$$
$$\epsilon_0, \ldots \epsilon_0^{\epsilon_0}, \ldots \epsilon_1, \ldots \epsilon_{\epsilon_0}, \ldots, \text{etc.}$$

Each ordinal is larger than all preceding ones, and is typically defined as the set of them all:

$$\omega = \text{the set of natural numbers}$$
$$\omega 2 = \omega \cup \{\omega + n | n \in \omega\}$$
$$\omega n = \cup_{i<n} \omega i$$
$$\omega^2 = \cup_{n \in \omega} \omega n$$
$$\omega^n = \cup_{i<n} \omega^i$$
$$\omega^\omega = \cup_{n \in \omega} \omega^n$$
$$\omega \uparrow n = \cup_{i<n} \omega \uparrow i$$
$$\epsilon_0 = \omega^{\epsilon_0} = \cup_{n \in \omega} \omega \uparrow n$$
$$\epsilon_0^{\epsilon_0} = \omega^{\epsilon_0^2}$$
$$\epsilon_1 = \cup_{n \in \omega} \epsilon_0 \uparrow n$$

The notation $\alpha \uparrow n$ represents a tower of n αs.

Infinite sets cannot provide a *notation* for ordinals. In Section 2 we look for bijections between natural classes of finite trees and initial segments of the countable ordinals.

Turing [1950] and Floyd [1967] suggested using ordinals for proving termination of programs. Earlier, in 1938, Gentzen used an ϵ_0 ordering to show that Peano Arithmetic is consistent, by showing the termination of a proof-tree transformation process. In Section 3, we give some examples of termination proofs that follow directly from tree representations of ordinals.

---

*Research supported in part by the U. S. National Science Foundation under Grants CCR-90-07195 and CCR-90-24271 and by a Meyerhoff fellowship at The Weizmann Institute of Science.

2 Trees as ordinals

Finite rooted trees correspond one-to-one with the ordinals up to ϵ_0: the one-node tree is 0; a tree with subtrees corresponding to $\alpha_1, \ldots, \alpha_n$ corresponds to the natural (commutative) sum $\omega^{\alpha_1} + \cdots + \omega^{\alpha_n}$. This ordering is natural in that trees are larger than their subtrees and replacing a subtree by a smaller one gives a smaller tree. Moreover, replacing a subtree with any finite number of smaller trees results in a smaller tree. Ordered this way, finite trees give all ordinals up to ϵ_0. (See [Dershowitz and Manna, 1979] for well-founded orderings of multisets.)

One can, alternatively, consider ordered trees and use the same interpretation, except for substituting noncommutative addition. This is not a bijection, but if, in addition, we insist that subtrees are listed in non-ascending order, then this is just another way of writing an ordinal less than ϵ_0 in Cantor normal form.

The standard correspondence between ordered trees and binary trees leads to the following interpretation of the latter: a tree is no smaller than either of its immediate subtrees; replacing one of the subtrees with one no larger, gives something no larger; if the left branch of tree t is larger than that of s and the whole of t is larger than the right branch of s, then t is larger than s. See Table 1 for some examples.

Going farther, one can associate the countable ordinals with infinite binary trees in which no path has infinitely many left turns. The empty binary tree is 0; if the right branch is infinite, the tree corresponds to the limit of the ordinals obtained by truncating the right branch at deeper and deeper points; otherwise, one gets $\omega^x + y$ for the binary tree whose left branch corresponds to x and right branch to y, unless $\omega^x + y = x$, in which case we add one. This is analogous to *tree ordinals* as defined in [Dennis-Jones and Wainer, 1983]: 0 is a tree ordinal; if α is then so is $\alpha + 1$; if α_n ($n \in \mathbb{N}$) are, then the ω-sequence $\alpha_0, \alpha_1, \ldots$ (representing their limit) also is.

Rational binary trees (trees with only finitely many different subtrees) can be represented finitely (as cyclic graph structures) and—with a natural extension of the ordering on finite trees—give all ordinals up to (and including) $\epsilon_{\epsilon_{...}}$. The effect is essentially the same as allowing leaves to be labeled by trees (themselves having such leaves). A leaf containing something is larger than trees with smaller leaves and corresponds to the epsilon number indicated by the contents of the leaf. In general, a tree corresponds to $\omega^x + y$, where x is the ordinal corresponding to the left branch and y corresponds to the right branch, unless x is an epsilon number ϵ_z, in which case one gets $x + y - z$ ($-$ is ordinal difference). An infinitely bifurcating rational tree corresponds to the critical ordinal $\epsilon_{\epsilon_{...}}$. See [Dershowitz and Reingold, 1992].

Labeled rooted trees also provide a natural notation for much larger ordinals. A *supertree* is a tree whose nodes can themselves be supertrees. Supertrees with identical roots are compared as were rooted trees above. But if tree s has a larger root than t, and s is larger than each of the subtrees of t, then s is larger than t. See Table 2.

Let $\phi^1(0), \phi^1(1), \ldots$ enumerate the epsilon numbers, and $\phi^\alpha(\beta)$ enumerate the fixpoints $\phi^\mu(\beta) = \beta$ that are common to all $\mu < \alpha$. (See [Schmidt, 1976].) Then we extend the mapping of trees to ordinals by making s greater than t if the root of s is greater than the root of t and s is greater than the subtrees of t. This maps a tree with root corresponding to α and subtrees $\beta_1, \ldots, \beta_n$ to $\phi^\alpha(\beta_1 + \cdots + \beta_n)$ (the sum is commutative), or to $\phi^\alpha(\beta_1 + \cdots + \beta_n + 1)$ when $\phi^\alpha(\beta_1 + \cdots + \beta_n) = \beta_1 + \cdots + \beta_n$ (that is, when $n = 1$ and $\beta_1 = \phi^\gamma(\delta)$, $\alpha < \gamma$).[1] This gives all (the predicative) ordinals up to Γ_0, the first ordinal whose definition requires "things infinite."

One can also consider ordered trees with ordinary nodes, treating its leftmost subtree as the root in the supertree ordering.

See Gallier [1991] for an exposition on properties of these ordinals.

---

[1] This patches the order-preserving mapping given in [Dershowitz, 1987]. An embedding of trees into Γ_0 is given by [Gallier, 1991] and others. It avoids supernodes, but ignores all subtrees but the two largest.

245

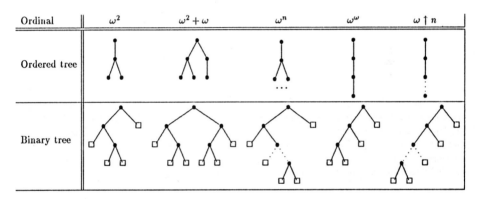

Table 1: Ordinals and trees

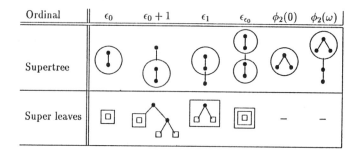

Table 2: Big ordinals and supertrees

Figure 1: Hercules versus Hydra.

All the orderings described in this section are simplification orderings [Dershowitz, 1982]: a tree is greater than any homeomorphically embedded tree. It has been shown [Okada and Steele, 1988] that all such orderings on finite trees are initial segments of Ackermann's notation (what we got with supertrees), which itself can be proved well-ordered by appealing to Kruskal's Tree Theorem. The well-orderings of rational and infinite trees are consequences of generalizations of the Tree Theorem, but their proof-theoretic strength is unknown.

3 Trees for termination

The contest "Hercules vs. Hydra" was designed [Kirby and Paris, 1982] to be terminating, but not provably so in Peano Arithmetic. Hydra is a bush-like creature with multiple heads. Each time Hercules hacks off a head of hers, Hydra sprouts many new branches identical to the weakened branch that used to hold the severed head, and adjacent to it. If he chops off a head coming straight out of the ground, no new branches result. It cannot be shown by elementary means that Hercules always defeats Hydra, reducing her to nothing, but it can be shown by ϵ_0 induction. See Figure 1.

The appendix contains code for doing arithmetic with ordinals up to ϵ_0, representing them as binary trees in the manner described in the previous section. The nth chop and regrowth steps reduces Hydra's value as an ordinal to its nth predecessor. The code can be used to calculate ordinals used in termination proofs.

Floyd [personal communication] gave the following problem on a Ph.D. qualifying exam at Carnegie-Mellon University in 1967 (expecting the students to use ordinals to solve it): Show that repeatedly applying the rules

$$
\begin{aligned}
D\,t &\rightarrow 1 \\
D\,a &\rightarrow 0 \\
D\,(x+y) &\rightarrow D\,x + D\,y \\
D\,(x\cdot y) &\rightarrow y\cdot D\,x + x\cdot D\,y \\
D\,(x-y) &\rightarrow D\,x - D\,y
\end{aligned}
$$

for symbolic differentiation to an arbitrary expression always ends with a term to which no rule applies. The proof of termination is complicated by the fact that one is allowed to apply a rule at any time to any subexpression of any of the given patterns, rewrite the subexpression accordingly. Termination follows by using the superleaf ordering, viewing expressions as operator trees, but with D as a leaf containing its argument.

The following transformation system was included as an example by Iturriaga [1967] (one of the students solving the above-mentioned "qual" question), but no proof of termination was given therein:

$$
\begin{aligned}
\neg\neg x &\rightarrow x \\
\neg(x \vee y) &\rightarrow \neg x \wedge \neg y \\
\neg(x \wedge y) &\rightarrow \neg x \vee \neg y \\
x \wedge (y \vee z) &\rightarrow (x \wedge y) \vee (x \wedge z) \\
(y \vee z) \wedge x &\rightarrow (y \wedge x) \vee (z \wedge x)
\end{aligned}
$$

To see that it terminates, use supertrees, viewing $\neg$ as 2, $\wedge$ as 1, $\vee$ and constants as 0.

Boyer used the following transformation in his theorem prover and circulated an electronic message (in 1977) soliciting proofs of its termination:

$$
if(if(x,y,z),u,v) \quad \rightarrow \quad if(x, if(y,u,v), if(z,u,v))
$$

This follows directly from Ackermann's original three-place notation. We can view $if(x,y,z)$ as a tree with x as its root and y and z as its two subtrees. The supertree ordering shows termination.

The following set of rewriting rules, an extension of the Hydra contest which allows the tree to grow in height as well as breadth, is designed to mimic Γ_0-induction:

$$
\begin{aligned}
G_n\overline{x} &\rightarrow G_{n+1}p_n x \\
p_n\langle x,y,z\rangle &\rightarrow \langle x,\overline{y},p_n z\rangle \\
p_{n+1}\langle A,y,z\rangle &\rightarrow \langle A,p_{n+1}y,r_n\langle B,\langle A,y,z\rangle,z\rangle\rangle \\
p_n\langle x,y,z\rangle &\rightarrow \overline{y} \\
p_n\langle B,y,z\rangle &\rightarrow r_n\langle B,y,z\rangle \\
r_{n+1}\langle B,y,z\rangle &\rightarrow \langle B,p_{n+1}y,r_n\langle B,y,z\rangle\rangle \\
r_n\langle x,y,z\rangle &\rightarrow \overline{z} \\
\langle x,\overline{y},\overline{z}\rangle &\rightarrow \overline{\langle x,y,z\rangle}
\end{aligned}
$$

"A nodes" are lexicographic; "B nodes" are sums, summands of which r duplicates for p to reduce; G stands for "Gremlin"; the bar keeps track of what p has done. Even bigger battles—and their associated ordinals—are described in [Okada, 1988].

4 Conclusion

We conclude with the function f of Figure 2 (a repaired riddle from [Dershowitz and Reingold, 1992]): Show that the sequence

$$
t \quad f(t) \quad f(f(t)) \quad \cdots \quad f^n(t) \quad \cdots
$$

always ends in a leaf starting with any finite binary tree t with foliage of two kinds: ♣ and ♠.

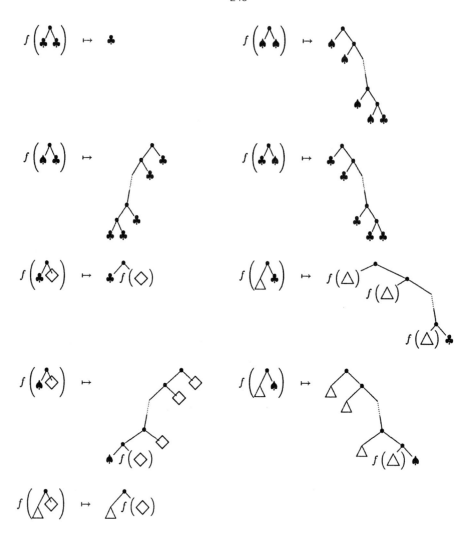

Figure 2: Hybrid tree (triangles and diamonds are arbitrary non-leaf trees)

(2) For every transition $\tau = (z, a, z_1 \ldots z_k)$ and z_j–computations ϕ_j of $A^{(2)}$ the following holds. Let J_i denote the set of all x_j where $\text{depth}(T_i(\phi_j)) \geq n \cdot |M|$ for $i = 1, 2$, and $J = J_1 \cup J_2$. Let $y_i = T_i(\tau)[v_{1i}, \ldots, v_{ki}]$ where $v_{ji} = x_j$ whenever $x_j \in J$ and $v_{ji} = T_i(\phi_j)$ otherwise. Assume $\#J > 1$. Consider the decompositions $y_i = z_i y_i'$ where z_i is the maximal x_1–prefix of y_i. Then J–substitutions θ_i, $i = 1, 2$, exist such that for every $j \in J$,
1. $x_j \in \{x_j\theta_1, x_j\theta_2\} \subseteq \tilde{T}_\Delta(x_j)$;
2. $y_1'\theta_2 = y_2'\theta_1$;
3. $(x_j\theta_1)T_1(\phi_j) = (x_j\theta_2)T_2(\psi_j)$.

M is of *weakly bounded difference (wbd)* iff for every z–computation ϕ of $A^{(2)}$, statement (1) must only hold provided depth $T_i(\phi) \geq n \cdot |M|$ for both $i \in \{1, 2\}$; and statement (2) only provided $J_1 \neq \emptyset \neq J_2$.

6   Characterizations

This section presents the main theorems of this paper. Theorem 9 states that the transduction of a reduced functional transducer M can be realized by a reduced deterministic one iff M has Properties (D0), (D1) and (D2). Theorem 10 is the corresponding version for realization by deterministic transducers. Here, the characterization only differs in that Property (D0) is replaced by Property (wD0).

Theorem 9. *Assume M is a reduced functional FST. Then the following three statements are equivalent:*

(1) $T(M)$ can be realized by a reduced deterministic transducer.
(2) M has Properties (D0), (D1) and (D2).
(3) M is of bounded difference.

It can be decided whether or not the transduction of an FST can be realized by a reduced deterministic one.

Proof. Let $M = (A, T)$ be a reduced functional FST where $A = (Q, \Sigma, \delta, Q_F)$ and $n = \#Q > 0$. We only give the construction showing that (3) implies (1). Assume that M is of bounded difference. We construct a reduced deterministic FST M_d realizing $T(M)$.

Let $A_0 = (Q_0, \Sigma, \delta_0, Q_{0,F})$ be the standard subset automaton for A, i.e., $Q_0 = 2^Q$; $Q_{0,F} = \{B \subseteq Q | B \cap Q_F \neq \emptyset\}$; and δ_0 consists of all transitions $(B, a, B_1 \ldots B_k)$ where $B = \{q \in Q | \forall j \exists q_j \in B_j : (q, a, q_1 \ldots q_k) \in \delta\}$.

The idea of the construction is the following. When starting the computation for some input tree t at the leaves, M_d behaves like A_0 but records for every accessible state q that part of the output of some q–computation of which it is not yet certain whether it will be part of the final output or not. This is similar as in the word case. The new difficulty that arises is to handle the start–up phase. Having accumulated sufficiently large possible output trees we have to find the right "end", i.e., that subtree which safely can be produced and leave variables at the right places. This choice is easy if for more than one of the subtrees at the present node large outputs can be produced (cf. Case 3). Otherwise, the size of the subtree's output must be large enough such that it can be uniquely detected (cf. Case 1).

Formally, we construct $M_d = (A_d, T_d)$ with $A_d = (Q_d, \Sigma, \delta_d, Q_{d,F})$ as follows.

Q_d is some set of mappings $\mu : B \to T_\Delta(x_1) \cup \{\bot\}$, $B \in Q_0$ such that $\mu(q)$ is a tree of depth less than $(2n+1) \cdot |M|$. $Q_{d,F}$ consists of all mappings $\mu \in Q_d$ which are defined for some $q \in Q_F$ where $T_d(\mu) = T(q)\mu(q)$, and $U(M_d) = \{\mu \in Q_d | \text{range}(\mu) \subseteq T_\Delta \cup \{\bot\}\}$.

The sets Q_d and δ_d are iteratively determined as the union of their "approximations", i.e., by

$$Q_d = \bigcup_{\nu \geq 0} Q^{(\nu)} \text{ and } \delta_d = \bigcup_{\nu \geq 0} \delta^{(\nu)}$$

where $Q^{(0)} = \emptyset$ and $\delta^{(0)} = \emptyset$. The construction will be done such that the following invariant holds:

(0) Assume $(\mu, u, s, \epsilon) \in T_d$, and B is the domain of μ. Then $(B, u, \epsilon) \in \delta_0$, and for every $q \in B$,
   - $(q, u, \mu(q)s, \epsilon) \in T$;
   - x_1 occurs in $\mu(q)$ iff x_1 occurs in $\mu(q')$ for every $q' \in B$;
   - If x_1 occurs in $\mu(q)$ then $\text{depth}(s) \geq (n+1) \cdot |M|$. Otherwise, $s = \bot$.

Assume $\nu > 0$ and the sets $Q^{(\nu-1)}$ and $\delta^{(\nu-1)}$ already have been defined. Let $\mu_1, \ldots, \mu_k \in Q^{(\nu-1)}$, B_j be the domains of μ_j, $j = 1, \ldots, k$, and $(B, a, B_1 \ldots B_k)$ a transition of the subset automaton A_0. We construct one map $\mu : B \to T_\Delta(x_1) \cup \{\bot\}$ such that $\mu \in Q^{(j)}$ and $\tau = (\mu, a, \mu_1 \ldots \mu_k) \in \delta^{(j)}$ and define $T_d(\tau)$.

By definition of δ_0, for every $q \in B$ some $\tau_q = (q, a, p_{q,1} \ldots p_{q,k}) \in \delta$ exists with $p_{q,j} \in B_j$ for all j. For $q \in B$ let $u_q = T(\tau_q)[\mu_1(p_{q,1})x_1, \ldots, \mu_k(p_{q,k})x_k]$, and let J_q denote the set of all j such that either $\mu_j(p_{q,j}) \in \tilde{T}_\Delta(x_1)$ or has depth $\geq n \cdot |M|$.

Case 1: $u_r \in T_\Delta$ for some $r \in B$.

According to claim (0) for $Q^{(\nu-1)}$, $u_q \in T_\Delta$ for all $q \in B$. If $\text{depth}(u_q) < (2n+1) \cdot |M|$ for all $q \in B$ then we define $\mu(q) = u_q$ and $T_d(\tau) = \bot$.

Otherwise, some $r \in B$ exists with $\text{depth}(u_r) \geq (2n+1) \cdot |M|$. We claim that

(1) $v \in T_\Delta$ and $w_q \in \tilde{T}_\Delta(x_1)$ exist such that for all $q \in B$,
   - $u_q = w_q v$;
   - $\text{depth}_{x_1}(w_q) < n \cdot |M|$;
   - w_q does not contain subtrees from T_Δ of depth $\geq (n+1) \cdot |M|$;
   - the maximal common x_1-suffix of $w_q, q \in B$, is x_1.

Under this assumption, we put $\mu(q) = w_q$ and $T_d(\tau) = v$.

Case 2: $\exists j : \mu_j(p_{r,j}) \in \tilde{T}_\Delta(x_1)$ for some $r \in Q$ and $\forall q \in B : \#J_q \leq 1$.

Then by claim (0) for $Q^{(\nu-1)}$, $\mu_j(p_{q,j}) \in \tilde{T}_\Delta(x_1)$ for every $q \in B$. Hence, $J_q = \{j\}$, and $\mu_{j'}(p_{q,j'}) \in T_\Delta$ for all $j' \neq j$. Therefore, $u_q \in \tilde{T}_\Delta(x_j)$ for every

$q \in B$. Moreover, u_q does not contain subtrees in T_Δ of depth $\geq (n+1) \cdot |M|$. Let $u_q = w_q y$ where y is the maximal common x_j–suffix of all u_q. We claim that

(2) For every $q \in B$, $\text{depth}_{x_1}(w_q) < n \cdot |M|$.

> Provided Claim (2) holds, we put $\mu(q) = w_q x_1$ and $T_d(\tau) = y$.
> Case 3: $\exists j : \mu_j(p_{r,j}) \in \tilde{T}_\Delta(x_1)$ and $\#J_r > 1$ for some $r \in B$.
> Again by Claim (0) for $Q^{(\nu-1)}$, $\mu_j(p_{q,j}) \in \tilde{T}_\Delta(x_1)$ for all $q \in B$. We claim:

(3) There exists exactly one $s \in T_\Delta(X_k)$ such that the following holds:
   - for all $q \in B$, $u_q = v_q s$ where $v_q \in \tilde{T}_\Delta(x_1)$ with $\text{depth}_{x_1}(v_q) < n \cdot |M|$ such that v_q does not contain subtrees from T_Δ of depth $\geq (n+1) \cdot |M|$;
   - s is maximal with this property.

Provided Claim (3) holds, we define $\mu(q) = v_q$ for every $q \in B$, and put $T_d(\tau) = s$. Observe that x_j occurs in s iff $\mu_j(p_{q,j}) \notin T_\Delta$ for some q. Therefore, (provided claim (0) for $Q^{(\nu-1)}$ holds) x_j occurs in $T_d(\tau)$ iff $\mu_j \notin U(M_d)$.
This finishes the construction. In order to prove its correctness we claim:

(4) Assume $(B, u, \epsilon) \in \delta_0$. Then $(\mu, u, s, \epsilon) \in T_d$ for some $\mu \in Q_d$ whose domain is B and where for every $q \in B$, $(q, u, \mu(q)s, \epsilon) \in T$.

> This claim together with claim (0) and the definition of $T_d|_{Q_{d,F}}$ show that $T(M_d) = T(M)$. Since M_d is reduced deterministic by construction we are done provided Claims (0) through (4) hold.
> Claims (0) through (4) must be proven together by induction on the depth of an input tree u. Note that termination of the construction is due to the second parts of claims (1) and (2). $\qquad\square$

Analogously to Theorem 9 we find:

Theorem 10. *Assume M is a reduced functional FST. Then the following three statements are equivalent:*

(1) $T(M)$ can be realized by a deterministic transducer.
(2) M has Properties (wD0), (D1) and (D2).
(3) M is of weakly bounded difference.

It can be decided whether or not the transduction of an FST can be realized by a deterministic one. $\qquad\square$

From Theorems 9 and Theorems 10 we conclude that the transduction of a deterministic transducer can be realized by a reduced deterministic one iff the corresponding reduced transducer has Property (D0). We have:

Corollary 11. *Assume M is a deterministic FST. Let M_r be a reduced functional transducer with $T(M) = T(M_r)$. Then the following two statements are equivalent:*

(1) $\mathcal{T}(M)$ can be realized by a reduced deterministic transducer.
(2) M_r has Property (D0).

It can be decided in polynomial time whether or not the transduction of a deterministic FST can be realized by a reduced deterministic one. □

Proof. If $\mathcal{T}(M_r)$ can be realized by a reduced deterministic transducer then by Prop. 4, M_r has Property (D0). Conversely, assume M_r has Property (D0). Since $\mathcal{T}(M_r)$ can be realized by a deterministic transducer (namely M), M_r has Properties (D1) and (D2) by Prop. 6 and 8. But then by Theorem 9, $\mathcal{T}(M_r)$ can be realized by a reduced deterministic transducer.

However, the general construction of the equivalent reduced deterministic transducer given in the proof of Theorem 9 can be replaced by a simpler construction here. Let $M_r = (A_r, T_r)$ be the reduced functional transducer with $\mathcal{T}(M_r) = \mathcal{T}(M)$ as constructed in the proof of 2. Since M was deterministic the set $D_r(u)$ of states derivable by some input tree u (w.r.t. A_r) always is a subset of $\{\langle q, 0\rangle, \langle q, 1\rangle\}$ where $(q, u, \epsilon) \in \delta$. Therefore, if $\langle q, 0\rangle \notin D_r(u)$ we safely can produce output whereas as long as $\langle q, 0\rangle \in D_r(u)$ we only produce $\perp$ and memorize a possible output provided $\langle q, 1\rangle \in D_r(u)$.

To implement this idea assume $M = (A, T)$ with $A = (Q, \Sigma, \delta, Q_F)$. We construct $M_d = (A_d, T_d)$ with $A_d = (Q_d, \Sigma, \delta_d, Q_{d,F})$ as follows. Q_d is some set of pairs $Q \times (\{\perp\} \cup T_\Delta \cup \{x_1\})$ such that

1. $\langle q, \perp\rangle \in Q_d$ iff $\langle q, 0\rangle \in Q_r$ but $\langle q, 1\rangle \notin Q_r$; i.e., the output for the presently processed subtree is irrelevant in all cases;
2. $\langle q, y\rangle \in Q_d$ with $y \in T_\Delta$ iff both $\langle q, 0\rangle \in Q_r$ and $\langle q, 1\rangle \in Q_r$; i.e., the output t produced so far possibly is relevant; whereas
3. $\langle q, x_1\rangle \in Q_d$ iff $\langle q, 0\rangle \notin Q_r$ but $\langle q, 1\rangle \in Q_r$; i.e., the output is definitively relevant and already has been produced.

$Q_{d,F}$ consists of all pairs $\langle q, y\rangle \in Q_d$ where $q \in Q_F$, and $U(M_d) = Q_d \cap (Q \times (\{\perp\} \cup T_\Delta))$.

The sets Q_d and δ_d are again iteratively defined as the union of their "approximations", i.e., by

$$Q_d = \bigcup_{\nu \geq 0} Q^{(\nu)} \text{ and } \delta_d = \bigcup_{\nu \geq 0} \delta^{(\nu)}$$

where $Q^{(0)} = \emptyset$ and $\delta^{(0)} = \emptyset$.

Assume $\nu > 0$ and $\langle q_1, y_1\rangle, \ldots, \langle q_k, y_k\rangle \in Q^{(\nu-1)}$. Let $\tau = (q, a, q_1 \ldots q_k) \in \delta$. We construct some $y \in \{\perp\} \cup T_\Delta \cup \{x_1\}$ such that $\langle q, y\rangle \in Q^{(\nu)}$ and $\tau_d = (\langle q, y\rangle, a, \langle q_1, y_1\rangle \ldots \langle q_k, y_k\rangle) \in \delta^{(\nu)}$, and define $T_d(\tau_d)$.

Case 1: $\langle q, 0\rangle \in Q_r$ and $\langle q, 1\rangle \notin Q_r$.

Note that then also for every j, $\langle q_j, 0\rangle \in Q_r$ and $\langle q_j, 1\rangle \notin Q_r$. Hence, all $y_j \in \{\perp\} \cup T_\Delta$. Therefore, we put $y = \perp$ and $T_d(\tau_d) = \perp$.

Case 2: $\langle q, 0\rangle \in Q_r$ and $\langle q, 1\rangle \in Q_r$.

Again, $y_j \in \{\perp\} \cup T_\Delta$ for all j. Moreover, $y_j \neq \perp$ whenever x_j occurs in $T(\tau)$. Therefore, $y = T(\tau)[y_1, \ldots, y_k]$ in deed is in T_Δ. Finally, we put $T_d(\tau_d) = \perp$.

Case 3: $\langle q, 0 \rangle \notin Q_r$ and $\langle q, 1 \rangle \in Q_r$.

This is the only case where we have to produce an output pattern different from $\bot$. Define $y'_j = x_j$ if $y_j = x_1$ and $y'_j = y_j$ otherwise. Then put $y = x_1$ and $T_d(\tau_d) = T(\tau)[y'_1, \ldots, y'_k]$.

It is easy to verify that the construction terminates, and that this construction produces a reduced deterministic transducer which is equivalent to M (or M_r). Especially for every $\langle q, y \rangle \in Q_d$, depth$(y) < \#Q \cdot |M|$.

7 Conclusion

We gave a characterization of functional tree transducers whose transduction can be realized by deterministic or even reduced deterministic transducers. It remained open whether or not these two characterizations can be decided even in polynomial time. At least we were able to prove that it can be decided in polynomial time whether or not the transduction of a deterministic transducer can be realized by a reduced deterministic one.

8 References

1. A.V. Aho, J.E. Hopcroft, J.D. Ullman: *The design and analysis of computer algorithms.* Addison–Wesley, 1974
2. J. Berstel: *Transductions and Context–Free Languages.* Teubner, Stuttgart, 1979
3. J. Engelfriet: Some open questions and recent results on tree transducers and tree languages. In: Formal Language Theory, ed. by R.V. Book, Academic Press 1980, pp. 241–286
4. Chr. Ferdinand, H. Seidl, R. Wilhelm: Tree automata for code selection. In: R. Giegerich, S.L. Graham (eds): *Code Generation – Concepts, Tools, Techniques.* Springer, Workshops in Computing, pp. 31–50, 1992
5. F. Gecseg, M. Steinby: Tree automata. Akademiai Kiado, Budapest, 1984
6. R. Giegerich, K. Schmal: Code selection techniques: pattern matching, tree parsing and inversion of derivors. Proc. of ESOP 1988, LNCS 300 pp. 245–268
7. C. Reutenauer: Subsequential Functions: Characterizations, Minimization, Examples. Proc. IMYCS 1990, LNCS 464, pp. 62–79
8. H. Seidl: Equivalence of finite–valued bottom–up finite state tree transducers is decidable. Proc. CAAP '90, LNCS 431, pp. 269–284, 1990; extended version to appear in: Math. Syst. Theory
9. H. Seidl: Single–valuedness of tree transducers is decidable in polynomial time. To appear in: TCS, special issue of CAAP 90
10. A. Weber, R. Klemm:: Economy of Description for Single–valued Transducers. Preprint J.W.Goethe–Universität, Frankfurt/Main, 1991
11. Z. Zachar: The solvability of the equivalence problem for deterministic frontier–to–root tree transducers. Acta Cybernetica 4 (1978), pp. 167–177

Automata on Infinite Trees with Counting Constraints

Danièle Beauquier[*]
LITP-IBP 4 Place Jussieu 75252 Paris Cedex 05 France

Damian Niwiński[†]
Institute of Informatics, University of Warsaw
ul.Banacha 2, 02 097 Warszawa, Poland

Abstract

We investigate finite automata on infinite trees with the usual Muller criterion for the success of an infinite computation path, but with the acceptance paradigm modified in that not all the computation paths need to be successful. Instead, it is required that the number of successful paths must belong to a specified set of cardinals Γ. We show that Muller automata with the acceptance constraint of the form "there are at least γ accepting paths" can be always simulated by tree automata with a weaker criterion for successful paths, namely Büchi acceptance condition. We also show that this is the most general class of constraints for which a simulation by Büchi automata is always possible. Next, we characterize the maximal class of constraints which can be simulated by classical Muller automata (known to be more powerful than Büchi automata) . The condition requiered of the set Γ there, is that the intersection with natural numbers forms a recognizable set. Finally, we exhibit a set of trees which is recognized by a classical Büchi automaton but fails to be recognized by any Muller automaton with a non trivial cardinality constraint (i.e., except for $\Gamma = 0$).

1 Introduction

The subject of automata on infinite objects (words or trees) has attracted the attention of computer scientists from both a practical and a theoretical point of view.

An essay by [E.A.EMERSON(1990)] gives an account of how the ideas of Büchi, originally conceived in context of mathematical logic, have later found

---

[*]Supported partially by ESPRIT-BRA working group ASMICS

[†]Supported partially by Polish KBN grant $n^0 211929101$

multiple applications in the reasoning about concurrent programs with ideally nonterminating behaviour, this including such issues as specification, mechanical synthesis and verification of such programs.

From a theoretical viewpoint, the interesting feature is that finite automata provide an essentially finite ("finite state") description of intrinsically infinite and often highly complicated objects, as e.g., strategies in infinite games. The subject is relevant to several topics, such as decidability of mathematical theories, expressiveness of logics, Borel and projective hierarchies of descriptive set theory, and determinancy of games (see [W. THOMAS(1990)] for a detailed survey).

The use of automata for reasoning about programs is based on the fact that, although the automata can accept highly undecidable sets of infinite objects due to infinite computations, yet still the emptiness problem for them is elementarily decidable ([M.O. RABIN(1969)], the actual complexity varies from polynomial to exponential time depending on the type of automata, c.f. [E.A. EMERSON AND C. JUTLA(1988)]). This fact has been used to show the elementary decidability of a variety of logics of programs. It is reported by [E.A.EMERSON(1990)] that automata *themselves* have also been proposed as a specification language for concurrent programs. In this context, the questions about different aspects of the expressive (or, defining) power of automata are of interest. In the present paper, we consider the question what kind of *counting* conditions can be expressed by automata.

The concept of "counting" is well known in computation theory. Generally speaking, it consists of a refinement of qualitative conditions like "there is a successful computation" or "each computation is successful" by giving a constraint on the *number* of successful computations as, e.g., "at least a half of possible computations is successful".

Recall that a classical concept of the acceptance of an infinite tree by a finite automaton is based on the notion of a *successful path* of computation. An automaton starts its computation at the root of an input tree and then simultaneously works down the paths of the tree, level by level. In a Büchi automaton, a computation path is successful simply if some *accepting state* is assumed infinitely often. Rabin automata, as well as Muller automata, have a more sophisticated acceptance condition that can be viewed as a Boolean combination of Büchi conditions. For all these automata, the acceptance paradigm is the same: a whole computation is successful if *all* its paths are successful.

The idea of introducing counting constraints for automata on infinite trees was suggested by M.Nivat and has been first investigated by [D. BEAUQUIER, M. NIVAT AND D. NIWIŃSKI(1992)] for the case of Büchi automata. The acceptance criterion is now altered in that not all the computation paths need to be successful. Instead, it is required that the number of successful paths must belong to a specified set of cardinals Γ. It is shown in that paper that Büchi automata with a constraint "there are at least γ accepting paths" can be simulated by ordinary Büchi automata while any other type of a constraint leads to a class of tree languages wich is incomparable with the class of Büchi recognizable sets of trees.

In the present paper we investigate the question how the counting constraints alter the power of Muller automata on infinite trees. [1]

We strengthen a result mentioned above by showing that any Muller automaton with a constraint "there are at least γ accepting paths" can be simulated by an ordinary Büchi automaton. This fact is of interest since the emptiness problem is considerably easier for Büchi automata (polynomial time vs. NP-hard, c.f. [E.A. EMERSON AND C. JUTLA(1988)]), while they are weaker than Muller automata in the expressive power. We complete this result to a full characterization, by showing that a Muller automaton with a constraint specified by a set of cardinals Γ can be simulated by a Büchi automaton if and *only if* Γ is of the form $\{\alpha : \gamma \leq \alpha\}$. Next we characterize those contraints Γ which can be simulated by (classical) Muller automata. The necessary and sufficient condition is that the intersection of Γ with the set of natural numbers (i.e., finite cardinals) should form a recognizable set. Finally, we address the question whether Muller automata with cardinality constraints are at least as powerful as classical Muller automata and answer this question negatively. Actually, we exhibit a set of trees that is recognized by a Büchi automaton but cannot be recognized by a Muller automaton with any counting constraint except for the trivial case $\Gamma = 0$ (i.e., "there are no accepting paths", which amounts to the acceptance by a dual automaton).

The remaining of the paper is organized as follows. In the introductory Section 2, we present some basic notions concerning trees and also prove two lemmas that are crucial for further results. In Section 3, we introduce automata on trees, first classically and then with the counting constraints. We also point out the relationship with monadic logic. Sections 4 and 5 are devoted to the characterizations of those counting constraints that can be simulated by Büchi and Muller automata respectively. Then, in Section 6, we exhibit a tree language that cannot be accepted by a Muller automaton with any nontrivial cardinality constraint. In the last section, we discuss some possible extensions of our results and try to place them in a more general context.

The *continuum hypothesis* is assumed throughout the paper, so the numbers in consideration are only the natural numbers, ω and the continuum (the cardinals greater than continuum are not relevant here). This assumption can be shown inessential by an argument of the descriptive set theory, since the sets in consideration (i.e., the sets of accepting paths) are Borel and the continuum hypothesis is known to be generally valid for such sets.

---

[1] We have chosen Muller automata rather than Rabin automata, that are maybe more commonly used in temporal logic, only for technical reasons. Muller automata are known to be effectively equivalent to Rabin automata in the expressive power (although the latter are in general more succinct) and the actual construction preserves not only the accepted sets but also the number of successful computation paths. All our results (and proofs) could be easily adapted to the case of Rabin automata.

2 Trees

The set of natural numbers $0, 1, \ldots$ is denoted by ω and identified with the first infinite cardinal number. We say that a set X is *countable* if its cardinality, $|X|$, is less than or equal to ω. The cardinality of the powerset of ω, is denoted c (continuum).

For a set X, X^* is the set of finite words over X, including the empty word λ. The *length* of a word w is denoted by $|w|$, note that $|\lambda| = 0$. The (proper) *initial segment relation* is denoted $\leq$ ($<$). The same symbols are occasionally used for the standard inequality relation on natural numbers, but confusion should not arise. The following relation will be also useful:

$$u \lhd v \text{ iff } not \ v \leq u$$

($\lhd$ is not an ordering). The concatenation of words $u, w \in X^*$ is presented by uw, this notation is also extended to sets of words $L, K \subseteq X^*$,

$$LK = \{uw : u \in L \text{ and } w \in K\}.$$

If $u = vw$, we occasionally write $w = v^{-1}u$.

A nonempty subset T of X^* closed under initial segments is called a *tree*. The elements of T are usually called *nodes*, the $\leq$-maximal nodes are *leaves* and λ is the *root* of T. If $u \in T$, $x \in X$ and $ux \in T$ then ux is an *immediate successor* of u in T. An infinite sequence $P = (w_0, w_1, \ldots)$ such that $w_0 = \lambda$ and, for each m, w_{m+1} is an immediate successor of w_m is called a *path* in T. We recall the celebrated *König's Lemma* (c.f., e.g., [K. KURATOWSKI AND A.MOSTOWSKI(1976)]).

> If $T \subseteq X^*$ is an infinite tree and each $w \in T$ has only a finite number of immediate successors in T then T has an infinite path.

If S is an arbitrary set and T is a tree then a mapping $t : T \to S$ is called an *S-valued* tree or shortly an *S-tree* ; in this context T is the *domain* of t denoted by $T = dom(t)$. We say "root of t", "path in t" etc., referring to the corresponding objects in $dom(t)$.

If $P = (w_0, w_1, \ldots)$ is a path in t, let

$$Inf(t, P) = \{s \in S : t(w_m) = s \text{ for infinitely many } m\}$$

Observe that if S is finite then $Inf(t, P)$ is always nonempty and there is some m_0, such that $(\forall m > m_0) \ t(w_m) \in Inf(t, P)$.

For an S-tree $t : dom(t) \to S$ and a node $v \in dom(t)$, the *subtree* of t induced by v is the S-tree denoted by $t.v$ and defined by

- $dom(t.v) = \{w : vw \in dom(t)\}$

- $t.v(w) = t(vw)$, for $w \in dom(t.v)$.

Now suppose that $A \subseteq dom(t)$ is an *antichain* with respect to $\leq$ (i.e. any two elements of A are incomparable) and let f be a function which associates an S-tree $f(w)$ with each $w \in A$. Then the *substitution $t[f]$* is the S-tree defined by

- $dom(t[f]) = \{w \in dom(t) : \forall w' \in A, w \triangleleft w'\} \cup \bigcup_{w \in A} w \, dom(f(w))$,

- $t[f](u) = \begin{cases} f(w)(v) & \text{if } u = wv, w \in A \\ t(u) & \text{otherwise} \end{cases}$

In the case when A is finite, say $A = \{w_1, \ldots, w_k\}$, we shall often express f explicitly, writing for example $t[w_1 : t_1, \ldots, w_k : t_k]$.

We also introduce the concepts of *limit* and *iteration*. Suppose $t_0, t_1, \ldots$ is a sequence of S-trees such that $dom(t_0) \subseteq dom(t_1) \subseteq \ldots$, and, for each $w \in \cup_{n < \omega} dom(t_n)$ there is some $m(w)$ such that $\forall m \geq m(w), t_m(w) = t_{m(w)}(w)$. Then we define the limit of the sequence t_n, $t = lim \, t_n$ by

- $dom(t) = \bigcup_{n < \omega} dom(t_n)$,

- $t(w) = t_{m(w)}(w)$, for $w \in dom(t)$.

Now let t be an S-tree and let v and w be nodes of t such that $v < w$ and $t(v) = t(w)$. Then we define the *iteration of t along the interval* $[v, w]$, in symbols $t^{[v,w]}$ as the limit of substitutions of $t.v$ into (subsequently created copies of) the node w. Formally, we define a sequence of trees t_n and the sequence of nodes of corresponding trees, w_n, as follows. Let $w = vu$. We set

- $t_0 = t$,

- $w_0 = w$,

- $t_{n+1} = t_n[w_n : t.v]$,

- $w_{n+1} = w_n u$.

Finally,

$$t^{[v,w]} =_{df} lim \, t_n$$

In this context we shall call the path containing the chain $w_0, w_1, \ldots$, a *trace of iteration*.

Since now on, for notational convenience, we shall focus on full binary trees over Σ, i.e. the Σ-trees with $dom(t) = \{1, 2\}^*$. Thus, any node $w \in dom(t)$ has exactly two successors $w1$ and $w2$. The extension of our results to n-ary trees (with $n \geq 2$) or ranked trees (where the number of successors of a node depends on the actual label) would present no difficulty.

We end this section by proving two useful lemmas about trees. The first one is a combinatorial observation that some "triangle-like" pattern must occur in a sufficiently large finite part of a tree. It is convenient to consider here finite rather than infinite trees. Let $\{1, 2\}^{\leq n} = \{w \in \{1, 2\}^* : |w| \leq n\}$.

Lemma 2.1 *Let S be a finite alphabet and let $K \geq |S|^2 + 1$. Let $t : \{1,2\}^{\leq K} \to S$ be a (finite) tree. Then there exist nodes $u, v, w \in \{1,2\}^{\leq K}$, such that $u < v$, $u < w$, w and v are incomparable, $t(u) = t(v) = t(w)$ and moreover $\{t(x) : u \leq x \leq v\} = \{t(x) : u \leq x \leq w\}$.*

Proof. By induction on $|S|$. For $|S| = 1$, the claim is obvious. Suppose that the lemma holds for alphabets with cardinality less than $|S|$ and let $t : \{1,2\}^{\leq K} \to S$ be a tree with $K \geq |S|^2 + 1$. Let $t(\lambda) = q$. Now consider two cases.

(1) For each w with $|w| = |S| + 1$, there exists $v \geq w$ with $t(v) = q$. In this case, by counting argument we are already done.

(2) There is some w with $|w| = |S| + 1$, such that $\forall v \geq w : t(v) \neq q$. Then the subtree $t.v$ is of the form $t.v : \{1,2\}^{\leq K - |S| - 1} \to S - \{q\}$ where $K - |S| - 1 \geq |S|^2 + 1 - |S| - 1 \geq (|S| - 1)^2 + 1$ (for $|S| > 1$). Then the claim follows from the induction hypothesis. $\square$

The second lemma of this section will be a core of the proof of our results concerning the cardinality c. Some preparation is needed.

Let S be a *finite* set and let $t : \{1,2\}^* \to S$ be a tree. Observe that, by simple counting argument, there is a subset $S' \subseteq S$ such that $Inf(t, P) = S'$, for a continuum of paths in t. We shall complete this observation, by showing that the set of nodes assuming the states from S' contains some tree-like structure. We call a set of nodes $D \subseteq \{1,2\}^*$ *dense* if $D \neq \emptyset$ and

$$(\forall x \in D \exists y, z \in D) x < y \,\&\, x < z \,\&\, y \text{ and } z \text{ are incomparable}$$

We state the following.

Lemma 2.2 *Let S be a finite set and let $t : \{1,2\}^* \to S$ be a tree. Let $S' \subseteq S$ be a set such that $Inf(t, P) = S'$, for a continuum of paths in t and let $s \in S'$. Then there exists a dense set $D \subseteq \{1,2\}^*$ such that $\forall x \in D : t(x) = s$ and*

$$(\forall x, y \in D) x < y \Rightarrow \{t(w) : x \leq w \leq y\} = S'$$

Proof. Call a node w s.t. $t(w) = s$ an *s-node*. Let Π be a set of paths P in t such that $Inf(t, P) = S'$. Call a node w_i of a path $P = (w_0, w_1, \ldots)$ in Π *terminal* for P if $\forall m \geq i : t(w_m) \in S'$. Call a node *super terminal* if it is terminal for a continuum of paths in Π. Clearly, each path in Π has a terminal s-node and, since there is only countably many nodes while $|\Pi| = 2^\omega$, there exists a super terminal s-node x.

We now show that, whenever x is a super terminal s-node, there also exist some super terminal s-nodes $y, z > x$ such that y and z are incomparable and

$$\{t(w) : x \leq w \leq y\} = \{t(w) : x \leq w \leq z\} = S'$$

Let $\Pi(x) \subseteq \Pi$ be the set of paths for which x is a terminal node. Let X be the set of s-nodes $x' > x$ such that x' occurs in some path in $\Pi(x)$ and $\{t(w) : x \leq w \leq x'\} = S'$. Notice that any path P in $\Pi(x)$ contains some node

x' in X (in fact, infinitely many), and such a node is terminal for P. So, if we write $\Pi(x, x')$ for the set of those paths in $\Pi(x)$ that contain a node x', we have $\Pi(x) = \bigcup_{x' \in X} \Pi(x, x')$, and, by the cardinality argument there must be some super terminal s-node in X, y say. By applying the same argument in turn to y and then repeating it *ad infinitum*, we obtain the existence of infinitely many super terminal nodes in X. In order to show that there exists a super terminal node $z \in X$, **incomparable** with y, suppose for the contrary that all super terminal nodes in X form a chain and so lie along a single infinite path. Then, except for this path, any path in $\Pi(x)$ belongs to some $\Pi(x, x')$, where x' is *not* super terminal and therefore $\Pi(x, x')$ is countable. Thus, $\Pi(x)$ is countable (as a countable union of countable sets), a contradiction with the choice of x. Thus the existence of the desired y and z is proved and, by repeating the same argument for y and z etc., we eventually obtain a set D satisfying the condition of the lemma. $\square$

3   Automata with Cardinality Constraints

We now fix a finite alphabet Σ. Let T_Σ be the collection of all full binary Σ-trees, i.e. the trees of the form $t : \{1, 2\}^* \to \Sigma$.

We recall the classical definition of an automaton on infinite trees with Muller acceptance condition.

A *Muller automaton* on Σ-trees (henceforth often called just automaton) is a tuple $\mathcal{A} = (Q, q_0, \mathit{Trans}, \mathit{Accept})$, where Q is a finite set of *states*, q_0 is an *initial state*, $\mathit{Trans} \subseteq Q \times \Sigma \times Q \times Q$ is a set of *transitions* and $\mathit{Accept} \subseteq 2^Q$ is a family of *successful sets* of states.

A q-*run* of the automaton $\mathcal{A}$ on a tree t is a Q-tree $r : dom(t) \to Q$ such that $r(\lambda) = q$ and for each node $w \in dom(t)$, $\langle r(w), t(w), r(w1), r(w2) \rangle \in \mathit{Trans}$. A q_0-run is called just a *run*. A *path* $P = (w_0, w_1, \ldots)$ of a run r is *accepting* if $\mathit{Inf}(r, P) \in \mathit{Accept}$. A *run* is accepting if *all* its paths are accepting. A *tree* t is *accepted* by an automaton $\mathcal{A}$ if there exists an accepting run of $\mathcal{A}$ on t. The set of trees accepted by $\mathcal{A}$ is denoted $L(\mathcal{A})$.

The notion of a *Büchi automaton* on Σ-trees differs from that of Muller automaton only in the acceptance condition that is actually simpler and can be identified with a set of states $F \subseteq Q$. A path P of a run r is accepting if $\mathit{Inf}(r, P) \cap F \neq \emptyset$. Clearly, a Büchi automaton can be presented as a Muller automaton, but the converse is not true. Let $\Sigma = \{a, b\}$ and let M be the set of trees $t \in T_\Sigma$ such that, any path P in t has only a finite number of occurrences of b (i.e. $\mathit{Inf}(t, P) = \{a\}$). It can be easily seen that M can be accepted by a Muller automaton, but [M.O. RABIN(1970)] showed that

Proposition 3.1 *There is no Büchi automaton that accepts M.*

Now let γ be a cardinal number. We say that a run of an automaton (of either type) is $\{\gamma\}$-*accepting* if it has precisely γ accepting paths. More generally, for a set of cardinals Γ, a run will be called Γ-*accepting* if it is $\{\gamma\}$-accepting for some $\gamma \in \Gamma$. The corresponding sets of Γ-*accepted* trees will be denoted by $L_\Gamma(\mathcal{A})$. (Notice that "ω-accepting" and "$\{\omega\}$-accepting" mean two different things.) Finally, let $\Gamma$$-$Muller$_\Sigma$ denote the class of all subsets of T_Σ that can be presented as $L = L_\Gamma(\mathcal{A})$, for some Muller automaton $\mathcal{A}$. We also use the notation Muller$_\Sigma$ and Büchi$_\Sigma$ to denote the families of classically Muller recognizable (resp. Büchi recognizable) sets of trees. We often omit the subscript Γ if the alphabet is known from the context or if the choice of a particular (finite) alphabet is irrelevant for the result. Let us remark that a run has at most c accepting paths. So, from now, **we only consider cardinals less than or equal to** c.

Examples. A run is ω-accepting if the number of accepting paths is finite; it is $\{\alpha : \alpha \geq \omega\}$-accepting or, equivalently, $\{\omega, c\}$-accepting if the number of accepting paths is infinite. Notice that $L_{\{c\}}(\mathcal{A})$ is, in general, different from $L(\mathcal{A})$. The tree language $L_{\{0\}}(\mathcal{A})$ coincides with the set accepted by the automaton *dual* to $\mathcal{A}$, i.e. the one that differs from $\mathcal{A}$ only in that its accepting condition is the complement of *Accept* (w.r.t. 2^Q).

We now recall the basic facts concerning the monadic second-order theory of trees.

Recall that a (non-labelled) full binary tree can be considered as a logical structure of the form

$$T = (\{1,2\}^*, \lambda, s_1, s_2, \leq)$$

where s_1 and s_2 are the left and the right successor functions over $\{1,2\}^*$ respectively, λ is the empty word (that can be viewed as a root of the tree) and $\leq$ is the prefix relation. The formulas of *monadic second order logic* over this structure use individual variables $x_0, x_1, \ldots$ (ranging over nodes of the tree) and the set-variables $X_0, X_1, \ldots$ (ranging over sets of nodes). The *atomic formulas* are $t_1 = t_2$, $t_1 \leq t_2$, and $X_i(t)$, where the t's are *terms* built from the individual variables, the constant λ and the functional symbols s_i, $i = 1, 2$. The other formulas are built as usual, using propositional connectives and quantifiers $\exists, \forall$ applied to both kinds of variables.

The formulas of *weak* monadic second order logic have the same syntax but differ in the semantics: the set-variables which are quantified are assumed to range over finite sets of nodes.

The (weak) monadic second order theory of the structure described above is usually abbreviated $(W)S2S$.

In the following definition, it is convenient to have a distinguished set of variables, say $Z_0, Z_1, \ldots$ that are supposed to range over finite sets of nodes only. (The introduction of these variables does not increase the expressive power of the theory $S2S$ since the property "X is finite" *is* expressible there). A formula of $S2S$ is called a Σ_1^1 formula if it is of the form

$$\exists Y_1 \ldots \exists Y_m \varphi(Y_1, \ldots, Y_m, X_1, \ldots, X_n)$$

where, in φ, all quantifiers (if any) are restricted to variables among $Z_0, Z_1, \ldots$.

Now, if the alphabet Σ can be embedded into $\{0, 1\}^k$, for suitable k, a tree $t \in T_\Sigma$ can be coded by a k-tuple of sets of nodes $X_1, \ldots, X_k$, such that $w \in X_i$ iff the i-th component of $t(w)$ is 1. (Conversely, a k-tuple of sets of nodes represents a tree over the alphabet $\{0, 1\}^k$.)

In this sense, a set of trees $L \subseteq T_\Sigma$ can be identified with a set of k-tuples of sets of nodes and therefore can be defined by a formula of S2S, $\phi(X_1, \ldots, X_n)$.

We recall the classical characterizations due to [M.O. RABIN(1970)].

Theorem 3.2 *A set of trees $L \subseteq T_\Sigma$ is recognizable by a (ordinary) Muller automaton iff it can be defined by an S2S formula.*

A set of trees $L \subseteq T_\Sigma$ is recognizable by a Büchi automaton iff it can be defined by a Σ_1^1 S2S formula.

4 Büchi Definable Constraints

In this section we examine the cardinality constraints of the form "there are *at least* γ accepting paths". We show that Muller automata with this kind of constraints can be always simulated by ordinary Büchi automata. We also show that this is the only kind of cardinality constraint having such a property.

Theorem 4.1 *Let γ be a cardinal number. Then*

$$\{\alpha : \alpha \geq \gamma\} - \text{Muller} \subseteq \text{Büchi}$$

Proof. Let us abbreviate $\{\alpha : \alpha \geq \gamma\} = [\gamma)$.

Let $\mathcal{A} = (Q, q_0, \text{Trans}, \text{Accept})$ be a Muller automaton. Observe first that *any* run is $[0)$-accepting and so it is easy to construct a suitable Büchi automaton (just set in $\mathcal{A}$, $F = Q$).

For $\gamma > 0$, it will be convenient to use the logical charcterization of Büchi automata mentioned in the previous section. In doing this, we use the standard method of coding a run of an automaton with m states by an m-tuple of sets of nodes (see, e.g., [W. THOMAS(1990)]). If γ is a finite cardinal (i.e. an integer), the construction of a suitable Σ_1^1 formula is easy. For $\gamma = \omega$, we use an observation that the existence of ω paths satisfying a given condition is equivalent to the existence of an infinite "comb" structure, i.e. an infinite antichain of nodes each of them lying on some path satisfying the condition in question. Such a figure can be described by a Σ_1^1 formula (a formal argument can be found in [D. BEAUQUIER, M. NIVAT AND D. NIWIŃSKI(1992)]. The case of $\gamma = c$ is the most interesting one. We use here 2.2 from the introductory section. Then the existence of c paths can be reduced to the existence of some dense set of full nodes. $\square$

One can ask whether the inclusions in the above theorem are proper. It is indeed the case and we shall see an actually stronger result in Section 5.

Another natural question is whether the class of constraints Γ considered above is a maximal one for the inclusion $\Gamma - \textit{Muller} \subseteq \textit{Büchi}$, or an apparently weaker result $\Gamma - B\ddot{u}chi \subseteq B\ddot{u}chi$, holds. It turns out that it is indeed the case, i.e., the special form of Γ considered in the theorem above is necessary.

Let $\Sigma = \{a, b\}$. Consider a Büchi automaton defined as follows: $\mathcal{A} = (\{q_a, q_b\}, q_a, \{(q, s, q_s, q_s) : q \in \{q_a, q_b\}, s \in \{a, b\}\}, \{q_b\})$. It is easy to see that the accepted set $L(\mathcal{A})$ consists of all trees in T_Σ such that any path P of t contains infinitely many b's (i.e. $b \in Inf(t, P)$). Moreover, a tree is $\{\gamma\}$-accepted by $\mathcal{A}$ if it has exactly γ paths with infinitely many b's.

Lemma 4.2 *Let Γ be a set of cardinals. Then $L_\Gamma(\mathcal{A}) \in$ Büchi iff $\Gamma = [\gamma)$, for some cardinal number γ.*

We need an auxiliary result for the proof of this lemma.

Let $\mathcal{B} = (Q, q_0, Trans, Accept)$ be a Büchi automaton. Suppose r is a q-run of $\mathcal{B}$ on a tree t. A *demonic triangle* for r is a triple of nodes (u, v, w) such that v and w are incomparable and both greater than u, $r(u) = r(v) = r(w) \in Accept^2$ and there are some $u < w_1 < v$ and $u < w_2 < w$ such that $t(w_1) = t(w_2) = b$.

Now, for $m \geq 1$, we define a tree $h^{(m)}$ similar to that used in [M.O. RABIN(1977)]. The tree $h^{(m)}$ is b-labelled at nodes $\lambda, 2^{n_1}1, 2^{n_1}12^{n_2}1, \ldots,$ $2^{n_1}12^{n_2}1 \ldots 2^{n_m}1$ for all $n_1, \ldots, n_m > 0$ and a-labelled at other nodes. The following lemma is proved in [D. BEAUQUIER, M. NIVAT AND D. NIWIŃSKI(1992)].

Lemma 4.3 *If $\mathcal{B}$ is a Büchi automaton with m states and r is an accepting q-run of $\mathcal{B}$ on $h^{(m)}$, then there exists a demonic triangle for r.*

Proof of Lemma 4.1

We have to prove the "only if " part. Let us suppose that there are two cardinals α and β such that $\alpha \in \Gamma$, $\beta \notin \Gamma$, $\alpha < \beta \leq c$. We claim that $L_\Gamma(\mathcal{A}) \notin$ Büchi. Suppose that there is a Büchi automaton $\mathcal{B}$ with m states such that $L_\Gamma(\mathcal{A}) = L(\mathcal{B})$. Fix some tree f in $L_\Gamma(\mathcal{A})$ and let $h^{(m)}$ be the tree defined above. We combine these two trees into a tree t such that $t(\lambda) = a$ (for definiteness), $t.1 = f$ and $t.2 = h^{(m)}$. Clearly, $t \in L_\Gamma(\mathcal{A})$. Let r be an accepting run of $\mathcal{B}$ on t. Applying Lemma 4.2 to the subtree $t.2$, we obtain a demonic triangle of r, say (u, v, w).

We have three cases to consider: $\beta < \omega$, $\beta = \omega$, $\beta = c$.

- $\beta < \omega$

  Then, we can suppose without loss of generality that $\beta = \alpha + 1$. Let $t' = t^{[u,w]}$ and $r' = r^{[u,w]}$. Since (u, v, w) is a demonic triangle, r' is an accepting run of $\mathcal{B}$ on t'. On the other hand, $t' \in L_{\alpha+1}(\mathcal{A})$ since we have created in t' a new path which has an infinite number of b. So, $t' \notin L_\Gamma(\mathcal{A})$, a contradiction with the hypothesis.

- $\beta = \omega$

---

[2]Recall, that for a Büchi automaton, *Accept* is a set of states.

In the tree t' defined above, let us consider, for $i > 0$, the nodes u'_i and v'_i defined in the following way:

$u'_i = u(u^{-1}w)^i$ and $v'_i = u'_i(u^{-1}v)$.

Let t'' be the limit of the sequence of trees $t'^{[u'_1,v'_1]}$, $t'^{[u'_1,v'_1][u'_2,v'_2]}$, ..., $t'^{[u'_1,v'_1]\ldots[u'_i,v'_i]}$, ... The tree t'' is still accepted by $\mathcal{B}$, and t'' has exactly ω paths with an infinite number of b's. Then, $t'' \notin L_\Gamma(\mathcal{A})$, a contradiction.

- $\beta = c$

  We apply the following iteration construction to the triangle (u, v, w). Let $v = uv'$, $w = uw'$. Replace in t the two subtrees $t.v$ and $t.w$ by $t.u$, in the result replace the four subtrees induced by the nodes vv', vw', wv', ww' again by $t.u$ and so on infinitely many times. The similar iteration is applied to the run r. Clearly the resulted tree is not in $L_\Gamma(\mathcal{A})$ since it has a continuum set of paths with an infinite number of b's, and nevertheless it is in $L(\mathcal{B})$, a contradiction. $\square$

Clearly, the above result holds for any alphabet $\Sigma' \supset \Sigma$. Then, we can state the following.

Corollary 4.4 *Let Σ have at least two elements and let Γ be a set of cardinals. Then $\Gamma - $ Muller $\subseteq$ Büchi iff $\Gamma - $ Büchi $\subseteq$ Büchi iff $\Gamma = \{\alpha : \alpha \geq \gamma\}$, for some ordinal γ.*

5 Muller Definable Constraints

In this section we consider the question: for what sets Γ, $\Gamma - $ Muller $\subseteq$ Muller .

Call a set of integers $A \subseteq \omega$ *recognizable* if it is recognizable by a finite automaton when identifying the integers with strings over one letter alphabet (c.f.[D.Perrin(1990)]).

Theorem 5.1 *Let the alphabet Σ have at least two elements. Then $\Gamma - $Muller $\subseteq$ Muller iff $\Gamma \cap \omega$ is recognizable.*

Proof. "only if". Without loss of generality, we can set $\Sigma = \{a, b\}$. Suppose $\Gamma - $ *Muller* $\subseteq$ *Muller*. We shall construct an automaton $\mathcal{A}$ such that the Muller recognizability of $L_\Gamma(\mathcal{A})$ will imply the recognizability of $\Gamma \cap \omega$. Let $\mathcal{A} = (Q, q_0, Trans, Accept)$, where

- $Q = \{q, \tilde{q}, q_a, \tilde{q}_a, q_b, \tilde{q}_b\}$

- $q_0 = q$

- $Trans = \{(q, a, q, q_a), (q_a, a, \tilde{q}_a, q_a), (\tilde{q}_a, a, \tilde{q}_a, \tilde{q}_a), (q, b, q_b, q_b), (q_b, b, q_b, q_b)\}$

- $Accept = \{\{q_a\}\}$

The automaton $\mathcal{A}$ is deterministic and so, for any tree $t \in T_\Sigma$, there exists at most one run on t. Notice that the automaton $\mathcal{A}$ admits a run on a tree t only in the case when either $t(w) = a$ for all w, or, there exists an $m_0 > 0$ such that, for all $w \in \{1,2\}^*$, $t(1^{m_0}w) = b$ and $t(v) = a$ otherwise. In this latter case, $t \in L_\Gamma(\mathcal{A})$ iff $m_0 \in \Gamma$. Indeed, the only accepting paths are of the form $(\lambda, 1, 11, \ldots, 1^m, 1^m2, 1^m22, 1^m222, \ldots)$, where $m \geq 0$ provided that $t(1^m) = a$ (and, consequently, all the nodes of the path are labelled by a), so the number of accepting paths corresponds to the number of integers less than m_0. Let us denote a tree in the form considered above by t_{m_0}.

Now suppose that the set $L_\Gamma(\mathcal{A})$ is recognized by a Muller automaton $\mathcal{B}$. We shall construct a finite automaton $\mathcal{C}$ running on finite words over a single letter alphabet.

Let t_a be defined by $(\forall w \in \{1,2\}^*)t(w) = a$ (the similar for t_b). Without loss of generality we can assume that the tree t_a is not in L_Γ (otherwise, we could take the tree language $L_\Gamma(\mathcal{A}) - \{t_a\}$ that should be Muller recognizable as well). Let S be the set of states of $\mathcal{B}$. For $s \in S$, we shall use notation $s \models t$ to mean "there is an accepting s-run (i.e. a run starting from s) of $\mathcal{B}$ on t". We let the set of states of $\mathcal{C}$ be S and the initial state be the same as in $\mathcal{B}$. A pair (s, s') is a transition of $\mathcal{C}$ (we omit the single letter of the alphabet) if there is a transition (s, a, s', s'') of $\mathcal{B}$ for some s'' such that $s'' \models t_a$. Finally, s is an accepting state of $\mathcal{C}$, if $s \models t_b$. It is straightforward to see that there is an accepting finite run of $\mathcal{C}$ on an integer k (considered as string over one letter alphabet) iff there is an accepting run of $\mathcal{B}$ on a tree t_{k+1} which in turn is equivalent to $k + 1 \in \Gamma$. Then the set $\{k : k + 1 \in \Gamma\}$ is recognizable and clearly, this induces that the set Γ itself is recognizable.

This completes the proof of the implication "only if" of the theorem.

We shall now prove the "if" implication.

We have $L_\Gamma(\mathcal{A}) = \mathcal{L}_{-\cap\omega}(\mathcal{A}) \cup \mathcal{L}_{-\cap[\omega)}(\mathcal{A})$.

Since $L_{[\omega)}(\mathcal{A})$ and $L_c(\mathcal{A})$ are in *Büchi*, *Büchi* $\subset$ *Muller* and the family *Muller* is closed under boolean operations, we have only to prove that $L_{\Gamma\cap\omega}(\mathcal{A}) \in$ *Muller*.

Recall that a recognizable set of integers can be always presented as a finite union of sets of the form $\{p + na : n \in \omega\}$, for some p, a.

Without loss of generality, we can assume that Γ itself is a set of integers in the above form. For notational simplicity, we let $\Gamma = \{p + 2n \mid n \in \omega\}$. Observe first that a run r of $\mathcal{A}$ on a tree t is $\{\gamma\}$-accepting for some integer γ iff there is an antichain X consisting of γ elements such that:

1) for each successful path P, $X \cap P \neq \emptyset$
2) for each $x \in X$, there is a unique successful path P such that $x \in P$.

Now, in order to express the property that a run is Γ accepting, it is enough to show that a property "X is a finite antichain the cardinality of which belongs to Γ" is expressible by an S2S formula. This fact is well known but we sketch the argument for the sake of completeness. Finiteness may be expressed by saying that there exists an antichain Y which majorizes X and each infinite path intersects Y. Next, we have to say that X is a disjoint union of, say, X_1, X_2 such that X_1 has p elements and the cardinality of X_2 is divisible by 2. The first is obvious (remember that p is fixed). Now observe that the lexicographical order $\prec$ on X can be expressed by an S2S formula. Then, $|X_2|$ is even iff either X_2 is empty or

    i) X_2 is a disjoint union $X^{(0)} \cup X^{(1)}$

    ii) the minimal (w.r.t. $\prec$) element of X_2 exists and belongs to $X^{(0)}$

    iii) the maximal element of X_2 exists and belongs to $X^{(1)}$

    iv) for each $x \in X^{(0)}$ (resp. $X^{(1)}$) not equal to the maximal element of X_2, its successor in X_2 (w.r.t. $\prec$) is in $X^{(1)}$ (resp. $X^{(0)}$).

Clearly the above clauses are expressible in the S2S. So the proof is done. □

6 Counterexample

We start with the following observation:

Proposition 6.1 $\{0\} - Muller = $ Muller

Proof. For any of the inclusions, a suitable automaton can be obtained by complementing the family of accepting sets of states of the original automaton. □

We shall see that for any $\Gamma \neq \{0\}$, the situation is different. Let $\Sigma = \{a, b\}$ and let L be the set of trees in T_Σ such that any path P of t contains infinitely many b's (i.e. $b \in Inf(t, P)$). We have already considered this language in Section 4, where we observed it is recognized by a Büchi automaton. On the other hand, we prove the following.

Theorem 6.2 *For any set of cardinals* $\Gamma \neq \{0\}$ *,* $L \notin \Gamma - $ Muller.

Proof.

Let us fix some $m \geq 1$ and define a tree t by

$$t(w) = \begin{cases} b & \text{if } |w| = k(m+2), \ k < \omega \\ a & \text{otherwise} \end{cases}$$

We first state the following.

Lemma 6.3 *Let* A *be a Muller automaton with* m *states. Suppose that there exists a run of* A *on the tree* t *with* α *accepting paths, where* α *is a cardinal number greater than 0. Then there exists a tree* $t' \in T_\Sigma$ *not in* L *and a run* r' *of* A *on* t' *which has also precisely* α *accepting paths.*

Suppose that $L = L_\Gamma(A)$, for some Muller automaton A, with m states.

Let r be a γ-accepting run of A on the tree t (as defined above), $\gamma \in \Gamma$. If $\gamma > 0$, a contradiction follows immediately from the lemma above.

If $\gamma = 0$, choose $\delta \in \Gamma$, $\delta > 0$ (remember $\Gamma \neq \{0\}$). We shall construct a tree t' not in L and a run r' of $\mathcal{A}$ on t' that will have δ accepting paths. The argument splits into three cases, depending on whether δ is finite, ω, or c.

Suppose first that δ is finite. Choose k such that $2^{k(m+2)} > \delta$ and select δ different nodes of length $k(m+1)$, say $v_1, \ldots, v_\delta$. Then, for each $i = 1, \ldots \delta$, choose w_i', w_i'' such that $v_i < w_i' < w_i''$, $(\forall u) w_i' \leq u \leq w_i'' \Rightarrow t(u) = a$ and $r(w_i') = r(w_i'')$. Observe that, for each $i = 1, \ldots, \delta$, the set $Q_i =_{df} \{r(u) : w_i' \leq u \leq w_i''\}$ is an accepting set of $\mathcal{A}$, (otherwise we could apply an iteration along $[w_i', w_i'']$ and obtain a run with 0 accepting path on a tree which is not in L.) Then apply the iteration to all pairs $[w_i', w_i'']$. The resulted run $r^{[w_1', w_1''], \ldots, [w_\delta', w_\delta'']}$ has δ successful paths, but the $\{\delta\}$-accepted tree $t^{[w_1', w_1''], \ldots, [w_\delta', w_\delta'']}$ is clearly not in L.

If $\delta = \omega$, the argument is essentially the same, but the corresponding selected nodes $v_0, v_1, \ldots$ cannot now, of course, be of the same length. Rather we can choose, for example, $v_k = 2^{(k+1)(m+2)-1}1$, $k = 0, 1, \ldots$. The rest of the argument is similar, we omit the details.

The case when $\delta = c$ is slightly more difficult. (Notice that a consideration of this case is necessary, since Γ can be just $\{0, c\}$.) Let $\tilde{t}$ be a tree defined as t above, but with replacing m by $m^2 + 1$, and $\tilde{r}$ be a run of $\mathcal{A}$ on $\tilde{t}$ having 0 accepting paths. By applying Lemma 2.1 from the introductory section to the initial segment of this tree, we find that there exists a "triangle" u, v, w, such that $|u|, |v|, |w| \leq m^2 + 1$, $u < v, u < w$, v and w are incomparable, $t(u) = t(v) = t(w)$ and $\{t(x) : u \leq x \leq v\} = \{t(x) : u \leq x \leq w\}$. Let us denote this last set by Q'. Now consider two cases.

If Q' is a nonaccepting set of $\mathcal{A}$ then we can apply iteration to, e.g., the segment $[u, v]$. The resulted run $\tilde{r}^{[u,v]}$ has still 0 accepting paths but $\tilde{t}^{[u,v]} \notin L$.

If Q' is accepting, we apply the iteration construction to the triangle. (More precisely, let $v = uv', w = uw'$. Replace in $\tilde{t}$ the two subtrees $\tilde{t}.v$ and $\tilde{t}.w$ by $\tilde{t}.u$. Then, in the result, replace the four subtrees induced by the nodes $vv', vw', wv'ww'$ again by $\tilde{t}.u$ and so on. The construction can be easily formalized similarly as it has been done for the iteration along a single segment in the introductory section; we omit the details. The similar iteration is applied to the run $\tilde{r}$.) The resulted tree is not in L but the resulted run clearly has c accepting paths.

This completes the proof of the theorem. $\square$

7 Conclusion

From a broader perspective, where, as we have mentioned in the introduction, automata on infinite trees can be viewed as a formalism for specification and verification of program properties, automata with counting constraints may prove to be useful for expressing those properties that explicitly refer to the cardinality. For example, we can express the fact that the number of computation paths satisfying a fairness requierement is finite, or infinite, or continuum. From some point of view, the results of the paper may appear rather pessimistic: as pointed out by Theorems 4.1 and 6.1, the expressive power of these automata is rather limited. On the positive side, we belive that automata with counting constraints may be sometimes more convenient to use since they specify the property more directly and are in general more succint than the corresponding Muller or Büchi automata. Yet still, in view of the characterizations provided by Corollary 4.1 and Theorem 5.1, for large classes of counting constraints, the new automata can be simulated by classical ones and, since the proofs of simulations are constructive, the standard techniques known for classical automata (as e.g., decision procedures for emptiness or containement) can apply.

Acknowledgments

Most of this work was done while the second author visited LITP (Laboratoire d'Informatique Théorique et Programmation) in June and July 1992. Thanks go to the Laboratory members for this invitation and a stimulating working atmosphere. We also thank Jacques Sakarovitch for helpful ideas and A.A.Muchnik for enlightening remarks.

References

[D. BEAUQUIER, M. NIVAT AND D. NIWIŃSKI(1992)] The Effect of the Number of Successful Paths in a Büchi Tree Automaton, to appear in *Int. Jour. of Alg. and Comp.*

[E.A.EMERSON(1990)] The Role of Büchi's Automata in Computing Science, *in:* MacLane and Siefkes, eds., The Collected Works of J.R.Büchi, Springer Verlag, Berlin, 18-22.

[E.A. EMERSON AND C. JUTLA(1988)] The complexity of tree automata and logics of programs, *Proc. 29th IEEE Symp. on Foundations of Computer Science*, N.Y.,328-337.

[F. GECSEG AND M. STEINBY(1984)] Tree Automata, Akademiai Kiado, Budapest.

[K. KURATOWSKI AND A.MOSTOWSKI(1976)] Set Theory, *North-Holland.*

[D.PERRIN(1990)] Finite Automata, *in:* Handbook of Theoretical Computer Science, vol.B (J.van Leeuven,ed.), 1-57.

[M.O. RABIN(1969)] Decidability of second-order theories and automata on infinite trees, *Trans.Amer.Soc.*141, 1-35.

[M.O. RABIN(1970)] Weakly definable relations and special automata, *in:* Mathematical Logic in Foundations of Set Theory (Y.Bar-Hillel,ed.), 1-23.

[M.O.RABIN(1972)] Automata on infinite objects and Church 's problem, *Amer. Math.Soc.*, 1-22.

[M.O. RABIN(1977)] Decidable theories, *in:* Handbook of Mathematical Logic (J.Barwise, ed.).

[W. THOMAS(1990)] Automata on infinite objects *in:* Handbook of Theoretical Computer Science, vol.B (J. van Leeuven, ed.), 133-191.

[M.Y. VARDI AND P.L.WOLPER(1986)] Automata-theoretic techniques for modal logics of programs, *J. Comput. System Sci.* 32, 183-221.

Directed Column-Convex Polyominoes by Recurrence Relations

Elena Barcucci   Renzo Pinzani   Renzo Sprugnoli

Dipartimento di Sistemi e Informatica
Firenze, Italy

Abstract. In the literature most counting problems for directed column-convex polyominoes are solved by using Schutzenberger's method. In this paper, we use the traditional recurrence relation approach in order to count the number of directed column-convex polyominoes with a given area, the number of their columns and the number of directed column-convex polyominoes having at most k cells in the first column. This approach allows us to state a very simple algorithm for the random generation of directed column-convex polyominoes. Furthermore, directed column-convex polyominoes are considered to be structures for storing and retrieving information in a computer, and their average internal path length is then evaluated.

1 Introduction

In the vast literature concerning polyominoes, attention has been given to the so-called *directed column-convex polyominoes, dcc-polyominoes* or *dcc-animals* for short. Many counting problems (see Viennot [7] for an exhaustive survey) for these structures were solved by Delest and Dulucq [4] and by Barcucci, Pinzani, Rodella and Sprugnoli [1]. In the general setting of polyominoes, the qualification *directed column-convex* refers to the following characteristics: i) they are *directed* in the sense that they can be built by starting with a single cell (the *origin*) and then by adding new cells on the right or on the top of an existing cell; ii) in this construction, every column must be formed by contiguous cells.

The *area* of a dcc-polyomino is the number of its cells. In fig. 1 all the dcc-polyominoes having area $n = 1$, 2, 3, 4 are shown.

Undoubtedly, the dcc-polyominoes are one of the simplest and easiest subclasses of polyominoes to study. They are also an interesting combinatorial object and their study can constitute a first step in the analysis of many properties of polyominoes. Furthermore, they can serve as a structure for storing and retrieving information in a computer. The above-mentioned authors used Schutzenberger's method; this consists in looking for an unambiguous, context-free language, whose words have a 1−1 correspondence with dcc-polyominoes; it is then possible to derive their counting generating functions from the formal grammar. For n-area dcc-polyominoes, a very simple language can be defined by:

$$A ::= \epsilon \mid aA$$
$$B ::= \epsilon \mid bB$$
$$C ::= AcB$$
$$M ::= \epsilon \mid CM$$
$$P ::= MaA$$

It is a simple matter to show that the language $L(P)$ has a 1–1 correspondence with the set of dcc-polyominoes. Every column in a dcc-polyomino (except the last one) corresponds to a (possibly empty) sequence of a, followed by a c, followed by a (possibly empty) sequence of b. Every letter corresponds to a cell and the letter c denotes the cell from which the next column starts. The last column is only composed by a. Therefore, the 13 dcc-polyominoes of area 4 correspond to the words {$aaaa$, $cbba$, $acba$, $aaca$, $cbaa$, $acaa$, $cbca$, $acca$, $caaa$, $ccba$, $caca$, $ccaa$, $ccca$} (according to the ordering in Fig. 1). From this grammar, several counting problems can be easily solved.

Fig. 1 - Dcc-polyominoes with area $n = 1, 2, 3, 4$.

In this paper, we follow a different approach. We only deal with dcc-polyominoes of a given area and derive recurrence relations in order to solve our problems. In particular these relations allow us to state a very simple linear time random generation algorithm for this kind of polyominoes. This algorithm is much simpler and more direct than the ones which can be obtained by the general algorithm proposed for regular grammars [5] or by the methods of [2, 3]. The first two results are already known, but all the others seem to be new. In Section 1, we find recurrence relations for the number of dcc-polyominoes, for the number of their columns and for the number of dcc-polyominoes having area n and k columns. In Section 2, we find the number of dcc-polyominoes having area n and k cells in the first column; this allows us to state a simple algorithm to generate random dcc-polyominoes in linear time. Finally in Section 3, we find the average internal path length of the dcc-polyominoes with area n.

2 How to Count Dcc-Polyominoes

As we shall see, the number of dcc-polyominoes and many other related quantities are strictly connected to the Fibonacci numbers $\{0, 1, 1, 2, 3, 5, 8, \ldots\}$. We denote by F_n the nth Fibonacci number whose generating function is:

$$\mathcal{G}\{F_n\} = F(t) = \frac{t}{1-t-t^2}$$

Note that by applying the bisection rules we find:

$$\mathcal{G}\{F_{2n}\} = \frac{t}{1-3\,t+t^2} \qquad\qquad \mathcal{G}\{F_{2n+1}\} = \frac{1-t}{1-3\,t+t^2}$$

The basic result of Delest and Dulucq [4] concerns the number V_n of dcc-polyominoes with area n. We get the same result by using the following recurrence relation:

Theorem 2.1: The number V_n of dcc-polyominoes with area n is given by the recurrence relation:

$$V_n = 1 + \sum_{k=1}^{n-1} k\, V_{n-k}$$

having the initial condition $V_0 = 1$, given by the empty polyomino. Hence, we obtain the generating function:

$$V(t) = \frac{1-2\,t}{1-3\,t+t^2}$$

and the closed formula $V_n = F_{2n-1}$, for every $n > 0$.

Proof: Since it is obvious that $V_1 = 1$, let us suppose that $n > 1$. There is only one dcc-polyomino having a single column with n cells. For every $1 \leq k < n$, let k be the number of cells in the first column. The other $n-k$ cells constitute a dcc-polyomino which can be attached to every cell in the first column. Therefore, we have:

$$V_n = 1 + \sum_{k=1}^{n-1} k\, V_{n-k}$$

dcc-polyominoes, and this is our recurrence. The sum can be extended from 0 to n, provided we subtract the n resulting from $k = n$ (and hence $V_{n-k} = V_0 = 1$). So we have:

$$V_n = 1 + \sum_{k=0}^{n} k \, V_{n-k} - n$$

and for the generating functions:

$$V(t) = \frac{1}{1-t} + \frac{t}{(1-t)^2} V(t) - \frac{t}{(1-t)^2}$$

This can be solved in $V(t)$

$$V(t) = \frac{1-2t}{1-3t+t^2}$$

Finally, we observe that $1 + t \mathcal{G}\{F_{2n+1}\} = V(t)$ and this means that $V_n = F_{2n-1}$, for every $n > 0$. □

In much the same way we can count the number of dcc-polyominoes having area n and k columns:

Theorem 2.2: The number of n-area dcc-polyominoes having exactly k columns is:

$$V_{n,k} = \binom{n+k-2}{n-k}$$

Proof: The numbers $\{V_{n,k} \mid n, k \in \mathbb{N}, k \leq n\}$ constitute a triangle:

$n \backslash k$	0	1	2	3	4
0	1				
1	0	1			
2	0	1	1		
3	0	1	3	1	
4	0	1	6	5	1
	.	.	.	.	. . .

If $V_k(t)$ denotes the generating function of column k, we obviously have $V_0(t) = 1$ and $V_1(t) = \frac{t}{(1-t)}$. As in the proof of Theorem 2.1, we can now show that for $k > 0$:

$$V_{n,k+1} = \sum_{j=1}^{n-1} j \, V_{n-j,k} = \sum_{j=0}^{n} j \, V_{n-j,k}$$

In terms of generating functions, this is equivalent to:

$$V_{k+1}(t) = \frac{t}{(1-t)^2} \, V_k(t)$$

By using $V_1(t)$ and the induction principle, we easily find:

$$V_k(t) = \frac{t^k}{(1-t)^{2k-1}}$$

Finally, we can extract the coefficient of t^n:

$$V_{n,k} = [t^n] \, V_k(t) = [t^n] \frac{t^k}{(1-t)^{2k-1}} = \binom{-2\,k+1}{n-k}(-1)^{n-k} = \binom{n+k-2}{n-k}$$

In fact, this formula is valid for any $n, \ k \in \mathbb{N}$, except when $n = 1, \ k = 0$. $\square$

It is worth noting that Theorems 2.1 and 2.2 imply $\sum_{k=1}^{n} \binom{n+k-2}{n-k} = F_{2n-1}$; hence, by first setting $h = k-1$ and then $m = n-1$, we obtain a combinatorial proof of the identity:

$$\sum_h \binom{m+h}{m-h} = F_{2m+1}$$

As it will be illustrated in the next section, an important quantity is the average number of columns in the n-area polyominoes. To find this value, let us begin by counting the total number of columns in all the n-area polyominoes.

Lemma 2.3: The total number D_n of columns in all the n-area polyominoes is defined by the recurrence:

$$D_n = 1 + \sum_{k=1}^{n-1} k(D_{n-k} + V_{n-k})$$

having the initial condition $D_0 = 0$. Hence, we have the generating function:

$$D(t) = \frac{t\,(1-t)^3}{(1-3\,t+t^2)^2}$$

and the closed formula:

$$D_n = \frac{2\,n-1}{5} F_{2n} = \frac{n-5}{5} F_{2n-1}$$

Proof: It is obvious that $D_0 = 0$ and $D_1 = 1$. Since there is only one dcc-polyomino with a single column of n cells for $n > 1$, let us consider the dcc-polyominoes with the first column of k cells, for $1 \leq k < n$. We can attach a dcc-polyomino of area $n-k$ to every cell of the first column, for a total of

$k D_{n-k}$ columns. The contribution of the first column is $k V_{n-k}$, and so we obtain the recurrence:

$$D_n = 1 + \sum_{k=1}^{n-1} (k D_{n-k} + k V_{n-k})$$

As in Theorem 2.1, we can extend the sum from 0 to n, provided we take into account the extra quantities we introduce. So we have:

$$D_n = 1 + \sum_{k=0}^{n} k D_{n-k} + \sum_{k=0}^{n} k V_{n-k} - n - \delta_{n0}$$

and for the generating functions:

$$D(t) = \frac{1}{1-t} + \frac{t}{(1-t)^2} D(t) + \frac{t}{(1-t)^2} V(t) - \frac{t}{(1-t)^2} - 1$$

Since $V(t)$ is known, we obtain:

$$D(t) = \frac{t(1-t)^3}{(1-3t+t^2)^2}$$

and by means of very simple computations or by using a computer algebra system:

$$D_n = -\frac{n}{5} F_{2n+2} + \frac{4}{5}(n-1) F_{2n} + \frac{8}{5} F_{2n} - F_{2n-2} = \frac{2n-1}{5} F_{2n} - \frac{n-5}{5} F_{2n-1}$$

This is the closed formula for D_n. □

Finally, the average number of columns is given by the following:

Theorem 2.4: The average number d_n of columns in the n-area dcc-polyominoes is:

$$d_n \sim \frac{\sqrt{5}}{5} n + \frac{9-\sqrt{5}}{10}$$

Proof: For $n > 0$, we have:

$$d_n = \frac{D_n}{V_n} = \frac{2n-1}{5} \frac{F_{2n}}{F_{2n-1}} - \frac{n-5}{5} \sim \frac{2n-1}{5} \phi - \frac{n-5}{5} = \frac{\sqrt{5}}{5} n + \frac{9-\sqrt{5}}{10}$$

where $\phi = (\sqrt{5}+1)/2$ is the golden ratio. □

The value is accurate for a small n, too. For example, for $n = 4$ the true value is $d_4 = 32/13 = 2.46153846$ and the approximate value is 2.46524758, with an error of 0.15%.

3 The Random Generation of Dcc-Polyominoes

The aim of this section is to find a method of generating a random dcc-polyomino in linear time. In other words, we wish to find out an algorithm which receives an integer n as input and gives a dcc-polyomino of area n, selected at random (with probability $1/V_n$) among all the possible n-area dcc-polyominoes, as output. We begin by counting the number of n-area dcc-polyominoes with the first column containing at most k cells.

Theorem 3.1: The number of n-area dcc-polyominoes whose first column contains exactly k cells is $c_{n,k} = k V_{n-k}$ for $k = 1, 2, \ldots, n-1$ and $c_{n,n} = 1$. The number of n-area dcc-polyominoes whose first column contains at most k cells is:

$$G_{n,k} = V_n - V_{n-k-1} - (k+1) F_{2n-2k-2}$$

for $k = 1, 2, \ldots, n-1$ and $F_{n,n} = V_n$.

Proof: The first part is obvious, since, as we have already observed, if the first column contains k ($k < n$) cells, we can attach a dcc-polyomino of area $n-k$ to every one of these cells and thus obtain a total of $k V_{n-k}$ different n-area dcc-polyominoes. For the second part, we have:

$$G_{n,k} = \sum_{j=1}^{k} c_{n,k} = \sum_{j=1}^{k} j V_{n-j} = \sum_{j=0}^{k} j V_{n-j} = \sum_{j=n-k}^{n} (n-j) V_j =$$

$$= \sum_{j=0}^{n} (n-j) V_j - n \sum_{j=0}^{n-k-1} V_j + \sum_{j=0}^{n-k-1} j V_j$$

We can now evaluate these three sums by using partial fraction expansion:

$$\sum_{j=0}^{n} (n-j) V_j = [t^n] \frac{t}{(1-t)^2} \frac{1-2t}{1-3t+t^2} = [t^n]\left(\frac{t}{(1-t)^2} - \frac{2}{1-t} + \frac{1-2t}{1-3t+t^2}\right) =$$

$$= V_n + n + 1 - 2 = V_n + n - 1$$

$$\sum_{j=0}^{n-k-1} V_j = [t^{n-k-1}]\frac{1}{1-t} \frac{1-2t}{1-3t+t^2} = [t^{n-k-1}]\left(\frac{1}{1-t} + \frac{t}{1-3t+t^2}\right) = 1 + F_{2n-2k-2}$$

$$\sum_{j=0}^{n-k-1} j V_j = [t^{n-k-1}]\frac{t}{1-t} \frac{d}{dt}\frac{1-2t}{1-3t+t^2} = [t^{n-k-1}]\frac{t-2t^2+2t^3}{(1-t)(1-3t+t^2)^2} =$$

$$= [t^{n-k-1}]\left(\frac{1}{1-t} - \frac{1-2t}{1-3t+t^2} + \frac{t(1-t^2)}{(1-3t+t^2)^2}\right) = 1 - V_{n-k-1} + (n-k-1) F_{2n-2k-2}$$

In the last sum, we used the fact that:

$$\mathcal{G}\{k\,F_{2k}\} = t\frac{d}{dt}\frac{t}{1-3\,t+t^2} = \frac{t(1-t^2)}{(1-3\,t+t^2)^2}$$

By putting everything together, we eventually find:

$$G_{n,k} = V_n + n - 1 - n - n\,F_{2n-2k-2} + 1 - V_{n-k-1} + (n-k-1)\,F_{2n-2k-2} =$$

$$= V_n - V_{n-k-1} - (k+1)\,F_{2n-2k-2}$$

For $k = n$, we obviously have $G_{n,n} = V_n = F_{2n-1}$ $(n > 0)$ $\square$

It is easy for us to go from frequencies to probabilities:

$$p_{n,k} = 1 - \frac{V_{n-k-1}}{V_n} - (k+1)\,\frac{F_{2n-2k-2}}{V_n} \qquad 1 \le k \le n$$

and $p_{n,0} = 0$, $p_{n,n} = 1$. This is the probability that an n-area dcc-polyomino's first column contains k or less cells. This result suggests a simple algorithm for generating random dcc-polyominoes. We begin by extracting a uniformly distributed random number p in the range $[0, 1)$, and decide that the first column of the dcc-polyomino to be generated contains exactly k cells iff $p_{n,k-1} \le p \le p_{n,k}$. If $k = n$, we have finished; otherwise, we extract a random integer number a such that $1 \le a \le k$, and this is the cell which the rest of the dcc-polyomino has to be attached to. We go on to apply the same procedure recursively to generate a random dcc-polyomino having area $n-k$. Obviously, the dcc-polyomino is uniquely determined by the list of pairs $\{(c_1, g_1), (c_2, g_2), \ldots, (c_{b-1}, g_{b-1}), (c_b, 0)\}$, where c_i is the number of cells in the i-th column, and g_i is the cell which the next column is attached to minus 1. In Fig. 2, we show a random dcc-polyomino with area 30 generated by the algorithm and corresponding to the list $\{(2, 0), (2, 0), (2, 0), (1, 0), (1, 0),$ $(1, 0), (3, 2), (1, 0), (2, 1), (3, 1), (3, 0), (1, 0), (3, 0), (1, 0), (2, 1), (2, 0)\}$.

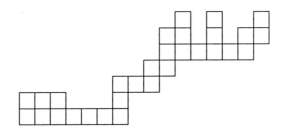

Fig. 2 - A random dcc-polyomino with area 30

To be more precise, we formulate the algorithm as a pseudo-Pascal procedure, to be called *column(n)* if we want to generate a random dcc-polyomino having area *n*:

```
procedure column (n: integer);
var g, c: integer; p: real;
begin   p := random;
        c := findlevel (n, p);
        if (c = n) or (c = 1) then append (c, 0)
        else begin  g := random (c); append (c, g) end;
        if c < n then column (n−c)
end {column};
```

In most Pascal compilers there is a *random* function which generates uniformly distributed pseudo-random numbers in the interval $[0, 1)$; the same function, called with an integer argument *k*, generates a random integer in the range $0 \ .. \ k-1$. The procedure *append* is a simple routine which appends the pair formed by its arguments to a global list; the list will eventually contain the result of our generation and is to be initialized before calling *column* for the first time. Finally, the *findlevel* function is used for finding the number of cells in the column to be generated. A possible formulation is as follows:

```
function findlevel (n: integer; p: real): integer;
var v, z: real; k: integer;
begin if n = 1 then k := 1 else begin
        v := dccpoly (n); q := v*p; k := 0;
        repeat   k := k+1;
                 if k = n then z := v else
                 z := v−dccpoly (n−k−1)−(k+1)*fibo (2*n−2*k−2)
        until z > q end;
        findlevel := k
end {findlevel};
```

Obviously, the *fibo* and *dccpoly* functions compute the nth Fibonacci number and the number of the *n*-area dcc-polyominoes, respectively. Actually, *dccpoly* is reduced to a call to *fibo*, except for $n = 0$ when the result is 1.

We now want to show that this program generates a dcc-polyomino in $O(n)$ time. We must study the number of calls to three routines: *random*, *append* and *fibo*, which are all executed in constant time, say t_r, t_a, t_f time units, respectively. Let us observe that:

$$F_n = round \left(\frac{\phi^n}{\sqrt{5}} \right) = floor \left(\frac{1}{\sqrt{5}} \ exp \, (n \, log \, \phi) + 0.5 \right);$$

this takes a long time compared to *random* and *append*, but when we have fixed the precision, the evaluation time does not depend on *n*. If the three routine are called A_r, A_a, A_f times during the generation of a dcc-polyomino, then the total time will be:

$$T = A_r t_r + A_a t_a + A_f t_f + C$$

where C is the time taken by housekeeping operations and t_r, t_a, t_f may embody the time for loop control execution if necessary.

Let us begin by determining A_f, the number of calls to the routine *fibo*. According to the *findlevel* program above, the variable v is computed once for every column in the resulting dcc-polyomino. The variable z, instead, is computed once for every cell in a column, and then for every cell in the dcc-polyomino. So if the generated dcc-polyomino has area n and c columns, we have $A_f = c + 2n$. Note that when the last column has only one cell, there is no call to *fibo* because of the initial condition in *findlevel*. The number V'_n of n-area dcc-polyominoes with the last column containing a single cell is easily evaluated. Since without this last cell we have a dcc-polyomino of area $n-1$, we find $V'_n = V_n - V_{n-1}$. By means of these facts and Lemma 2.3, we obtain the total number of calls to *fibo* for generating all the V_n dcc-polyominoes of area n: $D_n + 2n V_n - V_n + V_{n-1}$. Therefore, we have:

Theorem 3.2: The average number $\overline{A}_f$ of calls to the routine *fibo* to generate a random n-area dcc-polyomino is

$$\overline{A}_f \sim n\left(2 + \frac{\sqrt{5}}{5}\right) - \frac{\phi}{5} + \frac{1}{\phi}$$

Proof: By using the expression for D_n found in Lemma 2.3 and dividing by V_n, we find:

$$\overline{A}_f \sim \frac{2n-1}{5}\phi - \frac{n-5}{5} + 2n - 1 + \frac{1}{\phi} = n\left(2 + \frac{2\phi}{5} - \frac{1}{5}\right) - \frac{\phi}{5} + \frac{1}{\phi}$$

The constant multiplying n is about 2.4472135955. $\qquad\square$

Theorem 3.3: The average number $\overline{A}_a$ of calls to the routine *append* to generate a random n-area dcc-polyomino is:

$$\overline{A}_a \sim \frac{\sqrt{5}}{5}n + \frac{9 - \sqrt{5}}{10}$$

Proof: The *append* routine is exactly called once for every column in the generated dcc-polyomino. Therefore, we have $\overline{A}_a = d_n$ and the result follows from Theorem 2.4. $\qquad\square$

Let us now determine the value of A_r, the number of calls to the routine *random*. The evaluation of the variable p in *column* is made once for every column in the generated dcc-polyomino. However, the evaluation of g is performed only when the column is not the last one and contains at least two cells. As a result, we have to determine the number $H_{n,k}$ of the k-cell columns in all the n-area dcc-polyominoes. We have the infinite triangle $\{H_{n,k} \mid n, k \in \mathbb{N}, k \le n\}$:

	1	2	3	4	5
1	1				
2	2	1			
3	6	3	1		
4	18	9	4	1	
5	53	28	12	5	1
.	.	.	.	.	.

In order to determine a recurrence relation for $H_{n,k}$ ($k \leq n$), let us consider for $j = 1, 2, \ldots, n$ the n-area dcc-polyominoes having j cells in the first column. We find a total of $\sum_{j=1}^{n-1} j\, H_{n-j,k}$ columns containing k cells; when $j = k$, we also have to count the first columns, which contribute for a total of $k\, V_{n-k}$. Hence:

$$H_{n,k} = \sum_{j=1}^{n-1} j\, H_{n-j,k} + k\, V_{n-k}$$

This completely defines the above triangle but we are only interested in the one cell columns:

Lemma 3.4: The total number H_n of one-cell columns in all the n-area dcc-polyominoes is:

$$H_n = \frac{3\,n-4}{5} F_{2n} - \frac{4\,n-10}{5} F_{2n-1}$$

Proof: By setting $k = 1$, the above recurrence becomes

$$H_n = \sum_{j=1}^{n-1} j\, H_{n-j} + V_{n-1}$$

Since $H_0 = 0$, the sum can be extended to $j = 0$ through n and we can go on to the generating functions:

$$H(t) = \frac{t}{(1-t)^2} H(t) + t\, V(t)$$

By solving in $H(t)$ and using partial fraction expansion:

$$H(t) = \frac{t(1-t)^2(1-2\,t)}{(1-3\,t+t^2)^2} = \frac{t}{5}\left(\frac{17-10\,t}{1-3\,t+t^2} - \frac{(4-11\,t)(3-2\,t)}{(1-3\,t+t^2)^2}\right)$$

By extracting the coefficient of t^n, after some easy computations, we find:

$$H_n = \frac{17}{5} F_{2n} - 2 F_{2n-2} - \frac{4}{5} n F_{2n+2} + \frac{11}{5}(n-1) F_{2n} = \frac{3n-4}{5} F_{2n} - \frac{4n-10}{5} F_{2n-1}$$

$\square$

We are now able to give the value for A_r:

Theorem 3.5: The average number $\overline{A}_r$ of calls to the *random* routine for generating a random n-area dcc-polyomino is:

$$\overline{A}_r \sim n\frac{\phi+2}{5} + \frac{2\phi}{5} - \frac{1}{\phi}$$

Proof: As we have already observed, the total number of calls to *random* for generating all the V_n n-area dcc-polyominoes is given by $D_n+(D_n-H_n-V_{n-1})$. In fact, H_n is the total number of one-cell columns and V_{n-1} represents the number of the last columns containing at least two cells. We divide by V_n and for $n > 0$ we find:

$$\overline{A}_r \sim \frac{4n-2}{5}\phi - \frac{2n-10}{5} - \frac{3n-4}{5}\phi + \frac{4n-10}{5} - \frac{1}{\phi} = n\frac{\phi+2}{5} + \frac{2\phi}{5} - \frac{1}{\phi} \quad \square$$

Obviously, the quantities t_r, t_a, t_f and C depend on the particular implementation of the algorithm, but we have now proved that the execution time is $O(n)$ and most time is spent in computing Fibonacci numbers. Some improvements can be easily conceived of. For example as predefined lists, we can code all the dcc-polyominoes having an area less than or equal to $n_0 = 5$ (say) and extract a random list whenever *column* is called with $n \leq n_0$. This and other "tricks" of the same kind, however, go beyond the aim of the present paper.

4 The Average Internal Path Length

Yuba and Hoshi [8] proposed directed polyominoes under the name of Binary Search Networks (BSN) as a structure for storing and retrieving information in a computer. The idea was to use VLSI hardware for searching in parallel along the directed, linear paths of the structure in order to minimize retrieval time. Parallelism is essential because in a traditional serial computer, BSN's cannot favourably compare with other well-known structures, such as binary search trees, with which BSN's share a common retrieving methodology. It is well-known (see, e.g., Knuth [6]) that binary search trees have an average retrieval time of order $O(\log n)$, if n is the total number of data contained in the tree. It is evident that for BSN's, the average retrieval time is much worse and is situated somewhere between $O(\sqrt{n})$ and $O(n)$. As far as we know, nobody has been able to find out the exact order, but computer experiments [2] show that it is about $O(n^{0.82})$. In the case of dcc-polyominoes, we are able to give the exact value of the average retrieval time when all the dcc-polyominoes are considered as equally probable. This value, however, cannot be extrapolated to all directed polyominoes.

We use the common terminology for binary search trees and define the *internal path length* (IPL) of a cell in a dcc-polyomino as the minimal number of steps necessary for reaching the cell starting at the origin and going from one cell to any one of the two adjacent cells. It is easy to show that there are several minimal paths of this kind, but every path contains the same number of steps. In Fig. 3, we give an example with the internal path length of every cell in the dcc-polyomino.

	6		8
3	5	6	7
2	4		
1	2	3	

Fig. 3 - The internal path length in a dcc-polyomino

It is not very difficult to find a recurrence relation for the total IPL relative to all the n-area dcc-polyominoes. Let P_n be this quantity. By Fig. 1, we can easily find the first values: $P_1 = 1$, $P_2 = 6$, $P_3 = 29$, $P_4 = 122$ and state the following:

Theorem 4.1: The total internal path length P_n of all the V_n n-area dcc-polyominoes satisfies the recurrence relation:

$$P_n = \sum_{k=1}^{n-1} k\, P_{n-k} + n \sum_{k=1}^{n-1} \frac{k(k+1)}{2} V_{n-k} + \frac{n(n+1)}{2}$$

and then it is defined by the generating function:

$$P(t) = \frac{t}{(1-t)(1-3\,t+t^2)} + \frac{2\,t^2}{(1-t)(1-3\,t+t^2)^2} + \frac{3\,t^3-2\,t^4}{(1-t)(1-3\,t+t^2)^3}$$

Proof: First, let us observe that if the dcc-polyomino is reduced to a single column, then its total internal path length is $n(n+1)/2$. Let us assume that the first column contains k cells with $1 \leq k \leq n$, and let r ($1 \leq r \leq k$) be the position of the cell which the rest of the dcc-polyomino is attached to. Therefore:

i) the first column contributes for $k(k+1)/2$ to the total IPL of all the dcc-polyominoes, and it must be taken into account for each of the V_{n-k} dcc-polyominoes making up the rest of our dcc-polyomino;

ii) these V_{n-k} dcc-polyominoes have a total internal path length equal to P_{n-k};

iii) since every one of them is attached to the cell in position r, the IPL of each of their cells is increased by r, for a total contribution of $r(n-k) V_{n-k}$.

Therefore we have :

$$P_n = \frac{n(n+1)}{2} + \sum_{k=1}^{n-1} \sum_{r=1}^{k} \left(\frac{k(k+1)}{2} V_{n-k} + P_{n-k} + r(n-k) V_{n-k} \right) =$$

$$= \frac{n(n+1)}{2} + \sum_{k=1}^{n-1} \left(k P_{n-k} + \frac{k^2(k+1)}{2} V_{n-k} + (n-k) V_{n-k} \frac{k(k+1)}{2} \right) =$$

$$= \frac{n(n+1)}{2} + \sum_{k=1}^{n-1} k P_{n-k} + n \sum_{k=1}^{n-1} \frac{k(k+1)}{2} V_{n-k}$$

and this is the recurrence we are looking for. Obviously, $P_0 = 0$. At this point, it is not difficult to extend the sums from 0 through n, recalling that $V_0 = 1$. By adding and subtracting suitable quantities, we find:

$$P_n = \sum_{k=0}^{n} k P_{n-k} + n \sum_{k=}^{n} \frac{k(k+1)}{2} V_{n-k} + \frac{(n-1)n(n+1)}{2}$$

We can now go on to generating functions. We observe that:

$$\mathcal{G}\left\{ \sum_{k=0}^{n} k P_{n-k} \right\} = \frac{t}{(1-t)^2} P(t)$$

$$\mathcal{G}\left\{ \sum_{k=0}^{n} \binom{k+1}{2} V_{n-k} \right\} = \frac{t^2}{(1-t)^3} V(t) = \frac{t^2(1-2t)}{(1-t)^3(1-3t+t^2)}$$

$$\mathcal{G}\left\{ n \sum_{k=0}^{n} \binom{k+1}{2} V_{n-k} \right\} = t \frac{d}{dt} \frac{t^2}{(1-t)^3} V(t) =$$

$$= \frac{t(1+2t)(1-2t)}{(1-t)^4(1-3t+t^2)} + \frac{t^2(1-2t+2t^2)}{(1-t)^3(1-3t+t^2)^2}$$

$$\mathcal{G}\left\{ \binom{n+1}{3} \right\} = \frac{t^2}{(1-t)^4}$$

and these relations imply:

$$P(t) = \frac{t}{(1-t)^2} P(t) + \frac{t(1-4t^2)}{(1-t)^4(1-3t+t^2)} + \frac{t^2(1-2t+2t^2)}{(1-t)^3(1-3t+t^2)^2} - \frac{3t^2}{(1-t)^4}$$

By solving in $P(t)$ we find:

$$P(t) = \frac{t(1-4\,t^2)}{(1-t)^2(1-3\,t+t^2)^2} + \frac{t^2(1-2\,t+2\,t^2)}{(1-t)\,(1-3\,t+t^2)^3} - \frac{3\,t^2}{(1-t)^2\,(1-3\,t+t^2)}$$

Now we use partial fraction expansions to obtain:

$$\frac{t-4\,t^3}{(1-t)^2(1-3\,t+t^2)^2} = \frac{5-12\,t}{(1-3\,t+t^2)^2} - \frac{7-5\,t}{1-3\,t+t^2} + \frac{5}{1-t} - \frac{3}{(1-t)^2}$$

$$\frac{t^2-2\,t^3+2\,t^4}{(1-t)\,(1-3\,t+t^2)^3} = \frac{7-18\,t}{(1-3\,t+t^2)^3} - \frac{8+t}{(1-3\,t+t^2)^2} + \frac{2-t}{1-3\,t+t^2} - \frac{1}{1-t}$$

$$\frac{3\,t^2}{(1-t)^2\,(1-3\,t+t^2)} = \frac{3\,t}{1-3\,t+t^2} - \frac{3}{(1-t)^2} + \frac{3}{1-t}$$

Finally, by putting all these together:

$$P(t) = \frac{7-18\,t}{(1-3\,t+t^2)^3} - \frac{3+13\,t}{(1-3\,t+t^2)^2} - \frac{5-t}{1-3\,t+t^2} + \frac{1}{1-t}$$

which is the generating function we were looking for. □

We can now extract the coefficient of t^n from the generating function and thus obtain a closed form for the total IPL referring to all the n-area dcc-polyominoes. For $n > 0$, the number of cells in all these polyominoes is $n\,F_{2n-1}$, and by dividing by this quantity, we get the average IPL referring to n-area dcc-polyominoes.

Theorem 4.2: The total IPL relative to all the n-area dcc-polyominoes is:

$$P_n = \frac{n^2}{10}\left(F_{2n} + 2\,F_{2n-1}\right) + \frac{7\,n}{10}\,F_{2n} - F_{2n-1} + 1$$

and therefore the average internal path length is:

$$p_n \sim \frac{\phi+2}{10}\,n + \frac{7\,\phi}{10} - 1$$

Proof: The formula for P_n is a tedious exercise in coefficient extraction. In the proof of Lemma 2.3 we found:

$$[t^n]\,\frac{3-2\,t}{(1-3\,t+t^2)^2} = (n+1)\,F_{2n+4}$$

By differentiating, we obtain:

$$\frac{d^2}{d\,t^2}\,\frac{1}{1-3\,t+t^2} = \frac{16-18\,t+6\,t^2}{(1-3\,t+t^2)^3}$$

and therefore:

$$[t^n]\,\frac{16-18\,t+6\,t^2}{(1-3\,t+t^2)^3} = (n+1)(n+2)\,F_{2n+6}$$

By using these formulas, we can expand the terms of $P(t)$ into partial fractions and extract the coefficients of t^n:

$$\frac{7-18\,t}{(1-3\,t+t^2)^3} = \frac{1}{10}\,\frac{(7+18\,t)(16-18\,t+6\,t^2)}{(1-3\,t+t^2)^3} + \frac{1}{5}\,\frac{(9-24\,t)(3-2\,t)}{(1-3\,t+t^2)^2} - \frac{48}{5}\,\frac{1}{1-3\,t+t^2}$$

and then

$$[t^n]\,\frac{7-18\,t}{(1-3\,t+t^2)^3} = \frac{7}{10}\,(n+1)(n+2)\,F_{2n+6} - \frac{9}{5}\,n(n+1)\,F_{2n+4} +$$

$$+ \frac{9}{5}\,(n+1)\,F_{2n+4} - \frac{24}{5}\,n\,F_{2n+2} - \frac{48}{5}\,F_{2n+2}$$

Analogously:

$$\frac{3+13\,t}{(1-3\,t+t^2)^2} = \frac{(7-9\,t)(3-2\,t)}{(1-3\,t+t^2)^2} - \frac{18}{1-3\,t+t^2}$$

or:

$$[t^n]\,\frac{3+13\,t}{(1-3\,t+t^2)^2} = 7\,(n+1)\,F_{2n+4} - 9\,n\,F_{2n+2} - 18\,F_{2n+2}$$

Finally, we have:

$$[t^n]\,\frac{5-t}{1-3\,t+t^2} = 5\,F_{2n+2} - F_{2n}$$

At this point, by putting everything together and repeatedly using the recurrence relation for Fibonacci numbers $F_n = F_{n-1} + F_{n-2}$, we easily obtain the formula for P_n. The last formula is obtained dividing by $n\,F_{2n-1}$ considering that $F_{2n}/F_{2n-1} \sim \phi$ and by ignoring the lower order terms. $\square$

For dcc-polyominoes, the IPL is linear in n, which is worse than for directed polyominoes in general.

References

1. E. Barcucci, R. Pinzani, E. Rodella, R. Sprugnoli: A Characterization of Binary Search Networks. In: L. Budach (ed.): Foundamentals of Computation Theory. Lecture Notes in Computer Science 529. Berlin: Springer 1991, pp. 126-135

2. E. Barcucci, R. Pinzani, R. Sprugnoli: Génération Aléatoire des Animaux Dirigés. In: J. Labelle, J.-G. Penaud (eds.): Atelier de Combinatoire Franco-Québecois. Publications du LACIM. Montréal 1991, pp.17-25

3. E. Barcucci, R. Pinzani, R. Sprugnoli: The Random Generation of Underdiagonal Walks. In: P. Leroux, C. Reutenauer (eds.): Séries Formelles et Combinatoire Algébrique. Publications du LACIM 11. Montréal 1992, pp. 17-32

4. M. P. Delest, S. Dulucq: Enumeration of Directed Column-convex Animals with Given Perimeter and Area. Rapport LaBRI 87-15. Université de Bordeaux I 1987

5. T. Hickey, J. Cohen: Uniform Random Generation of Strings in a Context-Free Language. SIAM J. Comput. 12, 645-655 (1983)

6. D. E. Knuth: The Art of Computer Programming, Vol. I-III. Addison-Wesley, Reading, Ma, 1968-1973

7. X. G. Viennot: A Survey of Polyomino Enumeration. In: P. Leroux, C. Reutenauer (eds.): Séries Formelles et Combinatoire Algébrique. Publications du LACIM 11. Montréal 1992, pp. 399-420

8. T. Yuba, M. Hoshi: Binary Search Networks: a New Method for Key Searching. Information Processing Letters 24, 59-65 (1987)

Object Organisation in Software Environments for Formal Methods

Jun Han and Jim Welsh

Software Verification Research Centre
Department of Computer Science
University of Queensland, Qld 4072, Australia

Abstract. Software development by formal methods involves an overwhelming amount of technical and managerial detail. Systematic organisation of this information in a method's support environment is an important engineering concern. In this paper, we introduce a model for object organisation in software environments for formal methods, with particular emphasis on easy construction, modification, review and reuse of software objects. We demonstrate how the model can be instantiated to individual methodologies to obtain the object organisation architectures for their support environments.

1 Introduction

The value of formal methods in the development of reliable software systems is increasingly recognised. Because of its complexity, software development by formal methods requires computer-aided support. There have been many efforts to develop computer-based support systems for software development by formal methods. However, most of them concentrate on demonstrating the feasibility of automated semantic support while providing limited clerical and syntactic assistance. Few of them provide systematic support for software development from the software engineering viewpoint.

One of the major engineering concerns in providing environment support for software development by formal methods is the organisation of software objects. In principle, these objects and their organisation should record the development results, reflect the development process, and conform to the user's conceptual model of software development in the given formal method. In this paper, we introduce a model for object organisation in software environments for formal methods, with particular emphasis on easy construction, modification, review and reuse of software objects. This model provides an architectural framework for developing environments supporting software development by formal methods.

The paper is organised as follows. Section 2 overviews our approach to methodology modelling. Based on this approach, section 3 introduces our model for object organisation. Sections 4 to 6 present examples of instantiating the model to individual methodologies. Section 7 reviews related work. Finally, section 8 concludes this paper with a few further remarks on environment support.

2   An Approach to Methodology Modelling

Systematic software development requires that the software engineer follow well-established methodologies. To facilitate environment support for such methodologies, methodology models are required to capture their support requirements.

A software development methodology concerns software products and the software processes that produce these products. In modelling software development methodologies, we adopt an object-oriented approach. A software product is regarded as an object upon which various operations are performed in the course of its development. In this sense, the process or sequence of development operations permitted in the production of a software artifact is held to be inherent in the product itself. A software object is usually developed in a context composed of a large number of other software objects. These software objects are related to each other as the given methodology permits.

A software development environment supports the manipulation of the software objects and their relations allowed by the supported methodology. A methodology model defines the software objects, their relations and their manipulation as allowed by a range of methodologies.

Instantiating a model to a given methodology captures its requirements for environment support. In the instantiation process, methodology-specific meanings are assigned to the model features, and the constraints that the methodology imposes on these features are recognised. The result is an environment support architecture for the given methodology.

In our approach, environment support for methodologies' structural aspect can be achieved in a generic fashion, i.e. the support provided by a generic system according to the model can be specialised to meet the requirements of individual methodologies. Environment support for their semantic aspect is provided by additional methodology-specific tools.

3   An Object Organisation Model

Based on the above approach, we introduce a model for object organisation in software environments for formal methods. Software development by formal methods has program refinement and theorem-proving as two major sub-tasks. We first analyse each of them in its own right, and then discuss their relationships in the context of software development by formal methods.

3.1   Theorem-Proving

Proof Theory System. An interactive theorem-proving system maintains the information useful in constructing and understanding proofs. The user updates the information from time to time. Since a system is usually developed to support theorem-proving in different application domains, the information is divided into domain-specific groups. The information in one group forms *a proof theory*, and all the proof theories constitute the *proof theory system*.

Between the proof theories, there exist relations capturing the fact that one application domain is a sub-domain of, or similar to, another application domain. If the application domain of theory A contains the application domain of theory B, the information in B may all be included in A. To retain the fact that they are two separate theories and to achieve maximum reuse and consistency, an inter-theory relation may be introduced to indicate that theory A inherits all the information of theory B. We call this relation *an inheritance reference* from theory A to theory B. Concrete examples can be found in Demo2 [12], HOL [4] and Mural [7].

If theory C's domain has features similar to those of theory D's domain, certain information in D may be used in C. To realise this, an inter-theory relation of another kind may be introduced to indicate that theory C can access certain information of theory D upon translation. We call this relation *a morphism reference* from theory C to theory D. Concrete examples can be found in Mural [7].

The inheritance and morphism reference relations are called *theory dependence relations* from *child theories* to *parent theories*. The proof theory system records the individual theories and the dependence relations between them.

Proof Theory. A proof theory provides a logical context for proof problems in the concerned application domain. This logical context contains, as *elements*, symbols, axioms, definitions, theorems, inference rules, tactics, and so on. Between these elements, there exist relations capturing the fact that one element refers to another element for definitional or inferential purposes. For instance, a function may be used in stating an inference rule, and an axiom may be referred to when justifying assertions in a theorem's proof. We call such relations *reference relations* between proof theory elements. A proof theory records the theory elements and the reference relations between them.

Proof Theory Elements. A proof theory element usually has a number of *components*. Most of these components have a very simple structure. The most complicated element components are proofs of theorems.

Proof. Constructing a proof involves an inference process aimed at establishing the validity of an assertion which expresses a proof problem. This inference process is usually composed of a number of inference steps. Each step relates an assertion to other assertions according to an inference rule, in the hope that establishment of these latter assertions guarantees establishment of the former assertion. The relation from the former assertion to each of the latter assertions is called *a use relation* between assertions. This inference process continues until all the assertions involved either have immediate proof or have been related to other assertions.

A proof records each of the assertions involved and the information relevant to each proof step. The use relations between assertions are embedded in their corresponding proof step information, and reflect the proof's construction process.

Proof Object Hierarchy. We call all the objects involved in the proof process *proof objects*, including the proof theory system, proof theories, theory elements, element components (e.g. proofs), assertions and proof step information. The inclusion relations among these objects tailor them into a proof object hierarchy. The dependence relations between proof theories, the reference relations between proof theory elements and the use relations between assertions are also structural features of interactive theorem-proving that we are interested in. These relations are embedded in the relevant proof objects.

3.2 Program Refinement

As in theorem-proving, an interactive program refinement system assists the user in manipulating all the objects involved in the refinement process, which we call *refinement objects*. By analogy, a hierarchy of refinement objects may also be formulated as an object organisation model for interactive program refinement.

Refinement Theory System. Corresponding to the proof theory system, we have the *refinement theory system* which contains all the information useful in developing and understanding refinements. This information is divided into groups specific to application domains of program refinement. Each group forms *a refinement theory*. There exist inheritance and morphism reference relations between refinement theories to capture the fact that one application domain is a sub-domain of, or similar to, another application domain. The refinement theory system records the individual refinement theories and the dependence relations between them.

Refinement Theory. A refinement theory is composed of different kinds of *elements* useful for program refinement in the concerned application domain, such as function definitions, refinement rules, applications, and so on. An application encapsulates the development of a software system in a way similar to that in which a theorem encapsulates the proof of an assertion. It has a name, a statement which specifies the targeted software system, and a refinement which records the refinement results and process of the system.

There exist reference relations between elements of a refinement theory for definitional or refinement purposes. For instance, an application's statement may be defined using functions, and its refinement steps use refinement rules.

A refinement theory records the theory elements and the reference relations between them.

Refinement Theory Elements. Elements of a refinement theory have a number of *components*. Most of these components have a very simple structure. The most complicated components are refinements of applications.

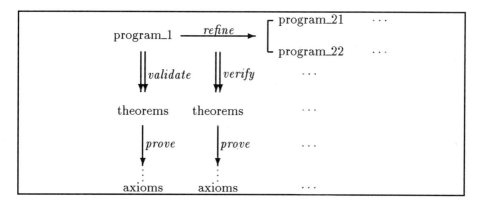

Fig. 1. Relationship between refinements and proofs

Refinement. Developing a software system in a formal method involves formal specifications and program code. In our discussion, specifications and programs are not distinguished, and they are all referred to as programs. Therefore, a program is a specification segment, a code segment or a mixture of both. A program may have additional validation obligations stating its properties.

The development of an application usually involves a number of design or refinement steps. Each step relates a program to other programs according to a refinement rule. Under the specific semantic relation determined by the refinement rule, these latter programs constitute a refinement of the former program. The relation from the former program to each of the latter programs is called *a use relation* between programs. Among the information relevant to a refinement step are the verification obligations stating the conditions that the step has to satisfy. This refinement process continues until all the programs involved are either efficient code segments or have been related to other programs.

A refinement records each of the programs involved and the information relevant to each refinement step. The use relations between programs are embedded in their corresponding refinement step information, and reflect the refinement's construction process.

3.3 Software Development by Formal Methods

As discussed above, program refinement gives rise to validation and verification obligations, which are theorems to be proved. This relationship between refinements and proofs is shown in Fig. 1.

Conceptually, program refinement (excluding the establishment of proof obligations) and theorem-proving are separate tasks. Therefore, we retain the refinement and proof object hierarchies in the support environment. They constitute the overall software object hierarchy for software development by formal methods, rooted at the *development theory system*, as shown in Fig. 2.

To realise the above relationship between refinements and proofs on this overall hierarchy, we introduce reference relations from proof obligations of programs

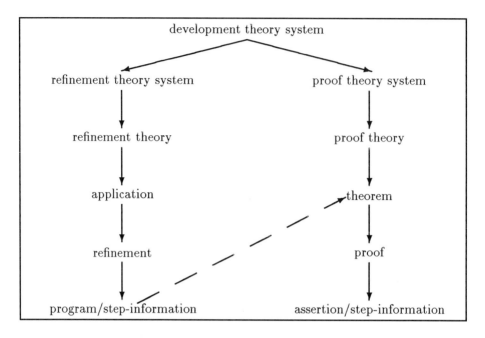

Fig. 2. Hierarchical relationship among software objects

and refinement steps on the refinement sub-hierarchy to theorems on the proof sub-hierarchy (see Fig. 2). These reference relations are called *proof allocation relations*. Under a proof allocation relation, the proof obligation concerned is regarded as being discharged by the proof of the referred theorem.

The above structural organisation of software development by formal methods supports the user's conceptual model in that the distinction between the program refinement task and the theorem-proving task is maintained by separation of refinement theories from proof theories and that the close relationship between refinements and their proofs is supported by proof allocation relations. In general, this approach gives an object organisation model for the entire software development task, which is conceptually natural and structurally simple.

This object organisation model has been instantiated to a number of theorem-proving and program refinement methodologies, to obtain their environment support architectures [5]. They include Demo2 [12], Mural [7], HOL [4], Nuprl [3], B [14] and the refinement calculus [8]. The model is also applicable to other methodologies such as VDM [6] and RAISE [9]. In the following three sections, we concentrate on the instantiations to the refinement calculus and the Demo2 theorem-proving system. We also discuss the refinement-proof relationships in using Demo2 to meet the theorem-proving requirements of the refinement calculus.

theory name	inheritance references (to)	elements
root		$< elements \ldots >$
fol	root	$< elements \ldots >$
func_logic	fol	$< elements \ldots >$
computation	func_logic	$< elements \ldots >$
arithmetic	computation	$< elements \ldots >$
$\vdots$	$\vdots$	$\vdots$

Fig. 3. A Demo2 proof theory system

4 Demo2

Demo2 is an interactive proof editor developed based on a *window inference* approach [10, 12]. Proofs, proof theory elements, proof theories and the proof theory system in our model largely correspond to proofs, theory elements, theories and the theory hierarchy in Demo2, respectively.

4.1 Proof Theory System

The proof theory system in our model corresponds to the theory hierarchy in Demo2. Structurally, the proof theory system is composed of the model theories which correspond to the Demo2 theories on the hierarchy. All the dependence relations between theories in Demo2 are inheritance relations in our model. Except for the theory **root** which does not have parent theories, all other theories have exactly one parent theory.

Figure 3 shows an example proof theory system in Demo2. The theory **root** contains the basic facts about theorem-proving. The theory **fol** is a theory of first order logic. The theory **func_logic** is a theory of functional logic [11]. The theory **computation** is a theory of computation in functional logic. The theory **arithmetic** is a theory of arithmetic. The inheritance relations between these theories are also shown in Fig. 3.

4.2 Proof Theory

A theory in Demo2 comprises the information available for proof construction in a particular application domain. A proof theory in our model corresponds to a Demo2 theory, and may contain additional information such as tactics. The following are some typical theory elements: primitive and defined quantifiers, primitive and defined functions, window opening rules, hypothesis splitting rules, simplification rules, axioms, theorems, and tactics.

Reference relations exist among elements of a proof theory, including the inferential reference relations among axioms, theorems and inference rules. Demo2 enforces strict "proof-before-use", i.e. only axioms and theorems with complete proofs can be used to prove other theorems and to introduce inference rules.

```
theory name: arithmetic          inheritance references (to): computation

theory elements:
```

name	type	contents
is_int	prim_fun	(1,default,A)
+	prim_fun	(2,500,yfx)
*	prim_fun	(2,490,yfx)
<	prim_fun	(2,520,xfx)
>	def_fun	(2,520,xfx); $[x_1, x_2]$, $x_2 < x_1$
$\geqslant$	def_fun	(2,520,xfx); $[x_1, x_2]$, $(x_1 > x_2) \vee (x_1 = x_2)$
ltsucc	axiom	$\text{is\_int}(A) \Rightarrow A < A + 1$
posinc	axiom	$A \geqslant 0 \Rightarrow A + 1 \geqslant 1$
geonem	axiom	$A < B \wedge C \geqslant 1 \Rightarrow A < B * C$
th	theorem	$\text{is\_int}(S) \wedge S \geqslant 0 \Rightarrow$ $(S \geqslant 0) \wedge (S < (S + 1) * (S + 1)) \quad < proof... >$
$\vdots$	$\vdots$	$\vdots$

Fig. 4. Demo2 theory arithmetic

Figure 4 shows some elements of the Demo2 theory arithmetic, where the theorem proofs are omitted. Note that a primitive function has, as its contents, an arity, a precedence and an associativity. A defined function has, in its contents, an additional definition term preceded with a list of object variables. An axiom has a statement as its contents. A theorem has a statement and a proof as its contents. The use of the defined function $\geqslant$ in the statement of the theorem th is an example of definitional references between proof theory elements. In the next subsection, we will see examples of inferential references.

4.3 Proof

The construction of a proof in Demo2 is carried out primarily by a sequence of goal-directed equivalence transformations in a logical window. Each transformation is either simple or complex. If the user transforms a window from one version to another version by a simple operation such as appealing to an axiom or a hypothesis, this transformation is classified as simple. On the other hand, a complex transformation achieved by transforming a term relevant to the current window version requires justification of how the term transformation is performed. The justification itself is a proof carried out in a nested subwindow and is composed of a sequence of simple and complex transformations.

A proof in our model corresponds to a Demo2 proof, with assertions corresponding to window versions and proof steps to transformation steps. Therefore, a model proof for Demo2 is composed of a linear sequence of proof steps. Except for the initial window version, all other assertions are generated from proof steps. An assertion has a focus F, a goal G, a number of hypotheses H, and an

1_1^1: $\vdash ((\text{is\_int}(S) \wedge S \geqslant 0 \Rightarrow (S \geqslant 0) \wedge (S < (S+1) * (S+1))) \Leftrightarrow \text{true})$

openwin on $(S \geqslant 0) \wedge (S < (S+1) * (S+1))$

2_1^1: $\text{is\_int}(S), S \geqslant 0 \vdash ((S \geqslant 0) \wedge (S < (S+1) * (S+1)) \Leftrightarrow \text{true})$

openwin on $S \geqslant 0$ of focus

3_1^1: $\text{is\_int}(S), S \geqslant 0, S < (S+1) * (S+1) \vdash ((S \geqslant 0) \Leftrightarrow \text{true})$

trans focus by hyp 2

3_1^2: $\text{is\_int}(S), S \geqslant 0, S < (S+1) * (S+1) \vdash (\text{true} \Leftrightarrow \text{true})$

closewin

2_1^2: $\text{is\_int}(S), S \geqslant 0 \vdash ((S < (S+1) * (S+1)) \Leftrightarrow \text{true})$

lemma proof $S < S+1$

3_2^1: $\text{is\_int}(S), S \geqslant 0 \vdash ((S < S+1) \Leftrightarrow \text{true})$

trans_true focus by ltsucc and hyp 1

3_2^2: $\text{is\_int}(S), S \geqslant 0 \vdash (\text{true} \Leftrightarrow \text{true})$

closelemma

2_1^3: $\text{is\_int}(S), S \geqslant 0, 1 : S < S+1 \vdash ((S < (S+1) * (S+1)) \Leftrightarrow \text{true})$

lemma proof $S+1 \geqslant 1$

3_3^1: $\text{is\_int}(S), S \geqslant 0, S < S+1 \vdash ((S+1 \geqslant 1) \Leftrightarrow \text{true})$

trans_true focus by posinc and hyp 4

3_3^2: $\text{is\_int}(S), S \geqslant 0, S < S+1 \vdash (\text{true} \Leftrightarrow \text{true})$

closelemma

2_1^4: $\text{is\_int}(S), S \geqslant 0, 1 : S < S+1, 1 : S+1 \geqslant 1$

$\vdash ((S < (S+1) * (S+1)) \Leftrightarrow \text{true})$

trans_true focus by geonem, hyp 3 and hyp 8

2_1^5: $\text{is\_int}(S), S \geqslant 0, 1 : S < S+1, 1 : S+1 \geqslant 1 \vdash (\text{true} \Leftrightarrow \text{true})$

closewin

1_1^2: $1 : \text{is\_int}(S) \wedge S \geqslant 0 \Rightarrow (S < S+1), 1 : \text{is\_int}(S) \wedge S \geqslant 0 \Rightarrow (S+1 \geqslant 1)$

$\vdash (\text{true} \Leftrightarrow \text{true})$

Fig. 5. th's Demo2 proof

equivalence relation $\equiv$. It defines an intention to prove that given the hypotheses, the focus and the goal are equivalent according to the equivalence relation: $H \vdash (F \equiv G)$. The focus, goal and hypotheses are all logical terms. The equivalence relation can be logical equivalence, arithmetic equality, and so on. The information attached to a proof step records the proof command applied, including references to theory elements such as axioms and theorems. A complex proof step also has a nested justification proof.

Figure 5 shows a Demo2 proof of the theorem th in the theory arithmetic in a condensed form. At the beginning of the proof, the initial assertion labelled 1_1^1 is introduced. The proof is carried out top-down, and is recorded with assertions to the left and (explanations of) proof operations to the right in an interleaved manner. Because the proof operations are self-explanatory, we shall not go through the proof process step by step. Note that the use of the axiom ltsucc in the above proof is an example of inferential references between theory elements.

The modelling exercise in this section shows that the organisation require-

theory name	inheritance references (to)	elements
⋮	⋮	⋮
list	...	< elements ... >
arith	list	< elements ... >
sorting	list	< elements ... >
UI	...	< elements ... >
language	arith, sorting	< elements ... >
environment	language, UI	< elements ... >

Fig. 6. A refinement theory system for the refinement calculus

ments of Demo2 can be naturally met by our model. Like the current Demo2 system, our model supports object construction. In addition, the modelling suggests improvements as to easy editing, checking, review, replay and reuse of proof objects by recording the object structures and inter-object relations.

5 Refinement Calculus

The refinement calculus is a formal method for software development, developed primarily by Back, Morgan and Morris. In the following discussion, we follow Morgan's presentation of the method in [8].

Experimental tools have been developed to support the refinement calculus [2, 13, 1]. Because of their experimental nature, these tools concentrate on the support for the core refinement activities, and give little consideration to the object organisation issue. Instead of modelling an existing system, therefore, we propose an object organisation system for the refinement calculus.

5.1 Refinement Theory System

The refinement theory system for the refinement calculus is composed of individual refinement theories specific to application domains. For simplicity, only inheritance relations between these theories can be introduced to allow one theory to inherit all the information of another theory.

Figure 6 shows a refinement theory system for the refinement calculus and contains a number of refinement theories: list for list-processing, arith for arithmetics, sorting for sorting algorithms, UI for user interface applications, language for processing programming languages, and environment for developing programming environments. The inheritance relations between these theories are also shown in Fig. 6.

5.2 Refinement Theory

A refinement theory for the refinement calculus contains the information available for program refinement in a particular application domain, and is composed

theory name: `arith`		inheritance references (to): `list`

theory elements:

name	type	contents
$+$	prim_fun	$(2, 500)$; $\mathbb{R} + \mathbb{R} : \mathbb{R}$
$*$	prim_fun	$(2, 490)$; $\mathbb{R} + \mathbb{R} : \mathbb{R}$
$\sqrt{\ }$	def_fun	$(1, 480)$; $\sqrt{\mathbb{R}} : \mathbb{R}$; $\sqrt{a} = b$ **iff** $b \geqslant 0 \wedge b * b = a$
$\lfloor\ \rfloor$	def_fun	$(1, 480)$; $\lfloor \mathbb{R} \rfloor : \mathbb{Z}$; $\lfloor a \rfloor = b$ **iff** $b \leqslant a < b + 1$
assn$_1$	rule	**if** $pre \Rightarrow post[w \backslash E]$, **then** $w, x : [pre, post] \sqsubseteq w := E$
sqrt	app	$\lvert\lvert$ **var** $r, s : \mathbb{N} \bullet r : [\mathbf{true}, r = \lfloor \sqrt{s} \rfloor] \rvert \rvert$
		$< refinement \ldots >$
$\vdots$	$\vdots$	$\vdots$

Fig. 7. Refinement theory `arith`

of various elements. The following are some typical elements in a refinement theory: primitive functions, defined functions, refinement rules and applications. Definitional and refinement reference relations exist among these elements. For example, the primitive and defined functions may be used to define other functions and to write programs involved in applications. The refinement rules are used to carry out refinement steps of applications. One application may be used in another application's refinement as part of the development.

Figure 7 shows some of the elements in the refinement theory `arith`, where the refinements of applications are omitted. Note that a primitive function has, as its contents, an arity-precedence pair and a concrete syntax in terms of the types of the function's parameters and result. A defined function has an additional definition in its contents. A refinement rule has a rule statement as its contents. An application has a statement (i.e. an abstract program) and a refinement as its contents. The use of $\lfloor\ \rfloor$ in the statement of the application `sqrt` is an example of definitional reference between refinement theory elements. An example of refinement references can be found in the next subsection.

5.3 Refinement

Constructing a refinement in the refinement calculus involves many steps. Each step refines a program by applying a refinement rule, and generates a number of other programs. The refinement records all the programs and refinement steps.

The refinement calculus embeds a specification mechanism, the *specification statement*, in Dijkstra's Guarded Command Language. As such, a program in the refinement calculus may contain both abstract and executable constructs, and is a simple or complex statement[1]. A simple statement is an assignment statement

---

[1] For simplicity, we only consider those programs that do not contain validation obligations or advanced language features such as procedures and modules.

or a specification statement. The specification statement has the form:

$$w : [pre, post]$$

where w is the *frame* containing the variables whose values may be changed by the statement, *pre* is the *precondition* describing the initial state of the program, and *post* is the *postcondition* describing the final state of the program. A complex statement is composed of a number of statements organised by one of the following constructs: sequential composition (;), alternation (**if fi**), iteration (**do od**) and local block (|[ ]|). A local block may contain variable (**var**), invariant (**and**) and logical constant (**con**) declarations. A program in our model corresponds to a program in the refinement calculus, except that a model program may have an *environment* to record the declaration information of its enclosing context when it is isolated from this context: [*environment*] *statement*.

A refinement step in the refinement calculus is carried out by application of a refinement rule, and may generate verification obligations. A step which isolates some components of a program without functional refinement is also regarded as a refinement step. For instance, the body of an iteration may be isolated from the overall iteration. The refinement operation applied and the verification obligations generated (if any) constitute the information attached to the refinement step. The refinement operation contains, among other things, a reference to the refinement rule applied.

To demonstrate the modelling of refinements in the refinement calculus, we consider an example taken from [8]. The refinement problem is that we are given a natural number s and required to set the natural number r to the greatest integer not exceeding $\sqrt{s}$. It is formulated as the application sqrt in the refinement theory **arith** (see Fig. 7). The abstract program specifying this problem is

$$|[\textbf{var } r, s : \mathbb{N} \bullet r : [\textbf{true}, r = \lfloor \sqrt{s} \rfloor]]| \tag{1}$$

It is the initial program of the refinement and is introduced at the beginning of the refinement process. After a number of refinement steps, this abstract program is refined to code (see pages 70-73 of [8] for details):

$$
\begin{aligned}
&|[\textbf{var } r, s : \mathbb{N} \bullet \\
&\quad |[\textbf{var } q : \mathbb{N} \bullet \\
&\qquad q, r := s + 1, 0; \\
&\qquad \textbf{do } r + 1 \neq q \longrightarrow \\
&\qquad\quad |[\textbf{var } p : \mathbb{N} \bullet \\
&\qquad\qquad p := (q + r) \text{ div } 2; \\
&\qquad\qquad \textbf{if } s < p^2 \longrightarrow q := p \\
&\qquad\qquad [\!] \ s \geq p^2 \longrightarrow r := p \\
&\qquad\qquad \textbf{fi} \\
&\qquad\quad]| \\
&\qquad \textbf{od} \\
&\quad]| \\
&]|
\end{aligned}
\tag{2}
$$

Due to space limitation, we shall not give all the details of the refinement process (see [5]). The following is one of the refinement steps. Program (3):

$$[\textbf{var } q, r, s : \mathbb{N}] q, r : [\textbf{true}, r^2 \leqslant s < q^2] \tag{3}$$

is refined to program (4):

$$[\textbf{var } q, r, s : \mathbb{N}] q, r := s + 1, 0 \tag{4}$$

using the refinement rule $\textbf{assn}_1$ (see Fig. 7). The verification obligation of this refinement step is

$$[\textbf{var } q, r, s : \mathbb{N}] \textbf{ true} \Rightarrow 0 \leqslant s < (s+1)^2 \tag{$3.O_1$}$$

Note that the use of the refinement rule $\textbf{assn}_1$ in this step is an example of refinement references between theory elements.

As with the modelling of Demo2, the modelling exercise in this section shows that our model can effectively meet the organisation requirements of the refinement calculus.

6   Refinement Calculus and Demo2

The above refinement example has shown that applying certain refinement rules gives rise to verification obligations. In general, validation obligations may also be stated against programs. According to our model, discharging these proof obligations is a theorem-proving task and should be carried out in proof theories.

If we choose Demo2 as the theorem-proving system for the refinement calculus, its development theory system is composed of a refinement theory system for the refinement calculus and a proof theory system for Demo2. For example, we may combine the refinement theory system and the proof theory system given in previous examples, into a development theory system.

In a development theory system for the refinement calculus and Demo2, the proof obligations of refinements may be discharged by proving theorems in Demo2 theories. The relationships between them are captured by proof allocation relations. For instance, we may introduce a proof allocation relation from the verification obligation $(3.O_1)$ of $\texttt{sqrt}$'s refinement in the refinement theory $\texttt{arith}$ to the theorem $\texttt{th}$ in the Demo2 theory $\texttt{arithmetic}$. Proving this theorem (as shown earlier) discharges the verification obligation $(3.O_1)$.

Carrington and Robinson's refinement editor [2] uses Bill Pugh's demonstration proof editor $\textbf{pv}$ for theorem-proving, while Back's refinement diagram editor [1] is developed on top of the HOL proof generating system. The distinction between program refinement and theorem-proving tasks is not fully supported in either of these two systems. In contrast, Vickers' refinement editor [13] separates program refinement from theorem-proving completely. The natural relationship between refinements and their proofs is lost.

7   Related Work

Our object organisation model for software development by formal methods is developed based on investigations into existing theorem-proving and program refinement methodologies/systems. Many theorem-proving systems have a mechanism to organise proof information into proof theories. In particular, Mural provides one of the most advanced organisation mechanisms called the theory store, which corresponds to the proof theory system in our model. The concept of proof theories as a basic mechanism for organising proof information has also inspired us to organise refinement information into refinement theories.

In dealing with the relationships between theorem-proving and program refinement, there have been two major approaches. One is to separate them, and the close relationship between refinements and their proofs is not supported. The other is to regard them as a single task based on theorem-proving, and the distinction between the program refinement task and the theorem-proving task is not recognised. As our model suggests, we argue that both the close relationship between refinements and their proofs and the distinction between the program refinement and theorem-proving tasks should be supported to conform to the user's conceptual model. Mural provides such support to a certain degree by relating programs/refinement-steps to proof theories.

Most of the existing systems provide methodology-specific object organisation. The issues involved are not addressed systematically. In particular, there are very limited provisions for easy modification, review and reuse of software objects, and no provisions for refinement organisation by refinement theories.

8   Conclusions

In this paper, we have introduced a model for object organisation in software environments for formal methods. It centres on a hierarchy of software objects, including two related sub-hierarchies for program refinement and theorem-proving. Proof allocation relations are introduced to capture the structural relationships between program refinement and theorem-proving. They tailor the two sub-hierarchies into the overall hierarchy in a simple and consistent manner. The software objects record the development results and reflect the development processes. Their definition and organisation conform to the user's conceptual model of software development in given formal methods.

The proposed model has been systematically instantiated to a number of theorem-proving and program refinement methodologies. These instantiations have captured the relevant methodologies' object organisation requirements, and have consequently reflected their environment support architectures. To this end, our model provides an architectural framework for developing generic and methodology-specific environments supporting software development by formal methods.

A more comprehensive account of the model can be found in [5]. It contains detailed definition of object structures, operations and consistency, and also deals with object presentation. After some prototype experiment [5] and a feasibility study, we are currently developing a generic, methodology-based environment for software development by formal methods.

Acknowledgements

We would like to thank David Carrington, Ian Hayes, Peter Lindsay, Peter Robinson, John Staples and Nigel Ward for their comments and help.

References

1. R.J.R. Back. Refinement diagrams. In *Proc. 4th BCS-FACS UK Refinement Workshop*, pages 125–137, Cambridge, UK, January 1991.
2. D. Carrington and K. Robinson. A prototype program refinement editor. In *Proc. 3th Australian Software Engineering Conf.*, pages 45–63, Canberra, Australia, May 1988.
3. R.L. Constable, S.F. Allen, et al. *Implementing Mathematics with the Nuprl Proof Development System*. Prentice-Hall, Englewood Cliffs, NJ, 1986.
4. M.J.C. Gordon. HOL: A proof generating system for higher-order logic. In *VLSI Specification, Verification and Synthesis*, pages 73–128. Kluwer Academic Publishers, Boston, MA, 1988.
5. J. Han. *A Structural Model for Methodology-based Interactive Rigorous Software Development*. PhD thesis, University of Queensland, St. Lucia, Australia, 1992.
6. C.B. Jones. *Systematic Software Development using VDM*. Prentice-Hall International, London, second edition, 1990.
7. C.B. Jones, K.D. Jones, P.A. Lindsay, and R. Moore. mural: *A Formal Development Support System*. Springer-Verlag, London, 1991.
8. C. Morgan. *Programming from Specifications*. Prentice-Hall International, London, 1990.
9. M. Nielsen, K. Havelund, K.R. Wagner, and C. George. The RAISE language, method and tools. *Formal Aspects of Computing*, 1(1):85–114, 1989.
10. P.J. Robinson and J. Staples. Formalising the hierarchical structure of practical mathematical reasoning. Technical Report 138, Department of Computer Science, University of Queensland, St. Lucia, Australia, December 1989.
11. J. Staples. Functional logic for program verification: Introductory lectures. Technical Report 168, Department of Computer Science, University of Queensland, St. Lucia, Australia, July 1990.
12. T.G. Tang, P.J. Robinson, and J. Staples. The demonstration proof editor Demo2. Technical Report 175, Department of Computer Science, University of Queensland, St. Lucia, Australia, April 1991.
13. T. Vickers. An overview of a refinement editor. In *Proc. 5th Australian Software Engineering Conf.*, pages 39–44, Sydney, Australia, May 1990.
14. T. Vickers. An overview of a theorem proving assistant. In *Proc. 13th Australian Computer Science Conf*, pages 402–411, Melbourne, Australia, February 1990.

Monads, Indexes and Transformations

Françoise Bellegarde* and James Hook**

Pacific Software Research Center
Oregon Graduate Institute of Science & Technology
19600 N.W. von Neumann Drive
Beaverton, OR 97006-1999
{bellegar,hook}@cse.ogi.edu

Abstract. The specification and derivation of substitution for the de Bruijn representation of λ-terms is used to illustrate programming with a function-sequence monad. The resulting program is improved by interactive program transformation methods into an efficient implementation that uses primitive machine arithmetic. These transformations illustrate new techniques that assist the discovery of the arithmetic structure of the solution.

Introduction

Substitution is one of many problems in computer science that, once understood in one context, is understood in all contexts. Why, then, must a different substitution function be written for every abstract syntax implemented? This paper shows how to specify substitution once and use the monadic structure of the specification to instantiate it on different abstract syntax structures. It also shows how to interactively derive an efficient implementation of substitution from this very abstract specification.

Formal methods that support reasoning about free algebras from first principles based on their inductive structure are theoretically attractive because they have simple and expressive theories. However, in practice they often lead to inefficient algorithms because they fail to exploit the "algebras" implemented in computer hardware. This paper examines this problem by giving a systematic program development and then describing a series of (potentially) automatic program transformations that may be used to achieve an efficient implementation.

The particular program development style employed is based on the categorical notion of a *monad*. This approach to specification has been advocated by Wadler[8] and is strongly influenced by Moggi's work on semantics[6]. The substitution algorithm for λ-calculus terms represented with de Bruijn indexes serves as the primary example. The development of the specification is a refinement of an example in Hook, Kieburtz and Sheard[5]. It is noteworthy because a non-standard category is used; the earlier work did not identify this category.

The specification is transformed into first-order equations using techniques implemented in the partial evaluator Schism[4]. It is then refined to an equivalent first-

---

* Bellegarde is currently at Western Washington University, Bellingham, WA 98225.
** Both authors are supported in part by a grant from the NSF (CCR-9101721).

The first thing to observe about the sequence is that its general shape is $\sigma_{i+1}0 = 0$ and $\sigma_{i+1}(n+1) \approx \sigma_i n$. To make it exact it is necessary to increment all global variables in $\sigma_i n$ without incrementing the local variables. This is done by another sequence of functions:

$$f_0 n = n + 1 \qquad f_1 0 = 0 \qquad f_2 0 = 0$$
$$f_1(n+1) = n+2 \qquad f_2 1 = 1$$
$$f_2(n+2) = n+3$$

Observe that in the example a single application of f_1 to the body of $\sigma_1 1$ accounts for $\lambda . 0 \, 1$ being adjusted to $\lambda . 0 \, 2$. In general the f_i are generated by $f_{i+1}0 = 0$ and $f_{i+1}(n+1) = (f_i n) + 1$. So, assuming a *map* that applies a family of functions, the family of substitution functions, $(\sigma_0, \sigma_1, \ldots)$, is given by the initial substitution, σ_0, and the recurrence $\sigma_{i+1}0 = 0$ and $\sigma_{i+1}(n+1) = map \, (f_0, f_1, \ldots) \, (\sigma_i n)$. Given the sequence of functions, $(\sigma_0, \sigma_1, \ldots)$, mapping indexes to terms, the *map* function for sequences can be used to apply the sequence of substitution functions. This, however, results in terms of terms, since every variable has replaced its index by a term. This is not a problem, however, because the *Term* type constructor developed below is designed to be a monad; monads have a polymorphic function, *mult*, which performs the requisite flattening.

2 Monads

A *monad* is a concept from category theory that has been used to provide structure to semantics[6] and to specifications[8]. In the computer science setting a monad is defined by a parametric data type constructor, T, and three polymorphic functions: $map : (\alpha \rightarrow \beta) \rightarrow T\alpha \rightarrow T\beta$, $unit : \alpha \rightarrow T\alpha$, and $mult : TT\alpha \rightarrow T\alpha$. The *map* function is required to satisfy $map \, id_\alpha = id_{T\alpha}$ and $map \, (f \circ g) = map \, f \circ map \, g$. The polymorphic functions *unit* and *mult* must satisfy $mult_\alpha \circ unit_{T\alpha} = id_{T\alpha}$, $mult_\alpha \circ (map \, unit_\alpha) = id_{T\alpha}$ and $mult_\alpha \circ mult_{T\alpha} = mult_\alpha \circ (map \, mult_\alpha)$. A simple example of a monad is *list*. For lists, *map* is the familiar `mapcar` function of Lisp, *unit* is the function that produces a singleton list, and *mult* is the concatenate function that flattens a list of lists into a single list. Other examples of monads are given by Wadler[8].

Several categorical concepts are implicit above. The functional programming category has types as objects and (computable) functions as arrows. (Values are viewed as constant functions—arrows from the one element type.) The requirements on *map* specify that the type constructor T and the *map* function together define a *functor*. The polymorphic types of *unit* and *mult* implicitly require them to be *natural transformations*. The three laws given for them are the *monad laws*.

Monads have been used to structure specifications (and semantics) because it is often possible to characterize interesting facets of a specification as a monad. Algorithms to exploit the particular facet may frequently be expressed in terms of the *map*, *unit* and *mult* functions with no explicit details of the type constructors. Finally, the many facets are brought together by composing the type constructors.

3 The Term Monad

The development in Sect. 1 suggests that the specification of the substitution operation will be straightforward in a monadic data type with an appropriate *map*. To be
monadic, the data type must be parametric. The following simple type declaration
is sufficient[2]:

$$\textbf{datatype } Term(\alpha) = Var(\alpha)$$
$$| \; Abs(Term(\alpha))$$
$$| \; App(Term(\alpha) * Term(\alpha))$$

Using techniques developed in earlier work, it is possible to automatically generate *map*, *mult* and *unit* functions for this type realizing a monadic structure[5].
Unfortunately, the *map* function obtained with those techniques does not work with
families of functions.

To accommodate the function sequences a new category, FUNSEQ, is used. The
objects are data types, as before, but the morphisms are sequences of functions
(formally $\text{HOM}(A, B) = (B^A)^\omega$). Identities are constant sequences of identities from
the underlying category; composition is pointwise, i.e. $(f_i)_{i\in\omega} \circ (g_i)_{i\in\omega} = (f_i \circ g_i)_{i\in\omega}$.

The *map* function for *Term* exploits the new structure by shifting the series of
functions whenever it enters a new context. Its definition is given as a functional
program:

$$map \; (f_0, f_1, \ldots) \; (Var \; x) \quad = Var((f_0, f_1, \ldots) \; x)$$
$$map \; (f_0, f_1, \ldots) \; (Abs \; t) \quad = Abs(map \; (f_1, f_2, \ldots) \; t)$$
$$map \; (f_0, f_1, \ldots) \; (App(t, t')) = App(map \; (f_0, f_1, \ldots) \; t, map \; (f_0, f_1, \ldots) \; t')$$

It is easily verified that (*Term*, *map*) satisfy the categorical definition of a functor.

Looking at these definitions, it is clear how to insert an ordinary function or value
into the category, and it is straightforward to insert the families of functions needed
for the example by giving the initial element of the sequence and the functional that
generates all others. However, it is also necessary to define the mapping that pulls
a computation from FUNSEQ back into the category of functional programs. This
is accomplished by taking the first element of the function sequence. Thus, one way
to realize the *map* function of FUNSEQ in a functional programming setting is with
the *map_with_policy* function introduced in Hook, Kieburtz and Sheard[5]:

$$map\_with\_policy \; Z \; f \; (Var \; x) \quad = Var(fx)$$
$$map\_with\_policy \; Z \; f \; (Abs \; t) \quad = Abs(map\_with\_policy \; Z \; (Zf) \; t)$$
$$map\_with\_policy \; Z \; f \; (App(t, t')) = App(map\_with\_policy \; Z \; f \; t,$$
$$map\_with\_policy \; Z \; f \; t')$$

In this encoding Z is the functional that generates the sequence and f is the seed
value. That is, $(map \; (f, Zf, Z^2f, \ldots))_0 = map\_with\_policy \; Z \; f$. Note the projection

---

[2] This is a simplified form of the Term data type in Hook, Kieburtz and Sheard[5]. An
anonymous referee has pointed out that an alternative structure can be used instead.
The argument to *Abs* may be given the type $Term(1 + \alpha)$ (where $+$ is interpreted as
a discriminated union). While this structure is very interesting, it is not possible to
express the map function for this type in the Standard ML type system. Preliminary
results indicate this structure can be used to specify substitution.

of the first element from the family of functions on the left hand side indicated by the subscript 0.

The *unit* and *mult* functions automatically generated for *Term* can be lifted to FUNSEQ. Simple inductions show that they satisfy the monad laws.

With these definitions in place the complete definition of substitution is given in Fig. 1. Note that the algorithm makes no explicit mention of the data constructors. It only uses the information about the type implicit in the definition of *map_with_policy*, *unit* and *mult*.

$$
\begin{aligned}
&\textbf{fun } apply\_substitution\ \sigma_0\ M = \\
&\quad \textbf{let } \textbf{fun } succ\ x = x + 1 \\
&\qquad \textbf{fun } transform\_index\ f \\
&\qquad\quad = \lambda n\ .\ \textbf{if } n = 0 \textbf{ then } n \textbf{ else } 1 + f(n-1) \\
&\qquad \textbf{fun } transform\_substitution\ \sigma \\
&\qquad\quad = \lambda n\ .\ \textbf{if } n = 0 \textbf{ then } unit\ 0 \\
&\qquad\qquad\qquad \textbf{else } map\_with\_policy\ transform\_index\ succ\ (\sigma(n-1)) \\
&\quad \textbf{in }\quad mult(map\_with\_policy\ transform\_substitution\ \sigma_0\ M) \\
&\quad \textbf{end}
\end{aligned}
$$

Fig. 1. Substitution function

4 Transformation to a First-Order Set of Equations

To obtain a practical algorithm, the substitution function *apply_substitution* in Fig. 1 must be made more efficient. This section shows how this transformation can be done automatically. Program transformation systems operate on systems of first-order equations. To apply them to the specification of substitution the higher-order facets must be translated into first-order structures. A partial evaluation system is used to accomplish this.

The software allowing a complete automatic transformation is not yet written. The transformations below have been performed with the Schism partial evaluator [4] and the Astre program transformation system [1], which are not yet integrated and do not use the same language.

4.1 Transformation of the *map_with_policy* Operator

The first step is to rewrite the program using the *map_with_policy* operator for the type $Term(\alpha)$ as a system of first-order functions. A partial evaluator can be used to specialize higher-order functions decreasing their order level. For example, consider the particular function σ_0 in the example in Sect. 1, and the call *apply_substitution* σ_0. A partial evaluator produces a program that does not contain *apply_substitution* in its full generality; it specializes the definition of *apply_substitution* for the particular constant σ_0. This specialization, called *apply_substitution_σ_0*, does not have a function as an argument, so it is first-order.

Unfortunately, this technique is insufficient for processing calls of *map_with_policy*, which is called twice in the program in Fig. 1. The specialization of *map_with_policy* for a particular policy function K and seed function g_0 gives the following function *Mwp_g*:

$$Mwp\_g\ (g, Var(n))\ \ \ = Var(g(n))$$
$$Mwp\_g\ (g, Abs(t))\ \ \ = Abs(Mwp\_g(K\ g, t))$$
$$Mwp\_g\ (g, App(t, t')) = App(Mwp\_g(g, t), Mwp\_g(g, t'))$$

The function *Mwp_g* has a function as an argument. But if it is specialized for a particular function g_0, the partial evaluator has to specialize the internal call $Mwp\_g(K\ g, t)$; it loops on this attempt. Fortunately, the partial evaluator is able to detect this circumstance, allowing it to select another technique. The alternative technique translates the higher-order functions into a system of first-order functions. This standard encoding, which is due to Reynolds [7], is outlined below.

1. The first step constructs a data type that encodes how the higher-order arguments are manipulated and applied. In this case the functions to be encoded are g_0 and $K\ g$. For the constant function, g_0, a constant C is introduced as a summand in the data type *Func*. The argument $K\ g$ cannot be encoded by a simple constant value because it contains g as a free variable. Since g is a higher-order parameter, it will already be represented by a value of type *Func*. Hence the new constructor, F, representing the application of K, must have type $Func \rightarrow Func$. This gives the data type *Func*, defined **datatype** $Func = C \mid F(Func)$.. The introduction of this type is a rediscovery of the sequence of functions $g_0, g_1, \ldots$ because it encodes each function in the family. The function g_0 is encoded by C, and the function g_3, for example, is encoded by $F(F(F(C)))$, which is written F^3.

2. The functions appearing as actual arguments are replaced by their encodings. The argument functions do not exist anymore—they are replaced by first-order data. In the call $Mwp\_g(g_0, M)$, g_0 is no longer a function but a first-order value, $\lceil g_0 \rceil$, of type *Func*. The definition of *Mwp_g* leads to the new function *Mwp_g'*:

$$Mwp\_g'(\lceil g \rceil, Var(n))\ \ \ = Var(\lceil g \rceil(n))$$
$$Mwp\_g'(\lceil g \rceil, Abs(t))\ \ \ = Abs(Mwp\_g'(F(\lceil g \rceil), t))$$
$$Mwp\_g'(\lceil g \rceil, App(t, t')) = App(Mwp\_g'(\lceil g \rceil, t), Mwp\_g'(\lceil g \rceil, t'))$$

But since $\lceil g \rceil$ is not a function, the application $\lceil g \rceil(n)$ is nonsense.

3. To make sense of the applications of functional parameters in the original programs "application" functions are introduced. Specifically the function *apply_g*, defined below, decodes applications of the form $\lceil g \rceil(n)$.

$$apply\_g(C, n) = g_0(n)$$
$$apply\_g(F(\lceil g \rceil), n) = (K\ \lambda n\ .\ apply\_g(\lceil g \rceil, n))(n)\ . \tag{4}$$

Note that *apply_g* is a first-order function because its argument, $\lceil g \rceil$, is an element of the type *Func*. The partial evaluator unfolds the definition of the policy function K to get a first-order expression of $apply\_g(F(\lceil g \rceil), n)$. The definition of Mwp_g' can be completed into:

$$Mwp\_g'(\lceil g \rceil, Var(n)) = Var(apply\_g(\lceil g \rceil, n))$$
$$Mwp\_g'(\lceil g \rceil, Abs(t)) = Abs(Mwp\_g'(F(\lceil g \rceil), t))$$
$$Mwp\_g'(\lceil g \rceil, App(t, t')) = App(Mwp\_g'(\lceil g \rceil\, t), Mwp\_g'(\lceil g \rceil, t'))$$

Recall that this encoding is done with respect to a specific call of map_with_policy $Z\ g_0\ M$. In the program in Fig. 1 there are two such calls. If the partial evaluator succeeds in the transformation of (4), then the new functions corresponding to Mwp_g and $apply\_g$ will constitute a first-order program equivalent to the functions generated by map_with_policy. This step of the transformation can be automated using a partial evaluator.

4.2   Application to $apply\_substitution$

Using the preceding techniques, the function $apply\_substitution$ is successfully transformed into the first-order program in Fig. 2. The data type $Subst$ and the data type $Fseq$ are introduced using the techniques above for the encodings of $transform\_index$ and $transform\_substitution$.

$$\textbf{datatype } Subst = S0 \qquad\qquad \textbf{datatype } Fseq = SUCC$$
$$\mid SUBST(Subst) \qquad\qquad\qquad\qquad \mid FSEQ(Fseq)$$

```
fun apply_substitution_σ₀(M) =
  let  fun apply_f(SUCC, n)        = s(n)
       |   apply_f(FSEQ(f), n)     = if n = 0 then 0
                                     else s(apply_f(f, n − 1))
       fun Mwp_f(f, Var(n))        = Var(apply_f(f, n))
       |   Mwp_f(f, Abs(t))        = Abs(Mwp_f(FSEQ(f), t))
       |   Mwp_f(f, App(t, t'))    = App(Mwp_f(f, t), Mwp_f(f, t'))
       fun apply_σ(S0, n)          = σ₀(n)
       |   apply_σ(SUBST(σ), n)    = if n = 0 then unit(0)
                                     else Mwp_f(Succ, (apply_σ(σ, n − 1)))
       fun Mwp_σ(σ, Var(n))        = Var(apply_σ(σ, n))
       |   Mwp_σ(σ, Abs(t))        = Abs(Mwp_σ(SUBST(σ), t))
       |   Mwp_σ(σ, App(t, t'))    = App(Mwp_σ(σ, t), Mwp_σ(σ, t'))
  in   mult(Mwp_(σ)(S0, M))
  end
```

Fig. 2. First-order Program

These two data types are isomorphic to the data type Nat^3 which is implemented efficiently in the hardware. However, the specialized function Mwp_σ does not exploit

---

[3] The constructors for the data type Nat are 0 and s, i.e. $\textbf{datatype } Nat = 0 \mid s(Nat)$.

the efficient implementation since it uses the (essentially unary) representation of the data type instead. Thus, the function $apply\_\sigma$ must peel off all of the data constructors each time Mwp_σ is applied to $Var(n)$. For example, after three levels of abstraction, σ_3 is represented by $SUBST(SUBST(SUBST(S0)))$. (The same is also true of the function Mwp_f.) To eliminate this inefficiency, which was present in the calling behavior of the original specification, the data types $Subst$ and $Fseq$ must be changed to the uniform data type Nat. This transformation can be performed automatically by Astre. Ultimately the explicit use of Nat will facilitate the use of primitive arithmetic in the program.

5 Simple Transformations

The following two simple transformations are performed automatically by Astre after introducing new function symbols. The first one introduces indexes to count the level of abstractions. The second replaces the composition of Mwp with the function $mult$ by a single function. The order of these transformations does not matter; they can be done simultaneously.

For technical reasons recursive definitions of the form $g(n) = \mathbf{if}\, n = 0\,\mathbf{then}\, e_1\,\mathbf{else}\, e_2$ are manipulated more effectively by Astre in the equivalent form $g(0) = e_1[0/n]$ and $g(s(n)) = e_2[s(n)/n]$. The notation $c[e'/x]$ denotes the substitution of expression e' for x in e. This restriction of the form of equations ensures the termination of the rewriting used by Astre to unfold the definition of g.

5.1 Introduction of Indexes

The isomorphism between the automatically generated type $Subst$ and the natural numbers is made explicit by introducing the function $iso\_\sigma : Nat \rightarrow Subst$:

$$\mathbf{fun}\ \mathbf{fun}\ iso\_\sigma(s(i)) = SUBST(iso\_\sigma(i))$$
$$|\ iso\_\sigma(0)\quad = S0$$

The functions $apply\_\sigma$ and Mwp_σ are replaced by the new functions $\sigma(i, n)$ (for $\sigma_i(n)$) and Mwp_σ', respectively. These functions satisfy $\sigma(i, n) = apply\_\sigma(iso\_\sigma(i), n)$ and $Mwp\_\sigma'(i, n) = Mwp\_\sigma(iso\_\sigma(i), n)$. Using these new equations, the Astre system implements the data type $Subst$ using the data type Nat. New functions to implement the data type $Fseq$ using Nat are also provided to the Astre system which then gives the program in Fig. 3. The program in Fig. 3 does not improve the performance of the program in Fig. 2. However, its explicit use of numbers is key to the improvements presented in the next section.

5.2 Composition Step

The transformation continues with a simple (automatic) step that replaces the composition of $mult$ with Mwp_σ' by a single function.[4] This is accomplished by introducing a function symbol, Ewp, which is equated to the composition of $mult$ with

---

[4] This composition is often called the *Kleisli star* or *natural extension*. Ewp is a mnemonic for extension with policy.

```
fun apply_substitution_σ₀(M) =
    let  fun f(0, n)              = s(n)
         | f(s(i), 0)            = 0
         | f(s(i), s(n))         = s(f(i, n))
         fun Mwp_f'(i, Var(n))    = Var(f(i, n))
         | Mwp_f'(i, Abs(t))      = Abs(Mwp_f'(s(i), t))
         | Mwp_f'(i, App(t, t'))  = App(Mwp_f'(i, t), Mwp_f'(i, t'))
         fun σ(0, n)              = σ₀(n)
         | σ(s(i), n)            = unit(0)
         | σ(s(i), s(n))         = Mwp_f'(0, σ(i, n))
         fun Mwp_σ'(i, Var(n))    = Var(σ(i, n))
         | Mwp_σ'(i, Abs(t))      = Abs(Mwp_σ'(s(i), t))
         | Mwp_σ'(i, App(t, t'))  = App(Mwp_σ'(i, t), Mwp_σ'(i, t'))
    in   mult(Mwp_σ'(0, M))
    end
```

Fig. 3. Program with indexes

Mwp_σ', i.e., $Ewp(0, M) = mult(Mwp\_\sigma'(0, M))$. Astre gives a program which uses neither $mult$, nor Mwp_σ' that includes the following definition of Ewp:

```
fun Ewp(i, Var(n))     = σ(i, n)
  | Ewp(i, Abs(t))     = Abs(Ewp(s(i), t))
  | Ewp(i, App(t, t')) = App(Ewp(i, t), Ewp(i, t'))
```

The main body of the function is then replaced by $Ewp(0, M)$. The functions $mult$ and Mwp_σ', which have become useless, are removed. Since the Mwp_σ' has now been eliminated, Mwp_f' is renamed Mwp to simplify the nomenclature below.

6 Transformation of the Sequence of the σ Functions

The transformations in this section exploit the arithmetic arguments introduced above to replace the expensive and redundant recursive calculations in σ and Ewp with index arithmetic.

The function $\sigma(i, n)$ of the transformed program is a rediscovery of the series of functions $\sigma_i(n)$ of Sect. 1. To further refine this program a specific instance of $apply\_substitution$ σ_0 must be specified. In what follows, the substitution function σ_0, needed for the contraction described in Sect. 1, is used to illustrate the specialization. Recall that σ_0 replaces variables of index 0 with the term $\lambda . 0\,1$, which is represented by $Abs(App(Var(0), Var(1)))$. Thus, $\sigma_0(0) = Abs(App(Var(0), Var(1)))$ and $\sigma_0(s(n)) = unit(n)$. Unfolding these equations yields a complete definition of $\sigma(i, n)$:

$$\sigma(0, 0) = Abs(App(Var(0), Var(1)))$$
$$\sigma(0, s(n)) = unit(n)$$
$$\sigma(s(i), 0) = unit(0)$$
$$\sigma(s(i), s(n)) = Mwp(0, \sigma(i, n)) \tag{5}$$

Since the equational program is complete with respect to *Nat* * *Nat*, the computation of any instance of $\sigma(i, n)$ results in a ground constructor term. For example, $\sigma(4, 2)$ yields:

$$\sigma(s(s(s(s(0)))), s(s(0))) \rightarrow \tag{6}$$
$$Mwp(0, \sigma(s(s(s(0))), s(0))) \rightarrow \tag{7}$$
$$Mwp(0, Mwp(0, \sigma(s(s(0)), 0))) \rightarrow^* Var(s(s(0)))$$

Rewrites (6) and (7) are unfoldings by equation (5). Computation of any instance of $\sigma(i, n)$ by naturals can begin with unfoldings using (5) until a subterm, $\sigma(u, v)$, in which u *and/or* v are equal to 0 is obtained.

This suggests a target program of the form:

$$\sigma(i, n) = \text{if } i > n \text{ then } e_1 \text{ else if } i = n \text{ then } e_2 \text{ else } e_3$$

where e_1, e_2, and e_3 are expressions. The transformation will be beneficial if these expressions are efficient. This step introduces a form of function definition by a conditional (instead of structural induction) that violates the technical restriction on programs used to assure termination of rewriting as required by the Astre system. Presently, Astre does not perform this part of the transformation. Moreover, the transformation does not directly generate the conditional; instead it generates the complete definition: $\sigma(s(i) + k, k) = u_1$, $\sigma(k, k) = u_2$ and $\sigma(k, s(n) + k) = u_3$.

6.1 First Transformation Step

The general strategy of the two transformation steps that follow is to discover arithmetic operations implicit in the recursion structure of programs. The first step in this process is a definition that makes the iteration structure of functions explicit.

Definition 1. Let x be a variable of type α, let y_i be a term of type β_i for each $i = 1, \cdots, n$, and let φ be a function of type $\beta_1 * \cdots * \alpha * \cdots * \beta_n \rightarrow \alpha$. The function $\hat{\varphi}$ of type $Nat * (\beta_1 * \cdots * \alpha * \cdots * \beta_n) \rightarrow \alpha$ is defined by:

$$\hat{\varphi}(s(k), (y_1, \cdots, x, \cdots, y_n)) = \varphi(y_1, \cdots, \hat{\varphi}(k, (y_1, \cdots, x, \cdots, y_n)), \cdots, y_n)$$
$$\hat{\varphi}(0, (y_1, \cdots, x, \cdots, y_n)) = x$$

Proposition 2.

$$\hat{\varphi}(k, (y_1, \cdots, \varphi(y_1, \cdots, y, \cdots, y_n), \cdots, y_n)) = \varphi(y_1, \cdots, \hat{\varphi}(k, (y_1, \cdots, y, \cdots, y_n)), \cdots, y_n)$$

Proof. By induction on k.

An immediate consequence of Definition 1 is $\hat{\varphi}(1, x) = \varphi(x)$, where $x : \beta_1 * \cdots * \alpha * \cdots * \beta_n$.

Having made the iteration structure of functions explicit, the next theorem helps program transformations exploit that structure. To simplify the exposition, consider the case in which $\varphi : \alpha \rightarrow \alpha$. In this case $\hat{\varphi} : Nat * \alpha \rightarrow \alpha$ and $\hat{\varphi}(k, n) = \varphi^k(x)$, where φ^k denotes k applications of φ. Suppose now that $f : Nat * Nat \rightarrow \alpha$ satisfies the equation: $f(s(i), s(n)) = \varphi(f(i, n))$; then $f(4, 7) = \varphi^4(f(0, 3)) = \hat{\varphi}(4, f(0, 3))$. More generally, $f(i + k, n + k) = \hat{\varphi}(k, f(i, n))$, which is the result expressed by Theorem 3.

Theorem 3. *Assume f of type $Nat^n \to \alpha$, let y_i be a term of type β_i for each $i = 1, \cdots, n$, and let φ be a function of type $\beta_1 * \cdots * \alpha * \cdots * \beta_n \to \alpha$. The following are equivalent:*

1. $f(s(x_1), \cdots, s(x_n)) = \varphi(y_1, \cdots, f(x_1, \cdots, x_n), \cdots, y_m)$
2. $\hat{\varphi}(k, (y_1, \cdots, f(x_1, \cdots, x_n), \cdots, y_n)) = f(x_1 + k, \cdots, x_n + k)$

Proof. That *1* implies *2* is obvious by instantiating k to 1. The converse is proved by induction on k.

To apply this theorem to (5), let $Mwp0(x)$ be $Mwp(0, x)$ and introduce the equation: $\widehat{Mwp0}(k, \sigma(i, n))) = \sigma(i + k, n + k)$. This gives the equational definition of $\sigma(i, n)$:

$$\sigma(s(i) + k, k) = \widehat{Mwp0}(k, unit(0))$$
$$\sigma(k, k) = \widehat{Mwp0}(k, Abs(App(Var(0), Var(1))))$$
$$\sigma(k, s(n) + k) = \widehat{Mwp0}(k, unit(n))$$

This definition can be rewritten in the conditional form described at the beginning of the section with $e_1 = \widehat{Mwp0}(n, unit(0))$, $e_2 = \widehat{Mwp0}(i, Abs(App(Var(0), Var(1))))$ and $e_3 = \widehat{Mwp0}(i, unit(n - i - 1))$.

6.2 Second Transformation Step

The second transformation step transforms the expressions e_1, e_2 and e_3. The definition of $\widehat{Mwp0}$ of type $Term \to Term$, obtained by Definition 1, refers to the (inefficient) function $Mwp0$. To get an efficient program an alternative (but equivalent) definition of $\widehat{Mwp0}$ that does not refer to $Mwp0$ must be generated. Theorem 4 addresses this issue.

To introduce Theorem 4, consider the function $upto$. Informally, $upto(i, n) = [i, i + 1, \cdots, n]$. The function $upto$ satisfies $upto(s(i), s(n)) = map\ s\ upto(i, n)$. Let map_s be the specialization of the definition of map by s:

$$map\_s\ [] = []$$
$$map\_s\ (x :: xs) = s(x) :: (map\_s\ xs)$$

The operators $[]$ and $::$ are the constructors of the data type $List(\alpha)$. By Theorem 3,

$$(\widehat{map\_s})\ (k, upto(i, n)) = (map\_s)^k\ (upto(i, n)) = upto(i + k, n + k)$$

Theorem 4 will yield the following recursive definition of $(map\_s)^k$, (that is of $\widehat{map\_s}$); it does not refer to map_s.

$$(map\_s)^k\ [] = []$$
$$(map\_s)^k\ (x :: xs) = s^k(x) :: ((map\_s)^k\ xs)$$

Note, in this definition $(map\_s)^k$ is the function being defined. It is to be regarded atomically; map_s is neither defined nor referred to.

Theorem 4. *Let y_i be a term of type β_i for each $i = 1, \cdots, n$, let φ be a function of type $\beta_1 * \cdots * \alpha * \cdots * \beta_n \rightarrow \alpha$, and let C be a constructor of type α. The following are equivalent:*

1. $\varphi(y_1, \cdots, C(x_1, \cdots, x_n), \cdots, y_n) = C(\varphi_1(x_1), \cdots, \varphi_n(x_n))$
2. $\hat{\varphi}(k, (y_1, \cdots, C(x_1, \cdots, x_n), \cdots, y_n)) = C(\widehat{\varphi_1}(k, x_1), \cdots, \widehat{\varphi_n}(k, x_n))$

Proof. That *1* implies *2* is obvious by instanciating k to 1. The converse is proved by induction on k.

If C is a constructor of arity zero, Theorem 4 degenerates to the two equations $\varphi(y_1, \cdots, C, \cdots, y_n) = C$ and $\hat{\varphi}(k, (y_1, \cdots, C, \cdots, y_n)) = C$.

To apply this result to $\widehat{Mwp0}$, recall that $Mwp0(x) = Mwp(0, x)$ and that:

$$
\begin{aligned}
Mwp(i, Var(n)) &= Var(f(i, n)) \\
Mwp(i, Abs(t)) &= Abs(Mwp(s(i), t)) \\
Mwp(i, App(t, t')) &= App(Mwp(i, t), Mwp(i, t')).
\end{aligned}
$$

Introduction of the specializations $f_0(x) = f(0, x)$, and $Mwp1(x) = Mwp(1, x)$ allows the application of Theorem 4, producing:

$$
\begin{aligned}
\widehat{Mwp0}(k, Var(n)) &= Var(\widehat{f_0}(k, n)) \\
\widehat{Mwp0}(k, Abs(t)) &= Abs(\widehat{Mwp1}(k, t)) \\
\widehat{Mwp0}(k, App(s, t)) &= App(\widehat{Mwp0}(k, s), \widehat{Mwp0}(k, t)).
\end{aligned}
$$

It is easy to show that $\widehat{f_0} = \hat{s}$ because $f(0, x) = s(x)$, and that $\hat{s}(k, a) = a + k$ by induction on k. Therefore $\widehat{Mwp0}(k, Var(n)) = Var(\widehat{f_0}(k, n))$, which is equivalent to $Var(\hat{s}(k, n))$, which can be rewritten $Var(n + k)$. Although this appears to have progressed, it is incomplete because $\widehat{Mwp1}$ is still defined in terms of $Mwp1$. Attempts to define $\widehat{Mwp1}$ by this method, however, will require the function $\widehat{Mwp2}$; this would continue forever. Fortunately, there is another way in which Theorem 3 may be applied to (5), yielding the equation $\widehat{Mwp}(k, (0, \sigma(i, n))) = \sigma(i + k, n + k)$. Applying the same transformation as above produces another conditional definition of $\sigma(i, n)$ with $e_1 = unit(n)$, $e_2 = \widehat{Mwp}(i, (0, Abs(App(Var(0), Var(1)))))$ and $e_3 = unit(n-1)$. Application of Theorem 4 produces a recursive definition of $\widehat{Mwp}$ that does not refer to Mwp:

$$
\widehat{Mwp}(k, (i, Var(n))) = Var(\hat{f}(k, (i, n))) \tag{8}
$$
$$
\widehat{Mwp}(k, (i, App(s, t))) = App(\widehat{Mwp}(k, (i, s)), \widehat{Mwp}(k, (i, t)))
$$
$$
\widehat{Mwp}(k, (i, Abs(t))) = Abs(\widehat{Mwp}(k, (s(i), t)))
$$

The transformation is not yet finished. Equation (8) remains to be improved by finding a recursive definition of $\hat{f}$ that does not refer to the function f.

6.3 Transformation of $\hat{f}$

Recall the equations for f:

$$f(0, n) = s(n) \tag{9}$$
$$f(s(i), 0) = 0 \tag{10}$$
$$f(s(i), s(n)) = s(f(i, n)) \tag{11}$$

Applying Theorem 4 to (11) yields:

$$\hat{f}(k, (s(i), s(n))) = s(\hat{f}(k, (i, n))) . \tag{12}$$

This suggests attempting a conditional definition for $\hat{f}$. Using equations (9), (10), (11), Theorem 4, Theorem 3, and Definition 1 produces:

$$\hat{f}(k, (0, s(n))) = s(\hat{s}(k, n)) = s(n + k) \tag{13}$$
$$\hat{f}(k, (s(i), 0)) = 0 \tag{14}$$
$$\hat{f}(k, (0, 0)) = k \tag{15}$$

Applying Theorem 3 to (12) gives: $\hat{f}(k, (i+p, n+p)) = \hat{s}(p, \hat{f}(k, (i, n))) = \hat{f}(k, (i, n)) + p$. Applying that to equations (13), (14), (15) produces

$$\hat{f}(k, (s(i) + p, p)) = p$$
$$\hat{f}(k, (p, s(n) + p)) = n + 1 + k + p$$
$$\hat{f}(k, (p, p)) = k + p$$

This equational definition is equivalent to the program:

$$\hat{f}(k, (i, n)) = \text{if } i > n \text{ then } n \text{ else if } i = n \text{ then } n + k \text{ else } n + k.$$

The program simplifies to: $\hat{f}(k, (i, n)) = \text{if } i > n \text{ then } n \text{ else } n + k$. By unfolding $\hat{f}$ and by a well known property of the conditional, equation (8) becomes: $\widehat{Mwp}(k, (i, Var(n))) = \text{if } i > n \text{ then } Var(n) \text{ else } Var(n + k)$. Including the transformed form of σ, which comes from above, produces the program in Fig. 4 which does not perform redundant computations for σ_i and f_i. The transformation involved in this section has been done manually. However the transformation process is systematic and involves equational reasoning using Theorem 3 and Theorem 4. It shows implicitly how to automatically transform a function of type $Nat * Nat \rightarrow Nat$ into a more efficient conditional form.

7 Directions

The paper has presented a clearly motivated and correct specification for a subtle representation of λ-terms, the implementation of which has, in the second authors experience, been prone to "off by one" errors. It has taken this abstract specification, with its extensive use of higher-order concepts, reduced it to a first-order program,

```
fun apply_substitution_σ₀(M) =
    let  fun M̂wp(k, (i, Var(n)))      = if i > n then Var(n) else Var(n + k)
         | M̂wp(k, (i, Abs(t)))        = Abs(M̂wp(k, (s(i), t)))
         | M̂wp(k, (i, App(t, t')))    = App(M̂wp(k, (i, t)), M̂wp(k, (i, t')))
         fun σ(i, n)                   = if i > n then unit(n)
                                         else if i = n then
                                                M̂wp(i, (0, Abs(App(Var(0), Var(1)))))
                                         else unit(n − 1)
         fun Ewp(i, Var(n))            = σ(i, n)
         | Ewp(i, Abs(t))             = Abs(Ewp(s(i), t))
         | Ewp(i, App(t, t'))         = App(Ewp(i, t), Ewp(i, t'))
    in   Ewp(0, M))
    end
```

Fig. 4. Final result

introduced index arithmetic and produced an efficient algorithm that exploits computer arithmetic.

This development illustrates several new techniques. First, it makes the monadic structure in the development of the specification explicit by showing that it is a monad in FUNSEQ. It supports this structure with new program transformation techniques which allow the implicit use of arithmetic to be "rediscovered" formally. Finally, it demonstrates the feasibility of integrating tools for monadic programming and specification, which tend to be higher-order, with relatively standard program transformation technology, which is strictly first-order. The importance of partial evaluation technology in bridging this gap cannot be overstated.

7.1 Technology

Currently our technology is a tower of Babel. Automatic support for monadic programming, including automatic program generation, exists in CRML, a Standard ML derivative developed by Sheard. The partial evaluator, Schism, uses its own (typed) dialect of Scheme as its object language. Astre, Bellegarde's program transformation system, is written in CAML. It uses a very simple first-order language as its object language.

In this environment, claims that the development is automatable mean that we have automated the process "piecewise", translating between the formalisms in a nearly mechanical fashion. It is, of course, our vision that one day these tools will all work in concert, allowing a development to proceed from specification to efficient realization with human intervention only when necessary.

7.2 Reuse

Although this paper has focused on the λ-calculus, the specification can be applied to virtually any abstract syntax with a regular binding structure provided its type can be expressed as a monad and the appropriate definition of *map_with_policy* can be given. For example, adding boolean constants and a conditional has no effect on the specification of substitution and only changes *map_with_policy* by defining it to apply f recursively on the components of the conditional without applying Z. Adding *let* is also trivial; again, no changes need to be made to the specification of substitution—only to *map_with_policy*. In this case, *map_with_policy* must apply Z to f when it enters the component in which the bound variable has been introduced. This ability to reuse specifications is one of the strongest arguments for the adoption of monads as a tool to structure program specification and development.

But what about the transformations? Can we reuse program improvements? Here we have less experience, however the decisions that are required to improve programs for the different scenarios outlined above are substantially the same. It appears that a transformation system that records its development may be able to replay the development and obtain similar improvements.

References

1. Françoise Bellegarde. Program transformation and rewriting. In *Proceedings of the fourth conference on Rewriting Techniques and Applications*, volume 488 of *LNCS*, pages 226–239, Berlin, 1991. Springer-Verlag.
2. N. G. de Bruijn. Lambda calculus notation with nameless dummies, a tool for automatic formula manipulation, with application to the Church-Rosser theorem. *Indagaciones Mathematische*, 34:381–392, 1972.
3. N. G. de Bruijn. Lambda calculus with namefree formulas involving symbols that represent reference transforming mappings. In *Proc. of the Koninklijke Nederlandse Akademie van Wetenschappen*, pages 348–356, Amsterdam, series A, volume 81(3), September 1978.
4. Charles Consel. The Schism Manual. Technical report, Oregon Grad. Inst., 1992.
5. James Hook, Richard Kieburtz, and Tim Sheard. Generating programs by reflection. Technical Report 92-015, Oregon Grad. Inst., July 1992.
6. Eugenio Moggi. Notions of computations and monads. *Information and Computation*, 93(1):55–92, July 1991.
7. John C. Reynolds. Definitional interpreters for higher-order programming languages. In *ACM National Conference*, pages 717–740. ACM, 1972.
8. Philip Wadler. The essence of functional programming. In *POPL '92*. ACM Press, January 1992.

A Technique for Specifying and Refining TCSP Processes by Using Guards and Liveness Conditions

R. Peña

Departamento de Informática y Automática
Universidad Complutense de Madrid
E-28040 Madrid. Spain
e-mail: ricardo@dia.ucm.es

Luis M. Alonso

Departamento de Lenguajes y Sistemas Informáticos
Universidad del Pais Vasco
E-20080 San Sebastian. Spain
e-mail: alonso@gorria.if.ehu.es

Abstract

A technique for the specification of TCSP processes based upon the concepts of *guards* and *liveness rules* is presented. It is shown how safety and liveness properties can be proved for processes specified in this way. A technique related to bisimulations is proposed to prove refinements correct. The technique is extended to handle the concealment of events in the implementing process. The refinement relation preserves the safety and liveness properties already proved for the specification. Parallel composition of specifications is also defined preserving the failures semantics. To illustrate the technique, an example is used throughout the paper.

1   Introduction

The *failures* model [5,6,9] has proved to be a successful theoretical and practical tool for the specification and verification of parallel systems. Other related algebraic theories and calculus of processes are those by Milner [12,13], Hennessy [8], and Bergstra and Klop [4]. The notion of *trace* of the process, i.e. the sequence of actions already performed by the process, plays in TCSP a central role. The so called *refusal sets* provide a means to define the inmediate liveness of the process after a given trace.

Starting with these concepts, the authors proposed in [15] a technique for TCSP process specification. Valid traces were defined by partial abstract types, as described in [7]. These ideas evolved in [2,3] where the notion of state for defining TCSP processes was made explicit in the form of *state variables*. States corresponding to legal traces were characterized by means of *invariants*, much in the sense of data representation invariants defined in [10].

The present paper represents the culmination of these ideas. Its main contribution is a change in the technique for building specifications and proving refinements correct. State variables are retained, but now process behaviour is specified by two sets of conditions: *safety* requirements and *liveness* requirements. The first one takes the form of a family of *guards* and defines the allowed traces for the process. The second one consists of a collection of set expressions, defining the mandatory events in each state.

Specifications with this technique are shorter and more abstract than those presented in the previous papers. Proving refinements correct and proving that a specification satisfies a liveness predicate, are also easier.

The organization of the paper is as follows: Section 2 defines the concept of *process specification with safety and liveness conditions*, first by using an example and then formally. Its semantics is given in terms of the failures model. Section 3 explains how safety and liveness properties can be proved for processes specified in this way. In Section 4 we characterize the notion of refinement of a process by another. Concealment of events in the implementing process is also considered. In Section 5, we define the parallel composition of process specifications. Finally, Section 6 provides a short conclusion. In this paper, we provide neither the proofs of the propositions nor meaningful examples. The interested readers are addressed to [1].

2 Process Specification Using Safety and Liveness Conditions

The technique used in [9] for specifying processes consisted of a predicate $S(tr, X)$ with free variables tr (for traces) and X (for *refusal sets*). A process is said to satisfy a specification, denoted P sat $S(tr, X)$, if every legal trace tr of P and every refusal set X of P after engaging in the trace tr, satisfy the predicate $S(tr, X)$, i.e.:

$$P \text{ sat } S(tr, X) \triangleq \forall (tr, X) \in P.S(tr, X)$$

Here, we are assuming that a non divergent *TCSP* process is a subset of $\mathcal{L}^* \times \mathcal{P}(\mathcal{L})$, $\mathcal{L}$ being the alphabet of the process. A trace tr represents a possible event history for P and a refusal X represents a menu of events such that P *may* deadlock if the external environment of P offers that menu.

Also in [9], a set of proof rules for verifying the sat relation was given. These are based on the syntactic structure of P and take the form of deduction rules such as the following one:

$$P \text{ sat } S(tr, X) \wedge Q \text{ sat } T(tr, X) \Rightarrow P \sqcap Q \text{ sat } S(tr, X) \vee T(tr, X)$$

where $\sqcap$ is the internal choice *TCSP* operator. In case P is recursive, some form of induction is needed to verify the desired property. In general, the proofs of realistic specifications using these rules tend to be very hard and they have an *ad hoc* look as they heavily depend on the specific syntax of the involved processes.

In this section we propose both a technique for defining *TCSP* processes using a syntactical *normal form,* and a method for proving the sat relation in a more systematic way. In fact, the technique can be seen as a way of structuring the $S(tr, X)$ predicate according to some simple rules, giving as result a process satisfying the predicate.

First, it is worthy to note that $S(tr, X)$ can be split into two predicates, one on traces establishing which are the allowed traces for the process, and another one establishing the *future* of the process after a legal trace. In the *TCSP* jargon, it is traditional to say that the first one specifies the *safety* properties of the system while the second one expresses its *liveness* properties, i.e.,

$$S(tr, X) = Safe(tr) \wedge Live(tr, X)$$

Example 1 A mutual exclusion arbiter for n users

Let us assume a system in which n users synchronize with an arbiter by means of the events req_i (user i asks for permission to use the resource), ack_i (the arbiter gives the permission to user i) and rel_i (user i has finished using the resource). The safety predicate for a robust arbiter can be defined as follows:

$$
\begin{aligned}
&Safe(tr)\overset{\Delta}{=} \quad\quad\quad\quad\quad\quad\quad\quad\quad\quad\quad\quad\quad\quad\quad\quad\quad\quad (1)\\
&\forall i \in U.\#(tr{\uparrow}rel_i) \leq \#(tr{\uparrow}ack_i) \leq \#(tr{\uparrow}req_i) \leq \#(tr{\uparrow}rel_i) + 1\\
&\wedge\\
&(Ni : i \in U.\#(tr{\uparrow}rel_i) < \#(tr{\uparrow}ack_i)) \leq 1
\end{aligned}
$$

where $tr{\uparrow}e$ means the projection of the trace tr over the alphabet $\{e\}$, N is the counting quantifier, $\#$ denotes the number of events of a trace and $U = \{1 \ldots n\}$.

Another way of specifying $Safe(tr)$ is to define it as the following inductively generated set of traces:

- $Safe(<>)$

- $Safe(tr) \wedge thinking_i(tr) \Rightarrow Safe(tr^\frown req_i)$

- $Safe(tr) \wedge eating_i(tr) \Rightarrow Safe(tr^\frown rel_i)$

- $Safe(tr) \wedge hungry_i(tr) \wedge \neg eaters(tr) \Rightarrow Safe(tr^\frown ack_i)$

where

$$
\begin{aligned}
thinking_i(tr) &\overset{\Delta}{=} \#(tr{\uparrow}req_i) = \#(tr{\uparrow}rel_i)\\
hungry_i(tr) &\overset{\Delta}{=} \#(tr{\uparrow}ack_i) < \#(tr{\uparrow}req_i)\\
eating_i(tr) &\overset{\Delta}{=} \#(tr{\uparrow}rel_i) < \#(tr{\uparrow}ack_i)\\
eaters(tr) &\overset{\Delta}{=} \exists i \in U.eating_i(tr) = true
\end{aligned}
$$

That is, for every legal trace tr and every event e, we state the boolean condition $G_e(tr)$ under which it is *safe* to allow the event e to be added to tr. In what follows, we will use the term *guard* when referring to those conditions G_e.

This way of defining $Safe(tr)$ gives us directly an operational definition of a safe process: let us imagine a process having, as internal state, a variable of type *trace*

process $MutEx_s$
 alphabet req_i, ack_i, rel_i
 state variables
  $s : \mathcal{L}^* := <>$
 transition rules
  on $req_i \Rightarrow s := s^\frown req_i$
  on $ack_i \Rightarrow s := s^\frown ack_i$
  on $rel_i \Rightarrow s := s^\frown rel_i$
 requirements .
  $req_i \Rightarrow thinking_i(s)$
  $ack_i \Rightarrow hungry_i(s) \wedge \neg eaters(s)$
  $rel_i \Rightarrow eating_i(s)$
end process $MutEx_s$

Figure 1: Chaotic mutual exclusion arbiter specified by using traces

where it *stores* the trace performed by it up to a particular moment. It can use the guards G_e (which are boolean functions on traces) to know the set of safe events in which it can engage at that moment. It then makes a nondeterministic choice and decides either to engage in one of these events or to stop. If it decides to engage in one event, then updates its internal state, recording that this event is now part of the trace (in fact it is the last event). The description of such a process for example 1 is shown in figure 1. The boolean condition after the expression $e \Rightarrow$ in the "requirements" section, is the guard G_e. It is understood that $i \in U$ and that a free i in a line means the replication of that line for all $i \in U$.

This kind of process with internal memory starts its execution with the empty trace as initial state and, in every state, it behaves like what we can call a *safe chaotic* process, in short *safe chaos*. It is the most nondeterministic process of those that satisfy $Safe(tr)$. Every safe process is *included* in it.

If we have the predicate $Safe(tr)$ explicitly defined and we want to prove that a process P built with guards satisfies it, it is enough to think of $Safe(tr)$ as an invariant of P. We must prove that $Safe(tr)$ holds for the empty trace and that it is preserved by every safe transition. This technique is explained in detail in section 3.

We turn now to the liveness conditions. The **stop** process and, in general, any process that stops after executing a legal trace, are included among the safe ones. Usually, we would like to require a process to accept certain (safe) events in some states. In *TCSP* , refusal sets are used to impose obligations on a process. In [2,3] the authors used a (perhaps more explicit) *menu relation* to specify the set of nondeterministic menus offered by the process in any state. The translation from menus to refusals is immediate. If a particular event is included in *all* the menus associated to a particular state, then the process is forced to engage in this event if the environment insists. In other words, the event is deterministic. Otherwise, it is nondeterministic. Of course, there must be a consistency between the safety and the liveness conditions imposed on a process.

Here, we have chosen to define the obligations of a process by means of *liveness rules.* A liveness rule is a (total) function from states to sets of events. Its semantics, formally given below, is that in every state the process must be able to engage in at least one of the events of (the evaluation of) the liveness rule in that state. If there exist several liveness rules, the process must satisfy the obligations imposed by all of them.

The mutual exclusion arbiter with liveness rules can be built by adding to figure 1 the following liveness rules:

$$\forall i \in U.Req_i(s) \triangleq \{req_i \mid thinking_i(s) = true\}$$
$$\forall i \in U.Rel_i(s) \triangleq \{rel_i \mid eating_i(s) = true\}$$
$$Ack(s) \triangleq \{ack_i \mid hungry_i(s) \wedge \neg eaters(s)\}$$

In this specification we require that the events req_i and rel_i be deterministic whenever user i is respectively *thinking* or *eating*. Also, one of the events ack_i for all *hungry* users i, is compulsory in states such that no user is *eating*. When an event e is both safe and compulsory in a state, we will use the abbreviation $e \Leftrightarrow G_e$. This is equivalent to defining the guard G_e and the following liveness rule

$$\text{if } G_e(tr) \text{ then } \{e\} \text{ else } \emptyset$$

A specification with guards and liveness rules defines, as we will see, a unique process in the failures model. Proving that it satisfies an explicit predicate $S(tr, X) = Safe(tr) \wedge Live(tr, X)$ is a straightforward task (see section 3). The advantage of the proposed method is that we have not only built an abstract specification, but also an actual system to start the design process with. The rest of the task consists of *refining* the system and proving that the refinements are correct.

Before proceeding to the formal definitions, let us now introduce the concept of *state variables* as defined in [3]. In the example of figure 1, it is obvious that the information kept by the process in its internal memory is excessive. In most of the examples, to record the relevant data about the past of the process, it is enough to have a finite set of "small" variables. Based on this information, the process can take exactly the same decisions as if it had the complete trace stored. In the example, the only variables that are needed are the individual states st_i of the users, where:

$$st_i : UserState \quad \text{and} \quad UserState \triangleq \{thinking, hungry, eating\}$$

For all $s \in \mathcal{L}^*$, we want to preserve the following invariant relation:

$$\begin{aligned}
Safe(s) \Rightarrow \quad & \forall i \in U. & (2)\\
& thinking_i(s) \Leftrightarrow st_i = thinking \\
\wedge \quad & hungry_i(s) \Leftrightarrow st_i = hungry \\
\wedge \quad & eating_i(s) \Leftrightarrow st_i = eating
\end{aligned}$$

The translation of the arbiter specified with traces to an arbiter specified with state variables st_i, is shown in figure 2. There, the predicate *eaters* can be defined in terms of the new state variables as:

$$(Ni.st_i = eating) > 0 \tag{3}$$

process *MutEx*
    alphabet req$_i$, ack$_i$, rel$_i$
    state variables
    st_i: UserState := *thinking*
    transition rules
    on req$_i$$\Rightarrow$$st_i$:= *hungry*
    on ack$_i$$\Rightarrow$$st_i$:= *eating*
    on rel$_i$$\Rightarrow$$st_i$:= *thinking*
    requirements
    req$_i$$\Leftrightarrow$$st_i$ = *thinking*
    ack$_i$$\Rightarrow$$(st_i = hungry) \wedge \neg eaters$
    rel$_i$$\Leftrightarrow$$st_i$ = *eating*
    $Ack \triangleq \{ack_i \mid st_i = hungry \wedge \neg eaters\}$
end process *MutEx*

Figure 2: Mutual exclusion arbiter with state variables st_i

We regard the state variables of a process as *observer* functions on traces. Each state variable conveys some relevant information about the past history of the process. The transition rules can be looked at as the definitions of these observer functions. They explain how the observation changes as we concatenate a new event to the trace. Let us note that these observer functions are partial functions over $\mathcal{L}^*$ and total ones over *traces(P)*. The same happens to the guards and liveness rules since they are expressed in terms of the primitive observers st_i.

Now we proceed to the formal definitions. For the rest of the paper, we assume the existence of some predefined data domains $\mathcal{D}_{t_1} \dots \mathcal{D}_{t_n}$ with type names $t_1 \dots t_n$.

We will use a tuple $x_1 \dots x_n$ of *state variables* to represent the set of states. Any state σ may be seen as an assignment $\{x_1 \leftarrow \kappa_1, \dots, x_n \leftarrow \kappa_n\}$ of values from the appropriate data domains to state variables. In particular, the initial state of the process is given by an *initial assignment* σ_0. From now on, given a set of state variables $\mathcal{V} = \{x_1, \dots, x_n\}$, we will denote by $Ass(\mathcal{V})$ the set of all possible assignments $\sigma : \mathcal{V} \longrightarrow \mathcal{D}$ of values to variables in $\mathcal{V}$.

The state transitions are described giving expressions $E_{e,x}$ for every pair of event e and state variable x. If $\sigma \xrightarrow{e} \sigma'$ is a transition, the value of x in σ' is defined as the value of $E_{e,x}$ in σ.

Definition 2 A *process specification with safety and liveness conditions*, in short a *process specification*, is given by a tuple $SP = (\mathcal{L}, \mathcal{V}, \sigma_0, \mathbf{TR}, \mathbf{G}, \mathbf{L})$ where:

- $\mathcal{L}$ is a nonempty *alphabet* of events

- $\mathcal{V} = \{x_1 \dots x_n\}$ is a finite set of typed variables, called *state variables*

- σ_0, the *initial assignment*, associates to every state variable x an appropiate value, denoted $\sigma_0(x)$

- **TR** is a $\mathcal{L}$-indexed family $(TR_e)_{e \in \mathcal{L}}$ of *transition rules*. A transition rule TR_e associates to every state variable x a properly formed expression $E_{e,x}$, with free variables in $\mathcal{V}$.

- **G** is a $\mathcal{L}$-indexed family $(G_e)_{e \in \mathcal{L}}$ of boolean expressions with free variables in $\mathcal{V}$, called *guards*.

- **L** is a set $\{L_i(\mathcal{V})\}$ of expressions, with free variables in $\mathcal{V}$. The type of each of them is "set of events of $\mathcal{L}$". Each L_i is called a *liveness rule*.

Very often, expressions defining transition or liveness rules will use auxiliary functions defined in some suitable formalism. For simplicity, in the rest of the paper we shall assume that such functions are totally defined over $Ass(\mathcal{V})$. As we will immediately see, not every state in $Ass(\mathcal{V})$ is a state *reachable* by the process.

Let $\sigma \in Ass(\mathcal{V})$ and let $E(\mathcal{V})$ be an expression with free variables in $\mathcal{V}$. We will denote by $\overline{\sigma}(E(\mathcal{V}))$, in short $\overline{\sigma}(E)$, the evaluation of the expression E after assigning values to variables by σ. Let $TR_e = \{E_{e,x_1} \dots E_{e,x_n}\}$, be a transition rule, we will denote by $TR_e \circ \sigma$ the following assignment:

$$TR_e \circ \sigma = \{x_i \leftarrow \overline{\sigma}(E_{e,x_i}), x_i \in \mathcal{V}\}$$

Last, given a predicate $\mathcal{P}$ with free variables in $\mathcal{V}$, we will denote by $TR_e(\mathcal{P})$ the predicate obtained by substituting E_{e,x_i} for every occurence of variable x_i in $\mathcal{P}$. In what follows, we shall assume the implicit existence of a process specification:

$$SP = (\mathcal{L}, \mathcal{V}, \sigma_0, \mathbf{TR}, \mathbf{G}, \mathbf{L})$$

Definition 3 The set of *reachable* states of SP, denoted Σ_{SP}, is the following inductively generated set of assignments:

1. $\sigma_0 \in \Sigma_{SP}$

2. $\forall \sigma \in \Sigma_{SP}, \forall e \in \mathcal{L}.(\overline{\sigma}(G_e) = true \Rightarrow TR_e \circ \sigma \in \Sigma_{SP})$

Definition 4 The *transition relation* of SP, denoted $\longrightarrow_{SP}$, abbreviated $\longrightarrow$, is the following inductively generated set of triples $\sigma \overset{t}{\longrightarrow} \sigma' \in \Sigma_{SP} \times \mathcal{L}^* \times \Sigma_{SP}$:

1. $\forall \sigma \in \Sigma_{SP}.\sigma \overset{<>}{\longrightarrow} \sigma$

2. $\forall \sigma_1, \sigma_2 \in \Sigma_{SP}, \forall t \in \mathcal{L}^*, \forall e \in \mathcal{L}.(\sigma_1 \overset{t}{\longrightarrow} \sigma_2 \wedge \overline{\sigma}_2(G_e) = true \Rightarrow \sigma_1 \overset{\frown{t}e}{\longrightarrow} TR_e \circ \sigma_2)$

Definition 5 The set of *traces* of SP, denoted $traces(SP)$, is defined from $\longrightarrow_{SP}$ as the following set:

$$traces(SP) = \{t \in \mathcal{L}^* \mid \exists \sigma_t \in \Sigma_{SP}.\sigma_0 \overset{t}{\longrightarrow} \sigma_t\}$$

We will denote by σ_t the state reached by SP after executing the trace t. Let us note that the mapping defined by $\sigma(t) = \sigma_t$ is not, in general, an injection and always is a surjection over Σ_{SP}.

Definition 6 The set of *possible* events of SP after the trace t, is defined as:

$$next(t) = \{e \in \mathcal{L} \mid \bar{\sigma}_t(G_e) = true\}$$

Definition 7 A pair (t, m), where $t \in traces(SP)$ and $m \subseteq \mathcal{L}$ *satisfies* SP, denoted (t, m) **sat** SP, if

- $m \subseteq next(t)$, and

- $\forall L \in \mathbf{L}.(\bar{\sigma}_t(L) \neq \emptyset \wedge \bar{\sigma}_t(L) \subseteq next(t) \Rightarrow m \cap \bar{\sigma}_t(L) \neq \emptyset)$

This definition expresses the semantics we want for our specifications. Let us emphasize the following aspects:

- in a state σ_t, if a liveness rule L gives rise to a non empty set of events $\bar{\sigma}_t(L)$, and all these events are safe in that state, then all the menus m of the process in state σ_t must include at least one event of $\bar{\sigma}_t(L)$.

- if all liveness rules $L \in \mathbf{L}$ give rise to empty sets in a state $\bar{\sigma}_t$, then any subset of $next(t)$, even the empty set, satisfies SP. We say that SP behaves as a *safe chaos* in that state.

- if a liveness rule L imposes a partially unsafe set of events in a state, then it has no effect in that state. (This is an arbitrary decission but it has proved to be useful in the examples the authors have tried.)

- if $next(t) = \emptyset$ in a state, then the only menu satisfying SP in that state is $\emptyset$. This will be a deadlock state.

- if $next(t) - \bigcup_{L \in \mathbf{L}} \bar{\sigma}_t(L) \neq \emptyset$, all the events in this difference can be chosen by the process in a non deterministic way. They are neither mandatory, nor forbidden in that state.

Expressing this desired semantics into the failures model is immediate:

Definition 8 The *failures semantics* of SP, denoted $[\![SP]\!]$, is the following inductively generated subset of $\mathcal{L}^* \times \mathcal{P}(\mathcal{L})$:

1. $\forall t \in traces(SP), \forall m \subseteq \mathcal{L}.(t, m)$ sat $SP \Rightarrow (t, \overline{m}) \in [\![SP]\!]$

2. $\forall t \in traces(SP), \forall X_1, X_2 \subseteq \mathcal{L}.(t, X_1) \in [\![SP]\!] \wedge X_2 \subseteq X_1 \Rightarrow (t, X_2) \in [\![SP]\!]$

Proposition 9 Given a process specification $SP = (\mathcal{L}, \mathcal{V}, \sigma_0, \mathbf{TR}, \mathbf{G}, \mathbf{L})$, $[\![SP]\!]$ is a process, in particular a non divergent one, in the failures model.

3 Proving Properties

As it has been said, in [9] the specification of a process takes the form of a predicate with free variables tr and X denoting any trace and refusal set of the process. The expression P sat $S(tr, X)$, is formalized by:

$$\forall tr, X.tr \in traces(P) \wedge X \in refusals(P/tr) \Rightarrow S(tr, X)$$

In our context, safety properties can be expressed as a predicate over the process state variables, i.e. as a predicate $Safe$ with free variables in $\mathcal{V}$. Given the corresponding predicate on traces, its statement using state variables is usually immediate.

To prove a safety property written in terms of state variables, it must be shown that it holds for all values of state variables corresponding to *legal* traces of the process. The assignments corresponding to reachable states must then be characterized.

Definition 10 We shall denote by $Reach_{SP}$ the strongest predicate, with free variables in $\mathcal{V}$, satisfying the following conditions:

- $\bar{\sigma}_0(Reach_{SP}) = true$

- $G_e \wedge Reach_{SP} \Rightarrow TR_e(Reach_{SP})$, holds for all $e \in \mathcal{L}$.

Then the proof of any safety property $Safe$, would reduce to prove the following implication:

$$Reach_{SP} \Rightarrow Safe$$

Usually, we do not need to know exactly $Reach_{SP}$. In most situations, it suffices proving that $Inv_{SP} \Rightarrow Safe$ holds, for some predicate Inv_{SP} weaker than $Reach_{SP}$ which is invariant in the following sense:

Definition 11 A predicate Inv, with free variables in $\mathcal{V}$, is an SP-*invariant* if:

- $\bar{\sigma}_0(Inv) = true$

- $G_e \wedge Inv \Rightarrow TR_e(Inv)$, holds for all $e \in \mathcal{L}$.

The reader can easily prove that the following predicate is an invariant of the mutual exclusion arbiter of figure 2:

$$(Ni \in U.st_i = eating) \leq 1 \tag{4}$$

We will discuss now the analysis of liveness properties. The relevant definitions are:

Definition 12 A specification SP is *well formed* if there exists an SP-invariant Inv_{SP} such that

$$Inv_{SP} \Rightarrow \forall L \in \mathbf{L}.L \subseteq next_{SP}$$

where $next_{SP}(\mathcal{V})$ is a set-of-events expression defined in terms of state variables as $\{e \mid e \in \mathcal{L} \wedge G_e(\mathcal{V})\}$. It represents the set of safe events the process can engage in after each state.

Well formedness removes the need to check in all the proofs whether the liveness requirements are in contradiction or not with the safety ones.

Definition 13 Given a well formed specification SP, an SP-invariant Inv_{SP}, and a liveness expression $S(\mathcal{V}, m)$, in terms of state variables $\mathcal{V}$ and menu m, SP *satisfies* $S(\mathcal{V}, m)$, denoted SP **sat** $S(\mathcal{V}, m)$, if

$$Inv_{SP} \wedge m \subseteq next_{SP} \wedge (\forall L \in \mathbf{L}.(L = \emptyset) \vee (m \cap L \neq \emptyset)) \Rightarrow S(\mathcal{V}, m)$$

In our context, liveness properties must be expressed as set expressions depending on the state variables and on a free variable m representing the possible menus of the process in any valid state.

For instance, an explicit liveness expression for the mutual exclusion example of figure 2 would be the following one:

$$
\begin{aligned}
S(\mathcal{V}, m) \overset{\text{def}}{=} \quad & (\forall j \in U.st_j = thinking \Rightarrow req_j \in m) \\
\wedge \quad & (\forall j \in U.st_j = eating \Rightarrow rel_j \in m) \\
\wedge \quad & ((Nj \in U.st_j = hungry) > 0 \wedge \neg eaters \Rightarrow \\
& \exists k \in U.st_k = hungry \wedge ack_k \in m)
\end{aligned}
$$

Using invariant 4 and definition 13, the reader can prove that this property is satisfied by the arbiter of figure 2. From this property, weaker ones can be deduced. For instance, that if only one user k is *hungry* and no user is *eating*, then the event ack_k is mandatory for the system. Also, deadlock freedom expressed as $S(\mathcal{V}, m) \overset{\text{def}}{=} (m \neq \emptyset)$, can easily be proved.

4 Refinements

The *TCSP* refinement relation $\sqsubseteq$ preserves the safety and liveness properties of processes. Following the approach taken in TCSP, we say that a specification $SPEC$ is refined by another specification IMP if any possible trace of IMP is also allowed by $SPEC$, and if for every trace, any set of events that $SPEC$ is forced to offer, is also offered by IMP.

Definition 14 Given two specifications with the same alphabet, $SPEC$ and IMP, we say that IMP *is a refinement of* $SPEC$, denoted by $SPEC \sqsubseteq IMP$, if $[\![SPEC]\!] \sqsubseteq [\![IMP]\!]$.

The failures model enjoys a rich set of algebraic axioms to prove both equality and refinements of processes. For example, for any two processes P and P':

$$P \sqsubseteq P' \Leftrightarrow P \sqcap P' = P$$

The use of the algebraic laws to prove correctness of refinements has been shown elsewhere and will not be discussed here. The explicit modeling of process states by means of state variables allows us to compare guards and liveness rules in corresponding states i.e., in states reached after the same trace. To carry out this comparison, we establish some relation between states that takes the form of a predicate with free variables of $\mathcal{V}_{sp}$ and $\mathcal{V}_{imp}$; this relation shall hold initially and be preserved by transitions. This proving technique has strong similarities with the concept of *bisimulation* introduced by Park [14] in the framework of *CCS*. The use of bisimulations to compare *TCSP* processes has been studied in other works [11].

In what follows, we assume as given two well-formed specifications with disjoint sets of state variables:

$$SPEC = (\mathcal{L}_{spec}, \mathcal{V}_{spec}, \sigma_{0,spec}, \mathbf{TR}_{spec}, \mathbf{G}_{spec}, \mathbf{L}_{spec})$$
$$IMP = (\mathcal{L}_{imp}, \mathcal{V}_{imp}, \sigma_{0,imp}, \mathbf{TR}_{imp}, \mathbf{G}_{imp}, \mathbf{L}_{imp})$$

Definition 15 Given two well-formed specifications $SPEC$ and IMP, with $\mathcal{L} = \mathcal{L}_{spec} = \mathcal{L}_{imp}$, and predicates $Spec(\mathcal{V}_{spec})$ and $Imp(\mathcal{V}_{imp})$, which are $SPEC$-invariant and IMP-invariant respectively, we say that predicate ϕ, with free variables in $\mathcal{V}_{spec} \cup \mathcal{V}_{imp}$, is a *refinement relation* with respect to $SPEC$ and IMP if the following conditions hold:

1. $\overline{\sigma_0}(\phi) = true$ with $\sigma_0 = \sigma_{0,spec} \cup \sigma_{0,imp}$

2. $\forall e \in \mathcal{L}.Spec(\mathcal{V}_{spec}) \wedge Imp(\mathcal{V}_{imp}) \wedge G_e^{spec} \wedge G_e^{imp} \wedge \phi \Rightarrow TR_e(\phi)$
   with:
   $$TR_e = TR_e^{spec} \cup TR_e^{imp}$$

for any values of state variables in $\mathcal{V}_{spec}$ and $\mathcal{V}_{imp}$.

Proposition 16 Given two well-formed specifications $SPEC$ and IMP with $\mathcal{L} = \mathcal{L}_{spec} = \mathcal{L}_{imp}$,
$$SPEC \sqsubseteq IMP$$
if there are predicates $Spec(\mathcal{V}_{spec})$, $SPEC$-invariant, and $Imp(\mathcal{V}_{imp})$, IMP-invariant, and refinement relation ϕ with respect to $SPEC$ and IMP, satisfying the following conditions:

safety: $\forall e \in \mathcal{L}.Spec(\mathcal{V}_{spec}) \wedge Imp(\mathcal{V}_{imp}) \wedge \phi \wedge G_e^{imp} \Rightarrow G_e^{spec}$

liveness: $Spec(\mathcal{V}_{spec}) \wedge Imp(\mathcal{V}_{imp}) \wedge \phi \Rightarrow \mathbf{L}$
   where:

$$\mathbf{L} \stackrel{\Delta}{=} \forall L(\mathcal{V}_{spec}) \in \mathbf{L}_{spec}. \, L(\mathcal{V}_{spec}) \neq \emptyset \Rightarrow$$
$$\exists L'(\mathcal{V}_{imp}) \in \mathbf{L}_{imp}. L'(\mathcal{V}_{imp}) \neq \emptyset \wedge L'(\mathcal{V}_{imp}) \subseteq L(\mathcal{V}_{spec})$$

for any values of state variables in $\mathcal{V}_{spec}$ and $\mathcal{V}_{imp}$.

When refining some specification by another we define a more deterministic system, more amenable for practical implementation, possibly by adding and/or removing some state variables, while keeping unchanged the alphabet of events. If we are interested in designing distributed systems, we will eventually face the task of specifying a network of communicating subsystems, so that abstracting from internal activities, it becomes a refinement of the given system specification. Concealing a set of events in a *TCSP* process may produce divergence, if there is the possibility for infinite chattering to occur. The technique for proving divergence freedom is established below.

Definition 17 Given a process specification SP, with alphabet $\mathcal{L} \cup \mathcal{L}_h$, SP *is divergence free with respect to* $\mathcal{L}_h$ if the $TCSP$ process $[\![SP]\!]\backslash\mathcal{L}_h$ is not divergent.

Proposition 18 Given a process specification SP, with alphabet $\mathcal{L} \cup \mathcal{L}_h$, SP *is divergence free with respect to* $\mathcal{L}_h$ if there exist a SP-invariant Inv, and a *variant* integer expression Ω with free variables in $\mathcal{V}$, satisfying the following conditions:

1. $Inv \Rightarrow \Omega \geq 0$

2. $\forall e \in \mathcal{L}_h.Inv \wedge G_e \Rightarrow TR_e(\Omega) < \Omega$

for any values of state variables in $\mathcal{V}$.

Definition 19 Given two well-formed specifications $SPEC$ and IMP with $\mathcal{L}_h = \mathcal{L}_{imp} - \mathcal{L}_{spec}$, IMP *is an implementation of SPEC with respect to* $\mathcal{L}_h$ if:

1. IMP is divergence free with respect to $\mathcal{L}_h$

2. $SPEC \sqsubseteq IMP\backslash\mathcal{L}_h$

Definition 20 Given two well-formed specifications $SPEC$ and IMP, with $\mathcal{L}_h = \mathcal{L}_{imp} - \mathcal{L}_{spec}$, and given predicates $Spec(\mathcal{V}_{spec})$, $SPEC$-invariant, and $Imp(\mathcal{V}_{imp})$, IMP-invariant, the predicate ϕ with free variables in $\mathcal{V}_{spec} \cup \mathcal{V}_{imp}$, is an *abstraction relation* with respect to $SPEC$, IMP and $\mathcal{L}_h$if:

1. $\overline{\sigma}_0(\phi) = true$, with $\sigma_0 = \sigma_{0,spec} \cup \sigma_{0,imp}$

2. $\forall e \in \mathcal{L}_{spec}.Spec(\mathcal{V}_{spec}) \wedge Imp(\mathcal{V}_{imp}) \wedge G_e^{spec} \wedge G_e^{imp} \wedge \phi \Rightarrow TR_e(\phi)$ where:

$$TR_e = TR_{e,spec} \cup TR_{e,imp}$$

3. $\forall s \in \mathcal{L}_h.Spec(\mathcal{V}_{spec}) \wedge Imp(\mathcal{V}_{imp}) \wedge G_s^{imp} \wedge \phi \Rightarrow TR_s^{imp}(\phi)$

for any values of state variables in $\mathcal{V}_{spec}$ and $\mathcal{V}_{imp}$.

Proposition 21 Given well-formed specifications $SPEC$ and IMP, with $\mathcal{L}_h = \mathcal{L}_{imp} - \mathcal{L}_{spec}$, IMP is an implementation of $SPEC$ with respect to $\mathcal{L}_h$ if IMP is divergence free with respect to $\mathcal{L}_h$ and there are predicates $Spec(\mathcal{V}_{spec})$, $SPEC$-invariant, and $Imp(\mathcal{V}_{imp})$, IMP-invariant, and an abstraction relation ϕ with respect to $SPEC$, IMP and $\mathcal{L}_h$, satisfying the following conditions:

safety: $\forall e \in \mathcal{L}_{spec}.Spec(\mathcal{V}_{spec}) \wedge Imp(\mathcal{V}_{imp}) \wedge G_e^{imp} \wedge \phi \Rightarrow G_e^{spec}$

liveness: $Spec(\mathcal{V}_{spec}) \wedge Imp(\mathcal{V}_{imp}) \wedge Stable(\mathcal{V}_{imp}) \wedge \Phi \Rightarrow \mathbf{L}$
where $\mathbf{L}$ and $Stable$ are defined as

$$\mathbf{L} \stackrel{\triangle}{=} \forall L \in \mathbf{L}_{spec}.(L \neq \emptyset \Rightarrow \exists L' \in \mathbf{L}_{imp}.L' \neq \emptyset \wedge L' - \mathcal{L}_h \subseteq L)$$
$$Stable \stackrel{\triangle}{=} \forall L' \in \mathbf{L}_{imp}.(L' \neq \emptyset \Rightarrow L' - \mathcal{L}_h \neq \emptyset)$$

for any values of state variables in $\mathcal{V}_{spec}$ and $\mathcal{V}_{imp}$.

5 Parallel composition of process specifications

Once we have shown that the desired network exhibits the intended behaviour, we are in position to determine the specifications for the component subsystems. For every subsystem, the design process is resumed and new decisions are taken to define new refinements and, possibly, new implementations. Eventually, the whole system is constructed in a hierarchical way. To achieve this goal, parallel composition of specifications with state variables must be defined.

If we restrict our attention to deterministic processes, this is done in a straightforward way. In deterministic processes, liveness rules may be omitted since they are given by the guards. Also, state variables in every subsystem either evolve according to their own transition rules, or remain unchanged when the event is performed solely by the other subsystem. If they synchronize in one event, the guard of that event is obtained by the conjunction of the guards for that event in both subsystems. Otherwise, the guard is imported from the corresponding subsystem. These ideas are reflected in the following definition:

Definition 22 Given two deterministic specifications,

$$SP_1 = (\mathcal{L}_1, \mathcal{V}_1, \sigma_{0_1}, \mathbf{TR}_1, \mathbf{G}_1)$$
$$SP_2 = (\mathcal{L}_2, \mathcal{V}_2, \sigma_{0_2}, \mathbf{TR}_2, \mathbf{G}_2)$$

with disjoint sets of state variables, *the parallel composition of SP_1 and SP_2*, denoted by $SP_1 \| SP_2$, is given by the tuple, $(\mathcal{L}, \mathcal{V}, \sigma_0, \mathbf{TR}, \mathbf{G})$ where:

1. $\mathcal{L} = \mathcal{L}_1 \cup \mathcal{L}_2$

2. $\mathcal{V} = \mathcal{V}_1 \cup \mathcal{V}_2$

3. $\sigma_0 = \sigma_{0_1} \cup \sigma_{0_2}$

4. $\mathbf{TR}$ is the family of transition rules indexed by $\mathcal{L} \times \mathcal{V}$ and defined by:

$$E_{e,x} \stackrel{\Delta}{=} \begin{cases} E_{e,x}^1 & \text{if } e \in \mathcal{L}_1 \wedge x \in \mathcal{V}_1 \\ E_{e,x}^2 & \text{if } e \in \mathcal{L}_2 \wedge x \in \mathcal{V}_2 \\ x & \text{if } (e \notin \mathcal{L}_1 \wedge x \in \mathcal{V}_1) \vee (e \notin \mathcal{L}_2 \wedge x \in \mathcal{V}_2) \end{cases}$$

5. $\mathbf{G}$ is the family of deterministic guards indexed by $\mathcal{L}$ and defined by:

$$G(e) \stackrel{\Delta}{=} \begin{cases} G_1(e) & \text{if } e \in \mathcal{L}_1 - \mathcal{L}_2 \\ G_2(e) & \text{if } e \in \mathcal{L}_2 - \mathcal{L}_1 \\ G_1(e) \wedge G_2(e) & \text{if } e \in \mathcal{L}_1 \cap \mathcal{L}_2 \end{cases}$$

This tuple actually defines a deterministic specification.

Fact 23 Given two deterministic specifications SP_1 and SP_2, then

$$[\![SP_1 \| SP_2]\!] = [\![SP_1]\!] \| [\![SP_2]\!]$$

Using this definition we are in position to analyze some interesting parallel and distributed algorithms but it is worthwhile extending the above ideas to cover the most general situation, i.e. the composition of non-deterministic systems.

Unfortunately, the definition of the parallel composition of nondeterministic process specifications is rather cumbersome and not very useful. The authors have found more interesting in practice to have criteria to *decompose* a given specification, representing a complex system, into a number of smaller specifications in a such way that, composing in parallel these specifications, we get a behaviour identical to that of the complex system. The details cannot be given here due to lack of space. They can be found in [1].

6   Conclusions

A technique for the specification and verification of *TCSP* processes has been presented, establishing a method with a sound mathematical basis for the hierarchical development of communicating systems. The authors have extensively tried the method in a number of examples that cover distributed arbitration systems and other synchronization problems, like the dinning and drinking philosophers, or distributed message routing systems. For more details, interested readers are addressed again to [1].

References

[1] L.M. Alonso. *Técnicas formales para el desarrollo jerárquico de sistemas concurentes.* PhD thesis, Universidad del País Vasco, 1992.

[2] L.M. Alonso and R. Peña. Acceptance automata: a framework for specifying and verifying TCSP parallel systems. In E.H.L. Aarts, J. van Leeuwen, and M. Rem, editors, *PARLE'91: Parallel Architectures and Languages Europe*, pages 75–91, Springer-Verlag, 1991.

[3] L.M. Alonso and R. Peña. Using state variables for the specification and verification of TCSP processes. *Internal report DIA-UCM-92.3, Dep. Informática y Automática, Univ. Complutense de Madrid, Spain*, 1–26, 1992.

[4] J.A. Bergstra and J.W. Klop. Algebra of communicating processes with abstraction. *Theoretical Computer Science*, 37:77–121, 1985.

[5] S.D. Brookes. *A Model for Communicating Sequential Processes.* PhD thesis, Oxford University, 1983.

[6] S.D. Brookes, A.W. Roscoe, and C.A.R. Hoare. A theory for communicating sequential processes. *Journal of the ACM*, 31:560–599, 1984.

[7] M. Broy and M. Wirsing. Partial abstract types. *Acta Informatica*, 18:47–64, 1982.

[8] M. Hennessy. *Algebraic Theory of Processes.* MIT Press, London, 1989.

[9] C.A.R. Hoare. *Communicating Sequential Processes*. Prentice-Hall, London, 1985.

[10] C.A.R. Hoare. Proof of correctness of data representations. *Acta Informatica*, 1:271–281, 1972.

[11] H. Jifeng. Process simulation and refinement. *Formal Aspects of Computing*, 1:229–241, 1989.

[12] R. Milner. *A Calculus of Communicating Systems*. Volume 92 of *Lecture Notes in Computer Science*, Springer-Verlag, Berlin, 1980.

[13] R. Milner. *Communication and Concurrency*. Prentice-Hall, London, 1989.

[14] D. Park. Concurrency and automata on infinite sequences. In E.H.L. Aarts, J. van Leeuwen, and M. Rem, editors, *Proceedings 5th GI Conf. of Theoretical Computer Science*, pages 245–251, Springer-Verlag, 1981. Lecture Notes in Computer Science.

[15] R. Peña and L.M. Alonso. Specification and Verification of TCSP Systems by Means of Partial abstract Types. In J. Diaz; F. Orejas, editor, *TAPSOFT'89: Theory and Practice of Software Development, Vol. 2*, pages 328–344, Springer-Verlag, 1989. Lecture Notes in Computer Science no. 352.

Applications of Type Theory

Bernd Mahr

Fachbereich Informatik
Technische Universität Berlin

Abstract. The paper discusses the setting of type theory and proposes a uniform framework for disciplines of declarations and types. The framework combines fundamental concepts found in the setting of type theory and supports both its denotational and its constructive view. In the denotational view $\in$-structures are introduced as semantic models and in the constructive view the general forms of judgements and rules are given. Finally applications are discussed which build on the ideas of this framework, namely models of untyped λ-calculus which truly solve the equation of reflexive domains, and $\in_T$-logic, a first-order theory of propositions with selfreference and impredicative quantification allowing for intensional models of truth.

1 Introduction

Types and typing not only apply in the foundations of mathematics (see Russell [Ru 08] and Martin-Löf [ML 84]) and the study of functions and propositions (see Church [Ch 40], Curry and Feys [CF 58], Girard [Gi 71] and Howard [Ho 69]), but, equally important, also in correctness of programs (see Reynolds [Re 74] and Milner [Mi 78]), formal specification and programming (see Martin-Löf [ML 80] and Nordström [No 81], [NPS 90]), terminological modelling (see [BHR 90] for an overview) and in the constructive foundation of functional programming (see Thompson [Th 91] for example).

The notion of type has no rigid definition. It is intentional by nature and has a fixed meaning only in the context of a given discipline, formalism or system. As such, types may be indices, sorts, categories, kinds, sets, domains, propositions, specifications and the like. Types always indicate some form of classification, and typing - the attachment of types to entities - provides type information that can be used for control in building expressions and formation of concepts, for verification of well-formedness and consistency, in specification and in the declaration of ontologies and truth.

Though types and typing have various forms and uses, there is a common underlying setting which we call the *setting of type theory*. In the following we discuss this setting and applications in it, and derive a unified *framework for declaration and type disciplines*.

2 Type Propositions

The origins of type theory date back to ancient philosophy and to the still vivid question whether all objects are of one kind or not, i.e. that "there are properties which can be meaningfully predicated of certain objects but not of others" (see [FBL 84] p 188 ff). Though there are many formalizations and formalisms based on concepts like kind, class, category or type (as geometry distinguishes points, lines and planes, and logic distinguishes orders of predication), untyped languages are still in favor for their orthogonality and self-similarity properties (like LISP and some object oriented languages for example).

Russell used typing in [Ru 08] to avoid impredicative set formation (i.e. the set to be defined appears in the range of a quantifier that is used to define that set). By attaching indices to variables which indicate a certain level in the hierarchy of sets and by restricting membership and quantification accordingly, he ruled out antinomies that were found in naive set theory. As a consequence the paradoxical, $S = \{x \mid x \notin x\}$ which satisfies $S \in S \longleftrightarrow S \notin S$ and therefore contradicts Cantors conception that it be determined whether or not an object is a member of a given set, can no longer be expressed.

Other approaches to solve the foundational problems of mathematics have later made use of this idea of hierarchical types. For its naturalness Church introduced in [Ch 40] simply typed λ-calculus with typed variables, abstractions and applications

$$x^a$$
$$(E^a \longrightarrow {}^bF^a)^b$$
$$(\lambda x^a E^b)^a \longrightarrow b$$

for any type expressions of the form a, b and a → b.

With similar motivations Herbrand had earlier introduced sorts into first order logic [He 30], which was later extended to subsorts, and was adopted in universal algebra by Higgins [Hi 63], leading to the notion of heterogeneous or many-sorted algebra, which focus the basic concept of algebraic specification (see [EM 85] for example).

Common in these cases of introducing types into a formalism is, that formation of expressions becomes restricted by type constraints. An expression in the typed formalism therefore contains type information, be it explicitly stated or implicit in the property of well-formedness. This type information in expressions creates a fragment of their meaning.

However, different in these cases is the effect the introduction of types has on the formalism's expressive power: Untyped first order logic is equivalent to many-sorted first order logic, which was already shown by Herbrand. Many-sorted algebra with equational specifications is more powerful than unsorted algebra. Russell's Type Theory is obviously restricting naive set theory, and so is simply typed λ-calculus less powerful than untyped λ-calculus (it actually forms a decidable theory of total functions that have at most superexponential complexity).

Fundamental in the setting of type theory is the notion of *type proposition*. A type proposition provides type information and is written uniformly as

$$a : A$$

with a and A being *expressions*. In the locality of a given type proposition we call the expression a an *entity* and the expression A its *type*.

A type proposition is a proposition and therefore may be found or declared to be true or false. A type proposition has one or more *readings*. These readings articulate certain *interpretations* which are substantiated either by the *rules of a type system* in which the particular type proposition is admissible, or by the meaning of the type proposition in some *model*. Both ways, which actually belong to different views on formalization and mathematics, give semantics to the formal expression of a type proposition.

For example:

In the type proposition

$$5 : nat$$

5 may denote an element of the set of natural numbers denoted by nat. This type proposition makes an assertion about 5 (rather than nat) and has an obvious modeltheoretic interpretation.

In the type proposition

$$f{:}A \rightarrow B$$

A and B may denote sets and $A \rightarrow B$ may denote the set of functions from the set denoted by A to the set denoted by B. Again there is an obvious modeltheoretic interpretation. Another reading could be to regard A and B as propositions and $A \rightarrow B$ as an implication in intuitionistic logic. Then f represents a proof for $A \rightarrow B$ which is a method to construct from every proof for A a proof for B. While this reading does not have an obvious appropriate modeltheoretic interpretation, it is typical for type systems based on the 'Curry-Howard-Isomorphism', which stands for the concept of 'propositions as types', that these systems support with their rules both readings: $A \rightarrow B$ denoting the function space and $A \rightarrow B$ expressing a proposition.

Similarily with the type proposition

$$(w, p) : (\exists\, x{:}A.P(x))$$

which can be regarded as the assertion that the type ∃ x:A.P(x) which is the sum of types P(x), indexed over the entities of A is inhabited and therefore exists, and at the same time as the assertion that the proposition ∃ x:A.P(x) is provable and has the pair (w, p) consisting of a witness w for the quantifier and a proof p for P(w) as a proof (see [Th 91] for example).

Finally, in the type proposition

$$a : true$$

the focus is on the attachment of the type true to the entity a. A possible reading is to say that a denotes a proposition which is a member of the set of all true propositions denoted by true. This reading can indeed be supported by an appropriate modeltheoretic interpretation (see [Str 92]).

3   The Constructive View

Constructive mathematics and intuitionism have a major influence in type theory. They constitute, as we call it, *the constructive view* in the setting of type theory. The meaning of type propositions under this constructive view is declared by the rules of a type system, which determine what type propositions exist and how they are to be handled.

Simply typed λ-calculus is a first and good example. Moreover, it is the starting point for a great number of systems which have been designed for various purposes: to obtain a powerful theory of total functions which is decidable, to formalize type inference in programming, to support the reading of 'propositions as types' in a constructive theory of propositions, or to provide a constructive foundation to mathematics, that is consistent. Among these systems is the system F by Girard [Gi 71] which extends simply typed λ-calculus to second order typed λ-calculus allowing quantifications over type variables. A similar system was independently invented by Reynolds to "permit the definition of polymorphic procedures" in typed programming languages (see [Re 74]). Other systems are intuitionistic type theory by Martin-Löf (see [ML 71] and [ML 84]) and the calculus of constructions by Coquand and Huet (see [Co 85] and [CH 88]).

Most of these systems are built under the paradigm of 'proposition as types' and therefore not only support the dual reading of type propositions, but can also be seen as constructive theories of propositions. Understanding propositions as types was first exhibited by Curry and Howard (see [CF 58] and [Ho 69]) and then developed further by many authors (see Barendregt [Ba 90] for a summary of results). The idea of propositions as types originates in the similarities between the building-rules for typed λ-abstraction and application in simply typed λ-calculus on one side, and the rules for introduction and elimination of → in natural deduction systems of propositional logic (see Gentzen [Ge 69]) on the other.

The setting of type theory under the constructive view is based on rules and calculi which control the building of expressions and type propositions *(construction)*, which determine what type propositions can be stated *(declaration)*, and what type propositions can be inferred from others *(inference)*. Rules, in this context, are sets of *judgements* (see [ML 84]) in which one judgement is distinguished *(conclusion)* from the others *(premisses)*. The judgements of a rule usually have a certain *form* that is characteristic for the system in which this rule occurs.

Fundamental questions in the setting of type theory under the constructive view are consistency, existence of principal types, and normalization properties, which concern the expressive power of a system. Still under discussion is the question, whether or not *impredicativity* in type propositions should be admissible. While Russell's type theory and simply typed λ-calculus excluded impredicativity, second order typed λ-calculus, Martin-Löf's first system, and the calculus of constructions admitted impredicativity by quantification over propositions. In combination with a universal type 'type' (which is inhabited by itself, i.e. type:type is true) Martin-Löfs first system is inconsistent. In intuitionistic type theory impredicativity is therefore excluded. On the other hand, it seems meaningful to allow for impredicativity in the propositional fragment of a type system, since it is not by itself a source for inconsistency and occurs naturally if not banned (see also Luo [Luo 90]).

4 The Denotational View

Tarskis perception of semantics is to provide meaning to syntactic objects by giving models in which these objects can be interpreted. Since type propositions are expressed by syntactic objects, a modeltheoretic interpretation requires appropriate mathematical structures which allow to capture their underlying intention. While this is obvious in the case of the simply typed λ-calculus, for example, in which every expression can be interpreted as a total function of a kind expressed in the expression's type, it is less trivial for other type systems and may even lead back to the foundational problems of mathematics in which circularity was discarded for reasons of consistency. Furthermore, the question of what we want to accept as a model of a type system has not clearly been answered yet. It is discussed in [Mey 82] for the untyped λ-calculus, but has been revised again for type calculi (see the discussion of this topic in the various contributions of [Hue 90]).

Fundamental in the setting of type theory under the denotational view is *the interpretation of a type proposition as a certain relationship* that holds between the interpretation of its entity on one side and of its type expression on the other i.e. the equation

$$[\![\,a{:}A\,]\!] = [\![\,a\,]\!] \; [\![:]\!] \; [\![A]\!]$$

The actual nature of $[\![\,a\,]\!]$, $[\![A]\!]$ and $[\![:]\!]$ is determined by the model in which these items are defined. $[\![:]\!]$ is in any case a binary relationship that is usually uniformly understood as some kind of *"membership"*. The relations between the expression a and the object $[\![\,a\,]\!]$ and between A and

⟦A⟧ depends, at least in most of the familiar uses on the structure of a and A. This dependency can appropriately be expressed by *"denotational constraints"* which formulate the conditions to hold for ⟦a⟧ and ⟦A⟧ as interpretations of a and A respectively.

For example, the expression f(a) which is obtained by application of the function symbol f to the argument expression a, has the denotational constraint C(f(a)) which requires that

"⟦f(a)⟧ is the result of applying the function ⟦f⟧ to the argument ⟦a⟧ "

In many formalisms with modeltheoretic semantics, like algebra or logic for example, these denotational constraints are implicit in the archetecture of the formalism (signature, term structure, algebraic structure, evaluation homomorphism).

5 A Framework for Declaration and Type Disciplines under the Denotational View

The components we have identified as fundamental in the setting of type theory can now be combined into a uniform framework. This framework provides under the denotational view general concepts for model theoretic semantics of type propositions and declarations, and fixes under the constructive view the forms of rules which control construction, declaration and inference of type propositions.

The focus of this framework is on the notion of type proposition and declaration, where declarations are sets of type propositions. Following the basic observation that modeltheoretic semantics has to provide an interpretation of type propositions, the framework avoids to use signatures as classifiers for structures and instead models the attachement of a type proposition; namely, if a:A is a type proposition, ⟦a:A⟧ represents a pair

$$(⟦a⟧, ⟦A⟧)$$

of objects from the domain in which expressions are evaluated, where the evaluation of expressions obeys the denotational constraints associated with the expressions. Signature information, however, is not discarded , but is coded in type propositions and denotational constraints like any other informations that appears in a declaration.

More formally we define the following:

An $\in$-*structure* $M = (M, \in)$ consists of a nonempty set M of objects and a binary relation on M.

By $\in$-*logic* we refer to classical first order logic with equality and a single binary predicate $\in$. Atomic $\in$-formulas are of the form $x = y$ or $x \in y$ for variables x and y (note, this logic is customary for axiomatic set theory, see Quine [Qu 63] for example, and $\in$-structures are the natural interpretations of $\in$-formulas).

A *declaration* or *type discipline*

$$D = (\text{Expr, C, Decl})$$

then consists of

- Expr   a set of entities, called *expressions*
- $C : \text{Expr} \longrightarrow \in\text{-Form (Expr)}$ a mapping which assigns to each expression an $\in$-formula over the set of expressions as variables, called *denotational constraint*.
- Decl   a class of sets of type propositions e:E with e and E being expressions in Expr; Decl is called the class of *admissible declarations*

Given a discipline $D = (\text{Expr, C, Decl})$ and an admissible declaration $\Delta \in \text{Decl}$, let $\text{Expr}(\Delta)$ be the set of all expressions $e \in \text{Expr}$ which either occur in the type propositions of Δ or in their denotational constraints , and let $(M, \in)$ be an arbitrary $\in$-structure, and

$$[\![\ ]\!] : \text{Expr} \longrightarrow M$$

be such that

- $((M, \in), [\![\ ]\!]) \models C(e)$
  for all expressions e in $\text{Expr}(\Delta)$
- $((M, \in), [\![\ ]\!]) \models a \in A$
  for all type propositions a:A in Δ

then $((M, \in), [\![\ ]\!])$ is a *model of* Δ.

The notion of a discipline together with its modeltheoretic semantics is very general. It turns out that about all known declaration and type disciplines can be "reconstructured" in this framework in a uniform way. In addition, even new disciplines can be designed which allow for circularity like selfreference and selfapplication. The following simple example might illustrate the style of semantics typical for $\in$-structures.

Take as a declaration Δ in some suitable discipline D the following

$$\text{id} : A \longrightarrow A$$
$$\text{id} : A$$
$$x : A$$
$$(\text{id}(x) = x) : \text{true}$$

which can be interpreted as declaring a self-applicable identity function id. Assume, that the discipline D implies the following denotational constraints:

$C(A \longrightarrow A) \equiv$ "A $\longrightarrow$ A is the set of all functions from A to A"

$C(\text{true}) \equiv$ "the only member of true is T"

$C(\text{id}(x)) \equiv$ "id(x) is the unique object y such that $(x, y) \in$ id"

$C(x = y) \equiv$ "x and y are equal"

and for all other expressions in Δ, namely x, id, and A, the denotational constraints are void, i.e. of the form x = x for some variable x (note, that these constraints can be expressed in $\in$-logic). Then the following $\in$-structure $(M, \in)$, represented by the graph

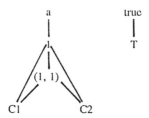

with $[\![\ ]\!]$ assigning

$[\![\ \text{id}\ ]\!] = 1$
$[\![\ A\ ]\!] = a$
$[\![\ A \longrightarrow A\ ]\!] = a$
$[\![\ x\ ]\!] = 1$
$[\![\ \text{id}(x) = x\ ]\!] = T$
$[\![\ \text{TRUE}\ ]\!] = \text{true}$

is a model of Δ, in which 1 is indeed the selfapplicable identity, seen as a set of pairs, with pairs coded after Kuratowski (see [MSU 90]) .

$\in$-structures form a theory of non-wellfounded sets similar to the one given by Aczel in [Acz 88]. A major difference, however, is the fact that objects in an $\in$-structure, which are regarded as sets, are not identified with their extension, but instead have an extension only associated. Accordingly, the axiom of extension is not valid, if not explicitly required, and the possibility of circles is not ruled out. The exact relationship between $\in$-sets and Aczel-sets has been studied by Sträter [Str 92a] where it is shown that, roughly speaking, every Aczel set can be obtained as a quotient of an $\in$-set, factorized by the strongest extension conform equivalence relation (which is closely related to bisimulation).

The set theoretic interpretation of objects in $\in$-structures not only leads to a new set theory in which sets are viewed as collections of "statements of memberships", but also allows for semantic models with circularity properties, not constructible under conventional set theory like ZF. Such models have not only been constructed for investigating modeltheoretic semantics in natural language processing, but also for untyped λ-calculus.

In [Po 92] the idea of selfapplicable functions, which is already in the above example, is used to define $\in$-structures which contain objects, say D, that solve the domain equation

$$D = (D \longrightarrow D)$$

for some set of functions from D to D correctly, while regarding functions in a conventional way as sets of ordered pairs. Based on this conception, an environment model of the λ-calculus is defined which, under an appropriate notion of homomorphism, is initial in the class of all generated models.

6 A Framework for Declaration and Type Disciplines under the Constructive View

What we accept as an admissible declaration in a discipline D = (Expr, C, Decl) is only listed in the class Decl. But in most of the known declaration and type disciplines declarations satisfy internal completeness and consistency conditions and are constructable from inductive definitions (signature, terms, axioms, specifications). Following the setting of type theory under the constructive view, we use rules in this framework for the design of declarations. Such *rules have the following general form.*

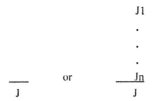

with J, J1, ..., Jn being judgements. Proofs and derivations are conventionally defined and give rise to the notion of *consequence*

$$R \triangleright J$$

where R is a set of rules and J is a judgement that can be derived using the rules of R. *Judgements* are uniformly assumed to *have one of the following forms*:

c ident   (construction)

$\triangle$ decl   (declaratios)

$\triangle$ ⊩ a:A   (construction)

$\triangle$ ⊢ a:A   (inference)

This choice of forms is motivated from the observation that rules in the setting of type theory under the constructive view generally fulfill one of the tasks: construction, declaration or inference. Furthermore, we can restrict ourselves to type propositons as the only entity which creates judgements (note, that the judgements c ident and $\triangle$ decl are actually type propositions, just written differently). The particular choice of rules and judgements appropriate for a particular discipline does very much depend on the underlying intention. But generally, if a *judgement of declaration,*$\triangle$ decl, is made, $\triangle$ is assumed to be a declaration, i.e. a set of type propositions. The *judgement of construction,* $\triangle$ ⊩ a:A, expresses that there is enough information in $\triangle$ to construct a:A. The *judgement of inference,* $\triangle$ ⊢ a:A , expresses that the type proposition a:A is a consequence of $\triangle$, thereby assuming that every model of $\triangle$ is also a model of a:A. We can now say that a discipline D = (Expr, C, Decl) is *constructive*, if a set of rules R exists such that for every $\triangle \in$ Decl we have R ▷ $\triangle$ decl.

The following set of rules, to give a simple example, allows to derive algebraic signatures

$$\frac{\qquad\qquad}{c\ ident}$$ (introducing an identifier)

$$\frac{\qquad\qquad}{\varnothing\ decl}$$ (introducing the empty declaration)

$$\frac{\triangle \Vdash e:E}{\triangle \cup \{e:E\}\ decl}$$ (building of declarations)

$$\frac{\triangle \Vdash e:E}{\triangle \cup \{f:F\}\ decl}$$
$$\triangle \cup \{f:F\} \Vdash e:E$$ (monotonicity of construction)

$$\frac{\triangle\ decl}{s\ ident}$$
$$\triangle \Vdash s : sort$$ (constructing a sort)

$$\frac{c\ ident}{\triangle \Vdash s : sort}$$
$$\triangle \Vdash c : s$$ (constructing a constant)

Γ ident

$\Delta \Vdash s1 : sort$

$\underline{\Delta \Vdash sn+1 : sort}$

$\Delta \Vdash f : s1...sn \longrightarrow sn+1$ (constructing an n-ary operation symbol)

In [MSU 90] further rules are given which allow for the construction of algebraic specifications and the inference of equational logic.

Constructive disciplines are usually more liberal than those defined in conventional ways, which is due to the fact that in this framework there are no means to produce information that restricts the use of identifiers.

A so called *standard discipline* has been designed in [Um 91] which is presently under revision. It includes logic, set theoretic operators and functions. Based on this discipline, an implementation of this framework, called *calculus of declarations*, has been given in [BD 91].

A major investigation has been made in a discipline of first order propositions in Sträters thesis [Str 92], which leads to a theory of truth with total truth predicates. This theory, called $\in$ T-logic, allows for self reference, like the liar paradox

$$(x = (x : false)) : true$$

and impredicative quantification over propositions. Both, self reference and impredicativity appear naturally if intensional equality (proposition x says the same as proposition y) and quantification are admitted. A complete calculus for this logic is given and, based on the ideas of $\in$-structures, noncyclic extensional and intensional models are constructed which satisfy the Tarski biconditionals (expressing that a proposition about the model that is true is also true in the model, and vice versa) thereby proving the conjecture, ascribed to Tarski, false that such models with total truth predicates can not be built.

References

[Acz 88]   Aczel, P.: Non-Wellfounded Sets, CSLI Lecture Notes 14, 1988

[Ba 90]   Barendregt, H.: Introduction to Generalized Type Systems, Tech. Report 90-8, Univ. of Nijmegen, 1990.

[BD 91]   Ballmann, S., Dunker, G.: Entwurf und Implementierung für den Kalkül getypter Deklarationen, students thesis, Fachbereich 20, TU Berlin 1991

[BHR 90]   Bläsius, K.H., Hedtstück, U., Rollinger, C.R. (eds): Sorts and Types in Artificial Intelligence, LNAI 418, Springer, 1990

354

[CF 58]	Curry, H.B., Feys, R.: Combinatory Logic, North Holland, 1958
[Ch 40]	Church, A.: A formulation of the simple Theory of Types, J. Symb. Log. 5, 1940, 56-68
[CH 88]	Coquand, Th., Huet, G.: The Calculus of Constructions, Information and Computation 76, 2/3, 1988, 95-120
[Co 85]	Coquand, Th.: Une théorie des constructions, Thèse, Université Paris VII, 1985
[EM 85]	Ehrig, H., Mahr, B.: Fundamentals of Algebraic Specification 1, Springer-Verlag, 1985
[FBL 84]	Fraenkel, A.A., Bar-Hillel, Y., Levy, A.: Foundations of Set Theory, North-Holland, 1984
[Ge 69]	Gentzen, G.: The collected Papers of Gerhard Gentzen. ed E. Szabo, North Holland, 1969
[Gi 71]	Girard, J.Y.: Une extension de l'interprétation de Gödel à l'analyse et son application à l'élimination des conpures dans l'analyse et dans le théorie des types, Proc. of the Zud Scandinavian Logic Symposium (ed. J.E. Fenstad), North Holland, 1971, 63-92
[He 30]	Herbrand, J.: Investigations in Proof Theory (1930) in: Logical Writings, ed. W.D. Goldfarb, Reidel, 1971
[Hi 63]	Higgins, P.J.: Algebra with a scheme of operators, Mathematische Nachrichten, Z7, 1963, 115 - 132
[Ho 69]	Howard, W.A.: The formulae-as-Types notion of construction, in: To H.B. Curry: Essays on Combinatory Logic, Lambda Calculus and Formalism, ed. J.P. Seldin and J.R. Hindley, Academic Press, 1980, 479-490
[Luo 90]	Luo, Z.: An Extended Calculus of Constructions, Dept. of Comp. Science, Univ. of Edinburgh, 1990
[Mey 82]	Meyer, A.R.: What is a model of Lambda Calculus? in: Information and Control 52, 1982, 87-122
[Mi 78]	Milner, R.: A Theory of Type Polymorphism in Programming, J.C.S.S. 17, 1978, 384-375
[ML 71]	Martin-Löf, P.: A Theory of Types, Report 71-3, Dept. of Math., Univ. of Stockholm, 1971
[ML 80]	Martin-Löf, P.: Constructive Mathematics and Computer Programming, Logic, Methodology and Philosophy of Science 6, 1980, 153-175
[ML 84]	Martin-Löf, P.: Intuitionistic Type Theory, Bibliopolis, 1984
[MSU 90]	Mahr, B., Sträter, W., Umbach, C.: Fundamentals of a Theory of Types and Declarations, KIT-Report 82, TU Berlin, Fachbereich 20, 1990
[No 81]	Nordström, B.: Programming in Constructive Set Theory: Some Examples. Proc. ACM Conf. of Funct. Prog. Lang. and Comp. Arch., ACM, 1981, 141-154
[NPS 90]	Nordström, B., Petersson, K., Smith, J.M.: Programming in Martin-Löfs` Type Theory, Clarendon Press, 1990
[Po 92]	Pooyan, L.: ∈−structures as Semantic Models of the λ-calculus, Diploma Thesis, Fachbereich Informatik, TU Berlin, 1992

[Qu 63]   Quine, W.O.: Mengenlehre und ihre Logik, Vieweg, 1973, First published in 1963

[Re 74]   Reynolds, J.C.: Towards a Theory of Type Structure, LNCS 19, Springer-Verlag, 1974, 408-425

[Ru 08]   Russell, B.: Mathematical Logic as based on the theory of types, Am. J. Math. 30, 1908, 222 - 262

[Str 92]   Sträter, W.: $\in_T$ Eine Logik erster Stufe mit Selbstreferenz und totalem Wahrheitsprädikat, KIT-Report 98, TU Berlin, Fachbereich 20, 1992

[Str 92a]   Sträter, W.: Internal notes on non wellfounded sets, Fachbereich 20, TU Berlin, 1992

[Th 91]   Thompson, S.: Type Theory and Functional Programming, Addison-Wesley, 1991

[Um 91]   Umbach, C.: A standard discipline in the calculus of declarations, Internal notes, Fachbereich 20, TU Berlin, 1991

Feature Automata and Recognizable Sets of Feature Trees

Joachim Niehren* and Andreas Podelski

German Research Center for Artificial Intelligence (DFKI)
Stuhlsatzenhausweg 3, 6600 Saarbrücken 11, Germany
niehren@dfki.uni-sb.de

Digital Equipment Corporation, Paris Research Laboratory (PRL)
85, Avenue Victor Hugo, 92563 Rueil-Malmaison, France
podelski@prl.dec.com

Abstract. Feature trees generalize first-order trees whereby argument positions become keywords ("features") from an infinite symbol set $\mathcal{F}$. Constructor symbols can occur with any argument positions, in any finite number. Feature trees are used to model flexible records; the assumption on the infiniteness of $\mathcal{F}$ accounts for dynamic record field updates.

We develop a universal algebra framework for feature trees. We introduce the classical set-defining notions: automata, regular expressions and equational systems, and show that they coincide. This extension of the regular theory of trees requires new notions and proofs. Roughly, a feature automaton reads a feature tree in two directions: along its branches and along the fan-out of each node.

We illustrate the practical motivation of our regular theory of feature trees by pointing out an application on the programming language LIFE.

1 Introduction

In this section, we will give some background and motivation ("the task") and then outline the rest of the paper ("the method").

The Task. We describe a specific formalism of data structures called feature trees. They are a generalization of first-order trees, also called constructor trees or the elements of the Herbrand universe. Since trees have been useful, *e.g.*, for structuring data in modern symbolic programming languages like Prolog and ML, this gives the more flexible feature trees an interesting potential. Precisely, feature trees model record structures. They form the semantics of record calculi like [AK86], which are used in symbolic programming languages [AKP91b] and in computational linguistics (*cf.*, the book [Car92]). In the logical framework for record structures of [BS92], they constitute the interpretation of a completely axiomatizable, and hence decidable, first-order theory.

As graphs, feature trees are easily described as finite trees whose nodes are labeled by constructor symbols, and whose edges are labeled by feature symbols, all those edges outgoing from the same node by different ones. Thus, symbolic keywords called features

---

* partially supported by Graduierten-Kolleg Informatik der Universität des Saarlandes.

denote the possible argument positions of a node. They access uniquely the node's direct subtrees. All constructor symbols can label a node with any features attached to it, in any, though finite, number.

Although thoroughly investigated [AK86, Smo92, BS92, AKPS92], also in comparison with first-order trees [ST92], feature trees have never been characterized as composable elements in an algebraic structure, *i.e.*, with operations defined on them. Also, up to now, there has been no corresponding notion of automata. This device has generally proven useful for dealing efficiently with systems calculating over sets of elements.

In our case, the practical motivation consists of the possibility of defining a hierarchy of types denoting sets of feature trees, as a Boolean lattice. For its use in a logical programming system employing feature trees such as LIFE [AKP91b], we need to compute efficiently the intersection of two types (roughly, for unification). Concurrent systems, in connection with control mechanisms such as residuation or guards [AKP91a], require furthermore an efficient test of the subset relation (matching). Thus, we need to provide a formalism defining the types in a way which is expressive enough and yet keeps the two problems decidable. Such a formalism can be given, for example, as a system of equations and a corresponding automata notion with Boolean closure properties and decidable emptyness problem.

A major difficulty of an algebraic framework for feature trees[2] comes from the fact that the set $\mathcal{F}$ of features, *i.e.*, of possible argument positions of a node accessing its direct subtrees, is infinite. The infiniteness of $\mathcal{F}$ is, however, an essential ingredient of the formal frameworks modeling flexible record structures. A practical motivation is the need to account for dynamic record field updates. It turns out that this semantical point of view has advantages in efficiency as well. Namely, the correctness of the algorithms for entailment and for solving negated constraints on feature trees [AKPS92] relies on the infiniteness of $\mathcal{F}$.

The Method. The first step in solving the problem described above is to build an appropriate algebraic framework. Such a framework is provided by universal algebra in the case of first-order trees. Formally, these are the elements of the free algebra over a given signature of function symbols (finite or infinite, *cf.*, [Mah88]). This framework yields immediately a "good" notion of automata.

In fact, as Courcelle has shown in [Cou89, Cou92], universal algebra provides a framework for a rich variety of trees. Clearly, it is that work that inspired our notion of the algebra underlying feature trees. We introduce this notion in Section 2. Informally speaking, the operation composing feature trees in the algebra takes a record value and adds a record field containing another value to it. In a special case, this amounts to Nivat's notion of 'sum of trees' [Niv92]; thus, incidentally, we obtain an algebraic formalization hereof.

To define feature automata as algebras, it is useful to consider the class of all finite trees whose nodes are labeled by constructor symbols, and whose edges are labeled by feature symbols. We call these multitrees.[3] Multitrees are of interest on their own, namely for representation of knowledge with set-valued attributes [Rou88]. Thus, feature trees are

---

[2] ... with the property that automata and equational systems coincide (let us note that the expressiveness of tree automata is equal to the one of equational systems for the free term algebras over finite signatures; it is strictly weaker in the case of infinite signatures for all tree species, also those considered in [Cou89, Cou92])

[3] The unranked unordered trees studied in [Cou89] (the number of arguments of the nodes is not

multitrees with the restriction that features are "functional," *i.e.*, all edges outgoing from the same node are labeled with different features. Feature automata recognize languages of multitrees, which are then cut down to recognize languages of feature trees.

In Section 3, we will define feature automata and show the basic properties of this notion: closure under the Boolean operations and decidability of the emptyness problem. In order to restrict our study to finitely presentable automata and yet to account for the infiniteness of the set of features $\mathcal{F}$, we introduce the notion of a **finitary automaton**: the number of states is finite, and the evaluation of the automaton can be specified not only on single symbols, but also on finite sets or on complements of finite sets of symbols. Thus, say: on f for $f \in F$, or: on f for $f \notin F$, where $F \subseteq \mathcal{F}$ finite.

Roughly, a feature automaton reads a feature tree in two directions: along its branches (from the frontier to the root) and along the fan-out of each node (along all argument positions). This is necessary in order to account for the flexibility in the depth as well as in the out-degree of the nodes of feature trees. The first direction is standard for all automata over trees. In order to study its behavior in the latter direction, or what we call the local structure of the recognized language, we consider recognizable sets of feature trees of depth 1, called flat feature trees.

In Section 4, we define a class of logical formulas, called **counting constraints**. The name comes from the fact that they express threshold- or modulo counting of the subtrees which are accessed via features from a finite or co-finite set of features.

The main technical result of this paper is a theorem saying that counting constraints characterize exactly the recognizable sets of flat feature trees. The proof takes up Sections A and B. The theorem essentially links counting and the finitary-condition; in all of the set-defining devices presented here, either of these two notions accounts for the infiniteness of $\mathcal{F}$.

Counting constraints can express that certain features exist in the flat feature tree (labeling edges from the root), and that others do not.[4] As a consequence, one can show that the set of first-order trees, with fixed arity assigned to constructor symbols, and recognizable subsets of these, are sets recognized by feature automata.

In Sections 5 and 6 we give two alternative ways to define recognizable sets of feature trees which are more practical than automata: regular expressions and equational systems. In the first one, the sets are constructed by union, substitution and star (and, optionally, complement or intersection). In the second, they are defined as solutions of equations in a certain form. For both, counting constraints can be used to define the base cases. Thanks to the main theorem in Section 4, we are able to show that either class of defined sets is equal to the one for feature automata. Moreover, the devices can be effectively translated one into another. These results, together with the previous ones, are necessary to present a complete regular theory of feature trees and to offer a solution to the practical problem of computing with types denoting sets of feature trees as described above.

---

restricted, and the arguments are not ordered) are a special case of multitrees, namely with just one feature. In the framework of [Cou89], however, recognizability by automata is strictly weaker than definability by equational systems, even if the set of node labels is finite.

[4] In [ST92, Smo92], these correspond to the constraints xF, $xf{\downarrow}$ or their negations, where $F \subseteq \mathcal{F}$ finite and $f \in \mathcal{F}$.

2 The Algebra $\mathcal{J}$

In this section we will introduce feature trees and the more general multitrees as elements of an algebra that we define, called $\mathcal{J}$. This yields the notion of a $\mathcal{J}$-automaton. This section follows the approach of [Cou89] and [Cou92].

In the following we will assume a given set $\mathcal{S}$ of constructor symbols (also called sorts, referred to by A, B, etc.) and a given set $\mathcal{F}$ of feature symbols (also called attributes, or record field selectors, referred to by f, g, etc.).

Formally, **multitrees** are trees (*i.e.*, finite directed acyclic rooted graphs) whose nodes are labeled over $\mathcal{S}$, and whose edges are labeled over $\mathcal{F}$. Or, the set $\mathcal{MT}$ of multitrees over $\mathcal{S}$ and $\mathcal{F}$ can be introduced as $\mathcal{MT} = \bigcup_{n \geq 0} \mathcal{MT}_n$ where (let $\mathbb{N}$ denote the set of all natural numbers, and $\mathbb{N}^M_{finite}$ the set of finite multisets with elements from the set M):

$$\mathcal{MT}_0 = \{(A, \emptyset) \mid A \in \mathcal{S}\},$$
$$\mathcal{MT}_n = \{(A, E) \mid A \in \mathcal{S}, E \in \mathbb{N}^{\mathcal{F} \times \mathcal{MT}_{n-1}}_{finite}\} \cup \mathcal{MT}_{n-1}.$$

$\mathcal{MT}_n$ contains the multitrees of depth $\leq n$.

Feature trees are multitrees such that all edges outgoing from the same node are labeled by different features. $\mathcal{FT}$ denote the set of all feature trees (and $\mathcal{FT}_n$ all those of depth $\leq n$).

We introduce two sorts MT and F for multitrees and features, respectively, and define the $\{MT, F\}$-sorted signature:
$$\Sigma = \{\Rightarrow\} \uplus \mathcal{F} \uplus \mathcal{S}$$
where $\Rightarrow$ is a function symbol of profile: $MT \times F \times MT \mapsto MT$, and the symbols in $\mathcal{F}$ and $\mathcal{S}$ are constants of sort F and of sort MT, respectively.

The **algebra of multitrees** $\mathcal{J}$ is defined as a Σ-algebra. Its two domains are $D_{MT} = \mathcal{MT}$ and $D_F = \mathcal{F}$ of the sorts MT and F, respectively. The function symbol $\Rightarrow$ is interpreted in $\mathcal{J}$ as the operation which composes two multitrees t, $t' \in \mathcal{MT}$ via a feature $f \in \mathcal{F}$ to a new multitree composed of t and t' with an edge labeled f from the root of t to the root of t'. Or (where $\sqcup$ denotes multiset union),

$$\Rightarrow^{\mathcal{J}} ((A, E), f, t) = (A, E \sqcup \{(f, t)\}).$$

Borrowing the 'tree sum' notation from [Niv92], we might write $\Rightarrow^{\mathcal{J}} (t, f, t')$ more intuitively as $t + ft'$. In fact, for the special case where $\mathcal{F} = \{1, 2\}$ (the two features denoting left and right successors), we obtain an algebraic reading of the notation of [Niv92].

The interpretation of the constants is given by $f^{\mathcal{J}} = f$ and $A^{\mathcal{J}} = (A, \emptyset)$.

It is easy to verify that the algebra $\mathcal{J}$ satisfies the **order independence** (OIT), *i.e.*, the following equation is valid in $\mathcal{J}$.

$$\Rightarrow (\Rightarrow (x, f_1, x_1), f_2, x_2) = \Rightarrow (\Rightarrow (x, f_2, x_2), f_1, x_1) \tag{1}$$

In the 'tree sum' notation this expresses the commutativity[5] of +, in the sense that $t + f_1 t_1 + f_2 t_2 = t + f_2 t_2 + f_1 t_1$. Of course, always $t + f_1 t_1 + f_2 t_2 \neq t + f_1 (t_1 + f_2 t_2)$.

We use T_Σ to denote the free algebra of terms over the signature Σ.

---

[5] In a sense which can be made formal (*cf.*, Section A), also the associativity holds for +; this justifies dropping the parenthesis.

Lemma 1. *The algebra of multitrees $\mathcal{J}$ is isomorphic to the quotient of the free term algebra over Σ with the least congruence generated by the order-independence equation (1),*

$$\mathcal{J} = \mathcal{T}_{\Sigma/OIT}.$$

It is well-known that, given any system of equations $\mathcal{E}$, $\mathcal{T}_{\Sigma/\mathcal{E}}$ is the initial object in the category of all Σ-algebras satisfying the equations $\mathcal{E}$.

A $\mathcal{J}$-automaton is a tuple $(\mathcal{A}, h, Q_{\text{final}})$ consisting of a finite Σ-algebra $\mathcal{A}$, a homomorphism $h : \mathcal{J} \mapsto \mathcal{A}$ and the subset $Q_{\text{final}} \subseteq D_{MT}^{\mathcal{A}}$ of values of sort MT ("final states") where the number of values of sort MT and of sort F ("states") is finite. A $\mathcal{J}$-automaton corresponds to the "more concrete" notion of a (finite deterministic bottom-up) tree automaton over the terms of $\mathcal{T}_{\Sigma}$ such that all terms which are equal modulo OIT are evaluated to the same state. This means that any representation of a multitree t as a term in $\mathcal{T}_{\Sigma}$ can be chosen in order to calculate the value of t.

3   Feature Automata

Given any many-sorted signature Σ with a finite number of non-constant function symbols $c \in)\Sigma - \Sigma_s^0$ for every sort s, we define a Σ-algebra $\mathcal{A}$ to be **finitary** if, for each sort s and each value $q \in D_s^{\mathcal{A}}$ of sort s, the set:

$$\{c \in \Sigma_s^0 \mid c^{\mathcal{A}} = q\}$$

of constant symbols in Σ of sort s which are valued to q is finite or co-finite.

We now return to the particular $\{MT, F\}$-sorted signature Σ introduced above; clearly, the definitions below can be made in general framework as well.[6]

A **feature automaton** $\mathcal{A}$ is defined as a finitary $\mathcal{J}$–automaton. The set of multitrees recognized by $\mathcal{A}$ is the set:

$$L_{MT}(\mathcal{A}) = \{t \in MT \mid h(t) \in Q_{\text{final}}\},$$

and the set of feature trees recognized by $\mathcal{A}$ is the set: $L_{FT}(\mathcal{A}) = L_{MT}(\mathcal{A}) \cap FT$. The families $Rec_{MT}(\mathcal{J})$ and $Rec_{FT}(\mathcal{J})$ of **recognizable** sets of multitrees and feature trees are defined accordingly.

Remark. If (and only if) the set of features is infinite, the set of all feature trees is not a recognizable language of multitrees (with respect to $\mathcal{J}$).

Example. We will construct a feature automaton $\mathcal{A}$ that recognizes the set of natural numbers. These are coded into the feature trees of the form $(0, \{(succ, (0, \{(succ, (..., \{(0, \emptyset)\})\})\})\})$, with n edges labeled $succ$ for the natural number n. As elements in the quotient term algebra $\mathcal{T}_{\Sigma/OIT}$, they would be written as the singleton congruence classes $\{\Rightarrow (0, succ, \Rightarrow$

---

[6] Also, the finitary-condition: finite or co-finite, could be made more general such that the proof of Theorem 2 still holds.

$(0, succ, \Rightarrow (..., 0)))\}$. The feature automaton $\mathcal{A}$ has the states $Q = \{q_{nat}, q_{other}\}$ and $P = \{p_{succ}, p_{other}\}$ of sort MT and F, respectively. The evaluation is given by:

$$0^{\mathcal{A}} = q_{nat},$$
$$A^{\mathcal{A}} = q_{other} \quad \text{if } A \neq 0,$$
$$succ^{\mathcal{A}} = p_{succ},$$
$$f^{\mathcal{A}} = p_{other} \quad \text{if } f \neq succ,$$
$$\Rightarrow^{\mathcal{A}} (q_{nat}, p_{succ}, q_{nat}) = q_{nat},$$
$$\Rightarrow^{\mathcal{A}} (q_1, p, q_2) = q_{other} \quad \text{otherwise.}$$

As final state set we choose $Q_{final} = \{q_{nat}\}$. It is clear that $\mathcal{A}$ respects the order independence theory and the finitary-condition. Of course, it will be more practical to define this set by regular expressions or equational systems.

The following theorem and corollary states that the standard properties of recognizable languages are valid for the sets in $Rec_{\mathcal{FT}}$ as well.

Theorem 2.

1. *The family of recognizable languages of feature trees $Rec_{\mathcal{FT}}$ is closed under the Boolean operations. The corresponding feature automata can be given effectively.*

2. *The emptiness problem ($L_{\mathcal{FT}}(\mathcal{A}) \stackrel{?}{=} \emptyset$) is decidable for each feature automaton $\mathcal{A}$.*

Proof. The known constructions for Boolean operations on automata are still valid for $\mathcal{J}$-automata. To see that the finitary-condition is preserved, simply note that the system of finite and co-finite sets is Boolean closed and, for two states q_1 and q_2 of the feature automata $\mathcal{A}_1$ and $\mathcal{A}_2$, respectively,

$$\{c \in \Sigma_s^0 \mid c^{(\mathcal{A}_1, \mathcal{A}_2)} = (q_1, q_2)\} = \{c \in \Sigma_s^0 \mid c^{\mathcal{A}_1} = q_1\} \cap \{c \in \Sigma_s^0 \mid c^{\mathcal{A}_2} = q_2\}.$$

Since $\mathcal{J} = T_{\Sigma}/\text{OIT}$, each $\mathcal{J}$-automaton $\mathcal{A}$ corresponds to a tree automaton $\mathcal{A}_T$ over terms in T_{Σ}, and:

$$L_{\mathcal{FT}}(\mathcal{A}) = \emptyset \text{ iff } L_{T_{\Sigma}}(\mathcal{A}_T) = \emptyset,$$

it suffices to decide the emptiness problem for the tree automaton $\mathcal{A}_T$. As usually, this can be done by checking all terms of depth smaller than the number of states of $\mathcal{A}_T$. Let C be some finite set of constants c such that $c^{\mathcal{A}} = q$ for each state q which is a value of some constant. Iff L is not empty, it contains a term of bounded depth that is constructed with constants of C and non-constant function symbols. But there are only finitely many terms of this kind.

A finitary automaton can be finitely represented. From such a representation one can calculate some set C as described above. This yields an algorithm for testing $L_{\mathcal{MT}}(\mathcal{A}) = \emptyset$. In the case of $L_{\mathcal{FT}}(\mathcal{A})$ the algorithm checks only terms representing feature trees. $\square$

We conclude the section by defining non-deterministic feature automata which are needed in Sections 5 and 6.

Definition 3. A **non-deterministic feature automaton** $\mathcal{A} = (Q, P, h, Q_{\text{final}})$ is a tuple such that:

Q is the set of states of sort MT, P the states of sort F and $Q_{\text{final}} \subseteq Q$ is the set of final states, h is composed of the functions $h : S \rightarrow 2^Q$ and $h : \mathcal{F} \rightarrow 2^P$ and the transition function $\Rightarrow^{\mathcal{A}} : Q \times P \times Q \rightarrow 2^Q$,

$\mathcal{A}$ satisfies the OIT-theory, i.e., for all states q, p_1, q_1, p_2, q_2,

$$\Rightarrow^{\mathcal{A}} (\Rightarrow^{\mathcal{A}} (q, p_1, q_1), p_2, q_2) \;=\; \Rightarrow^{\mathcal{A}} (\Rightarrow^{\mathcal{A}} (q, p_2, q_2), p_1, q_1),$$

$\mathcal{A}$ satisfies the finitary-condition, i.e., for all states p and q, the sets $\{f \in \mathcal{F} \mid p \in f^{\mathcal{A}}\}$ and $\{A \in S \mid q \in A^{\mathcal{A}}\}$ are finite or co-finite.

The evaluation of the term $t \in T_{\Sigma}$ by $\mathcal{A}$, i.e., the set $h(t) \subseteq Q$ is defined inductively by:

$$h(\Rightarrow (t_1, f, t_2)) \;=\; \Rightarrow^{\mathcal{A}} (h(t_1), h(f), h(t_2)).$$

If t_1 and t_2 are congruent modulo OIT, we have $h(t_1) = h(t_2)$. Thus, $h([t]) = h(t)$ is well defined for all congruence classes $[t]$. The language of multitrees recognized by $\mathcal{A}$ is:

$$L_{MT}(\mathcal{A}) \;=\; \{\, [t] \mid h([t]) \cap Q_{\text{final}} \neq \emptyset \,\},$$

and the language of feature trees recognized by $\mathcal{A}$ is $L_{FT}(\mathcal{A}) = L_{MT}(\mathcal{A}) \cap \mathcal{FT}$. Each feature automaton is also a non-deterministic feature automaton.

Lemma 4. *Given a non-deterministic feature automaton $\mathcal{A}$, an equivalent (deterministic) feature automaton $\mathcal{A}^d$ can be constructed effectively.*

Proof We apply the usual subset construction on a given non-deterministic feature automaton $\mathcal{A}$ of the form above, yielding the equivalent automaton $\mathcal{A}^d$ as follows: $Q^d = 2^Q$, $P^d = 2^P$, $A^{\mathcal{A}^d} = A^{\mathcal{A}}$, $f^{\mathcal{A}^d} := f^{\mathcal{A}}$, and:

$$\Rightarrow^{\mathcal{A}^d} (q_1^d, p^d, q_2^d) \;=\; \bigcup \{\Rightarrow^{\mathcal{A}} (q_1, p, q_2) \mid (q_1, p, q_2) \in q_1^d \times p^d \times q_2^d\}.$$

We define the final states of $\mathcal{A}^d$ by: $Q_{\text{final}}^d = \{q^d \mid q^d \cap Q_{\text{final}} \neq \emptyset\}$.

Clearly, the algebra $\mathcal{A}^d$ satisfies the OIT-theory. The equality: The finitary-condition is preserved, since:

$$\{A \mid A^{\mathcal{A}^d} = q^d\} \;=\; \bigcap_{q \in q^d} \{A \mid q \in A^{\mathcal{A}}\} \cap \bigcap_{q \notin q^d} \{A \mid q \in A^{\mathcal{A}}\}^C$$

shows that the finitary-condition is preserved, too. $\qquad\qquad\square$

4 Counting Constraints

In this section we characterize recognizable languages of flat feature trees using formulae of a certain from, called counting constraints. The proof of this characterization, which is the main technical result of this paper, will be done in Sections A and B.

The syntax of **counting constraints** C (written $C(x)$ to indicate that x is the only free variable) is defined in the BNF style as follows (where F a finite or co-finite sets of features, $n, m \in \mathbb{N}$ are natural numbers, and T is a finite or co-finite subset of S).

$$C(x) ::= \quad card \{\varphi \in F \mid \exists y. (x\varphi y \wedge Ty)\} = n \bmod m$$
$$\mid Sx$$
$$\mid C(x) \wedge C(x) \qquad\qquad (2)$$
$$\mid \neg C(x)$$

The counting constraint $C(x) \equiv card \{\varphi \in F \mid \exists y. (x\varphi y \wedge Ty)\} = n \bmod m$ holds for the multitree x if the number of all edges in x which: (1) go from the root to a node labeled by a symbol in T and (2) are labeled by a feature φ in F, is equal to $n \bmod m$.[7] The cardinality operator $card$ applies on a multiset of features, *i.e.*, counts their double occurrences.

The counting constraint $C(x) \equiv Sx$ holds for the multitree x if the root of x is labeled by some symbol in S.

We note the following fact (*cf.*, [Eil74]).

Fact 5 *A language of natural numbers is recognizable iff it can be decomposed into a finite union of sets of the form:* $\{n + k \cdot m \mid k \in \mathbb{N}\}$, *with* $n, m \in \mathbb{N}$.

Thus, we can define the syntax of counting constraints equivalently in the form (where N is a set of natural numbers which is recognizable in the monoid $(\mathbb{N}, +, 0)$; S, and T, a finite or co-finite subset of S; F a finite or co-finite sets of features):

$$C(x) ::= \quad card \{\varphi \in F \mid \exists y. (x\varphi y \wedge Ty)\} \in N$$
$$\mid Sx$$
$$\mid C(x) \wedge C(x) \qquad\qquad (3)$$
$$\mid C(x) \vee C(x)$$

Note that also under this definition, counting constraints are closed under negation. Indeed, $\neg \, card \{\varphi \in F \mid \exists y. (x\varphi y \wedge Ty)\} \in N$ is equivalent to $card \{\varphi \in F \mid \exists y. (x\varphi y \wedge Ty)\} \in N^c$, and $\neg \, Tx$ is equivalent to $T^c x$.

Some important feature constraints can be expressed by our new constraints. For example, in the syntax of [Smo92], for $F \subseteq \mathcal{F}$ finite, for $f \in \mathcal{F}$, and for $A \in S$: xF ("for exactly the features f in F there exists one edge labeled f from the root"), $xf \downarrow$ ("there exists no edge labeled f from the root"), and Ax ("the root is labeled by A").

$$xF \equiv \bigwedge_{f \in F} card\{\varphi \in \{f\} \mid \exists y. x\varphi y\} \in \{1\}$$

---

[7] We define $n \bmod 0 = n$, although this is not quite standard. That is, "counting" means here threshold- and modulo counting.

$$\land \quad card\{\varphi \in F^c \mid \exists y.\, x\varphi y\,\} \in \{0\}\,,$$

$$xf \downarrow \equiv card\{\varphi \in \{f\} \mid \exists y.\, x\varphi y\} \in \{0\}\,,$$

$$Ax \equiv \{A\}x\,.$$

Each constraint $C(x)$ defines the set $L_{MT}(C)$ of multitrees x for which the constraint $C(x)$ holds. Accordingly, we define: $L_{FT}(C) = L_{MT}(C) \cap \mathcal{FT}$, $L_{MT_1}(C) = L_{MT}(C) \cap \mathcal{MT}_1$, and $L_{FT_1}(C) = L_{FT}(C) \cap \mathcal{FT}_1$. The languages of flat multitrees of the form $L_{MT_1}(C)$, or of flat feature trees $L_{FT_1}(C)$, are called **counting-definable**.

The following theorem holds for multitrees instead of feature trees, as well.

Theorem 6. *A language of flat feature trees is counting-definable iff it is recognizable (in $\mathcal{J}$, by a feature automaton).*

Proof Sketch. A flat multitree can be represented as a finite multiset over $(\mathcal{F} \cup \{root\}) \times \mathcal{S}$. The operation $\Rightarrow^{\mathcal{J}}$ corresponds to the union of such multisets. In Section A we study the algebra $\mathcal{M}$ of finite multisets of pairs. It is three-sorted, the sorts denoting $\mathcal{F} \cup \{root\}$, $\mathcal{S}$ and $\mathcal{MT}$, respectively. We show that $\mathcal{J}$- and $\mathcal{M}$-recognizability coincide.

In Section B, we consider counting constraints $D(x)$ for multisets x of $\mathcal{M}$. They are of the form:

$$D(x) \equiv card\{(f, A) \in x \mid f \in F,\ A \in T\} \in N\,,$$

or conjunctions or disjunctions of these. Again F and T are finite or co-finite subsets of $\mathcal{F}$ and $\mathcal{S}$ and N is a recognizable set of natural numbers.

We show that definability of languages of multisets by these constraints and $\mathcal{M}$-recognizability coincide. The main idea is that the mapping:

$$x \mapsto card\{(f, A) \in x \mid f \in F,\ A \in T\}$$

is essentially a homomorphism from $\mathcal{M}$ into $\mathbb{N}$. □

The theorem above expresses that feature automata can count features either threshold or modulo a natural number.

5 Kleene's Theorem

We define regular expressions over feature trees. In generalization of the standard cases, the atomic constituents of these are not just constants (denoting singletons or trees of depth 1), but expressions which denote sets of feature trees of depth ≤ 1.

As usual, we need construction variables labeling the nodes where the substitution and the Kleene star operations can take place. These variables are taken from a set Y which is assumed given (disjoint from $\mathcal{S}$). It is infinite; the definition of each regular language, of course, uses only a finite number of construction variables. We call a syntactic expression C of the form (2) a **counting-expression** if T ranges over finite or co-finite subsets of $\mathcal{S} \cup Y$.

Its denotation is defined as the set of all feature trees of depth ≤ 1 which satisfy it as a counting constraint over the extended alphabet of sorts.

A **regular expression** R over $\mathcal{F}$ and $\mathcal{S} \cup Y$ is of the form given by:

$$
\begin{array}{lll}
R ::= & C & C \text{ is a counting-expression} \\
& \mid R \cdot_y R & \text{concatenation (where } y \in Y) \\
& \mid R^{*y} & \text{Kleene star (where } y \in Y) \\
& \mid R \cup R & \text{union}
\end{array}
$$

Complement and intersection are optional operators, which, as we will see, do not properly add expressiveness.

The definition of the language $L_{\mathcal{FT}}(R)$ of feature trees (or $L_{\mathcal{MT}}(R)$ of multitrees) denoted by the regular expression R is by straightforward induction. For concatenation and Kleene star for sets of multitrees: If L_1 and L_2 are sets of feature trees, then $L_1 \cdot_y L_2$ is obtained by replacing the construction variable y in the leaves of the trees of L_1 by (possibly different) trees of L_2. The Kleene star operation on a set is an iterated concatenation of a set with itself. Formally, for a set L of feature trees, $L_y^1 = L$, $L_y^n := L_y^{n-1} \cdot_y L$, and $L^{*y} = \bigcup_{n \geq 1} L_y^n$.

The languages of feature trees (or multitrees) denoted by regular expressions are called **regular languages**.

Theorem 7 Kleene. *A language of feature trees (or multitrees) is regular iff it is recognizable.*

Proof. It is sufficient to prove the theorem for multitrees. We show by induction over the structure of the regular expressions that the language of each regular expression over $\mathcal{S} \cup Y$ and $\mathcal{F}$ is recognizable. The base case $R = C$ is handled by Theorem 6. Union is captured by the Boolean closure properties in Theorem 2. Substitution and star are established using the equivalence of deterministic and non deterministic feature automata. For the other direction, we use the standard McNaughton/Papert induction technique, the base case being handled again by Theorem 6. $\qquad\square$

6 Equational Systems

The next possibility to define recognizable sets of feature trees (or multitrees) in a convenient way uses equational systems. These systems again generalize the constituents from singletons of trees of the form a or $f(y_1, \ldots, y_n)$, for $a \in \Sigma_0$ and $f \in \Sigma_n$ in the case of a ranked signature for first-order trees, to counting-expressions denoting (unions of) sets of flat feature trees.

The extra symbols $y \in Y$ in these counting expressions now correspond to set variables of the equations.

We write $C(y_1, \ldots, y_n)$ instead of C if the set variables of C are contained in the set $\{y_1, \ldots, y_n\}$. These variables are not to be confused with the logical variable x used in $C = C(x)$ as a logical formula.

An **equational system** is a finite set $\mathcal{E}$ of equations of the form (where C_i is a counting-expression, for $i = 1, \ldots, n$):

$$
y_i = C_i(y_1, \ldots, y_n).
$$

Given an assignment, *i.e.*, a mapping $\alpha : Y \mapsto 2^{\mathcal{FT}}$, the equations in $\mathcal{E}$ are interpreted such that $C_i(y_1, \ldots, y_n)$ denotes the set:

$$L_{\mathcal{FT}}(C_i) \cdot_{y_1} \alpha(y_1) \cdot_{y_2} \ldots \cdot_{y_n} \alpha(y_n).$$

A solution of $\mathcal{E}$ is an assignment α satisfying $\mathcal{E}$. Each equational system has a least solution. The existence follows with the usual fixed point argument. Namely, an equational system is considered as an operator over the lattice of assignments α and the least solution is obtained in ω iteration steps of this operator, starting with the assignment $\alpha(y_i) = \emptyset$ for $i = 1, \ldots, n$.

A language of feature trees is called **equational** if it is the union of some of the sets $\alpha(y_i)$ for the least solution α of $\mathcal{E}$. The notion is defined accordingly for multitrees.

Theorem 8. *A language of feature trees (or multitrees) is equational iff it is recognizable.*

Proof Since $\mathcal{J}$-recognizability corresponds to the characterization by congruence relations, and Theorem 6 covers the case of feature trees of depth ≤ 1, the proof can be done following the standard one for first-order trees (*cf.*, [GS84]). $\qquad\square$

7 Conclusion and Further Work

The results of this paper together present a complete regular theory of feature trees. They offer a solution to the concrete practical problem of computing with types denoting sets of feature trees as described in the introduction.

Now, it is interesting to investigate where, in the wide range of applications of first-order trees, feature trees can be useful in replacing or extending those. Since tree automata play a major role, either directly or just by underlying some other formalism, the regular theory of feature trees developed here is a prerequisite for this investigation.

A more speculative application might be conceived as part of the compiler optimizer of the programming language LIFE [AKP91b]. Namely, unary predicates over feature trees defined by Horn clauses without multiple occurrences of variables define recognizable sets of feature trees. Now, satisfiability of the conjunction of two such predicates corresponds to non-emptyness of the intersection of the defined sets. When used in deep guards, entailment of a predicate by others of this kind corresponds to the subset relation on the defined sets of feature trees.

We are curious to extend the developed theory in the following ways. First, we would like to find a logical characterization of the class of recognizable feature trees, extending the results of Doner, Thatcher/Wright and Courcelle [Don70, TW67, Cou90]. It will be interesting to combine second-order logic and the counting constraints introduced here, in order to account for the flexibility in the depth as well as in the out-degree of the nodes of feature trees.

Also, in order to account for circular data structures, like, *e.g.*, circular lists, it is necessary to consider infinite (rational) feature trees. Thus, it would be useful to construct a regular theory of these.

Finally, in [CD91] it is shown that the first-order theory of a tree automaton is decidable (in the case of a finite signature). More precisely, it is possible to solve first-order formulas built up from equalities between first-order terms and membership constraints of the form $x \in q$, where q denotes a set defined by a tree automaton. Since we have established the corresponding automaton notion, we may hope to obtain the corresponding result for feature trees. For the special case of the set of all feature trees, this is the decidability of first-order feature logic. A proof for infinite feature trees can be found in [BS92]. Can the techniques of that proof be combined with the ones of [CD91]?

We add the fact, suggested by one of the referees, that the first-order theory of multitrees is not decidable. This can be shown by employing a proof technique by Ralf Treinen [Trei92].

Acknowledgements

We are grateful to Hassan Aït-Kaci and Gert Smolka for first arousing our individual interest in the idea of using tree automata for feature constraint solving and then bringing us together. We also thank Hubert Comon, Helmut Seidl and Ralf Treinen for encouraging discussions. Finally, we thank the anonymous referees for their helpful and intriguing comments.

References

[AK86]   Hassan Aït-Kaci. An algebraic semantics approach to the effective resolution of type equations. *Theoretical Computer Science*, 45:293–351, 1986.

[AKP91a]   Hassan Aït-Kaci and Andreas Podelski. Functional constraints in LIFE. PRL Research Report 13, Digital Equipment Corporation, Paris Research Laboratory, Rueil-Malmaison, France, 1991.

[AKP91b]   Hassan Aït-Kaci and Andreas Podelski. Towards a meaning of LIFE. In J. Maluszyński and M. Wirsing, editors, *Proceedings of the 3rd International Symposium on Programming Language Implementation and Logic Programming*, Springer LNCS vol. 528, pages 255–274. Springer-Verlag, 1991.

[AKPS92]   Hassan Aït-Kaci, Andreas Podelski, and Gert Smolka. A feature-based constraint system for logic programming with entailment. In *Proceedings of the 5th International Conference on Fifth Generation Computer Systems*, pages 1012–1022, Tokyo, Japan, June 1992. ICOT.

[BS92]   Rolf Backofen and Gert Smolka. A complete and recursive feature theory. Research Report RR-92-30, German Research Center for Artificial Intelligence (DFKI), Stuhlsatzenhausweg 3, 6600 Saarbrücken 11, Germany, September 1992.

[Car92]   Bob Carpenter. *The Logic of Typed Feature Structures*, volume 32 of *Cambridge Tracts in Theoretical Computer Science*. Cambridge University Press, Cambridge, UK, 1992.

[CD91]   Hubert Comon and Catherine Delors. Equational formula with membership constraints,. Rapport de recherche 648, LRI, Universit de Paris Sud, March 1991. To appear in *Information and Computation*.

[Cou89]   Bruno Courcelle. On recognizable sets and tree automata. In Hassan Ait-Kaci and Maurice Nivat, editors, *Resolution of Equations in Algebraic Structures, Algebraic Techniques*, volume 1, chapter 3, pages 93–126. Academic Press, 1989.

[Cou90]   Bruno Courcelle. The monadic second-order logic of graphs I: Recognizable sets of finite graphs. *Information and Computation* 85, pages 12-75, 1990.

[Cou92]   Bruno Courcelle. Recognizable sets of unrooted trees. In Maurice Nivat and Andreas Podelski, editors, *Tree Automata, Advances and Open Problems*. Elsevier Science, 1992.

[Don70]   John E. Doner. Tree Acceptors and some of their applications. *Journal of Comp. System Sci.* 4, pages 406-451, 1970.

[Eil74]   Samuel Eilenberg. *Automata, Language and Machine*, volume A of *Applied and Pure Mathematics*. Academic Press, 1974.

[GS84]   F. Gécseg and M. Steinby. *Tree Automata*. Akadémiai Kiadó, Budapest, 1984.

[Mah88]   Michael J. Maher. Complete axiomatizations of the algebras of finite, rational and infinite trees. In *LICS*, pages 348–457, July 1988.

[Niv92]   Maurice Nivat. Elements of a theory of tree codes. In Maurice Nivat and Andreas Podelski, editors, *Tree Automata, Advances and Open Problems*. Elsevier Science, 1992.

[Rou88]   William C. Rounds. Set values for unification-based grammar formalisms and logic programming. Report CSLI-88-129, 1988.

[Smo92]   Gert Smolka. Feature constraint logics for unification grammars. *Journal of Logic Programming*, 12:51–87, 1992.

[ST92]   Gert Smolka and Ralf Treinen. Records for logic programming. In *Proceedings of the 1992 Joint International Conference and Symposium on Logic Programming*, Washington, DC, November 1992. The MIT Press, to appear.

[TW67]   J. W. Thatcher and J. B. Wright. Generalized finite automata theory with an application to a decision problem of second-order logic. *Mathematical Systems Theory*, 2(1):57–81, August 1967. Published by Springer-Verlag NY Inc.

[Trei92]   Ralf Treinen. A New Method for Undecidability Proofs of First Order Theories. *Journal of Symbolic Computation*, 14:437-457, 1992.

APPENDIX

A   The Algebra of Multisets

We will reduce $\mathcal{J}$-recognizability for languages of flat multitrees to a notion of recognizability of finite multisets of pairs. The idea is to identify a flat multitree with a finite multiset of pairs,

$$(A, E) \equiv \{(root, A)\} \sqcup E$$

where *root* is considered like an extra feature. Roughly, the operation of adding edges corresponds to the union operation on multisets.

In all generality, we introduce the algebra $\mathcal{M} = \mathcal{M}(\mathcal{U}_1, \ldots, \mathcal{U}_n)$ of finite multisets over n-tuples with components in given sets $\mathcal{U}_1, \ldots, \mathcal{U}_n$, for some $n \geq 1$. (Later, we will instantiate $\mathcal{U}_1 = \mathcal{F} \cup \{root\}$ and $\mathcal{U}_2 = \mathcal{S}$.) $\mathcal{M}$ is $n+1$-sorted, over the the the sorts $s_1, \ldots, s_n$ and *FMS* which denote, respectively, the domains $D_{s_1} = \mathcal{U}_1, \ldots, D_{s_n} = \mathcal{U}_n$, and $D_{FMS} = \mathbb{N}_{finite}^{\mathcal{U}_1 \times \ldots \times \mathcal{U}_n}$ (where $\mathbb{N}_{finite}^{M}$ denotes the set of finite multisets over M).

The operations of $\mathcal{M}$ are the (associative and commutative) union $\sqcup^{\mathcal{M}}$ of multisets and the creation of a singleton multiset from n elements, one for each component, *i.e.*, $\langle u_1, \ldots, u_n \rangle^{\mathcal{M}} = \{(u_1, \ldots, u_n)\}$. Thus, they are mappings $\sqcup^{\mathcal{M}} : D_{FMS} \times D_{FMS} \mapsto D_{FMS}$, and $\langle \, \rangle^{\mathcal{M}} : \mathcal{U}_1 \times \ldots \times \mathcal{U}_n \mapsto D_{FMS}$.

Formally, $\mathcal{M}$ is an algebra over the $\{s_1, \ldots, s_n, FMS\}$-sorted signature:

$$\Sigma_{\mathcal{U}_1, \ldots, \mathcal{U}_n} = \mathcal{U}_1 \uplus \ldots \uplus \mathcal{U}_n \uplus \{\langle ., \ldots, . \rangle, \sqcup\}$$

where the constants of sort s_i are just the elements of $\mathcal{U}_i$, and the two function symbols have the profile: $\sqcup : FMS \times FMS \mapsto FMS$, and $\langle \, \rangle : s_1 \times \ldots \times s_n \mapsto FMS$.

Lemma 9. *The algebra $\mathcal{M}$ is isomorphic to the quotient of the term algebra with the congruence generated by the associativity and commutativity laws for $\sqcup$,*

$$\mathcal{M} = T_{\Sigma u_1, \ldots, u_n}/AC \cdot$$

We define a subset of D_{FMT} of multisets of n-tuples to be *recognizable* if it is recognized by a *finitary* $\mathcal{M}$-automaton.

It is important to note that the notions of recognizability in $\mathcal{M} = \mathcal{M}(\mathcal{U}_1, \ldots, \mathcal{U}_n)$ and $\mathcal{M}(\mathcal{U}_1 \times \ldots \times \mathcal{U}_n)$ can be different, namely if $n \geq 2$ and one of the $\mathcal{U}_i$ is infinite.[8]

Now, we consider the special case where $\mathcal{U}_1 = \mathcal{F} \cup \{root\}$ and $\mathcal{U}_2 = \mathcal{S}$, i.e.,

$$\mathcal{M} = \mathcal{M}(\mathcal{F} \cup \{root\}, \mathcal{S}).$$

Thus, the domains of $\mathcal{M}$ are $D_{s_1}^{\mathcal{M}} = \mathcal{F} \cup \{root\}$, $D_{s_2}^{\mathcal{M}} = \mathcal{S}$, and $D_{FMS}^{\mathcal{M}} = FMS(\mathcal{F} \cup \{root\} \times \mathcal{S})$.

We define the injection:

$$I : \mathcal{M}T_1 \to \mathbb{N}_{finite}^{(\mathcal{F} \cup \{root\}) \times \mathcal{S}}$$

by $I((A, E)) = \{(root, A)\} \sqcup E$. Thus (writing the operator $\sqcup^{\mathcal{M}}$ infix):

$$I(\Rightarrow^{\mathcal{J}} (t, f, A)) = I(t) \sqcup^{\mathcal{M}} \langle f, A \rangle^{\mathcal{M}}.$$

Lemma 10 Reduction Lemma. *A language L of flat multitrees is recognizable in $\mathcal{J}$ iff the language $I(L)$ of multisets of pairs is recognizable in $\mathcal{M}$.*

Proof The difficult direction is from left to right. Given a finitary $\mathcal{J}$-automaton $(\mathcal{A}, h, Q_{final})$, where $D_{\mathcal{A}}^{MT} = Q$ and $D_{\mathcal{A}}^{F} = P$, we construct a finitary $\mathcal{M}$-automaton $(\mathcal{A}^\star, h^\star, Q_{final})$ such that, for all flat multitrees t:

$$h^\star(I(t)) = h(t). \tag{4}$$

This is sufficient to show the recognizability of $I(L)$, since $I(L) = h^{-1}(\mathcal{A}) \cap I(\mathcal{M}T_1)$, and $I(\mathcal{M}T_1)$ is a recognizable set in $\mathcal{M}$.

We set $D_{s_2}^{\mathcal{A}^\star} = Q$, $D_{s_1}^{\mathcal{A}^\star} = P \cup \{p_{root}\}$, and (where *Func* denotes the set of functions generated by the functions $\Rightarrow^{\mathcal{J}} (\,.\,, p, q)$; *i.e.*, the smallest set containing these and closed under composition):

$$D_{FMS}^{\mathcal{A}^\star} = Func \uplus Q \uplus \{q_\perp\}.$$

---

[8] Generally, the finiteness condition for $\mathcal{M}(\mathcal{U}_1 \times \ldots \times \mathcal{U}_n)$-automata is weaker then the one for $\mathcal{M}$-automata. It may be strictly weaker since cartesian products of finite and co-finite sets need neither be finite nor co-finite. For example, suppose $\mathcal{U}$ to be an infinite set. The cartesian product $\mathcal{U} \times \{1\}$ is neither finite nor co-finite as subset of $\mathcal{U} \times \{0, 1\}$. Thus, the language of the singleton subsets of $\mathcal{U} \times \{1\}$ is not recognizable in the algebra $\mathcal{M}(\mathcal{U} \times \{0, 1\})$, but it is with respect to $\mathcal{M} = \mathcal{M}(\mathcal{U}, \{0, 1\})$.—In fact, it is this finitary-condition which makes the proofs that complicated and non-standard.

The evaluation of $\mathcal{A}^\star$ is defined by (we write $\cdot^{\mathcal{A}^\star}$ instead of $h^\star(\cdot)$ and use the more intuitive infix notation):

$$\langle p, q \rangle^{\mathcal{A}^\star} = \Rightarrow^{\mathcal{A}} (\,.\,, p, q),$$
$$\langle p_{root}, q \rangle^{\mathcal{A}^\star} = q,$$
$$h_1 \sqcup^{\mathcal{A}^\star} h_2 = h_1 \circ h_2,$$
$$q \sqcup^{\mathcal{A}^\star} h = h(q),$$
$$h \sqcup^{\mathcal{A}^\star} q = h(q),$$
$$q \sqcup^{\mathcal{A}^\star} \tilde{q} = q_\perp.$$

Every function in the interpretations taking $q_\perp$ as argument is again mapped to $q_\perp$. Precisely:

$$q_\perp \sqcup^{\mathcal{A}^\star} h = q_\perp,$$
$$h \sqcup^{\mathcal{A}^\star} q_\perp = q_\perp,$$
$$q_\perp \sqcup^{\mathcal{A}^\star} q = q_\perp,$$
$$q \sqcup^{\mathcal{A}^\star} q_\perp = q_\perp,$$
$$\langle p, q_\perp \rangle^{\mathcal{A}^\star} = q_\perp,$$
$$\langle p_{root}, q_\perp \rangle^{\mathcal{A}^\star} = q_\perp.$$

Clearly, $\mathcal{A}^\star$ is an AC-automaton, $i.e.$, the operation $\sqcup^{\mathcal{A}^\star}$ is associative and commutative. The associativity is trivial for functions as arguments. The commutativity for functions follows from the OIT-theory, and the associativity for functions by:

$$\Rightarrow^{\mathcal{A}} (\,.\,, p, q) \sqcup^{\mathcal{A}^\star} \Rightarrow^{\mathcal{A}} (\,.\,, p_1, q_1) = \Rightarrow^{\mathcal{A}} (\Rightarrow^{\mathcal{A}} (\,.\,, p_1, q_1), p, q)$$
$$= \Rightarrow^{\mathcal{A}} (\Rightarrow^{\mathcal{A}} (\,.\,, p, q), p_1, q_1)$$
$$= \Rightarrow^{\mathcal{A}} (\,.\,, p_1, q_1) \sqcup^{\mathcal{A}^\star} \Rightarrow^{\mathcal{A}} (\,.\,, p, q).$$

The proof for all possible cases is now easily established.

The identity (4) is now easily verified. Finally, we note that the finitary-condition is preserved from $\mathcal{A}$ to $\mathcal{A}^\star$.

For the other direction, given a finitary $\mathcal{M}$-automaton $\mathcal{A}^\star$, we will construct a finitary $\mathcal{J}$-automaton $\mathcal{A}$ satisfying (4). This is sufficient, now, since $\mathcal{MT}_1$ is a recognizable set in $\mathcal{J}$. In fact, we will construct an automaton in another algebra.[9] Next, we will introduce this algebra. We resume this proof after having proven Lemma 12.

The algebra $\mathcal{J}_{local}$ of flat multitrees is obtained from the algebra $\mathcal{J}$ by restricting the domain of the third argument from $\mathcal{MT}$ to $\mathcal{S}$ ($\ldots = \mathcal{MT}_0$), and the domain of the first from $\mathcal{MT}$ to $\mathcal{MT}_1$, $i.e.$, to to flat multitrees instead of arbitrary ones.

That is, the algebra $\mathcal{J}_{local}$ is three-sorted with sorts MT_1, F and S. The domains are given by $D_{MT_1} = \mathcal{MT}_1, D_F = \mathcal{F}, D_S = \mathcal{S}$. The operation is given by (where E is a finite multiset over pairs in $\mathcal{F} \times \mathcal{S}$):

$$\Rightarrow^{\mathcal{J}_{local}} ((A_1, E), f, A_2) = (A_1, E \sqcup \{(f, A_2)\})$$

(which is equal to $\Rightarrow^{\mathcal{J}} ((A_1, E), f, A_2)$). The signature of $\mathcal{J}_{local}$ is the disjoint union:

$$\Sigma_{local} = \mathcal{S} \uplus \mathcal{F} \uplus \mathcal{S} \uplus \{\Rightarrow\}.$$

---

[9] The motivation for the construction of yet another algebra is, roughly, the fact that a symbol $A \in \mathcal{S}$ occurs as a root-labeling as well as a leave-labeling; these two roles are distinguished in $\mathcal{J}$-automata, but not in $\mathcal{M}$-automata.

Here, the symbols in S appear twice: they are supposed to be renamed apart. Firstly, they are constants of sort MT_1, and secondly, they are constants of sort S. The different functionality is made clear syntactically by writing A_{MT_1} and A_S, with interpretations $(A_{MT_1})^{\mathcal{J}_{local}} = (A, \emptyset) \in MT_0 \subseteq MT_1$ and $(A_S)^{\mathcal{J}_{local}} = A \in S$.

The features are constants of sort F and interpreted freely. The profile of the function symbol in $\mathcal{J}_{local}$ is $\Rightarrow: MT_1 \times F \times S \to MT_1$.

The algebra $\mathcal{J}_{local}$ satisfies the order independence theory (OIT); namely, for all flat multitrees t, features f and symbols A the following holds.

$$\Rightarrow^{\mathcal{J}_{local}} ((\Rightarrow^{\mathcal{J}_{local}} (t, f_1, A_1), f_2, A_2) = \Rightarrow^{\mathcal{J}_{local}} ((\Rightarrow^{\mathcal{J}_{local}} (t, f_2, A_2), f_1, A_1)$$

The following lemma states that we can use the more concrete notion of tree automata.

Lemma 11. $\mathcal{J}_{local}$ *is isomorphic to a quotient term algebra,*

$$\mathcal{J}_{local} = T_{\Sigma_{local}}/OIT \quad .$$

Again, we define recognizability in $\mathcal{J}_{local}$ in terms of finitary automata.

Lemma 12. *A language of flat multitrees is recognizable in $\mathcal{J}$ iff it is recognizable in $\mathcal{J}_{local}$.*

Proof We will first modify a finitary $\mathcal{J}$-automaton $\mathcal{A}$, where $D_{\mathcal{A}}^{MT} = Q$ and $D_{\mathcal{A}}^F = P$, in order to obtain a finitary $\mathcal{J}_{local}$-automaton $\mathcal{A}^1$ such that the two automata (with the same set of final states) will recognize the same languages of flat multitrees. We define the domains of $\mathcal{A}^1$ by:

$$D_S^{\mathcal{A}^1} = Q,$$
$$D_{MT_1}^{\mathcal{A}^1} = Q,$$
$$D_F^{\mathcal{A}^1} = P,$$

and we define the evaluation of $\mathcal{A}^1$ by (for all $A \in S, f \in \mathcal{F}$, and for all $q, q' \in Q$ and $p \in P$):

$$(A_{MT_1})^{\mathcal{A}^1} = A^{\mathcal{A}},$$
$$(A_S)^{\mathcal{A}^1} = A^{\mathcal{A}},$$
$$f^{\mathcal{A}^1} = f^{\mathcal{A}},$$
$$\Rightarrow^{\mathcal{A}^1} (q, p, q') = \Rightarrow^{\mathcal{A}} (q, p, q').$$

Clearly the finitary-condition and the order independence theory are preserved between $\mathcal{A}^1$ and $\mathcal{A}$.

For the other direction, given a finitary $\mathcal{J}_{local}$-automaton $\mathcal{A}^2$ (with final states Q_{final}^2, of sort MT_1), we will define a finitary $\mathcal{J}_{local}$-automaton $\mathcal{A}^1$ that recognizes the same language, but has the two properties: $D_{MT_1}^{\mathcal{A}^1} = D_S^{\mathcal{A}^1}$, and, for all symbols A in S, $(A_{MT_1})^{\mathcal{A}^1} = (A_S)^{\mathcal{A}^1}$. Thanks to these, one can define a $\mathcal{J}$-automaton $\mathcal{A}$ that accepts the same flat multitrees as $\mathcal{A}^1$. Again, this is sufficient since the language MT_1 is recognizable with respect to $\mathcal{J}$.

We define the domains of $\mathcal{A}^1$ by:

$$D_{MT_1}^{\mathcal{A}^1} = D_{MT_1}^{\mathcal{A}^2} \times D_S^{\mathcal{A}^2},$$

$$D_S^{\mathcal{A}^1} = D_{MT_1}^{\mathcal{A}^2} \times D_S^{\mathcal{A}^2},$$

$$D_F^{\mathcal{A}^1} = D_F^{\mathcal{A}^2},$$

and, after having fixed an arbitrary element $r_{fix} \in D_S^{\mathcal{A}^2}$, we define the evaluation of $\mathcal{A}^1$ by (for all $A \in \mathcal{S}, f \in \mathcal{F}$, and for all $q, \tilde{q} \in D_{MT_1}^{\mathcal{A}^2}, p \in D_F^{\mathcal{A}^2}$ and $r, \tilde{r} \in D_S^{\mathcal{A}^2}$):

$$(A_{MT_1})^{\mathcal{A}^1} = ((A_{MT_1})^{\mathcal{A}^2}, (A_S)^{\mathcal{A}^2}),$$

$$(A_S)^{\mathcal{A}^1} = ((A_{MT_1})^{\mathcal{A}^2}, (A_S)^{\mathcal{A}^2}),$$

$$f^{\mathcal{A}^1} = f^{\mathcal{A}^2},$$

$$\Rightarrow^{\mathcal{A}^1} ((q,r), p, (\tilde{q}, \tilde{r})) = (\Rightarrow^{\mathcal{A}^2} (q, p, \tilde{r}), r_{fix}).$$

As final states of $\mathcal{A}^1$ we choose:

$$Q_{final}^1 = \{(q, r) \mid q \in Q_{final}^2 \text{ and } r \in D_S^{\mathcal{A}^2} \}.$$

Again, the finiteness condition and the order independence theory are preserved. This concludes the proof of Lemma 12. $\square$

End of Proof of Reduction Lemma 10

Given a finitary $\mathcal{M}$-automaton $\mathcal{A}^\star$, we construct a finitary $\mathcal{J}_{local}$-automaton $\mathcal{A}$ such that $(I(t))^{\mathcal{A}^\star} = t^{\mathcal{A}}$ for all flat multitrees t. The domains of $\mathcal{A}$ are: $D_S^{\mathcal{A}} = D_{s_2}^{\mathcal{A}^\star}, D_F^{\mathcal{A}} = D_{s_1}^{\mathcal{A}^\star}$ and $D_{MT_1}^{\mathcal{A}} = D_{FMS}^{\mathcal{A}^\star}$.

The evaluation of $\mathcal{A}$ is defined by (where q, p and r are states of $\mathcal{A}$ of sorts MT_1, F and S):

$$(A_S)^{\mathcal{A}} = A^{\mathcal{A}^\star},$$

$$f^{\mathcal{A}} = f^{\mathcal{A}^\star},$$

$$(A_{MT_1})^{\mathcal{A}} = \langle root^{\mathcal{A}^\star}, (A_S)^{\mathcal{A}^\star} \rangle^{\mathcal{A}^\star},$$

$$\Rightarrow^{\mathcal{A}} (q, p, r) = q \sqcup^{\mathcal{A}^\star} \langle p, r \rangle^{\mathcal{A}^\star}.$$

Since $\mathcal{A}^\star$ satisfies (AC), $\mathcal{A}$ satisfies (OIT). The finitary-condition is preserved, as well. $\square$

B Counting in Multisets

Again in the general framework where $\mathcal{M} = \mathcal{M}(\mathcal{U}_1, \ldots, \mathcal{U}_n)$, We will characterize recognizability in $\mathcal{M}$, i.e., of languages of finite multisets, by appropiate counting constraints.

We define $\mathcal{M}$-counting constraints C (written $C(x)$ to indicate that x is the only free variable—logically, a multiset variable) to expressions of the following form:

$$C(x) ::= \quad card \{(u_1, \ldots, u_n) \in x \mid u_i \in U_i \text{ for all } i\} \in N$$
$$| \; C(x) \cap C(x)$$
$$| \; C(x) \cup C(x).$$

Here, N is a recognizable set of natural numbers with respect to the monoid $(\mathbb{N}, +, 0)$, and the sets $U_i \subset \mathcal{U}_i$ are finite or co-finite. The counting constraint

$C(x) \equiv card\,\{(u_1, \ldots, u_n) \in x \mid u_i \in U_i \text{ for all } i\} \in N$ holds for the multiset x if the number of tuples $(u_1, \ldots, u_n)$ in x such that $u_i \in U_i$ for all $i = 1, \ldots, n$ is an element of N. The cardinality operator $card$ applies on a multiset of tuples, $i.e.$, counts double occurrences.

The language defined by an $\mathcal{M}$-counting constraint $C(x)$ is the set of all finite multisets x that satisfy $C(x)$. It is denoted by $L_\mathcal{M}(C)$.

Theorem 13. *The family of languages defined by $\mathcal{M}$-counting constraints is exactly the family of languages of multisets recognizable in $\mathcal{M}$.*

Proof. Given an $\mathcal{M}$-counting constraint of the form: $C = card\,\{(u_1, \ldots, u_n) \in x \mid u_i \in U_i \text{ for all } i\} \in N$, we will show the recognizability of $L_\mathcal{M}(C)$.

We can define a homomorphism $h : \mathcal{M}(\mathcal{U}_1 \ldots, \mathcal{U}_n) \rightarrow \mathcal{M}(\{1\}, \ldots, \{1\})$ by setting $h(u_i) = \{1\}$ for $u_i \in U_i$, and $h(u_i) = \emptyset$ otherwise.

Furthermore, the homomorphism $J : \mathbb{N}_{finite}^{\{1\} \times \ldots \times \{1\}} \rightarrow \mathbb{N}$, given by $J(\{(u_1, \ldots, u_n)\}) = 1$ if $(u_1, \ldots, u_n) = (1, \ldots, 1)$, and $\ldots = 0$, otherwise, identifies a multiset consisting of k tuples $(1, \ldots, 1)$ with $k \in \mathbb{N}$.

Thus, for all finite multisets of n-tuples $x \in D_{FMT}$,

$$J(h(x)) = card\,\{(u_1, \ldots, u_n) \in x \mid u_i \in U_i \text{ for all } i\}.$$

Hence, $L_\mathcal{M}(C) = h^{-1}(J^{-1}(N))$. The finitary-condition is invariant under inverse images of homomorphisms. Thus, $L_\mathcal{M}(C)$ is recognizable in $\mathcal{M}$.

For the reverse inclusion, suppose that L is recognized by a finitary $\mathcal{M}$-automaton $(\mathcal{A}, h, Q_{final})$ with, say, the set $D_{FMS} = \{q_1, \ldots, q_n\}$ of states of sort FMS.

The evaluation of the multiset t by $\mathcal{A}$ leads to the state (written in a notation which is justified by the fact that $\mathcal{A}$ satisfies (AC), even if $\sqcup^\mathcal{A}$ is taken over the empty multiset):

$$t^\mathcal{A} = \bigsqcup_{(u_1, \ldots, u_n) \in t}^{\mathcal{A}} \langle u_1^\mathcal{A}, \ldots, u_n^\mathcal{A} \rangle^\mathcal{A}.$$

We define the natural numbers: $a_i(i) = card\,\{(u_1, \ldots, u_n) \in t \mid \langle u_1^\mathcal{A}, \ldots, u_n^\mathcal{A} \rangle^\mathcal{A} = q_i\}$ and obtain (again thanks to (AC) being satisfied):

$$t^\mathcal{A} = \bigsqcup_{i=1}^{n}{}^\mathcal{A} \bigsqcup_{j=1}^{a_i(i)}{}^\mathcal{A} q_i.$$

We define a mapping $\nu_t : \{1, \ldots, n\} \rightarrow \{1, \ldots, n\}$ such that $q_{\nu_t(i)} = \bigsqcup_{j=1}^{a_i(i)}{}^\mathcal{A} q_i$. If $t \in L_\mathcal{M}(\mathcal{A})$, then:

$$\bigsqcup_{i=1}^{n}{}^\mathcal{A} q_{\nu_t(i)} \in Q_{final}, \qquad (5)$$

Generally, for a mapping $\mu : \{1, \ldots, n\} \to \{1, \ldots, n\}$, we define, for $i = 1, \ldots, n$, the set of natural numbers:

$$N_\mu^i = \{m \in \mathbb{N} \mid \bigsqcup_{j=1}^{m}{}^{\mathcal{A}} q_i = q_{\mu(i)} \}.$$

We note that $a_t(i) \in N_{\nu_t}^i$, for $i = 1, \ldots, n$. That is, t is an element of the language defined by the $\mathcal{M}$-counting constraint:

$$\bigwedge_{i=1}^{n} a_x(i) \in N_{\nu_t}^i.$$

Vice versa, for each mapping μ satisfying the property (5), the language of the $\mathcal{M}$-counting constraint:

$$\bigwedge_{i=1}^{n} a_x(i) \in N_\mu^i$$

is contained in L. We get $L = L(R)$ where R is the $\mathcal{M}$-counting constraint:

$$R = \bigvee_{\substack{\mu \\ \text{with (5)}}} \bigwedge_{i=1}^{n} a_x(i) \in N_\mu^i .$$

Since the number of mappings μ with (5) is finite, it only remains to show that the constraints used in R are of the defined form. The constituents $a_i(x)$ are admissible by the finitary-condition of $\mathcal{A}$. Finally, we have to proof that the sets N_μ^i are recognizable with respect to $(\mathbb{N}, +, 0)$. We will construct appropiate automata $\mathcal{A}_\mu^i$ from $\mathcal{A}$. We set $D^{\mathcal{A}_\mu^i} = Q$, $0^{\mathcal{A}_\mu^i} = \emptyset^{\mathcal{A}}$, $1^{\mathcal{A}_\mu^i} = q_i$ and interpret the addition by $\sqcup^{\mathcal{A}}$. As final states we take the singleton $\{q_{\mu(i)}\}$. Then, $\mathcal{A}_\mu^i$ recognizes N_μ^i. $\square$

Proof of Theorem 6.

For each language L of flat multitrees defined by a counting constraint C we will find an $\mathcal{M}$-counting constraint C' that defines $I(L)$, and *vice versa*.

Given a counting constraint for flat multitrees of the form:

$$C(x) = \operatorname{card}\{\varphi \in F \mid \exists y. (x\varphi y \wedge Ty\} \in N,$$

we set:

$$C'(x) = \operatorname{card}\{(\varphi, y) \in x \mid \varphi \in F \wedge y \in T\} \in N$$
$$\cap \operatorname{card}\{(\operatorname{root}, y) \in x \mid y \in \mathcal{F}\} = 1.$$

The case $C = Tx$ is obvious, as well as conjunction and disjunction.

For the other direction, given an $\mathcal{M}$-counting constraint C' for finite multisets, we will give a constraint C such that $L_{\mathcal{MT}_1}(C_x) = I^{-1}(L_{\mathcal{M}}(C'))$, or, equivalently, $L_{\mathcal{MT}_1}(C) = L_{\mathcal{M}}(C') \cap I(\mathcal{MT}_1)$. We note that the languages of the form $I(L)$ are the multisets containing exactly one pair with first component root. Given the $\mathcal{M}$-counting constraint:

$$C' = \operatorname{card}\{(\varphi, y) \in x \mid \varphi \in F \wedge y \in T\} \in N,$$

we have to distinguish the two cases *root* $\notin F$ and *root* $\in F$. In the first case we set:

$$C = card\{\varphi \in F \mid \exists y. (x\varphi y \wedge Ty\} \in N.$$

In the second case, we note that the set: $N - 1 = \{n - 1 \mid n \in N \text{ and } n \geq 1\}$ is recognizable with respect to $(\mathcal{N}, +, 0)$, and set:

$$\begin{aligned}C = \quad &card\{\varphi \in F - \{root\} \mid \exists y. (x\varphi y \wedge Ty)\} \in N - 1 \\ &\cap Tx.\end{aligned}$$

In either case C has the required property.

This concludes the proof of Theorem 6, since the reduction lemma (Lemma 10, page 14) and the above theorem (Theorem 13) close the cycle from counting-definable languages L of flat feature trees to those recognizable in $\mathcal{J}$ by feature automata. Namely, according to the above correspondence between counting- and $\mathcal{M}$-counting constraints, via $\mathcal{M}$-counting-definable languages $I(L)$, which, according to Theorem 13, are exactly the ones recognizable in $\mathcal{M}$, back to L according to Lemma 10. □

About the Theory of Tree Embedding

Alexandre Boudet and Hubert Comon

LRI, CNRS URA 410
Université Paris-Sud, Centre d'Orsay
91405 Orsay Cedex, France

Abstract. We show that the positive existential fragment of the theory of tree embedding is decidable.

1 Introduction

Symbolic Constraints, i.e. formulae interpreted in some term structure, have been revealed to be extremely useful in logic programming and theorem proving. Among such constraints, the *ordering constraints* can be used in expressing ordered strategies at the formula level instead of the inference level. This allows to cut further the search space, while keeping the completeness of the strategy [7]. Solving ordering constraints also allows for a nice lifting of orderings from the ground level to the terms with variables: define $s > t$ by $\forall \vec{x}.s > t$ where $\vec{x}$, the variables of s, t, range over all ground terms. This provides with more powerful orderings for termination proofs in rewriting theory.

Up to now, the satisfiability of ordering constraints has been studied for some orderings on terms: Venkataraman showed that the existential fragment of the theory of the subterm ordering is decidable, while the Σ_3 fragment is undecidable [10]. These results have been extended recently to infinite trees [9]. Comon showed that the existential fragment of the theory of any total lexicographic path ordering is decidable [1]. This result has been extended to any recursive path ordering over a total precedence by Jouannaud and Okada [6]. On the other hand, the Σ_4 fragment of the theory of any partial recursive path ordering is undecidable (provided that the signature is rich enough) [8].

All these works have left some open questions, among which the decidability of the existential theory of a partial recursive path ordering. Among the partial recursive path orderings, the *tree embedding* is the simplest one: the precedence is assumed to be empty. Actually the tree embedding is contained in all (partial) recursive path orderings. We do not solve here the decidability problem in its full generality, but we hope to contribute to the general solution: we show that the *positive* existential fragment of the theory of tree embedding is decidable.

The proof is carried out by elementary techniques which are quite different from those in [10, 9, 1, 6]. Indeed, for subterm problems, [10, 9] use some "test sets" showing that, if there is a solution, there is some solution which has a "small" size. They also use normal forms of inequations systems in which all inequations $s \geq t$ have a variable on the left. As we will see, it is not possible to follow this technique with the embedding relation. On the other hand, [1, 6, 7] use the linearity of the ordering in many places: the main problem is the expression of the *successor* function on the term level. Of course, we cannot use such a technique with the embedding which is not a linear ordering.

First, we set up precisely the problem in section 2. Then we give some obvious transformation rules in section 3. Using some stability properties of the set of solutions, we derive some additional rules reported in section 4. In section 5, we introduce more syntactic constructions in order to express easily strategies and we solve the problem of multiple upper bounds. We give section 6 the last rule which allows to break *non-trivial cycles* which necessarily occur in problems that are irreducible w.r.t. the other rules. Then we show that the whole set of rules terminates, thus leading to the decidability result.

2 Syntax and Semantics

Terms are built on the finite (ranked) alphabet F of function symbols and a set of variable symbols X. The resulting algebra is denoted $T(F, X)$ (Or $T(F)$ when X is empty). We use mainly the notations of [3]. For example, the result of replacing a term t with a term u at position p in s is denoted $s[u]_p$. This notation is also used in order to indicate that u occurs at position p in s. The root position (empty string) is denoted by Λ.

The *tree homeomorphic embedding* (or simply *embedding*) is the reduction relation associated with the rewrite system consisting of all rules

$$f(x_1, \ldots, x_n) \to x_i$$

for $i \in \{1, \ldots, n\}$ and $f \in F$ ($x_1, \ldots, x_n$ are variables). Embedding is a well ordering on terms [4]; it will be denoted $\trianglelefteq$ (more precisely, $s \trianglelefteq t$ if $t \xrightarrow{*} s$ using the above rules).

More operationally, we can use the following definition:

$$s \equiv f(s_1, \ldots, s_n) \trianglelefteq g(t_1, \ldots, t_m) \equiv t \qquad \text{iff}$$
$$\exists i, s \trianglelefteq t_i$$
$$\text{or} \quad f = g \text{ and } \forall i, s_i \trianglelefteq t_i$$

Inequational formulae are disjunctions of existentially quantified conjunctions of either inequations $s \leq t$ or equations $s = t$ where $s, t \in T(F, X)$. The set of variables of an inequational formula I is denoted by $Var(I)$. $\top$ and $\bot$ respectively denote the trivial and the unsatisfiable inequational problem.

I is interpreted as follows: a ground assignment σ (i.e. a mapping associating each variable of I with a term in $T(F)$) *satisfies* $s \leq t$ if $s\sigma \trianglelefteq t\sigma$. Similarly, it satisfies $s = t$ if $s\sigma \equiv t\sigma$ ($\equiv$ is the identity of terms). This interpretation extends to inequational formulae in the usual way. If all solutions of an inequational formula I are also solutions of an inequational formula J, we will write $I \models J$.

The problem we address here is the satisfiability of inequational problems. "Most" of the problems are satisfiable. Let us show some examples of unsatisfiable problems in increasing complexity. In all examples, f, h are binary function symbols, g, k are unary function symbols and a, b are constants.

Example 1.

$g(y) \leq x \wedge g(x) \leq y$ is not satisfiable since we can deduce $g(g(y)) \leq y$, which is unsatisfiable. This illustrates the *monotonicity* of embedding. We also used the fact that embedding contains the subterm ordering.

Example 2.

$g(y) \leq x \wedge x \leq f(y, g(g(a))) \wedge b \leq f(x,y)$ is not satisfiable since, from the first two inequations, we can conclude that $g(y)$ must be embedded in $g(g(a))$. It follows that y is either a or $g(a)$. Next, x must be embedded in $f(g(a), g(g(a)))$. Then $b \leq f(x,y)$ cannot be satisfied. This illustrates the fact that *only finitely many terms are embedded in a given term*.

Example 3.

$x \leq g(k(y)) \wedge x \leq k(g(y)) \wedge k(y) \leq x \wedge g(y) \leq x$ is not satisfiable. Indeed, either $x = g(x_1)$, or $x = k(x_1)$ for some x_1, or the top symbol of x is neither g nor k.

- In the first case, we deduce from the second inequation that $g(x_1) \leq g(y)$, hence $x_1 \leq y$. From the third inequation, we deduce that $k(y) \leq g(x_1)$, hence $k(y) \leq x_1$. Now there is a contradiction: $x_1 \leq y \wedge k(y) \leq x_1$ is unsatisfiable as in example 1.
- The second case ($x = k(x_1)$) is symmetric of the first one.
- In the last case (the top symbol of x is neither g nor k), we can deduce from the first inequation that $x \leq y$ which, together with $k(y) \leq x$ leads to a contradiction.

This example illustrates the problem of "multiple upper bounds": if some term t is embedded in both $g(u)$ and $h(v)$, then it must be embedded in either u or v.

3   A first set of transformation rules

The technique we will use for deciding the satisfiability of inequational formulae is now classical (see [2, 5]): it consists of rewriting the formula, using some rules which preserve the satisfiability, until the problem becomes trivially decidable.

Our first set of rules is quite straightforward to derive. It is displayed in figure 1. Let us call $\mathcal{R}_0$ this set of rules. All formulae are assumed to be kept in disjunctive normal form. Then the rules of figure 1 transform an inequational formula into an inequational formula.

Lemma 1. *All rules in $\mathcal{R}_0$ preserve the set of solutions of inequational formulae. Moreover, $\mathcal{R}_0$ is terminating and irreducible inequational formulae are disjunctions of conjunctions of equations and inequations whose at least one member is a variable.*

Actually, after one normalization w.r.t. $\mathcal{R}_0$, equations become useless. Discarding them preserves the satisfiability. Hence, for sake of simplicity, we assume now that inequational formulae do not contain any equation. We can assume this property along all other transformations. Also, every disjunction can be treated separately (there is no interaction between them). For this reason, we will sometimes forget that inequational problems contain disjunctions.

Embedding Rules (**Emb**)

$$f(s_1, \ldots, s_n) \le g(t_1, \ldots, t_m) \rightarrow \bigvee_{i=1}^{m} f(s_1, \ldots, s_n) \le t_i$$
$$\text{if } f \ne g$$

$$f(s_1, \ldots, s_n) \le f(t_1, \ldots, t_n) \rightarrow (\bigwedge_{i=1}^{n} s_i \le t_i) \vee \bigvee_{i=1}^{n} f(s_1, \ldots, s_n) \le t_i$$

Unification Rules (**Unif**)

$$f(s_1, \ldots, s_n) = g(t_1, \ldots, t_m) \rightarrow \bot$$
$$f(s_1, \ldots, s_n) = f(t_1, \ldots, t_n) \rightarrow s_1 = t_1 \wedge \ldots \wedge s_n = t_n$$
$$x = s \wedge P \rightarrow x = s \wedge P\{x \mapsto s\}$$
$$\text{if } x \notin Var(s), \ x \in Var(P), \text{ and}$$
$$\text{if } s \in X, \text{ then } s \in Var(P)$$
$$s = s \rightarrow \top$$
$$x = s[x]_p \rightarrow \bot$$
$$\text{if } p \ne \Lambda$$

Occur Check Rules (**Check**)

$$x \le t[x] \rightarrow \top$$
$$t_1[x_1]_{p_1} \le x_2 \wedge \ldots \wedge t_n[x_n]_{p_n} \le x_1 \rightarrow \bot$$
$$\text{if } p_i \ne \Lambda \text{ for some } i$$

$$x_1 \le x_2 \wedge \ldots \wedge x_n \le x_1 \wedge P \rightarrow P\{x_2 \mapsto x_1, \ldots, x_n \mapsto x_1\} \wedge \bigwedge_{i=2}^{n} x_i = x_1$$

Removing ground terms occurring on the right (**Ground 1**)

$$x \le t \wedge P \rightarrow \bigvee_{u \trianglelefteq t} x = u \wedge P\{x \mapsto u\}$$
$$\text{if } t \in T(F)$$

Fig. 1. The set $\mathcal{R}_0$ of rules

4 Basic Properties of Inequational Problems

In this section, we state the basic (crux) properties of inequational problems.

Lemma 2. *The set of solutions of an inequational problem is stable by homomorphism i.e. given any tree-morphism θ from $T(F)$ into itself if $\sigma \models I$, then $\theta \circ \sigma \models I\theta$.*

For example, if there is no constant occurring in I, and $a \in F$ is a constant, then the set of solutions is stable under the morphism $\{a \mapsto t\}$ for any ground term t.

We can also take advantage of the following straightforward remark:

Lemma 3. *If I is a conjunction of inequations of the form $x \leq t$ where x is a variable and t is a non-ground term, then, for any ground term u, the substitution σ_u mapping every variable of I on u is a solution of I.*

As a corollary, the following rule preserves the satisfiability:

Separate

$I_1 \wedge I_2 \wedge s_1 \leq t_1 \wedge \ldots \wedge s_n \leq t_n \quad \longrightarrow \quad I_1$

If $Var(I_2) \cap (Var(s_1, \ldots, s_n) \cup Var(I_1)) = \emptyset$, and

for every i, $Var(t_i) \not\subseteq Var(I_1) \cup Var(s_1, \ldots, s_n)$, and

I_2 consists of inequations $x \leq s$ where x is a variable and s is a non-ground term.

Indeed, if σ is a solution of I_1, then the substitution $\sigma \circ \sigma_u$ is a solution of $I_1 \wedge I_2 \wedge s_1 \leq t_1 \wedge \ldots \wedge s_n \leq t_n$ for some large enough u. Actually, it is sufficient to choose for u a term larger than $s_1\sigma, \ldots, s_n\sigma$. This is always possible, except if F contains two distinct constants and no function symbol of arity larger or equal to 2. This latter case is discarded now: the case of unary function symbols can be solved by means of automata.

The above remarks also suggest to remove inequations $s \leq x$ from I when s is a ground term. Indeed, if σ is a solution of the remainder of the problem, then it will be enough to compose σ with a well chosen homomorphism ($\{a \mapsto s\}$ for example), leading to a solution of I. This is not completely correct as the remainder of I may contain occurrences of constants (and hence be modified by the morphism). So, we will "freeze" the inequations $s \leq x$ when the variables of s only occur on the left, waiting until the rest of the problem is solved. Then, either $s \leq x$ has become ground along the transformation (leading to either $\top$ or $\bot$) or else we will be able to construct a solution out of a solution of the non-frozen part, thanks to the stability by homomorphism. Let us show an example:

Example 4.
Let I be $g(a) \leq x \wedge x \leq f(a, y) \wedge x \leq f(y, a) \wedge y \leq x$. We freeze $g(a) \leq x$. The two inequations $x \leq f(a, y) \wedge x \leq f(y, a)$ are equivalent to $x \leq f(a, a) \vee x \leq y$ (see the next sections). In the first case, using the $\mathcal{R}_0$-normalization, we get a contradiction with the frozen part $g(a) \leq x$ which has become ground: $g(a) \leq f(a, a)$. In the second case, we get $y = x$. From any substitution $\sigma = \{x \mapsto s; \ y \mapsto s\}$ (which is a solution of the hot part) we get a solution $\theta \circ \sigma$ of I, by composition with the morphism $\theta = \{b \mapsto g(a)\}$ where b is any constant occurring in s.

Let us consider a new syntactic construction (for strategic purposes only) in inequational formulae: conjunctions of inequations may be surrounded by brackets $\{\}$ in which case, the inequations are *frozen*. This will be managed by the following rule:

> **Freeze**
> $\{I_1\} \wedge s \leq t \wedge I_2 \quad \rightarrow \quad \{I_1 \wedge s \leq t\} \wedge I_2$
> If there is no variable in s occurring in some right hand side of an inequation of I_2

The non-frozen part of a conjunction of inequations I will also be called the *hot part* of I and written $H(I)$.

5 Elimination of multiple upper bounds

The **Separate** rule allows to eliminate variables which occur only in right sides of inequations (take $I_2 = \emptyset$). **Freeze** eliminates (from the hot part) variables which occur only on the left. It is also possible to eliminate the variables which are bound only once; the rule:

> **Eliminate**
> $\{P\} \wedge Q \wedge x \leq s \quad \rightarrow \quad \{P\{x \mapsto s\}\} \wedge Q\{x \mapsto s\}$
> If x does not occur in s nor in any left member of an inequation of P or Q

preserves the satisfiability. Indeed, if σ is a solution of $\{P\} \wedge Q \wedge x \leq s$, consider the substitution θ which is identical to σ, except on x where $x\theta \equiv s\sigma$. Of course, θ still satisfies any inequation in which x does not occur. It also obviously satisfies $x \leq s$. Then, it only remains to consider inequations in which x occurs on the right. Let $y \leq t$ be such an inequation. Then $y\theta \equiv y\sigma \triangleleft t\sigma \triangleleft t\theta$ since $x\sigma \triangleleft s\sigma \equiv x\theta$. Hence θ is also a solution of $y \leq t$.

The problem is now illustrated by example 3: some variable may be bounded twice by "incompatible" terms. In order to express that x is bounded by both s and t, we write $x \in s\&t$. This will be useful for keeping track of the deductions we already considered.

Let $\mathcal{E}$ be the set of terms in $T(F \cup \{\&\}, X)$ where $\&$ is assumed to be associative-commutative and is used in infix notation. Ground expressions $e \in \mathcal{E}$ are interpreted as finite sets of terms as follows:

$$[\![s\&t]\!] \stackrel{\text{def}}{=} [\![s]\!] \cap [\![t]\!]$$
$$[\![f(s_1, \ldots, s_n)]\!] \stackrel{\text{def}}{=} [\![s_1]\!] \cup \ldots \cup [\![s_n]\!] \cup \{f(t_1, \ldots, t_n) \mid \forall i, t_i \in [\![s_i]\!]\}$$
$$\mathcal{I}(f(s_1, \ldots, s_n)) \stackrel{\text{def}}{=} \{f(t_1, \ldots, t_n) \mid \forall i, t_i \in \mathcal{I}(s_i)\}$$
$$\mathcal{I}(s\&t) \stackrel{\text{def}}{=} [\![s\&t]\!]$$

For example, $\mathcal{I}(g(f(a, g(a))\&h(b, g(a)))) = \{g(a), g(g(a))\}$: the first g cannot be erased, whereas the other occurrences of g (below $\&$) can be erased. Let us emphasize that $[\![\cdot]\!]$ stands for the set of all terms embedded in the expression, whereas $\mathcal{I}$, which is only used above the first occurrence of a $\&$, imposes that no symbol is erased until an $\&$ is reached.

Then, we introduce a new predicate symbol $\in$ with the following meaning: the solutions of $s \in e$, where $s \in T(F, X)$ and $e \in \mathcal{E}$ is the set of ground substitutions σ such that $s\sigma \in \mathcal{I}(e\sigma)$. For example, the solutions of $x \in g(k(y))\&k(g(y))$ are the substitutions $\{x \mapsto g(s); \; y \mapsto s\}$ for some ground term s and the substitutions $\{x \mapsto k(s); \; y \mapsto s\}$ for some ground term s.

The *occur-check relation* is the smallest reflexive-transitive relation $\leq_{oc}^{I}$ on the variables of an inequational problem I such that:

– if $u[x] \leq y$ is in I, then $x \leq_{oc}^{I} y$
– if $x \in y\&e$ is in I, then $x \leq_{oc}^{I} y$

Gathering together the bounds of a variable x is expressed using the new predicate symbol:

Bounds

$x \leq s_1 \wedge \ldots \wedge x \leq s_n \quad \longrightarrow \quad x \in s_1 \& \ldots \& s_n$

if x is maximal w.r.t. $\leq_{oc}$ among the variables occurring in inequations of the hot part of the problem, and $s_1, \ldots, s_n$ are all the terms occurring on the right of an inequation whose left member is x, and $n \geq 2$.

The correctness of this rule is quite straightforward. "Deciphering" membership conditions consists in replacing $x \in e$ with a conjunction of inequations; for $e \in \mathcal{E}$, we define $\mathcal{D}(s \in e)$ as the set of inequations $s \leq t$ where t is any normal form of e w.r.t the rewrite system

$$u\&v \longrightarrow u$$
$$u\&v \longrightarrow v$$

Now, we are ready to give the additional rules dealing with the new syntactic constructions. They are given in figures 2 and 3.

The rule system $\mathcal{R}_1$ acts on normal forms w.r.t. $\mathcal{R}_0$. It consists of all rules of figures 2, 3 and of the rule **Bounds**. The new rules **Separate** and **Freeze** which are displayed in this figure are generalizations of the previous ones (hence we do not have to give new names), incorporating the new syntactic construction.

Lemma 4. *All rules of* $\mathcal{R}_1 - \{$**Separate**, **Unbounded-Var**$\}$ *preserve the satisfiability of inequational problems.*

This is mostly a mechanical verification. Note however that, for $e \in \mathcal{E}$, we always have $\mathcal{I}(e) \subseteq [\![e]\!]$, but the converse is false when the top symbol of e is not $\&$. Consequently, the **Ground 2** rule or the second **Freeze** rule which replaces $x \in e$ with $\mathcal{D}(x \in e)$ may, locally, add solutions. But they don't add solutions to the original inequational problem as the additional solutions can be found in another disjunct.

Eliminate

$$\{P\} \wedge Q \wedge x \le s \rightarrow \{P\{x \mapsto s\}\} \wedge Q\{x \mapsto s\}$$
    if x does not occur in s nor in any left member of an inequation of P or Q

Ground 2

$$x \in e \rightarrow \mathcal{D}(x \in e)$$
        if there is an inequation $x \le t$ with t ground in $\mathcal{D}(x \in e)$

&-normalization

$$x \in e[f(t_1, \ldots, t_n) \& g(s_1, \ldots, s_m)] \rightarrow \bigvee_{i=1}^{n} x \in e[t_i \& g(s_1, \ldots, s_m)] \vee$$
$$\bigvee_{i=1}^{m} x \in e[f(t_1, \ldots, t_n) \& s_i]$$
$$\text{if } f \ne g$$

$$x \in e[f(t_1, \ldots, t_n) \& f(s_1, \ldots, s_n)] \rightarrow x \in e[f(s_1 \& t_1, \ldots, s_n \& t_n)] \vee$$
$$\bigvee_{i=1}^{n} x \in e[t_i \& f(s_1, \ldots, s_n)] \vee$$
$$\bigvee_{i=1}^{n} x \in e[f(t_1, \ldots, t_n) \& s_i]$$

Ground 2

$$x \in e \rightarrow \mathcal{D}(x \in e)$$
        if there is an inequation $x \le t$ with t ground in $\mathcal{D}(x \in e)$

Check-&

$$x \in e[u[x]_p \& s] \rightarrow x \in e[s]$$
            if there is no $\&$ symbol along the path p

Check-∈

$$P \wedge x_0 \in x_1 \& e_1 \wedge \ldots \wedge x_n \in x_0 \& e_{n+1} \rightarrow x_0 = x_1 \wedge \ldots \wedge x_0 = x_n$$
$$\wedge x_0 \in e_1 \& \ldots \& e_{n+1}$$
$$\wedge P\{x_1 \mapsto x_0; \ldots; x_n \mapsto x_0\}$$

Fig. 2. The set $\mathcal{R}_1$ of rules. Part I

Separate

$$\bigwedge_{i \in \mathcal{I}} x_i \in e_i \wedge \bigwedge_{j \in \mathcal{J}} y_j \in e'_j \wedge \bigwedge_{k \in \mathcal{K}} s_k \leq t_k \wedge P_{-V} \rightarrow \bigwedge_{j \in \mathcal{J}} y_j \in e'_j \wedge P_{-V}$$

If 1. no rule from $\mathcal{R}_0$, **&-normalization**, **Ground 2** can be applied to the problem on the left
2. V is a subset of the variables occurring in the problem on the left
3. For all $i \in \mathcal{I}$, $Var(x_i, e_i) \subseteq V$
4. For all $j \in \mathcal{J}$, $Var(e'_j) \cap V \neq \emptyset$
5. For all $k \in \mathcal{K}$, $Var(s_k) \cap V = \emptyset$ and $Var(t_k) \cap V \neq \emptyset$
6. $Var(P_{-V}) \cap V = \emptyset$.

Unbounded-Var

$$x \in t[u[y]_p \& v]_q \rightarrow x \in t[v]_q$$
$$x \in t[y]_p \rightarrow \top$$

 If y doesn't occur in any left side of a membership condition or an inequation, there is no & along the path p, and the **&-normalization** rules cannot be applied.

Freeze

$$\{I_1\} \wedge s \leq t \wedge I_2 \rightarrow \{I_1 \wedge s \leq t\} \wedge I_2$$

 If there is no variable in s which occurs in either some right hand side of an inequation of I_2 or in some right side of a membership condition of I_2.

$$\{I_1\} \wedge x \in e \wedge I_2 \rightarrow \{I_1 \wedge \mathcal{D}(x \in e)\} \wedge I_2$$

If x does not occur in e nor in I_2.

Fig. 3. The set $\mathcal{R}_1$ of rules. Part II

Also, we need an extension of lemma 3 in order to prove the correctness of the **Separate** rule:

Lemma 5. *Assume that I consists of membership conditions $x \in e$ only and that I is irreducible w.r.t. **&-normalization** and **Ground 2**. Then, for every ground term t, there is a solution σ of I such that, for every variable x of I, $t \trianglelefteq x\sigma$.*

Proof. Replace every atom $x \in t_x[z_1 \& e_1, \ldots, z_n \& e_n]$ in the inequational problem I with $\exists x_1, \ldots, x_n . x = t_x[x_1, \ldots, x_n] \wedge x_1 \in z_1 \& e_1 \ldots \wedge x_n \in z_n \& e_n$ where t_x doesn't contain any occurrence of & (this is of course correct). We get an equational part I_1 and a conjunction I_2 of atoms of the form $x \in z \& e$ where z is a variable (by irreducibility w.r.t. **&-normalization**). Then, for every ground term u, σ_u is a solution of I_2. We prove this result by induction on the sum of sizes of all expressions occurring on the right of the membership conditions of I_2.

If all membership conditions are of the form $x \in t$ where t does not contain any $\&$, this is a consequence of lemma 3. In the same way, if the only occurrences of $\&$ are in expressions $z_1 \& \ldots \& z_n$ where $z_1, \ldots, z_n$ are variables, then σ_u is obviously a solution.

Now, assume that there is a condition $x \in z_1 \& \ldots \& z_n \& e$ where e is not a variable. Then, by irreducibility w.r.t. **&-normalization**, e can be written $u[y_1 \& e_1, \ldots, y_k \& e_k]$ $(k \geq 0)$ where u does not contain any occurrence of $\&$ and $y_1, \ldots, y_k$ are variables. Moreover, there is an index i such that **Ground 2** would not apply on $x \in y_i \& e_i$. (For, otherwise, **Ground 2** would apply on $x \in z_1 \& \ldots \& z_n \& e$). Applying the induction hypothesis to I_2 in which $x \in z_1 \& \ldots \& z_n \& e$ is replaced with $x \in y_i \& e_i$, we get the result that σ_u is a solution of this new membership system. But, if $x\sigma_u \in [\![y_i \sigma_u \& e_i \sigma_u]\!]$, then, a fortiori, $x\sigma_u \in [\![z_1 \sigma_u \& \ldots \& z_n \sigma_u \& e \sigma_u]\!]$.

We conclude the proof by considering the substitutions θ_u which assign to each $x \in Var(I)$ the term $t_x[x_1, \ldots, x_n]\sigma_u$: θ_u is a solution of I and $u \trianglelefteq x\theta_u$. $\square$

Lemma 6. *The rules* **Separate** *and* **Unbounded-Var** *preserve the satisfiability of inequational problems.*

Lemma 7. *Assume that ϕ is $\in$-free and $\phi \xrightarrow[\mathcal{R}_1]{*} \psi$. Then all variables occurring as left members of membership conditions in ψ do not occur in any left hand side of an inequation of ψ.*

This is a consequence of the maximality conditions on x in the **Bounds** rule.

Lemma 8. *Considering $\mathcal{R}_1$ as acting on normal forms w.r.t. $\mathcal{R}_0$ (i.e. we assume an $\mathcal{R}_0$-normalization after each $\mathcal{R}_1$-reduction), we get a terminating reduction.*

Indeed, if we only consider the hot part of inequational problems, the number of variables occurring in left sides of inequations is not increasing. No rule can introduce variables in left hand sides of inequations, except the rules which replace a variable with some other variable in the whole problem (with the **Check** and **Check-$\in$** rules) and the **Ground 2** rule. In the former case, the number of variables occurring in left sides of inequations is not increasing. In the latter case, by $\mathcal{R}_0$-normalization, x must be replaced everywhere with a ground term, which means that it does no longer occur in a left side of an inequation. Now, by lemma 7, the number of variables occurring in left sides of inequations of the hot part is strictly decreasing as soon as **Bounds** is applied.

Now, if there is no occurrence of **Bounds** in the reduction sequence, the &-normalization alone terminates (and is independent of the other rules), **Ground** rules eliminate variables and all other rules reduce the size of the problem.

6 Eliminating Cycles

In this section, we restrict our attention to the hot part ϕ of an inequational problem I irreducible for $\mathcal{R}_0 \cup \mathcal{R}_1$. The transformation rules that we have given so far yield problems whose hot parts are either $\top$ or $\bot$, or problems involving some *non-trivial cycles* as defined below. For studying the properties of such cycles, we associate a weighted, oriented graph G^ϕ with an inequational problem ϕ, irreducible for $\mathcal{R}_0 \cup \mathcal{R}_1$. Examining this graph will give us both the application conditions of our last rule and the termination proof.

6.1 Interpreting Inequational Problems into Graphs

The vertices of G^ϕ are the variables of ϕ. The graph G^ϕ has two different kind of arcs, and several arcs may connect two vertices:

Definition 9. Let ϕ be an inequational problem, irreducible for $\mathcal{R}_0 \cup \mathcal{R}_1$. The graph G^ϕ has the variables of ϕ for vertices and

- There is an arc $x \overset{p}{\Longleftarrow} y$ if and only if there is an inequation $u[x]_p \leq y$ in ϕ, where the *weight* $\mid p \mid$ of the arc is the length of position p.
- There is an arc $x \overset{p}{\longleftarrow} y$ if and only if there is an atom $x \in e$ in ϕ, and $x \leq t[y]_p$ belongs to $\mathcal{D}(x \in e)$, where the *weight* $\mid p \mid$ of the arc is the length of position p.

A *non-trivial cycle* is a cycle (*i.e.*, a non-trivial path with the same target and origin) involving arcs of the form $x \overset{p}{\Longleftarrow} y$ and arcs of the form $x \overset{p}{\longleftarrow} y$. The weight of an arc in superscript will be dropped if irrelevant.

It turns out that if an inequational problem, irreducible for $\mathcal{R}_0 \cup \mathcal{R}_1$ is not $\top$ or $\bot$, then the associated graph G^ϕ will contain a non-trivial cycle.

It follows from the lemma 7 that if there is an arc $x \overset{p_i}{\longleftarrow} x_i$ in G^ϕ, then all the in-going arcs of x are of the form $x \overset{p_j}{\longleftarrow} x_j$, and they all come from the same atom $x \in e[x_1, \ldots, x_n]$ of ϕ.

In case G^ϕ contains no arcs of the form $x \overset{p}{\Longleftarrow} y$, then **Separate** applies with $V = Var(\phi)$, turning the hot part of the problem into $\top$. We have the following straightforward lemma:

Lemma 10. *Let ϕ be an inequational problem, irreducible for $\mathcal{R}_0 \cup \mathcal{R}_1$. Then G^ϕ has at least one arc of the form $x \overset{p}{\Longleftarrow} y$.*

We can now restrict our attention to the problems involving arcs of the form $x \overset{p}{\Longleftarrow} y$. Now, a crucial property of G^ϕ will locate where to apply our last rule:

Lemma 11. *Let ϕ be an inequational problem, irreducible for $\mathcal{R}_0 \cup \mathcal{R}_1$. If G^ϕ contains an arc $x \overset{p}{\Longleftarrow} y$ with $p \neq \Lambda$, then there is a vertex $z \geq_{oc} y$ whose in-going arcs are all of the form $z \overset{q}{\longleftarrow} z'$ with $\mid q \mid \neq 0$.*

Proof. Consider a maximal (*i.e.* without any in-going arcs) strongly connected component C of G^ϕ. Let $Var(C)$ be the set of vertices of C. C cannot be reduced to a singleton $\{x\}$ since **Unbounded-Var**, **Separate**, or **Eliminate** would apply. Indeed, in this case, x having no in-going arc could not appear anywhere in a left-hand side of an inequation or a membership condition.

We assume now that $Var(C)$ is not a singleton, and we first show, by contradiction that C contains an arc of the form $x \overset{p}{\Longleftarrow} y$ with $p \neq \Lambda$. Assume the converse. Then there is no inequation in ϕ of the form $u[x]_p \leq y$ with $p \neq \Lambda$ and $x \in Var(C)$ because if $y \in Var(C)$, then the edge $x \overset{p}{\Longleftarrow} y$ would belong to C and otherwise, C would have an in-going arc. Let $Atom(C)$ be the set of atoms of ϕ containing a variable of $Var(C)$. The atoms of $Atom(C)$ are then of one of the following forms:

- $x \in e$, where $x \cup Var(e) \subseteq Var(C)$,
- $s \leq x$, where $x \in Var(C)$ and $Var(s) \cap Var(C) = \emptyset$,
- $x \in e$, where $x \notin Var(C)$ and $Var(e) \cap Var(C) \neq \emptyset$.

In this case, $Var(C)$ matches the application conditions of **Separate**, a contradiction.

Consider now an arc $x \overset{p}{\Longleftarrow} y$ of C and let z be a variable, such that $z \geq_{oc} y$, z being maximal for the occur-check relation. C having no in-going arc, z belongs to C. Since z is maximal for $\geq_{oc}$, its only in-going arcs are of the form $z \overset{q}{\Longleftarrow} z_i'$, with $q \neq \Lambda$.□

The previous lemma shows that one of the following rules can be applied to a problem ϕ irreducible for $\mathcal{R}_0 \cup \mathcal{R}_1$, whenever ϕ contains an inequation.

Explode
$$x \in t[e_1, \ldots, e_n]_{p_1, \ldots, p_n} \wedge \psi \quad \longrightarrow$$
$$\exists \vec{z}\ x = t[z_1, \ldots, z_n]_{p_1, \ldots, p_n} \wedge \bigwedge_{i=1}^{n} z_i \in e_i \wedge \psi\{x \mapsto t[z_1, \ldots, z_n]_{p_1, \ldots, p_n}\}$$
if no rule of $\mathcal{R}_0 \cup \mathcal{R}_1$ applies, and x is maximal for $\leq_{oc}$, and there is an inequation $u[y]_p \leq x'$ with $p \neq \Lambda$ in ψ, and $x \geq_{oc} x'$, and $p_1 \neq \Lambda, \ldots, p_n \neq \Lambda$, where $e_1, \ldots, e_n$ are the maximal subterms of t with top function symbol $\&$.

The rule **Explode** preserves the sets of solutions, according to the semantics of the predicate $\in$. Note in addition that the proof of lemma 11 shows that if G^ϕ contains an edge $x \overset{p}{\Longleftarrow} y$ with $p \neq \Lambda$, then it contains a non-trivial cycle since both an edge $x \overset{p}{\Longleftarrow} y$ and an edge $x' \overset{q}{\Longleftarrow} y'$ belong to the same strongly connected component. The partial correctness of our algorithm is given by the following lemma:

Lemma 12. *If the hot part ϕ of an inequational problem $I \not\equiv \perp$, irreducible for $\mathcal{R}_0 \cup \mathcal{R}_1$, is not $\top$, then the rule* **Explode** *applies.*

Indeed, such a problem must contain an inequation $u[y]_p$ with $p \neq \Lambda$, otherwise **Separate** would apply, reducing the hot part of the problem to $\top$. In this case, lemma 11 shows that **Explode** applies.

We are left to show that the process of applying **Explode** and re-normalizing the problem with $\mathcal{R}_0 \cup \mathcal{R}_1$ terminates.

6.2 Termination

We prove the termination by defining a well-founded ordering $>_W$ on graphs such that if **Explode** is applied to a problem ϕ and the resulting problem is re-normalized for $\mathcal{R}_0 \cup \mathcal{R}_1$, yielding a problem ψ, then $G^\phi >_W G^\psi$.

Definition 13. Let $Path(G^\phi)$ be the set of maximal paths of G^ϕ of the form $x \overset{p_1}{\Longleftarrow} y_1 \overset{p_2}{\Longleftarrow} y_2 \overset{p_3}{\Longleftarrow} y_3 \cdots y_{n-1} \overset{p_n}{\Longleftarrow} y_n$, which do not contain twice a same arc (by *maximal* we mean that there is no further arc $y_n \overset{p_{n+1}}{\Longleftarrow} y_{n+1}$).
With a path $\mathcal{P} = x \overset{p_1}{\Longleftarrow} y_1 \overset{p_2}{\Longleftarrow} y_2 \overset{p_3}{\Longleftarrow} y_3 \cdots y_{n-1} \overset{p_n}{\Longleftarrow} y_n \in Path(G^\phi)$, we associate the weight $W(\mathcal{P}) = (\mid p_1 \mid, n \cdot \mid p_n \mid \cdot \mid p_{n-1} \mid \cdots \mid p_2 \mid)$. The ordering $>_W$ on graphs is the multiset extension of the ordering obtained by comparing lexicographically the weights of the paths of $Path(G^\phi)$, using the usual ordering on natural numbers for the first component, and alphabetic[1] ordering on words of natural numbers for the second component.

Lemma 14. *Let ϕ be an inequational problem, irreducible for $\mathcal{R}_0 \cup \mathcal{R}_1$. Assume **Explode**, is applied to ϕ, followed by a normalization for $\mathcal{R}_0 \cup \mathcal{R}_1$, yielding a problem ψ. Then $G^\phi >_W G^\psi$.*

Proof. (Sketched) Assume that **Explode** is applied to $x \in t[u_1, \ldots, u_n]_{p_1, \ldots, p_n}$ in ϕ, the variable x being replaced by $t[z_1', \ldots, z_n']_{p_1, \ldots, p_n}$, where the z_i's are new variables. The resulting problem is then normalized for $\mathcal{R}_0 \cup \mathcal{R}_1$, yielding the problem ψ. The atoms involving x before **Explode** is applied to the atom $x \in t$ are of one of the following forms:

- $x \in t[u_i[z_j]_{q_{i,j}}]_{p_i}$
- $v_k \in t'[x]_{q_k}$
- $u[y]_r \le x$
- $y \le s[x]$

The last inequation is irrelevant for our measure. Note that the p_is are different from Λ by the application conditions of **Explode** (and lemma 11), and that x cannot occur in a left-hand side of an inequation. The corresponding arcs, (including a possible additional path going through x and leading to an arc $w' \Longleftarrow w$) are as follows:

---

[1] The alphabetic ordering is not well-founded (there are infinite descending sequences $1 > 0 \cdot 1 > 0 \cdot 0 \cdot 1 \cdots$), but our ordering is well-founded since the first integer in a word is its length.

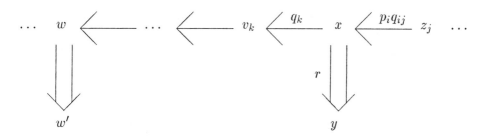

After applying **Explode**, the atom $x \in t$ has disappeared, and there are new atoms of the form $z_i' \in u_i[z_j]_{q_{ij}}$. The atoms of the form $v_k \in t'[x]_{q_k}$ have become $v_k \in t'[t[z_i']_{p_i}]_{q_k}$. They are normalized using the rules of **&-Normalization** into $v_k \in t''[z_i']_{q_{ki}'}$ with $\mid q_{ki}' \mid \leq \mid q_k \mid + \mid p_i \mid$. The inequation $u[y]_r \leq x$ has become $u[y]_r \leq t[z_i']_{p_i}$ which has to be re-normalized. This does not increase the weight since no rules (except the unification rules that will never be applied again) may introduce a variable in a left-hand side of an inequation, and the embedding rules may only decrease the depth of the variables in the left-hand sides of inequations, which decreases the first component of the weight of the paths starting with y, or yield an inequation of the form $u[y]_r \leq z_i'$. In the first case, (that is if the rule $f(s_1, \ldots, s_n) \leq f(t_1, \ldots, t_n) \rightarrow \bigwedge_{i=1}^{n} s_i \leq t_i$ of **Emb** is applied), then the paths starting from y have been replaced by paths of smaller weight (on the first component). Otherwise, the normalization yields an inequation of the form $u[y]_r \leq z_i'$. The inequation $y \leq s[x]$ has become $y \leq s[[z_1', \ldots, z_n']_{p_1, \ldots, p_n}]$, which is still irrelevant for our measure. The graph G^{ψ} is then as follows:

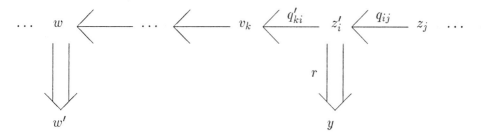

The paths of $Path(G^{\phi})$ going to y, (or to some w') trough x have been replaced by paths of the same length (and same weight in the first component) going through the z_i's, but the arcs from the z_js to x labeled with $p_i q_{ij}$ have been replaced by arcs from the z_js to the z_i's labeled by q_{ij} with $p_i \neq \Lambda$, all smaller on the second component of their weight. $\square$

We can now state our main result, following by lemmas 12 and 14.

Theorem 15. *The positive existential fragment of the first-order theory of homeomorphic embedding is decidable.*

7 Conclusion

We gave the first decidability result for the satisfiability of partial path orderings. We need however to go beyond:

- we wish to investigate the full existential fragment of the theory of embedding.
- we wish to investigate the full positive theory of embedding.
- we wish to investigate the extension to the positive existential fragment of any recursive path ordering. This is not straightforward, since, for example, $x \leq t$ where t is ground, needs not to have only finitely many solutions.

All these works are first steps towards the study of the theory of arbitrary partial recursive path orderings (for which we recall that only the Σ_4 fragment is known to be undecidable). Finally, we would like to understand better the relationships with automata theory and, in particular, the combination of ordering constraints and sort constraints expressed in terms of the membership to recognizable tree languages.

References

1. Hubert Comon. Solving symbolic ordering constraints. *International Journal of Foundations of Computer Science*, 1(4), 1990.
2. Hubert Comon. Disunification: a survey. In Jean-Louis Lassez and Gordon Plotkin, editors, *Computational Logic: Essays in Honor of Alan Robinson*. MIT Press, 1991.
3. Nachum Dershowitz and Jean-Pierre Jouannaud. Rewrite systems. In J. van Leeuwen, editor, *Handbook of Theoretical Computer Science*, volume B, pages 243–309. North-Holland, 1990.
4. Graham Higman. Ordering by divisibility in abstract algebras. *Proceedings of the London Mathematical Society*, 2(3):326–336, September 1952.
5. Jean-Pierre Jouannaud and Claude Kirchner. Solving equations in abstract algebras: A rule-based survey of unification. In Jean-Louis Lassez and Gordon Plotkin, editors, *Computational Logic: Essays in Honor of Alan Robinson*. MIT-Press, 1991.
6. Jean-Pierre Jouannaud and Mitsuhiro Okada. Satisfiability of systems of ordinal notations with the subterm property is decidable. In *Proc. 18th Int. Coll. on Automata, Languages and Programming, Madrid, LNCS 510*, 1991.
7. R. Nieuwenhuis and A. Rubio. Theorem proving with ordering constrained clauses. In Deepak Kapur, editor, *Proc. 11th Int. Conf. on Automated Deduction, Saratoga Springs, NY, LNCS 607*. Springer-Verlag, June 1992.
8. Ralf Treinen. A new method for undecidability proofs of first order theories. Tech. Report A-09/90, Universität des Saarladandes, Saarbrücken, May 1990.
9. Sauro Tulipani. Decidability of the existential theory of infinite terms with subterm relation. To appear in *Information and Computation*, 1991.
10. K. N. Venkataraman. Decidability of the purely existential fragment of the theory of term algebras. *Journal of the ACM*, 34(2):492–510, 1987.

Linear Unification of Higher-Order Patterns

Zhenyu Qian[*]

Universität Bremen

Abstract

Higher-order patterns are simply typed λ-terms in η-long form where free variables F only occur in the form $F(x_1, \cdots, x_k)$ with $x_1, \cdots, x_k$ being distinct bound variables. It has been proved in [6] that in the simply typed λ-calculus unification of higher-order patterns modulo α, β and η reductions is decidable and unifiable higher-order patterns have a most general unifier.

In this paper a unification algorithm for higher-order patterns is presented, whose time and space complexities are proved to be linear in the size of input.

1 Introduction

Lambda calculi are suitable frameworks for succinctly representing logical languages with bound variables. This is not only because they can be directly and intuitively used in encoding logical terms and formulae, but also because some of them have been turned into computational realities, e.g. in the logic programming languages λProlog [8] and Elf [14], and in the generic theorem prover Isabelle [12], due to the pioneer work on unification of simply typed λ-terms by Huet [3].

However, unification of simply typed λ-terms is a complex operation since the problem is in general undecidable [2], and unifiable terms may have infinite independent unifiers. Even when one is only interested in the existence of unifiers, where Huet's insight was that terms with free variables at heads are always unifiable and thus need not be further dealt with [3], the unification process could be expensive in time and space because it may be nondeterministic and nonterminating. This has led to search for special classes of λ-terms on which unification is decidable and unifiable terms has a most general unifier.

Miller discovered such a class and gave a unification algorithm to compute the most general unifiers [6]. The terms in the class are those where certain restrictions are placed on occurrences of free variables. Nipkow used the results in the context of higher-order rewriting, reformulated the unification algorithm [9] and presented a functional program for the unification [10]. Pfenning adapted the results for his logic programming language Elf [13] and extended them to the Calculus of Constructions [15]. We follow Nipkow and call these terms *higher-order patterns* (short: *patterns*).

Unification of patterns is a proper compromise of the full unification of simply typed λ-terms [7]: Taking a higher-order logic programming language L_λ based on patterns as proposed in [6], the full unification of simply typed λ-terms can be coded as a L_λ program axiomatizing only the notions of equality and substitution of simply typed λ-terms in a direct and declarative way. The rest of the full unification is addressed by unification of patterns and a backtracking strategy implemented in a L_λ interpreter.

However, unification of patterns may be extremely inefficient in its worst case since so may be unification of first-order terms ([11, 4]) and first-order terms are just special patterns. The purpose of this paper is to tackle unification of patterns from a computational complexity point of view. More precisely, an algorithm for unification of patterns is proposed

---

[*]FB Informatik, Universität Bremen, 2800 Bremen 33, Germany. E mail: qian@informatik.uni-bremen.de
Research partially supported by ESPRIT Basic Research WG *COMPASS* 6112.

whose time and space complexities are both linear in the size of the input. The structure of our algorithm has some similarities with Martelli and Montanari's one [4, 5], but ours is not a direct extension of theirs. The features needed in our machine are manipulation of pointers, comparison of labels and random access of array components.

The rest of this paper is organized as follows: In Section 2 basic notions of λ-calculus are reviewed and unification of patterns is presented at a fairly high level. In Section 3 some problems with extending the first-order linear unification algorithms in [11, 4, 5] to unification of patterns are discussed. A linear algorithm for unification of patterns is proposed in Section 4, and its linearity is proved in Section 5. We conclude in Section 6.

2 Preliminaries

Given a set $\mathcal{T}_0$ of *base types*, the set $\mathcal{T}$ of (*simple*) *types* is constructed as usual. For every type $\alpha \in \mathcal{T}$ there exist a set C_α of *constants* and a countably infinite set $\mathcal{V}_\alpha$ of *variables* such that $C_{\alpha_1} \cap \mathcal{V}_{\alpha_2} = \{\}$ for any $\alpha_1, \alpha_2 \in \mathcal{T}$ and $C_{\alpha_1} \cap C_{\alpha_2} = \mathcal{V}_{\alpha_1} \cap \mathcal{V}_{\alpha_2} = \{\}$ if $\alpha_1 \neq \alpha_2$. Let $C = \bigcup_{\alpha \in \mathcal{T}} C_\alpha$ and $\mathcal{V} = \bigcup_{\alpha \in \mathcal{T}} \mathcal{V}_\alpha$. Constants and variables are also called *atoms*.

The set $\mathcal{L}_\alpha$ of *terms of type* $\alpha \in \mathcal{T}$ is constructed as usual. Let $\mathcal{L} = \bigcup_{\alpha \in \mathcal{T}} \mathcal{L}_\alpha$. A term of the form $(s\ t)$ is called an *application*, and $\lambda x.s$ an *abstraction*. The topmost part λx in $\lambda x.s$ is called a λ-*binder* of x, and the term t is said to be *covered* by or *in the scope* of λx. *Free* and *bound* variable occurrences are defined as usual. We use the following abbreviations: $\lambda \overline{x_n}.s$ stands for $\lambda x_1.\dots.\lambda x_n.s$; $a(\overline{u_n})$ stands for $(\dots((a\ u_1)\ u_2)\dots u_n)$.

The *size of a term* t is defined as the total number of occurrences of atomic subterms and λ-binders in t.

Terms are only compared modulo α-conversion. Thus we assume from now on that in a term no variable is bound more than once and no variable occurs both bound and free. The set of all bound (or free) variables in a syntactic object O is denoted by $\mathcal{BV}(O)$ (or $\mathcal{FV}(O)$).

Reductions on terms are the usual β and η-reductions, denoted by $\longrightarrow_\beta$ and $\longrightarrow_\eta$, resp. Define $\longrightarrow_{\beta\eta}$ as $\longrightarrow_\beta \cup \longrightarrow_\eta$. Let $\mathcal{X} \in \{\beta, \eta, \beta\eta\}$. We use $\longrightarrow_\mathcal{X}^*$ to denote the reflexive and transitive closure, and $=_\mathcal{X}$ the equivalence relation induced by $\longrightarrow_\mathcal{X}$.

Every term s can be $\mathcal{X}$-reduced to a unique $\mathcal{X}$-*normal form* $s\downarrow_\mathcal{X}$. A term t is a β-normal form if and only if t is of the form $\lambda \overline{x_k}.a(\overline{t_n})$ with $a \in C \cup \mathcal{V}$ and each t_i being a β-normal form. The atom a is called the *head*. Let $t = \lambda \overline{x_k}.a(\overline{t_n})$ be a β-normal form as above. Then t is called *flexible* if $a \in \mathcal{FV}(t)$, *rigid* if not. Furthermore, t is called an η-*long form* if $a(\overline{t_n})$ is of a base type and each t_i is a η-long form. Every term s has a unique η-long form $s\downarrow_{l_\eta}$ such that $s\downarrow_{l_\eta} \longrightarrow_\eta^* s\downarrow_\beta$. For single variable x, $x\downarrow_{l_\eta}$ may still be written as x.

A *substitution* θ is defined as usual and denoted by $\{x_1 \mapsto t_1, \dots, x_n \mapsto t_n\}$ or $\{\overline{x_n \mapsto t_n}\}$. The *domain* of θ is $\mathcal{D}om(\theta) = \{x_1, \dots, x_n\}$, and the *range* $\mathcal{R}an(\theta) = \{t_1, \dots, t_n\}$. It is always assumed that before applying θ to a term s in $\theta(s)$, all bound variables in s have been α-converted so that $\mathcal{BV}(s) \cap \mathcal{FV}(\mathcal{R}an(\theta)) = \{\}$. It is also assumed that $\mathcal{BV}(s) \cap \mathcal{D}om(\theta) = \{\}$, hence $\theta(\lambda x.s) = \lambda x.\theta(s)$ holds automatically.

The *restriction* of a substitution θ to a set $\mathcal{W}$ of variables is a substitution $\theta_{|\mathcal{W}} = \{x \mapsto \theta(x) \mid x \in \mathcal{W}\}$. Let σ and θ be substitutions. Then the *composition* $\sigma \circ \theta$ is a substitution defined by $(\sigma \circ \theta)(x) = \sigma(\theta(x))$ for every $x \in \mathcal{V}$. Let $\sigma =_{\beta\eta} \theta$ denote $\sigma(x) =_{\beta\eta} \theta(x)$ for each $x \in \mathcal{V}$. Then σ is said to be *more general than* θ, denoted as $\sigma \leq_{\beta\eta} \theta$, if there is a substitution σ' such that $\sigma' \circ \sigma =_{\beta\eta} \theta$.

A substitution θ is called a *unifier* of terms s and t if $\theta(s) =_{\beta\eta} \theta(t)$. In this case s and t are said to be *unifiable*. Define a *unification pair* $s =^? t$ as an unordered pair of terms s and t of the same type. A *unification problem* P is a finite multiset of unification pairs. Two unification problems are said to be *equivalent* if they have the same unifiers.

For $\theta = \{\overline{x_n \mapsto t_n}\}$, define $[\theta] = \{\overline{x_n =^? t_n}\}$. Obviously θ is a most general unifier of $[\theta]$. If $\mathcal{D}om(\sigma) \cap \mathcal{D}om(\theta) = \{\}$ then $[\sigma \circ \theta]$ and $[\sigma] \cup [\theta]$ are equivalent.

In the sequel, we use s, t, u and v to denote terms, a and b atoms, c, d and f constants, x, y and z bound variables, X, Y, Z, F, G and H free variables, σ and θ substitutions.

2.1 Higher-order patterns and higher-order pattern unification

Higher-order patterns (short: *patterns*) are η-long forms in which free variables F only occur in the form $F(\overline{x_k})$ with $x_1, \cdots, x_k$, $k \geq 0$, being distinct bound variables. For example, the terms $\lambda xyz.F(y, x)$ and $\lambda xy.y(\lambda z.F(z, y), F(x, y), G(y))$ are patterns, provided that they are η-long forms, whereas $\lambda x.F(c, x)$, $\lambda xy.F(x, x)$ and $\lambda x.F(G(x))$ are not patterns.

Lemma 2.1 *([6]) It is decidable whether two arbitrary patterns are unifiable. Furthermore, a substitution whose range contains only patterns can always be computed as the most general unifier of two arbitrary unifiable patterns.*

From now on we only consider patterns and substitutions whose ranges contain only patterns. Note that for such a substitution σ if t is a pattern then so is $\sigma(t){\downarrow}_\beta$.

We represent here an algorithm by Nipkow [9]. The algorithm is given by the following five transformation rules on pairs of substitutions and unification problems, where unification problems are viewed as lists instead of multisets of unification pairs and @ denotes the concatenation operation of lists. The algorithm starts with the pair $\langle \{\}, P \rangle$ for any unification problem P and terminates with $\langle \sigma, \{\} \rangle$ if P is unifiable, in which case σ is the most general unifier of P. It is assumed that a unification pair is always automatically α-converted so that both sides always have the same sequence of outermost λ-binders.

Rule (Rep) propagates solutions.

$$\langle \sigma, \{\lambda\overline{x_k}.F(\overline{x_k}) \stackrel{?}{=} t\}@P \rangle \implies \langle \sigma' \circ \sigma, \sigma'(P){\downarrow}_\beta \rangle \tag{Rep}$$

if $F \notin \mathcal{FV}(t)$, where $\sigma' = \{F \mapsto t\}$.

Rule (Dec) breaks a unification pair into simpler ones.

$$\langle \sigma, \{\lambda\overline{x_k}.a(\overline{s_n}) \stackrel{?}{=} \lambda\overline{x_k}.a(\overline{t_n})\}@P \rangle \implies \langle \sigma, \{\overline{\lambda\overline{x_k}.s_n \stackrel{?}{=} \lambda\overline{x_k}.t_n}\}@P \rangle \tag{Dec}$$

if $a \in \mathcal{C} \cup \{\overline{x_k}\}$.

Rule (Bin) finds a partial binding for a head variable.

$$\langle \sigma, \{\lambda\overline{x_k}.F(\overline{y_n}) \stackrel{?}{=} \lambda\overline{x_k}.a(\overline{t_m})\}@P \rangle \implies \langle \sigma' \circ \sigma, \{\overline{\lambda\overline{x_k}.H_m(\overline{y_n}) \stackrel{?}{=} \lambda\overline{x_k}.t_m}\}@\sigma'(P){\downarrow}_\beta \rangle \tag{Bin}$$

if $F \notin \mathcal{FV}(\overline{t_m})$ and $a \in \mathcal{C} \cup \{\overline{y_n}\}$, where $H_1, \cdots, H_m$ are new variables and $\sigma' = \{F \mapsto \lambda\overline{y_n}.a(\overline{H_m(\overline{y_n})})\}$.

Rule (FF-1) finds a unifier of a unification pair of flexible terms with distinct heads.

$$\langle \sigma, \{\lambda\overline{x_k}.F(\overline{y_n}) \stackrel{?}{=} \lambda\overline{x_k}.G(\overline{z_m})\}@P \rangle \implies \langle \sigma' \circ \sigma, \sigma'(P){\downarrow}_\beta \rangle \tag{FF-1}$$

if F and G are distinct free variables, where $\sigma' = \{F \mapsto \lambda\overline{y_n}.H(\overline{v_p}), G \mapsto \lambda\overline{z_m}.H(\overline{v_p})\}$, $\{v_1, \cdots, v_p\} = \{\overline{y_n}\} \cap \{\overline{z_m}\}$ and H is a new free variable.

Rule (FF-2) finds a unifier of a unification pair of flexible terms with the same head.

$$\langle \sigma, \{\lambda\overline{x_k}.F(\overline{y_n}) \stackrel{?}{=} \lambda\overline{x_k}.F(\overline{z_n})\}@P \rangle \implies \langle \sigma' \circ \sigma, \sigma'(P){\downarrow}_\beta \rangle \tag{FF-2}$$

where $\sigma' = \{F \mapsto \lambda\overline{y_n}.H(\overline{v_p})\}$, $\{\overline{v_p}\} = \{y_i \mid y_i = z_i, 1 \leq i \leq n\}$ and H is a new free variable.

Inversing the preconditions to the above rules yields the following failure cases. The first case may be described as $\lambda\overline{x_k}.a(\overline{s_n}) =^? \lambda\overline{x_k}.b(\overline{t_m})$, where $a, b \in \mathcal{C} \cup \{\overline{x_k}\}$ with $a \neq b$, and is called *clash*. The second and third cases may be described as $\lambda\overline{x_k}.F(\overline{y_n}) =^? \lambda\overline{x_k}.a(\overline{s_m})$, where $F \in \mathcal{FV}(\overline{s_m})$ or $a \in \{\overline{x_k}\} - \{\overline{y_n}\}$. The case $F \in \mathcal{FV}(\overline{s_m})$ is called *cycle* and the case $a \in \{\overline{x_k}\} - \{\overline{y_n}\}$ *bound variable capture*.

Theorem 2.2 *([9])There are no infinite sequences of transformations by the above rules. A unification problem P is unifiable if and only if every sequence of transformations starting with $\langle \{\}, P \rangle$ terminates with $\langle \sigma, \{\} \rangle$, in which case $\sigma_{|\mathcal{FV}(P)}$ is a most general unifier of P.*

In the first-order case, rules (Rep), (Bin) and (FF-1) degenerate into rule (Rep'), and rules (Dec) and (FF-2) into (Dec') as follows:

$$\langle \sigma, \{F \overset{?}{=} t\} \cup P \rangle \implies \langle \sigma' \circ \sigma, \sigma'(P) \rangle \tag{Rep'}$$

if $F \notin \mathcal{FV}(t)$, where $\sigma' = \{F \mapsto t\}$.

$$\langle \sigma, \{a(\overline{s_n}) \overset{?}{=} a(\overline{t_n})\} \cup P \rangle \implies \langle \sigma, \overline{\{s_n \overset{?}{=} t_n\}} \cup P \rangle \tag{Dec'}$$

if $a \in \mathcal{A}$.

Most first-order unification algorithms can be derived from rules (Rep') and (Dec'). In particular, the linear unification algorithms by Paterson and Wegman ([11]) and by Martelli and Montanari ([4, 5]) can be derived from these two rules, where terms are represented by *directed acyclic graphs* (short: *DAGs*), unification problems may be re-organized by the following merging rule

$$\{s \overset{?}{=} t, s \overset{?}{=} u\} \cup P \implies \{s \overset{?}{=} t, t \overset{?}{=} u\} \cup P$$

and the unification pair, to which rule (Rep') is applied at each stage, is always so selected that no substitutions have to be applied to the rest unification problem.

3 Problems with Extending the First-Order Linear Unification Algorithms

In this section we discuss some problems with extending the linear unification algorithms in [11, 4, 5] to higher-order patterns.

The first problem is due to the propagation of outermost λ-binders in rule (Dec). For example, a unification pair $\lambda \overline{x_k}.f(\overline{a_k}) =^? \lambda \overline{x_k}.f(\overline{b_k})$ of length $O(k)$ may be transformed into $\{\lambda \overline{x_k}.a_1 =^? \lambda \overline{x_k}.b_1, \cdots, \lambda \overline{x_k}.a_k =^? \lambda \overline{x_k}.b_k\}$ of length $O(k^2)$. Making a copy of the λ-binders $\lambda \overline{x_k}$ for each subproblem $s_i =^? t_i$ would lead to at least quadratic space complexity.

Our solution to the problem is to require that whenever rule (Dec) is applied, it should be applied repeatedly to each newly yielded unification pair of two rigid terms. Not all old outermost λ-binders, but only those that do bind some occurrences of bound variables in a flexible term need to be carried over to a final resulting unification pair. All occurrences of bound variables that do not occur in a flexible term have to be eliminated in the further unification process anyway; otherwise the original problem is not unifiable.

For example, unifying $\lambda \overline{x_k}.g(f(F(x_1)), c_1, \cdots, c_k) =^? \lambda \overline{y_k}.g(f(y_2), c_1, \cdots, c_k)$ should directly yield $\lambda x_1.F(x_1) =^? \lambda y_1.y_2$. The unnecessary intermediate unification problem

$$\{\lambda \overline{x_k}.f(F(x_1)) \overset{?}{=} \lambda \overline{y_k}.f(y_2), \lambda \overline{x_k}.c_1 \overset{?}{=} \lambda \overline{y_k}.c_1, \cdots, \lambda \overline{x_k}.c_k \overset{?}{=} \lambda \overline{y_k}.c_k\}$$

will not be really created at all. Note that now the total size of all unification pairs yielded is always linear in the size of the original unification pair. For, each newly created sequence of λ-binders corresponds uniquely to a flexible subterm in the original unification pair and is shorter than the flexible subterm. Continue the unification process for $\lambda x_1.F(x_1) =^? \lambda y_1.y_2$ in the above. Since the occurrence of y_2 is not covered by a corresponding λ-binder, a failure will arise. Intuitively, the failure corresponds to a bound variable capture in unifying $\lambda \overline{x_k}.F(x_1) =^? \lambda \overline{y_k}.y_2$.

The second problem is due to the time required for renaming subterms of bound variables possibly needed before a merging step. For example, in order to merge the unification pairs $\lambda \overline{x_k}.F(x'_k) =^? \lambda \overline{x_k}.s$ and $\lambda \overline{x_k}.F(y'_k) =^? \lambda \overline{x_k}.t$, the second unification pair may first have to be converted into an equivalent one $\lambda \overline{x_k}.F(x'_k) =^? \lambda \overline{x_k}.\phi(t)$ with $\phi = \{y'_k \mapsto x'_k\}$. Now a merging step may be performed and result in $\lambda \overline{x_k}.F(x'_k) =^? \lambda \overline{x_k}.s$ and $\lambda \overline{x_k}.s =^? \lambda \overline{x_k}.\phi(t)$. The renaming operation in $\phi(t)$ is a possible source of nonlinear behaviors, since an occurrence of a bound variable in t may be involved in many merging steps in the entire unification process and thus need to be renamed many times. Consider the unification problem

$$P_1 = \{\lambda xy.y(F(x, y), F(y, x)) \overset{?}{=} \lambda xy.s_1\},$$

where $s_i = y(x(G_i(x,y), G_i(y,x)), s_{i+1}), i = 1, \ldots, n-1$, and $s_n = y(x(G_n(x,y), G_n(y,x)),$ $y(c,c))$. Obviously, P_1 has the size $O(n)$. By rule (Dec), P_1 may be transformed into

$$\{\lambda xy.F(x,y) \overset{?}{=} \lambda xy.x(G_1(x,y), G_1(y,x)), \lambda xy.F(y,x) \overset{?}{=} \lambda xy.s_2\}.$$

Now $\lambda xy.F(y,x) =^? \lambda xy.s_2$ may be converted into $\lambda xy.F(x,y) =^? \lambda xy.t_2$, where t_2 denotes $\{x \mapsto y, y \mapsto x\}(s_2)$, and the resulting unification pairs may be merged into

$$\{\lambda xy.F(x,y) \overset{?}{=} \lambda xy.x(G_1(x,y), G_1(y,x)), \lambda xy.x(G_1(x,y), G_1(y,x)) \overset{?}{=} \lambda xy.t_2\}.$$

The first unification pair may be solved by rule (Rep), where no substitution need to be applied to the rest unification problem

$$P_2 = \{\lambda xy.x(G_1(x,y), G_1(y,x)) \overset{?}{=} \lambda xy.t_2\}.$$

Continue the unification process with P_2 in the same way as above, it is easy to see that the total number of renaming x and y in the entire unification process is $O(n^2)$.

The merging step in the above example is also necessary when terms are denoted by De Bruijn's representations. So a naive extension of the first-order linear unification algorithms with De Bruijn's representations of patterns has at least quadratic time complexity.

Our solution to the problem is to avoid renaming subterms of bound variables whenever possible. Indeed, such renaming operations would be unnecessary if no attempts are made to keep both sides of a unification pair have the same sequence of outermost λ-binders. In merging $\lambda \overline{x_k}.F(\overline{x_k'}) =^? \lambda \overline{x_k}.s$ and $\lambda \overline{x_k}.F(\overline{y_k'}) =^? \lambda \overline{x_k}.t$, since $\lambda \overline{x_k}.\phi(t) = \lambda \phi^{-1}(\overline{x_k}).t$ by α-conversion, where $\phi = \{\overline{y_k'} \mapsto \overline{x_k'}\}$, the second unification pair may also be converted into $\lambda \overline{x_k}.F(\overline{x_k'}) =^? \lambda \phi^{-1}(\overline{x_k}).t$. Due to our solution to the first problem, the size of a sequence of outermost λ-binders, i.e. $\lambda \overline{x_k}$ in this case, is linear in the size of a flexible term, i.e. $F(\overline{x_k'})$ in this case. Thus the time for renaming the sequence, i.e. $\phi^{-1}(\overline{x_k})$ in this case, may be linear in the size of the flexible term. Since a merging step is only applied when the free variable in the flexible term will be solved by rule (Rep) directly afterwards, the flexible term cannot be charged for time expenses in renaming other sequences of outermost λ-binders. Since the flexible term is a subterm in the original unification problem, our solution may be linear.

Now a unification pair may have terms with different sequences of outermost λ-binders. So subterms of bound variables can only be compared modulo α-conversion. This means that for example, in unifying $\lambda \overline{x_k}.x(\cdots) =^? \lambda \overline{y_k}.y(\cdots)$, we need to check whether the λ-binders λx and λy occur at the same position in $\lambda \overline{x_k}$ and $\lambda \overline{y_k}$, resp. Thus each sequence of outermost λ-binders should be implemented by a data structure, where the position of a given λ-binder can be computed in a constant time. However, maintaining such a data structure for each sequence of outermost λ-binders in the entire unification process is nonlinear, since λ-binders may be discarded, and since the same (named) λ-binders may occur in different sequences.

Our solution is to delay the checking operations: Instead of performing a checking operation when and where required, all conditions to be checked are first collected. Afterwards, all bound variables in the collected conditions are replaced by their positions in the corresponding sequences of outermost λ-binders. If some bound variables that should be α-equivalent are replaced by different positions, a failure arises. In fact, this kind of failures correspond to clashes in the original unification problem.

4 A Linear Unification Algorithm for Higher-Order Patterns

4.1 Representations of patterns, multiequations and systems of multiequations

The linearity of first-order unification heavily depends on the DAG representation of terms where only one data structure is dynamically created for a variable and all occurrences of the variable are implemented as pointers to the data structure. We do the similar things for free variables in patterns. The difference is that now a free variable may have arguments of bound variables. Formally, a pattern can be representated as a DAG such that

1. each occurrence of an atom corresponds to a node labeled with the name of the atom and having no out-arcs,

2. each application $a(\overline{t_n})$ corresponds to a node labeled with the special symbol @ and having $n + 1$ ordered out-arcs going to the nodes corresponding to $a, t_1, \cdots, t_n$, resp.,

3. each abstraction $\lambda x.t$ corresponds to a node labeled with λ and having 2 ordered out-arcs leading to the nodes corresponding to x and t,

4. different occurrences of subterms correspond to different nodes, except that occurrences of the same free variable correspond to the same node.

Obviously the root node has no father nodes, and any other node that does not correspond to a free variable has exactly one father node.

We extend the notions of *multiequation* and of *system of multiequations* in [4] as follows: A *multiequation* is a pair $U =^? M$ of a nonempty set U of flexible patterns and a set M of patterns. Usually, patterns in M are rigid. A multiequation $\{s\} =^? M$ may be written as $s =^? M$, and $U =^? \{t\}$ as $U =^? t$. A multiequation $U =^? M$ denotes a unification problem $\{s =^? t \mid t \in U \cup M\}$ where s is some term in U. A *system of multiequations* is defined as (T, S) with T being a sequence of multiequations, called the *solved* part, and S a set of multiequations, called the *unsolved* part, such that

1. the right-hand side of each multiequation in T and S contains at most one term,

2. the left-hand side of each multiequation in T consists of one flexible term, and the right-hand side, if nonempty, consists of a term of the same type,

3. the free variable in the left-hand side of a multiequation in T may only occur in the right-hand sides of preceding multiequations in T and nowhere else.

A DAG representation of a system (T, S) can be obtained by creating a node for each multiequation with out-arcs to all its terms, a node for T (and a node for S) with out-arcs to all its multiequations, and a node for (T, S) with two out-arcs to T and S, resp., where all nodes of the same free variable are identified.

Intuitively, a system of multiequations corresponds to a pair of a substitution and a unification problem in Subsection 2.1. For any given set S_0 of multiequations, our algorithm starts with a system $(\langle \rangle, S_0)$, attempts to transfer multiequations from the unsolved to solved part while preserving the unifiers of the whole system and terminates with a system $(T_f, \{\})$ if S_0 is unifiable.

In the first-order case [4], a multiequation $U =^? M$ in S may be moved to T if no free variables in U occur in $S - \{U =^? M\}$. The same thing cannot be directly done in higher-order case, since some information about free variables in M may be lost. Consider

$$S = \{\lambda xy.F(x) \overset{?}{=} \lambda xy.a(G(x,y))\} \cup S'$$

with $F \notin \mathcal{FV}(S')$ as an example. Intuitively the multiequation should not be directly moved to T since it has a left-hand side not equal to F and thus is not directly a substitution of F.

The nature of the problem is that a unifier θ of $\lambda xy.F(x) =^? \lambda xy.a(G(x,y))$ maust satisfy that y does not occur in $\theta(G)(x,y){\downarrow}_\beta$. In fact, we may add an additional multiequation $\lambda xy.G(x,y) =^? \lambda xy.H(x)$ to the above S, where H is a new free variable. By rules (Bin) and (FF-1) in Subsection 2.1, the resulting S is equivalent to the original one when restricted to the original free variables. Now the multiequation $\lambda xy.F(x) =^? \lambda xy.a(G(x,y))$ can be moved from S to T since the information that would have been lost in the above is kept by the additional multiequation. Note that the name of H is immaterial. Therefore we may write $\lambda xy.G(x,y) =^? \lambda xy.H(x)$ as $\lambda y[\lambda x.G(x,y) =^? \{\}]$, where the λy outside the square bracket $[\cdots]$ means that no substitutions of $\lambda x.G(x,y)$ in the unification process may contain y.

In general, the form $\lambda \overline{x_k}.[U =^? M]$ denotes two multiequations

$$\{\lambda \overline{x_k}.s \mid s \in U\} \stackrel{?}{=} \{\lambda \overline{x_k}.t \mid t \in M\} \quad \text{and} \quad \lambda \overline{y_n}.F(\overline{y_n}) \stackrel{?}{=} \lambda \overline{y_n}.H(\overline{z_m})$$

where $F(\overline{y_n})$ is a subterm in U and $\{\overline{z_m}\} = \{\overline{y_n}\} - \{\overline{x_k}\}$. Note that the ordering of λ-binders in $\lambda \overline{x_k}$ may be arbitrary. The form $\lambda \overline{x_k}.[U =^? M]$ can be simplified into $U =^? M$ if all subterms of each x_i in U and M can be recognized as occurrences of bound variable on its own. In this paper bound variables are denoted by lower-case letters x, y, z.

In the sequel, we allow the above extended multiequations in systems of multiequations. The outermost λ-binders in U or M are sometimes called *remaining λ-binders*.

In the above example, the multiequation $\lambda xy.F(x) =^? \lambda xy.a(G(x,y))$ is first rewritten into $\lambda x.F(x) =^? \lambda x.a(G(x,y))$ and then moved to the solved part, while an additional $\lambda x.G(x,y) =^? \{\}$ is created in the unsolved part.

Assume $T_f = \langle U_m =^? M_m \rangle$ in a system $(T_f, \{\})$. Let θ_i, $i = 1, \cdots, m$, be defined as

$$\begin{aligned}
\theta_m &= \{F \mapsto t\} && \text{if } U_m = \{\lambda \overline{x_k}.F(\overline{x_k})\} \text{ and } M_m = \{t\} \\
\theta_i &= \{\} && \text{if } M_i = \{\} \\
\theta_i &= \{F \mapsto \theta_{i+1}(t)\downarrow_\beta\} && \text{if } U_i = \{\lambda \overline{x_k}.F(\overline{x_k})\} \text{ and } M_i = \{t\}.
\end{aligned}$$

Then a most general unifier of T_f can be constructed as $\theta = \theta_1 \cup \cdots \cup \theta_m$. In fact, T_f is a factorized form of θ.

From a given unification pair $\lambda \overline{x_k}.s =^? \lambda \overline{x_k}.t$ a set of multiequations can be constructed as follows: If at least one of $\lambda \overline{x_k}.s$ and $\lambda \overline{x_k}.t$ is flexible then the set consists of one multiequation $U =^? M$, where $U = \{u \in \{\lambda \overline{x_k}.s, \lambda \overline{x_k}.t\} \mid u$ is flexible$\}$ and $M = \{\lambda \overline{x_k}.s, \lambda \overline{x_k}.t\} - U$; Otherwise the set consists of two multiequations $U_1 =^? M_1$ and $U_2 =^? M_2$, where $U_1 = U_2 = \{\lambda \overline{x_k}.H(\overline{x_k})\}$ with H being a new free varviable, $M_1 = \{\lambda \overline{x_k}.s\}$ and $M_2 = \{\lambda \overline{x_k}.t\}$. For a unification problem P, the starting set S_0 of multiequations consists of the multiequations constructed from all unification pairs in P. Obviously P and S_0 are equivalent when restricted to $\mathcal{FV}(P)$.

4.2 The algorithm

Our algorithm *Unify* is given below. At each stage, when S is nonempty, the algorithm first selects a set MS of multiequations from S, where no free variables in the left-hand sides of the multiequations in MS occur in $S - MS$ or in the right-sides in MS (line 8). Note that no resulting substitutions of unifying MS need to be applied to the rest of the system. A stack ST is used to keep the sets of multiequations that have been looked at but do not satisfy the condition required in the above. To unify MS the algorithm first merges all multiequations in MS into a multiequation $U =^? M$ (line 9). Then flexible terms in U are unified and the results are put into T (line 10), where B is a set consisting of the original positions of all remaining λ-binders in U after unification. Note that now U contains one term. If M is empty, then nothing has to be done; Otherwise the terms in M are unified w.r.t. the information in B (line 11), and, when no failure arises, a multiequation as a fragment of the final solution with U on the left and the common top layer of all terms in M on the right will be obtained and put into T, and a set of smaller multiequations as a part of the rest unification problem is created and put into S and ST. All sets in the algorithm are implemented as lists, so that sometimes we may talk about "the first (or last) element" in a set. Procedure parameters of complex data structures like lists are implemented as pointers to these data structures.

(1) **Algorithm** *Unify*
(2) **input** A system of multiequations $(\langle\rangle, S)$;
(3) **output** A system of multiequations $(T, \{\})$;
(4) **begin**
(5)   Create an empty stack ST;
(6)   **while** S is nonempty **do**
(7)   **begin**
(8) $Select(ST, S, MS)$;
(9) $Merge(MS, U =^? M)$;
(10) $UnifyL(U, T, B)$;
(11)   **if** M is nonempty **then** $UnifyR(U, M, B, T, S, ST)$
(12)   **end**
(13) **end**

The procedure *Select* is given in the appendix. It can be seen as an easy extension of its first-order counterpart in [5]. For more details see also [16].

4.3 Merge the selected multiequations

The procedure $Merge(MS, U =^? M)$ merges all multiequations in MS into a multiequation $U =^? M$. To begin with, all flexible terms in each left-hand side in MS are α-converted so that they have the same outermost λ-binders (line B-3). Then the procedure takes an arbitrary multiequation in MS as the first $U =^? M$, and starts to merge all other multiequations $U' =^? M'$ in MS one by one into the current $U =^? M$.

First, all left-hand sides are merged. For simplicity, we may factorize the common remaining λ-binders and write $\{\lambda\overline{x_k}.t_1, \cdots, \lambda\overline{x_k}.t_n\}$ as $\lambda\overline{x_k}.\{t_1, \cdots, t_n\}$. Let $U = \lambda\overline{x_k}.V$ and $U' = \lambda\overline{y_m}.V'$ with $F(\overline{x_n'}) \in V$ and $F(\overline{y_n'}) \in V'$. Then a mapping $\phi = \{y_n' \mapsto x_n'\}$ may be created (line B-7). Note that $x_i' \notin \{\overline{x_n}\}$ or $y_i' \notin \{\overline{y_m}\}$ means x_i' or y_i', resp., has been required to be eliminated somewhere. We may compute the common remaining λ-binders for both multiequations modulo α-conversion (line B-8). Now U' may be α-converted and merged into U (line B-9), where it is assumed that all bound variables in V' that are not in $\{\overline{y_n'}\}$ do not occur in V; otherwise we may add an additional renaming operation here.

The resulting left-hand side then consists of terms with a common sequence of remaining λ-binders. The fact that some λ-binders have been discarded in merging the left-hand sides implies that the λ-binders at the same positions in the corresponding right-hand sides should also be discarded (line B-14). The right-hand side is merged in line B-15, where the order of λ-binders are so changed as though the left-hand sides were originally covered by $\lambda\overline{x_k}$.

(B-1) **procedure** $Merge(MS, \mathbf{var}\ U =^? M)$
(B-2) **begin**
(B-3)   For each $\{\lambda\overline{x_k^1}.t_1, \cdots, \lambda\overline{x_k^n}.t_n\} =^? M$ in MS, replace each $\lambda\overline{x_k^i}.t_i$ by $\lambda\overline{x_k^1}.\{x_k^i \mapsto x_k^1\}t_i$;
(B-4)   Assume $MS = \{U_1 =^? M_1, \cdots, U_h =^? M_h\}$; $U := U_1$;
(B-5)   **for** $i = 2$ to h, assume $U = \lambda\overline{x_k}.V$, $U_i = \lambda\overline{y_m}.V'$, $F(\overline{x_n}) \in V$ and $F(\overline{y_n}) \in V'$, **do**
(B-6)   **begin**
(B-7)   Let ϕ_i be $\{y_n' \mapsto x_n'\}$;
(B-8)   Let $\{x_{p_1}, \cdots, x_{p_g}\} = \{\overline{x_k}\} \cap \{\phi_i(y_m)\}$ be a set with $p_j < p_l$ for $j < l$;
(B-9) $U := \lambda x_{p_1} \cdots \lambda x_{p_g}.(V \cup \phi_i(V'))$
(B-10)   **end**;
(B-11) $M := \{\}$; Assume $U = \lambda\overline{x_k}.V$; Let ϕ_1 be the identity map, $\phi_2, \cdots, \phi_h$ as above;
(B-12)   **for** $i = 1$ to h, assume $U_i = \lambda\overline{y_m}.V'$ and $M_i = \{\lambda\overline{z_m}.t\}$, **do**
(B-13)   **begin**
(B-14)   Let $\{p_1, \cdots, p_k\}$ be such that $\phi_i(y_{p_j}) = x_j$; (*$j \leq l$ may not imply $p_j \leq p_l$.*)
(B-15) $M := M \cup \{\lambda z_{p_1} \cdots \lambda z_{p_k}.t\}$

(B-16)   end;
(B-17) end

As an example, consider

$$MS = \{ \ \{\lambda x_1 x_2 x_3.F(x_1, x_2, x_4, x_3), \lambda x_1 x_2 x_3.G(x_1, x_2, x_3)\} \quad =^? \quad \lambda x_1' x_2' x_3'.s,$$
$$\{\lambda y_1 y_2 y_3.F(y_2, y_1, y_3, y_4), \lambda y_1 y_2 y_3.G(y_2, y_3, y_1)\} \quad =^? \quad \lambda y_1' y_2' y_3'.t \ \}.$$

Let $i = 2$ in line B-5. Then $\phi_2 = \{y_2 \mapsto x_1, y_1 \mapsto x_2, y_3 \mapsto x_4, y_4 \mapsto x_3\}$ in line B-7, $\{x_{p_1}, \cdots, x_{p_q}\} = \{x_1, x_2\}$ in line B-8 and $U = \lambda x_1 x_2.\{F(x_1, x_2, x_4, x_3), G(x_1, x_2, x_3),$ $G(x_1, x_4, x_2)\}$ in line B-9. Furthermore, we have $x_1 = \phi_2(y_2), x_2 = \phi_2(y_1)$ in line B-14. Thus the final M is constructed in line B-15 as $\{\lambda x_1' x_2'.s, \lambda y_2' y_1'.t\}$.

4.4   Unify the left-hand side

Unification of flexible terms corresponds to applications of rules (FF-1) and (FF-2) in Subsection 2.1. Note that U is of the form $\lambda \overline{x_k}.V$. In lines C-6 and C-7, the procedure *UnifyL* computes the bound variables which should be preserved when applying rules (FF-1) and (FF-2). When the **for**-structure from line C-4 to C-8 is finished, a new set X of remaining λ-binders has been found. Now all free variables in U are replaced by a new variable H with arguments from X. In order to adjust the λ-binders in the right-hand side w.r.t. the set X, the procedure also returns a set B of original positions for all λ-binders with bound variables in X.

(C-1)   **procedure** *UnifyL*(**var** U, **var** T, **var** B)
(C-2)   **begin**
(C-3)   Assume $U = \lambda \overline{x_k}.V$ and let $X = \{\overline{x_k}\}$;
(C-4)   **for each** $F \in \mathcal{FV}(U)$ with $F(\overline{y_n^1}), \cdots, F(\overline{y_n^m})$ being all subterms in U with F **do**
(C-5)   **begin**
(C-6)   Let $\{p_1, \cdots, p_q\} = \{i \mid y_i^1 = \cdots = y_i^m\}$ with $p_j < p_l$ for $1 \leq j < l \leq q$;
(C-7) $X := X \cap \{y_{p_1}^1, \cdots, y_{p_q}^1\}$
(C-8)   **end**;
(C-9)   Let H be a new variable;
(C-10)   **for each** $F \in \mathcal{FV}(U)$, assume $F(\overline{y_n}) \in V$, **do**
(C-11)   append $\lambda \overline{y_n}.F(\overline{y_n}) =^? \lambda \overline{y_n}.H(\overline{X})$, marked as 'visited", to the end of T;
(C-12) $U := \{\lambda \overline{X}.H(\overline{X})\}$; $B := \{i \mid x_i \in X\}$
(C-13) **end**

As an example, consider the result of the previous example

$$U = \lambda x_1 x_2.\{F(x_1, x_2, x_4, x_3), G(x_1, x_2, x_3), G(x_1, x_4, x_2)\}.$$

Considering $G(x_1, x_2, x_3), G(x_1, x_4, x_2)$ we have $X = \{x_1\}$ in line C-7. The multiequations that are put into T in line C-11 are $\lambda \overline{x_4}.F(\overline{x_4}) =^? \lambda \overline{x_4}.H(x_1)$ and $\lambda \overline{x_3}.G(\overline{x_3}) =^? \lambda \overline{x_3}.H(x_1)$. As outputs we have $U = \{\lambda x_1.H(x_1)\}$ and $B = \{1\}$.

4.5   Unify the right-hand side

The procedure *UnifyR* unifies the terms in the right-hand side $M = \{\lambda \overline{x_k^1}.t_1, \cdots, \lambda \overline{x_k^n}.t_n\}$. First, a global array $\Lambda[i]$ is created for noting each sequence of the initial λ-binders $\lambda \overline{x_k^i}$. Let Λ be an array with components $\Lambda[1], \cdots, \Lambda[n]$. Note that the number of arrays in Λ, denoted by $width(\Lambda)$, is fixed as n within a call to *UnifyR*, whereas the number of λ-binders in each array $\Lambda[i]$, denoted by $length(\Lambda[i])$, may increase, since additional λ-binders may be appended at the end of $\Lambda[i]$.

Two procedures *SimpUnifyR1* and *SimpUnifyR2* are called in lines D-6 and D-7. The procedure *SimpUnifyR1* constructs a scheme C of the common top part of all terms in M, and a set Q of schemes of multiequations, which are the rest unification problems obtained when factorizing C from the terms. We call the outputs "schemes" because they contain some "scheme variables", which need to be made precise in the procedure $SimpUnifyR2$, where some conditions of clashes and bound variable captures are also checked.

As mentioned in Section 3, not all initial λ-binders need to be left in the rest unification problem. For computing actual remaining λ-binders, the procedure $SimpUnifyR1$ appends all λ-binders it encounters to Λ, and notes the requirements of other changes of actual remaining λ-binders. The global variable K created in line D-4 will be used to enumerate the requirements of changes. The procedure $SimpUnifyR1$ uses the global variable BS created in line D-5 to store the requirements, and also all conditions to be checked. The procedure $SimpUnifyR2$ will really compute the actual sequences of remaining λ-binders w.r.t. the requirements stored in BS, and check all conditions stored in BS.

Assume that $SimpUnifyR2$ returns C and Q successfully. Let M be as above and $B = \{p_1, \cdots, p_m\}$ with $p_i < p_j$ for $i < j$. Then the multiequation $U =^? \lambda x^1_{p_1} \cdots \lambda x^1_{p_m}.C$ is a fragment of the final most general unifier (line D-9). The set Q of smaller multiequations is a part of the rest unification problem and put back to S and some of them to ST by the procedure call $AddS(Q, ST, S)$ (line D-10). The procedure $AddS$ is given in the appendix.

(D-1)   **procedure** $UnifyR(U, \{\lambda \overline{x^1_k}.t_1, \cdots, \lambda \overline{x^n_k}.t_n\}, B, \textbf{var } T, \textbf{var } S, \textbf{var } ST)$

(D-2)   **begin**

(D-3)   Create a global array $\Lambda[1..n]$ of arrays with initial $\Lambda[i] = \overline{x^i_k}$, $i = 1, \ldots, n$;

(D-4)   Let K be a global variable with initial $K = 1$;

(D-5)   Create a global empty set BS;

(D-6) $SimpUnifyR1(\{(t_1, 1), \cdots, (t_n, n)\}, C, Q)$;

(D-7) $SimpUnifyR2(B, C, Q)$;

(D-8)   Assume $B = \{p_1, \cdots, p_m\}$ with $p_i < p_j$ for $i < j$;

(D-9)   Append the multiequation $U =^? \lambda x^1_{p_1} \cdots x^1_{p_m}.C$ to the end of T;

(D-10) $AddS(Q, ST, S)$

(D-11) **end**

The procedure $SimpUnifyR1$ considers mainly the following cases:

If all terms in N are abstractions (line E-4) then the outermost λ-binder of each term is appended to the corresponding component array of Λ (line E-6). In addition, a requirement of extending the actual remaining λ-binders is noted (line E-7). Then the subterms are considered (line E-8). Before leaving the procedure, a requirement of recovering the old remaining λ-binders is noted (line E-9).

A procedure $NewBinders$ to note a requirement of changing the actual remaining λ-binders may be defined as follows:

    procedure $NewBinders((D_1, D_2))$

    begin $K := K + 1$; Put (D_1, D_2, K) into BS **end**

In the case that all terms in N are rigid (line E-11), topmost atoms should be equivalent modulo α-conversion and bound by the actual remaining λ-binders. However, checking these conditions at this place may be expensive in the worst case since the procedure has to find the corresponding λ-binders from Λ for the bound variables. We delay the checking here: The conditions are put into BS in line E-13 and to be checked in the procedure $SimpUnifyR2$.

In the case that there is a flexible term in N (line E-17), the flexible term will be first removed from N and the procedure continues to unify the rest of N. Multiequations in [4] may have right-hand sides consisting of arbitrary number of terms. So a corresponding procedure in [4] terminates as long as one of the input terms is flexible, and returns a single multiequation having all flexible input terms on the left and all other input terms on the right. In our case, however, the right-hand side can contain at most one term. Therefore, even when N contains a flexible term, other terms in N have to be further unified (line E-23), until N becomes a singleton (line E-3). The final resulting Q (in line E-25) returned in our case is a set consisting of all multiequations in Q' returned by the further unification process in line E-23 and a multiequation with the flexible term on the left and the common part of other terms of N on the right.

The strange notation $\Gamma(F, (\overline{y_n}, p), p_1)$ in line E-20 is one of the so-called scheme variables. It will be replaced by a term of the form $F(\overline{y'_n})$ in the procedure $SimpUnifyR2$, where $\overline{y'_n}$ are obtained from $\overline{y_n}$ by renaming all bound variables in $\Lambda[p]$ into corresponding ones in $\Lambda[p_1]$. We delay the renaming here since finding the positions of λ-binders in $\Lambda[p]$ is expensive at the moment. The reason for this renaming is that the procedure $SimpUnifyR1$ agrees to return a common part with bound variables corresponding to the λ-binders in the first term of N. Note that p_1 is the index of the first term in N (line E-19). The choices of λz_1 in line E-9, a_1 in line E-15, q in line E-25, and $\lambda x^1_{p_1} \cdots x^1_{p_m}$ in line D-9 of the procedure $UnifyR$ are based on this agreement.

The strange notation $\lambda\Gamma((\overline{y_n}, p), K)$ in line E-21 is also a scheme variable. Assume that $\Lambda[p] = \lambda\overline{x_m}$. Let $x_{q_1}, \ldots, x_{q_h}$ be all bound variables in $\{\overline{y_n}\}$ which occur the K-th computed sequence of remaining λ-binders. Then the scheme variable will be replaced by $\lambda\overline{x_{q_h}}$ in $SimpUnifyR2$. The situation is similar for the scheme variables $\lambda\Gamma((\overline{y_n}, p), K)$ and $\lambda\Gamma((\overline{y_n}, q), K)$ in line E-25. Note that the K's in lines E-21 and E-25 may be distinct but the sequences of actual remaining λ-binders are always identical.

When N contains a flexible term, new remaining λ-binders should be computed, as noted in line E-20 by $NewBinders((+, (\overline{y_n}, p)))$. Before leaving $SimpUnifyR1$ the old remaining λ-binders should be recovered, as noted by $NewBinders((-, (\overline{y_n}, p)))$ in line E-27.

If the original input M to $UnifyR$ contains only one term then the condition in line E-3 can never be true. In this case, $SimpUnifyR1$ simply serves to prepare the conditions which will be used by $SimpUnifyR2$ to check failures of bound variable captures in the term.

```
(E-1)   procedure SimpUnifyR1(N, var C, var Q)
(E-2)   begin
(E-3)     if N = {(t, p)} and width(Λ) > 1 then (C, Q) := (t, {})
(E-4)     else if N = {(λz₁.s₁, p₁), ···, (λzₙ.sₙ, pₙ)} then
(E-5)       begin
(E-6)         Add zᵢ to the end of Λ[i], i = p₁, ..., pₙ;
(E-7)         Let L = length(Λ[p₁]);   NewBinders((+, L));
(E-8)         SimpUnifyR1({(s₁, p₁), ···, (sₙ, pₙ)}, C', Q');
(E-9)         NewBinders((−, L));   C := λz₁.C';   Q := Q'
(E-10)      end
(E-11)    else if N = {(a₁(s¹₁, ···, s¹ₘ), p₁), ···, (aₙ(sⁿ₁, ···, sⁿₘ), pₙ)} then
(E-12)      begin
(E-13)        Put ({(a₁, p₁), ···, (aₙ, pₙ)}, K) into BS;
(E-14)        for i = 1 to m do SimpUnifyR1({(s¹ᵢ, p₁), ···, (sⁿᵢ, pₙ)}, Cᵢ, Qᵢ);
(E-15)        C := a₁(C̄ₘ);   Q := ⋃ᵢ₌₁ᵐ Qᵢ
(E-16)      end
(E-17)    else if there is some (F(ȳₙ), p) ∈ N then
(E-18)      begin
(E-19)        Assume (s, p₁) be the first element in N;
(E-20)        C := Γ(F, (ȳₙ, p), p₁);   NewBinders((+, (ȳₙ, p)));
(E-21)        if N − {(F(ȳₙ), p)} is empty then Q := {λΓ((ȳₙ, p), K).F(ȳₙ) =? {}}
(E-22)        else begin
(E-23)          SimpUnifyR1(N − {(F(ȳₙ), p)}, C', Q');
(E-24)          Assume (t, q) be the first element in N − {(F(ȳₙ), p)};
(E-25)          Q := Q' ∪ {λΓ((ȳₙ, p), K).F(ȳₙ) =? λΓ((ȳₙ, q), K).C'}
(E-26)        end;
```

(E-27) $NewBinders((-,(\overline{y_n},p)))$;

(E-28) **end**

(E-29) **else** failure

(E-30) **end**

As an example, assume that $UnifyR$ is called with $M = \{\lambda\overline{x_3}.x_3(\lambda x.t), \lambda\overline{y_3}.y_3(\lambda y.G(y_2)),$ $\lambda\overline{z_3}.F(z_1,z_3)\}$ and $B = \{2,3\}$. An array $\Lambda[1..3]$ is then created with $\Lambda[1] = \overline{x_3}$, $\Lambda[2] = \overline{y_3}$ and $\Lambda[3] = \overline{z_3}$. The procedure $SimpUnifyR1$ will be recursively called with $N = \{(x_3(\lambda x.t),1),$ $(y_3(\lambda y.G(y_2)),2),(F(z_1,z_3),3)\}$ in line D-6, with $N = \{(x_3(\lambda x.t),1),(y_3(\lambda y.G(y_2)),2)\}$ in line E-23, with $N = \{(\lambda x.t,1),(\lambda y.G(y_2),2)\}$ in line E-14, with $N = \{(t,1),(G(y_2),2)\}$ in line E-8 and with $N = \{(t,1)\}$ in line E-23. The final results are $\Lambda[1] = \overline{x_3}x$, $\Lambda[i] = \overline{y_3}y$, $\Lambda[3] = \overline{z_3}$, $K = 7$, $BS = \{(+,(z_1z_3,3),2),(\{(x_3,1),(y_3,2)\},2),(+,4,3),(+,(y_2,2),4),$ $(-,(y_2,2),5),(-,4,6),(-,(z_1z_3,3),7)\}$, $C = \Gamma(F,(z_1z_3,3),1)$ and $Q = \{\lambda\Gamma((y_2,2),4).G(y_2)$ $=^? \lambda\Gamma((y_2,1),4).t, \lambda\Gamma((z_1z_3,3),6).F(z_1,z_3) =^? \lambda\Gamma((z_1z_3,1),6).x_3(\lambda x.\Gamma(G,(y_2,2),1))\}$.

The tasks of $SimpUnifyR2$ are to check the conditions of clashes (line F-10) and of bound variable captures (line F-18) in BS and to replace the scheme variables in C and Q by concrete symbols (lines F-8 and F-20). Note that not only clashes of bound variables at heads but also other kinds of clashes, e.g. when the heads are distinct constants, or partly bound variables and partly constants, are checked here. The procedure finds the positions of λ-binders for occurrenes of bound variables (line F-7), and also computes the positions of all actual remaining λ-binders (lines F-14 – F-17). Note that the symbol $\otimes$ in line F-14 may be either $+$ or $-$, and in F-15 denotes the the usual plus or minus operation of integers.

The positions of actual remaining λ-binders are marked in TB. Remaining λ-binders at different places may use different marks. The variable I keeps the mark for the current remaining λ-binders and may be changed in line F-15.

(F-1) **procedure** $SimpUnifyR2(B, \textbf{var } C, \textbf{var } Q)$

(F-2) **begin**

(F-3) Let max be the maximum of all $length(\Lambda[i])$; Assume $\{1,\ldots,max\} \cap (C \cup V) = \{\}$;

(F-4) **for** $p = length(\Lambda)$ **to** 1, assume $\Lambda[p] = \overline{x_m}$, **do**

(F-5) **begin**

(F-6) Let $\phi = \{x_1 \mapsto 1, \cdots, x_m \mapsto m\}$;

(F-7) Replace each $(\overline{y_n},p)$ in BS, C or Q by $(\phi(\overline{y_n}),p)$;

(F-8) Replace each $\Gamma(F,(\overline{p_n},p'),p)$ in C or Q by $F(\phi^{-1}(\overline{p_n}))$

(F-9) **end**;

(F-10) **if** there is $(CLA,K) \in BS$ with $(a,i),(b,j) \in CLA$ and $a \neq b$ **then** failure (clash);

(F-11) Create an array $TB[1..max]$ with $TB[i] = 1$ if $i \in B$ and $TB[i] = 0$ if $i \notin B$; $I := 1$;

(F-12) **for** $K' = 2$ **to** K **do**

(F-13) **begin**

(F-14) **if** there is $(\otimes,(\overline{p_n},p),K')$ in BS **then**

(F-15) **begin for** $j = 1$ **to** n **do if** $TB[p_j] = I$ **then** $TB[p_j] := I \otimes 1$; $I := I \otimes 1$ **end**;

(F-16) **if** there is $(+,L,K')$ in BS **then** $TB[L] := I$;

(F-17) **if** there is $(-,L,K')$ in BS **then** $TB[L] := 0$;

(F-18) **if** there is $(CLA,K') \in BS$ with $(q,p) \in CLA$ such that

(F-19) $q \in \{1,\ldots,max\}$ and $TB[q] = I$ do not hold **then** failure (capture)

(F-20) Replace each $\lambda\Gamma((\overline{p_n},p),K')$ in C or Q by $\lambda\overline{x_{q_h}}$ where $\Lambda[p] = \lambda\overline{x_m}$ and $q_1,\ldots,q_h$

(F-21) are all in $\{\overline{p_n}\}$ such that $1 \leq q_j \leq max$, $TB[q_j] = I$ and $q_j < q_l$ for $j < l$

(F-22) **end**

(F-23) **end**

Continuing to compute the previous example with the procedure $SimpUnifyR2$, we will have $BS = \{(+,(13,3),2),(\{(3,1),(3,2)\},2),(+,4,3),(+,(2,2),4),(-,(2,2),5),(-,4,6),$ $(-,(13,3),7)\}$, $C = F(x_1,x_3)$ and $Q = \{\lambda((13,3),6).F(z_1,z_3) =^? \lambda((13,1),6).x_3(\lambda x.G(x_2)),$

$\lambda((2,2),4).G(y_2) =^? \lambda((2,1),4).t\}$ at line F-10. As the results of the procedure we have $C = F(x_1, x_3)$ and $Q = \{\lambda z_3.F(x_1, z_3) =^? \lambda x_3.x_3(\lambda x.G(x_2)), G(y_2) =^? t\}$.

Theorem 4.1 *For any input* $(\{\}, S_0)$, *the algorithm Unify is terminating. Furthermore,* S_0 *is unifiable if and only if Unify terminates with* $(T_f, \{\})$, *where* S_0 *and* T_f *have the same set of unifiers when restricted to the free variables in* S_0.

Proof Proof can be found in [16]. □

5 Our Algorithm is Linear

It is assumed that all data structures involved in the algorithm are dynamically created and possibly connected through pointers. Since in principle the space required cannot exceed the running time in such a machine, we will mainly concentrate on the time complexity.

A data structure can always be marked in some way. Changing and checking the mark of a given data structure need only constant time.

As mentioned, systems of multiequations are implemented by DAG's in the usual way, i.e. nodes by dynamically created data structures connected through pointers as required by directed arces. A node of a free variable has a list of father nodes. Each of other nodes has at most one father node.

Sets, multisets or stacks are all implemented as lists. Let us recall that eliminating or inserting an element in a list need only constant time when the element to be inserted and the place where the eliminating or inserting operation should be performed are known (see e.g. [1]).

Each bound variable in the starting system may be coded as a unique integer. So an array can be created with indices being (the integers corresponding to) all bound variables in the starting system such that for a given bound variable the corresponding component in the array can always be visited in a constant time. It suffices to allocate a place of a (large enough but) fixed size for each component. Then the size of the array is obviously linear in the size of the starting system.

Using the above array, the time needed in computing the intersection of two sets of bound variables is linear in the total size of the two sets (see e.g. [1]).

First of all, the procedure *Select* is linear since it visits each node in the starting system at most once, and only a fixed number operations may be performed w.r.t. each node. The situation is similar to its first-order counterpart in [5].

The procedure *Merge* is linear since the time required for each call $Merge(MS, U =^? M)$ is linear in the total size of the left-hand sides in MS. Indeed, after this call, all terms on the left will be unified and put into the solved part so that they can never be visited again.

The execution time for the call $UnifyL(U, T, B)$ is linear in the size of U. This can be proved in the similar way as above. Note that the new free variables introduced in line C-9 cannot be more than the original free variables.

Now let us consider the procedure $UnifyR$. The creation of a global array Λ is obviously linear in the size of M. Therefore we need only to prove the linearity of $SimpUnifyR1$, $SimpUnifyR2$ and $AddS$.

Intuitively, the procedure $SimpUnifyR1$, like the procedure *Select*, visits each node of the starting system at most once. Remember that in a call $SimpUnifyR1(N, C, Q)$ all nodes in N are from the right-hand sides of some multiequations in the unsolved part. During the procedure call, the nodes in N that have been visited are either simply dropped or moved to the left-hand sides of some multiequations in Q. So these nodes cannot be visited again by $SimpUnifyR1$ in the entire unification process. Furthermore, it can be observed that the time required for each operation during the procedure call is always linear in the size of the current nodes being visited. Note that the additional space for the newly created nodes in Λ, BS, C, the remaining outermost λ-binders and the left-hand sides in Q is also linear in the total size of the visited nodes of N.

To prove the linearity of the procedure *SimpUnifyR2* we assume a list of pointers for each p with $1 \leq p \leq width(\Lambda)$, which connects all pairs of the form $(\overline{y_n}, p)$ and all scheme variables of the form $\Gamma(F, (\overline{p_n}, p'), p)$ in BS, C and Q, as required in lines F-7 and F-8. In fact this list can be easily created during the process of creating BS, C and Q in *SimpUnifyR1*. Furthermore it is also assumed that in the process of creating BS, C and Q in *SimpUnifyR1*, a list of pointers for each K' with $1 \leq K' \leq K$ has also been created, which connects all $(\otimes, (\overline{p_n}, p), K')$, $(\otimes, L, K')$, (CLA, K') and $\lambda\Gamma((\overline{p_n}, p), K')$ as required in lines F-14, F-16, F-17, F-18 and F-20. In a call *SimpUnifyR2*(B, C, Q), the nodes in Λ, BS, C, in the outermost λ-binders and in the left-hand sides in Q will be visited along the above two lists. The time for the operations associated to a node being visited is always linear in the size of the node.

The time required for the procedure call $AddS(Q, S, ST)$ is linear in the number of multiequations in Q. We need only to partition the time into contant time segments and to assign them to the terms in the left-hand sides in Q. No other executions of $AddS$ may be assigned to the same terms since $AddS$ only handles multiequations in Q, which are yielded in unifying some right-hand sides.

Theorem 5.1 *The algorithm Unify is linear in the size of its input system.*

6 Conclusion

We have presented a unification algorithm for patterns whose time and space costs are both linear in the size of input. This result may be used as a basis for analyzing computational complexities of higher-order logic programming and higher-order proof systems. The ideas we have used in avoiding potential sources of nonlinear behaviors are also very useful in guiding the design of practical unification algorithms for patterns.

ACKNOWLEDGEMENT

We thank Tobias Nipkow for discussions and the anonymous referees for comments.

References

[1] A. Aho, J. Hopcroft, and J. Ullman. *The Design and Analysis of Computer Algorithms.* Addison-Wesley Publishing Company, 1974.

[2] W. Goldfarb. The undecidability of the second-order unification problem. *Theoretical Computer Science*, 13:225–230, 1981.

[3] G. Huet. A unification algorithm for typed λ-calculus. *Theoretical Computer Science*, 1:27–57, 1975.

[4] A. Martelli and U. Montanari. An efficient unification algorithm. *ACM TOPLAS*, 4(2):258–282, 1982.

[5] A. Martelli and U. Montanari. *Unification in linear time and space: A structured presentation.* Technical Report, Internal Rep. B76-16, Ist. di Elaborazione delle Informazione, Consiglio Nazionale delle Ricerche, Pisa, Italy, 1976.

[6] D. Miller. A logic programming language with lambda-abstraction, function variables, and simple unification. *Journal of Logic and Computation*, 1(4):497 – 536, 1991.

[7] D. Miller. Unification of simply typed lambda-terms as logic programming. In P. K. Furukawa, editor, *Proc. 1991 Joint Int. Conf. on Logic Programming*, MIT Press, 1991.

[8] G. Nadathur and D. Miller. An overview of λProlog. In R. A. Kowalski and K. A. Bowen, editors, *Proc. 5th Int. Logic Programming Conference*, MIT Press, 1988.

[9] T. Nipkow. Higher-order critical pairs. In *Proc. 6th LICS*, pages 342–349, 1991.

[10] T. Nipkow. *Practical Unification of Higher-Order Patterns.* Draft, Technische Universität München, 1991.

[11] M. Paterson and M. Wegman. Linear unification. *J. Computer and System Sciences*, 16:158–167, 1978.

[12] L. Paulson. Isabelle: the next 700 theorem provers. In P. Odifreddi, editor, *Logic and Computer Science*, pages 361–385, Academic Press, 1990.

[13] F. Pfenning. Elf: a language for logic definition and verified meta-programming. In *Proc. 4th LICS*, pages 313–322, IEEE Computer Society Press, June 1989.

[14] F. Pfenning. Logic programming in the LF logical framework. In G. Huet and G. D. Plotkin, editors, *Logical Frameworks*, Cambridge University Press, 1991.

[15] F. Pfenning. Unification and anti-unification in the Calculus of Constructions. In *Proc. 6th LICS*, pages 74–85, IEEE Computer Society Press, July 1991.

[16] Z. Qian. *Unification of Higher-Order Patterns in Linear Time and Space*. Technical Report, Forschungsbericht 5/92, FB3 Informatik, Universtät Bremen, 1992.

Appendix

(A-1) **procedure** $Select(\textbf{var } ST, \textbf{var } S, \textbf{var } MS)$
(A-2) **begin**
(A-3)   **if** ST is nonempty **then** pop ST to MS
(A-4)   **else begin** $MS := \{E\}$ for an "unvisited" multiequation E; Mark E as "visited" **end**;
(A-5)   **while** there is an "unvisited" $F(\overline{x_k}) \in \mathcal{U}(MS)$ **do**
(A-6)   **begin**
(A-7)   **if** there is another "unvisited" occurrence $F(\overline{y_k})$
(A-8)   **then begin**
(A-9)   Mark $F(\overline{y_k})$ as "visited";
(A-10)   **if** $F(\overline{y_k}) \in \mathcal{U}(E)$ for some multiequation E **then**
(A-11)   **if** E is "unvisited" **then**
(A-12)   **begin** Mark E as "visited"; $MS := MS \cup \{E\}$ **end**
(A-13)   **else begin if** E is in ST **then** failure (cycle) **end**
(A-14)   **else begin**
(A-15) $Node := F(\overline{y_k})$;
(A-16)   **repeat** $Node := Father.Node$; Mark N as "visited"
(A-17)   **until** $N \in \mathcal{M}(E)$ for some multiequation E;
(A-18)   **if** E is "visited" **then** failure (cycle);
(A-19)   Push MS in ST; Mark E as "visited"; $MS := \{E\}$
(A-20)   **end**
(A-21)   **end**
(A-22)   **else** mark $F(\overline{x_k})$ as "visited"
(A-23)   **end**;
(A-24) $S := S - MS$
(A-25) **end**

(G-1) **procedure** $AddS(Q, \textbf{var } ST, \textbf{var } S)$
(G-2) **begin**
(G-3) $S := S \cup Q$;
(G-4)   **if** some $U' =^? M' \in Q$ with some "visited" $t \in U' \cup M'$ **then**
(G-5)   **begin**
(G-6)   Mark $U' =^? M'$ as "visited";
(G-7)   **if** $t \in U'$ **then**
(G-8)   **begin** Pop ST to MS; $MS := MS \cup \{U' =^? M'\}$; Push MS in ST **end**;
(G-9)   **if** $t \in M'$ **then** push $\{U' =^? M'\}$ into ST
(G-10)   **end**
(G-11) **end**

A Theory of Requirements Capture and Its Applications

Wei   Li

Department of Computer Science
Beijing University of Aeronautics and Astronautics
100083 Beijing, P.R. China

Abstract

A theory of requirements capture is developed. Some concepts, such as new law, user's rejection, and reconstruction of a specification are defined; the related theorems are proved. The concepts of capture process and the limit of a capture process are further established. It is proved that, given a user's model and a specification, there is a procedure that all processes generated from the procedure and starting with the specification are convergent, and their limit is the truth of the model. Some computational aspects of reconstructions are studied. Some applications of the theory are briefly discussed, especially, an editor called SpecReviser is introduced.

1 Introduction

Formal approaches to program development usually focus on the problems of how to develop programs from a given specification and how to verify them to meet the specification ([BG77], [BJ 83], [EM 85], [NS 84] and [ST 88]).

In this paper, we study another problem, i.e., how to build a formal specification from some informal requirements. Let us call it the requirements capture. It is the first stage of the software development cycle. A requirement capture is a process describing the evolution of specifications. This process is usually non-trivial since no one can accomplish an appropriate specification of a problem at one stroke. In the process, there is a lot of interactions between the clients and software engineers in order to evaluate and develop an appropriate specification.

The purpose of this paper is to introduce the necessary concepts used in this area, study their computational aspects, prove the related theorems, and show some applications of the theory to software tools. Before going to the technical details, let us study a simple example and see what kind of concepts will be needed in the theory.

Example 1.1 Reverse function.
Consider how a student builds a specification for the reverse function. For simplicity, we assume that a first order language is used as our formal language.

Let L, K, P, Q denote the lists and Nil be the empty list. Let a, b, c denote the elements of a list.

$append : list \times list \rightarrow list$ is the concatenation function.

$reverse : list \times list \rightarrow bool$ is an atomic formula.

At the beginning, the student captured his first law: $A_1 = reverse(Nil, Nil)$ easily. Thus, his specification is

$$\Gamma_1 = \{A_1\} = \{reverse(Nil, Nil)\}.$$

He then found the fact that if K is the reverse of L, then, for any element a, the list $append(\{a\}, K)$ is the reverse of the list $append(L, \{a\})$. He then generalized this fact, and obtained his second law:

$$A_2 \equiv \forall K, L, P : list.(reverse(K, L) \supset reverse(append(P, K), append(L, P))).$$

Since A_2 is logically independent of Γ_1, in other words, neither A_2 nor $\neg A_2$ can be deduced from Γ_1, he added A_2 into Γ_1. Thus, the revised specification became:
$$\Gamma_2 = \{\Gamma_1, A_2\}.$$

After having tried some examples for Γ_2, he realized that Γ_2 is a wrong specification because he found a counter examples: Let:

$$\begin{aligned} L_1 &\equiv K_1 \equiv & c.nil \\ P_1 &\equiv & a.b.nil \\ Q_1 &\equiv & b.a.nil \end{aligned}$$

then

$$\begin{aligned} append(P_1, K_1) &= & a.b.c.nil \\ append(L_1, P_1) &= & c.a.b.nil \end{aligned}$$

$reverse(K_1, L_1) = true$, but

$$reverse(append(P_1, K_1), append(L_1, P_1)) = false.$$

L_1, K_1 and P_1 together are called a user's rejection of A_2, and A_2 is said to be rejected by the user. Thus, he deleted A_2 from Γ_2. The revised specification denoted by Γ_3 becomes $\{A_1\}$ again. In fact, a user's rejection is a model (counter example) which falsifies A_2. To continue the process, he then tried the law:

$$A_3 \equiv \forall L, K, P, Q : list.(reverse(L, K) \supset (reverse(P, Q) \\ \supset reverse(append(P, L), append(K, Q)))).$$

Obviously, A_3 is logically independent of $\Gamma_3 = \{A_1\}$. It is called a new law for Γ_3. He added A_3 into Γ_3 and captured Γ_4. The reconstruction of Γ_3 is:

$$\Gamma_4 = \{\Gamma_3, A_3\}.$$

The sequence of specifications: Γ_1, Γ_2, Γ_3, Γ_4, $\cdots$ describes the evolution of specifications given by the student. It is called a process of requirements capture for the reverse function. □

The conclusions which we have reached from this example are:

1. The processes of requirements capture for a specific problem can be expressed by a sequence of specifications: $\Gamma_1, \cdots, \Gamma_n, \cdots$, where Γ_{n+1} is a reconstruction of Γ_n. A specification must be revised if a new law or a user's rejection can be found.

2. A new law denoted by A for a given specification Γ is a formula which is logically independent of Γ. The reconstruction of the specification, in this case, is obtained by adding A into Γ.

3. The only way to check whether a specification Γ meets the user's requirements is to *deduce* some result (theorem) B from Γ (including the formulas contained in Γ) using logical inference rules, and to see whether B meets the user's requirements. There are two possibilities:

   (a) Every B matches user's requirements. Then, the specification is accepted.

   (b) There exists a B which meets a user's rejection (a counter-example). Then, the specification must be revised. All formulas contained in Γ have to be checked; those (minimal) subsets which have caused the user's rejection must be found and rectified.

4. A process of requirements capture is non-monotonic if a user's rejection arises after the reconstruction of a specification for a new law. For instance, in the example 1.1 we have: $\Gamma_1 \subseteq \Gamma_2 \nsubseteq \Gamma_3$.

In this paper, the concepts and ideas mentioned in this section will be formalized and expanded step by step.

2 New laws and user's rejections

We assume that the specification language used in the paper is a first order language L defined in [Gall 87]. More precisely, L is a set of strings of symbols formed by a BNF like grammar over an alphabet consisting of logical connectives including $\neg$, $\wedge$, $\vee$, $\supset$, $\forall$, $\exists$, and $\doteq$, a countable set **Var** of variables ranged over by $x, y, z \cdots$, a countable set **FS** of function symbols ranged over by $f, g, h \cdots$, a countable set **CS** of constants ranged over by $a, b, c \cdots$, and a countable set **PS** of predicate symbols ranged over by the capital letters $P, Q \cdots$.

A and Γ are used to denote a formula and a sequence of formulas respectively. $Th(\Gamma)$ is used to denote the set of all theorems deduced from Γ.

A sequent is a form of $\Gamma \vdash A$. It should be mentioned that we follow [Paul 87], use the symbol $\vdash$ to replace the symbol $\rightarrow$ in [Gall 87], and use $\Gamma \vdash A$ as an object language assertion (see [Paul 87]).

In this paper, we employ the proof rules of sequent calculus given in [Paul 87]. Thus, we will treat a sequence of formulas as a set of formulas if it is needed.

The concepts of validity, satisfiability, falsifiability, provability and consistency used in this paper are defined in [Gall 87]. The proof system (inference rules) is *sound and complete*.

A model **M** is a pair $< M, I >$, where M is a domain and I is an interpretation. We use $\mathbf{M} \models \Gamma$ to denote $\mathbf{M} \models A$ for all A in Γ. Intuitively, a model can be viewed as an instantiation of a specification.

Definition 2.1 Semantic consequence

A is a semantic consequence of Γ denoted by $\Gamma \models A$ iff, for any model **M**, if $\mathbf{M} \models \Gamma$ then $\mathbf{M} \models A$.

Definition 2.2 Specification

A sequence Γ of closed formulas is called a specification, if Γ is consistent and is not empty. The closed formulas contained in Γ are called the laws of Γ.

In terms of mathematical logic, a specification discussed in this paper is a sequence of non-logical axioms, or a closed formal theory. The condition that Γ is not empty means that only the non-logical axioms are interested and can be rejected by the user. The definition of new law is:

Definition 2.3 New law.

A is called a new law for Γ iff there exist two models **M** and $\mathbf{M'}$ such that

$$\mathbf{M} \models \Gamma \qquad \text{and} \qquad \mathbf{M} \models A$$

$$\mathbf{M'} \models \Gamma \qquad \text{and} \qquad \mathbf{M'} \models \neg A$$

Theorem 2.1 A is a new law for Γ iff A is logically independent of Γ, that is neither $\Gamma \vdash A$ nor $\Gamma \vdash \neg A$ is provable.

Proof: straightforward from soundness and completeness. $\square$

Corollary 2.1 If A is a new law for Γ, then both the sequences $\{\Gamma, A\}$ and $\{\Gamma, \neg A\}$ are consistent.

Definition 2.4 User's rejection

Let $\Gamma \models A$. A model **M** is a user's rejection of A iff $\mathbf{M} \models \neg A$.

Let $\Gamma_{M(A)} \equiv \{A_i \mid A_i \in \Gamma, \quad \mathbf{M} \models A_i, \quad \mathbf{M} \models \neg A\}$.

M is an **ideal user's rejection** of A iff $\Gamma_{M(A)}$ is *maximal* in the sense that there is no another user's rejection $\mathbf{M}'$ such that

$$\Gamma_{M(A)} \subset \Gamma_{M'(A)}.$$

An ideal user's rejection of A is denoted by $\overline{M}(A)$. There may exist many ideal user's rejection of A. Let

$$\mathcal{R}(\Gamma, A) \equiv \{\Gamma_{\overline{M}(A)} \mid \overline{M} \text{ is an ideal user's rejection of } A\}$$

The user's rejection meets the tradition that whether a specification Γ of a problem is acceptable depends only on whether all deduced results from Γ agree with the user's intuition about the problem; and it has to be rejected if there is a counter example. Anyhow, the acceptance of the specification has nothing to do with the logical inference rules of the first order logic.

The ideal user's rejections model the tradition of scientific research (Occam's razor): if some particular result deduced from a specification is rejected by the user, then only the minimal subsets of laws (contained in the specification) that cause the rejection have to be checked and rectified, and the rests (the maximal subsets) of the laws are *temporarily* retained.

The following definition is a generalized version of revision given in [Gär 88] by Gärdenfors, where the revision is defined in propositional logic.

Definition 2.5 Revision of a specification

Let $\Gamma \vdash A$. A revision Λ of Γ about $\neg A$ is a maximal consistent subset (or subsequence) of Γ, and is consistent with $\neg A$.

Let $\mathcal{A}(\Gamma, A)$ be the set of all revisions of Γ about $\neg A$.

The following theorems show that the proof-theoretic concept of ideal user's rejection is revision, and vice versa.

Theorem 2.2 R-soundness

If $\Lambda \in \mathcal{A}(\Gamma, A)$, then there exists an ideal user's rejection of A, $\overline{M}$, such that $\Gamma_{\overline{M}(A)} = \Lambda$.

Proof: Since $\Lambda \in \mathcal{A}(\Gamma, A)$ is consistent and is also consistent with $\neg A$, $\{\Lambda, \neg A\}$ is satisfiable. Thus, there exists a model $\mathbf{M}'$ such that $\mathbf{M}' \models \Lambda$ and $\mathbf{M}' \models \neg A$. So, $\mathbf{M}'$ is a user's rejection of A. $\mathbf{M}'$ is maximal, since if there exists another $\mathbf{M}''$ such that $\mathbf{M}'' \models \neg A$ and $\Gamma_{M''(A)} \supseteq \Gamma_{M'(A)} \supseteq \Lambda$, then $\Gamma_{M''(A)} \subseteq \Lambda$ because it is a consistent subset of Γ which is consistent with $\neg A$. $\square$

Theorem 2.3 R-completeness
    If $\overline{M}$ is an ideal user's rejection of A, then there exists a revision Λ of Γ about $\neg A$, such that $\Lambda = \Gamma_{\overline{M}(A)}$.

Proof: Straightforward. $\square$

Corollary 2.2 $\mathcal{R}(\Gamma, A) = \mathcal{A}(\Gamma, A)$

Example 2.1 Let
$$\Gamma \equiv \{A, A \supset B, B \supset C, E \supset F\}$$
be a specification. We have $\Gamma \vdash C$. Assume that C meets a user's rejection, then there are three revisions of Γ about $\neg C$. The $\mathcal{A}(\Gamma, C)$ consists of:

$$\{A, A \supset B, E \supset F\} \quad \{A, B \supset C, E \supset F\} \quad \{A \supset B, B \supset C, E \supset F\}.$$

3 Processes of requirements capture

In this section, we deal with the problem of how to reconstruct a specification when a new law or a user's rejection arises, and will define what a process of requirements capture is.

Definition 3.1 Reconstruction of a specification.
    Let A be a new law for Γ. The N-reconstruction of Γ for the new law A is the set $\{\Gamma, A\}$.
    Let $\Gamma \models A$ and A have met a user's rejection. An R-reconstruction of Γ for the user's rejection of A is $\Gamma_{\overline{M}(A)}$, where $\overline{M}$ is an ideal user's rejection of A.
    A specification Γ' is a reconstruction of Γ iff Γ' is either an N-reconstruction of Γ for a new law A or an R-reconstruction of Γ for a user's rejection of A.

From theorem 2.3 we know that an R-reconstruction of Γ for the user's rejection of A is a revision of Γ about $\neg A$. Having defined the reconstructions of a specification, we can study the concept of process of requirements capture.

Definition 3.2 Process of requirements capture.
    A specification sequence $\Gamma_1, \Gamma_2, \cdots, \Gamma_n, \cdots$ is called a process of requirements capture iff Γ_{i+1} is a reconstruction of Γ_i for $i \geq 1$.
    The process is *increasing* iff $\Gamma_n \subseteq \Gamma_{n+1}$ for all n; it is *decreasing* iff $\Gamma_n \supseteq \Gamma_{n+1}$ for all n. The process is *monotonic* iff it is either increasing or decreasing; otherwise it is *non-monotonic*.

Since, for a given user's rejection of A, there may be many R-reconstructions ($\mathcal{A}(\Gamma_n, A)$ contains more than one element), the evolution of a specification should be represented by a *tree*, each branch of which is a process of requirements capture.

Theorem 3.1 Monotonicity

A process of requirements capture $\{\Gamma_n\}$ is increasing iff for any $n \geq 1$, Γ_{n+1} is an N-reconstruction of Γ_n for some new law A.

A process of requirements capture $\{\Gamma_n\}$ is decreasing iff for any $n \geq 1$, Γ_{n+1} is an R-reconstruction of Γ_n for user's rejection of some A.

Theorem 3.2 Non-monotonicity

A process of requirements capture is non-monotonic iff, for some $n > 1$, Γ_{n+1} is an R-reconstruction of Γ_n for a user's rejection, and Γ_n is an N-reconstruction of Γ_{n-1} for a new law; or Γ_{n+1} is an N-reconstruction of Γ_n for a new law, and Γ_n is an R-reconstruction of Γ_{n-1} for a user's rejection.

Proof: Straightforward from the definition. □

The above theorem tell us that non-monotonicity is a characteristic of a process of requirements capture where a user's rejection arises after a new law, or vice versa.

4   The Limits

If a process of requirements capture (or 'capture process' for short) is finite, it means that after finite steps of explorations, we build an appropriate specification. For the infinite capture processes, we need to introduce the concept of limits. In this section, we will build a procedure, and will prove that, given a user's model about a problem and a specification, all processes generated from the procedure and starting with the specification are convergent, and their limit is the truth of the model of the problem. In fact, this theorem is an improved version of the theorem given in [Li 92-2].

In the rest of this paper, we assume that two sentences P and Q are the same sentence iff $P \equiv Q$ (that is $(P \supset Q) \wedge (Q \supset P)$ is a tautology).

Definition 4.1 Limit

Let $\{\Gamma_n\}$ be a capture process. The sequence of formulas:

$$\Gamma^* \equiv \bigcap_{n=1}^{\infty} \bigcup_{m=n}^{\infty} \Gamma_m$$

is called the *upper limit* of the capture process $\{\Gamma_n\}$. The sequence of formulas:

$$\Gamma_* \equiv \bigcup_{n=1}^{\infty} \bigcap_{m=n}^{\infty} \Gamma_m$$

is called the *lower limit* of the capture process $\{\Gamma_n\}$. A capture process is *convergent* iff

$$\Gamma_* = \Gamma^*.$$

The lower limit (and also the upper limit) is called the *limit* of a convergent capture process $\{\Gamma_n\}$. This limit is denoted by $\lim_n \Gamma_n$.

Lemma 4.1 $A \in \Gamma^*$ iff there exist infinite many $\{k_n\}$ such that $A \in \Gamma_{k_n}$. $A \in \Gamma_*$ iff there exists an N such that $A \in \Gamma_m$ for $m > N$.

There are some capture processes which have no limit. Intuitively, such processes indicate that the specification is not an appropriate description of a problem. For example, let $\Gamma_1 = \{A\}$ where A is the statement "tossing a coin and getting tails". Obviously, any capture process starting with Γ_1 has no limit. An appropriate description should be "tossing a coin, the probability of getting tails is 50%".

Definition 4.2 $\wp$, $L_\wp$ *and* $\mathbf{M}_\wp$.
Given a specific problem $\wp$, $L_\wp$ is a subset of L containing countablly infinite (include finite) constant, function and predicate symbols representing the problem $\wp$. A user model of $\wp$ denoted by $\mathbf{M}_\wp$ is a model of $L_\wp$.

Intuitively, a user model of $\wp$ may be considered to be a description of the problem $\wp$ in the real world.

Definition 4.3 $\mathcal{T}_{M_\wp}$
For a given user model $\mathbf{M}_\wp$, $\mathcal{T}_{M_\wp}$ is the set of all sentences of $L_\wp$ valid in $\mathbf{M}_\wp$, i.e.,

$$\mathcal{T}_{M_\wp} \equiv \{A \mid A \in L_\wp, \; FV(A) = \emptyset, \; \mathbf{M}_\wp \models A\}.$$

where $FV(A)$ denotes the set of all free variables occurring in A.

According to its definition, the set $\mathcal{T}_{M_\wp}$ is countable. We represent it as a sequence $\{A_m\}$ (for example, in the lexicographical order).

The following definition gives a procedure to generate the capture process $\{\Gamma_n\}$. The basic idea is: given a user's model $\mathbf{M}_\wp$ and a specification Γ, enumerate all A_i contained in $\mathcal{T}_{M_\wp}$; if A_i is a theorem of Γ_n, then pass it; if A_i is a new law, then take it in, i.e., $\Gamma_{n+1} = \{A_i, \Gamma_n\}$; if $\neg A_i$ is a theorem, that is, $\neg A_i$ has met a user's rejection, then Γ_{n+1} is taken to be an R-reconstruction of Γ_n.

Definition 4.4 Given an user model $\mathbf{M}_\wp$ and a specification Γ, an $\mathbf{M}_\wp$ capture process of Γ denoted by $\{\Gamma_n\}$ is defined as follows:

1. $\Gamma_1 = \Gamma$. Let $\mathcal{T}_{M_\wp} = \{A_m\}$ and $A_{k_1} = A_1$. Let $\{\Theta_n\}$ be a sequence of specifications, and $\Theta_1 = \emptyset$.

2. Γ_{n+1} is defined as below:

(a) If $\Gamma_n \vdash A_{k_n}$ is provable, then put A_{k_n} into Θ_n, that is $\Theta_n :=$ $\{\Theta_n, A_{k_n}\}$, and consider $\Gamma_n \vdash A_{k_n+1}$.

(b) If neither $\Gamma_n \vdash A_{k_n}$ nor $\Gamma_n \vdash \neg A_{k_n}$ is provable, then $\Gamma_{n+1} = \{A_{k_n}, \Gamma_n\}$. Let $\Theta_{n+1} = \Theta_n$.

(c) If $\Gamma_n \vdash \neg A_{k_n}$ is provable, then do the following two steps consecutively:

    i. $\Gamma_{n+1} = \{\Lambda\}$ where $\Lambda \in \mathcal{A}(\Gamma_n, \neg A_{k_n})$, and $A_{k_i} \in \Lambda$ hold for $i = 1, \cdots, n-1$. Let $\Theta_{n+1} = \Theta_n = \{C_1, ..., C_l\}$. .

    ii. $\Gamma_{n+2} = \{A_{k_n}, \Gamma_{n+1}\}$. Let $j = 2$. For $i = 1$ to l do the loop: If $\Gamma_{n+j} \vdash C_i$ is provable, then do nothing. If neither $\Gamma_{n+j} \vdash C_i$ nor $\Gamma_{n+j} \vdash \neg C_i$ is provable, then delete C_i from Θ_{n+j}, and take $A_{k_{n+j}} = C_i$; let $j := j+1$ and construct Γ_{n+j} using the sub-item 2-(b).

    Note: Let Γ_m be the last specification constructed by this loop, then either $A_i \in \Gamma_m$ or $\Gamma_m \vdash A_i$ holds for $i = 1, \cdots, k_m$.

It should be mentioned that when an R-reconstruction is taken in response to a user's rejection, some information may be lost. For example, let $\Gamma = \{A \wedge B\}$, we have that both $\Gamma \vdash A$ and $\Gamma \vdash B$ are provable. Assume that A has met a user's rejection, then the maximal consistent subset of Γ which is consistent with $\neg A$ is the empty set. Thus, after the R-reconstruction of Γ for A, B is missing! In order to repair the loss, in the definition we introduce a "stack" called Θ. For any n, Θ_n collects those A_m, $m < k_n$, which can be deduced from Γ_i for some $i < n$. When a user's rejection arises, we execute the sub-item 2-(c)-ii, check all A_m contained in Θ_n, and pick up the lost ones back as new laws. Since, for any n, Θ_n is always finite, the execution of sub-item 2-(c)-ii will always be terminated.

Theorem 4.1 Given an user model $\mathbf{M}_\wp$, and a specification Γ, if Γ does not contain any formula which is logically independent of $\mathcal{T}_{M_\wp}$, then every $\mathbf{M}_\wp$ capture process of Γ denoted by $\{\Gamma_n\}$ is convergent, and

$$Th(\lim_n \Gamma_n) = \mathcal{T}_{M_\wp}.$$

Proof: Let $\{\Gamma_n\}$ be an $\mathbf{M}_\wp$ capture process of Γ. We prove $Th(\lim_n \Gamma_n) = \mathcal{T}_{M_\wp}$ in the following two steps:

1. $\mathcal{T}_{M_\wp} \subseteq Th(\Gamma_*)$. For any $A_i \in \mathcal{T}_{M_\wp}$, by the construction of $\{\Gamma_n\}$, there must exist an n such that either $A_i \in Th(\Gamma_n)$ or $A_i \notin Th(\Gamma_n)$ and $A_i \in \Gamma_{n+1}$.

(a) For the first case, by definition 4.4, there must be an l such that $A_i \in Th(\Gamma_m)$ for $m \geq l$, since T_{M_p} is consistent. For each $m \geq l$, there is a finite subset of Γ_m denoted by $\Delta_m = \{B_{m_1}, \cdots, B_{m_j}\}$ and $\Delta_m \vdash A_i$.

For each k, $1 \leq k \leq j$, either $B_{m_k} \in \bigcap_{n=l}^{\infty} \Gamma_n$ or $(\bigcap_{n=l}^{\infty} \Gamma_n) \vdash B_{m_k}$, otherwise by definition 4.4, $B_{m_k} \in \Gamma$, and there must exist an $m' \geq m$ such that $\Gamma_{m'}$ contains $\neg B_{m_k}$, thus $B_{m_k} \notin Th(\Gamma_{m'})$ which is a contradiction. Thus $A_i \in Th(\bigcap_{m=l}^{\infty} \Gamma_m)$ holds. Therefore

$$A_i \in Th(\bigcup_{n=1}^{\infty} \bigcap_{m=n}^{\infty} \Gamma_m) = Th(\Gamma_*).$$

(b) For the second case, by the definition 4.4, $A_i \in \Gamma_m$ for any $m > n$. Thus,
$$A_i \in \bigcup_{n=1}^{\infty} \bigcap_{m=n}^{\infty} \Gamma_m = \Gamma_*.$$

2. $\Gamma^* \subseteq T_{M_p}$. Assume that there is a closed formula A such that $A \in \Gamma^*$ and $A \notin T_{M_p}$. There are only two possibilities:

(a) neither $T_{M_p} \vdash A$ nor $T_{M_p} \vdash \neg A$ is provable, but this contradicts that Γ does not contain any logically independent formula w.r.t. T_{M_p}.

(b) $\neg A \in T_{M_p}$. This is also impossible, if so, there must be i such that $\neg A = A_i$, then there must be n such that $\neg A \in \Gamma_n$. Thus $\neg A \in \Gamma_m$ for all $m > n$. this is $\neg A \in \Gamma^*$, a contradiction.

Thus, we have
$$\Gamma^* \subseteq T_{M_p} \subseteq Th(\Gamma_*)$$

and so $\Gamma_* = \Gamma^*$. Hence, the theorem has been proved. $\square$

It is not difficult to see that the theorem still holds without the condition: Γ does not contain logically independent laws of T_{M_p}, because the similar techniques given in the above proof can be used to eliminate those laws from Γ. Furthermore, if we replace the sub-items 2-(a) and 2-(b) in definition 4.4 by the following sentence: if A is consistent with Γ then $\Gamma_{n+1} = \{A_{k_n}, \Gamma_n\}$, the theorem also holds.

The proof of the theorem shows that the capture processes will always converge on the same limit, if they are generated in the way that for any Γ_n which has met a user's rejection of some A, we *arbitrarily* choose a maximal consistent subset of Γ_n which is consistent with $\neg A$ and contains $A_{k_1}, \cdots, A_{k_n}$. Thus, the uniqueness of revision discussed in [Gär 88] seems unnecessary.

In practice, since a user usually may not know the mathematical model of a problem at the beginning of a capture process, the theorem cannot be applied.

However, to build a reconstruction does not need the user to know the whole model of the problem. There is a *criterion of modification*. It says that a theory must be modified if its logical consequences fail to agree with the practice; and a statement must be replaced by another one if neither itself or its negation agrees with the practice. If the user follows the criterion, then he can approach an appropriate specification of the problem by making the reconstructions given in the proof of the theorem.

We can view a program written in a language (or a block of machine codes) as a specification. If so, all the versions of a software in their given order form a capture process, since for every version, its succedent version is obtained from this version either by adding some new pieces of programs (new laws) or by correcting some mistakes (which can be decomposed to making some R-reconstructions followed by taking some N-reconstructions). Then, the above theorem says that a software will eventually approach the goal by producing the versions. Therefore, an important task for software engineers is to discover those procedures that their generated capture processes are convergent as fast as possible.

5 Computational aspects of revisions

From the definitions and theorems about new laws and ideal user's rejections, we know that the key point for building a reconstruction of specification Γ is to find a maximal consistent subset of Γ which is consistent with some given formula A. The following two theorems show that it is not an easy task.

Theorem 5.1 For propositional logic, if every specification contains finite laws (propositions) only, then building a reconstruction of a specification is an NP-hard problem.

Proof: The proof follows directly from Cook's theorem ([GJ 79]).

Theorem 5.2 For the first order language L, building a reconstruction of a specification is a undecidable problem.

Proof: It is proved by Gödel's second incompleteness theorem [Shoen 67].

In computer science, we are interested in what circumstances a reconstruction can be efficiently built. In this section, we give a simple case. Assume that the language L is restricted to be without equality $\doteq$.

Definition 5.1 $\Gamma_{-\{A\}}$ *and* $\Gamma_{+\{A\}}$.
Assume that A is contained in Γ. $\Gamma_{-\{A\}}$ is the subsequence of Γ obtained by eliminating all A_i containing any predicate symbols in common with A. $\Gamma_{+\{A\}}$ is the subsequence of Γ obtained by eliminating all A_j contained in $\Gamma_{-\{A\}}$.

Definition 5.2 Simple user's rejection
Given $\Gamma \models A$, a user's rejection is called simple iff there exists a model **M** such that

$$\mathbf{M} \models A_i \quad \text{for all } A_i \text{ in } \Gamma_{-\{A\}} \quad \text{and} \quad \mathbf{M} \models \neg A.$$

Lemma 5.1 If $\Gamma \models A$ and A has met a simple user's rejection, then any R-reconstruction of Γ for A contains $\Gamma_{-\{A\}}$.

The concept of simple user's rejection allows us to apply the well-known Davis-Putnam procedure to find the maximal consistent subsets. In fact, we can use the following procedure to build a R-reconstruction:

formula: a well-formed first order formula
F-sequence: sequence of closed formals

```
procedure R-REVISE(Γ: F-sequence; A: formula; var    T: sequence);
    begin
        T := Γ_{A}
        for every B contained in Γ_{+{A}} do
            if {T, ¬A, B} is consistent
            then T := {T, B}
            else  skip
        endfor
    end
```

Recently, Gu claimed that he built some efficient algorithms based on optimization theory to solve SAT problem [Gu 92]. It may bring about some hope to build reconstruction practically for a large class of problems.

6   Specification revisers

At the end of section 4, we briefly discussed the role of theorem 4.1 in the software development. Since a new version of a software is always made by some editors, the theory suggests that for the different levels of specifications we need different editors. The editors which we have used are syntax directed editors and synthesizers (including type and proof editors). They can check the syntactic or static errors of the inputs automatically, and they work interactively with the user.

The theory given in this paper inspires us to build some editors for the requirement capture. Let us call them specification reviser. It checks the consistency of the newly added laws with respect to a specification which has been stored. It also detects the fallibility of a specification when a user's rejection exists, and points out the rejected laws. The editor will further provide all possible

R-reconstructions for a rejected law, and ask the user to select their preferred revision (theorem 4.1 guarantees that the user will eventually approach the goal). It allows the user to mark some laws which cannot be rejected, even if some facts contradict them. Thus, the editor will direct the user to capture an appropriate specification while keeping the consistency of revised specifications at every stage in a process. Finally, it works interactively with the user. Here, we give an outline of the main procedures of the editor called SpecReviser [LW 92]:

function MINIMAL(A: formula, Γ: F-sequence);

For a given formula A, and a consistent F-sequences Γ, the function MINIMAL outputs *all* the sets $\Gamma - \Lambda$ where $\Lambda \in A(\Gamma, \neg A)$. If every such set contains marked laws and A is not marked, then Γ is not revised and outputs "A contradicts the marked laws". If every such subset contains marked laws and A is marked, then outputs "Please remark the marked laws".

procedure SPEC-REVISER(A: formula; *var* Γ: F-sequence);
    var Δ: F-sequence;
    begin
        $\Delta := \emptyset$
        loop do
            begin
                input a formula A;
                if CONSISTENT(Γ, A)
                    then begin
                        $\Gamma := \{\Gamma, A\}$;
                        output:"A is accepted";
                        if A is marked *then* $\Delta := \{\Delta, A\}$
                        end
                    else begin
                        output:"A is not consistent with Γ";
                        MINIMAL(A, Γ);
                        the user makes a choice, say Γ';
                        $\Gamma := \Gamma - \Gamma'$;
                        if A is marked *then* $\Delta := \{\Delta, A\}$
                        end;
            end
        end loop
    end

7 Related work

From a view point of logic, our theory (see [Li 91, 92-1 and 92-2]) is close to the *theory of knowledge in flux* given by Gärdenfors in the sense of setting up a "theory for modeling the dynamics of epistemic states" (see [Gär 88]). For example, he defined the proof-concepts: expansions of Γ by A and the revisions of Γ by A, whose corresponding model-theoretic concepts are our N-reconstruction of Γ for a new law A (with a minor difference) and R-reconstructions of Γ for a user's rejection of A respectively. For defining the revisions, he introduced the principle of informational economy which is essentially the same as Occam's razor which we use to set up ideal user's rejection.

The main differences between Gärdenfors's theory and ours are:

1. He set up a formal theory of expansions and revisions of belief sets. In contrast, we built a theory of sequences and limits of belief sets (or specifications called in this paper).

2. He studied all the concepts in propositional logic, and define them proof-theoretically. In contrast, we study these concepts in first order logic, and define them both proof-theoretically and model-theoretically. We introduced the model-theoretic concepts such as new laws and user's rejections to describe the interactions between logical inference (logical information) and user's practice (empirical information).

3. We introduced some concepts and obtained some results which are new to his theory. For example, we defined the capture processes and the limit of a capture process, advanced to build procedures for generating capture processes, and proved that the processes, generated from the procedure in section 4, are convergent, and their limit is the truth of the user's model of the given problem. The proof of the about limit theorem shows that the uniqueness of revision needed in his theory seems unnecessary.

It should be mentioned that much work remains to be done. For example, when a user's rejection arises, there are, in practice, many ways to revise a specification . For instance, we could change the concepts, or replace the formal language or even change the paradigm of thinking. Here, we only provide a simple solution – the R-reconstructions.

Finally, it should also be pointed out that the concepts and results proved in this paper can be applied to any formal languages with a complete proof system, and that the theory has many other potential applications, such as machine learning, knowledge base maintenance and diagnostic techniques.

Acknowledgement

I would like to thank Günter Hotz and Reinhard Wilhelm for the encouragements, and thank Zhou Chaochen and referees for correcting some mistakes in the earlier versions of the paper. The work is supported by the National High-Tech Programme of China.

tion of functions is sufficient to describe the Ok-codomain; the Ok-values are those generated by the safe operations. As pointed out in [Ber86][BBC86], bounded data structures cannot be specified in this framework. For example, $succ$ and $+$ are not safe for bounded natural numbers; consequently the Ok-part of the sort Nat would be reduced to 0.

This problem is solved in [BBC86] where exception names are reflected by *labels*, a special label Ok being reserved for Ok-values. The labels are carried by values: the predicate $v \in TooLarge$ means that the value v is labelled by $TooLarge$. This approach allows us to specify bounded data structures; unfortunately, certain recoveries lead to write inconsistent specifications:

Example 1 Let us assume that every value of the form $succ^i(0)$ $(i \geq 9)$ is labelled by $TooLarge$.[1] Let us consider an exception handler that recovers every $TooLarge$-value on $succ^8(0)$. A possible way of expressing this recovery is *"if the operation succ raises the exception TooLarge, then do not perform it."* It is formally specified as:

$$succ(n) \in TooLarge \implies succ(n) = n$$

As the term $succ^9(0)$ is recovered on $succ^8(0)$, they have the same value; thus both of them are labelled by $TooLarge$. By applying the axiom with the assignment $n = succ^7(0)$ we get then the inconsistency[2] $succ^8(0) = succ^7(0)$. The point here is that, even if the *terms* $succ^9(0)$ and $succ^8(0)$ have the same *value*, they should not carry the same labels. Notice that subsorting [FGJM85] gives rise to a similar paradox because sorts are attached to values. Two terms having the same value must share the same subsorts; consequently $succ^8(0)$ and $succ^9(0)$ cannot be distinguished, and this example would lead to the same inconsistency.

This is indeed the case for all existing algebraic framework for exception handling, because exception names (if provided) are always carried by values.

Example 1 reveals the difference between "exception handling" and "error handling." The term $succ^9(0)$ is not erroneous but it is exceptional; even if the term $succ^9(0)$ is recovered on $succ^8(0)$, the exception name $TooLarge$ should not be propagated to $succ^8(0)$. Exception names should be carried by terms, not by values. Roughly speaking, exception handling requires a special "typing" of *terms* (according to our terminology distinguishing exception handling from error handling). We shall call *labels* these special "types." Labels will form a third component of the signature. From this point of view, label algebras are an extension of more standard algebraic approaches with "multityping" such as order sorted algebras [Gog78b][FGJM85]. Some other extensions of order sorted algebras are: Equational Type Logic [MSS90], unified algebras [Mos89] or G-algebras [Meg90]. All of them attach types (or subtypes) to values while, in our approach, labels are attached to terms (see also [BL91a]). In [Ber86][BBC86], only the label Ok is carried by terms, and in a restricted manner. This leads to complicated semantics and Example 1 cannot be treated.

---

[1] $succ^i(0)$ stands for $succ(succ(\ldots(succ(0))\ldots))$, the operation $succ$ being applied i times.

[2] Indeed, this inconsistency propagates in the same way, and all values are equal to 0.

The rest of this paper is devoted to label algebras, label specifications and their applications to exception handling.

4 Label algebras

4.1 Introduction

Usually, algebras are (heterogeneous) sets of values [GTW78][EM85]. Let us remember that a signature is usually a couple $< S, \Sigma >$ where S is a finite set of sorts (or type names) and Σ is a finite set of operation names with arity in S^*; an object (algebra) of the category $Alg(\Sigma)$ is a heterogeneous set A, partitioned as $A = \{A_s\}_{s \in S}$, and with, for each operation name "$f : s_1 \dots s_n \to s$" in Σ $(0 \leq n)$, a total function $f_A : A_{s_1} \times \dots \times A_{s_n} \to A_s$; the morphisms of $Alg(\Sigma)$ (Σ-morphisms) being obviously the sort preserving, operation preserving applications.

As a consequence of our approach, (labelled) terms must also be considered as "first class citizen objects." Given an algebra A, the satisfaction relation must be defined using terms (the usual definition only involves values). A simple idea could be to consider both A and T_Σ (the ground term algebra). Unfortunately, finitely generated algebras (i.e. such that the initial Σ-morphism from T_Σ to A is surjective) are not powerful enough to cope with enrichment, parametrization or abstract implementations. How is one to deal with both terms and unreachable values ? This question is solved by the free Σ-term algebra $T_\Sigma(A)$.

Notation 1 *Given a heterogeneous "set of variables" $V = \{V_s\}_{s \in S}$, the* free Σ-term algebra with variables in V *is the least Σ-algebra $T_\Sigma(V)$ (with respect to the preorder induced by Σ-morphisms) such that $V \subseteq T_\Sigma(V)$.*

Since V is not necessarily finite or enumerable, we can consider in particular $T_\Sigma(A)$ for every algebra A. An element of $T_\Sigma(A)$ is a Σ-term such that each leaf can contain either a constant of the signature, or a value of A.

The main technical point underlying our framework is to systematically use $T_\Sigma(A)$. Intuitively, a term reflects the "history" of a value; it is a "sequence of calculations" which results in a value. Several histories can provide the same value. This is the reason why labelling is more powerful than typing: it allows us to "diagnose" the history in order to apply a specific treatment or not. The canonical evaluation morphism $eval_A : T_\Sigma(A) \to A$, deduced from the Σ-algebra structure of A, relates each term to its final value. Of course, *in the end*, the satisfaction of an equality must be checked on values; thus, $eval_A$ is a crucial tool. However, the considered assignments can be precisely restricted to certain kinds of terms/histories *before* checking equalities on values, and consequently, all the inconsistencies mentioned before can be solved via label algebras.

Notation 2 *We note $\overline{A} = T_\Sigma(A)$, and for every Σ-morphism $\mu : A \to B$, $\overline{\mu} : \overline{A} \to \overline{B}$ denotes the canonical Σ-morphism which extends μ to the corresponding free algebras.*

4.2 Definitions and results

For lack of space, the results are not proved here. Complete proofs can be found in [BL91b][LeG93].

Definition 1 *A label signature is a triplet $\Sigma L = < S, \Sigma, L >$ where $< S, \Sigma >$ is a (usual) signature and L is a (finite) set of labels.*

A ΣL-algebra is a couple $\mathcal{A} = (A, \{l_A\}_{l \in L})$ where A is a Σ-algebra, and $\{l_A\}_{l \in L}$ is a L-indexed family such that, for each l in L, l_A is a subset of $\overline{A}$.

There are no conditions about the subsets l_A: they can intersect several sorts, they are not necessarily disjoint and their union $(\bigcup_{l \in L} l_A)$ does not necessarily cover $\overline{A}$.

Definition 2 *Let $\mathcal{A} = (A, \{l_A\}_{l \in L})$ and $\mathcal{B} = (B, \{l_B\}_{l \in L})$ be two ΣL-algebras. A ΣL-morphism $h : \mathcal{A} \to \mathcal{B}$ is a Σ-morphism from A to B such that: $\forall l \in L, \overline{h}(l_A) \subseteq l_B$. The category of all ΣL-algebras is denoted by $Alg_{Lbl}(\Sigma L)$.*

When there is no ambiguity about the signature under consideration, ΣL-algebras and ΣL-morphisms will be called *label algebras* and *label morphisms*, or even algebras and morphisms.

Not surprisingly, a "label specification" will be defined by a label signature and a set of well formed formulae (axioms):

Definition 3 *Given a label signature ΣL, a ΣL-axiom is a well formed formula built on:*

- atoms: *atoms are either equalities $(u = v)$ such that u and v are Σ-terms with variables, u and v belonging to the same sort, or labelling atoms $(w \in l)$ such that w is a Σ-term with variables and l is a label belonging to L,*

- connectives *belonging to $\{\neg, \wedge, \vee, \Rightarrow\}$.*

(Every variable is implicitly universally quantified.)[3]

A ΣL-axiom is called positive conditional *if and only if it is of the form $a_1 \wedge \ldots \wedge a_n \Rightarrow a$ where the a_i and a are positive atoms (if $n = 0$ then the axiom is reduced to a).*

The predicate " ϵ " should be read "*is labelled by*".

Definition 4 *A label specification is a couple $SP = < \Sigma L, Ax >$ where ΣL is a label signature and Ax is a set of ΣL-axioms. SP is called* positive conditional *iff all its axioms are positive conditional.*

The *satisfaction relation* is indeed the crucial definition. It is of first importance to consider assignments with range in $\overline{A} = T_\Sigma(A)$ (terms) instead of A (values):

Definition 5 *Let $\mathcal{A} = (A, \{l_A\}_{l \in L})$ be a ΣL-algebra.*

- *$\mathcal{A}$ satisfies $(u = v)$, where u and v are two terms in $\overline{A}$, means that $eval_A(u) = eval_A(v)$ [the symbol "$=$" being the set-theoretic equality in the carrier of A].*

---

[3] Allowing existential quantifiers is not difficult [LeG93], but this extension is not required for defining exception algebras.

- $\mathcal{A}$ *satisfies* $(w \in l)$, *where* $w \in \overline{A}$ *and* $l \in L$, *means that* $w \in l_A$ *[the symbol "$\in$" being the set-theoretic membership].*

- *Given a* ΣL-*axiom* φ, $\mathcal{A}$ *satisfies* φ *means that for all assignments* $\sigma : V \to \overline{A}$ *(V covering all the variables of* φ*),* $\mathcal{A}$ *satisfies* $\sigma(\varphi)$ *according to the "atomic satisfaction" defined above and the truth tables of the connectives.*

A label algebra satisfies a label specification SP if and only if it satisfies all its axioms. The full subcategory of $Alg_{Lbl}(\Sigma L)$ *containing all the algebras satisfying SP is denoted by* $Alg_{Lbl}(SP)$.

The classical results of [GTW78] can be extended to the framework of label algebras:

Theorem 1 *Let SP be a positive conditional* ΣL-*specification. Let* $\mathcal{X}$ *be a* ΣL-*algebra. Let R be a binary relation over X compatible with the sorts of the signature (i.e. R is a subset of* $\bigcup_{s \in S} X_s \times X_s$*). There is a least* ΣL-*algebra* $\mathcal{Y}$ *in* $Alg_{Lbl}(SP)$ *such that there exists a label morphism* $h_Y : \mathcal{X} \to \mathcal{Y}$ *and* $(\mathcal{Y}, h_Y)$ *is compatible with R (i.e.* $\forall x, y \in X, x\ R\ y \Rightarrow h_Y(x) = h_Y(y)$*).*

Corollary 1 *If SP is positive conditional, then* $Alg_{Lbl}(SP)$ *has an initial object* $\mathcal{T}_{SP}$.

Corollary 2 *Let* SP_1 *and* SP_2 *be two positive conditional label specifications such that* $SP_1 \subseteq SP_2$ *(i.e.* $S_1 \subseteq S_2$, $\Sigma_1 \subseteq \Sigma_2$, *etc.).*
The forgetful functor $U : Alg_{Lbl}(SP_2) \to Alg_{Lbl}(SP_1)$ *exists and has a left adjoint functor* $F : Alg_{Lbl}(SP_1) \to Alg_{Lbl}(SP_2)$.

As usual, the adjunction unit $I_A : \mathcal{A} \to U(F(\mathcal{A}))$ can be used to define *hierarchical consistency* (i.e. the "no-collapse" property) and *sufficient completeness* (i.e. the "no-junk" property) for structured specifications. In addition, pushouts and colimits exist (from Theorem 1), thus parameterization can be handled without difficulty.

5 Exception signatures and exception algebras

The framework of exception algebras is a specialization of the one of label algebras, where the labels are used for exception handling purposes.

5.1 Label algebras and exception algebras

The particular label Ok will be distinguished to characterize the normal cases; exception names and error messages will be reflected by the other labels. This allows us to take exception names into account in the axioms; thus, an extremely wide spectrum of exception handling and error recovery cases can be specified. Intuitively, in an exception algebra $\mathcal{A}$, $t \in l_A$ with $l \neq Ok$ will mean that the calculation defined by t leads to the exception name l; and $t \in Ok_A$ will mean that the calculation defined by t is a "normal" calculation (i.e. it does not need an exceptional treatment and the calculation is successful).

As shown in Section 3, when specifying a data structure with exception handling features, the specifier has first to declare the desired Ok-part. Let us assume for example that all the terms $succ^i(0)$ with $i \leq 8$ are labelled by Ok and that the specification contains also the following "normal axiom:" $pred(succ(n)) = n$. Then, for instance, the term $pred(succ(0))$ should also belong to the Ok-domain because its calculus does not require any exceptional treatment and leads to the Ok-term 0 via the previous normal axiom. By the terseness principle, labelling by Ok must be *implicitly* propagated through the axioms kept for normal cases. These axioms will be called Ok-axioms, and this implicit propagation rule will be an important component of their semantics, as described in Section 6. Since label algebras have no implicit aspects, the semantics of exception specifications must be more elaborated than the semantics of label specifications.

Another important implicit aspect is the "common future" property. Let us consider $\mathcal{A}$ reflecting the natural numbers bounded by 8, the terms $succ^i(0)$ with $i \leq 8$ being labelled by Ok. Let us assume that $succ^9(0)$ is recovered on $succ^8(0)$. Once this recovering is done, we want everything to happen as if the exception $succ^9(0)$ were never raised; this is the very meaning of the word recovery. The same succession of operations applied to $succ^8(0)$ or to $succ^9(0)$ should return the same value and raise the same exception names. If $succ^9(0)$ is labelled by $TooLarge$, then the term $t = succ^{10}(0)$ should also be labelled by $TooLarge$, since $succ^9(0) = t[succ^9(0) \leftarrow succ^8(0)]$. [4]

In a label algebra $\mathcal{A}$, $eval_A(u) = eval_A(v)$ implies that, for every term t containing u as strict subterm, t and $t[u \leftarrow v]$ have the same value, but it does not imply that they have the same labels. On the contrary, such a property will be required for exception names in exception algebras.

5.2 Exception signature and exception algebras

Definition 6 *An* exception signature ΣExc *is a label signature* $< S, \Sigma, L >$ *such that Ok does not belong to L. The elements of L are called* exception labels *or* exception names. *In the sequel, $\tilde{L}$ will denote $L \cup \{Ok\}$, and $\Sigma\tilde{L}$ will be the label signature $< S, \Sigma, \tilde{L} >$.*

Example 2 $NatExc =< \{Nat\}, \{succ_-, pred_-\}, \{Negative, TooLarge\} >$ *is a possible exception signature for an exception specification of bounded natural numbers.*

Definition 7 *Let $\mathcal{A}$ be a label algebra and l a label. $\mathcal{A}$ satisfies the* common future property *for l if and only if, for all terms u and v of $\overline{A}$ such that $eval_A(u) = eval_A(v)$, we have for all terms t with u as a strict subterm:*
$$t \in l_A \iff t[u \leftarrow v] \in l_A$$
("strict" means that u is a subterm of t distinct from t; in this case, t is called a future of u.)

Definition 8 *An* exception algebra *over the exception signature ΣExc is a label*

---

[4] The term $t[u \leftarrow v]$ is the term of $\overline{A}$ obtained by replacing the occurrence of u in t by v.

algebra $\mathcal{A}$ over the signature $\Sigma\tilde{L}$ that satisfies the common future property for all exception labels $l \in L$.

We have carefully excluded the term u from the set of all the futures of u by considering only strict subterms. If we accept $t = u$ as a future of u then everything happens exactly as if labelling were attached to values. We have shown in Example 1 that this is not suitable. The common future property is a weaker constraint than the labelling of values. For instance Example 1 does not lead to inconsistencies with our formalism (see Section 7.1).

Remark 1 The label Ok is not concerned with the common future property. Otherwise, if $pred(0)$ is recovered on 0 and if $succ(pred(x)) = x$ is an Ok-axiom, we would have: $succ(pred(0))$ is an Ok-term. This would lead to the inconsistency $succ(0) = 0$. Clearly, the term $succ(pred(0))$ is recovered but it must remain exceptional because an exceptional treatment has been required in its history (see also Section 6).

Example 3 According to the exception signature $NatExc$ defined above, we can consider the exception algebra $\mathcal{A} = (A, \{l_A\}_{l\in\tilde{L}})$ defined by:

$$A = \{\ldots, -2, -1, 0, 1, 2, \ldots, 8\}$$

$succ_A$ and $pred_A$ being defined as usual on integers with the restriction $succ_A(8) = 8$; $Negative_A$ is given by the set:

$$\left\{\begin{array}{l} \ldots, \quad \ldots, \quad pred(pred(0)), \quad pred(0), \quad succ(pred(0)), \quad \ldots, \\ \ldots, \quad -3, \quad -2, \quad -1, \quad succ(-1), \quad succ(succ(-1)), \\ \ldots, \quad \ldots, \quad succ(-3), \quad succ(-2), \quad succ(succ(-2)), \quad \ldots, \end{array}\right\}$$

$Negative_A$ contains here at the same time negative values and terms. All these terms have a negative value by classical evaluation in the set of integers or else have at least a subterm which would have a negative value by evaluation.

$$TooLarge_A = \{succ^9(0), succ(8), succ(succ(8)), \ldots\}$$

$$Ok_A = \left\{\begin{array}{l} \ldots, \quad succ(0), \quad succ(1), \quad \ldots, \\ 0, \quad 1 \quad 2, \quad 3, \\ pred(1), \quad pred(2), \quad pred(3), \quad \ldots, \end{array}\right\}$$

Definition 9 *Given an exception signature ΣExc, an exception morphism $\mu : \mathcal{A} \to \mathcal{B}$ is a $\Sigma\tilde{L}$-morphism from $\mathcal{A}$ to $\mathcal{B}$. The category of all ΣExc-algebras is denoted by $Alg_{Exc}(\Sigma Exc)$.*

Theorem 2 *Let ΣExc be an exception signature. Let $SP_{\Sigma\tilde{L}}$ be the positive conditional label specification which contains all the $\Sigma\tilde{L}$-axioms of the form:*

$$x_1 = y_1 \wedge \ldots \wedge x_n = y_n \wedge f(x_1, \ldots, x_n) \in l \implies f(y_1, \ldots, y_n) \in l$$

where f is any (non-constant) operation of Σ, x_i and y_i are variables of sorts given by the arity of f, and l is any exception label of L.

The label specification $SP_{\Sigma \tilde{L}}$ specifies the ΣExc-algebras, i.e. $Alg_{Exc}(\Sigma Exc) = Alg_{Lbl}(SP_{\Sigma \tilde{L}})$.

Consequently, $Alg_{Exc}(\Sigma Exc)$ has an initial object, denoted $\mathcal{T}_{\Sigma Exc}$.

6   Exception specifications and semantics

Following the arguments given in Section 2, the axioms of an exception specification will be separated in two parts in order to preserve clarity and terseness.

The first part, called $GenAx$, is mainly devoted to exception handling. Its first purpose concerns labelling of terms. The axioms with a conclusion of the form $t \in Ok$ (resp. $t \in l$ with $l \in L$) mean that t is a normal term (resp. the heading function of the term t raises the exception name l). The second purpose of $GenAx$ is to handle the exceptional cases, in particular to specify recoveries, according to the previous labelling of terms. The corresponding axioms will have a conclusion of the form $u = v$.

As the axioms of $GenAx$ concern all terms, exceptional or not, the satisfaction of such axioms will simply be the same as for label axioms.

The second part, called $OkAx$, is entirely devoted to the normal cases, and will only concern terms labelled by Ok. The semantics of $OkAx$ must be carefully restricted to Ok-assignments, in order to avoid inconsistencies. It will both treat equalities between Ok-terms and carefully propagate labelling by Ok through these equalities (following the arguments given in Section 5.1).

Two examples of exception specifications are given in Section 7.

Definition 10 *Let ΣExc be an exception signature. A set of generalized axioms is a set $GenAx$ of positive conditional label axioms with respect to the label signature $\Sigma \tilde{L}$.*

An exception algebra $\mathcal{A}$ satisfies $GenAx$ if and only if its underlying label algebra satisfies $GenAx$, regarded as a set of label axioms.

Definition 11 *Let ΣExc be an exception signature. A set of Ok-axioms is a set $OkAx$ of positive conditional $\Sigma \tilde{L}$-axioms with a conclusion of the form: $v = w$.*

Definition 12 *Let ΣExc be an exception signature. An exception algebra $\mathcal{A}$ satisfies an Ok-axiom of the form $P \Rightarrow v = w$, where P is the premise,[5] if and only if for all assignments σ with range in $\overline{A}$ (covering all the variables of the axiom) which satisfy the premise (i.e. $\mathcal{A}$ as $\Sigma \tilde{L}$-algebra satisfies $\sigma(P)$ as "ground" label axiom), the two following properties hold:*

1. *Ok-propagation: if at least one of the terms $\sigma(v)$ or $\sigma(w)$ belongs to Ok_A and the other one is of the form $f(t_1, \ldots, t_p)$ with all the t_i belonging to Ok_A (p may be equal to 0), then both $\sigma(v)$ and $\sigma(w)$ belong to Ok_A.*

---

[5] P may be empty.

2. *Ok-equality: if $\sigma(v)$ and $\sigma(w)$ belong to Ok_A then $eval_A(\sigma(v)) = eval_A(\sigma(w))$.*

$\mathcal{A}$ satisfies $OkAx$ if and only if $\mathcal{A}$ satisfies all the Ok-axioms of $OkAx$.

The first property of the definition reflects a propagation of the label Ok (which starts from the Ok-terms declared in $GenAx$); a term can be labelled by Ok through an Ok-axiom only if all the arguments of its heading function are already labelled by Ok. This rule allows us to carefully propagate the label Ok. Intuitively, such an innermost evaluation reflects an implicit propagation of exceptions: if t is not an Ok-term then $f(\ldots t \ldots)$ cannot be turned into an Ok-term via the Ok-axioms. (However f is not necessarily a strict function; lazyness can be specified via the generalized axioms, where $f(\ldots t \ldots)$ can be recovered.)

The second property specifies the equalities that must hold for the normal cases. Two terms can get the same evaluation through an Ok-axiom only if they are both labelled by Ok.

Definitions 13 *An exception specification is a triplet $SPEC = < \Sigma Exc, GenAx, OkAx >$ where ΣExc is an exception signature, $GenAx$ a set of generalized axioms and $OkAx$ a set of Ok-axioms.*

A ΣExc-algebra $\mathcal{A}$ satisfies $SPEC$ if and only if it satisfies $GenAx$ and $OkAx$, as sets of generalized axioms and Ok-axioms respectively.

We denote by $Alg_{Exc}(SPEC)$ the full subcategory of $Alg_{Exc}(\Sigma Exc)$ containing all the algebras satisfying $SPEC$.

Lemma 1 *Let ΣExc be an exception signature. Let α be an Ok-axiom. There is a set of positive conditional $\Sigma \tilde{L}$-axioms, $Tr(\alpha)$, such that for every ΣExc-algebra $\mathcal{A}$, $\mathcal{A}$ satisfies the Ok-axiom α if and only if the underlying $\Sigma \tilde{L}$-algebra of $\mathcal{A}$ satisfies $Tr(\alpha)$.*

$Tr(\alpha)$ is obtained from α by adding certain premises reflecting Definition 12; $Tr(\alpha)$ may thus contain a great number of label axioms (related to the number of operations of $\Sigma \tilde{L}$).

Theorem 3 *Let $SPEC = < \Sigma Exc, GenAx, OkAx >$ be an exception specification. Let $Tr(SPEC)$ be the label specification defined by the label signature $\Sigma \tilde{L}$ and the set of label axioms containing: the axioms of $SP_{\Sigma \tilde{L}}$ (defined in Theorem 2), $GenAx$ and all the $Tr(\alpha)$ for $\alpha \in OkAx$ (mentioned in Lemma 1 above). We have $Alg_{Exc}(SPEC) = Alg_{Lbl}(Tr(SPEC))$. $Tr(SPEC)$ is called the translation of $SPEC$ into a label specification.*

$Tr(SPEC)$ only contains positive conditional axioms. Thus, from Corollary 1 we have:

Theorem 4 *Let $SPEC$ be a ΣExc-specification. $Alg_{Exc}(SPEC)$ has an initial object $\mathcal{T}_{SPEC}$.*

Remark 2 Given two exception specifications $SPEC_1$ and $SPEC_2$ such that $SPEC_1 \subseteq SPEC_2$, the forgetful functor $U : Alg_{Exc}(SPEC_2) \rightarrow Alg_{Exc}(SPEC_1)$ exists and has a left adjoint functor F.

7 Examples

Section 7.1 contains an example with "intrinsic" exceptional cases and bounds. Section 7.2 contains an example with bounds and "dynamic" exceptional cases. Thus, all the classes of exceptional cases, as classified in Section 1, are covered.

7.1 A short example

Let $NatExc = < \{Nat\}, \{succ\_, pred\_\}, \{TooLarge, Negative\} >$ be the exception signature given in Section 5.2. An exception specification of natural numbers bounded by 8 is given below:

GenAx : $succ^8(0) \epsilon Ok$
$\qquad succ(n) \epsilon Ok \implies n \epsilon Ok$
$\qquad succ^9(0) \epsilon TooLarge$
$\qquad pred(0) \epsilon Negative$
$\qquad succ(n) \epsilon TooLarge \implies succ(n) = n$
OkAx : $pred(succ(n)) = n$
Where : $n : Nat$

The first two axioms of $GenAx$ specify the Ok part of Nat. It is not necessary to declare *all* the Ok-terms (the label Ok will be automatically propagated to terms such as $pred(succ(0))$ via the Ok-axiom). It is only desirable to declare at least one term for each intended Ok-value. The meaning of the third and fourth generalized axioms is that the operation $succ$ (resp. $pred$) raises the exception $TooLarge$ (resp. $Negative$) when applied to $succ^8(0)$ (resp. 0). The last generalized axiom recovers $succ^9(0)$ on $succ^8(0)$ (as well as all its successors, from the common future property). The inconsistency described in Example 1 does not occur any more, as $succ^8(0)$ is not labelled by $TooLarge$. Then, $OkAx$ only has to specify the operation $pred$ in all normal cases; it is actually terse and clear.

Let us note that we operate in a total framework; however this does not force to always define a recovery condition. For example, the previous specification does not imply for $pred(0)$ to be equal to an Ok-term; consequently, in the initial model, it denotes an exceptional value that can be understood as an error exit.

Moreover, the instance $pred(succ^8(0)) = pred(succ^9(0)) = succ^8(0)$ is no longer an instance of the Ok-axiom because $succ^9(0)$, and therefore $pred(succ^9(0))$, is not required to be an Ok-term in our framework (even though $eval_A(succ^9(0)) = eval_A(succ^8(0))$). Thus, $pred(succ^9(0)) = succ^8(0)$ is *not* a consequence of $OkAx$. This is a good example of our restricted propagation of the label Ok through the Ok-axioms; it shows how the semantics of Ok-axioms reflect an implicit propagation of exceptions.

Let us note that the exception algebra described in the Section 5.2 satisfies this specification.

7.2 A more elaborated example

We give a specification of bounded arrays of natural numbers,[6] where a new array is not initialized. The specifications of natural numbers and booleans are not given in this example; it is not difficult, for instance, to complete the specification of Section 7.1 with the operations eq and $\leq$.

S : $Array$

Σ : $create\_\_$: $Nat\ Nat \to Array$

            $store\_\_\_$: $Nat\ Array\ Nat \to Array$

            $fetch\_\_$: $Array\ Nat \to Nat$

            $lower\_$: $Array \to Nat$

            $upper\_$: $Array \to Nat$

L : $BadRange,\ OutOfRange,\ NonInitialized$

GenAx:

$low \in Ok \wedge up \in Ok \wedge low < up = true \implies create(low, up) \in Ok$

$a \in Ok \wedge ind \in Ok \wedge x \in Ok \wedge lower(a) \leq ind = true \wedge ind \leq upper(a) = true \implies$
$$store(x, a, ind) \in Ok$$

$low < up = false \implies create(low, up) \in BadRange$

$ind < lower(a) = true \implies store(x, a, ind) \in OutOfRange$

$upper(a) < ind = true \implies store(x, a, ind) \in OutOfRange$

$ind < lower(a) = true \implies fetch(a, ind) \in OutOfRange$

$upper(a) < ind = true \implies fetch(a, ind) \in OutOfRange$

$lower(a) \leq ind = true \wedge ind \leq upper(a) = true \implies$
$$fetch(create(low, up), ind)) \in NonInitialized$$

$eq(ind1, ind2) = false \wedge fetch(a, ind1) \in NonInitialized \implies$
$$fetch(store(x, a, ind2), ind1) \in NonInitialized$$

OkAx :

$lower(create(low, up)) = low$

$upper(create(low, up)) = up$

$lower(store(x, a, ind)) = lower(a)$

$upper(store(x, a, ind)) = upper(a)$

$store(x, store(y, a, ind), ind) = store(x, a, ind)$

$eq(ind1, ind2) = false \implies$
$$store(x, store(y, a, ind1), ind2) = store(y, store(x, a, ind2), ind1)$$

$fetch(store(x, a, ind), ind) = x$

Where : $low,\ up,\ ind,\ ind1,\ ind2,\ x,\ y : Nat$; $a : Array$

The term $create(low, up)$ creates a new array of range $[low, up]$. Notice that if low or up is exceptional, then $create(low, up)$ is exceptional too (exception propagation). The operations $lower$ and $upper$ retrieve the acceptable range of an array. The exception name $OutOfRange$ is raised when a $store$ or a $fetch$ is performed outside of the acceptable range. Thus, the label $OutOfRange$ intersect several sorts ($Array$ and Nat).

---

[6] For simplicity, both indexes and elements of arrays are of sort Nat.

8   Conclusion

We have introduced a distinction between what we call "exception handling" and "error handling." We have shown that *exception handling* requires a refined notion of the satisfaction relation for algebraic specifications. The scope of an axiom should be restricted to carefully chosen patterns, because a satisfaction relation based on assignments with range in *values* often raises inconsistencies. A more elaborated notion of assignment is considered: assignment with range in *terms*. This allows us to restrict the scope of an axiom to certain suitable patterns, and solves the inconsistencies raised by exception handling.

We have also shown that exception names, or error messages, should be carried by terms, and that they are advantageously reflected by *labels*. Labels must not go through equational atoms; thus, two terms having the same value do not necessarily carry the same labels. We have first defined the framework of *label algebras*, that defines suitable semantics for labels. The scope of a label axiom is carefully delimited by labels which serve as special marks on terms.

Then, we have proposed a new algebraic framework for exception handling, based on label algebras, which is powerful enough to cope with all suitable exception handling features such as implicit propagation of exceptions, possible recoveries, declaration of exception names, etc. All the usual exceptional cases can easily be specified ("intrinsic" exceptions of an abstract data type, "dynamic" exceptional cases and bounded data structures). This approach solves some weaknesses of existing frameworks (see Section 3) and succeeds with respect to *clarity* and *terseness*, that are two crucial criteria for formal specifications with exception handling.

Although we have introduced the theory of label algebras as a general frame for exception handling purpose, the application domain of label algebras seems to be much more general than exception handling. Indeed, labels provide a great tool to express several other features developed in the field of (first order) algebraic specifications. We have mentioned in Section 3 that label algebras can be shown as an extension of more standard algebraic approaches based on "multityping." Similarly to exception handling, partial functions [BW82] or observability issues [Hen89][BB91] can also be described in the same way by some well chosen forms of label specifications. However, all the specific applications of label algebras require certain *implicit* label axioms in order to preserve clarity and terseness. Thus, the framework of label algebras provides us with "low level" algebraic specifications: in a generic way, the specific semantical aspects of a given approach (e.g. observational specifications or exception specifications) can be specified by a well chosen set of label axioms.

Intuitively, labels are unary predicates on terms. In order to facilitate certain applications of label algebras, we plane to generalize labels to "labels of strictly positive arity." Several other extensions, such as higher order label specifications, may be dealt with in future works.

Acknowledgements: We would like to thank Pierre Dauchy and Anne Deo-Blanchard for a careful reading of the draft version of this paper. This work has been partially supported by CNRS GRECO de Programmation and EEC Working Group COMPASS.

References

[BB91]   Bernot G., Bidoit M. *Proving the correctness of algebraically specified software: Modularity and Observability issues.* Proc. of AMAST-2, Second Conference of Algebraic Methodology and Software Technology, Iowa City, Iowa, USA, May 1991.

[BBC86]   Bernot G., Bidoit M., Choppy C. *Abstract data types with exception handling : an initial approach based on a distinction between exceptions and errors.* Theoretical Computer Science, Vol.46, n.1, pp.13-45, Elsevier Science Pub. B.V. (North-Holland), November 1986. (Also LRI Report 251, Orsay, Dec. 1985.)

[Ber86]   Bernot G. *Une sémantique algébrique pour une spécification différenciée des exceptions et des erreurs : application à l'implémentation et aux primitives de structuration des spécifications formelles.* Thèse de troisième cycle, Université de Paris-Sud, Orsay, February 1986.

[BL91a]   Bernot G., Le Gall P. *Label algebras : a systematic use of terms.* "8th International Workshop on Abstract Data Types", Dourdan, August 1991. LNCS 655 p 144-163. (also LRI Report 719, Orsay, Dec. 1991.)

[BL91b]   Bernot G., Le Gall P. *Label algebras and exception handling.* Draft Version (also in Habilitation Thesis of Bernot G., University of Orsay, Paris XI, Feb. 1992.)

[Bid84]   Bidoit M. *Algebraic specification of exception handling by means of declarations and equations.* Proc. 11th ICALP, Springer-Verlag LNCS 172, July 1984.

[BW82]   Broy M., Wirsing M. *Partial abstract data types.* Acta Informatica, Vol.18-1, Nov. 1982.

[EM85]   Ehrig H., Mahr B. *Fundamentals of Algebraic Specification 1. Equations and initial semantics.* EATCS Monographs on Theoretical Computer Science, Vol.6, Springer-Verlag, 1985.

[FGJM85] Futatsugi K., Goguen J., Jouannaud J-P., Meseguer J. *Principles of OBJ2.* Proc. 12th ACM Symp. on Principle of Programming Languages, New Orleans, january 1985.

[GDLE84] Gogolla M., Drosten K., Lipeck U., Ehrich H.D. *Algebraic and operational semantics of specifications allowing exceptions and errors.* Theoretical Computer Science 34, North Holland, 1984, pp.289-313.

[GM89]   Goguen J.A., Meseguer J. *Order-sorted algebra I: equational deduction for multiple inheritance, overloading, exceptions and partial operations.* Technical Report SRI-CSL-89-10, SRI, July 1989.

[Gog78a] Goguen J.A. *Abstract errors for abstract data types.* Formal Description of Programming Concepts, E.J. NEUHOLD Ed., North Holland, pp.491-522, 1978.

[Gog78b]   Goguen J.A. *Order sorted algebras: exceptions and error sorts, coercion and overloading operators.* Univ. California Los Angeles, Semantics Theory of Computation Report n.14, Dec. 1978.

[GTW78]   Goguen J.A., Thatcher J.W., Wagner E.G. *An Initial Algebra Approach to the Specification, Correctness, and Implementation of Abstract Data Types.* Current Trends in Programming Methodology, ed. R.T. Yeh, Printice-Hall, Vol.IV, pp.80-149, 1978. (Also IBM Report RC 6487, October 1976.)

[Gut75]   Guttag J.V. *The specification and application to programming.* Ph.D. Thesis, University of Toronto, 1975

[Hen89]   Hennicker R. *Implementation of Parameterized Observational Specifications.* TapSoft, Barcelona, LNCS 351, vol.1, pp.290-305, 1989.

[LeG93]   Le Gall P. *Les algèbres étiquetées : une sémantique fondée sur une utilisation systématique des termes. Application au test de logiciel avec traitement d'exceptions.* forthcoming thesis, University of Orsay, 1993.

[LZ75]   Liskov B., Zilles S. *Specification techniques for data abstractions.* IEEE Transactions on Software Engineering, Vol.SE-1 n.1, March 1975.

[McL71]   Mac Lane S. *Categories for the working mathematician.* Graduate texts in mathematics, 5, Springer-Verlag, 1971

[Meg90]   Mégrelis A. *Algèbre galactique - Un procédé de calcul formel, relatif aux semi-fonctions, à l'inclusion et à l'égalité.* Ph.D. Thesis, University of Nancy I, Sept. 1990.

[Mos89]   Mosses P. *Unified algebras and Institutions.* Proc. of IEEE LICS'89, Fourth Annual Symposium on Logic in Computer Science, June 1989, Asilomar, California.

[MSS90]   Manca V., Salibra A. and Scollo G. *Equational Type Logic.* Conference on Algebraic Methodology and Software Technology, Iowa City, IA, May 1989, TCS 77, p 131-159.

[Poi87]   Poigné A. *Partial algebras, subsorting, and dependent types* Recent Trends in Data Type Specification, 5th Workshop on Specification of Abstract Data Types, Gullane, Scotland, September 1987. LNCS 332, p 208-234.

[Sch91]   Schobbens P.Y. *Clean algebraic exceptions with implicit propagation.* Proc. of AMAST-2, Second Conference of Algebraic Methodology and Software Technology, Iowa City, Iowa, USA, May 1991.

Gate Splitting in LOTOS Specifications Using Abstract Interpretation [*]

Fosca Giannotti and Diego Latella

CNR, Ist. CNUCE, via S.Maria 36, I56126 Pisa Italy
email: fosca@cnuce.cnr.it latella@fdt.cnuce.cnr.it [**]

Abstract. In this paper[1] a technique for an efficient solution to the problem of gate splitting in LOTOS specifications is presented. The transformation problem is part of a design methodology based on the specification language LOTOS. The problem is formally defined. The technique is based on Abstract Interpretation which is used for approximating the sets of possible values which LOTOS value expressions can evaluate to. The originality of the proposed approach stems from the fact that the abstract domain as well as abstract functions are generated *automatically* from the LOTOS specification to be transformed. The abstract interpretation as well as the transformation are proved correct.

1 Introduction

A software development methodology based on the ISO standard specification language LOTOS [2, 3, 20] and on the notion of *correctness preserving transformations* [18] has been developed as a major result of the ESPRIT-LOTOSPHERE Project [14, 15, 16, 17].

Gate splitting is a simple, yet useful, transformation which, given a specification P, hereafter called the *input specification*, returns a specification Q insisting on a set of gates different from that of the input specification but preserving the information on the behaviour of P. In other words the transition systems of P and Q are isomorphic; they share the same non-deterministic structure and the actions of Q are obtained via an injective renaming of those of P. The gates of Q are obtained from those of P by means of *splitting*: a certain gate g in P can be *split* into different gates $g_1, g_2, ..., g_k$ in Q. For each action occurring in each g_i in Q, there will be a uniquely determined action of P occurring in g, which can be recognized by interaction parameters and vice-versa. Thus, no information on P is lost in Q.

There are different motivations for this transformation at different steps of the development trajectory from abstract specification to concrete realization [14] including the need of splitting an abstract interaction point into a set of communication

---

[*] This work has been done within the ESPRIT Project Ref. 2304 - LOTOSPHERE and has been partially funded by the CNR-NATO Advanced Fellowships Program.

[**] Current address of Diego Latella: Univ. of Twente, Dept. of Comp. Science, PO BOX 217, 7500 AE Enschede, The Netherlands email: latella@cs.utwente.nl

[1] An extended abstract of the present paper has already been published in the Proceedings of the "Workshop on Static Analysis" LaBRI - Univ. of Bordeaux I 23-25 Sept. 1992.

channels when the specification is matched against an implementation architecture or when the implementation language imposes constraints on communication channels (e.g. forcing them to be *typed*). Finally, splitting a gate can facilitate increasing potential parallelism, to be obtained by means of other transformations [22, 13, 18].

In the present paper we show how *Abstract Interpretation* (AI) can be used in order to get an efficient solution to the gate splitting problem, when the input specification satisfies some syntactical constraints. Such constraints give the abstract data type (ADT) part of the specification a functional programming language style.

AI of programs is a static analysis technique aimed at gathering information about the dynamic behaviour of a program or specification, to be used by compilers, partial evaluators and debuggers, or merely as documentation [1, 4, 5, 6, 7]. AI consists in assigning language constructs non-standard (i.e. *abstract*) meaning which *approximate* standard semantics.

The original contribution of this paper stems from the fact that the abstract domain for abstract interpretation as well as abstract functions are *automatically* generated from the input specification and heavily depend on it. With respect to this, speaking about *Abstract Compilation*, more than AI would be more appropriate. This is quite uncommon in traditional use of AI where the definition of abstract domains and functions is left to the user of the technique who is usually forced to rely on "ad hoc" solutions.

In this paper it is assumed the reader is familiar both with LOTOS and with AI. We believe that the key ideas for the above mentioned automatic construction of the abstract domain are largely independent from LOTOS and therefore can be applied to different languages. Nevertheless, we shall make explicit reference to LOTOS here in order to show them working on a real specification language.

In Sect.2 a possible formalization of the gate splitting problem is given and a solution is informally introduced. A formal solution to the problem is discussed in Sect.3. The solution is proved correct. The details of the proofs are omitted here, the interested reader being referred to [9]. Finally, in Sect.4 several improvements to our solution are briefly discussed.

2   The problem of Gate Splitting

In this paper we shall assume that a gate can be split only according to the values exchanged throughout it. Thus the *Gate Rearrangement Criterion* (GRC) will be specified as a function $\mathcal{R} : Gates \rightarrow Values \rightarrow Gates$ where *Gates* and *Values*, denote respectively the set of LOTOS *gate identifiers* and *data values*. Moreover, in order for the transformation to make sense, we shall require that $range(\mathcal{R})$ be finite.

Consider for example the following LOTOS process definition[2]:

---

[2] In the sequel no distinction will be made between *process definitions* and *specifications*. Also, the syntax of the ADT part is slightly different from that of standard LOTOS. The details on such a syntax will be given in Sect.3.1. Moreover, *currying* will be often used for functions [8] in the meta-notation.

```
process P[a]: noexit :=
choice x in Nat
 (a!RQ(x);
 (is_0(x)--> a!BLOB;stop [] not(is_0(x))--> a!RS(m2(x));P[a])
where type SP_type is
sorts
Nat, Bool, SP
constrs
 0     :-->Nat            s     :Nat-->Nat
 BLOB :-->SP              RQ,RS:Nat-->SP
 tt,ff:-->Bool
functns
 is_0:Nat-->Bool         not:Bool-->Bool        m2:Nat-->Nat
 is_0(0)  =tt            not(tt)=ff             m2(0)    =0
 is_0(s(x))=ff           not(ff)=tt             m2(s(0)) =s(0)
                                                m2(s(s(x))=m2(x)

endtype
endproc
```

Process P computes a function $m2$ on any positive natural number n received as a request $RQ(n)$ on gate a and returns the result $RS(m2(n))$ on the same gate. If the input value is 0 the process returns the constant $BLOB$ and stops. Suppose now we want to split gate a in such a way that all the request actions will occur at either gate $r0$ or r, according to the fact the input value is zero or a positive number. Moreover we want the $BLOB$ action occur on the customized gate b. Finally, if the result of the computation is 0 then the response action must occur on gate $s0$, otherwise it will occur on gate s. Such informal criterion corresponds to the following GRC $\mathcal{G}$, which is defined only on gate a:

$$\mathcal{G} \text{ a v} = \text{ if (is\_BLOB v) then b}$$
$$\text{else if (is\_RQ v) then if (is\_0(URQ v)) then r0}$$
$$\text{else r}$$
$$\text{else if (is\_0(URS v)) then s0}$$
$$\text{else s}$$

The above definition uses some functions defined as follows:

```
URQ,URS:SP-->Nat   is_BLOB:SP-->Bool   is_RQ:SP-->Bool    is_RS:SP-->Bool
URQ(RQ(x))=x       is_BLOB(BLOB)=tt    is_RQ(RQ(x))=tt    is_RS(RS(x))=tt
URS(RS(x))=x       is_BLOB(RQ(x))=ff   is_RQ(BLOB)=ff     is_RS(BLOB)=ff
                   is_BLOB(RS(x))= ff  is_RQ(RS(x))=ff    is_RS(RQ(x))=ff
```

So, the first step of our methodology consists in defining the GRC in terms of functions defined in the ADT part of the specification, possibly extended with some auxiliary functions[3].

In order to formalize the transformation *correctness requirement* we need the following definitions, which extend the notion of *strong bisimulation equivalence* [11].

---

[3] Notice that the GRC itself is *not* part of the ADT specification because, in the general case it might contain tests on the *type* of data values, which cannot be defined *within* the LOTOS specification itself.

Definition 1 Labeled Transition System. A *Labeled Transition System* is a 4-tuple $< S, A, T, s >$, where S is a set of *states*, A is a set of action *labels*, T is a set of *transition relations*: given $a \in A$ the transition relation $\xrightarrow{a}$ is a binary relation over S. We shall often write $s_1 \xrightarrow{a} s_2$ for $< s_1, s_2 > \in \xrightarrow{a}$. Finally $s \in S$ is the *initial state*.

Definition 2 ϕ-bisimulation relation. Let $Sys_1 = < S_1, A_1, T_1, s0_1 >$ and $Sys_2 = < S_2, A_2, T_2, s0_2 >$ be labeled transition systems. Let $\phi : A_1 \longrightarrow A_2$ be a *bijection*. A *ϕ-bisimulation relation* is any relation $R_\phi \subseteq S_1 \times S_2$ such that:
$\forall a_1 \in A_1, a_2 \in A_2, s_1 \in S_1, s_2 \in S_2$ with $< s_1, s_2 > \in R_\phi$

1. $s_1 \xrightarrow{a_1} s_1' \Rightarrow \exists s_2' : s_2 \xrightarrow{\phi\, a_1} s_2'$ and $< s_1', s_2' > \in R_\phi$
2. $s_2 \xrightarrow{a_2} s_2' \Rightarrow \exists s_1', a_1 : s_1 \xrightarrow{a_1} s_1'$ and $a_2 = \phi\, a_1$ and $< s_1', s_2' > \in R_\phi$

Definition 3 Φ-bisimulation equivalence. B_1 and B_2 are *Φ-bisimulation equivalent*, written $B_1 \sim_\Phi B_2$, iff there exists a *ϕ-bisimulation* R_ϕ such that $B_1 R_\phi B_2$

Proposition 4. $\sim_\Phi$ *is an equivalence relation.*

Our transformation problem can then be formalized as follows, where for all process definitions B $Gates(B)$ returns the set of gates which textually occur within B and LTS_B stands for the labeled transition system denoted by B:
Given a process definition P and a GRC $\mathcal{R}$ we want to get a process definition Q such that $Gates(Q)=\mathcal{R}(Gates(P)\times\ Values)$ and $LTS_P \sim_\Phi LTS_Q$.

A possible solution for our sample process definition and GRC is the following one:

```
process Q[b,r0,r,s0,s]:noexit :=
choice x : Nat []
 (r0!RQ(0);b!BLOB;stop
   []
   r!RQ(x)[not(is_0(x))];(s0!RS(m2(x))[is_0(m2(x))];Q[b,r0,r,s0,s]
                          []
                          s!RS(m2(x))[not(is_0(m2(x)))];Q[b,r0,r,s0,s]
                         )
 )
where ....
```

A close look at the above process Q reveals that it is extremely useful for the transformation to have knowledge about the *possible output values* of the GRC when it is applied to values denoted by LOTOS value expressions. In fact, knowing that $\mathcal{G}\, a\, BLOB = b$ we can translate $a!BLOB$; *stop* into $b!BLOB$; *stop*. On the other hand, since $m2(x)$ may be any natural number *and* the set of possible values for $\mathcal{G}\, a\, RS(n)$, for any natural number n is $\{s0, s\}$, we shall translate $a!RS(m2(x));...$ into a *choice expression* like the following one:

```
(s0!RS(m2(x))[is_0(m2(x))];..)
[]
(s!RS(m2(x))[not(is_0(m2(x)))];..)
```

where the appropriate alternative will be selected by a *selection predicate* consistent with the definition of the GRC (for instance $is\_0(m2(x))$ in the first alternative). Notice that complete lack of knowledge on the possible output values of $\mathcal{G}$ a $RS(n)$ would have resulted in a choice expression with *five* alternatives instead of *two*, one for *each* member of the codomain of $\mathcal{G}$, i.e. $\{b, r0, r, s0, s\}$.

Essentially the transformation acts on *action prefix* changing it into a choice expression where each alternative is an action prefix guarded by a selection predicate, the treatment of other constructs being mainly implied by these main changes. The number of alternatives of such choice expressions depend both on "how much" the GRC depends on actual data values and on the amount of knowledge on that which can be acquired from a static analysis of the input specification. In Sect. 3, we shall develop a technique for computing such a knowledge and for using it within the transformation.

3 A Solution to the Problem of Gate Splitting

In this section we shall describe in detail the solution we propose for the gate splitting problem. A major emphasis will be put on the static analysis technique we use for getting suitable knowledge on the GRC behaviour. The transformation itself is quite straightforward.

The key point is to get statically computable information on the *possible values* which the GRC as well as LOTOS *value expressions* can evaluate to in a given specification. AI can be used for finitely approximating the sets of those values. The level of uncertainty present in those approximations is determined by the amount of the information on both the "data flow" and the behaviour of functions defined in the ADT part of a specification which can be deduced by a static analysis of the specification.

In our example function $m2$ is defined on Nat. The set $\{0, s(0), s(s(\bot_{Nat}))\}$ can be chosen as a representation for Nat, where 0 and $s(0)$ are represented explicitly and $s(s(\bot_{Nat}))$ represents $s(s(0)), s(s(s(0))), s(s(s(s(0))))$... Notice that the above representation is *finite* (it contains only three elements) and *complete* (every term in Nat is represented). Also, it is an *abstraction* of Nat (the term $s(s(\bot_{Nat}))$ intuitively stands for *any natural number greater than 1*). Moreover, it gives 0 and $s(0)$ a "special status" of *distinguished elements*; this is because those two terms are the only terms which occur explicitly in the text of the process definition.

Starting from $\{0, s(0), s(s(\bot_{Nat}))\}$ we can use its *power set* as an abstraction for the set of sets on Nat. We must keep in mind that the elements of such an *abstract domain*, i.e. the *abstract terms*, are just approximations of sets on natural numbers in the sense that not all sets are explicitly represented. Some of them are only approximated by terms which represent sets in which they are included.

The *abstract version* f^A of a function f is a function which gives information on the possible outcomes of f when applied to sets of possible input values. f^A is defined on abstract terms and is then a finite function. Finally, the information on the *possible values* of value expressions is obtained via an *abstract evaluation function* $\mathcal{V}$, which maps LOTOS *value expressions* into abstract terms.

In the following we shall describe the details of our technique for the automatic construction of the abstract domain and the procedure for getting the abstract functions out of the definition of their concrete counterpart.

3.1 Abstract Framework

In the sequel we shall assume that in the ADT part of the input specification *constructor names* will be kept separated from *function names*. Given the term $n(t_1, \ldots, t_n)$, we shall call it a *constructor term* if n is constructor name and we shall call it a *functor term* if n is a function name. Only functor terms may occur in the left-hand-side of equations. For the sake of notational simplicity, in this paper conditional equations are not dealt with and we also require that for each term t of a given sort s and function $f : s \rightarrow s'$ there is *exactly* one equation in the definition of f the left-hand-side of which matches with t (this implies that the technique presented here does not deal with "error-driven" default values for functions as well as "overlapping patterns"). Let S and Σ respectively be the *sorts set* and the *signature* of the input specification. The word algebra over Σ will be denoted by T_Σ. $T_{\Sigma \cup Var}$ denotes the algebra of terms with (sorted, free) variables. T_{Σ_c} will denote the subset of T_Σ containing only terms made up of constants and constructors applied to them recursively[4]. A_s will denote the *carrier* of sort s in the Σ-algebra A. We say that a sort s is *basic* if whenever $K : s_1, \ldots, s_n \rightarrow s$ is a constructor of sort s, then $s_1 = \ldots = s_n = s$. In this paper we shall consider only specifications in which the ADT part has at least one basic sort. The above notation will be used also for families of *sets*.

Abstract Domains The starting point for the construction of the abstract domains is the notion of *partial term*.

Definition 5 Partial term posets:$< ((\Pi_\Sigma)_s, \preceq_s)|s \in S >$. For all sorts s the set of *partial terms* of sort s is defined as the smallest set $(\Pi_\Sigma)_s$ such that:
1. $\perp_s \in (\Pi_\Sigma)_s$
2. for all constants $c :\rightarrow s, c \in (\Pi_\Sigma)_s$ and
3. for all constructors $k : s_1, \ldots, s_n \rightarrow s$ and partial terms $t_i \in (\Pi_\Sigma)_{s_i}$, $i = 1 \ldots n, k(t_1, \ldots, t_n) \in (\Pi_\Sigma)_s$.

The partial order relation $\preceq_s$ is defined as the *reflexive, anti-symmetric* and *transitive* closure of relation $\leadsto_s$, which is the smallest set in $(\Pi_\Sigma)_s \times (\Pi_\Sigma)_s$ such that:
1. $\perp_s \leadsto_s t$ for all $t \in (\Pi_\Sigma)_s$
2. $k(t_1, \ldots, t_n) \leadsto_s k(r_1, \ldots, r_n)$ iff $t_i \leadsto_{s_i} r_i$, for all $i = 1, \ldots, n$.

As usual, $x \preceq_s y$ and $x \neq y$ will be denoted by $x \prec_s y$. Also, the subscript s will be omitted when this will not give raise to ambiguities.

---

[4] Notice that due to the restriction of not having equations for constructors T_{Σ_c} correctly represents T_Σ modulo the equations for the functions in the ADT definition.

Definition 6 Partial terms generators: π_s. For all sorts s
$\pi_s : (T_{\Sigma \cup Var})_s \to (\Pi_\Sigma)_s$ is defined as follows:

$$\pi_s(c) \qquad\qquad = c \text{ for all constants } c :\to s$$
$$\pi_s(x) \qquad\qquad =\perp_s \text{ for all variables of sort } s$$
$$\pi_s(k(t_1,\ldots,t_n))= k(\pi_{s_1}(t_1),\ldots,\pi_{s_n}(t_n)) \text{ for all constructor terms}$$
$$\pi_s(f(t_1,\ldots,t_n))=\perp_s \qquad\qquad\qquad \text{for all functor terms}$$

Intuitively, given a sort s, a partial term is a finite representation for a subset of $(T_\Sigma)_s$ and is obtained from a term in $(T_{\Sigma \cup Var})_s$ where variables and functor terms are replaced by a special symbol, $\perp$, representing *all* values in $(T_\Sigma)_{s'}$ for some proper sort s'. Any ground term t simply represents the singleton $\{t\}$. For instance, in our example, 0 represents $\{0\}$, $\perp_{Nat}$ represents $\{0, s(0), s(s(0)), s(s(s(0))), ...\}$, $s(\perp_{Nat})$ represents $\{s(0), s(s(0)), s(s(s(0))), ...\}$ and so on. The intuitive meaning of the ordering relation is that $t_1 \preceq t_2$ if t_1 is "less specified", or "more partial" than t_2, or, equivalently, the set of terms represented by t_2 is included in that represented by t_1.

It is also natural to think at different sets of partial terms as representations of different subsets of $(T_\Sigma)_s$.

For instance, $\{0, s(s(\perp_{Nat}))\}$ will represent $\{0, s(s(0)), s(s(s(0))), ...\}$. On the other hand, a given subset of $(T_\Sigma)_s$ could be represented in many different ways. For instance, the following are alternative representations for $(T_\Sigma)_{Nat}$ itself:$\{\perp_{Nat}\}$, $\{0, s(\perp_{Nat})\}$. It is worth noting that the second set differs from the first one only because it keeps the representation of 0 separated from the one of all the other values. A much more refined representation would be $\{0, s(0), s(s(\perp_{Nat}))\}$ where a special status is granted to $s(0)$ too. Finally, notice that in $\{0, s(\perp_{Nat}), s(s(\perp_{Nat}))\}$ there is a kind of redundancy since $s(\perp_{Nat}) \preceq s(s(\perp_{Nat}))$.

The following definition allows to characterize *all* finite representations of $(T_\Sigma)_s$ made up out of partial terms which do not suffer of the above unpleasant redundancy and which differ only in the set of terms which have an explicit representation, i.e. in their "grain".

Definition 7 Cuts. Given a partial order $(D, \preceq)$, $C \subseteq D$ is a *cut* of D iff both the following conditions hold:
1. $\forall x, y \in C x \not\prec y \wedge y \not\prec x$
2. $\forall x \in D \exists y \in C$ such that $x \preceq y \vee y \preceq x$

The following definitions will make it possible to automatically generate a finite representation AB_s for each sort s in the data type part of any given LOTOS specification. All terms textually occurring in the LOTOS specification will be explicitly represented in AB_s. This is crucial since any static information on the behaviour of the GRC will in the end necessarily depend upon such terms.

Definition 8 Raw Abstract Bases: RAB_s. Let s be a *basic* sort. The *Raw Abstract Base* of sort s, RAB_s is the set of all partial terms $\pi_s(t)$ such that $t \in (T_{\Sigma \cup Var})_s$ is a term which textually occurs in the LOTOS specification. Moreover, $\perp_s \in RAB_s$ is also required.

If s is non-basic, then let RAB'_s be the set defined as above. Then RAB_s will the smallest set which includes RAB'_s and such that all partial terms $k(t_1, \ldots, t_n)$ such that contructor $k : s_1, \ldots, s_n \to s$ occurs in RAB'_s and $t_i \in RAB_{s_i}$, with RAB_{s_i} basic, belong to RAB_s too.

In our running example we have:
$RAB_{Nat} = \{\perp_{Nat}, 0, s(\perp_{Nat}), s(s(\perp_{Nat}))\}$
$RAB_{Bool} = \{\perp_{Bool}, tt, ff\}$
$RAB_{SP} = \{\perp_{SP}, RQ(\perp_{Nat}), RS(\perp_{Nat}), RQ(0), RS(0), RQ(s(\perp_{Nat})), RS(s(\perp_{Nat})),$
$RQ(s(s(\perp_{Nat}))), RS(s(s(\perp_{Nat})))\}$

Definition 9 Abstract Bases: AB_s. The *Abstract Base* of sort s, AB_s is the smallest cut C of $(\Pi_\Sigma)_s$ such that $\forall x \in RAB_s \exists y \in C$ such that $x \preceq y$

For Nat, $Bool$, SP, we have:
$AB_{Nat} = \{0, s(0), s(s(\perp_{Nat}))\}$
$AB_{Bool} = \{tt, ff\}$
$AB_{SP} = \{RQ(0), RS(0), RQ(s(0)), RS(s(0)), RQ(s(s(\perp_{Nat}))), RS(s(s(\perp_{Nat})))\}$

Lemma 10. *For all s, AB_s is finite.*

Definition 11 Abstract Domain :ABS. The *Abstract Domain* of sort s, ABS_s, is defined as $2^{(AB_s)}$ with standard set inclusion partial ordering.
The *Abstract Domain*, ABS, for a given data type definition is defined as the $\perp-coaleshed\ sum$[5] of the abstract domains for all the sorts in the type definition.

As we shall see later, intuitively the empty set, i.e. the bottom of ABS, denotes the undefined value, i.e. a computation which *definitely fails* to terminate. Any other abstract term denotes computations which *may* terminate and it gives information on the set of the possible values they can yield.

Abstract Functions In this section we shall show how to compute the abstract version of any function defined within an abstract data type definition T. To that purpose we need to define what does it mean for an abstract term to *approximate* a *set of* partial terms, which in term represents a set of possible values. We need some additional definitions:

Definition 12 Min, Max. Given a partial order $(D, \preceq)$ and $X \subseteq D$
$Min(X) = \{m | m \in X, \not\exists x \in X\ x \preceq m\}$
$Max(X) = \{m | m \in X, \not\exists x \in X\ m \preceq x\}$

Definition 13 ∇. Given a partial order $(D, \preceq)$ and $d \in D$, ∇_d is the partial order with set of elements $X = \{x | d \preceq x\}$ and ordering relation $\preceq \cap X \times X$.

---

[5] By $\perp-coaleshed\ sum$ of $D_1, \ldots D_n$ we mean the coaleshed sum [12] of $D_1, \ldots, D_n$ thought as posets rather than lattices; i.e. $\perp_1, \ldots, \perp_n$ collapse into an unique element, $\perp$ in the $\perp-coaleshed$ sum of $D_1, \ldots, D_n$, whereas the top elements of $D_1, \ldots, D_n$ remain distinct elements of the sum, which is no longer a lattice, but only a c.p.o.

Definition 14 Approximation. Given a partial order $(D, \preceq)$, $d \in D$, and $W \subseteq D$
1. W *generates* d iff $\exists\, x \in W : x \preceq d$
2. W *represents* d iff $\exists\, X \subseteq W : X$ is a *cut* for ∇_d
3. W *approximates* d iff W generates $d \vee W$ represents d

Definition 15 Approximation Function:$\aleph_s$. For all $X \subseteq (\Pi_\Sigma)_s$:

$$
\begin{aligned}
\aleph_s(\{\}) \quad&= \{\}\\
\aleph_s(\{\bot_s\}) \quad&= AB_s\\
\aleph_s(\{c\}) \quad&= \bigcup Min(\{a | a \in ABS_s, a \text{ approximates } c\})\\
&\quad \text{for all constants } c\\
\aleph_s(\{k(p_1, \ldots, p_n)\}) \quad&= \aleph_s(\{x | x = k(x_1, \ldots, x_n), \bigwedge_{i=1}^{n} x_i \in \aleph_{s_i}(\{p_i\})\})\\
&\quad \text{for constructor terms}\\
\aleph_s(\{p_1, \ldots, p_n\}) \quad&= \bigcup_{i=1..n} \aleph_s(\{p_i\})
\end{aligned}
$$

We shall use only *finite, non-empty* sets of partial terms, in which case function $\aleph$ is certainly effectively computable and total. In our running example we have for instance $\aleph(\{\bot_{Nat}\}) = \{0, s(0), s(s(\bot_{Nat}))\}$, $\aleph(\{s(s(0))\}) = \{s(s(\bot_{Nat}))\}$, $\aleph(\{0, s(s(0))\}) = \{0, s(s(\bot_{Nat}))\}$.

The reason why we need the approximation function will be clear later, when we shall describe how to get the abstract version of functions from their definition. Moreover notice that when the ADT has n-ary constructors, with $n > 1$, then more then one abstract term could be a "best" approximation of a set of partial terms. Consider for instance a constructor $K : S, S \to S$ for a type with a constant a. Assuming
$$ABS = \{a, K(a, \bot_S), K(\bot_S, a), K(K(\bot_S, \bot_S), \bot_S), K(\bot_S, K(\bot_S, \bot_S))\}$$
we have that both $\{K(a, \bot_S)\}$ and $\{K(\bot_S, a)\}$ would be "best" approximations for $\{K(a, a)\}$. We take $\aleph(\{K(a, a)\}) = \{K(a, \bot_S), K(\bot_S, a)\}$. Such an approximation is not as "good" as any of $\{K(a, \bot_S)\}$ and $\{K(\bot_S, a)\}$ but it has the advantage of making $\aleph$ be a *function* rather than a relation. In fact , a possible alternative could be to let $\aleph$ return the *set* of best approximations and then select one on the basis of some a priori criterion (i.e. lexicographic ordering). This would make safety harder to proof and it is left for further study.

Lemma 16. *For all* $X, Y \subseteq (\Pi_\Sigma)_s$ $\aleph(X \cup Y) = \aleph(X) \cup \aleph(Y)$

Lemma 17. *For all* $X, Y \subseteq (\Pi_\Sigma)_s$ *if* $X \subseteq Y$ *then* $\aleph(X) \subseteq \aleph(Y)$

Function Abstraction Procedure In order to compute the abstract version of all the functions defined in T, we generate a new system of equations starting from those in T and let such abstract functions be its minimal solution.

For the sake of simplicity, in the following we shall deal with unary functions only. All definitions and results can easely be extended to n-ary functions.

For each function $f : s' \to s$, the set of equations defining its abstract version f^A is composed by two parts. The first one does not depend on the equations which define f, and it is the following one, where $p_i \in AB_{s'}$:

1. $f^A(\{\})$ $= \{\}$
2. $f^A(\{p_1, \ldots, p_n\}) = \bigcup_{i=1\ldots n} f^A(\{p_i\})$

In order to complete the definition of f^A we have to introduce the equations for f^A when applied to singletons. The right hand side of $f^A(\{p\})$ is obtained by selecting the equation of f's definition the left-hand-side of which *matches* with the partial term p, if any. Pattern matching is easely extended to partial terms simply considering $\bot$ as an additional constant. If no equation can be selected then the equation for $f^A(\{p\})$ is the following:

3. $f^A(\{p\}) = AB_s$

Otherwise it will be the following one:

4. $f^A(\{p\}) = AS[\![rhs(p)]\!]$

where $rhs(p)$ is the right-hand-side of the *unique* equation for f which has been selected, properly instantiated according to the bindings induced by pattern-matching Function AS is defined as follows:

4.1) $AS[\![c]\!]$ $= \aleph(\{c\})$, for all constants $c :\to s$, or $c = \bot$
4.2) $AS[\![k(e_1, \ldots, e_n)]\!] = \aleph(\{x | x = k(x_1, \ldots, x_n), \bigwedge_{i=1}^{n} x_i \in AS[\![e_i]\!]\})$,
$\qquad$ for all constructor terms
4.3) $AS[\![f(e)]\!]$ $= f^A(AS[\![e]\!])$, for all functor terms.

Notice that $f^A(AS[\![e]\!])$ is to be intended as a *syntactical* function application, i.e. *functor term*, here.

$\qquad$ The relevant equations obtained for function $m2$ follow:

$m2^A(\{0\})$ $= \{0\}$
$m2^A(\{s(0)\})$ $= \{s(0)\}$
$m2^A(\{s(s(\bot_{Nat}))\}) = m2^A(\{0, s(0), s(s(\bot_{Nat}))\})$

Proposition 18. *Existence of solution*

Proof. The left-hand-side of the equations for the abstract functions is made up of constants (rules 1 and 3), constant functions (rules 4.1 and 4.2) and continuous operators like function application and set union (rules 2 and 4.3). Thus the existence of the least-fixed-point for the functional associated to the set of equations is guaranteed. $\qquad\qquad\square$

Finally, the abstract version of the GRC is obtained by substituting in its definition all the user-defined functions and predicates with their abstract version and the *if then else* operator with the following, abstract, one:

$if^A(\{\}, a, b)$ $= \{\}$
$if^A(\{tt\}, a, b)$ $= a$
$if^A(\{ff\}, a, b)$ $= b$
$if^A(\{tt, ff\}, a, b) = a \cup b$

Remark. It is worth noting that, due to *finiteness* of all the objects involved in the computation of the abstract version of the GRC the former can be performed in finite time.

In the following table the abstract versions is_0^A and $m2^A$ of functions is_0 and $m2$ of our sample specification are given. In the third column the values for g^A are given, where g is defined by $g(x) = s(m2(x))$. Notice that those values are obtained via function $\aleph$, the use of which essential from the third row on. The keypoint here is that since the term $s(s(0))$ does *not* occur textually in the specification we are dealing with, it does not deserve a "distinguished" representation in ABS_{Nat}. On the other hand we have $g(s(0)) = s(s(0))$ so we need an approximation for $s(s(0))$ in our abstract domain. Such an approximation could be $\{0, s(0), s(s(\perp_{Nat}))\}$, which abstractly represent *any natural number* (i.e. is the result of $\aleph(\{\perp_{Nat}\})$), but *a better* approximation is certainly $\{s(s(\perp_{Nat}))\}$ which is the *best* indeed, given the amount of static information available.

	is_0^A	$m2^A$	g^A
$\{\}$	$\{\}$	$\{\}$	$\{\}$
$\{0\}$	$\{tt\}$	$\{0\}$	$\{s(0)\}$
$\{s(0)\}$	$\{ff\}$	$\{s(0)\}$	$\{s(s(\perp_{Nat}))\}$
$\{s(s(\perp_{Nat}))\}$	$\{ff\}$	$\{0, s(0)\}$	$\{s(0), s(s(\perp_{Nat}))\}$
$\{0, s(0)\}$	$\{tt,ff\}$	$\{0, s(0)\}$	$\{s(0), s(s(\perp_{Nat}))\}$
$\{0, s(s(\perp_{Nat}))\}$	$\{tt,ff\}$	$\{0, s(0)\}$	$\{s(0), s(s(\perp_{Nat}))\}$
$\{s(0), s(s(\perp_{Nat}))\}$	$\{ff\}$	$\{0, s(0)\}$	$\{s(0), s(s(\perp_{Nat}))\}$
$\{0, s(0), s(s(\perp_{Nat}))\}$	$\{tt,ff\}$	$\{0, s(0)\}$	$\{s(0), s(s(\perp_{Nat}))\}$

It is interesting to point out the kind of *don't know* information provided by the abstract version of predicates. Such information is represented by the abstract term $\{tt,ff\}$. So, for instance, $is\_0^A(\{0, s(0), s(s(\perp_{Nat}))\}) = \{tt,ff\}$ means that no information can be statically inferred on the behaviour of the test on 0 when no information is available on the argument which the test is applied to, except that it is a natural number. On the other hand, from $is\_0^A(\{s(0), s(s(\perp_{Nat}))\}) = \{ff\}$ we know that the test on 0 will yield ff on any number greater then 0. This kind of uncertainty, once generated by means of an abstract evaluation of what textually occurs in the LOTOS specification and propagated through the abstractions of the functions used by the GRC, may give raise to uncertainty in the value of the GRC itself, so bringing to the use of choice and selection predicates in the transformation. The table below shows some interesting values of $\mathcal{G}^A \{a\}$

	$\mathcal{G}^A\{a\}$
$\{RQ(0)\}$	$\{r0\}$
$\{RQ(s(0))\}$	$\{r\}$
$\{RQ(s(s(\perp_{Nat})))\}$	$\{r\}$
$\{RQ(0), RQ(s(0)), RQ(s(s(\perp_{Nat})))\}$	$\{r0, r\}$
$\{RS(0), RS(s(0))\}$	$\{s0, s\}$

From the above table it should be clear that if no information is available on n in actions like $< a, RQ(n) >$ then all that can be said about the possible outcomes of the GRC on those values is that they are $r0$ and r. Some uncertainty is still present but this is better then saying that the set of possible outcomes is $\{b, r0, r, s0, s\}$ which would be the case when no information at all is available on the values passing through a, except their type (namely $\mathcal{G}^{\mathcal{A}}\{a\}\ AB_{SP}$, not shown in the table).

Finally, it is worth noting that $m2^{\mathcal{A}}(\{0, s(0), s(s(\perp_{Nat}))\}) = \{0, s(0)\}$ essentially tells us which is the co-domain of $m2$. When such information for any function $f : s1 \to s2$ cannot be computed statically, one will get $f(AB_{s1}) = AB_{s2}$.

The last step before defining the transformation is the definition of a function, $\mathcal{V}$, which maps LOTOS *value expressions* into their abstract values. It takes a *veriable identifier/abstract-value* binding function (*environment*) as well.

Definition 19 Abstract Data Evaluation. $\mathcal{V}_s : Vex_s \to AEnv \to ABS_s$ where: $AEnv = VIdentifiers \to ABS_s$

$$
\begin{aligned}
\mathcal{V}[\![c]\!]\rho &= \aleph(\{c\}), \text{ for all constants } c :\to s \\
\mathcal{V}[\![x]\!]\rho &= \rho(x), \text{ for all variables } x :\to s \\
\mathcal{V}[\![k(e_1, \ldots, e_n)]\!]\rho &= \aleph(\{x | x = k(x_1, \ldots, x_n), \bigwedge_{i=1}^{n} x_i \in \mathcal{V}[\![e_i]\!]\rho\}), \\
&\quad \text{for all constructor terms} \\
\mathcal{V}[\![f(e)]\!]\rho &= f^{\mathcal{A}}(\mathcal{V}[\![e]\!]\rho), \text{ for all functor terms.}
\end{aligned}
$$

Notice that $f^{\mathcal{A}}(\mathcal{V}[\![e]\!]\rho)$ denotes the *result* of the application of the actual function $f^{\mathcal{A}}$, as defined by the appropriate system of equations, to $\mathcal{V}[\![e]\!]\rho$.

Correctness of the Abstract Interpretation In this section we shall prove that the abstract interpretation obtained according to the technique defined in the previous sections is *safe*, that is it provides correct information. We shall proceed according to the approach known as *logical relation* [1]; other approaches [4, 5, 6, 7] use Galois insertions as safety criterion. We shall first define the correctness requirement. Then we shall prove that the abstraction function $\aleph$ meets such requirement. Finally we shall prove the main proposition which states that correctness is preserved by abstract functions. It is worth pointing out that correctness is proved w.r.t. a fixpoint semantics of LOTOS abstract data types, which is *not* the standard one. The relation between the two semantics is not investigated here. Anyway the data types definition part of LOTOS is likely to be changed into a functional-like one [19].

We start by extending our concrete semantic sets with the undefined elements and by defining the proper partial orders.

Definition 20 Concrete semantic domains. For all sorts s
$\omega_s \in (T_{\Sigma_c})_s$ and $\omega_s \in (\Pi_\Sigma)_s$
For all $p_1, p_2 \in (\Pi_\Sigma)_s$ $p_1 \sqsubseteq p_2$ iff $p_1 = \omega$ or $p_1 = p_2$ $\qquad\qquad \Box$

We shall assume natural extension for all functions, i.e. for all $f : s \to s'$ $f(\omega_s) = \omega_{s'}$. Moreover, for all (finite) sets $P \subseteq (\Pi_\Sigma)_s$ we define $\aleph(P \cup \{\omega\}) = \aleph(P)$. Thus $\aleph(\{\omega\}) = \{\}$.

Definition 21 Concretization Function:γ_s.
$$\gamma_s(\{\}) \quad\quad =\{\omega_s\}$$
$$\gamma_s(\{p_1,\ldots,p_n\})= \bigcup_{i=1..n} \gamma_s(\{p_i\})$$
$$\gamma_s(\{p\}) \quad\quad =Max(\nabla_p)$$

Lemma 22. *For all $a_1, a_2 \in ABS_s$ $\gamma(a_1 \cup a_2) = \gamma(a_1) \cup \gamma(a_2)$*

Lemma 23. *For all $a_1, a_2 \in ABS_s$ if $a_1 \subseteq a_2$ then $\gamma(a_1) \subseteq \gamma(a_2)$*

Lemma 24. $(T_{\Sigma_c})_s \subseteq \gamma(AB_s)$

It is interesting to point out that $\omega \in \gamma(a)$ for any abstract term a. So the empty set abstractly represents all those computations the result of which is undefined (i.e. those computations which *definitely fail* to terminate) whereas any other abstract term a represents computations the result of which may be not undefined (i.e. they *may* terminate) in which case it also gives some information on the possible output values.

Definition 25 Correctness relation: C (read "correctly represents"). For all $a \in ABS_s, t \in (T_{\Sigma_c})_s$ aCt iff $t \in \gamma(a)$

So, essentially, a correctly represents t if and only if t can be generated from a via instantiation of some partial term in a

Lemma 26. *For all $p \in (\Pi_\Sigma)_s, t \in (T_{\Sigma_c})_s$, if $p \preceq t$ then $t \in \gamma(\aleph(\{p\}))$*

Corollary 27. *For all $t \in (T_{\Sigma_c})_s$ $\aleph(\{t\})Ct$, i.e. the abstraction function is correct.*

Lemma 28. *If a_iCt_i for $i = 1\ldots n$ then $\aleph(\{k(x_1,\ldots,x_n)|x_i \in a_i\})Ck(t_1,\ldots,t_n)$*

Proposition 29 Safety of the abstract interpretation. *For all $a \in ABS_s, t \in (T_{\Sigma_c})_s f : s \rightarrow s'$ with $f^A : ABS_s \rightarrow ABS_{s'}$ defined according to the abstraction procedure , the following holds: $aCt \Rightarrow f^A(a)Cf(t)$*

Proof. We make use both of computational and structural induction. Letting g_i denote the i-th approximation of the minimal fixpoint for the equations for function g, it has to be proved that for all i it holds $aCt \Rightarrow f_i^A(a)Cf_i(t)$. The (computational) induction step requires induction *on the structure* of a in turn. Finally it must be proved that if the proposition holds for all approximations of the minimal fixpoint then it holds also for the fixpoint itself. The details of the proof are given in [9]. $\square$

3.2 Definition of the Transformation

The transformation is defined as a function $TB : Bex \rightarrow Ac \rightarrow AEnv \rightarrow Bex$. In [9] the function is formally defined by structural induction on the set of all LOTOS behaviour expressions ($: Bex$) and takes the abstract version of a GRC abstract environment (:AEnv) as extra arguments. It obviously returns a behaviour expression as result. $\mathcal{TB}$ acts mainly on action prefix, propagating throughout the whole specification the changes which it makes and also performing some simplifications, on the basis of static "data-flow" information recorded in the abstract environment. In the sequel she shall discuss the behaviour of $\mathcal{TB}$ only on "input" action prefix $g!e; B$ and in an informal way.

Let $\mathcal{R}$ be a GRC. Let also ρ the abstract environment collecting all the static information on the possible values which variables can be bound to *in the context* in which $g!e; B$ is to be transformed. Now, if for this particular occurrence of g, it is statically decidable that the GRC gives only one value g' as result, i.e. $\mathcal{R}^{\mathcal{A}} \{g\} (\mathcal{V}[\![e]\!]\rho) = \{g'\}$, then $\mathcal{TB}[\![g!e; B]\!]\mathcal{R}^{\mathcal{A}}\rho = g'!e; \mathcal{TB}[\![B]\!]\mathcal{R}^{\mathcal{A}}\rho$. If, on the other hand, $\mathcal{R}^{\mathcal{A}}\{g\}(\mathcal{V}[\![e]\!]\rho) = \{g_1, g_2, \ldots, g_k\}$, then $\mathcal{TB}[\![g!e; B]\!]\mathcal{R}^{\mathcal{A}}\rho = $
$g_1!e[p_1(e)]; \mathcal{TB}[\![B]\!]\mathcal{R}^{\mathcal{A}}\rho$
$[]$
$g_2!e[p_2(e)]; \mathcal{TB}[\![B]\!]\mathcal{R}^{\mathcal{A}}\rho$
$\vdots$
$[]$
$g_k!e[p_k(e)]; \mathcal{TB}[\![B]\!]\mathcal{R}^{\mathcal{A}}\rho$
where p_j is the unique predicate such that $p_j(v) \Rightarrow \mathcal{R} g v = g_j$[6].

In conclusion, given a process definition whose behaviour expression is B, with type definitions T (with sorts $s_1, \ldots, s_k$) and local process definitions $P_1, \ldots, P_n$, and a GRC $\mathcal{R}$ the transformed process definition is given by $\mathcal{TB}[\![B]\!]\mathcal{R}^{\mathcal{A}} \Omega$ where $\Omega x = AB_{s_i}$ for all variable identifiers x of sort s_i. Obviously the transformation has to be applied to all P_i in turn.

Proposition 30 Correctness of the transformation. *For any behaviour expression B and GRC $\mathcal{R}$, $B \sim_\Phi \mathcal{TB}[\![B]\!]\mathcal{R}^{\mathcal{A}} \Omega$ provided that for all $g1, g2 \in Gates$, $v1, v2 \in Value$: $\mathcal{R} g1 v1 = \mathcal{R} g2 v2 \Rightarrow (v1 = v2 \Rightarrow g1 = g2)$*

Proof. Under the assumption that the above requirement is met, it is trivial to prove that the function given below is a bijection from the set of actions of P to that of Q:
$\phi (x < v >) = (\mathcal{R} x v) < v >$ with $x \notin \{i, \delta\}$[7]
$\phi (i) = i$
$\phi (\delta < v >) = \delta < v >$
The second step is to show that for all *behaviour expressions B*, the pair $< B, \mathcal{TB}[\![B]\!]\mathcal{R}^{\mathcal{A}} \Omega >$ is in some ϕ-*bisimulation* relation, which can be proved by structural induction on B, using the definition of $\mathcal{TB}$. In [10] the proof is given in detail, under the simplifying assumption that $\mathcal{R}$ does not depend on the actual value of its second argument but only on its sort. The extension to the more general case does not introduce any conceptual complication. $\square$

---

[6] p_j can easely be derived from the definition of $\mathcal{R}$. Notice that such a predicate may contain a test on the *sort* of v, which must obviously be removed in the selection predicate.

[7] i and δ denote LOTOS *internal*, respectively, *successful termination* actions.

4 Further Work

Further work is required in order to improve our technique. For instance, since the transformation is very much sensitive to the particular way in which the GRC is defined, reasonable guidelines or even further syntactical/static semantics restrictions on the GRC meta-notation are needed in order to get real advantage of available static information.

Moreover, the transformation itself can be improved in many ways. Better simplifications can be achieved by means of using abstract interpretation of boolean expressions in *selection predicates* and *guards* and then using the abstract values for properly modify the environment in order to keep track of the abstract data flow.

An analysis which keeps track of the abstract values of the parameters present at every instantiation could make it possible to discover that the abstract value of all the actual parameters associated to a given formal parameter in all the instantiations of a process definition within a given behaviour expression are the same, so allowing forther optimizations in the associated *process definition.*

The current, simplified, implementation of the transformation in the *LOTOS Integrated Tool Environment - LITE* [21] imposes that the GRC cannot depend on the actual values exchanged throughout a given gate but only on their *sorts*. We are now starting developing a new version of the tool where such a requirement is removed and the abstract domain construction presented in this paper is implemented.

Finally, we are thinking at further applications of our technique. An interesting application of the analysis technique we have described in the present paper is to use it in order to study the dependence on data of a system's behaviour or of those aspects of the behaviour one is interested in. Suppose for instance we are interested in studying safety or liveness properties of a communication protocol. It is then likely that for our purposes we can just abstract away from everything in the protocol which has to do with "user-data" and just concentrate on "control-data" since they influence the behaviour of the protocol w.r.t. the properties we want to reason about. In this way we can reduce the complexity of the problem and probably move from an infinite object, i.e. the "whole" protocol, defined on user data too, towards a finite object which represents the "control part" of the protocol. Then suitable tools (usually working only on finite objects) can be used for checking. We think our technique can profitably be used for studying such dependence on data of both the LOTOS specification and the particular (modal) logic formula which expresses the desired property.

5 Acknowledgments

The intuitive ideas behind the technicalities described in this paper come from discussions with Elie Najm and Rom Langerak during an unforgettable ESPRIT-LOTOSPHERE meeting in Venice, March 1991.

References

1. S. Abramsky, C. Hankin, ed.: Abstract Interpretation of Declarative Languages. Computers and their Applications. Ellis Horwood, Chichester, U.K. 1987

2. T. Bolognesi, E. Brinksma: Introduction to the ISO specification language LOTOS. Computer Network and ISDN Systems - Vol. 14, No 1, 1987
3. E. Brinksma (Ed.): LOTOS - A formal description technique based on the temporal ordering of observational behaviour. ISO IS8807, February 1989, ISO, Geneva
4. P. Cousot, R. Cousot: Static determination of dynamic properties of programs. Proc. of the 2nd Int. Symp. on Programming Languages. Dunod, Paris 1976
5. P. Cousot, R. Cousot: Abstract Interpretation: a unified lattice model for static analysis of programs by construction or approximation of fixpoints. Proc. of the 4th ACM Symp. on Principles of Programming Languages
6. P. Cousot, R.Cousot: Static determination of dynamic properties of recursive procedures. Proc. of IFIP Conf. on Formal Description of Programming Concepts. North-Holland 1977
7. P. Cousot, R.Cousot: Abstract Interpretation Frameworks. Journal of Logic and Computation, 1992 (to appear)
8. H. B. Curry, R. Feys: Combinatory Logic. Vol. I. North Hollnad, 1968
9. F. Giannotti, D. Latella: Gate Splitting in LOTOS Specifications By Using Abstract Interpretation. CNUCE Internal Report C92-13
10. D. Latella: Correctness of the IPR transformation. ESPRIT Project 2304 - LotoSphere, ref. Lo/WP1/T1.2/CNUCE/N0021- 1991
11. R. Milner: A Calculus of Communicating Systems. Lecture Notes in Computer Science vol. 92, Springer-Verlag, 1980
12. J. Stoy: Denotational Semantics: the Scott-Strachey Approach to programming languages Theory. The MIT Press 1979
13. J. Schot, L. Pires (eds.): Final deliverable of the PANGLOSS Architectural Task - Results of the ESPRIT/PANGLOSS project - ref. P/AT/137, part II, section 4.3.4.1. University of Twente, Enschede, Netherlands, December 1989
14. L. Pires (Ed.): The LotoSphere Design Methodology - I: Basic Concepts. ESPRIT Project 2304 - LotoSphere, Task 1.1 Deliverable, ref. Lo/WP1/T1.1/N0045/V03 - 1992
15. The LotoSphere Design Methodology - I: Guidelines. ESPRIT Project 2304 - LotoSphere, Task 1.1 Deliverable, ref. Lo/WP1/T1.1/N0044/V03 - 1992
16. The LotoSphere Design Methodology - I: Illustrations. ESPRIT Project 2304 - LotoSphere, Task 1.1 Deliverable, ref. Lo/WP1/T1.1/N0046/V03 - 1992
17. G. Yadan: (Ed.) The LotoSphere Design Methodology - I: Experience in industrial environment. ESPRIT Project 2304 - LotoSphere, Task 1.1 Deliverable, ref. Lo/WP1/T1.1/N0047/V03 - 1992
18. T. Bolognesi (Ed.): Catalogue of LOTOS Correctness Preserving Transformations ESPRIT Project 2304 - LotoSphere, Task 1.2 Deliverable, ref. Lo/WP1/T1.2/N0045/V03 - 1992
19. LOTOS Enhancements. ESPRIT Project 2304 - LotoSphere, Task 1.4 Final Deliverable - 1992
20. P.H.J. van Eijk, C. A. Vissers, M. Diaz (Ed.): The Formal Description Technique LOTOS. North-Holland
21. P.H.J. van Eijk: Tool demonstration: The LotoSphere Integrated Tool Environment Lite. Proc. FORTE'91, North-Holland, 1992
22. K. Warkentyne: The Application of Transformations in T3.2 (MiniMail+ISDN). ESPRIT Project 2304 - LotoSphere, ref. WP1/T11/ASCOM/N0015, Feb. 1992

Constructing Systems as Object Communities *

Hans-Dieter Ehrich
Grit Denker
Abteilung Datenbanken, Technische Universität, Postfach 3329
W–3300 Braunschweig, GERMANY

Amilcar Sernadas
Computer Science Group, INESC, Apartado 10105
1017 Lisbon Codex, PORTUGAL

Abstract

We give a survey of concepts for system specification and design based on the viewpoint that a system is a community of objects. Objects are self-contained units of structure and behavior capable of operating independently and cooperating concurrently. Our approach integrates concepts from semantic data modeling and concurrent processes, adopting structuring principles partly developed in the framework of object-orientation and partly in that of abstract data types. A theory of object specification based on temporal logic is briefly outlined.

1   Introduction

The components of large software systems often do not fit together well. The *impedance mismatches* between programming languages, database systems and operating systems are notorious. And extending or adapting a software system is, if feasible at all, expensive and error-prone.

One of the deeper reasons for this state of affairs is that appropriate formal methods are missing which are powerful and versatile enough for handling the many facets of large software systems in a coherent way.

For instance, information systems are usually designed by modeling and specifying the static structure and the dynamic behavior by independent, often incompatible formalisms. Consequently, there is no uniform formal description of the entire system. Without such a uniform model, correctness assertions concerning the whole system cannot even be formulated, let alone proved [Sa92].

There are three successful modeling domains, each supported by languages and tools: abstract data types, concurrent processes and persistent data collections. For

---

*This work was partly supported by the EC under ESPRIT BRA WG 3023/6071 IS-CORE and WG 3264/6112 COMPASS, by DFG under Sa 465/1-1 and Sa 465/1-2, and by JNICT under PM-CT/C/TIT/178/90 FAC3 contract.

the first two, we have rich bodies of theory. Each of these modeling domains addresses essential aspects of software systems, but none of them is broad enough to cover all aspects in an adequate way.

For abstract data types, we have two lines of development, the algebraic approach and the model based approach. [CHJ86] gives an introduction to both. Theoretical treatments of the algebraic approach can be found in [EGL89, EM85]. Relevant textbooks for diverse approaches to process theory are [He88, Ho85, Mi89, Re85]. Persistent data collections are at the heart of conceptual modeling [Bo91, CY91, GKP92, Gr91, HK87, RBPEL91, RC92, SF91].

Our approach is a combination of ideas from these three fields, drawing especially from experience in information systems modeling and design. The ideas have been mainly developed in the ESPRIT Working Group IS-CORE: employing objects as a unifying concept and aiming at a conceptually seamless methodology from requirements to implementation [EGS91, EGS92, ES91, ESS92, FSMS92, SE91, SF91, SJE92].

There are many languages, systems, methods and approaches in computing which adopt the object paradigm, among them programming languages, database systems, and system development methods. Our intention is to provide high-level system specification languages with in-the-large features, backed by a sound theory and a coherent design methodology.

Because of space limitations, we cannot go into much detail. In the next section, we give an intuitive survey of our concepts so that the casual reader can get an idea of what our approach is about. Then we take a closer look at the most important issues: templates, schemata involving classes, specialization, generalization, aggregation, interfacing and interaction, and finally reification and modularization.

2 Concepts

We view a system as a community of objects. Objects are self-contained units of structure and behavior capable of operating independently and cooperating concurrently. Objects store and manipulate data, and they interact by exchanging data in messages. Messages are transmitted via channels which can be viewed as shared subobjects.

In our opinion, data and objects are different kinds of entities: data are more like messages, namely signals to be processed, and objects are like processors processing the signals. Unifying these concepts as in Smalltalk is possible, but introduces unnecessary conceptual complication and confusion.

Data values like integer '7' or text 'abc' are global and unchangeable. It is standard practice to organize data into abstract types, each encapsulating a domain of values and offering an interface with a specific set of operations on these values. There are well understood techniques and tools for specifying and designing appropriate universes of data types.

Because they are unchangeable items, also object identities are considered as data. For conceptual modeling, it is practical to utilize the facilities of abstract data type specification for structuring the identities into several types, allowing for application specific operations combining identities to form new identities.

Objects, in contrast, are time-varying entities, albeit with individual identities which do not change. An object encapsulates all its relevant static and dynamic properties: it has an individual behavior and an internal state changing in time. Objects can be composed to form complex objects, they can be related by different forms of inheritance, they can be interfaces of other objects, and they can interact with each other.

Objects are usually organized into object classes having a time-varying population of (usually similar) objects as members. Object classes can be viewed as particular kinds of complex objects.

An object community is a complex object designed for modeling the system at hand. It usually contains many object classes and individual objects.

A conceptual schema – or schema for short – is a formal specification of an object community.

The basic unit of a schema is a *template*. A template encapsulates the structural and behavioral properties of a specific kind of object or object class – or just an aspect of it. The core parts of a template describe which attributes can be observed, which actions can be performed, how attributes change when actions happen, under which conditions actions may happen, under which conditions actions are obliged to happen, etc.

Example 2.1: As an example, consider the following specification of a simple clock template. We use OBLOG-TROLL style pseudocode [SSE87, CSS89, JSHS91].

```
template  CLOCK
   attributes
      hr:      [0..23]
      min:     [0..59]
      alarm?:  {yes,no}
   actions
      *create(alarm:{yes,no})
      +destroy
      tic !
   valuation
      [create(a)]hr = 0
      [create(a)]min = 0
      [create(a)]alarm? = a
      [tic]hr = if min<>59 then hr else if hr=23 then 0 else hr+1
      [tic]min = if min<>59 then min+1 else 0
   permission
      {create}tic
      {tic}destroy
   obligation
      {warranty=valid} ⇒ tic
end CLOCK
```

Please note that the specification is not complete: in order to keep the example intuitive, we use a warranty attribute in the obligation section, and in order to keep the example small, we do not specify it in the attributes and valuation sections.

The specification says that a CLOCK is a kind of object with three attributes, hr, min and alarm?, giving rise to the following possible observations:

hr=0,..., hr=23, min=0,..., min=59, alarm?=yes, alarm?=no.

The third attribute indicates whether the clock has an alarm facility or not.

The action section says that a clock can be created (∗ indicates a birth event), giving as a parameter whether it has an alarm facility or not, or that it can be destroyed (+ indicates a death event), or that it can tick. The symbol ! indicates initiative, i.e., that the clock can actively perform the action by its own initiative[1].

The valuation section specifies the effects of actions on attributes in an obvious way. The permission section specifies preconditions for actions to happen, i.e. safety constraints: a clock can only tick after creation, and it can only be destroyed after it has ticked (at least once). The obligation section specifies that a clock must tick if – and as long as – there is a warranty.

There is no specification about how the tic action affects the alarm? attribute: we assume a frame default rule saying that an attribute doesn't change unless explicitly specified otherwise.   □

The conceptual schema of an object community has to specify not only templates, but also *relationships* between templates. Such relationships comprise several kinds of interaction (action calling or sharing, synchronously or asynchronously), ways of how objects can be put together to build complex objects (aggregation of parts), ways of how aspects can give different views of the same object (specialization, roles) or a unified abstract view of different objects specified before (generalization), and ways of abstracting only part of the features specified (interfacing, hiding).

Example 2.2:   Referring to our clock example, we might want to specify an alarm clock as a specialization of CLOCK. We inherit the specification given above and add the special alarm clock items in a specification like this:

```
template  ALARM-CLOCK
   special CLOCK where alarm?=yes
      ...
end ALARM-CLOCK
```

We omit the details. In a similar way, we may further specialize to specify a snoozer-alarm-clock, various clock versions, say, with different styles of showing the time (English, German, ...), etc.

The specialization given above is static in the sense that it is determined by the alarm? attribute which is set at creation time and cannot change during lifetime. Often, an object can enter and leave special roles during lifetime, like persons becoming patients for a while. We could have modeled a dynamic alarm clock which enters this role, say, by pressing the alarm-on button, and becomes a usual clock again by pressing the alarm-off button:

```
template  DYNAMIC-ALARM-CLOCK
   role of CLOCK
      ...
   actions
      *alarm-on
      +alarm-off
      ...
end DYNAMIC-ALARM-CLOCK
```

---

[1]The other actions are passive, i.e. they can only occur by some other object's initiative via interaction. Therefore, these services should probably be called *passions*.

Here, * and + indicate role entry and exit rather than birth and death. The attributes and actions specified here apply only during the alarm phase, otherwise they are not enabled. Again, we omit the details.

In another specification section, we might want to specify how clocks are put together from parts. To this end, we would probably like to reuse specifications set up before, for instance that of a battery.

Somewhere in the same or another specification section, we might want to specify how the parts interact and cooperate to perform the desired function. We might also want to specify how clocks interact with their environment, e.g., their users.

Later on, we might be interested in reusing part of our clock design to specify the generalized concept of a device for weights and measures, generalizing clocks, pairs of scales, etc.

Another abstraction we might want to specify is putting an interface, or view, on our clock, hiding the inner mechanism and showing only the observable display. Maybe another object uses just this, triggering its operation by the time observed. In general, hiding introduces nondeterminism: the clock changes its time while the reason for this is not apparent from the interface actions (of course, we are used to looking at clocks as being among the most deterministic devices ever, although we do not see the inner mechanism; but still... think about it!). □

All inter-template relationships mentioned in the example can be based on the concept of incorporating one template into another one, like clock into alarm-clock. We elaborate on this idea in the next section.

Having set up a specification for an object community, we would like to understand precisely what it means. Roughly speaking, the semantics describes all possible actual populations and all possible dynamic behaviors of such populations. An actual population consists of a set of object instances, structured in a way permitted by the schema. At any point in time, a single object instance is in some state, given by the current values of its attributes, the set of currently enabled actions, the set of actions currently happening, and the execution state of its process. We do not presume that larger aggregations of objects, nor the entire object community, have a definable state: if there is no system-wide clock synchronizing everything, the concept of global state may be inadequate.

If we have completed the specification of an object society and understood it thoroughly, the work is not yet done: we might want to implement it.

To this end, we reify our specification, i.e., give a more detailed description on a lower level of abstraction, using a given implementation platform. In particular, specification level (concurrent) actions will be reified to implementation level (serialized) transactions. If the system is large and the gap between abstraction levels is big, we would like to reify in pieces and steps, addressing a manageable portion of the whole task at a time. For verification purposes, we would like to make the relationship between the specified abstract interface and that of the implementation platform very precise. And we would like to know whether the entire system is correctly implemented if we have made the single tasks right, parallel steps (horizontal composition) as well as subsequent steps (vertical composition).

For reusing work done before, we would like to encapsulate, and probably parameterize, typical modules that have an abstract 'top' interface and a concrete 'bottom' one, putting the abstract interface into operation once the services of the concrete one are provided. The other way round, if we have a library of such modules available, we would like to find the ones we need in an effective way and integrate them easily into our design.

In the sections to follow, we give more details on the concepts mentioned above. The salient feature of our approach is to integrate concepts from semantic data modeling and concurrent processes, adopting structuring principles partly developed in the framework of object-orientation, and partly in that of abstract data types.

3   Templates

Templates represent structure and behavior patterns for kinds of objects. Example 2.1 shows a typical template specification: structure is described by attributes, and dynamic behavior by actions. Axioms express, among others, the effects of actions on attributes and the permissible and obliged occurrences of actions.

Since we envisage objects to appear in multiple specializations or roles, we will have to cope with several templates for one kind of object, each one describing some *aspect* of the object. Examples 2.1 and 2.2 show CLOCK as an aspect of ALARM-CLOCK. Also for composite objects, we will have to cope with several interrelated templates for describing one object: the composite template incorporates the templates of the parts. Therefore, it is essential to study not only templates, but also appropriate relationships between templates.

We distinguish between templates and types. In a sense, templates are like types: they give critera for the kind of object accepted in a certain context. In another sense, however, templates are different from types: they do not provide a domain of possible instances. For that, we must add a domain of identities [ESS89, JSHS91].

We already made the distinction between templates and classes: the latter describe time-varying populations of (usually similar) objects as members. Object classes can be viewed as particular kinds of complex objects. So we also have templates for classes, as we will see in the next section.

Technically speaking, templates are adequately modeled as processes endowed with data. We give a particularly simple template model where enabled and occurring actions as well as data observations are uniformly treated as facts: sets of facts describe situations, finite or countably infinite sequences of situations describe life cycles, and sets of life cycles describe template processes. Amazingly enough, this simple model is powerful enough to serve as a semantic basis for languages like TROLL [JSHS91, Ju93].

A template defines a set of actions and a set of attributes with their value domains. For each action α, we have two *facts* (propositions): $\triangleright\alpha$ (α is enabled), and $\odot\alpha$ (α occurs). For each attribute a and each value v in its domain, we have a fact $a = v$ with obvious meaning. This way, a template defines a set of facts F which we take as our abstract notion of signature.

Definition 3.1 : A *template signature* is a set F of facts.

At any point in time, we observe that some facts hold true: some actions are enabled, some occur, and attributes have certain values. A *situation over F* is a set of facts $\sigma \subseteq F$. Usually, not every subset of F represents a meaningful situation. For instance, we expect that actions are enabled when they occur, that each attribute has at most one value, etc. We do not elaborate on this point here.

Taking the facts as atomic formulas of a propositional logic, we obtain a *situation logic* for talking about static object situations conforming with the template at hand.

Given a set F of facts, a *life cycle* $\lambda = (\sigma_1, \sigma_2, \sigma_3, \dots)$ *over* F is a finite or infinite sequence of situations over F. It represents a specific run of an object conforming with the template. Our process model is a set Λ of life cycles over F: a process represents all possible runs of an object conforming with the template.

An appropriate logic for talking about template dynamics is *temporal logic* [Pn77, Se80, FM92, SSC92]: adding modalities *always* $\Box$, *sometime* $\Diamond$ and *next* $\bigcirc$ extends our situation logic to what we call our *template logic TL*. TL is similar to *OSL* [SSC92] and to the logic used in [Ju93].

In the rest of this section, we give precise definitions for the most fundamental concepts in our approach: template specifications and template specification morphisms, together with their formal semantics.

Definition 3.2 : A *template specification* is a pair $\Theta = (F, \Psi)$ where F is a template signature, and Ψ is a set of axioms, i.e., formulas of *TL*.

The *models* of template logic are life cycles $\lambda = (\sigma_1, \sigma_2, \sigma_3, \dots)$ where $\sigma_i, i = 1, 2, \dots$, are situations. The semantics $[\Theta]$ of a template specification is the set of all its models, i.e., a process. That is, we employ a loose semantics describing the template's possible behavior in a most liberal way: every system run is permitted as long as it does not violate axioms. If $\Psi = \emptyset$, we write $[F]$ instead of $[\Theta]$.

For studying relationships among templates, we use maps $h : F_1 \to F_2$ between sets of facts as *signature morphisms*. In practical cases, signature morphisms will send facts to "similar" facts (enablings to enablings, occurrences to occurrences, etc.), but the theory works – and is a lot simpler! – without making such assumptions.

Let $h : F_1 \to F_2$ be a signature morphism. Using this map in the reverse direction, we can translate each life cycle $\lambda_2 = (\sigma_{21}, \sigma_{22}, \sigma_{23}, \dots)$ over F_2 to the life cycle $\lambda_1 = (\sigma_{11}, \sigma_{12}, \sigma_{13}, \dots)$ over F_1 by defining $\sigma_{1i} = \{f \in F_2 \mid h(f) \in \sigma_{2i}\}$ for all $i = 1, 2, \dots$

This defines a reduction map $h^\flat : [F_2] \to [F_1]$.

If h is an inclusion, $h^\flat$ restricts each λ_2 to F_1. Referring to examples 2.1 and 2.2, each ALARM-CLOCK life cycle is reduced to a CLOCK life cycle by just keeping the CLOCK facts and omitting the others.

Definition 3.3 : Let $\Theta_1 = (F_1, \Psi_1)$ and $\Theta_2 = (F_2, \Psi_2)$ be template specifications. A *template specification morphism* $h : \Theta_1 \to \Theta_2$ is a signature morphism $h : F_1 \to F_2$ such that Ψ_2 entails $h^\sharp(\Psi_1)$.

$h^\sharp(\Psi_1)$ is the obvious translation of formulas, applying h to facts and leaving the rest unchanged. If h is an inclusion, $h^\sharp$ is just the identity map.

The semantics of a template specification morphism is a reduction map $h^\flat : [\Theta_2] \to [\Theta_1]$ preserving models: $h^\flat$ sends each life cycle satisfying Ψ_2 to one satisfying Ψ_1.

We note in passing that template logic as outlined above forms an institution [GB92] (cf. also [SCS92]).

4   Schemata

A schema is a formal specification of an object community. Its semantics is given by the permissible populations of the community, the permissible interactions between its members, the permissible behaviors of its members, and their possible states.

Template specifications are the atomic units of a schema, but they rarely occur in isolation. The predominant description units are template clusters, specification "molecules" so to speak, interrelated in a characteristic way. We explain the most important of these clusters: classes, specialization, generalization, aggregation, interfacing, and interaction.

Classes. There is some confusion around the class concept in object-oriented approaches. In programming, a class is considered to be like a template in our sense. In the database field, a class is considered to be an abstraction of the *file* concept: it represents a time-varying collection of members (*records*). We follow this latter concept.

A class is specified by giving a template together with a naming mechanism for the members of the class. The template specification gives the "record schema" describing the permissible members, and the rest of the class specification describes the permissible structure and dynamics of the collection. Often, most of the latter is a hidden "standard package" which the user doesn't specify: it provides actions for insertion, deletion and update, and attributes like the current set of members, its cardinality, etc. In TROLL, the specifier has to provide only the domain of identities for members. For more details, the reader is referred to [JSHS91, ES91, ESS92, SJE92].

The semantics of a class specification is given by its expansion to a template specification, making the above mentioned class structure and behavior explicit.

Thus, a class is a particular kind of object – or, rather, *aspect*! Indeed, classes are subject to the structuring principles to be explained below: they can be specializations or roles or generalizations of other classes, etc.

Specialization. By specialization we mean what often is called "inheritance": we specify a specialization of a template by inheriting the latter. But there is too much confusion around inheritance, so we avoid this term altogether.

Example 2.2 gives an example of how specialization is handled in TROLL. This example also shows our concept of roles, i.e., dynamic specialization.

Specialization (static and dynamic) is formally described by a template specification morphism which is an inclusion. Referring to example 2.2, the morphism includes the CLOCK specification textually into that of ALARM-CLOCK (or DYNAMIC-ALARM-CLOCK, respectively).

The semantics is a reduction of (dynamic) alarm clock life cycles to pure clock life cycles by omitting the special facts, as explained in the previous section.

This way, an alarm clock (any kind) can be viewed as a clock, i.e., it can be treated as a clock in any context where a clock is expected. For instance, it can be a member in some class of clocks, together with other special kinds of clocks, giving the class concept a polymorphic flavor although it is formally monomorphic.

As for dynamic specialization: it is not obvious how the semantics of objects which run through phases should be, and how to reason about them. For instance, consider a person with an attribute weight running through a patient phase. Suppose that the patient template has special actions changing the weight, like surgery. After terminating the patient phase, this action is no longer in the scope of that person, it is unknown to her or him. But it left its effect as a change of weight behind which is now unexplainable from visible actions. For specifying the person template, this means that we cannot adopt the frame default rule mentioned in example 2.1: the weight can change "spontaneously". Reasoning is a problem, too: how can we prove anything about the person's weight? Should it be possible to reason with actions outside the current scope? Or should we choose the union of all possible phases as scope of reasoning? The interplay between multiple specializations and roles of the same object is a delicate point in itself. These problems need further study.

The object aspects specified in a specialization cluster must be present in any state: an alarm clock *is a* clock at any time, and a patient *is a* person at any time. This is in contrast to the meaning of aggregation clusters to be explained below.

Generalization. Generalization is the reverse of specialization: if we have already specified several special templates, we want to recognize and specify an aspect common to all of them. For instance, if we already have patients and employees in our schema, we might want to specify persons, integrating properties common to both patients and employees.

In a sense, this is reminiscent of view integration studied extensively in conceptual modeling and database design.

Logically and semantically, the situation is similar to specialization. We cannot go into further detail here.

Aggregation. Aggregation concepts are standard in many languages and modeling approaches: objects are aggregated to form complex objects.

The template of a complex object incorporates those of its parts in much the same way as a specialization incorporates an aspect. In fact, on the template level, there is no difference between specialization and aggregation: both are formalized by template morphisms which are inclusions or injections, respectively. The difference is with the intended interpretation. The parts of an aggregated template are to be interpreted by *different* objects, not by aspects of the same object. The parts relationship may be dynamic: a complex object may insert and delete components.

Complex objects may share parts: whatever happens in a shared part affects all objects sharing it. For example, consider two persons sharing a job. If the job gets better paid, both persons are happy.

While the syntax of aggregation is textual inclusion, its semantics is given by parallel composition. For instance, if $\Theta_1 = (F_1, \Psi_1)$ and $\Theta_2 = (F_2, \Psi_2)$ are templates and $\Theta_1 + \Theta_2 = (F_1 + F_2, \Psi_1 + \Psi_2)$ is their aggregation (disjoint union), then $[\Theta_1 + \Theta_2] = [\Theta_1] \| [\Theta_2]$ where $\|$ denotes disjoint parallel composition, i.e., the set of all life cycles whose projections are in $[\Theta_1]$ and in $[\Theta_2]$, respectively [ES91].

Interfacing. The concept of interfacing is well known, e.g., from database views. On the template level, an interface to an object is like a generalization of this object, it provides part of the services and hides the rest. The semantics, however, is different: the interface is intended to be a separate object with its own identity.

Also the pragmatics of interfacing is different. While generalizations of deterministic objects are most often intended to be still deterministic, this is not the case with interfacing. Like in read-only database views, we accept and expect behavior which is determined by hidden actions so that the interface shows "spontaneous" moves in a nondeterministic way. While our logic and semantics are powerful enough to capture nondeterminism (this is not obvious, but we cannot explain it here), reasoning in such a framework is not an easy problem.

Interaction. Interaction is essential for an object community to cooperate in a meaningful way. For specification and modeling, there are several concepts available: synchronous or asynchronous interaction, and symmetric or directed interaction.

In our approach, we adopt synchronous symmetric interaction by *event sharing* and synchronous directed interaction by *event calling*.

The easiest way to give interaction a formal semantics in our framework is via constraints: synchronous calling $a_1 \gg a_2$ of action a_2 by action a_1 is captured by the constraint that, whenever a_1 occurs in some situation in a life cycle, a_2 must occur in the same situation in the same life cycle. Synchronous sharing is easily treated as mutual calling.

Also asymmetric forms of interaction can be given a precise meaning in our theory, namely via lifeness constraints. We did not exploit this so far.

More elaborate forms of interaction can be described via shared components: they can act as channels synchronizing all objects sharing the actions happening in the channel. Also interaction via "shared memory" can be treated this way, by sharing attributes as well. The formal semantics of interaction by sharing coincides with that of aggregation with shared parts.

5 Reification

Reification means implementation: an abstract object is reified by describing it in more detail on a lower level of abstraction, using the features of a given base object (which will typically be composite). The purpose is that, once the services of the base object are provided, the abstract object is put into operation.

The problem has been studied extensively in algebraic data type theory [EGL89, EM90] and in the theory of processes [REX89, Br91]. In our approach, aspects of both theories are involved [SJE92, SGS92].

For example, consider the reification of an object class EMPLOYEE by a relational database relation EMP_REL plus appropriate transactions. If address is an attribute of an EMPLOYEE, we may implement it by several attributes in EMP_REL like street, number, city, zipcode, etc. If, say, fire is an action for an EMPLOYEE, its implementation will be a transaction consisting of a series of deletions, insertions and updates, probably distributed over several database relations.

For describing reification, we have to combine three objects: the abstract object, the (composite) base object, and a "middle" object specifying how to bridge the gap, i.e., how the abstract services depend on the base services. That is, the middle object consists of an aggregation of the two others, enriched by a specification how to reify abstract attributes by base "data structures" (combinations of base attributes), and abstract actions by (possibly concurrent) base transactions.

In order to show correctness of an implementation, we need to know which base data structures represent which abstract attributes. Let Θ_a denote the abstract template, and let Θ_b denote the base template. Let $F_b^{\wedge}$ be the set of finite conjunctions of facts in F_b. We capture correct representation by an *abstraction function* [Ho72], i.e., a partial surjective map $\alpha : F_b^{\wedge} \to F_a$ sending conjunctions of base attribute–value facts to abstract attribute–value facts. For example, each meaningful combination of street, number, city, zipcode, etc. data is mapped to one abstract employee address, and each of the latter should be represented by some such combination of data. Please note that α is always undefined on action enablings and occurrences.

Unless α is injective, the inverse image α^{-1} may associate more than one alternative base representation with an abstract attribute–value fact. Such alternative representations often occur in practice. As an example, consider buffers: many internal representations represent one and the same abstract queue state.

The middle template is of the form $\Theta_m = \Theta_a + \Theta_b + \Theta_c$ where Θ_c describes how the abstract items in Θ_a are "programmed" on top of the base items in Θ_b. Given abstraction map α, the correctness criteria are given by a set $\mathcal{A}$ of formulas saying that each middle situation must contain some base representation for each abstract attribute–value fact. For each such fact $a = v \in F_a$, its inverse image $\alpha^{-1}(a = v) = \{\rho_1, \ldots, \rho_r\}$ gives the set of its alternative representations. Then we have $\mathcal{A} = \{$ $\Box(a = v \Rightarrow \rho_1 \vee \ldots \vee \rho_r) \mid a = v \in F_a\}$. as theorems to be proved in the middle template.

As for the semantics: each middle life cycle contains an abstract and a base life cycle where it can be projected to by the corresponding reduction maps. The criteria $\mathcal{A}$ make sure that the middle life cycles coordinate the abstract and base actions in such a way that, at any moment, the observable attribute–value facts are in correct interrelationship.

There is, however, one problem: it is not practical to assume that the abstract and base life cycles are in perfect step-to-step synchronization. On the contrary, one abstract action will usually be reified by a base *trans*action consisting of many single actions extending over some span of time. We capture this by allowing for empty situations being interspersed in life cycles, as appropriate. These empty situations serve as placeholders, i.e., as "virtual" steps where nothing is observable, nothing is enabled, and nothing happens. By this *life cycle stretching*, the "real" situations in an abstract life cycle can be positioned into any place and synchronized with their corresponding representations in the base life cycles.

Of course, the logics and semantics of templates has to be reconsidered carefully in view of life cycle stretching. For instance, the temporal next operator $\bigcirc$ becomes somewhat problematic, but this is inevitable anyway when it comes to reification. Another problem is the frame default rule mentioned in example 2.1, but this rule has to be reconsidered anyway in view of nondeterminism as introduced by interfacing. Please note that the correctness criteria $\mathcal{A}$ defined above are vacuous for virtual abstract situations, so they are trivially satisfied there. This allows for base intermediate steps whithout correct representation requirements, a feature badly needed in practice.

With the logics and semantics worked out appropriately, we obtain a general abstract serializability criterion, leaving much freedom for implementing any practical transaction management system.

As pointed out in section 2, it is most important that a reification concept displays horizontal and vertical composability. We are confident that our approach indeed enjoys these properties.

Term Rewriting in CT_Σ

Andrea Corradini*

Università di Pisa
Dipartimento di Informatica
Corso Italia 40, 56125 Pisa, Italy
andrea@di.unipi.it

Abstract. We extend the classical theory of term rewriting systems to infinite and partial terms (i.e., to the elements of algebra CT_Σ), fully exploiting the complete partially ordered structure of CT_Σ. We show that redexes and rules, as well as other operations on terms, can be regarded as total functions on CT_Σ. As a consequence, we can study their properties of monotonicity and continuity. For rules, we show that non-left-linear rules are in general not monotonic, and that left-infinite rules are in general not continuous. Moreover, we show that the well-known Church-Rosser property of non-overlapping redexes holds for monotonic redexes. This property allows us to define a notion of parallel application of a finite set of monotonic redexes, and, using standard algebraic techniques, we extend the definition to the infinite case. We also suggest that infinite parallel term rewriting has interesting potential applications in the semantics of *cyclic term graph rewriting*.

1 Introduction

Term Rewriting is a model of computation that is employed in various areas of computer science, including symbolic algebraic computation, functional and logic programming, automated theorem proving, and execution of algebraic specifications. The 'computations' of a term rewriting system consist of repeatedly replacing subterms of a given expression with equal terms, until the simplest form possible is obtained. The theory of rewriting systems is nowadays well established within Theoretical Computer Science, at least for what concerns the rewriting of *finite* terms (see [DJ90, Kl91] for two recent surveys).

For a long time (at least to our knowledge) the extension of term rewriting to infinite terms has not been considered in the literature, probably because of the lack of motivations and/or interesting applications. Only recently this topics has become the target of an intense research activity, carried on by many research groups ([FRW88, FW89, DKP89, DK89, KKSV90]). The main motivation for the recent interest in infinite term rewriting is undoubtedly the need of extending the theory of term rewriting in order to provide a satisfactory interpretation for *cyclic term graph rewriting*.

* Research partially supported by the COMPUGRAPH Basic Research Esprit Working Group n. 7183

Acyclic term graph rewriting (i.e., the issue of representing finite terms with directed, acyclic graphs, and of modelling term rewriting via graph rewriting) has been addressed in a number of places [Ra84, BvEGKPS87, Ke87, HP91, CR93], and is now well understood. The main advantage of this approach (with respect to classical term rewriting) is that the sharing of common subterms can be represented explicitly in the graph. Therefore the rewriting process is speeded up, because the rewriting steps do not have to be repeated for each copy of an identical subterm. For example, the rewrite rule $R : f(x) \rightarrow g(x)$ can be applied twice to term $t \equiv k(f(a), r(f(a)))$, yielding in two steps term $t' \equiv k(g(a), r(g(a)))$. If instead t is represented as a graph, and the two identical subterms are shared (as in graph G of Fig. 1), then a single application of the rule is sufficient to reduce it to graph G' of Fig. 1, which clearly represents term t'. Thus a single graph rewriting step may correspond to n term rewriting steps, where n is the 'degree of sharing' of the rewritten subterm.

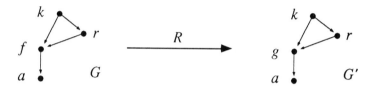

Fig. 1. An example of term graph rewriting

During the last years, many authors considered the extension of term graph rewriting to the cyclic case, allowing (finite, directed) cyclic graphs as well. The first consequence of this extension is that infinite terms (or, more precisely, *rational* terms, i.e., infinite terms with a finite number of distinct subterms) can be represented as well, exploiting cycles. The second effect is that a single graph rewriting step may now correspond to some infinite term rewriting. Consider for example rule R above: by applying it to graph H of Fig. 2 one obtain graph H' (in any reasonable definition of graph rewriting). Clearly, H represents the infinite term $f^\omega \equiv f(f(f(\ldots)))$, while H' represents term g^ω. There are (at least) two possible ways of interpreting the rewriting of term f^ω to term g^ω via some number of applications of rule R:

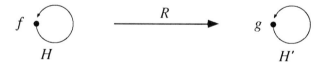

Fig. 2. An example of cyclic term graph rewriting

1. g^ω is the limit of an infinite sequence of applications of R, i.e., $f^\omega \rightarrow_R g(f^\omega) \rightarrow_R g(g(f^\omega)) \rightarrow_R \ldots \leadsto_\omega g^\omega$.

2. g^ω is the result of the simultaneous application of R to an infinite number of redexes in f^ω: in a single step all the occurrences of f in f^ω are replaced by g.

The relevant fact is that, unlike the example of Fig. 2, there are cases where these two interpretations lead to different results. This happens, for example, when *collapsing* rules are considered, i.e., rules having a variable as right-hand side. The most famous collapsing rule is the rule for identity, $R_I : I(x) \rightarrow x$, and the pathological case (considered already by many authors) is the application of R_I to I^ω. Using the first interpretation above, we have that $I^\omega \rightarrow_{R_I} I^\omega \rightarrow_{R_I} \cdots$, and clearly the limit of this sequence is I^ω itself. On the other hand, if we follow the second interpretation, all the occurrences of I in I^ω are deleted in a single step, and thus we should obtain as result a term not containing function symbols, i.e., some sort of 'undefined' term. It is worth stressing that *both* interpretations are meaningful from the point of view of cyclic term graph rewriting, and they correspond to two different choices of the graph rewriting algorithm.

In fact, if one uses the term graph rewriting model defined in [BvEGKPS87], the 'circular-I' (i.e., graph G_I in Fig. 3, representing I^ω) rewrites via R_I to itself: therefore the first interpretation must be used. This is the approach followed in [FRW88, FW89, DKP89, DK89, KKSV90], where they elaborated a theory of *transfinite term rewriting*, showing its adequacy for modelling finite, cyclic graph rewriting. In essence, a finite graph derivation has the 'same effect' of a converging transfinite term rewriting sequence: for the notion of convergence they used the well-known topological structure of (possibly infinite) terms, which, equipped with a suitable notion of distance, form a complete ultra-metric space [AN80].

If instead one uses as term graph rewriting model the so-called 'algebraic' or 'double-pushout' approach [EPS73], as done for the acyclic case in [HP91, CR93], the circular-I rewrites via R_I to a graph consisting of a single node. The situation is summarized in the lower part of Fig. 3. This is the approach taken by the author in a forthcoming paper with Frank Drewes. In order to explain this result from the perspective of term rewriting, the second of the above interpretations must be used. In this case the theory of transfinite term rewriting is no more helpful, because it cannot justify this result. We need instead some notion of 'infinite parallel rewriting', that could explain the fact that all the occurrences of the operator I in I^ω are deleted in a single step.

The notion of infinite parallel rewriting can be defined in a satisfactory way (as shown in this paper) by exploiting the well-known algebraic structure of (possibly infinite, possibly partial) terms over a signature Σ, which form a complete partial ordering (CPO) denoted CT_Σ. CT_Σ has a least element denoted $\bot$ (the undefined term), and the order relation is defined as $t < t'$ if t is a partial term that is 'less defined' than t'. CT_Σ enjoys several nice algebraic properties, which are studied in depth in the seminal work by the ADJ group, [ADJ77].

We show informally how the algebraic structure of CT_Σ can be exploited to show that I^ω rewrites via R_I to $\bot$ (by the way, this also gives a precise interpretation of the unlabelled node of Fig. 3: it denotes the undefined term

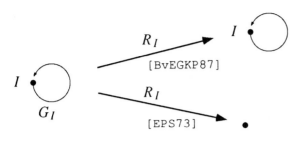

Fig. 3. The two possible results of applying R_I to the 'circular-I'

$\perp$). The infinite term I^ω is the least upper bound of an infinite chain of finite, partial terms of CT_Σ: in fact, $I(\perp) \leq I(I(\perp)) \leq \ldots \leq I^n(\perp) \leq \ldots \quad \rightsquigarrow_\omega I^\omega$. Now, if we apply rule R_I to each term of the chain as many times as possible, all those terms reduce to $\perp$ (in particular, $I^n(\perp)$ reduces to $\perp$ in n steps, or, and we prefer this interpretation, in a single finite parallel step, where the rule is applied simultaneously to the n occurrences of I). Therefore, after applying rule R_I as many times as possible, the above chain is reduced to $\perp \leq \perp \leq \ldots$: we define the least upper bound of this chain (i.e., $\perp$ itself) as the result of the infinite parallel rewriting of I^ω via R_I.

The last example shows that the CPO structure of (infinite) terms can be exploited fruitfully in the framework of term rewriting systems. But, as far as we know, the algebraic structure of CT_Σ has never been taken into account in the term rewriting literature. Therefore one of the goals of this paper is to revisit some definitions and some results of the classical theory of term rewriting, extending them to the case of infinite or partial terms, and taking care of the CPO structure of CT_Σ.

As expected, except for the original definition of infinite parallel rewriting in Section 5, no really new results come out from this reworking of well-known notions. Nevertheless, we think that our presentation sheds new light on some concepts which are a bit obscure in the term rewriting literature, like, for example, the real nature of non-left-linear rules, and why they behave so badly with respect to Church-Rosser properties. Moreover, the presence of partial terms and the CPO structure of CT_Σ allow us to define rewrite rules, redexes, and also basic operations like subterm selection and subterm replacement in an original way as *total* functions operating on terms. Like for every function on a CPO, we can ask ourselves if those functions are monotonic or continuous: in this way we can classify the rules of a term rewriting system w.r.t. to their algebraic properties. An interesting result shows that the classical Church-Rosser property of independent redexes always holds for *monotonic* rewrite rules; *continuous* rules are instead required for a correct definition of infinite parallel rewriting. These results are reconciled with the traditional Church-Rosser properties of orthogonal (i.e., left-linear, left-finite, non-overlapping) term rewriting systems by a proposition that shows that all left-linear rules are monotonic, while all left-linear and left-finite rules are continuous.

The paper is organized as follows. In Section 2 we introduce the CPO structure of terms and some basic operations on terms, regarding them as (continuous) total functions. Next in Section 3 we introduce term rewriting of (possibly partial) terms: the main contribution here is an extension of the definition of redex and of redex application which takes into account the possibility that the left-hand side of a rule matches just partially the term to be rewritten. In Section 4 we study the properties of monotonicity and continuity of rewrite rules, showing, among other things, that the customary discrimination against not left-linear rules is fully justified in this clean algebraic setting, because they are even not monotonic (at least in general). Furthermore, we present the natural extension of the Church-Rosser theorem for orthogonal TRS's to the case of partial, infinite terms, showing that it holds for all monotonic rules. The Church-Rosser theorem is then exploited in Section 5 in order to define the notion of *finite* parallel rewriting via the application of two monotonic rules to two independent redexes in a term. In the same section we introduce our original definition of *infinite* parallel rewriting for continuous rules, which is defined via a suitable limit construction: the well-definedness of the definition and its consistency with the finite case are the main results of the section. Finally, Section 6 summarizes the main results of the paper and suggests some topics for future research. Because of space limitations, most of the proofs are not included in the paper.

2 The complete partial ordering of partial, infinite terms

We introduce here the notion of possibly partial, possibly infinite terms, borrowing their definition from [ADJ77], where they are called Σ-trees.

Definition 1 (occurrences). Let ω^* be the set of all finite strings of natural numbers. Elements of ω^* are called **occurrences**. The empty string is denoted by λ. The set ω^* is equipped with a binary relation (which is obviously a partial ordering), defined as $u \leq w$ iff u is a prefix of w. Two occurrences u, w are called *disjoint* (written $u|w$) if they are incomparable w.r.t. $\leq$. The *length* of an occurrence w, denoted $|w|$, is defined as $|\lambda| = 0$ and $|wi| = |w| + 1$ for $w \in \omega^*$ and $i \in \omega$.

Definition 2 (terms). Let Σ be a (one-sorted) signature, i.e., a ranked alphabet of operator symbols $\Sigma = \cup_n \Sigma_n$, and let X be a set of variables. A **term over** (Σ, X) is a partial function $t : \omega^* \to \Sigma \cup X$, such that for all $w \in \omega^*$ and all $i \in \omega$, the domain of definition of t, $\mathcal{O}(t)$, satisfies the following:

- $wi \in \mathcal{O}(t) \Rightarrow w \in \mathcal{O}(t)$
- $wi \in \mathcal{O}(t) \Rightarrow t(w) \in \Sigma_n$ and $i \leq n$ for some $n > 0$.

Set $\mathcal{O}(t)$ is also called the **set of occurrences** of t. We will denote by $\mathcal{O}_X(t)$ the *set of occurrences of variables* of t, i.e., $\mathcal{O}_X(t) = \{v \in \mathcal{O}(t) \mid t(v) \in X\}$, and by $\mathcal{O}_\Sigma(t)$ the *set of occurrences of operators* of t, i.e., $\mathcal{O}_\Sigma(t) = \{v \in \mathcal{O}(t) \mid t(v) \in \Sigma\}$. The set of variables of a term t, $var(t)$, is defined as $var(t) = \{x \in X \mid \exists v \in \mathcal{O}(t) . t(v) = x\}$.

A term t is **finite** if $\mathcal{O}(t)$ is finite. The **depth** of a term t is defined only if t is finite; in this case, $depth(t) \equiv max\{|w| \mid w \in \mathcal{O}(t)\}$. A term t is **total** if $t(w) \in \Sigma_n \Rightarrow wi \in \mathcal{O}(t)$ for all $0 < i \leq n$. The set of terms over (Σ, X) is denoted by $CT_\Sigma(X)$ (with the convention that CT_Σ stays for $CT_\Sigma(\emptyset)$).

Throughout the paper we will often use (for finite terms) the equivalent and more usual representation of terms as operators applied to other terms. Partial terms are made total in this representation by introducing the undefined term $\perp$ (called *bottom*), which represents the empty function $\perp : \emptyset \to \Sigma \cup X$. Thus, for example, if $x \in X$, $t = f(\perp, g(x))$ is the term such that $\mathcal{O}(t) = \{\lambda, 2, 21\}$, $t(\lambda) = f \in \Sigma_2$, $t(2) = g \in \Sigma_1$, and $t(21) = x \in X$.

We introduce now the relevant algebraic structure of terms ([ADJ77]).

Definition 3 ($CT_\Sigma(X)$ as ω-complete lower semi-lattice). Given two terms $t, t' \in CT_\Sigma(X)$, t **approximates** t' (written $t \leq t'$) iff t is less defined than t' as partial function. In the proofs throughout the paper, we will use the following characterization of term approximation:

$$t \leq t' \quad \Leftrightarrow \quad \forall w \in \mathcal{O}(t) . t(w) = t'(w)$$

Equivalently, relation '$\leq$' can be defined as the minimal relation such that $\perp \leq t$ for all t; $x \leq x$ for all $x \in X$; and $f(t_1, ..., t_n) \leq f(t'_1, ..., t'_n)$ if $t_1 \leq t'_1, ..., t_n \leq t'_n$, for all $f \in \Sigma_n$.

An ω-**chain** $\{t_i\}_{i<\omega}$ is an infinite sequence of terms $t_0 \leq ... \leq t_n \leq ...$. Every ω-chain $\{t_i\}_{i<\omega}$ in $CT_\Sigma(X)$ has a **least upper bound** (*lub*) $\cup_{i<\omega}\{t_i\}$ characterized as follows:

$$t = \cup_{i<\omega}\{t_i\} \quad \Leftrightarrow \quad \forall w \in \omega^* . \exists i < \omega . \forall j \geq i . t_j(w) = t(w)$$

Formally this means that $CT_\Sigma(X)$ is ω-**complete**.

Given two terms t and t', their **greatest lower bound** $t \cap t'$ is uniquely characterized by the property $(t \cap t' \leq t) \wedge (t \cap t' \leq t) \wedge (\forall t'' . (t'' \leq t) \wedge (t'' \leq t') \Rightarrow t'' \leq t \cap t')$. It can be proved that $t \cap t'$ exists for all $t, t' \in CT_\Sigma(X)$, and that it is defined as follows. Let $D = \{w \mid w \in \mathcal{O}(t) \cap \mathcal{O}(t') \wedge t(w) = t'(w)\}$ be the subset of the intersection of the domains of t and t' where their values agree, and let $D' \subseteq D$ be the largest prefix-closed subset of D, i.e., such that $wi \in D' \Rightarrow w \in D'$. Then $t \cap t'$ is defined as

$$t \cap t'(u) = \begin{cases} t(u) & \text{if } u \in D' \\ \perp & \text{otherwise.} \end{cases}$$

Finally, $CT_\Sigma(X)$ has a least element w.r.t. $\leq$, which is $\perp$ (bottom). All this amounts to say that $CT_\Sigma(X)$ is an ω-**complete lower semilattice**.

Definition 4 (monotonic and continuous functions). A function $f : D \to D'$ between ω-complete partial orderings D and D' is said **monotonic** if $d \leq d' \Rightarrow f(d) \leq f(d')$. It is ω-**continuous** if for all ω-chain $\{d_i\}_{i<\omega} \subseteq D, \cup_{i<\omega}\{f(d_i)\} = f(\cup_{i<\omega}\{d_i\})$, i.e., the lub of ω-chains are preserved.

In the rest of the paper we will omit the 'ω-' qualification of chains, completeness, and continuity. We introduce now two well-known operations on terms, namely *subterm selection* and *subterm replacement*. We define them in an original way: by exploiting the existence of partial terms, we can turn them into *total functions* on terms. We also state that, as functions on CT_Σ, both operations are continuous.

Definition 5 (subterm selection). Given an occurrence $w \in \omega^*$ and a term $t \in CT_\Sigma(X)$, the **subterm of** t **at** *(occurrence)* w is the term t/w defined as $t/w(u) = t(wu)$ for all $u \in \omega^*$. Using the alternative representation of terms, t/w is equivalently defined by the following clauses:

- $\perp/w = \perp$
- $t/\lambda = t$
- $x/iw = \perp$ if $x \in X$
- $f(t_1, ..., t_n)/iw = t_i/w$ if $f \in \Sigma_n$ and $i \leq n$
- $f(t_1, ..., t_n)/iw = \perp$ if $f \in \Sigma_n$ and $i > n$.

It is easy to check that $t/w = \perp$ iff $w \notin \mathcal{O}(t)$.

Proposition 6 (subterm selection is continuous). *For all $w \in \omega^*$, the function* $\_/w : CT_\Sigma(X) \to CT_\Sigma(X)$ *mapping t to t/w is continuous.*

Definition 7 (subterm replacement). Given terms $t, s \in CT_\Sigma(X)$ and an occurrence $w \in \omega^*$, the **replacement of** s **in** t **at** *(occurrence)* w, denoted $t[w \leftarrow s]$, is the term defined as $t[w \leftarrow s](u) = t(u)$ if $w \not\leq u$ or $t/w = \perp$, and $t[w \leftarrow s](wu) = s(u)$ otherwise. Equivalently, it can be defined as follows:

- $t[w \leftarrow s] = t$ if $t/w = \perp$ (i.e., if $w \notin \mathcal{O}(t)$)
- $t[\lambda \leftarrow s] = s$ if $t \neq \perp$
- $f(t_1, ..., t_n)[iw \leftarrow s] = f(t_1, ..., t_i[w \leftarrow s], ..., t_n)$ if $i \leq n$.

The first clause also implies that $\perp[w \leftarrow s] = \perp$ for all w, s (even if $w = \lambda$).

Proposition 8 (subterm replacement is continuous). *For all $w \in \omega^*$, the function* $\_[w \leftarrow \_] : CT_\Sigma(X) \times CT_\Sigma(X) \to CT_\Sigma(X)$ *mapping (t, s) to $t[w \leftarrow s]$ is continuous, that is, it is continuous in the two arguments separately.*

The next statement collects some equalities relating subterm selection and subterm replacement. They follow directly from the definitions. The names are taken from [Hu80].

Proposition 9 (properties of subterm replacement and selection). *The following equalities hold for all occurrences w, v, and for all terms t, s, and s':*

[*commutativity*] $t[w \leftarrow s][v \leftarrow s'] = t[v \leftarrow s'][w \leftarrow s]$ *if $w|v$;*
[*dominance*] $t[wv \leftarrow s][w \leftarrow s'] = t[w \leftarrow s']$;
[*distributivity*] $t[wv \leftarrow s]/w = t/w[v \leftarrow s]$.

Definition 10 (substitutions). Let X and Y be two sets of variables. A **substitution** *(from X to Y)* is a function $\sigma : X \to CT_\Sigma(Y)$ (used in postfix notation). The collection of all substitutions from X to Y is denoted by $Subs_\Sigma(X, Y)$. A substitution $\sigma \in Subs_\Sigma(X, Y)$ uniquely determines a function (also denoted by σ) from $CT_\Sigma(X)$ to $CT_\Sigma(Y)$, which extends σ as follows

- $\perp\sigma = \perp$,
- $f(t_1, ..., t_n)\sigma = f(t_1\sigma, ..., t_n\sigma)$.

The partial ordering on terms can be extended to elements of $Subs_\Sigma(X, Y)$ as follows: $\sigma \leq \sigma'$ iff for all $x \in X$, $x\sigma \leq x\sigma'$. $Subs_\Sigma(X, Y)$ is an ω-complete lower semilattice under this ordering. If $\sigma \in Subs_\Sigma(X, Y)$ and $\sigma' \in Subs_\Sigma(Y, Z)$, then their composition $\sigma' \circ \sigma$ is a substitution from X to Z defined as $x(\sigma' \circ \sigma) = (x\sigma)\sigma'$ for all $x \in X$.

If X is finite, a substitution $\sigma \in Subs_\Sigma(X, Y)$ will be represented sometimes as a finite set of the form $\{x_1/t_1, ..., x_n/t_n\}$ with $t_i = x_i\sigma$ for all $1 \leq i \leq n$.

Proposition 11 (substitution is continuous). *Every substitution σ from X to Y, regarded as a function from $CT_\Sigma(X)$ to $CT_\Sigma(Y)$, is continuous. Moreover, for all sets of variables X, Y, and Z, the composition of substitutions $\_ \circ \_ :$ $Subs_\Sigma(X, Y) \times Subs_\Sigma(Y, Z) \to Subs_\Sigma(X, Z)$ is continuous, i.e., it is continuous separately on both arguments.*

Proof. See [ADJ77].

3   Term rewriting systems: basic definitions

In this section we introduce some basic definitions about term rewriting systems, like rules, redexes, and the application of a redex to a term, taking into account the rich algebraic structure of CT_Σ.

Definition 12 (rewrite rule, term rewriting system). A **rewrite rule** $R = (l, r)$ is a pair of terms of $CT_\Sigma(X)$, where $var(r) \subseteq var(l)$, and l is not a variable. Terms l and r are called the left- and the right-hand side of R, respectively. A rule is called *left-linear* if no variable occurs more than once in l. A rule is *left-finite* if l is finite, and it is *total* if l and r are total terms (see Definition 2). In the paper we will consider total rules only. A **term rewriting system R** is a finite set of rewrite rules, $\mathbf{R} = \{R_i\}_{i<n}$.

A *redex* (for *REDucible EXpression*) is usually defined in the literature as an occurrence of the left-hand side of a rule in a given term at a certain occurrence. We will use a slightly different definition, which does not involve any term: a redex is just a pair $\Delta = (w, R)$ where w is an occurrence and R is a rewrite rule. Then given any term t, a redex $\Delta = (w, R)$ can be *total* in t (if the subterm of t at w matches the left-hand side of R), or *partial* in t (if the matching is only partial), or *null* in t (if there is no matching at all). This definition allows us to regard a redex as a total function from terms to terms, whose behaviour on a term is determined by its type w.r.t. that term. More precisely, when a redex $\Delta = (w, R)$ is applied to a term t, there are three possible effects: if Δ is total in t, then the result is the usual one, i.e., the application of rule R to t at occurrence w; if Δ is null in t, then the result is t itself; and finally if Δ is partial in t, then the result of the application of Δ to t is the best approximation we can determine of the actual result. For the sake of simplicity (and without loss of generality) we consider just the rewriting of ground terms (i.e., elements of CT_Σ): the same definitions can be applied to the rewriting of terms of $CT_\Sigma(X)$ as well, because the variables in the term to be rewritten play no role during rewriting.

Definition 13 (redex). Given a term rewriting system **R**, a **redex** Δ (w.r.t. **R**) is a pair $\Delta = (w, R)$ where $w \in \omega^*$ is an occurrence, and $R : l \to r \in \mathbf{R}$ is a rule. Given a term $t \in CT_\Sigma$, a redex $\Delta = (w, R)$ can be of three kind w.r.t. t:

- Δ *is* **total** *in* t if there exists a substitution $\sigma : var(l) \to CT_\Sigma$ such that $t/w = l\sigma$. In this case we say that *substitution σ makes Δ total in t.*
- Δ *is* **partial** *in* t if there is no σ such that $t/w = l\sigma$, but there exists a term $l' < l$ and a substitution $\sigma' : var(l') \to CT_\Sigma$ such that $t/w = l'\sigma'$. In this case we say that *the pair (l', σ') makes Δ partial in t.*
- Δ *is* **null** *in* t if it is neither total nor partial in t.

For a given rule R, we will often denote the redex (λ, R) improperly by R itself.

Example 1 (redexes). Given the rule $R : f(g(x), y) \to h(x)$, the redex $\Delta = (1, R)$ is made total in $k(f(g(\perp), b))$ by substitution $\{x/\perp, y/b\}$ and in $f(g(\perp), \perp)$ by substitution $\{x/\perp, y/\perp\}$; it is made partial in $k(f(\perp, \perp))$ by pairs $(f(\perp, \perp), \{\})$ and $(f(\perp, y), \{y/\perp\})$; and it is null in $k(f(k(a), b))$. Notice that, by the definition, Δ is also made partial in term c by the pair $(\perp, \{\})$.

Consider now the redex $\Delta' = (\lambda, R')$, where $R' : f(g(x), x) \to h(x)$ is a non-left-linear rule. Then Δ' is made total in $f(g(k(\perp)), k(\perp))$ by substitution $\{x/k(\perp)\}$; it is made partial in $f(\perp, k(\perp))$ by pair $(f(\perp, x), \{x/k(\perp)\})$; and it is null in $f(g(k(\perp)), k(a))$.

Proposition 14 (characterization of the kind of rexedes). *Let $\Delta = (w, R : l \to r)$ be a redex and $t \in CT_\Sigma$ be a term.*

1. *The kind of Δ in t (i.e., total, partial, or null) is uniquely determined.*
2. *Δ is total in t iff the following two conditions are satisfied:*
   (a) *for each occurrence $v \in \mathcal{O}_\Sigma(l)$, $t(wv) = l(v)$.*
   (b) *for each pair of distinct occurrences of variables $v, v' \in \mathcal{O}_X(l)$ such that $l(v) = l(v')$, $t/wv = t/wv'$.*

   Moreover, the unique substitution $\sigma : var(l) \to CT_\Sigma$ making Δ total in t (i.e., such that $l\sigma = t/w$) is determined as $x\sigma = t/wv$, if $x \in var(l)$ and v is any occurrence in $\mathcal{O}_X(l)$ such that $l(v) = x$.

3. Δ *is partial in* t *iff the following three conditions are satisfied:*

   (a) *for each occurrence* $v \in \mathcal{O}_\Sigma(l)$, *either* $t(wv) = l(v)$ *or* $t(wv) = \bot$;

   (b) *for each pair of distinct occurrences of variables* $v, v' \in \mathcal{O}_X(l)$ *such that* $l(v) = l(v')$, *either* $t/wv = t/wv'$, *or* $t/wv = \bot$, *or* $t/wv' = \bot$;

   (c) *there exists an occurrence* $v \in \mathcal{O}_\Sigma(l)$ *such that* $t(wv) = \bot$, *or there exist two occurrences* $v, v' \in \mathcal{O}_X(l)$ *such that* $l(v) = l(v')$, *and* $t/wv \neq t/wv'$.

   As a consequence, for every occurrence w *and rule* R, *if* $w \notin \mathcal{O}(t)$ *then the redex* (w, R) *is partial in* t.

4. Δ *is null in* t *iff one of the following conditions hold:*

   (a) *there exists an occurrence* $v \in \mathcal{O}_\Sigma(l)$ *such that* $t(wv) \neq \bot$ *and* $t(wv) \neq l(v)$,

   (b) *there exist two distinct occurrences* $v, v' \in \mathcal{O}_X(t)$, *with* $l(v) = l(v')$, $t/wv \neq \bot$, $t/wv' \neq \bot$, *and* $t/wv \neq t/wv'$.

It is worth stressing that the conditions characterizing total, partial, and null redexes can be simplified in the case of left-linear rules. In fact, if R is left-linear then the second condition of the characterization of total and partial redexes always holds (it is vacuous), while condition 4.b and the second part of condition 3.c cannot be satisfied. Exploiting this fact it is possible to prove the following lemma.

Lemma 15 (properties of left-linear rules). *Let* R *be a left-linear rule. If* $t \leq t'$, *then*

1. *if* (w, R) *is total in* t, *then it is total in* t';
2. *if* (w, R) *is null in* t, *then it is null in* t';
3. *if* (w, R) *is partial in* t', *then it is partial in* t.

We define now what does it mean to apply a redex to a term t. As expected, the result of this operation depends on the kind of the redex in t.

Definition 16 (redex application). Given a redex $\Delta = (w, R : l \to r)$, the result of its **application** to a term t, denoted $\Delta(t)$, is defined by the following clauses:

   - $\Delta(t) = t[w \leftarrow r\sigma]$ if σ makes Δ total in t (i.e., $l\sigma = t/w$);
   - $\Delta(t) = t[w \leftarrow (l' \cap r)\sigma]$ if (l', σ) makes Δ partial in t (i.e., $l' < l$ and $l'\sigma = t/w$);
   - $\Delta(t) = t$ if Δ is null in t.

We also write $t \to_\Delta s$ to mean $\Delta(t) = s$, and we say that t **rewrites to** s **via** Δ. Recalling that R also denotes the redex (λ, R) (see Definition 13), it follows that $R(t)$ denotes the result of the application of R to the topmost operator of t.

The second clause of the last definition may be not obvious. The idea is that as far as we have just a partial matching of the lhs of a rule with a term, we cannot specify completely the term resulting from the application of the redex: we should wait for additional information about the term, which can either complete the matching successfully (and then the first clause is applied) or can cause a clash (in this case the third clause is applied). Thus if the matching is just partial, we can specify the result just as far as the first and the third clauses agree: this is expressed by the term $(l' \cap r)\sigma$ obtained by applying the matching substitution to the largest term included both in the approximation l' of the left-hand side, and in its right-hand side r (see Definition 3 for the definition of $t \cap t'$).

In order to prove the well-definedness of the last definition, we need the following technical lemma.

Lemma 17. *Let l', l'' be two terms and let $\sigma' : var(l') \to CT_\Sigma$, $\sigma'' : var(l'') \to CT_\Sigma$ be two substitutions. If $l'\sigma' \leq l''\sigma''$ and l' and l'' have a common upper bound (i.e., $l' \leq l$ and $l'' \leq l$ for some l), then for each term r it holds $(l' \cap r)\sigma' \leq (l'' \cap r)\sigma''$.*

Proposition 18 (redex application is well-defined). *The application of a redex Δ to a term t is well-defined, that is, $\Delta(t)$ is uniquely determined. Thus Δ is a total function $\Delta : CT_\Sigma \to CT_\Sigma$.*

Proof. By Proposition 14.1 the three clauses of Definition 16 are applicable in mutually disjoint cases. The fact that $\Delta(t)$ is uniquely determined is obvious if Δ is total or null in t (if it is total, the substitution σ making it total is unique, as stressed in Proposition 14.2)

If the second clause is applied, we have to show that if (l', σ') and (l'', σ'') make Δ partial in t, then $(l' \cap r)\sigma' = (l'' \cap r)\sigma''$. But the fact that (l', σ') and (l'', σ'') make Δ partial in t means that $l', l'' < l$ and that the two substitutions $\sigma' : var(l') \to CT_\Sigma$ and $\sigma'' : var(l'') \to CT_\Sigma$ are such that $l'\sigma' = t/w = l''\sigma''$. Then $(l' \cap r)\sigma' = (l'' \cap r)\sigma''$ follows by two applications of Lemma 17. Therefore $\Delta(t)$ is well-defined also when Δ is partial in t.

The following statement stresses some properties of rule application which will be helpful later on. The listed properties can easily be checked by a careful inspection of the corresponding definitions.

Proposition 19 (properties of rule application). *The following properties hold for every rule R, for all t, $s \in CT_\Sigma$, and v, $w \in \omega^*$:*

1. $(vw, R)(t) = t[v \leftarrow (w, R)(t/v)]$
   If $w = \lambda$, this simplifies to $(v, R)(t) = t[v \leftarrow R(t/v)]$.
2. $(wv, R)(t[w \leftarrow s]) = t[w \leftarrow (v, R)(s)]$.
3. If $\Delta = (w, R)$ and $v|w$ then $\Delta(t)/v = t/v$.

4   On monotonicity and continuity of rules

Since redexes are just functions from CT_Σ to itself (as shown in Proposition 18), it makes sense to talk about *monotonic* and *continuous* redexes. These notions may be extended to rules in an obvious way.

Definition 20 (monotonic and continuous rules). A redex Δ is *monotonic* (*continuous*) if so is the corresponding function $\Delta : CT_\Sigma \to CT_\Sigma$. A rewrite rule R is **monotonic (continuous)** if for every occurrence $w \in \omega^*$, (w, R) is monotonic (continuous).

The following proposition shows that in order to check the continuity (or monotonicity) of a rewrite rule, it is sufficient to examine its effect when applied at the topmost occurrence of a term.

Proposition 21 (rules and topmost redexes). *A rewrite rule R is monotonic (continuous) iff redex (λ, R) is monotonic (continuous).*

Proof. The *only if* part is obvious. For the *if* part, by Proposition 19.1 we have that for every occurrence $w \in \omega^*$, $(w, R)(t) = t[w \leftarrow (\lambda, R)(t/w)]$. Therefore (w, R) is a suitable composition of subterm selection $(\_/w)$, of subterm replacement $(\_[w \leftarrow \_])$, and of the redex (λ, R). Then the thesis follows by observing that for all $w \in \omega^*$, functions $\_[w \leftarrow \_]$ and $\_/w$ are continuous (see Propositions 6 and 8).

The next interesting result shows that the classification of rewrite rules (regarded as functions) with respect to their algebraic properties is consistent with the usual classification based on the properties of the left-hand side. In fact, left-linearity and left-finiteness of rules are proved to be strictly related to monotonicity and continuity.

Theorem 22 (characterization of monotonic and continuous rules). *Let $R : l \to r$ be a rewrite rule. Then*

1. *If R is left-linear then it is monotonic.*
2. *If R is left-linear and left-finite then it is continuous.*
3. *If R is not left-linear, then it is monotonic iff $l = r$.*
4. *If R is not left-finite, then it is continuous iff $l = r$.*

Example 2 (non-monotonic and non-continuous rules). Let $R = f(x, x) \to k$ be a non-left-linear rule. Consider the terms $t_1 = f(g(\bot), g(\bot))$ and $t_2 = f(g(b), g(c))$. Clearly, $t_1 < t_2$, $t_1 \to_R k$ and $t_2 \to_R f(g(b), g(c))$, but $k \not\sqsubseteq f(g(b), g(c))$. Thus R is not monotonic.

Let $R = f(f(f(\ldots))) \to k$ be a left-infinite rule, let $f^n(\bot) = f(f^{n-1}(\bot))$ for each $1 < n < \omega$, and let $f^1(\bot) = f(\bot)$. Then $f^n(\bot) \to_R \bot$ for all n, but $f^\omega \to_R k$. Thus R is not continuous.

We restate now the well-known Church-Rosser theorem for independent, finite set of redexes (see for example [Ros73, Kl91]). We show that the Church-Rosser property holds for *monotonic* rules. It is worth stressing that, as for redexes, also the definition of *independence of redexes* presented below is given in a way which is independent of the actual term to be rewritten, unlike the related literature. The Church-Rosser theorem will allow us to define in the next section the parallel rewriting of a term via a finite set of independent redexes.

Definition 23 (independent redexes). Two redexes $(w, R : l \to r)$ and $(w', R' : l' \to r')$ are **independent** if their left hand sides do not overlap on occurrences of operators, that is, if $w \cdot \mathcal{O}_\Sigma(l) \cap w' \cdot \mathcal{O}_\Sigma(l') = \emptyset$ (if V is a set of occurrences and w is an occurrence, by $w \cdot V$ we denote the set $\{wv \mid v \in V\}$).

Theorem 24 (Church-Rosser property for monotonic redexes). *Let* $R : l \to r$ *and* $R' : l' \to r'$ *be two monotonic rules, and let* $\Delta = (w, R)$ *and* $\Delta' = (w', R')$ *be two independent redexes. For every term* $t \in CT_\Sigma$ *there exist two natural numbers* $1 \leq n, n' < \omega$ *and occurrences* $v_1, ..., v_n, v'_1, ..., v'_{n'}$ *such that* $(v_1, R) \circ ... \circ (v_n, R) \circ \Delta'(t) = (v'_1, R') \circ ... \circ (v'_{n'}, R') \circ \Delta(t)$. *Moreover, if* $w \not\succ w'$ *(i.e.,* $w|w'$ *or* $w < w'$*, because* $w \neq w'$ *by independence of* Δ *and* Δ'*), then the last statement holds for* $n = 1$ *and* $v_1 = w$ *(that is, there exists a number* $1 \leq n' < \omega$ *and occurrences* $v'_1, ..., v'_{n'}$ *such that* $\Delta \circ \Delta'(t) = (v'_1, R') \circ ... \circ (v'_{n'}, R') \circ \Delta(t)$*).*

5 Infinite Parallel Rewriting

Exploiting the Church-Rosser theorem presented in the last section, it is easy to define a notion of parallel term rewriting. To this aim, we need to stress that the theorem not only shows that one can build the classical 'diamond' when two different (monotonic, independent) redexes are applied to a term, but it also shows that the term 'closing the diamond' can be characterized easily as $\Delta \circ \Delta'(t)$, provided that $w|w'$ or $w < w'$ (symmetrically, if instead $w > w'$, then the term closing the diamond is $\Delta' \circ \Delta(t)$). We will use the Church-Rosser diamond to define in an obvious way the parallel application of two redexes to a term. Actually, we consider the parallel application of any *finite* set of independent, monotonic redexes.

Definition 25 (parallel redexes). A **parallel redex** Φ is a (possibly infinite, necessarily countable) set of *monotonic*, mutually independent redexes. The set of *root occurrences* of a parallel redex Φ is defined as $\mathcal{O}_{rt}(\Phi) = \{w \in \omega^* \mid \exists R . (w, R) \in \Phi\}$. A parallel redex Φ is *continuous* if all the redexes in Φ are continuous. If $t \in CT_\Sigma$ and Φ is a parallel redex, then the parallel redex $\Phi \cap t$ is defined as the subset of Φ including all redexes whose occurrence is an occurrence of t, i.e., $\Phi \cap t = \{\Delta \in \Phi \mid \Delta = (w, R) \wedge w \in \mathcal{O}(t)\}$.

Definition 26 (application and composition of finite parallel redexes). Let $\Phi = \{\Delta_1, ..., \Delta_n\}$ be a *finite* parallel redex with $\Delta_i = (w_i, R_i)$ for all $1 \leq i \leq n$. Then Φ is also a function (called *finite parallel redex application*)

$\Phi : CT_\Sigma \longrightarrow CT_\Sigma$, defined as $\Phi = \Delta_{i_1} \circ \ldots \circ \Delta_{i_n}$, where $(\Delta_{i_1}, \ldots, \Delta_{i_n})$ is any permutation of Φ such that for all $1 \leq j \leq k \leq n$, $w_{i_j} \not> w_{i_k}$ (i.e., either $w_{i_j} | w_{i_k}$ or $w_{i_j} \leq w_{i_k}$). If Φ and Φ' are two parallel redexes, their *parallel composition* is the parallel redex $\Phi || \Phi' = \{\Delta \mid \Delta \in \Phi \text{ or } \Delta \in \Phi'\}$, and it is defined only if all redexes in $\Phi \cup \Phi'$ are mutually independent.

The well-definedness of finite parallel redex application is ensured by the next result.

Proposition 27 (finite parallel redex application is well-defined). *Let $\Phi = \{\Delta_1, \ldots, \Delta_n\}$ be a finite parallel redex. Then the finite parallel redex application $\Phi : CT_\Sigma \longrightarrow CT_\Sigma$ is well defined. That is, if $(\Delta_{i_1}, \ldots, \Delta_{i_n})$ and $(\Delta_{l_1}, \ldots, \Delta_{l_n})$ are two permutations of Φ such that for all $1 \leq j \leq k \leq n$ both $w_{i_j} \not> w_{i_k}$ and $w_{l_j} \not> w_{l_k}$, then $\Delta_{i_1} \circ \ldots \circ \Delta_{i_n} = \Delta_{l_1} \circ \ldots \circ \Delta_{l_n}$.*

Fact 28 (monotonicity and continuity of parallel redexes). *If Φ is a finite parallel redex, then $\Phi : CT_\Sigma \longrightarrow CT_\Sigma$ is monotonic. Moreover, if all the redexes in Φ are continuous, then function Φ is continuous as well. This follows directly from the definitions, because Φ, regarded as a function, is a suitable compositions of all the redexes it contains.*

We are now ready to extend the definition of application of parallel redexes to the infinite case. Since in the finite case the application of a parallel redex is defined as the sequential application of all contained redexes (in a suitable order), a naive extension to infinity wouldn't work, because it would correspond to an infinite composition of functions. We propose therefore a definition which makes use of a suitable limit construction. The main result of this section (Theorem 32 below) proves that the definition is well-given and consistent with the definition of finite parallel redex application, provided that all the involved redexes are continuous. Thus we restrict the definition to *continuous* parallel redexes.

Definition 29 (parallel redex application). Let Φ be a continuous, possibly infinite parallel redex, and let $t \in CT_\Sigma$. Let $\{t_i\}_{i<\omega}$ be any chain of terms such that $t = \bigcup_{i<\omega}\{t_i\}$, and such that for all $i < \omega$ the parallel redex $\Phi_i \equiv \Phi \cap t_i$ is finite. Then the *application* of Φ to t is defined as $\Phi(t) = \bigcup_{i<\omega}\{\Phi_i(t_i)\}$.

In order to prove the well-definedness of the last definition, we need two technical lemmas that state some important properties of parallel redexes.

Lemma 30 (some properties of parallel redexes).

1. *Let Φ and Φ' be two finite, parallel redexes, such that all redexes in $\Phi \cup \Phi'$ are mutually independent. If for all $w \in \mathcal{O}_{rt}(\Phi)$ and for all $w' \in \mathcal{O}_{rt}(\Phi')$ $w \not> w'$, then $\Phi || \Phi' = \Phi \circ \Phi'$.*
2. *If Φ is a finite parallel redex, then for all $t \in CT_\Sigma$, $\Phi(t) = (\Phi \cap t)(t)$.*
3. *If Φ is a parallel redex, $t \in CT_\Sigma$, and $\Phi \cap t$ is finite, then for all t' such that $t \leq t'$ and for all finite Φ' such that $\Phi \cap t \subseteq \Phi' \subseteq \Phi$, it holds $(\Phi \cap t)(t) \leq \Phi'(t')$.*

Lemma 31 (a property of continuous parallel redexes). *Let $t \in CT_\Sigma$ and let Φ be a continuous parallel redex such that $\Phi \cap t$ is finite. Then for all $v \in \mathcal{O}((\Phi \cap t)(t))$ there exists a finite term $t_v \leq t$ such that $(\Phi \cap t)(t)(v) = (\Phi \cap t_v)(t_v)(v)$.*

Theorem 32 (parallel redex application is well-defined). *Let Φ be a continuous, possibly infinite parallel redex.*

1. *If $\{t_i\}_{i<\omega}$ is any chain of terms such that $t = \cup_{i<\omega}\{t_i\}$, and such that for all $i < \omega$ the parallel redex $\Phi_i = \Phi \cap t_i$ is finite, then $\{\Phi_i(t_i)\}_{i<\omega}$ is a chain.*
2. *Definition 29 is well given, i.e., $\Phi(t)$ does not depend on the choice of the chain approximating t.*
3. *Definition 29 is consistent with the definition of finite parallel redex application (Definition 26).*

Proof. 1. We have to show that if $t \leq t'$ and both $\Phi \cap t$ and $\Phi \cap t'$ are finite, then $(\Phi \cap t)(t) \leq (\Phi \cap t')(t')$. This follows directly from Lemma 30.3, observing that $(\Phi \cap t) \subseteq (\Phi \cap t') \subseteq \Phi$.

2. Let $t \in CT_\Sigma$, and let $\{s_i\}_{i<\omega}$ and $\{t_i\}_{i<\omega}$ be two chains approximating t, such that for all $i < \omega$ both $\Phi \cap s_i$ and $\Phi \cap t_i$ are finite. Moreover, let $s' = \cup_{i<\omega}\{(\Phi\cap s_i)(s_i)\}$ and $t' = \cup_{i<\omega}\{(\Phi\cap t_i)(t_i)\}$ Then we have to show that $s' = t'$: we show just that $s' \leq t'$ (i.e., that $s'(v) = t'(v)$ for all $v \in \mathcal{O}(s')$), the converse being symmetrical.

Let $v \in \mathcal{O}(s')$. Since $s' = \cup_{i<\omega}\{(\Phi \cap s_i)(s_i)\}$, there exists a $k < \omega$ such that $v \in \mathcal{O}((\Phi \cap s_k)(s_k))$ and $(\Phi \cap s_k)(s_k)(v) = s'(v)$. By Lemma 31, there exists a finite term $\hat{s}_k \leq s_k \leq t$ such that $v \in \mathcal{O}((\Phi\cap\hat{s}_k)(\hat{s}_k))$ and $(\Phi\cap\hat{s}_k)(\hat{s}_k)(v) = (\Phi \cap s_k)(s_k)(v) = s'(v)$. Since $\hat{s}_k \leq t$ is finite, there exists an n such that $\hat{s}_k \leq t_n$, and therefore $(\Phi \cap \hat{s}_k)(\hat{s}_k) \leq (\Phi \cap t_n)(t_n)$ (by Lemma 30.3). As a consequence, $s'(v) = (\Phi \cap \hat{s}_k)(\hat{s}_k)(v) = (\Phi \cap t_n)(t_n)(v) = t'(v)$.

3. Let Φ be a finite, continuous parallel redex and let $t \in CT_\Sigma$. Let $t = \cup_{1\leq i<\omega}\{t_i\}$, and $t' = \cup_{i<\omega}\{(\Phi \cap t_i)(t_i)\}$ ($\Phi \cap t_i$ is clearly finite for all i). Then we have to show that $t' = \Phi(t)$. In fact, since Φ is finite there must exist a $k < \omega$ such that for all $k \leq j < \omega$, $\Phi \cap t_j = \Phi \cap t$. Thus $\Phi(t) = (\Phi\cap t)(t) = (\Phi\cap t_k)(\cup_{i<\omega}\{t_i\}) = (\Phi\cap t_k)(\cup_{k\leq i<\omega}\{t_i\}) = \cup_{k\leq i<\omega}\{(\Phi\cap t_k)(t_i)\} = \cup_{k\leq i<\omega}\{(\Phi \cap t_i)(t_i)\} = \cup_{i<\omega}\{(\Phi \cap t_i)(t_i)\} = t'$. $\square$

The next example shows that the continuity of Φ, required in the last theorem, is a necessary condition, at least for points 2 and 3.

Example 3. Let $\Phi = \{(\lambda, R)\}$ be a finite parallel redex, where $R = f(f(f(\ldots))) \to k$ is a left-infinite rule that, as shown in Example 2, is not continuous. Clearly, $\Phi(f^\omega) = R(f^\omega) = k$ using Definition 26. Now, let $t_i = f^\omega$ and $s_i = f^i(\bot)$ for all $1 \leq i < \omega$. Then, obviously, $\cup_{i<\omega}\{t_i\} = f^\omega = \cup_{i<\omega}\{s_i\}$, and $\Phi \cap t_i$ and $\Phi \cap s_i$ are finite for all i. Moreover, for all $i < \omega$, $\Phi(t_i) = k$ (because R is total in t_i) and $\Phi(s_i) = s_i \cap k = \bot$ (because R is partial in s_i). As a consequence, $\cup_{i<\omega}\{\Phi(t_i)\} = k$, but $\cup_{i<\omega}\{\Phi(s_i)\} = \bot$, showing that infinite parallel redex application is not well-defined if one wants to extend it to non-continuous redexes.

6   Conclusion and future work

In this paper we extended the theory of term rewriting systems to infinite and partial terms (i.e., the elements of algebra CT_Σ), fully exploiting the complete partially ordered structure of CT_Σ. By regarding redexes and rules, as well as the main operations on terms, as total functions, we studied their properties of monotonicity and continuity. For rules, we showed that non-left-linear rules are in general not monotonic, and that left-infinite rules are in general not continuous, unless the left- and right-hand sides are identical. Then we showed that the well-known Church-Rosser property of non-overlapping redexes always holds for monotonic rules. We exploited this property in order to give meaning to the parallel application of a finite set of monotonic redexes, and using standard algebraic techniques we extended the definition to the infinite case. Infinite parallel term rewriting, which is the main contribution of this paper, is well-defined if all the involved rewrite rules are continuous.

This paper is just a first step towards a complete theory of term rewriting in CT_Σ. A lot of work remains to be done in many directions. For example one should consider the extension of other classical notions of the term rewriting literature (like confluence and termination, just to mention two of them) to the setting described in this paper.

Coming back to the motivating example presented in the introduction, the author is currently working with Frank Drewes, Berthold Hoffmann and Detlef Plump of Bremen in order to show that infinite parallel term rewriting as defined here is adequate with respect to cyclic term graph rewriting. A single graph rewriting step would correspond to a single infinite parallel term rewriting step, where the same rule can be applied to an infinite ('rational') number of independent redexes. In our view this solution is more satisfactory than the one proposed for example in [KKSV90], for at least two reasons. First, finite graph derivations can be modelled by *finite* term reductions, while in [KKSV90] a finite graph derivation may correspond to an *infinite* term derivation. Second, the collapsing rules (like R_I in the Introduction) are handled in a completely uniform way in our approach, while in the mentioned paper they are treated in an ad hoc manner in many definitions and proofs.

7   Acknowledgements

The main ideas presented in this paper originated during a visit of the author at the Computer Science Department of Bremen, in stimulating discussions with Hans-Joerg Kreowski, Frank Drewes, Berthold Hoffman, and Detlef Plump. I want to thank all of them.

References

[ADJ77]   J.A. Goguen, J.W. Tatcher, E.G. Wagner, J.R. Wright, *Initial Algebra Semantics and Continuous Algebras*, JACM **24** (1), 1977, pp. 68–95.

[AN80]   A. Arnold, M. Nivat, *The metric space of infinite trees. Algebraic and topological properties*, Fundamenta Informatica, **4**, 1980, pp. 445–476.

[BvEGKPS87] H.P. Barendregt, M.C.J.D. van Eekelen, J.R.W. Glauert, J.R. Kennaway, M.J. Plasmeijer, M.R. Sleep, *Term graph reduction*, in Proc. PARLE, LNCS 259, 1987, pp. 141–158.

[CR93]   A. Corradini, F. Rossi, *Hyperedge Replacement Jungle Rewriting for Term Rewriting Systems and Logic Programming*, to appear in Theoretical Computer Science.

[DJ90]   N. Dershowitz, J.-P. Jouannaud, *Rewrite Systems*, Handbook of Theoretical Computer Science (ed. J. van Leeuwen), Vol. B, North Holland, 1990, pp. 243–320.

[DK89]   N. Dershowitz, S. Kaplan, *Rewrite, Rewrite, Rewrite, Rewrite, Rewrite ...*, Principles of Programming Languages, Austin 1989, pp. 250–259.

[DKP89]   N. Dershowitz, S. Kaplan, D.A. Plaisted, *Infinite Normal Forms (plus corrigendum)*, ICALP 1989, pp. 249–262.

[EPS73]   H. Ehrig, M. Pfender, H.J. Schneider, *Graph-grammars: an algebraic approach*, Proc, IEEE Conf. on Automata and Switching Theory, 1973, pp. 167–180.

[FRW88]   W.M. Farmer, J.D. Ramsdell, R.J. Watro, *A correcteness proof for combinator reduction with cycles*, Report M88-53, The MITRE Corporation, Massachussets, 1988.

[FW89]   W.M. Farmer, R.J. Watro, *Redex capturing in term graph rewriting*, in Computing with the Curry Chip, Report M89-59, The MITRE Corporation, Massachussets, 1989.

[HP91]   B. Hoffmann, D. Plump, *Implementing Term Rewriting by Jungle Evaluation*, in Informatique théorique et Applications/Theoretical Informatics and Applications, **25** (5), 1991, pp. 445–472.

[Hu80]   G. Huet, *Confluent Reductions: Abstract Properties and Applications to Term Rewriting Systems*, in Journal of the ACM, **27** (4), 1980, pp. 797–821.

[Ke87]   J.R. Kennaway, *On 'On Graph Rewritings'*, Theoretical Computer Science, **52**, 1987, pp. 37–58.

[KKSV90]   J.R. Kennaway, J.W. Klop, M.R. Sleep, F.J. De Vries, *Transfinite Reductions in Orthogonal Term Rewriting System*, Report CS-R9041, Centre for Mathematics and Computer Science, The Netherland, 1990.

[Kl91]   J.W. Klop, *Term rewriting systems*, to appear in Handbook of Logic in Computer Science (eds. S. Abramsky, D. Gabbay, and T. Maibaum), Vol I, Oxford University Press, 1991.

[Ra84]   J.C. Raoult, *On Graph Rewritings*, Theoretical Computer Science, **32**, 1984, pp. 1-24.

[Ros73]   B.K. Rosen, *Tree maninulating systems and Church-Rosser theorems*, JACM **20**, 1973, pp. 160–187.

Optimal Reductions in Interaction Systems*

Andrea Asperti

INRIA-Rocquencourt

Cosimo Laneve

Dip. di Informatica, Pisa

Abstract

Lamping's optimal graph reduction technique for the λ-calculus is generalized to a new class of higher order rewriting systems, called Interaction Systems. This provides a uniform description, in Lamping's style, of other basic computational constructs such as conditionals and recursion.

1 Introduction

At the end of 70's, Lévy fixed the theoretical performance of what should be considered as an optimal implementation of the λ-calculus. The optimal evaluator should always keep *shared* those redexes in a λ-expression that have a common origin (e.g. that are copies of the same redex). For a long time, no implementation achieved Lévy's performance (see [5] for a quick survey). Only recently Lamping and Kathail have solved independently the problem [14,9].

Unfortunately, both the theoretical studies by Lévy and Lamping-Kathail's evaluators take under consideration only the pure λ-calculus. This is a great limitation from the point of view of Computer Science, since essential operators as *conditionals* and *recursion* are left definitely out (in general, δ-rules: see [3], chapter 15).

The main aim of this paper is to provide optimal implementations for a much wider class of rewriting systems. In order to define the performance of the optimal evaluators of such a class we need to generalize the theoretical studies in [16]. This is particularly heavy. Here we prefer to survey rather briefly about this issue, focusing much more on the implementative aspects. See [2,15] for detailed presentations of the theory.

(*Interaction Systems*) The class of rewriting systems we are going to analyze in this paper became apparent to us by studying implementative issues. In particular, the remarkable settlement of Lamping's evaluator by Gonthier, Abadi and Lévy [7,8]. Roughly, these works establish a correspondence between Lamping's optimal implementation of λ-calculus and Girard's implementation of λ-calculus into *proof nets* [6], thus providing a (*linear*) logic foundation of Lamping's *control operators*. Such foundation made clear that λ-calculus could be split into two distinct parts: one, the *linear part*, defining the operators of the calculus (e.g. the arity, the "binding power", etc.) and the other taking care of the *management of resources* (or, better, of subexpressions). Therefore it seemed that Lamping-Gonthier's evaluation style could be *smoothly generalized* to a

---

*Supported in part by the ESPRIT Basic Research Project 6454 - CONFER

large class of systems just by replacing the "linear part" with an arbitrary linear (intuitionistic) calculus.

Let us explain the paradigm we have in mind. Take a generic set of logical operators. An intuitionistic presentation consists of a set of rules managing sequents of the shape $A_1, \cdots, A_n \vdash B$. Roughly, these rules are partitioned into two sub-classes, according to the introduction of the logical operator happens on the left of the entail or on the right. This partition is reflected in the *language of the proofs*, too. Thus, there are proofs operators which correspond to introduction of a logical connective to the left of the entail (*destructors*) and to the right (*constructors*). As it is well-known from the Curry-Howard analogy, a rule can be simplified by *eliminating cuts* (interactions between destructors and constructors of a logical connective). These simplifications are usually formalized by means of *rewriting rules*, where left hand sides (lhs's, in brief) mention exactly the destructor/constructor pair yielding the cut. The calculi that result have a higher order nature since functional symbols own a "binding power" over their arguments (think about λ-abstraction).

The *linear* versions of intuitionistic calculi have already been studied in literature by Lafont [11] and named *Interaction Nets* (shortened into IN's). Therefore, we are just dropping the linearity constraint of IN's. In order to recall this strict analogy, we have named our systems Interaction Systems (IS's, in brief).

The higher order nature of IS's makes them a sub-class of Klop's Combinatory Reduction Systems [10,1] (CRS's). In particular, IS's are CRS's where the Curry-Howard analogy still "makes sense". In [2] we have deepened the relations between Interaction Systems, Interaction Nets and CRS's.

(*Optimal evaluators*) The logical nature of Interaction Systems is at the basis of the optimal evaluators we shall provide. In particular, let L be the intuitionistic logic associated with an IS. We can define a "linear logic" version of L. That is, we may define a new system L_{LL} by just replacing the structural part of L with its "counterpart" in Linear Logic (i.e. giving to weakening and contraction a "logical status" by means the operators *why not* and *of course*). Then, L can be embedded into L_{LL} in essentially the same way that Intuitionistic Logic is embedded into (Intuitionistic) Linear Logic. So, by using the optimal implementation of *boxes* defined in [8], we get an optimal implementation of the original IS's.

A particular care is needed for implementing rewriting rules, since right hand sides (shortened into rhs's) must be "linearized" w.r.t. the metavariables. This is not a problem for the λ-calculus because the two metavariables occur exactly once in the rhs of the β-reduction. But, in general, this is false. For instance, as in the conditionals, a metavariable can be erased by the rule (it does not appear in the rhs). In order to preserve the *locality* of the (graph) rewriting, we must attach at the positive port of the metavariable a node performing the erasing. The rule defining the recursion operator duplicates a metavariable. Obviously, duplication invalidates optimality, since redexes internal to the expression represented by the metavariable are duplicated, too. Thus we must keep shared the duplicated expressions. The linear form of the rhs will be yielded by writing them in a substitution-free shape (by means of pseudo-operations of abstraction and application) and partially evaluating it.

We emphasize that the rewriting system describing the optimal implementation of an IS is an Interaction Net. That is, we are providing (optimal) implementations of IS's into IN's, thus eliminating variables from symbolic computations. This generalizes recent works of Burroni [4] and Lafont [12] to higher order rewriting systems.

As much as possible we shall avoid any reference to Interaction Nets and Linear Logic. However [8] is a prerequisite for a deep understanding of the evaluators.

2   Interaction Systems

An Interaction System is defined by a *signature* Σ and a set of *rewriting rules* R.

(**The signature**) The signature Σ consists of a denumerable set of *variables* and a set of *forms*. The set of forms is partitioned into two disjoint sets Σ^+ and Σ^-, representing *constructors* (ranged over by **c**) and *destructors* (ranged over by **d**). Variables will be ranged over by $x, y, z, \cdots$, possibly indexed. Vectors of variables will be denoted by $\vec{x}_i$ where i is the length of the vector (often omitted).

Each form can work as a binder. This means that in the arity of the form we must specify not only the number of arguments, but also, for each argument, the number of variables it is supposed to bind. Thus, the *arity* of a form **f**, is a finite (possibly empty) sequence of naturals (and not, as usual, a natural!). Moreover, we have the constraint that the arity of every destructor $\mathbf{d} \in \Sigma^-$ has a leading 0 (i.e., it cannot bind over its first argument). The reason for this restriction is that, in Lafont's notation [11], at the first argument we find the *principal port* of the destructor, that is the (unique) port where we will have interaction.

Expressions, ranged over by $t, t_1, \cdots$, are inductively generated by the two rules below:

a. every variable is an expression;

b. if **f** is a form of arity $k_1 \cdots k_n$ and $t_1, \cdots, t_n$ are expressions then
$\mathbf{f}(\vec{x}_{k_1}^1 . t_1, \cdots, \vec{x}_{k_n}^n . t_n)$ is an expression.

Free and bound occurrences of variables are defined in the obvious way. As usual, we will identify terms up to renaming of bound variables (α-conversion).

(**The rewriting rules**) Rewriting rules are described by using schemas or *metaexpressions*. A metaexpression is an expression built up also with *metavariables*, ranged over by $X, Y, \cdots$, possibly indexed (see [1] for more details). Metaexpressions will be denoted by $H, H_1 \cdots$.

A *rewriting rule* is a pair of metaexpressions, written $H_1 \rightarrow H_2$, where H_1 (the *left hand side* of the rule, lhs for short) has the following format

$$\mathbf{d}(\mathbf{c}(\vec{x}_{k_1}^1 . X_1, \cdots, \vec{x}_{k_m}^m . X_m), \cdots, \vec{x}_{k_n}^n . X_n)$$

and $i \neq j$ implies $X_i \neq X_j$ (*left linearity*). The arity of **d** is $0 k_{m+1} \cdots k_n$ and that of **c** is $k_1 \cdots k_m$.

The *right hand side* H_2 (rhs, for short) is every *closed* metaexpression, whose metavariables are already in the lhs and built up by the following syntax

$$H \quad ::= \quad x \quad | \quad \mathbf{f}(\vec{x}_{a_1}^1 . H_1, \cdots, \vec{x}_{a_j}^j . H_j) \quad | \quad X_i[^{H_1}/_{x_1^i}, \cdots, ^{H_{k_i}}/_{x_{k_i}^i}]$$

The expression $X[^{H_1}/_{x_1}, \cdots, ^{H_n}/_{x_n}]$ denotes a meta-operation of substitution, as in the λ-calculus.

Finally, the set of rewriting rules must be *non-ambiguous*, i.e. there exists at most one rewriting rule for every pair d-c.

Example 2.1 (The λ-calculus) We have a destructor @ of arity 00, and a constructor λ of arity 1. The only rewriting rule is β-reduction:

$$@(\lambda(x.X), Y) \rightarrow X[^Y/_x].$$ ■

Example 2.2 Interesting Interaction Systems can be defined by enriching the λ-calculus with "δ-rules". For instance, it is possible to extend the λ-calculus with an *if-then-else* operator $\natural$. Let T and F be two (new) constructors of arity ε, and $\natural$ be a destructor of arity 000. The rules for the conditional are described by the following interactions between $\natural$ and T or F:

$$\natural(\mathbf{T}, X, Y) \rightarrow X$$

$$\natural(\mathbf{F}, X, Y) \rightarrow Y$$

Note that we do not have any interaction between $\natural$ and λ.

A less trivial example is provided by the recursion operator μ. We may describe it as a destructor of arity 0, interacting with λ as follows:

$$\mu(\lambda(x.X)) \rightarrow X[^{\mu(\lambda(y.X[^y/_x]))}/_x]$$

Note that the μ and the λ in the rhs have nothing to do with those in the lhs. ■

2.1 Graphical representations

Expressions of Interaction Systems have graphical representations that are reminiscents of Lafont's Interaction Nets. In particular, a form $\mathbf{f}$ of arity $k_1 \ldots k_n$ is represented as a node of name $\mathbf{f}$ with $1 + \sum_{i=1}^n p_i$ ports (edges); $p_i = k_i + 1$ is the i-th *partition* of $\mathbf{f}$. The only port which does not belong to a partition is drawn with an outgoing arrow, and it is called the *principal port* of the form $\mathbf{f}$; the other entries are called *auxiliary ports* (see [11]). The i-th partition represents the connections between $\mathbf{f}$ and its i-th argument M. In particular, one connection is with the root of M, and k_i with the variables bound by $\mathbf{f}$. Observe that bound variables correspond to ports of the form $\mathbf{f}$. Thus our graphs are cyclic. If $\mathbf{f}$ is a constructor, the principal port is "at the root" of the form; if $\mathbf{f}$ is a destructor, its principal port is at its first argument (recall tha t no binding is possible over this argument). So, interaction between constructors and destructors takes place only at principal ports (local sequentiality).

The correspondence between ports, bound variables and body of the arguments is fixed once and for all for each form. Thi s means that all ports of a given form should be suitably "marked" (for the sake of readability, we shall generally omit to do that). For example the graphical representation of $\mathbf{c}(\langle x_1, x_2 \rangle. \mathbf{d}(x_1), \langle y \rangle. \mathbf{g}(y, y))$ is illustrated in Figure 1.(a). Variables which are not bound will be depicted as dangling edges whose ends are labeled by the name of the variables. This is the case for the variables u and v in the λ-term $(\lambda x.(xu)(xv))(\lambda y.y)$ depicted in Figure 1.(b). We recall that, in this way, several edges may have a common end, due to the multiple occurrence of a free variable in an expression.

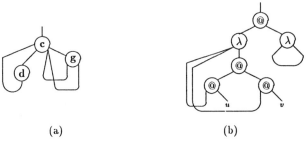

(a)   (b)

Figure 1: Graphical representations of expressions

The reader is referred to [2] for more details about the graphical representation. A lot of examples will be found in the following pages.

3   Labelling and the family relation

This section is devoted to the generalization of Lévy's labeling [16] from λ-calculus to arbitrary Interaction Systems. Labelling allows us to define the family relation, that is the kind of "optimal" sharing the implementation should support.

Definition 3.1 Let $L = \{a, b, \cdots\}$ be a countable set of *atomic labels*. The set **L** of *labels*, ranged over by $\alpha, \beta, \cdots$ is defined by the following rules:

$$L \mid \alpha\beta \mid (\alpha)_s$$

where $s \in I\!N^+$. The operation of concatenation $\alpha\beta$ will be assumed *associative*. ∎

Although its formalization is a bit entangled, the idea behind the following labeling is very simple. When a redex is fired, a label α is captured between the destructor and the constructor; this is the label associated with the redex. Then, the rhs of the rewriting rule must be suitably "marked" with α, in order to keep a trace of the history of the creation. Moreover, since in the rhs we may introduce new forms, we must guarantee a property similar to the initial labeling, where all labels are different. This means that all links in the rhs must be marked with a different function of α (and we shall use sequences of integers, for this purpose).

Let us come to the formal definition. Every IS (Σ, R) can be turned in a free way into a (*labeled*) CRS (Σ^L, R^L).

The forms of Σ^L are those in $\Sigma \cup L$ with the arity of every $\alpha \in L$ equal to 0. If

$$\mathbf{d}(\mathbf{c}(\vec{x}^{\,1}.X_1, \cdots, \vec{x}^{\,m}.X_m), \cdots, \vec{x}^{\,n}.X_n) \;\rightarrow\; H$$

is a rule in R then, for every i and for every i-tuple $\alpha_1, \cdots \alpha_i$, the rule

$$\mathbf{d}(\alpha_1(\cdots(\alpha_i(\mathbf{c}(\vec{x}^{\,1}.X_1, \cdots, \vec{x}^{\,m}.X_m)\cdots), \cdots, \vec{x}^{\,n}.X_n) \;\rightarrow\; \mathcal{L}^0_{\alpha_1 \cdots \alpha_i}(H)$$

belongs to R^L, where $\mathcal{L}^s_\alpha$ is defined over metaexpressions as follows

$$\mathcal{L}_\alpha^s(x) = (\alpha)_s(x)$$

$$\mathcal{L}_\alpha^s(\mathsf{f}(\vec{x}^0. H_0, \cdots, \vec{x}^m. H_m)) = (\alpha)_s(\mathsf{f}(\vec{x}^0. \mathcal{L}_\alpha^{s0}(H_0), \cdots, \vec{x}^m. \mathcal{L}_\alpha^{sm}(H_m))$$

$$\mathcal{L}_\alpha^s(X[^{H_0}/_{x_0}, \cdots, ^{H_n}/_{x_n}]) = (\alpha)_s(X[^{\mathcal{L}_\alpha^{s0}(H_0)}/_{x_0}, \cdots, ^{\mathcal{L}_\alpha^{sn}(H_n)}/_{x_n}])$$

Example 3.2 Consider again the λ-calculus. The β-reduction $@(\lambda(x.X), Y) \to X[^Y/_x]$ gives rise, in the labeled version, to the following rules:

$$@(\alpha_1(\cdots(\alpha_i(\lambda(x.X)\cdots), Y) \to \mathcal{L}_\ell^0(X[^Y/_x])$$

where $\ell = \alpha_1 \cdots \alpha_i$. Note that, by definition, $\mathcal{L}_\ell^0(X[^Y/_x]) = (\ell)_0(X[^{(\ell)_{00}(Y)}/_x])$, therefore, by replacing ℓ_0 with $\overline{\ell}$ and ℓ_{00} with $\underline{\ell}$, we easily recognize Lévy's labeling. ∎

Labeled expressions are depicted by the same standard as unlabeled ones, with the agreement to write labels besides edges connecting forms.

Let (Σ, R) be an IS and let (Σ^L, R^L) be the labeled CRS built in the way described above. Given a form f in Σ and an occurrence of it in a term t of Σ^L, we say that f has *label* $\alpha_1 \alpha_2 \cdots \alpha_i$ if, in the syntactic tree of t, $\alpha_1 \alpha_2 \cdots \alpha_i$ is the path towards the root which links f to the less outside form in Σ (or to the root). The *degree* of a redex u is the label of the constructor (i.e. the sequence of the labels between the pair of symbols d-c of the redex u).

Definition 3.3 Two redexes are *in a same family* if and only if their degrees are the same. ∎

This approach to the notion of redex-family based on labels does not give much insights about the intuitions that are behind. There are other equivalent approaches, suggested by the case of λ-calculus [16,17]. The relations among them have been discussed in detail in [2,15].

4 Sharing graphs

Let us switch to the optimal implementation of IS's. As remarked in the Introduction, the aim is to share along derivations redexes that are in the same family. This is yielded by enriching graphical representation of expressions with control operators. Such operators are described in Figure 2 and must be considered as forms. This means that each node has a principal port of

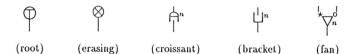

| (root) | (erasing) | (croissant) | (bracket) | (fan) |

Figure 2: The control operators

interaction. In Figure 2, the principal ports are always the lower edges.

To be formal, croissants brackets and fans are of two types, according to the polarity of their principal port. When the polarity of (the principal port of) the fan is negative then the node is called *fan-in*; when the polarity is positive, the fan is named *fan-out*. Fans are the main nodes for implementing sharing. Let us see an example. In Figure 3, we have depicted the λ-expression $@(@(M, N), @(M, N'))$ through a sharing graph. The reader should be wondering why this graph represents the expression $@(@(M, N), @(M, N'))$. Actually the reading back of the sharing graphs is the foremost problem. So let us try to retrieve the original expression. As usual with graphical representations, we start from the root and try to recover the expression by traveling along the graph. Well, the first node we meet is $@$. So the original expression must have the form $@(X, Y)$. In order to recover X, we travel along the left branch of the $@$. During this trip, we find the $\star$-branch of the fan-in. Keep this information in mind! Continue the trip (fan nodes are discarded by the read-back procedure: they do not appear in the syntactic expression). We reach a new node $@$, thus X has the form $@(X_1, X_2)$. The subexpression X_1 is found immediately in the left branch of the lower $@$: it is M. The expression X_2 is less obvious.

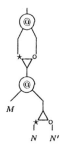

Figure 3: The sharing graph representation of a λ-expression

Traveling along the right branch of $@$ we reach a fan-out node. What branch we must choose? Well, remember that the last time we traversed a fan-in, we went into a $\star$-branch. So we decide that the right answer has to be "the $\star$-branch of the fan out". This answer gives N as second argument of the lower $@$ and, notice, this agrees with the original expression. Now we must determinate Y. By traveling along the right branch of the higher $@$, we are obliged to enter the o-branch of the fan-in. Now, it should be clear that, when we shall reach the paired fan-out, we shall choice the o-branch. Therefore we yield the original expression.

Summing up, the distinction between branches of fan-nodes is essential to recover correctly the original λ-expression. However it is not powerful enough to solve any possible situation that could rise computing λ-expressions (e.g. matching correctly fan-ins and fan-outs). Therefore the introduction of other control operators as brackets and croissants (see [14]).

Brackets and croissants have a simple linear logic explanation: the firsts implement boxes, the latters are used for disintegrating boxes. This should not scare too much the reader since we are encoding intuitionistic systems into linear logic systems, thus we need to implement every mechanism of the latters. An alternative way for understanding the meaning of brackets and croissants is as *context transformers*, i.e. as "transformers" of the information that is needed to travel correctly along the sharing graph. For example, the presence of indexes besides the operators indicates the *depth* where the transformation takes place. We strongly recommend the reading of Section 6 or the corresponding section in [13,14].

The rules governing the interactions between control operators are drawn in Figure 4.

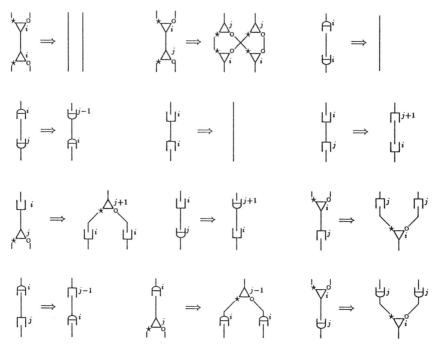

Figure 4: The control rules $(0 \leq i < j)$

The root and void nodes are respectively attached to the "important" and "unimportant" dangling edges of the graph. The important edges are the root and the free variables; the useless edges are those parts of the graph that have been discarded along the derivation. Indeed, the main purpose of erasing is to connect part of the graph that are erased by a contraction in order to preserve locality of the rewriting rules. We could add rules providing garbage collection (mainly involving the erasing node), but these do not eliminate all garbage and are not essential for correctness. So we omit them.

5   Implementation

Now we have all the preliminaries to provide the implementation of a generic IS. Actually, the evaluators are Interaction Nets. But we will not be fussy on this point. So, more genericly, the optimal implementations are graph rewriting systems where the nodes are the control operators and the forms of the IS. The translation of IS-expressions is discussed in Subsection 5.1 below. Subsection 5.2 will deal with the rewriting rules.

5.1 The translation of expressions

Let us translate an arbitrary expression in sharing graph. We shall essentially follow [8], that is particularly clear.

For simplicity, we shall only consider the paradigmatic case when constructors and destructors have respectively arity 1 and 01. The other cases are easily derived. The translation is a function $\mathcal{T}$, inductively defined in Figure 5. In this figure, the dangling edges in the bottom represent

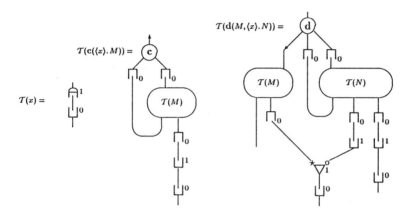

Figure 5: The translation function $\mathcal{T}$

generic free variables which are not bound by the forms **c** and **d**. In particular, the edge outgoing the 1-indexed fan-in, represents a free variable which is common to M and N. If some bound variable does not occur in the body, the corresponding port of the binder is a plug, as usually. The above translation is a clear consequence of the linear logic implementation in [8] and the use of a type $(!D) \multimap D$. For instance, a variable x represents an axiom whose negative edge has been derelicted. The composition of these two operations, according to [8], yields the sharing graph $\mathcal{T}(x)$ of Figure 5. The introduction of a form needs a previous step in which the body is "protected" by !. This because, unlike λ-calculus, the body of a binder can be used in a non linear way by the rewriting rule. Here a peculiarity deserves to be emphasized: the effect of !-introduction is not felt by bound variables. Actually, we are assuming the presence of a pseudo-binder in between the form and the body as drawn below:

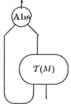

So, when we perform the !-introduction and the c-introduction, we yield:

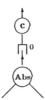

That is as the constructor had no bound variable! Since the pseudo-binder is a ghost, it disappears, the bracket traverses it and we obtain the translation of Figure 5. The reasons for this stuff will be clear when we will implement rewriting rules of the IS. In that moment the ghost-binder will become apparent and will play an essential role in the partial evaluation providing the correct rhs's.

Notice also that the first argument of the destructor is not inside an of-course operation. This because destructors always behave linearly w.r.t. their principal port (it will be the outermost form inside its first argument that will "take care" of its arguments).

5.2 The translation of rewriting rules

Rewriting rules may be classified in three groups.

Control Rules. These are the 12 rules in Figure 4

Interfacing Rules. These are the rules which describe the interaction between control operators and forms of the syntax. Therefore, for every form **f** and control operator there is a rule schema. They are drawn in Figure 6. Notice the constraint $i > 0$. It follows from the interpretation of forms

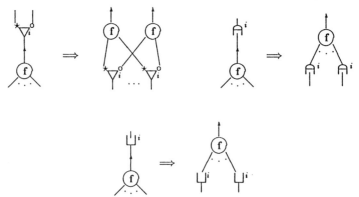

Figure 6: The interfacing rules between control operators and forms ($i > 0$)

as "generalized fans", namely forms properly combine the informations over their ports and "make connections" when they interact. This view completely fit with that in [7,8] where abstraction and application are 0-indexed fans. Lamping has a much more "syntactical" interpretation of forms, thus needing a further control operator in order to fulfil to correctness [13,14].

Proper Rules. These rules describe the interactions between destructors and constructors of the IS's. These are the only rules which are dependent from the particular Interaction System under investigation. We shall define the implementation of the rewriting rules in several steps.

Let R be an IS-rewriting rule. Foremost, we must put the rhs of R in a suitable form, in order to emphasize the "interface" between the new structure introduced in the rhs and the metavariables in its lhs.

(β-expansion) The first step is to β-expand all substitutions in the rhs. For this purpose we shall use two classes of *pseudo-forms*: abstraction $\mathbf{Abs}_n$ and application $\mathbf{App}_n$, for $n \geq 0$. These pseudo-forms must be considered similar to other forms of the syntax. $\mathbf{Abs}_n$ is a constructor of arity n whilst $\mathbf{App}_n$ is a destructor of arity 0^{n+1}. As the reader suspects, they generalize λ-calculus abstraction and application. This is clear looking at the rewriting rule:

$$\mathbf{App}_n(\mathbf{Abs}_n(\langle x_1, \cdots, x_n \rangle . X), Y_1, \cdots, Y_n) \longrightarrow X[^{Y_1}/_{x_1}, \cdots, ^{Y_n}/_{x_n}]$$

In the following we shall always omit the index 1 in $\mathbf{Abs}_1$ and $\mathbf{App}_1$.

So, the step of β-expansion consists simply of writing the rhs of the IS-rule without using the metaoperation of substitution and exploiting pseudo-forms $\mathbf{Abs}_n$ and $\mathbf{App}_n$.

Example 5.1 Consider the rewriting rule for μ:

$$\mu(\lambda(\langle x \rangle . X)) \to X[^{\mu(\lambda(\langle y \rangle . X[^y/_x]))}/_x]$$

The β-expansion of the rhs gives the following term:

$$\mathbf{App}(\mathbf{Abs}(\langle x \rangle . X), \mu(\lambda(\langle y \rangle . \mathbf{App}(\mathbf{Abs}(\langle x \rangle . X), y)))) \qquad \blacksquare$$

Note that, after the β-expansion, every metavariable is closed by a pseudo binders, i.e. they are into expressions of the shape $\mathbf{Abs}_n(\vec{x}. X)$.

(linearization) The next step relies on *linearizing* the rhs w.r.t. the occurrences of expressions $\mathbf{Abs}_n(\vec{x}. X)$. This is obtained by taking, for every metavariable X_i, a fresh *pseudo-variable* w_i and replacing every occurrence of $\mathbf{Abs}_n(\vec{x}^i. X_i)$ with w_i. In this way we yield a metaexpression T. Next T must be closed w.r.t. metavariables w_i's. So, let $w_{i_1}, \cdots, w_{i_k}$ be the metavariables *occurring* in T. The linearization step ends by giving the metaexpression

$$\mathbf{App}_k(\mathbf{Abs}_k(\langle w_{i_1}, \cdots, w_{i_k} \rangle . T), \mathbf{Abs}_{n_1}(\vec{x}^1. X_{i_1}), \cdots, \mathbf{Abs}_{n_k}(\vec{x}^k. X_{i_k}))$$

where n_j is the arity of the metavariable X_{i_j}.

Example 5.2 After the linearization step, the rhs of the recursion rule becomes:

$$\mathbf{App}(\mathbf{Abs}(\langle w \rangle . \mathbf{App}(w, \mu(\lambda(\langle y \rangle . \mathbf{App}(w, y))))), \mathbf{Abs}(\langle x \rangle . X)) \qquad \blacksquare$$

(**translation**) This step provides the graphical representation of the rhs of the rule. It is essential that, during the translation, we may consider each subexpression $\mathbf{Abs}_n(\vec{x}.X)$ as a "black-box". According to the linearization step, the expression that results will have the shape $\mathbf{App}_k(M, \mathbf{Abs}_{n_1}(\vec{x}^1.X_{i_1}), \cdots, \mathbf{Abs}_{n_k}(\vec{x}^k.X_{i_k}))$. The translation of this expression is drawn in Figure 7, where, for simplicity, we have assumed $n_i = 1$, for every i. Notice that metavariables

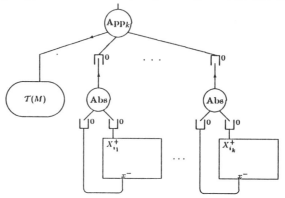

Figure 7: The translation step

are not inside boxes: they are already internal to boxes, due to the translation of expressions in Figure 5, and we use this box instead of building a new box around the argument of the application. In this way, no operation around the (unaccessible!) free variables of the instance of the metavariable can be performed.

Now it is possible to gain much more intuition about our translation in Figure 5. Let us see that the trick of the ghost-binder allows us to have a much efficient implementation (in terms of the amount of control operators that are used). Take an expression $\mathbf{Abs}(\vec{x}.X)$. The 0-indexed bracket along the principal edge of the **Abs** in Figure 7 must be considered as the "lifting" of the box that surround the metavariable. This means that the effect of the outermost box in X along the output of X and the bound ports must be undone. This is easy for the output, since it is enough to introduce a closed 0-indexed bracket along the auxiliary negative port of the **Abs**. Let us see what happens for the bound edges. Suppose to give up the "ghost-binders" in the translation of Figure 5. Then, the following sequence Υ of control operators should face the bound ports: an open 0-indexed bracket, an open 1-indexed bracket and a closed 0-indexed bracket. In order to cancel such sequence we should introduce a "dual" sequence of control operators and prove that the closed 0-indexed bracket in Υ disappears due to the interaction with a 0-indexed bracket in X. It is clear that the resulting translation step is less efficient (and less obvious).

The partial evaluation can begin as soon as we generalize the translation function $\mathcal{T}$ to pseudo abstractions and pseudo applications. The usual (call by name) interpretation of **Abs** and **App** can be found in Figure 8.

Remark the absence of brackets around the argument of **Abs**: in ordinary β-reduction, there is a linear use of the body of the abstraction.

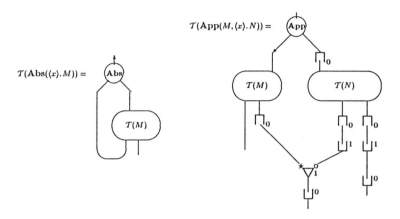

Figure 8: The generalization of the translation function $\mathcal{T}$

A final remark before discussing about the partial evaluation. Some metavariable in the lhs of the IS-rewriting rule could not occur in the rhs. That is the corresponding expression is erased by the rule. This is implemented by taking every metavariable X_r not appearing in the rhs and adding the graph in Figure 9.(a) to Figure 7. Figure 9.(b) shows what happens when an

(a)   (b)

Figure 9: Erasings performed by rewriting rules

expression t replacing a metavariable does not contain an occurrence of a bound variable x_i (so, the bound port of the corresponding binder is a plug). Namely, an erasing node is introduced which allows to erase every subexpression replacing x_i.

The final step is to partially evaluate the term we have obtained after the translation w.r.t. all pseudo operators. Recall that the reduction rule for pseudo application and abstraction is

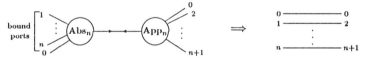

The case $n = 0$ is rather interesting. Here the rewriting rule simply consists of connecting the two edges coming into non principal ports of $\mathbf{Abs_0}$ and $\mathbf{App_0}$.

It is easy to show that the partial evaluation of the expressions yielded by the translation step strongly normalizes to a graph without pseudo-forms.

Example 5.3 By applying the previous technique (and some optimizations not worth discussing) we obtain the implementation of the rhs of the rule concerning μ illustrated in Figure 10.   ∎

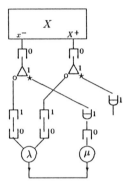

Figure 10: The graphical representation of the rhs of the rule firing μ-λ

Remark 5.4 The previous translation could (and must) be improved. Apart from studying optimization techniques for reducing the number of sharing operators, the translation should be *relativized* to the particular IS's under investigation. In particular, some operators of the syntax could make only a linear use of some of their arguments. For instance, this is the case of the λ-calculus, where the body of the abstraction is treated linearly in β-reduction. These linear arguments have a simpler translation, since there is no need to put them inside a "box". Furthermore, remark that the decision that some operator **f** behaves linearly over an argument needs the examination of *all* the interaction rules involving **f**. ■

6   Correctness and optimality

The evaluators we have defined are correct and optimal w.r.t. the Interaction Systems they implement. We have not space to deepen these issues, so, here, we will hint briefly to some problems we have found. We refer the reader to [15] or to the full paper for a complete discussion.

Let G be a sharing graph representing an IS-expression t. Correctness relies on showing that performing a graph-rewriting $G \rightarrow G'$ does simulate a set of IS-rewritings $t \longrightarrow t'$ such that t' is the expression represented by G'. It is clear that determinating the expression represented by a sharing graph is a prerequisite for any arguing about correctness. This is the so called *read-back* problem. It is solved in [13,7,8] by labeling edges of the sharing graphs through *contexts* and interpreting control operators (and forms in [7,8]) as *contexts transformers*. Expressions matching the sharing graphs are thus "unfoldings" of the graphs where only *consistent paths* are considered, that is paths that behave well w.r.t. contexts.

Due to the generality of the shape of IS-rewriting rules, the notion of consistent path must be further refined w.r.t. that in the λ-calculus. Actually, a contraction can create new forms and new edges (thus new paths). So, in general, a consistent path traversing a proper redex can be disconnected after a proper rewriting, thus invalidating any property of consistency. Therefore we have restricted consistent paths in order to avoid crossings of proper redexes. As a consequence, the read-back procedure $\mathcal{R}$ is more involved w.r.t. that in [14].

Theorem 6.1 The implementation $\mathcal{T}$ is correct. That is, if N is a graph yielded by a derivation starting at $\mathcal{T}(t)$ then:

(A) $N \longrightarrow N'$ implies $\mathcal{R}(N) \longrightarrow\!\!\!\!\rightarrow \mathcal{R}(N')$;

(B) N in normal form implies that also $\mathcal{R}(N)$ is in normal form. ∎

Optimality is proved by showing that, if two redexes yielded by a labeled derivation have the same label, then the read-back function identifies them, that is they have the same representation in the sharing graph. The proof goes along the same lines of that in [13].

Theorem 6.2 In every derivation no two redexes destructor-constructor have the same label. Therefore the graph implementation is optimal. ∎

7 Conclusions

We have generalized Lamping's optimal graph-reduction technique [14] to Interaction Systems, thus covering all the basic constructs of a real programming language. The main point of IS's w.r.t. optimality, is that it is particularly simple to "interface" the forms of the syntax with Lamping-Gonthier's control operators.

An interesting problem remains open: the efficiency. That is the amount of control operators that are used in the general approach suggested in this chapter (in order to linearize rewriting rules, in particular). These control operators cause an heavy overhead in terms of the number of control and interfacing reductions, that jeopardize optimality. For instance, take λ-calculus. According to our technique, the usual β-reduction, that does not exploits any control operator in [14,7,8], is turned into a rule with two control operators in between the external context and the functional part and six control operators in between the functional part and the argument part. That is, we gain in generality but we loose in efficiency. We suggest, case by case, to improve the translation (see also Remark 5.4).

An alternative approach relies on extending the *bus notation* ([7]) to IS's. Indeed, this notation is particularly appealing for an actual implementation, since it enormously reduces the number of "mutual crossing" between control operators.

Recently, Burroni [4] and Lafont [12] have refined usual term rewriting systems by explicitly managing variables with control operators. The advantage is that symbolic computations can be rid of variables. In this respect, our (optimal) graph implementations seem the natural generalization of Burroni-Lafont's works to higher order rewriting systems. The richer set of control operators is justifiable for coping with situations created by the mechanisms of binding and substitution.

Acknowledgements: We would like to thank J.J.Lévy and G.Gonthier for the interesting discussions and their relevant suggestions. Cosimo Laneve would like to thank INRIA for its warm hospitality during his permanence in Spring 1992.

References

[1] P. Aczel. A general church-rosser theorem. Draft, Manchester, 1978.

[2] A. Asperti and C. Laneve. Interaction systems 1: The theory of optimal reductions. Technical report n. 1748, INRIA-Rocquencourt, Septembre 1992.

[3] H.P. Barendregt. *The Lambda Calculus*. North-Holland, 1985.

[4] A. Burroni. Higher dimensional word problems. In *Category Theory and Computer Science*, volume 530 of *Lecture Notes in Computer Science*, pages 94 – 105. Springer-Verlag, 1991.

[5] J. Field. On laziness and optimality in lambda interpreters: tools for specification and analysis. In *Proceedings 17th ACM Symposium on Principles of Programmining Languages*, pages 1 – 15, 1990.

[6] J. Y. Girard. Linear logic. *Theoretical Computer Science*, 50, 1986.

[7] G. Gonthier, M. Abadi, and J.J. Lévy. The geometry of optimal lambda reduction. In *Proceedings 19th ACM Symposium on Principles of Programmining Languages*, page ??, 1992.

[8] G. Gonthier, M. Abadi, and J.J. Lévy. Linear logic without boxes. In *Proceedings 7th Annual Symposium on Logic in Computer Science*, page ??, 1992.

[9] V. Kathail. *Optimal Interpreters for lambda-calculus based functional languages*. PhD thesis, MIT, 1990.

[10] J. W. Klop. *Combinatory Reduction System*. PhD thesis, Mathematisch Centrum, Amsterdam, 1980.

[11] Y. Lafont. Interaction nets. In *Proceedings 17th ACM Symposium on Principles of Programmining Languages*, pages 95 – 108, 1990.

[12] Y. Lafont. Penrose diagrams and 2-dimensional rewritings. In *LMS Symposium on Applications of Categories in Computer Science*. Cambridge University Press, 1992.

[13] J. Lamping. An algorithm for optimal lambda calculus reductions. Technical report, Xerox PARC, 1989.

[14] J. Lamping. An algorithm for optimal lambda calculus reductions. In *Proceedings 17th ACM Symposium on Principles of Programmining Languages*, pages 16 – 30, 1990.

[15] C. Laneve. *Optimality and Concurrency in Interaction Systems*. PhD thesis, Dip. Informatica, Università di Pisa, December 1992.

[16] J.J. Lévy. *Réductions correctes et optimales dans le lambda calcul*. PhD thesis, Université Paris VII, 1978.

[17] J.J. Lévy. Optimal reductions in the lambda-calculus. In J.P. Seldin and J.R. Hindley, editors, *To H.B. Curry, Essays on Combinatory Logic, Lambda Calculus and Formalism*, pages 159 – 191. Academic Press, 1980.

Optimal Solutions to Pattern Matching Problems

Laurence Puel[1] and Ascánder Suárez[2]

[1] LRI. URA 410 du CNRS
bat 490, Université Paris Sud
91405 Orsay, FRANCE

[2] LIENS. URA 1327 du CNRS
Ecole Normale Supérieure
45, Rue d'Ulm
75005 Paris, FRANCE

Abstract. We define a *General Pattern Matching problem* and we show that several compiling problems in programming languages, like pattern Matching in ML and the calling mechanism of Prolog can be formalized as instances of the General Pattern Matching problem. As a consequence of this, the solutions of the general problem which are compiling algorithms can be instantiated into compiling algorithms for the instances. In particular, the proof of the decidability of the existence of optimal solutions is a proof of the decidability of the instances. This approach can be used for the meta-compilation of pattern-matching problems, for the implementation of languages or systems that contain different instances of the general problem and for the implementation of systems using *Call by Name* style of evaluation for which completeness and optimality are equivalent.

Introduction

In 1979 Huet and Lévy [1, 2] proposed a method for the compilation of pattern matching problem with linear non ambiguous patterns. In 1988 Laville[4, 5] adapted this result for the matching of linear pattern with priority rule for disambiguation. In 1990 Puel and Suárez [7] extended Huet and Lévy results for a family of terms called constrained terms in order to solve the call by pattern matching problem of the compilation of the language ML.

In this work, we propose a generalization of the pattern matching defined in [1] and a compilation algorithm. We define and prove properties of sequentiality and optimality of this algorithm. We check the correspondence between the notion of sequentiality in [1] and here.

After this theoretical results, we show how the problem addressed in [1] can be seen as a particular case of our general pattern matching problem. Finally, we show how to use this results in practice in order to build compilers of matching primitives of programming languages. Two kinds of instances of the matching problem are defined. Those based on the matching of terms and those based on unification. We check the inheritance of the general result of sequentiality and optimality for these instances.

1 Terms and Constraints

Definition 1 *Let Σ and X be two disjoint sets of symbols representing respectively variables and term constructors. The set T of terms is composed by:*

$$
\begin{array}{ll}
terms & \\
T ::= x & x \in X \\
\quad | F(t_1, \ldots, t_n) & F \in \Sigma, t_1, \ldots, t_n \in T \; n \geq 0
\end{array}
$$

Notation *In what follows, we abbreviate the sequence of terms $t_1, \ldots, t_n$ by $\overline{t_n}$. A linear term t is a term in which variable names are pairwise distinct. A substitution is a morphism over terms. A term t is more general than another term t' denoted $t \preceq t'$ if there exists a substitution s such that $s(t) = t'$; in this case we also say that t' is an instance of t. Two terms t and t' are compatible denoted $t \uparrow t'$ if there exists a substitution s such that $s(t) = s(t')$. A closed term is a term without variables.*

The occurrences O are sequences of pairs formed by a term constructor $F \in \Sigma$ and an integer i denoted F^i (notice that the sequence of integers represents the usual notion of occurrence). The empty sequence is denoted ϵ. Let t be a term, the set of occurrences of t, denoted $O(t)$, is the subset of O defined by

$$
\begin{array}{l}
O(F) = \{\epsilon\} \qquad F \in \Sigma \cup X \\
O(F(\overline{t_n})) = \{\epsilon\} \cup \{F^i.u | u \in O(t_i), 1 \leq i \leq n\}.
\end{array}
$$

The subterm of a term t at occurrence u, denoted t/u is defined by

$$
\begin{array}{l}
t/\epsilon = t \\
F(\overline{t_n})/F^i.u = t_i/u \; 1 \leq i \leq n.
\end{array}
$$

The label of a term t at occurrence u, denoted $t(u)$ is defined by

$$
\begin{array}{ll}
x(\epsilon) = x & if \; x \in X \\
t(\epsilon) = F & if \; t = F(\overline{t_n}), n \geq 0 \\
t(u) = (t/u)(\epsilon) & if \; u \neq \epsilon
\end{array}
$$

An occurrence v is a prefix of another occurrence u, denoted $v \leq_{\text{prefix}} u$ if and only if there exists an occurrence w such that $u = vw$. An occurrence u is incompatible with a term t if there exist two occurrences v and w such that $u = vw$, $v \in O(t)$, $t/v = F(\overline{t_n})$, $w = G^i.w'$ and $F \neq G$ or $i > n$. An occurrence u overpass a term t if there exists $v <_{\text{prefix}} u$ such that $v \in O(t)$ and $t(v) \in X$ (in other words, neither $u \in O(t)$ nor u is incompatible with t). The set $\text{Var}(t)$ of variables of a term t is $\{x \in X | \exists u \in O(t) \text{ such that } t(u) = x\}$.

Example 1 Let $\Sigma = \{f, g, a\}$, $x \in X$ and $t = f(g(a), x)$. $O(t) = \{\epsilon, f^1, f^2, f^1 g^1\}$, $t/\epsilon = t$, $t/f^1 = g(a)$, $t/f^1 g^1 = a$, $t/f^2 = x$. $f^2 g^1$ overpass t and $f^1 f^1$ is incompatible with t.

Definition 2 *Let A be a set. The* constraints *are predicate logic expressions with constants* true, false *and atoms $A \in \mathcal{A}$.*

$$\text{constraints}$$
$$
\begin{aligned}
C ::=\ & A & A \in \mathcal{A} & \quad \text{(Atomic constraints)} \\
& |\ \text{true}\ |\ \text{false} & & \\
& |\ c_1 \vee c_2 & c_1, c_2 \in C & \\
& |\ c_1 \wedge c_2 & c_1, c_2 \in C & \\
& |\ \neg c & c \in C &
\end{aligned}
$$

To each atomic constraint A is associated a subset of O denoted $U(A)$ and a valuation function $\mathcal{V}(A) : T \to C$. *The valuation* function of atoms is extended to any constraint as follows:*

$$
\begin{aligned}
\mathcal{V}(\text{true})(t) &= \text{true} \\
\mathcal{V}(\text{false})(t) &= \text{false}
\end{aligned}
$$

$$
\begin{aligned}
\mathcal{V}(c_1 \vee c_2)(t) &= \text{true}\ \ \textit{if}\ \mathcal{V}(c_1)(t) = \text{true} \\
& \qquad\qquad \textit{or}\ \mathcal{V}(c_2)(t) = \text{true} \\
\mathcal{V}(c_1 \vee c_2)(t) &= \text{false}\ \textit{if}\ \mathcal{V}(c_1)(t) = \text{false} \\
& \qquad\qquad \textit{and}\ \mathcal{V}(c_2)(t) = \text{false} \\
\mathcal{V}(c_1 \vee c_2)(t) &= \mathcal{V}(c_1)(t) \vee \mathcal{V}(c_2)(t) \\
& \qquad\quad \textit{otherwise}
\end{aligned}
$$

$$
\begin{aligned}
\mathcal{V}(c_1 \wedge c_2)(t) &= \text{true}\ \ \textit{if}\ \mathcal{V}(c_1)(t) = \text{true} \\
& \qquad\qquad \textit{and}\ \mathcal{V}(c_2)(t) = \text{true} \\
\mathcal{V}(c_1 \wedge c_2)(t) &= \text{false}\ \textit{if}\ \mathcal{V}(c_1)(t) = \text{false} \\
& \qquad\qquad \textit{or}\ \mathcal{V}(c_2)(t) = \text{false} \\
\mathcal{V}(c_1 \wedge c_2)(t) &= \mathcal{V}(c_1)(t) \wedge \mathcal{V}(c_2)(t) \\
& \qquad\quad \textit{otherwise}
\end{aligned}
$$

$$
\begin{aligned}
\mathcal{V}(\neg c)(t) &= \text{true}\ \ \textit{if}\ \mathcal{V}(c)(t) = \text{false} \\
\mathcal{V}(\neg c)(t) &= \text{false}\ \textit{if}\ \mathcal{V}(c)(t) = \text{true} \\
\mathcal{V}(\neg c)(t) &= \neg(\mathcal{V}(c)(t)) \\
& \qquad\quad \textit{otherwise}
\end{aligned}
$$

The instances *of a constraint C are the set $\text{Inst}(C) = \{t \in T | \mathcal{V}(C)(t) = \text{true}\}$. A constraint C* implies *a constraint D, denoted $C \Rightarrow D$, if $\text{Inst}(C) \subset \text{Inst}(D)$. Two constraints C and D are* equivalent, *denoted $C \equiv D$, if $\text{Inst}(C) = \text{Inst}(D)$. Two constraints C and D are* compatible, *denoted $C \uparrow D$, if $\text{Inst}(C) \cap \text{Inst}(D) \neq \emptyset$. Otherwise they are* incompatible, *denoted $C \not\uparrow D$. A constraint C is compatible with a set of constraints Π if there exists a constraint $D \in \Pi$ compatible with C.*

We define here a set of atoms frequently used below: the predicate $\text{Occ}(u)$ tests if u belongs to the set of occurrences of a term.

Definition 3 (Constraint $\text{Occ}(u)$**)** *To each* $u \in O$ *is associated the predicate* $\text{Occ}(u)$ *over terms such that* $U(\text{Occ}(u)) = \{u\}$ *and its valuation is defined by:*

$$\begin{aligned} \mathcal{V}(\text{Occ}(u))(t) &= \text{true} \quad \textit{if } u \in O(t) \\ &= \text{Occ}(u) \textit{ if } u \textit{ overpass } t \\ &= \text{false} \quad \textit{if } u \textit{ incompatible with } t \end{aligned}$$

2 General Pattern Matching Problem

We define pattern matching over constraints and check its correspondence with pattern matching over terms.

2.1 Match over constraints

Definition 4 *Let* $\Pi = \{M_1, \dots, M_n\}$ *be a set of pairwise incompatible constraints named patterns. The pattern matching partial function* Match_Π *over constraints is defined by* $\text{Match}_\Pi(C) = i$ *if and only if* $C \Rightarrow M_i$.

Let us show how a matching problem can be seen as a Matching over constraints.

— Atoms for matching and valuation:

  Definition 5 *Let* A *be the set of atoms of the form* $u \doteq F$ *(* $u \in O$*,* $F \in \Sigma$ *and* $U(u \doteq F) = \{u\}$*) whose valuation is defined by*

$$\begin{aligned} \mathcal{V}(u \doteq F)(t) &= \text{true} \quad \textit{if } u \textit{ incompatible with } t \\ \mathcal{V}(u \doteq F)(t) &= u \doteq l \quad \textit{if } u \textit{ overpass } t \\ \mathcal{V}(u \doteq F)(t) &= \text{true} && \textit{if } t(u) = F \\ \mathcal{V}(u \doteq F)(t) &= \text{false} \textit{ if } t(u) = G \\ &\quad\quad \textit{and } F \neq G \\ \mathcal{V}(u \doteq F)(t) &= u \doteq F && \textit{if } t(u) \in X. \end{aligned}$$

  These atoms correspond to primitive comparison operations between the label of a term at a given occurrence and a constant.

— To each term t is associated the constraint

$$\mathcal{C}(t) = \bigwedge_{\substack{u \,\in\, O(t), \\ t(u) \,=\, F}} u \doteq F$$

— **Lemma 1** *Let* t *and* t' *be two terms.* $t \preceq t'$ *if and only if* $\mathcal{C}(t') \Rightarrow \mathcal{C}(t)$.
  Proof: Clearly, if $t \preceq t'$, there exists a constraint D such that $\mathcal{C}(t') \equiv \mathcal{C}(t) \wedge D$ and thus, $\mathcal{C}(t') \Rightarrow \mathcal{C}(t)$. Conversely if $\mathcal{C}(t') \Rightarrow \mathcal{C}(t)$, as $\mathcal{V}(\mathcal{C}(t'))(t') = \text{true}$, for every $u \in O(t)$, such that $t(u) = F$, $\mathcal{V}(u \doteq F)(t') = \text{true}$, $u \in O(t')$ and $t'(u) = t(u)$, otherwise, there would exist $v \in O(t') \cap O(t)$ such that $t'(v) \neq t(v) (= G)$ and thus, $\mathcal{V}(v \doteq G)(t') \neq \text{true}$. In conclusion, $t \preceq t'$.

There are several algorithms to check the match of a constraint by a given set of patterns, named pattern matching algorithms. We will use *Search trees* to represent these algorithms. The nodes of these trees that are not leaves, have constraints as labels. The label of the root is true. The sons of a node with label C are $C \wedge D$ where D is either an atom or the negation of an atom and $C \wedge D$ is compatible with a pattern. The labels of the leaves are pairs (C, i) where C is a constraint and i is the integer such that $C \Rightarrow M_i$. The only freedom in the construction is the choice of the atom used to develop the subtrees. A pattern matching algorithm either associates to a given constraint a pattern or *fails*. The algorithm is said to recognize the constraint C if there exists a leaf (D, i) such that $C \Rightarrow D$.

Definition 6 *Let* $\Pi = \{\overline{M_n}\}$ *a set of pairwise disjoint constraints and s be a search tree corresponding to Π. A term t is recognized by s if it belongs to the instances of one of the leaves of s. The partial function* Search *that follows associates to a pair (s, t) an integer i such that $t \in \text{Inst}(M_i)$.*

$$\begin{aligned} \text{Search}((C, i), t) &= i \quad \text{if } t \in \text{Inst}(C) \\ \text{Search}(C(\overline{\tau_m}), t) &= \text{Search}(\tau_j, t) \\ &\qquad \text{if } t \in \text{Inst}(\text{label}(\tau_j)) \\ \text{Search}((C, i), t) &= \text{fail } \textit{otherwise.} \end{aligned}$$

2.2 Optimality and sequentiality

We are interested in optimal pattern matching algorithm in the following sense:

Definition 7 (Optimal Pattern Matching) *A pattern matching algorithm is optimal if it recognizes every term that is recognized by any other pattern matching algorithm.*

In the following we propose an algorithm that produces a search tree and prove the optimality of the corresponding pattern matching algorithm. In order to do that we introduce, following Huet and Lévy [1], the sequentiality of a pattern matching problem Π and we prove that the algorithm producing the search tree does not fail if and only if the problem is sequential and that the sequentiality of the problem is decidable and implies the optimality of the pattern matching algorithm.

Definition 8 (Set of Directions of a constraint C with respect to Π) *Let Π be a set of pairwise incompatible constraints. Let C be a constraint and $\Pi' = \{M \in \Pi \,|\, M \uparrow C\}$ the set of patterns compatible with C.*

$$\text{Dir}_\Pi(C) = \left\{ D \left| \begin{array}{l} D \in \text{Atom}(\Pi), C \not\Rightarrow D, \ C \not\Rightarrow \neg D, \\ \forall u \in U(D), C \Rightarrow \text{Occ}(u) \text{ and} \\ \forall M \in \Pi', \forall u \in U(D), M \wedge C \Rightarrow D \vee \neg D \end{array} \right. \right\}$$

Definition 9 (sequentiality) *Let Π be a finite set of pairwise incompatible constraints. The problem Π is sequential, if for every constraint C compatible with Π and such that every pattern $M \in \Pi$, $C \not\Rightarrow M$, $\text{Dir}_\Pi(C) \neq \emptyset$.*

The following algorithm built trees $ST_\Pi(\text{true})$ that we interpret as pattern matching algorithms for a given set of patterns Π.

Definition 10 (Search tree) *Let $\Pi = \{M_1, \ldots, M_n\}$ be a set of patterns and C be a constraint.*

$$
\begin{aligned}
&ST_\Pi(C) \\
&= \textbf{if } \text{Dir}_\Pi(C) \textit{ non empty } \textbf{then let} \\
&\qquad D \in \text{Dir}_\Pi(C), \\
&\qquad \Pi_1 = \{M \in \Pi \,|\, M \wedge C \wedge D \not\equiv \text{false}\} \textbf{ and} \\
&\qquad \Pi_2 = \{M \in \Pi \,|\, M \wedge C \wedge \neg D \not\equiv \text{false}\} \textbf{ in} \\
&\qquad C(ST_\Pi(C \wedge D), ST_\Pi(C \wedge \neg D)) \\
&\qquad\qquad\qquad\qquad\quad \textbf{if } \Pi_1 \neq \emptyset \textit{ and } \Pi_2 \neq \emptyset \\
&\qquad C(ST_\Pi(C \wedge D)) \quad \textbf{if } \Pi_1 \neq \emptyset \textit{ and } \Pi_2 = \emptyset \\
&\qquad C(ST_\Pi(C \wedge \neg D)) \textbf{ if } \Pi_1 = \emptyset \textit{ and } \Pi_2 \neq \emptyset \\
&= (C, i) \textit{ if } C \Rightarrow M_i \\
&= \textit{fail } \textbf{otherwise}
\end{aligned}
$$

We prove in lemma 3 that all the trees provided by this algorithm for a given set of patterns recognize the same set of patterns. Let us first show how this formalism can describe the usual pattern matching problem for terms.

2.3 Huet and Levy's original problem

To each term t is associated the constraint $C(t)$ defined above. The following notions correspond:

$$
\begin{aligned}
&\text{term } t \quad \text{and} \quad \text{constraint } \mathcal{C}(t) \\
&\{\tau \,|\, \exists \sigma \ \sigma(t) = \tau\} \quad \text{and} \quad \{\tau \,|\, \mathcal{V}(\mathcal{C}(t))(\tau) = \text{true}\} \\
&\text{match}_\Pi \quad \text{and} \quad \text{Match}_{\mathcal{C}(\Pi)} \\
&Dir_\Pi(t) \quad \text{and} \quad Dir_{\mathcal{C}(\Pi)}(\mathcal{C}(t))
\end{aligned}
$$

The equality between $\{\tau \,|\, \exists \sigma \ \sigma(t) = \tau\}$ and $\{\tau \,|\, \mathcal{V}(\mathcal{C}(t))(\tau) = \text{true}\}$ is a consequence of the fact that for every term t, $\mathcal{V}(\mathcal{C}(t))(t) = \text{true}$.

Let $\Pi = \{p_1, \ldots, p_n\}$ be a set of pairwise incompatible linear terms. Let $\mathcal{C}(\Pi) = \{\mathcal{C}(p_1), \ldots, \mathcal{C}(p_n)\}$ be the set of corresponding constraints. Let match_Π be the predicate defined by $\text{match}_\Pi(t) = \text{true}$ if there exists $p_i \in \Pi$ such that $p_i \preceq t$. A term t satisfies the predicate match_Π if and only if the function $\text{Match}_{\mathcal{C}(\Pi)}$ is defined for the corresponding constraint $\mathcal{C}(t)$, as a consequence of lemma 1.

Let $\Pi = \{p_1, \ldots, p_n\}$ be a set of pairwise incompatible linear terms. Let $\mathcal{C}(\Pi) = \{\mathcal{C}(p_1), \ldots, \mathcal{C}(p_n)\}$ be the set of corresponding constraints. Let t be a term compatible with a pattern $p \in \Pi$ such that $\text{match}_\Pi(t) = \text{false}$. Let us recall that $u \in Dir_\Pi(t)$ if and only if $u \in O(t)$, t/u is a variable and for every pattern $p \in \Pi$ compatible with t, $p/u \not\preceq t/u$. The following property is satisfied.

$$
u \in Dir_\Pi(t) \Leftrightarrow \exists D \in Dir_{\mathcal{C}(\Pi)}(\mathcal{C}(t))
$$
$$
\text{such that } u \in U(D).
$$

Let $u \in Dir_\Pi(t)$, there exists a pattern p compatible with t such that $p/u = F(\ldots)$. Let $D = u \dot{=} F$ and $U(D) = u$, $D \in Atom(\mathcal{C}(\Pi))$ and by definition $\mathcal{C}(t) \Rightarrow Occ(u)$. As t satisfies $\mathcal{C}(t)$ and t/u is a variable, $\mathcal{C}(t) \not\Rightarrow D$. As p is compatible with t there exists an instance τ of t such that $\tau/u = F(\ldots)$ and thus, $\mathcal{C}(t) \not\Rightarrow \neg D$. Finally let $M \in \Pi$ be a pattern compatible with t. $M/u \not\leq t/u$ implies $\mathcal{C}(M) \Rightarrow D \vee \neg D$. Conversely let $D = u \dot{=} F \in Dir_{\mathcal{C}(\Pi)}(\mathcal{C}(t))$. As $\mathcal{C}(t) \Rightarrow Occ(u)$, t/u is defined. t/u is a variable otherwise either $t(u) = F$ and $\mathcal{C}(t) \Rightarrow D$ or $t(u) = G$ with $G \neq F$ and $\mathcal{C}(t) \Rightarrow \neg D$. For every compatible pattern $p \in \Pi$, p/u is not a variable otherwise $\mathcal{C}(p) \not\Rightarrow D \vee \neg D$ because $\mathcal{V}(D \vee \neg D)(p) \neq$ true and $\mathcal{V}(\mathcal{C}(p))(p) =$ true.

3 Decidability of sequentiality. Optimality

As in the case of terms we prove that the pattern matching algorithm computed for a sequential set of constraints Π is optimal. First we prove that a finite set of patterns Π is sequential if and only if the set of constraints appearing in the labels of the search tree $ST_\Pi(\text{true})$ is sequential. This property implies the decidability of the sequentiality of a finite set of patterns .

Lemma 2 *Let Π be a finite set of constraints such that $ST_\Pi(\text{true})$ does not fail. For every constraint C compatible with a pattern $M \in \Pi$ there exists a label P in $ST_\Pi(\text{true})$ such that $C \Rightarrow P$ and for every label P', if $C \Rightarrow P'$ then $P \Rightarrow P'$. P is named the maximum prefix of C in $ST_\Pi(\text{true})$. Furthermore, if P is not a leaf, $Dir_\Pi(P) \cap Dir_\Pi(C) \neq \emptyset$.*
Proof: Let C be a constraint such that there exists a pattern $M \in \Pi$ compatible with C. Let $\mathcal{P}$ be the set of labels M in $ST_\Pi(\text{true})$ such that $C \Rightarrow M$. $\mathcal{P}$ is not empty because $C \Rightarrow$ true. All the elements of $\mathcal{P}$ belongs to the same branch of $ST_\Pi(\text{true})$ otherwise there exists a constraint D such that $C \Rightarrow D$ and $C \Rightarrow \neg D$ and thus, $C \equiv$ false that contradicts the fact $D \uparrow M$. Clearly there exists $P \in \mathcal{P}$ such that for every $P' \in \mathcal{P}$, $P \Rightarrow P'$.
Let $D \in Dir_\Pi(P)$ such that $P \wedge D$ or $P \wedge \neg D$ or both are labels of $ST_\Pi(\text{true})$. Knowing that $D \in Dir_\Pi(P)$ we prove that $D \in Dir_\Pi(C)$. $C \not\Rightarrow D$ otherwise $C \Rightarrow P \wedge D$ that contradicts the maximality of P if $P \wedge D$ is a label of $ST_\Pi(\text{true})$ and the compatibility of C with a pattern if not. The same argument proves $C \not\Rightarrow \neg D$. By definition of $ST_\Pi(\text{true})$, D is a direction of P and thus, $\forall u \in U(D)$, $P \Rightarrow Occ(u)$. As $C \Rightarrow P$, then $C \Rightarrow Occ(u)$. The last property is a consequence of the fact that $C \Rightarrow P$ implies $C \wedge M \Rightarrow P \wedge M$.

Lemma 3 (Equivalence of optimal Search Trees) *Let Π be a set of patterns. All the search trees built using the algorithm $ST_\Pi(\text{true})$ have the same set of leaves.*
Proof: Let T and T' be two search trees $ST_\Pi(\text{true})$ and F be a leaf of T. Notice that $Dir_\Pi(F) = \emptyset$, $Inst(F) \neq \emptyset$ and if $F' \neq F$ is a leaf of T, $Inst(F) \cap Inst(F') = \emptyset$. There exists by lemma 2 a leaf P' of T' such that $F \Rightarrow P'$. The same reasoning leads to the existence of a leaf F' of T such that $P' \Rightarrow F'$. Thus, $F = F'$.

We deduce from this lemma that all the different trees $ST_\Pi(\text{true})$ recognize the same set of constraints which allows us to use $ST_\Pi(\text{true})$ in order to denote one of them.

Theorem 1 *Let Π be a finite set of constraints. Π is sequential if and only if the algorithm $ST_\Pi(\text{true})$ terminates without any fail. Furthermore the sequentiality of a finite set of patterns is decidable.*

Proof: If Π is sequential each step in $ST_\Pi(\text{true})$ is such that either there exists a direction or a pattern matches the constraint. Conversely, let us suppose that $ST_\Pi(\text{true})$ does not fail. By lemma 2, for every constraint C compatible with Π such that for every $M \in \Pi$, $C \not\Rightarrow M$, there exists a maximal prefix P in $ST_\Pi(\text{true})$ such that $Dir_\Pi(P) \cap Dir_\Pi(C) \neq \emptyset$. Therefore $Dir_\Pi(C) \neq \emptyset$ and Π is sequential. The algorithm $ST\Pi(\text{true})$ terminates because the depth of the tree is bounded by the number of atoms in Π, and thus the sequentiality is decidable.

Lemma 4 *Let $\Pi = \{M_1, \ldots, M_n\}$ be a set of pairwise incompatible constraints. For every integer i and every constraint C such that $C \Rightarrow M_i$, there exist $F_1, \ldots, F_k$ leaves of $ST_\Pi(\text{true})$ such that $C \Rightarrow \bigvee_{1 \leq j \leq k} F_j \Rightarrow M_i$.*

Proof: Let C be a constraint such that $C \Rightarrow M_1$ for instance and P its maximum prefix in $ST_\Pi(\text{true})$. The proof is by induction over the size of the subtree of $ST_\Pi(\text{true})$ with root P. If P is a leave there exists a pattern M_i such that $C \Rightarrow P \Rightarrow M_i$ that implies $M_1 = M_i$ because patterns are incompatible. Otherwise, let $D \in Dir_\Pi(P)$ such that $P \wedge D$ or $P \wedge \neg D$ or both are labels of $ST_\Pi(\text{true})$. First notice that $C \equiv (C \wedge D) \vee (C \wedge \neg D)$ because $C \Rightarrow M_1 \Rightarrow D \vee \neg D$. As $C \wedge D$ (resp. $C \wedge \neg D$) satisfies the inductive hypothesis, $C \wedge D \Rightarrow \bigvee_{j \in J} F_j \Rightarrow M_1$ (resp. $C \wedge \neg D \Rightarrow \bigvee_{j \in J'} F_j \Rightarrow M_1$) where J (resp. J') is a subset of $[1, k]$. Thus, $C \Rightarrow \bigvee_{j \in J \cup J'} F_j \Rightarrow M_1$. The last part follows straightforwardly.

Theorem 2 *Let Π be a finite set of pairwise incompatible constraints. If Π is sequential then the search tree $ST_\Pi(\text{true})$ is optimal.*

Proof: The optimality is a consequence of lemma 4, by definition.

Definition 11 *Let $\Pi = \{\overline{M_n}\}$ a set of pairwise disjoint constraints and s be a search tree corresponding to Π. A term t is recognized by s if it belongs to the instances of one of the leaves of s. The partial function Search that follows associates to a pair (s, t) an integer i such that $t \in \text{Inst}(M_i)$.*

$$\text{Search}((C, i), t) = i \quad \text{if } t \in \text{Inst}(C)$$
$$\text{Search}(C(\overline{\tau_m}), t) = \text{Search}(\tau_j, t)$$
$$\text{if } t \in \text{Inst}(\text{label}(\tau_j))$$
$$\text{Search}((C, i), t) = \text{fail } otherwise.$$

We present now several instances of the general match problem which can be classed in two groups: Those based on the match operation and those based on the unification operation. The former can be used in term rewriting systems and in functional programming; the later group is oriented to the implementation of logic programming languages.

4 Compilation of Pattern Matching in ML

For the first group, let us consider different variants of the match construct of the ML language whose semantics can be defined by the following conditional rewriting rule in the style of [6].

Definition 12 (Semantics of match in ML) *Let E be a set of expressions of the ML language containing functions defined by cases "(**fun** $p_1 \to e_1 | \ldots | p_n \to e_n$)" and the match construct below that corresponds to the application of a function to an expression "**match** e **with** $p_1 \to e_1 | \ldots | p_n \to e_n \equiv ($**fun** $p_1 \to e_1 | \ldots | p_n \to e_n) e$" . The set P of language patterns and the relation $i = \text{match}_{\{\overline{p_n}\}}(v)$ where $\{\overline{p_n}\} \subset P$ will be defined for each of the proposed variants of the match construct. The substitution operation $e_i[p_i \leftarrow v]$ produces a partially evaluated expression in which the variables in pattern p_i are replaced by the corresponding parts of the value v. Finally, $e \Rightarrow v$ is the relation that holds if the value of expression e is v, which is defined on the structure of expressions and contains the rule*

$$\frac{e \Rightarrow v \quad i = \text{match}_{\{\overline{p_n}\}}(v) \quad e_i[p_i \leftarrow v] \Rightarrow v'}{\textbf{match } e \textbf{ with } p_1 \to e_1 | \ldots | p_n \to e_n \Rightarrow v'} \quad \text{(match)}$$

The goal of each of these presentations is to define, for each of the instances of the problem, a representation of patterns $\Pi_0 = \{\overline{p_n}\}$ as constraints $\Pi = \mathcal{C}(\Pi_0)$ which, by lemma 2, will lead to the definition of a search tree $s = \text{ST}_\Pi(\text{true})$ such that for any value v, $\text{match}_{\Pi_0}(v) = \text{Search}(s, v)$. Under these conditions, the rule above can be replaced by its equivalent compiled version.

$$s = \text{ST}_{\mathcal{C}(\overline{p_n})}(\text{true})$$

$$\frac{e \Rightarrow v \quad i = \text{Search}(s, v) \quad e_i[p_i \leftarrow v] \Rightarrow v'}{\textbf{match } e \textbf{ with } p_1 \to e_1 | \ldots | p_n \to e_n \Rightarrow v'} \quad \text{(match')}$$

4.1 Match of linear non ambiguous patterns

This is a restriction to the match construct of the ML language in which patterns must not have common instances. It correspond to the original work of Huet and Lévy [1]. For this instance of the problem the set P of language patterns is the set T of terms (definition 1); the evaluation of the match construct

$$\textbf{match } e \textbf{ with } p_1 \to e_1 | \ldots | p_n \to e_n \Rightarrow v'$$

is only defined for sets of patterns $\Pi = \{\overline{p_n}\}$ such that for any term $t \in T$, $p_i \preceq t$ and $p_j \preceq t$ if and only if $i = j$; finally, the match predicate is defined by $\text{match}_\Pi(v) = i$ if $p_i \preceq v$.

To each pattern $p \in P$ is associated the constraint

$$\mathcal{C}(p) = \bigwedge_{\substack{u \in O(p), \\ p/u = F(\overline{\tau_m})}} u \dot{=} F$$

The translation of a set Π_0 of patterns is defined by

$$\mathcal{C}(\Pi_0) = \{\mathcal{C}(p)|p \in \Pi_0\}$$

Example 2 Let e_0, e_1, e_2, e_3 be ML expressions :: be a binary constructor in infix notation, Nil, 1 be constants, x, y, z be variables and e be the expression

$$\textbf{match } e_0 \textbf{ with } (1 :: y :: z) \rightarrow e_1 \mid (x :: \text{Nil}) \rightarrow e_2 \mid \text{Nil} \rightarrow e_3.$$

The set of patterns of e is $\Pi_0 = \{1 :: y :: z, x :: \text{Nil}, \text{Nil}\}$. The translation of these patterns produces the constraints

$$
\begin{aligned}
C_1 &= \epsilon \doteq :: \wedge ::^1 \doteq 1 \wedge ::^2 \doteq ::, \\
C_2 &= \epsilon \doteq :: \wedge ::^2 \doteq \text{Nil}, \\
C_3 &= \epsilon \doteq \text{Nil and} \\
\Pi &= \{C_1, C_2, C_3\}.
\end{aligned}
$$

The optimal search tree associated to this problem is

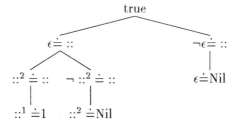

Another search tree for the same set of patterns could be

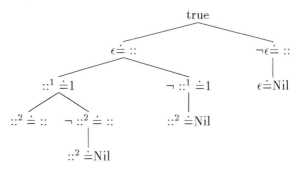

Compared to the optimal search tree below, this search tree has an additional step for instances of the second pattern, which means that there are instances of terms that can be recognized by the former and not by the later. That is the case of the term $x :: \text{Nil}$.

4.2 Match of linear patterns ordered by priority

This instance has been studied by its own by Laville[4] and by Puel and Suárez [7]. The presentation proposed here does not cover completely those works; in particular, the strictness characterization of a match problem is not treated here. This instance of the general match problem correspond to the original match construct of the ML language.

We keep in this instance the same set P of language patterns, and change the match predicate as follows:

$$\text{match}_\Pi(v) = i \quad \text{if } p_i \preceq v \text{ and for any } j < i, p_i \not\preceq v$$

To each pattern $p \in P$ is associated the constraint

$$\mathcal{C}(p) = \bigwedge_{\substack{u \in O(p), \\ p/u = F(\overline{\tau_m})}} u \doteq F$$

The translation of a set Π_0 of patterns is defined by

$$\mathcal{C}(\Pi_0) = \{\mathcal{C}(p_i) \wedge \bigwedge_{1 \leq j < i} \neg\mathcal{C}(p_j) | 1 \leq i \leq n\}$$

Example 3 Let e_0, e_1, e_2, e_3 be ML expressions, f be a constructor, a, b be constants and x, y be variables and e be the expression

match e_0 **with** $f(a, b) \rightarrow e_1 \mid f(c, x) \rightarrow e_2 \mid f(x, b) \rightarrow e_3$.

The translation of the patterns of this problem produces the constraints

$$C_1 = \epsilon \doteq f \wedge f^1 \doteq a \wedge f^2 \doteq b,$$
$$C_2 = \epsilon \doteq f \wedge f^2 \doteq b,$$
$$C_3 = \epsilon \doteq f \wedge f^2 \doteq b \wedge \neg f^1 \doteq a \wedge \neg f^1 \doteq c \text{ and}$$
$$\Pi = \{C_1, C_2, C_3\}.$$

The optimal search tree associated to this problem is

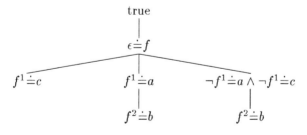

4.3 Match of non linear non ambiguous patterns

This is a variant of the match construct of ML in which variables in patterns might appear several times. The set P of language patterns in this instance is the set of non linear terms that can be represented with the notation (p with $x_1 = y_1, \ldots, x_m = y_m$) which indicates that in the linear pattern p variables x_i and y_i should correspond to the same value. The match predicate of this instance, defined only for non ambiguous sets of patterns is

$$\text{match}_\Pi(v) = i$$
$$\text{if } p_i = (p \text{ with } s),\ p \preceq v$$
$$\text{and for any pair } x = y \in s, x[p \leftarrow v] = y[p \leftarrow v]$$

We introduce now, new atoms that will represent the non linear part of patterns.

Definition 13 *Let A be the set of atoms of the form $u \dot= F$ as in definition 5 completed with equality constraints which are expressions of the form $u \dot\uparrow v$ where u and v are occurrences and $U(u \dot\uparrow v) = \{u, v\}$. The valuation function defined for terms as follows:*

$$\mathcal{V}(u \dot\uparrow v)(t) = \text{true } \textit{if } u \textit{ incompatible with } t$$
$$\textit{or } v \textit{ incompatible with } t$$
$$\mathcal{V}(u \dot\uparrow v)(t) = u \dot\uparrow v \textit{ if } u \textit{ overpass } t \textit{ or } v \textit{ overpass } t$$
$$\mathcal{V}(u \dot\uparrow v)(t) = \text{false } \textit{if } t/v = F(\ldots) \textit{ and } t/u \in \text{Var}(t/v)$$
$$\mathcal{V}(u \dot\uparrow v)(t) = \text{false } \textit{if } t/u = F(\ldots), t/v = G(\ldots) \textit{ and } F \neq G$$
$$\mathcal{V}(u \dot\uparrow v)(t) = \mathcal{V}(\wedge_{1 \leq i \leq n} u.F^i \dot\uparrow v.F^i)(t)$$
$$\textit{if } t/u = F(\overline{t_n}) \textit{ and } t/v = F(\overline{t'_n})$$
$$\mathcal{V}(u \dot\uparrow v)(t) = u \dot\uparrow v \textit{ otherwise.}$$

Equality constraints can be translated into a call to a general equality function often available in functional languages.

To each pattern "τ with $s \in P$" is associated the constraint

$$\mathcal{C}(\tau \text{ with } s) = \bigwedge_{\substack{u \in O(\tau), \\ \tau/u = F(\overline{\tau_m})}} u \dot= F \wedge \bigwedge_{\substack{x = y \in s, \\ \tau/u = x, \\ \tau/v = y}} u \dot\uparrow v$$

The translation of a set Π_0 of patterns is defined by

$$\mathcal{C}(\Pi_0) = \{\mathcal{C}(p) | p \in \Pi_0\}$$

Example 4 Let e_0, e_1, e_2, e_3 be ML expressions, f, g, h be constructors, x be a variable and e be the expression

$$\mathbf{match}\ e_0\ \mathbf{with}\ f(g(x), h(x)) \rightarrow e_1$$
$$\mid f(g(x), x) \rightarrow e_2$$
$$\mid f(x, x) \rightarrow e_3.$$

The original patterns associated to this example are

$$\Pi_0 = \left\{ \begin{array}{l} (f(g(x), h(y)) \text{ with } x = y), \\ (f(g(x), y) \text{ with } x = y), \\ (f(x, y) \text{ with } x = y) \end{array} \right\}.$$

The translation of these patterns produces the constraints

$$C_1 = \epsilon \dot{=} f \wedge f^1 \dot{=} g \wedge f^2 \dot{=} h \wedge f^1.g^1 {\uparrow} f^2.h^1,$$
$$C_2 = \epsilon \dot{=} f \wedge f^1 \dot{=} g \wedge f^1.g^1 {\uparrow} f^2,$$
$$C_3 = \epsilon \dot{=} f \wedge f^1 {\uparrow} f^2 \text{ and}$$
$$\Pi = \{C_1, C_2, C_3\}.$$

The optimal search tree associated to this problem is

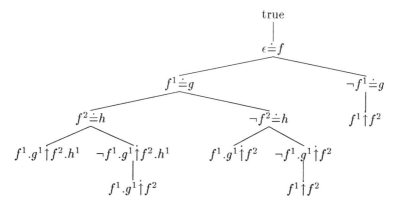

4.4 Match of non linear patterns ordered by priority

This is an extension of the match construct of ML in which both, priorities and non linear patterns are used. The constraints are defined on the set of atoms of definition 13.

To each pattern τ with $s \in P$ is associated the constraint

$$\mathcal{C}(\tau \text{ with } s) = \bigwedge_{\substack{u \in O(\tau), \\ \tau/u = F(\overline{\tau_m})}} u \dot{=} F \wedge \bigwedge_{\substack{x = y \in s, \\ \tau/u = x, \\ \tau/v = y}} u {\uparrow} v$$

The translation of a set Π_0 of patterns is defined by

$$\mathcal{C}(\Pi_0) = \{\mathcal{C}(p_i) \wedge \bigwedge_{1 \le j < i} \neg \mathcal{C}(p_j) | 1 \le i \le n\}$$

Example 5 Let e_0, e_1, e_2, e_3 be ML expressions, f be a constructor, x, y be variables and e be the expression

$$\textbf{match } e_0 \textbf{ with } f(x, y, y) \rightarrow e_1$$
$$\mid f(x, y, x) \rightarrow e_2$$
$$\mid f(x, x, y) \rightarrow e_3.$$

The translation of the patterns of this problem produces the constraints

$$C_1 = \epsilon \dot{=} f \wedge f^2 {\uparrow} f^3,$$
$$C_2 = \epsilon \dot{=} f \wedge f^1 {\uparrow} f^3 \wedge \neg f^2 {\uparrow} f^3,$$
$$C_3 = \epsilon \dot{=} f \wedge f^1 {\uparrow} f^2 \wedge \neg f^2 {\uparrow} f^3 \wedge \neg f^1 {\uparrow} f^3 \text{ and}$$
$$\Pi = \{C_1, C_2, C_3\}.$$

The optimal search tree associated to this problem is

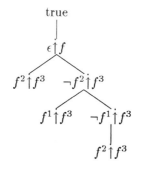

Another possible instance of the general match problem leading to the compilation of an extension of ML is the use of patterns of the form $(t \text{ with } s)$ in which s is any arbitrary predicate. The result will be a matching algorithm in which those predicates and the other matching operations are embedded and launched in the best possible order.

5   Compilation of Resolution in Prolog

The following examples represent different variants of the calling mechanism of logical programming languages. They are based on the unification as a pattern recognition operation.

Definition 14 (Semantics of the calling mechanism of Prolog) *Let $\Pi = \{\overline{p_n}\}$ be a set of patterns and $i = \text{match}_\Pi(t)$ be a relation representing the pattern matching operation that will be defined for each of the instances of the problem. A goal is a term (an element of T). The set Cl of Prolog clauses is defined by*

$$clauses$$
$$Cl ::= p :\!- q_1 \ldots q_n. \; p \in P, \overline{q_n} \in T, n \geq 0$$

The relation $\sigma = mgu(t, t')$ holds if the substitution σ is a most general unifier of terms t and t'. We note "$\Gamma \vdash g \Rightarrow g'$", a resolution step of a set of goals g given the set of clauses Γ producing a set of goals g'. This operation is defined by the conditional rewriting rule below in which $g, g_1 \ldots, g_n$ denote sets of terms representing goals

$$t(\epsilon) = F \quad \Gamma \Rightarrow F =_{\text{def}} (p_1 :- g_1 \ldots p_n :- g_n)$$

$$\frac{i = \text{match}_{\{\overline{p_n}\}}(t) \qquad \sigma = mgu(t, p_i)}{\Gamma \vdash \{t\} \cup g \Rightarrow \sigma(g_i) \cup \sigma(g)} \quad \text{(Resolv)}$$

Given an appropriate compilation function $\mathcal{C}$ for patterns, the predicate rule above can be replaced by a compilation rule for definitions of relations and a new rule for the resolution.

$$\frac{s = \text{ST}_{\mathcal{C}(\overline{p_n})}(\text{true})}{\Gamma, (F, p_1 :- g_1 \ldots p_n :- g_n) \Rightarrow} \quad \text{(Cmpl)}$$
$$\Gamma \cup \{F =_{\text{cmp}} (s, p_1, g_1, \ldots, p_n, g_n)\}$$

$$t(\epsilon) = F \quad \Gamma \Rightarrow F =_{\text{cmp}} (s, p_1, g_1, \ldots, p_n, g_n)$$

$$\frac{i = \text{Search}(s, t) \qquad \sigma = mgu(t, p_i)}{\Gamma \vdash \{t\} \cup g \Rightarrow \sigma(g_i) \cup \sigma(g)} \quad \text{(Resolv')}$$

5.1   Resolution with linear patterns ordered by priority

The first instance is variant of Prolog in which only linear patterns are allowed. A disambiguating rule, priority in this case, is necessary because unification as a pattern matching operation is intrinsicly ambiguous for terms that are prefixes (with respect to $\preceq$) of patterns.

In this instance of the general match problem, the set P of language patterns is the set T of terms and the match function is defined as follows:

t matches p if and only if p and t are unifiable
$\text{match}_\Pi(t) = i$ if p_i, matches t
and for any $j < i, t$ does not match p_j

The following atomic constraints will be used for the representation of patterns.

Definition 15 (Var Constraint) *To each $u \in O$ is associated a constraint $\text{Var}(u)$ defined by:*

$$\begin{aligned} \mathcal{V}(\text{Var}(u))(t) &= true & &\text{if } u \in O(t) \text{ and } t(u) \in X \\ &= \text{Var}(u) & &\text{if } u \text{ overpass } t \\ &= false & &\text{if } u \in O(t) \text{ and } t(u) \in \Sigma \end{aligned}$$

To each pattern $p \in P$ is associated the constraint

$$C(p) = \bigwedge_{\substack{u \in O(p), \\ p/u = F(\overline{\tau_m})}} (\text{Var}(u) \vee u \dot{=} F)$$

The translation of a set Π_0 of patterns is defined by

$$C(\Pi_0) = \{C(p_i) \wedge \bigwedge_{1 \leq j < i} \neg C(p_j) | 1 \leq i \leq n\}$$

Example 6 Let g_1, g_2 be sets of terms, g, h be constructors, x, y be variables and f be the Prolog predicate defined by

$$f(x, g(y)) :- g_1. \quad f(g(x), h(y)) :- g_2.$$

The constraints associated to this definition are

$$C_1 = (\text{Var}(\epsilon) \vee \epsilon \dot{=} f) \wedge (\text{Var}(f^2) \vee f^2 \dot{=} g),$$
$$C_2 = (\text{Var}(\epsilon) \vee \epsilon \dot{=} f) \wedge (\text{Var}(f^1) \vee f^1 \dot{=} g) \wedge$$
$$(\text{Var}(f_2) \vee f^2 \dot{=} h) \text{ and}$$
$$\Pi = \{C_1, C_2\}.$$

In order to save space in the representation of search trees, we will only represent nodes that are not implied by all of their sons. This convention lead to the representation of trees that are not binary. The optimal search tree associated to this problem is

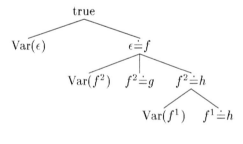

5.2 Resolution with non linear patterns ordered by priority

This instance of the general match problem correspond to the usual pure Prolog calling mechanism. As for pattern matching, we use the intermediate notation "τ with s" where $s = \{x_1 = y_1, \ldots, x_n = y_n\}, n \geq 0$ to note non linear patterns. The match function is defined for this instance as:

$$t \text{ matches } (\tau \text{ with } s) \text{ if and only if } \tau \text{ and } t \text{ are unifiable}$$
$$\text{and for any pair } x = y \in s,$$
$$x \text{ and } y \text{ are unifiable}$$
$$\text{match}_\Pi(t) = i \text{ if } p_i, \text{ matches } t \text{ and for any } j < i,$$
$$t \text{ does not match } p_j$$

Definition 16 (Unifiability Constraint) *An* unifiability constraint *is an expression of the form $u \mathbin{\dot{\Uparrow}} v$ where u and v are occurrences and $U(u \mathbin{\dot{\Uparrow}} v) = \{u, v\}$. The valuation function for unifiability constraints is defined as follows:*

$$\mathcal{V}(u \mathbin{\dot{\Uparrow}} v)(t) = \text{true} \quad \textit{if } u \textit{ incompatible with } t$$
$$\textit{or } v \textit{ incompatible with } t$$
$$\mathcal{V}(u \mathbin{\dot{\Uparrow}} v)(t) = \text{true} \quad \textit{if } u \textit{ overpass } t \textit{ or } v \textit{ overpass } t$$
$$\mathcal{V}(u \mathbin{\dot{\Uparrow}} v)(t) = \text{true} \quad \textit{if } t/u \in X \textit{ and } t/v \in X$$
$$\mathcal{V}(u \mathbin{\dot{\Uparrow}} v)(t) = \text{true} \quad \textit{if } t/u \in X, t/v = F(\overline{t_n})$$
$$\textit{and } t/u \notin \mathrm{Var}(t/v)$$
$$\mathcal{V}(u \mathbin{\dot{\Uparrow}} v)(t) = \text{true} \quad \textit{if } t/v \in X, t/u = F(\overline{t_n})$$
$$\textit{and } t/v \notin \mathrm{Var}(t/u)$$
$$\mathcal{V}(u \mathbin{\dot{\Uparrow}} v)(t) = \text{false} \quad \textit{if } t/u = F(\overline{t_n}), t/v = G(\overline{t_n})$$
$$\textit{and } F \neq G$$
$$\mathcal{V}(u \mathbin{\dot{\Uparrow}} v)(t) = \text{false} \quad \textit{if } t/v = F(\overline{t_n}) \textit{ and } t/u \in \mathrm{Var}(t/v)$$
$$\mathcal{V}(u \mathbin{\dot{\Uparrow}} v)(t) = \text{false} \quad \textit{if } t/u = F(\overline{t_n}) \textit{ and } t/v \in \mathrm{Var}(t/u)$$
$$\mathcal{V}(u \mathbin{\dot{\Uparrow}} v)(t) = \mathcal{V}(\wedge_{1 \leq i \leq n} u.F_i \mathbin{\dot{\Uparrow}} v.F_i)(t)$$
$$\textit{if } t/u = F(\overline{t_n})$$
$$\textit{and } t/v = F(\overline{t'_n})$$
$$\mathcal{V}(u \mathbin{\dot{\Uparrow}} v)(t) = u \mathbin{\dot{\Uparrow}} v \quad \textit{otherwise.}$$

Unifiability constraints can be implemented by a built-in unification procedure for terms called as an atomic operation.

To each language pattern is associated the constraint

$$\mathcal{C}(\tau \text{ with } s) = \bigwedge_{\substack{u \in O(p), \\ p/u = F(\overline{\tau_m})}} (\mathrm{Var}(u) \vee u \mathbin{\dot{=}} F) \wedge \bigwedge_{\substack{x = y \in s, \\ \tau/u = x, \\ \tau/v = y}} u \mathbin{\dot{\Uparrow}} v$$

The translation of a set Π_0 of patterns is defined by

$$\mathcal{C}(\Pi_0) = \{\mathcal{C}(p_i) \wedge \bigwedge_{1 \leq j < i} \neg \mathcal{C}(p_j) \mid 1 \leq i \leq n\}$$

Example 7 Let g_1, g_2, g_3 be sets of terms, a, b be constants, x, y be variables and f be the Prolog predicate defined by

$$f(x, b, x) :- g_1. \quad f(a, a, x) :- g_2. \quad f(x, a, y) :- g_3.$$

The constraints associated to this definition are

$$C_1 = \mathrm{Var}(\epsilon) \vee (\epsilon \mathbin{\dot{=}} f \wedge (\mathrm{Var}(f^2) \vee f^2 \mathbin{\dot{=}} b) \wedge f^1 \mathbin{\dot{\Uparrow}} f^3),$$
$$C_2 = (\mathrm{Var}(\epsilon) \vee (\epsilon \mathbin{\dot{=}} f \wedge (\mathrm{Var}(f^1) \vee f^1 \mathbin{\dot{=}} a) \wedge (\mathrm{Var}(f^2) \vee f^2 \mathbin{\dot{=}} a))) \wedge \neg C_1,$$
$$C_3 = (\mathrm{Var}(\epsilon) \vee (\epsilon \mathbin{\dot{=}} f \wedge (\mathrm{Var}(f^2) \vee f^2 \mathbin{\dot{=}} a))) \wedge \neg C_1 \wedge \neg C_2 \text{ and}$$
$$\Pi = \{C_1, C_2, C_3\}.$$

Finally, the optimal search tree associated to this problem is

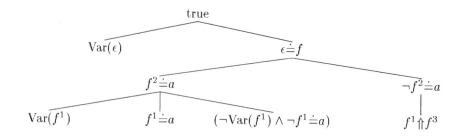

Conclusion

We have given in this work the tools needed for the application of the sequentiality methodology for the resolution of different matching problems. We showed that this is a practical approach for the meta-compilation of pattern matching constructs in programming languages by the development of different variants of the matching constructs of two different programming languages: ML and Prolog. As part of this work, we also developed two interesting and practical instances: the match of terms with non linear patterns and the use of unification as a pattern matching primitive.

References

1. G. Huet and J-J. Lévy. Call by need computations in non ambiguous linear term rewriting systems. Rapport IRIA Laboria 359, INRIA, Domaine de Voluceau, Rocquencourt BP105, 78153 Le Chesnay Cedex. FRANCE, 1979.
2. G. Huet and J-J. Lévy. Call by need computations in orthogonal term rewriting systems. In J.L. Lassez and G. Plotkin, editors, *Computational Logic*. MIT Press, 1991.
3. J.W. Klop and A. Middeldorp. Sequentiality in orthogonal term rewriting systems. *J. Symbolic Computation*, 12(2), 1991.
4. A. Laville. *Evaluation paresseuse des filtrages avec priorité. Application au Langage ML*. PhD thesis, Université Paris 7, 1988. Thèse.
5. A. Laville. Implementation of lazy pattern matching algorithms. In H. Ganzinger, editor, *ESOP'88*, pages 298–316. Lecture Notes in Computer Science 300, March 1988.
6. G. Plotkin. Call-by-name, call-by-value and the λ-calculus. In *TCS*, pages 125–159, 1975.
7. L. Puel and A. Suárez. Compiling pattern matching by term decomposition. In *acm conf. on Lisp and Functional Programming*, pages 273–281. acm Press, June 1990.

Testing for a Conformance Relation Based on Acceptance*

MingYu Yao and Gregor v. Bochmann

Département d'informatique et de recherche opérationnelle,
Université de Montréal, Montréal, Québec, Canada H3C 3J7
e-mail: (yao, bochmann)@iro.umontreal.ca

Abstract. Although the object-oriented paradigm has been gaining wide popularity in recent years, little work has been done on how to test object-oriented software systems. We believe that many special programming features found in the object-oriented paradigm will also play important roles during the testing phase. In this paper, we propose a conformance testing method for object-oriented software systems. The conformance relation that can be tested by this method is based on a modified version of the acceptance tree model and takes into account the special requirements imposed by the inheritance mechanism -- which we believe is the most important feature provided by the object-oriented paradigm. The proposed method allows us to test, under certain assumptions, whether an object instance implementation conforms to a given class specification by applying to the implementation the test cases derived from the given class specification.

1 Introduction

With the increasing complexity of software systems, *stepwise refinement* is becoming an important methodology for software development. The stepwise refinement approach starts from a formal specification of the functionality of the system on a high level of abstraction. This abstract *initial specification* is then transformed in a number of successive *refinement* or *implementation* steps, where each step produces a new specification reflecting certain design decisions. The transformation process terminates when a physical *realization* of the system is obtained. With such an approach, implementation and specification only have relative meanings. A refinement produced in an intermediate step is an implementation of the refinement in the previous step, while it also serves as a specification for the refinement in the next step. The stepwise development process must be such that the final realization, as well as the intermediate refinements, conform to the initial specification. Certainly, some criterion should be designated beforehand for specifying the meaning and conditions of "*conform*". Actually, there have been many criteria proposed for defining possible conformance relationships, such as *trace preorder, reduction, extension* and *conformance* of [5, 6, 7], *failure* of [9, 10], and *failure trace* and *generalized failure* of [12]. These relations have been proposed largely for conformance testing of distributed systems, particularly of communication protocols.

---

* This research was supported by a grant from the Canadian Institute for Tele-communications Research under the NCE program of the Government of Canada.

The object-oriented paradigm, which has been gaining wide popularity in recent years, directly supports the stepwise refinement approach. In an object-oriented system, the components called *objects* are usually organized into object *classes*. An object class is a set of objects which are called its *instances* [2]. An object class definition specifies a set of allowable behaviors that each object instance in that class may exhibit. Furthermore, the *inheritance* mechanism allows one to define a new class (called *subclass*) from existing classes (called *superclasses*). The subclass inherits a set of nonconflicting behaviors specified by its superclasses. As such, the subclass is a refinement of each superclass in the sense that certain implementation decisions -- the elimination of conflicting behaviors, have been made in the subclass. Thus the conformance problem also arises in object-oriented systems, such as the conformance of a subclass to its superclasses, and the conformance of a physical realization (implementation) of an object instance to its class definition. As pointed out in [4], the inheritance mechanism imposes some special requirements on the criteria for defining conformance relations in object-oriented systems.

The rest of the paper is organized as follows. In Section 2, we present a conformance relation for object-oriented systems. This conformance relation was originally proposed in [4]. Our presentation of this conformance relation will be given with a slightly different notation. The possibility of defining other conformance relations for object-oriented systems is also discussed. In Section 3, we propose a test case derivation method for checking this conformance relation. Finally, in Section 4, we give the conclusion and point out some future research directions.

2   A Conformance Relation for Object-Oriented Systems

An object class definition in an object-oriented system specifies a set of allowable behaviors that may be adopted by object instances in that class. Thus a class definition essentially serves as a common specification for the physical realizations or implementations of all the object instances in that class. The purpose of this section is to introduce a conformance relation between two class specifications and then to extend the definition of this conformance relation to cover the case of conformance between an implementation of an object instance and a class definition. The possibility of defining other conformance relations will also be discussed in this section.

2.1 Requirements on the Conformance Relation Imposed by Multiple Inheritance

A number of models are available for describing behavior specifications. For object-oriented systems, however, a specification model should be carefully selected for class definitions such that the conformance relation defined based on this model will satisfy the special requirements imposed by a multiple inheritance mechanism [4]. These special requirements can be summarized as follows.

Let $C_1, C_2, ..., C_n$ be n class definitions described in a specification model. We use $INH(C_1, C_2, ..., C_n)$ to represent the subclass definition which is obtained by multiple inheritance from these n given class definitions. Further, let *con* denote a conformance relation defined between two class definitions such that C *con* C' means the class definition C conforms to the class definition C'. Then a natural requirement on the conformance relation can be informally stated as: $INH(C_1, C_2, ..., C_n)$ is the "largest" subclass definition which conforms to each of the n class definitions C_1, $C_2, ..., C_n$. The precise meaning of this requirement is given as the following property.

Property 2.1: Requirements for conformance relation
(1) $INH(C_1, C_2, ..., C_n)$ *con* C_i, for i = 1, 2, ..., n;
(2)   If C *con* C_i, for i = 1, 2, ..., n, then C *con* $INH(C_1, C_2, ..., C_n)$.
                                                        [End of property]

Let *equ* be a relation between two class definitions such that C *equ* C' iff C *con* C' and C' *con* C. Then the following corollary follows directly from Property 2.1.

Corollary 2.2
If C_1 *equ* C_2 *equ* ...*equ* C_n, then $INH(C_1, C_2, ..., C_n)$ *equ* C_i, for i =1, 2, ..., n.
                                                        [End of corollary]

The intuitive explanation of this corollary is that if the class definitions $C_1, C_2, ...,$ C_n specify n sets of *equivalent* behaviors, then the set of behaviors specified by $INH(C_1, C_2, ..., C_n)$ is equivalent to each of those n sets of behaviors.

2.2 Conformance between Two Class Specifications

To ensure that our conformance relation satisfies the requirements stated in Property 2.1 (and Corollary 2.2), we adopt a behavior specification model [4] which is a modified version of the *acceptance tree* model [9, 10]. Throughout this paper, let $L =$ $\{a_1, a_2, ..., a_n\}$ be a set of observable actions (we do not consider internal actions). L should be *finite* but *sufficiently large* to include all those actions that may be of interest. Let $P(L)$ denote the powerset of L, i.e. the set of all subsets of L. Then a class specification which specifies the allowed behaviors is described in terms of a set of pairs $< t, A_t >$, where t is a sequence of actions taken from L and A_t is a subset of $P(L)$. An element A of A_t is a subset of L and represents a state in which an object instance of the class may be after it has executed the sequence t of actions, and in which the instance object can only accept the actions in A. As such, A_t gives the set of all possible states in which an object instance may be after the execution of the sequence t of actions. Therefore, this specification model is non-deterministic.

The conformance relation based on this specification model, denoted as $\leq_A$ throughout the paper, was first proposed in [4] and later further generalized to the *constraint* relation ($\leq_C$) in [3] where an action is allowed to have input and output parameters.

Definition 2.3

Let $S = \{ S_1, S_2, ..., S_m \}$ and $S' = \{S_1', S_2', ..., S_k'\}$ be two subsets of $P(L)$. Then we say that

S' *covers* S iff for each $S_i \in S$, there exists an $S_j' \in S'$, such that $S_i \subseteq S_j'$.

[*End of definition*]

Definition 2.4: $\leq_A$

Given two class specifications $C = \{< t, A_t >\}$ and $C' = \{< t, A_t'>\}$. We say that C *conforms to* C', written $C \leq_A C'$, iff for each action sequence t, if there is a $< t, A_t > \in C$, then there exists a $< t, A_t'> \in C'$, such that A_t' *covers* A_t.

[*End of definition*]

It is easy to prove that $\leq_A$ is a preorder, i.e., a reflective and transitive relation. So we can define a *conformance equivalence* relation, denoted as $\approx_A$, as follows.

Definition 2.5: $\approx_A$

Given two classes definitions C and C'. We say that C and C' are *conformance equivalent*, written $C \approx_A C'$, iff $C \leq_A C'$ and $C' \leq_A C$.

[*End of definition*]

According to Property 2.1, for the conformance relation $\leq_A$, $INH(C_1, C_2, ..., C_n)$, the multiple inheritance of the class definitions $C_1, C_2, ..., C_n$, should be the "largest" class definition which conforms to ($\leq_A$) each of its n superclasses $C_1, C_2, ..., C_n$. The following theorem shows how to calculate $INH(C_1, C_2, ..., C_n)$ under our specification model.

Theorem 2.6: Derivation of inheritance in respect to $\leq_A$

For a given set of class definitions

$$C_i = \{< t, A_t^i >\}, \quad i = 1, 2, ..., n,$$

multiple inheritance $INH(C_1, C_2, ..., C_n)$ in respect to the conformance relation $\leq_A$ of Definition 2.4 can be defined as follows:

$$INH(C_1, C_2, ..., C_n)$$

$$= \{ < t, A_t > \mid < t, A_t^i > \in C_i \text{ for } i = 1, 2,...n, \text{ and}$$

$$A_t = \{ A_1 \cap A_2 \cap ... \cap A_n \mid A_i \in A_t^i, i = 1, 2,...n\} \}.$$

This definition satisfies the Property 2.1.

[*End of theorem*]

The proof of this theorem is omitted since it is easy to prove that the so-defined $INH(C_1, C_2, ..., C_n)$ is really the "largest" class definition which conforms to ($\leq_A$) each of the given class definitions $C_1, C_2, ..., C_n$. It should be noted that the multiple inheritance $INH(C_1, C_2, ..., C_n)$ of a given set of class definitions $C_1, C_2, ..., C_n$ is unique under the conformance equivalence relation of Definition 2.5.

2.3 Conformance of an Object Instance Implementation to a Class Definition

For a given class definition C and a given object instance implementation O, the conformance of O to C is essentially the conformance of C' to C, where C' is an imagined specification which specifies a set of behaviors exactly implemented by the given implementation O. Therefore, the definition of the conformance relation $\leq_A$ can be extended such that $\leq_A$ is defined not only between two class definitions, but also between an implementation of an object instance and a class definition. We say that O conforms to C, written as $O \leq_A C$, iff $C' \leq_A C$, where C' is the imagined specification.

2.4 Other Possible Conformance Relations

Under our specification model, the conformance relation $\leq_A$ and the trace preorder $\leq_T$ are so far the only two relations known to satisfy the requirements stated in Property 2.1 (and Corollary 2.2). However, the trace preorder $\leq_T$ and its induced trace equivalence $\approx_T$ are often criticized for being too weak in the sense that they sometimes identify too many specifications which should be distinguished [12]. This is the reason that, in this paper, we choose $\leq_A$ as the conformance relation for object-oriented systems.

It should be noted that there may be other conformance relations suitable for object-oriented systems. In fact, Property 2.1 implies that, for a given relation, if we can define an inheritance semantics such that those requirements are satisfied, then the given relation can be used as a conformance relation for the object-oriented systems with that defined inheritance semantics. In one recent work [15], it has been proved that two given behavior specifications, described under the acceptance graph model or the label transition system model, can be merged to give a new behavior specification which satisfies the *extension* relation [5] with respect to each of the two given specifications. It can be shown that the requirements of Property 2.1 (and Corollary 2.2) are satisfied if that merging operation is taken as the inheritance semantics and the extension relation as the conformance relation. Therefore, the merging operation gives us another view of multiple inheritance.

3 The Testing of the Conformance Relation $\leq_A$

We have seen in Section 2.3 that, for an object instance implementation O and a given class definition C, $O \leq_A C$, iff $C' \leq_A C$, where C' is an imagined specification which specifies a set of behaviors exactly implemented by the given implementation O. In black-box testing, however, the implementation O is treated as a black-box and therefore C' is unknown. As such the checking whether $O \leq_A C$ should be based on the experimental observations from O instead of C'.

3.1 Testing Assumptions

There has been much work reported in the literature on testing distributed systems. The theories and methods developed for testing nondeterministic systems [5, 6, 7, 8] usually assume that :

(A1) the "reset" function is correctly implemented, which guarantees that the implementation O, also called the implementation under test (IUT), can be brought back to its initial state from any other state; and

(A2) the IUT exhibits certain complete testing assumption, such that when a trace of actions is repeatedly applied to the IUT for a number of times, all the different paths with the same trace will be exercised at least once.

Many known implementation relations, such as *failure preorder*, *testing equivalence* and *conformance* of [5, 6, 7] have been proved to be testable under these assumptions [5, 6, 7, 8]. However, the relation $\leq_A$ is not testable under the same assumptions, as demonstrated by the following counter example.

Example 3.1
Consider the following class specification C and two object implementations O_1 and O_2 as shown in Figure 1. Obviously $O_1 \leq_A C$, while $O_2 \not\leq_A C$. However, under the usual assumptions (A1) and (A2), it is not difficult to see that O_1 and O_2, when disposed as black boxes, will result in the same set of experimental observations. This implies that, based on this experimental observation set, we can neither accept nor reject $O_1 \leq_A C$ and $O_2 \leq_A C$.

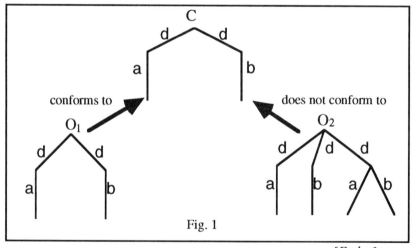

Fig. 1

[*End of example*]

This implies that some stronger assumptions should be made if we want to test $\leq_A$. For this purpose, we replace assumption (A1) by the following so-called *copying* assumption (A1').

(A1') The observer has the ability to take multiple copies of the object under test (OUT) at any stage of the test in order to independently experiment on each of these copies at a time.

Assumption (A1') has been adopted in certain testing methods [1, 13], where it was argued that this copying feature can be realized, in some situations, by a simple core dump procedure, and that it is applied in several kinds of fault tolerant systems. With assumption (A1'), we do not have to assume the correct implementation of the "reset" function, since this can be achieved with the assumed copying ability. As we will see in the following, under assumptions (A1') and (A2), we can develop test cases for verifying $\leq_A$.

3.2 Testing Language

The copying assumption (A1') actually allows us to use a testing language with the following syntax [cf. 13]:

$$\mathbf{e} ::= stop \mid a;\mathbf{e} \mid (\mathbf{e}_1, ..., \mathbf{e}_n)$$

where

(1)   *stop* has the same meaning as in Lotos [11];

(2) $a;\mathbf{e}$ (with $a \in L$) describes a test consisting of first applying the action a and in case of success proceeding with $\mathbf{e}$;

(3) $(\mathbf{e}_1, ..., \mathbf{e}_n)$ is a test which requires that n copies of the current state of the IUT are taken allowing all the tests $\mathbf{e}_1, ..., \mathbf{e}_n$ to be performed independently on the same state.

A test case can be formed by combining several constructs of the above three basic types. Any test case $\mathbf{E}$ used for checking a designated conformance relation (such as $\leq_A$) should be associated with a set $\mathbf{V}$ of *allowable observations* by which the experimenter can decide whether the implementation under test passes $\mathbf{E}$ based on the *actual observations* of the IUT to which $\mathbf{E}$ is applied. We use $(\mathbf{E}, \mathbf{V})$ to denote the test case $\mathbf{E}$ and its associated set $\mathbf{V}$ of allowable observations.

3.3 Test Derivation for $\leq_A$

Here we propose a test derivation method for testing the conformance relation $\leq_A$. This test derivation method will allow us to generate, from a given class definition C, a set of test cases which, when applied to an object instance implementation O, can check whether $O \leq_A C$.

Let $C = \{ <t, A_t> \}$ be a given class specification. For a $<t, A_t> \in C$, we construct a test case (E_t, V_t) where E_t is a test of the following format

$$E_t = t;(a_1;\textit{stop}, a_2;\textit{stop}, ..., a_n;\textit{stop}), \quad a_i \in L, \quad i = 1, 2, ..., n$$

and

$$V_t = A_t$$

is the set of allowed observations when E_t is applied to an implementation under test.

Suppose O is the implementation of an object instance under test. The test execution of O with E_t, i.e. a test run of E_t with O, goes in two phases:

Phase 1: we first experiment on O, in sequence, the actions in trace t. If this sequence of actions are successfully experimented, i.e. $O =t=> O'$, then goto phase 2; otherwise the result of this test run is inconclusive and we have to try a new test run.

Phase 2: n copies of O' are made. The i-th copy is experimented with a_i, for $i = 1, 2, ..., n$. we define the observation of this test run as
$$B = \{ a_i \mid \text{if i-th copy of } O' \text{ accepts } a_i \}$$
i.e., B consists of the actions that are acceptable by O after it executed the sequence of actions t.

Under the complete testing assumption (A2), we should be able to get, after a number of test runs of E_t with O, a set of all the *actual* experimental observations, which we write as

$$R_t(O) = \{ B \mid \text{each } B \text{ is an observation of a test run of } E_t \text{ with } O \}.$$

Definition 3.2
Let (E_t, V_t) be a test case and O an implementation of an object instance. We define that
O *passes* E_t iff V_t *covers* $R_t(O)$.

           [End of definition]

Then for the given class specification $C = \{ <t, A_t> \}$, a test suite TS_C, i.e. a set of test cases for checking the conformance relation $\leq_A$, can be constructed as follows:

$$TS_C = \{ (E_t, A_t) \mid \text{for each } <t, A_t> \in C \}.$$

The following theorem states that the so-constructed test suite checks that an object O conforms to the class definition C.

Theorem 3.3

$O \leq_A C$ iff   for each $(E_t, A_t) \in TS_C$, O *passes* E_t

[End of theorem]

It should be noted that when a given class definition C specifies a set of infinite behaviors, the so-constructed test suite TS_C is also infinite, that is, TS_C contains infinite number of test cases and therefore is not suitable for practical testing. A test derivation method was proposed in [8] which can be used to generate a finite test suite from a specification defining a set of infinite behaviors in terms of a (non-deterministic) finite state machine. The generated finite test suite can then be used, under certain appropriate assumptions, to check if an implementation satisfies the *failure preorder* in respect to the given specification. We believe that, following a similar approach to [8], we can also develop a test derivation method which will allow us to generate a *finite* test suite TS_C from an *infinite* class definition which can be modeled by a finite state machine, and the finite test suite TS_C allows us to test if an object implementation satisfies the conformance relation $\leq_A$ in respect to the given class definition.

4   Conclusions

We have proposed, in this paper, a conformance testing method for object-oriented software systems. The conformance relation that can be tested by this method is based on a modified version of the acceptance tree model [9, 10] and takes into account the special requirements imposed by the inheritance mechanism -- one of the primary strengths of the object-oriented paradigm. Under the *complete testing* and *copying* assumptions, the proposed method allows us to test whether an object instance implementation conforms to its class specification. Therefore this testing method applies at the *unit testing* level rather than at the *system testing* level.

How to test object-oriented software systems is a rather new research area. A lot of questions still remain open. One interesting question would be "*how to reuse tests*". Inheritance allows us to reuse the (behavior) specification of one object class in another object class specification. We believe that such a "*reuse*" relationship between two object classes also exists at the testing level, namely certain tests derived for one object class can also be reused as (part of) the tests of another object class. Actually, some work has been reported on the reuse of tests based on the deterministic input/output finite state machine model [14, 16]. In [16], it has been shown that the test suite generated from one finite state machine can be reused as a starting point for the incremental generation of a test suite for another finite state machine, provided that the latter has been obtained from the former by adding additional transitions. The conformance relation considered there is the *trace extension* which is one of the strongest relations for comparing deterministic finite state machines. It has also been pointed out in [14] that the test suites generated from two given finite state machines can be reused in the generation of the test suite for a third finite state machine which is the composition of the first two finite state machines, under the assumption that the first two finite state machines have no common behaviors.

Finally, we point out that it is also important to study the requirements imposed on testing by other object-oriented programming features, such as polymorphism and dynamic binding.

Acknowledgment: Special thanks go to Chen Wu, with whom the authors have had many useful discussions.

References

1. S. Abramsky: Observation equivalence as a testing equivalence, Theoretical Computer Science **53** (1987) 225-241.
2. A special issue on object-oriented design, Communication of the ACM **33** (9) (1990)
3. G. v. Bochmann and R. Gotzein: Specialization of object behaviors and requirement specifications, Technical Report (Draft) Département d'informatique et de recherche opérationelle, Université de Montréal (1992).
4. G. v. Bochmann: On the specialization of object behaviors, in J.Palsberg & M.I.Schwartzbach (eds.), Types, Inheritance and Assignments, a collection of position papers from the ECOOP'91 workshop W5, Geneva, Switzerland (July 1991).
5. E. Brinksma, et al: Lotos specification, their implementation and their tests, in B. Sarakaya and G. v. Bochmann (eds.), Protocol Specification, Testing, and Verification VI, North Holland, Amsterdam (1987) 349-360.
6. E. Brinksma: A theory for the derivation of tests, in S. Aggarwal (ed.), Protocol Specification, Testing, and Verification VIII, North Holland, Amsterdam (1988) 63-74.
7. E. Brinksma: A formal approach to testing distributed systems, draft version.
8. S. Fujiwara and G.v. Bochmann: Testing non-deterministic finite state machines with fault coverage, Proc. 4th International Workshop on Protocol Test Systems, Leidschendam, the Netherlands (October 15-17, 1991).
9. M. Hennessy: Acceptance trees, J. ACM **32** (4) (1985) 896-928.
10. M. Hennessy: Algebraic theory of processes, The MIT Press (1988).
11. ISO/DIS/8807, LOTOS - A formal description technique based on the temporal ordering of observational behavior, (1987).
12. R. Langerak: A testing theory for LOTOS using deadlock detection, in E. Brinksma, G. Scollo and C. A. Vissers (eds.), Protocol Specification, Testing, and Verification IX, North Holland, Amsterdam (1990) 87-98.
13. K. G. Larsen and A. Skou: Bisimulation through probabilistic testing, R88-29, Department of Math. and Compt. Sci., Aalborg University Center (1988).
14. E. H. Htite: Génération de tests pour le service de communication personnalisé, Mémoire de maîtrise ès sciences (M.Sc.), Département d'informatique et de recherche opérationelle, Université de Montréal, 1992.
15. F. Kendek and G.v. Bochmann: Merging Specification Behaviors, submitted for publication, 1992.
16. M. Yao, A. Petrenko and G.v. Bochmann: Conformance Testing of Protocol Machines without Reset, submitted for publication, 1992.

Testability of a communicating system through an environment

K. DRIRA[1], P. AZEMA[1], B. SOULAS[2] and A.M. CHEMALI[2]

[1] LAAS du CNRS, 7 avenue du Colonel Roche, F-31077 Toulouse Cedex
[2] EDF-DER, Renardières, BP1 F-77250 Moret sur Loing

Abstract. Testing of a component embedded in a whole system is addressed. The component is not as easy to check as when taken in isolation. The notion of conformance, as introduced by E. Brinksma and G. Scollo, is extended to formalize testing through an environment that does not allow some non conforming implementations to be discarded. A method enabling embedded systems testability to be characterized is proposed. It is based on the refusal graph whose arcs are labeled by events and nodes by subsets of events. An approach is presented to identify erroneous implementations. In particular, the least erroneous implementations discarded by testing through environment are defined and computed.

1 Introduction

Formal Description Techniques, and particularly, process algebra, like CCS [MI 80], CSP [HO 85], ACP [BK 85] and LoTos [LOT 88], are a well-known mathematical framework permitting communicating systems to be specified by composition and transformation of elementary behaviours. To verify the equivalence of two specifications of the same system, many algebraic relations have been proposed. The best known relations are presented and compared in [DN 87].

The use of formal specifications as a reference model to validate implementations, prompted the introduction of *testing equivalences* and especially *implementation relations* (validity or conformance) [AB 87, DH 84, LE 91]. This led, within the framework of LoTos, to a formal definition of conformance and a theory for the derivation of corresponding tests [BSS 87, BR 88]. From a system's specification a tester is generated. Applying this tester to an implementation ends with a verdict ('fail', 'pass') that distinguishes nonconforming implementations from the others.

This paper deals with the analysis of the testability of a system embedded in an environment. Such analyses are important because specific constraints are imposed for testing a module embedded whithin a system: The different components (processes or modules), that cooperate to implement the global behaviour, are specified. The delivered system comprises all the components already integrated. It can be shown, by testing, that the global behaviour conforms to the expected one. But what conclusion may be drawn about the conformance of a given component to its specifcation ?

Suppose we are particularly (or only), interested in a component whose implementation and specification are I and M respectively. The problem, to be solved here, can be summarized as follows: what can be decided about the conformance of this component to its specification, M, assuming the global system ('I within E', E being the environment: i.e. the other components are interconnected) passes the tests[3] of the specification 'M within E'. M testability through its environment, E, is said to be good, if testing the whole system ('I within E') discards as many nonconforming M implementations as direct testing of M (i.e. without environment) would.

Here an approach is proposed for the analysis of a component testability when it can only be tested within the whole system. Intuitively this testing is less powerful than the one that has direct access to the isolated component. In practice, this is expressed by non-detection of some erroneous implementations that would have been discarded by directly testing this system. This will be called *testability degradation*.

Testability analysis is easily understood in the idealistic case :
conformance is a total ordering, $\geq$, that places the specification M and its implementations[4] at the same axis: $\{I < M\} \cup \{M\} \cup \{I > M\}$;
testing an implementation I can lead to either of the conclusions: $I > M$ (I conforming) or $I < M$ (I nonconforming).
In this idealistic case, testability (degradation) analysis consists of searching the new reference model, $M'(\leq M)$, such that only '$I < M'$' can be checked when testing I through the environment. M' is called the *limit* of testability degradation (or shortly the limit of testability). Testability degradation is expressed by the widening of the margin of nonconforming implementations not detected through the environment: $\{I, M' < I < M\}$

This paper encompasses this introduction and three sections.

Section 2 describes conformance and other relations as defined in [BR 88] and characterizes erroneous implementations that conformance testing can discard. Testing through an environment is then presented. Testability analysis and related problems are detailed. Finally, the limits of testability are characterized.

Section 3 introduces a behaviour representation structure, referred to as "*Refusal graph*", providing composition and restriction operators together with testing relations ($conf$, red, $\approx_g$) consistent with those initially defined in [BR 88].

Section 4 provides a method for testability analysis based on the refusal graph. An ordered characterization of erroneous implementations allows identification of the least erroneous implementations that testing through an environment can discard.

---

[3] or part of these tests that aim at activating this component

[4] rather than physical implementations, we consider models of these implementations described in the same formalism as the specification. This allows us to compare implementations as well as implementation to a given specification. This identification is discussed in [LE2 91].

2 Conformance through environment

2.1 Preliminary Definitions

This section recalls conformance related definitions first introduced by Brinksma, Scollo and Steenbergen in [BSS 87]. The equivalent definitions used are also employed by Leduc in [LE 90]. This section also presents new relations dealing with non conformance.

Labeled Transition System

A finite Labeled Transition System (LTS) is a quadruple: $\mathcal{S} = (S, \Sigma, \Delta, s_0)$ where:

- S is a finite set of states, and s_0, $s_0 \in S$, is the initial state of $\mathcal{S}$.
- Σ is a finite set of visible actions, or labels
- $\Delta \subseteq S \times (\Sigma \cup \{\tau\}) \times S$: the transitions set, $\tau \notin \Sigma$ is called internal or invisible action. An element $(x, \mu, y) \in \Delta$ is denoted: $x \xrightarrow{\mu} y$

Another transition relation, $\{\xRightarrow{\mu}\}_{\mu \in \Sigma \cup \{\epsilon\}}$ is defined in a standard way by:

- $s \xRightarrow{\epsilon} s' : s = s'$ or $s \xrightarrow{\tau} s_1 \xrightarrow{\tau} \cdots \xrightarrow{\tau} s_n \xrightarrow{\tau} s'$
- $s \xRightarrow{\mu} s' : s \xRightarrow{\epsilon} s_1 \xrightarrow{\mu} s_1 \xRightarrow{\epsilon} s'$

The following notations are used:

- $s \xRightarrow{\mu}$ means $\exists s'\ s \xRightarrow{\mu} s'$. $s \xnRightarrow{\mu}$ means $\neg(s \xRightarrow{\mu})$.
- $out(s) = \{\mu \in \Sigma \mid s \xRightarrow{\mu}\}$ denotes the set of visible actions that can be performed by the system at the state s

This relation is extended to sequences (i.e. words or strings over Σ: $\sigma \in \Sigma^*$) by:

- if σ is the sequence $\mu_1 \cdots \mu_n$ write $s \xRightarrow{\sigma} s'$ when $s \xRightarrow{\mu_1} s_1 \xRightarrow{\mu_2} \cdots \xRightarrow{\mu_{n-1}} s_n \xRightarrow{\mu_n} s'$

The empty sequence is denoted ϵ. As in the case of a state output, "traces of a state" refer to the set of all sequences of visible actions, $\sigma \in \Sigma^*$, that can be performed from this state: $Tr(s) = \{\sigma \in \Sigma^* \mid s \xRightarrow{\sigma}\}$. The traces of LTS are those of its initial state.

Conforming implementations

In the sequel, A is a set of actions: $A \subseteq \Sigma$; σ is a sequence of actions: $\sigma \in \Sigma^*$. P (resp. P', I, M ...) denotes a behaviour expression associated with a finite Labeled
Transition System whose initial state is P (resp. P', I, M ...).

- $P\ ref\ A$ when $\forall a \in A\ P \xnRightarrow{a}$. P has no derivate by any action a among A. Then it is said that P refuses A. Note that if P refuses A then P refuses all subsets of A (i.e. $B \subseteq A$ implies $P\ ref\ B$)
- $P\ after\ \sigma = \{P' : P \xRightarrow{\sigma} P'\}$: set of all derivates of P via sequence σ. If $\sigma \notin Tr(P)$ then P has no derivate via σ and then $P\ after\ \sigma = \emptyset$.
- $(P\ after\ \sigma)\ ref\ A$ when $(\exists P' \in P\ after\ \sigma\ , P'\ ref\ A)$ at least one of the derivates of P refuses A.

When $\sigma \notin Tr(P)$, there exists no element in $(P\ after\ \sigma)$ and then $(P\ after\ \sigma)\ ref\ A$ has 'false' as logical value. This substanciates the equivalence of the following two definitions of the conformance relation.

- **conformance:** implementation I is said to be conforming to specification M when I deadlocks less often than M when placed in an environment whose traces

are limited to those of M. Formally $I \underline{conf} M \equiv_{df} \forall \sigma \in Tr(M) \cap Tr(I), \forall A \subseteq \Sigma$: if $(I \ after \ \sigma) \ ref \ A$, then $(M \ after \ \sigma) \ ref \ A$. Or equivalently:
$\forall \sigma \in Tr(M), \forall A \subseteq \Sigma$: if $(I \ after \ \sigma) \ ref \ A$, then $(M \ after \ \sigma) \ ref \ A$

• **reduction:** A reduction is a conforming implementation with less traces than the specification. Formally: $I \underline{red} M \equiv_{df} (I \underline{conf} M) \wedge Tr(I) \subseteq Tr(M)$

• **extension:** An extension is a conforming implementation that has more traces than the specification. Formally: $I \underline{ext} M \equiv_{df} (I \underline{conf} M) \wedge Tr(I) \supseteq Tr(M)$

• **improvement:** An improvement is a conforming implementation possessing the same traces as the specification. Formally: $I \geq M \equiv_{df} Tr(I) = Tr(M)$ and $I \underline{conf} M$. We also say that I is more deterministic than M. The symbol $\leq$ is used to denote $\geq^{-1}$: $I \leq M \stackrel{def}{\Longleftrightarrow} M \geq I$. $I \leq M$ means: I is less deterministic than M.

Note that $(I \geq M) \stackrel{def}{\Longleftrightarrow} (I \underline{red} M) \wedge (I \underline{ext} M)$.

• **testing equivalent** It is these implementations which are as deterministic as the specification. Formally: $I \underline{te} M$ iff $(I \underline{red} M) \wedge (M \underline{red} I)$.

Non conforming implementations

Definition 1 Distortion. Every nonconforming implementation with the same traces as the specification. I is said to be a distortion of M and is denoted $I \ dis \ M$ when $Tr(I) = Tr(M)$ and $I \ \neg conf \ M$.

Definition 2 Degradation. Every implementation (strictly) less deterministic than the specification. I is said to be a degradation of M and is denoted $I < M$ when $I \leq M$ and $\neg(M \underline{te} I)$. Equivalently: A degradation I of M is a distortion such that $M \underline{conf} I$.

Summary of the different relations

Let $\mathcal{I}$ denote the implementation set of a specification M. A conformance test splits $\mathcal{I}$ into two subsets:

• $\mathcal{I}^{\oplus}$ is the set of conforming implementations: $\{I \in \mathcal{I} : I \ conf \ M\} = Conf(M)$ (upper zone of Fig. 1). These implementations pass the conformance test.

• $\mathcal{I}^{\ominus}$ is the set of nonconforming implementations: $\{I \in \mathcal{I} : I \ \neg conf \ M\} = \neg Conf(M)$. (lower zone of Fig. 1). These implementations fail the conformance test.

On the other hand, $\mathcal{I}$ can be partitioned into the set of implementations whose traces are comparable to those of M (inside of the circles of Fig. 1), and its complementary: $\mathcal{I} = (A \cup B) \cup (\mathcal{I} \setminus (A \cup B))$ where

$A = \{I \in \mathcal{I} : Tr(I) \subseteq Tr(M)\}$ is the set of trace reductions of M. This set is denoted Red_tr(M) and is the left circle of Fig. 1.

$B = \{I \in \mathcal{I} : Tr(I) \supseteq Tr(M)\}$ is the set of trace extensions of M. This set is denoted Ext_tr(M) and is the right circle of Fig. 1.

Intersection of these different sets is summarized in the following tables and illustrated in Fig. 1.

2.2   Testing through an environment

Here *the test of a system through an environment* is formalized using Lotos operators as a basis for behaviour composition. The system is a finite Lotos

conformance zone: ⊕

designation	Symbol	Notation
Conforming	$\mathcal{I}^{\oplus}$	Conf(M)
Reductions	$A \cap \mathcal{I}^{\oplus}$	Red(M)
Extensions	$B \cap \mathcal{I}^{\oplus}$	Ext(M)
Improvements	$A \cap B \cap \mathcal{I}^{\oplus}$	Imv(M)

nonconformance zone : ⊖

designation	Symbol	Notation
Nonconforming	$\mathcal{I}^{\ominus}$	¬Conf(M)
Distortions	$A \cap B \cap \mathcal{I}^{\ominus}$	Dis(M)
Degradations	$\subseteq (A \cap B \cap \mathcal{I}^{\ominus})$	Deg(M)

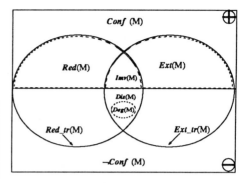

Fig. 1. Zones of the implementations domain

process (which can be represented by a finite LTS). The environment is the particular context $hide\ \Gamma\ in\ (\bullet|[\Gamma]|E)$, where E is finite Lotos process.

We suppose that the global implementation results from the composition of an implementation of M (i.e. another process I) with an environment identical[5] to E: Implementation under test is $hide\ \Gamma\ in\ (I|[\Gamma]|E)$

The conforming/nonconforming (pass/fail) verdict is considered as a verdict directly concerning M. In other words, a failure only involves the implementation of component M (which is then called component under test).

Definition 3 Conformance through an environment. An implementation I conforms to a specification M through E if $hide\ \Gamma\ in\ (I|[\Gamma]|E)$ conforms to $hide\ \Gamma\ in\ (M|[\Gamma]|E)$. This will be noted: $I\ conf_E\ M$

2.3 Testability Analysis

Analysis of M testability through environment E is tantamount to introducing, in the implementation domain zones, a new partition of $\mathcal{I}$ given by the conformance verdict when testing implementations through the environment. This leads us to compare M testability after embedding in environment E, and testability of isolated M.

Adopting the intuitive idea that testing through an environment can only degrade testability [6] leads to the following paradox: testing through an environment may evaluate as **nonconforming** some conforming implementations.

Indeed extensions (right upper half of the circle in Fig. 1) may become nonconforming when testing through an environment. This can be explained by considering the objective of conformance testing: conformance testing aims at

---

[5] This hypothesis can be relaxed without affecting the results : 'identical' can be replaced by 'observationally equivalent' or also another equivalence stronger than testing equivalence and which is a congruence w.r.t. hiding and composition operators ($hide$ and $||$).

[6] i.e. nonconforming implementations are erroneously evaluated as conforming

verifying the correct functioning of the implementation with respect to the specified behaviour: A conformance tester accepts implementations that extend the specification traces as soon as they conform to the specified behaviour. Without making any assumptions on the environment behaviour, the latter may have a superset of traces (relativeto synchronization actions) of the specification. The environment therefore participates in *robustness testing*[7] [BR 88]. And testing through this environment rejects conforming implementations that are not reductions of the specification.

This paradox vanishes when the synchronization traces of the environment are restricted to those of the specification.

On the other hand, without assuming that hiding synchronization actions creates no divergence, reductions as well as improvement might be evaluated as nonconforming when checked through an environment.

In Figure 2, the E-conformance boundaries (continuous line) cross the conformance boundaries (horizontal dashed line), which result from a test of the isolated component.

The general case, depicted in part (a) of Fig. 2, illustrates the incomparability of these two conformance tests, because some conforming implementations will be regarded as nonconforming when tested through the environment. These are nonconforming implementations depicted by the horizontally dashed regions in part (a) of the figure.

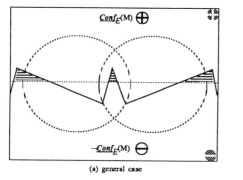

(a) general case

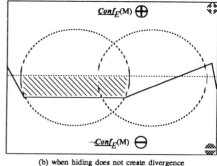

(b) when hiding does not create divergence

Fig. 2. Conformance through environment

Tracing regularity, in the trace inclusion zone, of part (b) of Fig. 2 shows that, in the absence of divergence, conforming implementations with at the most the same traces as the specification (reductions) remain conforming when tested through the environment. This expresses the so-called conformance preservation. It can be formalized as follows

---

[7] i.e. testing implementation against an environment that behaves incorrectly. This kind of test guarantees that the implementation does not possess unspecified traces.

Proposition 4. *conformance preservation*
In the absence of divergence:
• *If I red M then I red_E M (and then I $conf_E$ M) [LE 87]*
where I red_E M $\equiv_{df}$ (hide Γ in I||[Γ]|E) red (hide Γ in M|[Γ]|E),
Reductions are conforming implementations that remain conforming when tested through the environment.

2.4 Limits of testing through an environment

No proposition can be established about the existence of nonconformance detection limits by testing through an environment. This strongly depends on the specification of the component under test and on its environment. Nevertheless, they may have a meaning when they exist.

A limit is an erroneous implementation which may be detected when testing through the environment and such that: only 'more erroneous' implementations will be detected.

The 'more erroneous' relation will be expressed by the pre-order $\leq$; and I_1 is said to be more erroneous than I_2 when $I_1 \leq I_2$.

It can now be stated that the limits are the least erroneous implementations that testing through environment can discard:

An erroneous implementation, I, is a limit of nonconformance detection if
(i) nonconformance of I is detected (through the environment).
(ii) nonconformance of (strictly) less erroneous implementations (i.e. $I' > I$) is not detected (through the environment).

Assuming that hiding creates no divergence, the following proposition shows that implementations that are more erroneous than a detected erroneous implementation (and particularly a limit) will also be detected.

Proposition 5. *non conformance detection*
Given two implementations, I and I' , of specification M
if $(I \neg conf_E M)$ then $(I' \leq I) \Rightarrow (I' \neg conf_E M)$
if I is detected by testing through E, then all implementations, which are more erroneous than I, will also be detected.

3 Refusal Graphs for computing limits of testability

Labeled transition systems are the initial semantics of LOTOS. Another semantic model (Rooted Failure Tree with divergence) was defined in [LE 90] and proposed to interpret LOTOS specifications. This model was useful for enriching the basic model (Failure tree) of the theory for tests derivation of [BR 88] with *composition* and *restriction* (or *hiding*) operators. The model referred to as *Refusal Graph* presented here, makes the approach for the testability analysis (presented in the next section) operational.

In this section, the refusal graph structure is defined along with the composition and restriction operators. Finally, conformance (*conf*), reduction (*red*) and equivalence ($\approx_g$) relations are defined directly on the refusal graph structure. These relations are (bi)simulation-like defined [PA 81, MI 80] and therefore easier to check than the initial definitions on transition systems.

3.1 Refusal Graph

The Refusal Graph is a structure specifying the failures of a communicating system [HO 85] (a failure is a couple made up of a sequence of actions in which the system may engage, and a set of actions it can refuse after this sequence).

Definition 6 Refusal Graph. A refusal graph, denoted RG, is a bilabeled graph represented by a 5-tuple $(S, \Sigma, \Delta, Ref, s_0)$ where:
- S is a finite set of states, $s_0 \in S$ is an element of S called initial state.
- $\Sigma \subseteq L$ is a finite set of actions (edge labels), also called the alphabet of RG,
- $\Delta \subseteq (S \times \Sigma \times S)$ is a set of transitions. An element $(s, a, s') \in \Sigma$ is denoted: $s \overset{a}{\Rightarrow} s'$. Transitions described in Δ must verify the following determinism property:
$$\forall s \in S, \forall a \in \Sigma; \exists \text{ at the most one } s' \in S \text{ such that } s \overset{a}{\Rightarrow} s'.$$
- $Ref : S \longrightarrow \mathcal{P}(\mathcal{P}(L))$ is an application which defines for each state, the sets of actions that may be refused after the sequence leading to this state.

To avoid redundancy, refusal sets must be minimal w.r.t. set inclusion: $\forall s \in S, \forall X, Y \in Ref(s) : (Y \subseteq X) \Rightarrow (X = Y)$. Or equivalently $\not\exists X, Y \in Ref(s) : (X \neq Y) \wedge (Y \subseteq X)$.
i.e. no subset of an element of $Ref(s)$ is in $Ref(s)$. In other words, all elements of a refusal set are pairwise incomparable (w.r.t set inclusion $\subseteq$).

And to avoid describing imaginary systems, one of the following hypothesis is imposed on the refusal graph structure:
h1. $\forall X \in Ref(s), X \subseteq out(s)$. Only refused parts of the output[8] set are considered. Or
h2. $\forall X \in Ref(s), X \cup (L \setminus out(s)) \in Ref(s)$. Refused parts are saturated with respect to output complement. This second hypothesis is used in [BR 88, LE 90]

The changeover from a refusal set, R, built according to h1, to its representation according to h2 is possible by the completion transformation $complete(Ref(s)) = \{X \cup (L \setminus out(s)), X \in Ref(s)\}$. (The reverse changeover corresponding to the reverse transformation $uncomplete(R) = \{X \cap out(s), X \in Ref(s)\}$.)

Let $G_1 = (S_1, \Sigma_1, \Delta_1, Ref_1, s_0^1)$ and $G_2 = (S_2, \Sigma_2, \Delta_2, Ref_2, s_0^2)$ be two refusal graphs such that Ref_1 and Ref_2 are defined with respect to the completion hypothesis (h2.) with alphabet $L = \Sigma_1 \cup \Sigma_2$ as superset of Σ_1 and Σ_2. Let $\Gamma(\subseteq \Sigma_1 \cup \Sigma_2)$ be a set of actions such that $\Sigma_1 \cap \Sigma_2 \subseteq \Gamma$. [9]

Definition 7 refusal graph composition. The composition of G_1 and G_2 is the refusal graph $G = (S, \Sigma, \Delta, Ref, s_0)$ defined by:
- Set of states $S \subseteq S_1 \times S_2$ is such that $(s_0^1, s_0^2) \in S$, and every couple of elements

---

[8] $out(s) = \{a \in \Sigma, \exists s' \in S : s \overset{a}{\Rightarrow} s'\}$ is called output of state s.

[9] This hypothesis allows the definition of the composition operator to be simplified compared to the RFT model of [LE 90]. It is equivalent to assuming that only synchronization gates may have the same name in the system and environment specifications which is not restrictive in the framework of testing through an environment.

of S_1 and S_2 which may follow an element of S by one of the transition rules (i), (ii), (iii), given below, is an element of S,

- $\Sigma = \Sigma_1 \cup \Sigma_2$ is the set of actions,
- Δ is defined by: $\forall a \in \Gamma, \forall a \in (\Sigma_1 \setminus \Gamma), \forall b \in (\Sigma_2 \setminus \Gamma)$:

  (i) $\dfrac{s_1 \overset{a}{\Rightarrow} s_1', \; s_2 \overset{a}{\Rightarrow} s_2'}{(s_1,s_2) \overset{a}{\Rightarrow} (s_1',s_2')}$ (ii) $\dfrac{s_1 \overset{a}{\Rightarrow} s_1'}{(s_1,s_2) \overset{a}{\Rightarrow} (s_1',s_2)}$, (iii) $\dfrac{s_2 \overset{b}{\Rightarrow} s_2'}{(s_1,s_2) \overset{b}{\Rightarrow} (s_1,s_2')}$

- $(\forall (r,s) \in S) \; Ref((r,s)) = \{((X_1 \cup X_2) \cap \Gamma) \cup (X_1 \cap X_2), X_1 \in Ref_1(r), X_2 \in Ref_2(s)\}$
- $s_0 = (s_0^1, s_0^2)$ is the initial state.

To define the restriction operator on refusal graphs, it is assumed that the restriction creates no divergence. In the opposite case, only upper and lower bounds may be obtained as in [LE 90].

Given a refusal graph $G = (S, \Sigma, \Delta, Ref, s_0)$ and a set of actions $\Gamma \subseteq \Sigma$,
Definition 8 refusal graph restriction. The restriction of Γ in G, is the refusal graph $G' = (S', \Sigma', \Delta', Ref', s_0')$ denoted $G \setminus \Gamma$ and defined by:

- $s_0' = \{s_i : s_0 \overset{\gamma}{\Rightarrow} s_i, \gamma \in \Gamma^*\}$ is the initial state. It is the set of all the states reached from s_0 by a sequence of actions in the restriction set.
- $S' \subseteq \mathcal{P}(S)$: whose elements are defined by the series $(s_n')_{n \geq 0} : s_n' = \delta(s_{n-1}')$ where:

$\delta(s') = \bigcup_{s \in s'} \delta(s), \; \delta(s) = \bigcup_{a \in (\Sigma \setminus \Gamma)} \delta_a(s), \; \delta_a(s) = \{t \in S, \exists \gamma_1, \gamma_2 \in \Gamma^* : s \overset{\gamma_1 a \gamma_2}{\Rightarrow} t\}$

states of G' are sets of G states that may be reached from s_0' by a sequence where actions in Γ are considered as internal.

- $\Sigma' = \Sigma \setminus \Gamma$: the alphabet of G' is restricted to $\Sigma \setminus \Gamma$
- Δ' is such that: $\forall a \in (\Sigma \setminus \Gamma) \; s_1' \overset{a}{\Rightarrow} s_2'$ iff $\exists s_1 \in s_1', \exists s_2 \in s_2', \exists \gamma_1, \gamma_2 \in \Gamma^*$: $s_1 \overset{\gamma_1 a \gamma_2}{\Rightarrow} s_2$
- $Ref'(s') = \{X \setminus \Gamma, X \in Ref(s) \; et \; \Gamma \subset X, s \in s'\} \setminus \{Y \in Ref'(s') | \exists X \in Ref'(s') : Y \subset X\}$

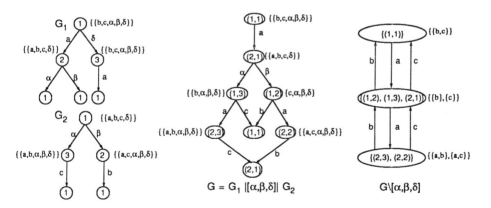

Fig. 3. composition and restriction

Notations: If L is a finite set, then

- $\mathcal{P}(L)$ denotes the power set of L, i.e. the set of subsets of L
- for $A \in \mathcal{P}(\mathcal{P}(L))$ we note $Min(A) = A \setminus \{X, \exists Y \in A : X \subseteq Y, et X \neq Y\}$.
- for $R \subseteq \mathcal{P}(\mathcal{P}(L))$ we note $Min(R) = \{Min(A), A \in R\}$.
- the minimal refusal sets on alphabet $L' \subseteq L$ are elements of $Min(\mathcal{P}(\mathcal{P}(L')))$
- for every minimal refusal set A, $X \in A \equiv_{df} \exists Y \in A : X \subseteq Y$.
- $A \sqsubset B \equiv_{df} \forall X, (X \in A) \Rightarrow (X \in B)$
- $A \sqsubset_s B \equiv_{df} (A \sqsubset B) \wedge (A \neq B)$
- Application Ref_I defines the refusal sets for the states of refusal graph I.
- Application Ref_E^I defines the refusal sets for the states of refusal graph $(I|[\Gamma]|E) \setminus \Gamma$.

3.2 Binary relations over refusal graphs

Consider two refusal graphs defined over the same alphabet[10] L: $I = (S_I, L, \Delta_I, Ref_I, I)$ and $M = (S_M, L, \Delta_M, Ref_M, M)$.

Definition 9 .
- conformance $I \, conf \, M \equiv_{df}$
    (i) $Ref_I(I) \sqsubset Ref_M(M)$
    (ii) $\forall a \in out(I) \cap out(M) : if \, I \overset{a}{\Rightarrow} I' \, then \, M \overset{a}{\Rightarrow} M' \, and \, I' \, conf \, M'$.
- reduction $I \, red \, M \equiv_{df}$
    (i) $Ref_I(I) \sqsubset Ref_M(M)$
    (ii) $\forall a \in L : if \, I \overset{a}{\Rightarrow} I' \, then \, M \overset{a}{\Rightarrow} M' \, and \, I' \, red \, M'$.
- testing equivalence $I \approx_g M \equiv_{df} I \, red \, M \, et \, M \, red \, I$

The refusal graph corresponding to a transition system is obtained by making deterministic the transition system considered as an automaton whose every state is terminal. This provides a mapping, *newState*, which associates each state of the refusal graph with a set of states of the transition system. The refusal sets of a state g are given by: $Ref(g) = Min(\{out(g) \setminus out(s), s \in newState(g)\})$.

Proposition 10 is related to the compatibility of the composition and restriction operators of the refusal graphs with those defined on transition systems. The latter are similar to basic LOTOS operators: a transition system is viewed as a set of processes, S, executing actions in $\Sigma \cup \{i = \tau\}$ according to the transition rules defined by Δ. The initial behaviour being the initial state of the transition system, i.e. s_0.

For any transition systems, S_1 and S_2, we have:

Proposition 10. *operator compatibility*
- *composition:* $rg(S_1|[\Gamma]|S_2) \approx_g rg(S_1)|[\Gamma]|rg(S_2)$
- *restriction:* $rg(hide \, \Gamma \, in \, S_1) \approx_g rg(S_1) \setminus \Gamma$

Relations $\geq$, $\leq$, and *dis* are also defined over refusal graphs, by replacing the definition of *conf* of transition systems by its dual relation of refusal graphs. For these two types of relations the same symbols are kept.

---

[10] in practice L is the union of the alphabets of the two refusal graphs

4 Testability through an environment

This section is dedicated to the use of the refusal graphs structure for computing the limits of nonconformance detection when testing through an environment.

4.1 Ordered erroneous implementations

This section introduces the transformations employed to simulate the three types of implementations presented earlier (paragraph 2.1), namely, *'improvements'*, *'degradations'*, and *'distortions'*[11].

With respect to testability analysis, we want particularly to order the erroneous implementations (degradations and distortions) such that they can then be classified in agreement with the degradation relation ($<$). Thus an approach, based on an ordered analysis of erroneous implementations, can be developed to identify the limits.

As illustrated in Fig. 4, testability analysis consists of tracing limits (painted ovals) of nondetection of degradations (and distortions) over the set of ordered erroneous implementations.

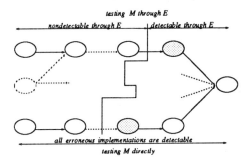

Fig. 4. testability Degradation

For every state, i, of the specification refusal graph, $M = (S, \Sigma, \Delta, Ref, s_0)$, a mapping, Ψ_i is defined associating with each refusal set, $A \in Min(\mathcal{P}(\mathcal{P}(out(i))))$, an erroneous implementation (degradation or distorsion), or a conforming implementation (improvement). Let $\mathcal{G}$ denote the set of implementations having the same refusal graph as M except for the refusal sets (i.e. the same state space, the same edge labels, but not the same state labels).

Let $(\mathcal{T}, \mathbb{C})$ denote the lattice $(Min(\mathcal{P}(\mathcal{P}(out(i)))), \mathbb{C})$. [12] And $\forall A \in \mathcal{T}$, $\forall \mathcal{E} \subseteq \mathcal{T}$

$\underline{A} = \{B \in \mathcal{T}, B \mathbb{C}_s A\}$, $\overline{A} = \{B \in \mathcal{T}, A \mathbb{C}_s B\}$ et $inf(\mathcal{E}) = \{A \in \mathcal{E}, \nexists B \in \mathcal{E}, B \mathbb{C}_s A\}$.

---

[11] For the latter, we consider only those which may not be captured as degradations.

[12] In practice it is possible to use the same ordered set $Min(\mathcal{P}(\mathcal{P}(\Sigma)))$, $\mathbb{C}$, for all the states.

$$\Psi_i : T \longrightarrow \mathcal{G}$$
$$A \longrightarrow \Psi_i(A) = (S, \Sigma, \Delta, Ref', s_0) \text{ such that:}$$
$$\begin{cases} \forall j \in S, j \neq i, Ref'(j) = Ref(j) \\ Ref'(i) = A \end{cases}$$

Thus a lattice $(\Psi_i(T), \geq)$ isomorphic to $(T, \sqsubseteq)$ is built. In particular we verify that: $B \sqsubseteq A$ iff $\Psi_i(B) \geq \Psi_i(A)$, meaning: $\Psi_i(B)$ is more deterministic than $\Psi_i(A)$. When $B \sqsubseteq_s A$ then $\Psi_i(B) > \Psi_i(A)$ and $\Psi_i(A)$ is a degradation of $\Psi_i(B)$.

- $I \in \Psi_i(Ref(i))$ implies $I > M$. *These are M improvements.*
- $I \in \Psi_i(\overline{Ref(i)})$ implies $I < M$. *These are M degradations.*
- $I \in \Psi_i(T \setminus (Ref(i) \cup \overline{Ref(i)} \cup \{Ref(i)\}))$ implies I *dis* M. *These are M distortions.*

By way of example, consider the state 2 of the refusal graph M represented by G_1 in the Fig. 3. $out(2) = \{\alpha, \beta\}$ et $Ref(2) = \{\{\}\}$

According to the lattice depicted in Fig. 5, M has four degradations [13]: $M_{1,1}$ is the one having $\{\{\alpha\}\}$ as refusal set at the state 2. $M_{2,1}$ has $\{\{\beta\}\}$ as refusal set. $M_{2,2} = M_{1,2}$ have $\{\{\alpha\}, \{\beta\}\}$ as refusal set. And finally $M_{2,3} = M_{1,3} = M_{min}$ have $\{\{\alpha, \beta\}\}$ (i.e. $\{out(2)\}$) as refusal set.

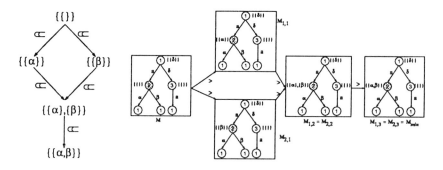

Fig. 5. Ordered refusal sets and induced Ordered degradations

4.2 Use of refusal graphs for limits location

Refusal graphs allow erroneous implementation characterization problem to be reduced to elementary operations on the refusal set structure. Just as in the case of testability degradation limit identification. Indeed, the definition on refusal graphs of the composition and restriction operators allows us to decide if an error is detectable through the environment by comparing (two) refusal sets w.r.t. order relation $\sqsubseteq$.

---

[13] to simplify we present refusal sets according to the first hypothesis h1 of refusal graphs definition

Let $Deg(i) = \overline{Ref_M(i)}$, $Imv(i) = Ref_M(i)$, $Dis(i) = T \setminus (Deg(i) \cup Imv(i) \cup \{Ref_M(i)\})$, and $Err(i) = Deg(i) \cup \overline{Dis(i)}$

Simulating an error related to state i, consists in replacing the refusal set at this state, $Ref_M(i)$, by one, say A, of the lower bounds of $Err(i)$.

To verify whether this error is a limit (of conformance testing through environment E) the following steps are executed:

- choose a state s of $(M\|[\Gamma]\|E) \setminus \Gamma$ which could have been "disturbed" by this error, and which includes a couple of the form $(i, *)$, ($*$ matching any E state).

- compute the new refusal set of s by replacing, $Ref_M(i)$ by the (completed) refusal set $complete(A)$.
- test whether the obtained set is included (in the sense of $\sqsubset$) in the initial refusal set. If it is not (the corresponding erroneous implementation is a limit), stop the exploration (of the matching states, s) and add this error to the set of limits sought. Remove A and all its successors (i.e. all sets B such that $A \sqsubset B$) from set of errors to be explored. The new set to explore is then $Err(i) \setminus (\overline{A} \cup \{A\})$.
  In the opposite case (the erroneous implementation corresponding to A cannot be detected in any state s), only A is removed from the set of errors to be explored.

Formalization: For every state, i, of the refusal graph, let (G, V) denote the oriented graph structure that represents the lattice $(Min(\mathcal{P}(\mathcal{P}(out(i)))), \sqsubset)$.

- G is a set of nodes representing the lattice elements.
These refusal sets are candidate for replacing the refusal set $Ref(i)$ that will be referred to as e_i.
- V is the set of edges representing the (strict) inclusion of two refusal sets.
- (G, V^*) is the transitive closure of (G, V).

For every couple of (distinct) nodes (e, e'),
- $(e, e') \in V$ means: $e \sqsubset e'$ and $\nexists e''$ such that $e \sqsubset_s e'' \sqsubset_s e'$
- $(e, e') \in V^*$ means: $\exists e_1, .., e_k : e \sqsubset_s e_1 \sqsubset_s \cdots \sqsubset_s e_k \sqsubset_s e'$

The search for the limits of degradations and distortions that cannot be detected when testing through the environment can be formalized by the calculus of the set **Limits** returned by the following algorithm:

```
Distortions := G \ {e_i} \ {e : (e, e_i) ∈ V* ,or, (e_i, e) ∈ V*}
Degradations := {e : (e_i, e) ∈ V*}
OrderedErrors := Distortions ∪ Degradations
Limits := ∅
PotLimits:= inf(OrderedErrors)
while PotLimits ≠ ∅ do
        forall e ∈ PotLimits do
                detected(e) := VerifyBySubstitution(i,e)
                if detected(e) then
                        OrderedErrors:= OrderedErrors\{e}\ {e_k : (e, e_k) ∈ V*}
                        Limits := Limits ∪{e}
```

```
            else
                OrderedErrors:= OrderedErrors\{e}
            endif
        done
        PotLimits:=inf(OrderedErrors)
done
```

Where:
- **VerifyBySubstitution**(i,e) is a procedure that returns **true** if the replacement of $Ref(i)$ by e in the calculus of $Ref_E^M(s)$ gives a refusal set r such that $r \not\sqsubseteq Ref_E^M(s)$.
where s is a state (of $M\|[\Gamma]\|E \setminus \Gamma$) containing a couple $(i, *)$.
- for $\mathcal{E} = \{e_1, e_2, .., e_n\} \subseteq G$, $\mathbf{inf}(\mathcal{E})$ returns the set $\{e \in \mathcal{E} : \not\exists e_k \in \mathcal{E} : (e, e_k) \in V\}$

$\forall e \in$ Limits, we have :
$\Psi_i(e) \neg conf \ M$, $\Psi_i(e) \neg conf_E \ M$
$\Psi_i(e)$ *is an erroneous implementation of M detectable by the test through E.*
$\forall e' \in G : e' \sqsubset_s e$ implies $\Psi_i(e') conf_E \ M$
No implementation less erroneous than $\Psi_i(e)$ can be detected through E.
$\forall e' \in G : e \sqsubset_s e'$ implies $\Psi_i(e') \neg conf_E \ M$
Any implementation more erroneous than $\Psi_i(e)$ can be detected through E.

5   Conclusion

In this paper, we have presented a formalization of the notion of degradation of the testablity of a system when the latter is embedded in an environment that prevents it from being directly tested. We relied on a formal definition of the conformance of an implementation to a given specification. This conformance definition supports automatic tests generation, for details see [BR 88, LE2 91]. We explained the testability degradation by the existence of nonconforming implementations (i.e. erroneous implementations which are discarded by conformance testing when no constraints are imposed by an environment) that the testing through an environment procedure cannot detect.

Assuming hiding synchronization actions creates no divergence, the notion of testability degradation limits was put forward. Limits was characterized as erroneous implementations before which nonconformance cannot be detected when testing through an environment. An original presentation of the conformance and related notions has been given. To simulate erroneous implementations and determine these limits, we proposed transformations by 'degradation' and 'distorsion' of the specification described by a bilabeled graph structure referred to as refusal graph. Note that characterizing ordered erroneous implementations can be used for more general purposes, e.g. for test selection. A framework for test selection, proposed in [BTV 91], assumes error characterization as we detailed in this paper.

The refusal graph structure yields composition and restriction operators that lead to an operational approach for the testability analysis. Furthermore, this structure, together with the bisimulation relation, $\approx_g$, defined on, facilitate checking of testing equivalence of two systems.

Finally an approach for simulation of erroneous implementations and computation of the so-called limits of testability has been presented.

Acknowledgment: We thank Guy Leduc of Université de Liège for his relevant comments on the draft version of this paper.

References

[AB 87] S. ABRAMSKY *Observation equivalence as a testing equivalence* Theoretical Computer Science 53 (1987), pp. 225-241.

[BK 85] J.A. BERGSTRA, J.W. KLOP *Algebra of Communicating Processes with Abstraction.* Theoretical Computer Science 37 (1985). 77-121

[BSS 87] E. BRINKSMA, G. SCOLLO AND C. STEENBERGEN *Lotos Specifications, their implementations and their tests.* Protocol Specification Testing and Verification, VI. B. Sarikaya and G.V. Bochmann (editors) Elsevier Science Publishers B.V. (North-Holland) 1987

[BR 88] E. BRINKSMA *A theory for the derivation of tests.* Protocol Specification Testing and Verification, VIII. S. Aggrawal and K.Sabani (editors) Elsevier Science Publishers B.V. (North-Holland) 1988.

[BTV 91] E. BRINKSMA, J. TRETMANS and L. VERHAARD *A Framework for Test Selection* Proceedings of the 11th international IFIP WG6.1 Symposium on Protocol Specification, Testing and Verification. Stockholm, June 17-20 1991.

[DH 84] R. DE NICOLA, M.C.B. HENNESSY *Testing equivalences for processes.* Theorical Computer Science 34 (1984). 83-133.

[DN 87] R. DE NICOLA *Extensional Equivalences for Transition Systems.* Acta Informatica 24, (1987), pp. 211-237.

[HO 85] C.A.R. HOARE *Communicating Sequential Processes.* Printice-Hall International series in computer science, New York 1985

[LE 87] G. LEDUC *The Interwriting of Data Types and Processes in LOTOS.* Protocol Specification Testing and Verification, VII. H. Rudin and C.H. West (editors) Elsevier Science Publishers B.V. (North-Holland) 1987

[LE 90] G. LEDUC *On the role of Implementation Relations in the Design of Distributed Systems using LOTOS.* dissertation d'agrégation, Université de Liège, Juillet 1990

[LE 91] G. LEDUC *A Framework based on implementation relations for implementing LOTOS specifications.* Computer Networks & ISDN Systems, 1991.

[LE2 91] G. LEDUC *Conformance relation, associated equivalence, and new canonical tester in LOTOS.* Proceedings of the 11th international IFIP WG6.1 Symposium on Protocol Specification, Testing and Verification. Stockholm, June 17-20 1991.

[LOT 88] INTERNATIONAL STANDARD Iso8807 *Information processing systems, Open systems interconnection, A formal description technique based on the temporal ordering of observational behaviour*

[MI 80] R. MILNER *A Calculus of Communicating System*, LNCS, Vol. 64, 1980.

[PA 81] D. PARK *Concurrency and Automata on Infinite Sequences*, LNCS, Vol. 104, 1981.

Automating (Specification ≡ Implementation) using Equational Reasoning and LOTOS

Carron Kirkwood*

Department of Computing Science, University of Glasgow
email: carron@dcs.glasgow.ac.uk

Abstract. We explore some of the problems of verification by trying to prove that some sort of relationship holds between a given specification and implementation. We are particularly interested in the decisions taken in the process of establishing and formalising the verification requirements and of automating the proof. Despite the apparent simplicity of the original problem, the verification is non-trivial.

The example chosen is an abstraction of a real communications problem. We use the formal description technique LOTOS [8] for specification and implementation, and equational reasoning, automated by the RRL term rewriting system [9], for the proof.

1 Introduction

The last few years has seen an increase in the use of formal methods in the design and analysis of computer systems. This has many benefits; one of which is being able to verify that certain properties hold of a system (or not, as the case may be). However, although formal methods are popular for specification, formal verification has not been taken up to the same extent, resulting in the situation where formal methods are used for specification but the implemented systems are tested in the conventional way. Three possible explanations for this are: 1) verification techniques are not as well understood as testing techniques, 2) there is little tool support for verification (making it less appealing), and 3) it is not always straightforward to express the properties to be verified. Our long term aim is to contribute to each of these areas by developing verification methods specifically for systems described using the formal description technique LOTOS [8]. In order to gain a better understanding of the problems of verification we undertook the study of the verification of the small communications problem presented in this paper.

A common problem in system development is showing that some sort of relationship holds between a given specification and implementation, i.e. the implementation *satisfies* the specification. The problem is compounded if, as here, the implementation is not formally derived from the specification. In the course of the verification we explore various ways of expressing the property to

* Funded by SERC grant gr/f 35371/ 4/1/1477, Verification Techniques for LOTOS.

be proved and consider several approaches to the proof. We also try to automate the proofs required (by tailoring a general purpose theorem prover).

The example is presented in section 2: an informal overview of the whole system is given, followed by formal and informal descriptions of the specification and implementation of the system. The formal descriptions given here are written in Basic LOTOS [8]. LOTOS was chosen because of its status as an international standard. Section 3 is concerned with a preliminary discussion of the interpretation of the verification requirements, and possible approaches to the proof that these are satisfied. The details are formalised in section 3.1. The process of automating these proofs, including the system used (the term rewriting system RRL [9]), is described in section 4.

Section 5 tells how initially we failed to meet the verifications requirements. In fact, we could show that the implementation did not satisfy the specification. Close examination of the proofs resulted in a deeper understanding of the requirements and the development of a different approach to the proof. The new approach hinges on adding some extra information in a modular way to the specification; we did this by adopting the constraint oriented style of specification [14]. This allowed the proof to be successfully completed. The new approach and the resulting specification are presented in section 5.3.

We recognise that the example as it stands is simple, so possible extensions to the case study are discussed in section 6. In section 7 we review our experience with LOTOS and RRL, making suggestions for improvements. Finally, we give our conclusions and ideas for further work arising from this study.

2 The Example

2.1 Informal Overview of the System

The example is an abstraction of a real communications problem involving four communicating processes at OSI Session level. It was first investigated as a case study for the "Verification Techniques for LOTOS" project.

There are four communicating entities: **A**, **B**, **C** and **D**, shown in figure 1. In the diagram, a box represents an entity, and a $\circ\!\!\longrightarrow$ represents a message mx (sent in the direction of the arrow). The meaning of the mx are also given in figure 1. Messages of the form px or nx (where x is a number) are positive and negative acknowledgements, respectively, to the corresponding mx messages.[2]

A requests a service from **B**; in order to satisfy that service, **B** must communicate with **C** and **D**. **B** has an internal timer which "times out" if **D** does not reply to its communication within a previously set time limit. **B** must send deallocation messages to **C** and **D** when they are no longer required.

---

[2] Note that some messages only require a positive acknowledgment, while others require both positive and negative acknowledgments (see figure 1) — this is to do with the nature of the messages which they acknowledge, e.g. it does not make any sense to allow **C** to respond in a negative way to the message $m6$ "Service terminated".

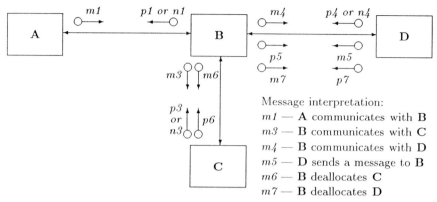

Fig. 1. The Processes and their messages

The original example [5] was supplied by Jeremy Dick, who worked for RACAL at the time. For reasons of security, we were given only the abstract description of the system as above; no indication of the real content or meaning of the messages was given. To help illuminate the system, we invented a possible interpretation of our own. This provides some intuition as to what happens in the system, although it is not an exact match. We view the system as follows: **A** is a user wishing to log-on to a system with a username and a password. **C** takes a username and checks that it is valid. **D** takes a valid username, acknowledges receipt of the name, and then returns the corresponding password. **B** co-ordinates these activities to ascertain if **A** is a valid user and has supplied the correct password.

Two possible descriptions of the system are given below: firstly, a group of protocols which make up the specification, and secondly a group of processes which make up the implementation. Note that inconsistencies may be found between the way the specification describes something and the way the implementation describes the same thing. This is because the implementation was not formally derived from the specification and one of the problems considered here is that of trying to reconcile any differences between the two.

The informal introductions to the specification and implementation are followed by their formal descriptions, given in Basic LOTOS. Only the process algebra part of LOTOS is used as no data types are required (see section 6 for extensions involving data types). The reader is assumed to be familiar with LOTOS or a related process algebra such as CCS [12]. The language constructs used for the descriptions are: **exit** denoting successful termination, ; denoting action sequencing, and [] denoting choice between two process expressions. Note that in the remainder of this document, the term *processes* will be used to refer to the implementation part of the example. LOTOS processes will be referred to as such, or as process expressions.

In these descriptions the simplifying assumptions that the carrier is faithful and no messages or acknowledgements are lost or corrupted are made.

2.2 Protocols

Communication in the system is governed by protocols $P1$, $P2$ and $P3$. Each protocol describes the interface between just two of the processes in the system, e.g. $P1$ describes the interface between **A** and **B**, ignoring **C** and **D**.

$P1$: **A** sends $m1$ to **B**, which must be acknowledged by $p1$ or $n1$.
$P2$: **B** sends $m3$ to **C** which must be acknowledged by $p3$ or $n3$. Following $p3$, **B** may or may not send $m6$ to **C** which must be acknowledged by $p6$.
$P3$: **B** sends $m4$ to **D** which must be acknowledged by $p4$ or $n4$. After $p4$, **D** may or may not send $m5$ to **B**. $m5$ must be acknowledged by $p5$. Also after $p4$, **B** may or may not send $m7$ to **D**. $m7$ is acknowledged by $p7$. Receipt of $m7$ removes the capability to send $m5$.

process P1 := m1; (n1; exit [] p1; exit) **endproc**
process P2 := m3; (n3; exit [] p3; (exit [] m6; p6; exit)) **endproc**
process P3 := exit [] m4; (n4; exit
　　　　　　　　　　　[] p4; (exit [] m7; p7; exit
　　　　　　　　　　　　　　　[] m5; p5; (exit [] m7; p7; exit))) **endproc**

Note that in a real system the protocols, and also the processes, would probably be described recursively, i.e. cycling over the same behaviour forever. This is ignored at the moment, the simpler finite case being dealt with first. Having finite LOTOS processes instead of recursive ones results in the initial **exit** branch of $P3$; this expresses the notion that the full $P3$ protocol is not always activated.

2.3 Processes

The implementation of the system is achieved by four interacting processes.

A: **A** sends $m1$ to **B**. After this message **B** sends either $p1$ or $n1$ to **A**, indicating success or failure of the transaction respectively.
C: **C** receives $m3$ from **B** to which it replies either $p3$ or $n3$. If $p3$ is sent then **C** expects an $m6$ deallocation message, to which it replies $p6$.
D: **D** receives $m4$ from **B**, to which it replies $p4$, and the transaction continues, or $n4$, and the transaction terminates. After $p4$, **D** sends $m5$ to **B**, expecting $p5$ in response, then deallocation by $m7$, to which **D** replies $p7$. The transaction may be terminated if **D** receives $m7$ before it sends $m5$, i.e. the timer has expired causing **B** to terminate the transaction.
B: In a successful execution **B** receives $m1$ from **A**, allocates **C** with $m3$ $p3$ and **D** with $m4$ $p4$, then sets a timer as **D** must send $m5$ within some time limit. When $m5$ arrives the timer is cancelled and **B** replies with $p5$. **C** and **D** are deallocated by $m6$ $p6$ and $m7$ $p7$ respectively. Finally **B** signals the success of the transaction by sending $p1$ to **A**.
This sequence of actions may fail in a number of ways: either **C** or **D** could refuse to participate by returning negative acknowledgments ($n3$ or $n4$), or

D might not send *m5* within the time period, in which case the timer "times out". In these cases **B** replies *n1* to **A**. Deallocation of C and **D** occurs if and only if they originally agreed to participate in the transaction, i.e. if they sent *p3* and *p4* respectively.

process A := m1; (n1; exit [] p1; exit) **endproc**
process C := m3; (n3; exit [] p3; m6; p6; exit) **endproc**
process D := exit [] m4; (n4; exit
                          [] p4; (m5; p5; m7; p7; exit
                                 [] m7; p7; exit)) **endproc**
process B :=
  m1; m3; (n3; n1; exit
          [] p3; m4; (n4; m6; p6; n1; exit
                     [] p4; set; (timeout; m6; p6; m7; p7; n1; exit
                                 [] m5; tcancel; p5; m6; p6; m7; p7; p1; exit)))
          endproc

Now we have the formal descriptions of the specification and the implementation we wish to verify that the implementation is correct with respect to the specification. The next section examines how that correctness can be evaluated.

3 Verification of the Example

The statement to be verified can be expressed as: does the implementation (the processes **A**, **B**, **C** and **D**) satisfy the specification (the protocols $P1$, $P2$ and $P3$)? The terms used above are deliberately vague, allowing exploration of different possible interpretations, discussed informally here and formally in section 3.1. Three terms have yet to be defined: "specification", "implementation" and "satisfies". The meaning of the first two ought to be straightforward since the protocols and the processes have been given, but these are only the bones of the description. For example, the protocols form the specification, but how they should be combined, or indeed *if* they should be combined, is not mentioned. The same is true of the processes and the implementation.

Suppose the protocols are to be combined to form the specification and the processes combined to form the implementation. The statement then becomes:

$$(A \mid B \mid C \mid D) \text{ satisfies } (P1 \mid P2 \mid P3) \qquad (1)$$

where the "|" operator denotes "combined with". Note that each instance of "|" may be replaced by a slightly different operator when the problem is made concrete. For example, the combinator used in A | B may be different from that used in C | D, or $P1$ | $P2$. These things will be formalised in section 3.1.

An alternative approach exploits the modular way in which the system has been defined: each facet of the interaction can be examined separately.

$$(A \mid B) \text{ satisfies } P1 \qquad\qquad (2)$$
$$(C \mid B) \text{ satisfies } P2 \qquad\qquad (3)$$
$$(D \mid B) \text{ satisfies } P3 \qquad\qquad (4)$$

As they stand, these equations are not quite correct since the language, i.e. the events, of the left-hand expression may not be the same as that of the right-hand expression, e.g. A | B will use events not mentioned in $P1$. Either these events will have to be hidden, or the interpretation of "satisfies" must take account of the extra events.

Since equations (2), (3) and (4) each yield a boolean, the results can be combined using a boolean operator. We choose & since we want all facets of the interaction to be satisfied, but we must also be sure that satisfying all equations is the same as satisfying the system as a whole. In this case, since $P1, P2$ and $P3$ are all concerned with distinct facets of the communication of the system, it seems likely that the verification can safely be split into parts. Note that this really depends on choosing the right methods of splitting up the system, hiding unimportant events, making individual proofs, and recombining the results.

3.1 Formalising the Verification Requirements

We should now give the formal interpretation of "|", the hiding of events, and "satisfies", again using LOTOS.

The general parallelism operator of LOTOS is used to combine both processes and protocols. This operator takes two process expressions and a list of events specifying the events on which the process expressions must synchronise. Variation of the events in this list give the subtly different combinations of the components of the system (as mentioned above). The syntax for this operator is $P \mid [eventlist] \mid Q$, where P and Q are process expressions.

The **hide** operator is used to restrict the processes to protocol events only. This operator takes a process expression and a list of events to be hidden. Hidden events are treated like the internal event i; they are unobservable and occur instantaneously. The syntax is **hide** *eventlist* in P.

There are many different possible interpretations for the "satisfies" relation. The particular sort of relation (e.g. equivalence or preorder) will depend on the sort of decisions made in the step between the specification and the implementation. For example, the implementation may resolve some choices left open in the specification, or it may add some information about how to perform a particular task, or it may substitute one method of performing a task for another. Some steps preserve the observable behaviour of the specification while others do not, therefore in some cases an equivalence or a congruence relation is appropriate, i.e. where the processes must implement *all* the alternatives set out in the protocols, while in other cases a preorder relation will suffice. Since in this example the implementation was not derived directly from the specification we cannot say anything about the sort of steps used, so we must examine a variety of LOTOS relations in more detail to determine which are most suitable. Starting with the strongest (i.e. makes fewer identifications):

Strong Bisimulation Equivalence This relation requires all events, including the internal event, to be matched exactly. Given the use of the **hide** operator which converts hidden events into the internal event, an equivalence which ignores these is required.

Weak Bisimulation Equivalence This relation requires all events except the internal event to be matched exactly. The internal event is given its status as a special, unobservable, event and can be matched by zero or more internal events. This relation does not preserve the substitution property in all LOTOS contexts, i.e. two process expressions may be weak bisimulation equivalent, but their internal structure could cause them to behave differently when in combination with other process expressions.

Weak Bisimulation Congruence This is the largest congruent relation contained in weak bisimulation equivalence. Most, but not necessarily all, of the internal events created by the use of **hide** can be removed by weak bisimulation congruence laws.

Testing Relations The basic testing relation for LOTOS is a preorder called **red**. B_1 **red** B_2 says that B_1 is a deterministic reduction of B_2, which may be interpreted as B_1 "implements" B_2. The equivalence generated by this preorder is not a congruence. To obtain congruence the **cred** relation, the largest congruent sub-relation of **red**, must be used.

Trace Equivalence This says that two process expressions are equivalent if their trace sets, i.e. their sequences of actions, are the same. This does not give a satisfactory interpretation of "satisfies" since deadlock properties are not preserved, i.e. two process expressions may be trace equivalent but one may deadlock after a trace s while the other does not.

In summary, trace equivalence is rejected because too many identifications are made, strong bisimulation equivalence because too few are made. Our system will probably have to interact with other systems, so it is important that it behaves in the same way in all contexts. This leads us to reject weak bisimulation equivalence and testing equivalence, leaving weak bisimulation congruence and testing congruence. We also have the testing preorders. Since there are no other criteria to take into account, any of these relations will suffice as an interpretation of "satisfies".

The next section describes the method and software used to automate the proofs of equivalence.

4 Proof: Technique and Application

Several software tools are currently available which can determine the equivalence/ordering of two process expressions, e.g. the Concurrency Workbench [3] and TAV [6]. These systems generate a finite state machine to represent the processes and apply some sophisticated algorithms to decide their relationship. This approach suffers from the state explosion problem and cannot handle infinite systems. Although the current example is unlikely to cause state explosion and is finite, our aim is to develop methods which may be applicable to other examples. For this reason we use *equational reasoning*, i.e. symbolic manipulation of terms, thus avoiding any special representations. This approach is also successfully used in [4, 11, 13].

Using term rewriting to implement equational reasoning, two terms are proved equivalent by reducing them to their normal forms and comparing these syntactically. If the normal forms are the same then the original terms are equivalent, otherwise not. The same technique is used to prove a preorder between two terms. This procedure relies on having a *complete* (i.e. confluent and terminating) set of rules (giving unique normal forms).

A brief description of the rule sets used for this case study follows; a more detailed presentation can be found in [10]. We split the rules according to their function, giving three sets:

1. Rules derived from the weak bisimulation congruence laws, including the **hide** expansion law, which are given in appendix B.2.2 of the LOTOS standard [8]. These rules remove instances of the **hide** operator (by converting events to be hidden into the internal event, **i**) and reduce terms with respect to weak bisimulation congruence.

2. Rules which "implement" the expansion law for parallelism, also found in appendix B.2.2 of the LOTOS standard. These rules remove instances of the parallel operator, converting the terms into equivalent ones which use only sequencing and choice operators.

3. Rules corresponding to the **cred** laws, which can be found in appendix B.3.2 of the LOTOS standard. Set 3, when used, is always an addition to Set 1, since one of the laws for **cred** states that all the laws of weak bisimulation congruence are also true for **cred**. These rules allow terms to be reduced with respect to the **cred** refinement relation.

Sets 1 and 2 also contain rules for basic data types, e.g. lists, sets etc.

The RRL term rewriting system [9] was used to perform the proofs. RRL features include Knuth-Bendix completion and proof by rewriting. RRL also handles rewriting and completion modulo associative-commutative operators. This was the main reason for choosing this system over others currently available.

The rule sets given above are not confluent and terminating, which means we have a semi-decision procedure for equivalence/ordering of LOTOS processes, i.e. normal forms are not unique. This means that if two terms can be shown to be equivalent/ordered by our rules, then they are equivalent/ordered in the LOTOS semantics, but if two terms cannot be shown to be equivalent/ordered by our rules, then they may or may not be equivalent/ordered in the semantics. No special techniques to cope with non-confluent rule sets are adopted; if two terms cannot be shown equivalent by RRL the proof is completed by hand.

The next section contains details of the proofs which were attempted, and some discussion of why some of those proofs failed.

5   Verification Proofs

In section 3 two possible approaches to proving that the implementation of the system satisfies its specification were discussed. One involved splitting the proof into three parts corresponding to the three protocols in the specification, while the other dealt with the system as a whole. The results of these approaches, successes and failures, in trying to prove automatically that the specification is satisfied by the implementation are given below.

5.1   Splitting the Proofs into Three Sections

Since each protocol describes the interface between just two of the processes, the idea of proving each interface is correct and deducing from that the correctness of the whole system is very appealing. Unfortunately, this approach turned out to be unsuccessful. Proofs about the relationship between the specification and the implementation could be completed, but the results were not strong enough to satisfy the correctness requirement. However, examining these proofs (successful or otherwise) helps illuminate the reasons for the failure of this approach. In the following, $\equiv_{wbc}$ denotes weak bisimulation congruence.

Weak Bisimulation Congruence We tried to prove the following equations.

$$P1 \equiv_{wbc} \textbf{hide } CDevents \textbf{ in } (A \mid[m1, p1, n1]\mid B) \tag{5}$$

$$P2 \equiv_{wbc} \textbf{hide } ADevents \textbf{ in } (C \mid[m3, p3, n3, m6, p6]\mid B) \tag{6}$$

$$P3 \equiv_{wbc} \textbf{hide } ACevents \textbf{ in } (D \mid[m4, p4, n4, m5, p5, m7, p7]\mid B) \tag{7}$$

where $P1, P2, P3$ and A, B, C, D are as defined in section 2 and the event lists to be hidden are:

$CDevents = [m3, \ p3, \ n3, \ m4, \ p4, \ n4, \ m5, \ p5, \ m6, \ p6, \ m7, \ p7\,]$
$ADevents = [m1, \ p1, \ n1, \ m4, \ p4, \ n4, \ m5, \ p5, \ m7, \ p7\,]$
$ACevents = [m1, \ p1, \ n1, \ m3, \ p3, \ n3, \ m6, \ p6\,]$

Equations (5), (6) and (7) cannot be proved using RRL. The proof was completed by hand to show that the equations do not hold in the LOTOS semantics. The full proof is not presented here, but may be found, together with the other proofs from this study, in appendix A of [10]. The next step was to try to show the equations hold for a weaker relation.

Testing Relations Taking the left and right hand sides of the equations as above, we substituted the **cred** relation for $\equiv_{wbc}$ and tried to show the new equations held either left-to-right or vice-versa (if they hold in both directions we get testing congruence).

$$P1 \textbf{ cred } \textbf{hide } CDevents \textbf{ in } (A \mid[m1, p1, n1]\mid B) \tag{8}$$

$$P2 \textbf{ cred } \textbf{hide } ADevents \textbf{ in } (C \mid[m3, p3, n3, m6, p6]\mid B) \tag{9}$$

$$P3 \textbf{ cred } \textbf{hide } ACevents \textbf{ in } (D \mid[m4, p4, n4, m5, p5, m7, p7]\mid B) \tag{10}$$

The proofs of equations (8) and (9) can be completed by RRL in the left-to-right direction, which means that the protocols are a deterministic reduction of the processes, i.e. the processes may have some nondeterminism not present in the protocols (which is not what may normally be expected). None of the equations holds in the right-to-left direction; equation (10) holds in neither direction.

At this point it appeared that trying to prove the verification requirement was satisfied was hopeless. However, we strongly believed that the processes were a valid implementation of the system and that therefore it was the approach to the proof which was incorrect. The strategy of splitting the proof into three parts did not work, or rather, some proofs could be completed, but they were not sufficient to satisfy the verification requirement. In particular, it seemed that the hiding of events caused the failure of the proofs by spotlighting apparently non-deterministic choices in the process expressions. These choices are not really non-deterministic; the choices are determined by factors in the other processes. For example, the right-hand process expression in equation (5) makes a non-deterministic choice between replying $p1$ and replying $n1$. However, we know that this choice really depends on the receipt of $m5$ (which is hidden). This problem affects proofs using weak bisimulation congruence or testing congruence. We observe that we are not the only ones to encounter this problem; the same phenomenon also causes problems for other authors, e.g. [1, 2].

We then went on to try the other approach to the proof, where the system is considered as a whole, thus avoiding the use of **hide**.

5.2   Proving the System as a Whole

No relationships between the processes all combined and the protocols all combined could be demonstrated because although the processes can be combined using parallelism, there is no meaningful way in which to combine the protocols.

There are two operators which could be used to combine the protocols. These are sequential composition of process expressions and interleaving (general parallelism synchronising on no events) since the protocols have no events in common. The former cannot be used because, for example, the events of $P1$ do not all precede the events of $P2$, and the latter cannot be used because the protocols contain no information about the relative ordering of events in different protocols. Interleaving results in a process expression which has a large number of traces which are meaningless in our example, given our informal description.

The reason the protocols cannot be combined in a way that reflects our intuition is that there is some information missing from the specification, leaving too large a step between it and the implementation. This may have occurred because the implementation was not derived from the specification, but it is also generally true that verification becomes harder as the distance between the specification and the implementation increases.

The missing information, which is implicit in the implementation, includes details of a timer, deallocation and what constitutes success or failure of the transaction. In the specification there is no information about any of these things.

Our solution was to add the information in the form of *constraints* giving a successful approach to the problem.

5.3 Adding Constraints to the Example

The constraint oriented style of specification [14] relies on the way in which the LOTOS general parallelism operator handles multi-way synchronisation, i.e. synchronisation between two or more actions. For example, if three LOTOS processes, all of which use the action *a*, are combined using general parallelism, synchronising on *a*, then all three must perform that event at the same time. This means that different process expressions can specify different aspects of a behaviour, interacting to give the whole specification. The effect is similar to using conjunction in a logical specification; each part must be satisfied for the whole to be satisfied.

Using this method, more LOTOS processes are defined which express other aspects of the specification not included in the protocols. These include a timer in **B** to determine how long it should wait for **D** to send the *m5* message, compulsory deallocation of **C** and **D**, ordering of events as mentioned in the informal overview of the system, and conditions dictating success or failure of the transaction as a whole. The following constraints are added to the specification:

Timer Constraints
```
process timer     := exit [] set; ( tcancel; exit [] timeout; exit) endproc
process timer_on := exit [] p4; set; exit endproc
process timer_off := exit [] set; ( m5; tcancel; p5; m7; exit
                                    [] timeout; m7; exit) endproc
```

Deallocation Constraints
```
process dealloc_C := p3; m6; p6; exit [] n3; exit endproc
process dealloc_D := exit [] m4; (p4; m7; p7; exit [] n4; exit) endproc
```

Success and Failure
```
process system :=   m5; p1; exit
                  [] n3; n1; exit
                  [] n4; n1; exit
                  [] timeout; n1; exit endproc
```

Ordering Constraints

process order13 := m1; m3; (n3; n1; exit
                 [] p3; (n1; exit [] p1; exit)) **endproc**

process order34 := m3; (n3; n1; exit
               [] p3; m4 (n4; n1; exit
                     [] p4; (n1; exit [] p1; exit))) **endproc**

process order457 := n3; n1; exit
               [] m4; (n4; n1; exit
                 [] p4; (m5; p5; m7; p7; p1; exit
                     [] timeout; m7; p7; n1; exit)) **endproc**

process order56 := n3; n1; exit
               [] n4; m6; p6; n1; exit
               [] timeout; m6; p6; n1; exit
               [] m5; p5; m6; p6; p1; exit **endproc**

process order67 := n3; n1; exit
               [] p3; (n4; m6; p6; n1; exit
                 [] p4; m6; p6; m7; p7; (n1; exit
                       [] p1; exit)) **endproc**

    As with the descriptions of the protocols and the processes, some **exit** branches are introduced to express the notion that a constraint may not be activated.

    Given these constraints, the equation to be proved by RRL becomes:

$(((\text{P1} \,|[p1,n1]|\, \text{system}) \,|[m1,p1,n1,n3]|\, \text{order13})$
    $|[p1,n1,m3,p3,n3,n4,m5,timeout]|$
$((((\text{P2} \,|[p3,n3,m6,p6]|\, \text{dealloc\_C})$
    $|[m3,p3,n3,m6,p6]|\, (\text{order34} \,|[p3,n3,p4,n4]|\, \text{order67}))$
    $|[p1,n1,n3,m4,p4,n4,m7,p7]|$
$(((\text{P3} \,|[m4,p4,n4,m7,p7]|\, \text{dealloc\_D}) \,|[m4,p4,\mathbf{n4},\mathbf{m5},\mathbf{p5},m7,p7]|\, \mathbf{order457})$
    $|[p4,m5,p5,m7,timeout]|$
$((\text{timer} \,|[set]|\, \text{timer\_on}) \,|[set,timeout,tcancel]|\, \text{timer\_off}))$
    $|[m5,p5,m6,p6,timeout]|\, \text{order56}))$
$\equiv_{wbc}$
$(((\text{A} \,|[m1,p1,n1]|\, \text{B}) \,|[m3,p3,n3,m6,p6]|\, \text{C})$
    $|[m4,p4,n4,m5,p5,m7,p7]|\, \text{D})$

    Although the order in which the process expressions are combined does not matter in the semantics, we add as much information as possible to each protocol before combining it with the others. This is because in performing the proof, our system can only deal with one parallel statement at a time, which means that the proof has to be built up gradually from small units. Adding as much information as early as possible helps to cut down the size of the intermediate terms in the proof.

    This equation can be proved to hold by RRL. This is an adequate proof of correctness since it means not only that the processes have the same observable behaviour as the protocols, but also that they behave in the same way in all contexts. The proof requires only the rules from set 2; no other rule sets are required. As the specification and implementation use no internal actions we may also deduce that the above equation holds for strong equivalence as well as for weak bisimulation congruence.

6 Extensions to the Example

The example as considered in this document is very simple; there are a number of ways in which it can be made more complex.

- A useful extension would be to add an "abort" message, call it $m2$. **A** can abort the service at any time by sending $m2$ to **B**, which should clean up by deallocating any resources held and then replying to **A** with $p2$.

  In LOTOS it would be simple to add $m2$ $p2$ as an abort sequence using the operator [> , which allows one process to take control from another. However, in this example the system is more complicated, requiring varying sequences of actions between $m2$ and $p2$, depending on the events which occurred before $m2$. The original solution could not be easily extended to include this new behaviour. This could indicate a fault in the solution to the original problem, perhaps it is not modular enough, or it could be that there is no simple, elegant way to extend the solution. Another possibility is that it is the form of this particular modification which is causing the problem, see section 7.
- Data types could be added to the messages, e.g. the login name and password of the informal interpretation of the example.
- The most obvious extension would be to introduce recursion. Work is in progress on the addition of recursion to the example. So far the proofs have not become any more complex, however, we felt that the example was simpler to present without recursion.

7 Review of the Tools Used

Although some degree of success was achieved in the case study, there were also many problems, not all of which arose from the example itself; some were due to either LOTOS or RRL. For example, in RRL we would have liked more control over the application of rules and more feedback on the rules RRL used in a reduction. The suggested improvements to LOTOS are given below.

LOTOS was not always suitable to describe the example. A major problem was revealed when attempting to extend the original problem to include the abort message. The [> operator was unsuitable for this purpose because it does not allow the abort sequence to be dependent on the state of execution before the abort message. One way round this is to write each abort possibility into the LOTOS processes as choice branches, which makes the specification rather cumbersome. What is required is an operator which allows the abort sequence to be flexible, perhaps allowing parameters to be passed from the interrupted to the interrupting process (as with sequential composition of processes).

Another feature which would have been useful was an operator to "wrap-up" several actions and make them behave as a single action, i.e. like a critical section in a mutual exclusion problem. For example, we wanted to be able to combine two process expressions using interleaving, but to have a section in one of the expressions which, once it had begun, had to finish without interleaving with the other process until after the last action was completed. This could have been solved with a mutual exclusion algorithm, but a language construct to do this would be more convenient. This problem is also identified in [7].

8   Conclusions and Further Work

After much experimentation, we succeeded in showing that the verification requirements of a small communications protocol were indeed satisfied. It must be noted that the given specification was not sufficient for our purposes and had to have more information added to enable the proofs to be carried out. The new information was added in a modular way however, and the text of the original specification was unaltered, although it must be admitted that the size of the new specification is greatly increased. Possible extensions to the problem are provided in section 6. It is hoped that these can also be made in a modular way.

In some ways, the initial failure to meet the verification requirements was perhaps more fruitful than the final proof, because we were able to identify problems in the verification process which need to be further researched. For example, the effect of **hide** on our proofs, introducing non-determinism and thus causing failure, and the difficulty in choosing between the different relations. There are many more equivalences defined in the process algebra literature than presented in this document, we merely chose some of the most well-known.

Another possible line of research is that of investigating alternative formulations of the verification requirements. Other situations may require different interpretations of the statement "specification satisfies implementation", e.g. one alternative is "prove the system satisfies certain temporal formulae", giving another way of looking at what constitutes specification and implementation.

The main result of our work on this case study is the demonstration that verification, even of such a small and simple system, is a difficult process; one which is full of opportunities to take the wrong decision and thereby to fail to prove the correctness of the system under investigation. In this study we only arrived at a successful proof because we persevered, having a strong belief that such a proof must exist. In more complex examples it would perhaps be less easy to hold such a belief.

Acknowledgements We would like to thank the members of the ERIL project group, in particular our colleagues at Glasgow, Muffy Thomas and Phil Watson, for many stimulating discussions on the issues and problems raised by this case study. Thanks also to the referees for their helpful comments, and to Deepak Kapur for supplying RRL.

References

1. J. Baillie. A CCS case study: a safety-critical system. *Software Engineering Journal*, pages 159–167, July 1991.

2. G. Bruns and S. Anderson. The Formalization and Analysis of a Communications Protocol. Technical Report ECS-LFCS-91-137, LFCS, University of Edinburgh, 1991.

3. R. Cleveland, J. Parrow, and B. Steffen. The Concurrency Workbench. In J. Sifakis, editor, *Automatic Verification Methods for Finite State Systems*, LNCS 407, pages 24–37. Springer-Verlag, 1989.

4. R. De Nicola, P. Inverardi, and M. Nesi. Using the Axiomatic Presentation of Behavioural Equivalences for Manipulating CCS Expressions. In J. Sifakis, editor, *Automatic Verification Methods for Finite State Systems*, LNCS 407, pages 54–67, 1989.

5. A.J.J. Dick. A Case Study for the ERIL Project. Private communication, 1990.

6. J.C. Godskesen, K.G. Larsen, and M. Zeeberg. TAV (Tools for Automatic Verification): Users Manual. Technical report, Aalborg University, 1989.

7. R. Gotzhein. Specifying Abstract Data Types with LOTOS. In B. Sarikaya and G.V. Bochmann, editors, *Protocol Specification, Testing, and Verification, VI*, pages 15–26. Elsevier Science Publishers B.V. (North-Holland), 1987.

8. International Organisation for Standardisation. *Information Processing Systems — Open Systems Interconnection — LOTOS — A Formal Description Technique Based on the Temporal Ordering of Observational Behaviour*, 1988.

9. D. Kapur and H. Zhang. *RRL : Rewrite Rule Laboratory User's Manual*, 1987. Revised May 1989.

10. C. Kirkwood. A Case Study for the ERIL Project. Technical Report 1992/R4, University of Glasgow, 1992.

11. C. Kirkwood and K. Norrie. Some Experiments using Term Rewriting Techniques for Concurrency. In J. Quemada, J. Mañas, and E. Vásquez, editors, *Formal Description Techniques, III*, pages 527–530. Elsevier Science Publishers B.V. (North-Holland), 1991. Extended Abstract.

12. R. Milner. *Communication and Concurrency*. Prentice-Hall International, 1989.

13. M. Nesi. Mechanizing a Proof by Induction of Process Algebra Specifications in Higher Order Logic. In K.G. Larsen and A. Skou, editors, *Proceedings of CAV 91*, LNCS 575, pages 288–298, 1992.

14. C.A. Vissers, G. Scollo, M. van Sinderen, and E. Brinksma. Specification styles in distributed systems design and verification. *Theoretical Computer Science*, 89:179–206, 1991.

On the Ehrenfeucht-Fraïssé Game in Theoretical Computer Science *
(Extended Abstract)

Wolfgang Thomas

Christian-Albrechts-Universität zu Kiel, Institut für Informatik und Praktische
Mathematik, D-W-2300 Kiel, Germany

Abstract. An introduction to (first-order) Ehrenfeucht-Fraïssé games
is presented, and three applications in theoretical computer science are
discussed. These are concerned with the expressive power of first-order
logic over graphs, formal languages definable in first-order logic, and
modal logic over labelled transition systems.

1 Introduction

The Ehrenfeucht-Fraïssé game is a convenient and flexible method to determine
the expressive power of logical formalisms (involving boolean connectives and
quantifiers). It was first introduced for first-order logic, but exists now in a
multitude of variants covering other logics occurring in computer science, such
as process logics, query languages, logics that capture complexity classes, and
regular-like expressions.

In this short note, we are not able to survey the recent developments in
sufficient detail. Instead we give an introduction to the nonspecialist, explaining
the basic case of first-order logic, and discuss three applications within first-order
logic that are relevant to computer science. Some selected references concerning
extensions of first-order logic are also mentioned. (The applications and the
subject of extended logics are treated in more depth in the full paper.)

The expressive power of a logic is measured by its ability to distinguish
between structures (of a form admitted by the respective semantics). Thus,
evaluating the expressive power of a logic means to describe the equivalence
between structures that holds if they are indistinguishable by formulas of this
logic. Instead of keeping track of all the formulas that could play a role in this
equivalence, one looks for a description of it which refers directly to the "algebraic" properties of the structures and thus is easier to handle. Since the logical
systems to be considered here cannot distinguish between isomorphic structures,
an algebraic formulation of logical indistinguishability will lead to a weakening
of isomorphism (or to isomorphism itself).

---

* The present work was supported by EBRA Working Group "Algebraic and Syntactic
Methods in Computer Science (ASMICS II)".

It was R. Fraïssé [Fr54] who introduced an algebraic notion (weakening isomorphism) which captures indistinguishability by first-order formulas of a relational signature. A. Ehrenfeucht [Ehr61] reformulated Fraïssé's algebraic treatment in game theoretic terminology and extended the method to weak monadic second-order logic (analyzing its power to distinguish between countable ordinals). Ehrenfeucht's paper helped much to spread the idea. Today we speak of "Ehrenfeucht-Fraïssé games". The game theoretic formulation is more intuitive, but in many concrete applications it is useful to work in an algebraic framework as Fraïssé originally developed.

The Ehrenfeucht-Fraïssé technique is one of the few methods from model theory which is applicable to finite structures, hence to many definability questions in computer science. Presently, in the rapidly developing area of *finite model theory*, Ehrenfeucht-Fraïssé games play a central role. Perhaps the method is used so frequently in theoretical computer science because it is applicable in a very transparent way over relational structures with relations of arity 1 and 2 only, like graphs, linear orderings, and partially ordered structures. Structures of this type are predominant in many fields of computer science (e.g., formal language theory, data base theory, semantics of concurrency).

In classical model theory, the emphasis is different: Its cornerstones are the the Löwenheim-Skolem Theorem and the Compactness Theorem, both meaningful only when infinite structures are admitted, and the algebraic applications (to groups, fields, etc.) require relational signatures involving higher arities. This may be a reason why there are relatively few textbooks where Ehrenfeucht-Fraïssé games are treated. We mention [EFT84, Chapter 11], [Ro82, Chapter 13], [Mo76, Chapter 26]; for (model theoretic) extensions of first-order logic see the survey volume [BF85].

In Section 2 we summarize basic facts on first-order Ehrenfeucht-Fraïssé games, guided by the exposition in [EFT84]. In Section 3, applications are outlined on the expressive power of first-order logic over graphs, on logical definability of formal languages, and on a system of modal logic over labelled transition systems.

2 Basics

2.1 m-Equivalence

In the sequel we consider a first-order language with equality and a simple signature S, consisting of unary relation symbols P_1, ..., P_k and binary relation symbols R_1, ..., R_l only. The restriction to unary and binary relations is inessential for the results but saves notation and covers all applications to be discussed below. Letters P and R will indicate unary, resp. binary relation symbols from S. Relational structures for this signature (S-*structures*) are of the form $\mathcal{A} = (A, P_1^A, \ldots, P_k^A, R_1^A, \ldots, R_l^A)$ where A is the structure's universe, $P_i^A \subseteq A$ for $1 \leq i \leq k$ and $R_j^A \subseteq A \times A$ for $1 \leq j \leq l$. Sometimes we expand such a structure by designated elements from its universe.

First-order formulas for the signature S (*S-formulas*) involve variables x_1, $x_2, \ldots$, and are built up from atomic formulas of the form $x_i = x_j$, Px_i, and Rx_ix_j by applying the boolean connectives $\neg$, $\vee$, $\wedge$, $\rightarrow$, $\leftrightarrow$ and the quantifiers $\exists$, $\forall$. For a tuple $\bar{x} = (x_1, \ldots, x_n)$ of variables, the notation $\varphi(\bar{x})$ indicates that φ is a formula in which at most $x_1, \ldots, x_n$ occur free. As a measure of complexity for formulas we use *quantifier-depth*: Define $qd(\varphi)$ inductively by setting

- $qd(\varphi) = 0$ for atomic φ, $qd(\neg\varphi) = qd(\varphi)$,
- $qd(\varphi \vee \psi) = qd(\varphi \wedge \psi) = qd(\varphi \rightarrow \psi) = qd(\varphi \leftrightarrow \psi) = max(qd(\varphi), qd(\psi))$
- $qd(\exists x\varphi) = qd(\forall x\varphi) = qd(\varphi) + 1$

Given an n-tuple $\bar{a} = (a_1, \ldots, a_n)$ of elements from the universe A of the S-structure $\mathcal{A}$ and a formula $\varphi(\bar{x})$, one writes $(\mathcal{A}, \bar{a}) \models \varphi(\bar{x})$ if φ holds in $\mathcal{A}$ when interpreting x_i by a_i for $1 \leq i \leq n$ (as well as symbols P and R by P^A and R^A, respectively).

Let $\mathcal{A}$, $\mathcal{B}$ be S-structures with universes A, B, and let $\bar{a}$, $\bar{b}$ be n-tuples of elements from A, B, respectively. Given $m \geq 0$ we say that $(\mathcal{A}, \bar{a})$ and $(\mathcal{B}, \bar{b})$ are *m-equivalent* (short: $(\mathcal{A}, \bar{a}) \equiv_m (\mathcal{B}, \bar{b})$) if

$$(\mathcal{A}, \bar{a}) \models \varphi(\bar{x}) \iff (\mathcal{B}, \bar{b}) \models \varphi(\bar{x})$$

for all S-formulas $\varphi(\bar{x})$ of quantifier-depth $\leq m$. For the case of empty sequences $\bar{a}$ and $\bar{b}$ this means that the two structures satisfy the same sentences (formulas without free variables) of quantifier-depth m.

2.2 m-Isomorphism

Our aim is to describe $\equiv_m$ as a weakening of isomorphism. First we do this for $m = 0$, where the notion of "partial isomorphism" turns out appropriate. Given S-structures $\mathcal{A}$ and $\mathcal{B}$ with universes A and B, we indicate a finite relation $\{(a_1, b_1), \ldots, (a_n, b_n)\} \subseteq A \times B$ by $\bar{a} \mapsto \bar{b}$. Such a relation is called a *partial isomorphism* if the assignment $a_i \mapsto b_i$ determines an injective (partial) function p from A to B (whose domain consists of the elements in $\bar{a}$), which moreover preserves all relations P^A, R^A under consideration, in the sense that

$$P^A a \iff P^B p(a) \quad \text{and} \quad R^A aa' \iff R^B p(a)p(a')$$

for all symbols P, R from S and all a, a' in the domain of p.

Let us verify that partial isomorphisms characterize $\equiv_0$-equivalence: We have

$$(\mathcal{A}, \bar{a}) \equiv_0 (\mathcal{B}, \bar{b})$$

iff any boolean combination of formulas $x_i = x_j$, Px_i, and Rx_ix_j is satisfied in $(\mathcal{A}, \bar{a})$ iff it is satisfied in $(\mathcal{B}, \bar{b})$

iff (by boolean logic) any of the atomic formulas $x_i = x_j$, Px_i, and Rx_ix_j is satisfied in $(\mathcal{A}, \bar{a})$ iff it is satisfied in $(\mathcal{B}, \bar{b})$

iff $a_i = a_j \Leftrightarrow b_i = b_j$ and $P^A a_i \Leftrightarrow P^B b_i$ and $R^A a_i a_j \Leftrightarrow R^B b_i b_j$ ($1 \leq i, j \leq n$).

Hence $(\mathcal{A}, \bar{a}) \equiv_0 (\mathcal{B}, \bar{b})$ iff $\bar{a} \mapsto \bar{b}$ is a partial isomorphism. As we may expect, this characterization does not extend to $\equiv_m$ for $m > 0$. Consider, for example, the linear orderings $(\mathbb{R}, <^{\mathbb{R}})$ and $(\mathbb{Z}, <^{\mathbb{Z}})$ of the integers, resp. the real numbers. Then $p_0 : (2,3) \mapsto (3,4)$ is a partial isomorphism (i.e., order preserving) but does not preserve truth of the formula $\exists x_3(x_1 < x_3 \wedge x_3 < x_2)$, which states that between the two considered elements there is a third one. In the terminology of partial isomorphisms, this means that $p_0 : (2,3) \mapsto (3,4)$ cannot be extended to a new partial isomorphism having for example $2\frac{1}{2}$ in its domain. The idea in Fraïssé's Theorem is that the possibility of extending partial isomorphisms m times (in both directions) characterizes the m-equivalence $\equiv_m$.

To describe this extension property, we introduce sets $I_1, I_2, \ldots, I_m$ of partial isomorphisms such that I_k contains partial isomorphisms which allow k-fold extension. Call $(\mathcal{A}, \overline{a})$ and $(\mathcal{B}, \overline{b})$ m-isomorphic (short: $(\mathcal{A}, \overline{a}) \cong_m (\mathcal{B}, \overline{b})$) if there are nonempty sets $I_0, \ldots, I_m$ of partial isomorphisms, each of them extending $\overline{a} \mapsto \overline{b}$, such that for all $k = 1, \ldots, m$

- *(back property)* $\forall p \in I_k \; \forall b \in B \; \exists a \in A$ such that $p \cup \{(a,b)\} \in I_{k-1}$
- *(forth property)* $\forall p \in I_k \; \forall a \in A \; \exists b \in B$ such that $p \cup \{(a,b)\} \in I_{k-1}$.

Fraïssé's Theorem. *For $m \geq 0$: $(\mathcal{A}, \overline{a}) \equiv_m (\mathcal{B}, \overline{b})$ iff $(\mathcal{A}, \overline{a}) \cong_m (\mathcal{B}, \overline{b})$.*

2.3 The Game Theoretic View

In the game theoretic view due to Ehrenfeucht, relations (such as partial isomorphisms) are configurations in a two-person game, and moves in this game perform extensions of relations. Consider two structures $(\mathcal{A}, \overline{a})$ and $(\mathcal{B}, \overline{b})$. A play of the associated *Ehrenfeucht-Fraïssé Game* $G_m((\mathcal{A}, \overline{a}), (\mathcal{B}, \overline{b}))$ consists of m rounds and is carried out as follows: The initial configuration is $\overline{a} \mapsto \overline{b}$. Given a configuration r, a round is composed of two moves: first player I picks an element a from A or b from B, and then player II reacts by choosing an element in the other structure, i.e. some b from B, resp. some a from A. The new configuration is $r \cup \{(a,b)\}$. After m rounds, player II has won if the final configuration is a partial isomorphism (otherwise player I has won). Instead of asking for a partial isomorphism at the end of the play, one may as well require partial isomorphisms during the whole play (because the final configuration is a partial isomorphism iff all configurations during the play are). While player II aims at a partial isomorphism at the end, player I tries to avoid this. (To emphasize this, [FSV92] introduce the suggestive names "spoiler" and "duplicator" instead of Ehrenfeucht's names "I" and "II".) We say that II *wins* the game $G_m((\mathcal{A}, \overline{a}), (\mathcal{B}, \overline{b}))$ if II has a strategy to win each play (we skip a formal definition of "strategy").

Ehrenfeucht's Theorem. *For $m \geq 0$:*

$$(\mathcal{A}, \overline{a}) \cong_m (\mathcal{B}, \overline{b}) \quad iff \quad II \text{ wins } G_m((\mathcal{A}, \overline{a}), (\mathcal{B}, \overline{b})).$$

The proof is straightforward, because sets of configurations which allow player II to win with k rounds ahead correspond to sets I_k in the definition of m-isomorphism, and the possibility for player II to stay within "winning" configurations corresponds to the assumption that the two extension properties (back and forth) hold.

2.4 Distributive Normal Form

The proof of Fraïssé's theorem proceeds by induction on m in both directions. The proof of m-equivalence given m-isomorphism is not difficult. For the converse direction

$$(\mathcal{A}, \bar{a}) \equiv_m (\mathcal{B}, \bar{b}) \;\Rightarrow\; (\mathcal{A}, \bar{a}) \cong_m (\mathcal{B}, \bar{b})$$

it is sufficient to describe the $\cong_m$-classes by formulas of quantifier-depth m. So we have to present for any structure $(\mathcal{C}, \bar{c})$ a formula $\varphi_{(\mathcal{C},\bar{c})}^m(\bar{x})$ of quantifier-depth m which is satisfied exactly by the structures which are m-isomorphic to $(\mathcal{C}, \bar{c})$. The suitable inductive definition is built on a formalization of $\equiv_0$-equivalence and of the two extension properties. Let, for a structure $(\mathcal{C}, \bar{c})$ with $\bar{c} = (c_1, \ldots, c_n)$

$$\varphi_{(\mathcal{C},\bar{c})}^0(\bar{x}) := \bigwedge_{\varphi(\bar{x}) \text{ atomic, } (\mathcal{C},\bar{c}) \models \varphi(\bar{x})} \varphi(\bar{x}) \wedge \bigwedge_{\varphi(\bar{x}) \text{ atomic, } (\mathcal{C},\bar{c}) \models \neg\varphi(\bar{x})} \neg\varphi(\bar{x})$$

$$\varphi_{(\mathcal{C},\bar{c})}^{m+1}(\bar{x}) := \bigwedge_{c \in C} \exists x_{n+1} \varphi_{(\mathcal{C},\bar{c},c)}^m(\bar{x}, x_{n+1}) \wedge \forall x_{n+1} \bigvee_{c \in C} \varphi_{(\mathcal{C},\bar{c},c)}^m(\bar{x}, x_{n+1})$$

To justify this definition in case the structure $\mathcal{C}$ is infinite, one has to observe that (due to the finite signature) there are only finitely many atomic formulas involving variables from $x_1, \ldots, x_n$, and that (as verified by induction on m) the number of logically nonequivalent formulas $\varphi_{(\mathcal{C},\bar{c})}^m(\bar{x})$ is finite (for any given length of tuples $\bar{c}$). Thus the disjunction and the conjunction (over $c \in C$) in the definition of $\varphi_{(\mathcal{C},\bar{c})}^{m+1}(\bar{x})$ both range only over finitely many formulas $\varphi_{(\mathcal{C},\bar{c},c)}^m(\bar{x}, x_{n+1})$ and thus specify first-order formulas.

The formulas $\varphi_{(\mathcal{C},\bar{c})}^m(\bar{x})$ go back to Hintikka [Hi53] and are sometimes called "Hintikka formulas". They are the basis of ⋯⋯ l form for first-order formulas. Obviously, the class of structures which sati͙ ͙en formula $\varphi(\bar{x})$ of quantifier-depth m must be a union of $\equiv_m$-classes, i ͙raïssé's Theorem, a union of $\cong_m$-classes. Each of these is defined by a Hi ͙rmula. Thus $\varphi(\bar{x})$ is logically equivalent to the (finite!) disjunction of tl ͙tikka formulas which define these $\cong_m$-classes. This representation is cal ͙ *distributive normal form* for first-order logic. For more details, variants of ͙a formulas, and applications see e.g. [Fl74], [Sc79].

3 Three Applications

3.1 Directed Graphs of Bounded Degre .

An S-structure $\mathcal{A} = (A, P_1^A, \ldots, P_k^A, R_1^A, \ldots, R_l^A)$, where the P_i^A form a partition of A and the R_j^A are disjoint relations, may be considered as a graph with labelled vertices and edges. The edge relation is $E = \bigcup_j R_j^A$, and the indices i, j represent the labels for the vertices, resp. edges. In the sequel, "graphs" are meant to be S-structures of this kind. A graph is of degree $\leq d$ if for any vertex a there are at most d vertices b with Eab or Eba. We want to determine the expressive power of first-order logic over graphs of bounded degree.

For $\mathcal{A}$ as above, $a \in A$, and $r \in \mathbb{N}$, the "sphere with radius r around a in $\mathcal{A}$" is the induced subgraph of $\mathcal{A}$ with vertices of distance $\leq r$ from a. (Here we assume that edges may be traversed in both directions.) This subgraph with designated center a is denoted $r-\mathrm{sph}(\mathcal{A}, a)$. Since we consider graphs of degree $\leq d$, there are, for any $r > 0$, only finitely many possible isomorphism types of r-spheres. For an isomorphism type σ of r-spheres, let $occ(\sigma, \mathcal{A})$ be the number of occurrences of spheres of type σ in $\mathcal{A}$. We shall see that any first-order formula is equivalent (over graphs of degree $\leq d$) to a statement on these occurrence numbers for finitely many types σ. Moreover, for any given formula the values $occ(\sigma, \mathcal{A})$ are relevant only up to a certain threshold $t \in \mathbb{N}$.

Formally, define $\mathcal{A} \sim_{r,t} \mathcal{B}$ if for any isomorphism type σ of spheres of radius r the numbers $occ(\sigma, \mathcal{A})$ and $occ(\sigma, \mathcal{B})$ are either both $> t$ or else coincide. The following "sphere lemma" states that $\sim_{r,t}$-equivalence (for suitable r, t) is fine enough to capture m-equivalence over graphs of degree $\leq d$.

Sphere Lemma. *For any $m \geq 0$ there are $r, t \geq 0$ such that for any two graphs $\mathcal{A}, \mathcal{B}$ (of degree $\leq d$) we have: If $\mathcal{A} \sim_{r,t} \mathcal{B}$ then $\mathcal{A} \equiv_m \mathcal{B}$.*

The proof, due to Hanf [Hf65], uses Fraïssé's Theorem: It suffices to ensure $\mathcal{A} \cong_m \mathcal{B}$ for suitable r, t. Set $r = 3^{m+1}$ and $t = m \cdot d^{3^{m+1}}$. The required sequence of sets $I_0, \ldots, I_m$ of partial isomorphisms is defined as follows: Let $p : (a_1, \ldots, a_{m-k}) \mapsto (b_1, \ldots, b_{m-k})$ belong to I_k iff

$$\bigcup_{i=1}^{m-k} 3^k - \mathrm{sph}(\mathcal{A}, a_i) \quad \cong \quad \bigcup_{i=1}^{m-k} 3^k - \mathrm{sph}(\mathcal{B}, b_i)$$

i.e., the two induced subgraphs formed from the 3^k-spheres around the a_i, resp. the b_i, are isomorphic. To verify e.g. the forth property, assume this condition holds for p and let $a(= a_{m-(k-1)}) \in A$. We have to find $b(= b_{m-(k-1)}) \in B$ such that

$$\bigcup_{i=1}^{m-(k-1)} 3^{k-1} - \mathrm{sph}(\mathcal{A}, a_i) \quad \cong \quad \bigcup_{i=1}^{m-(k-1)} 3^{k-1} - \mathrm{sph}(\mathcal{B}, b_i).$$

If $a \in \frac{2}{3} \cdot 3^k - \mathrm{sph}(\mathcal{A}, a_i)$ for some a_i, we may choose b from $\frac{2}{3} \cdot 3^k - \mathrm{sph}(\mathcal{A}, b_i)$ correspondingly; note that $3^{k-1} - \mathrm{sph}(\mathcal{A}, a)$ is contained in $3^k - \mathrm{sph}(\mathcal{A}, a_i)$ and thus $3^{k-1} - \mathrm{sph}(\mathcal{A}, b)$ in $3^k - \mathrm{sph}(\mathcal{A}, b_i)$. So $3^{k-1} - \mathrm{sph}(\mathcal{A}, a) \cong 3^{k-1} - \mathrm{sph}(\mathcal{B}, b)$ holds. Otherwise, $3^{k-1} - \mathrm{sph}(\mathcal{A}, a)$, say of type σ, is disjoint from all $3^{k-1} - \mathrm{sph}(\mathcal{A}, a_i)$, and it suffices to find a sphere of type σ in $\mathcal{B}$ which is disjoint from all spheres $3^{k-1} - \mathrm{sph}(\mathcal{B}, b_i)$. This will be possible if the number of occurrences of spheres of type σ in $\mathcal{B}$ is large enough. But this is guaranteed by the assumption $\mathcal{A} \sim_{r,t} \mathcal{B}$.

By the Sphere Lemma and the Distributive Normal Form, any first-order formula is equivalent (over graphs of degree $\leq d$) to a boolean combination of statements "there are $\geq k$ occurrences of spheres of type σ". So first-order logic can express only "local" graph properties and hence is too weak for many applications. (In the terminology of formal language theory, a first-order definable set of graphs of bounded degree is "locally threshold testable"; see [Th91].) This fact, which has also been shown by a different method (quantifier elimination) in [Ga82], has motivated the consideration of several extensions of first-order logic over graphs. Suitable extensions of the Ehrenfeucht-Fraïssé game serve to analyze their expressive power. Such an analysis has been carried out, for example, for existential monadic second-order logic ([Fag75], [FSV92]), for transitive closure logic (e.g. [Gr92]), and for different kinds of fixed point logic ([Bo92]).

3.2   Labelled Linear Orders and Congruence Lemmas

A word w over an alphabet $\Sigma = \{s_1, \ldots, s_k\}$ can be represented by the structure $\underline{w} = (\{1, \ldots, |w|\}, <, P_1^w, \ldots, P_k^w)$ with unary relations P_i^w, where $j \in P_i^w$ iff the j-th letter of w is s_i. A formal language $L \subseteq \Sigma^+$ is called first-order definable if there is a first-order sentence φ (in the signature $\{<, P_1, \ldots, P_k\}$) such that $L = \{w \in \Sigma^+ \mid \underline{w} \models \varphi\}$. Ehrenfeucht-Fraïssé games have been useful in clarifying the relation between first-order logic and definability notions from formal language theory, in particular concerning *star-free regular languages*. A language $L \subseteq \Sigma^+$ is called *star-free* if it can be constructed from finite languages by applications of boolean operations and concatenation. By a well-known result of McNaughton, a language is first-order definable iff it is star-free. The difficult direction is from left to right, and usually proved by induction on quantifier-depth (e.g. in [Lad77]). It turns out that the essential point of the induction step (concerning the existential quantifier) is the following claim:

Congruence Lemma. If $\underline{u} \equiv_m \underline{u}'$ and $\underline{v} \equiv_m \underline{v}'$, then $\underline{u} \cdot \underline{v} \equiv_m \underline{u}' \cdot \underline{v}'$.

The proof is straightforward if we refer to $\cong_m$ instead of $\equiv_m$ and think in terms of the Ehrenfeucht-Fraïssé game: The assumption tells us that player II has winning strategies for the games $G_m(\underline{u}, \underline{u}')$ and $G_m(\underline{v}, \underline{v}')$. An obvious composition of these two strategies ("on the segments u and u' use the first strategy, on the segments v and v' use the second strategy") guarantees her or him to win also the game $G_m(\underline{u} \cdot \underline{v}, \underline{u}' \cdot \underline{v}')$.

Congruence lemmas are a typical application of Ehrenfeucht-Fraïssé games; they have been proved also for other logics and over more complex structures than words. A congruence lemma states that properties of a structure as a whole are determined by (and hence can be composed from) properties of its parts. In [Th84], [Th87a], Ehrenfeucht-Fraïssé games are applied to obtain congruence lemmas for two modified versions of first-order logic: first-order formulas in prenex normal form with a fixed quantifier prefix type, and star-free regular expressions. A small but interesting difference between first-order logic and star-free expressions is worked out in [LT88], also via the game method.

Highly intricate examples of congruence lemmas were given by Shelah [Sh75], concerning the the monadic second-order theory of (arbitrary) linear orderings, and obtained by an extension of the Ehrenfeucht-Fraïssé technique. Later, congruence lemmas were proved also for tree structures, e.g. in [GS83] for monadic second-order logic or in [Th87b] for path-oriented logics. The extension of first-order logic over trees by "modulo counting quantifiers" was analyzed in [Pot92], again using appropriate Ehrenfeucht-Fraïssé games.

3.3 Labelled Transition Systems and Modal Logic

The notion of bisimulation was introduced by Park [Pa81] and related to modal logic by Hennessy and Milner ([HM85], [Mil90]). There is a close connection between bisimulations and Ehrenfeucht-Fraïssé games, although they were developed quite independently. Here we describe some aspects of this connection, but to avoid technical overhead we consider only a very restricted form of bisimulation and observational equivalence, in which the special role of the so-called "silent transition" is suppressed. (For a different approach to treat behavioral equivalences in first-order logic see [Og92].)

We refer to structures $\mathcal{A} = (A, R_1^A, \ldots, R_l^A)$, which serve as the model theoretic representation of "labelled transition systems" ([Mil90]): The elements of A are "states", and $R_1^A, \ldots, R_l^A$ are "transition relations". Hennessy-Milner Logic is a system of modal logic to be interpreted over labelled transition systems. We introduce this logic here directly as a fragment of first-order logic, given by special "admissible" formulas. An admissible formula has exactly one free variable. As basic atomic formulas we allow only $tt(x_i)$ (always true). Binary boolean connectives are applicable only to formulas with the same free variable, negation is always applicable, and quantifiers are allowed only in "R_j-relativized form", observing certain conditions on the indexing of variables: Given $\varphi(x_{i+1})$ one may proceed to $\psi(x_i)$ of the form $\exists x_{i+1}(R_j x_i x_{i+1} \wedge \varphi(x_{i+1}))$ or $\forall x_{i+1}(R_j x_i x_{i+1} \to \varphi(x_{i+1}))$. To normalize the indexing of variables, we finish the construction of a formula always with x_0 as free variable (to be interpreted by a designated element of a labelled transition system). In this framework, a formula such as

$$\Diamond_i \Box_i (\Diamond_j tt \wedge \Diamond_k tt)$$

of Hennessy-Milner Logic is written as the following admissible formula $\varphi(x_0)$:

$$\exists x_1(R_i x_0 x_1 \wedge \forall x_2(R_i x_1 x_2 \to (\exists x_3(R_j x_2 x_3 \wedge tt(x_3)) \wedge \exists x_3(R_k x_2 x_3 \wedge tt(x_3)))))$$

Define $(\mathcal{A}, a_0) =_m (\mathcal{B}, b_0)$ in the same way as $(\mathcal{A}, a_0) \equiv_m (\mathcal{B}, b_0)$, however referring to admissible formulas of quantifier rank $\leq m$. By the lack of equality and because of the restricted use of the symbols R_j, the appropriate notion of "partial isomorphism" is weaker than before; in particular, we do no more require that it represents an injective function: Let us call a relation $r : (a_0, \ldots, a_n) \mapsto (b_0, \ldots, b_n) \subseteq A \times B$ a *correspondence* if $R_j^A a_i a_{i+1} \Leftrightarrow R_j^B b_i b_{i+1}$ for $i = 0, \ldots, n-1$ and $j = 1, \ldots, l$. Finally, define $(\mathcal{A}, a_0) \simeq_m (\mathcal{B}, b_0)$ in the same way as $(\mathcal{A}, a_0) \cong_m (\mathcal{B}, b_0)$, with correspondences replacing partial isomorphisms. Now the proof of Fraïssé's Theorem, adjusted to this context, shows

$$(\mathcal{A}, a_0) =_m (\mathcal{B}, b_0) \quad \text{iff} \quad (\mathcal{A}, a_0) \simeq_m (\mathcal{B}, b_0).$$

This equivalence may be regarded as a restricted form of the Hennessy-Milner characterization of bisimilarity (as formulated, for example, in [Mil90, Theorem 5.2.5 (1)]). Two points should be mentioned: Usually, in semantics of concurrency one deals with one transition system only, i.e. one considers equivalences between structures $(\mathcal{A}, a_0)$ and $(\mathcal{A}, b_0)$. More important, in the theory of bisimulations one does not refer to the existence of some sequence $(I_0, \ldots, I_m)$ of sets of correspondences (as one does in the definition of "m-isomorphism"), but works with a fixed canonical sequence $(J_0, \ldots, J_m)$ of correspondence sets: J_0 contains just the universal relation, and J_{k+1} contains all relations which allow back and forth extensions in J_k. This does not change the equivalence result above, but it prevents the definition of specific winning strategies by the correspondence sets.

In the general framework of bisimulations and observational equivalences (see [HM85], [Mil90]), the considered "actions" in transition systems are more complex, consisting of sequences of R_j-transitions and depending in different ways on occurrences of a designated "silent" transition. This general situation suggests to include infinite signatures. A corresponding extension of first-order logic is the system $L^\omega_{\infty\omega}$, allowing infinite disjunctions and conjunctions (however only finitely many variables in each formula, which are reusable within a formula). The appropriate extension of the Ehrenfeucht-Fraïssé technique has been developed and applied in other fields of computer science, e.g. in complexity theory (Immerman [Im82]) and data base theory (Kolaitis and Vardi [KV90]). The topic of reusable variables is treated, using special Ehrenfeucht-Fraïssé games, in [IK89] and [Fl92].

References

[BF85] J.Barwise, S. Feferman (eds.), *Model-Theoretic Logics*, Springer-Verlag, Berin-Heidelberg, New York 1985.

[Bo92] U. Bosse, An "Ehrenfeucht-Fraïssé game" for fixpoint logic and stratified fixpoint logic, manuscript, Math. Inst., Universität Freiburg, 1992.

[EFT84] H.D. Ebbinghaus, J. Flum, W. Thomas, *Mathematical Logic*, Springer-Verlag, New York 1984 (revised and extended edition to appear 1993).

[Ehr61] A. Ehrenfeucht, An application of games to the completeness problem for formalized theories, Fund. Math. 49 (1961), 129-141.

[Fag75] R. Fagin, Monadic generalized spectra, Z. math. Logik u. Grundl. Math. 21 (1975), 123-134.

[FSV92] R. Fagin, L. Stockmeyer, M.Y. Vardi, A simple proof that connectivity separates existential and universal monadic second-order logic over finite structures, IBM Rep. RJ 8647, 1992.

[Fl74] J. Flum, First-order logic and its extensions, in: Proc. ISILC Logic Conf., Kiel, Springer Lect. Notes in Math. 499 (1975), 248-310.

[Fl92] J. Flum, On bounded theories, in: Computer Science Logic (E. Börger et al., eds.), Springer LNCS 626 (1992), 111-118.

[Fr54] R. Fraïssé, Sur quelques classifications des relations, basés sur des isomorphismes restreints, Publ. Sci. de l'Univ. Alger, Sér. A 1 (1954), 35-182.

[Ga82]   H. Gaifman, On local and non-local properties, in: *Proc. of the Herbrand Symposium*, Logic Colloquium '81 (J. Stern, ed.), North-Holland, Amsterdam 1982, pp. 105-135.

[Gr92]   E. Grädel, On transitive closure logic, in: Computer Science Logic (E. Börger et al., eds.), Springer LNCS 626 (1992), 149-165.

[GS83]   Y. Gurevich, S. Shelah, Rabin's uniformization problem, J. Symb. Logic 48 (1983), 1105-1119.

[Hf65]   W.P. Hanf, Model-theoretic methods in the study of elementary logic, in: *The Theory of Models* (J.W. Addison, L. Henkin, A. Tarski, eds.), North-Holland, Amsterdam 1965, pp. 132-145.

[HM85]   M. Hennessy, R. Milner, Algebraic laws for nondeterminism and concurrency, J. Assoc. Comput. Mach. 21 (1985), 137-161.

[Hi53]   J. Hintikka, *Distributive normal forms in the calculus of predicates*, Acta Philos. Fennica 6 (1953).

[Im82]   N. Immerman, Upper and lower bounds for first-order expressibility, J. Comput. System Sci. 25 (1982), 76-98.

[IK89]   N. Immerman, D. Kozen, Definability with a bounded number of bound variables, Inform. Comput. 83 (1989), 121-139.

[KV90]   Ph. Kolaitis, M. Vardi, On the expressive power of Datalog: Tools and a case study, Proc. 9th ACM Symp. on Principles of Database Systems, 61-71.

[Lad77]   R.E. Ladner, Application of model-theoretic games to discrete linear orders and finite automata, Inform. Contr. 33 (1977), 281-303.

[LT88]   D. Lippert, W. Thomas, Relativized star-free expressions, first-order logic, and a concatenation game, in: Semigroup Theory and Applications (H. Jürgensen et al. eds.), Springer Lect. Notes in Math. 1320 (1988), 194-204.

[Mil90]   R. Milner, Operational and algebraic semantics of concurrent processes, in: *Handbook of Theoretical Computer Science* (J. v. Leeuwen, ed.), Vol. B, Elsevier Science Publ., Amsterdam 1990, pp. 1201-1241.

[Mo76]   D. Monk, *Mathematical Logic*, Springer-Verlag, New York 1976.

[Og92]   H. Oguztüzün, A fragment of first-order logic adequate for observation equivalence, in: Computer Science Logic (E. Börger et al., eds.), Springer LNCS 626 (1992), 287-291.

[Pa81]   D. Park, Concurrency and automata on infinite sequences, in: Theoretical Computer Science (P. Deussen, ed.), Springer LNCS 104 (1981), 167-183.

[Pot92]   A. Potthoff, Modulo counting quantifiers over finite trees, in: CAAP'92 (J.C. Raoult, ed.), LNCS 581 (1992), 265-278.

[Ro82]   J.G. Rosenstein, *Linear Orderings*, Academic Press, New York 1982.

[Sc79]   D. Scott, A note on distributive normal forms, in: *Essays in Honour of Jaakko Hintikka* (E. Saarinen et al., eds.), Reidel, Dordrecht 1979, pp. 75-90.

[Sh75]   S. Shelah, The monadic theory of order, Ann. Math. 102 (1975), 379-419.

[Th84]   W. Thomas, An application of the Ehrenfeucht-Fraïssé game in formal language theory, Bull. Soc. Math. France, Mem. 16 (1984), 11-21.

[Th87a]   W. Thomas, A concatenation game and the dot-depth hierarchy, in: Computation Theory and Logic (E. Börger, ed.), LNCS 270 (1987), 415-426.

[Th87b]   W. Thomas, On chain logic, path logic, and first-order logic over infinite trees, Proc. 2nd LICS, Ithaca, N.Y. 1987, 245-256.

[Th91]   W. Thomas, On logics, tilings, and automata, in: Proc. 18th ICALP, Madrid (J. Leach Albert et al., eds.), Springer LNCS 510 (1991), 441-454.

On Asymptotic Probabilities in Logics That Capture DSPACE(log n) in Presence of Ordering

Jerzy Tyszkiewicz*

Institute of Informatics, University of Warsaw,
ul. Banacha 2, 02-097 Warszawa, Poland.
jurekty@mimuw.edu.pl

Abstract. We show that for logics that capture DSPACE(log n) over ordered structures, and for recursive probability distributions on the class of all finite models of the signature, the 0–1 law and the convergence law hold if and only if certain boundedness conditions are satisfied. As one of the consequences we get necessary and sufficient conditions of both laws for fixpoint logic and recursive distributions. This in turn allows us to consider a conjecture of Kolaitis and Vardi, stating that the 0–1 law for fixpoint logic holds iff the same law holds for infinitary logic $L^{\omega}_{\omega_1\omega}$.

1 Introduction

1.1 About the Theory of Asymptotic Probabilities

The problems considered in this paper belong to the research area called *random structure theory,* and, more specifically, to its logical aspect.

To explain (very imprecisely and incompletely) what it means, let us consider a class of some structures (say: finite ones over some fixed signature), equipped with a probability space structure. This probability is usually assumed to be only *finitely* additive. Then we draw one structure at random and ask:

- how does the drawn structure look like?
- does the drawn structure have some particular property?

Those questions are typical in random structure theory. To turn to the logical part of it, look at the drawn structure through the logical glasses: we can only notice properties definable in some particular logic. Then new questions become natural:

- does every property we can observe have a probability (is it measurable)?
- if so, what are the possible values of probabilities?
- can we compute this probability, and, eventually, how difficult is it?

It becomes clear from the above that the random structure theory is closely connected to combinatorics, finite model theory, mathematical logic, and, last but not least, computer science. An exposition of the logical part of the random structure theory may be found in a nice survey of Compton [1].

---

* Partially supported by KBN grant GR-71.

Generally, it seems that the emergence of the theories of asymptotic probabilities and of descriptive complexity reflect the same trend that was observed in continuous mathematics. Namely, in order to better understand the nature of the set of real numbers, mathematicians equipped it with various structures (such as the structure of probability space, topological space, field, Banach algebra, etc.), and studied the resulting object.

To better understand the expressive power of a logic over finite structures, logicians equip the set of finite models of the signature with various structures.

One of possible choices is to add the successor relation to the signature, and then every structure can be treated as a word, so that every sentence of the logic under consideration defines a language. The great discovery of the theory of descriptive complexity is that for most of natural logics the resulting families of languages naturally correspond to well known complexity classes.

The other choice is to add the structure of a (asymptotic) probability space. The resulting theory of asymptotic probabilities allows one to make some other nontrivial observations. One of them is, e.g., the connection between decidability of finite satisfiability problem for a prefix class $\mathcal{F}$ of first order formulas and uniform, labelled 0–1 law for the collection of existential second order formulas with first order part in $\mathcal{F}$: the class $\Sigma_1^1(\mathcal{F})$. More information about this result can be found in the paper [6] of Kolaitis and Vardi. Other examples are presented in Gurevich's article [3].

1.2   Aim of the Paper

In the current paper we are interested in 0–1 laws and convergence laws for logics with various forms of recursion. These include transitive closure logic, fixpoint logic and others. In general, all of them capture at least DSPACE($\log n$) in ordered finite structures. We develop a very general method for dealing with such problems. We present several applications of this method, presenting necessary and sufficient conditions of these laws for several logics, in particular solving open problem, in the form of the following conjecture of Kolaitis and Vardi:

Conjecture 1 (Kolaitis and Vardi [8]). *Let $\mathcal{A}$ be any class of finite structures and let μ_n, $n \geq 1$ be any sequence of probability measures on the structures of $\mathcal{A}$ with n elements. Then the 0–1 law holds for the infinitary logic $L_{\omega_1\omega}^{\omega}$ in $\mathcal{A}$ relative to the measures μ_n if and only if the 0–1 law holds for fixpoint logic in $\mathcal{A}$ relative to the measures μ_n.*

We show that the above conjecture is untrue in general. However, it becomes true when restricted to measures whose values can be approximated in recursive way with arbitrary precision.

We keep the paper on rather abstract level. In particular, we do not give complete definitions of the logics we consider, but use results about them. The reader, who is not familiar with them, will probably have to consult some textbooks. There are also no examples – we decided to use the limited space for more theorems and more details in the proofs, instead.

2 Formal Definitions

Throughout the paper we assume that we are dealing with logics over some fixed, finite signature σ (with equality). It is assumed to contain only relation symbols, and therefore eventual functions are represented as restricted relations. Let $\mathcal{A}$ be the set of *all* finite structures $\mathbf{A}$ over signature σ, such that the carrier set $|\mathbf{A}|$ of $\mathbf{A}$ is some initial segment of natural numbers. Let $\mathcal{A}(n)$ be the set of all structures $\mathbf{A} \in \mathcal{A}$ with carrier set (of cardinality) $|\mathbf{A}| = n = \{0, \ldots, n-1\}$.

Let there be a probability distribution μ_n on each $\mathcal{A}(n)$. Writing μ for $\{\mu_n\}_{n \in \mathbb{N}}$ we consider $\langle \mathcal{A}, \mu \rangle$ as *randomized set of finite structures,* and make it an object of our study. Since $\mathcal{A}$ is fixed, μ itself determines this randomized set, and therefore in the sequel we deal with distributions only.

Then for any subset $D \subseteq \mathcal{A}$ we define

$$\mu_n(D) = \mu_n(D \cap \mathcal{A}(n)).$$

We often consider D being the set of those structures in $\mathcal{A}$ that satisfy some sentence φ in the logic under consideration, and then we write $\mu_n(\varphi)$, instead of $\mu_n(D)$. We are interested in asymptotic properties of $\mu_n(\varphi)$, and especially whether the limit

$$\mu(\varphi) = \lim_{n \to \infty} \mu_n(\varphi)$$

exists, for φ being a sentence of the logic. If it exists, we call it an *asymptotic probability of φ.* If this is the case for every sentence of the logic L, we say that the *convergence law* holds (for L and μ). If, in addition, every sentence has probability either 0 or 1, we say that the *0-1 law* holds.

We fix some method of coding structures in $\mathcal{A}$ as natural numbers. The coding bijection $\mathcal{A} \to \mathbb{N}$ we denote by code, while its converse $\mathbb{N} \to \mathcal{A}$ by struct. They will be used to speak about recursive sets of elements of $\mathcal{A}$, first structure in a $D \subseteq \mathcal{A}$, etc. The particular choice of coding function is immaterial, except that we require it to satisfy: the function $a \mapsto |\text{struct}(a)|$ is recursive, and for a relation symbol R of arity k from σ and k-tuple $\mathbf{b} \in |\text{struct}(a)|^k$, it is decidable whether $\text{struct}(a) \models R(\mathbf{b})$.

The *representing relation* of a distribution μ is a ternary relation m_μ on natural numbers, defined as follows:

$$m_\mu(a, b, c) \qquad \text{iff} \qquad \mu_{|\text{struct}(a)|}(\{\text{struct}(a)\}) \le b/c.$$

More intuitive (but essentially equivalent to the above) is to take m_μ to be the relation

$$\mu_{|\mathbf{A}|}(\{\mathbf{A}\}) \le q$$

included in $\mathcal{A} \times \mathbb{Q}$. Now we have a uniform method of representing distributions, which is independent of the representation of the values of μ (which may be e.g. irrational), so we can speak about *complexity* of the distribution.

There is, however, one thing to consider before. Namely, a very simple (of very low complexity) distribution can be converted into a one of very high complexity by a perturbation that vanishes as $n \to \infty$. But, as we are interested in asymptotical properties of the resulting distribution only, it should be still regarded as simple. The formalisation of this idea is as follows:

Definition 2. We say that two distributions μ and μ' are *asymptotically equivalent* if and only if for every $D \subseteq \mathcal{A}$

$$\lim_{n \to \infty} \mu_n(D) - \mu'_n(D) = 0.$$

Now we define the *arithmetical complexity* of a distribution μ: for $k > 0$ we say that the distribution μ is Δ_k (Σ_k, Π_k, resp.) iff there exists a distribution μ', asymptotically equivalent to μ, and such that its representing relation $m_{\mu'}$ is Δ_k (Σ_k, Π_k, resp.). □

We are particularly interested in Δ_1 distributions, whose values can be approximated with arbitrary precision in recursive way.

First we prove a simple fact, stating that essentially the arithmetical hierarchy collapses to the Δ hierarchy for distributions:

Proposition 3. *If a distribution μ is Σ_k (Π_k, resp.), then it is Δ_k, as well. Moreover, there exists a distribution μ', asymptotically equivalent to μ, such that the function $\mathbf{A} \mapsto \mu'_{|\mathbf{A}|}(\{\mathbf{A}\})$ is rational valued and Δ_k.*

Proof. We consider only the case of $k = 1$ and Σ_1. The converse implication can be obtained by symmetric argumentation, while for $k > 1$ it suffices to replace Turing machines, appearing in the proof below, by Turing machines with suitable oracle.

Suppose that the distribution μ is Σ_1. We construct a distribution μ', which is asymptotically equivalent to μ, rational valued and, moreover, the function $\mathbf{A} \mapsto \mu'_{|\mathbf{A}|}(\{\mathbf{A}\})$ is recursive.

Let M be the Turing machine that enumerates all true inequalities of the form $\mu_{|\mathbf{A}|}(\{\mathbf{A}\}) \leq q$, $\mathbf{A} \in \mathcal{A}$, $q \in \mathbb{Q}$.

We construct machine N, computing function $\mathbf{A} \mapsto \mu'_{|\mathbf{A}|}(\{\mathbf{A}\})$.

Given input $\mathbf{A} \in \mathcal{A}(n)$, the machine N simulates the behaviour of M and stores all the inequalities it generates until the first moment there is a subset of them

$$\{\mu_n(\{\mathbf{B}\}) \leq q_\mathbf{B} \mid \mathbf{B} \in \mathcal{A}(n)\}$$

with the property

$$\sum_{\mathbf{B} \in \mathcal{A}(n)} q_\mathbf{B} \geq 1 - 1/n.$$

At that moment N outputs the value

$$\mu'_n(\{\mathbf{A}\}) = \begin{cases} 1 - \sum_{\mathbf{B} \in \mathcal{A}(n) \setminus \{\mathbf{A}\}} q_\mathbf{B} & \text{if } \mathbf{A} \text{ is the first element of } \mathcal{A}(n), \\ q_\mathbf{A} & \text{otherwise.} \end{cases}$$

The machine N always halts since the equality $\sum_{\mathbf{B} \in \mathcal{A}(n)} \mu_n(\{\mathbf{B}\}) = 1$ holds. The distribution μ' is clearly asymptotically equivalent to μ, as for every $D \subseteq \mathcal{A}$ we have $|\mu_n(D) - \mu'_n(D)| \leq 1/n$. □

It is quite natural to call Δ_1 distributions *recursive*, and we do so in the sequel.

3   The Main Theorem

The distribution μ is assumed to be fixed in this paragraph, and therefore all the notions we introduce should be understood to refer to the fixed pair $\langle \mathcal{A}, \mu \rangle$.

Now we introduce one more definition, being the crucial definition in our paper:

Definition 4. Let L be a logic, and let $Int(\mathbf{x})$, $Eq(\mathbf{x}, \mathbf{y})$, $Succ(\mathbf{x}, \mathbf{y})$ and $Edge(\mathbf{x}, \mathbf{y})$ be L–formulas with ℓ, 2ℓ, 2ℓ and 2ℓ free variables, respectively. Let $\mathcal{J}$ be the quadruple $\langle Int, Eq, Succ, Edge \rangle$, $D \subseteq \mathcal{A}$ be a class of finite structures, and let C be a complexity class. We say that L is C-*expressive in D for $\mathcal{J}$* if and only if:

1. In every structure $\mathbf{A} \in D$ the interpretation $Eq^{\mathbf{A}}$ of formula Eq is an equivalence relation, and the structure $\mathcal{J}(\mathbf{A}) = \langle Int^{\mathbf{A}}, Succ^{\mathbf{A}}, Edge^{\mathbf{A}} \rangle / Eq^{\mathbf{A}}$ is isomorphic to a graph with successor. The cardinality of this graph is denoted by $|\mathbf{A}|$.
2. For every set S of graphs with successor in C there exists a sentence φ in L such that for every $\mathbf{A} \in D$:

$$\mathbf{A} \models \varphi \quad \Leftrightarrow \quad \mathcal{J}(\mathbf{A}) \in S.$$

$\square$

The above definition generalizes in some aspect the notion of a logic that captures complexity class (see e.g. [5]), where the formulas Int, Eq, $Succ$ and $Edge$ were a *priori* chosen (to be atomic formulas) and fixed.

Namely, the standard notion is: one can express by sentences of L all those properties of a structure $\mathbf{A} \in D$ that are computable in C, and only those.

Our notion is: one has $\mathcal{J}$, which interprets in every $\mathbf{A} \in D$ another structure $\mathcal{J}(\mathbf{A})$ (being graph with successor). Then one is able to express all those properties of $\mathcal{J}(\mathbf{A})$ that are computable in C (with respect to size of $\mathcal{J}(\mathbf{A})$!).

We say that L *is almost surely C-expressive for $\mathcal{J}$* if and only if there is a subset $D \subseteq \mathcal{A}$ such that $\mu(D) = 1$ and L is C–expressive for $\mathcal{J}$ in D.

In this paper we focus our attention on $C = \text{DSPACE}(\log n)$. We do not need the edge relation in the sequel, and this is why we take $\mathcal{J}$ to be a 3–tuple, and $\mathcal{J}(\mathbf{A})$ to be, in general, isomorphic to an interval of natural numbers with successor.

First we need a simple complexity–theoretic fact:

Let us adopt that a recursive function $h : \mathbb{N} \to \mathbb{N}$ is called *space constructible* iff there exists an on-line Turing Machine M which computes h, and for some constant c_h and all $n \in \mathbb{N}$, machine M uses at most $c_h \cdot \text{length}(h(n))$ tape cells during computation with input n (input and output are represented as binary strings). Note that our definition is slightly more liberal than the usual one. The name is chosen to indicate that all space constructible (in standard sense) functions satisfy our definition.

Lemma 5. *If $h : \mathbb{N} \to \mathbb{N}$ is strictly growing and space constructible, then the binary relation $(k \leq h(m))$, of arguments k, m being natural numbers written in unary expansion, is in $\text{DSPACE}(\log k)$.*

Proof. Let the machine recognizing our relation first check whether $k \leq m$, given input (k, m). (It can be done without reading entire input, when $k < m$!) If this is the case, it decides that $k \leq h(m)$ (from strict monotonicity of h it follows that $k \leq m \leq h(m)$). Otherwise it first converts m into binary, and then tries to compute the value of $h(m)$ in $c_h \lceil \log k \rceil$ space cells. If it succeeds and the result is less than k, then $k \not\leq h(m)$; if either it does not succeed (due to lack of space), or it succeeds and the result is $\geq k$, then it decides that $k \leq h(m)$. The computation requires $c_h \lceil \log k \rceil + \lceil \log k \rceil + O(1)$ space cells, and so the relation is in DSPACE($\log k$). □

Now we are ready to state and prove the main result of the paper:

Theorem 6. *Let μ be a recursive distribution. Suppose that a logic L is almost surely DSPACE($\log n$)-expressive for $\mathcal{J}$. Then*

1. *If there is a constant $\alpha < 1$ such that for every natural d*

$$\liminf_{n \to \infty} \mu_n(\{A \in \mathcal{A} \mid |A|\} \leq d) < \alpha,$$

   then the convergence law does not hold for L and μ.
2. *If there is no natural d such that*

$$\mu(\{A \in \mathcal{A} \mid |A|\} \leq d) = 1,$$

   then the 0-1 law does not hold for L and μ.

Proof. Throughout the proof we will simply write DSPACE($\log n$) properties of $|A|$ as the formulas of L.

We start proving 1.

Without any loss of generality we may assume the distribution μ to be so that the function $A \mapsto \mu_{|A|}(\{A\})$ is rational valued and recursive. Moreover, we may also assume that whenever $\mu_{|A|}(\{A\}) > 0$, the structure $\mathcal{J}(A)$ is an interval with successor.

If for some $d \in \mathbb{N}$ the value

$$a(d) = \mu(|A| \leq d)$$

does not exist, we are done, since then the sentence in L expressing property $|A| \leq d$ has no asymptotic probability. (Recall that all finite sets are in DSPACE($\log n$).)

So for the rest of the proof we assume that the values $a(d)$ do exist. Then observe that $a(d)$ is nondecreasing function of d, bounded by 1, and therefore the limit

$$\lim_{d \to \infty} \mu(|A| \leq d)$$

exists (we denote it by a). Our assumption becomes now equivalent to $a < 1$.

So let $\delta > 0$ be a rational number, satisfying $1.5\delta > 1 - a > \delta$. Choose M large enough to have $1.5\delta > 1 - a(M) > \delta$, and N large enough to have $1.5\delta > 1 - \mu_n(|A| \leq M) > \delta$ for all $n > N$.

Now let $g : \mathbb{N} \to \mathbb{N}$ be defined as follows: $g(0) = 0$ and for $n > 0$

$$g(n) = 1 + (\text{the least number } m > g(n-1) \text{ such that } \mu_m(|A| > n) > \delta).$$

The function g is strictly growing and recursive since μ is rational valued and recursive.

Now let $\bar{g} : \mathbb{N} \to \mathbb{N}$ be strictly growing, space constructible function satisfying $\bar{g}(n) > (g(n))^{\ell}$. (Observe that always $|\mathbf{A}| \le |\mathbf{A}|^{\ell}$.) Then we define space constructible and strictly growing $f : \mathbb{N} \to \mathbb{N}$ to be

$$f(m) = \begin{cases} 1 & \text{if } m = 0, \\ \bar{g}\,\bar{g}f(m-1) & \text{if } m > 0. \end{cases}$$

Then the following property can be decided in DSPACE($\log n$), and hence also expressed by some L sentence (say ϑ) :

$$|\mathbf{A}| \ge M \wedge \bigwedge_{k=0}^{\infty} \left[(|\mathbf{A}| \ge f(k)) \;\to\; (|\mathbf{A}| \ge \bar{g}(f(k))) \right].$$

Let us make sure that ϑ is indeed a DSPACE($\log n$) property (recall that $n = |\mathbf{A}|$ is written in unary expansion). Indeed, it follows from strict monotonicity that $f(k) \ge k$, so ϑ is equivalent to

$$|\mathbf{A}| \ge M \wedge \bigwedge_{k=0}^{s-1} \left[(|\mathbf{A}| \ge f(k)) \;\to\; (|\mathbf{A}| \ge \bar{g}(f(k))) \right],$$

where s is a minimal number such that $f(s) > |\mathbf{A}|$. Now the quantified part of the above property can be verified in DSPACE($\log n$) by systematic checking of all $k < s$, according to lemma 5.

We claim that ϑ has no asymptotic probability.

A. For all sufficiently large k and $n = g(f(k))$ such that $n > N$ and $f(k) > M$ (there are infinitely many such n), we have that

$$\mu_n(|\mathbf{A}| \ge f(k)) \ge \delta,$$

and

$$\mu_n(|\mathbf{A}| \ge \bar{g}(f(k))) \le$$
$$\mu_n(|\mathbf{A}| > (g(f(k)))^{\ell}) =$$
$$\mu_n(|\mathbf{A}| > n^{\ell}) = 0.$$

Hence

$$\mu_n(\vartheta) \le$$
$$1 - \mu_n(|\mathbf{A}| < M) - \mu_n(|\mathbf{A}| \ge f(k)) \le$$
$$(1 - \mu_n(|\mathbf{A}| < M)) - \delta < 1.5\delta - \delta = 0.5\delta.$$

B. For all sufficiently large k and $n = g(\bar{g}(f(k)))$ such that $n > N$ and $\bar{g}(f(k)) > M$ (there are infinitely many such n), we have that

$$\mu_n(|\mathbf{A}| \geq \bar{g}(f(k)) > M) > \delta,$$

and

$$\mu_n(|\mathbf{A}| \geq f(k+1)) =$$

$$\mu_n(|\mathbf{A}| \geq \bar{g}(\bar{g}(k))) \leq$$

$$\mu_n(|\mathbf{A}| > (g(\bar{g}(k)))^\ell) =$$

$$\mu_n(|\mathbf{A}| > n^\ell) = 0.$$

Combining we get

$$\mu_n(\vartheta) > \delta.$$

We conclude that $\mu_n(\vartheta)$ cannot be convergent, since both inequalities $\mu_n(\vartheta) > \delta$ and $\mu_n(\vartheta) < 0.5\delta$ hold infinitely often, and $\delta > 0$.

To prove 2. suppose to the contrary that the 0–1 law holds, but there is no natural d such that $\mu(|\mathbf{A}| \leq d) = 1$. Then, as the 0–1 law holds and all properties $|\mathbf{A}| \leq d$ are L–definable, we conclude that for every d we have $\mu(|\mathbf{A}| \leq d) = 0$. But then the first part of the proof applies, and even the convergence law fails to hold, which yields a contradiction, and thus finishes the proof. □

The above theorem subsumes the results in [10] and [11], where it was assumed that the length of the defined interval should be estimated from the below by a non-decreasing, recursive function, with no too small probability. In particular, most of examples of applications presented there can now be formulated in stronger versions, and the proofs become easier.

4 The Consequences: Recursive Distributions

4.1 Fixpoint Logic and the Kolaitis and Vardi Conjecture

Before we turn to the Conjecture itself, let us recall basic definitions concerning fixpoint logic and infinitary logic $L_{\omega_1\omega}^\omega$.

The *infinitary logic* $L_{\omega_1\omega}^\omega$ is an extension of first order logic, where, except all first order formula formation rules, there is an infinitary rule: if Φ is an arbitrary countable set of $L_{\omega_1\omega}^\omega$ formulas such that only finitely many distinct variables occur in formulas in Φ, then the *infinitary disjunction* $\bigvee \Phi$ is a formula of $L_{\omega_1\omega}^\omega$. We can also define certain fragments of $L_{\omega_1\omega}^\omega$: e.g., the recursive (recursively enumerable, ...) fragment of $L_{\omega_1\omega}^\omega$ is obtained by restricting infinitary disjunctions to recursive (recursively enumerable, ...) sets of formulas.

The *fixpoint logic* is a logic obtained from first order logic by adding *fixpoint formulas* of the form φ^∞, where φ is a first order formula, has ℓ free variables (say $x_1, \ldots, x_\ell$), and a new ℓ-ary relation symbol $X^\ell \notin \sigma$ occurs *positively* (i.e. under even number of negations) in it. The set of formulas of fixpoint logic is the least set of expressions, containing all first order formulas, all fixpoint formulas and closed under standard first order formula formation rules: propositional connectives and quantification.

The semantics of a fixpoint formula φ^∞ is as follows: Let $\mathbf{A}$ be a finite σ-structure. Then there is an operator from ℓ-ary relations in $|\mathbf{A}|$ to ℓ-ary relations in $|\mathbf{A}|$, defined by

$$\Phi(R) = \{\mathbf{a} \in |\mathbf{A}|^\ell \mid \mathbf{A}, \mathbf{x}{:}\mathbf{a}, X^\ell{:}R \models \varphi.\}$$

Since X^ℓ occurs only positively in φ, the operator Φ is monotone: if $R \subseteq R'$, then $\Phi(R) \subseteq \Phi(R')$. Therefore it gives rise to an increasing sequence of *stages*, $\Phi(\emptyset) \subseteq \Phi(\Phi(\emptyset)) \subseteq \dots$ Elements of this sequence we denote $\Phi^1, \Phi^2, \dots$ Since $\mathbf{A}$ is finite, it follows that there exists a minimal m such that $\Phi^m = \Phi^{m+1}$. Moreover, the value of m cannot exceed $|\mathbf{A}|^\ell$. Φ^m is the *least fixed point of* Φ, and we denote it by Φ^∞. Now we define:

$$\mathbf{A}, \mathbf{x}{:}\mathbf{a} \models \varphi^\infty \quad \Leftrightarrow \quad \mathbf{A}, \mathbf{x}{:}\mathbf{a}, X^\ell{:}\Phi^\infty \models \varphi.$$

The value of m defined above we call the *closure ordinal of φ in* $\mathbf{A}$, and denote $|\mathbf{A}|_\varphi$.

We say that formula φ^∞ is *bounded in a class* $D \subseteq \mathcal{A}$ iff there is a constant d such that $|\mathbf{A}|_\varphi \leq d$ for every $\mathbf{A} \in D$. If this is the case for every fixpoint formula, we say that fixpoint logic is *bounded in* D. Either of these properties is said to hold almost surely iff, in addition, $\mu(D) = 1$.

It should be noted that if fixpoint logic is bounded in D, then, in particular, it collapses to first order logic in D. It is also known that fixpoint logic is essentially a sublogic of $L^\omega_{\omega_1\omega}$, as proved by Kolaitis and Vardi in [7].

The following theorem is the key one:

Theorem 7. *For an arbitrary fixpoint formula φ^∞ there exist fixpoint formulas Int_φ, $Succ_\varphi$ and Eq_φ, such that fixpoint logic is PTIME–expressive (and, in consequence, also DSPACE($\log n$)–expressive) for $\mathcal{J}_\varphi \equiv \langle Int_\varphi, Succ_\varphi, Eq_\varphi \rangle$ in $\mathcal{A}$.*

Observe that the above theorem is essentially an amalgamate of: Moschovakis Stage Comparison Theorem from [9], which provides point 1 of the definition, and, due to Immerman [4] and Vardi [12]: classical result stating that fixpoint logic captures PTIME in finite structures with standard successor, together with normal form theorem for fixpoint logic, the latter assuring that one can, on the semantical level, substitute formulas resulting from Moschovakis Theorem into the place of standard successor.

Theorem 8. *Let μ be arbitrary recursive probability distribution on the class $\mathcal{A}$ of all finite structures over the signature σ. Then:*

1. *The convergence law holds for the fixpoint logic relative to μ if and only if the same law holds for first order logic, and for every $\varepsilon > 0$ there is a subset $D \subseteq \mathcal{A}$ with $\mu(D) > 1 - \varepsilon$, and such that fixpoint logic is bounded in D.*
2. *The 0–1 law holds for the fixpoint logic relative to μ if and only if the same law holds for first order logic, and fixpoint logic is almost surely bounded in $\mathcal{A}$.*

Proof. We prove only the nontrivial direction: from left to right. According to theorem 7, premises of the theorem 6 are satisfied. It follows that:

1. if the fixpoint convergence law holds, then for every $\varepsilon > 0$, and for every formula φ^∞, there exists a subset $D \subseteq \mathcal{A}$ with $\mu(D) > 1 - \varepsilon$ in which φ^∞ is bounded.
2. if the fixpoint 0–1 law holds, then for every $\varepsilon > 0$, and for every formula φ^∞, there exists a subset $D \subseteq \mathcal{A}$ with $\mu(D) = 1$ in which φ^∞ is bounded.

It remains to be shown that we can exchange the quantifiers "for every formula" and "there exists a subset". This is a standard construction. Let us consider, e.g., the convergence law:

Let φ_1^∞, φ_2^∞, ... be any enumeration of all fixpoint formulas. Let M_j be a sequence of natural numbers such that

$$\lim_{n \to \infty} \mu_n(|\mathbf{A}|_{\varphi_j} \leq M_j) \geq 1 - \varepsilon/2^j.$$

Moreover, let n_i for $i = 1, 2, \ldots$ be a number such that

$$\mu_n(|\mathbf{A}|_{\varphi_j} \leq M_j) \geq 1 - (\varepsilon/2^j) - (1/i^2)$$

for all $j \leq i$ and all $n \geq n_i$.

Then we set

$$D = \{\mathbf{A} \in \mathcal{A} \mid \bigwedge_{j=1}^{\infty} (|\mathbf{A}| \geq n_j \to |\mathbf{A}|_{\varphi_j} \leq M_j)\}.$$

First observe that fixpoint logic is bounded on D. Indeed, for every fixpoint formula φ^∞, say $\varphi \equiv \varphi_i$, we have that φ^∞ is bounded on $\{\mathbf{A} \in D \mid |\mathbf{A}| > n_i\} \subseteq D$ by construction, and there are only finitely many other structures in D.

Now let $n_i \leq n < n_{i+1}$. We have

$$\mu_n(D) =$$

$$\mu_n(\{\mathbf{A} \in \mathcal{A} \mid n_i \leq |\mathbf{A}| < n_{i+1} \wedge \bigwedge_{j=1}^{\infty}(|\mathbf{A}| \geq n_j \to |\mathbf{A}|_{\varphi_j} \leq M_j)\}) =$$

$$\mu_n(\{\mathbf{A} \in \mathcal{A} \mid \bigwedge_{j=1}^{i} |\mathbf{A}|_{\varphi_j} \leq M_j\}) =$$

$$1 - \mu_n(\{\mathbf{A} \in \mathcal{A} \mid \bigvee_{j=1}^{i} |\mathbf{A}|_{\varphi_j} > M_j\}) \geq$$

$$1 - \sum_{j=1}^{i} \mu_n(\{\mathbf{A} \in \mathcal{A} \mid |\mathbf{A}|_{\varphi_j} > M_j\}) =$$

$$1 - \sum_{j=1}^{i}(1 - \mu_n(\{\mathbf{A} \in \mathcal{A} \mid |\mathbf{A}|_{\varphi_j} \leq M_j\})) \geq$$

$$1 - \sum_{j=1}^{i}(\varepsilon/2^j + 1/i^2)$$

$$\geq 1 - \varepsilon - 1/i.$$

It follows that D, with some structures eventually removed to make it measurable, satisfies $\mu(D) \geq 1 - \varepsilon$, as desired. $\square$

We can derive now several consequences, the first of them being proof of the Kolaitis and Vardi conjecture for recursive distributions. Before we cite here one deep result from their paper:

Theorem 9 (Kolaitis and Vardi [8], theorem 4.1). $L^\omega_{\omega_1\omega}$ *collapses to first order logic in a class* $D \subseteq \mathcal{A}$ *if and only if fixpoint logic is bounded in* D. $\square$

Theorem 10. *Let* μ *be arbitrary recursive probability distribution on the class* $\mathcal{A}$ *of all finite structures over the signature* σ. *Then:*

1. *The convergence law holds for the infinitary logic* $L^\omega_{\omega_1\omega}$ *relative to* μ *if and only if the convergence law holds for fixpoint logic relative to* μ.
2. *The same is true when "convergence law" is replaced by "0–1 law".*

Proof. Part 2 is immediate from theorems 8 and 9. Part 1 is almost immediate (once more we prove only the nontrivial direction): let $\varepsilon > 0$ be arbitrary; take $D \subseteq \mathcal{A}$ with $\mu(D) \geq 1 - \varepsilon$, in which fixpoint logic is bounded. Then $L^\omega_{\omega_1\omega}$ collapses to first order logic in D, by theorem 9. Since the convergence law for first order logic holds, it follows that for no φ in $L^\omega_{\omega_1\omega}$ the difference between $\limsup_{n\to\infty} \mu_n(\varphi)$ and $\liminf_{n\to\infty} \mu_n(\varphi)$ exceeds ε, which implies the thesis. $\square$

As a simple consequence we get the following

Corollary 11. *The same thesis as in theorem 10 holds for every logic whose expressive power over finite structures is between fixpoint logic and* $L^\omega_{\omega_1\omega}$. *These include, among others, partial fixed point logic, recursive fragment of* $L^\omega_{\omega_1\omega}$, *recursively enumerable fragment of* $L^\omega_{\omega_1\omega}$. $\square$

Now we turn to relationships between fixpoint logic and first order logic. The first consequence we derive is the following, having "excluded middle principle" flavour:

Corollary 12. *Let* μ *be arbitrary recursive probability distribution on the class* $\mathcal{A}$ *of all finite structures over the signature* σ. *Then if the fixpoint convergence law holds, then asymptotic probability of every sentence of fixpoint logic is a limit of a sequence of asymptotic probabilities of first order sentences.*

In particular, if first order 0–1 law holds, then either fixpoint 0–1 law holds, or even fixpoint convergence law fails to hold.

Proof. Let fixpoint 0–1 law hold for μ. Suppose that φ is any sentence of fixpoint logic.

Let D_m be any subset of $\mathcal{A}$ with $\mu(D_m) \geq 1 - 1/m$, and such that fixpoint logic is bounded in D_m. It exists by theorem 8. Let φ_m be any first order sentence equivalent to φ in D_m. Then we immediately get $|\mu(\varphi) - \mu(\varphi_m)| \leq 1/m$, and consequently, $\mu(\varphi) = \lim_{m\to\infty} \mu(\varphi_m)$. $\square$

The other consequence touches the problem of computing asymptotic probabilities of fixpoint properties:

Let us call the L *almost sure theory* the set of those formulas φ of the logic L, for which $\mu(\varphi) = 1$. We say that this theory is *recursively approximable* iff for every $\varepsilon > 0$ there exists a recursive set S of sentences of fixpoint logic such that if $\mu(\varphi) = 1$ then $\varphi \in S$, and if $\liminf_{n\to\infty} \mu_n(\varphi) < 1 - \varepsilon$, then $\varphi \notin S$.

We cite now a result from [11] (after conversion to our terminology):

Theorem 13. *Let* μ *be arbitrary (not necessarily recursive) probability distribution on the class* $\mathcal{A}$. *Suppose that the convergence law for first order logic holds. Then:*

1. *The fixpoint almost sure theory is recursive iff the first order almost sure theory is recursive and fixpoint logic is almost surely bounded.*
2. *The fixpoint almost sure theory is recursively approximable iff the first order almost sure theory is recursively approximable and for every $\varepsilon > 0$ there is a subset $D \subseteq \mathcal{A}$ with $\mu(D) > 1 - \varepsilon$, such that fixpoint logic is bounded in D.* $\square$

Now we can easily combine the above theorem with theorem 8, getting

Corollary 14. 1. *Let μ be a Δ_1 distribution such that the first order 0-1 law holds, and the first order almost sure theory is recursive. Then the fixpoint 0-1 law holds if and only if the fixpoint almost sure theory is recursive.*
2. *The same as above is true, when "the 0-1 law" is replaced by "the convergence law", and "recursive" by "recursively approximable".* $\square$

4.2 Deterministic Transitive Closure Logic

In this section we want to show (but in less details), that most of results from the previous section are true also for *deterministic transitive closure logic* (DTC, in short).

This logic allows formulas expressing transitive closure of relations (of even arity) definable in this logic, provided that they are single valued. Namely, we augment first order logic with the following formula formation rule: if $\varphi(\mathbf{x}, \mathbf{x}')$ is a formula (the length ℓ of $\mathbf{x}$ is equal to the length of $\mathbf{x}'$), then $\varphi^{DTC}(\mathbf{x}, \mathbf{x}')$ is also a formula. The least set of expressions containing all first order formulas and closed under such enriched family of formula formation rules is the DTC.

The semantics of DTC formulas is as follows: let $\mathbf{A}$ be any finite σ-structure. Then $\mathbf{A}, \mathbf{x} : \mathbf{a}, \mathbf{x}' : \mathbf{a}' \models \varphi^{DTC}$ iff the pair $(\mathbf{a}, \mathbf{a}')$ belongs to the *transitive closure* of the relation

$$R = \{(\mathbf{a}, \mathbf{a}') \in (|\mathbf{A}|^\ell)^2 \mid (\exists! \mathbf{b} \ \mathbf{A}, \mathbf{x} : \mathbf{a}, \mathbf{x}' : \mathbf{b} \models \varphi) \wedge \mathbf{A}, \mathbf{x} : \mathbf{a}, \mathbf{x}' : \mathbf{a}' \models \varphi\}.$$

To apply the proofs we presented in previous section, we need suitable substitutes of the closure ordinal related definitions, and of theorem 7. The closure ordinal $|\mathbf{A}|_\varphi$ is a straightforward construction: it is a diameter of the set $(|\mathbf{A}|^\ell)^2$ under the distance measured in number of arcs of the relation R, necessary to get from one tuple to the other. The substitute of theorem 7 is a simple exercise in the part of constructing a successor structure, while the part of expressing DSPACE($\log n$) properties (rather than PTIME ones) can be found in [5].

These constructions allow us to formulate and prove counterparts of theorems 8, and corollaries 12 and 14. The last of them, however, requires additional effort: it is also necessary to look at the paper [11] to see that the necessary and sufficient conditions of decidability and recursive approximability of the fixpoint almost sure theory can be easily transformed into ones for almost sure theory of DTC sentences.

However, counterparts of theorem 10 and corollary 11 do not hold. In fact, one of the examples presented by Grädel and McColm in [2] (namely, the one with hypercubes, in section 4 of that paper), shows that there are classes of finite structures in which deterministic transitive closure logic collapses to first order logic, while unrestricted transitive closure logic does not. The example can be suitably modified so that it gives a recursive distribution with the 0-1 law for deterministic transitive closure logic, but without convergence law for fixpoint logic. In particular, convergence law for $L^\omega_{\omega_1\omega}$ and this distribution also fails.

5 Nonrecursive Distributions

It is quite natural to ask now: "What about distributions which are not recursive?"

The answer is essentially (but implicitly) given in [11]: there exists a distribution for which neither of theses of theorems 6, 8, 9 holds. Of course this distribution is not recursive. We sketch briefly (after cf. [11]) the construction now to analyze its complexity.

Let for natural numbers $p < n$ the structure $A(p,n)$ be a directed graph with carrier set $\{0,\ldots,n-1\}$ and with edges $(i-1,i)$ for $1 \le i \le p$. Thus $A(p,n)$ contains one chain of length p and $n-p-1$ isolated points.

Let $F \subseteq \mathbb{N}$ satisfy the following condition: for every recursively enumerable subset $R \subseteq \mathbb{N}$ either $F \cap R$ is finite or $F \setminus R$ is finite. This set can be constructed by standard diagonalization technique, and then it is Σ_2.

Once we have defined F we define $f : \mathbb{N} \to \mathbb{N}$ by

$$f(n) = \max\{m \in F \mid n \ge 2m\}.$$

Now consider the distribution μ^f, defined by:

$$\mu^f_n(\{A\}) = \begin{cases} 1 & \text{if } A = A(f(n),n) \\ 0 & \text{otherwise.} \end{cases}$$

It is immediate that μ^f is Σ_2, like F, and hence by proposition 3 it is also Δ_2. Therefore the following theorem both falsifies the Kolaitis and Vardi Conjecture in it original formulation, and gives a tight (with respect to the arithmetical hierarchy) bound on the distributions for which it remains true.

Theorem 15 ([11]). *The fixpoint 0-1 law for the distribution μ^f holds, but even the $L^\omega_{\omega_1\omega}$ convergence law for μ^f does not hold.*

Proof. It is an easy observation that if φ is in $L^\omega_{\omega_1\omega}$ and has k variables (free and bound), and $n-p-1$, $m-p-1 \ge k$, then

$$A(p,n) \models \varphi \qquad \text{iff} \qquad A(p,m) \models \varphi,$$

which may be immediately proved by application of the infinitary Ehrenfeucht-Fraïssé game with k pebbles.

Moreover, it is easily observed that f is nondecreasing, unbounded, $f(n) \le n/2$, so $n - f(n) \ge n/2$. Therefore for every sentence φ in $L^\omega_{\omega_1\omega}$ with at most k variables, and for all sufficiently large n the validity of φ in $A(f(n),n)$ depends on the value $f(n)$, only. As we are interested in asymptotic properties of $\mu^f_n(\varphi)$, we may think that φ simply recognizes some set R of natural numbers – the lengths of chains in models of positive probability. The set of all chain lengths in models of positive probability is F.

Let φ be any sentence of fixpoint logic and let R be the set of chain lengths it recognizes. Clearly R is recursive. Then either $F \setminus R$ is finite, so $\mu_n(\varphi) = 1$ for all large n, or $F \cap R$ is finite, so $\mu_n(\varphi) = 0$ for all large n. Therefore the fixpoint 0–1 law holds for μ^f. This completes the first part of the thesis.

We construct now a sentence in $L^\omega_{\omega_1\omega}$ without asymptotic probability. Let first order sentence φ_m be:

$$\exists x(\exists y E(x,y) \wedge (\exists x E(y,x) \wedge (\exists y E(x,y) \wedge (\ldots \wedge (\exists \{x|y\} E(\{x|y\}, \{y|x\})) \ldots)))),$$

with $m + 1$ occurrences of quantifier "$\exists$". We take $\{u|v\}$ to be u if m is even and v if m is odd. Then, essentially, φ_m expresses the property "there exists a chain of length m".

Let R be an arbitrary infinite and coinfinite subset of F. Then the $L^\omega_{\omega_1\omega}$ sentence $\bigvee_{m \in R} \varphi_m \wedge \neg\varphi_{m+1}$ has no asymptotic probability. $\qquad\square$

On the other hand, the reader will easily guess how to prove the following theorem:

Theorem 16. *Let S be arbitrary subset of $\mathcal{P}(\mathbb{N}^3) \cup \mathcal{P}(\mathbb{N})$, closed under Turing reductions and complements. Then for arbitrary probability distribution μ on $\mathcal{A}$ such that m_μ is in S, one has*

1. *The convergence law holds for the S-fragment of the infinitary logic $L^\omega_{\omega_1\omega}$ relative to μ if and only if the convergence law holds for whole $L^\omega_{\omega_1\omega}$ relative to μ.*
2. *The same is true when "convergence law" is replaced by "0–1 law".* $\qquad\square$

Acknowledgment The author is pleased to thank Erich Grädel for carefully reading this text and for his numerous comments and remarks.

References

1. Compton, K.J. 0–1 laws in logic and combinatorics, *Proc. NATO Advanced Study Institute on Algorithms and Order* (I. Rival, ed.), Reidel, Dordrecht (1988).
2. Grädel,. E., and McColm, G.L., Deterministic versus nondeterministic transitive closure logic, in: *Proc. 7th IEEE Symp. on Logic in Computer Science, 1992*, pp. 58–63.
3. Gurevich, Yu., Zero-one laws, *Bull. EATCS*, Spring 1992, pp. 90–106.
4. Immerman, N.: Upper and lower bounds for first–order expressibility, *Journal of Computer and System Sciences* 25(1982), pp. 76–98
5. Immerman, N.: Languages that capture complexity classes, *SIAM Journal of Computing* 16(1987).
6. Kolaitis, Ph.G., and Vardi, M.Y., 0–1 laws for fragments of second order logic: an overview, *MSRI Workshop on Logic from Computer Science (ed. Y.N. Moschovakis), Berkeley 1989, to appear.*
7. Kolaitis, Ph., and Vardi, M.Y., On the expressive power of Datalog: tools and a case study, in: *Proc. 9th IEEE Symp. on Principles of Database Systems, 1990*, pp. 61–71.
8. Kolaitis, Ph., and Vardi, M.Y., Fixpoint logic vs. infinitary logic in finite–model theory, in: *Proc. 7th IEEE Symp. on Logic in Computer Science, 1992*, pp. 46–57.
9. Moschovakis, Y.N. *Elementary induction on abstract structures*, North Holland, 1974.
10. Tyszkiewicz, J., Infinitary queries and their asymptotic probabilities I: Properties definable in Transitive Closure Logic in: E. Börger et al. (eds.), Proc. *Computer Science Logic '91, LNCS 626, Springer Verlag, pp. 396–410.*

11. Tyszkiewicz, J., Infinitary queries and their asymptotic probabilities II: Properties definable in Least Fixed Point Logic *to appear in: A. Frieze et al. eds., Proc. Random Graphs '91, Wiley (?)*.

12. Vardi, M.Y.: Complexity of relational query languages, *14th Symposium on Theory of Computation* 1982, pp. 137–146.

A PROPOSITIONAL DENSE TIME LOGIC
(Based on nested sequences)

Mohsin Ahmed and G. Venkatesh

Department of Computer Science and Engineering,
Indian Institute of Technology, Bombay 76, India.
Email: {mosh,gv}@cse.iitb.ernet.in

Abstract

This paper extends propositional linear time temporal logic (PTL) to propositional dense time logic (PDTL). While a PTL model is a single sequence of states, a PDTL model, called an omega-tree, consists of a nested sequence of states. Two new operators, called *within* and *everywhere* are introduced to access nested sequences. Besides its application in describing activities for Artificial Intelligence, PDTL can be used to represent more naturally procedural abstractions in control flow. PDTL is shown to be decidable by a tableau based method, and a complete axiomatization is given.

PDTL's omega tree models allow a dense mix of events. By imposing a stability condition on the propositions we get a subset of the omega tree models called ordinal trees which are free of dense mix. This logic called Propositional Ordinal Tree Logic (POTL) is also shown to be decidable in exponential time. Ordinal tree models though based on dense points, represent interval based information which maybe refined to any finite level. Hence POTL is a good bridge between point based and interval based temporal logics.

Ordinal trees can be easily embedded as a temporal data structure in a conventional logic programming language and thus provide a framework for temporal logic programming.

Keywords: Temporal logic, dense time, ordinal trees.

1 Introduction

There is frequent need to qualify information with time, especially if we are talking about the real world and the events taking place in it. Consider, for example, the statement: "The ball hit the wall before rolling off into the drain." This describes a sequence of events, the first of which consists of the ball hitting the wall, the last event describes the ball falling into the drain, and the events in between describe the ball rolling. A convenient way of describing this information is to say what happened in each of three consecutive intervals: one for striking, one for rolling and one for falling. The rolling interval can be further refined to describe what occurs within it. While a rolling interval may not be particularly eventful, we could instead consider the example "After hitting the wall, the ball bounced on the ground before falling into the drain." Here, the intervening interval consists of a unknown number of bouncing events.

While there have been a number of studies in representing temporal information within a logical framework [6, 10, 12, 13, 19], many of these deal with a time model which is discrete (i.e. consists of a sequence of states). This does not allow us to refine the time between two states. In particular, we cannot interpolate an unbounded (or infinite) sequence of states between two states. Such a requirement also arises when we wish to compose specifications of systems [12]. This paper does not focus on this issue, but instead looks at the issue of representing dense time information.

We present a temporal logic based on a model of time which allows arbitrary nesting of sequences. To be more precise, our model consists of a sequence of states at the top level. Between any two states of a sequence, another sequence of states can be interpolated. This model can be represented as an infinite binary tree, and is called the *omega tree* model.

Two new operators are introduced into propositional linear time temporal logic (PTL) [10]. The new operators $\oslash$ (read *within*) and $\boxplus$ (read *everywhere*), allow us to refine an interval and describe it in more detail. The dual of $\boxplus$ is $\diamondsuit$ (read *somewhere*). This gives us the ability to represent dense time information. A behavior consisting of a sequence of events terminating in a limit point can also be expressed, for example a bouncing ball coming to rest can be represented by:

$$\oslash(\oslash U p \wedge \Box(\oslash U p \leftrightarrow \bigcirc \oslash Down)) \wedge (\bigcirc \boxplus Down) \wedge \boxplus(Down \leftrightarrow \neg Up),$$

where Up and $Down$ are propositions. This formula can be read as: "Within the first interval the ball is initially up, and it alternates between up and down. From the next interval onwards it remain down, and at every time point the ball is either up or down." Such a sequence can be nested in a bigger sequence of events, as in the statement "Every time he hit the ball, the ball bounced and came to rest." This statement can represented by $\Box(Hit \rightarrow \phi)$, where ϕ is the formula given before, and Hit is a new propositional symbol.

We show that the resulting logic, called Propositional Dense Time Logic (PDTL) is decidable in exponential time by a tableau based decision procedure similar to that used for deciding the satisfiability of PTL formulas [13, 19]. A simple axiomatization for PDTL is given and its completeness is shown.

Though PDTL is reducible to the Deterministic Propositional Dynamic Logic (D-PDL) [5] and hence its decidability follows from that of D-PDL [11], PDTL's *within* and *next* operators have a direct temporal interpretation in terms of nested sequences. Moreover the tableau based method is more appealing intuitively, and is a direct extension of the methods used for PTL [13, 19].

PDTL allows us to write a satisfiable sentence: $\boxplus(\diamondsuit P \wedge \diamondsuit \neg P)$, which describes a dense mix of states that satisfy P and $\neg P$. Such formulas contribute to unwieldy models and rarely occur in practice. To filter out such models, we define *stability* of propositions. Call a proposition p *stable* in an omega tree if there is no dense mixture of p and $\neg p$ in the omega tree. *Ordinal Trees* are omega trees where all the propositions are stable, and its logic is called Propositional Ordinal Tree Logic (POTL).

Ordinal trees are omega trees, which can be represented by finite binary trees with back-arcs allowed in a restricted way so that infinitely-nested sequences do not appear. The logic of formulas valid over ordinal trees (POTL) is shown to be decidable by extending PDTL's tableau based procedure. Here nodes which do not contain any ordinal tree models are also closed. Thus POTL is also decidable in exponential time, as compared to deciding it in non-elementary recursive time by interpreting it in *S2S* of Rabin [15, 16].

An ordinal tree can represent a nested infinite sequences of events such as $a \cdot b^\omega \cdot c^{\omega^2} \cdot b$, where a, b and c are some events, and a^k denotes a occurring k times. In [2] we describe an extension to prolog that uses ordinal trees for temporal logic programming. For example, the temporal query: "Was the janitor absent on Wednesday?", can be positively answered from the causal-rule: "Whenever it rained, the janitor was absent the next day." and the temporal-fact: "It rains every Tuesday."

Discrete time temporal logic programming has also been investigated by several researchers[1, 4, 8, 9, 14]. The theory of dense time logics has also been studied by a number of researchers [7, 17, 18]. Alur and Henzinger in [3] show a real time logic to be undecidable. Our method differs from others, in that we provide for the first time a dense time logic (POTL) that is:

- Theoretically interesting, since it is decidable in exponential time by a simple extension of the tableau method for PTL.
- Practically interesting, as it gives rise to a temporal data structure that is useful in a logic programming language[2].

Organization of the paper

Section 2 defines the language and section 3 defines the models and semantics of PDTL, along with some examples. The decidability of PDTL is covered in section 4 and section 5 covers the axiomatization and completeness of PDTL. In section 6 we look at ordinal trees models and their logic POTL, and section 7 gives a tableau based decision procedure for POTL. Finally section 8 concludes the paper.

2 The Language

Propositional Dense Time Logic (PDTL) is an extension of the usual PTL. The language of PDTL contains the usual propositional logic symbols: truth constants T (true) and F (false), set of propositions $PROP = \{p_1, \ldots, p_n\}$, logical connectives: $\neg$ (not), $\rightarrow$ (implies), the usual temporal operators: $\Box$ (henceforth), $\bigcirc$ (next), with the following new operators: $\boxplus$ (everywhere) and $\oslash$ (within). The *until* operator of PTL [10] is not considered in this paper.

Define the language of PDTL to be a set L_{PDTL} of formulas generated by L:

$$L ::= F | p_1 | \ldots | p_n | \neg L | L \rightarrow L | \Box L | \bigcirc L | \boxplus L | \oslash L$$

The new syntactic definitions are: $\Diamond \phi \stackrel{\text{def}}{=} \neg \Box \neg \phi$, $\Phi \phi \stackrel{\text{def}}{=} \neg \boxplus \neg \phi$.

Notation: $\mathcal{N}$ is the set of natural numbers. $\mathcal{N}^+$ is the set $\{(k_0, \ldots, k_n) | k_i \in \mathcal{N}, 0 \leq i \leq n\}$, and $\mathcal{N}^* = \mathcal{N}^+ \cup \{()\}$. An element of $\mathcal{N}^*$ will be denoted by $\overline{k} = (k_0, \ldots, k_n)$. $\overline{0}_i$ will denote an i-tuple of zeroes. The concatenation of $\overline{k}$ with i will be denoted by $\overline{k} \cdot i = (k_0, \ldots, k_n, i)$. The concatenation of $\overline{k}$ with $\overline{m} = (m_0, \ldots, m_j)$, will be $\overline{k} \cdot \overline{m} = (k_0, \ldots, k_n, m_0, \ldots, m_j)$.

3 Semantics

While the models of PTL are based on the natural numbers, the models of PDTL are based on nested sequences of natural numbers. The language and the semantics of PTL are extended so that we can talk about the truth of formulas in such a model.

A state is a subset of $PROP$. A ω-sequence of states (the usual model for PTL [10, 13]) is a sequence of states indexed by elements of $\mathcal{N}$. The model for PDTL is an infinitely nested sequence of states indexed by $\mathcal{N}^+$.

Definition 1 (Omega Tree) *An* omega-tree *model for PDTL is an infinite binary tree $T = (\mathcal{N}^+, 0, w, x, s)$, rooted at (0), with two successor functions: $w : \mathcal{N}^+ \mapsto \mathcal{N}^+$*

(within) and $x : \mathcal{N}^+ \mapsto \mathcal{N}^+$ (next), The valuation function $s : \mathcal{N}^+ \mapsto 2^{PROP}$, maps its nodes $(\mathcal{N}^+)$ to subsets of $PROP$.

The w-child of $(\overline{k})$ is $(\overline{k} \cdot 0)$ and the x-child of $(\overline{k} \cdot i)$ is $(\overline{k} \cdot i + 1)$, see figure 1. The omega tree rooted at $(k_0, \ldots, k_n)$ will be denoted by $T((k_0, \ldots, k_n))$.

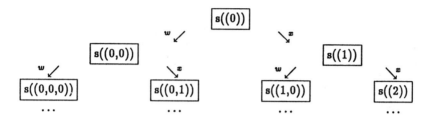

Figure 1: Omega-tree

The sequence of states $\ll s((0)), s((1)), \ldots \gg$ occurs as in a PTL model, but here the sequence of states $\ll s((0,0)), s((0,1)), \ldots \gg$ is a nested sequence between the states $s((0))$ and $s((1))$. This sequence is accessible from $s((0))$ by the $\oslash$ operator. The states can be temporally ordered as follows:

$$s(\overline{k}) =_t s(\overline{k} \cdot 0) \qquad\qquad \overline{k} \in \mathcal{N}^+$$
$$s(\overline{k} \cdot i) \leq_t s(\overline{k} \cdot i \cdot \overline{m}) <_t s(\overline{k} \cdot i + 1) \qquad \overline{k} \in \mathcal{N}^*, \ \overline{m} \in \mathcal{N}^+, \ i \geq 0$$

Since we identify the time point $s(\overline{k})$ with $s(\overline{k} \cdot 0)$, $s(\overline{k}) = s(\overline{k} \cdot 0)$. Truth of formulas in T is defined as follows:

$$
\begin{aligned}
T &\models \phi & &\overset{\text{def}}{=} & &T((0)) \models \phi \\
(T(\overline{k}) &\models p), \ p \in PROP & &\text{iff} & &p \in s(\overline{k}) \\
T(\overline{k}) &\not\models \mathcal{F} & & & & \\
T(\overline{k}) &\models \neg\phi & &\text{iff} & &\text{not } (T(\overline{k}) \models \phi) \\
T(\overline{k}) &\models \phi \rightarrow \psi & &\text{iff} & &\text{not } (T(\overline{k}) \models \phi) \text{ or } (T(\overline{k}) \models \psi) \\
T((k_1, \ldots, k_n)) &\models \bigcirc\phi & &\text{iff} & &T((k_1, \ldots, k_{(n-1)}, k_n + 1)) \models \phi \\
T((k_1, \ldots, k_n)) &\models \Box\phi & &\text{iff} & &\forall j \geq 0, \ T((k_1, \ldots, k_{(n-1)}, k_n + j)) \models \phi \\
T((k_1, \ldots, k_n)) &\models \Diamond\phi & &\text{iff} & &\exists j \geq 0, \ T((k_1, \ldots, k_{(n-1)}, k_n + j)) \models \phi
\end{aligned}
$$

$\oslash\phi$ asserts that ϕ holds in the w-child of the current state, and $\boxplus\phi$ asserts that ϕ holds everywhere below the current state in the omega-tree model.

$$
\begin{aligned}
T(\overline{k}) &\models \oslash\phi & &\text{iff} & &T(\overline{k} \cdot 0) \models \phi \\
T((k_1, \ldots, k_n)) &\models \boxplus\phi & &\text{iff} & &\forall j \geq 0, \forall \overline{m} \in \mathcal{N}^*, \ T((k_1, \ldots, k_{(n-1)}, k_n + j) \cdot \overline{m}) \models \phi \\
T((k_1, \ldots, k_n)) &\models {\diamondplus}\phi & &\text{iff} & &\exists j \geq 0, \exists \overline{m} \in \mathcal{N}^*, \ T((k_1, \ldots, k_{(n-1)}, k_n + j) \cdot \overline{m}) \models \phi
\end{aligned}
$$

Examples: In the examples below, we assume that time is divided into days at the top level so that the intervals $[s_0, s_1), [s_1, s_2), \ldots$ represent days.

'It is always hot': $\boxplus Hot$. 'There will be rain': ${\diamondplus}Rain$. 'The rain will last over a time interval': ${\diamondplus} \oslash \boxplus Rain$. 'It rains daily': $\Box \oslash {\diamondplus}Rain$. This does not mean that it rains the whole day, but that on everyday there is rain. In fact it is consistent with the next example. 'It never rains for a full day': $\Box \oslash {\diamondplus}\neg Rain$. 'Everyday the rains are followed by a flood': $\Box\oslash{\diamondplus}(\oslash{\diamondplus}\boxplus Rain \wedge \bigcirc{\diamondplus}\boxplus Flood)$. 'If he takes a walk everyday, then someday he will get wet in the rain': $\Box\oslash\blacklozenge Walk \rightarrow \Diamond\oslash\blacklozenge(Walk \wedge Rain)$. Note that this is not a theorem. Consider in contrast the next example. 'Even though it rains daily, it is possible for him to take a walk everyday and not get wet in the rain': $\Box\oslash(\blacklozenge Walk \wedge \blacklozenge Rain \wedge \boxplus(Walk \rightarrow \neg Rain))$.

PDTL offers us an interesting way of modeling qualitative temporal information 'event p occurred *many* times' in terms of $\oslash\Box p$, which deliberately identifies 'many occurrences' with 'infinitely many occurrences in finite time' [2]. We could also use this logic to reason more clearly about program executions. To represent that a property ϕ holds after one statement is executed we write $\bigcirc\phi$. If the statement is an abstraction of further statements (e.g. a procedure call), then the properties during the call can be written as $\oslash\bigcirc^i \psi$.

4 Satisfiability and Tableaux

Given a formula ϕ, we give a tableau method [13, 19] of deciding whether it is satisfiable or not. A tableau is a rooted directed graph, containing two kinds of nodes. A *state-Node* is a node containing only *literals* (propositions and their negations) and formulas of types: $\bigcirc\phi$ or $\oslash\phi$. A state-node η has two subnodes: the *within-subnode* $[\eta]_w$ and the *next-subnode* $[\eta]_x$. A empty-node is considered to be a state node. All other nodes are *logical-nodes*. A logical-node η has two subnodes $[\eta]_l$ and $[\eta]_r$.

4.1 Tableaux Building

We build a tableau for ϕ starting from the root node $\{\phi\}$. A leaf-node is expanded according to the type of formulas in it. On expansion, the leaf nodes generate subnodes to which it is linked by outgoing arcs. If a new subnode has the same formulas as an existing node μ, then the new sub-node is not created, instead η is linked to μ.

In a logical-leaf-node η, pick any expandable formula and call it the *principal formula* of η (denoted by $Pr(\eta)$). This formula will be expanded to generate subnodes according to table 1. Other formulas in η, called the side formulas are then copied unchanged to the subnodes. A state-leaf-node generates two subnodes:

	$Pr(\eta) \in \eta$	$[\eta]_l, ([\eta]_r = \mathcal{F})$
1	$\Box A$	$A, \bigcirc\Box A$
2	$\Diamond A$	$A \vee \bigcirc\Diamond A$
3	$\boxplus A$	$A, \bigcirc\boxplus A, \oslash\boxplus A$
4	$\blacklozenge A$	$A \vee (\bigcirc\blacklozenge A \vee \oslash\blacklozenge A)$
5	$\neg\bigcirc A$	$\bigcirc\neg A$
6	$\neg\oslash A$	$\oslash\neg A$
7	$\neg\Box A$	$\Diamond\neg A$
8	$\neg\Diamond A$	$\Box\neg A$
9	$\neg\boxplus A$	$\blacklozenge\neg A$
10	$\neg\blacklozenge A$	$\boxplus\neg A$

	$Pr(\eta) \in n$	$[\eta]_l$	$[\eta]_r$
11	$A \rightarrow B$	$\neg A$	B
12	$A \wedge B$	A, B	$\mathcal{F}$
13	$A \vee B$	A	B
14	$A \leftrightarrow B$	$\neg A, \neg B$	A, B
15	$\neg(A \rightarrow B)$	$A, \neg B$	$\mathcal{F}$
16	$\neg(A \wedge B)$	$\neg A$	$\neg B$
17	$\neg(A \vee B)$	$\neg A, \neg B$	$\mathcal{F}$
18	$\neg(A \leftrightarrow B)$	$\neg A, B$	$A, \neg B$
19	$\neg\neg A$	A	$\mathcal{F}$

Table 1: Expansion table for logical nodes

$[\eta]_w = \{\phi \mid \oslash\phi \in \eta\} \cup \{literal \in \eta\}$ and $[\eta]_x = \{\phi \mid \bigcirc\phi \in \eta\}$.

Let S be the set of formulas that appear in the tableau of $\{\phi\}$. We have $|S| < (4|\phi|)$, so number of nodes $< 2^{|S|} < 2^{4|\phi|}$ and the tableau expansion eventually halts.

4.2 Closing Nodes

A node is *closed* when we can show it is unsatisfiable, that is we can prove the negation of the node. A node which is not closed is called *open*. An empty node is considered open. If a node contains both A and $\neg A$ (or $\mathcal{F}$), then it is obviously unsatisfiable and therefore closed. However it is more difficult to give conditions for closing a node containing an unsatisfiable formula of the form $\Diamond A$ or $\Leftrightarrow A$.

If $\Diamond A$ is unsatisfiable at a node, it will be carried over only to every x-descendant of that node, that is, it will be indefinitely postponed. However if $\Leftrightarrow A$ is unsatisfiable at a node, it will be carried over separately to both its x and w descendant. Thus, we should close a node containing $\Diamond A$, if $\neg A$ holds at every node reachable from it by logical and x arcs. Similarly we close a node containing $\Leftrightarrow A$, if $\neg A$ holds at every reachable node.

Define R, Rx and Rxw to be the set of open descendants of a node as follows:

$R(\eta)$	$=$	$\{\eta\} \cup Rx([\eta]_l) \cup Rx([\eta]_r)$	if η is a logical node
$R(\eta)$	$=$	$\{\eta\}$	otherwise
$Rx(\eta)$	$=$	$\{[\eta]_l, [\eta]_r\} \cup Rx([\eta]_l) \cup Rx([\eta]_r)$	if η is a logical node
$Rx(\eta)$	$=$	$\{[\eta]_x\} \cup Rx([\eta]_x)$	if η is a state node
$Rwx(\eta)$	$=$	$\{[\eta]_l, [\eta]_r\} \cup Rwx([\eta]_l) \cup Rwx([\eta]_r)$	if η is a logical node
$Rwx(\eta)$	$=$	$\{[\eta]_x, [\eta]_w\} \cup Rwx([\eta]_w) \cup Rwx([\eta]_x)$	if η is a state node
x-leaf-scc(η)	iff	$\forall\mu(\mu \in Rx(\eta) \rightarrow \eta \in Rx(\mu))$	
wx-leaf-scc(η)	iff	$\forall\mu(\mu \in Rwx(\eta) \rightarrow \eta \in Rwx(\mu))$	

$R(\eta)$ is the set of logical descendants of η, that is, nodes reachable from η through logical arcs. $Rx(\eta)$ is the set of nodes reachable from η by a path of *logical* and *next* arcs; this set is a maximal x-strongly connected component when x-leaf-scc(η) is true. Similarly $Rwx(\eta)$ is the set of nodes reachable from η by any path, and this set is a wx-strongly connected component when wx-leaf-scc(η) is true.

Closing Algorithm:
repeat
      1. Construct $Rx(\eta)$ and $Rwx(\eta)$ for each open node η.
      2. Close any node η that satisfies any one of the conditions:
            2.1. $\psi, \neg\psi \in \eta$, (or $\mathcal{F} \in \eta$).
            2.2. All the logical children of η are closed.
            2.3. Either $[n]_x$ or $[n]_w$ is closed.
            2.4. $\Diamond\psi \in \eta$ and $\psi \notin \bigcup Rx(\eta) \cup \eta$
            2.5. $\Leftrightarrow\psi \in \eta$ and $\psi \notin \bigcup Rwx(\eta) \cup \eta$
until no more nodes can be closed.

Theorem 1 $\{\phi\}$ *is open iff it is satisfiable.*

Proof: ($\Leftarrow$) Let $\{\phi\}$ be closed, we show that it is unsatisfiable. Suppose $\{\phi\}$ is closed, later we show $\vdash \neg\phi$ in an axiom system Ax_{PDTL}. By soundness of the

Ax_{PDTL}, we have $\models \neg\phi$. Therefore ϕ is unsatisfiable. ∎

($\Rightarrow$) For the purpose of building models we need only the open state nodes. The tableau τ is shortened to a *state node tableau* Δ by removing the logical nodes as follows:

- The nodes of Δ are the open state nodes of τ.
- For $\mu_1, \mu_2 \in \Delta$, if $\mu_2 \in R([\mu_1]_x)$ is in τ, then an x arc is drawn from μ_1 to μ_2, similarly if $\mu_2 \in R([\mu_1]_w)$ then a w arc is drawn from μ_1 to μ_2. Note that a node in Δ may have many x and w children.

A omega tree model for the formulas in a node η can be extracted from the set of open state nodes in Δ. Define the mapping $m : \mathcal{N}^+ \to \Delta$ as follows:

Let $m((0)) := \eta, \quad \eta \in R(\{\phi\})$
If $m(\overline{k} \cdot k') = \mu$ then
    If not x-leaf-scc(μ) then
        Let $m(\overline{k} \cdot k' + 1)$ be any x-child of μ, and $m(\overline{k} \cdot k' \cdot 0)$ be any w-child of μ.
    If x-leaf-scc(μ) and not wx-leaf-scc(μ) then
        By the leaf condition there is a x-path $\ll \nu_0, \ldots, \nu_k \gg$ passing
        through every node in $Rx(\mu)$, such that $\mu = \nu_0 = \nu_k$, and
        ν_{j+1} is a x-child of ν_j, $\quad 0 \le j < k$.
        For $j := 0$ to k do
            Let $m(\overline{k} \cdot k' + j) := \nu_j$
            and let $m(\overline{k} \cdot k' + j \cdot 0)$ be any w-child of ν_j
    If wx-leaf-scc(μ) then
        By the leaf condition there is a wx-path $\ll \nu_0, \ldots, \nu_k \gg$ passing
        through every node in $Rwx(\mu)$, such that $\mu = \nu_0 = \nu_k$,
        and ν_{j+1} is a x-child or a w-child of ν_j, for $0 \le j < k$.
        Let $\overline{l} \cdot l' := \overline{k} \cdot k'$
        For $j := 0$ to $k - 1$ do
            if ν_{j+1} is a x-child of ν_j then
                Let $m(\overline{l} \cdot l' + 1) := \nu_{j+1}$ and let $m(\overline{l} \cdot l' \cdot 0)$ be any w-child of ν_j.
                Let $\overline{l} \cdot l' := \overline{l} \cdot (l' + 1)$
            otherwise let
                $m(\overline{l} \cdot l' \cdot 0) := \nu_{j+1}$ and let $m(\overline{l} \cdot l + 1)$ be any x-child of ν_j.
                Let $\overline{l} \cdot l' := \overline{l} \cdot l' \cdot 0$

The states of the omega tree can now be defined:

$$s(\overline{k}) \overset{\text{def}}{=} \bigcup_{i \ge 0} (m(\overline{k} \cdot \overline{0}_i) \cap PROP), \quad \overline{k} \in \mathcal{N}^+$$

It is easy to see that $T \models \phi$ by induction on the structure of ϕ. The important part is to verify that if $T(\overline{k} \cdot k') \models \Diamond\psi$ (respectively $T(\overline{k} \cdot k') \models \Leftrightarrow\psi$) then $T(\overline{k} \cdot k' + i) \models \psi$ for some $i \in \mathcal{N}$ (respectively $T(\overline{k} \cdot k' + i \cdot \overline{j}) \models \psi$ for some $i \in \mathcal{N}$ and $\overline{j} \in \mathcal{N}^*$). This can be shown using the fact $T(\overline{k} \cdot k')$ was constructed using every node of the x-leaf-scc (wx-leaf-scc respectively) [13]. ∎

Corollary 2 *PDTL is decidable in exponential time.*

Proof: The required strongly connected components can be constructed in time $O(|E| + |\tau|)$, where $|E|$ is the number of edges in τ. Therefore the whole tableau procedure takes $O(2^{c|\phi|})$ for some constant c. ∎

Example 1 The tableau for the unsatisfiable formula $\boxplus p \wedge \Leftrightarrow \neg p$ is given in figure 2. We close η_a because $\Leftrightarrow \neg p \in \eta_a$ and $\neg p \notin \bigcup Rwx(\eta_a) \cup \eta_a$.

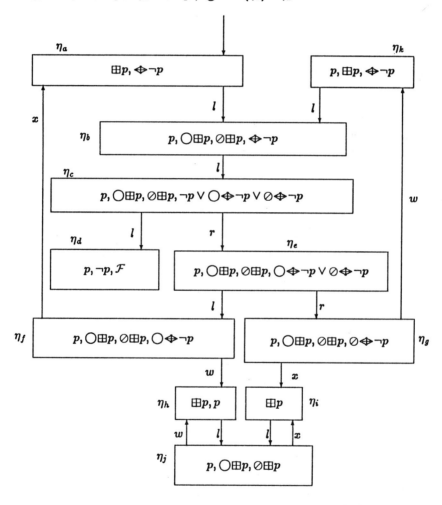

Figure 2: Tableau for $\{\boxplus p, \Leftrightarrow \neg p\}$

5 Completeness

Axioms (Ax_{PDTL}):

$Ax1$	$\Box(A \to B) \to (\Box A \to \Box B)$	$Ax2$	$\boxplus(A \to B) \to (\boxplus A \to \boxplus B)$
$Ax3$	$\bigcirc(A \to B) \to (\bigcirc A \to \bigcirc B)$	$Ax4$	$\oslash(A \to B) \to (\oslash A \to \oslash B)$
$Ax5$	$\bigcirc \neg A \leftrightarrow \neg \bigcirc A$	$Ax6$	$\oslash \neg A \leftrightarrow \neg \oslash A$
$Ax7$	$\Box A \to (A \wedge \bigcirc \Box A)$	$Ax8$	$\boxplus A \to (A \wedge \oslash \boxplus A \wedge \bigcirc \boxplus A)$
$Ax9$	$(A \wedge \Box(A \to \bigcirc A)) \to \Box A$	$Ax10$	$(A \wedge \boxplus(A \to (\bigcirc A \wedge \oslash A))) \to \boxplus A$
		$Ax11$	$p \leftrightarrow \oslash p, \quad \forall p \in PROP$

Rules of Inference:

$$PL : \frac{\vdash_{PL} A}{\vdash A}, \quad MP : \frac{\vdash A, A \to B}{\vdash B}, \quad RN : \frac{\vdash A}{\vdash \Box A}, \quad RE : \frac{\vdash A}{\vdash \boxplus A}$$

The rule PL allows all Propositional Logic tautologies to be theorems of PDTL.

Proposition 3 (Soundness) *The axioms are sound, and the rules of inference preserve soundness.*

Some Theorems of PDTL:

$T1$	$\vdash \quad \Box(A \wedge B) \leftrightarrow (\Box A \wedge \Box B)$	$T2$	$\vdash \quad \bigcirc(A \wedge B) \leftrightarrow (\bigcirc A \wedge \bigcirc B)$
$T3$	$\vdash \quad \boxplus(A \wedge B) \leftrightarrow (\boxplus A \wedge \boxplus B)$	$T4$	$\vdash \quad \oslash(A \wedge B) \leftrightarrow (\oslash A \wedge \oslash B)$
$T5$	$\vdash \quad \Box A \to \bigcirc A$	$T6$	$\vdash \quad \boxplus A \to (\oslash A \wedge \bigcirc A)$

Example 2 $\quad \vdash \boxplus A \to \Box A$

Proof:

$\vdash (\boxplus A \wedge A) \to (\bigcirc \boxplus A \wedge \bigcirc A)$	1	$Ax8, T6$
$\vdash (\boxplus A \wedge A) \to \bigcirc(\boxplus A \wedge A)$	2	$T2$
$\vdash \Box((\boxplus A \wedge A) \to \bigcirc(\boxplus A \wedge A))$	3	$RN, 2$
$\vdash (\boxplus A \wedge A) \to \Box(\boxplus A \wedge A)$	4	$Ax9, 3$
$\vdash \Box(\boxplus A \wedge A) \to (\Box \boxplus A \wedge \Box A)$	5	$T1$
$\vdash (\boxplus A \wedge A) \to \Box A$	6	$PL, 4, 5$
$\vdash \boxplus A \to A$	7	$Ax8$
$\vdash \boxplus A \to \Box A$	8	$PL, 6, 7$ ∎

Theorem 4 *If $\{\phi_1, \ldots, \phi_m\}$ is closed, then $\neg(\phi_1 \wedge \cdots \wedge \phi_m)$ is provable from the axioms.*

Proof: We prove this in the order in which the nodes are closed, so that at each step the theorem holds for nodes closed at a earlier stage. We use N to denote the conjunction of formulas in a node η. Consider the ways in which a node η is closed:

1. Node η contains both ϕ and $\neg \phi$ (or $\mathcal{F}$), then it is unsatisfiable, and $\vdash_{PL} \neg N$.
2. Logical node η is closed, because all its children are closed. Let L and R denote the conjunction of formulas in $[\eta]_l$ and $[\eta]_r$ respectively. From the expansion table for a logical node we get $\vdash N \to (L \vee R)$. Rules 1-10 in the expansion table follow from the axioms and definitions for PDTL, and rules 11-19 follow from PL. Assuming $\vdash (\neg L, \neg R)$, we get $\vdash \neg N$.

3. A state node η is closed because $[\eta]_x$ was closed, let X be the conjunction of formulas in $[\eta]_x$. Assuming $\vdash \neg X$, and applying $RE, T6, Ax5$, we get $\vdash \neg \bigcirc X$. Using $\vdash N \rightarrow \bigcirc X$, we derive $\vdash \neg N$.

4. State node η is closed because $[\eta]_w$ was closed. Let L be the conjunction of literals in η, and W be the conjunction of other formulas in $[\eta]_w$. Assuming $\vdash \neg(L \wedge W)$, and applying $RE, T6, Ax4$ we get $\vdash \neg \oslash (L \wedge W)$. Applying of $Ax11, T4$ on $\vdash N \rightarrow (L \wedge \oslash W)$, we get $\vdash N \rightarrow \oslash(L \wedge W)$. Now we can derive $\vdash \neg N$.

5. A node η was closed because $\Diamond A \in \eta$ has been indefinitely postponed. Let $P = \bigvee_{\eta_i \in Rx(\eta)}(N_i)$. We first show $\vdash P \rightarrow \neg A$.

   Let η' be an open node in $Rx(\eta)$ containing $\Diamond A$, it expands as

$$\begin{aligned} \eta' = \{\Diamond A, N'\} \;&\Rightarrow\; \{A, N'\} \quad\vee\quad \{\bigcirc\Diamond A, N'\} \\ &\Rightarrow\; \bigvee_{i=1}^{m}\underbrace{\{A, N_i'\}}_{\alpha_i} \vee \bigvee_{i=1}^{m}\underbrace{\{\bigcirc\Diamond A, N_i'\}}_{\beta_i} \end{aligned}$$

   where $N' = \bigvee_{i=1}^{i=m} N_i'$. Since $A \notin \cup Rx(\eta)$, all α nodes must be closed, and $\vdash N' \rightarrow \neg A$. Since this holds for all nodes in $Rx(\eta)$, $\vdash P \rightarrow \neg A$. Using the fact P is defined over a x-leaf-scc, we get $\vdash P \rightarrow \bigcirc P$, applying RN, $\vdash \Box(P \rightarrow \bigcirc P)$. Hence $\vdash N \rightarrow (P \wedge \Box(P \rightarrow \bigcirc P))$, applying the induction axiom $Ax9$ on it we get $\vdash N \rightarrow \Box P$. Now $Ax1$ gets us $\vdash N \rightarrow \Box \neg A$. Now $\vdash N \rightarrow \Diamond A$ leads to $\vdash \neg N$.

6. A node η was closed because $\Leftrightarrow A \in \eta$ has been indefinitely postponed. This can happen only if $\neg A$ holds in every descendant of η. Let

$$T \;=\; \bigvee_{\eta_i \in Rwx(\eta)}[\wedge(\eta_i - \{\Leftrightarrow A, \bigcirc\Leftrightarrow A, \oslash\Leftrightarrow A\})]$$

   It is so chosen because we do not need $\Leftrightarrow A$ to prove $\neg A$ and we need to show $T \rightarrow (\bigcirc T \wedge \oslash T)$.

   Let η' be an open node in $Rwx(\eta)$ containing $\Leftrightarrow A$, it expands as

$$\begin{aligned} \eta' = \{\Leftrightarrow A, N'\} \;&\Rightarrow\; \{A, N'\} \vee \{\bigcirc\Leftrightarrow A, N'\} \vee \{\oslash\Leftrightarrow A, N'\} \\ &\Rightarrow\; \bigvee_{i=1}^{m}\underbrace{\{A, N_i'\}}_{\alpha_i} \vee \bigvee_{i=1}^{m}\underbrace{\{\bigcirc\Leftrightarrow A, N_i'\}}_{\beta_i} \vee \bigvee_{i=1}^{m}\underbrace{\{\oslash\Leftrightarrow A, N_i'\}}_{\gamma_i} \end{aligned}$$

   Where $N' = \bigvee_{i=1}^{i=m} N_i'$. Proceeding as before $\vdash N' \rightarrow \neg A$.

   Let μ be a beta (respectively gamma) node of η, then $\Leftrightarrow A$ will not carry over to $[\mu]_w$ (respectively $[\mu]_x$). To prove $\neg A$ in the nodes of the $[\mu]_w$ (respectively $[\mu]_x$) subtree, we can use the nodes of the subtree at a gamma (respectively beta) node $\mu' \in Rwx(\eta)$ with the same formula as μ and where $\Leftrightarrow A$ is carried over. Hence $\neg A$ is provable in the subtree of μ also.

   Applying RE on: $\vdash T \rightarrow (\bigcirc T \wedge \oslash T)$ we get $\vdash \boxplus(T \rightarrow (\bigcirc T \wedge \oslash T))$. Using the induction axiom $Ax10$, we derive $\vdash N \rightarrow \boxplus T$. This along with the assumption $\vdash N \rightarrow \Leftrightarrow A$, gives $\vdash \neg N$. ∎

Corollary 5 (Completeness) $(\models \phi) \Rightarrow (\vdash \phi)$

6   Ordinal Trees and POTL

We consider a restricted set of omega tree models called ordinal trees and its logic: the Propositional Ordinal Tree Logic (POTL).

Definition 2 (Stability) *A proposition* $p \in PROP$ *is called* stable *in an omega tree* T *if* $\exists n \geq 0, \forall (k_0, \ldots, k_n) \in \mathcal{N}^+, \forall j \geq 0, \forall \overline{m} \in \mathcal{N}^* :$

$$p \in s(k_0, \ldots, k_n) \ \textit{iff} \ p \in s(k_0, \ldots, k_n + j, \overline{m})$$

Note that if a proposition p is stable in T then it follows:

$$\exists n \geq 0, \forall (k_0, \ldots, k_n) \in \mathcal{N}^+, \quad T((k_0, \ldots, k_n)) \models (\boxplus p \vee \boxplus \neg p)$$

Definition 3 (Recurrence) *A omega tree* T *is called* recurring *if:*

$$\forall \overline{k} \cdot k' \in \mathcal{N}^+, \exists k'' \geq k', m \geq 0, \ \forall i \geq 0, \quad T(\overline{k} \cdot (k'' + i)) = T(\overline{k} \cdot (k'' + i + m))$$

Definition 4 (Ordinal Tree) *A ordinal tree* T *model for POTL is an omega tree where all the propositions are stable in T and T is recurring.*

Ordinal trees are interval based rather than point based models. For example, the formula $\boxplus(\Diamond\!\!\!\!\Diamond A \wedge \Diamond\!\!\!\!\Diamond \neg A)$ has an omega tree model but no ordinal tree models. Figure 3 shows an ordinal tree for $PROP = \{p_1, p_2\}$. Ordinal trees are represented

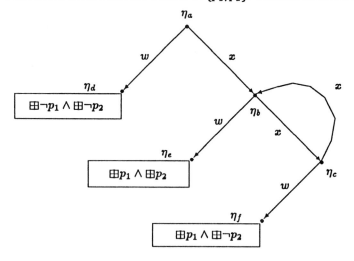

Figure 3: An ordinal tree

as finite binary trees possibly with back-x-arcs, with the following properties:
1. A back arc from node η' to η is allowed only if $\eta' \in Rx(\eta)$.
2. Each non-leaf node has two outgoing arcs, (x and w-arcs).
3. Each leaf node η is labeled by a formula $\zeta \in \Sigma$, where

$$\Sigma \ = \ \{\boxplus l_1 \wedge \ldots \wedge \boxplus l_n \,|\, l_i = p_i \text{ or } l_i = \neg p_i, 0 < i \leq n\}$$

Note that each leaf node $[\eta]_w$ represents an interval between η and $[\eta]_x$ and hence an ordinal tree represents a nested sequence of intervals. An ordinal tree T can be unrolled to get an omega tree as follows:
- A back arc from η to η' in T is unrolled by copying $T(\eta')$ below η.
- A leaf node η is replaced by the unique PDTL tree for η.

7 Tableau for POTL

The PDTL tableau procedure will be extended to check if the formula ϕ has any ordinal tree models. When we build a PDTL tableau τ for ϕ, a state node η will now have a third child $[\eta]_s$, called its *stable (s-)* child, besides the two usual children $[\eta]_w$ and $[\eta]_x$. If $\eta = \{\bigwedge_i l_i, \bigwedge_j \oslash\phi_j, \bigwedge_k \bigcirc\psi_k\}$ then $[\eta]_s = \{\bigwedge_i \boxplus l_i, \bigwedge_j \phi_j\}$.

Define $Rsxw$ descendants of a node as follows:

$$Rswx(\eta) = \{[\eta]_l, [\eta]_r\} \cup Rswx([\eta]_l) \cup Rswx([\eta]_r), \text{ if } \eta \text{ is a logical node.}$$
$$Rswx(\eta) = \{[\eta]_x, [\eta]_w\} \cup Rswx([\eta]_w) \cup Rswx([\eta]_x)$$
$$\text{if } \eta \text{ is a state node, and } [\eta]_s \text{ is closed}$$
$$Rswx(\eta) = \{[\eta]_x, [\eta]_w, [\eta]_s\} \cup Rswx([\eta]_w) \cup Rswx([\eta]_x) \cup Rswx([\eta]_s)$$
$$\text{if } \eta \text{ is a state node, and } [\eta]_s \text{ is open}$$
$$swx\text{-leaf-scc}(\eta) \text{ iff } \forall\mu(\mu \in Rswx(\eta) \to (\eta \in Rswx(\mu))) \text{ and}$$
$$\forall\mu(\mu \in Rswx(\eta) \wedge \mu \text{ is a state node } \to ([\mu]_s \text{ is open}))$$

$Rswx(\eta)$ is the set of open nodes reachable from η by any path, and this set is a swx-strongly connected component (with every state node in it having three children) when swx-leaf-scc(η) is true. The closing algorithm is applied is the same as that for PDTL for the closing conditions (1) to (4), however condition (5) now reads:

Close η if swx-leaf-scc(η) and $\diamondsuit\psi \in \eta$ and $\psi \notin \bigcup Rswx(\eta)$.

and the closing of a s-child does not effect its parent state node.

7.1 Marking Nodes

Nodes that have an ordinal tree model will be marked by a sequence of functions $\beta_i, i \geq 0$ defined on τ. A node η will be called *marked* at stage i, if $\beta_i(\eta)$ is defined, that is $\beta_i(\eta) \neq \bot$. The marking will proceed bottom up: first marking nodes in all swx-leaf-sccs, and then proceeding upwards marking nodes that can form ordinal trees from the nodes already marked.

The s-children ensure that all swx-leaf-scc nodes have ordinal tree models. That is, for any node $\eta \in \tau$: swx-leaf-scc(η) implies that $\bigcup Rswx(\eta)$ does not contain both p and $\neg p$ for all $p \in PROP$, and therefore η has an ordinal tree model that satisfies the formula $\sigma(\eta)$ given below:

$$\sigma(\eta) = \bigwedge \left(\begin{array}{cc} \{\boxplus p : p \in (PROP \cap \bigcup Rswx(\eta))\} & \cup \\ \{\boxplus\neg p : p \in (PROP - \bigcup Rswx(\eta)),\} & \end{array} \right)$$

The marking function β_i for a large enough i, maps a node of the tableau to an ordinal tree model for that node. The range of $\beta_i, i \geq 0$ is the language $\mathcal{L}$ (for a particular τ) given below:

- For $\eta \in \tau$, if swx-leaf-scc(η) then $\eta \in \mathcal{L}$.
- If $t_1, t_2 \in \mathcal{L}$ then $t_1 \cdot t_2 \in \mathcal{L}$.
- If $t \in \mathcal{L}$ then $t^\omega \in \mathcal{L}$.

Each string in $\mathcal{L}$ represents an ordinal tree model, for example the ordinal tree in figure 3 is represented by $\eta_d \cdot (\eta_e \cdot \eta_f)^\omega$. Initially nodes in swx-leaf-sccs are marked: $\beta_0(\eta) = \eta$ if swx-leaf-scc(η), otherwise $\beta_0(\eta) = \bot$. The initial marking β_0 is extended to $\beta_i, 0 < i \leq |\tau|$, such that:

- If $\beta_i(\eta) \neq \bot$ then $\beta_{i+1}(\eta) = \beta_i(\eta)$.
- If $[\eta]_l$ or $[\eta]_r$ is marked, then η is marked in the next stage.
- If $[\eta]_w$ (or $[\eta]_s$) and $[\eta]_x$ are marked, then η is marked in the next stage.

- If every node in an x-leaf-scc has a $[\eta]_w$ (or $[\eta]_s$) child that is marked, then all the nodes in that x-leaf-scc are marked simultaneously in the next stage.

Theorem 6 ϕ *has an ordinal tree model iff* $\beta_{|\tau|}(\{\phi\}) \neq \bot$, *where* $|\tau|$ *is the size of the tableau* τ *for* ϕ.

Proof: ($\Leftarrow$) The mark of the node at stage i (i.e. $\beta_i(\eta)$) itself represents an ordinal tree model starting at that node.
($\Rightarrow$) Let T be an ordinal tree model satisfying ϕ, without loss of generality we can assume T is minimal, i.e. there are no ordinal tree models with fewer nodes than T satisfying ϕ. T can be embedded in τ, since τ contains all the information regarding all the models of ϕ. For each $\eta \in T$, let (η) be the corresponding node in τ. A leaf node of T will correspond to a node in a leaf node of τ. It is easy to see that for any $\eta \in T$, $(\eta) \in \tau$ will get marked by the marking algorithm by stage i, where i is the length of the largest path (without loops) from η to a swx-leaf-scc in T. $\blacksquare$

Corollary 7 *The problem of testing whether a formula* ϕ *is satisfiable in POTL is decidable in exponential time.*

Proof: The complexity of the marking algorithm is $O(|E| + |\tau|)$, where $|E|$ is the number of edges in τ, $|\tau| \leq 2^{c|\phi|}$ and $|E| \leq 2^{2c|\phi|}$ for some constant c. $\blacksquare$

Example 3 (POTL tableau) The formula $\boxplus(p \vee \neg p)$ has an ordinal tree model, the stable leaf nodes of its tableau (figure 4) are η_c and η_f. The tableau has been simplified for exposition. The marking of its nodes is given below:

	η_a	η_b	η_c	η_d	η_e	η_f
β_0	$\bot$	$\bot$	η_c	$\bot$	$\bot$	η_f
β_1	$(\eta_c \cdot \eta_f)^\omega$	$(\eta_f \cdot \eta_c)^\omega$	η_c	$\bot$	$\bot$	η_f
β_2	$(\eta_c \cdot \eta_f)^\omega$	$(\eta_f \cdot \eta_c)^\omega$	η_c	$\eta_c \cdot (\eta_c \cdot \eta_f)^\omega$	$\eta_f \cdot (\eta_f \cdot \eta_c)^\omega$	η_f

Example 4 The formula $\boxplus(p \vee \neg p) \wedge \boxplus \Diamond p \wedge \boxplus \Diamond \neg p$ has no ordinal tree models, because it has no swx-leaf-sccs. In particular the nodes η_c and η_f of figure 4 will be closed because η_c (correspondingly η_f) form a swx-leaf-scc which does not satisfy $\neg p$ (respectively p).

8 Conclusion

We have presented a propositional dense time logic which allows us to reason about nested sequences of events. We showed that the logic is decidable in exponential time by a tableau based method and presented a complete axiomatization for it.

We next looked at an interesting subset of models called ordinal trees, where all the propositions are stable. The logic of ordinal trees, POTL was also shown to be decidable in exponential time by extending the tableau based decision procedure used in the first part. Ordinal trees are interval based as they allow only finite level of refinement, and they seem to be a good bridge between point based and interval based temporal logics.

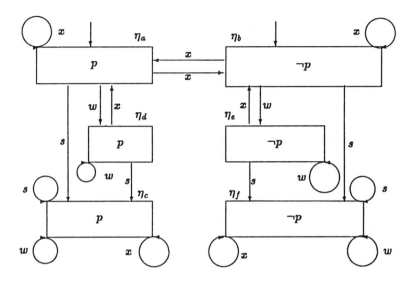

Figure 4: Ordinal tree tableau for $\boxplus(p \vee \neg p)$

Future work: We plan to axiomatize POTL and relate it to D-PDL with *converse*, *S2S* and other dense time logics. We will study if omega trees can be obtained as a limit of ordinal tree models.

We will also be considering logics dealing with finitely nested finite sequences of time points, i.e. we allow only finite subsequences of time points at each level. Each level of time could correspond to some natural periodic events, like 'hours', 'minutes', 'seconds' of a clock. For example, we could specify a day to consists of 24 hours, and make $\oslash \bigcirc^{24} \phi$ invalid or even better let $\oslash \bigcirc^{24} \phi \leftrightarrow \bigcirc \oslash \phi$. Such a representation is particularly useful in modeling synchronous digital circuits and in historical databases.

Acknowledgments: We thank Rohit Parikh, Madhavan Mukund, R. Ramanujam and Kamal Lodaya.

References

[1] M. Abadi and Z. Manna. Temporal logic programming. In *International Conference on Logic Programming San Fransisco, CA*, pages 4–16, 1987.

[2] M. Ahmed and G. Venkatesh. Dense time logic programming. In *Second Symposium on Logical Formalizations of Commonsense Reasoning, Austin, TX*, 1993.

[3] R. Alur and T. Henzinger. Real time logics: Complexity and expressiveness. In *Logic in Computer Science*, pages 390–401, 1990.

[4] M. Baudinet. Temporal logic programming is complete and expressive. In *16th POPL, Austin, TX*, pages 267–279, 1989.

[5] M. Ben-Ari, J. Y. Halpern, and A. Pnueli. Deterministic propositional dynamic logic: Finite models, complexity and completeness. *Journal of Computer and System Sciences*, 25:402–417, 1982.

[6] M. Ben-Ari, A. Pnueli, and Z. Manna. The temporal logic of branching time. *Acta Informatica*, 20:207–226, 1983.

[7] J. P. Burgess. Basic tense logic. In D. Gabbay and F. Guenther, editors, *Handbook of Philosophical Logic*, volume II, pages 89–133. D. Reidel, Dordrecht, Holland, 1984.

[8] D. Gabbay. Modal and temporal logic programming. In A. Galton, editor, *Temporal Logics and their applications*, pages 195–273. Academic Press, 1987.

[9] D. Gabbay. Modal and temporal logic programming - ii. In T. Dodd, editor, *Logic Programming*, pages 82–123. Intellect, Oxford, 1991.

[10] D. Gabbay, A. Pnueli, S. Shelah, and S. Stavi. The temporal analysis of fairness. In *7th POPL, Las Vegas, NE*, pages 163–173, 1980.

[11] D. Harel. Propositional dynamic logic. In D. Gabbay and F. Guenther, editors, *Handbook of Philosophical Logic*, volume II, pages 507–544. D. Reidel, Dordrecht, Holland, 1984.

[12] L. Lamport. Temporal logic of actions. TR 57, Digital, 1990.

[13] O. Lichtenstein, A. Pnueli, and L. Zuck. The glory of the past. In *Proc. Conf. Logics of Programs*, pages 196–218. Springer Verlag, 1985. LNCS 193.

[14] B. C. Moszkowski. *Executing Temporal Logic Programs*. Cambridge University Press, Cambridge, 1986.

[15] M. O. Rabin. Decidability of second order theories and automata on infinite trees. *Transactions of AMS*, 141:1–35, July 1969.

[16] W. Thomas. Automata on infinite trees. In J. V. Leeuwen, editor, *Handbook of Theoretical Computer Science*, volume B, pages 165–186. North Holland, Amsterdam, 1990.

[17] J. F. A. K. van Benthem. *The Logic of Time*. D. Reidel, Dordrecht, Holland, 1983.

[18] J. F. A. K. van Benthem. Time, logic and computation. In J. deBakker, W. deRoever, and G. Rozenberg, editors, *Linear Time, Branching Time and Partial Order in Logics and Models of Concurrency*. Springer Verlag, 1989. LNCS 354.

[19] P. Wolper. Temporal logic can be more expressive. *Information and Control*, 56:72–93, 1983.

La Vraie Forme d'un Arbre

J.Bétréma & A.Zvonkin

LaBRI, Université Bordeaux I
351, cours de la Libération, F33405 Talence
Unité associée CNRS 1304

1   Introduction

A.Grothendieck a observé, dans son mémoire [4], que pour toute carte combinatoire, il existe une surface de Riemann compacte de même genre, sur laquelle la carte peut être dessinée de façon canonique (à un automorphisme de cette surface près): c'est la théorie des *dessins d'enfants*.

Cette théorie implique, comme cas particulier, que *tout arbre plan possède un dessin canonique, à une similitude directe près*; de plus, elle fait apparaître une relation de *conjugaison* entre arbres plans, qui ne se réduit à aucune autre relation connue aujourd'hui, et une action du groupe de Galois sur ces arbres, avec pour orbites les classes de conjugaison.

Le calcul effectif des dessins, des classes de conjugaison, et des groupes de Galois associés, n'est pas facile, même pour de petits arbres, ce qui gêne la formulation et le test de conjectures. Le premier catalogue exhaustif pour les arbres avec au plus 8 arêtes, a été réalisé, à notre connaissance, par les auteurs au printemps 1992 [3]; son volume interdit de le reproduire ici; cet article présente les méthodes employées pour sa réalisation, illustrées sur le cas des arbres à 6 arêtes.

La section 2 donne les définitions et théorèmes fondamentaux de la théorie des dessins d'enfants appliquée aux arbres. La section 3 expose les principes des calculs, illustrés section 4; les Figs. 3 et 4 donnent les dessins canoniques des 14 arbres à 6 arêtes. La section finale résume l'état de l'art et les perspectives dans ce domaine de recherche.

Note sur les logiciels employés: nous avons utilisé `Maple` pour les calculs eux-mêmes. Il est vite apparu impossible, dans notre cas, de réaliser des dessins de qualité à partir des résultats produits par Maple, en utilisant les outils de dessin standard, comme la fonction `plot`; nous avons donc créé un logiciel de dessin spécialisé pour réaliser les dessins sous X-Windows, à l'aide de la boîte à outils `Xview`, pour OpenLook; les fichiers produits par Maple sont d'abord traités par un analyseur lexicographique simple, écrit en `lex`.

2   Arbres et Dessins d'enfants

2.1   Arbres Plans

Dans cet article, un *arbre* désignera un graphe connexe sans circuit, un *arbre plan* un arbre dessiné (plongé) dans le plan. Le dessin d'un arbre plan définit, pour chaque sommet de l'arbre, une permutation circulaire sur les sommets adjacents; un *isomorphisme* d'arbres plans est un isomorphisme d'arbres qui conserve ces permutations circulaires, et donc l'orientation; une classe d'isomorphisme d'arbres plans est appelée *arbre plan combinatoire*.

Pour fixer les idées, la Fig.1 présente les trois plus petits arbres (6 arêtes) possédant chacun deux dessins (numérotés *a* et *b*) non isomorphes.

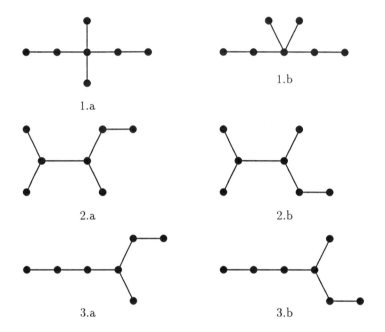

Fig. 1. Arbres plans non isomorphes

Les arbres plans combinatoires ont été énumérés dans [5], en utilisant le théorème de Pólya; la série énumératrice selon le nombre d'arêtes débute par:

$$1 + x + x^2 + 2x^3 + 3x^4 + 6x^5 + 14x^6 + 34x^7 + 95x^8 + 280x^9 + 854x^{10} \dots$$

à comparer avec celle des arbres:

$$1 + x + x^2 + 2x^3 + 3x^4 + 6x^5 + 11x^6 + 23x^7 + 47x^8 + 106x^9 + 235x^{10} \dots$$

2.2 Polynômes de Shabat

Considérons maintenant un polynôme à coefficients complexes $A(z)$, et soit a une racine (complexe) de A; l'image réciproque par A du segment réel $[0 \; \epsilon]$, pour ϵ petit, a l'aspect suivant:

avec un nombre de brins égal à la *multiplicité* de la racine a (ici 3). De même, soit b tel que $A(b) = 1$; l'image réciproque par A du segment $[1 - \epsilon, 1]$ a un aspect similaire, avec un nombre de brins égal à la multiplicité de la racine b pour le polynôme $B(z) = A(z) - 1$.

Un point u tel que $A'(u) = 0$ est appelé *point critique*; $v = A(u)$ est une *valeur critique*, et l'ordre du point critique u est égal par définition à son ordre de multiplicité en tant que racine du polynôme $A - v$; l'ordre de u est aussi la plus petite valeur de l'entier k tel que la dérivée $k^{\text{ème}}$ $A^{(k)}(u)$ soit non nulle. Notons Γ l'image réciproque par A du segment $[0\ 1]$:

$$\Gamma = A^{-1}([0\ 1])\ .$$

Si l'on suppose maintenant que les seules valeurs critiques de A sont 0 et 1 (autrement dit: tout point critique est racine de A ou de $A - 1$), Γ est constitué d'une collection de segments (courbes en général) qui relient les racines de A aux racines de $A - 1$, sans se couper (car deux segments ne peuvent se couper qu'en un point critique). Γ est donc le dessin d'un graphe planaire, dont les sommets sont alternativement racines de A et de $A - 1$, avec pour degrés les ordres de multiplicité de ces racines. On prouvera section 3 que Γ est en fait un arbre plan.

Dans la suite on appellera *noirs* (resp. *blancs*) les sommets correspondant aux racines de A (resp. $A - 1$). La théorie des dessins d'enfants, appliquée aux arbres, fournit la réciproque suivante:

Théorème 1. *Pour tout arbre plan Γ, il existe un polynôme $A(z)$, admettant pour valeurs critiques au plus 0 et 1, et tel que l'image réciproque du segment $[0\ 1]$ par A soit isomorphe à Γ; de plus A est unique, aux deux transformations suivantes près:*
   (i) changer z en $az + b$ (similitude directe)
   (ii) changer A en $1 - A$ (échange des couleurs des sommets).

Nous ne connaissons pas de preuve élémentaire de ce théorème. Suite aux travaux de G.Shabat [1, 6], nous appellerons dans la suite *polynôme de Shabat* d'un arbre plan Γ, tout polynôme A satisfaisant aux conditions du Théorème 1; l'image réciproque du segment $[0\ 1]$ par A est appelée *dessin canonique* de Γ. La Fig.2 montre ce dessin pour l'arbre 2.a de la Fig.1; les sections 3 et 4 expliquent comment obtenir ce dessin. Le polynôme de Shabat et le dessin canonique de Γ sont uniques à similitude directe, et échange des couleurs, près.

Note: Les seuls polynômes admettant pour unique valeur critique 0 ou 1 sont z^n et $z^n - 1$; tous les autres dans cet article admettent donc deux valeurs critiques, et deux seulement.

2.3 Arbres Conjugués et Action du Groupe de Galois

Le calcul des coefficients d'un polynôme de Shabat se ramène, comme on le verra sections 3 et 4, à la résolution d'un système d'équations algébriques à coefficients entiers; les coefficients d'un polynôme de Shabat peuvent donc être choisis dans un *corps de nombres algébriques* K. Comme un polynôme de Shabat est défini au changement de variable $z \to az + b$ près, K n'est pas unique; mais on a:

Théorème 2. *Soit Γ un arbre plan; il existe un corps algébrique minimal K de définition des coefficients d'un polynôme de Shabat associé à Γ.*

Le corps K défini par ce théorème est appelé *corps de définition* de Γ; il est impossible de donner dans cet article une preuve rigoureuse du Théorème 2, mais dans les calculs de la section 4, le corps de définition du dessin apparaît très naturellement.

Si K est le corps des rationnels $\mathbf{Q}$, c'est à dire si Γ possède un polynôme de Shabat à coefficients rationnels, l'arbre Γ lui-même sera dit *rationnel* – le risque de confusion avec l'emploi de ce mot dans le contexte de la théorie des langages d'arbres, semble minime.

Si le corps de définition est une extension algébrique propre de $\mathbf{Q}$, le calcul du polynôme de Shabat fait apparaître une famille de dessins *conjugués*, attachés aux diverses solutions de la même équation algébrique; et le *groupe de Galois*, qui agit sur ces solutions, agit donc sur ces dessins.

La théorie des dessins d'enfants associe aussi un corps de définition à toute carte combinatoire, bien que l'analogue du Théorème 2 ne soit plus valable sous la même forme dans le cas général. G.Belyi a démontré dans [2] que, pour tout corps de nombres K, il existe une carte dont K est le corps de définition; on ignore actuellement s'il en est de même en se restreignant aux arbres.

3 Calcul du Polynôme de Shabat

3.1 Polynômes avec Deux Valeurs Critiques

Donnons d'abord la preuve, annoncée section 2.2, de la proposition dont le Théorème 1 constitue la réciproque:

Proposition 1. *Soit A un polynôme non constant admettant pour seules valeurs critiques 0 et 1; autrement dit:*

$$A'(z) = 0 \ \text{implique} \ A(z) = 0 \ \text{ou} \ A(z) = 1 \ .$$

Alors $\Gamma = A^{-1}([0\ 1])$ est un arbre plan.

Preuve: Γ ne peut comporter de circuit, car la partie imaginaire d'une fonction polynomiale est harmonique, et ne peut donc être nulle sur un circuit sans être nulle dans toute la région bornée par ce circuit, ce qui est impossible pour un polynôme non constant. Donc Γ est un arbre ou une forêt; pour prouver que Γ est connexe, il suffit de compter arêtes et sommets.

Soit n le degré de A: c'est aussi le nombre d'arêtes de Γ; soit p (resp. q) le nombre de racines distinctes de A (resp. $A-1$), et $\alpha_1, \alpha_2, \ldots, \alpha_p$ (resp. $\beta_1, \beta_2, \ldots, \beta_q$) leurs multiplicités. On a évidemment:

$$\sum_{i=1}^{p} \alpha_i = \sum_{j=1}^{q} \beta_j = n \ .$$

Si $\alpha_i > 1$, la racine correspondante est aussi racine d'ordre $\alpha_i - 1$ de A'; idem pour les β_j; comme par hypothèse toutes les racines de A' sont des racines de A ou $A - 1$, on a:

$$\sum_{i=1}^{p}(\alpha_i - 1) + \sum_{j=1}^{q}(\beta_j - 1) = n - 1 \ .$$

Soit:

$$2n - (p + q) = n - 1 \text{ ou encore } p + q = n + 1 \ . \ \square$$

3.2 Assortiment des Degrés d'un Arbre Bicolorié

Tout arbre a une structure naturelle de graphe bipartite: on peut colorier alternativement les sommets en noir et blanc. Supposons choisi l'un des deux coloriages possibles; soit n le nombre d'arêtes de l'arbre, et soit $\alpha = \alpha_1, \alpha_2, \ldots, \alpha_p$ (resp. $\beta = \beta_1, \beta_2, \ldots, \beta_q$) la suite des degrés (ou *valences*) des sommets noirs (resp. blancs), ordonnée dans le sens décroissant. Comme toute arête joint un sommet blanc et un sommet noir, on a:

$$\sum_{i=1}^{p}\alpha_i = \sum_{j=1}^{q}\beta_j = n \ .$$

D'autre part l'arbre comporte p sommets noirs, et q sommets blancs, donc $p+q = n + 1$. On appellera *assortiment de degrés* d'un arbre bicolorié le couple (α, β), et pour abréger on dira que l'arbre est de *type* $< \alpha_1, \alpha_2, \ldots, \alpha_p; \beta_1, \beta_2, \ldots, \beta_q >$; par exemple l'arbre de la Fig.2 est de type $< 3\ 2\ 1; 3\ 1\ 1\ 1 >$. Réciproquement:

Proposition 2. *Soient deux partitions de l'entier n, avec respectivement p et q parts, telles que $p + q = n + 1$; il existe alors au moins un arbre bicolorié admettant ces partitions pour assortiment de degrés.*

Preuve (par récurrence): on vérifie facilement que les hypothèses impliquent que, pour $n \geq 2$, on a forcément $\alpha_1 > 1$ et $\beta_q = 1$ (ou l'inverse); par hypothèse de récurrence, il existe un arbre de type $< \alpha_1 - 1, \alpha_2, \ldots, \alpha_p; \beta_1, \beta_2, \ldots, \beta_{q-1} >$, et il suffit de relier le sommet de degré $\alpha_1 - 1$ à une nouvelle feuille blanche pour obtenir un arbre du type souhaité.

3.3 Système Associé à un Assortiment de Degrés

Le calcul du polynôme de Shabat associé à un arbre plan de type

$$< \alpha_1, \alpha_2, \ldots, \alpha_p; \beta_1, \beta_2, \ldots, \beta_q >$$

revient à trouver les valeurs des complexes:

$$\lambda, a_1, a_2, \ldots, a_p, b_1, b_2, \ldots, b_q$$

telles que l'on ait simultanément:

$$A(z) = \lambda(z - a_1)^{\alpha_1} \ldots (z - a_p)^{\alpha_p}$$

La Fig.4 montre les deux orbites d'arbres plans conjugués avec 6 arêtes; la première orbite, de taille 2, correspond aux arbres 2.a et 2.b de la Fig.1; les Figs. 3 et 4 fournissent donc la liste complète des dessins canoniques d'arbres avec 6 arêtes. Notons que dans le cas d'arbres conjugués, les positions mutuelles sont elles aussi canoniques.

5 Perspectives

Les calculs deviennent vite plus difficiles: pour certaines classes d'arbres à 7 ou 8 arêtes, le calcul produit plusieurs équations algébriques, et il faut employer les *bases de Gröbner*, ou une autre méthode sophistiquée, pour les résoudre. Au-delà, les calculs deviennent souvent impraticables, ce que l'argument suivant explique: les séries énumératrices des arbres plans et des partitions sont bien connues; en les comparant, on constate que le nombre moyen d'arbres plans, pour un assortiment de degrés donné, croît très rapidement: pour 24 arêtes, on peut s'attendre à ce que les coefficients du polynôme de Shabat soient racines d'équations de degré supérieur au million!

Les questions principales de cette théorie concernent le corps de définition d'un arbre, qu'on aimerait relier aux propriétés combinatoires de l'arbre; par exemple;

1. Comment caractériser les arbres rationnels?
2. Comment caractériser les arbres dont le corps de définition est quadratique?
3. Quand et comment une classe d'arbres, pour un assortiment de degrés donné, se scinde-t-elle en plusieurs classes de conjugaison?
4. Comment caractériser les arbres dont le corps de définition est cubique, et dont le groupe de Galois est le groupe cyclique C_3 (au lieu du groupe symétrique S_3)?

On a les réponses partielles suivantes:

Proposition 3. *Soit (α, β) un assortiment de degrés pour lequel il existe un seul arbre plan combinatoire Γ; alors Γ est rationnel.*

L'exemple 4.1 donne une idée de la preuve; des difficultés supplémentaires surgissent si le dessin ne possède pas de sommet célibataire; une preuve rigoureuse se trouve dans [1].

La réciproque est fausse, comme le prouve l'exemple 4.2. Nonobstant, N.Adrianov a réalisé une classification exhaustive des assortiments de degrés pour lesquels il existe un seul arbre plan combinatoire. Les cas les plus simples sont:

1. $< n; 1\ 1\ldots 1 >$: ce cas est celui du polynôme z^n, et le dessin correspondant possède comme sommets blancs les racines $n^{\text{èmes}}$ de l'unité, reliées à l'origine (sommet noir de degré n); voir dessin numéro 1, Fig.3.
2. $< 2\ 2\ldots 2; 2\ 2\ldots 2\ 1\ 1 >$ ou $< 2\ 2\ldots 2\ 1; 2\ 2\ldots 2\ 1 >$ selon la parité du nombre d'arêtes; l'arbre est une chaîne, et son polynôme de Shabat vaut: $(T_n + 1)/2$ où T_n désigne le polynôme de Tchebycheff de degré n, dont on

sait qu'il admet pour seules valeurs critiques -1 et 1, valeurs entre lesquelles il oscille à la manière d'une sinusoïde; voir dessin numéro 8, Fig.3.

La classification d'Adrianov comporte six classes d'arbres; vérifier que pour chaque cas il existe un seul dessin plan, à isomorphisme près, est assez direct; prouver que la classification est exhaustive est beaucoup plus difficile.

N.Adrianov et G.Shabat ont aussi montré d'une manière constructive:

Proposition 4. *Tout corps quadratique est le corps de définition d'un arbre plan.*

La proposition suivante répond partiellement à la question 3 ci-dessus:

Proposition 5. *Deux arbres conjugués ont même groupe d'automorphismes (en tant qu'arbres plans).*

Cette proposition explique que les deux arbres de l'exemple 4.2 ne soient pas conjugués, car l'un est invariant par rotation d'un demi-tour, et pas l'autre. Mais notre catalogue fournit l'exemple de la classe de l'assortiment de degrés $< 4\,2\,1\,;\,2\,2\,1\,1\,1 >$, qui comporte 4 arbres plans combinatoires; aucun n'admet d'automorphisme non trivial, et pourtant cette classe se scinde en deux classes de conjugaison d'ordre 2.

[8] contient un théorème d'existence en relation avec la question 4:

Proposition 6. *Il existe une classe de trois arbres conjugués admettant C_3 pour groupe de Galois.*

Terminons en signalant une question ouverte de dénombrement: quel est le nombre d'arbres plans combinatoires bicoloriés, connaissant leur assortiment de degrés? Il existe des réponses partielles dans [1, 7]. Il serait intéressant d'ajouter comme paramètre de l'énumération l'ordre de symétrie de l'arbre, à cause de la Prop.5.

Bibliographie

1. Adrianov, N., Shabat, G.: Dessins planaires à une face et polynômes avec deux valeurs critiques. Prépublication (en russe)
2. Belyi, G.: On the Galois extensions of the maximal cyclotomic field. Math. USSR Izvestia **14** (1980)
3. Bétréma, J., Péré, D., Zvonkin, A.: Plane trees and their Shabat polynomials. Catalog. Publication du LaBRI **92–75** (1992)
4. Grothendieck, A.: Esquisse d'un programme (1984)
5. Harary, F., Prins, G., Tutte, W.T.: The number of plane trees. Koninklijke Nederlandse Akademie Van Wetenschappen **67** (1964) 319–329.
6. Shabat, G., Voevodsky, V.: Drawing curves over number fields, *in* The Grothendieck Festschrift, vol.3 (1990) 199–227. Birkhäuser Verlag
7. Tutte, W.T.: The number of plane planted trees with a given partition. Amer. Math. Monthly **71** (1964) 272–277
8. Zvonkin, A.: Shabat polynomials for trees of diameter 4. International Conference on Dessins d'enfant, Luminy, April 19-24, 1993.

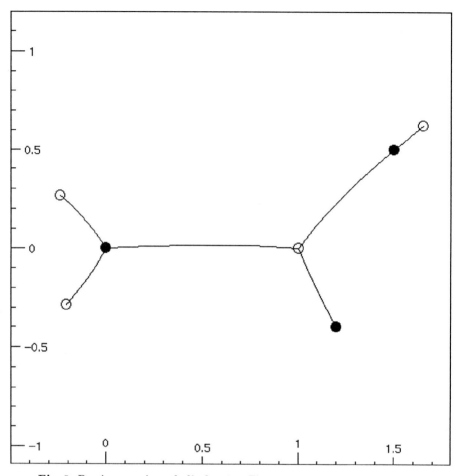

Fig. 2. Dessin canonique de l'arbre 2.a, Fig. 1

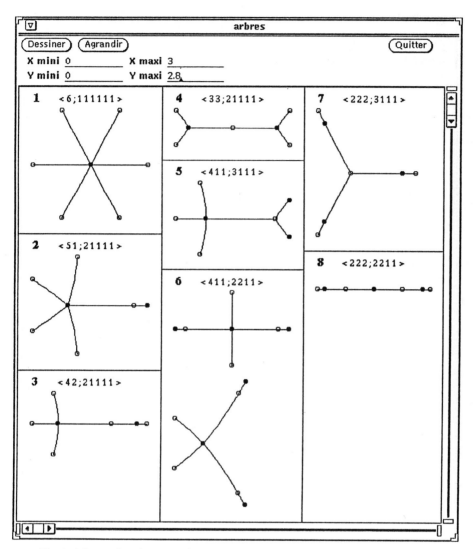

Fig. 3. Arbres rationnels avec 6 arêtes

612

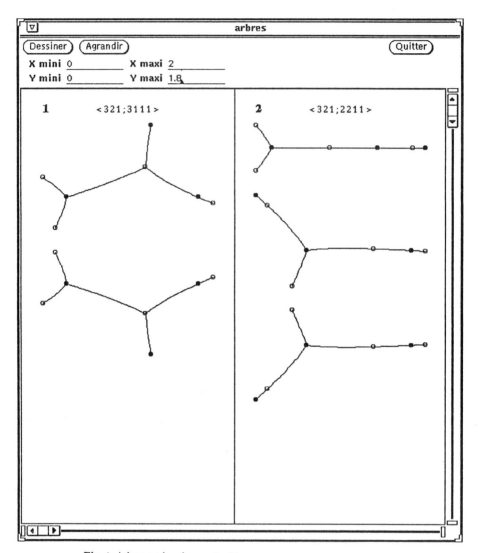

Fig. 4. Arbres conjugués avec 6 arêtes

Model Checking Using Net Unfoldings*

Javier Esparza

Institut für Informatik, Universität Hildesheim
Samelsonplatz 1, W-3200 Hildesheim, Germany.

Abstract. In [8], McMillan described a technique for deadlock detection based on net unfoldings. We extend its applicability to the properties of a temporal logic with a possibility operator. The algorithm is based on Linear Programming. It compares favourably with other algorithms for the class of deterministic concurrent systems.

1 Introduction

Model checking has become a well established paradigm for verifying that a concurrent program satisfies a temporal logic formula. It views the program as a structure on which to interpret the considered logic and evaluates the formula on this structure.

In most work on model checking, the structures are some sort of transition system obtained representing concurrency by arbitrary interleaving. It has been observed that this contributes to a state explosion problem, and that avoiding the enumeration of all interleavings could lead to more efficient algorithms.

Several researchers have proposed such algorithms. Some of them use partial order notions to reduce the size of the state space, such as the stubborn sets method of Valmari (see, for instance [12]) or the trace automaton method of Godefroid and Wolper (see, for instance, [5]). Others work directly on partial order structures, such as the behaviour machines of Probst and Li [10] and the Petri net unfoldings of McMillan [8]. We are particularly interested in the latter. McMillan's method is based on the net unfoldings introduced by Nielsen, Winskel and Plotkin in [9] as a partial order semantics of Petri nets (closely related to event structures) and further studied by Engelfriet in [3]. For verification purposes, these unfoldings have the problem of being infinite even for systems with a finite number of states. McMillan shows how to construct a finite prefix of the unfolding large enough to be able to detect deadlocks.

In this paper, we make deeper use of the theory of unfoldings to extend McMillan's approach to model checking: we propose a verification algorithm for a logic closely related to S_4 [7], which extends propositional logic with a possibility operator, and permits to express safety properties such as the reachability of a

---

*This work was partially supported by the Esprit Basic Research Action CALIBAN

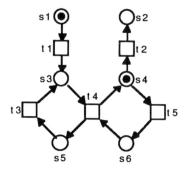

Figure 1: A finite 1-safe system.

state or the liveness of a transition.

Since the unfolding does not contain any explicit representation of the states of the system, our algorithm is very different from the traditional traversing algorithms of the state space. It uses Linear Programming to identify certain particularly important states.

Our algorithm is adequate for deterministic or nearly deterministic concurrent net systems, with applications to the design of asynchronous circuits. In the deterministic case (no conflicts) our algorithm is polynomial in the size of the prefix. For the class of conflict-free net systems [6,13] it is even polynomial in the size of the system, whereas the algorithms of [5,10,12] are either exponential or not applicable.

This paper is a shortened version of [4], where the proofs omitted here can be found. The paper generalises results of [1]. There, a model checker was given for the class of 1-safe Petri nets in which places have at most one input transition and at most one output transition. Here we generalise this model checker to arbitrary 1-safe Petri nets.

The paper is organised as follows. Section 2 is devoted to basic notations and results. Section 3 introduces the syntax and semantics of our logic. Section 4 shows how to reduce the model checking problem to two simpler problems. Algorithms for these problems are given in sections 5 and 6. Finally, Section 7 considers the case of deterministic concurrent systems.

2 Basic Notions

We assume that the reader is familiar with the basic notions and notations of Petri nets, as given for instance in [2]. We use finite 1-safe Petri nets as system models. We denote a Petri net by $\Sigma = (S, T, F, M_0)$, where (S, T, F) is a net and M_0 its initial marking. A place of a 1-safe Petri net can contain at most one token. In the sequel, we call 1-safe Petri nets 1-safe systems, or just systems. Figure 1 shows a 1-safe system.

Our execution model are Engelfriet's branching processes [3]. Branching processes are unfoldings of net systems containing information about both concurrency and conflicts.

Let (S, T, F) be a net and x_1, $x_2 \in S \cup T$. x_1 and x_2 are in *conflict*, denoted by $x_1 \# x_2$, if there exist distinct transitions t_1, $t_2 \in T$ such that $|{}^\bullet t_1| \cap |{}^\bullet t_2| \neq \emptyset$, and both (t_1, x_1), (t_2, x_2) belong to the reflexive and transitive closure of F. We define now occurrence nets, which are the nets underlying branching processes. To differentiate the system and execution levels, places of occurrence nets are called *conditions*, and their transitions are called *events*.

A net (B, E, F) is called *occurrence net* if

(i) for every $b \in B$, $|{}^\bullet b| \leq 1$,

(ii) the transitive closure of F is irreflexive, and

(iii) no event $e \in E$ is in conflict with itself (i.e., not $e \# e$).

Min(N) denotes the set of minimal elements of $B \cup E$ with respect to the transitive closure of F.

A *branching process* of a system $\Sigma = (S, T, F, M_0)$ is a pair $\beta = (N', p)$ where $N' = (B, E, F)$ is an occurrence net and $p: B \cup E \to S \cup T$ a labelling function of N' satisfying certain properties that make (N', p) an unfolding of the system [1]. Figure 2 shows a branching process of the system of Figure 1. The names of the events have been written within the boxes, while the transitions associated to them have been written close to them. The names of the conditions have been omitted to keep the picture simple.

In [3] an *approximation relation* is defined between branching processes. The exact definition is not necessary for the purpose of this paper. Intuitively, β_1 approximates β_2 if β_1 is isomorphic to an initial part of β_2. It was proved in [3] that a system has a unique maximal branching process (up to isomorphism) with respect to the approximation relation. The maximal branching process of the system of Figure 1 is infinite. Loosely speaking, it consists of a periodic repetition of the initial part of the branching process of Figure 2 obtained 'cutting' the net by a vertical line just to the right of the event e_4.

Let (B, E, F) be an occurrence net. By definition, the transitive closure of F is a partial order. We denote it by $\prec$. $\preceq$ denotes the reflexive and transitive closure of F. Given $x \in B \cup E$ and $X \subseteq B \cup E$, we say $x \prec X$ if there exists $x' \in X$ such that $x \prec x'$.

A subset $E' \subseteq E$ is a *configuration* if it is left-closed with respect to $\preceq$ and no two elements of E' are in conflict. In the branching process of Figure 2, the set $\{e_1, e_2\}$ is a configuration, while the sets $\{e_4\}$ and $\{e_1, e_3\}$ are not ($\{e_4\}$ is not left-closed, and $e_1 \# e_3$). $X \subseteq B$ is a co-set if $\forall x_1, x_2 \in X: \neg(x_1 \prec x_2) \wedge \neg(x_2 \prec x_1)$. A maximal co-set with respect to set inclusion is called a *cut*. It is well known [2,3] that if c is a cut of a branching process $\beta = (N', p)$, then $p(c)$ is a reachable marking of Σ. The converse holds for the maximal branching process.

---

[1] The exact definition is not relevant for this paper. It can be found in [3].

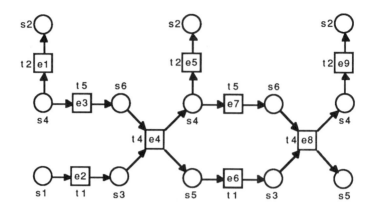

Figure 2: A branching process of the system of Figure 1

We associate to a configuration C a set of conditions $Cut(C)$ in the following way:

$$Cut(C) = (Min(N) \cup C^{\bullet}) \setminus {}^{\bullet}C$$

It is easy to prove that Cut is a bijection between the set of finite configurations of a branching process and its set of cuts.

Cuts will be used in the definition of the satisfaction relation of our logic. However, we shall mainly work with finite configurations, because they have a simpler mathematical structure, and cuts can always be retrieved via the Cut mapping.

3   A Modal Logic for 1-Safe Systems

We define in this section the syntax and semantics of a modal logic tailored for finite 1-safe systems.

We fix for the rest of the paper a finite 1-safe system $\Sigma = (S, T, F, M_0)$ such that every element of $S \cup T$ has a nonempty preset or a nonempty postset.

As pointed out in Section 2, Σ has a unique maximal branching process up to isomorphism. We fix a representative of the isomorphism class, denoted by

$$\beta_m = (B_m, E_m, F_m, p_m).$$

The logic is essentially S_4 [7] interpreted over the set of configurations of β_m, with elementary propositions tailored for Petri nets. The logic extends propositional logic with a possibility operator. The set of formulas over Σ is generated by the following grammar:

$$\phi ::= \textbf{true} \mid s \mid \neg\phi \mid \phi_1 \wedge \phi_2 \mid \Diamond\phi$$

The operator $\Box$ is defined by $\Box = \neg\Diamond\neg$. The logic S_4 is interpreted over a set of worlds having a preorder structure (or stronger). In our case, it is the set of finite configurations of β_m.

The satisfaction relation $\models$ is defined as usual for the propositional connectives. Moreover, for a finite configuration C we have:

$C \models s$ if $s \in p_m(Cut(C))$.

$C \models \Diamond\phi$ if   there exists a finite configuration $C' \supseteq C$ such that $C' \models \phi$.

Finally, we say that Σ satisfies ϕ, also denoted by $\Sigma \models \phi$, if $\emptyset \models \phi$.

Loosely speaking, $C \models s$ if after the occurrence of the events of C a marking is reached in which the place s contains a token. For instance, in the branching process of Figure 2, $\{e_1, e_2\} \models s_2$. We have $C \models \Diamond\phi$ if C can be extended to a configuration C' (lying therefore in the 'future' of C) such that C' satisfies ϕ. Notice that $\Diamond\phi$ means 'possibly ϕ' and not 'eventually ϕ'.

The logic permits one to express safety properties such as the reachability of a marking (the system of figure 1 satisfies $\Diamond(\neg s_1 \wedge s_2 \wedge \neg s_3 \wedge s_4 \wedge \neg s_5 \wedge \neg s_6)$ iff the marking $\{s_2, s_4\}$ is reachable), the liveness of a transition (the system satisfies $\Box\Diamond s_4$ iff transition t_5 is live) or the fact that a marking is a home state (the initial marking can always be reached again iff the system satisfies $\Box\Diamond(s_1 \wedge \neg s_2 \wedge \neg s_3 \wedge s_4 \wedge \neg s_5 \wedge \neg s_6))$.

We study in the sequel the model checking problem for this logic, i.e. whether $\Sigma \models \phi$ for a formula ϕ. It is immediate to see that the model checking problem reduces to the problem for formulas of the form $\Diamond\phi$ (formulas without modalities can be easily checked using directly the definition of $\models$).

We denote by $Sat(\phi)$ the set of configurations of β_m that satisfy ϕ. It follows easily from the definitions that $\Sigma \models \Diamond\phi$ iff $Sat(\phi) \neq \emptyset$. Therefore, the model checking problem further reduces to deciding for a formula ϕ if $Sat(\phi)$ is empty.

4   The Finite Prefix

The maximal branching process β_m may be infinite, and therefore unsuitable for verification. We define in this section a finite prefix of it. We say that a branching process $\beta = (B, E, F, p)$ of Σ is a prefix of β_m if β approximates β_m, and moreover $B \subseteq B_m$ and $E \subseteq E_m$.

The finite prefix β_f is chosen to ensure that all reachable markings of Σ are represented by cuts of β_f. This is necessary if we wish to base a model checker on β_f; otherwise, for the formula ϕ corresponding to the reachability of a marking not represented in β_f, we would have $Sat(\phi) \neq \emptyset$ but we could hardly decide it using information from β_f only.

The branching process β_f was defined and used for deadlock detection by McMillan in [8]. Its definition is based on the notion of set of causes of an event. Given a branching process $\beta = (B, E, F, p)$ and $e \in E$, the set $[e] = \{e' \in E \mid e' \preceq e\}$ is the set of causes of e (in β). In the branching process of Figure 2, we have $[e_5] = \{e_2, e_3, e_4, e_5\}$.

It follows immediately from the definitions that the set of causes of an event is a finite configuration. Moreover, for every configuration C, either C does not contain e or it includes $[e]$.

Definition 4.1 *The prefix β_f [8]*

An event e of β_m is called a cut-off event if there exists a set of causes $[e'] \subset [e]$ (proper inclusion) such that

$$p_m(\ Cut([e'])\ ) = p_m(\ Cut([e])\ )$$

(i.e. $[e']$ and $[e]$ correspond to the same reachable marking). β_f is the maximal prefix of β_m with respect to the approximation relation that contains no cut-off events.

E_f denotes the set of events of β_f. Given a cut-off event e, we denote by e^0 an arbitrarily selected event of $[e]$ such that

$$p_m(\ Cut([e^0])\ ) = p_m(\ Cut([e])\ )$$

This event exists by the definition of cut-off event. ∎ 4.1

The finiteness of β_f follows from the finiteness of the number of reachable markings of Σ [8]. Also, in [8] an algorithm is described for the construction of β_f. The algorithm searches for minimal cut-off events with respect to the relation $\prec$. When a minimal cut-off event is found, its succesors need not be explored, because they cannot be part of the prefix. The search is continued until all minimal cut-off events with respect to the relation $\preceq$ have been identified. The reader is referred to [8] for a detailed pseucode description of the algorithm and an evaluation of its performance.

The finite prefix of the system of Figure 1 is the one with $\{e_1, e_2, e_3, e_4, e_5, e_7\}$ as set of events as events (see Figure 3). The unique minimal cut-off event is e_6 (shaded in Figure 3). We take $e_6^0 = e_2$, because $e_2 \in [e_6]$, and

$$p(\ Cut([e_2])\ ) = \{s_3, s_4\} = p(\ Cut([e_6])\ )$$

(these two cuts are represented in Figure 3 by straight lines that cross the conditions of the cut).

Define $\Uparrow e$ as the branching process containing all nodes x of β_m such that for some $b \in Cut([e])$, $b \preceq x$ (it is routine to check that $\Uparrow e$ is a branching process). Loosely speaking, $\Uparrow e$ contains the events and conditions after $[e]$, or, in other words, the "future" of the system from the marking corresponding to $Cut([e])$. Since $Cut([e])$ and $Cut([e^0])$ correspond to the same markings, $\Uparrow e$ and $\Uparrow e^0$ are isomorphic branching processes. Using this fact, we can prove that every reachable marking is represented in β_f. For every reachable marking M of Σ, there exists some configuration C such that $p_m(Cut(C)) = M$. If C is a configuration of β_f, then we are done. Otherwise, C contains some cut-off event e. Since $\Uparrow e$ is isomorphic to $\Uparrow e^0$, there exists another configuration C' after e^0 with the same associated marking, and containing *less* events than C, because $|[e]| > |[e^0]|$. If C' is not a configuration of β_f, then we iterate the procedure.

4.1 Shifts

We introduce some notions that allow us to formalise arguments like the one of the previous paragraph.

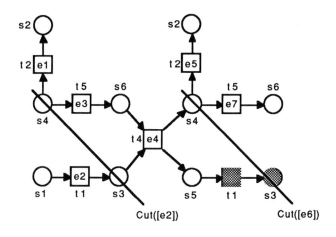

Figure 3: The finite prefix of the system of Figure 1

Definition 4.2 *Shift of a configuration*

Let e be a cut-off event of β_m and let I_e be an isomorphism from $\Uparrow e^0$ to $\Uparrow e$.
Let C be a configuration of β_m.
The e-shift of C, denoted by $\mathcal{S}_e(C)$, is the following configuration:

$$\mathcal{S}_e(C) = \left\{ \begin{array}{ll} C & \text{if } e^0 \notin C \\ [e] \cup I_e(C \setminus [e^0]) & \text{if } e^0 \in C \end{array} \right.$$

∎ 4.2

It is easy to prove that $\mathcal{S}_e(C)$ is a configuration, and therefore well defined. A configuration and its e-shift have associated the same reachable marking. In Figure 2, we have $\mathcal{S}_{e_6}(\{e_1, e_2\}) = [e_6] \cup I_{e_6}(\{e_1\}) = \{e_2, e_3, e_4, e_6\} \cup \{e_5\}$. Both $\{e_1, e_2\}$ and $\mathcal{S}_{e_6}(\{e_1, e_2\})$ have associated the marking $\{s_2, s_3\}$. We also have $|\mathcal{S}_e(C)| \geq |C|$, and the equality holds only if $\mathcal{S}_e(C) = C$.
For a set of configurations $\mathcal{C}$, we define $\mathcal{S}_e(\mathcal{C}) = \{\mathcal{S}_e(C) \mid C \in \mathcal{C}\}$.

We show that $Sat(\phi)$ can be generated from a subset of it, namely the set of configurations that satisfy ϕ and are contained in the finite prefix. Formally, we define $Sat_f(\phi) = Sat(\phi) \cap \mathcal{F}$, where $\mathcal{F}$ denotes the set of configurations of β_f This will reduce the model checking problem to deciding the emptyness of this subset.

Definition 4.3 *The mapping $\mathcal{S}$*

Let $\mathcal{C}$ be a set of configurations of β_m. The set of configurations $\mathcal{S}(\mathcal{C})$ is given by:

$$\mathcal{S}(\mathcal{C}) = \mathcal{C} \cup \bigcup_{e \in Off} \mathcal{S}_e(\mathcal{C})$$

where *Off* denotes the set of minimal cut-off events of β_m.
We define:

$$\mu S.C = \bigcup_{n \geq 0} S^n(C)$$

■ 4.3

Clearly, S is a monotonic function on the complete partial order of sets of configurations of β_m. It is easy to see that $\mu S.C$ is the least fixpoint of S containing C; this is the reason of the notation.

We can now state the first important result of the paper. Crudely speaking, it states that every configuration of $Sat(\phi)$ can be obtained by repeated shifting of some configuration of $Sat_f(\phi)$.

Theorem 4.4

Let ϕ be a formula. Then: $Sat(\phi) = \mu S.Sat_f(\phi)$.   ■ 4.4

In particular, we have $Sat(\phi) = \emptyset$ if and only if $Sat_f(\phi) = \emptyset$. That is, for every formula ϕ, if some configuration satisfies it, then some configuration of the finite prefix satisfies it as well. Therefore, the model checking problem can be reduced to deciding whether or not $Sat_f(\phi)$ is empty.

In Section 6, we shall show how to compute – using Linear Programming – the maximal elements of $Sat_f(\phi)$ for a simple subclass of formulas. In order to extend this to all the formulas of the logic, we obtain in the next section compositional equations for the maximal elements of $Sat_f(\phi)$.

4.2   Compositional equations

We introduce first a normal form for the formulas of our logic. It is a generalisation of the disjunctive normal form of propositional logic.

Definition 4.5 *Normal form*

A formula is in normal form if it is generated by the following grammar:

$$\gamma \quad ::= \quad \mathbf{true} \mid \mathbf{false} \mid s \mid \neg s \mid \gamma \wedge \gamma$$
$$\phi \quad ::= \quad \gamma \mid \phi \wedge \Diamond \phi \mid \phi \wedge \neg \Diamond \phi$$

■ 4.5

In the sequel, as was done in this definition, the symbol γ is used to denote conjunctions of literals.

Let $\phi_1 \equiv \phi_2$ be two formulas. ϕ_1 is equivalent to ϕ_2, denoted by $\phi_1 \equiv \phi_2$, if they have exactly the same models. We can prove the following proposition:

Proposition 4.6

Let ϕ be a formula. There exist formulas $\phi_1, \ldots, \phi_n$ in normal form such that $\phi \equiv \bigvee_{i=1}^{n} \phi_i$. ■ 4.6

By this result, $Sat(\phi) = \bigcup_{i=1}^{n} Sat(\phi_i)$ for a set of formulas $\{\phi_1, \ldots, \phi_n\}$ in normal form. It follows that deciding the emptyness of $Sat(\phi)$ for an arbitrary formula ϕ reduces to the problem of deciding the emptyness of $Sat(\phi)$ for a formula ϕ in normal form.

It must be remarked that the length of the conjunction of formulas in normal form equivalent to a given formula ϕ may be exponential in the length of ϕ. This makes our algorithm exponential in the length of the formula (however, as shown in [1], this cannot be avoided unless $P = NP$).

We show how to compositionally express $Sat(\phi)$ when ϕ is in normal form. First, we generalise the definition of $Sat(\phi)$ by introducing some more parameters.

Definition 4.7

Let C be a configuration and $\mathcal{C}$ a set of configurations. We say $C \leq \mathcal{C}$ if there exists $C' \in \mathcal{C}$ such that $C \subseteq C'$.

Let ϕ a formula and $\mathcal{C}_1$, $\mathcal{C}_2$ two sets of configurations. $C \in Sat(\mathcal{C}_1, \phi, \mathcal{C}_2)$ if $C \models \phi$, $C \not\leq \mathcal{C}_1$ and $C \leq \mathcal{C}_2$. ■ 4.7

Clearly, taking $\mathcal{C}_1$ as the empty set and $\mathcal{C}_2$ as the set of all configurations of β_m, we recover $Sat(\phi)$.

Before obtaining our set of equations, we need some properties of the relation $\leq$ defined above.

Lemma 4.8

Let C be a configuration and $\mathcal{C}_1$, $\mathcal{C}_2$ two sets of configurations.

(1) $C \models \Diamond\phi$ iff $C \leq Sat(\phi)$.

(2) $C \leq \mathcal{C}_1$ and $C \leq \mathcal{C}_2$ iff $C \leq \mathcal{C}_1 \bigtriangledown \mathcal{C}_2$, where

$$\mathcal{C}_1 \bigtriangledown \mathcal{C}_2 = \{C_1 \cap C_2 \mid C_1 \in \mathcal{C}_1, C_2 \in \mathcal{C}_2\}.$$

(3) $C \not\leq \mathcal{C}_1$ and $C \not\leq \mathcal{C}_2$ iff $C \not\leq \mathcal{C}_1 \cup \mathcal{C}_2$. ■ 4.8

We have now:

Theorem 4.9 *Compositional equations for $Sat(\mathcal{C}_1, \phi, \mathcal{C}_2)$*

Let $\mathcal{C}_1$, $\mathcal{C}_2$ be two sets of configurations of β_m, and let ϕ, ψ be two formulas.

$$Sat(\mathcal{C}_1, \phi \wedge \Diamond\psi, \mathcal{C}_2) = Sat(\mathcal{C}_1, \phi, \mathcal{C}_2 \triangledown Sat(\psi))$$
$$Sat(\mathcal{C}_1, \phi \wedge \neg\Diamond\psi, \mathcal{C}_2) = Sat(\mathcal{C}_1 \cup Sat(\psi), \phi, \mathcal{C}_2)$$

Proof: We only prove the $\supseteq$ inclusion of the first equation. The rest is similar. Let $C \in Sat(\mathcal{C}_1, \phi, \mathcal{C}_2 \triangledown Sat(\psi))$. By definition 4.7, $C \models \phi$, $C \not\leq \mathcal{C}_1$ and $C \leq \mathcal{C}_2 \triangledown Sat(\psi)$. By Lemma 4.8(2), $C \leq \mathcal{C}_2$ and $C \leq Sat(\psi)$. By Lemma 4.8(1), $C \models \Diamond\psi$. So $C \in Sat(\mathcal{C}_1, \phi \wedge \Diamond\psi, \mathcal{C}_2)$. ∎ 4.9

By exhaustively applying these equations, we can express $Sat(\phi)$ in terms of sets $Sat(\gamma)$ for conjunctions of literals γ.

It is easy to adapt these equations to $Sat_f(\phi)$. Instead of doing that, we shall go one step further. Since the set $Sat_f(\phi)$ can be large, and we are only interested in deciding if it equals the empty set, it suffices to compute its largest elements.

Definition 4.10 *Last sets of configurations*

Let $max\{\mathcal{C}\}$ denote the set of maximal elements of a set of configurations $\mathcal{C}$ with respect to set inclusion.
We define $Last(\phi) = max\{Sat_f(\phi)\}$.
More generally, let $\mathcal{C}_1$, $\mathcal{C}_2$ be two sets of configurations of β_f.
We define $Last(\mathcal{C}_1, \phi, \mathcal{C}_2) = max\{Sat_f(\mathcal{C}_1, \phi, \mathcal{C}_2)\}$. ∎ 4.10

Clearly, $Sat_f(\phi) = \emptyset$ if and only if $Last(\phi) = \emptyset$. Moreover, we have $Last(\phi) = Last(\emptyset, \phi, \mathcal{F})$. We obtain the following equations for $Last(\phi)$.

Theorem 4.11 *Compositional equations for $Last(\mathcal{C}_1, \phi, \mathcal{C}_2)$*

Let $\mathcal{C}_1$, $\mathcal{C}_2$ be two sets of configurations of β_f, and let ϕ, ψ be two formulas. Let $\mathcal{C} = \mu\mathcal{S}.Last(\psi) \triangledown \{E_f\}$.

$$Last(\mathcal{C}_1, \phi \wedge \Diamond\psi, \mathcal{C}_2) = Last(\mathcal{C}_1, \phi, max\{\mathcal{C}_2 \triangledown \mathcal{C}\})$$
$$Last(\mathcal{C}_1, \phi \wedge \neg\Diamond\psi, \mathcal{C}_2) = Last(max\{\mathcal{C}_1 \cup \mathcal{C}\}, \phi, \mathcal{C}_2)$$

∎ 4.11

This is the result we have been aiming for. Using these recursive equations, we can reduce the problem of deciding the emptyness of $Last(\phi)$ to the following two problems:

- Computing $\mu\mathcal{S}.\mathcal{C} \triangledown \{E_f\}$ for an arbitrary set $\mathcal{C} \subseteq \mathcal{F}$.

- Computing $Last(\mathcal{C}_1, \gamma, \mathcal{C}_2)$ for $\mathcal{C}_1, \mathcal{C}_2 \subseteq \mathcal{F}$ and a conjunction of literals γ.

Notice that, by definition of $\bigtriangledown$, the configurations of $\mu\mathcal{S}.\mathcal{C} \bigtriangledown \{E_f\}$ are subsets of E_f, and therefore contained in the finite prefix.

We give algorithms for these two problems in the following two sections. Let us first see how to compute, assuming these algorithms are available, if the formula $\square\Diamond s_2$ holds in the system of Figure 1.

The formula is equivalent to $\neg\Diamond\neg\Diamond s_2$. We check if $\Diamond\neg\Diamond s_2$ holds by deciding the emptyness of $Last(\neg\Diamond s_2)$.

First, we write $\neg\Diamond s_2$ as a disjunction of formulas in normal form. In this case, $\neg\Diamond s_2 \equiv (\mathbf{true} \wedge \neg\Diamond s_2)$, which is in normal form.

We compute $Last(\mathbf{true} \wedge \neg\Diamond s_2)$ by means of the second equation of Theorem 4.11. The first step is the computation of $Last(s_2)$.

We get

$$Last(s_2) = \{ \{e_1, e_2\}, \{e_2, e_3, e_4, e_5\} \}$$

Then, we have to compute $\mu\mathcal{S}_f.Last(s_2) \bigtriangledown \{E_f\}$. In this case, there exists one single cut-off event (e_6) and we obtain

$$\mu\mathcal{S}_f.Last(s_2) \bigtriangledown \{E_f\} = \{ \{e_1, e_2\}, \{e_2, e_3, e_4, e_5\}, \{e_2, e_3, e_4, e_7\} \} = max\{\mathcal{F}\}$$

Finally, we compute $Last(max\{\mathcal{F}\}, \mathbf{true}, \mathcal{F})$. Since $max\{\mathcal{F}\}$ is the set of the largest configurations of β_f, no configuration C of β_f satisfies $C \not\subseteq max\{\mathcal{F}\}$, and therefore we obtain $\emptyset$ as result. So $Last(\mathbf{true} \wedge \neg\Diamond s_2) = \emptyset$. Then, we have $\Sigma \not\models \Diamond\neg\Diamond s_2$ and, finally, $\Sigma \models \neg\Diamond\neg\Diamond s_2$.

5 Computing $\mu\mathcal{S}.\mathcal{C} \bigtriangledown \{E_f\}$

We start by showing how to compute the following mappings.

Definition 5.1 *Finite versions of the mappings $\mathcal{S}_e$ and $\mathcal{S}$*

Let $C \in \mathcal{F}$, and let e be a cut-off event. We define $\mathcal{S}_{fe}(C) = \mathcal{S}_e(C) \cap E_f$. Also, we define for a set of configurations $\mathcal{C}$

$$\mathcal{S}_f(\mathcal{C}) = \mathcal{C} \cup \bigcup_{e \in Off} \mathcal{S}_{fe}(C).$$

where Off denotes the set of minimal cut-off events of β_m.
Finally, we define

$$\mu.\mathcal{S}_f(\mathcal{C}) = \bigcup_{n \geq 0} \mathcal{S}_f^n(\mathcal{C})$$

∎ 5.1

Let I_e be an isomorphism between $\Uparrow e^0$ and $\Uparrow e$. When constructing the finite prefix β_f, it is easy to compute 'on the fly', for every cut-off event e, the pairs $(x, I_e(x))$ such that $I_e(x) \in E_f$. We start with the pairs (b, b') such that $b \in Cut([e^0])$, $b' \in Cut([e])$, $p_m(b) = p_m(b')$. Then, whenever we add a new node

$y' \in I_e(x)^\bullet$ to the prefix, we look for the node $y \in x^\bullet$ such that $p_m(y) = p_m(y')$, which exists and is unique. Then we add (y, y') to the set of pairs.

Using these pairs, $\mathcal{S}_{fe}(C)$ can be easily computed using the definition of $\mathcal{S}_e(C)$. We show now how to compute $\mu\mathcal{S}.\mathcal{C} \bigtriangledown \{E_f\}$.

Theorem 5.2

> For every set $\mathcal{C} \subseteq \mathcal{F}$ and every $n \geq 0$, $\mathcal{S}^n(\mathcal{C}) \bigtriangledown \{E_f\} = \mathcal{S}_f^n(\mathcal{C})$.
> In particular, $\mu\bar{\mathcal{S}}.\mathcal{C} \bigtriangledown \{E_f\} = \mu\mathcal{S}_f.\mathcal{C}$. ■ 5.2

The set $\mathcal{S}_f^n(\mathcal{C})$ can be stepwisely computed for increasing values of n.

Let C be a configuration of $\mathcal{S}_f^n(\mathcal{C}) \setminus \mathcal{S}_f^{n-1}(\mathcal{C})$ for $n > 0$. Then, C is obtained by shifting some configuration $C' \subseteq E_f$ and intersecting the result with E_f. This implies $|C| \geq |C'|$.

Since E_f is finite, we eventually reach an n such that $\mathcal{S}_f^{n+1}(\mathcal{C}) = \mathcal{S}_f^n(\mathcal{C})$. Once this point is reached, the computation can terminate, because $\mathcal{S}_f^m(\mathcal{C}) = \mathcal{S}_f^n(\mathcal{C})$ for every $m \geq n$, and therefore $\mu\mathcal{S}_f.\mathcal{C} = \mathcal{S}_f^n(\mathcal{C})$.

The size of the set $\mu\mathcal{S}_f.\mathcal{C}$ can grow quickly with the number of cut-off events; in turn, this number can be high if the system is very nondeterministic. This limits the applicability of our method to systems with an small amount of non-determinism, as is tipically the case in asynchronous circuits.

6   Computing $Last(\mathcal{C}_1, \gamma, \mathcal{C}_2)$

By the definition of $Last(\mathcal{C}_1, \gamma, \mathcal{C}_2)$, we have

$$Last(\mathcal{C}_1, \gamma, \mathcal{C}_2) = max\{ \bigcup_{C_2 \in \mathcal{C}_2} Last(\mathcal{C}_1, \gamma, \{C_2\}) \}.$$

Moreover, we have

$$C \in Last(\mathcal{C}_1, \gamma, \{C_2\}) \text{ iff } C \in Last(\emptyset, \gamma, \{C_2\}) \text{ and } C \not\leq \mathcal{C}_1.$$

$C \not\leq \mathcal{C}_1$ can be checked using the definition. So it suffices to solve the problem of computing $Last(\emptyset, \gamma, \{C_2\})$.

It is shown in [4] that the set $Last(\emptyset, \gamma, \{C_2\})$ contains at most one configuration. We show how to compute it (respectively, how to show that it does not exist) using Linear Programming. A Linear Programming problem is a set of linear inequations, or constraints, over a set of real variables, together with a linear function on the same variables called the optimization function. A feasible solution of the problem is an assignation of values to the variables which satisfies all the constraints. A feasible solution is optimal if the value of the optimization function applied to it is greater or equal than the value for any other feasible solution.

Definition 6.1 *The Linear Programming problem* $L(\gamma, C)$

Let C be a configuration of β_f and γ a conjunction of literals.
We associate to each event $e \in C$ a real variable $X(e)$. X denotes a the vector whose components are these variables.
For every condition b of $C^{\bullet}$, $^{\circ}b$ denotes the unique input event of b.
Similarly, for every condition b of $^{\bullet}C$, b° denotes the unique output event of b contained in C.
For every condition b of $Min(\beta_f) \cup C^{\bullet}$, $M(b)$ is a shortening for:

$$M(b) = \begin{cases} 1 & \text{if } b \in Min(\beta_f) \setminus {}^{\bullet}C \\ 1 - X(b^{\circ}) & \text{if } b \in Min(\beta_f) \cap {}^{\bullet}C \\ X(^{\circ}b) & \text{if } b \in C^{\bullet} \setminus {}^{\bullet}C \\ X(^{\circ}b) - X(b^{\circ}) & \text{if } b \in {}^{\bullet}C \cap C^{\bullet} \end{cases}$$

The Linear Programming problem $L(\gamma, C)$ consists of the following inequations:

(1) For every $e \in C$: $0 \leq X(e) \leq 1$.

(2) For every condition b of $^{\bullet}C \cap C^{\bullet}$: $X(^{\circ}b) \geq X(b^{\circ})$ (equivalently, $M(b) \geq 0$)

(3) For every literal s of γ, $\sum_{b \in B(s)} M(b) = 1$, where $B(s)$ is the set of conditions of $Min(\beta_f) \cup C^{\bullet}$ labelled by s.

(4) For every literal $\neg s$ of γ, $\sum_{b \in B(s)} M(b) = 0$.

and the optimization function: $\sum_{e \in C} X(e)$ ■ 6.1

By the inequations (1), the value of the optimizing function is not greater than $|C|$. It follows that if the problem has a feasible solution, then it has an optimal one.

Intuitively, the Linear Programming problem encodes in linear inequations the conditions that a vector has to satisfy in order to be the characteristic vector of a configuration satisfying γ. Also, it can be proved that the optimal solution of the problem, if it exists, is integer. Then, the group (1) ensures that the solution is in fact a characteristic vector; the group (2) that the set corresponding to the vector is left-closed, and therefore a configuration; the group (3) that the cut associated to the configuration contains some condition labelled s for every s of γ; finally, (4) ensures that this cut contains no condition labelled s for every $\neg s$ of γ.

Let us construct the system $L(s_4 \wedge \neg s_2, \{e_2, e_3, e_4, e_5\})$ for the finite prefix of Figure 3.

Group (1) $0 \leq X(e_i) \leq 1$ for $i = 2, 3, 4, 5$

Group (2) $X(e_2) \geq X(e_4)$, $X(e_3) \geq X(e_4)$, $X(e_4) \geq X(e_5)$

Group (3) $1 - X(e_3) + X(e_4) - X(e_5) = 1$

Group (4) $X(e_1) + X(e_5) = 0$

Maximize $X(e_2) + X(e_3) + X(e_4) + X(e_5)$

The optimal solution of this problem is

$$X(e_2) = 1 \quad X(e_3) = 1 \quad X(e_4) = 1 \quad X(e_5) = 0.$$

The reader can check that $\{e_2, e_3, e_4\}$ is the largest configuration contained in $\{e_2, e_3, e_4, e_5\}$ that satisfies $s_4 \wedge \neg s_2$.

Theorem 6.2

(1) If $L(\gamma, C_2)$ has no solution, then $Last(\emptyset, \phi, \{C_2\}) = \emptyset$.

(2) If $L(\gamma, C_2)$ has an optimal solution, then it is unique and it equals the characteristic vector in C_2 of the unique element of $Last(\emptyset, \phi, \{C_2\})$.

$$\blacksquare \ 6.2$$

By the polynomiality of Linear Programming, $Last(\emptyset, \gamma, \{C_2\})$ can be computed in polynomial time in the size of C_2. It is well know that the simplex algorithm has better average performance than the known polynomial algorithms, in spite of having exponential worst-case complexity. Some experiments performed by Thomas Thielke[2] using simplex indicate that the computation time is approximately $O(|C_2|^{2.7})$.

7   The Deterministic Case

We summarise in this section the results of [4] for the systems in which the finite prefix β_f has exactly one maximal configuration; they are systems in which, if two transitions are simultaneously enabled, then they are concurrent (there are no conflicts). Although this is a small subclass of Petri nets, they play an important rôle in the verification of asynchronous circuits. As pointed out in [11], the transition systems of the nets of this class are semimodular Muller-diagrams, the classical formal tool for the description of self-timed circuits. This makes the class a suitable modelling tool for these circuits.

It is shown in [4] that, in this particular case, $Last(\phi)$ has at most one element for every formula ϕ in normal form, and it can be computed solving a number of Linear Programming problems linear in the length of ϕ. This result proves that our model checker has linear complexity in the length of the formula and polynomial complexity in the size of the finite prefix.

---

[2]Personal communication.

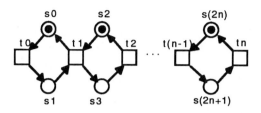

Figure 4: A simplified model of a concurrent buffer.

Conflict-free Petri nets are a class of net systems in which for every place s, $|s^\bullet| \leq 1$ or $s^\bullet \subseteq {}^\bullet s$. They have been thoroughly studied in several papers (see, for instance [6,13]).

The family of net systems shown in Figure 4 is conflict-free. They are very simple models of a concurrent buffer of length n. A token in s_{2i} means that the cell $i - 1$ is empty, while a token in s_{2i+1} means it is full. Items enter the buffer through the occurrence of t_0 and leave it through the occurrence of t_n.

Using a result of [13], it is easy to prove that the finite prefix of a 1-safe conflict-free system $\Sigma = (S, T, F, M_0)$ can be constructed in $O(|T|^2 \cdot |S|^2)$. We get as corollary that our model checker has polynomial complexity in the size of the system for this class of nets, in spite of the fact that 1-safe conflict free systems may have exponential state spaces (the family of Figure 4 has). In particular, for a buffer of length n we can check in polynomial time in n whether it is possible to reach a certain state (this is what has to be done in order to check that all cells can be simultaneously full) . However, Valmari's reduced state spaces [12] cannot be used to solve these problems in polynomial time; the reason is that for every state there is a formula which is true only of that state; therefore, no reduced state space is equivalent to the full state space for this logic. The algorithm of [5] faces a similar problem: in the worst case it has to completely generate the state space before the property can be decided, and it can be exponential. Finally, the approach of [10] is not applicable.

8 Conclusions

We have shown that it is possible to design model checkers that work on a net unfolding, a well-known partial order semantics of concurrent systems very close to event structures. A model checker of this kind has also been described in [10]; however, it uses a non-standard semantics and does not handle the whole set of properties of a logic. Our verification algorithm can check several important safety properties; reachability of a marking, coverability problems and liveness of transitions. We have shown that it is polynomial in the size of the system for a non-trivial class of systems with exponential state spaces, for which the algorithms of [5,10,12] are exponential or not applicable.

Verification algorithms for interleaving semantics usually traverse the state s-pace. In our approach there exists no explicit representation of the state space; we have used a new technique, in which we only compute some maximal states (in fact, maximal configurations) using Linear Programming.

It is pointed out in [8] that coverability problems can be solved 'on the fly' – i.e. while constructing the prefix. However, there existed so far no technique to reuse the prefix, once constructed, to solve new problems. This was annoying, because the size of the prefix can be much smaller than the computation time required to construct it. Our results solve this problem.

Acknowledgement. This paper generalises previous results obtained together with Eike Best. I am also very indebted to him for many fruitful discussions.

References

[1] E. Best and J. Esparza: Model Checking of Persistent Petri Nets. Computer Science Logic 91, LNCS 626, 35–52 (1991).

[2] E. Best and C. Fernández: Nonsequential Processes – A Petri Net View. EATCS Monographs on Theoretical Computer Science Vol. 13 (1988).

[3] J. Engelfriet: Branching processes of Petri nets. Acta Informatica Vol. 28, 575–591 (1991).

[4] J. Esparza: Model Checking Using Net Unfoldings. Hildesheimer Informatikfach-bericht 14/92 (October 1992).

[5] P. Godefroid and P. Wolper: Using Partial Orders for the Efficient Verification of Deadlock Freedom and Safety Properties. Computer Aided Verification, LNCS 575, 332–343 (1991).

[6] R. Howell and L. Rosier: On questions of fairness and temporal logic for conflict-free Petri nets. Advances in Petri Nets 1988, LNCS 340, 200–220, Springer, Berlin (1988).

[7] G.E. Hughes and M.J. Creswell: An Introduction to Modal Logic. Methuen and Co. (1968).

[8] K.L. McMillan: Using unfoldings to avoid the state explosion problem in the ver-ification of asynchronous circuits. 4th Workshop on Computer Aided Verification, Montreal, 164–174 (1992).

[9] M. Nielsen, G. Plotkin and G. Winskel: Petri Nets, Event Structures and Domains. Theor. Comp. Sci. Vol. 13, 1, pp. 85–108 (1980).

[10] D. K. Probst and H.F. Li: Partial-Order Model Checking: A Guide for the Per-plexed. Computer Aided Verification, LNCS 575, 322–332 (1991).

[11] M. Tiusanen: Some Unsolved Problems in Modelling Self-Timed Circuits Using Petri Nets. EATCS Bulletin Vol. 36, 152–160 (1988).

[12] A. Valmari: Stubborn Sets for Reduced State Space Generation. Advances in Petri Nets 1990, LNCS 483, 491–515 (1990).

[13] H. Yen: A polynomial time algorithm to decide pairwise concurrency of transitions for 1-bounded conflict-free Petri nets. Inf. Proc. Lett. 38, 71–76 (1991).

Reachability Analysis on Distributed Executions

Claire Diehl, Claude Jard, Jean–Xavier Rampon

IRISA,
Campus de Beaulieu,
F-35042 Rennes, FRANCE.
tel: (33) 99 84 71 00
(jard,rampon)@irisa.fr

Abstract. The paper presents basic algorithms for trace checking of distributed programs. In distributed systems, detecting global properties requires a careful analysis of the causal structure of the execution. Based on the on-the-fly observation of the partial order of message causality, we show how to build the lattice of all the reachable states of the distributed system under test. The regular structure of this graph makes it possible to build it with a quasi-linear complexity, which improves substantially the state-of-the-art.

1 Introduction

1.1 Problem statement

Progress in computer technology brings up parallelism and data distribution to an unavoidable level. However this is not a painless way: parallel and distributed programs are still complex objects. All the aspects of their development are not well mastered; observing their behaviors often reveals unexpected situations.

This motivates the interest of the scientific community on parallelism for distributed program debugging. Actually, we deal with verification techniques based on execution traces that we call "trace checking". For the goal of verification, the expected behavior or the suspected error of the system under test, is described by a global property (basically a global predicate on variables, or the possible occurrence orders of observable events). The problem is to verify whether this property is satisfied or not during the execution.

In the general context of asynchronous parallelism on distributed architectures that we are considering, the correct evaluation of global properties requires a careful analysis of the causal structure of the execution. The causal structure, induced by the message exchanges between processes in the distributed system, forms a partial order, as Lamport remarked in 1978. As a consequence, numerous questions about distributed executions refer to the notions of linear extensions and order ideals (also called consistent cuts). These consistent cuts define the notion of global state (snapshot) for a distributed execution. This allows to view the trace checking as a standard model checking of the set of reachable global states. Actually, one can based the testing method on a kind of reachability analysis which exactly builds the covering graph of the ideal lattice of the causality relation. In that context, testing must be performed on-the-fly, i.e. in parallel with the execution of the application under test.

1.2 Proposed approach

Trace checking rises several problems that must be solved:

- At the lowest level the runtime must provide the basic services of timestamping the communication actions. This gives information to decide causality between particular observable events. We use the classical Lamport's definition of message causality [15] and its "on the fly" coding given by Mattern and Fidge's vector clocks [9, 19]. Although all the communication events are modified at runtime, just a few significant observable events have to be traced for the goal of analysis. We slightly modify the timestamping mechanism to deal with observable events only.
- Deciding causality between events is not the most convenient way to represent the causality order. We show that in fact the covering relation (*i.e.* the transitive reduction of the order) can also be computed on the fly. For the goal of producing the immediate predecessors of an event when it occurs, we extend the vector clock with a bit array.
- Finally we show that the graph structure of the reachable states can be computed step by step at each event occurrence.

The last two algorithms are new. They allow to perform a reachability analysis in parallel with the considered computation. The time complexity is quasi-linear in the size of the state graph. Moreover, provided that observation preserves message causality, the construction is performed strictly on the fly: event by event with no additional delay. Thanks to the theory of orders which provides a good basis to deal with these problems. Trace checking is a particular case of model-checking. The reachability analysis builds the transition system associated to the considered distributed execution. Due to the lattice structure of these transition systems, reachability analysis can be performed almost linearly in time. Moreover, no doubt that existing methods to reduce the state explosion problem in standard model-checking (see [11] for example) will also apply in the near future.

1.3 Related work

Message causality is fundamental to many problems on distributed traces. Actually, it has been studied for different goals:

- determining consistent snapshots or consistent recovery points in the field of distributed debugging or distributed database management [4, 19];
- execution replay [16, 17];
- verifying logical properties in order to detect unexpected situations [7];
- getting performance measurements on global indicators [12, 5].

Most work in progress on the fundamentals of traces are based on the partial order defined by the causality relation [15]. To our knowledge, Cooper and Marzullo [7] were the first to perform a reachability analysis on the state space associated to a distributed execution. Their work however gives rise to the problem of the parallelism between the analysis process and the distributed computation. They require events to be considered level by level (the "level" is the number of predecessors). The analysis must then be blocked awaiting an event: in the worst case, where an isolated event occurs at the end of the trace, the analysis is postponed to the end of the trace. The basis of their algorithm is to enumerate all the possible nodes of the largest state space (p^n where p is the number of events per processor and n the number of processors), and then to remove nodes that are not reachable for the considered trace (by considering vector timestamps associated to the events).

We considerably improve the technique in allowing the analysis event by event: any linear extension can be processed. It can be referred as the "on the fly reachability analysis". This is made possible by actually computing on line the covering relation, rather than considering only vector stamps and makes best use of the lattice structure by a direct construction. More recently, a few algorithms have been published [10, 20, 18, 6] to detect some restricted classes of global properties. We think they could be explained and proved using the lattice structure of the state space.

2 Abstract causality order

2.1 Message causality between observable events

From an abstract point of view, a distributed program consists of n sequential processes $P_1, ..., P_n$ communicating solely by messages. The behavior of each process is completely defined by a local algorithm which determines its reaction towards incoming messages: local state changes and sending of messages to other processes. A distributed computation is the concurrent and coordinated execution of all these local algorithms. A standard way to deal with distributed computations is to consider that local actions are defined as events. Only a few of them are significant for the purpose of verification.

We will denote by $E = X \uplus \bar{X} \uplus O$ the finite set of events occurring during a computation. X contains all the sending events, $\bar{X}$ the corresponding receipts and O the internal events defined as observable by the user. We also consider that E is partitioned into disjoint subsets E_i of local events occurred on process P_i: $E = \uplus_{1 \leq i \leq n} E_i$.

Arguing from the fact that the only mean to gain knowledge for a process in a general distributed system is to receive messages from outside, one considers the receipt of a message as causally related to the corresponding sending. The causality between local events is defined by the local algorithm: a simple way is to consider the total ordering induced by the local sequentiality (denoted by $\prec_i$). The causality relation (defined by Lamport in [15]) in E^2 is the smallest relation $\prec$ satisfying:

1. $\forall i \in \{1..n\}, \forall x, y \in E_i, \ x \prec_i y \Longrightarrow x \prec y$

2. $\forall x \in X, \; x \prec \bar{x}$ ($\bar{x}$ the corresponding receipt of the sending event x)

3. $\prec$ is transitive

2.2 Definitions and preliminaries on partially ordered sets

A set P associated with a partial order relation (i.e. an antisymmetric, transitive and reflexive or irreflexive binary relation on P) is called a partially ordered set or a *poset*. If the relation is reflexive such a poset is written $\widetilde{P} = (P, \leq_{\widetilde{P}})$ else $\widetilde{P} = (P, <_{\widetilde{P}})$.

Let x and y be two elements of P:

We say that x and y are *comparable* in $\widetilde{P}$, when either $x \leq_{\widetilde{P}} y$ or $y \leq_{\widetilde{P}} x$. Otherwise, x and y are said to be *incomparable* in $\widetilde{P}$. If $x \leq_{\widetilde{P}} y$ holds, then x is a *predecessor* of y in $\widetilde{P}$ and y is a *successor* of x in $\widetilde{P}$.

We say that x is *covered* by y in $\widetilde{P}$, and we write $x -<_{\widetilde{P}} y$, if $x <_{\widetilde{P}} y$ and $\forall z \in P$, $(x <_{\widetilde{P}} z \leq_{\widetilde{P}} y) \Rightarrow (z = y)$; x is an *immediate predecessor* of y in $\widetilde{P}$ and y is an *immediate successor* of x in $\widetilde{P}$. The directed graph associated of this *covering relation* (i.e. the transitive reduction of $<_{\widetilde{P}}$) is the *covering graph* of $\widetilde{P}$ and is denoted by $Cov(\widetilde{P}) = (P, E_P)$.

Let A be a subset of P:

- $E_P(A)$ is the set of the edges corresponding to the subgraph of $Cov(\widetilde{P})$ on A.
- The *subposet* of $\widetilde{P}$ on A, $\widetilde{P}/_A = \widetilde{A} = (A, \leq_P)$ is the poset induced by $\widetilde{P}$ on A.
- For $|A| \geq 2$, if all elements of A are pairwise comparable (resp. incomparable) in $\widetilde{P}$, A is a *chain* (resp. an *antichain*) in $\widetilde{P}$. The *height* of $\widetilde{P}$, $h(P)$, is the maximum cardinality minus one of a chain in $\widetilde{P}$. The *width* of $\widetilde{P}$, $w(P)$, is the maximum cardinality of an antichain in $\widetilde{P}$. A *chain decomposition* of $\widetilde{P}$ is a partition $\{P_i\}_{i \in I}$ of P where each P_i is a chain in $\widetilde{P}$
- $Max(A, \widetilde{P}) = \{a \in A, \forall x \in A, (a \leq_{\widetilde{P}} x) \Rightarrow (a = x)\}$ is the *maximal* elements set of A in $\widetilde{P}$. Analogously, $Min(A, \widetilde{P}) = \{a \in A, \forall x \in A, (x \leq_{\widetilde{P}} a) \Rightarrow (a = x)\}$ is the *minimal* elements set of A in $\widetilde{P}$.
- $\downarrow_{\widetilde{P}}A] = \{x \in P, \exists a \in A, x \leq_{\widetilde{P}} a\}$ (resp. $\uparrow_{\widetilde{P}}A] = \{x \in P, \exists a \in A, a \leq_{\widetilde{P}} x\}$) is the *predecessor set* (resp. *successor set*) of A in $\widetilde{P}$.
- $\downarrow_{\widetilde{P}}A[= \downarrow_{\widetilde{P}}A] \setminus A$ (resp. $\uparrow_{\widetilde{P}}A[= \uparrow_{\widetilde{P}}A] \setminus A$) is the *strictly predecessor set* (resp. *strictly successor set*) of A in $\widetilde{P}$.
- $\downarrow_{\widetilde{P}}^{im}A = Max(\downarrow_{\widetilde{P}}A[, \widetilde{P})$ (resp. $\uparrow_{\widetilde{P}}^{im}A = Min(\uparrow_{\widetilde{P}}A[, \widetilde{P}))$ is the *immediate predecessor set* (resp. *immediate successor set*) of A in $\widetilde{P}$.
- If A is a singleton $\{x\}$, we shall simply write $\downarrow_{\widetilde{P}}x]$, $\uparrow_{\widetilde{P}}x]$, $\downarrow_{\widetilde{P}}x[$, $\uparrow_{\widetilde{P}}x[$, $\downarrow_{\widetilde{P}}^{im}x$ and $\uparrow_{\widetilde{P}}^{im}x$.

A *linear extension* of a poset $\widetilde{P}$ is a chain $\widetilde{C}$ on P that preserves $\widetilde{P}$, i.e.:
$x \leq_{\widetilde{P}} y \Rightarrow x \leq_{\widetilde{C}} y$.

A is an *ideal* of $\widetilde{P}$ iff it contains all its predecessors $\downarrow_{\widetilde{P}} A] = A$. $I(P)$ is the set of all ideals of $\widetilde{P}$ and $\widetilde{I(P)}$ is this set ordered by inclusion [1].

A has an *infimum* (resp. a *supremum*) in $\widetilde{P}$ if $|Max(\{x \in P, x \leq_{\widetilde{P}} y \ \forall y \in A\}, \widetilde{P})| = 1$ (resp. $|Min(\{x \in P, y \leq_{\widetilde{P}} x \ \forall y \in A\}, \widetilde{P})| = 1$).

$\widetilde{P}$ is a *lattice* iff any of its two elements subset has a supremum and an infimum in $\widetilde{P}$.

2.3 On the fly computation of causality

In order to characterize on the fly the message causality, Fidge and Mattern [9, 19] have developed a mechanism of logical clocks. Each event is stamped by a vector of $\mathbb{N}^n$ and the stamps ordering exactly codes the causality: it is an embedding of the causality order in $(\mathbb{N}^n, <_{\mathbb{N}^n})$ [2]. Formally, the timestamping is defined by the map [8]:

$$\delta : E \longrightarrow \mathbb{N}^n$$
$$e \longmapsto (| \downarrow_{\widetilde{E}} e] \cap E_i|)_{1 \leq i \leq n}$$

and we have the fundamental property:

$$\forall e, f \in E, e \prec f \iff \delta(e) <_{\mathbb{N}^n} \delta(f).$$

We modify the algorithm proposed by Fidge and Mattern to stamp only observable events. We compute the map:

$$\delta : O \longrightarrow \mathbb{N}^n$$
$$e \longmapsto (| \downarrow_{\widetilde{O}} e] \cap E_i|)_{1 \leq i \leq n}$$

which obviously codes $\widetilde{O}$. Stamps are growing slower because they count less events and, as we will see in the next section, computing the covering graph of $\widetilde{O}$ also simplifies our on the fly algorithm. The timestamping mechanism follows:

- Each processor P_i owns a logical clock $c_i \in \mathbb{N}^n$. Each c_i is initialized to $(0...0)$.
- Each message sent by P_i is stamped by the current value of c_i.
- When P_i receives a message stamped by c_m, P_i updates its clock[3]: $c_i := max(c_i, c_m)$.
- When an observable event e occurs on P_i, P_i increments the ith component of its clock: $c_i := c_i + (0..1_i..0)$ (only the ith component is incremented), and e is stamped by c_i: $\delta(e) := c_i$.

---

[1] For any I_1, I_2 in $I(P)$, $I_1 \cup I_2$ and $I_1 \cap I_2$ belong to $I(P)$. Moreover, $I_1 \cup I_2$ (resp. $I_1 \cap I_2$) is the smallest (resp. greatest) element of $I(P)$ including (resp. included in) both I_1 and I_2. Thus $\widetilde{I(P)}$ is a lattice.

[2] $<_{\mathbb{N}^n}$ is the canonical order on $\mathbb{N}^n$: $\forall x, y \in \mathbb{N}^n$, $x <_{\mathbb{N}^n} y \iff \forall i \in \{1..n\}, x[i] \leq y[i]$ and $\exists j \in \{1..n\}, x[j] < y[j]$

[3] $\forall x, y \in \mathbb{N}^n \ \forall i \in \{1..n\}, max(x, y)[i] = max(x[i], y[i])$

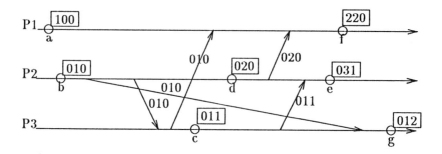

Fig. 1. Computation of message causality

The figure 1 shows an application of this algorithm. We only put the event stamps and the message stamps. This execution is used throughout the paper.

2.4 On the fly computation of the covering

We now present an algorithm based on the vector clock mechanism which computes on the fly the covering relation of the message causality order on observable events. It avoids an expensive computation stage: the computation of the covering relation from the vector stamp trace.

This new algorithm is based on the following remarks :

1. $\forall e \in O \cap E_i, \ \forall f \in O \setminus E_i, \ e \prec f \implies \delta(f)[i] = \delta(e)[i]$
   (When f occurs on P_j, the last event which P_j knows on P_i is necessary the $\delta(f)[i]^{th}$ on P_i.)
2. $\forall i \in \{1..n\}, \ \forall j \in \mathbb{N}, \ j \leq |O \cap E_i| \implies \exists! e \in O \cap E_i, \ \delta(e)[i] = j$
   ($\forall f \in O \cap E_i$, f is the $\delta(f)[i]^{th}$ observable event on P_i, hence it's unique.)

Therefore, in order to know the immediate predecessors of an event e, we only have to know both its stamp $\delta(e)$ and the processors where they occurred. Thus, in addition to δ, we have to compute the map:

$$\mu : O \longrightarrow \{\top, \bot\}^n$$
$$e \longmapsto \mu(e)$$

verifying: $\mu(e)[i] = (\downarrow^{im}_O e \cap E_i \neq \emptyset)$

Computation of μ goes with computation of logical clocks c_i. This is performed on the fly according to the following rules (see figure 2 for an example):

- Each processor P_i owns a boolean vector $m_i \in \{\top, \bot\}^n$ which indicates where the events currently covered occurred. For instance, if $m_i[j] = \top$ then an observable event currently covered by P_i has occurred on P_j. Each m_i is initialized to $(\bot..\bot)$.
- Each message sent by P_i is stamped by the current value of m_i.

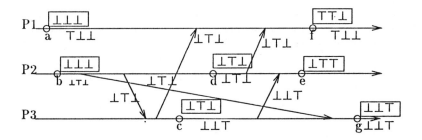

Fig. 2. On the fly computation of the covering

- When P_i receives a message stamped by $c_m \in \mathbb{N}^n$ and $m_m \in \{T, \perp\}^n$, P_i updates m_i. The new value of m_i depends on m_i, c_i, m_m and c_m.

$\forall j \in \{1..n\}$ if $c_m[j] > c_i[j]$ then $m_i[j] := m_m[j]$
else if $c_i[j] = c_m[j]$ then $m_i[j] := (m_i[j] \wedge m_m[j])$ ($\wedge$: logical and)

- When an observable event e occurs on P_i, e is stamped first ($\mu(e) := m_i$) and then P_i updates m_i: $m_i := (\perp ... T_i ... \perp)$ (only the ith component is equal to T: the only covered event is e).

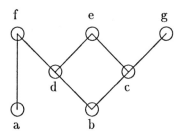

Fig. 3. The covering graph of our example

3 Associated state graph

3.1 State graph and the ideal lattice

Building the state graph associated to a distributed trace consists in "replaying" the trace, recording the changes of a global state vector. The only constraint during the replay is the causality preservation. We adopt the standard interleaving semantics for parallelism which considers only one move at a given time. The local state of a process P_i is picked up between two local events. In order to capture in the state all the messages in transit, we can identify the local state with the set of all the local events which have been already considered in the past of the process. To define the initial state, one can consider a minimal event $\emptyset$ in the past of all the observable events. The global state is the union of the local states for each process.

Notice that the causality constraint only produces global states being closed by the causality relation: the set of global states is isomorphic to the ideal lattice of the causality order. See figure 5 to have a look of the state graph of our example.

3.2 Fundamentals

Studies of correlations between poset properties and lattice properties are always of interest since the well known result of Birkhoff [1] on finite distributive lattices and posets. In the infinite case, an extension of this result and interesting properties can be found in Bonnet and Pouzet [2]. In the finite case, one of the most recent studies with an algorithmic point of view has been done by Bordat [14]. In this paper, we are only concerned by finite posets.

Since our goal is to compute on the fly the state graph of a distributed execution, we studied correlations between ideal lattices yielded by a poset and by one of its subposet when the missing vertex is a maximal one. Theorem 1 gives a complete characterization of correlations between these two lattices assuming that the initial poset has at least a maximal element.

For the proof of Theorem 1, we need the following lemma, saying that the ideals grow by adding one element at a time:

Lemma 1 *Let $\widetilde{Q}$ be a poset,*
$$\forall I, J \in I(Q), \ I \prec_{\widetilde{I(Q)}} J \Longleftrightarrow I \subset J \ and \ |J \setminus I| = 1$$

Proof: (*i*) Assume that $I \subset J$, then $I \prec_{\widetilde{I(P)}} J$. The result follows directly from the fact that $\forall Z, K \in I(P), \ Z \prec_{\widetilde{I(P)}} K \Longrightarrow Z \subset K$.

(*ii*) Assume that $I \prec_{\widetilde{I(Q)}} J$, then $I \subset J$. If $J \setminus I = \emptyset$ then $I = J$ which contradicts $I \prec_{\widetilde{I(Q)}} J$. If $|J \setminus I| \geq 2$, let $x, y \in J \setminus I$ with $x \neq y$. Without loss of generality, we can assume that $y \not<_{\widetilde{Q}} x$, then $I \prec_{\widetilde{I(Q)}} I \cup \downarrow_{\widetilde{Q}} x] \prec_{\widetilde{I(Q)}} J$ which contradicts again $I \prec_{\widetilde{I(Q)}} J$. $\square$

$J \setminus I$ is called the *label* of the edge $I \prec_{\widetilde{I(Q)}} J$.

Let $\widetilde{P}$ be a poset and x one of its maximal element. As one can see in Figure 4, $\widetilde{I(P)}$ is structured in three different parts. The upper part $IP(x)$ is formed with the ideals containing x: $IP(x) = \{I \in I(P) : I \cap \{x\} \neq \emptyset\}$. The medium part $I(x)$ is formed with the ideals containing the immediat predecessors of x and not containing x: $I(x) = \uparrow_{\widetilde{I(P)}}(\downarrow_{\widetilde{P}} x[) \setminus IP(x)$. $I(x)$ and $IP(x)$ are two isomorphic sublattices. The lower part is formed with the remaining ideals. This is formalized by Theorem 1.

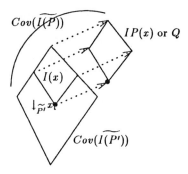

Fig. 4. Illustration of theorem 1

Theorem 1 *Let $\widetilde{P}$ be a poset, let $x \in Max(P, \widetilde{P})$, let $\widetilde{P'}$ be the subposet $P \setminus \{x\}$ and $Cov(\widetilde{I(P')}) = (I(P'), E_{I(P')})$. Let $I(x) = \uparrow_{\widetilde{I(P')}} (\downarrow_{\widetilde{P}} x[)]$. Let $G(Q) = (Q, E_Q)$ be an acyclic directed graph isomorphic to $Cov(\widetilde{I(x)})$ by a map ϕ.*
Then, the acyclic directed graph $G(Z) = (Z, E_Z)$ where $Z = Q \uplus I(P')$ and E_Z is defined by:

1. $\forall q_1, q_2 \in Q \times Q : q_1 q_2 \in E_Z \iff \phi(q_1)\phi(q_2) \in E_{I(P')}$

2. $\forall p, q \in I(P') \times Q : pq \in E_Z \iff q = \phi{-}1(p)$

3. $\forall p_1, p_2 \in I(P') \times I(P') : p_1 p_2 \in E_Z \iff p_1 p_2 \in E_{I(P')}$

is isomorphic to $Cov(\widetilde{I(P)})$ by the map φ:

$$\varphi : z \longmapsto \begin{cases} \phi(z) \cup \{x\} & \text{if } z \in Q \\ z & \text{otherwise} \end{cases}$$

Proof: Since $\widetilde{P}'$ is a subposet of $\widetilde{P}$ it is clear that $\varphi(Z) \subseteq I(P)$. For the same reason, for all $I \in I(P)$, if $x \notin I$ then $I \in I(P')$, otherwise $I \setminus \{x\} \in I(x)$ (moreover when $I_1 \neq I_2$ we have $I_1 \setminus \{x\} \neq I_2 \setminus \{x\}$). Thus $I(P) \subseteq \varphi(Z)$ and then φ is a bijection from Z to $I(P)$. It remains to show that φ is a morphism from $G(Z)$ to $Cov(\widetilde{I(P)})$.

Let us denote by $IP(x)$ the set $\{I \cup \{x\}, \ I \in I(x)\}$ (remark that $I(P) = I(P') \uplus IP(x)$). $\forall K \in IP(x)$ we have $K \not\lessdot_{\widetilde{I(P)}} I$, $\forall I \in I(P')$ (since $x \notin I$). It is then clear that the subgraph of $G(Z)$ on $I(P')$ is isomorphic by the corresponding restriction of φ to the subgraph of $Cov(\widetilde{I(P)})$ on $I(P')$.

Let ψ be a map from $I(x)$ to $IP(x)$ such that $\psi(I) = I \cup \{x\}$. Since ψ is bijective and since $\forall I, J \in I(x)$, $I \subset J \iff \psi(I) \subset \psi(J)$, the subgraphs of $Cov(\widetilde{I(P)})$ on $I(x)$ respectively on $IP(x)$ are isomorphic.

In order to conclude the proof it remains to study the edge connections between the subgraphs of $Cov(\widetilde{I(P)})$ on $I(P')$ and $IP(x)$. First we are going to show that $\forall I \in IP(x)$, $\exists! I' \in I(P')$ such that $I' \lessdot_{\widetilde{I(P)}} I$ and that $I' = I \setminus \{x\}$. By definition of $IP(x)$, $\forall I \in IP(x)$, $I \setminus \{x\} \in I(P')$ thus by Lemma 1 $I' \lessdot_{\widetilde{I(P)}} I$. For the unicity of I', assume that for $I \in IP(x)$ there exists $I_1', I_2' \in I(P')$ covered by I. Since $x \in I$ and x is neither in I_1' nor in I_2' then by Lemma 1 $I_1' = I \setminus \{x\}$ and $I_2' = I \setminus \{x\}$. Thus $I_1' = I_2'$. It remains to show that we have no other edge connections: since $\widetilde{P}'$ is a subposet of $\widetilde{P}$ it is clear that $\forall I \in I(P') \setminus I(x)$, $\exists K \in I(x)$ such that $I <_{\widetilde{I(P')}} K$ and thus $I <_{\widetilde{I(P)}} K <_{\widetilde{I(P)}} K \cup \{x\}$.

$\square$

To give an idea of the overall construction, let us take an example of poset $\widetilde{P}$, whose covering graph is given by Figure 3. We also suppose that elements are successively read in the order b, c, d, a, g, f, e which forms a linear extension of $\widetilde{P}$. For each element, we know its predecessor set.

The algorithm is illustrated in Figure 5. Black nodes denote nodes containing $\downarrow_P^{im} x$ and which will be duplicated when incorporating a new event x. Doted edges denote edges added between the duplicated subposet of $\widetilde{I(P)}$ and its corresponding copy. Assume that the first three steps have been performed. We have a lattice $\widetilde{I(P)}$ on $\{\emptyset, \{b\}, \{b,c\}, \{b,d\}, \{b,c,d\}\}$ and the new incoming vertex for $\widetilde{P}$, labeled "a", has for immediate predecessor set $D(a) = \emptyset$. Thus we have to:

1. duplicate the subposet of $\widetilde{I(P)}$ on all elements in $I(P)$ containing $D(a)$ (here the whole lattice). A new vertex "y" obtained from a vertex "x" has for label: $label(y) = (label(x) \cup \{a\}) \setminus D(a)$.

2. add a new edge xy between unconnected vertices x and y checking that y was obtained from x.

3.3   On the fly computation of the state graph

Assuming that the number of processes involved in a distributed computation is finite, using our previous theorem, we are now able to give an algorithm for an on the fly computation of a distributed execution state graph (assuming the knowledge of the covering causality relation).

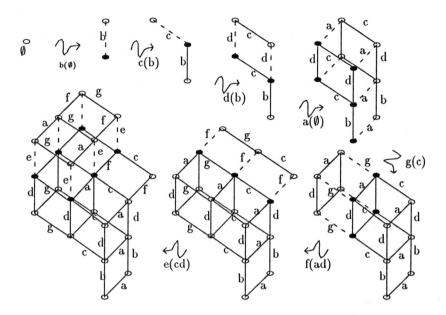

Fig. 5. On the fly computation of the state graph

Let $\widetilde{P}$ be an order, let $\{P_i\}_{1 \le i \le k}$ be a chain decomposition of $\widetilde{P}$ and let Δ be the map (which extends the vector clock coding of causality) defined by:

$$\Delta : I(P) \longrightarrow \mathbb{N}^k$$
$$I \longmapsto (\mid I \cap P_i \mid)_{1 \le i \le k}$$

This map embeds the lattice into the $(\mathbb{N}^k, \le_{\mathbb{N}^k})$ lattice.

Proposition 1 $\forall I, J \in I(P)$, the following properties are equivalent:

(i) $I \le_{\widetilde{I(P)}} J$

(ii) $\Delta(I) \le_{\mathbb{N}^k} \Delta(J)$

(iii) All maximal chains from I to J in $\widetilde{I(P)}$ have length
$lg(I, J) = \sum_{i=1}^{k}(\Delta(J)[i] - \Delta(I)[i])$. $\forall i \in \{1, \ldots, k\}$, $\Delta(J)[i] - \Delta(I)[i] \ge 0$. And there is at least one maximal chain.

Proof: Obviously $(iii) \Longrightarrow (ii)$.

$(ii) \Longrightarrow (i)$: For any ideal $A \in I(P)$ and for any $i \in \{1, \ldots, k\}$, if $|A \cap P_i| = \alpha_i \neq \emptyset$ then $A \cap P_i$ is a maximal subchain in $\widetilde{P}_i$ with α_i elements and containing the smallest element of $\widetilde{P}_i$. Thus, for any $i \in \{1, \ldots, k\}$ we have: $\Delta(I)[i] \leq_N \Delta(J)[i] \Longrightarrow I \cap P_i \subseteq J \cap P_i$. Consequently, $I = (I \cap (\bigcup_{1 \leq i \leq k} P_i)) \subseteq (J \cap (\bigcup_{1 \leq i \leq k} P_i)) = J$.

$(i) \Longrightarrow (iii)$: Since $I \leq_{\widetilde{I(P)}} J$, there exists a maximal chain from I to J in $\widetilde{I(P)}$. Let $(x_0 = I, x_1, \ldots, x_{\alpha-1}, x_\alpha = J)$ be such a chain. From Lemma 1 we have $|J| = |I| + \alpha$. Since I and J are ideals, $\forall i \in \{1, \ldots, k\}$ we have $I \cap P_i \subseteq J \cap P_i$ and then, $\forall i \in \{1, \ldots, k\}$ we have $\Delta(I)[i] \leq_N \Delta(J)[i]$ and thus $\Delta(J)[i] - \Delta(I)[i] \geq 0$. Then since $\{P_i\}_{1 \leq i \leq k}$ is a partition of P, it is clear that $lg(I, J) = \alpha$. Moreover, since $\widetilde{I(P)}$ is a distributive lattice, it is modular and thus graded. So all maximal chains have the same length. $\square$

The "granulation algorithm"

Input:

(1) The transitive reduction of $\widetilde{P}$ with a chain decomposition [4] $\{P_i\}_{1 \leq i \leq k}$.
(2) For any $y \in P$, $\delta(y) = (|\downarrow_{\widetilde{P}} y| \cap P_i|)_{1 \leq i \leq k}$ (same definition as in paragraph 2.3) and $i(y)$ such that $y \in P_{i(y)}$.
(3) A vertex $x \in Max(P, \widetilde{P})$ and the set $D(x) = \downarrow_{\widetilde{P}}^{im} x$.
(4) When $P' = P \setminus \{x\}$ and $\widetilde{P}/_{P'} = \widetilde{P'}$, $Cov(\widetilde{I(P')})$, such that:
   (a) Each $y \in P'$ is directly related to its corresponding $\downarrow_{\widetilde{P'}} y|$ in $Cov(\widetilde{I(P')})$.
   (b) Each edge yz in $Cov(\widetilde{I(P')})$ is labeled by $I_z \setminus I_y$ where I_y (resp. I_z) is the ideal of $\widetilde{P'}$ corresponding to the vertex y (resp. z) in $\widetilde{I(P')}$.
   (c) Outgoing edges of any vertices in $Cov(\widetilde{I(P')})$ are stored ordered by increasing index of the chain their label belong to.

Body:

(1) Find $\downarrow_{\widetilde{P'}} D(x)|$ in $Cov(\widetilde{I(P')})$.
(2) Build a directed graph $G(Q)$ isomorphic to $Cov(\widetilde{I(\downarrow x|)})$, by a map ϕ (where $I(\downarrow x|) = \{I \in I(P'), \downarrow_{\widetilde{P'}} D(x)| \leq_{\widetilde{I(P')}} I\}$).
(3) For any $I \in I(\downarrow x|)$, create the directed edge $(I, \phi^{-1}(I))$ with label x and store this edge according to the storage order.
(4) Create a link between x and $\phi^{-1}(\downarrow_{\widetilde{P'}} D(x)|)$.

Output:

The transitive reduction of $\widetilde{I(P')}$, such that:
   (a) Each $y \in P$ is directly related to its corresponding $\downarrow_{\widetilde{P}} y|$ in $Cov(\widetilde{I(P)})$.
   (b) Each edge yz in $Cov(\widetilde{I(P)})$ is labeled by $I_z \setminus I_y$ where I_y (resp. I_z) is the ideal of $\widetilde{P}$ corresponding to the vertex y (resp. z) in $\widetilde{I(P)}$.

---

[4] The chain decomposition on $\widetilde{P}$ is an extension of the chain decomposition on $\widetilde{P'}$, that is: $\forall i$, $i \leq i \leq k$ such that $i \neq i(x)$ we have $\{P_i\} = \{P_i'\}$ and $\{P_{i(x)}\}$ is $\{P_{i(x)}'\}$ with x added as maximal element.

(c) Outgoing edges of any vertices in $Cov(\widetilde{I(P)})$ are stored ordered by increasing index of the chain their label belong to.

Theorem 2 *The "granulation algorithm" runs in time complexity:*

$$O(((|\ I(P)\ |-|\ I(P')\ |)+|\ P'\ |)w(P')).$$

Proof: The correctness of the "granulation algorithm" is clearly achieved through Theorem 1. The time complexity analysis of the "granulation algorithm" can be perform step by step:

For step 1): Choose any y in $D(x)$, it is clear that $\Delta(\downarrow_{\widetilde{P'}} y) = \delta(y)$ and $\Delta(\downarrow_{\widetilde{P'}} D(x)) = \delta(x) - (0..1_{i(x)}..0)$. Then from proposition 1, we know there exists a chain in $Cov((\widetilde{I(P')}))$ from $\downarrow_{\widetilde{P'}} y)$ to $\downarrow_{\widetilde{P'}} D(x))$ with exactly $\Delta(\downarrow_{\widetilde{P'}} D(x))[i] - \Delta(\downarrow_{\widetilde{P'}} y)[i]$ edges belonging to $\widetilde{P_i}$. Thus starting from $\downarrow_{\widetilde{P'}} y)$, we choose an outgoing edge with label z and chain index j belonging to $Ind(y, D(x))$ where $Ind(y, D(x)) = \{i,\ \gamma(i) > 0\ with\ \gamma(i) = \Delta(\downarrow_{\widetilde{P'}} D(x))[i] - \Delta(\downarrow_{\widetilde{P'}} y)[i]\}$. Let $\gamma(j) = \gamma(j) - 1$, by induction on z we arrive in $\downarrow_{\widetilde{P'}} D(x))$ when $Ind(y, D(x)) = \emptyset$. Since the choice of such an z can be done in $O(w(P'))$, thus step 1) can be achieved in $O((|\ P'\ |)w(P'))$.

For step 2) and 3): Since the number of outgoing edges of any $I \in I(P')$ is bounded by $w(P')$, steps 2) and 3) can be achieved in $O((|\ I(P)\ | - |\ I(P')\ |)w(P'))$ (for example through a breadth first search algorithm).

Step 4 can be done in constant time during steps 2) and 3).

□

As consequence of this theorem, we are able to achieve the computation of the ideal lattice of a poset from any of its linear extensions [5].

Corollary 1 *Let $\widetilde{P}$ be a poset, $\widetilde{I(P)}$ can be computed in time complexity:*

$$O((|\ I(P)\ | + |\ P\ |^2)w(P)).$$

4 Conclusion

Trace checking for distributed programs is an important aspect of distributed debugging. The problem is complex since it requires a careful analysis of the causal structure of executions.

The use of the partial order theory is unavoidable to design efficient algorithms. As in classical verification methods for concurrent systems, the basis is a reachability analysis, *i.e* an exhaustive enumeration of the state space associated to the considered distributed execution. Furthermore, there is a need for the development of

---

[5] When $|\ I(P)\ |$ is in $\Omega(|\ P\ |^2)$, the computation of the ideal lattice of a poset from any of its linear extensions can be performed with the same time complexity than with the algorithm given by Bordat [3]. This last algorithm, which is up to our knowledge the most efficient one, is not accurate for the on the fly case (it is based on a depth first search of the all poset).

on–the–fly techniques which allows the trace analysis in parallel with its execution.

In this paper, we have presented such algorithms to build the states of a distributed execution. Obviously, for the purpose of verification, our algorithm must be coupled to a verifier which will attribute the states according to the properties that have to be checked.

Our proposal consists in two new algorithms. The first one builds the covering relation of causality between observable events: when an observable event occurs, we immediately know what are the observable events that just precede.

The second algorithm takes as input the covering relation event by event (*i.e.* any linear extension of the causality order) and gives a way to build (or search dependingly on the verification method) the state graph. This algorithm is based on theoretical results on lattices and orders. The regular structure of the graph makes it possible to build it with a quasi-linear complexity. Its on the fly characteristic and also its time complexity substantially improve the Cooper and Marzullo's contribution for detecting global predicates. The lattice seems also a good formal basis to prove specific algorithms for detecting restricted subclasses of global properties.

We have implemented our ideas in our favorite distributed environment Echidna [13]. Firstly, we have focussed our attention on visualization the covering relation and the state graph. Presently we are coupling the building of the graph to a verifier of properties expressed by automata and temporal logic formula.

Acknowledgments

Our understanding of distributed computation has been considerably enlighten by the study of the order theory. We would like to thanks those who stimulated our thoughts: B. Caillaud, B. Charron–Bost, M. Habib, F. Mattern and M. Raynal. This work has received a financial support from the french national project C^3 on concurrency, the french-israeli research cooperation and the research center of the french army (Celar).

References

1. G. Birkhoff. Rings of sets. *Duke Math J-3*, 311–316, 1937.
2. R. Bonnet and M. Pouzet. Linear extension of ordered sets. In I.Rival, editor, *Ordered Sets*, pages 125–170, D.Reidel Publishing Company, 1982.
3. J.P. Bordat. Calcul des idéaux d'un ordonné fini. *Recherche opérationnelle/Operations Research*, 25(3):265–275, 1991.
4. K. M. Chandy and L. Lamport. Distributed snapshots: determining global states of distributed systems. *ACM TOCS*, 3(1):63–75, 1985.
5. B. Charron–Bost. Combinatorics and geometry of consistent cuts: application to concurency theory. In Bermond and Raynal, editors, *Proceedings of the international workshop on distributed algorithms*, pages 45–56, Springer–Verlag, LNCS 392, France, Nice 1989.
6. B. Charron-Bost, C. Delporte, and H. Fauconnier. *Local and Temporal Predicates in Distributed Systems*. Research report 92-36, LITP - Paris 7, 1992.
7. R. Cooper and K. Marzullo. Consistent detection of global predicates. In *Proc. ACM/ONR Workshop on Parallel and Distributed Debugging*, pages 163–173, Santa Cruz, California, May 1991.
8. C. Diehl and C. Jard. Interval approximations of message causality in distributed executions. In Finkel and Jantzen, editors, *STACS*, pages 363–374, Springer–Verlag, LNCS 577, Cachan, february 1992.
9. J. Fidge. Timestamps in message passing systems that preserve the partial ordering. In *Proc. 11th Australian Computer Science Conference*, pages 55–66, february 1988.
10. Vijay K. Garg and Brian Waldecker. *Detection of Unstable Predicates in Distributed Programs*. Technical Report TR-92-07-82, University of Texas at Austin, march 1992.
11. P. Godefroid and P. Wolper. Using partial orders for the efficient verification of deadlock freedom and safety. In *Computer Aided Verification, LNCS 575*, pages 332–342, Aalborg, Denmark., 1991.
12. M. Habib, M. Morvan, and J.X. Rampon. Remarks on some concurrency measures. In *Graph–Theoretic Concepts in Computer Science*, pages 221–238, LNCS 484, june 1990.
13. C. Jard and J.-M. Jézéquel. ECHIDNA, an Estelle-compiler to prototype protocols on distributed computers. *Concurrency Practice and Experience*, 4(5):377–397, August 1992.
14. Bordat J.P. Sur l'algorithmique combinatoire d'ordres finis. Thèse de doctorat d'état, USTL Montpellier, 1992.
15. L. Lamport. Time, clocks and the ordering of events in a distributed system. *Communications of the ACM*, 21(7):558–565, July 1978.
16. T. Leblanc and J. Mellor-Crummey. Debugging parallel programs with instant replay. *IEEE Transactions on Computers*, C-36(4):471–482, April 1987.
17. E. Leu, A. Schiper, and A. Zramdini. Efficient execution replay techniques for distributed memory architectures. In Arndt Bode, editor, *Proc. of the Second European Distributed Memory Computing Conference, Munich*, pages 315–324, apr 1991.
18. Hurfin M., N. Plouzeau, and M. Raynal. *Détection de séquences atomiques de prédicats locaux dans les exécutions réparties*. Research report , IRISA, 1993.
19. F. Mattern. Virtual time and global states of distributed systems. In Cosnard, Quinton, Raynal, and Robert, editors, *Proc. Int. Workshop on Parallel and Distributed Algorithms Bonas, France, Oct. 1988*, North Holland, 1989.
20. R. Schwarz and F. Mattern. *Detecting Causal Relationships in Distributed Computations: In Search of the Holy Grail*. Technical Report 215/91, University of Kaiserslautern, 1991.

Property Preserving Abstractions under Parallel Composition[*]

Susanne Graf and Claire Loiseaux

IMAG, BP 53X, F-38041 Grenoble
e-mail : {graf,loiseaux}@imag.fr

Abstract. We study property preserving transformations for reactive systems. A key idea is the use of ϱ-simulations which are simulations parametrized by a relation ϱ, relating the domains of two systems. We particularly address the problem of property preserving abstractions of composed programs. For a very general notion of parallel composition, we give the conditions under which simulation is a precongruence for parallel composition and we study which kind of global properties are preserved by these abstractions.

1 Introduction

The investigation of property preserving abstractions of reactive systems has been the object of intensive research during the last years. However, the existing theoretical results are very fragmented. They strongly depend on the choice of the specification formalism and the underlying semantics.

Some results are given in the framework of linear time semantics as e.g., in [AL88,LT88b,Kur89] where the underlying semantics of as well programs as properties are languages traces. The notions of abstractions proposed are based on the use of structure homomorphisms.

In the framework of process algebras, the problem of combination of abstraction and composition is the problem of defining property preserving equivalence relations or preorders which are congruences, respectively precongruences for parallel composition and abstraction. This problem has been studied, for equivalences e.g., in [HM85,BK85,GS86,GW89,GS90b] and for preorders in [LT88a,Wal88,CS90,SG90,GL91].

The results presented here are based on those given in [BBLS92], where a general framework for property preserving abstractions is given. Program models are transition relations and abstractions are given by ϱ-simulations, which are parameterized by a relation ϱ between the domains of both systems. Thus, we do not restrict ourselves to abstractions defined by functions from the concrete to the abstract domain as cf. in [Kur89,CGL92].

In [BBLS92] the problem of compositional abstractions is not taken up at all. Here, we extend the results on property preservation to composed abstract programs, obtained by alternating steps of abstraction and composition. For a

---

[*] This work was partially supported by ESPRIT Basic Research Actions "SPEC" and "REACT"

general notion of parallel composition (expressed on program models), we give conditions under which composition of abstract programs preserves properties of fragments of branching-time μ-calculus.

Our program models are transition relations on some domain D and are represented symbolically. The validity of the given results does not depend on the symbolic representation, but their usability (computation of abstract programs) does. Program models may be composed by means of three composition operators, namely a synchronous, an asynchronous and a mixed one. With these three operators we can express most of the existing composition operators, for instance those of CSP [Hoa85], Lotos [ISO89], Unity [CM88], of S/R-models [KK86] and of I/O automata [LT88b].

The results presented in the paper are the following: for programs R_i and R_i', abstraction relations ϱ_i from the domains of R_i to the domains of R_i', we give conditions under which:

1. R_i ϱ_i-simulates R_i' implies $R_1 \odot R_2$ $(\varrho_1 \cap \varrho_2)$-simulates $R_1' \odot R_2'$ where $\odot$ is one of the three parallel operators.

   This result allows us, using the results of [BBLS92], to deduce that for any property f of the fragment $\Box L_\mu$ of the μ-calculus (defined in Section 5) such that all atomic predicates of f are preserved by ϱ (see Definition 14), then $R_1' \odot R_2$ satisfies f implies $R_1 \odot R_2$ satisfies f.

2. If $(R_i)_{\varrho_i}$ are reasonable ϱ_i-abstractions of R_i then, $(R_1)_{\varrho_1} \odot (R_2)_{\varrho_2}$ is a reasonable $(\varrho_1 \cap \varrho_2)$-abstraction of $R_1 \odot R_2$,

   where R_ϱ stands for the abstract program computed from R by means of the abstraction relation ϱ.

The conditions depend on the considered parallel operator $\odot$; but for all parallel operators studied here, it is not necessary that the processes are defined on independent domains. However, in order to have (2) for the asynchronous and also for the mixed parallel operator, the abstraction $\varrho_1 \cap \varrho_2$ must be decomposable so as the relation on the common domain is independent of the relations on the domains proper to each of the processes.

The paper is organized as follows. In the following section, we define the parallel operators. In Section 3, we present the results concerning composition and abstraction, which are illustrated by a small example in Section 4. In Section 5, we study which kind of properties are preserved by the abstractions defined in Section 3 and we illustrate these results in Section 6.

2 Parallel Composition and Abstraction Operators

First, we introduce some definitions and notations concerning intersections and unions of sets on different underlying domains.

Domains are as usual sets of valuations of program variables. We suppose a universal set of global program variables $\mathcal{V}$. Any domain is the set of valuations of some subset of program variables $V \subseteq \mathcal{V}$, denoted D_V. Thus, e.g., for $V = \{x, y\}$, $D_V = D_x \times D_y$.

Definition 1. concerning independency of domains and projection functions.

- For any V, W the domains D_V and D_W are called *independent* iff $V \cap W = \emptyset$, that means they are defined on separate variable sets.
- For any V, W, we denote by $\mathcal{R}(D_V, D_W)$, the set of binary relations from D_V to D_W. If $D_V = D_W$, we write $\mathcal{R}(D_V)$.
- For V, W such that $V \subseteq W$, we denote by π_V the projection function in $\mathcal{R}(D_W, D_V)$.

Now we can define intersections and unions of sets on different domains D_V and D_W as operators on $D_{V \cup W}$.

Definition 2. Let $D_V, D_{V_i}, D_W, D_{W_i}, i = 1, 2$ be domains, $X \subseteq D_V, Y \subseteq D_W$. Then we define,

- $X \cap Y = \{z \in D_{V \cup W} \mid \pi_V(z) \in X \wedge \pi_W(z) \in Y \}$
- $X \cup Y = \{z \in D_{V \cup W} \mid \pi_V(z) \in X \vee \pi_W(z) \in Y \}$

Consider binary relations $R_i \in \mathcal{R}(D_{V_i}, D_{W_i})$. Then, we define relations $R_1 \cap R_2 \in \mathcal{R}(D_{V_1 \cup V_2}, D_{W_1 \cup W_2})$ and $R_1 \times R_2 \in \mathcal{R}(D_{V_1} \times D_{V_2}, D_{W_1} \times D_{W_2})$, by

- $R_1 \cap R_2 = \{(z, z') \mid z \in D_{V_1 \cup V_2} \wedge z' \in D_{W_1 \cup W_2} \wedge (\pi_{V_1}(z), \pi_{W_1}(z')) \in R_1$
  $\wedge (\pi_{V_2}(z), \pi_{W_2}(z')) \in R_2 \}$
- $R_1 \times R_2 = \{(z, z') \mid z \in R_1 \wedge z' \in R_2\}$

We suppose that programs are represented by binary relations (transition relations) on some domain. This is a very general form of programs. We do not consider initial states since they are not necessary to obtain the results and it makes the representation of programs much simpler. In terms of TLA [Lam91], we consider programs consisting only of the invariant part.

Definition 3. Let be domains D_V, D_W and programs given by transition relations $R_1 \in \mathcal{R}(D_V)$ and $R_2 \in \mathcal{R}(D_W)$. Then, we define the transition relations of the composed processes in $\mathcal{R}(D_{V \cup W})$ by

- asynchronous composition :
  $R_1 \| R_2 = R_1 \times Id_{D_{W-V}} \cup Id_{D_{V-W}} \times R_2$
  where for any domain D, Id_D is the identity function on D.

- synchronous composition :
  $R_1 \otimes R_2 = R_1 \cap R_2$

- mixed composition :
  Consider transition relations R_i of the form $R_1 = \bigcup_{i \in I} R_{1i}$ and $R_2 = \bigcup_{j \in J} R_{2j}$. Let be $A \subseteq I \times J$, indicating which commands have to be executed synchronously, $A_1 = \{i \mid \exists j.(i, j) \in A\}$ and $A_2 = \{j \mid \exists i.(i, j) \in A\}$.

  $R_1 [A] R_2 = \bigcup_{(i,j) \in A} (R_{1i} \cap R_{2j}) \cup \bigcup_{i \in A_1} (R_{1i} \times Id_{D_{W-V}}) \cup \bigcup_{j \in A_2} (Id_{D_{V-W}} \times R_{2j})$

Comments :

- In the asynchronous composition, in each step one of the programs executes one of the currently enabled transitions and the other idle. This operator results in the "interleaving" of the component processes if they are defined on independent domains; if not, the execution of a transition of one of the processes may change the enabling conditions of the other one. This operator is exactly the union operator of Unity [CM88].

- In synchronous composition, in each step both programs execute exactly one action possible in this state, such that the changes on the common variables are consistent. This operator corresponds exactly to $\wedge$ applied on programs described by TLA formulas; it is also very similar to program composition of S/R models [KK86].
  If the domains of the component processes are independent, this operator is exactly the one introduced in [GL91]; since they use also the same preorder, their results are comparable to ours in the sense that they consider a logic, subset of ours, and the particular case of independent domains.
- Finally, in the mixed composition operator, some of the actions must be executed synchronously, whereas the others are executed asynchronously. This operator is not exactly the one in CSP [Hoa85] or LOTOS [ISO89], where all processes have distinct variable sets and communicate by exchanging values; however the here defined operator allows to simulate these operators. The results stated here are valid for any operator which can be considered as a special case of the here defined operator.

The first two operators need imperatively models with shared memory between processes in order to allow communication, whereas the third one allows also communication based only on action names without shared memory. Nevertheless, in practice, processes composed by the third operator share often at least some variables which are written by one of them and read by the other (this allows to simulate the Lotos operator $[\![\,]\!]$).

The mixed composition operator is the most general one as it allows to express the other ones as follows: $\|$ is equal to $[\![\emptyset]\!]$ and $\otimes$ is equal to $[\![I \times J]\!]$. We prefer however to keep these operators because they are interesting to be considered as subcases.

Lemma 4. Let $R_1 = \bigcup_{i \in I} R_{1i}$, and $R_2 = \bigcup_{j \in J} R_{2j}$, be transition relations and $A \subseteq I \times J$ as in Definition 3. Then,

- $R_1 \| R_2 = \bigcup_{i \in I}(R_{1i} \times \mathrm{Id}_{D_W - V}) \cup \bigcup_{i \in J}(\mathrm{Id}_{D_V - W} \times R_{2j})$
- $R_1 \otimes R_2 = \bigcup_{(i,j) \in I \times J}(R_{1i} \wedge R_{2j})$
- $R_1 [\![A]\!] R_2 = (\|_{(i,j) \in A} (R_{1i} \otimes R_{2j})) \| (\|_{i \notin A_1} R_{1i}) \| (\|_{j \notin A_2} R_{2j})$
  where we use the obvious n-ary extension of $\|$.
- $R_1 \| R_2 = R_1 [\![\emptyset]\!] R_2$
- $R_1 \otimes R_2 = R_1 [\![I \times J]\!] R_2$

The definition of ϱ-simulation is the same as in [BBLS92] and defines our notion of preorder on programs. First, we need to introduce the "predicate transformers" pre and $\tilde{pre}$.

Definition 5. Given a relation $\varrho \in \mathcal{R}(D, D')$, we define the functions $pre[\varrho], \tilde{pre}[\varrho] \in [2^{D'} \to 2^D]$ by,

- $\forall X \subseteq D' \,.\, pre[\varrho](X) = \{x \in D \mid \exists x' \in X \,.\, \varrho(x, x')\}$ defines the inverse image of X by ϱ.
- $\tilde{pre}[\varrho]$ is the dual of $pre[\varrho]$, i.e.,
  $\forall X \subseteq D' \,.\, \tilde{pre}[\varrho](X) = \overline{pre[\varrho](\overline{X})} = \{x \in D \mid \forall x' \in D' \,.\, \varrho(x, x') \Rightarrow x' \in X\}$

Definition 6. Let $R \in \mathcal{R}(D)$ and $R_a \in \mathcal{R}(D_a)$ be transition relations, and let ϱ be an abstraction relation in $\mathcal{R}(D, D_a)$. Then

$$R \; \varrho\text{-simulates } R_a \quad \text{iff} \quad pre[\varrho^{-1}] \circ pre[R] \circ \tilde{pre}[\varrho] \subseteq pre[R_a]$$

Notice that "there exists ϱ such that ϱ-simulates" defines a preorder on programs which is the same as the one defined in [GL91], and which is also the standard simulation preorder [Mil71]. If there exists ϱ such that R ϱ-simulates R_a, we say also that R simulates R_a or R_a is an abstraction of R.

Definition 7. Let be given a program by a transition relation $R = \bigcup_i R_i \in \mathcal{R}(D)$. For any abstraction relation $\varrho \in \mathcal{R}(D, D_a)$ we define an operator $_\varrho$ yielding an abstract program $R_\varrho \in \mathcal{R}(D_a)$, defined by the transition relation,

$$R_\varrho = \varrho^{-1} \circ R \circ \varrho = \bigcup_i \varrho^{-1} \circ R_i \circ \varrho$$

The following property justifies our motivation for computing abstract programs R_ϱ from R and ϱ: for a given abstraction relation ϱ we want to compute an abstract program R_ϱ with a reasonable cost and reasonably close to R, such that a maximum of properties that are satisfied on R are also satisfied on R_ϱ. In general the least abstract program R_a such that R ϱ-simulates R_a does not exist (since $pre[\varrho^{-1}] \circ pre[R] \circ \tilde{pre}[\varrho]$ does not necessarily distribute over $\cup$ and it is therefore not of the form $pre[R_a]$ for some relation R_a).
However, R_ϱ is **reasonable** in the sense that for any transition relation R_a, such that
R ϱ-simulates R_a and $R_a \subseteq R_\varrho$ and for any property f of the μ-calculus such that R satisfies f, we have R_a satisfies f iff R_ϱ satisfies f. This is expressed by the following proposition:

Proposition 8.

$$\frac{\exists R_a.\ R \leq_\varrho R_a,\ R_a \subseteq R_\varrho}{\forall f \in \square L_\mu,\ R_a \models_I f \iff R_\varrho \models_{I_A} f}$$

where I and $I_A = post[\varrho] \circ I$ are the interpretation functions on the concrete and abstract domains respectively.

Proof. given in the full paper.

Proposition 9. Let R be a transition relation on D, $\varrho \in \mathcal{R}(D, D_a)$ an abstraction relation total on D (i.e. $\tilde{pre}[\varrho] \subseteq pre[\varrho]$). Then

- R ϱ-simulates the abstract transition relation R_ϱ which defines a reasonable abstraction of R with respect to ϱ.
- If even $\tilde{pre}[\varrho] = pre[\varrho]$, i.e., ϱ is a total function from D into D_a, R_ϱ defines the least abstraction of R with respect to ϱ.

3 Abstraction of Composed Programs

When dealing with complex programs, it is interesting to construct abstractions as far as possible before composition. This allows to compute abstractions on smaller transition relations (and domains), and to compute the composition on the so obtained smaller abstract programs. Here we show in which cases one obtains an abstraction of the original composed program by proceeding this way, and furthermore, in which cases this can be done without losing too much with respect to the abstraction obtained proceeding the other way round.

We give conditions under which simulation is monotonic with respect to the different composition operators $\odot$, i.e.,

$$\frac{(R_1 \text{ simulates } R_1')\ \text{ and }\ (R_2 \text{ simulates } R_2')}{R_1 \odot R_2 \text{ simulates } R_1' \odot R_2'}$$

holds. We show also which kind of atomic predicates of the composed program are preserved.

Let $R_1 \in \mathcal{R}(D_V)$ and $R_2 \in \mathcal{R}(D_W)$ be transition relations and $\varrho_1 \in \mathcal{R}(D_V, D_{V_a})$, $\varrho_2 \in \mathcal{R}(D_W, D_{W_a})$ abstraction relations. For any composition operator $\odot$ of Definition 3 we have to find an abstraction relation $\varrho \in \mathcal{R}(D_{V \cup W}, D_{V_a \cup W_a})$ allowing to compute $(R_1)_{\varrho_1} \odot (R_2)_{\varrho_2}$ instead of $(R_1 \odot R_2)_\varrho$, i.e. such that $(R_1)_{\varrho_1} \odot (R_2)_{\varrho_2}$ is reasonably close to $(R_1 \odot R_2)_\varrho$.

We show that for all operators of Definition 3, R_i ϱ_i-simulates R'_i implies $R_1 \odot R_2$ $(\varrho_1 \cap \varrho_2)$-simulates $R'_1 \odot R'_2$ under some conditions on the abstraction relations ϱ_i.

Proposition 10. *Let be given transition relations $R_i \in \mathcal{R}(D_{V_i})$, $R'_i \in \mathcal{R}(D_{V_{ia}})$ and abstraction relations $\varrho_i \in \mathcal{R}(D_{V_i}, D_{V_{ia}})$ total on D_{V_i}, such that $\varrho_1 \cap \varrho_2$ is total on $D_{V_1 \cup V_2}$. Then,*

$$R_i \ \varrho\text{-simulates} \ R'_i, \ i = 1, 2 \quad \text{implies} \quad R_1 \otimes R_2 \ (\varrho_1 \cap \varrho_2)\text{-simulates} \ R'_1 \otimes R'_2$$

Proof. given in the full paper.

We are interested in the particular case that $R_1 \otimes R_2$ $(\varrho_1 \cap \varrho_2)$-simulates $R_{1_{\varrho_1}} \otimes R_{2_{\varrho_2}}$ and furthermore $R_{1_{\varrho_1}} \otimes R_{2_{\varrho_2}}$ is an abstraction reasonably close to $(R_1 \otimes R_2)_{\varrho_1 \cap \varrho_2}$.
It turns out that if the values in $D_{V_{1a} \cap V_{2a}}$ in ϱ_1 and in ϱ_2 depend only on $D_{V_1 \cap V_2}$ and if the projection of $\varrho_1 \cap \varrho_2$ on $\mathcal{R}(D_{V_1 \cap V_2}, D_{V_{1a} \cap V_{2a}})$ is a *function*, we have,

$$R_{1_{\varrho_1}} \otimes R_{2_{\varrho_2}} = (R_1 \otimes R_2)_{\varrho_1 \cap \varrho_2}$$

and it is certainly less expensive to compute $R_{1_{\varrho_1}} \otimes R_{2_{\varrho_2}}$ than $(R_1 \otimes R_2)_{\varrho_1 \cap \varrho_2}$.

Proposition 11. *Let be given programs by transition relations $R_i \in \mathcal{R}(D_{V_i})$, and $R'_i \in \mathcal{R}(D_{V_{ia}})$. Let be $W_1 = V_1 - V_2, W = V_1 \cap V_2, W_2 = V_2 - V_1$ and $W_{1a} = V_{1a} - V_{2a}, W_a = V_{1a} \cap V_{2a}, W_{2a} = V_{2a} - V_{1a}$. Let $\varrho_i \in \mathcal{R}(D_{V_i}, D_{V_{ia}})$ be abstraction relations, such that $\varrho_1 \cap \varrho_2$ total on $D_{V_1 \cup V_2}$, and such that ϱ_i can be put into the form $\varrho_i = \varrho_{i1} \cap \varrho_{i2}$, where $\varrho_{i1} \in \mathcal{R}(D_{W_i}, D_{W_{ia}})$ and $\varrho_{i2} \in \mathcal{R}(D_{V_i}, D_{W_a})$. Then,*

$$R_i \ \varrho\text{-simulates} \ R'_i, \ i = 1, 2 \quad \text{implies} \quad R_1 \parallel R_2 \ (\varrho_1 \cap \varrho_2)\text{-simulates} \ R'_1 \parallel R'_2$$

Proof. given in the full paper.

Remains to see in which cases $R_{1_{\varrho_1}} \parallel R_{2_{\varrho_2}}$ is a reasonable abstraction of $R_1 \parallel R_2$. It is easy to see that in general $R_{1_{\varrho_1}} \parallel R_{2_{\varrho_2}}$ and $(R_1 \parallel R_2)_{\varrho_1 \cap \varrho_2}$ are not comparable, but both reasonable abstractions.
In the case that $\varrho_1 \cap \varrho_2$ can be put into the form $\varrho_{11} \times \varrho \times \varrho_{21}$ such that $\varrho \in \mathcal{R}(D_W, D_{W_a})$ and $\varrho_{i1} \in \mathcal{R}(D_{W_i}, D_{W_{ai}})$ are functions, $R_{1_{\varrho_1}} \parallel R_{2_{\varrho_2}}$ and $(R_1 \parallel R_2)_{\varrho_1 \cap \varrho_2}$ coincide. If ϱ_{i1} are not functions, we have even $R_{1_{\varrho_1}} \parallel R_{2_{\varrho_2}} \subseteq (R_1 \parallel R_2)_{\varrho_1 \cap \varrho_2}$.

Proposition 12. *Let be given programs by transition relations $R_i = \bigcup_{I_i} R_{ij} \in \mathcal{R}(D_{V_i})$ and*
$R_i' = \bigcup_{I_i} R_{ij}' \in \mathcal{R}(D_{V_{ia}})$. *Let be $W_1 = V_1 - V_2, W = V_1 \cap V_2, W_2 = V_2 - V_1$*
and $W_{1a} = V_{1a} - V_{2a}, W_a = V_{1a} \cap V_{2a}, W_{2a} = V_{2a} - V_{1a}$. Let $\varrho_i \in \mathcal{R}(D_{V_i}, D_{V_{ia}})$
be abstraction relations, such that $\varrho_1 \cap \varrho_2$ total on $D_{V_1 \cup V_2}$, and such that ϱ_i
can be put into the form $\varrho_i = \varrho_{i1} \times \varrho_{i2}$, where $\varrho_{i1} \in \mathcal{R}(D_{W_i}, D_{W_{ia}})$ and $\varrho_{i2} \in$
$\mathcal{R}(D_W, D_{W_a})$. *Let be furthermore $A \subseteq I_1 \times I_2$ a synchronization set. Then,*

$$R_1 \llbracket A \rrbracket R_2 \ (\varrho_1 \cap \varrho_2)\text{-simulates } R_{1\varrho_1} \llbracket A \rrbracket R_{2\varrho_2}.$$

Proof. The fact that $R_1 \llbracket\ \rrbracket R_2$ can be expressed by using only $\otimes$ and $\parallel$ as given in Lemma 4 and that the condition of both of the preceding Propositions are satisfied is enough to prove the Proposition.

Proposition 13. *Let $R_1 \in \mathcal{R}(D_{V_1}), R_2 \in \mathcal{R}(D_{V_2})$ be transition relations.*

1. $R_1 \otimes R_2$ *ϱ-simulates R_1 for some ϱ such that*

$$\forall X \subseteq D_{V_1}. \ pre[\varrho](pre[\varrho^{-1}](X)) = X$$

2. R_1 *ϱ-simulates $R_1 \parallel R_2$ for some ϱ such that*

$$\forall X \subseteq D_{V_1}. \ pre[\varrho](pre[\varrho^{-1}](X)) = X$$

Proof. Let be $W = V_1 \cup V_2$. The required abstraction relations are

- $\varrho_1 = \{(d, d') \mid d \in D_W \wedge d' \in D_{V_1} \wedge \pi_{V_1}(d) = d'\} \in \mathcal{R}(D_W, D_{V_1})$ in case (1)
- $\varrho_2 = \{(d', d) \mid d' \in D_{V_1} \wedge d \in D_W \wedge \pi_{V_1}(d) = d'\} \in \mathcal{R}(D_{V_1}, D_W)$ in case (2)

Notice that ϱ_1 is a function but ϱ_2 is not.

By using the results given in [BBLS92], Proposition 13 allows to deduce that formulas of $\Box L_\mu$ (cf. Section 5) are preserved from an asynchronous product to its components, and from each component process to the synchronous product.

Now, we obtain from the preceding Propositions and the fact that $R \odot R = R$ for any transition relation and any parallel operator, the results of [GL91] as a particular case for the operator $\otimes$.

4 Example

In this section we illustrate the Propositions 11 and 12 with an example of a mobile moving on a grid.

The motion of a mobile on a grid is controlled by a controller so as to visit cyclically the points $CDACDA....$ Initially the mobile is within the rectangle defined by the points (A, B, C, D) (see figure 1). Its motion results of two independent motors.

The motor M_X makes the mobile move horizontally and M_Y vertically, the controller *Ctrl* gives orders to both motors. We describe processes with a set of guarded commands of the following form:

(*label*) *guard* → *command*

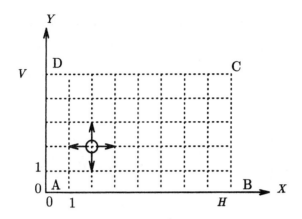

Fig. 1. Mobile

where the *label* identifies the guarded command and can be used for synchronization, the *guard* is a boolean condition which authorizes or not the execution of the *command*.

The motor M_X is defined on the variables:
- dir_X: a three-valued variable denoting the movement direction (Left, Right or Stop);
- X: a real number which denotes the position of the mobile on the horizontal axe.
- δ_X is a random input and is a positive real number.

Its transition relation is given by:

M_X: (right) $(dir_X = R) \wedge (X + \delta_X \leq H) \rightarrow X := X + \delta_X$
(left) $(dir_X = L) \wedge (X - \delta_X \geq 0) \rightarrow X := X - \delta_X$
(A) true $\rightarrow dir_X := R$
(C) true $\rightarrow dir_X := L$
(D) true $\rightarrow dir_X := S$

The motor M_Y is defined analogously.

M_Y: (up) $(dir_Y = U) \wedge (Y + \delta_Y \leq V) \rightarrow Y := Y + \delta_Y$
(down) $(dir_Y = D) \wedge (Y - \delta_Y \geq 0) \rightarrow Y := Y - \delta_Y$
(A) true $\rightarrow dir_Y := U$
(C) true $\rightarrow dir_Y := S$
(D) true $\rightarrow dir_Y := D$

The controller is defined on four variables:
- X, Y denote the current position of the mobile,
- X_C, Y_C are the coordinates of the previous visited control point.

$Ctrl$: (A) $(X_C = 0) \wedge (Y_C = V) \wedge (Y = 0) \rightarrow Y_C := 0$
(C) $(X_C = 0) \wedge (Y_C = 0) \wedge (X = H) \wedge (Y = V) \rightarrow X_C := H \wedge Y_C := V$
(D) $(X_C = H) \wedge (Y_C = V) \wedge (X = 0) \rightarrow X_C := 0$

The whole program is defined by $(M_X \parallel M_Y) \ |[(A, A), (C, C), (D, D)]| \ Ctrl$.

This system has an infinite number of states as the mobile can be in any position within the rectangle defined by the points A, B, C and D.

In order to verify that the mobile visits cyclically the points A, C and D, if it is correctly initialized, the only information we need is whether each coordinate X (respectively Y) is equal to 0, is between 0 an H (respectively V) or is equal to H (respectively V).

We propose the following abstraction relations consisting in replacing the co-ordinates X and Y by three-valued variables $x \in \{h_0, h_1, h_2\}$ and $y \in \{v_0, v_1, v_2\}$ and replacing in the controller the coordinates of the control point X_C and Y_C by a three-valued variable $Pcp \in \{A, C, D\}$ recording the previous visited control point.

ϱ_X: $(dir_X, X)\varrho_X(dir_X, x)$ iff
$\quad (x = h_0 \wedge X = 0) \vee (x = h_1 \wedge 0 < X < H) \vee (x = h_2 \wedge X = H)$
ϱ_Y: $(dir_Y, Y)\varrho_Y(dir_Y, y)$ iff
$\quad (y = v_0 \wedge Y = 0) \vee (y = v_1 \wedge 0 < Y < V) \vee (y = v_2 \wedge Y = V)$

ϱ_{Ctrl}: $(X_C, Y_C, X, Y)\varrho_{Ctrl}(Pcp, x, y)$ iff
$\quad [(x = h_0 \wedge X = 0) \vee (x = h_1 \wedge 0 < X < H) \vee (x = h_2 \wedge X = H)] \wedge$
$\quad [(y = v_0 \wedge Y = 0) \vee (y = v_1 \wedge 0 < Y < V) \vee (y = v_2 \wedge Y = V)] \wedge$
$\quad [(Pcp = A \wedge X_C = 0 \wedge Y_C = 0) \vee (Pcp = C \wedge X_C = H \wedge Y_C = V) \vee$
$\quad (Pcp = D \wedge X_C = 0 \wedge Y_C = V)]$

Note that the domains of M_X and M_Y are independent and so are the respective abstractions. We compute the following abstractions for the motors and the controller:

$(M_X)_{\varrho_X}$: (right) $(dir_X = R) \wedge (x = h_0) \rightarrow x := h_1$
$\quad\quad\quad$ (right) $(dir_X = R) \wedge (x = h_1) \rightarrow x := h_1$ or $x := h_2$
$\quad\quad\quad$ (left) $(dir_X = L) \wedge (x = h_2) \rightarrow x := h_1$
$\quad\quad\quad$ (left) $(dir_X = L) \wedge (x = h_1) \rightarrow x := h_0$ or $x := h_1$
$\quad\quad\quad$ (A) $\quad$ true $\quad\quad\quad\quad\quad\quad\quad \rightarrow dir_X := R$
$\quad\quad\quad$ (C) $\quad$ true $\quad\quad\quad\quad\quad\quad\quad \rightarrow dir_X := L$
$\quad\quad\quad$ (D) $\quad$ true $\quad\quad\quad\quad\quad\quad\quad \rightarrow dir_X := S$

We obtain an analogous abstract program for M_Y.

$(Ctrl)_{\varrho_{Ctrl}}$: (A) $(Pcp = D) \wedge (y_0 = v_0) \quad\quad\quad \rightarrow Pcp := A$
$\quad\quad\quad$ (C) $(Pcp = A) \wedge (x = h_2) \wedge (y = v_2) \rightarrow Pcp := C$
$\quad\quad\quad$ (D) $(Pcp = C) \wedge (x_0 = h_0) \quad\quad\quad \rightarrow Pcp := D$

From Propositions 11 and 12 and the fact that $\varrho_X \cap \varrho_Y \cap \varrho_{Ctrl} = \varrho_{Ctrl}$ we have that

P_A: $((M_X)_{\varrho_X} \parallel (M_Y)_{\varrho_Y}) \ |[(A, A), (C, C), (D, D)]| \ Ctrl_{\varrho_{Ctrl}}$ is an ϱ_{Ctrl}-abstraction of P.

5 Preservation of Properties

It is interesting to characterize the "global" properties preserved by the abstraction relation $\varrho_1 \cap \varrho_2$ on the compositions of abstract programs defined previously.

From the results given in [BBLS92] we have the following result on preservation of properties of $\Box L_\mu$, which is the fragment of the μ-calculus of [Koz83], consisting of the formulas without occurrences of negations and using only universal quantification on paths. $\Box L_\mu$ is strictly more expressive than linear time μ-calculus, and therefore contains all regular safety properties.

For a transition relation R, the meaning of formulas are subsets of the domain D of R, where the meaning of atomic predicates in $\mathcal{P}$ is given by an interpretation function $I : \mathcal{P} \rightarrow 2^D$.
We say R satisfies f or $R \models_I f$ if the meaning of f depending on the transition relation R and interpretation function I is equal to D.

In order to verify a property f of $\Box L_\mu$ on a program R on D with interpretation functions of atomic predicates $I : \mathcal{P} \rightarrow 2^D$ respectively $I_a : \mathcal{P} \rightarrow 2^{D_a}$, we can proceed as follows: find an abstraction relation ϱ and then,

(1) Verify $R_\varrho \models_{pre[\varrho^{-1}]\circ I} f$
or
(2) Verify $R_\varrho \models_{I_a} f$.

We know from [BBLS92] that in case (1), we have $R_\varrho \models_{pre[\varrho^{-1}]\circ I} f$ implies

$$R \models_{pre[\varrho]\circ pre[\varrho^{-1}]\circ I} f.$$

Thus, in order to obtain the initially required result, $R \models_I f$ we need for any predicate symbol p occurring in f

$$I(p) \subseteq pre[\varrho] \circ pre[\varrho^{-1}] \circ I \ (p) \quad (*)$$

As the opposite inclusion is always true, (*) equivalent to

$$pre[\varrho] \circ pre[\varrho^{-1}] \circ I \ (p) = I(p).$$

Analogously, in case (2) $R_\varrho \models_{I_a} f$ implies $R \models_{pre[\varrho]\circ I_a} f$.
As before, in order to be sure, that f is the same property on both interpretations, we need to know that all predicates p occurring in f,

$$pre[\varrho^{-1}] \circ pre[\varrho] \circ I_a \ (p) = I_a(p),$$

i.e. $I_a(p)$ is in the image of ϱ on which $pre[\varrho]$ defines an isomorphism from $image(\varrho)$ onto $image(\varrho^{-1})$ [Ore44].

Therefore, we already know which type of formulas we are allowed to verify on abstract programs. Here, we are interested in characterizing the set of predicates (considered as subsets of the domain D, respectively D') of the composed concrete program that can be used in these formulas, such that f is preserved in the way explained above.

Definition 14. Let be D, D_a domains, $I : \mathcal{P} \to 2^D$ respectively $I_a : \mathcal{P} \to 2^{D_a}$ interpretation functions of atomic predicates and ϱ an abstraction relation in $\mathcal{R}(D, D_a)$. Then we say for a predicate p that it is preserved by ϱ iff

$$pre[\varrho] \circ pre[\varrho^{-1}] \circ I\ (p) = I(p) \quad \text{respectively} \quad pre[\varrho^{-1}] \circ pre[\varrho] \circ I_a\ (p) = I_a(p).$$

Notice that this notion of preservation of predicates depends only on the abstraction relation ϱ, and not on the particular program (i.e. transition relation) under study.

In the following Proposition, we characterize a set of predicates on domains of programs of the form $R_1 \odot R_2$ that is preserved by relations of the form $\varrho_1 \cap \varrho_2$ as in the Propositions 10 to 12.

Proposition 15. Let $\varrho_i \in \mathcal{R}(D_{V_i}, D_{V_{ia}})$, $i = 1, 2$ be abstraction relations total on D_{V_i} and such that $\varrho_1 \cap \varrho_2$ is total on $D_{V_1 \cup V_2}$. Let p be a subset of $D_{V_1 \cup V_2}$ (interpretation of some atomic predicate) that can be put into the form $\bigcup_{i \in J} p_i^1 \cap p_i^2$ where $p_i^1 \subseteq D_{V_1}$ and $p_i^2 \subseteq D_{V_2}$ and J finite; let p_a be a subset of $D_{V_{1a} \cup V_{2a}}$ that can be put into the form $\bigcup_{i \in J'} p_{ai}^1 \cap p_{ai}^2$ where $p_{ai}^1 \subseteq D_{V_{1a}}$ and $p_{ai}^2 \subseteq D_{V_{2a}}$ and J' finite. Then,

- If all the p_i^j are preserved by ϱ_j (for $i \in J$ and $j = 1, 2$), p is preserved by $\varrho_1 \cap \varrho_2$.
- If all the p_{ai}^j are preserved by ϱ_j (for $i \in J'$ and $j = 1, 2$), p_a is preserved by $\varrho_1 \cap \varrho_2$.

Proof. $pre[\varrho](pre[\varrho^{-1}](\bigcup_i p_i)) = \bigcup_i pre[\varrho](pre[\varrho^{-1}](p_i))$ and $\forall i \in J$
$pre[\varrho_j](pre[\varrho_j^{-1}](p_i^j)) = p_i^j, j = 1, 2$ implies
$pre[\varrho_1 \cap \varrho_2](pre[\varrho_1^{-1} \cap \varrho_2](p_i^1 \cap p_i^2)) =$
$pre[\varrho_1](pre[\varrho_1^{-1}](p_i^1)) \cap pre[\varrho_2](pre[\varrho_2^{-1}](p_i^2)) = p_i^1 \cap p_i^2$.

Comment: Notice that not only sets of this form may be preserved by $\varrho_1 \cap \varrho_2$.

However, in the case that $\varrho_1 \cap \varrho_2$ is a product of independent relations, i.e., $\varrho_1 \cap \varrho_2 = \varrho_{11} \times \varrho \times \varrho_{22}$, as it has been required in Propositions 11 and 12, $pre[\varrho_1 \cap \varrho_2] \circ pre[\varrho_1^{-1} \cap \varrho_2]$ is of the form $(pre[\varrho_{11}] \circ pre[\varrho_{11}^{-1}]) \times (pre[\varrho] \circ pre[\varrho^{-1}]) \times (pre[\varrho_{22}] \circ pre[\varrho_{22}^{-1}])$.
Then, only sets p which can be put into the form

$$\bigcup_{i \in J} p_i^1 \cap p_i^x \cap p_i^2$$

where $p_i^1 \subseteq D_{V_1 - V_2}$, $p_i^x \subseteq D_{V_1 \cap V_2}$ and $p_i^2 \subseteq D_{V_2 - V_1}$ are preserved by $\varrho_1 \cap \varrho_2$ **iff** all the p_i^1 are preserved by ϱ_{11}, all the p_i^x are preserved by ϱ and all the p_i^2 are preserved by ϱ_{22}. That means instead of dealing with relations in $\mathcal{R}(D_{V_1 \cup V_2}, D_{V_{1a} \cup V_{2a}})$ we deal only with relations on subdomains.

6 Example Continued

From the results given in [BBLS92] we have that for any formula f in $\Box L\mu$ and any interpretation function I of atomic predicates on the abstract domain,

$$P_A \models_I f \text{ implies } P \models_{pre[\varrho] \circ I} f$$

The following CTL formula expresses the fact that the mobile, if it is correctly initialized and does effectively change control points, visits the control points A, C and D cyclically. This formula can be translated into a $\Box L\mu$ formula.

$$f = (Pcp = A) \text{ implies } \neg(Pcp = D) \text{ until } (Pcp = C) \wedge$$
$$(Pcp = C) \text{ implies } \neg(Pcp = A) \text{ until } (Pcp = D) \wedge$$
$$(Pcp = D) \text{ implies } \neg(Pcp = C) \text{ until } (Pcp = A)$$

In order to be sure that the formula is preserved, we have to verify that predicates that appear in the formula are preserved. The predicates involved in the formula appear only in ϱ_{Ctrl}, we verify:

$$pre[\varrho_{Ctrl}^{-1}](pre[\varrho_{Ctrl}](I(Pcp = A))) = I(Pcp = A)$$

This equality is obvious, and so are the equalities for the other predicates.

7 Discussion

We have studied property preserving abstractions of composed programs for a general notion of parallel composition. The results are close to those given in [Kur89] in the linear framework and are extensions of those given in [GL91].

A key idea is the parametrization of simulations by a relation ϱ which allows the computation of an abstract program (an idea which has been extensively used in the domain of abstract interpretation, cf. e.g. in [CC77]) and is good means to express composition of simulations.

The presented results are exploited in a tool which is currently being implemented. Its inputs are expressions using parallel and abstraction operators on boolean guarded command programs. The evaluation of such an expression results in guarded command program. Moreover, our tool verifies symbolically any μ-calculus formula on programs and allows to know whether basic predicates are preserved, in sense of Definition 14, by the applied abstractions.

Programs are represented by *sets* of relations instead of just a relation. Internally, each guarded command is implemented by a BDD ("Binary Decision Diagrams" [Bry86]) which is an efficient representation of boolean expressions. We never compute the BDD corresponding to the global transition relation as

- for the operator $[\![]\!]$, we need the transition relations of each guarded command.
- the space needed for representation in memory of a set of relations is likely to be much smaller than that needed to represent the global transition relation [HDDY92].

The tool will be connected to the Caesar tool [GS90a], which translates Lotos programs into Petri nets. For an important subclass of Lotos programs, these Petri nets can easily be translated into parallel compositions of boolean guarded command programs, which will allow to test the tool for important examples.

All the results obtained here are also valid if one represents programs by sets of functions and this should allow to obtain still smaller representations of programs as shown in [Fil91]. However, in case of functional representation, the abstract program cannot in all cases be computed as easily as R_ϱ for a program R and a relation ϱ. Experimentation is still necessary to compare the efficiencies of the two approaches.

Acknowledgements

We thank Saddek Bensalem and Joseph Sifakis for many helpful discussions and judicious remarks.

References

[AL88]   M. Abadi and L. Lamport. *The existence of refinement mappings*. Technical Report SRC-29, DEC Research Center, 1988.

[BBLS92]   A. Bouajjani, S. Bensalem, C. Loiseaux, and J. Sifakis. Property preserving simulations. In *Workshop on Computer-Aided Verification (CAV), Montréal*, To appear in LNCS, june 1992.

[BK85]   J. A. Bergstra and J.W. Klop. Algebra of communicating processes with abstraction. *TCS*, 37 (1), 1985.

[Bry86]   R. E. Bryant. Graph based algorithms for boolean function manipulation. *IEEE Trans. on Computation*, 35 (8), 1986.

[CC77]   P. Cousot and R. Cousot. Abstract interpretation: a unified lattice model for static analysis of programs by construction or approximation of fixpoints. In *4th POPL*, january 1977.

[CGL92]   E.M. Clarke, O. Grumberg, and D.E. Long. Model checking and abstraction. In *Symposium on Principles of Programming Languages (POPL 92)*, ACM, october 1992.

[CM88]   K. M. Chandy and J. Misra. *Parallel Program Design*. Addison-Wesley, Massachusetts, 1988.

[CS90]   R. Cleaveland and B. Steffen. When is "partial" adequate? a logic-based proof technique using partial specifications. In *LICS*, 1990.

[Fil91]   T. Filkorn. Functional extension of symbolic model checking. In *Workshop on Computer-Aided Verification 91, Aalborg (Denmark)*, LNCS Vol. 575, june 1991.

[GL91]   O. Grumberg and E. Long. Compositionnal model checking and modular verification. In J.C.M. Baeten and J.F. Groote, editors, *Concur '91, 2nd International Conference on Concurrency Theory*, pages 250–265, Springer-Verlag, august 1991.

[GS86]   S. Graf and J. Sifakis. A logic for the specification and proof of regular controllable processes of CCS. *Acta Informatica*, 23, 1986.

[GS90a]   Hubert Garavel and Joseph Sifakis. Compilation and verification of Lotos specifications. In L. Logrippo, R. L. Probert, and H. Ural, editors, *Proceedings of the 10th International Symposium on Protocol Specification, Testing and Verification (Ottawa)*, IFIP, North Holland, Amsterdam, june 1990.

[GS90b]   S. Graf and B. Steffen. Compositional minimisation of finite state processes. In *Workshop on Computer-Aided Verification, Rutgers*, LNCS 531, june 1990.

[GW89]   R.J. Van Glabbeek and W.P. Weijland. *Branching time and abstraction in bisimulation semantics (extended abstract)*. CS-R 8911, Centrum voor Wiskunde en Informatica, Amsterdam, 1989.

[HDDY92]   A.J. Hu, D.L. Dill, A.J. Drexler, and C.H. Yang. Higher-level specification and verification with bdds. In *4th Workshop on Computer-Aided Verification (CAV92), Montréal*, To appear in LNCS, Springer Verlag, june 1992.

[HM85] M. Hennessy and R. Milner. Algebraic laws for nondeterminism and concurrency. *Journal of the Association for Computing Machinery*, 32:137–161, 1985.

[Hoa85] C. A. R. Hoare. *Communicating Sequential Processes*. Prentice Hall International, 1985.

[ISO89] ISO. *IS ISO/OSI 8807 - LOTOS: a formal description technique based on the temporal ordering of observational behaviour*. International Standard, ISO, 1989.

[KK86] J. Katzenelson and B. Kurshan. S/R: A Language for Specifying Protocols and other Coordinating Processes. In *5th Ann. Int'l Phoenix Conf. Comput. Commun.*, pages 286–292, IEEE, 1986.

[Koz83] D. Kozen. Results on the propositional μ-calculus. In *Theoretical Computer Science*, North-Holland, 1983.

[Kur89] R.P. Kurshan. Analysis of discrete event coordination. In *REX Workshop on Stepwise Refinement of Distributed Systems, Mook*, LNCS 430, Springer Verlag, 1989.

[Lam91] L. Lamport. *The Temporal Logic of Actions*. Technical Report 79, DEC, Systems Research Center, 1991.

[LT88a] K. G. Larsen and B. Thomsen. Compositional proofs by partial specification of processes. In *LICS 88*, 1988.

[LT88b] N.A. Lynch and M.R. Tuttle. *An introduction to Input/Ouput Automata*. MIT/LCS/TM 373, MIT, Cambridge, Massachussetts, november 1988.

[Mil71] R. Milner. An algebraic definition of simulation between programs. In *Proc. Second Int. Joint Conf. on Artificial Intelligence*, pages 481–489, BCS, 1971.

[Ore44] O. Ore. Galois connexions. *Trans. Amer. Math. Soc*, 55:493–513, February 1944.

[SG90] G. Shurek and O. Grumberg. The Modular Framework of Computer-aided Verification: Motivation, Solutions and Evaluation Criteria. In *Conference on Automatic Verification (CAV), Rutgers, NJ*, LNCS 531, Springer Verlag, 1990.

[Wal88] D. J. Walker. Bisimulation and Divergence in CCS. In *3th Symposium on Logic in Computer Science (LICS 88)*, IEEE, 1988.

Types as Parameters[1]

Giuseppe Longo

LIENS (CNRS) et DMI, Ecole Normale Supérieure

45, Rue d'Ulm, 75005 Paris; longo@dmi.ens.fr

Abstract. This note is a brief survey and a discussion of recent ideas and open problems in the understanding of an important aspect of Type Theory: how terms may depend on types. This problem is at the core of the distinction between "ad hoc" and proper polymorphism and inspired the large amount of work on "parametricity".

Contents. 1 Types; 2 Parametricity; 3 Genericity; 4 Axiom C and Dinatural Transformations; 5 Axiom C and the Isomorphisms of Types; 6. Types as Parameters; 7. True type dependency or "ad hoc" polymorphism.

1 Types

In Mathematics, functions are typed. One always talks of functions from reals to reals, or from integers to reals, or from a given vector space to another, or of homomorphisms of groups and so on so forth.... In a sense, functions are always viewed as arrows with specific source and target, in the intended category. The objects of the category are the types. The formalization of mathematics in the frame of a type-free Set Theory was an oversimplification of Frege. A fruitful one, though, as it clarified matters and stimulated the design of a rigorous type-theoretic approach, after a simple inconsistency was pointed out by Russell.

The "mistake" was iterated by Curry and Church, in their functional approach to foundation. Again, this gave rise to a paradox, Curry's paradox, which is similar to Russell's when xx, self application, stands for $x \in x$. In this case though, the solution was twofold: one could add types, in Russell's style [Church41] or, by dropping negation, one could obtain a computationally very expressive type-free system, where Curry's paradoxical combinator was turned into the key tool for computing all partial recursive functions. And this was the type-free λ-calculus. Its many relevant properties are

---

[1] The presentation is directly endebted to joint work and many stimulating discussions with Giuseppe Castagna, Giorgio Ghelli, Roberto DiCosmo, Simone Martini, Kathleen Milsted, Sergei Soloviev. With Simone, in particular, I discussed of the dinatural interpretation (§.4), while Sergei and Roberto pointed out to me the connection to the isomorphisms of types in §.5.

discussed in [Bare84].

It is worth pointing out that this branching of the functional approach to foundation, which had no impact on the practice of mathematics, originated the relevant areas of type-free and typed functional programming languages and that, in computing, these two directions nicely interact. Ordinary typed languages, both in the case of type checking and of type assignement, deal with types at compile time, while computations are meant to be type free. As well known, one can reconstruct types for (typable) type-free terms and, conversely, erasing type information preserves the computational power of terms, an issue to be discussed later.

2 Parametricity

More richness has been embedded in programming by borrowing from higher order logic: just allow type variables, not just term variables, similarly as one considers set-variables or variables ranging over the objects of a category. In this case, terms may have several types, namely, all the instances of their type schema obtained by the use of type variables, and, hence, programs are (implicitly) *polymorphic* [Mil78]. When the analogy with higher order systems is more fully pursued, one considers quantified type variables and obtains *explicit* polymorphism (Girard's system F; [Gir71], [Rey74]).

Clearly, when type variables, X, Y, Z..., are allowed, then they naturally arise both in types and typed terms: $\lambda x{:}X.M$ is a term of type $X \to \rho$, where ρ is the type of M. But, then, terms, as functions, may depend on types. This is perfectly clear in explicit polymorphism, where one may abstract w.r.t. to type variables and terms may be applied to types: $P \equiv \lambda X.N$ of type $\forall X.\sigma$ and $P\tau$ of type $[\tau/X]\sigma$ are well formed. In particular, $\lambda X.N$ is an (explicitly) polymorphic functions from types to terms. Note the peculiar "dimension" (or type) of polymorphic functions: if constant types are objects in a category and terms are morphisms, then they are maps going from the objects of a category to the morphisms.

Several questions then come to the mind. Write $M[X]$ and $\sigma[X]$ in order to stress that X may occur in M and σ. Then the rule

$$M[X] : \sigma[X]$$

$$\overline{}$$

$$\lambda X.M[X] : \forall X.\sigma[X]$$

gives a uniform definition of the family of maps $\{M[X]\}_X$ with components $M[X]$. Note that this definining rule does not depend on the parameter X, or it is "uniform" in it.

Does the syntactic uniformity of the definition have some relevance in the computational meaning of M? Or, also, how do polymorphic terms, as functions from types to terms, actually behave?

What does it mean that types can be erased at compile time?

These questions are clearly related; the first two raise the issue of *parametricity*.

3 Genericity

The main motivation of this note is the need to relate the recent result in [LMS92] to (some of) the formal descriptions of how types act as parameters in functional languages. The result can be very easily stated. In a moderate extension of system F, the explicitly polymorphic calculus, types do not affect computations, in the sense that they are "generic" or "act like variables". More formally, call Fc the extension of F by "Axiom C" of the next section, then the following holds:

Theorem (Genericity) Let M, N :∀X.σ. If, for some type τ, Mτ = $_{Fc}$ Nτ, then M = $_{Fc}$ N.

The proof relies on a non trivial technique of generalizing the two terms M and N, to obtain a (well-typed) common term from which the two terms can be equated. The meaning (and the strength) of the theorem should be clear: if two polymorphic functions of the same type agree on *one* input, then they agree on all inputs. Note that the terms Mτ, Mρ,.... in general may live in different types, namely [τ/X]σ, [ρ/X]σ.... A suggestive pictorial representation of functions from types to terms, as parametric in types, may be the following:

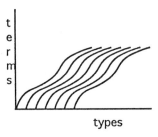

terms

types

Indeed, the Genericity Theorem tells us that different functions "never cross"; Reynolds' Abstraction Theorem (see §.6) tells us that polymorphic functions "preserve relations between inputs", or that they are "regular", in some precise sense to be discussed later.

The next two sections are meant to understand and justify the intended extension Fc of system F, by relating it to the semantics of F and the syntax of ML.

4   Axiom C and Dinatural Transformations

The Genericity Theorem is valid in a simple extension of system F, namely, Fc = F + Ax.C below. The idea is to impose that a polymorphic term, which outputs all values in the same type, is a constant function:

Ax.C If M : ∀X.σ, with X ∉ FV(σ), then Mρ = Mτ : σ, for any type ρ and τ.

This axiom is clearly compatible with F: the PER model, Girard's model over coherent domains and stable functions as well as other models realize it (see [LMS92]). More than this, Ax.C is truly in the spirit of system F: its negation, where MY ≠ MZ is interpreted by "they have a different erasure", yields a non normalizing system (see the remark in [Gir71] quoted in [LMS92]). We simply observe here that Ax.C is realized in all models where terms are understood as "dinatural transformations", defined below.

In §.2 we observed that the intended meaning of a polymorphic term λX.M is that of a function from the collection Ob$_C$ of objects of a category C to the collection of morphisms. However, types may contain type variables. Thus, they are maps from objects to objects, more than just objects. Functors do have this dimension, hence *natural transformations* between functors may seem to provide the right meaning to polymorphic terms. Natural transformations are collections of morphisms, indexed over objects: $v = \{v_A\}_{A\in Ob}$ is a natural transformation, between functors F and G, if for any morphism $f : A \to B$, one has:

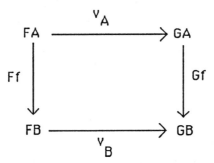

Thus, if $[\sigma]$ were the meaning of a type σ as object, the map v, with $v([\sigma]) = v_{[\sigma]}$, could interpret the polymorphic application of a term $\lambda X.M$ to a type σ. Unfortunately though, types are not functors, but just maps from Ob to Ob. The rub is that any type, in which the same variable occurs both at the right and the left of an "$\to$", should be at the same time a covariant and a contravariant functor. This is impossible, in general.

An interesting partial solution to this problem has been provided by [BFSS90] and further pursued by [GSS91], [FRR92]. The idea is that the interpretation of types, viewed as maps over the objects of a category, may be extended to functors, by distinguishing between the covariant and contravariant occurences of variables. Thus, an n-variable map is turned into a multivariant functor of $n\times n$ arguments. Over these kind functors, $F,G : C^n\times C^n \to C$, say, one may define *dinatural transformation* each family of morphisms $u = \{u_A : F\underline{A}\,\underline{A} \to G\underline{A}\,\underline{A} \mid \underline{A}\in C^n\}$ such that, for any vector of morphisms $f : \underline{A} \to \underline{B}$, one has:

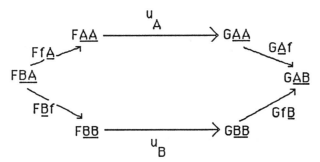

The problem here is that, in general, dinatural transformations do not compose. Thus, a category with all required properties to yield a model, cannot always interpret terms as dinaturals, simply because terms can be composed. However, in [BFSS90] and [GSS91], some interesting models are given, where dinatural transformations do compose. These models then yield the dinatural interpretation of terms.

It is easy now, to point out that Ax.C is realized in any model for dinatural transformations. Indeed, equivalently rewrite Ax.C as

Ax.C* If $\Gamma \vdash N : \sigma$, with $X \notin FV(\Gamma) \cup FV(\sigma)$, then $[\rho/X]N = [\tau/X]N : \sigma$

where the context Γ is explicitly mentioned (it was irrelevant before; the condition $X \notin FV(\Gamma)$ is required now in order to satisfy the side condition in the $(\forall I)$ rule of system F and obtain the equivalence with Ax.C). Then the intepretation of N is a dinatural transformation which goes from the interpretation of Γ, as a product functor, to the interpretation of σ. The point is that both Γ and σ do not contain X free, thus the exagon above collapses to a pair of parallel arrows. Or, the models of terms as dinaturals realize Ax.C*. (Note that Ax.C* can be stated also in the frame of implicit polymorphism, where type variables are allowed but no explicit quantification).

5 Axiom C and the Isomorphisms of Types

As already recalled, ML style languages allow type schemata. Namely, types may contain type variables and a term possesses as types all instances of its type schema. Indeed, an algorithm assigns to each typable term its most general type, from which all of its types may be derived, by instantiation. If preferred, explicit universal quantifications may be used, but, in the spirit of types as schemata, they can be only external.

It may seem obvious then that ML is strictly "weaker" than system F: only certain kinds of quantifications are allowed. In particular, provable isomorphisms of types in ML should be provable also in F (as for the relevance of isomorphisms of types, see [DiCoLo89] and [DiCo93]). This is not so and the difference is expressed by Ax.C.

To see this fact more closely, consider the extension $F_\times$ of F obtained by adding cartesian products (that is add product types, projections and surjective pairings axioms, since usual descriptions of ML include them). In [DiCo93] it is shown that the isomorphism

(Split) $\forall X.\sigma \times \tau \cong \forall X \forall Y.\sigma \times [Y/X]\tau$, for $Y \notin FV(\sigma)$,

can be derived in ML, but not in $F_\times$. This is so by the peculiar use of variable substitution as given by the "let... in..." variant of (β) reduction: one may allow different types for the same term, while performing the substitution. In particular, the type-free terms $\lambda x.x$ and $\lambda x.\langle p_1 x, p_2 x \rangle$, where the p_i are projections, yield the isomorphism in the implicitly polymorphic system, while their explicitly polymorphic versions, in system F, do not. Indeed, $\lambda z:(\forall X \forall Y.\sigma \times [Y/X]\tau).\lambda X.\langle p_1(zXX), p_2(zXX) \rangle$ and $\lambda z:(\forall X.\sigma \times \tau).\lambda X.\lambda Y.\langle p_1(zX), p_2(zY) \rangle$ only yield a retraction, in F, from $\forall X \forall Y.\sigma \times [Y/X]\tau$ into $\forall X.\sigma \times \tau$. Note that (Split) is the only isomorphism in the "difference" between ML and F (but, of course, $F_\times$ proves many more; see [DiCo93] for details).

The point here is that Ax.C fills the difference, as (Split) is provable in $F_\times c$. Observe first that, in Fc one has

(Iso.C) $\forall Y.\sigma \cong \sigma$, if $Y \notin FV(\sigma)$

where $\lambda x:(\forall Y.\sigma).xX$ and $\lambda z:\sigma.\lambda Y.z$ yield the isomorphism, by an explicit use of Ax.C. (Conversely, F extended by Iso.C, as given by the terms above, is equivalent to Fc.) Compute then

$$\forall X\forall Y.\sigma\times[Y/X]\tau \cong \forall X.(\forall Y.\sigma)\times(\forall Y.[Y/X]\tau) \text{ since } \forall Y.\sigma\times\rho \cong (\forall Y.\sigma)\times(\forall Y.\rho), \text{ in } F_\times,$$

$$\cong \forall X.\sigma\times(\forall Y.[Y/X]\tau) \text{ by Iso.C, as } Y\notin FV(\sigma),$$
$$\cong (\forall X.\sigma)\times(\forall X\forall Y.[Y/X]\tau) \text{ as above}$$
$$\cong (\forall X.\sigma)\times(\forall Y.[Y/X]\tau) \text{ by Iso.C,}$$
$$\cong (\forall X.\sigma)\times(\forall X.\tau) \text{ by renaming}$$
$$\cong \forall X.\sigma\times\tau .$$

In conclusion, we observed, following DiCosmo, that $F_\times$ is not an extension of ML, in spite of the popular belief (clearly, an isomorphism of types corresponds to the equations of two terms to the identity). We noticed though that Ax.C allows to overcome the difficulty and establishes, by this, a novel connection between the two systems. The observation is one more step towards justifying the usual practice in higher order functional programming, where types are not used at run-time. Indeed, in ML, types are only used at compile time. Programs are written as type free terms and an automatic type assignement system performs a partial correcteness check by assigning type schemas. Finally, programs run with no type information. This is perfectly fair in a programmming style where types are only used as a metalinguistic "dimensional control", at compile time. Why should running programs use no type information also in explicitly higher order systems such as Cardelli's Quest (see [CL91])? In those languages, types are first class citiziens of the language and they may be explicitly manipulated; why should the type erasures preserve the computational meaning of the intended computations, in these cases as well?

This is the core question discussed by the work on parametricity. Before getting into this issue, we note that the implicit use of Ax.C, by better establishing the theoretical connection to ML, already justifies the analogy at run time. As a matter of fact, in a recent investigation on the theoretical core of Quest, $F_\leq$ of [CMS91], a strong version of Ax.C is assumed. By the present remark, $F_\leq$ more closely relates to ML.

6   Types as Parameters

In the last two sections we introduced a preliminary understanding of the peculiar way in which terms depend on types in polymorphic functional languages and, at the same time, we justified the extension of system F by Ax.C. In particular, the meaning of terms as dinatural transformations sets an elegant connection to relevant areas of mathematics, where (di)naturality expresses a key categorical uniformity between functorial transformations. The validity of Ax.C in crucial models, see [LMS92], and in the dinatural intepretation, as well as its significance, shed some preliminary light on the "uniformity" of the dependence of terms from types.

A further insight into parametricity is given by a blending of two results, one of which has already been mentioned, the Genericity Theorem. The other is a syntactic understanding of Reynolds' work. In [Rey83] and [MaRey91] some abstract conditions are given such that, if a model satisfies them, then the intended meaning expresses a strong uniformity of terms w.r.t. types as inputs. In [ACC93] a syntactic treatment of Reynolds' approach is proposed. The advantage is given by a simpler presentation and by some relevant applications in the description of properties of programs (on the lines of [Wad89]). The key idea is the introduction of a (strong) extension of system F, system R, which deals with terms, types and *relations* between types. The main result, besides the applications to properties of programs, may be stated as follows (and it may be considered as a reunderstanding of Reynolds' "Abstraction Theorem"). In R, a type variable may be instantiated also by a relation R between types ρ and τ; this substitution, in a type σ, say, yields a relation $\sigma[R/X]$ between types $\sigma[\rho/X]$ and $\sigma[\tau/X]$.

Theorem (Abstraction) Let $M : \forall X.\sigma$. If a relation R is given between types ρ and τ, then $M\rho : \sigma[\rho/X]$ is related to $M\tau : \sigma[\tau/X]$ by $\sigma[R/X]$.

In other words, a polymorphic term takes related input types to related term values, in their output types (the result may be stated in a more general fashion by taking two related terms M and M' instead of one). The first point to be noted, now, is that R realizes Ax.C. Indeed, under the further condition $X \notin FV(\sigma)$, the relation $\sigma[R/X] \equiv \sigma$ collapses to the identity over $\sigma[\rho/X] \equiv \sigma \equiv \sigma[\tau/X]$. Thus, for any two types ρ and τ, whatever is the relation R between them, by the Abstraction Theorem, one has $M\rho = M\tau : \sigma$.

A most relevant application of parametricity, as described by the Abstraction Theorem, has been recently given by Hasegawa, [Hase93]. As well known, in intuitionistic second order logic implication and universal quantification, the type constructors of system F, are sufficient to form all other connectives. In particular, the absurdum, $\perp$, the existential quantifier $\exists$, *and* and *or* are all definable. However, all these definable connectives are weak, in the sense that $\perp$ (intuitively, the empty set or unprovable statement) is not initial and the others do not have the required projections or injections to be interpreted in all models as true existential, product and coproduct. The surprising result of Hasegawa is that the definable connectives have the right properties (initiality, projections...) exactly in those models of system F which are parametric, in the sense that they provide the relational frame for the Abstraction Theorem. Moreover, in [Hase93] it is shown that also initiality of free algebraic constructions holds exactly in presence of parametricity. In short, it is known that "free" algebraic types are representable in system F, see [BB85]: given an endofunctor G, $\forall X.((G(X) \rightarrow X) \rightarrow X)$ defines the algebraic type freely generated from G, (for example, $G(X) = 0+X$, for a terminal object 0, generates the natural numbers). So far so good, but, the crucial algebraic property of initiality is usually lost by this weak definition, inside system F. Well, parametricity gives it back and allows to embed algebraic definitions, in their full expressiveness, into all parametric models of system F. If nothing else could be said about the relevance of parametricity, this should be enough to convince the reader of the interest of this uniformity property of system F. Indeed, it tells us why lambda calculus, by uniformly coding proofs by terms, is much more than just the logical systems of their types as propositions.

One final remark. The Abstraction Theorem (or its instance, as presented here) is, in a way, "dual" to the Genericity Theorem. Given *one* term M of type $\forall X.\sigma$, if *two* input types ρ and τ are related, then so are the output values $M\rho$ and $M\tau$. Dually, Genericity says that, given *two* terms M and N of type $\forall X.\sigma$, if they coincide on *one* input type τ, then M and N are equal. Thus, the two results study the consequence of applying one term on two inputs vs two terms on one input. Jointly, they give some robust information on the parametric dependence of terms on types, as we tried to suggest, very informally, by the picture at the end of §.2: polymorphic functions never cross and are all similarly regular (or preserve relations, all in the same way). The difficulty (and the research issue) here, is that the Genericity Theorem does not hold in system $\mathbb{R}$. Indeed, $\mathbb{R}$ realizes Ax.C, but does not need to realize its implicative consequences. Namely, the equational theory of $\mathbb{R}$ is an equational variety and nothing is known, a priori, about the implications between equations that it realizes. A formal understanding of this problem or of the relations between the two theorems, by a unified frame for parametricity, would surely shed further light on this crucial property of lambda calculus.

7 True type dependency or "ad hoc" polymorphism

The results just mentioned stress the faithful correspondence of system F, the core of higher order functional programming, to constructive logical system. The intended meaning of a type, as formalized in intuitionistic type theories, is that of possibly infinite collection of individuals. Effective computations can only be carried on individuals or elements of types and cannot use the infinite amount of information implicit in the notion of type. Thus, a properly constructive second order system, where type or set variables are explicitly allowed, cannot compute with these variables nor with their instantiation by type symbols. In a sense, this justifies the practice of erasing type information at run-time: only the type, not the result of a computation can depend on type parameters.

However, in actual programming languages, types may be coded. After all, type symbols are countably many and programmers are not always very concerned by the intended interpretation of second order variables. Thus computations depending do exist in the practice of programming. Usually, though, true type dependency are resolved at compile-time. For example, the familiar overloaded functions of many imperative languages (or of imperative features of functional languages) are given different values, according to type information, before computing. Typical examples are the "+" or "print" functions in most running languages, where their overloaded meaning is decided when checking the type of the inputs, at compile-time. Usually these constructions are as untidy as low level code writing. Moreover, the early resolution of overloading has little expressivity and little mathematical relevance. However, this should not mislead us from this further expressivity of programming; as already mentioned, codes for types can be manipulated. Thus, in an even more constructive approach to reality, i.e., in actual programming, one may have functions whose output values depend on input types. As a matter of fact, "ad hoc" polymorphism is a powerful and useful feature and a further mathematical challenge. Too bad that it has been given a name with a negative connotation by the founding fathers of programming language theory; this name and their influential role may have diverted or delayed investigation from an important aspect of computing.

The point is to embed "ad hoc" polymorphism into a sound mathematical frame and turn it into a general, non ad hoc, programming tool.

We summarize here the proposal for the investigation of a true type dependency, viewed as overloading, made in [CGL92]. In that paper, a robust use of overloading is proposed in order to investigate some aspects of Object Oriented Programming in a functional frame. We directly borrow from [CGL92] a brief introduction to this typically "ad hoc" polymorphism.

The motivation come from considering overloading as a way to interpret message-passing in object-oriented programming, when methods are viewed as "global" functions:

they are named "outside" the objects and their (operational) value is specified as soon as the name of a global function is associated to an object. This value may entirely change according to the given object: overloading is not parametric in the sense of system F.

In short, in object-oriented languages computations evolve on objects. Objects are programming items grouped in classes and possess an internal state that is modified by sending messages to the object. When an object receives a message it invokes the method (i.e., code or procedure) associated to that message. The association between methods and messages is described by the class the object belongs to. In particular, objects are pairs (internal state , class_name).

The idea then is to consider messages as names of overloaded functions and message passing as overloaded application: according to the class (or more generally, the type) of the object the message is passed to, a different method is chosen (this is similar to programming in CLOS, for example). Thus, we pass objects to messages, similarly as types are passed as inputs to the polymorphic functions of system F. The crucial difference is that parametricity is lost by allowing a finitely branching choice of the possible code to be applied. And this choice will depend on types as inputs (or, more precisely, on the type of the inputs).

In the formalism designed in [CGL92], terms describe overloaded functions by "gluing up together" different "pieces of code". Thus the code of an overloaded function is formed by several branches of code. The branch to execute is chosen when the function is applied to an argument, according to a selection rule which uses the type of the argument.

A key feature of this approach is that the branch selection is not performed on the basis of the type the argument possesses at compile-time. As already mentioned this is a fundamental limitation of overloading as used in imperative languages (early binding). In the present approach, the selection is performed each time the overloaded application is evaluated during computation. Moreover, the branch selection can be performed only when the argument is fully evaluated, and depends on its "run-time type" (late binding) which may differ from the compile-time type.

For example, suppose that *Real* and *Nat* are subtypes of *Complex* and that *add* is an overloaded function defined on all of them, and suppose that x is a formal parameter of a function, with type *Complex*. Assume also that the compile-time type of the argument is used for branch selection (early binding). Then an overloaded function application (here denoted •), such as the following one

$$\lambda x : Complex.(...add \cdot x...),$$

is always executed using the *add* code for complex numbers; with late binding, each time the whole function is applied, the code for *add* is chosen only when the parameter x has been bound and evaluated. Thus the appropriate code for *add* is used on the basis of the run-time type of x and according to whether x is bound to a real or to a natural number.

In summary, in [CGL92] a simple extension of the typed lambda-calculus is designed, which is meant to formalize the behavior of overloaded functions with late binding in a type discipline with subtyping. The first point id to add to ordinary λ-terms, new terms such as $(M_1 \& ... \& M_n)$ that represent the overloaded function composed by the n branches M_i, for $i \leq n$. We extend then the ordinary functional application MN by an operation of overloaded application $M \cdot N$.

The types of the overloaded functions are finite lists of arrow types

$\{U_1 \to V_1, ..., U_n \to V_n\}$ (denoted by $\{U_i \to V_i\}_{i \in I}$ for a suitable set I), where every arrow type is the type of a branch. Overloaded types, though, must satisfy relevant consistency conditions, which, among others, take care, in our view, of the longstanding debate concerning the use of covariance or contravariance of the arrow type in its left argument. More precisely, the general arrow types will be given by contravariant "$\rightarrow$" in the first argument: this is an essential feature of (typed) functional programs, were type assignment (type-checking) helps avoiding run-time errors. Instead, the types of overloaded functions are covariant families of arrow types, as explained later.

We stress that the subtyping relation introduced is a complex, but expressive, feature of the calculus: it allows multiple choices, as a type may be a subtype of several types and subtyping is used to chose branches of overloaded terms. The blend of &-terms and subtyping makes this calculus an expressive and original mathematical formalism which shows, we claim, that "ad hoc" polymorphism may have also theoretical relevance. Here is a short survey of some basic idea in the calculus and its reduction rules.

The subtyping relation is defined as usual on arrow types. On overloaded types, it expresses that a type $T' = \{ U'_j \rightarrow V'_j \}_{j \in J}$ is smaller than another $T'' = \{ U''_i \rightarrow V''_i \}_{j \in I}$, if the programs in T' type check also when given as input an argument meant for programs in T'' (see the rule $[\rightarrow \text{ELIM}_{(\leq)}]$ below):

$$\frac{\text{for all } i \in I, \text{ there exists } j \in J \text{ such that } U''_i \leq U'_j \text{ and } V'_j \leq V''_i}{\{ U'_j \rightarrow V'_j \}_{j \in J} \leq \{ U''_i \rightarrow V''_i \}_{i \in I}}$$

Well-formed types are defined by using the (pre-)order on them (in case the preorder gives a set instead of a single element, e.g. the greatest lower bound, we choose a canonical one). The definition gives the structure of family of covariant types to overloaded types:

1. $A \in$ Types
2. if $V_1, V_2 \in$ Types, then $V_1 \rightarrow V_2 \in$ Types
3. if for all $i, j \in I$
   (a) $(U_i, V_i \in$ Types) and
   (b) $(U_i \leq U_j \Rightarrow V_i \leq V_j)$ and
   (c) If, when U_i and U_j have a common lower bound, there is a unique (or canonical) $h \in I$ such that $U_h = \inf \{U_i, U_j\}$, then $\{U_i \rightarrow V_i\}_{i \in I} \in$ Types

Terms are difined by adding &-terms and overloaded application:

$M ::= x^V \mid c \mid \lambda x^V. M \mid MM \mid M\&^V M \mid M \cdot M$

The crucial type-checking rules are the following. Note the type label over the &, in &-terms.

$[\rightarrow \text{ELIM}_{(\leq)}]$
$$\frac{\vdash M: U \rightarrow V \quad \vdash N: W \leq U}{\vdash MN: V}$$

$$\vdash M: W_1 \leq \{U_i \to V_i\}_{i \leq (n-1)} \qquad \vdash N: W_2 \leq U_n \to V_n$$

[{}INTPO]

$$\vdash (M \&^{\{U_i \to V_i\}_{i \leq n}} N): \{U_i \to V_i\}_{i \leq n}$$

$$\vdash M: \{U_i \to V_i\}_{i \in I} \qquad \vdash N: U \qquad U_j = \min_{i \in I} \{U_i \mid U \leq U_i\}$$

[{}ELIM]

$$\vdash M \cdot N: V_j$$

The last rule says that the output of an overloaded application lives in a type depending on the type of the input, namely the type V_j corresponding to the least U_i which contains the type of the input In a sense, U_i is the least type which allows the rule [$\to$ ELIM($\leq$)] to be applied (this is were subtyping blends with overloading in a crucial way). Indeed, the reduction rule below says that also the value depends on the type of the input, as the intended M_j is chosen inductively by using, again, the type of the input and the type label on the &.

β&) If $N: U$ is closed and in normal form and $U_j = \min \{U_i \mid U \leq U_i\}$ then

$$((M_1 \&^{\{U_i \to V_i\}_{i=1..n}} M_2) \cdot N) \mapsto \text{"if } j < n \text{ then } M_1 \cdot N, \text{ else } M_2 \cdot N \text{ for } j = n\text{"}$$

Clearly, the choice performed by the (β&) rule may give essentially different output values, as no restriction is set on the computation expressed by the terms. Iformally, one obtains a reduction $(M_1 \& ... \& M_n) \cdot N \mapsto M_j N$, for $j \leq n$ depending on the type of the input N. The motivations for the conditions on N are discussed in [CGL92]. (β) reductions are defined as usual (but [$\to$ ELIM $_{(\leq)}$] may let the type decrease during computations).

The non-obvious fact of this calculus is that it satisfies Strong Normalization and the Church-Rosser theorem, see [CGL92].

We believe that this sets on solid "functional" and non "ad hoc" grounds some aspects of Object Oriented Programming, when message passing is described as overloading. Much more is said in [CGL92 and 93]. We only wanted to mention here some motivations and a proposal for true type dependency or computations depending on input types. The approach though is just a preliminary attempt, as the goal would be to reach the smoothness and "uniformity" of higher order λ-calculi. The gluing together of terms given here is rather heavy. It takes care of many aspects, beyond type dependency, namely late binding and flexible subtyping, but it should be turned into an explicitly second order system, if ever possible. One should allow, say, notations such as $\lambda X.(...\&^X...)$ and still preserve the effectiveness (normalization?) of the present system (ongoing work of Castagna and Pierce is exploring this and other directions). Then we would really reach an alternative language to current functional approaches, restricted as they are by the limitations of parametricity.

References

[ACC93] M.Abadi, L. Cardelli, and P.-L. Curien, Formal parametric polymorphism. In *Proc. 20th ACM Symposium on Principles of Programming Languages*, 1993.

[Bare84] H. Barendregt, *The Lambada Calculus, its syntax and semantics*, North-Holland,Amsterdam, revised edition, 1984

[BB85] Berarducci and C. Boehm, Automatic synthesis of typed A-programs on term algebras, *Theoret. Comput. Sci.* 39 (1985) pp.135-154

[BFSS90] E.S. Bainbridge, P.J. Freyd, A. Scedrov, and P.J. Scott,. Functorial Polymorphism. *Theoretical Computer Science*, 70:35-64, 1990. Corresgendum *ibid.*, 71:431, 1990.

[Church41] A. Church, *The Calculi of Lambada Conversion*, Princeton University Press, Princeton

[CGL92] G. Castagna, G. Ghelli and G. Longo, A calculus for overloaded functions with subtyping **ACM Conference on LISP and Functional Programming**, San Francisco, Juillet 1992.

[CGL93] G. Castagna, G. Ghelli and G. Longo, The semantics for Lamda &-early: a calculus with overlaorading and early binding, Report LIENS.

[CL91] L. Cardelli and G. Longo, A semantic basis for Quest. In *Journal of Functional Programming* I(4), October 1991, pp.417-458.

[CMS91] L. Cardelli, J.C. Mitchell, S. Martini, and A. Scedrov, An extension of system F with Subtyping. To appear in *Information and Computation*. Extended abstract in T. Ito and A.R. Meyer (eds.), *Theoretical Aspects of Computer Software*, Springer-Verlag LNCS 526, 1991, pp. 750-770.

[DiCo92] R. DiCosmo, Deciding type isomorphisms in a type assignment framework. *Journal of Functional Programming*, To appear in the Special Issue on ML.

[DiCo93] R. DiCosmo, Isomorphisms of Types, PhD Thesis, Universita di Pisa.

[DiCoLo89] R. DiCosmo and G. Longo, Constructively equivalent propositions and isomorphisms of objects (or terms as natural transformations). *Workshop on Logic for Comptuer Science*, Moschovakis (ed), MSRI, Berkeley, November 1989.

[FrS92] P.J. Freyd and A. Scedrov, *Categories, Allegories*. Mathematical Library, North-Holland, 1990.

[FRR92] P.J. Freyd, E.P. Robinson, and G. Rosolini, Functorial parametricity. In *Proc. 7th Annual IEEE Symposium on Logic in Computer Science*, 1992.

[Gir71] J.-Y. Girard, Une extention de l'interprɔtation de Godel/l'analyse et la thɔorie et son application/l'ɔlimination des coupures dans l'analyse et la thɔorie des types, In *Proceedings of the Second Scandinavian Logic Symposium, Studies in Logic 63*, J.E. Fenstad (ed.), North-Holland, Amsterdam, pp.63-92.

[GLT89] J.-Y. Girard, Y. Lafont, and P. Taylor, *Proofs and Types*. Cambridge Tracts in Theoretical Computer Science, Cambridge University Press, 1989.

[GSS91] J.-Y. Girard, A. Scedrov, and P.J. Scott, Normal forms and cut-free proofs as natural transformations. In: Y.N. Moschovakis, editor, *Logic from Computer Science, Pro. M.S.R.I. Workshop, Berkeley, 1989*. M.S.R.I. Series Springer-Verlag, 1991.

[Hase93] R. Hasegawa, Categorical data types in parametric polymorphism, To appear in *Mathematical Structure in Computer Science*.

[LMS92] G. Longo, K. Milsted and S. Soloviev, The genericity theorem and the notion of parametricity in the plymorphic Lamda-calculus, Report LIENS 92-25 (submitted to LICS93).

[MaRey92] Q. Ma and J.C. Reynolds, Types, abstraction, and parametric polymorphism, Part 2. In S. Brookes *et al.*, editors, *Mathematical Fundations of Programming Semantics, Proceedings 1991*, Springer-Verlag LNCS 598, 1992, pp. 1-40.

[Mai 91] H. Mairson, Outline of a proof theory of parametricity. In *Proc. 5-th Intern. Symp. on Functional Programming and Computer Architecture*, 1991.

[Mil78] R. Milner, A theory of type polymorphism in programming. In *Journal of Computer and Systytem Science*, 17(3): 348-375, 1978.

[Mit88] J.C. Mitchell, Polymorphic type inference and containment. Information and Computation, 76(2/3): 211-249, 1988. Reprinted in *Logical Fundations of Functional Programming*, ed. G. Huet, Addison-Wesley, 1990, pp.153-194.

[Rey74] J.C. Reynolds, Towards a theory of type structure, in LNCS, Springer, Berlin, pp.408-425.

[Rey83] J.C. Reynolds, Types, abstraction, and parametric polymorphism. In R.E.A. Mason, editor, *Information Processing'83*, pp. 513-523. North-Holland, 1983.

[Wad89] P. Wadler, Theorems for free! in *4th internat. Symp. on FP Languages and Computer Architecture, London*, pp.347-359, ACM, 1989.

Polymorphic Type Inference with Overloading and Subtyping

Geoffrey S. Smith*

Cornell University†

Abstract. We show how the Hindley/Milner polymorphic type system can be extended to incorporate overloading and subtyping, by using constrained quantification. We describe an algorithm for inferring principal types and outline a proof of its soundness and completeness. We find that it is necessary in practice to simplify the inferred types, and we describe techniques for type simplification that involve shape unification, strongly connected components, transitive reduction, and the monotonicities of type formulas.

1 Introduction

Many algorithms have the property that they work correctly on many different types of input; such algorithms are called *polymorphic*. A polymorphic type system supports polymorphism by allowing some programs to have multiple types, thereby allowing them to be used with greater generality.

The popular polymorphic type system due to Hindley and Milner [5, 7, 2] uses universally quantified type formulas to describe the types of polymorphic programs. Each program has a best type, called the *principal type*, that captures all possible types for the program. For example, the program $\lambda f.\lambda x.f(fx)$ has principal type $\forall \alpha.(\alpha \rightarrow \alpha) \rightarrow (\alpha \rightarrow \alpha)$; any other type for this program can be obtained by instantiating the universally quantified type variable α appropriately. Another pleasant feature of the Hindley/Milner type system is the possibility of performing *type inference*—principal types can be inferred automatically, without the aid of type declarations.

However, there are two useful kinds of polymorphism that cannot be handled by the Hindley/Milner type system: *overloading* and *subtyping*. In the Hindley/Milner type system, an assumption set may contain at most *one* typing assumption for any identifier; this makes it impossible to express the types of an overloaded operation like multiplication. For $*$ has types $int \rightarrow int \rightarrow int$[1] and $real \rightarrow real \rightarrow real$ (and perhaps others), but it does not have type $\forall \alpha.\alpha \rightarrow \alpha \rightarrow \alpha$. So any single typing $* : \sigma$ is either too narrow or too broad. Subtyping cannot be handled in the Hindley/Milner system, because there is no way to express subtype inclusions such as $int \subseteq real$.

This paper extends the Hindley/Milner system to incorporate overloading and subtyping, while preserving the existence of principal types and the ability to do type inference. In order to preserve principal types, we need a richer set of type formulas. The key device needed is *constrained (universal) quantification,*

---

*This work was supported jointly by the NSF and DARPA under grant ASC-88-00465.

†Author's current address: Department of Computer Science and Information Systems, The American University, Washington, DC 20016–8116; geoffrey@gabriel.cas.american.edu

[1] Throughout this paper, we write functions in curried form.

in which quantified variables are allowed only those instantiations that satisfy a set of *constraints*.

To deal with overloading, we require *typing* constraints of the form $x : \tau$, where x is an overloaded identifier. To see the need for such constraints, consider a function $expon(x, n)$ that calculates x^n, and that is written in terms of $*$ and 1, which are overloaded. Then the types of $expon$ should be all types of the form $\alpha \rightarrow int \rightarrow \alpha$, provided that $* : \alpha \rightarrow \alpha \rightarrow \alpha$ and $1 : \alpha$; these types are described by the formula $\forall \alpha$ **with** $* : \alpha \rightarrow \alpha \rightarrow \alpha$, $1 : \alpha . \alpha \rightarrow int \rightarrow \alpha$.

To deal with subtyping, we require *inclusion* constraints of the form $\tau \subseteq \tau'$. Consider, for example, the function $\lambda f.\lambda x. f(f\ x)$ mentioned above; give this function the name *twice*. In the Hindley/Milner system, *twice* has principal type $\forall \alpha.(\alpha \rightarrow \alpha) \rightarrow (\alpha \rightarrow \alpha)$. But in the presence of subtyping, this type is no longer principal—if $int \subseteq real$, then *twice* has type $(real \rightarrow int) \rightarrow (real \rightarrow int)$, but this type is not deducible from $\forall \alpha.(\alpha \rightarrow \alpha) \rightarrow (\alpha \rightarrow \alpha)$. It turns out that the principal type of *twice* is $\forall \alpha, \beta$ **with** $\beta \subseteq \alpha . (\alpha \rightarrow \beta) \rightarrow (\alpha \rightarrow \beta)$.

A subtle issue that arises with the use of constrained quantification is the *satisfiability* of constraint sets. A type with an unsatisfiable constraint set is *vacuous*; it has no instances. We must take care, therefore, not to call a program well typed unless we can give it a type with a satisfiable constraint set.

1.1 Related Work

Overloading (without subtyping) has also been investigated by Kaes [6] and by Wadler and Blott [14]. Kaes' work restricts overloading quite severely; for example he does not permit constants to be overloaded. Both Kaes' and Wadler/Blott's systems ignore the question of whether a constraint set is satisfiable, with the consequence that certain nonsensical expressions are regarded as well typed. For example, in Wadler/Blott's system the expression *true + true* is well typed, even though + does not work on booleans. Kaes' system has similar difficulties.

Subtyping (without overloading) has been investigated by (among many others) Mitchell [8], Stansifer [12], Fuh and Mishra [3, 4], and Curtis [1]. Mitchell, Stansifer, and Fuh and Mishra consider type inference with subtyping, but their languages do not include a **let** expression; we will see that the presence of **let** makes it much harder to prove the completeness of our type inference algorithm. Curtis studies a very rich type system that is not restricted to *shallow* types. The richness of his system makes it hard to characterize much of his work; for example he does not address the completeness of his inference algorithm. Fuh and Mishra and Curtis also explore type simplification.

2 The Type System

The language that we study is the simple *core-ML* of Damas and Milner [2]. Given a set of *identifiers* $(x, y, a, \leq, 1, \ldots)$, the set of *expressions* is given by

$$e ::= x \mid \lambda x.e \mid e\ e' \mid \textbf{let}\ x = e\ \textbf{in}\ e'.$$

Given a set of *type variables* $(\alpha, \beta, \gamma, \ldots)$ and a set of *type constructors* (*int*, *bool*, *char*, *set*, *seq*, ...) of various arities, we define the set of (unquantified) *types* by

$$\tau ::= \alpha \mid \tau \to \tau' \mid \chi(\tau_1, \ldots, \tau_n)$$

where χ is an n-ary type constructor. If χ is 0-ary, then the parentheses are omitted. As usual, $\to$ is taken to be right associative. Types will be denoted by τ, π, or ρ. We say that a type is *atomic* if it is a type constant (that is, a 0-ary type constructor) or a type variable.

Next we define the set of quantified types, or *type schemes*, by

$$\sigma ::= \forall \alpha_1, \ldots, \alpha_n \text{ with } \mathcal{C}_1, \ldots, \mathcal{C}_m . \tau,$$

where each $\mathcal{C}_i$ is a *constraint*, which is either a typing $x : \pi$ or an inclusion $\pi \subseteq \pi'$. We use overbars to abbreviate sequences; for example $\alpha_1, \alpha_2, \ldots, \alpha_n$ is abbreviated as $\bar{\alpha}$.

A *substitution* is a set of simultaneous replacements for type variables:

$$[\alpha_1, \ldots, \alpha_n := \tau_1, \ldots, \tau_n]$$

where the α_i's are distinct. We write the application of substitution S to type σ as σS, and we write the composition of substitutions S and T as ST.

Now we give the rules of our type system. There are two kinds of assertions that we are interested in proving: typings $e : \sigma$ and inclusions $\tau \subseteq \tau'$. These assertions will in general depend on a set of *assumptions* A, which contains the typings of built-in identifiers (e.g. $1 : int$) and basic inclusions (e.g. $int \subseteq real$). So the basic judgements of our type system are $A \vdash e : \sigma$ ("from assumptions A it follows that expression e has type σ") and $A \vdash \tau \subseteq \tau'$ ("from assumptions A it follows that type τ is a subtype of type τ'").

More precisely, an *assumption set* A is a finite set of assumptions, each of which is either an identifier typing $x : \sigma$ or an inclusion $\tau \subseteq \tau'$. An assumption set A may contain more than one typing for an identifier x; in this case we say that x is *overloaded* in A. If there is an assumption about x in A, or if some assumption in A has a constraint $x : \tau$, then we say that x *occurs* in A.

The rules for proving typings are given in Figure 1 and the rules for proving inclusions are given in Figure 2. If C is a set of typings or inclusions, then the notation $A \vdash C$ represents

$$A \vdash \mathcal{C}, \quad \text{for all } \mathcal{C} \text{ in } C.$$

(This notation is used in rules ($\forall$-intro) and ($\forall$-elim).) If $A \vdash e : \sigma$ for some σ, then we say that e is *well typed* with respect to A.

Our typing rules (hypoth), ($\to$-intro), ($\to$-elim), and (let) are the same as in [2], except for the restrictions on ($\to$-intro) and (let), which are necessary to avoid certain anomalies. Because of the restrictions, we need a rule, ($\equiv_\alpha$), to allow the renaming of bound program identifiers; this allows the usual block structure in programs. Also ($\equiv_\alpha$) allows the renaming of bound type variables.

It should be noted that rule (let) cannot be used to create an overloading for an identifier; as a result, the only overloadings in the language are those given by the initial assumption set.[2]

---

[2] This is not to say that our system disallows user-defined overloadings; it would be simple to provide a mechanism allowing users to add overloadings to the initial assumption set. The only restriction is that such overloadings must have *global* scope; as observed in [14], *local* overloadings complicate the existence of principal typings.

(hypoth) $\quad A \vdash x : \sigma$, if $x : \sigma \in A$

($\rightarrow$-intro) $\quad \dfrac{A \cup \{x : \tau\} \vdash e : \tau'}{A \vdash \lambda x.e : \tau \rightarrow \tau'} \qquad (x \text{ does not occur in } A)$

($\rightarrow$-elim) $\quad \dfrac{\begin{array}{l} A \vdash e : \tau \rightarrow \tau' \\ A \vdash e' : \tau \end{array}}{A \vdash e\, e' : \tau'}$

(let) $\quad \dfrac{\begin{array}{l} A \vdash e : \sigma \\ A \cup \{x : \sigma\} \vdash e' : \tau \end{array}}{A \vdash \textbf{let } x = e \textbf{ in } e' : \tau} \quad (x \text{ does not occur in } A)$

($\forall$-intro) $\quad \dfrac{\begin{array}{l} A \cup C \vdash e : \tau \\ A \vdash C[\bar{\alpha} := \bar{\pi}] \end{array}}{A \vdash e : \forall \bar{\alpha} \textbf{ with } C . \tau} \quad (\bar{\alpha} \text{ not free in } A)$

($\forall$-elim) $\quad \dfrac{\begin{array}{l} A \vdash e : \forall \bar{\alpha} \textbf{ with } C . \tau \\ A \vdash C[\bar{\alpha} := \bar{\pi}] \end{array}}{A \vdash e : \tau[\bar{\alpha} := \bar{\pi}]}$

($\equiv_\alpha$) $\quad \dfrac{\begin{array}{l} A \vdash e : \sigma \\ e \equiv_\alpha e' \\ \sigma \equiv_\alpha \sigma' \end{array}}{A \vdash e' : \sigma'}$

($\subseteq$) $\quad \dfrac{\begin{array}{l} A \vdash e : \tau \\ A \vdash \tau \subseteq \tau' \end{array}}{A \vdash e : \tau'}$

Figure 1: Typing Rules

(hypoth) $\qquad A \vdash \tau \subseteq \tau'$, if $(\tau \subseteq \tau') \in A$

(reflex) $\qquad A \vdash \tau \subseteq \tau$

(trans) $\qquad \dfrac{\begin{array}{l} A \vdash \tau \subseteq \tau' \\ A \vdash \tau' \subseteq \tau'' \end{array}}{A \vdash \tau \subseteq \tau''}$

$((-) \rightarrow (+))$ $\qquad \dfrac{\begin{array}{l} A \vdash \tau' \subseteq \tau \\ A \vdash \rho \subseteq \rho' \end{array}}{A \vdash (\tau \rightarrow \rho) \subseteq (\tau' \rightarrow \rho')}$

$(seq(+))$ $\qquad \dfrac{A \vdash \tau \subseteq \tau'}{A \vdash seq(\tau) \subseteq seq(\tau')}$

Figure 2: Subtyping Rules

Rules (∀-intro) and (∀-elim) are unusual, since they must deal with constraint sets. These rules are equivalent to rules in [14], with one important exception: the second hypothesis of the (∀-intro) rule allows a constraint set to be moved into a type scheme only if the constraint set is satisfiable. This restriction, which is not present in the system of [14], is crucial in preventing many nonsensical expressions from being well typed. For example, from the assumptions $+ : int \rightarrow int \rightarrow int$, $+ : real \rightarrow real \rightarrow real$, and $true : bool$, then without the satisfiability condition it would follow that $true + true$ has type

$$\forall \text{ with } + : bool \rightarrow bool \rightarrow bool \, . \, bool$$

even though $+$ doesn't work on $bool$!

Inclusion rule (hypoth) allows inclusion assumptions to be used, and rules (reflex) and (trans) assert that $\subseteq$ is reflexive and transitive. The remaining inclusion rules express the well-known monotonicities of the various type constructors [10]. For example, $\rightarrow$ is antimonotonic in its first argument and monotonic in its second argument. The name $((-) \rightarrow (+))$ compactly represents this information. Finally, rule ($\subseteq$) links the inclusion sublogic to the typing sublogic—it says that an expression of type τ has any supertype of τ as well.

Given a typing $A \vdash e : \sigma$, other types for e may be obtained by extending the derivation with the (∀-elim) and ($\subseteq$) rules. The set of types thus derivable is captured by the *instance relation*, $\geq_A$.

Definition 1 $(\forall \bar{\alpha} \text{ with } C \, . \, \tau) \geq_A \tau'$ *if there is a substitution* $[\bar{\alpha} := \bar{\pi}]$ *such that*

- $A \vdash C[\bar{\alpha} := \bar{\pi}]$ *and*

- $A \vdash \tau[\bar{\alpha} := \bar{\pi}] \subseteq \tau'$.

Furthermore we say that $\sigma \geq_A \sigma'$ *if for all* τ, $\sigma' \geq_A \tau$ *implies* $\sigma \geq_A \tau$. *In this case we say that* σ' *is an* instance of σ *with respect to* A.

Now we can define the important notion of a *principal typing*.

Definition 2 *The typing* $A \vdash e : \sigma$ *is said to be* principal *if for all typings* $A \vdash e : \sigma'$, $\sigma \geq_A \sigma'$. *In this case* σ *is said to be a* principal type for e *with respect to* A.

We now turn to the problem of inferring principal types.

3 Type Inference

For type inference, it is useful to assume that the initial assumption set has certain properties. In particular, we disallow inclusion assumptions like $int \subseteq (int \rightarrow int)$, in which the two sides of the inclusion do not have the same 'shape'. Furthermore, we disallow 'cyclic' sets of inclusions such as $bool \subseteq int$ together with $int \subseteq bool$. More precisely, we say that assumption set A has *acceptable inclusions* if

- A contains only constant inclusions (i.e. inclusions of the form $c \subseteq d$, where c and d are type constants), and

$W_{os}(A, e)$ is defined by cases:

1. e is x

   if x is overloaded in A with $lcg\ \forall\bar{\alpha}.\tau$,
      return $([], \{x : \tau[\bar{\alpha} := \bar{\beta}]\}, \tau[\bar{\alpha} := \bar{\beta}])$ where $\bar{\beta}$ are new
   else if $(x : \forall\bar{\alpha}\ \textbf{with}\ C\ .\ \tau) \in A$,
      return $([], C[\bar{\alpha} := \bar{\beta}], \tau[\bar{\alpha} := \bar{\beta}])$ where $\bar{\beta}$ are new
   else *fail*.

2. e is $\lambda x.e'$

   if x occurs in A, then rename x to a new identifier;
   let $(S_1, B_1, \tau_1) = W_{os}(A \cup \{x : \alpha\}, e')$ where α is new;
   return $(S_1, B_1, \alpha S_1 \to \tau_1)$.

3. e is $e'e''$

   let $(S_1, B_1, \tau_1) = W_{os}(A, e')$;
   let $(S_2, B_2, \tau_2) = W_{os}(AS_1, e'')$;
   let $S_3 = unify(\tau_1 S_2, \alpha \to \beta)$ where α and β are new;
   return $(S_1 S_2 S_3, B_1 S_2 S_3 \cup B_2 S_3 \cup \{\tau_2 S_3 \subseteq \alpha S_3\}, \beta S_3)$.

4. e is $\textbf{let}\ x = e'\ \textbf{in}\ e''$

   if x occurs in A, then rename x to a new identifier;
   let $(S_1, B_1, \tau_1) = W_{os}(A, e')$;
   let $(S_2, B_1', \sigma_1) = close(AS_1, B_1, \tau_1)$;
   let $(S_3, B_2, \tau_2) = W_{os}(AS_1 S_2 \cup \{x : \sigma_1\}, e'')$;
   return $(S_1 S_2 S_3, B_1' S_3 \cup B_2, \tau_2)$.

Figure 3: Algorithm W_{os}

- the transitive closure of the inclusions in A is antisymmetric.

These restrictions imply that only types of the same 'shape' can be related by inclusion, and that the inclusion relation is a partial order.

Less significantly, we do not allow assumption sets to contain any typings $x : \sigma$ where σ has an unsatisfiable constraint set; we say that an assumption set has *satisfiable constraints* if it contains no such typings.

Henceforth, we assume that the initial assumption set has acceptable inclusions and satisfiable constraints.

Principal types for our language can be inferred using algorithm W_{os}, given in Figure 3. W_{os} is a generalization of Milner's algorithm W [7, 2]. Given initial assumption set A and expression e, $W_{os}(A, e)$ returns a triple (S, B, τ), such that

$AS \cup B \vdash e : \tau$.

Informally, τ is the type of e, B is a set of constraints describing all the uses made of overloaded identifiers in e as well as ·all the subtyping assumptions made, and S is a substitution that contains refinements to the typing assumptions in A.

$close(A, B, \tau)$:

let $\bar{\alpha}$ be the type variables free in B or τ but not in A;
let C be the set of constraints in B in which some α_i occurs;
if A has no free type variables,
    then if B is satisfiable with respect to A, then $B' = \{\}$ else *fail*
    else $B' = B$;
return $([], B', \forall \bar{\alpha} \text{ with } C . \tau)$.

Figure 4: A simple function *close*

Case 1 of W_{os} makes use of the *least common generalization* (*lcg*) [9] of an overloaded identifier x, as a means of capturing any common structure among the overloadings of x. For example, the *lcg* of $*$ is $\forall \alpha.\alpha \to \alpha \to \alpha$.

Case 3 of W_{os} is the greatest departure from algorithm W. Informally, we type an application $e'e''$ by first finding types for e' and e'', then ensuring that e' is indeed a function, and finally ensuring that the type of e'' is a *subtype* of the domain of e'.

Case 4 of W_{os} uses a function *close*, a simple version of which is given in Figure 4. The idea behind *close* is to take a typing $A \cup B \vdash e : \tau$ and, roughly speaking, to apply ($\forall$-intro) to it as much as possible. Because of the satisfiability condition in our ($\forall$-intro) rule, *close* needs to check whether constraint set B is satisfiable with respect to A; we defer discussion of how this might be implemented until Section 6.

Actually, there is a considerable amount of freedom in defining *close*; one can give fancier versions that do more type simplification. We will explore this possibility in Section 5.

4   Correctness of W_{os}

In this section, we outline the proof of correctness of W_{os}; complete proofs can be found in [11]. We begin with some useful properties of our type system.

Lemma 1 *If* $A \vdash e : \sigma$ *then* $AS \vdash e : \sigma S$. *If* $A \vdash \tau \subseteq \tau'$, *then* $AS \vdash \tau S \subseteq \tau' S$.

Let ($\forall$-elim$'$) be the following weakened ($\forall$-elim) rule:

$$(\forall\text{-elim}') \qquad \frac{(x : \forall \bar{\alpha} \text{ with } C . \tau) \in A \quad A \vdash C[\bar{\alpha} := \bar{\pi}]}{A \vdash x : \tau[\bar{\alpha} := \bar{\pi}].}$$

Write $A \vdash' e : \sigma$ if this typing is derivable in the system obtained by deleting the ($\forall$-elim) rule and replacing it with the ($\forall$-elim$'$) rule. In view of the following theorem, $\vdash'$ derivations may be viewed as a *normal form* for $\vdash$ derivations.

Theorem 2 $A \vdash e : \sigma$ *iff* $A \vdash' e : \sigma$.

Now we turn to the correctness of W_{os}. The properties of *close* needed to prove the soundness and completeness of W_{os} are extracted into the following two lemmas:

Lemma 3 *If $(S, B', \sigma) = close(A, B, \tau)$ succeeds, then for any e, if $A \cup B \vdash e : \tau$ then $AS \cup B' \vdash e : \sigma$.*

Lemma 4 *Suppose that A has acceptable inclusions and $AR \vdash BR$. Then $(S, B', \sigma) = close(A, B, \tau)$ succeeds and*

- *$B' = \{\}$, if A has no free type variables;*

- *free-vars$(\sigma) \subseteq$ free-vars(AS); and*

- *there exists T such that*

    1. $R = ST$,
    2. $AR \vdash B'T$, and
    3. $\sigma T \geq_{AR} \tau R$.

The advantage of this approach is that *close* may be given *any* definition satisfying the above lemmas, and W_{os} will remain correct.

The soundness of W_{os} is given by the following theorem.

Theorem 5 *If $(S, B, \tau) = W_{os}(A, e)$ succeeds, then $AS \cup B \vdash e : \tau$.*

Now we turn to the completeness of W_{os}. If our language did not contain **let**, then we could directly prove the following theorem by induction.

Theorem *If $AS \vdash e : \tau$, AS has satisfiable constraints, and A has acceptable inclusions, then $(S_0, B_0, \tau_0) = W_{os}(A, e)$ succeeds and there exists a substitution T such that*

    1. $S = S_0 T$, except on new type variables of $W_{os}(A, e)$,
    2. $AS \vdash B_0 T$, and
    3. $AS \vdash \tau_0 T \subseteq \tau$.

Unfortunately, the presence of **let** forces us to a less direct proof.

Definition 3 *Let A and A' be assumption sets. We say that A is stronger than A', written $A \succeq A'$, if A and A' contain the same inclusions and $A' \vdash x : \tau$ implies $A \vdash x : \tau$.*

Roughly speaking, $A \succeq A'$ means that A can do anything that A' can. One would expect, then, that the following lemma would be true.

Lemma *If $A' \vdash e : \tau$, A' has satisfiable constraints, and $A \succeq A'$, then $A \vdash e : \tau$.*

But the lemma appears to defy a straightforward inductive proof.[3] This forces us to combine the completeness theorem and the lemma into a single theorem that yields both as corollaries and that allows both to be proved simultaneously. We now do this.

---

[3] The key difficulty is that it is possible that $A \succeq A'$ and yet $A \cup C \not\succeq A' \cup C$.

Theorem 6 *Suppose that $A' \vdash e : \tau$, A' has satisfiable constraints, $AS \succeq A'$, and A has acceptable inclusions. Then $(S_0, B_0, \tau_0) = W_{os}(A, e)$ succeeds and there exists a substitution T such that*

1. *$S = S_0 T$, except on new type variables of $W_{os}(A, e)$,*

2. *$AS \vdash B_0 T$, and*

3. *$AS \vdash \tau_0 T \subseteq \tau$.*

Finally, we get the following principal typing result:

Corollary 7 *Let A be an assumption set with satisfiable constraints, acceptable inclusions, and no free type variables. If e is well typed with respect to A, then $(S, B, \tau) = W_{os}(A, e)$ succeeds, $(S', B', \sigma) = close(A, B, \tau)$ succeeds, and the typing $A \vdash e : \sigma$ is principal.*

5 Type Simplification

A typical initial assumption set A_0 will contain assumptions such as $int \subseteq real$, $if : \forall \alpha.bool \to \alpha \to \alpha \to \alpha$, $\leq : real \to real \to bool$, $\leq : char \to char \to bool$, and $car : \forall \alpha.seq(\alpha) \to \alpha$. Also, we need a typing for a least fixed-point operator fix, allowing us to express recursion: $fix : \forall \alpha.(\alpha \to \alpha) \to \alpha$.

Now let *lexicographic* be the following program:

$$fix\ \lambda leq.\lambda x.\lambda y.$$
$$if\,(null?\ x)$$
$$true$$
$$if\,(null?\ y)$$
$$false$$
$$if\,(=\ (car\ x)\ (car\ y))$$
$$(leq\ (cdr\ x)\ (cdr\ y))$$
$$(\leq\ (car\ x)\ (car\ y))$$

Function *lexicographic* takes two sequences x and y and tests whether x lexicographically precedes y, using $\leq$ to compare the elements of the sequences.

The computation

$$(S, B, \tau) = W_{os}(A_0, lexicographic);$$
$$(S', B', \sigma) = close(A_0, B, \tau).$$

produces a principal type σ for *lexicographic*. But if we use the simple *close* of Figure 4 we discover, to our horror, that we obtain the principal type

$\forall \alpha, \gamma, \zeta, \varepsilon, \delta, \theta, \eta, \lambda, \kappa, \mu, \nu, \xi, \pi, \rho, \sigma, \iota, \tau, \upsilon, \phi$ **with**

$$\left\{ \begin{array}{l} \gamma \subseteq seq(\zeta),\ bool \subseteq \varepsilon,\ \delta \subseteq seq(\theta),\ bool \subseteq \eta,\ \gamma \subseteq seq(\lambda), \\ \lambda \subseteq \kappa,\ \delta \subseteq seq(\mu),\ \mu \subseteq \kappa,\ \gamma \subseteq seq(\nu),\ seq(\nu) \subseteq \xi,\ \delta \subseteq seq(\pi), \\ seq(\pi) \subseteq \rho,\ \sigma \subseteq \iota,\ \leq\ :\ \tau \to \tau \to bool,\ \gamma \subseteq seq(\upsilon),\ \upsilon \subseteq \tau, \\ \delta \subseteq seq(\phi),\ \phi \subseteq \tau,\ bool \subseteq \iota,\ \iota \subseteq \eta,\ \eta \subseteq \varepsilon,\ (\xi \to \rho \to \sigma) \to \\ (\gamma \to \delta \to \varepsilon) \subseteq (\alpha \to \alpha) \end{array} \right\} . \alpha$$

Such a type is clearly useless to a programmer, so, as a practical matter, it is essential for *close* to simplify the types that it produces.

We describe the simplification process by showing how it works on *lexicographic*. The call $W_{os}(A_0, lexicographic)$ returns

$$([\beta, o := \xi \to \rho \to \sigma, \rho \to \sigma], B, \alpha),$$

where

$$B = \begin{cases} \gamma \subseteq seq(\zeta), \ bool \subseteq bool, \ bool \subseteq \varepsilon, \ \delta \subseteq seq(\theta), \ bool \subseteq \eta, \\ \gamma \subseteq seq(\lambda), \ \lambda \subseteq \kappa, \ \delta \subseteq seq(\mu), \ \mu \subseteq \kappa, \ \gamma \subseteq seq(\nu), \ seq(\nu) \subseteq \\ \xi, \ \delta \subseteq seq(\pi), \ seq(\pi) \subseteq \rho, \ \sigma \subseteq \iota, \ \leq : \ \tau \to \tau \to bool, \\ \gamma \subseteq seq(\upsilon), \ \upsilon \subseteq \tau, \ \delta \subseteq seq(\phi), \ \phi \subseteq \tau, \ bool \subseteq \iota, \ \iota \subseteq \eta, \\ \eta \subseteq \varepsilon, \ (\xi \to \rho \to \sigma) \to (\gamma \to \delta \to \varepsilon) \subseteq (\alpha \to \alpha) \end{cases}$$

This means that for any instantiation S of the variables in B such that $A_0 \vdash BS$, *lexicographic* has type αS. The problem is that B is so complicated that it is not at all clear what the possible satisfying instantiations are. It turns out, however, that we can make (generally partial) instantiations for some of the variables in B that are optimal, in that they yield a simpler, yet equivalent, type. This is the basic idea behind type simplification.

There are two ways for an instantiation to be optimal. First, an instantiation of some of the variables in B is clearly optimal if it is 'forced', in the sense that those variables can be instantiated in only one way if B is to be satisfied. The second way for an instantiation to be optimal is more subtle. Suppose that there is an instantiation T that makes B no harder to satisfy and that makes the body (in this example, α) no larger. More precisely, suppose that $A_0 \cup B \vdash BT$ and $A_0 \cup B \vdash \alpha T \subseteq \alpha$. Then by using rule ($\subseteq$), BT and αT can produce the same types as can B and α, so the instantiation T is optimal. We now look at how these two kinds of optimal instantiation apply in the case of *lexicographic*.

We begin by discovering a number of forced instantiations. Consider the constraint $\gamma \subseteq seq(\zeta)$ in B. By our restrictions on subtyping, this constraint can be satisfied only if γ is instantiated to some type of the form $seq(\chi)$; the partial instantiation $[\gamma := seq(\chi)]$ is forced. There is a procedure, *shape-unifier*, that finds the most general substitution U such that all the inclusions in BU are between types of the same shape.[4] In this case, U is

$$\left[\begin{array}{l} \gamma := seq(\chi), \\ \delta := seq(\psi), \\ \xi := seq(\omega), \\ \rho := seq(\alpha_1), \\ \alpha := seq(\delta_1) \to seq(\gamma_1) \to \beta_1 \end{array} \right]$$

The instantiations in U are all forced by shape considerations; making these forced instantiations produces the constraint set

$$\{seq(\chi) \subseteq seq(\zeta), \ bool \subseteq bool, \ bool \subseteq \varepsilon, \ seq(\psi) \subseteq seq(\theta), \ldots\}$$

and the body

$$seq(\delta_1) \to seq(\gamma_1) \to \beta_1.$$

We have made progress; we can now see that *lexicographic* is a function that takes two sequences as input and returns some output.

---

[4] Such a procedure is given in [4] with the name MATCH.

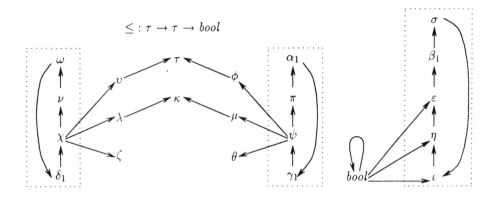

$$\text{body:} \quad seq(\delta_1) \rightarrow seq(\gamma_1) \rightarrow \beta_1$$

Figure 5: Atomic Inclusions for *lexicographic*

The new constraint set contains the inclusion $seq(\chi) \subseteq seq(\zeta)$. By our restrictions on subtyping, this constraint is equivalent to the simpler constraint $\chi \subseteq \zeta$. In this way, we can transform the constraint set into an equivalent set containing only *atomic inclusions*. The result of this transformation is shown graphically in Figure 5, where an inclusion $\tau_1 \subseteq \tau_2$ is denoted by drawing an arrow from τ_1 to τ_2. Below the representation of the constraint set we give the body.

Now notice that the constraint set in Figure 5 contains cycles; for example ω and ν lie on a common cycle. This means that if S is any instantiation that satisfies the constraints, we will have both $A_0 \vdash \omega S \subseteq \nu S$ and $A_0 \vdash \nu S \subseteq \omega S$. But since the inclusion relation is a partial order, it follows that $\omega S = \nu S$. In general, any two types within the same strongly connected component must be instantiated in the same way. If a component contains more than one type constant, then, it is unsatisfiable; if it contains exactly one type constant, then all the variables must be instantiated to that type constant; and if it contains only variables, then we may instantiate all the variables in the component to any chosen variable. We have surrounded the strongly connected components of the constraint set with dotted rectangles in Figure 5; Figure 6 shows the result of collapsing those components and removing any trivial inclusions of the form $\rho \subseteq \rho$ thereby created.

At this point, we are finished making forced instantiations; we turn next to instantiations that are optimal in the second sense described above. These are the monotonicity-based instantiations.

Consider the type $bool \rightarrow \alpha$. By rule $((-) \rightarrow (+))$, this type is *monotonic* in α: as α grows, a larger type is produced. In contrast, the type $\alpha \rightarrow bool$ is *antimonotonic* in α: as α grows, a smaller type is produced. Furthermore, the type $\beta \rightarrow \beta$ is both monotonic and antimonotonic in α: changing α has no effect on it. Finally, the type $\alpha \rightarrow \alpha$ is neither monotonic nor antimonotonic in α: as α grows, incomparable types are produced.

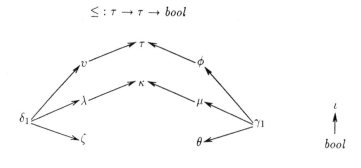

$$\leq : \tau \to \tau \to bool$$

body: $seq(\delta_1) \to seq(\gamma_1) \to \iota$

Figure 6: Collapsed Components of *lexicographic*

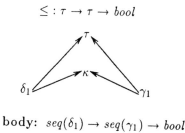

$$\leq : \tau \to \tau \to bool$$

body: $seq(\delta_1) \to seq(\gamma_1) \to bool$

Figure 7: Result of Shrinking ι, v, λ, ζ, ϕ, μ, and θ

Refer again to Figure 6. The body $seq(\delta_1) \to (seq(\gamma_1) \to \iota)$ is antimonotonic in δ_1 and γ_1 and monotonic in ι. This means that to make the body smaller, we must boost δ_1 and γ_1 and shrink ι. Notice that ι has just one type smaller than it, namely *bool*. This means that if we instantiate ι to *bool*, all the inclusions involving ι will be satisfied, and ι will be made smaller. Hence the instantiation $[\iota := bool]$ is optimal. The cases of δ_1 and γ_1 are trickier—they both have more than one successor, so it does not appear that they can be boosted. If we boost δ_1 to v, for example, then the inclusions $\delta_1 \subseteq \lambda$ and $\delta_1 \subseteq \zeta$ may be violated.

The variables v, λ, ζ, ϕ, μ and θ, however, do have unique predecessors. Since the body is monotonic (as well as antimonotonic) in all of these variables, we may safely shrink them all to their unique predecessors. The result of these instantiations is shown in Figure 7.

Now we are left with a constraint graph in which no node has a unique predecessor or successor. We are still not done, however. Because the body $seq(\delta_1) \to seq(\gamma_1) \to bool$ is both monotonic and antimonotonic in κ, we can instantiate κ arbitrarily, even to an incomparable type, without making the body grow. It happens that the instantiation $[\kappa := \tau]$ satisfies the two inclusions $\delta_1 \subseteq \kappa$ and $\gamma_1 \subseteq \kappa$. Hence we may safely instantiate κ to τ.

Observe that we could have tried instead to instantiate τ to κ, but this would

$close(A, B, \tau)$:

let A_{ci} be the constant inclusions in A,
B_i be the inclusions in B,
B_t be the typings in B;
let $U = shape\text{-}unifier(\{(\phi, \phi') \mid (\phi \subseteq \phi') \epsilon B_i\})$;
let $C_i = atomic\text{-}inclusions(B_i U) \cup A_{ci}$,
$C_t = B_t U$;
let $V = component\text{-}collapser(C_i)$;
let $S = UV$,
$D_i = transitive\text{-}reduction(nontrivial\text{-}inclusions(C_i V))$,
$D_t = C_t V$;
$E_i := D_i; \quad E_t := D_t; \quad \rho := \tau S$;
$\bar{\alpha} :=$ variables free in D_i or D_t or τS but not AS;
while there exist α in $\bar{\alpha}$ and π different from α such that
$$AS \cup (E_i \cup E_t) \vdash (E_i \cup E_t)[\alpha := \pi] \cup \{\rho[\alpha := \pi] \subseteq \rho\}$$
do $E_i := transitive\text{-}reduction(nontrivial\text{-}inclusions(E_i[\alpha := \pi]))$;
$E_t := E_t[\alpha := \pi]$;
$\rho := \rho[\alpha := \pi]$;
$\bar{\alpha} := \bar{\alpha} - \alpha$
od
let $E = (E_i \cup E_t) - \{\mathcal{C} \mid AS \vdash \mathcal{C}\}$;
let E'' be the set of constraints in E in which some α in $\bar{\alpha}$ occurs;
if AS has no free type variables,
    then if $satisfiable(E, AS)$ **then** $E' := \{\}$ **else** $fail$
    else $E' := E$;
return $(S, E', \forall \bar{\alpha} \text{ with } E'' . \rho)$.

Figure 8: Function $close$

have violated the overloading constraint $\leq : \tau \to \tau \to bool$. This brings up a point not yet mentioned: before performing a monotonicity-based instantiation of a variable, we must check that all overloading constraints involving that variable are satisfied.

At this point, δ_1 and γ_1 have a unique successor, τ, so they may now be boosted. This leaves us with the constraint set

$$\{\leq : \tau \to \tau \to bool\}$$

and the body

$$seq(\tau) \to seq(\tau) \to bool.$$

At last the simplification process is finished; we can now apply ($\forall$-intro) to produce the principal type

$$\forall \tau \text{ with } \leq : \tau \to \tau \to bool . seq(\tau) \to seq(\tau) \to bool,$$

which is the type that one would expect for $lexicographic$.

The complete function $close$ is given in Figure 8. One important aspect of $close$ that has not been mentioned is its use of $transitive\ reductions$. This provides an efficient implementation of the guard of the **while** loop in the case where a variable α must be shrunk: in this case, the only possible instantiation for α is its unique predecessor in E_i, if it has one. Similarly, if α must be boosted, then its only possible instantiation is its unique successor, if it has one.

6 Satisfiability Checking

We say that a constraint set B is *satisfiable* with respect to an assumption set A if there is a substitution S such that $A \vdash BS$. Unfortunately, this turns out to be an undecidable problem, even in the absence of subtyping [11, 13]. This forces us to impose restrictions on overloading and/or subtyping.

In practice, overloadings come in fairly restricted forms. For example, the overloadings of $\leq$ would typically be

$$\leq \; : char \rightarrow char \rightarrow bool,$$
$$\leq \; : real \rightarrow real \rightarrow bool,$$
$$\leq \; : \forall \alpha \text{ with } \leq \; : \alpha \rightarrow \alpha \rightarrow bool.$$
$$seq(\alpha) \rightarrow seq(\alpha) \rightarrow bool$$

Overloadings of this form are captured by the following definition.

Definition 4 *We say that x is overloaded by constructors in A if the lcg of x in A is of the form $\forall \alpha. \tau$ and if for every assumption $x : \forall \bar{\beta}$ with $C . \rho$ in A,*

- $\rho = \tau[\alpha := \chi(\bar{\beta})]$, *for some type constructor χ, and*

- $C = \{x : \tau[\alpha := \beta_i] \mid \beta_i \epsilon \bar{\beta}\}$.

In a type system with overloading but no subtyping, the restriction to overloading by constructors allows the satisfiability problem to be solved efficiently.

On the other hand, for a system with subtyping but no overloading, it is shown in [15] that the satisfiability problem is NP-complete.

In our system, which has both overloading and subtyping, the restriction to overloading by constructors is enough to make the satisfiability problem decidable [11]. But to get an efficient algorithm, it will be necessary to restrict the subtype relation.

7 Conclusion

This paper gives a clean extension of the Hindley/Milner type system that incorporates overloading and subtyping. The algorithms in this paper have been implemented and tried on a number of examples, usually producing the expected types. For example, the type inferred for *mergesort* is

$$\forall \alpha \text{ with } \leq : \alpha \rightarrow \alpha \rightarrow bool . seq(\alpha) \rightarrow seq(\alpha)$$

This experience gives confidence that this approach has the potential to be useful in practice.

7.1 Acknowledgements

I am grateful to David Gries and to Dennis Volpano for many helpful discussions of this work.

References

[1] Pavel Curtis. *Constrained Quantification in Polymorphic Type Analysis.* PhD thesis, Cornell University, January 1990.

[2] Luis Damas and Robin Milner. Principal type-schemes for functional programs. In *9th ACM Symposium on Principles of Programming Languages*, pages 207–212, 1982.

[3] You-Chin Fuh and Prateek Mishra. Polymorphic subtype inference: Closing the theory-practice gap. In *TAPSOFT '89*, volume 352 of *Lecture Notes in Computer Science*, pages 167–183. Springer-Verlag, 1989.

[4] You-Chin Fuh and Prateek Mishra. Type inference with subtypes. *Theoretical Computer Science*, 73:155–175, 1990.

[5] J. Roger Hindley. The principal type-scheme of an object in combinatory logic. *Transactions of the American Mathematical Society*, 146:29–60, December 1969.

[6] Stefan Kaes. Parametric overloading in polymorphic programming languages. In H. Ganzinger, editor, *ESOP '88*, volume 300 of *Lecture Notes in Computer Science*, pages 131–144. Springer-Verlag, 1988.

[7] Robin Milner. A theory of type polymorphism in programming. *Journal of Computer and System Sciences*, 17:348–375, 1978.

[8] John C. Mitchell. Coercion and type inference (summary). In *Eleventh ACM Symposium on Principles of Programming Languages*, pages 175–185, 1984.

[9] John C. Reynolds. Transformational systems and the algebraic structure of atomic formulas. *Machine Intelligence*, 5:135–151, 1970.

[10] John C. Reynolds. Three approaches to type structure. In *Mathematical Foundations of Software Development*, volume 185 of *Lecture Notes in Computer Science*, pages 97–138. Springer-Verlag, 1985.

[11] Geoffrey S. Smith. *Polymorphic Type Inference for Languages with Overloading and Subtyping.* PhD thesis, Cornell University, August 1991.

[12] Ryan Stansifer. Type inference with subtypes. In *Fifteenth ACM Symposium on Principles of Programming Languages*, pages 88–97, 1988.

[13] Dennis M. Volpano and Geoffrey S. Smith. On the complexity of ML typability with overloading. In *Conference on Functional Programming Languages and Computer Architecture*, volume 523 of *Lecture Notes in Computer Science*, pages 15–28. Springer-Verlag, August 1991.

[14] Philip Wadler and Stephen Blott. How to make *ad-hoc* polymorphism less *ad hoc*. In *16th ACM Symposium on Principles of Programming Languages*, pages 60–76, 1989.

[15] Mitchell Wand and Patrick O'Keefe. On the complexity of type inference with coercion. In *Conference on Functional Programming Languages and Computer Architecture*, 1989.

Type Reconstruction with Recursive Types and Atomic Subtyping

Jerzy Tiuryn*
Institute of Informatics
Warsaw University
Banacha 2, 02-097 Warsaw
Poland
tiuryn@mimuw.edu.pl

Mitchell Wand[†]
College of Computer Science
Northeastern University
360 Huntington Avenue, 161CN
Boston, MA 02115, USA
wand@flora.ccs.northeastern.edu

Abstract

We consider the problem of type reconstruction for λ-terms over a type system with recursive types and atomic subsumptions. This problem reduces to the problem of solving a finite set of inequalities over infinite trees. We show how to solve such inequalities by reduction to an infinite but well-structured set of inequalities over the base types. This infinite set of inequalities is solved using Büchi automata. The resulting algorithm is in *DEXPTIME*. This also improves the previous *NEXPTIME* upper bound for type reconstruction for finite types with atomic subtyping. We show that the key steps in the algorithm are *PSPACE*-hard.

1 Introduction

John Mitchell, in his seminal paper [8, 9], considered a system for type reconstruction for λ-terms in which the set of types is augmented with a partial order (the subtype order), and the type inference rules are augmented with the *subsumption rule*

$$\frac{A \vdash M : s \quad s \leq t}{A \vdash M : t}$$

In this case the type reconstruction problem reduces to the problem of solving a set of inequalities over the set of types. Mitchell showed that if the partial order is generated by a set of *atomic coercions* on the base types, it reduces to the problem of solving a set of inequalities over the base types [9].

This paper has been the source of a considerable body of work [5, 7, 17, 14]. Such a system is an important component of a type-checking system for object-oriented programming. However, a good model of object-oriented programming must include *recursive* types, which correspond to infinite trees [2, 3], but Mitchell's algorithm applies only to well-founded types, which correspond to finite trees.

---

*This work was partly supported by NSF grants CCR-9002253 and CCR-9113196 and by Polish KBN grant No. 2 1192 91 01

†Work supported by the National Science Foundation under grants CCR-9002253 and CCR-9014603.

In this paper we show how to extend Mitchell's algorithm to handle recursive types. Instead of solving inequalities over finite trees, we will need to solve inequalities over possibly infinite trees. Instead of reducing tree inequalities to a finite set of "flat" inequalities over the base types, we will get an infinite but *regular* set of flat inequalities. Instead of solving these inequalities in the base order (as in [17] or [7]) by nondeterministic choice, we solve them by reducing to the emptiness problem for Büchi automata. The resulting algorithm is in $DEXPTIME$. By contrast, the best previously-known upper-bound for type reconstruction with atomic subtyping, in the case of well-founded types, is $NEXP$-$TIME$; our algorithm can be used for this case also. Last, we show that the key steps in the algorithm are $PSPACE$-hard.

Definitions are given in Section 3, along with the basic properties of the order on infinite trees. The decision problems are posed in Section 4. Then, in Section 5, we begin the development of the algorithm. The algorithm has four main steps:

1. Reduce the type reconstruction problem to a set of inequalities over finite trees. This is the same as for the finite case. We sketch this familiar reduction in Section 5.

2. Find the shapes of the solutions via unification. The algorithm is presented in Section 6.1.

3. Enumerate the frontiers of the shapes to generate an infinite but *regular* set of flat inequalities. This step is presented in Section 6.2.

4. Solve inequalities over the partial order on the base types. This is done in Section 7 by reduction to Büchi automata, whose emptiness problem is solvable in polynomial time [15].

We note that our definition of types includes non-regular as well as regular trees; we obtain as a corollary that if an expression has any typing at all then it has one in which all the types are regular.

The resulting algorithm is in $DEXPTIME$, as all the steps are polynomial except for the reduction to Büchi automata, which is $2^{O(n)}$. On the other hand, when C is discrete, then C-TR reduces to unification on infinite trees and is therefore in $PTIME$.

We then present some lower bounds in Section 8. We show that C-REG-SAT is $PSPACE$-hard for every non-trivial poset C by reduction from quantified boolean formulas to the termination problem for a class of automata called autonomous reading pushdown automata (ARPDA), and then from ARPDA termination to C-REG-SAT.

2   Related Work

Mitchell [8, 9] introduced the problem of type reconstruction with coercions, including atomic coercions, and sketched the main algorithms for the case of well-founded types. This work concentrated on generating the set of atomic coercions that must hold among the base types. Fuh and Mishra [5] expanded these algorithms and introduced the variant in which the set of atomic coercions was either fixed or was part of the input.

Wand and O'Keefe [17] showed that type reconstruction when the set of atomic coercions was part of the input was NP-hard if certain constants were allowed in the terms to be typed. Mitchell and Lincoln [7] improved this result by establishing NP-hardness without constants, and by systematically considering the various versions of the problem.

Tiuryn [14] considered the problem of satisfiability of subtype inequalities (what we call *C-TREE-SAT*, but over finite trees only) and showed that for some classes of posets, the problem is *PSPACE*-hard, but for others it is polynomial-time.

All this work concerned well-founded (finite) types only. Amadio and Cardelli [1] considered a related problem for infinite types. They considered the validity problem for expressions denoting regular types, but with a rather different order, in which there were elements $\perp$ and $\top$ which were bounds for all types. This order may be related to the "partial types" of Thatte [13], which have a top (but not a bottom element). The decidability of type reconstruction for this type discipline was shown for the well-founded case by O'Keefe and Wand [10]. Kozen, Palsberg, and Schwartzbach [6] gave an $O(n^3)$ algorithm both for finite types and for recursive types under the partial-type ordering.

3 Definitions

3.1 Trees

Given a set C of labels, the set $Trees_C$ is the set of binary trees with leaf labels chosen from C; that is, the set of non-empty partial functions $t : \{0,1\}^* \to (C \cup \{\to\})$ such that

1. the domain of t is prefix-closed,

2. if $t(\alpha) = $ "$\to$" then $t(\alpha 0)$ and $t(\alpha 1)$ are both defined, and

3. if $t(\alpha) \in C$ then neither $t(\alpha 0)$ nor $t(\alpha 1)$ is defined.

Given a tree, its *shape* is its domain, that is, the set of nodes or paths in the tree. We will occasionally refer to a string in $dom(t)$ as a "path" or an "address". We say π is a *leaf* of t if it is in $dom(t)$, but neither $\pi 0$ nor $\pi 1$ is in $dom(t)$.

We will write $t{\downarrow}w$ for the subtree of t rooted at address w, that is the tree defined by $dom(t{\downarrow}w) = \{\pi \mid w\pi \in dom(t)\}$ and $(t{\downarrow}w)(\pi) = t(w\pi)$. The set $Regtrees_C$ of *regular* trees is the set of trees with only finitely many distinct subtrees $t{\downarrow}w$. Such trees can be thought of as being generated by a finite automaton.

3.2 Partial Order on Trees

We assume we are given a partial order $\leq_C$ on the label set C. This relation is extended to trees as follows:

1. $t \leq_0 t'$ for all t, t'.

2. For each $n \geq 0$, $\leq_{n+1}$ is defined as follows:

$$\frac{c \leq_C c'}{c \leq_{n+1} c'}$$

$$\frac{s' \leq_n s \quad t \leq_n t'}{(s \to t) \leq_{n+1} (s' \to t')}$$

3. $s \leq t$ iff $s \leq_n t$ for all $n \geq 0$.

This definition replaces the usual "bottom up" definition for $\leq$ on finite trees by a "top-down" definition. The subscripts essentially require that $s \leq_n t$ iff $s \leq t$ down to n levels; by quantifying over n, we require that $s \leq t$ for all levels. This intuition is made precise by the following lemmas.

The same-shape property, familiar from finite trees, extends to infinite trees as well:

Lemma 1 *If $t \leq t'$, then $dom(t) = dom(t')$.*

Proof: This is done by induction on the length of addresses, using the following lemma: for all $n \geq 0$, if $t \leq_n t'$ and $|\pi| \leq n$, then $\pi \in dom(t)$ iff $\pi \in dom(t')$. This is an easy induction on n. The base case uses the fact that tree domains always contain ϵ. $\square$

Let *POS* denote the regular set of strings in $\{0,1\}^*$ with an even number of 0's, and let *NEG* denote the corresponding set with an odd number of 0's. The following easy lemma will also be useful:

Lemma 2 *Let $t \leq t'$ and $\pi \in POS$ (resp. NEG). If $\pi \in dom(t)$ then $t{\downarrow}\pi \leq t'{\downarrow}\pi$ (resp. $t'{\downarrow}\pi \leq t{\downarrow}\pi$).*

Lemma 3 *$t \leq t'$ iff $dom(t) = dom(t')$ and for every leaf π of t either*

1. $\pi \in POS$ and $t(\pi) \leq_C t'(\pi)$

2. $\pi \in NEG$ and $t'(\pi) \leq_C t(\pi)$

4   The decision problems

4.1   *C-TR*

Let the set of types be $Trees_{C \cup X}$ for some set C of base types and some set X of type variables.

The problem *C-TR* has as input a triple (A, M, t), where A is a map from a finite set of variables of the λ-calculus to regular types (represented as non-deterministic finite automata), M is a λ-term, and t is a type. The problem is to determine whether there exists a map B and a substitution $\sigma : X \to Trees_C$ such that $B \supseteq A$ and $B\sigma \vdash M : t\sigma$ is deducible in the following system:

$$A \vdash x : A(x)$$

$$\frac{A \vdash M : t \to t' \quad A \vdash N : t}{A \vdash (M\,N) : t'}$$

$$\frac{A[x : t] \vdash M : t'}{A \vdash (\lambda x.M) : t \to t'}$$

$$\frac{A \vdash M : t \quad t \le t'}{A \vdash M : t'}$$

Here t and t' range over $Trees_C$, and A and B range over maps from a finite set of variables of the λ-calculus to regular types (represented as non-deterministic finite automata).

This version of the problem does not include constants in the λ-terms. The problem including constants can be reduced to C-TR by including the types of the constants in A. When C is a discrete order ($c \le_C c'$ implies $c = c'$), this is the ordinary type reconstruction problem over infinite trees. Another variant of this problem has as input only A and M, and asks whether t exists; this problem reduces to C-$TREE$-SAT similarly.

All these questions can be asked when the types are finite trees (i.e. simple types) only; we denote the finite-tree version of C-TR by C-TR_F.

4.2 C-$TREE$-SAT

Given a partial order C on the constants, the problem C-$TREE$-SAT is: Given a finite set of inequalities of the form $t \le t'$ where t and t' range over terms of the form

$$t := c \mid x \mid t \rightarrow t'$$

is there a valuation $\sigma : Vars \rightarrow Trees_C$ that satisfies all the inequalities? When C is discrete, this is just unification on infinite trees, and it is well-known that it is decidable in polynomial time, and if a solution exists, then there is a solution in which all the trees are regular.

We will use Σ as a symbol to range over instances of C-$TREE$-SAT and similar problems. We use x, y, z as metavariables ranging over the variables in the inequalities. For C-REG-SAT below, we will introduce x_α as subscripted variables, and we will identify x and x_ϵ.

Let us consider an example, which we will use throughout to illustrate the pieces of the algorithm. Consider the inequality

$$x \le y \rightarrow (c \rightarrow x)$$

By repeatedly applying Lemma 2, it is easy to deduce that in any solution σ, we will have

$$\sigma y \le (\sigma x){\downarrow}0$$
$$c \le (\sigma x){\downarrow}10$$
$$(\sigma x){\downarrow}0 \le (\sigma x){\downarrow}110$$
$$(\sigma x){\downarrow}10 \le (\sigma x){\downarrow}1110$$

etc. Furthermore, since x and x_1 are known to be interior nodes, all of these addresses must be in the domain of any solution, and all of $(\sigma x){\downarrow}11^*10$ must be leaves comparable to c, forming an increasing chain. In general, we have

$$\{(\sigma x){\downarrow}\alpha 0 \le (\sigma x){\downarrow}\alpha 110 \mid \alpha \in 1^*\}$$

By more complex initial conditions, one can generate quite complex sets of constraints, with many interlocking chains of inequalities. Our goal is to reduce C-$TREE$-SAT to an infinite (but structured) set of constraints to be solved in the partial order C. This leads us to C-REG-SAT.

4.3 C-REG-SAT

Definition 1 *A set of constraints is* regular *iff it can be expressed as a finite union of sets of inequalities of the following forms:*

(1) $\{x_{w\pi} \le y_{w'\pi} \mid \pi \in R\}$ *for some regular set R.*

(2) $\{x_w \le c\}$ *for some constant c*

(3) $\{c \le x_w\}$ *for some constant c.*

Note that a regular set of constraints is a "flat" system: it contains no arrows, so we may consider solving it over C, not $Trees_C$.

The problem C-REG-SAT is: Given a regular set of constraints, with the regular sets R represented by nondeterministic finite automata, is there a valuation $\sigma : Vars \to C$ that satisfies all the inequalities?

We will show the decidability of C-REG-SAT by reducing it to the emptiness problem for Büchi automata.

The fragment of C-REG-SAT in which all the regular sets R are finite is denoted C-FIN-SAT.

5 Reducing C-TR to C-$TREE$-SAT

The reduction from ordinary type reconstruction to unification on finite trees is well-known (e.g. [16]). The same process can be used to reduce C-TR to C-$TREE$-SAT.

Given an instance (A, M, t) of C-$TREE$-SAT, assign a type variable to every subexpression of M and every binding occurrence of a variable in M. We write t_N for the type variable associated with subexpression N; technically we should distinguish different occurrences of N, but this will be clear from context.

Since $\le$ is a partial order, consecutive occurrences of the subsumption rule may be merged. Therefore, if σ is any solution to (A, M, t), then $A\sigma \vdash M : t\sigma$ has a derivation tree in which each "structural" step is followed by exactly one subsumption step. For example, for an application, the tree would look like:

$$\frac{\dfrac{A\sigma \vdash M : t_M\sigma \quad A\sigma \vdash N : t_N\sigma}{A\sigma \vdash (M\ N) : t} \quad t \le t_{(MN)}\sigma}{A\sigma \vdash (M\ N) : t_{(MN)}\sigma}$$

where t is some type. We can summarize this information by generating the inequalities

$$t_M = t_N \to t$$
$$t \le t_{(MN)}$$

where t is a fresh type variable.

Extending these considerations to the other cases gives the following set of rules:

For each	generate
x	$t_{A(x)} \leq t_x$
$\lambda x.M$	$t_x \rightarrow t_M \leq t_{\lambda x.M}$
(MN)	$t_M = t_N \rightarrow t_1$
	$t_1 \leq t_{(MN)}$

where $t_A(x)$ is the type variable associated with the binding occurrence of x and t_1 is a fresh type variable.

Each solution to the generated set of inequalities corresponds to a type inference tree, and vice versa. Hence $C\text{-}TR$ reduces to $C\text{-}TREE\text{-}SAT$.

6 Reducing $C\text{-}TREE\text{-}SAT$ to $C\text{-}REG\text{-}SAT$

6.1 Finding the shape of the solution

By Lemma 1, we can determine the shapes of any solution to $C\text{-}TREE\text{-}SAT$ by reducing to the familiar problem of unification over infinite trees. More precisely, given an instance Σ of $C\text{-}TREE\text{-}SAT$, we can produce an instance $Shape(\Sigma)$ of unification over infinite trees as follows:

1. Replace every constant appearing in Σ by a single constant c_0. For each term t, call the resulting term $\bar{t}$

2. Replace every inequality $t \leq t'$ in Σ by the equality $\bar{t} = \bar{t}'$.

Lemma 4 *If σ is any solution to Σ, then the map σ' defined by*

$$(\sigma'x)(\pi) = \begin{cases} c_0 & \text{if } (\sigma x)(\pi) \in C \\ (\sigma x)(\pi) & \text{otherwise} \end{cases}$$

is a solution to $Shape(\Sigma)$.

Proof: Obvious from Lemma 1. □

We say Σ is *shape-consistent* iff $Shape(\Sigma)$ is solvable.

Lemma 5 *If Σ is not shape-consistent, then Σ is unsatisfiable.*

Proof: Immediate from Lemma 4. □

By the familiar algorithm ([4], Theorem 4.9.2), we can determine if $Shape(\Sigma)$ is solvable and, if it is, we can construct a principal solution to $Shape(\Sigma)$, that is a map $\sigma_\Sigma : Vars \rightarrow Regtrees_{C \cup X}$ for some finite set X of new variables, such that the solutions to $Shape(\Sigma)$ are precisely the maps of the form $\sigma \circ \tau$, where τ is any map $X \rightarrow Trees_C$.

Therefore, for each variable x appearing in Σ, we can construct regular sets $L_\Sigma(x)$, $Int_\Sigma(x)$ and $C_\Sigma(x)$ with the following properties.

$$\pi \in L_{\Sigma}(x) \quad \Longleftrightarrow \quad \pi \in dom(\sigma_{\Sigma} x)$$
$$\Longleftrightarrow \text{ for every solution } \sigma \text{ of } Shape(\Sigma), \ \pi \in dom(\sigma x)$$

$$\pi \in Int_{\Sigma}(x) \quad \Longleftrightarrow \quad (\sigma_{\Sigma} x)(\pi) = \rightarrow$$
$$\Longleftrightarrow \text{ for every solution } \sigma \text{ of } Shape(\Sigma), \ (\sigma x)(\pi) = \rightarrow$$

$$\pi \in C_{\Sigma}(x) \quad \Longleftrightarrow \quad (\sigma_{\Sigma} x)(\pi) = c_0$$
$$\Longleftrightarrow \text{ for every solution } \sigma \text{ of } Shape(\Sigma), \ (\sigma x)(\pi) = c_0$$

Let us further define $Leaves_{\Sigma}(x) = L_{\Sigma}(x) - Int_{\Sigma}(x)$. Furthermore, any solution σ, and the functions L_{Σ}, Int_{Σ}, etc., can be extended to act on finite terms instead of just on variables by setting $L_{\Sigma}(s \rightarrow t) = L_{\Sigma}(s) \rightarrow L_{\Sigma}(t)$, etc. Then, if $(s = t) \in \Sigma$, we have $L_{\Sigma}(s) = L_{\Sigma}(t)$, etc.

For our example, we have $L_{\Sigma}(x) = 1^* \cup 1^*0$, $Int_{\Sigma}(x) = 1^*$, $Leaves_{\Sigma}(x) = 1^*0$, and $C_{\Sigma}(x) = (11)^*10$.

Lemma 6 *Let Σ be a shape-consistent instance of C-TREE-SAT. Then:*

1. *If $\pi \in L_{\Sigma}(x)$, then in any solution σ of Σ, $\pi \in dom(\sigma(x))$.*

2. *If $\pi \in Int_{\Sigma}(x)$, then in any solution σ of Σ, $(\sigma x)(\pi) = \rightarrow$.*

3. *If $\pi \in C_{\Sigma}(x)$, then in any solution σ of Σ, $(\sigma x)(\pi)$ is a constant.*

Proof: We will do part 3; the others are similar. Let $\pi \in C_{\Sigma}(x)$ and σ be any solution of Σ. Form σ' as in Lemma 4. Since σ' is a solution to $Shape(\Sigma)$, we know that $(\sigma' x)(\pi) = c_0$. But this implies that $(\sigma x)(\pi) = c$ for some $c \in C$, by the construction of σ'. $\square$

6.2 Enumerating the leaf inequalities

Now we can give the reduction from *C-TREE-SAT* to *C-REG-SAT*. For a shape-consistent instance Σ of *C-TREE-SAT*, we build an instance $Flat(\Sigma)$ of *C-REG-SAT* by the following process. We start with the set Σ of inequalities with variables x, y, etc., and build a new set of inequalities $\hat{\Sigma}$ over subscripted variables x_w for $w \in \{0, 1\}^*$; we identify x and x_{ϵ}.

1. For each inequality $(s \leq t) \in \Sigma$, consider each pair of strings (w, w') such that w is a leaf of s and ww' is a leaf of t.

2. Consider the case in which $s(w)$ is a variable (say x), and ww' is a leaf (either $t(ww') = c$ or $t(ww') = y$). If ww' is positive, insert in $\hat{\Sigma}$ the inequality $x_{w'} \leq c$ or $x_{w'} \leq y$. If ww' is negative, insert in $\hat{\Sigma}$ the inequality $c \leq x_{w'}$ or $y \leq x_{w'}$.

3. If $s(w)$ is a constant c, it must be that $w' = \epsilon$ (otherwise Σ would not be shape-consistent) so $t(w) = c'$ or $t(w) = y$. If w is positive, insert in $\hat{\Sigma}$ the inequality $c \leq c'$ or $c \leq y$. If w is negative, insert in $\hat{\Sigma}$ that inequality $c' \leq c$ or $y \leq c$.

4. Similarly for each pair of strings (w, w') where w is a leaf of t and ww' is a leaf of s.

This gives us a set of inequalities of the form $x_w \leq y$, $x \leq y_w$, $x_w \leq c$, $c \leq x_w$, and $c \leq c'$.

For our example, this process generates $\hat{\Sigma} = \{y \leq x_0, c \leq x_{10}, x_{11} \leq x\}$.

Lemma 7 *If Σ is shape-consistent, then Σ is satisfiable iff $\hat{\Sigma}$ is satisfiable.*

Proof: If Σ has a solution σ, define $\hat{\sigma}(x_w) = (\sigma x){\downarrow}w$. If $\hat{\sigma}$ is a solution to $\hat{\Sigma}$, define σx to be the smallest tree such that $(\sigma x)(ww') = (\hat{s}x_w)(w')$, by marking every prefix of w with $\to$. $\square$

The instance $Flat(\Sigma)$ of C-REG-SAT is defined as follows:

- For each inequality of the form $x_w \leq y$, include the regular constraints

$$\{x_{w\pi} \leq y_\pi \mid \pi \in C(y) \cap POS\}$$

and

$$\{y_\pi \leq x_{w\pi} \mid \pi \in C(y) \cap NEG\}$$

- Include each inequality of the form $x_w \leq c$ or $c \leq x_w$.

For our example $C_\Sigma(x) = (11)^* 10 \subseteq NEG$, and $C_\Sigma(y) = \emptyset$, so we get $Flat(\Sigma) = \{c \leq x_{10}, \{x_\pi \leq x_{11\pi} \mid \pi \in (11)^* 10\}\}$

Theorem 1 *If Σ is shape-consistent, then Σ is satisfiable iff $Flat(\Sigma)$ is satisfiable.*

Proof: ($\Rightarrow$): If σ satisfies Σ and $\pi \in C_\Sigma(x)$, then $(\sigma x)(\pi)$ is a constant. Hence the variables in $Flat(\Sigma)$ are all assigned values in C, and it is easy to see that all of the constraints in $Flat(\Sigma)$ are satisfied.

($\Leftarrow$): Given a solution σ to $Flat(\Sigma)$, construct a solution σ' to Σ as follows:

1. For each variable x in Σ, let $dom(\sigma'x) = dom(\sigma_\Sigma x) = L_\Sigma(x)$.

2. If $\pi \in Int_\Sigma(x)$, let $(\sigma'x)(\pi) = \to$.

3. If $\pi \in C_\Sigma(x)$, let $(\sigma'x)(\pi) = \sigma(x_\pi)$ We will prove that x_π is a variable in $Flat(\Sigma)$.

4. Choose a $c_0 \in C$. If $\pi \in Leaves(x) - C(x)$, let $(\sigma'x)(\pi) = c_0$.

Since Σ is shape-consistent, it follows that $Int_\Sigma(x) \cap C_\Sigma(x)$ is empty, so it is easy to see that this assigns a label to every address $\pi \in L_\Sigma(x)$.

We must show that σ is a solution to Σ. Let $(s \leq t) \in \Sigma$. Then $(\bar{s} = \bar{t}) \in Shape(\Sigma)$, so by the construction of σ', $dom(\sigma's) = dom(\sigma_\Sigma \bar{s}) = dom(\sigma_\Sigma \bar{t}) = dom(\sigma't)$. By Lemma 3, it is enough to show that for every leaf π of $dom(\sigma's)$, $(\sigma's)(\pi)$ and $(\sigma't)(\pi)$ are appropriately related.

If $\pi \in Leaves_\Sigma(s) - C_\Sigma(s)$, then $(\sigma's)(\pi) = (\sigma't)(\pi) = c_0$, so the condition of Lemma 3 is satisfied regardless of whether π is positive or negative.

The remaining case is that $\pi \in C_\Sigma(s) = C_\Sigma(t)$. Then there must be paths w_1, w_2, π_1, π_2 such that $\pi = w_1\pi_1$ and w_1 is a leaf of s, and $\pi = w_2\pi_2$ and w_2 is a leaf of t.

If $s(w_1)$ is a constant (say c), then $\pi_1 = \epsilon$. So $t(w_2)$ must either be some constant c', in which case $\pi_2 = \epsilon$, or some variable y. Consider the case in which $\pi = w_1$ is positive. Then $Flat(\Sigma)$ includes $c \leq c'$ or $c \leq y_{\pi_2}$. Since σ is solution to $Flat(\Sigma)$, we have $c \leq_C c'$ or $c \leq (\sigma y_{\pi_2})$. In either case we have $(\sigma's)(\pi) \leq (\sigma't)(\pi)$ as required. The case for π negative is symmetrical.

So assume that $s(w_1)$ is some variable x, and $t(w_2)$ is some variable y. Then we have $(\sigma's)(\pi) = (\sigma'x)(\pi_1)$ and $(\sigma't)(\pi) = (\sigma'y)(\pi_2)$.

Without loss of generality, assume that w_1 is a prefix of w_2, say $w_2 = w_1 w$. Then we have $w_1\pi_1 = \pi = w_2\pi_2 = w_1 w\pi_2$, so $\pi_1 = w\pi_2$.

We now have four cases, depending on the parity of w and π_2. We will do only the case where both are positive. Since w is positive, $\hat{\Sigma}$ must contain the inequality $x_w \leq y$. Now $\pi \in C_\Sigma(s)$, so $\pi_2 \in C_\Sigma(y)$, $w\pi_2 \in C_\Sigma(x)$, and $(x_{w\pi_2} \leq y_{\pi_2}) \in Flat(\Sigma)$. Therefore σ assigns a value from C to each of these variables, as desired. Furthermore, we observe $(\sigma's)(\pi) = (\sigma'x)(\pi_1) = (\sigma'x)(w\pi_2) = (\sigma x_{w\pi_2}) \leq (\sigma y_{\pi_2}) = (\sigma'y)(\pi_2) = (\sigma't)(\pi)$, establishing the necessary relation between $(\sigma's)(\pi)$ and $(\sigma't)(\pi)$. The other cases are similar, reversing the signs as needed. $\square$

7   Reducing C-REG-SAT to Büchi automata

A Büchi automaton is a nondeterministic automaton which walks down a possibly infinite tree in which every node has a label chosen from some alphabet A. A run associates each node with a state. The state at any node may depend non-deterministically on the state of the machine at the parent node, the label at the parent node, and the direction (0 or 1) taken from the parent node to the current node.

Formally, the automaton is specified by a tuple (Q, q_0, Δ, F), consisting of a finite set of Q states, an initial state $q_0 \in Q$, a transition relation $\Delta \subset Q \times A \times \{0, 1\} \times Q$ and a set $F \subset Q$ of final states. a run on a tree t is a labelled tree t' with the same domain as t, such that $t'(\epsilon) = q_0$ and for any address π in the interior of t, the tuple $(t'(\pi), t(\pi), a, t'(\pi a))$ is in the set for $a \in \{0, 1\}$. The run is successful if on each path, some final state occurs infinitely often. It is well-known that the emptiness problem for Büchi automata is decidable, and is in fact decidable in polynomial time [12, 15].

Given a regular set of inequalities over C, we will construct a Büchi automaton whose language is non-empty iff the set of inequalities is satisfiable. Our machines will in fact be deterministic.

The first step is to reverse all the indices in Σ. This gets us to a finite set of families of inequalities of the form

$$\{x_{\pi w} \leq y_{\pi w'} \mid \pi \in R\}$$

for some regular set R represented as a nondeterministic finite automaton. This transformation clearly preserves satisfiability. We call such a set of inequalities *reverse-regular*.

Theorem 2 *Given any reverse-regular set of inequalities Σ, one can construct a Büchi automaton $\mathcal{A}$ such that the set of trees accepted by $\mathcal{A}$ is non-empty iff Σ is satisfiable.*

Proof: Without loss of generality, we consider only families of the form

$$\{x_{\pi w} \leq y_\pi \mid \pi \in R\}$$

and

$$\{x_\pi \leq y_{\pi w'} \mid \pi \in R\}$$

The constraints constructed in the preceding reduction are of this form; in general, any set of the form $\{x_{\pi w} \leq y_{\pi w'} \mid \pi \in R\}$ can be replaced by $\{x_{\pi w} \leq z_\pi \mid \pi \in R\}$, and $\{z_\pi \leq y_{\pi w'} \mid \pi \in R\}$, for some new variable z.

Assume that there are n unsubscripted variables $x^1, x^2, \ldots x^n$ in Σ, that is, the variables in Σ are of the form x_w^i for some $i \in \{1 \ldots n\}$. We will run our automaton over complete binary trees labelled by elements of C^n.

Such a tree will correspond to a solution of the set of inequalities. These trees are not quite solutions to the original set of inequalities over trees, because the indices have been reversed.

Each family of inequalities

$$\{x_\pi^i \leq x_{\pi w}^j \mid \pi \in R\}$$

can be represented by the tuple $(i, j, w, +, R)$. Similarly, each family of inequalities $\{x_{\pi w}^i \leq x_\pi^j \mid \pi \in R\}$ can be represented by the tuple $(j, i, w, -, R)$. In each case the first element of the tuple indicates the variable with the shorter subscript. The sign indicates whether the "later-found" element is larger or smaller than the "earlier-found" one. We refer to these as the *original items*.

Each inequality $c \leq x_w^i$ can be represented by the tuple $(c, i, w, +)$, and each inequality $x_w^i \leq c$ can be represented by the tuple $(c, i, w, -)$ We refer to these tuples collectively as *items*.

We construct an automaton $\mathcal{A}$ whose states are either (a) a distinguished failure state or (b) a finite set of items. The initial state will be the set of items corresponding to the constraints of the form $c \leq x_w^i$ and $x_w^i \leq c$. The accepting states will be all sets other than the failure state.

Once in the failure state, the machine will stay in the failure state forever. Otherwise, at every node the machine splits into two states, one for each branch. We refer to these states as the 0-successor state and the 1-successor state, respectively.

To construct the set of items for the two successor states, add items according to the following rules, beginning with the empty set:

1. For each original item $(i, j, aw, +, R)$, if the current address is in R then put the item $(c^i, j, w, +)$ in the a-successor state. Similarly for each item of the form $(i, j, aw, -, R)$.

2. For each original item $(i, j, \epsilon, +, R)$, if the current address is in R then check to see if $c^i \leq c^j$. If not, then make each a-successor state ($a = 0$ or 1) the failure state. (If $c^i \leq c^j$, then this constraint is satisfied at this address, so no item need be inserted.) Similarly for the original item $(i, j, \epsilon, -, R)$.

3. For each item $(c, i, aw, +)$ in the state, then the item $(c, i, w, +)$ will be in the a-successor state $(a = 0$ or $1)$.

4. For each item $(c, i, aw, -)$ in the state, then the item $(c, i, w, -)$ will be in the a-successor state.

5. For each item $(c, i, \epsilon, +)$ in the state, let c^i be the i-th component of the label at the current node. If $c^i \not\leq c$, then make both successor states the failure state. (If $c^i \leq c$, then the constraint coded by this item has been satisfied, so the item can be deleted). Similarly for each item $(c, i, \epsilon, -)$.

For each family of inequalities, represented by $(i, j, w, \pm, R)$, the automaton $\mathcal{A}$ keeps track of the current address in the tree and check to see whether it is in the regular set R. If the current address is in R, then we create an item $(c, j, w, \pm)$ that will walk down along the path w and check to see if the j-th component at that location satisfies the necessary inequality.

Each item $(c, j, w, \pm)$ walks down the tree from its creation point π, following path w to the tree address πw. It then compares the value of the y component at πw to c and either succeeds or fails, depending on the value of the $\pm$. If the constraint is violated, then the machine enters a failure state and rejects the input. Otherwise, the machine continues.

We next count the number of possible items $(c, j, w, \pm)$. Let the system Σ have k groups of inequalities, each of the form $\{c \leq x_{w_i}\}$, $\{x_{w_i} \leq c\}$, $\{x_\pi \leq y_{\pi w_i} \mid \pi \in R\}$, or $\{y_{\pi w_i} \leq x_\pi \mid \pi \in R\}$. Then the number of possible items obtained from one such group is at most $|C| \cdot |w_i|$. So the total number of items is at most

$$|C| \cdot (|w_1| + \ldots + |w_k|) \leq |C| \cdot |\Sigma|$$

Thus the number of possible items is $O(|\Sigma|)$, so $\mathcal{A}$ has at most $2^{O(|\Sigma|)}$ states.

We next show that this machine accepts some tree iff the reverse-regular set Σ of inequalities is satisfiable. If $\sigma : Vars(\Sigma) \to C$ is a solution to Σ, construct a tree $t : \{0, 1\} \to C^n$ by setting $t(\pi) = (c_1, \ldots c_n)$, where $c_i = \sigma(x_\pi^i)$ if $x_\pi^i \in Vars(\Sigma)$ and $c_i = c_0$ (some fixed constant) otherwise. This tree will be accepted by $\mathcal{A}$, since it will never send $\mathcal{A}$ to the failure state.

Conversely, if $t : \{0, 1\} \to C^n$ is accepted by $\mathcal{A}$, then for each $x_\pi^i \in Vars \Sigma$ let $\sigma(x_\pi^i)$ be the i-th component of $t(\pi)$. Since no run of $\mathcal{A}$ on t enters the failure state, it follows that all the partial-satisfaction conditions together with the component inequalities are satisfied, that is, this is a solution of Σ. $\square$

Theorem 3   1. Given a reverse-regular set of inequalities Σ, it is decidable in deterministic exponential time whether Σ is satisfiable.

2. C-REG-SAT is decidable in DEXPTIME.

Proof: By the polynomial decidability of the emptiness problem for Büchi automata and the observation that the size of $\mathcal{A}$ is $2^{O(|\Sigma|)}$. $\square$

Note by contrast that C-FIN-SAT is in NP, for every C.

We can summarize the sequence of reductions as follows:

Theorem 4   *1. The problem C-TREE-SAT is decidable in deterministic exponential time.*

2. The problem C-TR is decidable in deterministic exponential time.

3. If Σ is an instance of C-TR that has a solution, then it has a solution in which all the types are regular trees.

Proof: (i) Use nondeterministic finite automata to represent the regular sets in the solution of $Shape(\Sigma)$; then all the reductions except the last are polynomial.

(ii) All the reductions except the last are polynomial.

(iii) Because if the language accepted by a Büchi automaton is nonempty, then it includes some regular tree. □

Theorem 5 *The problem C-TR$_F$ is decidable in deterministic exponential time.*

Proof: To use this algorithm for type reconstruction with atomic subtyping in the case of well-founded types, merely test each set $L_\Sigma(x)$ for finiteness. This can be done in polynomial time. □

This result improves the upper bound for C-TR_F from $NEXPTIME$ to $DEXTIME$.

8   Lower Bounds

We show that if C is any nontrivial partial order (ie it has two unequal but comparable elements), then C-REG-SAT is $PSPACE$-hard. We will do this by defining a class of automata called *autonomous reading PDA's* (ARPDA's). Then we show that the ARPDA termination problem is PSPACE-hard, and that ARPDA termination reduces to C-REG-SAT over any nontrivial partial order.

An ARPDA consists of a finite set Q of states and a pushdown stack over the alphabet $\{0,1\}$, so an instantaneous description of a machine state is a pair (q, w) with $q \in Q$ and $w \in \{0,1\}^*$; we depict the top of the stack as being at the right-hand end of w. The machine has an initial state q^0 and a final state q^f, and its behavior is specified by a set Δ of *transitions*. Each transition is of one of two forms:

1. A *pds transition* $((p, a) \mapsto (q, b))$, where $p, q \in Q$ and $a, b \in \{0, 1, \epsilon\}$.

2. A *pds query* $((p, R) \mapsto q)$, where $p, q \in Q$, and $R \subseteq \{0,1\}^*$ is a regular set, represented as a nondeterministic finite automaton.

An ARPDA is a nondeterministic machine. Its behavior relation $\rightarrow$ is defined as follows:

- If $((p, a) \mapsto (q, b)) \in \Delta$, then $(p, ua) \rightarrow (q, ub)$ for any $u \in \{0, 1\}^*$.

- If $((p, R) \mapsto q) \in \Delta$, then $(p, u) \rightarrow (q, u)$ whenever $u \in R$.

The ARPDA termination problem is: Given an ARPDA M, does $(q^0, \epsilon) \xrightarrow{*} (q^f, \epsilon)$?

Theorem 6 *The ARPDA termination problem is PSPACE-hard.*

Proof: By reduction from evaluation of quantified boolean formulae. Let $(Q_1 x_1)\ldots(Q_n x_n)\Phi$ be a quantified boolean formula; that is, each Q_i is a quantifier ($\forall$ or $\exists$) and Φ is a boolean formula in disjunctive normal form over the variables $\{x_1, \ldots x_n\}$. We construct a ARPDA M that terminates iff this formula is true. The machine works by traversing a backtracking search tree over $\{x_1, \ldots x_n\}$. It maintains its position in the tree by keeping the values of $x_1, \ldots, x_n$ on the stack. It keeps track of its direction of travel (down or up) and its current level in $\{0, \ldots n+1\}$ in its control state Q. The initial state is (down, 1), and the final state is (up, 0).

The machine maintains the invariant that in state (up, i), the stack contains a valuation $x_1, \ldots, x_i$ that makes the formula $(Q_{i+1} x_{i+1})\ldots(Q_n x_n)\Phi$ true.

We next describe what happens at each state (d, i), when the machine is at level i travelling in direction d, and at the same time show that the machine maintains this invariant.

(down, i) On this visit, the machine is searching down in the tree. If $i \le n$ and Q_i is $\forall$, push a 0 on the stack. If $i \le n$ and Q_i is $\exists$, nondeterministically choose a value for x_i and push it on the stack. In either case go to state (down, $i + 1$).

If $i > n$, we have a complete set of values for $\{x_1, \ldots x_n\}$ on the stack. Evaluate the formula Φ using these values; this is possible by encoding Φ as a nondeterministic finite automaton and using the ability of M to check whether its stack matches an arbitrary regular set. If the formula is true, go to state (up, n). If not, then loop.

(up, i). According to the invariant, the stack contains a valuation $x_1, \ldots, x_i$ that makes the formula $(Q_{i+1} x_{i+1})\ldots(Q_n x_n)\Phi$ true. If Q_i is $\exists$, then the current value of x_i is the witness that shows that $x_1, \ldots, x_{i-1}$ makes $(Q_i x_i)(Q_{i+1} x_{i+1})\ldots(Q_n x_n)\Phi$ true. So pop the stack and go to state (up, $i - 1$).

If Q_i is $\forall$ and $x_i = 0$, this is the "infix" visit to this node: set $x_i = 1$ (by changing the topmost cell on the stack from 0 to 1), and go to the state (down, $i + 1$). If Q_i is $\forall$ and $x_i = 1$, this is the "postfix" visit to this node; at this point we have succeeded in evaluating the formula at this node, so go to state (up, $i - 1$).

Hence if we reach the state (up, 0), the stack will be empty and the original formula must have been true. Furthermore, it is clear that the machine M explores the entire subtree, so if the formula is true, all the needed witnesses will be found. $\square$

Theorem 7 *The ARPDA termination problem is polytime reducible to* C-REG-SAT *over any nontrivial poset C.*

Proof: Let $M = (Q, q^0, q^J, \Delta)$ be an ARPDA. We denote the initial and final states with superscripts to avoid conflicts with the subscripted variables of C-REG-SAT. Let C be a non-trivial poset with $a \le b$, $a \ne b$ holding in C. We will construct an instance Σ_M of C-REG-SAT such that Σ_M is unsatisfiable iff M halts.

The variables of Σ_M are Q. The inequalities are

$$p_{wa} \le q_{wb}$$

for every $w \in \{0,1\}^*$ and $((p,a) \mapsto (q,b)) \in \Delta$,

$$p_w \leq q_w$$

for $((p,R) \mapsto q) \in \Delta$ and $w \in R$, and the two inequalities

$$b \leq q^0, \quad q^f \leq a$$

It is clear that in M, (p,w) reduces to (q,u) in at most k steps iff the assertion $p_w \leq q_u$ is deducible from Σ_M in at most k applications of transitivity. Hence M halts iff $q^0 \leq q^f$ is deducible from Σ_M.

We claim that M halts iff Σ_M is unsatisfiable. Assume M halts and Σ_M is satisfiable with solution σ. Then we have $b \leq \sigma(q^0) \leq \sigma(q^f) \leq a$, so $a = b$, contradicting our assumption that $a \neq b$.

If M does not halt, construct a solution σ to Σ_M as follows: If (q,w) is reachable from the initial state (q^0, ϵ), assign $\sigma(q_w) = b$. Otherwise assign $\sigma(q_w) = a$. It is easy to show that this assignment satisfies all the inequalities in Σ_M. $\square$

It should be noted that C-REG-SAT exhibits dramatically different behavior than its fragment C-FIN-SAT which consists of finite instances of C-REG-SAT. As we remarked earlier, C-FIN-SAT is always in NP. It follows from the results of [11] that there are finite posets for which C-FIN-SAT is actually NP-complete. Our results of this paper indicate that C-REG-SAT is always between $PSPACE$ and $DEXPTIME$, for all posets C which are not discrete. Over discrete C, C-REG-SAT is clearly in $PTIME$.

9 Conclusions

We have shown how to extend Mitchell's algorithm for type reconstruction in a type system with atomic subtyping to handle recursive types. This extension is necessary to do type reconstruction for object-oriented systems with self. The resulting algorithm is in $DEXPTIME$, which also improves the previous $NEXPTIME$ algorithm for atomic subtyping on finite types.

References

[1] Roberto M. Amadio and Luca Cardelli. Subtyping Recursive Types. In *Conf. Rec. 18th ACM Symposium on Principles of Programming Languages*, pages 104–118, 1991.

[2] Kim B. Bruce. A Paradigmatic Object-Oriented Programming Language: Design, Static Typing and Semantics. Technical Report CS-92-01, Williams College, January 1992.

[3] William R. Cook, Walter L. Hill, and Peter S. Canning. Subtyping is not Inheritance. In *Conf. Rec. 17th ACM Symposium on Principles of Programming Languages*, pages 125–135, 1990.

[4] Bruno Courcelle. Fundamental Properties of Infinite Trees. *Theoretical Computer Science*, 25:95–169, 1983.

[5] Y.-C. Fuh and P. Mishra. Type Inference with Subtypes. In *Proceedings European Symposium on Programming*, pages 94–114, 1988.

[6] Dexter Kozen, Jens Palsberg, and Michael I. Schwartzbach. Efficient Inference of Partial Types. Technical Report DAIMI PB-394, Computer Science Department, Aarhus University, April 1992.

[7] Patrick Lincoln and John C. Mitchell. Algorithmic Aspects of Type Inference with Subtypes. In *Conf. Rec. 19th ACM Symposium on Principles of Programming Languages*, pages 293–304, 1992.

[8] John C. Mitchell. Coercion and Type Inference (summary). In *Conf. Rec. 11th ACM Symposium on Principles of Programming Languages*, pages 175–185, 1984.

[9] John C. Mitchell. Type Inference with Simple Subtypes. *Journal of Functional Programming*, 1:245–285, 1991.

[10] Patrick M. O'Keefe and Mitchell Wand. Type Inference for Partial Types is Decidable. In Bernd Krieg-Brückner, editor, *European Symposium on Programming '92*, volume 582 of *Springer Lecture Notes in Computer Science*, pages 408–417. Springer-Verlag, 1992.

[11] Vaughn Pratt and Jerzy Tiuryn. Satisfiability of Inequalities in a Poset. to appear, 1992.

[12] Michael O. Rabin. Weakly Definable Relations and Special Automata. In Y. Bar-Hillel, editor, *Mathematical Logic and the Foundations of Set Theory*, pages 1–23, Amsterdam, 1970. North-Holland.

[13] Satish Thatte. Type Inference with Partial Types. In *Proceedings International Colloquium on Automata, Languages, and Programming '88*, pages 615–629, 1988.

[14] Jerzy Tiuryn. Subtype Inequalities. In *Proc. 7th IEEE Symposium on Logic in Computer Science*, pages 308–315, 1992.

[15] Moshe Y. Vardi and Pierre Wolper. Automata-Theoretic techniques for modal logics of programs. *J. Comp. Sys. Sci.*, 32:183–221, 1986.

[16] Mitchell Wand. A Simple Algorithm and Proof for Type Inference. *Fundamenta Informaticae*, 10:115–122, 1987.

[17] Mitchell Wand and Patrick M. O'Keefe. On the Complexity of Type Inference with Coercion. In *Conf. on Functional Programming Languages and Computer Architecture*, 1989.

mapping, the so-called weight function. *For a given tree $T \in \mathcal{F}_t$, the weight $w_{a,g}(T)$ is recursively defined by*

$$w_{a,g}(T) := \text{if } T=\square \quad \text{then} \quad 0$$
$$\text{else} \quad \sum_{1 \leq i \leq t} [a\, w_{a,g}(T_i) + g(m_i, d_i)],$$

where subtree T_i of T is a d_i-tree, $d_i \in \{0, t\}$, with m_i nodes, $1 \leq i \leq t$.

Choosing appropriate weight functions g and real numbers a, the resulting weights $w_{a,g}(T)$ of a tree $T \in \mathcal{F}_t$ correspond to well known parameters like
  - the total path length (choose $g(m, d) := m$, $a := 1$),
  - the total degree path length (choose $g(m, d) := tm$, $a := 1$).

The following relation holds (see [6]):

Proposition 2. *Let $t \in \mathbb{N}$, $t \geq 2$, $\mathcal{F}_t$ be the family of trees with the characteristics $Q_{j,l}(z)$, $l \in \{0, t\}$, $1 \leq j \leq t$, let $a \in \mathbb{R}$, and g be a given weight function. Furthermore, let $E(z) := \sum_{n \geq t+1} \mathbb{E}[w_{a,g}(n)] z^n$ be the generating function of the average weight $\mathbb{E}[w_{a,g}(n)]$ over the family $\mathcal{F}_t(n)$. Then*

$$E(z) \odot Q_t(z) = \sum_{1 \leq j \leq t} \frac{Q_t(z)}{z + Q_{j,t}(z)}[g(1,0)z + \{a\,E(z) + G_t(z)\} \odot Q_{j,t}(z)], \quad (3)$$

where $G_t(z) = \sum_{n \geq t+1} g(n, t) z^n$, and $h_1(z) \odot h_2(z)$ denotes the Hadamard product of the two series $h_i(z) = \sum_{n \geq 0} h_{in} z^n$, $i \in \{1, 2\}$, which is defined by $h_1(z) \odot h_2(z) := \sum_{n \geq 0} h_{1n} h_{2n} z^n$. $\square$

Choosing appropriate characteristics, it is possible to describe well known probability models such as (see [6]):
  - Binary search trees (choose $Q_{1,2}(z) = Q_{2,2}(z) := \frac{z^3}{1-z^2}$),
  - t-ary digital search trees (choose $Q_{1,t}(z) = \ldots = Q_{t,t}(z) := z\exp(z^t) - z$),
  - Patricia trees (choose $Q_{1,2}(z) = Q_{2,2}(z) := \frac{1}{2}(\exp(z^2) - 1) - z$),
  - Regularly distributed t-ary trees (choose $Q_{1,2}(z) = \ldots = Q_{t,t}(z) := T(z) - z$,
    where $T(z)$ denotes the enumerator of the family $\mathcal{F}_t$).

For instance, in [2], R. Casas, J. Díaz and C. Martínez presented a probability model for simple families of trees, under which balanced trees are more likely than long skinny trees. Under this *Balanced Probability Model* (*BPM*), the average behaviour of two parameters, a so-called *occupancy* and the size of the intersection of two trees, are analyzed and compared with the uniform probability model. In order to get a better feeling about the concepts introduced above, let us summarize from [2] the basic definitions of the *BPM* in the following

Example 1. Let $\mathcal{F}$ be an arbitrary family of simply generated trees [10]. For any tree $T \in \mathcal{F}$, in which the degree of the root $r(T)$ is equal to $k \in \mathbb{N}_0$, the "frequency" $f(T)$ is recursively defined as follows:

$$f(T) := \text{if } T = \square \quad \text{then} \quad 1$$
$$\text{else} \quad \frac{1}{|T|}\, f(T_1) \cdots f(T_k),$$

where $|T|$ denotes the number of internal nodes and $T_1, \ldots, T_k$ denote the k subtrees of T.

In order to obtain a probability distribution over the subfamily of $\mathcal{F}$ of trees with the same number of internal nodes as T has, the probability $p(T)$ of T is defined by $p(T) := \frac{f(T)}{\sum_{\tau \in \mathcal{F}, |\tau| = |T|} f(\tau)}$. Furthermore, let $F^{(t)}(z) = \sum_{T \in \mathcal{F}_t} f(T) z^{|T|} = \sum_{r \geq 0} f_r^{(t)} z^r$, $t \geq 2$, be the "frequency" - generating function of the trees $T \in \mathcal{F}_t$. Then, the frequency - function is given by $F^{(t)}(z) = (1 - (t-1)z)^{-\frac{1}{t-1}}$. For $t = 2$, the BPM coincides with the BST-model. $\qquad \square$

A full average case analysis of additive weights of unlabelled rooted planar t-ary trees with polynomial weight functions under the BPM is presented in [11], using the characteristics $Q_{1,t}(z) = \ldots = Q_{t,t}(z) = zF^{(t)}(z^t) - z$.

In the sequel let $[z^r]T(z)$ denote the r-th coefficient of the series of $T(z)$ around $z = 0$. Symbols like $\mathcal{L}$ or $\mathcal{F}$ are always used to denote families of trees with some probability distribution.

2. Deformation of the BST - Model

Let L_r be the list - tree with r internal nodes, in which each internal node (with the exception of the root) is the right son of its father. Furthermore, let $\mathcal{L}_2(2r + 1)$ be the family of binary trees of size $2r + 1$, $r \in I\!N_0$, in which the linear list - tree L_r appears with probability 1 and all other trees appear with probability 0. This "$\mathcal{L}$ - model" is induced by the classical binary tree insertion algorithm, if the probability that r distinct keys are already sorted, is equal to 1. The average total path length $pl(2r + 1)$ over the family $\mathcal{L}_2(2r + 1)$ is equal to $pl(L_r) = r(r + 1)$. This rather trivial result can also be obtained by the methods presented above:

Proposition 3. *Let* $Q_{1,0}(z) = Q_{2,0}(z) := z$, $Q_{1,2}(z) :\equiv 0$ *and* $Q_{2,2}(z) := \frac{z^3}{1-z^2}$ *be given characteristics. Then the probability model induced by these characteristics coincides with the $\mathcal{L}$-model, and, under this model, the expected total path length $pl(2r + 1)$ of a tree of size $2r + 1, r \in I\!N_0$, is equal to the total path length $pl(L_r)$ of the linear list - tree L_r, which is equal to $r(r + 1)$.*

Proof. The generating function $Q_2(z)$, which is defined in Proposition 1, is equal to $Q_{2,2}(z)$. This means, that the probability $p_2(2r + 1, (1, 2r - 1), (0, d_2))$, that a tree of size $2r + 1$ is of type $< (2r + 1, 2); (1, 0), (2r - 1, d_2) >$ (the left subtree consists of one leaf, the right subtree has $2r - 1$ nodes), is equal to 1. With $G_2(z) := \sum_{r \geq 1} (2r + 1) z^{2r+1}$, we find by relation (3) of Proposition 2:

$$E(z) = \frac{z}{1 - z^2} \sum_{r \geq 1} 2r\, z^{2r} = \frac{z^2}{1 - z^2} \frac{\partial}{\partial z} \frac{z^2}{1 - z^2} = \frac{2z^3}{(1 - z^2)^3}.$$

The expected total path length $pl(2r + 1)$ is then equal to the coefficient $[z^{2r+1}]E(z)$ of z^{2r+1} of the generating function $E(z)$, hence, equal to $r(r + 1)$. $\qquad \square$

The $\mathcal{L}$-model is a "worst case" - model, which differs from the BST - model by the fact that $Q_{1,2}(z) \equiv 0$ instead of $\frac{z^3}{1-z^2}$. This observation leads to the following

Definition 3. Let c be a nonnegative real number. Let $Q_{1,0}(z) = Q_{2,0}(z) := z$ and $Q_{2,2}(z) := \frac{z^3}{1-z^2}$ be characteristics.

I) Let the $BST^{(I)}(c)$ - model be defined by choosing $Q_{1,2}(z) := \dfrac{cz^3}{1-z^2};$

II) Let the $BST^{(II)}(c)$ - model be defined by choosing $Q_{1,2}(z) := \dfrac{z}{1-cz^2} - z;$

III) Let the $BST^{(III)}(c)$ - model be defined by choosing $Q_{1,2}(z) := \dfrac{z}{(1-z^2)^c} - z.$

Obviously, if $c = 0$, all models coincide with the $\mathcal{L}$ - model, and, if $c = 1$, all models correspond to the traditional BST - model.

Using Formula (1) in Definition 1, it is a simple matter to obtain expressions for the probability $p_2(2r+1, (2r_1+1, 2r_2+1), (d_1, d_2))$, that a tree of size $2r+1$, $r \geq 2$, has $2r_1 + 1$ nodes in its left subtree and $2r_2 + 1$ nodes in its right subtree, a parameter, which makes the nature of each particular model clear:

Proposition 4. Let c be a nonnegative real number. Then the probability $p_2(2r + 1, (2r_1+1, 2r_2+1), (d_1, d_2))$, $r \geq 2$, $d_1, d_2 \in \{0, 2\}$, that a tree of size $2r + 1$ has a left subtree of size $2r_1 + 1$ and a right subtree of size $2r_2 + 1$, under the three models defined above, is given by:

I) $p_2(2r + 1, (2r_1 + 1, 2r_2 + 1), (d_1, d_2)) = \dfrac{c^{1-\delta_{r_1,0}}}{1 + c(r-1)},$

II) $p_2(2r + 1, (2r_1 + 1, 2r_2 + 1), (d_1, d_2)) = \dfrac{1-c}{1-c^r} c^{r_1},$

III) $p_2(2r + 1, (2r_1 + 1, 2r_2 + 1), (d_1, d_2)) = \dfrac{\Gamma(r)\Gamma(c+1)}{\Gamma(c+r)} \dfrac{\Gamma(c+r_1)}{\Gamma(r_1+1)\Gamma(c)},$

where r_1 can range from 0 to $r - 1$. Here δ denotes the Kronecker symbol and Γ denotes the Gamma function [1].

Proof. In each of the cases we have to compute $Q_2(z)$ and to plug the required coefficients into formula (1):

I) $Q_2(z) = \dfrac{z^3}{1-z^2} + \dfrac{cz^5}{(1-z^2)^2} = \sum_{r\geq 1}(1 + c(r-1)) z^{2r+1}$. The coefficient $q_1(2r_1 + 1, d_1)$ is equal to $c^{1-\delta_{r_1,0}}$, and $q_2(2r_2 + 1, d_2) = 1$.

II) Here, $Q_2(z) = z^3 \dfrac{1}{1-z^2} \dfrac{1}{1-cz^2} = \sum_{r\geq 1} \dfrac{1-c^r}{1-c} z^{2r+1}$, and $q_1(2r_1 + 1, d_1) = c^{r_1}$.

III) By [1, formula 6.1.21],

$$Q_2(z) = \sum_{r \geq 1} \frac{\Gamma(c+r)}{\Gamma(r)\Gamma(c+1)} \, z^{2r+1}, \text{ and } Q_{1,2}(z) = \sum_{r \geq 1} \frac{\Gamma(c+r)}{\Gamma(r+1)\Gamma(c)} \, z^{2r+1}. \qquad \square$$

Corollary 1. *Let c be a nonnegative real number. The probability $p_{s,r}^{(\circ)}(c)$ $\left(p_{l,r}^{(\circ)}(c)\right)$, $\circ \in \{I, II, III\}$, that, under the $BST^{(\circ)}(c)$ - model, the first of $r \geq 2$ distinct keys is the smallest (largest) one, is given by:*

I) $\quad p_{s,r}^{(I)}(c) \quad = \dfrac{1}{1+c(r-1)}, \quad \left(p_{l,r}^{(I)}(c) \; = c \, p_{s,r}^{(I)}(c)\right);$

II) $\quad p_{s,r}^{(II)}(c) \quad = \dfrac{1-.c}{1-c^r}, \quad \left(p_{l,r}^{(II)}(c) \; = c^{r-1} p_{s,r}^{(II)}(c)\right);$

III) $\quad p_{s,r}^{(III)}(c) \quad = \dfrac{\Gamma(r)\Gamma(c+1)}{\Gamma(c+r)}, \quad \left(p_{l,r}^{(III)}(c) = \dfrac{c}{c+r-1}\right).$

Proof. The corollary follows from Proposition 4 by setting $r_1 := 0$ $(r_1 := r - 1)$. $\square$

Note that $p_{s,r}^{(\circ)}(0) = 1$ and $p_{l,r}^{(\circ)}(0) = 0$, $\circ \in \{I, II, III\}$, because if $c = 0$, a given sequence of r distinct keys is assumed to be already sorted. If $c = 1$, we find that $p_{s,r}^{(\circ)}(1) = p_{l,r}^{(\circ)}(1) = \frac{1}{r}$, $\circ \in \{I, II, III\}$, which corresponds to the traditional BST - model, under which all $r!$ permutations of r distinct are assumed to be equally likely $(p_{s,r}^{(II)}(1) = \frac{1}{r}$ follows by Hospital's rule). Clearly, if $r = 1$, then all the probabilities defined in Corollary 1 are equal to 1.

Figure 1 shows the graphs of the probability functions $p_{\bullet,5}^{(\circ)}(c)$, $(\bullet, \circ) \in \{s, l\} \times \{I, II, III\}$. The functions $p_{s,5}^{(\circ)}(c)$ are monotonically decreasing, the functions $p_{l,5}^{(\circ)}(c)$ are monotonically increasing, $\circ \in \{I, II, III\}$. As the graph shows, model $BST^{(II)}(c)$ causes the strongest deformation, an observation which we shall verify in the next section. For instance, consider the $BST^{(I)}(c)$ - model, and let $c = \frac{1}{2}$. Furthermore, let the r distinct keys be choosen from $\{i \mid 1 \leq i \leq r\}$. A short computation shows, that the probability, that the first key is 1, is equal to $\frac{2}{r+1}$. The probability, that the first key is i, $i \in [2 : r]$, is equal to $\frac{1}{r+1}$. This causes a "deformation" of the BST - model "to the right side".

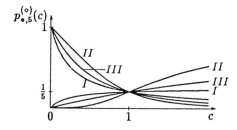

Figure 1. The monotonically decreasing probability functions $p_{s,5}^{(\circ)}(c)$ and their corresponding monotonically increasing probability functions $p_{l,5}^{(\circ)}(c)$, $\circ \in \{I, II, III\}$.

3. The Expected Total Path Length

In this section, we shall consequently make use of relation (3) of Proposition 2. In each particular case, the function $Q_2(z)$ can be picked from the corresponding proof of Proposition 4. We shall focus our attention to the main order of growth of the total path length, because the equations that are satisfied by the intervening generating functions cannot always be solved explicitly.

3.I. The $BST^{(I)}(c)$ - model

The main result is, that, unless $c = 0$, the value of c has no influence upon the dominant term of the asymptotic equivalent to the expected total path length:

Theorem 1. *Let c be a positive real number. Then, under the $BST^{(I)}(c)$ - model the expected total path length $\underline{pl}(2r+1)$ of a tree of size $2r+1$, $r \to \infty$, is asymptotically given by:*

$$\underline{pl}(2r+1) = 4r\log(r) + O(r).$$

Proof. Plugging the characteristics $Q_{i,j}(z)$, $i \in \{1, 2\}$, $j \in \{0, 2\}$, the function $Q_2(z)$ and the function $G_2(z) := \sum_{r \geq 1}(2r+1)\, z^{2r+1}$ into Formula (3), dividing the whole resulting expression by z, replacing z^2 by z, setting $e_r := \underline{pl}(2r+1)$ and using the identity $\sum_{r \geq 1}(2r+1)\, z^r = \frac{2z}{(1-z)^2} + \frac{z}{1-z}$, we obtain by a lengthy computation:

$$cz H'(z) + \frac{1 - c - 2z + z^2 - cz^2}{1 - z} H(z) = \frac{2z(1 - z + 2cz)}{(1-z)^3}, \qquad (4)$$

where $H(z) := \sum_{r \geq 1} e_r\, z^r$, with $H(0) = 0$.

The solution of the homogeneous equation (4) is a $\frac{e^{z(\frac{1}{c}-1)}z^{1-\frac{1}{c}}}{(1-z)^2}$, where a is an arbitrary constant. The classical *variation of constant* - method [4, p. 99] yields

$$H(z) = a\,\frac{e^{z(\frac{1}{c}-1)}z^{1-\frac{1}{c}}}{(1-z)^2} + \frac{e^{z(\frac{1}{c}-1)}z^{1-\frac{1}{c}}}{(1-z)^2}\,\frac{2}{c}\int \frac{e^{z(1-\frac{1}{c})}z^{\frac{1}{c}-1}(1 - z + 2cz)}{1 - z}\,dz, \qquad (5)$$

where the constant a must be set to 0, because $H(z)$ is equal to 0 and analytic at $z = 0$. Unfortunately, there doesn't seem to be a closed solution of (5) for an arbitrary value of c. However, it is not hard to see, that the integrand has exactly one simple pole at $z = 1$. The expansion of the integrand around this dominant singularity is of the form $2ce^{(1-\frac{1}{c})}(1 - z)^{-1} + O(1)$. Hence, $H(z)$ has a singular expansion of the form

$$H(z) = \frac{4}{(1-z)^2}\log\left(\frac{1}{1-z}\right) + O\left(\frac{1}{(1-z)^2}\right).$$

The theorem follows by the fact that $[z^r]\frac{1}{(1-z)^2}\log(\frac{1}{1-z}) = (r+1)(H_{r+1} - 1)$, where H_r denotes the r-th harmonic number $H_r := \sum_{1 \leq i \leq r} \frac{1}{i}$ (see [3, Eq. 7.43]). $\qquad \square$

It would be nice to have a better estimate of the O-term, however, this would require the knowledge about the coefficient of $(1 - z)^0$ in the expansion of the solution of the integral around $z = 1$.

3.II. The $BST^{(II)}(c)$ - model

As we shall see, this model resembles to the $\mathcal{L}$ - model, if $c \neq 1$:

Theorem 2. *Let c be a nonnegative real number, $c \neq 1$. Then, under the $BST^{(II)}(c)$ - model, the expected total path length $\underline{pl}(2r + 1)$ of a tree of size $2r + 1$, $r \to \infty$, is asymptotically given by:*

$$
\underline{pl}(2r + 1) = \begin{cases} (1 - c)r^2 + O(r), & \text{if } c < 1, \\[2mm] (1 - \frac{1}{c})r^2 + O(r), & \text{if } c > 1. \end{cases}
$$

Proof. Let $c < 1$. By an analogous computation as in the proof of Theorem 1, we find with $H(z) := \sum_{r \geq 1} e_r \, z^r$:

$$
H(z) = \frac{2(1 - c)z(1 - cz^2)}{(1 - z)^3(1 - cz)} + \frac{(1 - cz)^2}{(1 - z)^2} H(cz).
$$

Iterating this equation $i \in I\!N$ times yields

$$
H(z) = H(c^i z)\frac{(1 - c^i z)}{(1 - z)^2} + \frac{2z(1 - c)}{(1 - z)^2} \sum_{0 \leq s \leq i-1} \frac{c^s(1 - c^{2s+1}z^2)}{(1 - c^s z)(1 - c^{s+1}z)},
$$

and for $i \to \infty$ we obtain

$$
H(z) = \frac{2z(1 - c)}{(1 - z)^2} \left[\frac{1 - cz^2}{(1 - z)(1 - cz)} + \sum_{s \geq 1} \frac{c^s(1 - c^{2s+1}z^2)}{(1 - c^s z)(1 - c^{s+1}z)} \right].
$$

The first part of the theorem follows by Darboux's Theorem [4].

For $c > 1$, we repeat the whole procedure, but now with $H(cz)$ instead of $H(z)$. □

3.III. The $BST^{(III)}(c)$ - model

In this section we first derive a difference differential equation, using relation (3). This equation turns out to be an ordinary m-th order differential equation, if c is equal to some positive integer m. An asymptotic solution of this differential equation can be found for odd m or for $m = 2$.

Lemma 1. *Let $F(c, z)$ be the generating function $F(c, z) := \sum_{r \geq 1} e_r \frac{\Gamma(c+r)}{\Gamma(1+r)} z^r$, where $e_r := \underline{pl}(2r + 1)$ is the unknown expected total path length under the $BST^{(III)}(c)$ - model. Then, if $c > 0$, the function $F(c, z)$ satisfies the following equation:*

$$
\frac{\partial}{\partial z}F(c, z) = \frac{\Gamma(c + 1)2(1 + cz)}{(1 - z)^{2+c}} + \frac{c}{1 - z} F(c, z) + \frac{\Gamma(c + 1)}{(1 - z)^c} F(1, z). \quad (7)
$$

Proof. The lemma follows by relation (3) with [1, Formula 6.1.21]. □

Corollary 2. *Let c be equal to some positive integer $m \geq 1$, and let $H(z)$ be the generating function $H(z) := \sum_{r \geq 1} e_r z^{r+m-1}$. Then, under the $BST^{(III)}(c)$ - model, $H(z)$ satisfies the following ordinary differential equation (ODE):*

$$\frac{\partial^m}{\partial z^m} H(z) - \frac{m}{(1-z)} \frac{\partial^{m-1}}{\partial z^{m-1}} H(z) - \frac{m!}{(1-z)^m z^{m-1}} H(z) = \frac{2\, m!\, (1+mz)}{(1-z)^{m+2}}. \quad (8)$$

Proof. The proof follows from Formula (7) by repeated applications of the Gamma Function's recurrence formula $\Gamma(z+1) = z\Gamma(z)$ (see [1, Formula 6.1.15]) and the fact that $\Gamma(z+1) = z!$, if z is an integer value. $\qquad\square$

If $m = 1$, the solution of ODE (8) is (see[6]):

$$H(z) = \frac{4}{(1-z)^2} \log\left(\frac{1}{1-z}\right) - \frac{2z}{(1-z)^2},$$

and the expected total path length $\underline{pl}(2r+1)$ of a tree of size $2r + 1$ is

$$\underline{pl}(2r+1) = 4(r+1)(H_{r+1} - 1) - 2r.$$

For larger values of m, there doesn't seem to be a closed expression for the solution of ODE (8), with the exception of $m = 2$:

Theorem 3. *Let $m = 2$. Then, under the $BST^{(III)}(2)$ - model, the expected total path length $\underline{pl}(2r+1)$ of a tree of size $2r + 1$, $r \to \infty$, is asymptotically given by:*

$$\underline{pl}(2r+1) = 4r \log(r) + O(r).$$

Proof. Two linear independant solutions of the homogeneous equation of ODE (8) are given by:

$$h_1(z) := \frac{z}{(1-z)^2} \quad \text{and} \quad h_2(z) := \frac{z}{(1-z)^2}\left(z - \frac{1}{z} - 2\log(z)\right).$$

The corresponding Wronski - Determinant $w(z)$ is given by $(1-z)^{-2}$. By the *variation of constant* - method, we find that the solution of ODE (8) for $m = 2$ is:

$$H(z) = a_1 h_1(z) + a_2 h_2(z) + 2\frac{2z \log\left(\frac{1}{1-z}\right) - 1 - 4z - 2z\log(z)}{(1-z)^2},$$

where a_1 and a_2 are some well choosen numbers. This means that the local expansion of $H(z)$ around $z = 1$ is of the form

$$H(z) = \frac{4}{(1-z)^2} \log\left(\frac{1}{1-z}\right) + \frac{b_1}{(1-z)^2} + \frac{4}{1-z} \log\left(\frac{1}{1-z}\right) + O\left(\frac{1}{1-z}\right),$$

where b_1 is a constant depending on a_1 (we need not worry about a_2, because $h_2(z)$ is analytic at $z = 1$). $\qquad\square$

Note that under the $BST^{(III)}(2)$ - model, the dominant term of the expansion of $H(z)$ is the same as under the BST - model. This is not the case for larger m, m odd. However, before we shall prove this, let us first state the following lemma, which can be proved by elementary computations.

Lemma 2. *Let a be an arbitrary constant, and let $L^{[m]}$ be the linear operator*

$$L^{[m]}[A(z)] := \frac{\partial^m}{\partial z^m}A(z) - \frac{m}{1-z}\frac{\partial^{m-1}}{\partial z^{m-1}}A(z) - \frac{m!}{(1-z)^m z^{m-1}}A(z), \quad m \in \mathbb{N}.$$

Then the following identities hold:

a) $L^{[m]}\left[\frac{az^{m-1}}{(1-z)^2}\log\left(\frac{1}{1-z}\right)\right] = a\frac{(m-1)!(1+mH_{m-1})}{(1-z)^{m+2}} + \sum_{3\leq\nu\leq m+1}\frac{a_\nu}{(1-z)^\nu}$,

where H_r is the r-th harmonic number and the a_ν are computable constants;

b) $L^{[m]}\left[\frac{az^{m-1}}{(1-z)^2}\right] \equiv 0$; \qquad c) $L^{[m]}\left[\frac{az^{m-1}}{1-z}\right] = -a\frac{m!}{(1-z)^{m+1}}$;

d) $L^{[m]}\left[az^{m-1}(1-z)^k\right] = -a\frac{m!}{(1-z)^{k-m}} + \sum_{-1\leq\nu\leq k}b_{k,\nu}(1-z)^\nu, \quad 0 \leq k \leq m-2$,

where the $b_{k,\nu}$ are computable constants;

e) $L^{[m]}\left[az^{m-1}(1-z)^{m-1}\right] = \begin{cases} -a\dfrac{2m!}{1-z} + \displaystyle\sum_{0\leq\nu\leq m-1}c_{o,\nu}(1-z)^\nu, & m \text{ odd}, \\[2ex] \displaystyle\sum_{0\leq\nu\leq m-1}c_{e,\nu}(1-z)^\nu, & m \text{ even}, \end{cases}$

where the $c_{\bullet,\nu}$, $\bullet \in \{o, e\}$, are computable constants;

f) $L^{[m]}\left[az^{m-1}(1-z)^k\right] =$

$$= a\left((-1)^m\prod_{2-m\leq i\leq 1}(k+i) - m!\right)(1-z)^{k-m} + \sum_{k-m+1\leq\nu\leq k-1}d_{k,\nu}(1-z)^\nu,$$

where $k \geq m$, and where the $d_{k,\nu}$ are computable constants. $\qquad\square$

With Lemma 2 we are able to construct approximations to a particular solution of ODE (8), if m is odd, and from these approximations we obtain the following

Theorem 4. *Let $m \geq 3$ be an odd integer. Then, under the $BST^{(III)}(m)$ - model, the expected total path length $\underline{pl}(2r+1)$ of a tree of size $2r+1$, $r \to \infty$, is asymptotically given by:*

$$\underline{pl}(2r+1) = \frac{2m(m+1)}{1+mH_{m-1}}r\log(r) + O(r),$$

where H_r denotes the r-th harmonic number.

Proof. Readers who are unfamiliar with the theory of ODE's are referred to relevant books like [5,12]. We find that the homogeneous equation of ODE (8) has a so-called "regular-singular" point at $z = 1$. The corresponding "indicial equation in α" is:

$$(\alpha + 1)\alpha(\alpha - 1)\ldots(\alpha - m + 2) \;=\; 1, \text{ if } m \text{ is even,}$$
$$(\alpha + 1)\alpha(\alpha - 1)\ldots(\alpha - m + 2) \;=\; -1, \text{ if } m \text{ is odd.}$$

Similar equations appear in [9]. The solutions of them have the following properties:
- $\alpha = -2$ is always a solution, $\alpha = m - 1$ is a solution, if m is even;
- other solutions are conjugated complex numbers with real part larger than -2;
- if m is odd, no pair of solutions differs by an integer.

This means, that, if m is odd, the general solution of ODE (8) is of the form:

$$H(z) \;=\; \sum_{1 \le i \le m} \frac{e_i}{(1 - z)^{\alpha_i}} \sum_{\nu \ge 0} f_{i,\nu}(1 - z)^{\nu} \;+\; P(z),$$

where the e_i and the $f_{i,\nu}$, $i \in [1 : m]$, are constants, the α_i, $i \in [1 : m]$, are the m solutions of the indicial equation, and $P(z)$ is a particular solution of ODE (8). If m is even, we do not know, whether this is true, because, if two solutions of the indicial equation differ by an integer, there could be non-logarithm-free solutions of the homogeneous equation of ODE (8). Therefore, let m be odd for the rest of the proof.

In order to obtain a particular solution of ODE (8), we have to solve

$$I^{[m]}[P(z)] \;:=\; L^{[m]}[P(z)] - \frac{2(m + 1)!}{(1 - z)^{m+2}} + \frac{2m\, m!}{(1 - z)^{m+1}} \;=\; 0. \tag{9}$$

Approximations to the solution $P(z)$ of (9) can be constructed step by step using Lemma 2. In each step j, $j \in \mathbb{N}_0$, we have to achieve cancellation of the coefficient of $\frac{(1-z)^j}{(1-z)^{m+2}}$ left by the step $j - 1$.

The construction algorithm works as follows:
  i) set $j := -1$; and set $P_j(z) :\equiv 0$;
  ii) set $j := j + 1$;
  iii) compute $I^{[m]}[P_{j-1}(z)]$, and extract its coefficient of $\frac{(1-z)^j}{(1-z)^{m+2}}$;
  iv) depending on j, set $R(z)$ to:
      $\frac{z^{m-1}}{(1-z)^2} \log\left(\frac{1}{1-z}\right)$, if $j = 0$, and $z^{m-1}(1 - z)^{j-2}$, if $j \ge 1$;
  v) set $P_j(z) := P_{j-1}(z) + aR(z)$, where the constant a
      is choosen such that the coefficient of $\frac{(1-z)^j}{(1-z)^{m+2}}$ in $I^{[m]}[P_j(z)]$ vanishes;
  vi) goto ii).

The theorem follows by the fact that $P(z) = P_\infty(z)$. $\qquad\square$

Note that the algorithm doesn't work for even m, because case e) of Lemma 2 shows, that we cannot achieve cancellation of the coefficient of $\frac{1}{1-z}$. Note also that Theorem 4 remains valid for $m = 1$ and $m = 2$, because the 0-th harmonic number H_0 is equal to 0.

4. Algorithms

The first three sections are molded by mathematical considerations. At this point, it is worth summarizing the process employed above and giving an interpretation of our models and results.

We started with the traditional model of binary search trees BST. Under this model, all $r!$ permutations of r distinct keys are assumed to be equally likely. For instance, if $r = 3$, the 6 permutations are $(1,2,3)$, $(1,3,2)$, $(2,1,3)$, $(2,3,1)$, $(3,1,2)$, $(3,2,1)$, and the probabilities of the resulting search trees are given by the first line of Figure 2. The probability, that the left tree is of size $2r_1 + 1$, $0 \leq r_1 \leq r - 1$, is equal to $\frac{1}{3}$ in this special case, and $\frac{1}{r}$ in the case of r distinct keys. This term $\frac{1}{r}$ can be viewed as the *granularity of the tree type probability distribution*, where the term *tree type* is used in the sense of Definiton 1.

The BST - model can be described by generating functions, the characteristics. Using an external nonnegative real number c, one of these characteristics has been deformed. The deformation induces a deformation of the distribution of the tree type probabilities.

For instance, let us consider the $BST^{(I)}(c)$ - model, and let $c = \frac{1}{m}$ or $c = m$, where $m \in I\!N$ is an arbitrary positive integer. In the case $c = \frac{1}{m}$, the probability that a tree of size $2r+1$, $r \geq 2$, has a left subtree of size 1 is equal to $\frac{m}{m+r-1}$, and the probability that the left subtree is of size $2r_1 + 1$, $1 \leq r_1 \leq r - 1$, is equal to $\frac{1}{m+r-1}$.

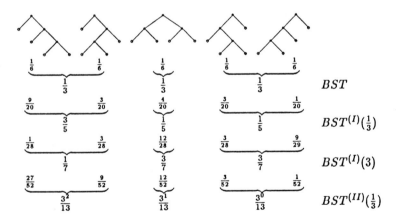

Figure 2. Binary search trees built from multisets of permutations of $\{1, 2, 3\}$ together with their probabilities and "tree type probabilities" under various models.

This recursive "splitting law on tree types" can be translated in a natural way into an algorithm. For a given a real number $c = \frac{1}{m}$, $m \in I\!N$, Program 1 generates a multiset of permutations of r distinct integer keys, such that the probability distribution over the resulting family of binary search trees is equal to that under the $BST^{(I)}(\frac{1}{m})$ - model, provided that all permutations of this multiset are choosen equally likely. In this program, the data type "permutation of length l", $l \in I\!N_0$, is an object of the form $(l, i_1, \ldots, i_l)$, where the $i_j \in I\!N$ are pairwise distinct integers. [1]

If we start Program 1 with $m := \frac{1}{3}$ and $keyset := \{1, 2, 3\}$, we finally obtain the following multiset ("$i * (\ldots)$" means, that permutation $(\ldots)$ occures i times):

$$\{1 * (3, 2, 1), 3 * (3, 1, 2), 1 * (2, 3, 1), 3 * (2, 1, 3), 3 * (1, 3, 2), 9 * (1, 2, 3)\},$$

and this induces the probability distribution given in the second line of Figure 2. This means, that the probability that the left subtree is of size 1, is equal to $\frac{3}{5}$, and the probability, that it is of size $2r_1 + 1$, $r_1 \in \{1, 2\}$, is equal to $\frac{1}{5}$, a finer granularity than under the BST - model.

```
program models;

type pset = multiset of permutation;
     iset = set of integer;

function model (m: integer; keyset: iset): pset;

var j,r: integer;
    ptmp: pset;

begin r := |keyset|;

        if r = 0 then model := {(0)};
        else if keyset = {k_1} then model := {(1,k_1)}
             else begin

                    model := Ø;
                    sort the r keys k_{i_j} of keyset, such that k_1 < k_2 < ... < k_r;

                    for j:=1 to r do begin
                        ptmp := model (m, keyset\{k_j});
                        ptmp := m^{δ_{j,1}} copies of ptmp;  *)
                        for each (r - 1, k_{i_1}, ..., k_{i_{r-1}}) ∈ ptmp do
                            model := model ∪ {(r, k_j, k_{i_1}, ..., k_{i_{r-1}})}
                    end
                end
end;

var modelset: pset;
    keyset: iset;

begin keyset := {k | 1 ≤ k ≤ r};
      modelset := model (m, keyset)
end.
```

Program 1 generates a multiset of key sequences inducing the $BST^{(I)}(\frac{1}{m})$ - model.

---

[1] The purpose of the first (additional) l is to improve the readability of the program. The resulting multiset of permutations is finally to be understood without the l.

If we replace the star-marked line of Program 1 by the line

$$ptmp := m^{1-\delta_{j,1}} \text{ copies of } ptmp; \ ,$$

then we obtain the $BST^{(I)}(m)$ - model, and, if $m = 3$, this leads to the probability distribution presented in the third line of Figure 2, and its granularity is $\frac{1}{7}$.

In both cases, $c = \frac{1}{m}$ and $c = m$, we observe that, with the exception of the case $r_1 = 0$, the probability that a tree of size $2r + 1$, $r \geq 3$, has a left subtree of size $2r_1 + 1$ and a right subtree of size $2r_2 + 1$, $r_2 \geq 1$, is equal to the probability that the left subtree is of size $2(r_1 + 1) + 1$ and the right subtree is of size $2(r_2 - 1) + 1$. In other words, with the exception of the case that the first key is the smallest one, the "tree type probabilities" remain equally distributed under the $BST^{(I)}(\circ)$ - model, $\circ \in \{\frac{1}{m}, m\}$. This is the reason for the fact, that the expected total path length doesn't increase significantly, as $r \to \infty$.

Under the $BST^{(II)}(\frac{1}{m})$ - model, we are faced with a totally different situation. An algorithm, which corresponds to this model, can be constructed by replacing the star-marked line of Program 1 by the line

$$ptmp := m^{r-j} \text{ copies of } ptmp; \ .$$

Instead of making m copies of the recursively computed multiset of permutations of $r - 1$ distinct keys, iff the key, which has been splitted off, is the smallest one, as the original Program 1 does, the modified program now makes m^{r-j} copies, iff the key, which has been splitted off, is the j-th smallest one.

If we start the modified program with $m := 3$ and $keyset := \{1, 2, 3\}$, we finally obtain the multiset

$$\{1 * (3, 2, 1), 3 * (3, 1, 2), 3 * (2, 3, 1), 9 * (2, 1, 3), 9 * (1, 3, 2), 27 * (1, 2, 3)\},$$

and the resulting probability distribution is given in the last line of Figure 2. We observe, that the tree type probability grows exponentially in the size of the right subtree instead of remaining constant, as it is the case under the $BST^{(I)}(\frac{1}{m})$ - model (with the one exception mentioned above), which causes the $O(r^2)$ order of growth of the expected total path length.

If we replace the star-marked line of Program 1 by the line

$$ptmp := m^{j-1} \text{ copies of } ptmp; \ ,$$

we obtain the $BST^{(II)}(m)$ - model, which behaves symmetrically to the $BST^{(II)}(\frac{1}{m})$ - model.

Finally, let us consider the $BST^{(III)}(m)$- model, $m \in I\!N$. An inspection of Proposition 4 shows, that the probability, that a tree of size $2r + 1$, $r \in I\!N$, has a left subtree of size $2r_1 + 1$, $r_1 \in I\!N_0$, and a right subtree of size $2r_2 + 1$, $r_2 \in I\!N_0$, is given by:

$$p_2(2r + 1, (2r_1 + 1, 2r_2 + 1), (d_1, d_2)) = \frac{m}{r} \prod_{1 \leq k \leq m-1} \frac{r_1 + k}{r + k}.$$

This formula translates into the star-marked program line

$$ptmp := \prod_{0 \leq k \leq m-2}(j + k) \text{ copies of } ptmp; \quad .$$

This means, that the tree type probability grows polynomially in the size of the left subtree, where the degree of the polynomial is equal to $m - 1$, a moderate growth, compared with the $BST^{(II)}(m)$ - model, causing only a modification of the dominant coefficient of the asymptotic equivalent to the expected total path length, but not a general modification of the order itself.

5. Concluding Remarks

We introduced three new probability models by choosing different characteristics. Clearly, the choice of these characteristics is artificial, and many other characteristics can be selected. However, as we have seen in Section 4, the three characteristics used in this paper represent three totally different probability distributions, while they are simple enough, so that we are able to compute the resulting expected path length. They give us a feeling about the question, what must happen to the BST - model in order to get "bad". Note that although we are relatively free in the selection of a characteristics, the choice must be done carefully. For instance, we cannot use $Q_{1,2}(z) := \frac{z^3}{c-z^2} - (1 - c)z$, $0 < c < 1$, because its expansion is $Q_{1,2}(z) = (c-1)z + \sum_{r \geq 1} c^{-r} z^{2r+1}$, but Definition 1 requires that $Q_{1,2}(z)$ is of the form $Q_{1,2}(z) = \sum_{r \geq 1} a_r z^{2r+1}$.

References

[1] Abramowitz, M., Stegun, I.A.: *Handbook of Mathematical Functions*. New York: Dover Publications, (1970)

[2] Casas, R., Díaz, J., Martínez, C.: *Average-case Analysis on Simple Families of Trees Using a Balanced Probability Model*. Series Formelles Et Combinatoire Algebrique, Actes de Colloque, 133-143, Bordeaux, (2.-4. Mai 1991)

[3] Graham, R.L., Knuth, D.E., Patashnik, O.: *Concrete Mathematics*. Addison-Wesley, Reading, Mass., (1988)

[4] Henrici, P.: *Applied and Computational Complex Analysis, Vol. 2*. Wiley Interscience, New York, (1977)

[5] Kamke, E.: *Differentialgleichungen*. Akademische Verlagsgesellschaft Geest & Portig K.-G., Leipzig, (1967)

[6] Kemp, R.: *Additive Weights of Non-Regularly Distributed Trees*. Annals of Discrete Mathematics 33, 129-155, (1987)

[7] Kemp, R.: *The Expected Additive Weight of Trees*. Acta Inf. 26, 711-740, (1989)

[8] Knuth, D.E.: *The Art of Computer Programming, Vol. 1, (2nd ed.)*. Addison-Wesley, Reading, Mass., (1973)

[9] Mahmoud, H., Pittel, B.: *Analysis of the Space of Search Trees Under the Random Insertion Algorithm*. Journal of Alg. 10, 52-75, (1989)

[10] Meir, A., Moon, J.W.: *On the Altitude of Nodes in Random Trees*. Can. J. Math. 30, 997-1015, (1978)

[11] Trier, U.: *Additive Weights Under the Balanced Probability Model*. Johann Wolfgang Goethe Universität Frankfurt, Fachbereich Informatik (20), Preprint, (1992)

[12] Wasow, W.: *Asymptotic Expansions for Ordinary Differential Equations*. Wiley Inter- science, New York, (1965)

Trie Size in a Dynamic List Structure

G. Louchard

Université Libre de Bruxelles, Département d'Informatique-CP 212
Boulevard du Triomphe - 1050 Brussels, Belgium

Abstract

This paper considers a classical binary tree implementation of a set of keys: the trie. The trie size properties in a static environment are well known: the size is asymptotically Gaussian when the keys number gets large. In this paper we analyze the trie in a dynamic environment, where the trie is allowed to grow and shrink in a probabilistic way. It appears that the trie size can be described by a stochastic process which is asymptotically non-Markovian Gaussian. This also allows the complete asymptotic analysis of the trie size maximum and the trie size integrated cost.

1 Introduction

List structures are well known dynamic objects in Computer Science. Let us mention dictionaries, priority queues, symbol tables, linear lists, stacks, tries, etc.

Many of them have already been analysed in the literature: see for instance Flajolet et al. [7], [6], Louchard [11], Louchard et al. [13]. Here we analyze the dynamic trie (which is a classical binary tree implementation of a set of keys), i.e. a trie initially of size 0 and returning to size 0 at step $2n$, on which insertions and deletions are performed. We want to characterize the trie size, i.e. the trie internal node number N as a stochastic process. N has already been statically investigated (i.e. with a fixed total keys number n) in Regnier, Jacquet [8] : it appears that N is asymptotically equivalent ($n \to \infty$) to a Gaussian random variable. For the dynamic trie size, we obtain here a Gaussian non-Markovian process. This also allows the analysis of two crucial variables in random structure complexity: the trie size maximum and the trie size cost (total integrated size on $[0, 2n]$).

Apart from the Knuth model (see [14]), this is the first time we meet a dynamic list structure with a non-Markovian behaviour.

The paper is organized as follows: Section 2 recalls trie definition and keys structure properties. Section 3 and 4 analyze the effects of an insertion and a deletion. Section 5 is devoted to a sequence of n insertions: several variables of interest are investigated. Section 6 deals with the covariance in the case of consecutive insertions. Section 7 gives a complete characterization of the trie size process. Section 8 deals with trie size maximum and section 9 with the trie size cost function. Section 10 concludes the paper.

The tools we use here are quite different from those we used in [12] (and of course different from classical combinatorial analysis). There, we were dealing with

Laplace's asymptotic method on functional space. Here we view the trie as a partition of $[0, 1]$ into intervals with exactly 1 or 0 key in each interval and we study the various (conditional) probabilities of m keys falling into such intervals. Each key has a uniform $[0, 1]$ distribution. This can be seen as an urn model, with dynamically varying urn sizes, where we study the occupancy distributions (For the classical occupancy problem, see Johnson and Kotz [10]). We mainly use difference equations on characteristic functions and detailed analysis of (conditioned) urn behaviour.

All detailed proofs and computations can be found in Louchard [15].

2 Binary trie and histories

Let us consider a classical binary trie where bits in the keys are 0 with probability p (and 1 with probability q): the set of keys is represented by a binary tree where edges are labelled by 0 or 1 and leaves contain the keys. The access path from the root to a leaf is a minimal prefix of the corresponding key.

In this paper, we consider the symmetric case: $p = q = 1/2$. We will use the trie to implement a dynamic list structure starting from 0 key at time 0 and returning to 0 at step (or time) $2n$.

Following Louchard [11] notations, let us first study the pos function for a classical keys structure with insertions (I) (each key has a uniform $[0, 1]$ density) and deletions (D) (each deleted key is choosen among n existing keys with equal probability $1/n$). The possibility function (defined for each request) is given by (n is the number of keys).

pos(n)

I	D	Q^+	Q^-
1	n	0	0

Indeed no order is requested here: the trie only depends on key *values*. Moreover the insertion and deletion policy insures that the trie can be seen, at each time t (with n keys) as being constructed on n independent keys. The process describing the number of keys n at time t is thus asymptotically equivalent to a priority queue $P.Q.$ so that Theor. 5.3 from [11] gives the associated Gaussian process.

3 Insertions

In this section, we analyze the effect of an insertion I on the configuration of the trie. The asymptotic distribution of a successful search in a trie is well known: see [12], [16] and [8].

Let us analyse the random variable (R.V.) i: increase in the internal nodes number N (N is the trie size).

Assume first that we have no information about the trie, apart from its keys total number n. We shall use the same approach as in [12] Sec.6. The trie can be seen as a partition of $[0, 1]$ into intervals (of size $1/2^j$) with exactly *1 or 0 key* in each interval.

Each interval $1/2^j$ possess one "buddy" of the same size. For instance a leaf $\boxed{*}$ of the trie is represented as follows (the interval is pictured as a rectangular box).

i) Assume that the inserted key • falls into such an interval. It is clear that the new trie depends on which buddy (after successive bisections) will contain the new key •. By symmetry, only one case must be considered (the new key is pictured with a •).

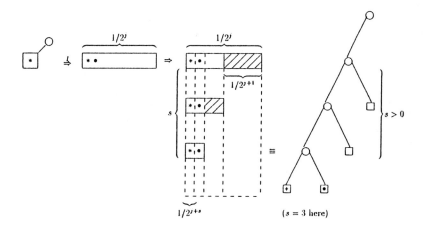

We obtain $Pr[i = s] = (\frac{1}{2})^s, s > 0$. Note that we have created $(s - 1)$ new empty leaves.

Apart from the inserted key •, there are n keys in the trie. The probability that none of these keys falls into an interval of size $1/2^j$ is given by a binomial. In first approximation this binomial is asymptotically Poisson, with probability $e^{-n/2^j}$. However we will not use the Poissonization argument as in [12] and [17]: we should then have to de-Poissonize our results. We shall instead correct the Poisson approximation when necessary.

Case i) corresponds to ($\Diamond$ means that the exact status of this node is unimportant)

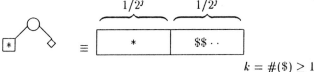

$$k = \#(\$) \geq 1$$

ii) the other subcase is related to

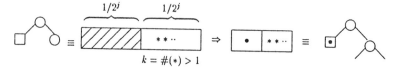

$$k = \#(*) > 1$$

In case ii), increase $i \equiv 0$.

So we obtain for the two above-mentioned cases

i)

$$Pr[i = s] \sim \left\{ \sum_{j=1}^{\infty} e^{-n/2^j} \frac{n}{2j} [1 - e^{-n/2^j}] \right\} \left(\frac{1}{2} \right)^s, s > 0$$

ii)

$$Pr[i = 0] \sim \left\{ \sum_{j=1}^{\infty} e^{-n/2^j} \left[1 - e^{-n/2^j} \left[1 + \frac{n}{2^j} \right] \right] \right\} \tag{1}$$

From these formula's we can deduce *unconditional* mean $\bar{i}$ and variance σ_i^2.

Let us now define the real problem. At time t, we know only the keys total number n and the trie size N. But the insertion process is Markovian if we know also all key *values* (or at least the exact partition of $[0,1]$). We can't deduce them from n and N. Moreover, after increasing by one key, the new trie must have the same unconditional probabilistic properties as a trie build on $(n+1)$ independent keys. It is proved in [8] and [9] that the trie size N after only n insertions is asymptotically Gaussian. The explicit values of mean and variance of N are given in [17].

4   Deletions

This section deals with the effect of a deletion D on the trie's configuration. The R.V. d (decrease in the internal nodes number N) is investigated. Assume first that we have no information about the trie apart from its key number n.

i) If the deleted key $\bullet$ is such that its leaf is like:

$$k = \#(*) > 1$$

then we observe no effect on the trie size $N, d = 0$.

ii) If the deleted key ● is such that (◇ means that the exact status of this node is unimportant):

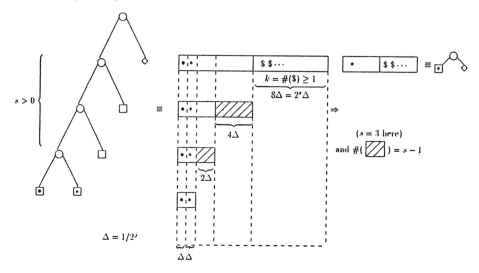

We see that $d = -s$. Apart from the deleted key ●, there are $n - 1$ other keys in the trie. Again, the probability that none of these keys falls into an interval of size $1/2^j$ is asymptotically given by $e^{-(n-1)/2^j}$.

iii) So we obtain for the above-mentioned cases

$$Pr[d = 0] \sim \left\{ \sum_{j=1}^{\infty} e^{-(n-1)/2^j} \left[1 - e^{-(n-1)/2^j} \left[1 + \frac{(n-1)}{2^j} \right] \right] \right\}$$

$$Pr[d = -s] \sim \left\{ \sum_{j=k+1}^{\infty} e^{-(n-1)/2^j} \left[e^{-(n-1)/2^j} \frac{(n-1)}{2^j} \right] e^{-\frac{(n-1)}{2^j} 2[2^{s-1}-1]} \right.$$
$$\left. \left[1 - e^{\frac{-(n-1)}{2^j} \cdot 2^s} \right] \right\}$$

with $s > 0$. From these formula's, we can deduce $\bar{d}$ and σ_d^2 (*unconditioned* values).

Again we meet the Markovian problem. If we only know n and N, we can't deduce the exact partition of $[0, 1]$.

5   A sequence of n insertions

In this section, we study the effect of a sequence of n insertions on several variables of interest: the total number S_n^e of empty leaves, D_n^e: the empty part of $[0, 1]$ (i.e. the total size of empty leaves), D_n^f (full leaves). We rediscover (by another method) the asymptotic properties of S_n^e (already analysed in [17]). This analysis also paves the way to all subsequent covariance computations.

Let us first set a few notations:

- $\#^f(\ell) :=$ number of *full* leaves (i.e. with *one* key) of size $1/2^\ell$

- $\#^e(\ell) :=$ number of *empty* leaves (i.e. with 0 key) of size $1/2^\ell$

- $c^\bullet(\ell) := E[\#^\bullet(\ell)]$

- $D^\bullet = \sum_j \#^\bullet(j)\frac{1}{2^j}$
  i.e. $D^e :=$ empty part of $[0,1]$
  $\quad\ D^f :=$ full part of $[0,1]$
  Off course $D^e + D^f = 1$.

- $S^\bullet = \sum_j \#^\bullet(j)$. For any quantity Q, $Q_n := Q$ *after n insertions* .

  Obviously $S_n^f \equiv n$ and the total *internal* node number N_n is given by:

$$N_n = S_n^e + S_n^f - 1 = n + S_n^e - 1 \tag{2}$$

Some expectations can now be considered. By (1) we know $c_n^\bullet$. Indeed, we deduce

$$\begin{cases} c_n^f(j)\frac{1}{2^j} = E\left[\#_n^f(j)\frac{1}{2^j}\right] \sim e^{-n/2^j}\frac{n}{2^j}[1 - e^{-n/2^j}] \\[2mm] c_n^e(j)\frac{1}{2^j} = E\left[\#_n^e(j)\frac{1}{2^j}\right] \sim e^{-n/2^j}\left[1 - e^{-n/2^j}\left[1 + \frac{n}{2^j}\right]\right] \end{cases}$$

So that, for instance

$$\begin{cases} E(D_n^e) \sim \sum_{j=1}^\infty \left\{e^{-n/2^j}\left[1 - e^{-n/2^j}\left[1 + \frac{n}{2^j}\right]\right]\right\} \\[2mm] E(S_n^e) \sim \sum_{j=1}^\infty 2^j \left\{e^{-n/2^j}\left[1 - e^{-n/2^j}\left[1 + \frac{n}{2^j}\right]\right]\right\} \end{cases} \tag{3}$$

A few difference equations can now be established. Let $\Delta_n c_n^\bullet(\ell) := c_{n+1}^\bullet(\ell) - c_n^\bullet(\ell)$. Then we derive

$$\begin{cases} \Delta_n c_n^f(\ell) = \sum_{j=1}^{\ell-1}\left(c_n^f(j)\frac{1}{2^j}\right)\frac{1}{2^{\ell-j}}\cdot(2) + \left(c_n^f(\ell)\frac{1}{2^\ell}\right)\cdot(-1) + c_n^e(\ell)\frac{1}{2^\ell}\cdot(1) \\[2mm] \Delta_n c_n^e(\ell) = \sum_{j=1}^{\ell-1}\left(c_n^f(j)\frac{1}{2^j}\right)\sum_{k=\ell-j+1}^\infty \frac{1}{2^k}\cdot(1) + \left(c_n^e(\ell)\frac{1}{2^\ell}\right)\cdot(-1) \end{cases} \tag{4}$$

From (4), we derive

$$\begin{cases} \Delta_n[E(S_n^f)] = E(D_n^f) + E(D_n^e) = 1 \qquad \text{(as it should)} \\[2mm] \Delta_n[E(S_n^e)] = E(D_n^f) - E(D_n^e) = 1 - 2E(D_n^e) \\ \quad \text{(this can be checked against (3))} \end{cases} \tag{5}$$

To obtain the distribution of S^e and D^e, let us analyze $\varphi_n(w_1) := E_n[e^{iw_1 S_n^e}]$. We obtain the difference equation

$$
\begin{aligned}
\Delta_n \varphi_n(w_1) &= E\left\{ D_n^f \left(\sum_{s=1}^{\infty} \frac{1}{2^s} e^{iw_1(s-1)} \right) e^{iw_1 S_n^e} + D_n^e e^{-iw_1} e^{iw_1 S_n^e} - e^{iw_1 S_n^e} \right\} \\
&= E\left\{ D_n^f \frac{1}{2} \frac{e^{iw_1 S_n^e}}{1 - e^{iw_1}/2} + D_n^e e^{-iw_1} e^{iw_1 S_n^e} - e^{iw_1 S_n^e} \right\}
\end{aligned}
$$

Expanding, we derive

$$
iw_1 : \Delta_n[E(S_n^e)] = E(D_n^f) - E(D_n^e) \qquad \text{(which confirms (5))}
$$

$$
\frac{-w_1^2}{2} : \Delta_n[E[(S_n^e)^2]] = 2E(D_n^f S_n^e) + 3E(D_n^f)
$$
$$
-2E(D_n^e S_n^e) + E(D_n^e) \qquad (6)
$$

We now turn to the asymptotic analysis of $E(D_n^e)$, $E(S_n^e)$ and $VAR(S_n^e)$. We obtain the following result

Theorem 5.1

$$
E(D_n^e) \sim 1 - \frac{1}{2ln2} + \beta_0(n)
$$
$$
E(D_n^f) \sim \frac{1}{2ln2} - \beta_0(n)
$$
$$
E(S_n^e) \sim n[\alpha_0 + \beta_1(n)]
$$

with $\alpha_0 = \frac{1}{ln2} - 1$ and $\beta_\bullet(n)$ are (small) periodic function of $\log_2 n$

$$
VAR(S_n^e) \sim n\alpha_2
$$

with $\alpha_2 := 1 - \frac{3}{2ln2} - \alpha_0^2 + 2\sum_{\ell=1}^{\infty} \frac{\delta}{1+\delta}/ln2$, and $\delta := 1/2^\ell$.

Proof The detailed proof, based on somewhere delicate urn sizes analysis, is given in [15].

$\square$

We now turn to the asymptotic distribution of S_n^e. We obtain the following theorem (the Gaussian character of S_n^e is proved in [8] and [9] by a different method).

Theorem 5.2 S_n^e is asymptotically Gaussian with mean $\sim \alpha_0 n$ and $VAR \sim n\alpha_6$.

Our proof is again based on some difference equation properties (the details are given in [15]).

6 Covariances - The case of consecutive insertions

This section is devoted to the case of ν consecutive insertions: we analyze the covariance between $S_{n_1}^e$ et $S_{n_2}^e$. This covariance is given by the following theorem.

Theorem 6.1 *Let* $COV(S_{n_1}^e, S_{n_2}^e) \sim \Psi(t_1, t_2)n$, *with* $n_1 = nt_1, n_2 = nt_2, n_2 = n_1 + \nu, (\nu \geq 0)$.

Then $\Psi(t_1, t_2) = \Pi(\frac{t_2}{t_1}) \cdot t_2$ *where*

$$
\begin{aligned}
\Pi(z) =\ & -\sum_{\ell=1}^{\infty} \delta[\delta^3 z - 3\delta^3 z^2 + 2\delta^3 z^3 - 4\delta^2 z + \delta^2 + 2\delta^2 z^4 + 3\delta^2 z^2 - 2\delta^2 z^3 \\
& - 3\delta\ z^2 - \delta\ z + 4z^3\delta - 1 + z^2]/[(1 + \delta\ z)(1 + \delta)(z + \delta)(1 + \delta\ z - \delta)z\ln(2)] \\
& - \frac{1}{2}\frac{(\ln(2)z - 2\ln(2) + \ln(2)z^2 + 2 - 2z^2)}{\ln(2)^2(z + 1)z} + \alpha_2
\end{aligned}
$$

(α_2 as given in Theor. 5.1, $\delta := 1/2^\ell$).

Proof The detailed proof is again given in [15].

□

7 Trie size in a dynamic structure

This section contains the main result of this paper: a complete characterization of the trie size process. We first recall the keys structure characteristics. Then we analyse a static structure, with I as first operation. D is described next. The static structure covariance is computed and finally the full dynamic structure covariance is obtained.

7.1 Key total number process

From Louchard [11] Theorem 5.3, it is known that the priority queue Y describing the number of keys at time nt is such that

$$
\frac{Y([nt]) - nf_1(t)}{\sqrt{n}} \Rightarrow X(t), \qquad 0 \leq t \leq 2 \tag{7}
$$

where we assume that we start with an empty structure at time 0 and we return to an empty structure at time $2n$. We have obtained in [11]:

$$
f_1(t) = \frac{1}{2}t(2 - t)
$$

$X(t)$ is a Markovian Gaussian process with covariance

$$
\begin{aligned}
f_2(s, t) &= \gamma(s)\gamma(2 - t), & s \leq t \\
&= \gamma(t)\gamma(2 - s), & s \geq t
\end{aligned}
$$

and $\gamma(v) = v^2/2$.

The error term in (7) can be deduced from the various expansions in [11]: it appears that the relative error in the density is $O(\frac{1}{\sqrt{n}})$. In the sequel, we will always use the denotation *structure* for the process (7). Keys total number is usually denoted by n_1, n_2, n_t. If we denote by n_1, n_2 the number of keys at time t_1, t_2, we have

$$E[e^{i(\zeta_1 n_1 + \zeta_2 n_2)}] \sim$$
$$\exp\left[n\left\{i[\zeta_1 f_1(t_1) + \zeta_2 f_1(t_2)]\right.\right.$$
$$\left.\left. -\frac{1}{2}[\zeta_1^2 f_2(t_1, t_1) + 2\zeta_1\zeta_2 f_2(t_1, t_2) + \zeta_2^2 f_2(t_2, t_2)]\right\}\right] \tag{8}$$

For further use, we denote

$$n_1^* := n f_1(t_1),$$
$$n_2^* := n f_1(t_2)$$

7.2   Non-random static structure

Let us start with a non-random (NR) static structure, following a path fixed by $n f_1(t)$. Let us divide the $2n$ steps into $2n/m$ groups of m steps, when m is large and $m = o(n)$. For instance, choose Dt small such that $m = n(Dt)$. It is well known (see Louchard [11], Lemma 5.1) that the probability p_I of an insertion is asymptotically constant on such an interval and is given by

$$p_I \sim \frac{1}{2}(1 + f_1'(t)) = 1 - t/2$$

similarly

$$p_D \sim \frac{1}{2}(1 - f_1'(t)) = t/2$$

The total number of insertions (deletions) on Dt is given by $n_I = m p_I$ ($n_D = m p_D$). Choose an interval $\Delta(= 1/2^j)$ in $[0, 1]$ such that $n_t^* \Delta = O(1) \cdot (n_t^* = n f_1(t))$. As the number of inserted keys in Δ (or deleted keys) is very small compared with $n_t^* \Delta$, we see that, asymptotically, insertions and deletions perform independently on Δ. Assume that, among the n_t^* keys, n_Δ stay in Δ. The probability that ν_Δ^D of these keys are removed is given by

$$\frac{\dbinom{n_\Delta}{\nu_\Delta^D}\dbinom{n_t^* - n_\Delta}{n_D - \nu_\Delta^D}}{\dbinom{n_t^*}{n_D}}$$

By Stirling's formula, this probability is seen to be, asymptotically

$$\dbinom{n_\Delta}{\nu_\Delta^D} p^{\nu_\Delta^D}(1 - p)^{n_\Delta - \nu_\Delta^D}$$

with $p = \frac{n_D}{n_t^*} = \frac{p_D(Dt)}{f_1(t)}$.

This is a Binomial with very small p ($\mathcal{B}$in law).

Also ν_Δ^I: the number of keys among the n_I inserted keys, which fall inside Δ is asymptotically given by a Poisson law ($\mathcal{P}$ law)

$$e^{-n_I \Delta}\frac{(n_I \Delta)^{\nu_\Delta^I}}{(\nu_\Delta^I)!}$$

with very small parameter $n_I \Delta = p_I n \Delta (Dt)$. We are thus led to a classical birth and death process, with birth rate $\lambda(t) := n\Delta(1 - t/2)$ and death rate $\mu(t) := \frac{1}{2-t}$. The survival probability between times t_1 and t_2 is given by $ps_{2,1} = e^{-\int_{t_1}^{t_2} \mu(s)ds} = \frac{2-t_2}{2-t_1}$ and $\lim_{t_2 \to t_1} ps_{2,1} = 1$. The total number of inserted keys (into Δ), between t_1 and t_2, which have not been deleted at t_2 is Poisson with parameter $n_{2,1}$ given by

$$n_{2,1} = \int_{t_1}^{t_2} \lambda(u)e^{-\int_u^{t_2} \mu(s)ds} du = n\Delta(1 - \frac{t_2}{2})(t_2 - t_1)$$

which can also be written as

$$n_{2,1} = \tilde{\gamma}_{2,1} y$$

and

$$
\begin{aligned}
y &= n_1^* \Delta \\
\tilde{\gamma}_{2,1} &= \frac{(2 - t_2)(t_2 - t_1)}{t_1(2 - t_1)}
\end{aligned}
$$

Of course $\lim_{t_2 \to t_1} \tilde{\gamma}_{2,1} = 0$.

If, at time t_1, we have a fixed number n_Δ of keys inside Δ, the total number of keys at t_2 in Δ is given by

$$Bin[n_\Delta, ps_{2,1}] + \mathcal{P}[n_{2,1}]$$

If, at time t_1, we have a random $\mathcal{P}[n_1^*\Delta]$ number of keys inside Δ, it is easy to check that we are led to $\mathcal{P}[n_2^*\Delta]$ keys in Δ at time t_2. This is also obvious from probabilistic arguments. For further use, set

$$\frac{n_2^*}{n_1^*} = 1 + \gamma_{2,1} = \frac{t_2(1 - t_2/2)}{t_1(1 - t_1/2)}$$

To ease notations, we shall write $\tilde{\gamma}, \gamma$ and ps (without indices).

We are now ready to analyse the covariance $COV_{NR}(S_{t_1}^e, S_{t_2}^e) = \Psi_{NR}(t_1, t_2)n$ say. We must consider two subcases: starting with an insertion or with a deletion. Each subcase leads to a function $f_3^I(t_1, t_2)$ (or $f_3^D(t_1, t_2)$) that we have obtained in [15] as rather complicated integrals. The differential equation for $\Psi_{NR}(t_1, t_2)$ (Non-random structure) can be written as follows. As in Sec.6, we now obtain $\partial_{t_1}\Psi_{NR}(t_1, t_2) = f_{3,NR}(t_1, t_2)$ where

$$f_{3,NR}(t_1, t_2) = p_I f_3^I(t_1, t_2) + p_D f_3^D(t_1, t_2) \tag{9}$$

with $p_I = 1 - t_1/2, p_D = t_1/2$.

And we finally obtain the following theorem

Theorem 7.1 *In a non-random structure, the covariance*
$COV(S_{t_1}^e, S_{t_2}^e) \sim \Psi_{NR}(t_1, t_2)n$ *with*

$$\Psi_{NR}(t_1, t_2) = -\int_{t_1}^{t_2} f_{3,NR}(u, t_2)du + \alpha_2 f_1(t_2)$$

and f_3 is given by (9).

Up to now, we have been unable (even with MAPLE) to get a close expression for $\Psi_{NR}(t_1, t_2)$. However, the behaviour of Ψ_{NR} for $t_2 \to t_1$ can be computed. Indeed, we can derive that

$$\lim_{t_2 \to t_1} f_3^I(t_1, t_2) = \frac{\alpha_3}{2} + E(D^e) + 3E(D^f) - \alpha_0^2$$

(10)

$$\lim_{t_2 \to t_1} f_3^D(t_1, t_2) = -\frac{\alpha_3}{2}$$

with $\alpha_3 := -5((2ln2) + 2\sum_{\ell=1}^{\infty} \frac{\delta}{1+\delta}/ln2$. Note that this can also be obtained from Sec.6.

Indeed, by simple probabilistic reasoning, we must have

$$f_3^I(t_1, t_1) = \partial_{t_1} \Psi(t_1, t_1) = f_3(0)$$
$$f_3^D(t_1, t_1) = -\partial_{t_2} \Psi(t_1, t_1) = -[\alpha_2 - f_3(0)]$$

which lead to (10). This gives

$$\partial_{t_1} \Psi_{NR}(t_1, t_2)|_{t_1=t_2} = p_I f_3^I(t_1, t_1) + p_D f_3^D(t_1, t_1) = f_1' \frac{\alpha_3}{2} + \frac{1}{2}(1 + f_1')(m_2 - \alpha_0^2)$$

$$\partial_{t_2} \Psi_{NR}(t_1, t_2)|_{t_1=t_2} = p_I(-f_3^D(t_1, t_1)) + p_D(-f_3^I(t_1, t_1))$$
$$= f_1' \frac{\alpha_3}{2} - \frac{1}{2}(1 - f_1')(m_2 - \alpha_0^2)$$

(11)

This last result is of course compatible with Theor.7.1.

7.3 The trie size in a dynamic structure

Let $N([ns])$ be the size of the trie at time s. By (2), we know that $N([ns]) = n + S^e_{[ns]} + 1$.

We know that, at t_1, t_2, the size n_1, n_2 of the underlying structure is characterized by (7), i.e. we can write

$$n_1 \sim n\left[f(t_1) + \frac{\theta_1}{\sqrt{n}} \right] + O(1), n_2 \sim n\left[f(t_2) + \frac{\theta_2}{\sqrt{n}} \right] + O(1)$$

(12)

where θ_1, θ_2 are Gaussian R.V., with mean 0 and covariance $f_2(t_1, t_2)$.

Given n_1, n_2, the size of the structure at $v \in (t_1, t_2)$ is given by $nz(v)$ where

$$z(v) = f_1(v) + \varphi_1(t_1, t_2, v) \frac{\theta_1}{\sqrt{n}} + \varphi_2(t_1, t_2, v) \frac{\theta_2}{\sqrt{n}} + \frac{\chi(v)}{\sqrt{n}} + O\left(\frac{1}{n}\right)$$

where φ_1, φ_2 can be computed as in Louchard [11] Sec.4.5.2 and $\chi(v)$ is a Gaussian process, with mean 0, $\chi(t_1) = \chi(t_2) = 0$ and a covariance that can be deduced from f_2. After carefully checking the effect of these modification on our computations, it appears that, *conditionally on n_1, n_2*, the covariance $COV_C(S^e_{n_1}, S^e_{n_2})$ is given by $n\Psi_C(t_1, t_2)$, with

$$\Psi_C(t_1, t_2) = \Psi_{NR}(t_1, t_2) + \overline{\varphi}_1(t_1, t_2) \frac{\theta_1}{\sqrt{n}} + \overline{\varphi}_2(t_1, t_2) \frac{\theta_2}{\sqrt{n}} + O\left(\frac{1}{n}\right)$$

(13)

10 Conclusion

We have characterized, as a Gaussian non-Markovian process, the trie size in a dynamic list structure. The limiting process is a superposition of a deterministic function (of order n) and a Gaussian process (of order $\sqrt{n}$). As a further work, we intend to analyze the asymmetric trie ($p \neq q$). The m-any trie should also be studied (see Pittel [16]). In cooperation with D. Gardy, we are also presently considering some other applications of the techniques introduced here, notably to join sizes in dynamic relational data bases, which is an important open problem.

Acknowledgments

The author is indebted to R. Schott for suggesting the problem we have investigated here. C. Kenyon made some useful comments on an earlier version of the paper. We are grateful to Ph. Flajolet and C. Lefèvre for several discussions on this topic.

References

[1] CSAKI, E., FÖLDES, A. and SALMINEN, P. On the Joint Distribution of the Maximum and its Location for a Linear Diffusion; Ann. Inst. Henri Poincaré, 1987, **23**, 2, 179-194.

[2] DANIELS, H.E. and SKYRME, T.H.R. The Maximum of a Random Walk whose Mean Path has a Maximum; Adv. Appl. Prob., 1985, **17**, 85-99.

[3] DANIELS, H.E. The Maximum of a Gaussian Process whose mean Path has a Maximum, with an Application to the Strength of Bundles of Fibres; Adv. Appl. Prob., 1989, **21**, 315-333.

[4] DURBIN, J. The First-Passage Density of a Continuous Gaussian Process to a General Boundary; J. Appl. Prob., 1985, **22**, 99-122.

[5] FLAJOLET, PH., REGNIER, M., SEDGEWICK, R., Some uses of the Mellin integral transfrom in the analysis of algorithms, INRIA - Rapport de recherche **398**, Mai 1985.

[6] FLAJOLET, PH., PUECH, C. and VUILLEMIN, J. The Analysis of Simple List Structures, Inform. Sci., 1986, **38**, 121-146.

[7] FLAJOLET, PH., FRANÇON, J. and VUILLEMIN, J. Sequence of operations analysis for dynamic data structures, J. Algorithms, 1980, **1**, 111-141.

[8] JACQUET, P. and REGNIER, M., Limiting distributions for trie parameters; INRIA, Report **502**.

[9] JACQUET, P. and REGNIER, M., Trie partitioning process: limiting distributions; Proceedings CAAP'86, LNCS **214**, 196-210.

[10] JOHNSON, N.L. and KOTZ, S., Urn models and their application; Wiley, 1977.

[11] LOUCHARD, G., Random walks, Gaussian processes and list structures; TCS, 1987, **53**, 99-124.

[12] LOUCHARD, G., Brownian Motion and algorithms complexity; B.I.T., 1986, **26**, 17-34.

[13] LOUCHARD, G., SCHOTT, R. and RANDRIANARIMANANA, B. Dynamic Algorithms in D.E. Knuth's Model : a Probabilistic Analysis; Theor. Comp. Sc., 1992, **93**, 201-225.

[14] LOUCHARD, G., SCHOTT, R. Probabilistic analysis of some distributed algorithms; Proceedings CAAP'90, LNCS **431**, 239-253 and Random Structures and Algorithms, 1991, **2**, 2, 151-185.

[15] LOUCHARD, G. Trie size in a dynamic list structure, Laboratoire d'Informatique Théorique, **TR-252**, 1992.

[16] PITTEL, B., Paths in a random digital tree: limiting distributions; Adv. Appl. Prob., 1986,**18**, 139-155.

[17] REGNIER, M. and JACQUET, P., New results on the size of tries; IEEE-Tr. Inf. Theor., 1989, **35**, 1, 203-205.

A Fully Parallel Calculus of Synchronizing Processes *

Diego Latella[†]   Paola Quaglia[‡]

[†] CNR Ist. CNUCE, Pisa, email: latella@fdt.cnuce.cnr.it **
[‡] Dip. di Informatica, Università degli Studi di Pisa, email: quaglia@di.unipi.it

Abstract. We propose a fully parallel calculus of synchronizing processes. The calculus was deeply inspired by LOTOS, of which it inherits *multi-party synchronization* in process parallel composition. On the other hand, its semantics is *not* interleaving whereas LOTOS one is. The model we propose is somehow in between Milner's SCCS and ASCCS in that independent actions are performed simultaneously, whereas synchronization is achieved by means of delay. Also, delay is controlled in the sense that no process can delay an action if the environment allows that action to be performed.

The calculus we propose here was originally designed as a first step towards a probabilistic one. Nevertheless we think that the pure version of the calculus has some features which are interesting on their own. As an example we use it to describe a quite simple system which may be thought of as a possible fault tolerant architecture for a hardware component.

We also provide a set of equational laws based on a notion of *strong bisimulation*.

1 Introduction

In this paper we present a fully parallel calculus of synchronizing processes. The calculus was originally designed as a first step towards a probabilistic one [11]. Several probabilistic models have been proposed in the literature [2,4,5,6,8,13,18,21,22]. They are derived mostly from SCCS [15] which, contrary to CCS [14], has a non-interleaving semantics.

In fact, in order to reason about probabilistic systems, it is a crucial point to have a direct correspondence between *choice operators* in behaviour expressions and the *branching structure* of the transition systems those expressions denote. This is so because on the syntactical level probabilities are associated *only* to the alternatives of choice expressions. On the other hand, from a semantic point of view, the transitions leaving from any state must define, *all together*, a stochastic experiment, which implies all of them being labeled by both an event and a probability value, so that the transition system can be thought of as a Markov system. This is not the case

---

* This work has been done within the ESPRIT Project Ref. 2304 - LOTOSPHERE and has been partially funded by CPR (Consorzio Pisa Ricerche) and the CNR-NATO Advanced Fellowships Program.

** Current address: Univ. of Twente, Dept. of Comp. Science - PO BOX 217 - 7500 AE Enschede - NL email: latella@cs.utwente.nl

with interleaving semantics since there are branches in transition systems which do not come from non-deterministic choice, but rather from parallel composition.

All the proposals for probabilistic process calculi mentioned above do not allow for *multi-party* synchronization, which is a main feature of CSP [1] and LOTOS [7] and is essential for modeling multi-/broad-casting. The only proposals for dealing with multi-party synchronization for probabilistic processes we know about are [3, 20]. Anyway they both are based on interleaving semantics and force to assign the same (fictitious!) probability to all transitions of branches generated by parallel expressions.

In our calculus, like in LOTOS, parallel composition looks like $B1|G|B2$, where $B1$ and $B2$ are *behaviour expressions* (i.e. processes) which can proceed in parallel but are compelled to simultaneously execute those actions belonging to the list G.

Departing from LOTOS standard semantics, we require (as in SCCS) that every transition corresponds to the *simultaneous* execution of an action by *every* component of the system. So the notion of a single atomic action at a time is replaced by the notion of *as soon as possible* and *composite event*, the latter being denoted by a multi-set. In other terms an action must be executed as soon as the environment makes it possible. For instance, being ';' the prefixing operator, the process $a; stop|[]|b; stop$ performs $\{\{a, b\}\}$ and becomes $stop|[]|stop$ (using '$\{\{$' and '$\}\}$' as multi-set brackets).

The situation is quite similar to Milner SCCS in that independent actions are executed simultaneously, but the actual action each process performs depends *both* on the actions it is able to perform *and* the synchronization constraints imposed by the parallel context in which it is put, i.e. its environment. In particular, when a process is ready to perform an action which is *not* allowed by the environment, the former is *delayed* and the action will be executed *if* and *as soon as* the synchronization constraints will allow it. In the meanwhile, the process will be forced to *idle*.

With this respect the model is similar to Milner's ASCCS [15] in that it does not force the specifier to explicitly insert idle actions in the specification in order to get the processes synchronized. On the other hand, it differs from the above mentioned calculus since delay is controlled: no process can delay an action if the environment allows that action to be performed. For instance consider the behaviour expression $B1|[a]|B2 = (a; stop)|[a]|(b; a; stop)$. When $B2$ performs b, process $B1$, whose initial action is a synchronization one, namely a, is delayed and executes the special *idling* action λ:

$$B1|[a]|B2 \xrightarrow{\{\{\lambda, b\}\}} B1'|[a]|B2' = (a; stop)|[a]|(a; stop) .$$

Now both $B1'$ and $B2'$ can perform action a, so:

$$B1'|[a]|B2' \xrightarrow{\{\{a, a\}\}} (stop|[a]|stop) .$$

In conclusion, we call our model *fully parallel* in the sense that it expresses the highest level of parallelism of actions which is allowed by synchronization constraints (i.e. everything which *can* be done *must* be done).

We formalize the concept of delay by means of an operational semantics which defines transition relations parametrized by *delay sets*, i.e. sets of actions which must be delayed. Given any finite set $\Delta \subseteq Gates$ ($Gates$ being the set of observable actions), $B \xrightarrow{\alpha}_\Delta B'$ informally means that B can produce the event α and transform in B' when all the actions belonging to Δ are delayed. Given a behaviour expression its semantics is then the one generated by letting $\Delta = \emptyset$, the intended meaning being obvious. The reason why we do not consider only the transition relation $\longrightarrow_\emptyset$ is that, when a behaviour expression is put in a synchronization context, the delay set Δ is computed according to synchronization constraints. In other terms, in order to deduce $B1|G|B2 \xrightarrow{\alpha}_\emptyset B'$, we need to know $B1 \xrightarrow{\alpha1}_{\Delta1} B1'$ and $B2 \xrightarrow{\alpha2}_{\Delta2} B2'$ for suitable $\Delta1$ and $\Delta2$, as we shall see later.

The rest of the paper is organized as follows. In Section 2 we discuss the formal semantics of the calculus. An example of its application is given in Section 3. In Section 4 we provide a notion of *strong bisimulation equivalence* and a set of equational laws. Section 5 contains directions for future work.

For the sake of simplicity we consider here only a subset of the calculus [1] consisting of *inaction, action prefix, choice, parallel composition, hiding, relabeling,* and *process instantiation*. A process B has the following sintax:

$$ B ::= stop \mid \mu;B \mid B[]B \mid B|G|B \mid hide\ g1,\dots,gn\ in\ B \mid B[a1/f1,\dots,an/fn] \mid $$
$$ P[a1,\dots,an] $$

where $\mu, gj, aj, fj \in Gates$ for $1 \leq j \leq n$.

We collect now some notational conventions which are used throughout the paper. Given any synchronization list G, we let G denote also the set with the same elements of the list, furthermore $\alpha, \alpha1, \alpha2, \beta, \beta1, \beta2 \in \mathcal{E}v$ which is the set of the events, i.e. of the finite multi-sets on $Gates \cup \{\lambda\}$ where $\lambda \notin Gates$. $\{\{a\}\}^+$ denotes the multi-set which contains only a finite, non-zero number of occurrences of a while $\#(a, \alpha)$ denotes the number of occurrences of a in the multi-set α. ∇ is the union operator over multisets and finally $\alpha[a1/f1,\dots,an/fn]$ denotes the multi-set obtained by simultaneously replacing in α all the occurrences of any fj with aj and, if $\Gamma = \{g1,\dots,gn\}$, we use $\alpha[a/\Gamma]$ as a shorthand for $\alpha[a/g1,\dots,a/gn]$.

In the sequel we shall assume the absence of unguarded recursion. Moreover, for the sake of notational simplicity, we shall often let the same symbol denote both a multiset and the set of its elements, the intended meaning being clear from the context.

2 Operational Semantics

We define the operational semantics [17] of the fully parallel calculus by means of an auxiliary set of axioms and deduction rules (Fig.1) [2] which define the relations $\longrightarrow_\Delta$. Let BE be the set of the behaviour expressions; formally $\longrightarrow_\Delta \subseteq (BE \times \mathcal{E}v \times BE)$ where Δ is a finite subset of $Gates$. Then the semantics of a behaviour expression (i.e. the transition relation $\xrightarrow{\alpha}$) can be derived only by means of the following rule:

$$ \frac{B \xrightarrow{\alpha}_\emptyset B'}{B \xrightarrow{\alpha} B'} $$

In the sequel we shall suppose that $B, B1, B1', B2$ e $B2'$ range over BE. Also, $B \xrightarrow{\alpha}_\Delta$ is a shorthand for $\exists B' : B \xrightarrow{\alpha}_\Delta B'$.

---

[1] The reader interested in the whole calculus is referred to [11].

[2] A first, simpler, version of this semantics is presented in [10], there it is also shown that such a simple version is indeed unable to express external nondeterminism.

$(st) \qquad stop \xrightarrow{\{\{\lambda\}\}}_\Delta stop$

$(a1) \qquad \mu;B \xrightarrow{\{\{\mu\}\}}_\Delta B \ , \ if \ \mu \notin \Delta$

$(a2) \qquad \mu;B \xrightarrow{\{\{\lambda\}\}}_\Delta \mu;B \ , \ if \ \mu \in \Delta$

$(c1) \qquad B1 \xrightarrow{\alpha}_\Delta B1' \ , \ \alpha \notin \{\{\lambda\}\}^+ \qquad implies \qquad B1[]B2 \xrightarrow{\alpha}_\Delta B1'$

$(c2) \qquad B2 \xrightarrow{\alpha}_\Delta B2' \ , \ \alpha \notin \{\{\lambda\}\}^+ \qquad implies \qquad B1[]B2 \xrightarrow{\alpha}_\Delta B2'$

$\qquad \ \ B1 \xrightarrow{\alpha 1}_\Delta B1' \ , \ \cdot B2 \xrightarrow{\alpha 2}_\Delta B2' \ , \ \alpha 1, \alpha 2 \in \{\{\lambda\}\}^+ \qquad implies \qquad B1[]B2 \xrightarrow{\{\{\lambda\}\}}_\Delta B1'[]B2'$

$(pld) \qquad B1 \xrightarrow{\alpha 1}_{G\cup\Delta} B1', \ B2 \xrightarrow{\alpha 2}_{G\cup\Delta} B2', \ Del_\Delta(B1,G,\alpha 2)$
$\qquad\quad implies \qquad B1|G|B2 \xrightarrow{\alpha 1 \triangledown \alpha 2}_\Delta B1'|G|B2'$

$(prd) \qquad B1 \xrightarrow{\alpha 1}_{G\cup\Delta} B1', \ B2 \xrightarrow{\alpha 2}_{G\cup\Delta} B2', \ Del_\Delta(B2,G,\alpha 1)$
$\qquad\quad implies \qquad B1|G|B2 \xrightarrow{\alpha 1 \triangledown \alpha 2}_\Delta B1'|G|B2'$

$(p\_b) \qquad B1 \xrightarrow{\alpha 1}_{Cant_\Delta(B1|G|B2)\cup\Delta} , \ B2 \xrightarrow{\alpha 2}_{Cant_\Delta(B1|G|B2)\cup\Delta} ,$
$\qquad\quad B1 \xrightarrow{\beta 1}_{Cant_\Delta(B1|G|B2)\cup\Delta\cup\Gamma 1} B1' \ , \ B2 \xrightarrow{\beta 2}_{Cant_\Delta(B1|G|B2)\cup\Delta\cup\Gamma 2} B2' \ ,$
$\qquad\quad B_\Delta(B1,B2,G,\alpha 1,\alpha 2,\beta 1,\beta 2)$
$\qquad\quad implies \qquad B1|G|B2 \xrightarrow{\beta 1 \triangledown \beta 2}_\Delta B1'|G|B2'$
$\qquad\quad where \qquad \Gamma 1 = (\alpha 1 \cap G) \setminus \alpha 2 \ , \qquad \Gamma 2 = (\alpha 2 \cap G) \setminus \alpha 1$

$(h) \qquad B \xrightarrow{\alpha}_{\Delta \setminus \{g1,...,gn\}} B' \qquad implies \qquad hide \ g1,...,gn \ in \ B \xrightarrow{\alpha[i/g1,...,i/gn]}_\Delta hide \ g1,...,gn \ in \ B'$

$(r) \qquad B \xrightarrow{\alpha}_\Gamma B' \qquad implies \qquad B[a1/f1,...,an/fn] \xrightarrow{\alpha[a1/f1,...,an/fn]}_\Delta B'[a1/f1,...,an/fn]$
$\qquad where \qquad \Gamma = (\Delta \setminus \{f1,...,fn\}) \cup \{fj : aj \in \Delta\}$

$(p) \qquad B[a1/f1,...,an/fn] \xrightarrow{\alpha}_\Delta B' \qquad implies \qquad P[a1,...,an] \xrightarrow{\alpha}_\Delta B'$
$\qquad where \qquad P[f1,...,fn] = B$

Fig. 1. Operational Semantics

The axiom (st) says that $stop$ does not perform any action letting time pass.

The axioms for $action \ prefix$ simply say that the atomic action μ, which is the only one ready to be executed, can actually be executed $(a1)$ only if it is not requested to be delayed. If it is not the case $(a2)$, then an $idle$ action λ is performed and the process remains unchanged, so that the same action will be ready for execution later.

The interpretation of the rules for hiding, relabeling and process instantiation is straightforward. We simply want to point out that the language of our calculus has indeed also a special $unobservable$ action i which we omitted in the presentation above for the sake of simplicity. It corresponds to the τ action of CCS and can never belong to a synchronization list. So in our framework, without making the notation dull, it is sufficient to know that any delay set can never contain i. And in fact the rule for hiding is such that the behaviour of $hide \ g1,...,gn \ in \ B$ w.r.t. Δ is derived by the one of B w.r.t. a delay set which does not contain the actions of $\{g1,...,gn\}$ which, just as the unobservable action i, have never to be delayed.

As far as relabeling is concerned, simply notice that, in order to infer the behaviour of $B[a1/f1, \ldots, an/fn]$ when delayed on Δ, what we must know is the behaviour of B when delayed on those elements belonging to Δ that will not be relabeled and those elements that will be relabeled by gates of Δ.

The semantics for the choice operator is such that the following requirements are met:

- in order for an alternative to be selected for execution it must *not* be the case it is *completely delayed* on Δ, i.e. it must produce an event which is *not* labeled by λs only ($(c1)$, $(c2)$);
- if both alternatives are completely delayed then the choice expression itself is delayed ($c3$).

For instance the *only* possible transitions of

$$B = (a; stop|[]|a; stop)[](b; stop|[]|b; stop)$$

when delayed respectively on $\emptyset$, $\{a\}$, and $\{a, b\}$, are the following ones:
$B — \{\{a, a\}\} \rightarrow_\emptyset (stop|[]|stop)$ and $B — \{\{b, b\}\} \rightarrow_\emptyset (stop|[]|stop)$,
$B — \{\{b, b\}\} \rightarrow_{\{a\}} (stop|[]|stop)$,
$B — \{\{\lambda\}\} \rightarrow_{\{a,b\}} B$.
The expression B above performs two transitions of size two when delayed on $\emptyset$ but it executes only one transition w.r.t. the delay sets $\{a\}$ and $\{a, b\}$ (respectively of size two and one).

Observation 1. An increase in the size of the delay set may induce a decrease on the number of transitions of a choice expression as well as the size of the involved events. The size of an event is to be intended as the potential *degree of parallelism* of the event, i.e. the number of processes contributing to its realization. The actual degree of parallelism is of course given by the number of non-λ actions in the event.

•

In order to explain the rules for parallel composition we need to introduce the function $Init_\Delta$ (see Fig.2). $Init_\Delta(B)$ is recursively defined on the structure of behaviour expressions and contains [3] all the observable actions which B may perform in its first step when delayed on Δ. For instance $Init_\emptyset((c; stop[]b; stop)|[a, b]|(a; stop[]b; stop)) = \{c, b\}$ and in fact we do not expect that the parallel composition can perform a since a is a synchronization action and one of the partners cannot execute it.

Using $Init_\Delta$ we can now establish (Def.2) which are the synchronization actions that $B1|G|B2$ is not enabled to perform.

Definition 2. $\forall B1, B2 \in BE$, $\forall G$ synchronization list, $\forall \Delta \subseteq Gates$,
$Cant_\Delta(B1|G|B2) = G \setminus (Init_\Delta(B1) \cap Init_\Delta(B2))$. •

Since $B1|G|B2$ cannot execute actions in $Cant_\Delta$, in order to infer the behaviour of the parallel composition when delayed on Δ, we take under consideration *only* the transitions of $B1$ and $B2$ when they are delayed (at least) on $\Delta \cup Cant_\Delta(B1|G|B2)$.

---

[3] It can be proved [19] that $\forall \mu \in Gates$, if $\mu \in Init_\Delta(B)$ then $\exists \alpha \in Ev : B \xrightarrow{\alpha}_\Delta$ and $\mu \in \alpha$.

$$Init_\Delta(stop) = \emptyset$$

$$Init_\Delta(\mu; B) = \{\mu\} \setminus \Delta$$

$$Init_\Delta(B1[]B2) = Init_\Delta(B1) \cup Init_\Delta(B2)$$

$$Init_\Delta(B1|G|B2) = (Init_\Delta(B1) \cap G \cap Init_\Delta(B2)) \cup (Init_\Delta(B1) \cup Init_\Delta(B2)) \setminus G$$

$$Init_\Delta(hide\ g1,\ldots,gn\ in\ B) = (Init_{\Delta \setminus \{g1,\ldots,gn\}}(B))[i/\{g1,\ldots,gn\}]$$

$$Init_\Delta(B[a1/f1,\ldots,an/fn]) = (Init_\Gamma(B))[a1/f1,\ldots,an/fn]$$
$$\text{where } \Gamma = (\Delta \setminus \{f1,\ldots,fn\}) \cup \{fj : aj \in \Delta\}$$

$$Init_\Delta(P[a1,\ldots,an]) = Init_\Delta(B[a1/f1,\ldots,an/fn])$$
$$\text{where } P[f1,\ldots,fn] = B$$

Fig. 2. $Init_\Delta(B)$

How can we combine such transitions? There are essentially three cases to handle; we are going to discuss them letting

$$B1 \xrightarrow{\alpha1} Cant_\Delta(B1|G|B2) \cup \Delta \quad \text{and} \quad B2 \xrightarrow{\alpha2} Cant_\Delta(B1|G|B2) \cup \Delta$$

First case. Consider the following parallel expression and let $\Delta = \emptyset$:

$$(a; stop)|[a, b]|(b; stop)$$

Both $B1$ and $B2$ are completely delayed by $Cant_\Delta(B1|G|B2) \cup \Delta$. In such a case also $B1|G|B2$ must be completely delayed. This behaviour can be obtained by pairing transitions of $B1$ and $B2$ delayed at least on $Cant_\Delta(B1|G|B2) \cup \Delta$.

$\otimes$

Second case. Both $\alpha1$ and $\alpha2$ are events not in $\{\{\lambda\}\}^+$. In such a case we can infer the behaviour of $B1|G|B2$ by combining transitions of the partners *provided* that such transitions are 'compatible'. More precisely, it *must not* be allowed to pair different synchronization actions of $B1$ and $B2$.

Take for instance the following expression with $\Delta = \emptyset$:

$$(a; stop[\,]b; stop)|[a, b]|(a; stop[\,]b; stop)$$

Of course we do not want to pair $\alpha1 = \{\{a\}\}$ and $\alpha2 = \{\{b\}\}$. Then the only transitions which we are allowed to take under consideration are those obtained augmenting the delay set of $B1$ and of $B2$ respectively by

$$\Gamma1 = (\alpha1 \cap G) \setminus \alpha2 \quad \text{and} \quad \Gamma2 = (\alpha2 \cap G) \setminus \alpha1$$

which are the sets of synchronization actions belonging to $\alpha1$ and not to $\alpha2$ or vice-versa (with a bit of overloading in the use of the variables αj which actually denote multisets).

Now recall the rules for choice expressions. For any delay set Γ, a choice expression may execute the same event performed by one of its components *only if* such a partner is not completely delayed by Γ. Thus augmenting Γ may result in 'dropping away' one alternative (or even both) of the choice expression (see Obs.1).

This is just the case for $(a; stop[\,]b; stop)|[a, b]|(a; stop[\,]b; stop)$ with $\Delta = \emptyset$, $\alpha 1 = \{\{a\}\}$ and $\alpha 2 = \{\{b\}\}$. In fact we have, for instance, $\Delta \cup \mathcal{C}ant_\Delta(\,(a; stop[\,]b; stop)|[a, b]|(a; stop[\,]b; stop)) \cup \Gamma 1 = \{a\}$ and $(a; stop[\,]b; stop) - \{\{b\}\} \to_{\{a\}}$. Such a transition has nothing to do with the event $\alpha 1$ previously considered and so we want to find a way for not picking it! Notice that the reason why we got such a 'wrong' transition was that the alternative $\alpha 2$.was such that $\alpha 1$ resulted completely delayed.

So we want to augment the delay set by $\Gamma 1$ (and respectively $\Gamma 2$) and *besides this* we require that $\Gamma 1$ $(\Gamma 2)$ does not completely delay the alternative of a choice expression which possibly takes part in the execution of the event $\alpha 1$ $(\alpha 2)$. Letting

$$B1 \xrightarrow{\beta 1} \mathcal{C}ant_\Delta(B1|G|B2) \cup \Delta \cup \Gamma 1 \quad \text{and} \quad B2 \xrightarrow{\beta 2} \mathcal{C}ant_\Delta(B1|G|B2) \cup \Delta \cup \Gamma 2$$

we infer a transition for $B1|G|B2$ by pairing $\beta 1$ and $\beta 2$ only if the above requirement is met. We would like the condition $(\beta 1 = \alpha 1[\lambda/\Gamma 1]$ *and* $\beta 2 = \alpha 2[\lambda/\Gamma 2])$ hold. Actually this is not possible due to the fact that the number of λs can decrease when delay sets grow (see Obs.1). So we have to define a new relation, $\preceq$, which accounts for this (Def.3).

Definition 3. $\forall \alpha, \beta \in \mathcal{E}v$, $\beta \preceq \alpha$ iff $\forall \mu \in Gates$,
$\#(\mu, \beta) = \#(\mu, \alpha)$ *and* $\#(\lambda, \beta) \leq \#(\lambda, \alpha)$. $\qquad\qquad\bullet$

$\beta \preceq \alpha$ informally means that β is essentially the same as α except for the fact that it may contain less λs than α. So the above requirement can be formalized as follows:

$$\beta 1 \preceq \alpha 1[\lambda/\Gamma 1] \quad \text{*and*} \quad \beta 2 \preceq \alpha 2[\lambda/\Gamma 2]$$

$$\otimes$$

Third case. Consider the following expression and let $\Delta = \emptyset$, $\alpha 1 = \{\{c\}\}$:

$$(c; stop[\,](a; stop[\,]b; stop))|[a, b]|(a; stop[\,]b; stop)$$

$\alpha 1$ contains observable actions (i.e. $\alpha 1 \notin \{\{\lambda\}\}^+$), and they are not involved in synchronization (i.e. $\alpha 1 \cap G = \emptyset$); on the other hand $B2$ can only synchronize (i.e. $Init_\Delta(B2) \subseteq G$).

In such a case we expect $B2$ to be completely delayed and the whole process to perform all the actions belonging to $\alpha 1$. Such a behaviour cannot be obtained as above, since the method used in the 'second case' does not work now. It is too weak, so to speak. It lacks of a global view on *all* the alternatives of the partner which must be delayed. In fact, looking at the transitions of $B2$ one at a time ($\alpha 2 = \{\{a\}\}$ and $\alpha 2 = \{\{b\}\}$), we find them, one at a time, completely delayed. In fact we have $\beta 2 \not\preceq \alpha 2$ in both cases, so that no transition of the parallel composition can be inferred for $\alpha 1 = \{\{c\}\}$.

In the present case, and in the symmetric one, the correct behaviour is obtained, indeed, by pairing transitions of $B1$ and $B2$ delayed on $G \cup \Delta$. In fact under the above assumptions $G \cup \Delta$ completely delays the component which is only able to synchronize ($B2$ in the example) but it does not delay the actions which the other partner can perform alone. Thus the above expression executes the event $\{\{c, \lambda\}\}$.

$\otimes$

As a result of the above discussion we may handle parallel composition by means of three rules. Two of them, which are symmetric, are devoted to situations like those described in the third case. Such rules are (pld), i.e. 'parallel left delayed', and (prd), i.e. 'parallel right delayed'. They have, among the hypotheses, a predicate (Def.4) which establishes whether the rule is suitable for the case under consideration, that is it says whether a process (partner of a parallel composition) is completely delayed by a given event α (chosen by the other component, which is not delayed), relative to synchronization list G.

Definition 4. $\forall B \in BE$, $\forall G$ synchronization list, $\forall \alpha \in \mathcal{E}v$, $\forall \Delta \subseteq Gates$,
$Del_\Delta(B, G, \alpha) = \alpha \notin \{\{\lambda\}\}^+$ _and_ $\alpha \cap G = \emptyset$ _and_ $Init_\Delta(B) \subseteq G$. $\bullet$

Finally, the last rule ((p_b), i.e. 'parallel both') deals simultaneously with the first and the second cases discussed above. Also this rule has a boolean condition (Def.5) among its hypotheses. It just formalizes our previous discussion.

Definition 5.
$\forall B1, B2 \in BE$, $\forall G$ synchronization list, $\forall \Delta \subseteq Gates$, if
$B1 \xrightarrow{\alpha 1}_{Cant_\Delta(B1|G|B2)\cup\Delta}$, $B2 \xrightarrow{\alpha 2}_{Cant_\Delta(B1|G|B2)\cup\Delta}$,
$\Gamma 1 = (\alpha 1 \cap G) \setminus \alpha 2$, $\Gamma 2 = (\alpha 2 \cap G) \setminus \alpha 1$,
$B1 \xrightarrow{\beta 1}_{Cant_\Delta(B1|G|B2)\cup\Delta\cup\Gamma 1}$, $B2 \xrightarrow{\beta 2}_{Cant_\Delta(B1|G|B2)\cup\Delta\cup\Gamma 2}$, then
$B_\Delta(B1, B2, G, \alpha 1, \alpha 2, \beta 1, \beta 2) = \underline{not}\ Del_\Delta(B1, G, \alpha 2)\ \underline{and}$
$\underline{not}\ Del_\Delta(B2, G, \alpha 1)\ \underline{and}$
$(\beta 1 \preceq \alpha 1[\lambda/\Gamma 1]\ \underline{and}\ \beta 2 \preceq \alpha 2[\lambda/\Gamma 2])$

$\bullet$

It can be proven [19] that if one of the three conditions $Del_\Delta(B1, G, \alpha 2)$, $Del_\Delta(B2, G, \alpha 1)$, and $B_\Delta(B1, B2, G, \alpha 1, \alpha 2, \beta 1, \beta 2)$ is true then the others are false. Moreover, if $\alpha 1$ and $\alpha 2$ make all the three predicates above false then we *must* deduce *no* transition for $B1|G|B2$. In fact, under that hypothesis, $\alpha 1$ and $\alpha 2$ are such that $(\beta 1 \preceq \alpha 1[\lambda/\Gamma 1]\ \underline{and}\ \beta 2 \preceq \alpha 2[\lambda/\Gamma 2])$ does not hold. Therefore at least one of the two transitions (or a choice sub-component) would be completely delayed by the selection of the other, even if it is not the case that one (or both) partner(s) of the parallel composition has (have) to be delayed. This simply means that the particular pairing $\alpha 1$, $\alpha 2$ is not allowed, like $\{\{a\}\}$, $\{\{b\}\}$ in $(a; stop[]b; stop)|[a, b]|(a; stop[]b; stop)$.

We conclude this section with a remark pertaining to the fact that idling gives rise to transitions, a questionable choice 'a priori'. Indeed the presence of transitions labeled by λs only has the major advantage that *any* process *always*, i.e. w.r.t. any delay set, performs an event. Vice-versa, if we remove $\{\{\lambda\}\}^+$ from $\mathcal{E}v$, then any behaviour expression B such that $Init_\Delta(B) = \emptyset$ executes *no* event when delayed on Δ. As a result of this, idling transitions could be removed from our model only at the price of having more rules for parallel composition. In fact, on the one hand, rules (pld) and (prd) would need only some refinements; for instance (prd) should become something like $B1 \xrightarrow{\alpha 1}_{G\cup\Delta} B1'$, $Init_\Delta(B2) \subseteq G$ implies $B1|G|B2 \xrightarrow{\alpha 1}_\Delta B1'|G|B2$.

But, on the other hand, there should be three different 'versions' of rule (p_b). Such versions should cope with the distinct situations which could arise out of the addition of $\Gamma1$ and, respectively, $\Gamma2$ to $Cant_\Delta(B1|G|B2) \cup \Delta$. In fact it could be the case that both $B1$ and $B2$ give rise to a transition w.r.t. the new delay sets, as well as the case that *only* $B1$ (or *only* $B2$) can perform an event w.r.t. $Cant_\Delta(B1|G|B2) \cup \Delta \cup \Gamma1$ $(Cant_\Delta(B1|G|B2) \cup \Delta \cup \Gamma2)$.

3 An Example

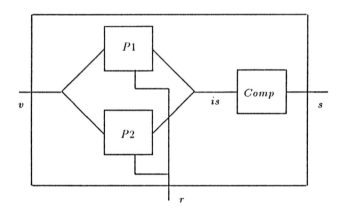

Fig. 3. Overall system

In this section a simple system is described. Its topology is shown in Fig.3. The overall system may be thought of as a possible fault tolerant architecture for a hardware component.

The sub-systems $P1$ and $P2$ are such that each of them, on request from outside (r) reads a value w which has been broadcasted to them via gate v and sends it back on gate is. However, this last value is non-deterministically affected by errors ek (Fig.4). We are using here a slightly richer version of the language in which we allow to deal with data values too. Anyway, we assume type IV of values received by the two processes, as well as type OV of their output values, be finite. Under this assumption the specification using data values can be proven equivalent to one without data values.

The third component of the system is a comparator $Comp$ (Fig.5). It receives values w_1 and w_2 from $P1$ and $P2$ respectively and compares them. If $|w_1 - w_2|$ is smaller than or equal to e, for suitable e, then it returns w_1, otherwise it returns $FAIL$.

Finally the formal specification of the overall system is given in Fig.6 whereas Fig.7 shows the labeled transition system of the overall system under the simplifying assumption $IV = \{1,2\}, OV = \{1,2,3\}, m = 1, c1 = 1, e = 0$.

```
process P1[r,v,is] =
 r;v?x1:IV;
 (    i;is!x1?x2:OV;P1[r,v,is]
   [] i;is!(x1+e1)?x2:OV;P1[r,v,is]
   [] i;is!(x1+e2)?x2:OV;P1[r,v,is]
   ...
   ...
   [] i;is!(x1+em)?x2:OV;P1[r,v,is]
 )
endproc

process P2[r,v,is] =
 r;v?x2:IV;
 (    i;is?x1:OV!x2;P2[r,v,is]
   [] i;is?x1:OV!(x2+e1);P2[r,v,is]
   [] i;is?x1:OV!(x2+e2);P2[r,v,is]
   ...
   ...
   [] i;is?x1:OV!(x2+em);P2[r,v,is]
 )
endproc
```

Fig. 4. Specification of processes $Pj, j = 1, 2$

```
process Comp[is,s]
 is?w1:OV;w2:OV;
 ( [|w1-w2|<=e] --> s!w1;Comp[is,s]
   []
   [|w1-w2|> e] --> s!FAIL;Comp[is,s] )
endproc
```

Fig. 5. Specification of process *Comp*

4 Strong Bisimulation Equivalence

In the sequel we propose an adaptation of the notion of *strong bisimulation equivalence* [14,16] to our model.

In our calculus the minimal observational unit is the composite event, then:

Definition 6. A symmetric binary relation $\mathcal{R} \subseteq BE \times BE$ is a *strong bisimulation* iff $B1\mathcal{R}B2$ implies that $\forall \alpha \in \mathcal{E}v$,
if $B1 \xrightarrow{\alpha} B1'$ then $\exists B2' : B2 \xrightarrow{\alpha} B2'$ and $B1'\mathcal{R}B2'$.   •

Definition 7. $B1$ and $B2$ are strong bisimulation *equivalent*, $B1 \sim B2$, iff exists a strong bisimulation $\mathcal{R}$ containing $(B1, B2)$.   •

```
process PP[r,v,s]
 hide is in
  (P1[r,v,is]|[r,v,is]|P2[r,v,is])|[is]|Comp[s,is]
endproc
```

Fig. 6. Specification of the overall system

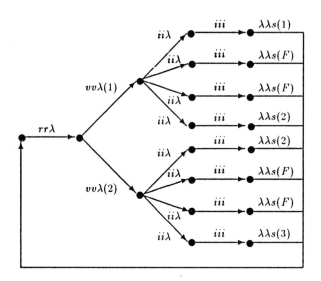

Fig. 7. Labeled Transition System of PP

Then $\sim = \bigcup \{\mathcal{R} | \mathcal{R}$ is a strong bisimulation$\}$. In order to prove such an assertion we have to define a function $\mathcal{F}$ on the relations $\mathcal{R}$ such that $(B1, B2) \in \mathcal{F}(\mathcal{R})$ iff Def.6 holds. $\mathcal{F}$ is monotone and $\mathcal{R}$ is a strong bisimulation iff $\mathcal{R} \subseteq \mathcal{F}(\mathcal{R})$, therefore $\sim$ is the greatest fixed point of $\mathcal{F}$ under set inclusion. Moreover, in [19] the following lemmata have been proven:

Lemma 8. *The relation* $\sim$ *is a congruence.* •

Lemma 9. *The following laws hold.*

$B1[]B2 \sim B2[]B1$
$B1[](B2[]B3) \sim (B1[]B2)[]B3$
$B1|G|B2 \sim B2|G|B1$
$B1|G|B2 \sim B1|G'|B2$ if $G = G'$
$hide\ g1, \ldots, gn\ in\ B \sim hide\ g1', \ldots, gn'\ in\ B$ if $\{g1, \ldots, gn\} = \{g1', \ldots, gn'\}$
$hide\ g1, \ldots, gm\ in\ hide\ g1', \ldots, gn'\ in\ B \sim hide\ f1, \ldots, fh\ in\ B$
   if $\{f1, \ldots, fh\} = \{g1, \ldots, gm\} \cup \{g1', \ldots, gn'\}$
$hide\ g1, \ldots, gn\ in\ g; B \sim g; hide\ g1, \ldots, gn\ in\ B$ if $g \notin \{g1, \ldots, gn\}$

$hide\ g1, \ldots, gn\ in\ g; B \sim i; hide\ g1, \ldots, gn\ in\ B$ if $g \in \{g1, \ldots, gn\}$

$hide\ g1, \ldots, gn\ in\ B1[]B2) \sim (hide\ g1, \ldots, gn\ in\ B1)[](hide\ g1, \ldots, gn\ in\ B2)$

$hide\ g1, \ldots, gn\ in\ (B1|G|B2) \sim (hide\ g1, \ldots, gn\ in\ B1)|G|(hide\ g1, \ldots, gn\ in\ B2)$

if $\{g1, \ldots, gn\} \cap G = \emptyset$

$stop[S] \sim stop$

$(\mu; B)[S] \sim \mu[S]; B[S]$

$(B1[]B2)[S] \sim B1[S][]B2[S]$

$B[S] \sim B$ if $[S]$ is the identity on the set of label of B

$P[a1, \ldots, an] \sim B[a1/f1, \ldots, an/fn]$ if $P[f1, \ldots, fn] = B$

●

All the laws of the above list have a counterpart in standard LOTOS, but our notion of bisimulation is too strong, for instance, to get an absorption law. This is due to the fact that the equivalence is sensitive to the number of occurrences of the idling action in the performed events. As an example notice that $B = a; stop|[a, b]|b; stop$ and $B[]B = (a; stop|[a, b]|b; stop)[](a; stop|[a, b]|b; stop)$ are not bisimilar, since B— $\{\{\lambda, \lambda\}\} \rightarrow B$ while $B[]B$—$\{\{\lambda\}\} \rightarrow B[]B$. Thus the absorption law, as well as a law equating $B[]stop$ and B, could be recovered by a weaker notion of bisimulation abstracting from idle moves. Such a bisimulation should be still stronger than the usual *weak bisimulation*.

We conclude the section with some remarks on the possibility of stating an expansion law. Indeed, in order to get it, we should include composite events as arguments of the prefixing operator. But this is not enough. Let us consider, for instance, the expression $B = a; stop|[]|b; stop$. Of course we would equate it to the process $\{\{a, b\}\}; (stop|[]|stop)$. On the other hand, consider the parallel composition $B|[a, b]|(a; stop[]b; stop)$. Due to synchronization constraints such a process can only perform the events $\{\{a, \lambda, a\}\}$ and $\{\{\lambda, b, b\}\}$. So, in order to be able to state an expansion of the whole behaviour, it should hold the equality $B = \{\{a, \lambda\}\}; (stop|[]|b; stop))[]\{\{\lambda, b\}\}; (a; stop|[]|stop)$, instead of the above one. As a result, stating an expansion law is really far from obvious, it would seem that 'auxiliary' expansion laws (unfortunately depending upon delay sets) are needed. In other words, in the bisimulation semantics, as well as in the operational one, the interaction of non-determinism and parallelism turns out to be intrinsically intricate.

5 Future work

In view of its synchrony, the proposed model seems to be quite appropriate for describing real-time systems or, to some extent, hardware systems, rather than distributed programs.

Anyway as we have already mentioned before, this work is a part of the definition of a probabilistic calculus [11] which can be considered as an extension of the language defined in this paper. In the complete work [12] also examples of applications as well as relation with Markov theory are presented.

With respect to the pure nondeterministic calculus we can refine the definition of the proposed operational semantics in order to represent synchronization with only one occurrence of the gate (in a way similar to LOTOS). We only need to redefine the rules for the parallel composition operator in such a way that multiple occurrences of any action occurring in G are replaced by a single occurrence of the same action. This should be of particular importance when the event is in $\{\{\lambda\}\}^+$ in order to equate all deadlock processes.

Finally, the proposed semantic model could be taken as a starting point for the development of a general framework for reasoning about parallelism degree. This would give raise to a *parallelism spectrum* the end-points of which would be the (standard LOTOS) interleaving semantics, where no parallelism at all is allowed, and the fully parallel semantics proposed in the present paper, where the only constraints imposed on parallelism are those implied by synchronization. A framework like this could be obtained by means of parameterizing the transition relation also with a number representing the maximal parallelism degree allowed by the system.

Acknowledgements. We would like to thank an anonymous referee whose stimulating observations led us to a more careful exposition of the topics of the paper.

References

1. S.D. Brookes, C.A.R. Hoare, A.W. Roscoe. A Theory of Communicating Sequential Processes. Journal of the ACM, Vol.31, No.3, pp. 560-599, 1984.
2. I. Christoff. Testing Equivalences and Fully Abstract Models for Probabilistic Processes. CONCUR 90, LNCS 458, Springer-Verlag, 1990.
3. I. Christoff. Testing Equivalences for Probabilistic Processes. Ph. D. Thesis, Dept. of Comp. Science, Uppsala Univ., ISSN 0283-0574, 1990.
4. A. Giacalone, C.C. Jou, S.A. Smolka. Algebraic reasoning for probabilistic concurrent systems. Proc. of Working Conference on Programming Concept and Methods IFIP TC 2, 1990.
5. R. van Glabbeek, S.A. Smolka, B. Steffen, C. Tofts. Reactive, Generative and Stratified Models of Probabilistic Processes. Proc. of 5th LICS, 1990.
6. H. Hansson, B. Jonsson. A Calculus for Communicating Systems with Time and Probabilities. IEEE RTSS, 1990.
7. ISO. Information processing systems - Open systems interconnection - LOTOS - A formal description technique based on the temporal ordering of observational behaviour. ISO 8807, 1989.
8. C.C. Jou, S.A. Smolka. Equivalences, congruences and complete axiomatizations for probabilistic processes. CONCUR 90, LNCS 458, Springer-Verlag, 1990.
9. J. Keilson. Markov Chain Models-Rarity and Exponentiality. Applied Mathematical Sciences, Vol.28, Springer-Verlag, 1979.
10. D. Latella, P. Quaglia. A fully parallel semantics for LOTOS. LotoSphere reference Lo/WP1/T1.2/CNUCE/N0023/V1, 1991.
11. D. Latella, P. Quaglia. A Proposal for a Calculus of Probabilistic Processes. Internal Report CNUCE-CNR C91-27, 1991.
12. D. Latella, P. Quaglia. A Calculus of Probabilistic Synchronizing Processes and Some Applications. Internal Report CNUCE-CNR C92-17, 1992.
13. K. G. Larsen, A. Skou. Bisimulation through probabilistic testing. Proc. POPL, 1989.
14. R. Milner. A Calculus of Communicating Systems. LNCS 92, Springer-Verlag, 1980.
15. R. Milner. Calculi for Synchrony and Asynchrony. Theoretical Computer Science, 25(3), 1983.
16. D. Park. Concurrency and automata on infinite sequences. Proc. 5th GI-Conference, LNCS 104, Springer-Verlag, 1981.

17. G. D. Plotkin. A Structural Approach to Operational Semantics. Technical Report DAIMI-FN-19, Comp. Science Dep., Aarhus University, 1981.
18. S. Purushothaman, P.A. Subrahmanyam. Reasoning about probabilistic behavior in concurrent systems. IEEE Trans. Software Engineering, Vol. SE-13, N.6, pp.740-745, 1987.
19. P. Quaglia. Proposta per una variante probabilistica di LOTOS. Tesi di Laurea in Scienze dell'Informazione, Universita' degli Studi di Pisa, 1991.
20. N. Rico, G.v. Bochmann. Performance description and analysis for distributed systems using a variant of LOTOS. Proc. of XI Int. IFIP Symp. on Protocol Specification, Testing and Verification, North Holland, 1991.
21. S.A. Smolka, B. Steffen. Priority as extremal probability. CONCUR 90, LNCS 458, Springer-Verlag, 1990.
22. C. Tofts. A synchronous calculus of relative frequency. CONCUR 90, LNCS 458, Springer-Verlag, 1990.

Generic Systolic Arrays :
A Methodology for Systolic Design

Pascal Gribomont

Vincent Van Dongen

Université de Liège
Institut Montefiore B28
4000 Liège Sart-Tilman (Belgium)

Centre de Recherche Informatique
1801 McGill College, Bureau 800
Montréal Canada H3A 2N4

Abstract. Several recent papers demonstrate the interest of viewing systolic algorithms as *while*-programs whose statements are synchronous multiple assignments. This approach is based on the classical invariant method and compares favourably with earlier ones, based on recurrence systems and space-time transformations. Our purpose is to use the particularities of the systolic paradigm to reduce the creativity needed to develop a systolic algorithm and its invariant. More precisely, two points are taken into account. First, the architecture is often chosen before the real beginning of the development and, second, the basic operations to be executed by individual cells are also partially known at the beginning. In fact, the development does not start from scratch, but from a "generic systolic array" (gsa), whose parameters have to be instantiated. Most systolic arrays are instances of a simple gsa that is introduced, investigated and illustrated in this paper.

1 Introduction to systolic array design

1.1 Systolic array

A *systolic array* is a regular network of similar processing units. These units, or *cells*, are connected by *channels*. Usually, each cell is connected with immediate neighbours only; this makes VLSI implementation more efficient [12].

The program executed by every cell is a loop, whose body is a finite, partially ordered set of statements. The statements specify three kinds of actions: receiving values (data) from some input channels, performing computations within the internal memory, transmitting values (results) to output channels.

The processing units act with high synchronism. This synchronism is often provided by a global, broadcasted clock, but this can lead to implementation problems. Another solution is the synchronization by communication, named *rendezvous*: a value can be transmitted from a cell to another one only when both cells are prepared to do so; there is no buffering mechanism.

Let us outline briefly the most classical application of systolic programming: the dot product of a matrix A by a vector x. The result y is described by the usual formula:

$$y_k = \sum_{j=1}^{p} A_{kj} x_j .\tag{1}$$

This is computed by the simple Pascal-like program

for $k := 1$ to p do $[\ y_k := 0\ ;$ for $j := 1$ to p do $y_k := y_k + A_{kj}x_j\ ]$.

The complexity of this algorithm is $O(p^2)$ since the assignment $y_k := y_k + A_{kj}x_j$ is executed p^2 times. However, as many of these operations may be executed concurrently, a systolic algorithm could be of linear complexity in time and space. Each cell will repeatedly execute the assignment with data received from the neighbouring cells and the outside, and transmit data and results to neighbouring cells or the outside. An adequate systolic algorithm for this application is presented in Section 3.2.

1.2 Space-Time transformation methodology

Many approaches have been developed for systolic array design. Some of them are presented in [6]; more recent ones are [15, 8, 2, 9, 14, 16, 17, 13, 18, 19]. We will outline a commonly used method. Classically, systolic design is concerned with the parallelization of algorithms. The algorithm to be mapped is specified as a set of equations attached to integral points, and mapped on the architecture using a regular time and space allocation scheme. This approach became the basis of many studies on the synthesis of systolic arrays. The main problems that were tackled were the scheduling of the computations, the mapping of the computations on regular architectures, the partitioning schemes for fixed size arrays, and the organization of multistep algorithms.

Let us summarize the basics of the *space-time transformation* methodology, illustrated with the matrix-vector multiplication algorithm. The methodology consists of four main steps: the *index localization*, the *uniformization*, the *space-time transformation*, and the *interface design*.

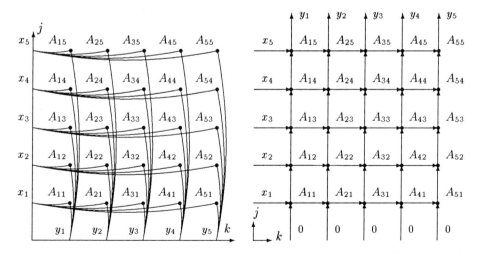

Fig. 1. The index localization, the basis of most mapping methodologies   (left)
  A uniform dependence graph for the matrix-vector multiplication algorithm (right)

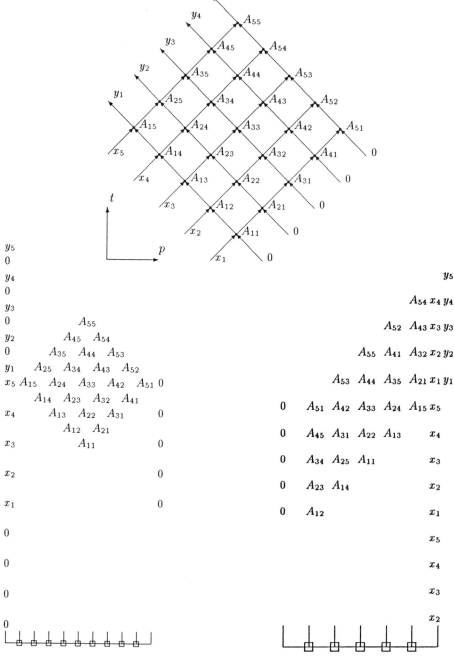

Fig. 2. Space-time diagram : when and where the computations are performed (top)
A classical array for the matrix-vector multiplication   (bottom left)
A new array for the matrix-vector multiplication   (bottom right)

1. *Index localization.* For the matrix-vector multiplication algorithm, the computations to be performed are defined by equation (1), which uses indices k and j. In the index localization, A_{kj} is attached to the point (k, j), x_j is attached to the point $(\_, j)$, and y_k is attached to the point $(k, \_)$. Figure 1 (left) shows graphically the result of this first step; the arcs of the graph represent the relations between the data.

2. *Uniformization.* Figure 1 (left) gives an indication on where the data need to be, and where the results are being produced. When a piece of data is needed at many places, the fan-out degree of the associated node is large. In the same way, when a result uses many data, the fan-in degree is large. The uniformization consists on reducing the fan-in and the fan-out degrees of these nodes, using the well known pipelining technique [4, 16]. In other words, step two transforms the initial algorithm into a set of *uniform recurrence equations.* Figure 1 (right) represents graphically the result of step two. At each node, the same set of computations needs to be performed:

$$y_{out} = y_{in} + A_{in} \times x_{in}, \quad x_{out} = x_{in}. \tag{2}$$

3. *Space-time transformation.* In this third step, a time and a processor allocation functions are being chosen. These two functions define respectively when and where the computations will be performed. Affine functions are well suited for the mapping of uniform recurrences on regular arrays [10]. Figure 2 (top) shows graphically the result of step three; the space-time diagram indicates when and where the computations are performed: the computation associated to the node (p, t) is performed at processor p at the time t.

4. *Interface design.* In this final step, the loading of the data and the unloading of the results are considered. There are two main techniques for doing so: either control signals are added with I/O lines, or the algorithm is slightly modified with the use of dummy variables. In the matrix-vector multiplication, we chose to propagate additional zeroes to avoid the use of control signals. The resulting classical circuit is shown in Figure 2 (bottom left), along with the data introduced in the circuit upon the time. The x_k's and the results are respectively introduced and produced at the leftmost cell. Zeroes are also introduced to the left to avoid the use of control signals for the initializations.

Many algorithms already were parallelized using this efficient technique. However, this methodology suffers from some drawbacks.
First, the algorithm must be specified as a set of recurrence equations, or nested do-loop instructions. This is not always easy to do. In particular, we will present an architecture that computes the greatest common divisor, but to which no recurrence equation is directly associated. Yet, the proof that the architecture performs the right result is given, using an invariant technique.
Second, a location in space is associated to each index value. This constraint is well suited for the synthesis of regular arrays: the data will be introduced in a regular order. However, this is not necessary and it eliminates the possibility of synthesizing other architectures. See for example the circuit described in Figure 2 (bottom right). The method used for its derivation is described hereafter;

no a priori assumption on the localization of the data was made. On the other hand, the above space-time approach could not derive such a circuit without using a very complex space-time transformation function.

The third drawback of the space-time transformation approach is the synthesis of the initializations. Here, additional zeroes were introduced to avoid the use of control signals. Thus, the initial algorithm (1) is now slightly modified; one should still use a proof technique to be sure that the results are not modified. In the technique presented hereafter, initializations are easily taken into account.

1.3 A program-oriented methodology

Various attempts have been made to overcome the drawbacks of the space-time transformation method. Those based (explicitly or not) on viewing systolic design as program design seem especially promising, for the reasons listed below.

- Most work has been done about formal methods for developing programs; these methods also apply to the development of systolic algorithms and, in particular, to the construction of an adequate while-loop.
- The notion of invariant, introduced for programs, happens to keep a prominent role in the design of systolic algorithm. (This is clearly demonstrated in [18]; an additional example is given in Section 4.2.)
- It is now widely accepted that operational notions should not appear in programming at the early design stages. For instance, control is left implicit in structured sequential programming (see e.g. [5]) and also in concurrent programming [3]. As space-time allocation is an operational notion, it is perhaps not adequate to base a method on this notion. In fact, space-time allocation should be deduced at the last stage of the design. Early introduction of operational notions often leads to exclude possible solutions of a problem.
- Time and space boundary conditions often are a problem in the design of systolic arrays; this problem is best handled with an invariant-based method.

To summarize, an adequate method of systolic design can be as follows. First, the specifications of the system are formalized with an input and an output predicates, just as in structured sequential programming. Second, a couple (program, invariant) is deduced in an incremental way from the specification. Third, the sequential while-program is further transformed into a systolic program; the statements of this program are concurrent assignments. Last, the systolic array is (easily) obtained from the systolic program. This approach (of some aspects of it) is presented and illustrated in several papers, including [2, 14, 7, 13, 18].

Such a method clearly inherits the usual problem in structured sequential programming: the development of a program together with its invariant is not easy, and some kind of creativity is often needed. Besides, further creativity is needed to transform a sequential program and its invariant into a systolic program and its invariant.

1.4 Generic systolic arrays

We propose to reduce the need of creativity by taking into account two facts about systolic arrays. First, most of systolic arrays presented in the literature are based on a common, very simple architecture. It is helpful to consider a systolic array as an instance of this architecture; systolic design is then reduced to parameter choosing. Second, the specifications of the problem frequently suggest all or part of the elementary operations to be performed by each cell; when this is the case, the remaining problem is to determine how and when data are to be pushed in the array, and when the results are to be collected out.

In this framework, the starting point will be neither a sequential algorithm, nor the description of a single process, but a *gsa* (generic systolic array), that is, some kind of partially specified systolic array (or piece of systolic array). This object is equally distant from the source problem and the target systolic implementation.

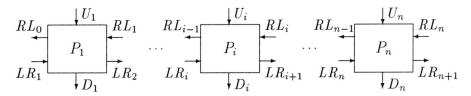

Fig. 3. The linear generic systolic array

We concentrate on one of the most common architectures. Processing units are connected in a linear array (Figure 3). Each cell is connected with its immediate neighbours; the extreme cells can exchange data and results with the outside. Furthermore, each cell can receive data from the top and transmit results to the bottom. For instance, cell P_i admits three input channels; P_i can receive data from P_{i-1} through channel LR_i (Left to Right), from P_{i+1} through RL_i, and from the outside through U_i (Up). Similarly, P_i has also three output channels, which allow transmission of results to the left and right neighbours and to the outside. In particular applications, some of these channels may be unused and suppressed. It is also possible to obtain 2-dimensional arrays by stacking several linear arrays and adequately connecting channels together. Ring, cylinder and torus arrays can be obtained in a similar way.

The *topological structure* of our gsa is fixed; it is still necessary to fix a *communication scheme*, that is, an order between the internal computation, the reception of data and the transmission of results. A simple scheme is as follows:

$$communication \; ; \; computation \qquad (3)$$

A generic systolic array is a systolic array whose computation part is left unspecified. The (generic) systolic arrays described here appear as particular CSP networks (see e.g. [15]). Recall that, if C is a transmission channel, the concurrent execution of the input statement $C?x$ and of the output statement $C!e$ implements the distributed assignment $x := e$.

This paper goes on as follows. In the next section, a formal model for the gsa is introduced; its properties are stated and proved. Two applications are presented in Sections 3 and 4, with emphasis on the critical design steps.

2 Properties of the linear generic systolic array

2.1 Description of the linear generic systolic array

The *linear* gsa is determined by the following points.
- The topology of the network is depicted on Figure 3.
- The scheme of communication is scheme (3).
- The internal memory of cell P_i contains six communication registers, denoted $A[i]$, $B[i]$, $C[i]$, $D[i]$, $E[i]$ and $F[i]$. The remaining part of the memory is denoted $M[i]$; its size is independent from the size n of the network.
- The communication phase for cell P_i consists in the concurrent execution of the following statements (Figure 4):

$$LR_i?A[i]\,,\ RL_{i-1}!B[i]\,,\ U_i?C[i]\,,\ D_i!E[i]\,,\ LR_{i+1}!F[i]\,,\ RL_i?G[i]\,.$$

- The internal computation phase is not restricted; it can be modelled by a function Φ. More specifically, the computation phase consists in executing the assignment $(F, E, B, M) := \Phi(A, C, G, M)$.

Comments. An *instance* of the linear gsa is obtained by replacing Φ by a total function (therefore, systolic algorithms are deterministic and never fail).
During the communication phase, only the *input registers* A, C and G are changed; during the computation phase, only the *storage register* M and the *output registers* B, D and F are changed. The registers can consist of a single memory cell, but also of any fixed amount of memory.

The linear gsa comprises four *logical* components, which are listed below:
- The *left-to-right* component contains LR_i, $A[i]$ and $F[i]$, for all i.
- The *right-to-left* component contains RL_i, $B[i]$ and $G[i]$, for all i.
- The *up-to-down* component contains U_i, D_i, $C[i]$ and $E[i]$, for all i.
- The *storage* component contains $M[i]$, for all i.

Incomplete instances of the linear gsa are obtained by omitting one or more logical components.

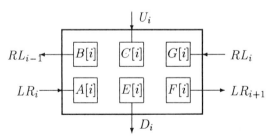

Fig. 4. A typical cell of the linear generic systolic array

Comment. The Warp machine [1] can be viewed as a gsa of size 10.

2.2 External behaviour of the linear gsa

From the outside, the linear gsa is seen as a "big cell". The input channels are $LR_0, U_0, \ldots, U_n$ and RL_n; the output channels are $RL_{-1}, D_0, \ldots, D_n$ and LR_{n+1}. The structure of the program executed by the array is

$$*(\alpha)[transmission\ phase;\ computation\ phase],$$

where "$*(0)P$" and "$*(\alpha+1)P$" respectively mean "$skip$" and "$P; *(\alpha)P$". A description of the transmission phase is given below:

$$LR_1?A[1] \parallel A[2:n] := F[1:n-1] \parallel LR_{n+1}!F[n] \qquad \text{Left-to-right,}$$
$$\parallel (\parallel_{k=1}^n U_k?C[k]) \parallel (\parallel_{k=1}^n D_k!E[k]) \qquad \text{Up-to-down,}$$
$$\parallel RL_0!B[1] \parallel G[1:n-1] := B[2:n] \parallel RL_n?G[n] \qquad \text{Right-to-left.}$$

The computation phase is modelled by

$$Cpt \;=\; \parallel_{r=1}^n \begin{cases} F[r] & := & S(A[r], C[r], G[r], M[r]) & \text{Left-to-right,} \\ E[r] & := & T(A[r], C[r], G[r], M[r]) & \text{Up-to-down,} \\ B[r] & := & V(A[r], C[r], G[r], M[r]) & \text{Right-to-left,} \\ M[r] & := & W(A[r], C[r], G[r], M[r]) & \text{Storage.} \end{cases}$$

The notation "$A[i:i+n] := B[j:j+n]$" stands for "$\parallel_{k=0}^n A[i+k] := B[j+k]$" ($skip$ if $n < 0$).

The gsa can work only when connected with an *environment*, providing data and collecting results. Data and results are organized in *streams*; a stream s is a sequence $(s(i) : i \in \mathbf{N}_0)$ of values. Data streams are called dL, dR and $dU_1, \ldots, dU_n$; result streams are rL, rR and $rD_1, \ldots, rD_n$ ("d"stands for "data" and "r" stands for "results"). The environment is modelled by a processing unit which executes the program

$$*(\alpha)[\; i := i+1\,; \qquad\qquad\qquad\qquad \text{Update counter,}$$
$$\qquad LR_1!dL(i) \parallel LR_{n+1}?rR(i) \qquad\qquad \text{Left-to-right,}$$
$$\parallel (\parallel_{k=1}^n U_k!dU_k(i) \parallel D_k?rD_k(i)) \qquad \text{Up-to-down,}$$
$$\parallel RL_0?rL(i) \parallel RL_n!dR(i) \qquad\qquad\quad \text{Right-to-left.}$$
$$\;].$$

The initial value of i is 0.

The parallel composition of the program executed by the network and the program executed by the array is an ordinary sequential program, since all communication statements appear in matching pairs, which reduce to assignments. This program is

$$*(\alpha)[\,i := i+1\,;$$
$$A[1] := dL(i) \parallel A[2:n] := F[1:n-1] \parallel rR(i) := F[n]$$
$$\parallel C[1:n] := dU_{1:n}(i) \parallel rD_{1:n}(i) := E[1:n]$$
$$\parallel rL(i) := B[1] \parallel G[1:n-1] := B[2:n] \parallel G[n] := dR(i)\,;$$
$$Cpt\,].$$

It has a very simple structure (single loop), and interesting knowledge can be gained about it, before instantiating the parameters S, T, V and W. This knowledge is conveniently summarized in the form of a recurrence system, which describes the effect of the execution of the loop body. Here is the recurrence system.

$$
\begin{aligned}
F_i[r] &= S(F_{i-1}[r-1], dU_r(i), B_{i-1}[r+1], M_{i-1}[r]) \\
E_i[r] &= T(F_{i-1}[r-1], dU_r(i), B_{i-1}[r+1], M_{i-1}[r]) \\
B_i[r] &= V(F_{i-1}[r-1], dU_r(i), B_{i-1}[r+1], M_{i-1}[r]) \\
M_i[r] &= W(F_{i-1}[r-1], dU_r(i), B_{i-1}[r+1], M_{i-1}[r])
\end{aligned}
\tag{4}
$$

The value of a register X of cell r, after the ith iteration, is denoted $X_i[r]$ (the symbol X stands for F, E, B or M). The ith element of the input stream dU_r is denoted $dU_r(i)$. The equations written above hold for all r in $\{1, \dots, n\}$ and for all $i > 0$, with the following additional conventions:

$$
F_{i-1}[0] = dL(i) \ ; \ \ B_{i-1}[n+1] = dR(i)
\tag{5}
$$

This recurrence system relates successive values of the output and storage registers; the output streams of the gsa are given by the following identities:

$$
rL(i) = B_{i-1}[1], \ \forall r : (\, rD_r(i) = E_{i-1}[r] \,), \ rR(i) = F_{i-1}[n].
\tag{6}
$$

2.3 Invariant of a recurrence system

An *invariant* of the recurrence system $X_{i+1} = f(X_i)$ is a predicate P such that $\forall Y [P(Y) \Rightarrow P(f(Y))]$, that is, an invariant of the associated program

$$
i := 0; \ \text{while } i < \alpha \ \text{do} \, (X_{i+1}, i) := (f(X_i), i+1).
$$

The knowledge of an adequate invariant of a recurrence system can be useful, especially when the system cannot be easily solved. The interesting fact about invariants is that they summarize substantial information under a concise form. An example will be given in paragraph 5.2.

3 Design of algorithms for linear systolic arrays

A *linear systolic array* is obtained by replacing the parameters S, T, V and W by actual functions in the linear gsa. These functions describe a specific algorithm for the array.

3.1 Outline of the method

The design problem consists in adapting the gsa to a specific task. This adaptation can be performed in several steps, enumerated below.

1. The linear generic systolic array is instantiated in a linear systolic array.

2. The behaviour of the array and its environment is formally stated as a set of recurrence equations.
3. The recurrence system is solved, or an adequate invariant is found.
4. The data and results streams of the array are interpreted as data and results of the problem.

Let us comment a little about these four steps. In the first step, the designer decides what will be the computation part *Cpt*. The linear gsa allows four logical components, described respectively by functions S, T, V and W but, for some applications, one or two logical components will be enough.

The second step is mechanical: the recurrence system corresponding to the array (and its environment) is obtained by mere instantiation of the generic recurrence system (4) introduced in paragraph 3.2.

The third step can be difficult. From the practical point of view, let us observe that the discovery of an adequate invariant can be easier than the discovery of the solution of the recurrence system. This point will be illustrated later (Section 4.2; see also [7]).

The fourth step is the interpretation step. It allows to determine where and when the data are transmitted into the array, and where and when the results are collected out. This determination is simpler than in the space-time method; it requires more carefulness than creativity, since rather little choice is left.

A classical application is presented in this section, in order to demonstrate the design method.

3.2 Matrix-vector product

As recalled in paragraph 1.1, the product y of a matrix A and a vector x is obtained by executing the assignments $y_k := y_k + A_{kj}x_j$ for all k, j in $\{1, \ldots, p\}$. The initial value of every y_k is 0. Assignments on y_k and $y_{k'}$ may be performed concurrently if and only if $k \neq k'$.

Classically, the design problem for this application consists in discovering an adequate time and processor allocation for the p^2 assignments. In this framework, an adequate allocation maps each assignment onto a processing unit, and also specifies when the assignment is performed. An adequate allocation should satisfy the concurrency constraint just mentioned and also an implementation constraint: a processing unit can perform only one assignment at a time.

Many adequate allocations exist. One of them is the purely sequential one: there is only one processing unit, and the assignment $y_k := y_k + A_{kj}x_j$ is performed at time $t(k, j) := p(k - 1) + j$. Interesting adequate allocations are *time-optimal* ones: due to the concurrency constraint, the time of computation is at least p, since each y_k is altered by p assignments. An optimum can be reached as follows. There are p processing units, each of them devoted to a single y_k. Each unit sequentially executes the assignment, for $j = 1, \ldots, p$.

This time-optimal allocation is not fully satisfactory. There are communication problems. Each x_j must be simultaneously broadcasted to all processing values. As broadcasting is generally not accepted in systolic arrays, the simple time-optimal allocation will be rejected.

The critical point of the design problem for this application is here: a trade-off between time-optimality and communication-optimality must be discovered.

Let us now come back to the linear gsa. The problem of finding such a trade-off disappears, since the communication scheme is already fixed. As a matter of fact, very little choice is left. Each cell will perform the assignment $a := a + b * c$, for some a, b and c. We have only to assign the three flows available in the gsa to these three values. We are interested in linear time algorithms or, at least, in algorithms of complexity better than quadratic, so the only acceptable b-flow (matrix coefficients) is the UD-flow. Indeed, the remaining flows LR and RL allow only one input at a time. They are assigned arbitrarily; for instance, LR is assigned to a (coefficients of y) and RL is assigned to c (coefficients of x). The storage logical unit is not used. This leads to the following parameters:

$$
\begin{aligned}
S(a,b,c) &= a + b * c, & LR\,, \\
T(a,b,c) &= b\,, & UD\,, \\
V(a,b,c) &= c\,, & RL\,.
\end{aligned}
$$

The corresponding recurrence system is:

$$
\begin{aligned}
\forall r : \ & F_i[r] = F_{i-1}[r-1] + dU_r(i) * B_{i-1}[r+1])\,, \\
\forall r : \ & E_i[r] = dU_r(i)\,, \\
\forall r : \ & B_i[r] = B_{i-1}[r+1]\,.
\end{aligned}
$$

We are interested in the result stream rR, which is obtained easily as follows

$$
\begin{aligned}
rR(i) &= F_{i-1}[n] \\
&= F_{i-2}[n-1] + dU_n(i) * B_{i-2}[n+1] \\
&= F_{i-3}[n-2] + dU_{n-1}(i-1) * B_{i-3}[n] + dU_n(i) * B_{i-2}[n+1] \\
&= \cdots \qquad \cdots \\
&= F_{i-n-1}[0] + \sum_{l=1}^{n} dU_{n-l+1}(i-l) * B_{i-l-1}[n-l+2] \\
&= F_{i-n-1}[0] + \sum_{l=1}^{n} dU_{n-l+1}(i-l) * B_{i-2l}[n+1] \\
&= dL(i-n) + \sum_{l=1}^{n} dU_{n-l+1}(i-l) * dR(i-2l+1)\,.
\end{aligned}
$$

Comment. The validity of the development is restricted by the range of the indices. The conditions are $i-n > 0$, $0 < n-l+1 \le n$, $i-l > 0$ and $i-2l+1 > 0$, for all l in $\{1, \ldots, n\}$. These conditions reduce to $i \ge 2n$. (For $0 < i < 2n$, the value $rR(i)$ depends on the initial values of the cells; as no condition is required about the initial values, this part of the result stream cannot be used.)

Let us emphasize the fact that, for the time being, the allocation implemented by the array is not known yet. Even the relation between the size n of the systolic array and the dimension p of the matrix and of the vector, must still be fixed. This is done in the fourth and last step of the design procedure.

The value $y_k = \sum_{r=1}^{n} A_{k,r} x_r$ must be extracted from the stream rR, for all k in $\{1, \ldots, n\}$. As the first useful value of the result stream is $rR(2n)$, the useful values could be $rR(2n)$, $rR(2n + 1)$, ..., $rR(3n - 1)$. More specifically, the identity

$$rR(2n - 1 + k) = \sum_{j=1}^{p} A_{kj} x_j$$

is matched, for $k \in \{1, \ldots, n\}$, with the identity

$$rR(2n - 1 + k) = dL(n - 1 + k) + \sum_{l=1}^{n} dU_{n-l+1}(2n - 1 + k - l) * dR(2n + k - 2l).$$

Several matchings are possible, and discovered easily. Obviously, n and p are equal and the dL flow must be 0. The dR contains the components of x. A simple solution consists in deliver these components in the natural order; let us choose $dL(j) = x_{j \bmod n + 1}$ ("+1" is introduced because the range of $j \bmod n$ is $\{0, \ldots, n - 1\}$, while the components of x are indexed in $\{1, \ldots, n\}$). This choice leads to:

$$rR(2n - 1 + k) = \sum_{l=1}^{n} dU_{n-l+1}(2n + k - l - 1) * x_{(2n+k-2l) \bmod n + 1}.$$

If n is odd, each component of x occurs exactly once in this sum. The last task consists in specifying the dU streams. The data $dU_{n-l+1}(2n + k - l - 1)$ should be the matrix component $A_{k, (2n+k-2l) \bmod n + 1}$. This allows the determination of $dU_i(j)$. The results are summarized below; a graphical representation is on Figure 2 (bottom right).

$$
\begin{aligned}
dL(j) &= 0 & & j \in \{n, \ldots, 2n - 1\}; \\
dU_i(j) &= A_{j-i-n+2, (j+i-n) \bmod n + 1} & & i \in \{1, \ldots, n\}, \\
& & & j \in \{n+i-1, \ldots, 2n+i-2\}; \\
dR(j) &= x_{j \bmod n + 1} & & j \in \{1, \ldots, 3n - 2\}.
\end{aligned}
\tag{7}
$$

Comments. Similar results can be obtained for even n.

Let us emphasize that the data are delivered to the systolic array in a rather strange way; moreover, the components of the vector x must be delivered twice or three times.

The components of x are output through rL_0, without modification, but with a delay of n time units.

The components of A are output through rD, without modification, but with a delay of one time unit; more specifically, $rD_r(j + 1) = dU_r(j)$.

The execution is completed after $3n - 1$ step.

The initial contents of the registers are arbitrary; so are the members of the input streams which do not occur in formulas (7).

4 More general systolic arrays

4.1 Formal description of generic arrays

Most systolic arrays can be obtained as combinations of linear arrays, whose communication channels are properly connected. Some important combinations are introduced now.

A *ring* consists in a single linear array whose left and right communications channels have been connected; this means that RL_0 and RL_n, on the one hand, and LR_1 and LR_{n+1} on the other hand, have been identified. A *rectangle* is obtained by stacking p identical linear arrays. Let these arrays be identified by a superscript. Channel D_i^{j+1} and channel U_i^j are identified, for $1 \leq i \leq n$ and $1 \leq j < p$. Further connections in a rectangle can lead to other interesting topologies. The *horizontal cylinder* is obtained by identifying U_i^p and D_i^1. The *vertical cylinder* is obtained transforming each linear array of a rectangle into a ring, and a *torus* is obtained by performing both up-down and left-right connections. A *square* is a rectangle where $n = p$.

The equations $(4, 5, 6)$ are a formal description of the generic linear systolic array. A similar description can be obtained for any architecture. This task is very simple for an architecture derived from the linear one. A single case, the ring, will be considered here.

The formal description of the ring is obtained from the description of the linear array in a straightforward way. First, the identities

$$rR(i) = dL(i) \qquad \text{and} \qquad rL(i) = dR(i)$$

are introduced in the equations $(4, 5, 6)$; second, the streams dL, dR, rL and rR are eliminated. The resulting equations are

$$
\begin{aligned}
F_i[r] &= S(F_{i-1}[r-1], dU_r(i), B_{i-1}[r+1], M_{i-1}[r]) \\
E_i[r] &= T(F_{i-1}[r-1], dU_r(i), B_{i-1}[r+1], M_{i-1}[r]) \\
B_i[r] &= V(F_{i-1}[r-1], dU_r(i), B_{i-1}[r+1], M_{i-1}[r]) \\
M_i[r] &= W(F_{i-1}[r-1], dU_r(i), B_{i-1}[r+1], M_{i-1}[r])
\end{aligned}
\tag{8}
$$

$$F_{i-1}[0] = F_{i-1}[n] \ ; \ B_{i-1}[n+1] = B_{i-1}[1]$$

$$\forall r : (\, rD_r(i) = E_{i-1}[r] \,)$$

4.2   Greatest common divisor

Let us consider a set $E = \{x_1, \ldots, x_n\}$ of positive integers. The greatest common divisor (gcd) of these numbers can be found by execution of the well known Euclidean algorithm:

> repeat until $x_i = x_j$ for all i, j:
>   select i, j such that $x_i > x_j$; replace x_i by $x_i - x_j$.

This algorithm always terminates and the common final value of the x_i is the requested gcd.

Let us try to implement this algorithm on a ring. The only data are the numbers; let us suppose that, initially, cell P_i contains x_i, for all i. Every cell will communicate the value it contains to, say, its right neighbour. (The right neighbour of P_n is P_1.) The computation part of cell P_i consists in comparing its value and the value received from P_{i-1} and in subtracting the smallest value from the greatest one; sooner or later, all the values in the array will become equal to the required gcd.

This very informal idea should be formalized according to the methodology presented in Section 4. The equations for the ring can be simplified, since only two logical components are needed: the LR component, to implement the circulation of data, and the storage component, since each cell should contain a value. The resulting equations are

$$\begin{aligned}
F_i[r] &= S(F_{i-1}[r-1], M_{i-1}[r]) \\
M_i[r] &= W(F_{i-1}[r-1], M_{i-1}[r]) \\
F_{i-1}[0] &= F_{i-1}[n]
\end{aligned} \tag{9}$$

The functions S and W are defined as follows:

$$S(x,y) := \text{if } x \neq y \text{ then } \max(x,y) - \min(x,y) \text{ else } x,$$
$$W(x,y) := \min(x,y).$$

Let us note that the following properties hold:

$$\forall x,y \in \mathbf{N} : gcd(S(x,y), W(x,y)) = gcd(x,y),$$
$$\forall x,y \in \mathbf{N} : [x \neq y \Rightarrow S(x,y) + W(x,y) < x + y].$$

The recurrence system reduces to:

$F_i[r] = \text{if } F_{i-1}[r-1] \neq M_{i-1}[r]$
$\qquad\qquad \text{then } \max(F_{i-1}[r-1], M_{i-1}[r]) - \min(F_{i-1}[r-1], M_{i-1}[r]) \text{ else } F_{i-1}[r-1],$
$M_i[r] = \min(F_{i-1}[r-1], M_{i-1}[r])$

with the convention $F_{i-1}[0] = F_{i-1}[n]$. The initial conditions are:

$$F_0[r] = M_0[r] = x_r, \quad r \in \{1, \ldots, n\}, \quad x_r \in \mathbf{N_0}.$$

Comment. Here is an example where the explicit solution of the recurrence system is not easily found (§3.1, point 3). Fortunately, such an explicit solution is not necessary, and it is sufficient to discover an adequate invariant instead. Let us introduce a notation:

$$E_i =_{def} \{F_i[1], M_i[1], F_i[2], \ldots, M_i[n-1], F_i[n], M_i[n]\}.$$

An interesting property of the (multi)set E_i is $gcd(E_i) = gcd(x_1, x_2, \ldots, x_n)$. The proof is by induction on i. The identity is obvious for $i = 0$. Let us suppose it is true for $i = k-1$. The identity $gcd(F_i[r], M_i[r]) = gcd(F_{i-1}[r-1], M_{i-1}[r])$ holds for all r: for all positive integers x and y, $gcd(x,y) = gcd(S(x,y), W(x,y))$. As a consequence,

$$gcd(E_i) = gcd(\bigcup_r \{F_i[r], M_i[r]\}) = gcd(\bigcup_r \{F_{i-1}[r-1], M_{i-1}[r]\}) = gcd(E_{i-1}).$$

Let us note Z_i the sum of the $2n$ members of the multiset E_i. The sequence $(Z_0, Z_1, \ldots, Z_n, \ldots)$ has three interesting properties. First, it is monotonically decreasing since, for all positive integer x, y, $S(x,y) + W(x,y) \leq x + y$. Second $Z_{i-1} = Z_i$ occurs if and only if $F_{i-1}[r-1] = M_{i-1}[r] = F_i[r] = M_i[r]$, for all r. Third, $Z_{i-1} = Z_i = Z_{i+1}$ occurs only if all the members of E_i are equal: the first identity implies $F_i[r] = M_i[r]$, the second one implies $F_i[r-1] = M_i[r]$, for all r.

As Z_i is always a positive integer, the sequence cannot decrease forever, and a stable state is reached after finitely many iterations.

Comments. The repetition number is still unknown. In practice, an additional circuit can be added to detect when all the registers F and M are identical; in this case, the common value is the gcd.

It is also possible to determine an adequate repetition number. With the simple definition we have adopted for S and W, it would be rather large. An improvement consists in replacing, in the definition of S, the expression "$\max(x, y) - \min(x, y)$" by "$\max(x, y) \bmod* \min(x, y)$", where "$\bmod*$" is the usual modulo operator, except that $(nA \bmod* A)$ is A instead of 0. In this case, $\alpha = \log_\phi(\Sigma)$ is an adequate repetition number, where $\phi = (1 + \sqrt{2})/2$ and $\Sigma = max_r x_r + 1$. (The Euclidean algorithm for the gcd is studied e.g. in [11].)

4.3 Other examples

Several examples have suggested that the instantiation of a generic systolic array is significantly easier than the design of a new array by the classical method. We did not encounter any example for which the instantiation method proposed here is more difficult than the space-time mapping method. However, the communication scheme considered in this paper (Equation 3) turned out to be rather restrictive and classical examples often require a slightly less elementary scheme, that is:

$$input \; ; \quad computation \; ; \quad output \,. \tag{10}$$

With the synchronous communication paradigm, "input" for a cell means "output" for some neighbour, so the global scheme really is

input for odd cells || output for even cells ,
computation for odd cells ,
input for even cells || output for odd cells ,
computation for even cells .

A rather frequent additional refinement is to dissociate cycles related to distinct communication flows; an example is

a-input and b-output for odd cells || a-output and b-input for even cells ,
a-computation for odd cells || b-computation for even cells ,
a-input and b-output for even cells || a-output and b-input for odd cells ,
a-computation for even cells || b-computation for odd cells .

The method we propose is easily adapted to any kind of communication scheme, but the choice of an adequate communication scheme is left to the designer. The solution is not unique; distinct schemes lead to distinct trade-off between the number of cells, the size of the memory and the time of a typical computation.

5 Conclusion

We presented in this paper the very simple but powerful concept of *generic systolic array*. Its properties have been stated and proved once for all, using CSP-like notations. A new methodology for the mapping of algorithms on systolic arrays is based on this concept. Because no a priori assumption is made on the localization of the data, circuits can be derived which are different from those obtained with a space-time transformation technique. Despite the fact that only simple algorithms have been derived here, this methodology is very promising.

References

1. M. Anaratone et al., "Warp architecture and implementation", Proc. 13th Int. Symp. on Computer Architecture, pp. 346-356, 1986
2. K.M. Chandy, J. Misra, "Systolic algorithms as programs", Distributed Computing 1, pp. 177-183 (1986)
3. K.M. Chandy, J. Misra, "Parallel Program Design : A Foundation", Addison-Wesley, Reading, Mass, 1988
4. M.C. Chen, "Synthesizing VLSI architectures: Dynamic programming solver", Proc. of the 1986 Int. Conf. on Parallel Processing, pp. 776-784, 1986
5. E.W. Dijkstra, "A discipline of programming", Prentice-Hall, New-Jersey, 1976
6. J.A.B. Fortes et al., "Systematic approaches to the design of algorithmically specified systolic arrays", IEEE Conf. ICASSP 85, vol. 1, pp. 300-302, 1985
7. P. Gribomont, "Proving systolic arrays", L.N.C.S. 299, pp. 185-199 (1988)
8. M. Hennessy, "Proving Systolic Systems Correct", ACM Toplas 8, pp. 344-387 (1986)
9. C.H. Huang, C. Lengauer, "An implemented method for incremental systolic design", L.N.C.S. 258, pp. 160-177 (1987)
10. R.M. Karp, R.E. Miller, S. Winograd, "The organization of computations for uniform recurrence equations", J.ACM 14, pp. 563-590 (1967)
11. D.E. Knuth, "The art of computer programming", vol. 1, Addison-Wesley, Reading, Mass, 1968
12. H.T. Kung, C.E. Leiserson, "Algorithms for VLSI processor arrays", in "Introduction to VLSI systems", Mead and Conway (Eds), Addison-Wesley, Reading, Mass, pp. 271-292, 1980
13. A.R. Martin, J.V. Tucker, "The concurrent assignment representation of synchronous systems", Parallel Computing 9, pp. 227-256 (1989)
14. C. Mongenet, G.-R. Perrin, "Synthesis of systolic arrays for inductive problems", L.N.C.S. 258, pp. 260-277 (1987)
15. M. Ossefort, "Correctness Proofs of Communicating Processes: Three Illustrative Examples from the Literature", ACM Toplas 5, pp. 620-640 (1983)
16. S.V. Rajopadhye, R.M. Fujimoto, "Systolic array synthesis by static analysis of program dependencies", L.N.C.S. 258, pp. 295-310 (1987)
17. M. Rem, "Trace theory and systolic computations", L.N.C.S. 258, pp. 14-33 (1987)
18. J.L.A. van de Snepscheut, J.B. Swenker, "On the Design of Some Systolic Algorithms", J.ACM 36, pp. 826-840 (1989)
19. V. Van Dongen, "Mapping uniform recurrences onto small size arrays" L.N.C.S. 505, pp. 191-208 (1991)

Index of Authors

Lecture Notes in Computer Science

For information about Vols. 1–595
please contact your bookseller or Springer-Verlag